How Arbitration Works

How Arbitration Works

by

Frank Elkouri
Professor of Law
University of Oklahoma

and

Edna Asper Elkouri
Juris Doctor With Honors
The George Washington University
Law School

THIRD EDITION

THE BUREAU OF NATIONAL AFFAIRS, INC.
WASHINGTON, D.C.

Second Printing June 1974
Third Printing January 1976
Fourth Printing March 1977
Fifth Printing March 1978
Sixth Printing June 1979
Seventh Printing February 1981

 13

Printed in the United States of America
Library of Congress Catalog Card Number: 72–95857
International Standard Book Number: 0-87179-180-3

TO AMERICA'S ARBITRATORS
Who Labor Earnestly and Ably

PREFACE TO THIRD EDITION

The Preface to the Second Edition serves well for the Third Edition also. Certainly, the rapid pace of development has continued. Thus, the updating of *How Arbitration Works* again presented a great challenge to the Authors, both as to time and effort. Even so, we have expanded the scope of the book by adding two new chapters, various new topics elsewhere in the book, and of course new developments throughout the book.

Frank Elkouri
Edna Asper Elkouri

PREFACE TO SECOND EDITION

The period since publication of the first edition of *How Arbitration Works* has witnessed a great outpouring of arbitration decisions as well as writings by arbitrators and students of arbitration. Thus, the past few years might well be termed a "classical" period in the history of arbitration. Much new thought has emerged, much previous thinking has been modified, and some of the old has departed. This is convincing evidence of the progressive and dynamic nature of arbitration in our industrial scheme of things today. The words of John Day Larkin, speaking as President of the National Academy of Arbitrators in 1956, effectively tell the story:

> "The work of arbitrators, like that of judges, is in one sense enduring and in another sense ephemeral. That which is erroneous is sure to perish. The good remains, the foundation on which new policies, practices and procedures will be built. That which is bad will be cast off in due time. Little by little, old and outworn doctrines are undermined, both through the process of negotiation by the parties and by the sounder reasoning of those called upon to interpret the language which the parties have hammered out in the heat of economic conflict, and through long hours of patient effort to reach an agreement." *

It is with the above thoughts in mind that the Authors offer the Second Edition of *How Arbitration Works* to arbitrators, students of arbitration, and especially to employers and employees.

Frank Elkouri
Edna Asper Elkouri

---

* Larkin, "Introduction: The First Decade," Critical Issues in Labor Arbitration viii, xv (BNA Incorporated, 1957).

FOREWORD TO FIRST EDITION

This study is a product of the graduate and research program of the University of Michigan Law School. The subject was selected on the basis of its current and increasing importance in the field of labor-management relations and as one which, partaking of many of the characteristics of a legal institution, is suitable for examination by lawyers as well as others.

Mr. Elkouri has sought from an examination of the reported arbitration cases themselves to throw new light on the procedural and substantive aspects of the arbitration process. He has modestly, and, in my opinion wisely, refrained on the whole from attempting to pass judgment on the wisdom and soundness of particular decisions and of general principles which appear to be emerging in the cases. Perhaps a study which undertakes such a critique will emerge in time, possibly from Mr. Elkouri himself. Meanwhile, what he has done is important enough.

It is still too early to determine the full impact of arbitration on collective bargaining. The next decade should disclose whether the recorded and published decisions of arbitrators have developed some generalized thinking about collective bargaining problems which has become an important part of the utilized knowledge of bargainers and of students of the subject. If experience with other bodies of accumulated knowledge is any criterion—and I can think of no valid reason why the field of labor relations should be set apart as an exception—we are likely to see just such a development. Some may view this prospect with alarm, based on a fear of stereotyped thinking and undue reverence for precedent. This attitude seems to me to show a lack of understanding of the judicial process. It is simply contrary to every canon of progress to refuse in this field or any other to conserve the accumulated wisdom and experience of the problems as sound judgment may dictate.

Russell A. Smith
Professor of Law
University of Michigan
1952

ACKNOWLEDGMENT, FIRST EDITION

I wish to acknowledge my deep indebtedness to Professor Russell A. Smith of the Michigan Law School, who, as my friend and Chairman of my Research Committee, contributed in so many ways to this book. I also wish to acknowledge my special indebtedness to the following persons, each of whom, in his respective way, contributed generously to make this book possible: E. Blythe Stason, Dean of Michigan Law School; Professor Lewis M. Simes, Director of Legal Research at Michigan Law School; Professor John E. Tracy, Professor Edgar N. Durfee, Professor L. Hart Wright and Professor Burke Shartel, all of Michigan Law School; Professor Hobart Coffey, Director of the Michigan Law School Library; Professor Coffey's Staff; Judge Frank P. Douglass and Mr. Leverett Edwards, both of the National Mediation Board; U.S. Senator Mike Monroney; Professor John B. Cheadle, Professor Victor H. Kulp and Professor Maurice H. Merrill, all of the University of Oklahoma Law School; Professor Sylvester Petro of New York University Law School; Professor George Wolbert of Washington and Lee Law School; Ford Motor Company Umpire Harry Shulman; Chrysler Motor Company Umpire David A. Wolff; Arbitrator Francis J. Robertson of Washington, D.C.; John D. Stewart, Executive Editor of The Bureau of National Affairs, Inc.; and, finally, the many arbitrators whose work has provided the basic material for this study.

Frank Elkouri

ACKNOWLEDGMENT, SECOND EDITION

In addition to the persons named above, the Authors wish to thank David Ross Boyd Professor George B. Fraser and Professor Mortimer Schwartz, both of the University of Oklahoma College of Law, for their valuable suggestions in connection with the Second Edition.

Frank Elkouri
Edna Asper Elkouri

SUMMARY TABLE OF CONTENTS

(See following pages for complete table of contents)

DETAILED TABLE OF CONTENTS

Chapter 1

ARBITRATION AND ITS SETTING

The labor dispute is a natural characteristic of our enterprise system in the context of worker organization and collective bargaining. Such disputes reflect the determination of labor and capital, respectively, to receive what each considers to be its "fair share" of industrial production.

Whether such conflict is an evil, and, if so, a necessary one, is not the concern here. What is important is that society and many disputants themselves recognize that production stoppages resulting from disputes should be minimized, and that an effective means of accomplishing this end is arbitration. This is recognized, too, as a matter of national policy. While he was a Justice of the U.S. Supreme Court, Arthur J. Goldberg underscored this policy: "In the United States Arbitration Act, the Labor-Management Relations Act [LMRA] and in numerous state statutes, our legislative bodies have voiced their conviction that voluntary arbitration of disputes is favored and has an important role in a society which seeks the peaceful, prompt and just disposition of controversies involving our citizens."[1] While a member of the National Labor Relations Board (NLRB), Joseph A. Jenkins declared: "I call arbitrators 'peacemakers' because they have it within their power to contribute more to the maintenance of good relations between conflicting forces in our society than any other group, whether public or private."[2]

This book deals with the workings of labor-management arbitration and with the numerous questions and problems that have confronted the parties and their arbitrators. The most realistic picture of how arbitration works and the most practical answers to its problems, it is believed, can be obtained through analysis of actual awards.

---

[1] Goldberg, "A Supreme Court Justice Looks at Arbitration," 20 Arb. J. 13, at 13 (1965).
[2] Jenkins, "The Peacemakers," 47 Georgetown L. J. 435, 436 (1959).

So it is to awards that the Authors turn for their primary source material.

Arbitration Defined—Historical Background

Arbitration, to use the words of one writer, is a "simple proceeding voluntarily chosen by parties who want a dispute determined by an impartial judge of their own mutual selection, whose decision, based on the merits of the case, they agree in advance to accept as final and binding."[3]

Submission of disputes to arbitration may be made compulsory by law. However, except as otherwise indicated, the use of the term "arbitration" in this book refers to voluntary arbitration. When parties voluntarily agree to arbitrate their differences, it thereafter becomes "obligatory" upon either party to arbitrate at the request of the other. Although both parties have voluntarily agreed to arbitrate, arbitration will not be resorted to unless at least one of them thereafter so wishes.

Arbitration as an institution is not new, having been in use many centuries before the beginning of the English common law.[4] Indeed, one court has called arbitration "the oldest known method of settlement of disputes between men."[5]

King Solomon was an arbitrator,[6] and it is interesting to note that the procedure used by him was in many respects similar to that used by arbitrators today. Another great man of history, George Washington, was a staunch believer in arbitration. Although he exercised all possible caution in writing his last will and testament, he did not overlook the possibility of disputes as to its intent. For this eventuality he specified arbitration:

> "But having endeavored to be plain and explicit in all the Devises—even at the expense of prolixity, perhaps of tautology, I hope, and trust, that no disputes will arise concerning them; but if contrary

---

[3] Chappell, "Arbitrate * * * and Avoid Stomach Ulcers," 2 Arb. Mag., Nos. 11–12, pp. 6, 7 (1944). For a similar definition by a court, see Gates v. Arizona Brewing Co., 95 P.2d 49, 50 (Arizona Sup. Ct., 1939).

[4] For some ancient sources and early developments of arbitration, see Murray, "Arbitration in the Anglo-Saxon and Early Norman Periods," 16 Arb. J. 193 (1961).

[5] McAmis v. Panhandle Pipe Line Co., 23 LA 570, 574 (Kan. City Ct. of App., 1954).

[6] Bible, 1 Kings, 3, 16–28.

to expectation the case should be otherwise from the want of legal expression, or the usual technical terms or because too much or too little; has been said on any of the devises to be consonant with law, my will and direction expressly is, that all disputes (if unhappily any should arise) shall be decided by three impartial and intelligent men, known for their probity and good understanding; two to be chosen by the disputants, each having the choice of one, and the third by those two.—which three men thus chosen, shall unfettered by Law, or legal constructions, declare their sense of the Testator's intention; and such decision is, to all intents and purposes to be as binding on the Parties as if it had been given in the Supreme Court of the United States."[7]

Commercial arbitration has long been used as a substitute for court action in the settlement of disputes between businessmen.[8] International arbitration has been used for the settlement of differences between nations, differences which, if not removed, might lead to war.[9] Development of labor arbitration in the United States began during the latter part of the nineteenth century, and its most rapid advance has been made since the United States became involved in World War II.[10]

Commercial arbitration grew up as an alternative to court action, while labor-management arbitration has evolved primarily as a substitute for strikes.

The development of labor-management arbitration generally has followed the development of collective bargaining. It has been most successful where collective bargaining has been successful. In the full-fashioned hosiery industry, for example, where the use of collective

---

[7] American Arbitration Association, Arbitration News, No. 2 (1963), where it is also explained that the quoted lines of the will are reproduced from a document published many years ago by the Federal Government.

[8] For the historical development of commercial arbitration, see Keller, Arbitration and the Legal Profession (Am. Arb. Assn., 1952).

[9] In 1970 the United States ratified the United Nations Convention on the Recognition and Enforcement of Foreign Arbitral Awards, under which courts of the signatory nations are to enforce arbitration clauses and awards on the same basis as they would domestic arbitration proceedings. For explanation and discussion, see McMahon, "Implementation of the UN Convention on Foreign Arbitral Awards in the U.S.," 26 Arb. J. 65 (1971).

[10] For the historical development of labor arbitration in the United States, see Fleming, The Labor Arbitration Process 1–30 (Univ. of Ill. Press, 1965); Stessin, Employee Discipline 8–12 (BNA Incorporated, 1960); Witte, "The Future of Labor Arbitration—A Challenge," The Profession of Labor Arbitration 1, 3–11 (BNA Incorporated, 1957); Witte, Historical Survey of Labor Arbitration (Univ. of Pa. Press, 1952); Keller, Arbitration and the Legal Profession (Am. Arb. Assn., 1952); Oliver, "The Arbitration of Labor Disputes," 83 U. of Pa. L. Rev. 206 (1934).

bargaining has been highly successful, over 1,500 disputes were decided over a 10-year period by the industry's impartial chairman without a single reported instance of noncompliance with or nonacceptance of an award.[11]

Collective Bargaining, Mediation, Fact-Finding, and Arbitration

The distinction between collective bargaining, mediation, fact-finding, and arbitration can be seen more clearly if one considers each a stage in the relationship between labor and management. Collective bargaining is the first stage and arbitration the last. Conciliation or mediation, and fact-finding, occupy intermediate stages.

Conciliation or mediation may be resorted to as an aid to negotiations.[12] Technically, conciliation is carried on without the intervention of a third party, while mediation implies the intervention of an outside person; but the two terms are commonly used interchangeably.[13] The essence of mediation and conciliation is compromise. The mediator does not make a decision. Rather, his aim is to persuade negotiators, by proposals or arguments, to come to voluntary agreement.[14]

"Fact-Finding," as the term is most commonly used, refers to a method of handling labor-management disputes which prohibits strikes and lockouts until an official agency, usually a fact-finding board, has had opportunity to investigate and report. Changes in the status quo, except when made by mutual consent of the parties, are prohibited during the "cooling-off" period which runs concurrently with the period of investigation and report. The function of fact-finders is to investigate and assemble all facts surrounding disputes. After the investigation, a report is made which may include recom-

---

[11] Millis, How Collective Bargaining Works 460 (1942). For a comprehensive summary of the development of collective bargaining and its effect upon arbitration, see Millis, id. at 871–907.

[12] Another possible device is the private use of independent third parties as neutral "consultants" or participants in the collective bargaining process itself. See Chamberlain, "Neutral Consultants in Collective Bargaining," Collective Bargaining and the Arbitrator's Role 83–116 (BNA Incorporated, 1962); Wirtz, "Role of Federal Government in Labor Relations," 51 LRRM 70, 78 (1962); Hildebrand, "The Use of Neutrals in Collective Bargaining," Arbitration and Public Policy 135 (BNA Incorporated, 1961).

[13] Millis & Montgomery, Organized Labor 719, n. 2 (1945).

[14] An excellent treatise on mediation is Simkin, Mediation and the Dynamics of Collective Bargaining (The Bureau of National Affairs, Inc., 1971). A shorter study is Fuller, "Mediation—Its Forms and Functions," 44 S. Calif. L. Rev. 305 (1971).

mendations (except under the emergency dispute provisions of the LMRA) and which, unlike the findings of an arbitrator, the disputants have a choice of accepting or rejecting.[15]

In arbitrating, parties are compelled by their own agreement to accept the decision of an arbitrator as final and binding. The objective of arbitration is adjudication, not compromise. Resort to arbitration usually occurs after the techniques of conciliation or mediation (and possibly fact-finding) have failed to produce agreement.

Arbitration as a Substitute for Work Stoppages

It has been said that the "most important difference between civilization and savagery is the habitual willingness of civilized men and nations to submit their differences of opinion to a factual test," and that "it is a mark of civilization to present reasons rather than arms."[16] Again, "industrial peace is not a God-given product. It must be cultivated and worked for constantly. * * * Conciliation, mediation and voluntary arbitration are the marks of civilization. They are the enemies of distrust and force. They do away with the fang and the claw."[17] Moreover, "if the rules and standards of orderly social behavior accepted for society at large are to be valid also for industrial relations, it would seem that settlement of labor disputes on rights should be sought as far as possible through judicial methods rather than through strikes and lockouts."[18] One method of settling labor-management differences without resort to strike or lockout is voluntary arbitration. As recognized by the U.S. Supreme Court, arbitration "is the substitute for industrial strife."[19]

In the United States the right to strike is looked upon as an essential economic freedom. Like all freedoms, however, it can be abused; it can be used unwisely and without sufficient justification.

---

[15] For a discussion of fact-finding, see Simkin, "Fact-Finding: Its Values and Limitations," Arbitration and the Expanding Role of Neutrals 165 (The Bureau of National Affairs, Inc., 1970).
[16] Boland, "Labor Disputes: The Preventive and Cure," Arbitration in Action 6 (Dec. 1943).
[17] McGrady, "Industrial Peace: A Joint Enterprise," 2 Arb. J. 339, 343 (1938).
[18] Spielmans, "Labor Disputes on Rights and on Interests," Am. Ec. Rev. 299 (June, 1939).
[19] United Steelworkers v. Warrier & Gulf Navigation Company, 80 S.Ct. 1347, 1351 (1960).

Many times, for example, strikes or lockouts have occurred not because of a real difference between the parties, but because one of them could not, or would not, of his own volition recede from a position irrevocably taken.[20] Here, of course, there is no social justification for a work stoppage. Even where a real difference exists, possibilities for a peaceful solution may make resort to force uncalled for. A difference that looms large to disputants may be relatively free of complexities when viewed by a disinterested observer. A basic tenet of arbitration is that the arbitrator will be able to look at the issue objectively; accordingly, a reasonable decision based upon the true merits of the dispute can be expected.

An agreement to arbitrate effects a complete surrender of any right of the employer to determine the controversy by unilateral action and of any right of both parties to support their contentions by a show of economic strength.[21] This surrender on occasion has been the basis of distrust of arbitration. One management argument against arbitration is that it substitutes for the experienced, responsible judgment of management the judgment of an outsider who lacks the responsibility for conducting the business. Labor, in turn, sometimes feels that giving up its freedom to strike, in reliance upon the understanding of an outsider who might prove to be not so understanding, involves too great a risk.

The answer to such fears is that the initially uninformed outsider is soon enlightened, for both parties have adequate opportunity to inform him as to their views, and he carries a responsibility for his decision akin to that of a judge in a court of law. Thus, parties sometimes have been urged to place complete trust in arbitration.[22]

Contracts that make arbitration the final step in the grievance procedure generally prohibit strikes and lockouts over arbitrable issues.[23] Moreover, the U.S. Supreme Court has held that a no-strike

---

[20] For views on use of arbitration for purposes of "face saving," see Eaton, "Labor Arbitration in the San Francisco Bay Area," 48 LA 1381, 1389–1390 (1967); Warren & Bernstein, "A Profile of Labor Arbitration," 16 LA 970, 979 (1951).

[21] Pan American Airways, Inc., 5 LA 590, 594–595 (Cahn, 1946).

[22] See Chappell, "Arbitrate * * * and Avoid Stomach Ulcers," 2 Arb. Mag., Nos. 11–12, p. 6 (1944). Also see Zack, Arbitration of Labor Disputes 21 (1947).

[23] Of 1,717 contracts analyzed in one study, 1,527 contained restrictions on strikes and lockouts. Many of these specified an absolute ban, but many limited the ban to disputes subject to grievance and/or arbitration procedures;

obligation is implied in those issues which are subject to binding arbitration under the agreement, and that a strike over such an issue violates the agreement despite the absence of an express no-strike clause.[24]

There is an increasing disposition on the part of labor and management to provide, as the final grievance step, for the arbitration of contract interpretation and application disputes. A study made by the U.S. Bureau of Labor Statistics in 1966 indicated that 94 percent of the collective bargaining agreements in the nation's important industries provided for arbitration as the terminal point of the grievance machinery.[25] Studies made by the Bureau in 1944, 1949, and 1952 showed percentages of 73, 83, and 89, respectively.[26] Even where employees are not represented by a union, recognition of the contribution that arbitration can make toward a healthy employer-employee relationship has led some employers to provide impartial arbitration machinery for the grievances of their unorganized employees.[27]

In contrast to the overwhelming acceptance of arbitration for contract interpretation and application disputes, the proportion of collective agreements with specific provision for the arbitration of contract negotiation disputes continued to hover at about 2 percent from 1949 to 1966.[28] In some quarters, however, it is suspected that the

---

some permitted strikes after exhaustion of the grievance procedure where there was no provision for arbitration or where mutual consent was required for arbitration. Major Collective Bargaining Agreements: Arbitration Procedures 83 (U.S. Dept. of Labor Bull. No. 1425-6, 1966). A 1970 study by BNA revealed similar results (90 percent frequency of no-strike clauses). "Basic Contract Patterns: No-Strike, No Lockout Pledges," 75 LRR 199 (1970), where it is also noted that some agreements limit union liability for violation of the no-strike pledge, particularly in regard to unauthorized strikes which the union makes sincere effort to terminate. As to thus limiting the union's liability, also see West Penn Power Co., 11 LA 166, 176 (Dash, 1948). That the no-strike ban and the no-lockout ban are not always coextensive is well illustrated by General Electric Co., 54 LA 660, 673 (Wildebush, 1969).

[24] Local 174 Teamsters v. Lucas Flour Co., 82 S.Ct. 571, 49 LRRM 2717 (1962).

[25] Major Collective Bargaining Agreements: Arbitration Procedures 5 (U.S. Dept. of Labor Bull. No. 1425-6, 1966), where 1,717 agreements were analyzed for arbitration clauses.

[26] Ibid. Also see Moore & Nix, "Arbitration Provisions in Collective Agreements, 1952," 76 Monthly Lab. Rev. 261 (Bureau of Lab. Stat., 1953).

[27] For example, see Arbitrator Leach in 52 LA 688, 690, 693 and in 48 LA 299, 301–302; Dworkin in 49 LA 370, 371–372; McKelvey in 49 LA 290, 291.

[28] Major Collective Bargaining Agreements: Arbitration Procedures 95 (U.S. Dept. of Labor Bull. No. 1425-6, 1966). There are marked differences between the United States and Great Britain in the use of arbitration. "In Great Britain arbitration is used to a significant extent to settle disputes over the terms of

strike is becoming outmoded even for contract negotiation disputes and that the use of voluntary arbitration with proper safeguards may be preferable.[29]

Advantages of Arbitration Over Litigation

Arbitration claims among its advantages the expertise of a specialized tribunal and the saving of time, expense, and trouble. While it is true that the courts of some jurisdictions have recognized that parties to collective agreements have legally enforceable rights thereunder, the costly, prolonged, and technical procedures of courts are not well adapted to the peculiar needs of labor-management relations. Arbitration, on the other hand, is more satisfactory "where a speedy decision by men with a practical knowledge of the subject is desired."[30]

The U.S. Supreme Court has acknowledged that arbitration, rather than court litigation, is the superior method of resolving disputes under collective agreements:

> "The labor arbitrator performs functions which are not normal to the courts; the considerations which help him fashion judgments may indeed be foreign to the competence of courts. * * * The parties expect that his judgment of a particular grievance will reflect not only what the contract says but, insofar as the collective bargaining agreement permits, such factors as the effect upon productivity of a particular result, its consequence to the morale of the shop, his judgment whether tensions will be heightened or diminished. For the parties' objective in using the arbitration process is primarily to further their common goal of uninterrupted production under the agreement, to make the agreement serve their specialized needs. The ablest judge cannot be expected to bring the same experience and competence

---

new agreements, but is used only rarely to settle minor disputes." Morrison and Marjorie Handsaker, "Arbitration in Great Britain," 1 Industrial Relations 117, 135 (1961). Also see Fairweather, "American and Foreign Grievance Systems," Developments in American and Foreign Arbitration 1 (The Bureau of National Affairs, Inc., 1968).

[29] See Handsaker, "Changing Role of Arbitration and Changing Issues," Proceedings of N.Y.U. Fourteenth Annual Conference on Labor 183, 197–198 (1961); Taylor, "Making Arbitration Work," Challenges to Arbitration 101, 104–107 (BNA Incorporated, 1960). In 1970 the AFL-CIO announced a joint labor-management effort, under the aegis of the American Arbitration Association, to explore the possibility of voluntary arbitration as a substitute for strikes in bargaining. "Labor-Management Plans for Voluntary Arbitration Study," 75 LRR 280 (1970).

[30] Webster v. Van Allen, 216 N.Y.S. 552, 554 (N.Y. Sup. Ct. App. Div., 1926).

to bear upon the determination of a grievance, because he cannot be similarly informed."[31]

Parties to an industrial dispute must "live with" the judgment or award rendered by the adjudicator. Courts of general jurisdiction are not often versed in labor relations problems. This recognized, some countries have established labor courts as a part of their judicial system. Scholars have noted that European labor courts serve different and broader purposes than do American arbitration tribunals, and they have advised that labor courts do not offer a ready alternative to grievance arbitration in America.[32] However, one of the similarities between the two systems should be noted: like labor courts, arbitrators are presumed to be familiar with the needs and techniques of industrial relations, so parties generally will be able to "live with" their awards.

The parties can make arbitration, as compared to litigation, relatively quick and inexpensive. Sometimes it takes only a few days from the appointment of the arbitrator until the issuance of his award, although in the bulk of the cases several weeks or even several months are required. The issues taken to arbitration have become increasingly complex and the time required for arbitration has naturally tended to increase as a result of this complexity of issues. Also, it frequently happens that the arbitrator chosen by the parties cannot be quickly available due to existing commitments to other parties. Nor are the parties themselves always quickly available for the arbitration hearing.

---

[31] United Steelworkers v. Warrior & Gulf Navigation Company, 80 S.Ct. 1347, 1352–1353 (1960). Not everyone agrees that arbitration is the superior process for grievances. In 1964 U.S. Court of Appeals Judge Paul R. Hays (a former arbitrator) launched a massive assault on the institution of labor arbitration. Hays, Labor Arbitration: A Dissenting View (Yale Univ. Press, 1966), the 1964 Storrs Lectures on Jurisprudence. For responses to the critics of arbitration, see Luskin, "The Presidential Address: Arbitration and Its Critics," Developments in American and Foreign Arbitration 125 (The Bureau of National Affairs, Inc., 1968); Smith, "The Presidential Address," Problems of Proof in Arbitration 74 (The Bureau of National Affairs, Inc., 1967); Straus, "Labor Arbitration and its Critics," 20 Arb. J. 197 (1965). An overwhelming majority of union and management officials contacted in one survey prefer the arbitration process to the available alternatives as a method of ultimate resolution of grievance disputes. Jones & Smith, "Management and Labor Appraisals and Criticisms of the Arbitration Process: A Report with Comments," 62 Mich. L. Rev. 1115, 1116–1117 (1964).

[32] Aaron, "Labor Courts: Western European Models and Their Significance for the United States," 16 U.C.L.A. L. Rev. 847, 876 (1969); Fleming, "The Presidential Address: The Labor Court Idea," The Arbitrator, the NLRB, and the Courts 229, 246 (The Bureau of National Affairs, Inc., 1967). For earlier discussions of labor courts, see Handsaker, "Labor Courts in Germany," 8 Arb. J. (N.S) 131 (1953); Lenhoff, "Some Basic Features of American and European Labor Law: A Comparison," 26 Notre Dame Law 389 (1951).

Nonetheless, arbitration continues to be relatively speedy as compared to litigation.[33]

Since the parties arbitrate voluntarily, prompt compliance with the award is obtained in most cases. Only infrequently is court action required for the enforcement or vacation of awards.[34]

Arbitration of Public Employee Disputes

With the tremendous growth of employee organization and collective bargaining in the public sector in the 1960's has come the rapidly expanding use of arbitration for public employee disputes. This development has been particularly important since federal and state employees continue to be restricted by the traditional prohibition against strikes by public employees. Neutral dispute settlement machinery is essential in the public sector if organizational and bargaining rights are to have any real substance.[35]

In 1962 federal employees were granted organizational and bargaining rights by President Kennedy's Executive Order 10988. These rights were further advanced by President Nixon's Executive Order 11491 of 1969, which made certain changes to coordinate, strengthen, and clarify the program.

Executive Order 10988 permitted the use of advisory (not binding) arbitration, and such arbitration was in fact used for representation, bargaining unit, and grievance issues in federal employment.[36]

---

[33] For statistics and discussions of the time required for arbitration, see Fleming, The Labor Arbitration Process 57-77 (Univ. of Ill. Press, 1965); "Survey of Arbitration in 1964," Proceedings of 18th Annual Meeting of National Academy of Arbitrators 246, 253-254 (BNA Incorporated, 1965); "Survey of Arbitration in 1962," Labor Arbitration—Perspectives and Problems 297, 315-316 (BNA Incorporated, 1964); Fleming, "The Labor Arbitration Process: 1943-1963," Labor Arbitration—Perspectives and Problems 43-46, 54 (1964); Ross, "The Well-Aged Arbitration Case," 11 Ind. & Lab. Rel. Rev. 262 (1958).

[34] For statistics, see Chapter 2, Legal Status of Arbitration.

[35] Concerning the continued prohibition against strikes, see Sullivan, "How Can the Problem of the Public Employees Strike be Resolved?" 19 Okla. L. Rev. 365, 380 (1966). On the special need for neutral dispute machinery, see Zack, "Why Public Employees Strike," 23 Arb. J. 69 (1968); Triborough Bridge & Tunnel Authority, 49 LA 1212, 1224-1228 (Wolf, Feinberg & Stockman, 1968). For a discussion of foreign experience, see Panel Discussion, "Foreign Experience in Public Employee Disputes," Arbitration and the Expanding Role of Neutrals 125 (The Bureau of National Affairs, Inc., 1970).

[36] See Rehmus, "Arbitration of Representation and Bargaining Unit Questions

Under Executive Order 11491, provision is made for representation disputes, grievances, and contract-negotiation disputes as follows:[37]

Provision is made for representation elections under the supervision of the Assistant Secretary of Labor for Labor-Management Relations, and this official decides questions as to the appropriate unit.

Negotiated procedures may provide for arbitration of employee grievances and of disputes over the interpretation or application of collective agreements between federal agencies and labor organizations. Either party may file exceptions to an arbitrator's award with the Federal Labor Relations Council.

Arbitration or third-party fact-finding may be used to resolve negotiation impasses, but only when authorized or directed by the Federal Service Impasses Panel (which itself may choose to make a final decision on the impasse).[38]

The labor relations problems of state and municipal employees are not covered by federal statutes or regulations. Following the federal lead, however, a sizeable number of states and some municipalities have acted to authorize organizational and bargaining activities by state and municipal employees (some provisions cover limited classes of employees such as teachers, firemen, and/or policemen, while other provisions apply to broad classes such as "state employees" or "municipal employees").[39]

---

in Public Employment Disputes," The Arbitrator, the NLRB, and the Courts 251, 252–256 (The Bureau of National Affairs, Inc., 1967); Rock, "Role of the Neutral in Grievance Arbitration in Public Employment," id. at 260, 262–268. For a general discussion of Executive Order 10988, see Craver, "Bargaining in the Federal Sector," 19 Lab. L. J. 569 (1968). For examples of advisory arbitration under Order 10988, see Arbitrator Koven in 51 LA 336; Dash in 50 LA 143; Kesselman in 49 LA 784. On Executive Order 11491, see Arbitrator Dworkin in 55 LA 236, 238–239.

[37] §§ 6, 10, 14, 17.

[38] For discussion of the Executive Orders and of federal labor relations in general, see Weber, "Federal Labor Relations: Problems and Prospects," Arbitration and the Public Interest 148 (The Bureau of National Affairs, Inc., 1971).

[39] See Smith, Merrifield, & St. Antoine, Labor Relations Law 790–792 (4th Ed., 1968); Weisenfeld, "The Philosophy of Bargaining For Municipal Employees," 22 Arb. J. 40 (1967); Sullivan, "How Can the Problem of the Public Employees Strike be Resolved?" 19 Okla. L. Rev. 365 (1966); Stutz, "Collective Bargaining by City Employees," 15 Lab. L. J. 696 (1964). For related articles, see Wellington & Winter, "Limits of Collective Bargaining in Public Employment," 78 Yale L. J. 1107 (1969); Smith, "State and Local Advisory Reports on Public Employment Labor Legislation: A Comparative Analysis," 67 Mich. L. Rev. 891 (1969); White, "Rights and Responsibilities in Municipal Bargaining," 22 Arb. J. 31 (1967).

Since 1960 there has been a significant increase in the use of fact-finding for state and municipal employee disputes.[40] There likewise has been a significant increase in the use of arbitration. Concerning the use of arbitration, state and municipal provisions vary widely as to classes of employees covered, the subjects which may be arbitrated, whether arbitration is to be voluntary or compulsory, and whether the award is to be binding or only advisory.[41]

In the state and municipal area there has been some use of arbitration for representation issues[42] and for new contract disputes;[43] and it has been used extensively for the resolution of grievances.[44] Grievance arbitration, in particular, is growing rapidly at the state and local level and will continue to do so.[45]

---

[40] For discussion of the authorization and use of fact-finding in the public sector, see "The Use of Fact-Finding in the Public Employee Dispute Settlement," Arbitration and Social Change 95-133 (The Bureau of National Affairs, Inc., 1970), which includes articles by labor (Wurf), employer (Saxton), and neutral (Anderson) spokesmen; Jossen, "Fact-Finding: Is It Adjudication or Adjustment?" 24 Arb. J. 106 (1969). For examples of fact-finding in the public sector, see Fact-Finders Kerrison in 52 LA 1169; Teple in 52 LA 800, 802; Young in 51 LA 1134; Saltonstall in 51 LA 208; Bickal in 51 LA 58; McFadden, Gould, & Karnow in 49 LA 1229; Feinberg & Stockman in 49 LA 1212.

[41] See Staudohar, "Voluntary Binding Arbitration in Public Employment," 25 Arb. J. 30 (1970); Howlett, "Arbitration in the Public Sector," Southwest Legal Foundation 15th Annual Institute on Labor Law 231, 262–268 (1969); Teele, "Characteristics of Public Employment Arbitration Under a Massachusetts Law," 24 Arb. J. 239 (1969); Sullivan, "How Can the Problem of the Public Employees Strike Be Resolved?" 19 Okla. L. Rev. 365 (1966).

[42] See Rehmus, "Arbitration of Representation and Bargaining Unit Questions in Public Employment Disputes," The Arbitrator, the NLRB, and the Courts 251, 256–260 (The Bureau of National Affairs, Inc., 1967). An example is Rochester Board of Education, 49 LA 1004 (McKelvey, 1967).

[43] For examples of contract-negotiation arbitration, see Arbitrator Gillingham in 53 LA 361; Schmidt in 52 LA 1301; McDermott in 52 LA 233; Florey in 51 LA 994; Handsaker in 51 LA 879; Siegel in 50 LA 1036. Many other cases are cited in Chapter 18.

[44] In 1969 the American Arbitration Association reported that "virtually every collective bargaining agreement in the public sector, as in private industry, provides for arbitration of grievances. Hundreds of grievance arbitration cases have already resulted from recently negotiated collective bargaining agreements." Arbitration News, No. 3, March 1969. For proposals concerning what should be included in public employee grievance arbitration clauses, see Worcester Teachers' Assn., 54 LA 796, 805–806 (Fact-Finder Seidenberg, 1970); Lowell School Committee, 48 LA 1044, 1049–1050 (Fact-Finder Wallen, 1967).

[45] See Krislov & Peters, "Grievance Arbitration in State and Local Government: A Survey," 25 Arb. J. 196 (1970); Teele, "Characteristics of Public Employment Arbitration Under A Massachusetts Law," 24 Arb. J. 239, at 239 (1969); Rock, "Role of the Neutral in Grievance Arbitration in Public Employment," The Arbitrator, the NLRB, and the Courts 260, 268–283 (The Bureau of National Affairs, Inc., 1967).

Studies of grievance arbitration indicate that most issues in public sector arbitration do not differ from private sector issues and that arbitrators tend to apply the same standards in both areas.[46] In this general regard, the authors of one study have declared:

"Commentators on labor-management relations frequently stress the 'differences' between the public sector and the private sector. They conclude that labor relations in the public sector must, therefore, be different from that developed in the private sector. This study of the emerging patterns of grievance arbitration in state and local governments does not support this conclusion.

"On the contrary, the parties in state and local government have leaned heavily upon private industry's arbitration experience. A formidable case could be made that the parties have virtually adopted the grievance arbitration mechanism from private industry."[47]

Other Important Roles of Arbitration

We have noted that arbitration is a substitute for work stoppages and for litigation. But it is much more than a substitute. Professor Harry Shulman declared:

"To consider * * * arbitration as a substitute for court litagation or as the consideration for a no-strike pledge is to take a foreshortened view of it. In a sense it is a substitue for both—but in the sense in which a transport airplane is a substitute for a stagecoach. The arbitration is an integral part of the system of self-government. And the system is designed to aid management in its quest for efficiency, to assist union leadership in its participation in the enterprise, and to secure justice for the employees. It is a means of making collective bargaining work and thus preserving private enterprise in a free government."[48]

Professor George W. Taylor has observed that "In a very real sense, the parties who establish their own labor arbitration machinery

[46] See Krislov & Peters, "Grievance Arbitration in State and Local Government: A Survey," 25 Arb. J. 196, 205 (1970); Howlett, "Arbitration in the Public Sector," Southwest Legal Foundation 15th Annual Institute on Labor Law 231, 268–269 (1969). Also see Teele, "Characteristics of Public Employee Arbitration Under a Massachusetts Law," 24 Arb. J. 239, 248 (1969).

[47] Krislov & Peters, ibid.

[48] Shulman, "Reason, Contract, and Law in Labor Relations," 68 Harv. L. Rev. 999, 1024 (1955), reprinted in Management Rights and the Arbitration Process 169, 198 (BNA Incorporated, 1956).

create a judicial procedure where none has existed."[49] In this connection, not all jurisdictions hold that collective bargaining agreements give rights which are enforceable in the courts. Moreover, the National Labor Relations Board (NLRB) lacks jurisdiction over contract-interpretation disputes which do not involve unfair labor practice aspects, and it may refuse to exercise jurisdiction over interpretation disputes which do involve unfair labor practice allegations if the dispute is covered by an arbitration clause.[50]

Then, too, insofar as contract-negotiation disputes are concerned arbitration provides essentially the only available tribunal for the final and binding resolution of such disputes after negotiations and mediation have failed to produce a settlement. Thus, it is obvious that even aside from any consideration of work stoppages and their avoidance, cases are taken to arbitration simply to obtain an answer to the dispute.

Another role of arbitration was recognized by the U.S. Supreme Court in emphasizing that the "processing of even frivolous claims may have therapeutic values."[51] This role has been described by Professor Louis L. Jaffe in such manner as also to portray realistically the spirit of the arbitration hearing:

"Arbitration * * * is a school, an arena, a theater. Everyone both participates and observes. The whole company of actors—arbitrator, union and employer officials, the griever, and the witnesses (mostly employees)—sits at one table. Argument, assertion, testimony, charge and countercharge, even angry abuse—sometimes spontaneous, sometimes 'for the record'—flow freely in quick, continuous intercourse. The arbitrator may let the discussion take its head for a moment, then rein it in; an occasional question, a request for clarification. Because the process is relatively free, it may assume many forms, some quiet and orderly, some volatile and discordant. The form is in fact a function of the general labor relations—of the maturity, the degree of mutual understanding and respect, the intelligence, of the opposing officials. * * *

"Arbitration takes its stand in the very current of industrial life. The scene, the dramatis personae, the vocabulary, being familiar, raise

---

[49] Statement by Professor Taylor in Preface to Freidin, Labor Arbitration and the Courts (1952).

[50] For discussion of the Board's policy and practice in regard to deferring to arbitration, see Chapter 10, subtopic titled "The NLRA, the Arbitrator, and the NLRB."

[51] United Steelworkers of America v. American Manufacturing Co., 80 S.Ct. 1343, 1346–1347 (1960).

no barriers to comprehension. The worker sees his case analyzed by his leaders, among whom I include employer as well as union officials. They reveal the clashing propositions at the heart of the grievance. The arbitrator relates his answer to basic industrial premises. * * *"[52]

Finally, it may be noted that a union might arbitrate a dispute because the employees or subordinate union officers directly involved simply could not be convinced that they were wrong; the company might do likewise in regard to its own subordinate officials. In either instance, higher officials may find it preferable to let an arbitrator make it clear to such persons that they were wrong.[53]

Arbitration and National War Labor Board

A great impetus in the use of arbitration was given by the National War Labor Board during World War II. The work of the Board constitutes an extensive experience in the use of arbitration. It was created by executive order in 1942 and was given statutory authority by the War Labor Disputes Act in 1943. Most of the 20,000 labor dispute cases determined by the Board during the war emergency were disputes over the terms of collective agreements. Of special importance was the Board's policy of requiring the use of clauses providing for arbitration of future disputes over the interpretation or application of the agreement. This policy of the Board laid the foundation for the popular practice today of terminating the contract grievance procedure with the final step of arbitration.[54]

Recommendations of the President's National Labor-Management Conference of 1945

The President's National Labor-Management Conference of 1945 was called for the purpose of laying the groundwork for industrial peace by studying the major causes of industrial strife and possibilities for their elimination. It was attended by delegates representing the American Federation of Labor, the United States Chamber of Commerce, the Congress of Industrial Organizations, the National

---

[52] Jaffe, "Labor Arbitration and the Individual Worker," The Annals of the American Academy of Political and Social Science 34, 40–41 (May, 1953).

[53] See Ahner, "Arbitration: A Management Viewpoint," The Arbitrator and the Parties 76, 80 (BNA Incorporated, 1958); Killingsworth, "Arbitration: Its Uses in Industrial Relations," 21 LA 859, 865 (1953).

[54] See Freidin & Ulman, "Arbitration and the War Labor Board," 58 Harv. L. Rev. 309 (1945).

Association of Manufacturers, the United Mine Workers of America, and the Railway Brotherhoods.

In regard to the setting of new contract terms the Conference recommended that parties first undertake good-faith collective bargaining and therafter, if necessary, conciliation and consideration of voluntary arbitration. It recommended, however, that, before voluntary arbitration is accepted, the parties should agree upon the precise issues to be decided, the terms of the submission, and principles or factors by which the arbitrator is to be governed.[55]

As to the settlement of grievances or disputes involving the interpretation or application of the agreement, the Conference recommended:

"4. The parties should provide by mutual agreement for the final determination of any unsettled grievances of disputes involving the interpretation or application of the agreement by an impartial chairman, umpire, arbitrator, or board. In this connection the agreement should provide:

"(a) A definite and mutually agreed-upon procedure of selecting the impartial chairman, umpire, arbitrator, or board;

"(b) That the impartial chairman, umpire, arbitrator, or board should have no power to add to, subtract from, change, or modify any provision of the agreement, but should be authorized only to interpret the existing provisions of the agreement and apply them to the specific facts of the grievance or dispute;

"(c) That reference of a grievance or dispute to an impartial chairman, umpire, arbitrator, or board should be reserved as the final step in the procedure and should not be resorted to unless the settlement procedures of the earlier steps have been exhausted;

"(d) That the decision of the impartial chairman, umpire, arbitrator, or board should be accepted by both parties as final and binding;

"(e) That the cost of such impartial chairman, umpire, arbitrator, or board should be shared equally by both parties.

"5. Any question not involving the application or interpretation of the agreement as then existing but which may properly be raised pursuant to agreement provisions should be subject to negotiation, conciliation, or such other means of settlement as the parties may provide."[56]

---

[55] The President's National Labor-Management Conference, Nov. 5–30, 1945 (U.S. Dept. of Labor, Div. of Labor Standards, Bull. No. 77, pp. 42–43, 1946).
[56] Id. at 46–47.

Compulsory Arbitration

Although there are obvious and fundamental differences between voluntary and compulsory arbitration, many of the considerations involved in the use of compulsory arbitration are helpful in an analysis of voluntary arbitration. These considerations help define the area of desirable use of voluntary arbitration. They also indicate pitfalls that may be faced in the use of arbitration generally.

Compulsory arbitration has been defined by the Department of Labor to mean a "process of settlement of employer-labor disputes by a government agency (or other means provided by government) which has power to investigate and make an award which *must* be accepted by all parties concerned."[57] Stated otherwise, compulsory arbitration "is that required by law."[58]

Thus, even where neither party wishes to arbitrate, both may be required to do so under compulsory arbitration. At times there has been agitation for legislation to subject all types of labor-management disputes to compulsory arbitration where settlement by any but a peaceful procedure would result in severe loss or hardship to third persons or the general public. While there is considerable support for use of compulsory arbitration in such situations, its use otherwise is generally opposed by labor and management alike.[59]

The principal argument in favor of compulsory arbitration is that unions and industries have grown so large and our economy has become so intermeshed that one strike can paralyze a large part of the nation. This consideration is particularly urgent where the strike interferes with national defense. Moreover, local critical disputes, such

---

[57] "Should the Federal Government Require Arbitration of Labor Disputes in All Basic American Industries?" 26 Cong. Dig. 193, 195 (1947).

[58] C.C.H. Dictionary of Labor Terms. For discussions of the development of compulsory arbitration in the United States and abroad, see Northrup, Compulsory Arbitration and Government Intervention in Labor Disputes 9–50 (Labor Policy Association, 1966); Williams, "The Compulsory Settlement of Contract Negotiation Labor Disputes," 27 Texas L. Rev. 587 (1949).

[59] See statistics and views in Warren & Bernstein, "A Profile of Labor Arbitration," 16 LA 970, 972–973 (1951). The general opposition to compulsory arbitration also is reflected in, for example, Farmer, "Compulsory Arbitration—A Management Lawyer's View," 51 Va. L. Rev. 396 (1965); Feller, "Compulsory Arbitration—A Union Lawyer's View," 51 Va. L. Rev. 410 (1965); "Report of American Bar Association Sub-Committee on Labor Arbitration Law," 35 LA 949, 949–951 (1960).

as those in transportation and public utility enterprises, can severely burden the general public. Proponents of compulsory arbitration contend that in such cases governmental action is warranted to protect the general welfare; that, when collective bargaining, mediation, and all other steps have failed, the government should step in as a last resort to prevent ruinous strikes, and, as a *quid pro quo,* provide for the settlement of the issues on their merits.[60]

It has also been urged that compulsory arbitration is necessary in a relationship where workers are not free to engage in collective bargaining in its fullest sense, namely, in the area of public employment.[61]

The arguments against compulsory arbitration as revealed in literature on the subject are, broadly stated, that (A) it is incompatible with free collective bargaining, (B) it will not produce satisfactory solutions to disputes, (C) it may involve great enforcement problems, and (D) it will have damaging effects upon our economic structure.[62] These arguments in more detail, again as revealed in the aforementioned literature, are:

(A)   That compulsory arbitration is the antithesis of free collective bargaining. Each party will be reluctant to offer compromises

---

[60] "Should the Federal Government Require Arbitration of Labor Disputes in All Basic American Industries?" 26 Cong. Dig. 193, 208 (1947). Also see Richberg, "Industrial Disputes and the Public Interest—I," Institute of Ind. Rel., U. of Calif., 59, 60 (1947); Huebner, "Compulsory Arbitration of Labor Disputes," 30 J. Am. Jud. Soc. 123 (1946).

[61] Schwartz, "Is Compulsory Arbitration Necessary?" 15 Arb. J. 189, 200 (1960). "The most significant arguments against compulsory arbitration are inapplicable in the area of public employment." Id. at 194. Also see Seinsheimer, "What's so Terrible About Compulsory Arbitration?" 26 Arb. J. 219 (1971). Urging "last offer arbitration," see Garber, "Compulsory Arbitration in the Public Sector: A Proposed Alternative," 26 Arb. J. 226 (1971).

[62] For writings in which various of these and related arguments are asserted or noted, see Kennedy, "Freedom to Strike Is in the Public Interest," Harvard Business Review, July-Aug. 1970, 45; Farmer, "Compulsory Arbitration—A Management Lawyer's View," 51 Va. L. Rev. 396 (1965); Feller, "Compulsory Arbitration—A Union Lawyer's View," 51 Va. L. Rev. 410 (1965); Van de Water, "Involuntary Arbitration and National Defense," 18 Arb. J. 96 (1963); Keel, The Pros and Cons of Compulsory Arbitration 18–24 (N.Y. Chamber of Commerce, 1961); Dash, "The Academy and Public Opinion," Challenges to Arbitration 1, 8–12 (BNA Incorporated, 1960), summarizing arguments of George W. Taylor, John T. Dunlop, and Thomas Kennedy against compulsory arbitration; Schwartz, "Is Compulsory Arbitration Necessary?" 15 Arb. J. 189 (1960); "Should the Federal Government Require Arbitration of Labor Disputes in All Basic American Industries?" 26 Cong. Dig. 193, 203–221 (1947), where strong opposition to compulsory arbitration was voiced by high government, labor, and management officials.

in bargaining for fear that they may prejudice its position in arbitration. Elimination of the strike from collective bargaining will eliminate the strongest incentive which the parties now have to reach agreement. One or both of the parties may make only a pretense at bargaining in the belief that more desirable terms may be obtained through the arbitration which is assured if bargaining fails. Since compulsory arbitration will be used to resolve unknown future disputes, both sides may list many demands and drop few in bargaining, believing that little will be lost if some of the "chaff" is denied by an arbitrator (who the party may believe would then be more inclined to favor that party on major issues in order to appear fair).

(B) That compulsory arbitration is a dictatorial and imitative process rather than a democratic and creative one. The parties cannot select the arbitrator and cannot specify the standards or criteria for his decision. If terms of employment are determined by legislation or by arbitration required by law, rules may emerge for uniform application to all parties regardless of their individual character and needs. Compulsory arbitration means an imposed decision which will often fail to satisfy either party, rather than an acceptable settlement based upon a meeting of the minds.

(C) That compulsion generates resistance and is a source of further conflict. There may be serious difficulty of enforcement of compulsory orders, with the attendant danger of divulging the impotence of government.

(D) That compulsory arbitration means governmental—politically influenced—determination of wages, and will inevitably lead to governmental regulation of prices, production, and profits; it threatens not only free collective bargaining but also the free market and enterprise system.

The most extensive experience (over 60 years) with compulsory arbitration is that of Australia. Writers who have studied the Australian system are by no means in agreement as to its degree of success, but they all agree that it has not eliminated strikes.[63] Indeed, an extensive study of compulsory arbitration experience in various countries led to the unqualified conclusion that compulsory arbitration "Does

---

[63] See Northrup, Compulsory Arbitration and Government Intervention in Labor Disputes 35–44 (Labor Policy Assn., 1966); Sykes, "Labor Regulation by Courts: The Australian Experience," 52 Northwestern U. L. Rev. 462 (1957); Merrifield, "Wage Determination Under Compulsory Arbitration: Margins For Skill in Australia," 24 Geo. Wash. L. Rev. 267 (1956); Oxnam, "Industrial Arbitration in Australia," 9 Ind. & Lab. Rel. Rev. 610 (1956). Some work stoppages may be legal, as explained by Levinson, "The New Zealand Waterfront Industry Tribunal," 25 Arb. J. 261 (1970).

not insure industrial peace, but rather can breed strikes, especially short ones."[64]

In 1920 Kansas enacted a compulsory arbitration act which set up a court of industrial relations for disputes in industries affecting the public interest. Broad interpretation of the Kansas law led to its application to industries other than public utilities. In 1923 the U.S. Supreme Court declared the wage-fixing provisions of the statute unconstitutional as violating the "due process" clause of the Fourteenth Amendment.[65] In light of more recent decisions of the Supreme Court, however, it seems possible that the exercise of similar power by the states now would withstand constitutional challenge (apart from federal preemption).[66] The Pennsylvania Supreme Court has upheld that state's public employee (policemen and firemen), compulsory arbitration statute against challenge under the state and federal (Fourteenth Amendment) constitutions.[67]

Some states have enacted compulsory arbitration statutes for their public utilities. These statutes prohibit work stoppages and either provide for outright compulsory arbitration or require the use of settlement procedures which amount to compulsory arbitration. This legislation, much of which was adopted about 1947, evidenced a growing public concern over work stoppages which cause hardship to the general consuming public. However, in 1951 the United States Supreme Court held that state power in this field must fall where the state law conflicts with the Labor-Management Relations Act.[68] Thus the

---

[64] Northrup, Compulsory Arbitration and Government Intervention in Labor Disputes 206 (Labor Policy Assn., 1966), where Professor Northrup also states the conclusion that compulsory arbitration does not necessarily further the economic or social policies of government, but in fact may work against such policies; that it enhances union power and growth, especially through political action; and that it discourages collective bargaining.

[65] Chas. Wolff Packing Co. v. Court of Industrial Relations of Kansas, 43 S.Ct. 630 (1923).

[66] For a survey of decisions which bear upon the matter, see Fairview Hospitals v. Hospital Employees, 22 LA 279, 282–289 (Minn. Sup. Ct., 1954). See also Spruck, "Compulsory Arbitration of Labor Disputes," 47 Mich. L. Rev. 242 (1948).

[67] Harney v. Russo, 255 A.2d 560, 71 LRRM 2817 (Pa. Sup. Ct., 1969). The Wyoming statute was upheld under that state's constitution in State v. City of Laramie, 437 P.2d 295 (Wyo. Sup. Ct., 1968).

[68] Amalgamated Association etc. v. Wisconsin ERB, 71 S.Ct. 359, 27 LRRM 2385 (1951). A state "plant seizure" statue was similarly invalidated on federal preemption grounds in Division 1287 v. Missouri, 83 S.Ct. 1657, 53 LRRM 2394 (1963). For a discussion of experience under the state public utility statutes prior to these decisions, see Northrup, Compulsory Arbitration and Government

supremacy of federal regulation constitutes a potent barrier to the application of state compulsory arbitration laws to workers covered by the federal statute.

In 1963 Congress enacted its first peacetime compulsory arbitration law, providing for the compulsory arbitration of diesel firemen and crew consist issues in the railroad industry. The neutral members of that compulsory arbitration board expressed regrets that this Congressional action was required:

"We write this opinion as the neutral members of a statutory arbitration board—a board whose creation was virtually forced upon Congress as the only way of avoiding a nationwide railroad strike. Never before in peacetime has Congress found it necessary to take such action. We wish at the very outset to record our regret that in this case the leaders of the railroad industry and the railroad operating unions were unable to agree upon some method of resolving their differences which would avoid the need for Congressional intervention. The great virtue of arbitration as it has developed in this country's labor relations has been the fact that it was a *voluntary* procedure, created and shaped by the disputing companies and unions themselves and thus responsive to their peculiar problems, values, and needs. It is unfortunate that the parties in this case, though finally agreeing in principle to arbitration, failed to agree upon the terms and procedures of an arbitration agreement and thereby abandoned to Congress an opportunity and responsibility that should rightly have been theirs."[69]

Congress next enacted special legislation for the compulsory arbitration of a specific dispute (railroad shopcrafts) in 1967. This approach of using ad hoc compulsory arbitration by special Congressional action (and only infrequently) is viewed in some quarters as less damaging and potentially more beneficial than any general provision for compulsory arbitration.[70] A similar use of ad hoc compulsory arbitration would be to include it in a so-called "arsenal of weapons"

Intervention in Labor Disputes 24–33 (Labor Policy Assn., 1966). Some of the statutes have subsequently been repealed.

[69] Railroads v. Operating Brotherhoods, 41 LA 673, 680 (Aaron, Healy, & Seward, 1963). This dispute is discussed by Levinson, "The Locomotive Firemen's Dispute," 17 Lab. L. J. 671 (1966); Kaufman, "The Railroad Labor Dispute: A Marathon of Maneuver and Improvisation," 18 Ind. & Lab. Rel. Rev. 196 (1965).

[70] See Farmer, "Compulsory Arbitration—A Management Lawyer's View," 51 Va. L. Rev. 396, 405–406 (1965). But in other quarters the ad hoc approach is viewed as discriminatory and not to be preferred. See Wyle, "Compulsory Labor Arbitration and the National Welfare," 19 Arb. J. 98 (1964).

to be made available by Congress for use within the President's discretion in critical industrial disputes.

Arbitration Costs

A number of factors or elements may contribute to the ultimate cost of any given arbitration.[71] Some of the factors are largely within the control of the parties who, to this extent, have it within their power to reduce costs, as by avoiding unnecessary delays, making thorough preparation for the hearing, use of stipulations, nonuse of transcripts and briefs, and the like (this is not to suggest that the use of transcripts and briefs in proper cases is not justified and desirable).

The total cost of arbitration can be (and often is) considerably less than the cost of taking the dispute to court, just as the time required for arbitration can be (and often is) considerably less than would be required for court action. Of course, arbitration costs have increased with the increased complexity of issues being taken to arbitration. Then, too, arbitration costs have naturally risen along with the rise in the economic index. Nevertheless, arbitration continues to be well worth its dollar cost when considered in light of the great service (immediate and ultimate) which arbitration performs for employees and for the owners of the enterprise.

In some instances the arbitrator's fee and expenses will constitute the primary cost of arbitration. The parties and the arbitrator should always agree in advance, and usually do, as to his compensation or the basis upon which it is to be determined. Ad hoc arbitrators typically charge on a per diem basis for hearing time, travel time, and time spent studying the case and preparing the decision (permanent

---

[71] For discussion and statistics regarding the cost of arbitration, see Jaffee, "It's Your Money! Cutting the Cost of Labor Arbitration," 26 Arb. J. 161 (1971); Fleming, The Labor Arbitration Process 31–56 (Univ. of Ill. Press, 1965); Straus, "Charges Against and Challenges For Professional Arbitration," Labor Arbitration—Perspectives and Problems 214, 216–219 (BNA Incorporated, 1964); Jones & Smith, "Management and Labor Appraisals and Criticisms of the Arbitration Process: A Report with Comments," 62 Mich. L. Rev. 1115, 1141–1146 (1964); Fleming, "The Labor Arbitration Process," Labor Arbitration— Perspectives and Problems 33, 35–46 (1964); Bluestone, "Making Arbitration Work," Challenges to Arbitration 107–112 (BNA Incorporated, 1960); Aaron, "Labor Arbitration and Its Critics," 10 Lab. L. J. 605 (1959); "Procedural Aspects of Labor-Management Arbitration," 28 LA 933, 939–943 (1954 data); Warren & Bernstein, "A Profile of Labor Arbitration," 16 LA 970, 983–984 (1951).

arbitrators may be employed on a retainer basis).[72] The idea that there should be a fixed ratio of study days to hearing days is unrealistic:

> "The ratio theory has a surface plausibility; if the hearing lasts for only one day or less, it may seem reasonable to assume that the arbitrator will need no more than one or two days to dispose of it. Unfortunately for the theory and its proponents, however, the fact is that some of the knottiest problems are most easily presented. Again, two experienced practitioners can, in a day's time, by careful preparation, use of stipulations and skillful examination of witnesses, build a record that will keep the most conscientious arbitrator working for a week."[73]

If counsel is retained, then of course counsel fees are involved. Additional costs are also entailed when a transcript of the proceedings is desired.[74] However, there are no court costs.[75]

Arbitration costs, except for counsel fees, generally are shared by the parties. Even where the parties had reached no agreement as to costs, the arbitrator required equal division since such "is common practice in arbitration."[76] Occasionally the collective agreement will provide that the loser in arbitration shall pay all of the costs. This is contrary to the recommendation of the President's National Labor-Management Conference that the cost of the neutral "should be shared equally by both parties." It is highly undesirable from the standpoint of the arbitrator and, it would seem, from the standpoint of the best interests of the parties.[77]

---

[72] For related discussion, see Chapter 7, subtopic titled "Arbitrator's Charges When Case is Cancelled."

[73] Aaron, "Labor Arbitration and Its Critics," 10 Labor L. J. 605, 645 (1959).

[74] See Chapter 7, topic titled "Transcript of Hearing."

[75] Parties who use the services of the American Arbitration Association pay an administrative fee.

[76] P. P. Williams Co., 24 LA 587, 592 (Reynard, 1955). In Schott's Bakery, Inc., 61-3 ARB ¶ 8675 (1961), Arbitrator Angus McSwain ruled that, unlike a court, he did not have power to award costs against a party who had unnecessarily caused an increase in arbitration costs. Cf., Arbitrator Getman in 48 LA 40, 43.

[77] In some instances under such provisions the arbitrator has assessed the costs against one party as the loser. See Arbitrator Hon in 53 LA 1298, 1301; Jaffee in 52 LA 1023, 1026; Keefe in 48 LA 373, 379; Dworkin in 38 LA 385, 388–389. In other cases, however, the arbitrator divided the costs equally since neither party lost all aspects of the case. See Arbitrator Klein in 48 LA 1058, 1065; Horvitz in 40 LA 522, 526; Pollard in 27 LA 611, 613; Emery in 22 LA 484, 489, and in 16 LA 454, 457. In W. O. Larson Foundry Co., 42 LA 1286, 1293 (1964), Arbitrator Kates assessed his fee 80 percent against the union and 20 percent against the company.

National Academy of Arbitrators

The National Academy of Arbitrators (NAA) is a nonprofit, professional, and honorary association of arbitrators.[78] While many of our most experienced arbitrators are included among the NAA's members, the Academy is not an agency for the selection of arbitrators. Rather, it was founded in 1947 to establish and foster high standards of conduct and competence for labor-management arbitrators and to promote the study and understanding of the arbitration process. The Academy conducts an extensive and highly important educational program through its various committees, study groups, and annual meetings. The proceedings of the annual meetings, including all important committee reports, have been published by The Bureau of National Affairs, Inc., and thus are easily available to all persons interested in arbitration.[79]

Government Agencies Serving Arbitration

The Federal Mediation and Conciliation Service's (FMCS) "basic arbitration function has come to be the maintenance of a roster" from which the Service can nominate arbitrators to the parties, and "the suggesting of certain procedures and guides that [the Service believes] will enhance the acceptability of arbitration as an alternative to the use of economic force in the industrial arena."[80]

---

[78] The Academy's Constitution and By-Laws as amended in 1965 are published in Proceedings of the 18th Annual Meeting of the National Academy of Arbitrators 207–218 (BNA Incorporated. 1965). For full discussion of the Academy, see Larkin, "Introduction: The First Decade," Critical Issues in Labor Arbitration, viii–xvi. Also see "The National Academy After Twelve Years: A Symposium," Challenges to Arbitration 13–38 (BNA Incorporated, 1960).

[79] The Profession of Labor Arbitration (selected papers from 1948–1954 proceedings); Arbitration Today (1955 proceedings); Management Rights and the Arbitration Process (1956 proceedings); Critical Issues in Labor Arbitration (1957 proceedings); The Arbitrator and the Parties (1958 proceedings); Arbitration and the Law (1959 proceedings); Challenges to Arbitration (1960 proceedings); Arbitration and Public Policy (1961 proceedings); Collective Bargaining and the Arbitrator's Role (1962 proceedings); Labor Arbitration and Industrial Change (1963 proceedings); Labor Arbitration—Perspectives and Problems (1964 proceedings); Proceedings of the 18th Annual Meeting of the National Academy of Arbitrators (1965 proceedings); Problems of Proof in Arbitration (1966 proceedings); The Arbitrator, the NLRB, and the Courts (1967 proceedings); Developments in American and Foreign Arbitration (1968 proceedings); Arbitration and Social Change (1969 proceedings); Arbitration and the Expanding Role of Neutrals (1970 proceedings); Arbitration and the Public Interest (1971 proceedings).

[80] Finnegan, "Federal Mediation and Conciliation Service," Management Rights and the Arbitration Process 96 (BNA Incorporated, 1956).

The National Mediation Board (NMB) performs important functions in the promotion of arbitration and the selection of arbitrators for the railroad and airline industries under the Railway Labor Act (RLA). These functions are described in detail in Chapter 4.

The various state mediation agencies likewise perform services in the furtherance and assistance of arbitration. The New York State Board of Mediation, for instance, maintains a panel of private arbitrators, and the Board's members and staff also serve as arbitrators.

American Arbitration Association

The American Arbitration Association (AAA) is a private, non-profit organization which offers services and facilities for voluntary arbitration. It is an administrative agency solely, never acting as arbitrator. It maintains panels from which arbitrators may be selected, and it provides administrative personnel and procedures for cases being arbitrated under its rules.[81]

The AAA is "devoted to the development and extension of the use of arbitration for the settlement of disputes in all fields of human endeavor."[82] In this connection, the AAA conducts an extensive educational program through its various publications and through its promotion of arbitration conferences at colleges and universities.

The Labor Management Institute (a Division of the American Arbitration Association) offers services as a neutral secretariat in arranging for bargaining and advises parties on techniques for resolution of conflicts that have been developed through experience in other industries and in other parts of the country. The Institute is available to help parties evolve specialized machinery to solve their particular problem.[83]

---

[81] The AAA's Labor Arbitration Rules are published in full in 43 LA 1292. An earlier version is published in 30 LA 1086.

[82] Braden, "Policy and Practice of American Arbitration Association," Management Rights and the Arbitration Process 84, 93 (BNA Incorporated, 1956).

[83] For another reference to the Institute's activities, see "The Labor Management Institute," 20 Arb. J. 10 (1965).

CHAPTER 2

LEGAL STATUS OF ARBITRATION

By and large the law has played a relatively limited role in labor-management arbitration in the United States.[1] Fundamentally, arbitration has been and still is a product of private contract between labor and management,[2] although in a significant sense arbitration has become "federalized" as to legal status.[3]

Through the years private contract and custom have shaped the principal features of arbitration. Having chosen arbitration as the best means of resolving their differences, the parties in the vast majority of cases have honored their agreement to arbitrate by proceeding faithfully to arbitration, by presenting their case informally but fully to the arbitrator, and by carrying out his award as the final disposition of the dispute—probably giving little or no thought to the legal status of arbitration at any time during the entire process.[4] In any event, in only a very small percentage of cases has court action been instituted in connection with any aspect of the arbitration.[5]

---

[1] Except where expressly stated otherwise, the term "arbitration" wherever used in this book refers to voluntary arbitration.

[2] "The uniqueness enjoyed by arbitration as a system of industrial jurisprudence is that it is the creature of the parties. It is created by them, and its limits, rules and regulations are established and may be changed by them." McDermott, "Arbitrability: the Courts Versus the Arbitrator," 23 Arb. J. 18, 19 (1968).

[3] See this Chapter, topic titled "Federal Law." One authority concluded that court decisions have not changed "the fact that grievance arbitration is basically a private system of jurisprudence," though federal court decisions have had an important effect in making both the arbitration agreement and the award enforceable and have set the stage for the establishment of other rules by court action. Fleming, The Labor Arbitration Process 28 (U. of Ill. Press, 1965).

[4] "The efficacy of grievance arbitration is founded on the pledge of the disputing parties that the arbitrator's award would be final and binding." Major Collective Bargaining Agreements: Arbitration Procedures 73 (U.S. Dept. of Labor Bull. No. 1425–6, 1966).

[5] Over the years the percentage appears to have varied from less than 1 percent to 1.5 percent per year. See the NAA Committee on Law and Legislation estimate for five-year period through 1968, "Arbitration and Federal Rights Under Collective Agreements in 1968," Arbitration and Social Change 187,

In turn, the courts and the legislatures generally have honored the "private contract" nature of arbitration by wisely limiting their roles in the process.

Indeed, the role of the law has been largely limited to the preliminaries and the "postliminaries" of the arbitration process. That is, the law has been concerned primarily with the enforceability of agreements to arbitrate, at the outset, and with the review and enforcement of awards at the close. The heart of the arbitration process, from the time the arbitrator is selected until his award has been issued, has been left largely within the exclusive control of and determination by the parties and their arbitrator. The temperance of the law, avoiding undue interference with the arbitration process, has permitted the high degree of flexibility essential to the success of the process.

However, even the limited role of law in the arbitration process involves some complex problems. The present book deals primarily with that part of the arbitration process which falls largely within the exclusive determination of the parties and their arbitrator; it does not deal extensively with either the legal status of arbitration or the problems involved in determining that status precisely for any given case. The Authors, however, do offer the following brief presentation of these matters, and they cite numerous detailed studies for the use of persons seeking deeper insight into the legal status of arbitration.[6]

In the remainder of this Chapter separate topics have been utilized for federal law and for state law (common law and statute). A final topic considers the matter of determining which of these categories might apply to the given case.

Federal Law

Federal statutes of significance to arbitration are the Federal Arbitration Act (FAA), the LMRA, and the RLA. The RLA deals extensively with arbitration and is discussed elsewhere in this book.[7]

---

210 (The Bureau of National Affairs, Inc. 1970). Also see "Procedural Aspects of Labor-Management Arbitration," 28 LA 933, 939 (1954 statistics); Howard, "Labor-Management Arbitration: 'There Ought to be a Law'—Or Ought There?" 21 Mo. L. Rev. 1, 18–20 (1956). For an illustration of the parties' willingness to comply even with distasteful awards, see Killingsworth, "Arbitration: Its Uses in Industrial Relations," 21 LA 859, 861 (1953).

[6] Throughout other parts of the book, also, the Authors refer briefly to relevant decisional and statutory law.

[7] See Chapters 3 and 4.

While the FAA (also called the United States Arbitration Act) provides significant support for arbitration, the courts have disagreed as to whether the Act applies to collective bargaining agreements. The issue is whether the Act's exclusion of "contracts of employment" applies only to individual employment contracts or also to collective agreements.[8] The Frankfurter dissent in *Lincoln Mills* contrues the majority opinion as a "silent" rejection of the FAA's applicability to collective agreement arbitration clauses.[9] Even assuming that the Act is not directly applicable to labor arbitration, however, it should not be overlooked as a guide for the courts in fashioning the body of law for labor arbitration under the *Lincoln Mills* decision.[10]

The LMRA of 1947 lends policy support to arbitration by declaring in Section 203 that final adjustment by a method agreed upon by the parties is the most desirable way to settle disputes over the interpretation and application of collective agreements. Moreover, in the landmark *Lincoln Mills* case, discussed below, the United States Supreme Court held that the LMRA provides enforceable support for labor arbitration.

The "Lincoln Mills" Case

Section 301 of the LMRA authorizes suits in the federal courts for violation of collective agreements in industries affecting interstate commerce. In the *Lincoln Mills* case the U.S. Supreme Court held that §301 authorizes the federal courts to fashion a body of federal law for the enforcement of collective agreement provisions for arbitration.[11] The Court declared that it was clear "that Congress adopted a policy which placed sanctions behind agreements to arbitrate grievance disputes, by implication rejecting the common-law rule * * * against enforcement of executory agreements to arbitrate."[12]

---

[8] The Act was passed in 1925 and codified in 1947. 9 U.SC. §§ 1–14. For discussion of the Act and the conflict as to its coverage, see Burnstein, "The United States Arbitration Act—A Reevaluation," 3 Vill. L. Rev. 125; 9 Labor L. J. 511 (1958). Also see Cox, "Grievance Arbitration in the Federal Courts," 67 Harv. L. Rev. 591 (1954).

[9] Textile Workers v. Lincoln Mills of Alabama, dissenting opinion, 77 S.Ct. 923, 926 (1957).

[10] The FAA applies directly to commercial arbitration. Furthermore, the Act gives federal substantive rights rather than merely providing federal enforcement of state-created rights. See Coulson, "Prima Paint: An Arbitration Milestone," 22 Arb. J. 237 (1967), discussing Prima Paint Corp. v. Flood & Conklin Mfg. Co., 87 S.Ct. 1801 (1967).

[11] Textile Workers v. Lincoln Mills of Alabama, 77 S.Ct. 912, 40 LRRM 2113 (1957).

[12] 77 S.Ct. at 917.

As to the substantive law to be applied in §301 suits, the Court stated:

"We conclude that the substantive law to apply in suits under §301(a) is federal law which the courts must fashion from the policy of our national labor laws. * * * The Labor Management Relations Act expressly furnishes some substantive law. It points out what the parties may or may not do in certain situations. Other problems will lie in the penumbra of express statutory mandates. Some will lack express statutory sanction but will be solved by looking at the policy of the legislation and fashioning a remedy that will effectuate that policy. The range of Judicial inventiveness will be determined by the nature of the problem. * * * Federal interpretation of the federal law will govern, not state law. * * * But state law, if compatible with the purpose of §301, may be resorted to in order to find the rule that will best effectuate the federal policy. * * * Any state law applied, however, will be absorbed as federal law and will not be an independent source of private rights."[13]

The "Trilogy"

After the *Lincoln Mills* case came the so-called Trilogy of 1960.[14] Some of the significant teachings of these cases may be summarized as follows:

As to compelling arbitration: Unless the parties expressly provide that the arbitrator is to determine arbitrability, the determination rests with the courts (if such issue is presented for judicial determination). The courts must compel arbitration where the party seeking it is mak-

---

[13] Id. at 918. Included among the many articles on *Lincoln Mills* are Gregory, "The Law of the Collective Agreement," 57 Mich. L. Rev. 635 (1959); Kramer, "In the Wake of Lincoln Mills," 9 Labor L. J. 835 (1958); Bickel & Wellington, "Legislative Purpose and the Judicial Process: The Lincoln Mills Case," 71 Harv. L. Rev. 1 (1957); Feinsinger, "Enforcement of Labor Agreements—A New Era in Collective Bargaining," 43 Va. L. Rev. 1261 (1957); American Bar Association Committee on Arbitration, "Report on Labor Arbitration," 28 LA 913, 914–922 (1957).

[14] United Steelworkers of America v. American Manufacturing Co., 80 S.Ct. 1343, 34 LA 559 (1960); United Steelworkers of America v. Warrior & Gulf Navigation Co., 80 S.Ct. 1347, 34 LA 561 (1960); United Steelworkers of America v. Enterprise Wheel & Car Corp., 80 S.Ct. 1358, 34 LA 569 (1960). For an extensive survey of the impact of these and other Supreme Court decisions on arbitration, see Smith & Jones, "The Impact of the Emerging Federal Law of Grievance Arbitration on Judges, Arbitrators, and Parties," 52 Va. L. Rev. 831 (1966). Also see Smith & Jones, "The Supreme Court and Labor Dispute Arbitration: The Emerging Federal Law," 63 Mich. L. Rev. 751 (1965); Aaron, "Arbitration in the Federal Courts: Aftermath of the Trilogy," 9 U.C.L.A. L. Rev. 360 (1962); Gregory, "Enforcement of Collective Agreements by Arbitration," 48 Va. L. Rev. 883 (1962); Meltzer, "The Supreme Court, Arbitrability, and Collective Bargaining," 28 U. Chi. L. Rev. 464 (1961).

ing a claim which on its face is governed by the contract, even though the court might feel that the grievance is frivolous or baseless. Doubts over arbitrability should be resolved in the affirmative—arbitration should be compelled unless it may be said with "positive assurance" that the arbitration clause is not susceptible to an interpretation that covers the dispute.

As to review and enforcement of awards: The question of interpretation of the agreement is for the arbitrator, and the courts "have no business overruling him because their interpretation of the contract is different from his." However, an award "is legitimate only so long as it draws its essence from the collective bargaining agreement. When the arbitrator's words manifest an infidelity to this obligation, courts have no choice but to refuse enforcement of the award." But the Court also indicated that a court should not reject an award unless it is clear that the arbitrator has exceeded his authority—the Supreme Court is unwilling to "assume" that an arbitrator has "abused the trust the parties confided in him" or that he "has not stayed within the areas marked out for his consideration."[15]

As to the merits of disputes: Courts should not delve into the merits of grievances. The merits are not a subject for court inquiry in actions either to compel arbitration or to enforce awards.

As to modification of awards: The Supreme Court upheld the Court of Appeals' rejection of the early common-law rule that a court action to enforce an award must be dismissed in its entirety if any deficiency exists in the award. The Supreme Court held that an award need not be set aside for incompleteness merely because the arbitrator neglected to calculate the amount of back pay due grievant; the award was returned to the parties for a determination of back pay by arbitration.[16]

As to the response of the courts to these *Trilogy* teachings, thorough studies conducted by the Law and Legislation Committee of the NAA produced the following findings: "Because of the presumption favoring the arbitrability of labor disputes, courts have continued to compel arbitration in most cases where the arbitrability of the dispute has been challenged."[17] The Committee noted that "Most courts have adopted a strict approach in requiring clear and unambiguous

---

[15] Quoted language from *Enterprise* decision.

[16] For rejection of the common-law rule by the Court of Appeals, see Enterprise Wheel & Car Corp. v. United Steelworkers, 269 F.2d 327, 332 (CA 4, 1959).

[17] "Arbitration and Federal Rights Under Collective Agreements in 1967," Developments in American and Foreign Arbitration 201, 214–215 (The Bureau of National Affairs, Inc., 1968).

exclusionary language in the contract in order to exclude a dispute from arbitration."[18]

These studies also disclosed that the courts have enforced the vast majority of awards which were challenged in judicial proceedings, though in reviewing awards the courts have exercised much less restraint about delving into the merits than in the case of suits to compel arbitration.[19]

Under federal law, as under state common law, the issuance of an arbitration award generally bars any subsequent court action on the merits of the original claim.[20]

Other Supreme Court Decisions Affecting Arbitration

After the *Trilogy* came other United States Supreme Court decisions directly or indirectly affecting labor-management arbitration. A brief statement concerning each of these decisions follows.

---

[18] "Arbitration and Rights Under Collective Agreements," National Academy of Arbitrators 18th Annual Meeting 219, 233–234 (BNA Incorporated, 1965).

[19] See the Law and Legislation Committee reports in the following Bureau of National Affairs publications: Arbitration and Social Change 197–203 (1970); Developments in American and Foreign Arbitration 201, 216 (1968); Problems of Proof in Arbitration 366, 378–379 (1967); National Academy of Arbitrators 18th Annual Meeting 219, 235–236 (1965). For other studies and views concerning court review of awards under the *Trilogy*, see Meltzer, "Ruminations About Ideology, Law, and Labor Arbitration," The Arbitrator, the NLRB, and the Courts 1, 7 et seq. (The Bureau of National Affairs, Inc., 1967); Christensen, "Labor Arbitration and Judicial Oversight," 19 Stanford L. Rev. 671 (1967); Note, "Judicial Review of Labor Arbitration Awards After the Trilogy," 53 Cornell L. Rev. 136 (1967), surveying grounds on which courts have refused enforcement of awards; Note, "Judicial Review of Labor Arbitration Awards Which Rely on the Practices of the Parties," 65 Mich. L. Rev. 1647 (1967); Comment, "Judicial Enforcement of Labor Arbitrators' Awards," 114 U. of Pa. L. Rev. 1050 (1966). For a discussion of possibilities for achieving the review of arbitration decisions short of going to court, see Jones & Smith, "Management and Labor Appraisals and Criticisms of the Arbitration Process: A Report with Comments," 62 Mich. L. Rev. 1115, 1119–1127 (1964). For actual efforts along this line by arbitrators or parties, see Arbitrator Jones in 47 LA 1075, 1078; Stix in 44 LA 1139 at 1139, and in 43 LA 824, 832; Sullivan in 42 LA 193, 212–213, 219–220.

[20] See Piper v. Neco. Inc., 412 F.2d 752 (CA 6, 1969); Haynes v. United States Pipe and Foundry Co., 362 F.2d 414 (CA 5, 1966); Howard v. U.S. Rubber Co., 36 LA 62 (USDC Mass., 1961); Rothlein v. Armour & Co., 57 LC ¶12,581 (CA 3, 1968), stating that an award ordinarily bars a §301 action on the merits, except where the union has violated its duty of fair representation or where the arbitration was a sham. As to suing under Title VII of the Civil Rights Act of 1964 after losing in arbitration, it has been held that there is no right to sue after an arbitrator has issued a final and binding award. Dewey v. Reynolds Metals Co., 429 F.2d 324 (CA 6, 1970), affirmed by the Supreme Court by an equally divided (4–4) vote and without an opinion. Dewey v. Reynolds Metals Co., 91 S.Ct. 2186 (1971).

Dowd Box: LMRA §301 did not divest state courts of jurisdiction over suits to enforce the collective agreement. State and federal courts have concurrent jurisdiction over such suits (this of course includes enforcement of the arbitration clause).[21]

Lucas Flour: Although both state and federal courts can enforce collective agreements, state courts exercising jurisdiction over cases within the purview of §301 must apply principles of federal substantive law rather than state law. This case also held that a no-strike obligation will be implied as to those issues which are subject to arbitration.[22]

Wiley & Sons: Once it is determined that the subject matter of a dispute is arbitrable, procedural questions which grow out of the dispute and bear on its final disposition should be left to the arbitrator. The Court stated that procedural questions, such as whether the preliminary steps of the grievance procedure have been exhausted or excused, ordinarily cannot be answered without consideration of the merits of the dispute.[23]

Drake Bakeries: Section 301 suits for damages must be stayed by the court pending arbitration where the arbitration clause is sufficiently broad to contemplate submission of the issue to an arbitrator—in this instance the issue was the employer's claim for damages for breach of a no-strike clause.[24]

Atkinson v. Sinclair: An employer's damage suit for breach of a no-strike clause may not be dismissed or stayed pending arbitration where the agreement limits arbitration to employee grievances.[25]

Needham Packing: Breach of a no-strike clause was not such a repudiation of the agreement as to relieve the employer of his obligation to arbitrate grievances over discharge of the strikers.[26]

---

[21] Dowd Box Co. v. Courtney, 368 U.S. 502, 49 LRRM 2619 (1962).

[22] Local 174, Teamsters v. Lucas Flour Co., 82 S.Ct. 571, 49 LRRM 2717 (1962).

[23] John Wiley & Sons v. Livingston, 84 S.Ct. 909, 55 LRRM 2769 (1964), in which the Court also held that under appropriate circumstances the successor employer must honor the arbitration agreement of a company acquired by merger. The successor, however, was not required to honor the entire agreement of the predecessor employer in NLRB v. Burns International Security Services, Inc., 92 S.Ct. 1571 (1972).

[24] Drake Bakeries, Inc. v. Bakery Workers Local 50, 82 S.Ct. 1346, 50 LRRM 2440 (1962).

[25] Atkinson v. Sinclair Refining Co., 82 S.Ct. 1318, 50 LRRM 2433 (1962), also holding that where a union is liable for such breach of contract, its officers and members are not liable.

[26] Packinghouse Workers, Local 721 v. Needham Packing Co., 84 S.Ct. 773; 55 LRRM 2580 (1963), in which the Court implied a different result might be reached in other instances, saying that it did not decide "whether a fundamental and long-lasting change in the relationship of the parties prior to the demand for arbitration would be a circumstance which, alone or among others, would release an employer from his promise to arbitrate." As to this point, also see Drake Bakeries, Inc. v. Bakery Workers Local 50, 82 S.Ct. 1346 (1962).

Boys Markets: Strikes which breach the collective agreement no-strike clause may be enjoined despite the Norris-LaGuardia Act, but only within the bounds of certain principles which the Supreme Court adopted:

> "When a strike is sought to be enjoined because it is over a grievance which both parties are contractually bound to arbitrate, the District Court may issue no injunctive order until it first holds that the contract *does* have that effect; and the employer should be ordered to arbitrate, as a condition of his obtaining an injunction against the strike. Beyond this, the District Court must, of course, consider whether issuance of an injunction would be warranted under principles of equity—whether breaches are occurring and will continue, or have been threatened and will be committed; whether they have caused or will cause irreparable injury to the employer; and whether the employer will suffer more from the denial of an injunction than will the union from its issuance."[27]

Smith v. Evening News: NLRB authority to deal with unfair labor practice conduct which also violates a collective agreement is not displaced by §301, but it is not exclusive and does not destroy the jurisdiction of the courts in §301 suits. This case also held that individual employees can sue under §301 to enforce their collective agreement rights (there was no arbitration clause); the Court overruled its prior holding that §301 does not apply to the enforcement of "uniquely personal" rights of employees under the agreement.[28]

Maddox: An employee must attempt to exhaust the contractural grievance and arbitration procedure (if any) prior to resorting to court action under §301.[29]

---

[27] Boys Markets, Inc. v. Retail Clerks Union, Local 770, 90 S.Ct. 1583, 1594, 74 LRRM 2257, 2264 (1970), in which the Supreme Court expressly overruled its decision in Sinclair Refining Co. v. Atkinson, 82 S.Ct. 1328 (1962), which had held that the Norris Act did bar federal court injunctive relief against a strike, in breach of the collective agreement no-strike clause, over a dispute which was subject to the arbitration clause. In the interim between these two decisions the Court had held in Avco Corp. v. Aero Lodge 735 IAM, 88 S.Ct. 1235, 67 LRRM 2881 (1968) that the union could have a state court injunction suit removed to federal court, which had the practical effect (when coupled with *Sinclair*) of ousting state courts of jurisdiction to enjoin strikes in breach of the no-strike obligation. In *Boys Markets* the Court agreed that Congress did not intend such restriction upon the states, and the Court concluded, furthermore, that the literal terms of Norris Act §4 must be accommodated to the subsequently enacted LMRA §301(a) and the purposes of arbitration, and that within the limits stated in *Boys Markets* the federal courts likewise are not barred from granting injunctive relief.

[28] Smith v. Evening News Association, 83 S.Ct. 267, 51 LRRM 2646 (1962).

[29] Republic Steel Corporation v. Maddox, 85 S.Ct. 614, 58 LRRM 2193 (1965). The "Maddox" rule was extended to railroad employees in Andrews v. Louisville & Nashville Railroad Company, 92 S.Ct. 1562 (1972). Cf., Glover v. St. Louis-San Francisco Railway Co., 89 S.Ct. 548, 70 LRRM 2097 (1969). The "Maddox" rule does not apply to a seaman's wage claims, which can be

Vaca v. Sipes: State courts have not been preempted from entertaining suits by employees against their union for refusing to arbitrate their grievance; but in such suits the state court must apply federal law, under which a breach of the statutory duty of fair representation occurs only when the union's conduct is arbitrary, discriminatory, or in bad faith. The Court noted that the courts will be compelled to decide whether there has been a breach of the duty of fair representation in the context of many §301 breach of contract actions against the employer, and the Court suggested that in these cases both the employer and the union might be held liable.[30]

Riss: An award of a joint labor-management grievance committee, though the procedure is not styled "arbitration," is enforceable by court action under §301 *if* the award was to be final and binding under the terms of the collective agreement.[31]

Carey v. Westinghouse: The use of arbitration to resolve work-assignment jurisdictional disputes which involve questions of representation is not barred by the superior authority of the NLRB, though the Board's processes may be invoked at any time and a Board decision would control in the event of disagreement with that of the arbitrator. In requiring the employer to arbitrate upon demand by one of the unions the Court noted "the blurred line" that often exists between work-assignment disputes and representation disputes, and the Court stated: "If it is a work assignment dispute, arbitration conveniently fills a gap and avoids the necessity of a strike to bring the matter to the Board. If it is a representation matter, resort to arbitration may have a pervasive, curative effect even though one union is not a party. * * * The superior authority of the Board may be invoked at any time. Meanwhile the therapy of arbitration is brought to bear in a complicated and troubled area."[32]

---

taken directly to federal court under an early statute or to arbitration under §301. U.S. Bulk Carriers, Inc. v. Arguelles, 91 S.Ct. 409 (1971). The question whether direct court action on a grievance alleging violation of the Fair Labor Standards Act would be proper even if the grievance were subject to the grievance and arbitration provisions of the agreement was left undecided in Iowa Beef Packers, Inc. v. Thompson, 92 S.Ct. 859 (1972).

[30] Vaca v. Sipes, 87 S.Ct. 903, 64 LRRM 2369 (1967). In Humphrey v. Moore, 84 S.Ct. 363, 55 LRRM 2031 (1964), the Supreme Court held that federal and state courts had concurrent jurisdiction under §301 of an employee's suit for alleged breach of a collective agreement by a joint union-employer committee in dovetailing the seniority lists of two companies. The improper representation claim against the union could be resolved as part of the §301 breach of contract claim against the employer. Even if an unfair labor practice within the NLRB's jurisdiction was involved, the courts could entertain the §301 suit.

[31] General Drivers, Local 89 v. Riss and Company, 83 S.Ct. 789, 52 LRRM 2623 (1963).

[32] Carey v. Westinghouse Electric Corp., 84 S.Ct. 401, 55 LRRM 2042 (1964).

The *Strong, Acme,* and *C & C Plywood* Cases: These cases teach that while the courts and arbitrators are the principal sources of contract interpretation and enforcement, the NLRB may interpret and give effect to the terms of a collective agreement if necessary to the adjudication of an unfair labor practice.[33]

State Law

State arbitration law is derived either from state common law or state statute, or from both.[34] While most states have some type of arbitration statute, many of them do not apply to labor arbitration. Moreover, many of those that do apply are very general in nature, leaving many details to be supplied by court decisions under the common law. Even where the case is covered by state statute it has usually been held that the statute does not abrogate but supplements the common law.[35]

One state, Washington, has held that its statute completely supersedes the common law, but the court recognized the contractual nature of arbitration and indicated that the parties may elect to establish arbitration procedures of their own in lieu of using the statutory procedures.[36]

---

[33] NLRB v. Strong, 89 S.Ct. 541 (1969); NLRB v. Acme Industrial Co., 87 S.Ct. 565, 64 LRRM 2069 (1967); NLRB v. C & C Plywood Corp., 87 S.Ct. 559, 64 LRRM 2065 (1967). *Acme* held that the employer must furnish information to the union to aid it in deciding whether to process a grievance; the Court stated that the NLRB's action in requiring the employer to provide information "was in aid of the arbitral process," which "can function properly only if the grievance procedures leading to it can sift out unmeritorious claims." 87 S.Ct. at 569.

[34] The concept of "common law" has been explained as follows: "When the courts have no written law [constitution or statute] on which to base its decision in a particular controversy, it decides the case on the basis of custom and general principles of right and wrong. These decisions create precedents or rules, which are applied to similar future controversies. The body of law created in this fashion is spoken of as the common law." Kagel, Anatomy of a Labor Arbitration 139 (BNA Incorporated, 1961).

[35] See Jones, "Judicial Review of Arbitral Awards—Common-Law Confusion and Statutory Clarification," 31 S. Cal. L. Rev. 1, 2 (1957); Gregory & Orlikoff, "The Enforcement of Labor Arbitration Agreements," 17 U. of Chi. L. Rev. 233, 254–255 (1950); Williston on Contracts §1927 (Rev. Ed., 1938).

[36] Puget Sound Bridge & Dredging Co. v. Lake Washington Shipyards, 96 P.2d 257, 259, 261 (1939). This right of election was reaffirmed in Greyhound Corp. v. Motor Coach Employees, 22 LA 555 (Wash. Sup. Ct., 1954). In Pennsylvania the common law applies unless the parties elect to come under the statue. Guille v. Mushroom Transportation Co., 229 A.2d 903, 904 (Pa. Sup. Ct., 1967), the court noting that where neither the agreement nor the arbitration conducted pursuant thereto made any reference to the state statute, "rules governing common law arbitration are applicable * * * except to the extent that these rules themselves have been pre-empted by federal common labor law."

State Common Law

While the common law of any given jurisdiction might not always accord in all respects with that of other jurisdictions, a general summary of common law arbitration and its relation to statutory arbitration has been provided by the U.S. Department of Labor:

> "Common law arbitration rests upon the voluntary agreement of the parties to submit their dispute to an outsider. The submission agreement may be oral and may be revoked at any time before the rendering of the award. The tribunal, permanent or temporary, may be composed of any number of arbitrators. They must be free from bias and interest in the subject matter, and may not be related by affinity or consanguinity to either party. The arbitrators need not be sworn. Only existing disputes may be submitted to them. The parties must be given notice of hearings and are entitled to be present when all the evidence is received. The arbitrators have no power to subpoena witnesses or records and need not conform to legal rules of hearing procedure other than to give the parties an opportunity to present all competent evidence. All arbitrators must attend the hearings, consider the evidence jointly and arrive at an award by a unanimous vote. The award may be oral, but if written, all the arbitrators must sign it. It must dispose of every substantial issue submitted to arbitration. An award may be set aside only for fraud, misconduct, gross mistake, or substantial breach of a common law rule. The only method of enforcing the common law award is to file suit upon it and the judgment thus obtained may be enforced as any other judgment. Insofar as a State arbitration statute fails to state a correlative rule and is not in conflict with any of these common law rules, it may be said that an arbitration proceeding under such statute is governed also by these rules."[37]

The common law provides very little support for executory agreements to arbitrate (executory in the sense that the arbitration has not proceeded as far as issuance of an award). Either party may repudiate or withdraw from arbitration at any time prior to issuance of an award since executory agreements to arbitrate future disputes have no binding effect and will not be enforced either by way of damages or specific enforcement, and since executory agreements to arbitrate existing disputes likewise will not be specifically enforced (although in some jurisdictions breach of the latter agreements may be the basis of suit for damages, usually nominal only).[38] This common

---

[37] Ziskind, Labor Arbitration Under State Statutes 3 (U.S. Dept. of Labor, 1943). As noted elsewhere in this Chapter, many jurisdictions hold, both under the common law and under statute, that awards ordinarily may not be set aside for a mistake of law.

[38] See Freidin, Labor Arbitration and the Courts 2 (1952); Gregory &

law rule against enforceability of executory agreements to arbitrate still prevails in many states.[39]

Although executory agreements to arbitrate are not specifically enforceable at common law, once an arbitration proceeding has been conducted and an award issued the courts will take jurisdiction to enforce or vacate the award.[40] A party who is dissatisfied with an award may initiate action for court review or may challenge the award when the satisfied party seeks court enforcement.[41]

At common law the issuance of an award generally bars any subsequent action on the original claim, but suit may be filed for enforcement of the award itself to the same extent as any contract.[42]

The grounds for attacking awards at common law are generally limited to:[43]

1. Fraud, misconduct, or partiality by the arbitrator, or gross unfairness in the conduct of the proceedings.
2. Fraud or misconduct by the parties affecting the result.
3. Complete want of jurisdiction in the arbitrator. Also, failure of the arbitrator to stay within his jurisdiction or to carry it out fully—that is, he decides too much or too little.

Orlikoff, "The Enforcement of Labor Arbitration Agreements," 17 U. of Chi. L. Rev. 233, 236, 241 (1950).

[39] American Bar Association Committee on Arbitration, "Report on Labor Arbitration," 28 LA 913, 929 (1957); Gregory & Orlikoff, "The Enforcement of Labor Arbitration Agreements," 17 U. of Chi. L. Rev. 233, 234, 254 (1950).

[40] Since the arbitrator's authority terminates under the common law upon issuance of his award, any review and enforcement of his award must be left to the courts, except to the extent that the parties or applicable statute give him authority to interpret or otherwise deal with the award after its issuance. Regarding termination of the arbitrator's authority, see Chapter 7, topic titled "Clarification or Interpretation of Award," and see Updegraff, Arbitration and Labor Relations 279–283 (The Bureau of National Affairs, Inc., 1970); Updegraff & McCoy, Arbitration of Labor Disputes, 1st Ed. pp. 120–124 (1946), 2d Ed. pp. 211–215 (1961), discussing also the question of power in the arbitrator to correct obvious mistakes and clerical errors in the award.

[41] See Justin, "Arbitration: Proving Your Case," 10 LA 955, 967 (1948); Updegraff, Arbitration and Labor Relations 285 (The Bureau of National Affairs, Inc., 1970); Updegraff & McCoy, Arbitration of Labor Disputes, 1st Ed. p. 125 (1946), 2d Ed. p. 216 (1961).

[42] Williston on Contracts §1927 (Rev. Ed., 1938). For additional discussion, see Dowell, "Judicial Enforcement of Arbitration Awards in Labor Disputes," 3 Rutgers L. Rev. 65, 70–72 (1949).

[43] See "When May an Arbitrator's Award Be Vacated?" 7 DePaul L. Rev. 236 (1958); Rothstein, "Vacation of Awards for Fraud, Bias, Misconduct and Partiality," 10 Vanderbilt L. Rev. 813 (1957); Freidin, Labor Arbitration and the Courts 31 (1952); Updegraff, Arbitration and Labor Relations 275, 278, 288–289 (The Bureau of National Affairs, Inc., 1970); Updegraff & McCoy, Arbitration of Labor Disputes, 1st Ed. pp. 116, 120, 126–127 (1946), 2d Ed. pp. 208, 210–211, 216–217 (1961).

4. Violation of public policy as by ordering the commission of an unlawful act.[44]

Under the common law awards generally will not be set aside for mistake of law or fact. As the Pennsylvania Supreme Court has stated, "Unless they are restricted by the submission, the arbitrators are the final judges of both law and fact and their award will not be disturbed for a mistake of either."[45]

State Arbitration Statutes

State arbitration statutes are of three general types: (1) general statutes designed primarily for commercial disputes, but some of which may be used for labor disputes; (2) special labor arbitration statutes, which contain some detail as to procedure; and (3) statutes which merely "promote" arbitration by charging a state agency to encourage its use.[46]

One of the most detailed and most utilized statutes is that of New York, which was amended in 1940 for the specific purpose of covering labor cases, and which was revised and modernized in 1963.[47] The California statute, enacted in 1961, supplanted an earlier act and introduced a number of innovations.[48] Examples of other important industrial states with modern arbitration statutes applicable to labor arbitration are Michigan, Ohio, Massachusetts, Illinois, and New Jersey.

In 1955 a proposed Uniform Arbitration Act was promulgated by the National Conference of Commissioners on Uniform Laws.[49]

---

[44] Regarding the latter ground, see Sturges, Commercial Arbitrations and Awards §61, p. 202 (1930). Also see Smith & Jones, "The Supreme Court and Labor Dispute Arbitration: the Emerging Federal Law," 63 Mich. L. Rev. 751, 803–807 (1965); Cox, "The Place of Law in Labor Arbitration," The Profession of Labor Arbitration 76, 78–79 (BNA Incorporated, 1957).

[45] Newspaper Guild, Etc. v. Philadelphia Daily News, Inc., 164 A.2d 215, 220 (1960). For large collections of cases to the same general effect, see 6 C.J.S., Arbitration and Award, §105, p. 251; 3 Am. Jur., Arbitration and Award, §92, pp. 923–924. Regarding the use of substantive law in arbitration, see Chapter 10.

[46] See Ziskind, Labor Arbitration Under State Statutes (U.S. Dept. of Labor, 1943). Also see Matto, "The Applicability of State Arbitration Statutes to Proceedings Subject to LMRA Section 301," 27 Ohio State L. J. 692 (1966); Lillard, "State Arbitration Statutes Applicable to Labor Disputes," 19 Mo. L. Rev. 280, 282–286 (1954). For an extensive list of citations to state arbitration statutes, see Updegraff, Arbitration and Labor Relations 385–388 (The Bureau of National Affairs, Inc., 1970).

[47] See "An Outline of Procedure Under the New York Arbitration Law," 20 Arb. J. 73 (1965); "The New York Arbitration Law," 18 Arb. J. 132 (1963).

[48] See "Report of NAA Committee on Law and Legislation," Collective Bargaining and the Arbitrator's Role 249, 252–253 (BNA Incorporated, 1962).

[49] The Act is published in 24 LA 886–889. The Act as amended in 1956 is published in 27 LA 909–912. Alaska, Arkansas, Arizona, Indiana, Illinois,

As of 1970 a majority of the states had some sort of "modern" arbitration statute.[50] There is no absolute uniformity among these statutes, and a detailed presentation of their provisions is beyond the scope of this book. However, it may be noted that provisions along the following general lines are frequently found in the modern statutes (many of the listed provisions are included, for instance, in the New York and California statutes, and in the Uniform Act):

1. Agreements to arbitrate existing and future disputes are made valid and enforceable.
2. Courts are given jurisdiction to compel arbitration, or to stay arbitration if no agreement to arbitrate exists.
3. Courts are given jurisdiction to stay litigation when one party to an arbitrable dispute attempts to take it to court instead of arbitrating.
4. Courts are authorized to appoint arbitrators where the parties fail to provide a method for appointment.
5. Majority action by arbitration boards is authorized.
6. Provision is made for oath by the arbitrator and/or witnesses, unless waived by the parties.
7. Default proceedings (in the absence of a party) are authorized under certain circumstances.
8. Provision is made for continuances and adjournments of hearings.
9. Limitation is placed upon the effect of waivers of the right to be represented by counsel.
10. Arbitrators are given the subpoena power.
11. Awards are required to be in writing and signed by the arbitrator, and some limitation is stated regarding the time within which awards must be rendered.
12. Arbitrators are granted limited authority to modify or correct awards upon timely application by a party, and the Uniform Act additionally permits the arbitrator to clarify his award by application from a party.
13. A summary procedure is provided for (1) court confirmation of awards, (2) court vacation of awards on limited grounds stated by the statute, (3) court modification or correction of awards on limited grounds stated by the statute.
14. Courts are authorized to enter judgment upon awards as confirmed, modified, or corrected; the judgment is then enforceable as any other judgment.
15. Provision is made for appeals from court orders and judgments under the statute.

The limited grounds for setting aside awards under many of the state statutes (and under the FAA) are along the following general

---

Maine, Maryland, Massachusetts, Minnesota, Texas, and Wyoming are included among states adopting the Uniform Act.
[50] Not all of these statutes apply to labor disputes.

lines, which differ little from the common law grounds:[51]

1. The award was procured by corruption, fraud, or other undue means.
2. The arbitrator was guilty of evident partiality, corruption, or misconduct (some statutes expressly limit the impartiality requirement to neutrals).[52]
3. The arbitrator refused to postpone the hearing upon sufficient cause shown, or refused to hear material evidence; or otherwise so conducted the hearing as to prejudice substantially the rights of a party.
4. The arbitrator exceeded his powers, or so imperfectly executed them that a mutual, final, and definite award upon the subject matter submitted was not made.[53]
5. There was no valid agreement to arbitrate (and it has not been determined otherwise by an action to compel or stay arbitration), and objection to that fact was properly raised.

The Uniform Act and the statutes of New York, California, Florida, and some other states provide that upon vacation of an award the court may order a rehearing before new arbitrators, or in some cases before the original arbitrators.

Some state statutes, and the FAA, authorize the courts to modify or correct awards on grounds essentially as follows (some statutes also authorize the arbitrator to modify or correct his award on these grounds):[54]

1. Where there was an evident miscalculation of figures, or an evident mistake in the description of any person, thing, or property referred to in the award.

---

[51] See Uniform Arbitration Act, 27 LA 909, 910–911; Federal Arbitration Act, 9 U.S.C. §10; Lillard, "State Arbitration Statutes Applicable to Labor Disputes," 19 Mo. L. Rev. 280, 293 (1954).

[52] The U.S. Supreme Court has stated, under the FAA, that the arbitrator "must not only be unbiased but must avoid even the appearance of bias." Commonwealth Coatings Corp. v. Continental Casualty Co., 89 S.Ct. 337, 340 (1968).

[53] Some of the statutes, such as California, provide for vacation of the award where the arbitrator exceeded his powers and the award cannot be corrected without affecting the merits of the decision.

[54] See Matto, "The Applicability of State Arbitration Statutes to Proceedings Subject to LMRA Section 301," 27 Ohio State L. J. 692, 713–714 (1966); Lillard, "State Arbitration Statutes Applicable to Labor Disputes," 19 Mo. L. Rev. 280, 294 (1954); Uniform Arbitration Act, 27 LA 909, 911; Federal Arbitration Act, 9 U.S.C. §11. Courts acting only under state common law may not be permitted to modify awards. See Updegraff, Arbitration and Labor Relations 289 (The Bureau of National Affairs, Inc., 1970); Updegraff & McCoy, Arbitration of Labor Disputes, 1st Ed. p. 127 (1946), 2d Ed. pp. 217–218 (1961); Enterprise Wheel & Car Corp. v. United Steelworkers, 269 F.2d 327, 332 (CA 4, 1959).

2. Where the arbitrators have awarded upon a matter not submitted to them, not affecting the merits of the decision upon the matter submitted.
3. Where the award is imperfect in a matter of form not affecting the merits of the controversy.

It is obvious from the above summaries that the state statutes generally provide no right of court review for errors of law or errors as to finding of fact.[55]

The Applicable Law

State common law and/or state statutory law governs the arbitration of labor-management disputes involving concerns not affecting interstate commerce and thus not falling within the purview of LMRA §301. State law likewise applies to disputes involving employees of state and local governments or involving other workers excluded from coverage of the federal statute. If such cases reach a court, it will ordinarily be a state court. Even if the case is taken to federal court, however, the case must be decided on the basis of state law when the federal court has jurisdiction only by virtue of diversity and not by virtue of any federal statute providing for arbitration; "the federal court enforcing a state-created right in a diversity case is * * * 'only another court of the State.' "[56]

The bulk of labor-management arbitrations no doubt do fall within the purview of LMRA §301. As we have noted, such cases are to be governed by federal substantive law, both in federal and state courts.[57] Although state courts have concurrent jurisdiction over suits covered by §301, "Congress intended doctrines of federal labor law uniformly to prevail over inconsistent local rules."[58]

Following the *Lincoln Mills* decision the federal courts have decided many §301 arbitration cases; thus these courts have commenced

---

[55] Also see Justin, "Arbitration: Proving Your Case," 10 LA 955, 967 (1948).

[56] Bernhardt v. Polygraphic Company of America, 76 S.Ct. 273, 276, 25 LA 693, 695 (1956), holding that enforceability of agreements to arbitrate must be decided by state law in such diversity cases.

[57] See this Chapter, topic titled "Federal Law." A clause stating that a contract was to be governed by New York law was held of no effect in a §301 action. Carey v. General Electric Co., 50 LRRM 2119 (USDC N.Y., 1962), modified on other grounds, 52 LRRM 2662 (CA 2, 1963).

[58] Local 174, Teamsters v. Lucas Flour Co., 82 S.Ct. 571, 577 (1962). Cases may be removed from state to federal court by virtue of §301 coverage. Johnson v. England, 356 F.2d 44 (CA 9, 1966); Kracof v. Retail Clerks, 244 F. Supp. 38 (USDC Pa., 1965).

the slow process of fashioning a body of federal law for this field. By the nature of the legal process, however, decades will be required to develop a basically complete and uniform body of federal law as ordered by the Supreme Court. Only by an outpouring of decisions by that Court, or by the enactment of a detailed federal statute for labor arbitration, can the process be accelerated.[59] In the meantime, the lower courts will be free to range widely in determining what is the federal labor policy on issues which have not been resolved by the Supreme Court, and in determining what local rules are consistent with that policy.[60]

The *Lincoln Mills* decision teaches that the "federal law" of labor arbitration is to be derived from the LMRA, from other federal statutes, and from state law; it also teaches that "The range of judicial inventiveness will be determined by the nature of the problem."[61]

The principles developed under state common law to prevent abuse of powers by arbitrators have been incorporated in many state statutes; numerous other common features appear in the modern arbitration statutes, in the Uniform Arbitration Act, and in the FAA.[62] A number of states have legislated such modern statutes since *Lincoln Mills,* and some since the *Trilogy.* It is not unreasonable to expect resort to these sources by both federal and state courts in developing the federal common law under *Lincoln Mills.* In any event, there is obvious validity in the comment that the "grant of concurrent jurisdiction gives the state courts an important role in assisting in the formulation of the federal substantive law under section 301."[63]

---

[59] In 1959 a committee of the NAA proposed a United States Labor Arbitration Act. The proposed Act is published in 34 LA 941.
[60] That significant questions may for years remain unanswered with finality is illustrated by the lower court conflict as to whether the Federal Arbitration Act applies to collective agreement arbitration clauses. This question has not been clearly resolved by the United States Supreme Court (the 1957 *Lincoln Mills* decision under LMRA §301 has of course reduced the significance of this particular question).
[61] Textile Workers v. Lincoln Mills of Alabama, 77 S.Ct. 912, 918 (1957).
[62] See this Chapter, topic titled "State Law."
[63] Smith and Clark, "Reappraisal of the Role of the States in Shaping Labor Relations Law," 1965 Wisc. L. Rev. 411, 421 (1965), where those authors add: "Furthermore, it may be that procedural and remedial matters in the enforcement of labor agreements remain to be determined by the law of the forum." In Local 1416, I.A.M. v. Jostens, Inc., 250 F.Supp. 496 (USDC Minn., 1966), the court stated that while the *Lincoln Mills* mention of resort to state law was undoubtedly referring to principles of substantive law, there should be no impediment to the use of state procedure, in the absence of a contrary or inconsistent federal statute or rule. In IAM v. Geometric Tool Co., 70 LRRM

As concerns reactions of state courts, there have been cases in which the state court expressly recognized that it must apply substantive rules compatible with federal policy.[64] However, while noting that "the controlling substantive law is Federal law," the Minnesota Supreme Court emphasized that "state law, if compatible with the purposes of §301, may be resorted to in order to find the rule that will best effectuate the Federal policy."[65]

No doubt some arbitration cases will be taken to state court and resolved there without issue being raised (or if raised, without actually being resolved) as to coverage by LMRA §301 and/or compatibility of state law with the federal labor policy.[66] Indeed, three possibilities have been recognized as to application of state statutes in cases covered by LMRA §301: (1) Per se application of the particular state statute, no attention being given to federal labor policy; (2) nonapplication, the court not applying the statute of the particular state but evaluating all state statutes in general to determine what the uniform federal rule should be; (3) prima facie application, the particular state provision being applied unless it conflicts with the federal labor policy.[67]

228, 51 LA 1156 (CA 2, 1968), a 60-day time limit specified by state statute for rendering awards was deemed contrary to federal labor policy and could not be strictly enforced where the case was covered by LMRA §301.

[64] See, for example, Butchers' Union Local 229 v. Cudahy Packing Co., 428 P.2d 849 (Calif. Sup. Ct., 1967).

[65] Fischer v. Guaranteed Concrete Co., 151 N.W. 2d 266, 269 (1967).

[66] It has been observed, for instance, that state courts "have not faced the problem of the applicability of their arbitration statutes to proceedings subject to section 301 to any great extent," that observer suggesting that the reason may be that "It is easy to look to the state statute and not attempt to determine what the federal policy is and whether any conflict exists." Matto, "The Applicability of State Arbitration Statutes to Proceedings Subject to LMRA Section 301," 27 Ohio State L. J. 692, 699 (1966). This excellent article discusses certain common features of state arbitration statutes and evaluates their compatibility with the federal labor policy.

[67] Id. at 694–702, where each of the possibilities is discussed in detail. That observer recommended prima facie application because it duly notes the Supreme Court's comments concerning state law as a source of federal law and would be consistent with the federal policy of encouraging labor arbitration. Id. at 717.

CHAPTER 3

SCOPE OF LABOR ARBITRATION

While many labor disputes are clearly suitable for arbitration, one of the potential hazards of labor arbitration has been said to be an "overoptimistic estimate" of its effective scope, "which tends to consider it an all-purpose tool or panacea for the resolution of any and all disputes which the parties fail to settle privately."[1]

Even if a dispute is of a type generally suitable for arbitration and is arbitrable under the collective agreement, judgment must be exercised in deciding whether to arbitrate the particular dispute. Included among the factors to be considered in this regard are the merits of the case, the importance of the issue, the effect of winning or losing, the possibilities of settlement, internal policies and politics within the union and the company, psychological and face saving considerations, and the like.[2]

Certainly, not all disputes are equally suitable for arbitration. The most popular use of labor arbitration concerns disputes involving the interpretation or application of the collective agreement. There is much less enthusiasm for its use, even on a voluntary basis, as a means of resolving disputes over terms of new or renewal contracts.[3]

There are some matters, too, which are so delicate or are considered to belong so intimately to one or the other of the parties, that

---

[1] Davey, "Hazards in Labor Arbitration," 1 Ind. and Lab. Rel. Rev. 386, 387 (1948). Later Mr. Davey indicated his "impression" that "an increasing number of companies are avoiding excessive arbitration in an intelligent and discriminating fashion." Davey, "Labor Arbitration: A Current Appraisal," 9 Ind. and Lab. Rel. Rev. 85, 90 (1955).

[2] See "Prehearing Arbitration Problems: A Panel Discussion," The Arbitrator, the NLRB and the Courts 341–352 (The Bureau of National Affairs, Inc., 1967); Fleming, The Labor Arbitration Process 205–208 (U. of Ill. Press, 1965); Kagel, Anatomy of a Labor Arbitration 14–15, 23 (BNA Incorporated, 1961).

[3] For extent of acceptance of the various uses of arbitration, see survey by Warren & Bernstein, "A Profile of Labor Arbitration," 16 LA 970, 971–973 (1951). Also see "Basic Patterns in Labor Arbitration Agreements," 34 LA 931, 939 (1960).

they are not too readily submitted to arbitration.[4] This has been suggested as a reasonable explanation for many of the specific exclusions from arbitration clauses studied by the U.S. Department of Labor in one survey:

"The reasons for such exclusions usually were not indicated by the agreements and, although they may have been fully understood by the parties, they are not always clear to outsiders reading the agreements. Some exclusions undoubtedly were intended to preserve certain management prerogatives, others to preserve union prerogatives. Some were necessary because the parties had agreed upon other methods of handling certain problems, and possibly some were motivated by a mutual desire not to overburden the arbitration machinery with trivialities. Exclusions in some cases appeared to represent a signal to workers in the bargaining unit that it would be pointless to raise a grievance over the designated issue. It seems reasonable to assume, however, that underlying many exclusions was a strongly held belief of one or both parties that the issue in question was too important or too subtle to be entrusted to a decision of a third party."[5]

Management naturally hesitates to submit to arbitration issues involving its normal prerogatives in the conduct of the business, such as the determination of methods of operation, operation policies, and finances. Labor usually considers that the settlement of an internal union conflict is "a matter in which management should not be permitted to participate, and it would be undesirable to permit the company to become involved in this question indirectly or in any manner whatsoever."[6] Improper activities of union officials in the administration of grievances have been held to be improper subjects for arbitration, since a contrary approach "might well result in a form of policing of internal union affairs by a third party who clearly was not intended nor competent to accomplish such a purpose. * * * The remedy lies with the union membership, which has the ultimate power, through democratic means, to control the selection of their representatives."[7]

---

[4] See Moore & Mix, "Arbitration Provisions in Collective Agreements," 76 Monthly Lab. Rev. 261–264 (1953); Lapp, Labor Arbitration 44 (1942). For surveys of matters which might be excluded from the collective agreement arbitration clause, see Major Collective Bargaining Agreements: Arbitration Procedures 6–22 (U.S. Dept. Labor Bull. No. 1425–6, 1966); "Basic Patterns in Labor Arbitration Agreements," 34 LA 931, 939 (1960).
[5] Major Collective Bargaining Agreements: Arbitration Procedures 11 (U.S. Dept. Labor Bull. No. 1425–6, 1966).
[6] Babcock & Wilcox Co., 8 LA 58, 61 (Dworkin, 1947).
[7] Spencer Kellogg & Sons, Inc., 1 LA 291, 294 (Miller, 1945). Cf., North American Aviation, Inc., 17 LA 199, 204 (Komaroff, 1951).

It may be noted, however, that internal union disputes do sometimes reach arbitration between company and union.[8] Furthermore, internal union disputes may be arbitrated without management involvement,[9] and such arbitration has been used widely for interunion jurisdictional disputes.[10] Similarly, intermanagement disputes may be arbitrated without labor involvement.[11]

Labor ordinarily would not consider its statutory right to strike a proper subject for arbitration. However, the right to strike is frequently arbitrated in the construction of contractural no-strike clauses, and in such proceedings the question of the right to strike under statute may be brought into play.[12]

Some doubt exists as to the suitability of labor-management arbitration for resolving racial discrimination grievances, but proposals have been made which "would modify in large part the voluntary and private nature of labor arbitration" to adapt it to the needs of racial discrimination grievances.[13]

While it has been suggested that "Arbitration is most effective when used sparingly,"[14] it has also been suggested that "it would hardly be right to judge the effectiveness or worth of an arbitration

---

[8] See Publishers' Association of New York City v. New York Mailers' Union, 317 F.2d 624 (CA 2, 1963), involving union action against a member who as company foreman had disciplined another union member. Similarly, Houston Chronicle Publishing Co. v. Houston Typographical Union, 272 F.Supp. 974 (DC Texas, 1966). Both of these cases involved broad arbitration clauses. For a case involving arbitration of a union welfare trust fund dispute, see Arbitrator Kates in 45 LA 222.

[9] See Royal Industrial Union, 51 LA 642 (Johnson, 1968); Screen Extras Guild, Inc., 46 LA 169 (Bernstein, 1966).

[10] E.g., Arbitrator Cole in 46 LA 28; Taft in 45 LA 69; Cole in 23 LA 827. For a general discussion, see Cole, Feinsinger & Dunlop, "Arbitration of Jurisdictional Disputes," Arbitration Today 149–165 (BNA Incorporated, 1955). The United States Supreme Court has upheld the use of arbitration for resolving representation disputes; "the therapy of arbitration" may thus be brought to bear, though any subsequent decision by the NLRB would take precedence over that of the arbitrator. Carey v. Westinghouse Electric Corp., 84 S.Ct. 401, 409 (1964).

[11] Plumbing, Heating and Piping Employers Council, 39 LA 513 (Ross, 1962).

[12] See General Electric Co., 42 LA 1255, 1264–1266 (Koretz, 1964).

[13] See Gould, "Labor Arbitration of Grievances Involving Racial Discrimination," 24 Arb. J. 197 (1969).

[14] Davey, "Labor Arbitration: A Current Appraisal," 9 Ind. and Lab. Rel. Rev. 85, 90 (1955).

system or the health of a labor-management relationship by the number of cases" arbitrated each year.[15]

Disputes on "Rights" and "Interests"

The distinction between "rights" and "interests" is basic in the classification of labor disputes and in views as to arbitrability. Disputes as to "rights" involve the interpretation or application of laws, agreements, or customary practices, whereas disputes as to "interests" involve the question of what shall be the basic terms and conditions of employment. This nomenclature is derived from the Scandinavian countries, which have treated the distinction between rights and interests as basic in their labor legislation. Sweden, for instance, has permanent national labor courts whose jurisdiction is carefully restricted to disputes concerning "rights" under collective agreements.[16]

The U.S. Supreme Court has explained the fundamental distinction between "interests" and "rights" disputes:

"The first relates to disputes over the formation of collective agreements or efforts to secure them. They arise where there is no such agreement or where it is sought to change the terms of one, and therefore the issue is not whether an existing agreement controls the controversy. They look to the acquisition of rights for the future, not to assertion of rights claimed to have vested in the past.

"The second class, however, contemplates the existence of a collective agreement already concluded or, at any rate, a situation in which no effort is made to bring about a formal change in terms or to create a new one. The dispute relates either to the meaning or proper application of a particular provision with reference to a specific situation or to an omitted case. In the latter event the claim is founded upon some incident of the employment relation, or asserted one, independent of those covered by the collective agreement * * *. In either case the claim is to rights accrued, not merely to have new ones created for the future."[17]

---

[15] Comment by Harry H. Platt in "The Chrysler-UAW Umpire System," The Arbitrator and the Parties 111, 142–143 (BNA Incorporated, 1958), where Umpire Platt asserted that labor relations at Ford were "at least as good as at Chrysler" even though Ford arbitrated many more cases than Chrysler; Umpire Platt offered explanations and justifications for the heavier caseload at Ford.

[16] Spielmans, "Labor Disputes on Rights and on Interests," 29 Am. Econ. Rev. 299 (1939).

[17] Elgin, J. & E. Ry. Co. v. Burley, 65 S.Ct. 1282, 1290, 16 LRRM 749 (1945), involving the Railway Labor Act. The Court noted that the two basic

Disputes as to "rights" are adjudicable under the laws or agreements on which the rights are based, and are readily adaptable to settlement by arbitration. Disputes as to "interests," on the other hand, involve questions of policy which, for lack of predetermined standards, are not generally regarded as justiciable or arbitrable. Yet, many "interests" disputes are settled by arbitration, and, as was seen in Chapter 1, some states have concluded that public utility "interests" disputes involve such serious risk of public harm that a requirement of compulsory arbitration of such disputes is justified. Sometimes laws are passed which settle specific contested economic issues; and in such cases there is, of course, a transfer of the contested matter from the zone of "interests" to that of "rights."[18]

It is highly important that the distinction between these two basic types of disputes be recognized and preserved in considering methods of settlement. This distinction was recognized early in the full-fashioned hosiery industry, which adopted one method of procedure for "rights" disputes and another for "interests" disputes. This has been explained:

> "The jurisdiction of the Impartial Chairman does not extend to disputes regarding the general level of wages in the industry. Since decisions of this type would involve changing all the rates specified in the Agreement, they are excluded from his jurisdiction by the provision which denies him the right to change any of the terms of the contract. Furthermore, the parties have established in the Agreement a special procedure for handling disputes over general wage-level changes. The 'flexibility clause' permits either party to seek a change in the general wage level at any time during the life of the agreement and provides for the establishment of a special wage tribunal in case the parties cannot agree on the percentage change to be made."[19]

The industry considered that, because there is no uniformly accepted body of principles for determining wage levels, one or both of the parties will be likely to feel that a given "interests" decision is grossly inequitable. Recognition of this fact gives special point to

---

types of disputes are traditionally called "major" and "minor" disputes in the railroad industry. Ibid. The Railway Labor Act is discussed herein below.
[18] For a splendid article on this subject, see Spielmans, "Labor Disputes on Rights and on Interests," 29 Am. Econ. Rev. 299 (1939).
[19] Kennedy, Effective Labor Arbitration 37 (1948). This is a comprehensive treatise on the Impartial Chairmanship of the Full-Fashioned Hosiery Industry. As to this industry, also see Fleming, The Labor Arbitration Process 10-11 (U. of Ill. Press, 1965).

the use of one set of machinery for the arbitration of "rights" disputes and another for "interests" disputes in permanent umpire or permanent chairman systems. Ill feeling against an arbitrator after an "interests" decision may be so general and so severe that one decision will destroy his usefulness to the industry.

Of the first six arbitrators chosen to determine general wage-level changes under the flexibility clause in the hosiery industry, not one was invited to serve a second time. Since it is not easy to find a person who combines the specialized knowledge of the industry and the type of personality which is necessary for success as an Impartial Chairman, the parties decided not to risk the loss of a good Impartial Chairman by asking him to decide general wage-level cases which can be handled by other arbitrators.[20] The same problem is recognized in respect to other new contract issues.[21]

Railroad labor legislation of the United States has also come to recognize the distinction between "rights" and "interests" disputes. The first three federal acts did not differentiate between them,[22] but the Transportation Act of 1920 provided for special treatment of the two types of disputes. Since then the distinction has been sharpened.

The Railway Labor Act of 1926, as amended in 1934, created the National Railroad Adjustment Board (NRAB), which, upon submission of a complaint by either party, takes jurisdiction over "disputes between an employee or group of employees and a carrier or carriers growing out of grievances or out of the interpretation or application of agreements concerning rates of pay, rules, or working conditions * * *" after they have been "handled in the usual manner up to and including the chief operating officer of the carrier designated to handle such disputes." On the other hand, disputes concerning "changes in rates of pay, rules, or working conditions not adjusted by the parties in conference" and "any other dispute not referable to the National Railroad Adjustment Board and not adjusted in conference between the parties or where conferences are refused" are handled by the National Mediation Board.

The function of the NRAB is to interpret and apply collective agreements, not to make or modify them. The NMB, on the other

[20] Kennedy, Effective Labor Arbitration 38-39 (1948).
[21] Id. at 39.
[22] Acts of 1888, 1898, and 1913.

hand, is directed to help the parties, through mediation, to reach agreement on the terms of collective agreements and, upon failure to bring about an agreement, to attempt to induce the parties to submit their dispute to voluntary arbitration.[23]

Recognizing the important distinction between the arbitration of "rights" and "interests" disputes, the various appointing agencies consider the type of dispute when requested by the parties to provide assistance in the selection of an arbitrator.[24]

While most disputes clearly fall into one of the two categories, basically involving "rights" or basically involving "interests," some disputes involve elements of both and cannot be clearly classified as falling exclusively within either of the categories. Arbitrability of the latter cases depends, as in other cases, upon whether the arbitration clause or submission is broad enough to cover the dispute.

Purpose and Subjects of "Interests" Arbitration

It is generally believed that the best labor-management contracts are those that are negotiated through collective bargaining without outside assistance. There are frequent instances, however, where the parties find it difficult or impossible to reach agreement by direct negotiation. In these instances, they may choose to settle the conflict by a test of strength, making use of the strike or lockout. But this can be costly and injurious to both parties. Moreover, a suspension of operations may bring great hardship upon others, as in the case of a cessation of public utility activities, for which neither labor nor management may wish to risk public censure.

In these situations voluntary arbitration is a way out of the dilemma.[25] One arbitration board, which was itself determining the

---

[23] For thorough treatment of this matter, see Lecht, Experience Under Railway Labor Legislation (1955); Jones, Handling of R.R. Labor Disputes 1888–1940 (1941).

[24] For instance, see policy statement of the United States Conciliation Service, U.S. Dept. of Lab. Rel. S. 47–152 (1946).

[25] For general examination of "interests" arbitration and a recommendation for its use after direct negotiations and mediation have failed, see Handsaker, "Arbitration and Contract Disputes," Challenges to Arbitration 78 et seq. (BNA Incorporated, 1960). For an extensive survey of past use of voluntary "interests" arbitration, its acceptability to the parties, and the potential for its future use, see Stieber, "Voluntary Arbitration of Contract Terms," Arbitration and the

provisions to be included in a utility renewal contract, stated the case for arbitration as follows: "Arbitration should be a last resort and not an easy pillow on which to fall just because difficulties are encountered. There is some evidence that in the transit industry there has not been the fullest utilization of collective bargaining just because there has existed a ready alternative. But, on the other hand, it cannot be denied that even some minor over-use of arbitration is preferable to long and costly strikes in this vital utility."[26] With this comment the arbitration board denied the request of one party for deletion of a provision, contained in the prior agreement, for arbitration of new contract terms.[27]

Arbitration of "interests" disputes may be viewed more as an instrument of collective bargaining than as a process of adjudication. In this connection it may be noted that this kind of arbitration is most frequently found in industries where collective bargaining is well established. In fact, Professor Charles O. Gregory has suggested that the compulsory arbitration of "interests" should be called "compulsory collective bargaining" rather than arbitration.[28]

An objection commonly urged against the arbitration of "interests" issues is the absence of definite principles or standards to govern the decision. This belief is not entirely justified, however. There are a number of standards which, while not as adequate as may be desired, are available and applied in the arbitration of such disputes. These standards are discussed in Chapter 18. Moreover, it is not uncommon for parties to agree upon general principles to be observed by the

---

Expanding Role of Neutrals 71 (The Bureau of National Affairs, Inc., 1970). For a related discussion, see Bryan, "Advisory Arbitration of New Contracts: A Case Study," id. at 55.

[26] Reading Street Railway Co., 6 LA 860, 871 (Simkin, 1947). Wage arbitration is well established in the local transit industry. Port Authority of Allegheny County, 45 LA 58, 58-59 (Crawford, 1965).

[27] Reading Street Railway Co., 6 LA 860, 872 (Simkin, 1947). Also denying such a request, Arbitrator Scheiber in 27 LA 309, 318. However, in Pacific Neo-Gravure, 51 LA 14, 25 (1968), Arbitrator Platt refused to continue a contractual provision for "interests" arbitration against the wishes of one party, Arbitrator Platt stating that to rule otherwise would in effect order compulsory arbitration contrary to our system of free collective bargaining. Accord, Arbitrator Haughton in 13 LA 115, 125. Arbitrator Mann postponed decision on this problem in 50 LA 700, 716.

[28] Gregory, "The Enforcement of Collective Labor Agreements by Arbitration," 13 U. Chi. L. Rev. 445, 469–470 (1946). For various possible uses of neutrals in bargaining negotiations, see "Current Problems of Arbitration," 35 LA 963, 965–966 (1961).

arbitrator, leaving to him only the task of applying these principles in the light of evidence.

The subject matter of "interests" arbitration can be as extensive and varied as the parties choose to make it. Any subject comprehended by collective bargaining can be placed in the agreement by arbitration. In determining over 20,000 labor-management disputes, most of which were over the terms of new agreements, the National War Labor Board of World War II traversed practically the entire range of collective bargaining issues.

Wage issues, as would be expected, constitute the most common subject of "interests" arbitration.[29] Among other "interests" issues that have been submitted to arbitration or to emergency boards are those involving: holidays,[30] vacations,[31] sick leave,[32] health and hospitalization benefits,[33] life insurance plans,[34] pension and retirement benefits,[35] benefits to curb the impact of automation,[36] meal periods,[37] rest periods,[38] seniority rules,[39] work schedules and shifts,[40] length of workday or workweek,[41] subcontracting restrictions,[42] union shop,[43] checkoff,[44] and length of contract term.[45]

The frequency of submitting issues to "interests" arbitration is no doubt affected by the economic conditions of the times and by

---

[29] For many cases involving the arbitration of wage issues, see Chapter 18.

[30] E.g., 48 LA 289, 47 LA 482, 37 LA 3, 27 LA 728, 25 LA 352, 18 LA 290, 16 LA 933.

[31] E.g., 48 LA 289, 45 LA 905, 39 LA 249, 28 LA 182, 24 LA 835, 21 LA 494, 17 LA 353.

[32] E.g., 52 LA 233, 48 LA 289, 47 LA 482, 17 LA 559, 16 LA 749, 14 LA 574, 13 LA 103, 11 LA 450.

[33] E.g., 44 LA 514, 26 LA 303, 25 LA 352, 22 LA 392, 21 LA 356, 16 LA 933, 11 LA 450.

[34] 28 LA 600, 22 LA 392, 21 LA 310, 16 LA 749, 13 LA 46.

[35] E.g., 52 LA 233, 37 LA 719, 33 LA 862, 29 LA 101, 25 LA 54, 19 LA 538, 18 LA 5, 14 LA 321, 13 LA 702, 11 LA 1037.

[36] 36 LA 44.

[37] 47 LA 482, 17 LA 353, 16 LA 749, 11 LA 166, 9 LA 577, 4 LA 548, 2 LA 663.

[38] 17 LA 353, 7 LA 845, 6 LA 98, 2 LA 227.

[39] 32 LA 945.

[40] 11 LA 501, 6 LA 860, 5 LA 269, 3 LA 804, 2 LA 10.

[41] E.g., 47 LA 482, 43 LA 875, 39 LA 249, 28 LA 600, 27 LA 343, 25 LA 54, 21 LA 307, 19 LA 538, 18 LA 903.

[42] 33 LA 451.

[43] E.g., 45 LA 801, 18 LA 112, 16 LA 611, 14 LA 574, 13 LA 620, 11 LA 501.

[44] 17 LA 833, 14 LA 574, 11 LA 501, 8 LA 149.

[45] E.g., 47 LA 482, 45 LA 905, 45 LA 58, 33 LA 451, 27 LA 468, 21 LA 356, 18 LA 174, 15 LA 871.

the prevailing political climate. The nature of the issue and the current relations of the parties are of obvious significance. Some of the above issues have been submitted to "interests" arbitration fairly frequently, but others only infrequently. Then, too, there have been periods of scanty use of "interests" arbitration, though wage issues have been submitted rather consistently.

Indiscriminate use of "interests" arbitration is to be avoided, for such use may impede healthy development of the labor-management relationship. In particular, parties who abdicate to arbitrators the responsibility of writing the bulk of the collective agreement risk serious disappointment.

Leaving too many "interests" issues to be resolved by neutrals has been severely criticized by the neutrals themselves[46] and has produced some pronounced disappointments of dispute settlement efforts.[47]

Arbitrator's Function in "Interests" Disputes

While various authorities have expressed generally similar views about the arbitrator's function in "interests" disputes, there are nuances which are worthy of note and which are illustrated by the comments quoted below.

In a definite sense the function of an "interests" arbitrator is to legislate for the parties. As explained by Arbitrator Emanuel Stein:

"The task is more nearly legislative than judicial. The answers are not to be found within the 'four corners' of a pre-existing document which the parties have agreed shall govern their relationship. Lacking guidance of such a document which confines and limits the authority of arbitrators to a determination of what the parties had agreed to when they drew up their basic agreement, our task here is to search for what would be, in the light of all the relevant factors and circumstances, a fair and equitable answer to a problem which the parties have not been able to resolve by themselves."[48]

---

[46] See Consumers Power Co., 18 LA 686, 688–689 (Fact-Finding Board, 1952); Pan-American World Airways, Inc., 17 LA 878, 881 (Emergency Board, 1952).
[47] New England Transportation Co., 15 LA 126, 133 (Company Dissent, 1950); Duquesne Light Co., 6 LA 470, 487, 492, 498 (Company and Union Dissents, 1947).
[48] New York Shipping Assn., 36 LA 44, 45 (1960). Contrast the function as viewed by Arbitrator Flagler in Des Moines Transit Co., 38 LA 666, 671 (1962).

In a similar sense, the function of the "interests" arbitrator is to supplement the collective bargaining process by doing the bargaining for both parties after they have failed to reach agreement through their own bargaining efforts. Possibly the responsibility of the arbitrator is best understood when viewed in that light. This responsibility and the attitude of humility that appropriately accompanies it have been described by one arbitration board speaking through its chairman, Whitley P. McCoy:

"Arbitration of contract terms differs radically from arbitration of grievances. The latter calls for a judicial determination of existing contract rights; the former calls for a determination, upon considerations of policy, fairness, and expediency, of what the contract rights ought to be. In submitting this case to arbitration, the parties have merely extended their negotiations—they have left it to this board to determine what they should, by negotiation, have agreed upon. We take it that the fundamental inquiry, as to each issue, is: what should the parties themselves, as reasonable men, have voluntarily agreed to? * * * We believe that an unusual demand, that is, one that has not found substantial acceptance in other properties, casts upon the union the burden of showing that, because of its minor character or its inherent reasonableness, the negotiators should, as reasonable men, have voluntarily agreed to it. We would not deny such a demand merely because it had not found substantial acceptance, but it would take clear evidence to persuade us that the negotiators were unreasonable in rejecting it. We do not conceive it to be our function to impose on the parties contract terms merely because they embody our own individual economic or social theories. To repeat, our endeavor will be to decide the issues as, upon the evidence, we think reasonable negotiators, regardless of their social or economic theories might have decided them in the give and take process of bargaining. We agree with the company that the interests of stockholders and the public must be considered, and consideration of their interests will enter into our conclusions as to what the parties should reasonably have agreed on."[49]

In concluding its opinion, the board said:

"We render this award not with pride but with some humility. The parties have placed upon us a tremendous task. In judging the results reached and deciding whether the award as a whole is fair, we invite the parties to consider whether, if an offer embodying this entire award

---

[49] Twin City Rapid Transit Co., 7 LA 845, 848 (1947). Similar views have been expressed by other highly respected arbitrators. See North American Aviation, Inc., 19 LA 76, 77 (Cole, Aaron, Wirtz, 1952).

had been made in bargaining, it would have been accepted as a reasonable compromise of many demands. If it would have been, we have performed the function we set for ourselves at the outset, namely, to determine what the parties, as reasonable men, should themselves have agreed to at the bargaining table."[50]

A highly realistic statement of the "interests" arbitrator's function has been offered by Arbitrator Harry H. Platt:

"[A]rbitrators in private wage disputes do not always conceive their function to be merely to discover what the parties would have agreed upon in negotiations and to decide accordingly. Quite often they view their function to be to fix a wage rate that will be fair and equitable to all concerned. Indeed, it is questionable whether any practical objective method exists of measuring the parties' bargaining strength—even when they bargain to a conclusion. In reality, an arbitrator's determination of what the parties would have agreed upon in negotiations if they had not arbitrated is his own opinion of what they should have agreed upon."[51]

Sometimes it is possible for the parties to agree upon the criteria to be observed by an arbitrator in deciding the issues submitted to him. But even with agreed-upon points of reference, the discretion of the arbitrator can be expected to be quite broad. "Interests" arbitration, as a part of the collective bargaining process, is essentially dynamic and fluid. The aggressor seeks to move into a new field, to expand the limits of an old area, or to reduce rights previously granted. It can be expected that something new will come from the arbitrator and that there will be some substitution of his judgment for that of the respective parties. It must be recognized that if the strike is to be relegated to a position of being the "very last resort," reasonable innovations must be possible through the arbitration process. Otherwise either progress would be unduly slowed or strikes invited, or both."[52]

Of course, in carrying out his function as "legislator" or "bargainer" for the parties, the "interests" arbitrator must strive to achieve a workable solution. It has been well said:

"[The arbitrator is] not a superior sort of dictator, dispensing justice from on high, but an agent of the two sides to the collective

---

[50] Twin City Rapid Transit Co., 7 LA 845, 858 (1947). Arbitrator McCoy also used "reasonable compromise" terminology in 29 LA 7, 10 (1957).
[51] Port Authority of Allegheny County, 50 LA 1103, 1109 (1968). For a similar view, see Arbitrator Heliker in 33 LA 451, 454.
[52] San Diego Electric Ry. Co., 11 LA 458, 461 (Kerr, 1948).

bargain. His job is to reach a solution that will be satisfactory enough to both sides to be workable. He has to take into consideration their relative strength and their relative necessities. He has to remember not to depart so far from a possible compromise, consistent with the respective power and desires of the parties, that one or the other of them will be likely next time to prefer open hostility to peaceful settlement. He has also to remember that a decision is useless if it cannot be enforced and that the power and ability of the respective parties to administer a decision successfully is an integral part of the decision itself.

"A decision which cannot be carried into effect or which will create lasting dissatisfaction is not really a decision at all. On this account a wage arbitration is not an exercise in pure reason, and a summary of merely logical arguments, accompanied by the opinion accompanying the decision, does not tell the whole story. Arbitrators frequently do not, of course, fully understand these limitations, but the more successful ones do so."[53]

Finally, we note that distinctions may be drawn between the role of emergency boards and that of the "interests" arbitrator. One emergency board, for instance, explained:

"The present Board, comprised solely of neutrals, is not empowered to make a final and binding award. Its Report, including recommendations, is designed to facilitate the subsequent and further collective bargaining of the parties. This Report is not intended to write the precise language of the collective bargaining agreement nor to determine the exact terms of settlement of the disputes between the parties. Rather, it is designed to suggest a relatively narrow area of settlement which the parties should explore constructively. The purpose of the Board is to present the facts, appropriate standards, and suggestions, in the hope that these will persuade the parties voluntarily to reach an agreement."[54]

---

[53] Soule, Wage Arbitration 6–7 (1928). While this statement was made in reference to wage issues, it would appear equally applicable to other "interests" matters.

[54] Railroads v. Nonoperating Unions, 34 LA 517, 522 (Dunlop, Aaron, and Sempliner, 1960). The Board also emphasized its responsibility to clarify the public interest in the dispute, to explain the dispute to the public, and thus "to bring to the bargaining table a further measure of public interest." Ibid. Another board explained that some emergency boards make recommendations only on the major subjects in dispute, while other boards deal with each submitted item. "Whatever technique is used, however, the underlying assumption is the same. The parties, following receipt of the Board's report, will be in a position to enter into a new collective bargaining contract which finally disposes of all requests of both employer and union." Pan American World Airways, Inc. v. Flight Engineers, 36 LA 1047, 1051 (Dash, Lynch, and Stark, 1961).

"Interests" Arbitration and Contract Clauses

Specific Provision for "Interests" Arbitration

Occasionally, a collective agreement will provide specifically for arbitration, at its expiration, of unsettled disputes over the terms of a new agreement.[55] A collective agreement clause providing for arbitration of future "interests" disputes may, for example, be as follows:

"Any differences that may arise between the company and the local union concerning wage reviews at dates specified in the agreement, or concerning amendments to the agreement at any termination date, which the representatives of the company and the local union are unable to settle, shall be submitted at the request of either party to a Board of Arbitration to be selected in a manner as specified hereinafter. The company and the local union agree that the majority decision of such Board shall be final and binding on both parties."[56]

More often, however, parties do not reach any agreement to arbitrate new contract terms until the old contract has expired and an impasse in negotiations has been reached.[57]

It may be noted that court decisions are in conflict as to whether LMRA §301 covers agreements to arbitrate future "interests" disputes so as to empower the courts to enforce collective agreement provisions for such arbitration.[58]

Clauses Equivocal as to "Interests" Disputes

Some collective agreements contain provisions which on their face indicate a very broad scope of arbitration, without providing a clue as to whether the process was intended to be limited to disputes involv-

---

[55] Of 1717 agreements covered by one study, less than 2 percent provided for arbitration of such disputes. Major Collective Bargaining Agreements: Arbitration Procedures 95 (U.S. Dept. Labor Bull. No. 1425-6, 1966). Five hundred of the agreements contained "reopening" clauses, and of these about 15 percent provided for arbitration if negotiations failed. Id. at 101.

[56] Agreement between San Diego Gas & Electric Co. and IBEW (agreement has expired). For other examples, see Major Collective Bargaining Agreements: Arbitration Procedures 98–103 (U.S. Dept. Labor Bull. No. 1425-6, 1966).

[57] For the type of instrument that may be used in such cases, see A. S. Abell Co., 45 LA 801, 806–807 (Cluster, 1965); River Valley Tissue Mills, 3 LA 245, 246 (Blair, 1946).

[58] Cases pro and con are collected in Winston Salem Printing Pressman and Assistant's Union v. Piedmont Publishing Co. of Winston Salem, 393 F.2d 221, 67 LRRM 2939 (CA 4, 1968), in which the court answered the question in the affirmative.

ing the interpretation of the agreement or was intended to include also disputes not arising under the agreement. Such provisions may state that "any grievance or complaint" or "any difference" or "any dispute over wages, hours, or other conditions of employment" may be arbitrated. In some instances arbitrators have held "interests" type disputes to be arbitrable under such *broad* arbitration clauses,[59] but in other instances arbitrators have ruled to the contrary.[60]

In one case the arbitrator held that while a provision for arbitration of "all" unsettled disputes made a demand for amendment of the contract arbitrable in the procedural sense that the arbitrator could rule upon it, the fact that granting the demand would alter the contract was good reason for its denial, since it would be unsound and unwise for him to impose his judgment where the appropriate course of action is bilateral negotiation and agreement.[61]

Efforts of a party to arbitrate pure "interests" issues under *narrow* arbitration clauses have often failed. For instance, under a clause providing only for arbitration of disputes involving the interpretation or application of the agreement, the fact that the agreement permitted reopening for consideration of general wage adjustments did not oblige the parties to agree on wage increases or, upon failing to agree, to permit an arbitrator to decide for them.[62]

But the fact that a contract excepts general wage increases from arbitration does not prevent arbitration of the question of whether the wage reopening clause permits more than one reopening during the contract term, since this issue involves the interpretation of the contract, rather than a general wage increase as such.[63]

---

[59] See Arbitrator Kates in 49 LA 40, 44; Duff in 48 LA 600, 603; Joseph in 48 LA 425, 427; Pope in 7 LA 685, 686; Brissenden in 6 LA 639, 641. For court decisions holding "interests" type disputes arbitrable under such broad clauses, see Beech Nut Packing Co., 23 LA 125 (N.Y. Sup. Ct., 1954); Textile Workers Union v. Cheney Bros., 22 LA 512 (Conn. Sup. Ct., 1954); Northland Greyhound Lines v. Amalgamated Ass'n., 3 LA 887 (U.S. Dist. Ct., 1946).

[60] See Arbitrator Gregory in 41 LA 1169, 1174–1176; Wallen in 12 LA 475, 478; Lehoczky in 9 LA 656, 657.

[61] Dictograph Products, Inc., 8 LA 1033, 1038 (Kaplan, 1947). Also see Chapter 7, topic titled "Recommendations by Arbitrator."

[62] In re Berger, 9 LA 1048 (N.Y. Sup. Ct., 1948), aff'd, 10 LA 929 (N.Y. App. Div., 1948). Accord, Arbitrator Aaron in 36 LA 1125, 1128; McCoy in 24 LA 741, 744; Livingston in 10 LA 528, 530. Also see Reynard in 24 LA 587, 589–591. Cf., Kerr in 20 LA 106, 107–108; Donnelly in 14 LA 1055, 1058.

[63] F. H. Hill Co., 8 LA 223, 225 (Blair, 1947). To similar effect, Arbitrator Piercey in 22 LA 261, 263–264; Stein in 7 LA 748, 749.

Subject Matter of "Rights" Arbitration

The sources of the subject matter of "rights" disputes are usually agreements, laws, and customary practices. Among the infinite number of matters that may be the subject of "rights" arbitration are questions with respect to seniority rights, vacations, holidays, discharge and discipline, layoffs, job classification, and the like.

But not all issues that are taken to arbitrators fall into such commonly recognized categories. This is illustrated by the "Case of the Lady in Red Slacks." A Ford Motor Company employee was reprimanded and docked one-half hour because she wore slacks described as bright red in color. The objection was to the color, not to the slacks, which female employees were required to wear. The issue was whether a lady's red slacks constituted a production hazard because of a tendency to distract male employees. Umpire Shulman stated that "it is common knowledge that wolves, unlike bulls, may be attracted by colors other than red and by various other enticements in the art and fit of female attire." The reprimand was expunged and the employee was reimbursed for the pay that she had been docked.[64]

Arbitrator's Function in "Rights" Disputes

The function of the "rights" arbitrator in the interpretation and application of collective agreements is treated in detail in Chapter 9 of this book, particularly in the topics titled "Ambiguity" and "Legislation vs. Interpretation." The reader is urged to consult those topics concerning the arbitrator's function in "rights" disputes.

Observers will probably agree that, on the whole, the function of the "rights" arbitrator is quite similar to that of a court in construing contracts.[65] The function is basically that of adjudication rather than legislation. Indeed, the parties very frequently provide that the arbitrator shall have no power to add to, subtract from, or

---

[64] Shulman, Opinions of the Umpire, Opinion A-117 (1944). Other disputes about female attire were resolved by Arbitrator Ryder in 45 LA 1071, 1073 (female could not be punished for wearing "short shorts"); Davis in 28 LA 83, 87.
[65] One survey revealed general (but not unanimous) agreement regarding this similarity. See Eaton, "Labor Arbitration in the San Francisco Bay Area," 48 LA 1381, 1383, 1391 (1967).

modify any provision of the agreement.[66] Nonetheless, the boundary line between interpretation and legislation cannot be drawn absolutely, and it is inevitable that the line will be crossed, in greater or lesser degree, fairly often. As is true of a court, an arbitrator may apply either a liberal or a strict construction to the provisions of an agreement, depending upon the question and circumstances involved, the attitude of the parties, and, of course, the general attitude of the arbitrator.

Helpful insight into "rights" arbitration, and in particular in regard to the function of the arbitrator, is provided by observing one of the nation's most extensive experiences in such arbitration—the NRAB. The RLA gives the Adjustment Board jurisdiction over "disputes between an employee or group of employees and a carrier or carriers growing out of grievances or out of the interpretation or application of agreements concerning rates of pay, rules, or working conditions * * *." While the word "Adjustment" in the Board's name might suggest that under this grant of jurisdiction the Board was intended to serve as an extension and continuation of the bargaining process,[67] in actual practice the function of the Board is much like true adjudication:

> "In hearing and deciding the cases which come before the Board [the Board members] do not act as negotiators or adjusters. Whatever may have been the intent of the law in setting up an Adjustment Board, there has been no trace in the history of the Board of any view on its part that its function is to iron out differences by taking into account the situation and needs of the parties and the practical effect of their respective demands, and on the basis of such consideration making concessions to one party in return for concessions by it for the good of the industry as a whole. The Board has never taken this view of its function. Instead it has assumed with the strictest legalistic viewpoint that the loosely drawn and often vague terms of

---

[66] Of 400 agreements included in one study, 88 percent so restricted the arbitrator. See "Basic Patterns in Labor Arbitration Agreements," 34 LA 931, 939 (1960).

[67] The labor members of the Board at one time expressed the view that this was the intended function of the Board. See statement of labor members submitted to the Attorney General's Committee on Administrative Procedure, in Railway Labor, 9–10 (1940), reprinted in Jones, Natl. R.R. Adjustment Board, 226 (1941). Those "who were mainly responsible for the statutory creation of the Board in 1934 hoped and doubtless believed that the Board would grow up to live chiefly as a collective bargaining agency * * * rather than as a real arbitration tribunal of last resort. * * * this hope has not been fulfilled for many years * * *" Daugherty, "Arbitration by the National Railroad Adjustment Board," Arbitration Today, 93, 94 (BNA Incorporated, 1955).

the schedules and agreements which come before it have a rigid technical meaning, and that this meaning is to be discovered by a process of purely technical reasoning. The most cursory examination of the nature of the arguments put up to the Board and the grounds of its decisions, where these are given, conclusively demonstrates that it regards its function as one of strict legal interpretation rather than compromise and adjustment."[68]

Probably most persons familiar with the activities of the NRAB would agree that the just-quoted statement is basically accurate and applies with equal force today. Certainly, when a referee is called in to sit as a member of the Board in deadlocked cases, the function of the Board is adjudication. But even in adjudication some rule making is inevitable:

"Even on the assumption that the Adjustment Board is strictly confined to the interpretation and application of existing rules, it is inescapable, particularly in deadlocked cases, that it will exercise a greater or less influence on the nature and scope of agreements between carriers and labor organizations. The Constitution of the United States is a small compact document; but one can gain no appreciation of its meaning and scope without examining the thousands of decisions in which the Supreme Court, in its interpretation, has molded and modified it. In a similar manner, it is inevitable that the Adjustment Board, subject to judicial review, will mold and modify railway collective agreements."[69]

In industries that use the permanent umpire or chairman device, the function varies. The jurisdiction of the Impartial Umpire for the Ford Motor Company and the United Auto Workers (UAW) has been limited generally to "alleged violations of the terms" of the parties' agreements. By specific provision he has been denied the power to "add to or subtract from or modify any of the terms of any agreement"; or to "substitute his discretion for the company's discretion in cases where the company is given discretion" by any agreement; or to "provide agreement for the parties in those cases where they have in their contract agreed that further negotiations shall or may provide for certain contingencies to cover certain subjects."[70] The 1968

---

[68] Railway Labor, ibid. The quotation is the statement of a carrier spokesman before the Attorney General's Committee.

[69] Spencer, The National Railroad Adjustment Board 31 (1938), reprinted in Jones, National R.R. Adjustment Board, p. 181 of appendix (1941).

[70] See Ford Motor Co., 6 LA 952, 953 (Shulman, 1944). The quoted provisions were continued in the 1967 Ford-UAW agreement. The jurisdiction of the Chrysler Appeal Board is somewhat similar to that of the Ford umpire. See Wolff, Crane & Cole, "The Chrysler-UAW Umpire System," The Arbitrator and the Parties 111, 114 (BNA Incorporated, 1958).

General Motors-UAW agreement states that the Umpire "shall have no power to add to or subtract from or modify any of the terms" of the agreement; the agreement further states that "Any case appealed to the Umpire on which he has no power to rule shall be referred back to the parties without decision." However, the agreement gives the Umpire "full discretion" in certain discipline cases.[71]

On the other hand, the Impartial Chairman of the full-fashioned hosiery industry has been given authority to determine all disputes except those involving new or renewal contract terms. In this industry, all disputes arising during the life of the contract "including but not limited to the interpretation, construction or application of the terms of this agreement" are "submitted to the Impartial Chairman for final and binding decision by him." He is denied the power to "alter, modify, or change" the "Agreement or any of the terms or provisions thereof," but there is no denial of power to add to the agreement, and the grant of power to decide issues not covered by the agreement can be viewed as giving him authority to add, by decisions, to the agreement.[72]

This subject should not be discussed without noting the view, as expressed by George W. Taylor, former Chairman of the National War Labor Board and a former Impartial Chairman for the full-fashioned hosiery industry, that grievance settlement often becomes an integral part of agreement-making. In an address before the NAA, he said:

> "A third important characteristic of grievance arbitration should be mentioned. Contrary to the views of many arbitrators, grievance settlement is not simply a process of contract interpretation. * * * [T]he difficult grievances arise because the labor contract reflects only a partial or an inconclusive meeting of minds. It doesn't give the reasonably clear answer to a dispute. In such cases, grievance settlement becomes an integral part of agreement-making. At any event, the manner in which the grievances are settled provides understandings that are as durable, or more so, than the actual terms of the labor

---

[71] The General Motors-UAW agreement is published in full (as is the Ford agreement) in CCH Labor Law Reporter, ¶59,000 specimen union contracts. One General Motors Umpire has commented that General Motors and the UAW have "needed and expected a so-called 'legalistic' approach to arbitration." Alexander, "Impartial Umpireships: The General Motors-UAW Experience," Arbitration and the Law 157 (BNA Incorporated, 1958).

[72] Kennedy, Effective Labor Arbitration 34–36 (1948).

contract themselves. No one need amplify to this audience the weight of 'established practices.' "[73]

The Taylor view has been approved by some but severely criticized by others.[74]

In one utterance the U.S. Supreme Court appears to have considered arbitration a part of "the continuous collective bargaining process":

> "Apart from matters that the parties specifically exclude, all of the questions on which the parties disagree must therefore come within the scope of the grievance and arbitration provisions of the collective agreement. The grievance procedure is, in other words, a part of the continuous collective bargaining process. It, rather than a strike, is the terminal point of a disagreement.

> "The labor arbitrator performs functions which are not normal to the courts; the considerations which help him fashion judgments may indeed be foreign to the competence of courts. * * *

> "The labor arbitrator's source of law is not confined to the express provisions of the contract, as the industrial common law—the practices of the industry and the shop—is equally a part of the collective bargaining agreement although not expressed in it. The labor arbitrator is usually chosen because of the parties' confidence in his knowledge of the common law of the shop and their trust in his personal judgment to bring to bear considerations which are not expressed in the contract as criteria for judgment. * * * The ablest judge cannot be expected to bring the same experience and competence to bear upon the determination of a grievance, because he cannot be similarly informed."[75]

---

[73] Taylor, "Effectuating the Labor Contract Through Arbitration," The Profession of Labor Arbitration 20, 21 (BNA Incorporated, 1957). In Standard Gravure Corp., 62-3 ARB ¶8927 (1962), the company urged that the arbitrator's function was adjudication while the union urged that it was an instrument of collective bargaining. Arbitrator Platt responded: "But in the Chairman's opinion, neither approach alone adequately represents the arbitration function in manning cases; together they mark the bounds within which an award should fall."

[74] For various reactions to the Taylor view, see O'Connell, "Should the Scope of Arbitration Be Restricted," Proceedings of the Eighteenth Annual Meeting of the National Academy of Arbitrators 102, 103–110 (BNA Incorporated, 1965); Garrett, "Some Potential Uses of the Opinion," Labor Arbitration—Perspectives and Problems 114, 122 (BNA Incorporated, 1964); Garrett, "The Role of Lawyers in Arbitration," Arbitration and Public Policy 102, 115–122 (BNA Incorporated, 1961).

[75] United Steelworkers v. Warrior & Gulf Navigation Co., 80 S.Ct. 1347, 1352–1353 (1960). For extensive discussion of past practice in arbitration, see Chapter 12, particularly the topic titled "Custom and Practice as Part of the Contract."

But in another utterance, contemporaneous with the statement quoted above, the Supreme Court bluntly confined arbitrators to the function specified by the parties:

> "When an arbitrator is commissioned to interpret and apply the collective bargaining agreement, he is to bring his informed judgment to bear in order to reach a fair solution of a problem. This is especially true when it comes to formulating remedies. * * * Nevertheless, an arbitrator is confined to interpretation and application of the collective bargaining agreement; he does not sit to dispense his own brand of industrial justice. He may of course look for guidance from many sources, yet his award is legitimate only so long as it draws its essence from the collective bargaining agreement. When the arbitrator's words manifest an infidelity to this obligation, courts have no choice but to refuse enforcement of the award."[76]

In apparently denying that there can be "a single generalized concept of the arbitration process which would be valid for all purposes," Impartial Chairman Sylvester Garrett explained:

> "There is infinite variety among arbitrators and arbitration systems, just as there are all kinds of judges and other tribunals. What one man will believe proper and practical in the interpretation of language will seem visionary to another under the same circumstances. One man's flair for mediation can be matched by another's distaste for it."[77]

Chairman Garrett explained further that some judges, like some arbitrators, have sought to induce settlements; he stated that critics of the "judicial process" theory of grievance arbitration have proceeded on the false assumption that all judges take a mechanical and sterile approach to agreement interpretation.[78]

"Rights" Arbitration Contract Clauses

Broad arbitration clauses utilize terminology such as "all disputes" or "any difference" between the parties. Such clauses often expressly exclude stated types of "interests" disputes, and sometimes exclude stated types of "rights" disputes.[79] Apart from express exclu-

---

[76] United Steelworkers v. Enterprise Wheel & Car Corp., 80 S.Ct. 1358, 1361 (1960).
[77] Garrett, "The Role of Lawyers in Arbitration," Arbitration and Public Policy 102, 122 (BNA Incorporated, 1961).
[78] Id. at 114, 120, 122.
[79] A clause excluding disputes concerning the "general subject of wages, hours and working conditions" was construed to exclude "interests" disputes

sions, *broad* clauses permit the arbitration of a wide variety of "rights" disputes, including those which do not involve the interpretation or application of the agreement.[80]

Of 1609 collective agreements studied by the U.S. Department of Labor in one survey, about one third contained *broad* arbitration clauses, while about two thirds contained *narrow* clauses restricting arbitration to disputes involving interpretation or application of the agreement.[81]

Narrow clauses restrict arbitration to disputes involving the interpretation or application of the agreement. Agreements with narrow clauses typically restrict the arbitrator's authority further by expressly prohibiting him from adding to, subtracting from, or altering the agreement. Sometimes additional restrictions are added by the express exclusion of stated types of interpretation or application disputes.

Under narrow arbitration clauses a dispute may be held non-arbitrable unless it involves rights traceable to the agreement.[82] How-

---

but not "rights" disputes. Standard Oil Co., 52 LA 151, 153 (Koven, 1968).

[80] Examples of disputes held arbitrable though not involving interpretation or application of the agreement are: *claim against employer for assault upon employee by employer's agent,* Goldstein v. Corbin, 63 LRRM 2248 (N.Y. Sup. Ct. 1966); *compulsory retirement,* Communications Workers v. Southwestern Bell Telephone Co., 415 F.2d 35 (CA 5, 1969); *claim based upon alleged oral agreement,* United Engineering & Foundry Employees Assn. v. United Engineering and Foundry Co., 389 F.2d 479 (CA 3, 1967); *right to Christmas bonus,* Newspaper Guild v. Tonawanda Corp., 55 LRRM 2222 (N.Y. Sup. Ct. 1964); *damage claim for secondary boycott,* Old Dutch Farms, Inc. v. Teamsters, 59 LRRM 2745 (USDC 1965). For other examples, but involving arbitrability rulings by arbitrators, see Arbitrator Handsaker in 22 LA 482, 483–484; Ryder in 22 LA 769, 771; Jaffee in 19 LA 872, 874; Gilden in 17 LA 81, 84; Lane in 8 LA 306; Abernethy in 7 LA 202, 217; Whiting in 6 LA 661, 662–663. In Operating Engineers v. Flair Builders, Inc., 80 LRRM 2441 (1972), the U.S. Supreme Court broadly interpreted the term "any difference." However, in Atkinson v. Sinclair Refining Co., 82 S.Ct. 1318 (1962), the Supreme Court held that employer grievances were not included within a clause defining grievances as "any difference regarding wages, hours or working conditions between the parties hereto or between the employer and an employee"; the Court held that since the employer's claim for damages for breach of a no-strike clause would not be arbitrable, he could seek damages in court.

[81] Major Collective Bargaining Agreements: Arbitration Procedures 6, 10 (U.S. Dept. Labor Bull. No. 1425-6, 1966). Of the 433 broad clauses, 93 excluded one or more issues from arbitration. Of the 1173 narrow clauses, 255 expressly excluded one or more issues.

[82] Where arbitration was limited to "alleged violation of the terms of the agreement," and where the agreement was silent on subcontracting, a grievance protesting subcontracting was not arbitrable. Independent Petroleum Workers v. American Oil Co., 324 F.2d 903 (CA 7, 1963), affd. by equally divided Court, 379 U.S. 130 (1964). Where the agreement limited arbitration to griev-

ever, disputes are sometimes held arbitrable under such clauses even though the agreement contains no specific provision on the subject of the alleged "right," as where the claimed "right" may be inherent in clauses on other subjects.[83] Furthermore, the "presumptive arbitrability" standard of the U.S. Supreme Court must be kept in mind in considering whether a court or an arbitrator might hold any given dispute to be arbitrable.[84]

Pre-Contract and Post-Contract Grievances

Under the narrow "interpretation and application" arbitration clauses, disputes which arise prior to execution of the agreement have been held nonarbitrable, even though the grievance is filed after execution of the agreement.[85]

Grievances that arise in the interim between the expiration of one collective agreement and the execution of a new one are nonarbitrable unless it is established that the parties extended the old agreement to span the gap.[86]

---

ances involving "the interpretation and application of the specific provisions of this agreement," a grievance over the employer's decision to discontinue the distribution of Christmas turkeys was held nonarbitrable. Boeing Co. v. Auto Workers, 349 F.2d 412 (CA 3, 1965). Also see Flintkote Co. v. Textile Workers Union, 60 LRRM 2071 (USDC 1965). For cases in which arbitrators have denied or dismissed grievances as being beyond the scope of their authority, see Chapter 7, topic titled "Recommendations by Arbitrator."

[83] See Arbitrator Marshall in 23 LA 228; Donnelly in 13 LA 747; Wallen in 9 LA 757. Also see Arbitrator Shister in 25 LA 50; Kaplan in 3 LA 259. In Camden Industries Co. v. Carpenters Union, 60 LRRM 2183 (USDC 1965), the court took the view that arbitration should be ordered if there is a possibility that an arbitrator may be able to resolve the dispute by interpreting existing provisions of the agreement; if the arbitrator subsequently finds that the dispute cannot be resolved by interpreting existing provisions, it is his responsibility then to hold the dispute to be nonarbitrable.

[84] See Chapter 2, subtopic titled "The Trilogy," and Chapter 6, topics titled "Determination by the Courts" and "Determination by the Arbitrator." Matters which are expressly excluded from the arbitration clause will ordinarily be held nonarbitrable. See United Mine Workers v. Chris-Craft Corporation, 385 F.2d 946 (CA 6, 1967). But see Los Angeles Paper Bag Co. v. Printing Specialties and Paper Products Union, 345 F.2d 757 (CA 9, 1965).

[85] See Arbitrator Wettach in 25 LA 772, 773; Platt in 20 LA 850, 851–852; Millar in 20 LA 207, 210; McCoy in 8 LA 66, 67; Marshall in 6 LA 460, 461. Cf., Shister in 33 LA 390. Similarly, a promise made to persons before they became covered by the collective agreement was not arbitrable under an "interpretation and application" clause. Ranco, Inc., 50 LA 269, 273 (Klein, 1968).

[86] Teamsters v. Kroger Co., 411 F.2d 1191 (CA 3, 1969); I.B.E.W. v. Wadsworth Electric Mfg. Co., 240 F.Supp. 292 (DC 1965); Procter & Gamble Independent Union v. Procter & Gamble, 312 F.2d 181 (CA 2, 1962), cert. den., 374 U.S. 830 (1963). Accord, United Parcel Service, Inc., 55 LA 443, 444–445 (Forsythe, 1970). As to arbitrability of the question whether the agree-

However, grievances which do arise during the term of a contract present a different matter. Once vested, rights under a collective agreement may be enforced through the grievance procedure and/or arbitration although the agreement has expired (and, under some decisions, even where the claim is first asserted after such expiration) or although the grievants are no longer employees.[87] Of course, the right to prosecute a grievance may be lost by failure to meet applicable time limits.[88]

Another situation which may be noted involved employees who returned to work after a new agreement was executed and who were then discharged for alleged misconduct as strikers during the interim between agreements; the discharges could be arbitrated since the grievance was the action of the employer in discharging the employees, not the employer's reason for that action.[89]

---

ment has in fact terminated, compare, Teamsters v. Kroger Co., 411 F.2d 1191 (CA 3, 1969); Burt Bldg. Materials Corp. v. Teamsters, 277 N.Y.S. 2d 399 (N.Y. Ct. App., 1966). Concerning the NLRA duty to bargain and union demands for arbitration during the interim between agreements, compare, Taft Broadcasting Co., 185 NLRB No. 68 (1970); Sterling Drug, Inc., 185 NLRB No. 58 (1970).

[87] Piper v. Meco, Inc., 302 F.Supp. 926 (DC, 1968), affd., 412 F.2d 752 (CA 6, 1969); General Tire & Rubber Co. v. Rubber Workers, 191 F.Supp. 911 (DC, 1961), affd., 294 F.2d 957 (CA 1, 1961). Accord, Arbitrator Gibson in 51 LA 837, 839; Dworet in 40 LA 847, 848; Mintzer in 38 LA 1175, 1176–1177; Rock in 36 LA 65, 67–70; Kelliher in 23 LA 298, 300; Rosenfarb in 19 LA 365, 368; Stutz in 19 LA 234, 236; Ingle in 5 LA 175, 177. But see Cheney in 5 LA 148, 150. As to the right of a union to arbitrate grievances after the union has lost its majority status or has been decertified, see Machinists v. International Aircraft Services, 49 LRRM 2976 (CA 4, 1962); Trumbull Asphalt Co., 38 LA 1093 (Elson, 1962). Also see note, "Union's Right to Assert Grievances Subsequent to Its Decertification and Change of Corporate Employers," 16 Kan. L. Rev. 552 (1968).

[88] See Chapter 5, topic titled "Time Limitations."

[89] Boeing Co. v. Machinists, 381 F.2d 119 (CA 5, 1967).

CHAPTER 4

THE ARBITRATION TRIBUNAL

Several types of tribunals are available for parties who wish to arbitrate. Also available are a variety of methods for selecting the arbitrator. Parties may choose in general between the use of a "temporary" arbitrator or the use of a "permanent" arbitrator. They also have a choice as to the number of arbitrators to be used, either single or multiple. The choice exercised in these matters may be of great importance to the success of the arbitration.

Single Arbitrator v. Arbitration Board

The parties have a choice as to the number of arbitrators to be used for their case. Over-all, the most common practice is to use a single neutral arbitrator, though in a given industry the most common practice may be to use arbitration boards.[1] When an arbitration board is used, it may be composed entirely of neutrals or it may be tripartite in its membership. Of the two types of boards, the tripartite board is used much more frequently than the board of neutrals.[2]

When a board of neutrals is used it will ordinarily have three members. Sometimes an alternate is also designated.[3] Under one variation in the use of neutral boards, only one member hears the case

---

[1] Of 1609 agreements studied in one survey by the United States Department of Labor, 858 specified use of a single arbitrator, 670 specified a tripartite board, 42 gave the parties an option to use one or the other, 26 specified use of a single arbitrator for some issues and a board for others, and 13 were silent on the matter. Major Collective Bargaining Agreements: Arbitration Procedures 33 (U.S. Dept. Labor Bull. No. 1425-6, 1966). Also see statistics in "Basic Patterns in Labor Arbitration Agreements," 34 LA 931, 938 (1960 survey); "Procedural Aspects of Labor-Management Arbitration," 28 LA 933, 934–935 (1954 survey).

[2] For discussion of tripartite boards, see "Tripartite Arbitration Boards," below.

[3] As in Southern Bell Telephone & Telegraph Co., 25 LA 85, 86 (Alexander, McCoy, Schedler & Whiting, 1955).

and makes findings of fact; then a decision based upon such findings is made by the full board.[4] Under another arrangement the case is heard by a board of two neutrals, with a third neutral to be selected subsequently if the first two cannot agree on a decision.[5]

"Temporary" or "Ad Hoc" Arbitrators

The "temporary" or "*ad hoc*" arbitrator is selected after the dispute arises.[6] He is named to arbitrate a specific dispute or a specific group of disputes, and there is no commitment to select him again. Most "interests" arbitrations involve temporary arbitrators. In a high percentage of "rights" arbitrations, too, temporary arbitrators are used. Most of the latter arbitrations are conducted pursuant to an arbitration clause in the collective agreement. The details of such clauses vary considerably from agreement to agreement, but it is customary to state at least: (1) what grievances may be submitted to arbitration; (2) the procedure for selecting the arbitrator; and (3) the scope of the arbitrator's jurisdiction and the binding effect of his award.

(a) Advantages

The possibility of easy change of arbitrators is one of the chief advantages of the use of temporary arbitrators. At the same time, as long as an arbitrator continues to be satisfactory to the parties, he can be selected again and again, if available, for cases as they arise. When parties first begin to arbitrate, the use of temporary arbitrators makes experimentation possible. Thus they may become acquainted with arbitration and, at the same time, better determine their particular needs in regard to its use. Later, the parties might graduate to the use of a permanent system.

For those parties who find themselves in the happy situation of having relatively few disputes, the appointment of arbitrators only as needed generally is more satisfactory, and especially so from the standpoint of economy.

---

[4] Ibid.

[5] As in Fairmont Auto Supply Co., 43 LA 369, at 369 (Lugar and Furbee, 1964), where the two neutrals who heard the case did agree on a decision.

[6] Over four fifths of the agreements in the aforementioned survey by the Department of Labor provided for selection of the arbitrator on an *ad hoc* basis. Major Collective Bargaining Agreements: Arbitration Procedures 33 (U.S. Dept. Labor Bull. No. 1425-6, 1966).

Use of temporary arbitrators permits the selection, in each case, of an arbitrator who has special qualifications for deciding that particular dispute. While the use of a specialist, as such, may not be required often, some issues are of such technical nature that it is advisable to select an arbitrator who has special training or knowledge in regard thereto.

Finally, it is probable that a temporary arbitrator, not being personally acquainted with either party, will not be swayed too far by the personalities of the parties. In other words, brief tenure in office makes it unlikely that a temporary arbitrator will acquire a bias in favor of either party.

(b) Disadvantages

The selection of an arbitrator after a dispute has arisen may involve as much difficulty as the dispute itself. Much time and effort may be lost because parties who are no longer friendly find themselves unable to agree upon an arbitrator, or even upon a method of selecting one. In the meantime the dispute remains unsettled, which may result in additional damage to the parties' relationship.

The arbitrator who is chosen for only one dispute, or a specific group of disputes, usually will not be familiar with the general circumstances of the parties. He will know little of the background of the dispute or the setting in which the collective agreement operates. At best, the parties may seek to educate him as to these matters, and even if additional hearing time is spent in his enlightenment, the arbitrator's knowledge of the parties' relationship will be shallow. The most successful arbitration is that which sets a smooth course for future operations. Thorough knowledge of the past relationship of the parties is an invaluable aid to one who would pursue this end. Moreover, since temporary arbitrators sometimes are selected on something of an emergency basis, the parties may not have adequate opportunity to check the qualifications of the arbitrator. Thus there is additional hazard that the parties may have to accept a decision which leaves their relationship in a weaker condition than existed prior to the rendition of the award.

Another disadvantage of the use of temporary arbitrators is that when several arbitrators render interpretations of the same contract, there is a real danger that conflicting decisions may create more differences than have been settled. In fact, it is not uncommon for a losing party to take the very same issue to arbitration again if it is thought that there is any possibility of obtaining a different ruling. An award by one temporary arbitrator may have so little precedential force as viewed by a subsequent arbitrator that the latter will decide contra.

Because it is easy to change temporary arbitrators, losing parties frequently will demand a change of arbitrators even though there may be no reasonable cause for a change. Thus the parties may be deprived of future valuable service of the eliminated arbitrator. Moreover, frequent and indiscriminate change of arbitrators permits none to become truly acquainted with the needs of the parties. This means that the parties may deprive themselves of the best possible arbitration services.[7]

"Permanent" Arbitrators

A "permanent" arbitrator is one who is selected to serve for a period of time, rather than for just one case or specific group of cases. He may be selected to serve for the term of the collective agreement, for some other specific period, or even at the pleasure of the parties.[8] His responsibilities and functions are determined by the contract by which his office is created. (The terms of permanent-arbitrator contracts vary widely, especially as to the precise jurisdiction of the arbitrator, since each such contract is carefully tailored to meet the special needs and wishes of the parties.) He may be employed on a full-time basis, but more often he is employed on a part-time basis, subject to call when needed. The use of a permanent arbitrator in an industry is evidence that labor-management relations have reached a relatively high degree of maturity.

The permanent arbitrator usually is called either "Impartial Umpire" or "Impartial Chairman." The Impartial Umpire usually sits

---

[7] For an excellent discussion of the advantages and disadvantages of using temporary arbitrators, see Simkin & Kennedy, Arbitration of Grievances (U.S. Dept. of Labor, Div. of Labor Standards, Bull. No. 82, 1946). Also see Warren & Bernstein, "A Profile of Labor Arbitration," 16 LA 970 (1951); "Labor Arbitration Today: Accomplishments and Problems," 16 LA 987 (1951).

[8] The permanent umpire under the 1968 General Motors-UAW agreement "shall serve for one year from date of appointment provided he continues to be acceptable to both parties." The umpire under the 1967 Ford-UAW agreement "shall continue to serve only so long as he continues to be acceptable to both parties." For factors which might affect the tenure or "survival" of a permanent arbitrator, see Fleming, The Labor Arbitration Process 219–220 (Univ. of Ill. Press, 1965).

alone. His function is similar to that of the temporary arbitrator, except that he is appointed to consider all arbitrable disputes which arise during his tenure. The Umpire generally is not commissioned to mediate, his function being quasijudicial in the sense that it is one of contract interpretation and application.[9]

The Impartial Chairman, on the other hand, usually sits as the only impartial member of an arbitration board. Often the Impartial Chairman is commissioned to be something more than an arbitrator, although his functions vary considerably from industry to industry. He may be authorized to mediate, and, where such is the case, he will arbitrate only after other methods fail, making it a last-resort solution. But when the Impartial Chairman does find it necessary to assume the role of an arbitrator, he too may then be restricted to contract interpretation and application.

The type of situation to which use of the permanent arbitrator is especially well adapted is indicated in the recommendation of a fact-finding board appointed by the Secretary of Labor to serve in connection with an International Harvester Company dispute:

> "While the Board believes that a permanent umpire system of arbitration would be more desirable here because of the complexity of the issues involved in the numerous grievances which have arisen under the recently expired contract, as witnessed by cases involving these grievances which have come before the National War Labor Board, we hesitate to recommend provision for a permanent umpire system in the contract unless by agreement of the parties. We recommend that the parties give serious consideration to naming an arbitrator in the contract, whose term of office would extend for the life of the agreement unless otherwise changed by mutual agreement. We believe that the value of the services of an arbitrator to the industrial relations welfare of the parties may be considerably enhanced by the experience gained through more frequent contact with the shop practices prevailing in the various International Harvester plants and the characteristics of the company's wage and incentive system than would be possible under an ad hoc arrangement."[10]

Accepting the above recommendation, the parties established a permanent umpire system at International Harvester, and one in-

---

[9] An interesting variation is the "Impartial Advisor," whose authority is not only restricted to agreement interpretation but is also limited to making findings and recommendations only. New York City Transit Authority, 27 LA 838 (Stark, 1955).

[10] International Harvester Co., 1 LA 512, 522 (Marshall, Spencer & Holly, 1946).

formed observer has been quoted as saying that it "proved to be the turning point in bringing order out of chaos in the field of contract interpretation."[11]

The use of permanent labor-management arbitrators is not new in the United States. Some industries have had umpire systems since the turn of the century. The anthracite coal industry, for instance, established a permanent system in 1903. Increase in the use of permanent arbitrators was gradual at first, but since 1935 it has been fairly rapid. Permanent-arbitrator provisions occur most frequently in collective agreements within the automobile, aircraft, meat-packing, steel, rubber, apparel, and transportation equipment industries.[12] Sometimes a permanent arbitrator is selected for an entire industry, as, for instance, in the full-fashioned hosiery industry.[13]

The Chrysler Corporation uses an Appeal Board which consists of two representatives of each of the parties and an Impartial Chairman. The partisan members of the Appeal Board first attempt to settle all grievances properly referred to the board. If the partisan members are unable to settle a matter, it is decided by the Impartial Chairman.[14]

Sometimes permanent umpire panels are maintained, as, for instance, in the case of the Bethlehem and United States Steel Companies.[15] Umpires are called in turn from these panels. Sometimes,

---

[11] Reilly, "Arbitration's Impact on Bargaining," 16 LA 987, 990 (1951).

[12] See Major Collective Bargaining Agreements: Arbitration Procedures 33 (U.S. Dept. Labor Bull. No. 1425-6, 1966); Arbitration Provisions in Union Agreements 3 (U.S. Dept. Labor Bull. No. 780, 1944). For extensive discussion of some permanent arbitrator systems, see Killingsworth & Wallen, "Constraint and Variety in Arbitration Systems," Labor Arbitration—Perspectives and Problems 56–81 (BNA Incorporated, 1964); Davey, "The John Deere-UAW Permanent Arbitration System," Critical Issues in Labor Arbitration 161–192 (BNA Incorporated, 1957); Arbitration of Labor-Management Grievances (U.S. Dept. Labor Bull. No. 1159, 1954), a study of the Bethlelem Steel system.

[13] See Kennedy, Effective Labor Arbitration 20, 24 (1948).

[14] For a detailed discussion of the Appeal Board, see Wolff, Crane & Cole, "The Chrysler-UAW Umpire System," The Arbitrator and the Parties 111–136 (BNA Incorporated, 1958), which discussion is followed by comments comparing the Ford and General Motors umpire systems with that at Chrysler. Id. at 141–148. Also see Killingsworth & Wallen, "Constraint and Variety in Arbitration Systems," Labor Arbitration—Perspectives and Problems 56, 62–69 (BNA Incorporated, 1964), comparing Ford, Chrysler, and General Motors; "Chrysler Procedure," 29 LA 885 (1958).

[15] See Killingsworth, "Arbitration: Its Uses in Industrial Relations," 21 LA 859, 860 (1953).

too, recommended decisions are made by individual members of a panel, subject to approval by another member thereof.[16]

(a) Advantages

Many persons active as arbitrators or as students of arbitration feel that great value is to be realized from the use of the permanent arbitrator. Dr. George W. Taylor, for instance, urges that ad hoc arbitration should be looked upon, at best, as a transitory method and as entailing comparative disadvantages. "As a support for industrial relations stability, a permanent arbitrator is a prime requisite. Out of the continuing relationship, consistent policy and mutually acceptable procedures can gradually be evolved."[17]

Since the permanent arbitrator is appointed in advance, no time need be lost in selecting one after a dispute arises. Moreover, the advance selection of the arbitrator permits time for careful consideration of his qualifications of impartiality, skill, and knowledge of labor-management relations. The permanent arbitrator usually is selected by the highly desirable method of mutual choice of the parties, rather than by some outside person or agency.

The permanent arbitrator becomes familiar with the provisions of the parties' agreement. He comes to know the day-to-day relationships of the parties, their circumstances, their personalities, and their customary practices. The importance of this knowledge was emphasized by Umpire Harry Shulman:

> "An opportunity should be provided, if possible, for the arbitrator by continuous association with the parties, or at least by repeated association with the parties, to get to know them better. A good many disputes that come to arbitration are deceptive. * * * Some are deceptive even because they don't really portray what the parties are concerned about. They seem to be fighting about one thing, and actually it is something else which is bothering them. That kind of thing happens, at least in my experience, quite frequently. A grievance is filed partly as a sort of pressure technic. It is filed partly in order to lay a foundation for a claim subsequently to be made. An arbitrator who doesn't know and doesn't sense what he is getting into, what

---

[16] See, for instance, Bethlehem Steel Co., 47 LA 270 (Gill/Seward, 1966); Bethlehem Supply Co., 25 LA 366 (Springfield/Seward, 1955). In certain circumstances the parties waive the review and approval requirement. See Bethlehem Steel Co., 37 LA 143, 144 (Valtin, 1961). The newspaper industry utilizes a procedure for appellate review of local arbitrators' awards. See Newspaper Agency Corp., 43 LA 1233 (Platt, 1964).

[17] Taylor, "Effectuating the Labor Contract Through Arbitration," The Profession of Labor Arbitration 20, 40 (BNA Incorporated, 1957).

a decision one way or the other will lead to in the developing strategy, might find himself regretting subsequently, when he finds out what the parties were really after—regretting he made that kind of determination. And so an arbitrator who is in continuous association with the parties may be in a better position to realize what the parties are really fighting for rather than what they appear to be fighting for."[18]

In respect to the matter of costs, if the parties have a large number of disputes so as to require frequent resort to arbitration, the use of a permanent arbitrator is a definte advantage. Moreover, with increased knowledge of the parties' relationship, the permanent arbitrator is able to shorten hearings; from the outset, many details already will be known to him. He needs less time for making investigations since he is familiar with the parties and the industry in which they operate. For the same reason time is saved in the preparation of opinions. Naturally, the saving of time means a reduction of costs.

Permanent arbitrators make their awards available for the guidance of the parties. Cases which do not involve new issues or new situations are likely to be settled at early stages of the grievance procedure since the parties know how the arbitrator has decided similar disputes. Thus one effect of a decision covering a disputed point may be its application by the parties themselves to other disputes involving the same issue. The awards of a permanent arbitrator generally will be consistent with one another, thus avoiding the confusion that sometimes results from having two or more temporary arbitrators rule on similar issues.

The permanent arbitrator has special reason for concern regarding the ultimate effect of each decision. He expects to continue to serve the parties after each decision is rendered and expects to be confronted time and again by his own decisions. The situation is somewhat different with a temporary arbitrator, who, while in good conscience is eager to render a sound award, serves with the realization that he may never again have contact with the parties.

(b) Disadvantages

The difficulty of finding enough mutually acceptable and available grade "A" men is a problem, at least, if not a disadvantage, to be faced in the use of permanent arbitrators. Any arbitrator given

---

[18] Conference on Training of Law Students in Labor Relations, Vol. III, Transcript of Proceedings, 710–711 (1947).

tenure of office should be able to inspire a high degree of confidence in both parties, and he should be experienced. The field of choice is necessarily limited.

There is always a danger that the parties will be too quick to turn to the permanent arbitrator.[19] Once selected, he is easily available. There is temptation to take a short-cut route to dispute settlement. Arbitration should not be substituted for negotiation—harm results when the parties fail to exhaust all possibilities of settlement at the pre-arbitration steps of the grievance procedure. Moreover, there is a danger that some cases will be sent to the arbitrator just to make him earn his salary.

The use of a permanent arbitrator obligates the parties in advance of need to some expense. The arbitrator's retainer fee must be paid regardless of whether his services prove to be needed.[20]

Danger of Favoritism or of "Splitting" Awards

In deciding whether to use permanent or temporary arbitrators another matter should be considered. Both labor and management should be quick to disown any arbitrator who appears to be playing favorites or appears to have the faintest taint of prejudice in favor of either party. Permanent value can be had from arbitration only if decisions are rendered on the merits. In this regard there are two potential dangers. First, the arbitrator might acquire a bias in favor of one side or the other. Second, the arbitrator might go to the other extreme and, in his desire to please both parties, render approximately the same number of awards for each side. In common parlance this is known as "splitting" awards.[21]

Some persons believe that a temporary arbitrator is less likely to acquire a bias in favor of either side and is in a better position

---

[19] For the results of a serious effort to screen grievances headed for the umpire, see Dunne, "The UAW Board of Review on Umpire Appeals at General Motors," 17 Arb. J. 162 (1962).

[20] Sometimes a retainer is provided plus a certain sum per case. For a discussion of the pros and cons of the use of permanent arbitrators, see Simkin & Kennedy, Arbitration of Grievances (U.S. Dept. of Labor, Div. Of Labor Standards, Bull. No. 82, 1946).

[21] Arbitrators as a group reject any suggestion of splitting awards, though the possibility has been recognized. See comments by Jones & Smith, "Management and Labor Appraisals and Criticisms of the Arbitration Process: A Report with Comments," 62 Mich. L. Rev. 1115, 1148–1149 (1964).

to decide cases impartially on the merits. On the other hand, it is argued that the relative stability of the permanent arbitration relationship is the best insurance for decisions on the merits. It is recognized, however, that each of these conclusions is debatable.[22]

Possibly there has been too much concern over this matter. Faith in the integrity and sound judgment of arbitrators generally and in their ability to "see through" attempts to obtain decisions not based on the merits should be sufficient to eliminate initial concern at least. If adequate evidence is produced showing that an arbitrator is not deciding issues on the merits, the parties need lose no time in terminating his services. This matter was given special consideration by the late Harry Shulman. His splendid analysis and expression of views leaves little more to be said:

> "Another, and perhaps less lofty thought, should be expressed. There seems to be a feeling on the part of some that a party can win a greater number of cases if it presents a greater number for decision, the assumption being that some purposeful percentage is maintained. There are many reasons why this point of view is wholly unsound. No Umpire should be retained in office if he is really believed to be making decisions on such a basis. An Umpire should be employed only so long as he renders decisions on the basis of his best and honest judgment on the merits of the controversies presented, and only so long as both parties believe that he does so. If he is believed to be making his decisions on a percentage basis, the remedy is to put him out of office rather than to give him more cases for arbitrary decision.

> "Moreover, as anyone concerned with industrial relations thoroughly knows, there is a great deal of room in the relation between a company and its employees for honest and reasonable differences of opinion on important questions of interpretation and application. If only such questions were brought to an Umpire, their normal, honest determination could fairly be expected in proper course to fall on both sides of the line. A purposeful percentage would be as unnecessary as it would be dishonest.

---

[22] Davey, "Hazards in Labor Arbitration," 1 Ind. & Lab. Rel. Rev. 386, 394, n. 22 (1948). One survey indicated that among those parties who do believe that cases are not always decided on their merits, "the fear of excessive compromise is greatest in a series of cases tried in succession before the same arbitrator, or where there is a permanent arbitrator." Eaton, "Labor Arbitration in the San Francisco Bay Area," 48 LA 1381, 1387 (1967). Danger of splitting awards has been rejected as grounds for resisting the simultaneous arbitration of several grievances before the same arbitrator. Koehring Div., 46 LA 827, 830 (King, 1966).

"From the selfish point of view of a party, there is a great advantage in appealing only cases believed to be entirely good rather than appealing indiscriminately many cases for the purpose of winning a percentage. When a party brings only strong cases, it breeds in others a feeling of confidence in its judgment and in its reasonableness which may tip the scales in cases of doubt and give it a considerable advantage at the start. If, on the other hand, a party brings cases carelessly, without substantial evidence and without apparent judgment in selection, it tends to breed in others a lack of confidence in its judgment which starts it off with a considerable disadvantage. This is particularly true in the 'did or didn't he' type of case here mentioned. For in such cases, [speaking of cases in which the evidence is not conclusive] as already stated, there is little to go on except the conflicting testimony of witnesses and the confidence in the parties developed over a period of time as a result of the record of their own selections."[23]

Mediation by Permanent Arbitrators

As we have noted, Impartial Chairmen often are commissioned to try to bring about settlement of differences through mediation. Sometimes an Impartial Umpire also exercises this function. The Impartial Chairman for the full-fashioned hosiery industry has acted as a mediator as well as an arbitrator.[24] The Impartial Chairman for the men's clothing industry in New York City has had the duty of continuing negotiations concerning disputes brought to him and of deciding issues only if agreement is not reached through such negotiations.[25]

During his tenure with the Ford Motor Company, Umpire Harry Shulman performed some mediation functions, as he once explained:

"The Umpire's contractural jurisdiction is limited to the interpretation, application or alleged violation of the terms of the parties' written agreements, with few exceptions. But, as the parties and I came to know each other better, my actual functions were greatly

---

[23] Ford Motor Company, 1 ALAA ¶67,274, p. 67,620 (1945). Also see comments by Arbitrator Ferguson in Servel, Inc., 1 LA 163, 165 (1945). For a broad discussion of the need for joint acceptability of arbitrators by the parties and its influence upon the arbitration process, see Ryder, "The Impact of Acceptability on the Arbitrator," Developments in American and Foreign Arbitration 94–124 (The Bureau of National Affairs, Inc., 1968), where the subject is also discussed by other observers.

[24] Kennedy, Effective Labor Arbitration 57 (1948).

[25] Morgan, Arbitration in the Men's Clothing Industry in New York City 1, 5 (1940).

expanded. With the full consent of both sides, I conferred with the parties separately and jointly on diverse problems outside that contractual jurisdiction, sat with them as mutual friend and adviser in their negotiations of amendments and supplements, spoke at educational classes and other union meetings, and was generally available for such help as a well-intentioned mutual friend could give in the interest of the total enterprise."[26]

Umpire Shulman also observed that sometimes the parties may press the umpire to decide issues which might be left undecided or at least delayed until time and experience provide greater assurance of wise judgment; in "cases of this character, and others in which the arbitrator conscientiously feels baffled, it may be much wiser to permit him to mediate between the parties for an acceptable solution."[27]

One of the strongest advocates of mediation by permanent arbitrators has been Dr. George W. Taylor. It has been his belief that collective bargaining should be carried on through the arbitration step and that the essential task of most chairmen is to bring about a meeting of minds if possible.[28] His view of the Impartial Chairman's office has been expressed as follows:

"An impartial chairman, then, is first of all a mediator. But he is a very special kind of mediator. He has a reserve power to decide the case either by effectuating his own judgment or by joining with one of the partisan board members to make a majority decision, depending upon the procedure designated by the agreement. A new reason for labor and management to agree is introduced—to avoid a decision. By bringing in a fresh viewpoint, moreover, the impartial chairman may be able to assist the parties in working out their problem in a mutually satisfactory manner. To me, such a result has always seemed to be highly preferable to a decision that is unacceptable to either of the parties. What's wrong per se about an agreement when agreeing is the essence of collective bargaining?"[29]

Dr. Taylor has recognized the widespread belief among industrial relations people that an arbitrator should not mediate, and he has hastened to warn that the Impartial Chairman approach is not uni-

---

[26] Shulman, Opinions of the Umpire, p. 3 of Preface (1943–1946).
[27] Shulman, "Reason, Contract, and Law in Labor Relations," 68 Harv. L. Rev. 999, 1022–1023 (1955), reprinted in Management Rights and the Arbitration Process 169, 195–197 (BNA Incorporated, 1957).
[28] Taylor, "Effectuating the Labor Contract Through Arbitration," The Profession of Labor Arbitration 20, 35 (BNA Incorporated, 1957).
[29] Ibid.

versally applicable; "it is only usable when both parties see eye-to-eye on the point."[30] It is interesting to note that over one third of all problems presented to Dr. Taylor as Impartial Chairman of the full-fashioned hosiery industry were settled by agreement of the parties.[31] A criticism of that office since Dr. Taylor stepped down has been in regard to the decreased number of such voluntary settlements.[32]

Combination of arbitration and mediation functions has been criticized by those who believe that there should be a clear distinction between the two and that the arbitrator's usefulness is reduced when he attempts to mediate.[33]

In some umpire systems neither party wishes the umpire to act as a mediator at any time.[34] Furthermore, an umpire system might utilize mediation for a time but the parties might ultimately come to favor the adjudication approach to decision-making rather than the mediation approach, as is said to be true both at General Motors and at Ford.[35]

As concerns temporary arbitrators, it appears reasonably clear that the majority of parties ordinarily prefer that the arbitrator not attempt mediation.[36]

---

[30] Id. at 36.

[31] Kennedy, Effective Labor Arbitration 28 (1948).

[32] Id. at 216.

[33] For a collection of views expressed in opposition to Dr. Taylor's, see Braden, "The Function of the Arbitrator in Labor-Management Disputes," 4 Arb. J. (N.S.) 35 (1949). For very strong criticism of the Taylor view, see O'Connell, "Should the Scope of Arbitration be Restricted," Proceedings of Eighteenth Annual Meeting of National Academy of Arbitrators 102, 103–104 (BNA Incorporated, 1965).

[34] See, for instance, Davey, "The John Deere-UAW Permanent Arbitration System," Critical Issues in Labor Arbitration 161, 162, 185 (BNA Incorporated, 1957).

[35] See Killingsworth & Wallen, "Constraint and Variety in Arbitration Systems," Labor Arbitration—Perspectives and Problems 56, 64, 68, 75–76 (BNA Incorporated, 1964).

[36] For statistical surveys of views on the desirability of mediation by arbitrators, see Eaton, "Labor Arbitration in the San Francisco Bay Area," 48 LA 1381, 1384 (1967); Warren & Bernstein, "A Profile of Labor Arbitration," 16 LA 970, 981–982 (1951). For further discussion of the pros and cons of mediation by arbitrators, see Simkin, Mediation and the Dynamics of Collective Bargaining 301–312 (The Bureau of National Affairs, Inc., 1971); Panel Discussion, "The Arbitration Hearing—Avoiding a Shambles," Proceedings of 18th Annual Meeting of National Academy of Arbitrators 75, 94–101 (BNA Incorporated, 1965); Fuller, "Collective Bargaining and the Arbitrator," Collective Bargaining and the Arbitrator's Role 8, 24–54 (BNA Incorporated, 1962); Raffaele, "Needed: A Fourth Party in Industrial Relations," 13 Labor L. J. 230 (1962). Also see "Symposium on Arbitration," 15 LA 966, 967–969 (1950). Attempts at mediated

Tripartite Arbitration Board

The tripartite arbitration board, which may be either temporary or permanent, is one made up of one or more members selected by management, an equal number selected by labor, and a neutral member who serves as chairman.[37] The labor and management members generally are partisans and act as advocates for their respective sides.[38] The Code of Ethics for Arbitration does not impose an obligation of strict neutrality upon the party members of tripartite boards.[39]

Thus, the impartial member is in some respects a single arbitrator, and it is something of a misnomer to call the partisan members "arbitrators." Some writers believe it would be more realistic to call them "representatives in arbitration" or use some other such title to acknowledge that the dispute is to be submitted to the neutral member, who is to act as sole arbitrator.[40] In this connection, some agreements provide that the party representatives shall be "advisory" members without voting rights, thus leaving the decision solely to the neutral.[41]

Tripartite boards do not often reach unanimous decisions.[42] In this regard, the collective agreements, statutes, and other instruments under which tripartite boards are established usually provide that a

---

settlements are certainly not rare, but many arbitrators appear reluctant to undertake mediation. See "Survey of Arbitration in 1962," Labor Arbitration—Perspectives and Problems 292, 314 (BNA Incorporated, 1964).

[37] For extensive discussion of tripartite boards, see Davey, "The Uses and Misuses of Tripartite Boards in Grievance Arbitration," Developments in American and Foreign Arbitration 152–179 (The Bureau of National Affairs, Inc., 1968). For the views of other observers, see "The Uses and Misuses of Tripartite Boards in Grievance Arbitration: Workshop Sessions," id. at 180–197.

[38] Sometimes they even present the evidence and argument for their respective sides, no other representatives being used. As in Pfeiffer Brewing Co., 16 LA 89, 90 (Smith, 1951). When they thus serve as counsel, they might agree to make the neutral the sole arbitrator. As in United Tavern, 16 LA 210, 211 (Slavney, 1951).

[39] 15 LA 961, 962–963, 965. Some state arbitration statutes expressly limit the impartiality requirement to neutrals. Similarly, party members of tripartite boards under the Railway Labor Act "are not in legal contemplation, or in fact, supposed to be neutral arbitrators." Arnold v. United Air Lines, Inc., 296 F.2d 191, 195 (CA 7, 1961).

[40] Updegraff & McCoy, Arbitration of Labor Disputes 27 (1946). Also see Reynard, "Drafting of Grievance and Arbitration Articles of Collective Bargaining Agreements," 10 Vanderbilt L. Rev. 749, 757 (1957).

[41] See "Tri-Partite Arbitration: Comment From Readers," 15 Arb. J. 49, 95 (1960). Also see Fleming, "Reflections on the Nature of Labor Arbitration," 61 Mich. L. Rev. 1245, 1267–1268 (1963).

[42] See statistics in "Procedural Aspects of Labor-Management Arbitration," 28 LA 933, 935 (1954 statistics).

majority award of the board shall be final and binding.[43] The side whose position is favored by the neutral member generally joins him in a majority award.

Some agreements give the neutral member the right and responsibility of making the final decision, regardless of whether it is a majority award.[44] Even where the agreement does not given the neutral this right, the parties may agree at the hearing that he alone shall write the opinion and award and that same shall be final and binding upon the parties (the right to dissent may be reserved) ;[45] or they may agree that if no majority award is reached, the award of the neutral shall be final and binding.[46] Indeed, when arbitration commences the parties frequently agree to waive the collective agreement provision for a tripartite board, and they agree that the neutral is to act as sole arbitrator from the outset.[47]

When the neutral member of a tripartite board is not given authority to render a binding award without a majority vote, he might be faced with the necessity of compromising his own views or even accepting the extreme position of one side or the other in order to have a majority award.[48] Sometimes neither party will vote with him in favor of an award based upon the true merits of the case.

---

[43] Thus, in most cases the common law rule requiring a unanimous decision does not apply.

[44] For views on this, see Warren & Bernstein, "A Profile of Labor Arbitration," 16 LA 970, 977 (1951). Similarly, a fairly common provision is that the decision of a majority of the board, or of the neutral member if a majority decision cannot be reached, shall be final and binding. See, Major Collective Bargaining Agreements: Arbitration Procedures 76 (U.S. Dept. Labor Bull. No. 1425-6, 1966).

[45] See Arbitrator Bothwell in 51 LA 41, 42; Hebert in 46 LA 140 at 140; Reynard in 24 LA 116, 117; Ferguson in 20 LA 684 at 684; Feinsinger in 16 LA 501 at 501; Ralston in 15 LA 608 at 608.

[46] See Arbitrator Maggs in 35 LA 249, 250; Howard in 23 LA 429, 430; Livengood in 21 LA 456, 457.

[47] See Arbitrator Geissinger in 46 LA 115, 116; Yagoda in 46 LA 111, 112; King in 46 LA 70 at 70; Stutz in 42 LA 446 at 446; Abernethy in 19 LA 658, 659; Slavney in 16 LA 210, 211. This was also done in Food Employers Council, 20 LA 724, 725, 730 (Van de Water, 1953), but the neutral was also authorized to call upon counsel for the parties for a joint discussion of the issues brought out at the hearing. Where the agreement called for a tripartite board but where the neutral acted throughout as sole arbitrator without a waiver of the board requirement, a court refused to enforce the award of the neutral as sole arbitrator. Local 227, Hod Carriers v. Sullivan, 221 F.Supp. 696 (DC, 1963).

[48] In Publishers' Assn. of New York City, 36 LA 706, 711–712 (1961), Arbitrator Seitz thus had to compromise his own best judgment. In Remington Rand, Inc., 20 LA 799, 800 (1953), Arbitrator Lehoczky withdrew his first proposed award (reported in 20 LA 271) and issued an amended award which attained a majority vote.

(a) Advantages

One advantage of using a tripartite board is that the neutral member may get valuable advice and assistance from the partisan members.[49] The usual practice is for the parties to select persons from their own ranks who are familiar with the background of the dispute. The technical assistance that such persons may give to the neutral member may be of special value. Moreover, use of the tripartite board gives the parties a better opportunity to keep the neutral arbitrator informed as to their real positions, which may not be exactly the same as their formal positions.

The tripartite board has its greatest utility in the arbitration of "interests" disputes.[50] In this regard, the tripartite composition of the National War Labor Board was considered in reality to be a substitute for the lack of completely satisfactory guiding principles and points of reference.[51] In the arbitration of contract-negotiation disputes, it is of the utmost importance that clear understanding of the underlying needs and requirements of the parties be obtained. To this end the neutral member of a tripartite board has the assistance of the partisan members, which may serve to prevent serious errors of judgment.[52]

Awards of tripartite boards, when they are unanimous, tend to be more acceptable than awards by single arbitrators. As one workshop discussion concluded:

"A principal feature of the tripartite system, as expressed during the workshop discussion, is that it promotes acceptability of the award on the part of both management and union and provides an opportunity for practical compromise. This result was not viewed as objectionable, and several responsible industry and union representatives voiced the opinion that compromise is not improper in some cases.

---

[49] See, for instance, Arbitrator Seward in Diamond State Telephone Co., 32 LA 200, 212 (1959); Arbitrator Day in Bell Aircraft Corp., 13 LA 813, 820–821 (1950).

[50] See discussion by Freidin, Labor Arbitration and the Courts 44–46 (U. of Pa. Press, 1952).

[51] See Taylor, "The Arbitration of Labor Disputes," 1 Arb. J. (N.S.) 409, 413 (1946).

[52] See Davey, "Hazards in Labor Arbitration," 1 Ind. & Lab. Rel. Rev. 386, 399 (1948). The same precaution is served by tripartite boards for grievances. See Davey, "The Uses and Misuses of Tripartite Boards in Grievance Arbitration," Developments in American and Foreign Arbitration 152, 190–192 (The Bureau of National Affairs, Inc., 1968), where other advantages of tripartite boards for grievances are enumerated.

It guards against an award which, although correct, may be impracticable for reasons not readily apparent to the neutral member."[53]

(b) Disadvantages

Tripartite boards often cause delay not only in the initial appointment of the partisan members, but also both at hearings and afterwards.[54] The members selected by the parties may insist upon complete reargument of the case after the hearing is concluded, which can lead to unduly extended sessions. Also, time may be lost in waiting for dissenting opinions to be written. Any additional time required necessarily adds to the costs.

The task of the impartial member can be unhappy and difficult. Too frequently he must act as conciliator for the other members, and, as has been seen, he may be forced to compromise his own best judgment in order to secure a majority vote, where such vote is required.

Because of such disadvantages, many parties prefer not to use tripartite boards for "rights" disputes. Although a survey of 1609 agreements indicated that roughly one third specified use of tripartite boards,[55] there is evidence that the actual ultimate use of tripartite boards does not reach nearly so high a percentage.[56]

Procedure Following the Hearing

The inherent nature of tripartite boards brings certain procedural matters into special consideration, particularly in regard to the extent

---

[53] "The Uses and Misuses of Tripartite Boards in Grievance Arbitration: Workshop Sessions," Developments in American and Foreign Arbitration 180, 193 (The Bureau of National Affairs, Inc., 1968).

[54] Regarding the problem of delay and possibilities of minimizing it, see Bell Aircraft Corp., 13 LA 813, 820–821 (Day, 1950).

[55] Major Collective Bargaining Agreements: Arbitration Procedures 41 (U.S. Dept. Labor Bull. No. 1425-6, 1966).

[56] See Davey, "The Uses and Misuses of Tripartite Boards in Grievance Arbitration," Developments in American and Foreign Arbitration 152, 155–157 (The Bureau of National Affairs, Inc., 1968). Davey in his article is generally critical of the use of tripartite boards for grievances, though he did offer suggestions for improving their workings. Id. at 172–174. Some other observers, however, see real utility in tripartite boards for grievances. See "The Uses and Misuses of Tripartite Boards in Grievance Arbitration: Workshop Sessions," id. at 180–197. Strong criticism of use of tripartite boards for grievances has been voiced by Reynard, "Drafting of Grievance and Arbitration Articles of Collective Bargaining Agreements," 10 Vanderbilt L. Rev. 749, 755–760 (1957); Braden, "Recurring Problems in Grievance Arbitration," Preparing and Presenting Arbitration Cases 28, 33–34 (1954).

of consultation and discussion between the impartial chairman and the partisan members following the arbitration hearing.[57]

The members of tripartite boards in many cases meet in executive session to discuss the case sometime after the hearing has been completed.[58] There is no fixed approach to be taken by the neutral in conducting executive sessions. Rather, he is free to choose the course of procedure and to vary his approach in accordance with his evaluation of the parties, the circumstances of the case, and the time when the session is held.[59]

Customarily the impartial chairman of the board will inquire as to the wishes of the partisan members in regard to meeting in executive session. In some cases it will be specifically agreed that there will be no executive session and that the neutral will write the opinion and award with each party reserving the right to file a dissent.[60] When this procedure is followed it also may be agreed that if the award prepared by the neutral does not receive a majority vote, the board will then meet in executive session to discuss the case further.[61] Another procedure is for the neutral to prepare a tentative opinion and award, the executive session then to be held to review the tentative decision.[62]

Often tripartite boards meet in executive session prior to the preparation of any proposed award. But while the session ordinarily gives the neutral a better insight into the dispute, only infrequently does it produce a unanimous decision. Often when the executive session fails to resolve the dispute, it will be understood that the neutral will prepare a proposed award without further conference or communication with the partisan members other than to submit the award to them for concurrence or dissent.[63]

---

[57] For discussion of arbitration procedure generally, see Chapter 7.

[58] Sometimes it is agreed that counsel for the parties may attend the session, as in Safeway Stores, Inc., 22 LA 466, 467 (Hildebrand, 1954).

[59] See explanations by Arbitrators Stein, Haughton, Platt, and Wallen in "Procedural Problems in the Conduct of Arbitration Hearings: A Discussion," Labor Arbitration—Perspectives and Problems 1, 14–16 (BNA Incorporated, 1964).

[60] As in Texas Co., 24 LA 240, 241 (White, 1955).

[61] See Kraft Foods Co., 15 LA 38, 39 (Updegraff, 1950). Similarly, Hillbro Newspaper Printing Co., 48 LA 1304, 1321 (Jones, 1967).

[62] As in Northwest Airlines, Inc., 41 LA 360, 361 (Rohman, 1963).

[63] See, for example, Arbitrator Tatum in 26 LA 477, 478; Dworkin in 21 LA 367, 369; Larking in 17 LA 335, 341.

Usually the neutral prepares an opinion to accompany his proposed award but it is commonly understood that a partisan member in signing an award does not necessarily indicate concurrence with any or all of the statements made by the neutral in his opinion.[64] Even where an executive session produces a unanimous decision, the responsibility for preparing a supporting opinion may be placed solely in the neutral member.[65]

Under some circumstances, at least, the neutral member of a tripartite board might not be compelled to meet in executive session with the partisan members even though the latter members have not expressly waived such session. For instance, in arbitration by a tripartite board under the Railway Labor Act a U.S. District Court declared that the provisions of said Act "necessarily recognize that the partisan members [of the tripartite board] will champion the position of their respective employers," and where all members of the board attended the arbitration hearing the Court held that the failure of the neutral member to call the board together after his proposed findings had been submitted to them should, at most, "be considered as a mere irregularity and not sufficient to vitiate the action of the majority of the Board." There was no showing that the members of the board ever conferred or consulted together as to the findings or as to the award to be made, nor that such consultation was requested by either party. About this the Court said: "The amenities of the situation might well have suggested to the Chairman that the other two members be advised that he would call the Board together for a conference if it was deemed desirable after the draft of the findings and award had been submitted to them. But, realistically considered, it must be recognized that such gesture would have accomplished nothing." The neutral's findings and award, when submitted to the partisan members, were concurred in by the company member and accordingly became the binding award by a majority of the board.[66]

---

[64] Sometimes the neutral himself emphasizes the latter fact. See Arbitrator Seitz in 48 LA 705 at 705; Davey in 44 LA 1057, 1059, 1089; Dash in 23 LA 177 at 177; Smith in 20 LA 625 at 625; Pension in 17 LA 152, 153.

[65] As in Shenango Valley Transit Co., 21 LA 356, 357 (Brecht, 1953).

[66] In re Duluth, Missabe and Iron Range Railway Co., 124 F.Supp. 923, 928–929 (D. Minn., 1954). Also see Railroad Trainmen v. Chicago, M., St.P. & P. R. Co., 237 F.Supp. 404, 423–424 (Dist. Colum., 1964). The opposite result was reached under state law in Simons v. News Syndicate, Inc., 26 LA 281 (N.Y. Sup. Ct., 1956). Failure of the neutral to call an executive session prior to issuance of his proposed award was strongly criticized by one party in Northwest Airlines, Inc., 29 LA 541, 545–546 (1957).

Neither the refusal of a partisan member of a tripartite board to attend the board's executive session nor the resignation or withdrawal of a partisan member prior to issuance of the award has been held to defeat the proceedings or prevent the issuance of a binding majority award by the other members of the board.[67]

Even if the common law rule which permits either party to withdraw from arbitration at any time prior to issuance of an award is otherwise applicable, it is said that where an arbitrator orally "announces what his decision will be, it is doubtful whether a party could withdraw between the time of that announcement and the formal written rendition."[68]

Methods of Selecting Arbitrators

Selection of an arbitrator satisfactory to both parties often entails difficulties. No part of the arbitration process is more important than that of selecting the person who is to render the decision. Fortunately, a variety of selection methods are available.

It is generally assumed that selection by mutual agreement of the parties is the most desirable method. This may be true in terms of insuring acceptance of the award, although there is no inherent reason why an equally if not more competent arbitrator might not be selected by a third party. However, there does appear to be more justification for mutual selection of permanent arbitrators since they ordinarily have some tenure of office.

Collective agreements often provide for selection by the parties[69] and, at the same time, alternative methods to be used if they fail

---

[67] See Publishers' Assn. of New York City v. Stereotypers' Union, 181 N.Y.S. 2d 527 (N.Y. Sup. Ct., 1959); Shoeworkers Assn. v. Federal Shoe, Inc., 24 LA 573, 576 (Maine Sup. Ct., 1955); Street Ry. Employees v. Connecticut Co., 24 LA 107, 108–110 (Conn. Sup. Ct., 1955). Cf., Fromer Foods, Inc. v. Edelstein Foods, Inc., 181 N.Y.S. 2d 352 (N.Y. Sup. Ct., 1959), involving death of a partisan member. Also see West Towns Bus Co. v. Division 241, 168 N.E.2d 473 (Ill. App. Ct., 1960); Consumers Power Co., 24 LA 581, 582 (Smith, Howlett & Sorensen, 1955). For a related discussion, see Chapter 7, topic titled "Default Awards."

[68] Updegraff & McCoy, Arbitration of Labor Disputes 122 (1946). To similar effect, Updegraff, Arbitration and Labor Relations 280 (The Bureau of National Affairs, Inc., 1970). For related matter, see Chapter 2, Legal Status of Arbitration.

[69] Under some circumstances this step may be held to have been waived. See Barbet Mills, Inc., 16 LA 563 (Livengood, 1951). But see Hartford Gas Co., 49 LA 630, 631–633 (Summers, 1967).

to agree within a specified time. Provision for alternative methods of appointment always should be made in the agreement. Otherwise, proposed arbitration might be defeated for want of an effective means of selecting the arbitrator.[70] This need not be the result, however, under the modern arbitration statutes which specify court appointment of an arbitrator if the parties cannot agree upon one or upon a method of appointment.[71]

The neutral member, or members, of tripartite boards may be selected by the members appointed by the parties. Agreements often provide that each party shall choose one or more arbitrators and that those so chosen shall select a neutral chairman. The partisan members, however, may fail to agree upon the neutral, so here too the agreement should provide alternate methods of selection.

Aid from an outside agency, whether requested at the outset or after the parties have failed to agree upon an arbitrator, generally takes one of two forms: (1) A list is submitted from which, often by a process of elimination, the parties select an arbitrator;[72] or (2) direct appointment of the arbitrator by the agency. An agreement may designate the FMCS, a state agency, the AAA, a judge, some public official, or any other impartial agency.[73]

The type of aid rendered by the FMCS depends upon the nature of the dispute and the authority vested in the service by the parties.

---

[70] See discussion by board of inquiry in Rochester Transit Corp., 19 LA 538, 558 (Tolley, McKelvey & Turkus, 1952). For a survey of collective agreement provisions on selecting the arbitrator, see Major Collective Bargaining Agreements: Arbitration Procedures 36–46 (U.S. Dept. Labor Bull. No. 1425-6, 1966). While many agreements provide alternative methods of appointment, this precaution is by no means universal. Id. at 36.

[71] For example, the New York statute provides: "If the arbitration agreement does not provide for a method of appointment of an arbitrator, or if the agreed method fails or for any reason is not followed, or if an arbitrator fails to act and his successor has not been appointed, the court, on application of a party, shall appoint an arbitrator." 75 CPLR §7504.

[72] For an explanation as to how the FMCS and the AAA decide what names to place on the list for a given case, see Jones & Smith, "Management and Labor Appraisals and Criticisms of the Arbitration Process: A Report and Comments," 62 Mich. L. Rev. 1115, 1138–1139 (1964). Also see "Report by FMCS, AAA on Arbitration Panels," 1967 Labor Relations Yearbook 225, 226 (The Bureau of National Affairs, 1968).

[73] For statistics as to the use of various appointing agencies, see "Survey of Arbitration in 1964," Proceedings of Eighteenth Annual Meeting of National Academy of Arbitrators 243, 245, 251–252 (BNA Incorporated, 1965); "Survey of Arbitration in 1962," Labor Arbitration—Perspectives and Problems 292, 296 (BNA Incorporated, 1964); Warren & Bernstein, "A Profile of Labor Arbitration," 16 LA 970, 974–975 (1951).

The FMCS encourages the parties to make their own selection from a list of qualified arbitrators. In this regard, FMCS regulations state:

"Two possible methods of selection from a panel are—(1) at a joint meeting, alternately striking names from the submitted panel until one remains, and (2) each party separately advising the Service of its order of preference by numbering each name on the panel. In almost all cases, an arbitrator is chosen from one panel of names. However, if a request for another panel is made, the Service will comply with the request, providing that additional panels are permissible under the terms of the agreement or the parties so stipulate."[74]

Under the rules of the AAA, parties may select the arbitrator as they please. However, in order to facilitate selection, the association sends lists of names to the parties. They have the privilege of crossing off names objected to. The association then makes the appointment from the names remaining on the lists, in order of preference.[75] If the parties fail to agree upon any of the names submitted, they may request additional lists. If they still cannot agree, the association appoints an arbitrator whose name has not appeared on the lists.[76]

While the rules of the FMCS and the AAA provide for direct appointments by the agency,[77] both agencies much prefer selection by the parties. It is said that the agencies will make the selection "only when the parties are adamant."[78]

---

[74] Section 1404.6(c), FMCS: Arbitration Policies, Functions, and Procedures (the Regulations were revised in 1967 and amended in 1968).

[75] AAA Rule 12. The Association may aid in the selection of the arbitrator even where it is not administering other aspects of the case, as in Celotex Corp., 24 LA 369, 370 (Reynard, 1955).

[76] Labor Arbitration 14–15 (AAA, 1957). The Association's formal rules do not actually provide for additional lists. See 43 LA 1292, 1293 (1965 Rules); 28 LA 908, 909 (1952 Rules).

[77] Section 1404.7 of the FMCS regulations states: "The Service will make a direct appointment of an arbitrator based upon a joint request, or upon a unilateral request when the applicable collective bargaining agreement so authorizes." Rule 12 of the AAA regulations states: "If the parties fail to agree upon any of the persons named or if those named decline or are unable to act, or if for any other reason the appointment cannot be made from the submitted lists, the Administrator shall have power to make the appointment from other members of the Panel without the submission of any additional lists."

[78] "Basic Patterns in Labor Arbitration Agreements," 34 LA 931, 939 (1960), where it is also noted that the FMCS makes the selection in less than 3 percent of the cases which it handles. The direct appointment percentage for the AAA is also low, being only about 5 percent in some years. See "Procedural Aspects of Labor-Management Arbitration," 28 LA 933, 935 (1957). Also see Murphy, "Free Choice of Arbitrators Is Still the American Way in Labor Arbitrations," 3 Arb. J. (N.S.) 234 (1948).

Arbitrator's Acceptance or Withdrawal

The Code of Ethics for Arbitrators includes the following statement on acceptance, refusal, or withdrawal from office: "The arbitrator, being appointed by voluntary act of the parties, may accept or decline the appointment. When he accepts he should continue in office until the matter submitted to him is finally determined. When there are circumstances which, in his judgment, compel his withdrawal, the parties are entitled to prompt notice and explanation."[79]

American Arbitration Association Rule 18 provides that if any arbitrator should resign, die, withdraw, refuse, or be unable or disqualified to perform the duties of his office, the AAA shall declare the office vacant and the vacancy shall be filled in the same manner as that governing the original appointment, the matter to be reheard by the new arbitrator.[80]

Arbitrators and Their Qualifications

Background, Training, and Supply of Arbitrators

With the rapid expansion of labor-management arbitration during and since World War II, there has emerged a large group of persons experienced and available for arbitration service. No special educational or technical training is required for arbitrators except as may be specifically required by the parties. It is not surprising, then, that arbitrators come from a wide variety of backgrounds. Indeed, the group includes professors, lawyers, judges, public office holders, ministers, accountants, economists, professional arbitrators, and others.[81]

---

[79] 15 LA 961, 963 (Part I, §6).

[80] 43 LA 1292, 1293.

[81] For "vital statistics" concerning arbitrators (education, background, arbitration training, arbitration income, and the like), see "Survey of the Arbitration Profession in 1969," Arbitration and the Public Interest 275–303 (The Bureau of National Affairs, Inc., 1971); "Survey of the Arbitration Profession," The Profession of Labor Arbitration 176–182 (BNA Incorporated, 1957); "Survey of Arbitration in 1962," Labor Arbitration—Perspectives and Problems 292–294, 304–316 (BNA Incorporated, 1964); "Procedural Aspects of Labor-Management Arbitration," 28 LA 933, 936 (1954 statistics); Warren & Bernstein, "A Profile of Labor Arbitration," 16 LA 970, 973–974 (1951). For general discussions of arbitrators and the qualities essential to their success, see Kelliher, "The Presidential Address," Proceedings of 18th Annual Meeting of National Academy of Arbitrators 66, 68–71 (BNA Incorporated, 1965); Loucks," Arbitration—A Profession?" Challenges to Arbitration 20–31 (BNA Incorporated, 1960); Cole, Freidin & Oliver, "The Status and Expendability of the Labor Arbitrator," The Profession of Labor Arbitration 42–65 (BNA Incorporated, 1957).

Although there are many experienced arbitrators who are readily acceptable to the parties, there is a shortage of such arbitrators. The problem was stated by a committee of the NAA:

"Since experience is unquestionably the best teacher in this field, as in so many others, and since there are many potentially able arbitrators whose services are not being used, the problem of maintaining an adequate supply of arbitrators now and in the future is to a large extent a problem of promoting the acceptability of newcomers * * *."[82]

Subsequently a committee of the American Bar Association (ABA) noted the absence of any institution comparable to the National War Labor Board, which served as the training ground for many arbitrators, and the committee added that both management and labor "are understandably reluctant to permit unknown men to experiment with their affairs."[83]

To help alleviate the problem, the AAA, the FMCS, and the NAA have cooperated in programs to aid in giving training, experience, and acceptability to new arbitrators.[84]

Qualifications Set Forth in Agreement

The parties may, by the collective agreement, specify qualifications which must be possessed by the arbitrator.[85] The selection of an arbitrator may be hampered seriously, however, by an attempt

---

[82] "Report on the Education and Training of New Arbitrators," The Profession of Labor Arbitration 170, 173 (BNA Incorporated, 1957). For another discussion as to why there is a shortage of acceptable arbitrators, see Davey, "Restructuring Grievance Arbitration Procedures: Some Modest Proposals," 54 Iowa L. Rev. 560, 561–564 (1969). Also see Hill, "The Presidential Address: The Academy and the Expanding Role of Neutrals," Arbitration and the Expanding Role of Neutrals 187, 190–194 (The Bureau of National Affairs, Inc., 1970), for figures as to the supply of arbitrators and the scope of demand for their services.

[83] "Report of the Committee on Labor Arbitration," Collective Bargaining and the Arbitrator's Role 242, 243 (BNA Incorporated, 1962).

[84] For descriptions and explanations of these programs and indications as to their degree of success, see "The Development of New Arbitrators: Report of Committee, 1970–1971," Arbitration and the Public Interest 305–321 (The Bureau of National Affairs, Inc., 1971); "Replenishment of Professional Arbitrators," Labor Arbitration—Perspectives and Problems 317 (BNA Incorporated, 1964); "Survey of Arbitration in 1962," Id. at 292, 309; Jones & Smith, "Management and Labor Appraisals and Criticisms of the Arbitration Process: A Report with Comments," 62 Mich. L. Rev. 1115, 1132–1140 (1964); "The Development of Qualified New Arbitrators," Collective Bargaining and the Arbitrator's Role 205 (BNA Incorporated, 1962); Zack, "An Evaluation of Arbitration Apprenticeships," Challenges to Arbitration 169 (BNA Incorporated, 1960).

[85] This is not the usual practice. See Major Collective Bargaining Agreements: Arbitration Procedures 50–51 (U.S. Dept. Labor Bull. No. 1425-6, 1966).

to fix qualifications rigidly in the agreement. It may be impossible to secure an arbitrator who meets the qualifications so specified. Although the determination of qualifications generally is left to the parties, a few state arbitration statutes do prescribe qualifications designed to insure impartiality.

Impartiality

No qualification is more important than that of impartiality. It may well be that no man can be absolutely free from bias or prejudice of any kind, but it is not too much to expect an arbitrator to be able to divest himself of any personal inclinations, and to be able to stand between the parties with an open mind. This does not mean, however, that an arbitrator should decide contrary to his own best judgment. Indeed, the element of honesty is not satisfied unless the arbitrator fully believes that he is doing what is right. To be an arbitrator worthy of the name, one must always be able and ready to "call 'em as he sees 'em." As long as both parties believe that an arbitrator is doing just that, they will respect him whether or not they "see 'em" the same way he does.[86]

Integrity

The integrity of arbitrators generally can be expected to be of the highest. Appointed judges sometimes are criticized for allegedly receiving political "plums." Elected judges sometimes are accused of being politicians. Arbitrators generally are not open to such criticism since they are selected by free choice of the parties or their agent. But how may a prospective arbitrator be tested for integrity and impartiality? Careful consideration of his personal and business background and affiliations is enlightening in this respect. Has the arbitrator any financial or business interest in the affairs of either party?[87]

---

[86] Some parties remain unconvinced that the typical arbitrator always "calls 'em as he sees 'em." See Jones & Smith, "Management and Labor Appraisals and Criticisms of the Arbitration Process: A Report With Comments," 62 Mich. L. Rev. 1115, 1146–1147 (1964). However, many parties apparently believe that awards are generally fair and objective. See Eaton, "Labor Arbitration in the San Francisco Bay Area," 48 LA 1381, 1387 (1967).

[87] Arbitrators must disclose to parties any dealings that might create an impression of possible bias. Commonwealth Coatings Corp. v. Continental Casualty Co., 89 S.Ct. 337 (1968). The Code of Ethics for Arbitrators states that it is "incumbent upon the arbitrator at the time of his selection to disclose to the parties any circumstances, associations or relationships that might reasonably raise any doubt as to his impartiality or his technical qualification for the particular case." 15 LA 961, 963 (Part I, §3). For an extensive survey of views

Has there been any such interest in the past? Does he have any personal affiliations, either directly or indirectly, with either of the parties? Does he have strong opinions in favor of either labor or management?[88] What has been his past record as an arbitrator?[89] The parties may review some past awards of the arbitrator, but the number of awards rendered in favor of each side should not be used as a test of impartiality. An arbitrator who deliberately tries to please both sides by "splitting" awards is not one who decides cases objectively. It is the arbitrator's fairness and good judgment, as indicated by his past awards and by his general reputation, that the parties should be concerned with.

Ability and Expertise

Naturally, extensive arbitration experience is one indication of ability. But at the outset a labor-management arbitrator should have a broad background of social and economic study or experience. He should have an analytical mind and should be able to orient himself quickly when dealing with new subject matter. Maturity of judgment is indispensable. Diplomacy helps too.

Must an arbitrator be something of a specialist in the subject matter which he is to consider? Generally speaking, no. While neither side cares to appoint persons completely unfamiliar with industrial matters, an arbitrator generally will not be disqualified merely because he is not an expert in the subject of the dispute. An acceptable expert may be difficult or impossible to secure. Moreover, the parties often prefer an arbitrator who has general business or financial experience or who is versed in law. Arbitrators, as judges, generally should be selected for their ability to understand all sorts of problems. But in

---

concerning the scope of the arbitrator's duty to disclose information concerning his background, associations, previous and current contacts with a party, and the like, see Sherman, "The Duty of Disclosure in Labor Arbitration," 25 Arb. J. 73 (1970). Also see Sherman, "Arbitrator's Duty of Disclosure—A Sequel," Arbitration and the Public Interest 203–233 (The Bureau of National Affairs, Inc., 1971); Elson, "Ethical Responsibilities of the Arbitrator," Id. at 194–203.

[88] A New York court was upheld in removing an arbitrator it had appointed but who, the court later learned, was partisan toward labor, although his integrity and honesty were not questioned. Western Union v. Selly, 2 LA 688 (N.Y. Ct. App., 1946). Also see In re Steuben, 14 LA 541 (N.Y. Sup. Ct. 1950); In re Culinary Bar & Grill Employees, 11 LA 1119 (N.Y. Sup. Ct., 1949).

[89] For helpful suggestions to aid parties in obtaining information concerning any particular arbitrator and suggestions to aid in evaluating his thinking and methods, see Jaffee, "Have Gavel, Will Travel," 18 Arb. J. 235 (1963).

some disputes a specialist may be considered essential.[90] Thus the parties may seek an industrial engineer, or a doctor, or some other type of specialist, depending upon the technical matter involved.

The desire of appointing agencies to accommodate the special needs of parties is illustrated by the following statement in an FMCS memorandum (seeking to establish a roster of arbitrators experienced in public employee disputes) sent to all arbitrators on the FMCS National Roster:

> "[We are] anxious to insure that our arbitration services continue to be responsive to the particular needs of those who normally utilize our services. For example, we make every effort to accommodate the parties when it comes to an arbitrator's geographical location, his experience or educational background or his particular specialty. Our national roster of arbitrators is maintained in such a way that we can now provide this tailored service. We now wish to refine our service even more by establishing a separate list of arbitrators who have had some experience in the public sector."[91]

Legal Training

Persons trained in law often make able arbitrators, although legal training is not indispensable. Many labor-management arbitrators are lawyers. Many parties prefer lawyers as arbitrators,[92] and lawyers are considered especially desirable for the position of neutral chairman of arbitration boards.[93]

Legal training helps an arbitrator to be objective. It improves his ability to analyze and evaluate facts. This means that the arbitrator who has had legal training may be less likely to be moved by personal bias or by extraneous evidence. By no means, however, do all lawyers make good arbitrators. Especially ineffective is the lawyer who is so concerned with technical rules of evidence and procedure that the

---

[90] For pros and cons as to use of arbitrators with "specific expertise" for the given dispute, see Eaton, "Labor Arbitration in the San Francisco Bay Area," 48 LA 1381 at 1381 (1967). Regarding need for technical expertness of arbitrators, see Warren & Bernstein, "A Profile of Labor Arbitration," 16 LA 970, 975 (1951). Some agreements provide for specialists for certain types of cases, or for employment of technical experts to assist the arbitrator when needed. See Major Collective Bargaining Agreements: Arbitration Procedures 47–50 (U.S. Dept. Labor Bull. No. 1425-6, 1966).

[91] January 10, 1969, Memorandum from the FMCS General Counsel to all arbitrators on the National Roster.

[92] See Eaton, "Labor Arbitration in the San Francisco Bay Area," 48 LA 1381 at 1381 (1967).

[93] See Gotshal, "The Lawyer's Place in Arbitration," 1 Arb. J. (N.S.) 367 (1946).

arbitration process is made unduly complicated. Such concern also may result in an award which fails to give sufficient consideration to the real merits of the dispute. Legal training alone is not enough to make an able arbitrator, but if a person possesses the other qualifications, legal training will make him even better.

Arbitrator's Immunity From Civil Liability

An arbitrator acting in his official capacity performs quasi-judicial duties and, like a judge, is immune from civil liability for acts done in his arbitral capacity.[94] In recognizing this immunity, it is considered that arbitrators "must be free from the fear of reprisals" and "must of necessity be uninfluenced by any fear of consequences for their acts."[95] Indeed, in light of the national policy which encourages arbitration it is said that the common-law rule protecting arbitrators from liability "ought not only to be affirmed, but, if need be, expanded."[96]

The Arbitrator's Accountability

Ordinarily a person must possess at least minimal qualifications in order to get his "first case" as an arbitrator. Regardless of his qualifications at the outset, the more important ultimate consideration is how well has he performed as an arbitrator. As is no doubt generally typical of the appointing agencies, it is the policy of the FMCS "to maintain on its roster only those arbitrators who are experienced, qualified, and acceptable, and who adhere to ethical standards."[97] Also as is no doubt typical, the FMCS evaluates the awards of arbitrators selected with its assistance "with a view to determining whether they meet the accepted professional standards as to form, clarity and logic."[98]

The arbitrator is indeed accountable, as was emphasized by a president of the NAA:

"The arbitrator functions in a glass bowl. The conduct of the hearing is closely observed by sophisticated, knowledgeable advocates.

---

[94] Cahn v. ILGWU, 311 F.2d 113, 51 LRRM 2186 (CA 3, 1962).
[95] Babylon Milk & Cream Co. v. Horvitz, 26 LA 121, 122 (N.Y. Sup. Ct., 1956).
[96] Hill v. Aro Corp., 363 F.Supp. 324 (DC, 1967). For related discussion, see Glick, "Bias, Fraud, Misconduct and Partiality of the Arbitrator," 22 Arb. J. 161 (1967).
[97] FMCS Regulations, Section 1404.2
[98] FMCS Regulations, Section 1404.11

An arbitrator who exhibits a lack of understanding of the process and who fails to conduct a hearing in an orderly fashion will usually find himself unacceptable to the parties for a subsequent hearing. The *ad hoc* arbitrator has no tenure; an umpire has limited tenure, and nothing is so impermanent as the permanent arbitrator. The arbitrator is selected by the parties either directly or through the offices of the AAA, the FMCS, or state mediation agencies. His decisions are read and reread, not only by the parties, but by hundreds of company and union representatives who have access to his awards through their own systems of distribution. Awards that are not based upon logical, sound interpretation of the provisions of the agreement will very quickly make the arbitrator responsible unacceptable to companies and unions alike.

"Sophisticated companies and unions do not keep a box score. They are primarily concerned with the quality of decisions. The companies and unions which submit a dispute to arbitration have complete freedom of choice in the selection of the arbitrator. The arbitrator is almost never foisted upon the parties. We are all aware of the fact that unions and companies, and those who represent them, effectively utilize their private pipelines of information. An arbitrator's reputation precedes him, and a series of poorly reasoned or poorly written decisions will very quickly read that arbitrator out of the profession. Major companies and major unions have their own 'don't use' list. That is a fact of life * * *."[99]

Data on Arbitrators

Information concerning the qualifications of some of the more active arbitrators may be had by consulting the "Directory of Arbitrators" prepared by The Bureau of National Affairs, Inc., or the "Who's Who" (of arbitrators) prepared by Prentice-Hall, Inc. This information includes the name, age, address, education, occupation, affiliations, experience, articles or books written, awards published, and other miscellaneous information concerning the arbitrator.

The FMCS provides biographical data on the arbitrators whose names are supplied to the parties for selection, and most other designating agencies follow the same practice.

---

[99] Luskin, "The Presidential Address: Arbitration and its Critics," Developments in American and Foreign Arbitration 125, 134 (The Bureau of National Affairs, Inc., 1968). For various factors which parties might consider in accepting or rejecting an arbitrator, see Eaton, "Labor Arbitration in the San Francisco Bay Area," 48 LA 1381, 1382 (1967); Fleming, The Labor Arbitration Process 209–210 (Univ. of Ill. Press, 1965).

Tribunals Under Railway Labor Act

One of the nation's most extensive experiences in labor-management arbitration has resulted from the arbitration provisions of the Railway Labor Act of 1926.[100]

Since it sometimes has been suggested that arbitration tribunals of the RLA variety be used for other industries, consideration is given here to the basic features of those tribunals. As was seen in Chapter 3, the present railroad labor legislation of the United States recognizes the distinction between disputes as to "rights" and those as to "interests." The NMB is concerned primarily with "interests" disputes, while the NRAB is concerned with "rights" disputes.

Railroad "Interests" Disputes

The NMB has jurisdiction over any "dispute concerning changes in rates of pay, rules, or working conditions not adjusted by the parties in conference," or any "other disputes not referable to the National Railroad Adjustment Board and not adjusted in conference between the parties or where conferences are refused." Either party may invoke the services of the NMB, or the NMB may proffer its services if a labor emergency is found to exist. The primary function of the NMB is to help the parties, through mediation, to reach agreement. Upon failure to bring about an amicable settlement through mediation, however, the Board seeks to induce the parties to submit the controversy to voluntary arbitration.

Section 7 of the Act provides details for the organization of the arbitration tribunal. It provides that, whenever a controversy is not settled "either in conference between representatives of the parties or by the appropriate adjustment board or through mediation," it may, by agreement of the parties, be submitted "to the arbitration of a board of three (or, if the parties to the controversy so stipulate, of six) persons * * *." If the parties choose a board of three, then

---

[100] 45 U.S.C. §§151–163, 181–188; 1 LRR Man. 843. The arbitration provisions of the 1926 Act (44 Stat. 577) were amended and expanded in 1934 (48 Stat. 1185), in 1936 (49 Stat. 1189), and in 1966 (80 Stat. 208). For extensive discussion of the Act, see Lecht, Experience Under Railway Labor Legislation (Colum. Univ. Press, 1955). Also, "Procedures Under the Railway Labor Act: A Panel Discussion," Proceedings of 18th Annual Meeting of National Academy of Arbitrators 27 (BNA Incorporated, 1965).

each party selects one member and the two so selected choose the neutral member. If a board of six is desired, each side selects two members, and the four so selected choose the two neutral members. If the members selected by the parties cannot agree upon the neutral or neutrals, they are appointed by the NMB. The board of arbitration selects one of its members to serve as chairman and makes such rules as are necessary for conducting hearings. The members selected by the parties need not be impartial. Each party compensates its appointees and the NMB compensates neutrals.

The award of the board, when signed by a majority of the members, may be filed with the clerk of the federal district court for the district in which the controversy arose or the arbitration is entered into. When so filed, it is conclusive on the parties as to the merits and facts of the controversy, and, unless within ten days a petition to impeach it on grounds specifically set out in the Act is filed with the court, judgment will be entered on the award.

National Railroad Adjustment Board

Upon submission of a petition by either side, the National Railroad Adjustment Board takes jurisdiction over "disputes between an employee or group of employees and a carrier or carriers growing out of grievances or out of the interpretation or application of agreements concerning rates of pay, rules, or working conditions," after they have been "handled in the usual manner up to and including the chief operating officer of the carrier designated to handle such disputes." Thus it is seen that the NRAB handles "rights" disputes. It assumes jurisdiction only if at least one of the parties wishes it to do so.[101]

The NRAB is strictly bipartisan. It is composed of 34 members, 17 of whom are selected and compensated by the carriers and 17 by the railroad labor organizations.[102] The NRAB is organized into

---

[101] Railroad employees no longer have any option to take their grievance under the collective agreement to court without exhausting the NRAB remedy. Andrews v. Louisville & Nashville Railroad Co., 92 S.Ct. 1562 (1972). Cf., Glover v. St. Louis San Francisco Rwy. Co., 89 S.Ct. 548 (1969).

[102] Prior to amendment of the RLA in 1970 the Board had 36 members, 18 selected by each side. The 1970 amendment, Public Law 91-234, reduced from 10 to 8 the number of members on the Board's First Division. This was made necessary by the merger of four unions representing the trainmen, firemen, conductors, and switchmen into a single union, the United Transportation Union. Although each side now has four members on the First Division, only two members from each side are entitled to vote.

four Divisions, each Division having jurisdiction over specified classes of railroad employees. The NRAB functions almost entirely through the individual Divisions, and each Division for all practical purposes is independent of the others. Each Division really amounts to a distinct arbitration tribunal, bipartisan in nature, with equal representation from the carriers and the labor organizations. The First Division has eight permanent members,[103] the Second and Third Divisions have 10 each, and the Fourth Division has six.

When a dispute is referred to one of the Divisions a hearing is held, unless waived. At the hearing the parties may be heard either in person, by counsel, or by other representatives. After the hearing, the Division proceeds to decide the case. As a matter of practice the Divisions frequently hold successive hearings on a group of cases, then hold sessions for deliberation and decision of the cases. Since each Division is equally represented by labor and management and since the representatives of each side tend almost always to vote the same way, a unanimous vote generally is necessary to decide a case. While many cases do receive the required vote, numerous others do not. Deadlocks are inevitable and frequent. The RLA provides for the selection of referees in such cases. The referee sits with the Division as a temporary member and decides the cases for which he is appointed. Usually a referee's appointment will be for a group of cases. Deadlocked cases are set aside until a sufficient number have accumulated to warrant calling in a referee.

Initial responsibility for the selection of referees is upon the Divisions. If a Division, however, is unable to agree upon a neutral person to serve as referee, one is selected by the NMB. Within ten days after a Division certifies to the NMB the fact of inability to agree upon a referee, the NMB makes the appointment. The Divisions, generally speaking, have not been able to agree upon referees, so the primary responsibility for appointment of referees has been with the NMB. All referees are compensated by the NMB.

Cases assigned to a referee are presented to him by Division members. Occasionally, if request is made, some Divisions permit oral argument by the parties before the referee. Generally, however, the referee's knowledge of a case comes from the parties' written submissions and

---

[103] See explanation in prior footnote.

from briefs and arguments of Division members.[104] Each Division has both labor and management members highly skilled in presenting cases to the referees. The referee is given opportunity to study case records prior to meeting with Division members. Division members often present written briefs to the referee and always give him opportunity to ask questions.

The referee then takes the cases under advisement, makes his findings, and writes the proposed opinions and awards. Practice varies as to the length of opinions. The Third Division, for instance, expects its referees to write relatively long opinions. The First Division prefers brevity. The referee discusses proposed awards with the Division and voting follows. The side in whose favor an award is rendered generally will vote with the referee to provide the required majority vote.[105]

The RLA as amended in 1966 provides that Adjustment Board awards "shall be final and binding upon both parties to the dispute" [though, as noted hereinbelow, limited right of court review does now exist].[106] If a dispute arises over the interpretation of an award, the Act directs the Division to interpret the award upon request by either party.

If an award is in favor of the employees, the Division is directed by the Act to issue an order requiring the carrier to make the award effective. After such order is issued, the Division has nothing to do with its enforcement. When a denial award is issued, the Division

---

[104] The NRAB is essentially an appellate tribunal. The Chrysler Corporation Appeal Board, too, was an appellate tribunal for many years; however, its procedure of using only signed written statements as evidence was changed in 1963 to receive evidence in the manner customary in most arbitration proceedings. See Jones & Smith, "Management and Labor Appraisals and Criticisms of the Arbitration Process: A Report with Comments," 62 Mich. L. Rev. 1115, 1129 (1964). For an illustration of the Appeal Board's former practice, see Chrysler Corp., 32 LA 719, 721 et seq. (Wolff, 1959).
[105] For other studies and discussions of the Adjustment Board, see Mangum, "Railroad Grievance Procedures," 15 Ind. & Lab. Rel. Rev. 491 (1962); Kaufman, "Grievance Arbitration in the Railroad Industry," 9 Labor L. J. 244 (1958); Daugherty, Whiting & Guthrie, "Arbitration by the National Railroad Adjustment Board," Arbitration Today 93–127 (BNA Incorporated, 1955); Lecht, Experience Under Railway Labor Legislation 10–11, 83, 163, 171, 191–192 (1955); Jones, National Railroad Adjustment Board (1941); Spencer, The National Railroad Adjustment Board (1938); Garrison, "The National Railroad Adjustment Board; A Unique Administrative Agency," 46 Yale L. J. 567 (1937).
[106] Sec. 3(m). As to the permissible scope of court review under the language of the Act prior to the 1966 amendments, see Gunther v. San Diego & Arizona Eastern Ry. Co., 86 S.Ct. 368 (1965).

is directed by the Act to issue an order to the petitioner stating such determination.

Prior to the 1966 amendments only the winning party could take the award to court, which it could do for the purpose of seeking court enforcement. Under the amendments the loser, too, has a right to take the award to court, for review. In either instance the court may not set the award aside except on limited grounds.

If a carrier does not comply with an order implementing an award, the party in whose favor it stands may within two years sue upon it for enforcement by the appropriate federal district court. In such suit the findings and order of the Adjustment Board Division "shall be conclusive on the parties".[107] The court may, however, set the Division's order aside for any of the following reasons: (1) failure of the Division to comply with requirements of the Act, (2) failure of the Division to confine itself to matters within the scope of its jurisdiction, or (3) fraud or corruption by a member of the Division making the order.[108]

Under the 1966 amendments any party who is aggrieved by an NRAB award (that is, a loser, whether an employee or carrier) may obtain review thereof by petitioning the appropriate federal district court. Here again, the action must be instituted within two years and the findings and order of the Adjustment Board Division "shall be conclusive on the parties," except that the court may set the order aside or remand it to the Division for any of the three reasons noted in the paragraph immediately hereinabove.[109]

---

[107] Sec. 3(p). The two-year limitation is stated in Sec. 3(r).

[108] Sec. 3(p). These three grounds for setting awards aside are part of the 1966 amendments. As to the court's right to "interpret" awards, see Sweeney v. Florida East Coast Ry. Co., 67 LRRM 2263 (CA 5, 1968). The burden of seeking court enforcement of awards is reduced by a provision of the Act which relieves the petitioner from some of the court costs and which allows a petitioner who prevails in his action a reasonable attorney's fee.

[109] Sec. 3(q). Prior to the 1966 amendments the party against whom an award was directed had no right to take it to court for review. Essentially the only way an award could be tested was for it to be in favor of the employees, for the carrier to refuse to comply with the award, and for the employees then to take it to court for enforcement. Theoretically, the carrier needed no right to go to court on its own initiative since it could refuse to comply with an award in favor of employees and let them take it to court. However, employees at times chose to strike instead of suing to force carrier compliance, thus depriving the carrier of opportunity for court review. The carrier's right of court review was ultimately assured by the Supreme Court ruling that strikes cannot be used to enforce Adjustment Board awards, Brotherhood of Locomotive Engineers v.

Finally, it should be noted that sometimes neither party to a dispute will submit it to the Adjustment Board even though the distpute is a "rights" or "minor" dispute of the type for which the Board was established. The U.S. Supreme Court has held that railroad employees may not strike over disputes that are actually pending before the NRAB, and that the federal courts may enjoin such strikes.[110] However, strikes over such disputes apparently may not be enjoined if the dispute is not actually pending before the NRAB.[111]

Existing differences which neither party will submit to the Board may plague the parties year after year until finally a sufficient number will have accumulated to cause a strike. At this point the National Mediation Board sometimes induces the parties to accept arbitration by a three-man or six-man board, or to establish a special board of adjustment for the cases in question.

Railroad Special Boards of Adjustment

Even prior to the 1966 amendments the Railway Labor Act authorized the establishment of system, group, or regional boards of adjustment by mutual consent of the parties. The 1966 amendments added a provision for establishment of special boards of adjustment, at the request of either party, "to resolve disputes otherwise referable to the Adjustment Board, or any dispute which has been pending before the Adjustment Board for twelve months from the date" when the dispute was submitted to the NRAB. Thus disputes in some instances may be withdrawn from the NRAB and submitted to a special board.

Louisville & N.R. Co., 83 S.Ct. 1059 (1963), and by the 1966 amendment giving any party aggrieved by an NRAB award the right to take it to court for review (but still on very limited grounds).

[110] Brotherhood of Railroad Trainmen v. Chicago R. & I. R. Co., 77 Sup. Ct. 635, 39 LRRM 2578 (1957). The carriers sometimes submit disputes to the Board as a means of avoiding strikes. While strikes may thus be enjoined, however, the Supreme Court has held that the district court may impose conditions requiring maintenance of the status quo as the "price of relief" when the injunctive powers of the court are invoked; thus the employees would be protected against a harmful change in working conditions during pendency of the dispute before the Adjustment Board. Brotherhood of Locomotive Engineers v. M-K-T R. Co., 80 Sup. Ct. 1326, 46 LRRM 2429 (1960).

[111] A state court injunction against one such strike was vacated by the U.S. Supreme Court where the dispute was not pending before the Adjustment Board. Manion v. Kansas City Terminal Railway Company, 77 Sup. Ct. 706, 39 LRRM 2641 (1957).

The RLA directs the National Mediation Board to aid in the establishment of these special boards (which have three members) and in the designation of the neutral member.[112] The Act makes awards of the special boards of adjustment "final and binding upon both parties," and provides that the awards shall be enforceable in federal district courts in the same manner as awards of the NRAB.

Airline System Boards of Adjustment

Amendment of the Railway Labor Act in 1936 made provision for the establishment of a national board of adjustment for the airlines when it shall be necessary "in the judgment of the National Mediation Board." Pending establishment of such national board, the airlines and their employees are directed to establish system boards of adjustment for the resolution of grievances. System boards of adjustment have been established by each airline pursuant to this mandate and have functioned very effectively on the whole.[113] Awards of these airline boards are governed and enforceable by federal law, in the federal courts.[114]

The National Mediation Board aids in the designation of neutrals for service with airline system boards of adjustment. The parties compensate the neutrals who serve with airline system boards. In sharp contrast, the Railway Labor Act provides that the National Mediation Board shall compensate the neutrals who serve with the National Railroad Adjustment Board or with railroad special boards of adjustment. Requiring the parties to compensate the neutrals tends to reduce the

---

[112] The NMB's rules for setting up special boards of adjustment under the 1966 amendments are published in 29 C.F.R. Part 1207. The Mediation Board calls the special boards "PL Boards" under Public Law 89-456. For discussion of these special boards, see Atchison, Topeka & Santa Fe Ry. Co., 50 LA 1057 (Jones, 1968), which also contains rulings as to procedural matters before PL Boards; Western Pacific Railroad Co., 50 LA 1013 (Wyckoff, 1968). It has been held that a special board considering a case that has been withdrawn from the NRAB should not be limited to a consideration of the evidence contained in the parties' submissions to the NRAB—the parties may proffer such oral testimony or written evidence as they wish, and the special board may request additional evidence from either party. Illinois Northern Railway, 53 LA 767, 769–770 (Sembower, 1969).

[113] For general discussion of these boards, see Kahn, "Airline Grievance Procedures: Some Observations and Questions," 35 J. of Air Law & Commerce 313 (1969).

[114] International Ass'n of Machinists v. Central Airlines, Inc., 83 Sup. Ct. 956 (1963).

number of meritless grievances that will be taken to arbitration, and this in turn contributes significantly to the success of any dispute settlement program or tribunal.

Statutory Tribunals for Critical Industrial Disputes

Both the RLA and the LMRA of 1947 contain provisions for special tribunals for critical industrial disputes, and both Acts contain provisions for requiring the parties to maintain the *status quo* without work stoppages pending investigation and report by the special tribunal. These tribunals should be noted briefly in passing even though, technically speaking, they are not arbitration tribunals.

Section 10 of the RLA provides that if a dispute between a carrier and its employees is not settled by use of the Act's other machinery, and if the NMB finds that the dispute threatens a substantial interruption of interstate commerce, the President may in his discretion create an Emergency Board to investigate and report the facts and circumstances of the dispute and make recommendations as to its settlement.[115]

Section 206 of the LMRA of 1947 provides that in national emergency disputes imperiling the national health or safety the President may appoint a Board of Inquiry to inquire into the issues involved in the dispute and to make a written report which "shall include a statement of the facts with respect to the dispute, including each party's statement of its position but shall not contain any recommendations."[116]

Boards of Inquiry may also be established under state statute. The function of one such board, which had authority to make recom-

---

[115] For detailed discussion of these boards, see Railroads v. Nonoperating Unions, 17 LA 833, 841, 843 (Cole, Horvitz & Osborne, 1952); Kaufman, "Emergency Boards Under the Railway Labor Act," 9 Labor Law J. 910 (1958); Lecht, Experience Under Railway Labor Legislation 6, 11–12, 53–54, 176, 190–191 (1955). For statement of the functions of emergency boards, see Chapter 3, topic titled "Arbitrator's Function in 'Interests' Disputes."

[116] For the reports of some of these boards, see Board of Inquiry Members Taylor, Perkins & Lehoczky in 33 LA 236; Farmer, Frankenthaler & Sembower in 33 LA 255; Cole, Carman & Comey in 21 LA 189 and in 21 LA 489; Harris, Cheney & Levy in 19 LA 532. For general discussion, see Cole, "Major Labor Disputes—Reexamination and Recommendations," The Profession of Labor Arbitration 90 (BNA Incorporated, 1957).

mendations, was deemed by its members to "contain elements both of mediation and arbitration," since:

"Like a mediator, the Board must think about the acceptability of its proposals. Like an arbitrator, it is concerned with the weight of the evidence and with the merits of the questions before it. As a statutory Board appointed by the State of New York, the Board has the additional function of serving a public interest which is not necessarily present in private proceedings."[117]

While the parties are not legally compelled to accept the findings of emergency boards and boards of inquiry, public pressure may strongly motivate them to do so, especially where the board has authority to make recommendations and actually does so.

---

[117] Rochester Transit Corp., 19 LA 538, 542 (Tolley, McKelvey & Turkus, 1952). Also see statement of functions by Board of Inquiry in Steel Industry, 33 LA 236 at 236 (Taylor, Perkins & Lehoczky, 1959).

CHAPTER 5

GRIEVANCES—PRELUDE TO ARBITRATION

Arbitration generally is the last step or terminal point of dispute settlement under union contracts. A happy situation exists when the preliminary steps of dispute-settlement machinery function effectively, resulting in settlement of a high percentage of disputes prior to the arbitration stage. If the preliminary steps do not function smoothly, the arbitration tribunal may be overburdened with cases, which, in turn, may lead to a breakdown of the system. It is generally agreed that no dispute should be taken to arbitration until all possibilities of settlement at the negotiation stages of the grievance procedure have been exhausted. However, once the preliminary steps have been exhausted without success, resort to arbitration should be prompt.

The Grievance Procedure

It is said that collective bargaining is not confined to the making of an agreement once a year but is a day-to-day process in which the grievance procedure has a very important role.[1] "The grievance procedure is, in other words, a part of the continuous collective bargaining process."[2] Some writers declare the grievance procedure to be the core of the collective bargaining agreement.[3] Professor Harry Shulman expressed a similar view:

"In labor negotiations there are factors peculiar to them which affirmatively press for almost deliberate incompleteness and uncertainty in the agreement; but, even if it were otherwise, it surely is true that no collective agreement has been or can be written which covers in detail all the exigencies with which the parties may be confronted in the contract period, or which makes crystal-clear its meaning with

---

[1] Chrysler Corp., 10 War Lab. Rep. 551, 554 (1943).
[2] United Steelworkers v. Warrior & Gulf Navigation Co., 80 S.Ct. 1347, 1352 (1960).
[3] Hill & Hook, Management at the Bargaining Table 199 (1945).

respect to the matters that it does cover. * * * It is this that makes collective bargaining an unending process in labor relations, and it is this that makes the grievance procedure the heart of the collective agreement."[4]

The extreme importance of a good grievance procedure in large companies has been emphasized by Arbitrator Michael I. Komaroff, who called the grievance machinery the "life-blood of a collective bargaining relationship."[5] In the coal mining industry the grievance procedure "is seen to be the 'safety-valve' in industrial relations, the procedure which gives a vital flexibility to the whole system of collective bargaining."[6]

The President's National Labor-Management Conference of 1945 recommended that every collective bargaining agreement contain provision for an effective grievance procedure. The Conference outlined some of the standards which a grievance procedure, to be "effective," should meet:

"1. Collective bargaining agreements should contain provisions that grievances and disputes involving the interpretation or application of the terms of the agreement are to be settled without resort to strikes, lockouts, or other interruptions to normal operations by an effective grievance procedure with arbitration as its final step.

"2. To be effective, the procedure established for the settlement of such grievances and disputes should meet at least the following standards:

"(a) The successive steps in the procedure, the method of presenting grievances or disputes, and the method of taking an appeal from one step to another should be so clearly stated in the agreement as to be readily understood by all employees, union officials, and management representatives.

"(b) The procedure should be adaptable to the handling of the various types of grievances and disputes which come under the terms of the agreement.

"(c) The procedure should be designed to facilitate the settlement of grievances and disputes as soon as possible after they arise. To this end:

---

[4] Conference on Training of Law Students in Labor Relations. Vol. III, Transcript of Proceedings 669 (1947). The U.S. Supreme Court expressed a similar view in "Warrior & Gulf," supra, at 1352.

[5] North American Aviation, Inc., 16 LA 744, 747 (1951).

[6] Somers, Grievance Settlement in Coal Mining 43 (W. Va. Univ. Bull. Series 56, No. 12-2, 1956).

"(1) The agreement should provide adequate stated time limits for the presentation of grievances and disputes, the rendering of decisions, and the taking of appeals.

"(2) Issues should be clearly formulated at the earliest possible moment. In all cases which cannot be settled in the first informal discussions, the positions of both sides should be reduced to writing.

"(3) Management and union should encourage their representatives to settle at the lower steps grievances which do not involve broad questions of policy or of contract interpretation and should delegate sufficient authority to them to accomplish this end.

"(4) The agreement should provide adequate opportunity for both parties to investigate grievances under discussion.

"(5) Provision should be made for priority handling of grievances involving discharge, suspension, or other disciplinary action.

"(d) The procedure should be open to the submission of grievances by all parties to the agreement.

"3. Managements and unions should inform and train their representatives in the proper functioning of the grievance procedure and in their responsibilities under it. In such a program it should be emphasized:

"(a) That the basic objective of the grievance procedure is the achievement of sound and fair settlements and not the "winning" of cases;

"(b) That the filing of grievances should be considered by foremen or supervisors as aids in discovering and removing causes of discontent in their departments;

"(c) That any tendency by either party to support the earlier decisions of its representatives when such decisions are wrong should be discouraged;

"(d) That the willingness of management and union officials to give adequate time and attention to the handling and disposition of grievances and disputes is necessary to the effective functioning of the procedure;

"(e) That for the sound handling of grievances and disputes both management and union representatives should be thoroughly familiar with the entire collective bargaining agreement."[7]

Most collective bargaining agreements give recognition to some, at least, of these standards, and arbitrators of "interests" disputes have

---

[7] The President's National Labor-Management Conference, Nov. 5–30, 1945 (U.S. Dept. Labor, Div. of Labor Standards, Bull. No. 77, pp. 45–46, 1946).

been known to direct the parties to "spell out" the details of their grievance procedures in accordance with the recommendations of the National Labor Management Conference.[8]

Grievances Defined

What is a "grievance"? Comprehensively, it is that which the parties to a particular collective agreement say it is. Such a definition, of course, does no more than apprise one of the fact that labor relations authorities disagree widely as to the precise meaning of the term and that collective agreements reflect this lack of accord. The term connotes conflict and irritation, and thus could be defined as any "gripe" or any type of complaint by an employee or a union against the employer or by an employer against his employee or the union. It is generally understood, however, that disputes involving demands for changes in the terms of a collective bargaining agreement ("interests" disputes) and disputes arising out of representation issues are not grievances.

Grievances may arise from an infinite number of causes, which may be either real or imaginary. This suggests inquiry as to what determines when a person has a grievance. Must there have been a wrong done? One employer has urged that a grievance does not come into existence so as to be subject to the grievance procedure until some harmful or disciplinary action has been taken against the complainant. The arbitrator who considered this view rejected it as being too narrow. He said: "Whether a man has a grievance or not is primarily his own feeling about the matter. Generally speaking, if a man thinks he has a grievance, he has a grievance."[9]

From a more technical standpoint, however, Arbitrator Charles O. Gregory has stated that the term "grievance" as it appears in the

---

[8] See N.Y. Shipping Assn., 1 LA 80, 84, 87–88 (Davis, 1945). Also see comments of Arbitrator Maurice H. Merrill in 20 LA 211, 212. For general discussion of grievance procedures, see The Grievance Process (Mich. State Univ. Lab. & Ind. Rel. Center, 1956); Reynard, "Drafting of Grievance and Arbitration Articles of Collective Bargaining Agreements," 10 Vanderbilt L. Rev. 749 (1957).

[9] Cudahy Packing Co., 7 LA 645, 646 (Fisher, 1947). "A grievance, real or imaginary, is nevertheless a grievance." Vulcan Mold & Iron Co., 41 LA 59, 61 (Brecht, 1963). Inchoate harm from a new management policy sufficed for a "grievance." Northwest Airlines, Inc., 45 LA 565, 569–570 (Shister, 1965). Also see Standard Oil Co. of Texas, 62-3 ARB ¶8885 (Coffey, 1962); Wyandotte Chemical Corp., 35 LA 783, 786–787 (Wollett, 1960). Cf., Arbitrator Komaroff in 16 LA 744, 747–748.

average contract refers to "a formal complaint" by persons who believe they have been wronged.[10]

Attitude of Parties to the Grievance Procedure

The parties' attitude in handling grievances, probably more than in any other aspect of the labor-management relationship, indicates their good faith. Nowhere in that relationship is mutual good faith more important.[11] The attitude of the parties is even more important than the type of grievance provisions contained in the agreement.[12] This view has been shared by unions and management alike in most cases in which the grievance procedure has been considered successful and in the majority of cases in which the procedure has broken down.[13] Good grievance machinery is important, but such machinery alone will not insure success. The attitude, judgment, experience, and training of the individual involved are of prime importance. Moreover, a desire to settle grievances, rather than to win them, is essential.

No grievance should be presented unless there is a real basis for complaint or need for decision. Much responsibility belongs directly to the union stewards, and indirectly to the union, to screen out complaints that have no real merit. The United States Department of Labor has suggested that persons responsible for the preparation of stewards' manuals give serious thought to the inclusion of the following instructions to stewards:

> "* * * *Use your best judgment in deciding whether or not a grievance is justified.*—If you are convinced that the worker does not have a real case it is better to tell him so right from the beginning. Taking up a lot of poor cases will cost you the respect of all concerned. On the other hand, don't forget that you are the worker's representative. If the case is a borderline one but you feel that the worker has considerable justice on his side, tell him frankly that you are

---

[10] E. I. DuPont De Nemours & Co., 29 LA 646, 650 (1957). But Cf., Braniff Airways, Inc., 27 LA 892, 896–898 (Williams, 1957).

[11] Also see comments by Arbitrator Luskin, "The Presidential Address: Arbitration and Its Critics," Developments in American and Foreign Arbitration 125, 133 (The Bureau of National Affairs, Inc., 1968), and by Arbitrator Jenkins in Hunt Foods & Industries, Inc., 44 LA 664, 669 (1965).

[12] "Grievance Procedure Under Collective Bargaining," 63 Monthly Lab. Rev. 175 (U.S. Dept. of Labor, 1946).

[13] Ibid.

not sure what is the correct answer. Then take the case up and get a definite ruling through the grievance procedure."[14]

Suggestions have been made, too, concerning the responsibility of foremen:

> "Greater emphasis should be placed on training foremen in the human relations aspects of their jobs. Many times a man simply wants a relief hour or perhaps a sympathetic listener. Foremen must be given better training, on the importance of fully hearing out rather than prematurely debating with their employees. They must acquire the ability of [noting] *what* is being said, rather than the manner in which the problem is being presented. Only in this way can gripes be separated from grievances, or can gripes be kept from becoming grievances."[15]

Both parties should make every effort to settle grievances at the lowest step. Grievances become magnified in importance and increasingly difficult to settle as they progress toward the top.

Settlements at the first steps of the grievance procedure often will be facilitated by honest and open disclosure of each party's position and its basis.[16] Moreover, the U.S. Supreme Court has held that a company had a legal duty to provide information to explain certain of its actions and thus enable the union to determine whether to process a grievance, the Court explaining: "Arbitration can function properly only if the grievance procedures leading to it can sift out unmeritorious claims. For if all claims originally initiated as grievances had to be processed through to arbitration, the system would be woefully overburdened."[17]

When approached with the proper attitude, grievance machinery serves the mutual advantage of employer, employees, and the union. It helps management discover and correct sore spots in plant opera-

---

[14] Preparing a Steward's Manual 7 (U.S. Dept. of Labor, Div. of Labor Standards, Bull. No. 59, 1943). Also see Arbitrator Sembower in 41 LA 185, 188.
[15] Comments of management spokesman Harry W. Lacey, Proceedings of the Conference on Improving the Relations Between the Parties 29 (Univ. of Notre Dame Press, 1960).
[16] See comments of Arbitrator Seitz in Sperry-Rand Corp., 46 LA 961, 965–966 (1966).
[17] NLRB v. Acme Industrial Co., 87 S.Ct. 565, 569 (1967). In Vickers, Inc., 43 LA 1256, 1261 (Bothwell, 1964), the provisions of the grievance procedure were held to imply an obligation by the company to provide the union with certain minimum information relevant to the validity of a grievance.

tions before they cause serious trouble. Grievances constitute a channel of communication, informing top management of things concerning which employees or the union feel strongly.[18] It is to the employer's advantage to make it as easy as possible to present grievances, and employees should be encouraged, not only to present their complaints, but also to present them while they are still "warm." Grievance machinery provides the union a mechanism for enforcing the rules which it has worked for and achieved through collective bargaining.

Moreover, through use of grievance machinery the union performs a service to the employees, which will increase their loyalty to the union. "To the individual worker, grievance procedure provides the means of enforcing the terms of the contract and * * * a democratic method of appeal against any one person's arbitrary decision affecting his wages or working conditions. It protects the democratic rights of the individual in industry in the same way that our judicial system protects his democratic rights in civil life."[19]

Abuse and Misuse of Grievance Procedure

It has been said that an "irresistible impulse to file grievances" is not a dischargeable offense, though the purposeful filing of deliberately untruthful grievances may be.[20]

The more serious threat to the health and integrity of the grievance procedure (including arbitration) comes from other causes. A valuable study of distressed grievance procedures and their rehabilitation has been made by Arbitrator Arthur M. Ross. This study reveals various impediments to a healthy grievance procedure, including such factors as: failure to screen grievances; factional strife within the union; desire of union shop committee to perpetuate itself (indiscriminate filing of grievances); poor investigation of grievances; poor steward training; company hard line on practically all grievances; failure of top management to back up industrial-relations personnel, who become inclined to pass the buck to an arbitrator; overgenerous

---

[18] Hill & Hook, Management at the Bargaining Table 199 (1945).

[19] Settling Plant Grievances 1 (U.S. Dept. of Labor, Div. of Labor Standards, Bull. No. 60, 1943).

[20] National Lead Co. of Ohio, 37 LA 1076, 1079 (Schedler, 1962). Filing a deliberately untruthful grievance justified discharge in Chrysler Corp., 32 LA 719, 738–739 (Wolff, 1959). Persistent filing of grievances was annoying to supervision but was not cause for discipline in Anaconda American Brass Co., 52 LA 1221, 1226 (Larkin, 1969). Cf., Arbitrator Bradley in 54 LA 206, 211–213.

grievance pay; availability of free or subsidized arbitration.[21] Identifying another impediment, a management spokesman has stated that foremen are generally well trained but that they should be better trained in the human-relations aspects of their job and should not automatically assume a defensive attitude in favor of the company.[22]

Remedies for Distressed Grievance Procedures

Some of the remedial devices frequently mentioned by persons consulted in the aforementioned Ross study include mass grievance settlements, screening of grievances, direct negotiations between management and union officials at higher levels of authority, and procedural changes.[23] It is generally agreed that screening of grievances is a most beneficial remedy, though this remedy may not be fully available due to internal union politics and union fears of legal liability to employees for failure to process grievances.[24]

A caveat as to repair of the grievance procedure was offered by William E. Simkin while speaking as Director of the Federal Mediation and Conciliation Service:

"Grievance procedure repair is not a simple process. It is not a good subject matter for crisis bargaining. It can only be handled adequately in a noncrisis atmosphere, by a great deal of hard work and with an approach designed to correct the differing faults of each

---

[21] Ross, "Distressed Grievance Procedures and their Rehabilitation," Labor Arbitration and Industrial Change 104, 107–108 (BNA Incorporated, 1963).

[22] Comments of Harry W. Lacey, Proceedings of the Conference on Improving the Relations Between the Parties 29 (Univ. of Notre Dame Press, 1960).

[23] For the pros and cons of these and other suggested remedies, see Ross, "Distressed Grievance Procedures and their Rehabilitation," Labor Arbitration and Industrial Change 104, 111 et seq. (BNA Incorporated, 1963). Also dealing with revival of distressed procedures, see Luskin, "The Presidential Address: Arbitration and its Critics," Developments in American and Foreign Arbitration 125, 132–134 (The Bureau of National Affairs, Inc., 1968).

[24] See Jones & Smith, "Management and Labor Appraisals and Criticisms of the Arbitration Process: A Report with Comments," 62 Mich. L. Rev. 1115, 1152–1153 (1964). As to extent of concern, by union officials, regarding possible legal liability, see panel discussion, "A Colloquium on the Arbitration Process," Labor Arbitration—Perspectives and Problems 100–102, 106, 109 (BNA Incorporated, 1964). As noted hereinabove, the Supreme Court in "Acme" emphasized the necessity of sifting out unmeritorious claims. Furthermore, in Vaca v. Sipes, 87 S.Ct. 903 (1967), the Supreme Court held that a breach of the statutory duty of fair representation occurs only when a union's conduct (in "Vaca" it was refusal to take a grievance to arbitration) toward a member of the bargaining unit is arbitrary, discriminatory, or in bad faith. For an elaborate system for screening grievances, see Dunne, "The UAW Board of Review on Umpire Appeals at General Motors," 17 Arb. J. 162 (1962).

specific situation. The basic job of correction in the collective bargaining process must be done by the parties themselves * * *."[25]

Failure to Comply Strictly With Technical Requirements of Grievance Procedure

As a general proposition arbitrators expect parties to comply with the technical requirements of the grievance procedure.[26] While arbitrators have sometimes ruled that substantial compliance will suffice,[27] wholesale disregard of grievance procedure requirements will not be tolerated.[28]

Where parties have been very informal in past handling of grievances, clear notice must be given if a party intends to insist upon strict future compliance with the previously ignored procedural requirements.[29]

Should Grievance Machinery Be Open to All Complaints?

There is no strong reason why parties should place limitations upon the subject matter that may be taken to the grievance procedure, even though a complaint is ultimately rejected as constituting an attempt to amend the agreement. Complaints often shrink in importance and are easily disposed of once they are brought into the open, while employees who have no outlet for their complaints tend to magnify them far beyond their true importance. Harry Shulman urged that every grievance should be received, heard, and considered seriously and sympathetically and that, to the extent possible, every grievance should be made the occasion for additional education of the parties and for a little more smoothing out of the wrinkles in their relationship.[30]

---

[25] Quotation from National Academy of Arbitrators Newsletter for January 1968, p. 3.

[26] This fact is apparent from cases cited throughout this Chapter. Also see comments of Arbitrator Koven in Fibreboard Paper Products Corp., 39 LA 691, 695 (1962).

[27] See Arbitrator Boles in 45 LA 502, 504; Kates in 44 LA 507, 510–512; Berkowitz in 41 LA 182, 183. In Great Lakes Pipe Line Co., 34 LA 617, 622–623 (Howard, 1959), alleged procedural defects were held waived by failure to object until arbitration was scheduled.

[28] See Arbitrator Nichols in Byrd Plastics, Inc., 51 LA 79, 82–83 (1968).

[29] Whiteway Stamping Co., 41 LA 966, 968 (Kates, 1963). To similar effect, Arbitrator Sembower in 49 LA 817, 820–821. Contra, Arbitrator Koven in 39 LA 691, 695.

[30] Conference on Training of Law Students in Labor Relations, Vol. III, Transcript of·Proceedings 702–703 (1947).

Some agreements do open the door of the grievance machinery to any complaint. The clause to this effect may take the following form:

"In the event of any complaints, grievances, difficulties, disagreements or disputes arising between the Company, its employees within the collective bargaining unit hereinabove defined, or the Union, there shall be no suspension of plant operations but an earnest effort shall be made to settle such difference, complaints, grievances, difficulties, disagreements, or disputes forthwith in the following manner [grievance procedure then described]."[31]

Many agreements, however, limit the grievance procedure to complaints involving the "interpretation or application" of the agreement, or otherwise state exclusions from the grievance procedure.[32] Agreements which limit the subject matter that may be taken to the grievance procedure are most commonly found in newly organized industries, where the parties have not acquired sufficient mutual confidence to open the door to any and all complaints. Some agreements define "grievance" in a restrictive way, limiting the types of complaints that will be considered. Or the types of complaints that will be heard may be listed specifically, thus excluding those not listed. Some agreements spell out specific types of complaints which may *not* be taken to the grievance procedure, as, for instance, matters within the field of exclusive management functions.

The complexities of social insurance and pension plans have led some parties to require complaints arising out of their administration to be processed separately from the usual grievance procedure.[33]

The question whether a given complaint is subject to the grievance procedure may itself be processed through the grievance procedure and arbitration.[34]

The right of former employees to utilize the grievance procedure for grievances based upon their previous employment status has sometimes been at issue. In one such instance, Arbitrator Mark L. Kahn

---

[31] From an agreement between Windsor Mfg. Co. and Textile Workers Union.

[32] See Major Collective Bargaining Agreements: Arbitration Procedures 6, 9 (U.S. Dept. Labor Bull. No. 1425-6, 1966); Major Collective Bargaining Agreements: Grievance Procedures 2, 6 (U.S. Dept. Labor Bull. 1425-1, 1964).

[33] "Basic Patterns in Labor Arbitration Agreements," 34 LA 931 at 931 (1960).

[34] Southwestern Bell Telephone Co., 44 LA 545, 547–548, 551 (Altieri, 1965), where the initial complaint was held subject to the grievance procedure and the company was ordered to cooperate in its processing.

declared that the union not only has a right but also a duty to utilize the grievance procedure in behalf of the former employee.[35] But the right of former employees to use the grievance procedure has not always been upheld.[36]

The widow of an employee was not herself an "employee" with the right to use the grievance procedure, so she could not process her grievance concerning accrued vacation pay of her deceased husband even though the grievance was filed by the union.[37]

Company Grievances

Express provision is sometimes made for the initiation of management grievances at some stage of the grievance procedure.[38] Absent an express provision on the matter, the company's right to submit grievances depends upon the interpretation of the particular agreement.[39] The presence of a no-lockout clause may be a very significant factor in an arbitrator's conclusion that company grievances are permitted where the agreement does not deal expressly with the question.[40]

Some management spokesmen urge that every contract which provides for arbitration as the final step of the grievance procedure

---

[35] Hudson Tool & Machine Co., 21 LA 431, 433–434 (1953). A former employee could use the grievance procedure for rights allegedly accrued prior to his resignation in Dover Corp., 48 LA 965, 968 (Volz, 1966). In accord on this point, Arbitrator Murphy in 52 LA 837, 840–841.

[36] See Van Dyne-Crotty, Inc., 46 LA 338, 343–345 (Teple, 1966); Kelly v. Adler, Inc., 25 LA 214 (N.Y. Sup. Ct., 1955).

[37] United States Steel Corp., 34 LA 306 at 306 (Sherman, 1960). The agreement was subsequently amended to permit the processing of such claims. See Pittsburgh Steel Co., 43 LA 860, 863 (McDermott, 1964). For a case involving the right of the union to use the grievance procedure in behalf of a supervisor who was discharged instead of being returned to the bargaining unit, see Tin Processing Corp., 16 LA 48, 51 (Emery, 1951).

[38] Of 400 agreements examined in one survey, 18 percent provided for company grievances. "Basic Patterns in Labor Arbitration," 34 LA 931, 936 (1960).

[39] See Meletron Corp., 36 LA 315, 317–319 (Jones, 1961). Also see Chase Bag Co., 42 LA 153, 154 (Elkouri, 1963). Earlier cases appeared to require clear language authorizing company grievances in order to open grievance procedure doors to the company. See Bassick Co. v. Bassick Local 229, 24 LA 59 (USDC, 1954); Hinson Mfg. Co., 20 LA 688, 690 (Davey, 1953). By discussing a company grievance through the grievance procedure up to arbitration the union waived any right to object that the contract made no provision for company grievances. Whitlock Mfg. Co., 19 LA 234, 236 (Stutz, 1952).

[40] See Arbitrator Duff in 45 LA 225, 226–227; Elkouri in 42 LA 153, 154–155; Jones in 36 LA 315, 317–319.

should include machinery available to management for presenting grievances against the union.[41]

Identification and Signature of Individual Grievants; Group Grievances

Sometimes an agreement will require, either specifically or by implication, that employee grievances be signed or otherwise presented by the aggrieved employee or employees.[42] One purpose of such requirements is to aid the employer in evaluating and responding to the grievance.[43]

Where such requirements have been strictly enforced by arbitrators, complaints signed only by a union steward could not qualify as grievances.[44] In some of these cases the grievance was of a personal nature (as distinguished from a "policy" or a "general" grievance),

---

[41] Hill & Hook, Management at the Bargaining Table 216 (1945). Employer access to the grievance procedure determines whether claims against the union for breach of no-strike clause shall be taken to court or to an arbitrator. See Atkinson v. Sinclair Refining Co., 82 S.Ct. 1318; 50 LRRM 2433 (1962); Drake Bakeries, Inc., v. Local 50, 82 S.Ct. 1346, 50 LRRM 2440 (1962). An employer's right to discipline individual employees for work stoppages does not preclude his right to file a grievance against the union where the agreement authorizes company grievances. Wallace-Murray Corp., 53 LA 1171, 1173 (Kabaker, 1969).

[42] However, in many contracts it is not clear whether it is the employee or the steward who is authorized to launch the formal complaint. "Basic Patterns in Labor Arbitration Agreements," 34 LA 931 at 931 (1960). A requirement for the signatures of individual employees on grievances has been held not to be a mandatory subject of bargaining. Bethlehem Steel Co., 136 NLRB 1500 (1962), enforcement denied on other grounds, 320 F.2d 615 (CA 3, 1963).

[43] See comments by Arbitrator Morvant in Geigy Chemical Corp., 34 LA 102, 104–105 (1960), and by Arbitrator Updegraff in John Deere Harvester Works, 10 LA 778, 782 (1948). Where this purpose is otherwise adequately achieved an arbitrator might feel less strictly bound by the employee signature requirement. See Republic Steel Corp., 11 LA 691, 694–695 (McCoy, 1948).

[44] See Arbitrator Erbs in 54 LA 1118, 1120; Eigenbrod in 53 LA 1230, 1233–1234; Dybeck in 49 LA 278, 279–280; Lennard in 44 LA 76, 82; Seinsheimer in 41 LA 947, 952; Kahn in 38 LA 580, 582–583; Larkin in 37 LA 659, 661; Updegraff in 10 LA 778, 782; Shulman in 3 LA 840, 841. Also see Cole in 23 LA 64, 65. Where there are multiple grievants, each may be required to sign to be included. See Arbitrator Eigenbrod in 53 LA 1230, 1233–1234; Lennard in 44 LA 76, 82; Morvant in 34 LA 102, 104–105; Howlett in 28 LA 633, 634; Updegraff in 10 LA 778, 782. As to any need to verify the grievant's signature, see American Airlines, 46 LA 440, 442–443 (Sembower, 1966). In Sohio Chemical Co., 52 LRRM 1390 (1963), the NLRB strictly construed a provision for signature by "the employee or the employee and his steward" to require the assent of the aggrieved employee to the filing of a grievance.

but even policy grievances were held covered by the requirement for employee signatures in some cases.[45]

On the other hand, some arbitrators have viewed the provision for employee signatures or initiation of grievances as a mere formality,[46] or have otherwise indicated a strong inclination to find in favor of the union's right to initiate grievances.[47] For example, although agreement language implied that the grievance procedure applied only to individually authorized grievances, Arbitrator Philip E. Marshall held that grievances not personal in nature and those involving the whole of the bargaining unit could be filed by the union without specific authorizations. Arbitrator Marshall asserted that "industrial practice generally recognizes the fact that certain types of grievances involving conflicting interpretations of contractual provisions are frequently brought by union representatives in behalf of the entire membership."[48]

Somewhat conversely, under a clause permitting the union to file grievances which apply to "employees as a group," Arbitrator Maurice H. Merrill held that the union could file the grievance of an individual employee since the situation was one which could occur to any employee, and therefore the grievance did affect the employees as a group.[49]

In many cases the agreement has been construed to permit the union to file "group," "class," and/or "policy" grievances without the signatures of all specific individuals covered by the grievance (sometimes without any of their signatures), and, in some instances,

---

[45] See Arbitrator Seinsheimer in 41 LA 947, 952; Kahn in 38 LA 580, 582–583; Larkin in 37 LA 659, 661.

[46] See Von Weise Gear Co., 51 LA 714, 715 (Bernstein, 1968); Industrial Gasket & Packing Co., 45 LA 847, 848–849 (Coffey, 1965), holding omission of employee signature not be a defect as to substance and holding that signature by a union representative will suffice.

[47] See Arbitrator Dworkin in 55 LA 709, 714; Leach in 45 LA 1039, 1044; Willingham in 42 LA 376, 384; Seligson in 40 LA 652, 658 (stating that under public policy there is a presumption of union right to initiate grievances).

[48] Timken-Detroit Axle Co., 6 LA 926, 934 (1947). To similar effect, Arbitrator Warns in 32 LA 516, 518–519. Of course the parties may agree to arbitral resolution of an interpretation dispute without identification of any individual grievant or even without submission of any grievance, as in Western Employers Council, 49 LA 61 at 61 (McNaughton, 1967).

[49] Jonco Aircraft Corp., 22 LA 887 (1954).

without identification of all individuals covered by the grievance (sometimes without identification of any specific individual).[50]

Financial or other benefits under the award in such cases might apply to all affected employees though not identified in the grievance,[51] but this is not always so.[52] A grievance is more likely to be held to cover employees not specifically identified if the group nature of the claim is evident on its face or if the matter was treated as a group grievance in the parties' handling of the dispute.[53]

Waiver of Employee Rights or Signature Requirement

The questions arise (1) whether individual employees may waive their rights under the collective agreement, and (2) whether the employer may waive a contractual requirement that grievances be signed by the aggrieved employee or a requirement that he be named.

As to the latter question, waiver results from failure to make timely objection to noncompliance with the requirement.[54] Similarly, the requirement may be held unenforceable (for the case under advisement) by virtue of loose past practice.[55]

---

[50] For cases reflecting these variations, see Arbitrator Solomon in 49 LA 718, 721; Whyte in 49 LA 33, 36–37; Murphy in 46 LA 289, 290; Blumrosen in 42 LA 392, 402; Teple in 40 LA 13, 17; Peck in 37 LA 496, 498–499; Jaffee in 37 LA 458, 463; Thompson in 29 LA 518, 520; Wolff in 27 LA 448, 452–453; Stutz in 27 LA 386, 388–389; Williams in 25 LA 748, 749–750; Lennard in 25 LA 644, 648–649; Dworkin in 23 LA 481, 482; Kelliher in 14 LA 1049, 1053. Even where the contract called for specific identification on the individual grievants, the requirement was not strictly enforced for a grievance which was basically of a "group" nature and where the company "knew full-well who the grievants were and what the Union was driving at." Folding Carrier Corp., 53 LA 784, 788 (Gorsuch, 1969).

[51] See Arbitrator Solomon in 49 LA 718, 721, 726; Blumrosen in 42 LA 392, 402–403; Gill in 37 LA 134, 137; Wolff in 27 LA 448, 453; Lennard in 25 LA 644, 657; Dworkin in 23 LA 481, 487; Davey in 17 LA 330, 333. This was the result, even though the agreement expressly required identification of all grievants, where the employer had refused to provide the names of all affected employees. Jeffrey Mfg. Co., 34 LA 814, 821 (Kuhn, 1960).

[52] See Greer Steel Co., 50 LA 340, 343 (McIntosch, 1968); St. Louis Newspaper Publishers' Assn., 33 LA 471, 477 (Green, 1959), holding that additional names could not be added at the arbitration hearing.

[53] See Arbitrator Jaffee in 37 LA 458, 463; Duff in 30 LA 441, 444; Dworkin in 23 LA 481, 482; Updegraff in 20 LA 243, 245; Davey in 17 LA 330, 333; Grant in 11 LA 312, 314.

[54] See Arbitrator Dolnick in 50 LA 167, 169–170; Kates in 49 LA 1095, 1096–1097; Larkin in 43 LA 140, 144–145.

[55] See Arbitrator Dolnick in 50 LA 167, 169–170; Sembower in 49 LA 817, 818, 820–821; Fisher in 47 LA 224, 226; Larkin in 43 LA 140, 144–145.

As to waiver of agreement rights by individual employees, even where affected employees refused to file or prosecute a grievance,[56] or where they wished to withdraw after they had instituted their grievance,[57] the right of the union to file or prosecute the grievance was not denied.

Arbitrators have recognized a strong right of the union to police the agreement and have recognized that the interests of the union and of an individual employee do not always dovetail.[58] Thus, it has been considered that an employee may waive a purely personal right under the agreement (such as the right to a promotion), but that the employee may not waive other rights (which affect the interests of other employees or the union) against the wishes of the union.[59]

Steps in Grievance Procedure

Grievance machinery usually consists of a series of procedural steps to be taken within specified time limits.[60] The nature of the procedure will depend upon the structure of the company and on the needs and desires of the parties, but there is a tendency to follow a fairly definite pattern. Grievances ordinarily are taken by the aggrieved employee, either with or without a union representative, to the foreman,[61] and, if no settlement is reached, may be appealed through successive steps of the management hierarchy and, in most cases, to arbitration. The aggrieved may be represented successively

---

[56] Atlantic Seaboard Corp., 42 LA 865, 869 et seq. (Lugar, 1964). Also see Arbitrator Bernstein in 51 LA 714, 715; Garrett in 44 LA 168, 174.

[57] Whiteway Stamping Co., 41 LA 966, 968 (Kates, 1963); Baur Brothers Bakery, 36 LA 1422, 1423, 61-1 ARB ¶8275 (Joseph, 1961).

[58] See Eastern Shore Public Service Co., 39 LA 751, 756–758 (Frey, 1962), recognizing right to police; Great Western Sugar Co., 40 LA 652, 658 (Seligson, 1963), recognizing possible diverse interests. The agreement in both of these cases could be construed to authorize union grievances.

[59] United States Borax & Chemical Corp., 41 LA 1200, 1203 (Leonard, 1963). In the latter regard, also see Lady Baltimore Bakery Co., 47 LA 8, 10 (Koven, 1966). For related discussion, see Chapter 10, topic titled "Waiver and Estoppel."

[60] Precise pleadings in moving from step to step ordinarily should not be required. See Henry Vogt Machine Co., 46 LA 654, 657 (Stouffer, 1966). One arbitrator has taken the view that a grievance alleging violation of a prior agreement but filed during the term of the subsequent agreement is to be processed under the procedures designated in the prior agreement. Dover Corp., 48 LA 965, 968 (Volz, 1966).

[61] The absence of a readily accessible "first step" may lead an employee to resort to self help. See Millage Produce, Inc., 45 LA 211, 214–215 (Miller, 1965), where discharge for insubordination was set aside.

by the shop steward, the business agent, the union shop committee, and international union representatives.[62]

Small companies can be expected to have short, simple grievance procedures, sometimes with only one or two steps. Larger companies usually have multistep procedures. Three-step and four-step procedures probably are most common,[63] but procedures with five or six steps are sometimes used, especially in plants which are units of a multiplant company.[64] The employee often is represented by the union grievance committee at the intermediate steps and by an international union representative at the next to last step and also at the last step.[65] The more steps in a grievance procedure, the more formal it can be expected to be. There is such variation in multistep procedures that no one plan may be said to be really typical. An indication, however, of what might be found in a multistep procedure is provided by the following illustration:

> "Should any employee, subject to this agreement, believe he has been unjustly dealt with, or that any of the provisions of this agreement have been violated, he shall present his alleged grievance to the Foreman of his department within five (5) days of the occurrence of such grievance.
>
> "In case the grievance is not adjusted by the foreman it shall be reduced to writing upon forms provided by the Company and signed and dated by the aggrieved employee and his department committeeman and three copies furnished the foreman. The foreman will have inserted in the proper place on the form his disposition of the matter and will sign and date the same returning one (1) copy to the aggrieved employee and one (1) copy to the department committeeman representing the employee within five (5) days.
>
> "If satisfactory adjustment is not made the department committeeman or his representative shall then take up the grievance with the General Foreman and General Superintendent in their respective order, within ten (10) days.

---

[62] Also see "Basic Patterns in Labor Arbitration Agreements," 34 LA 931, 932 (1960). It has been suggested that the representative of each party at each succeeding step should be a different person, with higher authority than the representative at the preceding step. Manning, Maxwell & Moore, Inc., 37 LA 475, 480 (Stutz, 1961).

[63] See "Basic Patterns in Labor Arbitration Agreements," 34 LA 931, 934 (1960).

[64] "Grievance Procedure Under Collective Bargaining," 63 Monthly Labor Review 175, 179 (U.S. Dept. of Labor, 1946).

[65] Id. at 180.

"If no satisfactory adjustment is then reached it shall be submitted for consideration and handling to the Manager of Works, or his representative, by the duly authorized General Committee or their representative, within ten (10) days.

"If after such consideration by the General Committee and the management, the grievance shall be unsettled, then the question shall be jointly submitted to the Chief Executive of the Company and the Chief Executive of the Brotherhood of Railway Carmen of America (or their representative) for joint conference within ten (10) days."[66]

Advanced Step Filing

There are certain issues which by nature are not capable of being settled at the preliminary stages of the procedure. Fundamental issues concerning company policies, for instance, are of this type. Provision sometimes is made for filing such grievances at an advanced step of the procedure.[67]

The question might be raised whether, in the absence of such provision, it should be permissible to file grievances at an advanced step where it is obvious that they cannot be settled at preliminary steps. The view has been expressed that there should be strict conformity with the agreement lest the exception be used to short-circuit the first steps in all cases.[68]

But Arbitrator Robert J. Wagner expressed a different view, holding that a grievance concerning veterans' vacation rights was properly initiated at the third step of the grievance procedure without presentation to the foreman at an earlier step. While he denied the union's contention that it had the right to enter an advanced step "at any time they choose," nevertheless he held that it could do so in proper cases. He stated that it is well recognized in the practice of industrial

---

[66] From an agreement between the Pullman-Standard Car Mfg. Co. and Brotherhood of Railway Carmen.

[67] Bypassing of one or more steps in certain cases is permitted by 35 percent of the 400 agreements covered by one survey. "Basic Patterns in Labor Arbitration Agreements," 34 LA 931, 935 (1960), where types of cases included in these provisions are also indicated.

[68] Lapp, How to Handle Labor Grievances 95–96 (1945). Holding that all grievances must go the prescribed route, including group and policy grievances, Arbitrator Byron Abernethy stated that it is not for the arbitrator to say that required steps can be ignored. Tenneco Oil Co., 40 LA 707, 710–712 (1963). It seems obvious that in most cases serious effort should be made to adjust grievances at the lower steps. Failure to do so may overburden the higher steps with harmful consequences to grievance machinery and the parties' interests. See discussion, "Distressed Grievance Procedures and their Rehabilitation," Labor Arbitration and Industrial Change 138, 142–143 (BNA Incorporated, 1963).

relations that certain disputes of a general nature can only be resolved at a high union-management level. "Then, again, particular circumstances may make it impractical to begin processing a grievance at the first step." Arbitrator Wagner concluded: "It would seem to be quite proper for this grievance to be processed at the third-step level, for only at this level are all negotiators of the contract, those officers of company and union who knew the meaning and intent of the language of the contractual provision controlling, required to appear."[69]

In any event, the right to object to the lack of discussion of a grievance at a preliminary step may be held waived by failure to make a timely objection.[70]

Grievance Mediation

Some parties add a "grievance mediation" step to the grievance procedure.[71] When this is done, a neutral is called in to discuss the case with the parties immediately prior to the arbitration stage. This process can dispose of some cases that otherwise must be arbitrated, and it may well deserve more experimentation as an intermediate device in the future.[72]

Time for Holding Hearings

Agreements vary as to the time prescribed for holding hearings on grievances. Some agreements provide that differences are to be taken up "as soon as possible"; others simply provide that "grievances shall be first taken up by the grievant and the foreman," without specifying a time; still others provide that grievances may be adjusted

---

[69] Manion Steel Barrel Co., 6 LA 164, 168 (1947). For similar comments, see Arbitrator Markowitz in 44 LA 212, 215; Kates in 43 LA 695, 699. Advanced step filing under proper circumstances was also permitted by Arbitrator Gorsuch in 53 LA 784, 788–789; Prasow in 50 LA 645, 655 and in 27 LA 153, 155–156; Gibson in 48 LA 1234, 1237; Murphy in 46 LA 289, 290; Dworkin in 42 LA 449, 453; Kelliher in 14 LA 1049, 1053.

[70] See Arbitrator Callaghan in 28 LA 659, 663; Donnely in 28 LA 621, 622; Kelliher in 20 LA 618, 619; Jaffe in 17 LA 187, 189–190.

[71] As to the apparent extent of this practice, see "Basic Patterns in Labor Arbitration Agreements," 34 LA 931, 936–937 (1960), where it is also noted that grievance mediation was more extensively used prior to the broad emergence of arbitration, and that a few agreements still specify conciliation instead of arbitration as the final step of the grievance procedure.

[72] For informative discussion of grievance mediation, see McPherson, Grievance Mediation Under Collective Bargaining (Univ. of Ill. Institute of Lab. & Ind. Relations Reprint Series No. 44, 1956); "Grievance Mediation," The Grievance Process 53–54, 59 (Mich. State Univ. Lab. & Ind. Relations Center, 1956).

with the foreman "at the end of the working day." Reason should be exercised in determining when to present grievances. It has been held, for instance, that when the number of employees involved in a grievance is so great that their absence from the job would interfere with production and upset morale and discipline, the shop steward has a clear duty to give management an opportunity to adjust the grievance without an interruption of work. Accordingly, a shop steward who took six or seven men off the job to discuss a grievance, without having made advance arrangements with management, was held to have been properly admonished not to do so again.[73]

Similar results have been reached in other such cases where employees or their representative interfered with production and disregarded the need for orderly presentation of grievances in seeking to rush the hearing of their complaint.[74]

Advanced-step hearings generally are scheduled more definitely. Many plants hold regularly scheduled meetings at specified intervals to negotiate appealed grievances.[75] Such meetings are usually held weekly during working hours, but may be held monthly or at other intervals.

Sometimes, however, these meetings are not regularly scheduled, but are made subject to "call," to be held whenever necessary. "Call" meetings may be preferred because they provide the necessary flexibility for more prompt disposition of complaints, and the number of meetings can be adjusted to the number of cases. On the other hand, some parties prefer regularly scheduled meetings because of the assurance that grievances will be considered within a definite period.

---

[73] Dwight Mfg. Co., 10 LA 786, 792 (McCoy, 1948).

[74] See Arbitrator Jones in 49 LA 944, 947; Platt in 21 LA 220, 221–222; Komaroff in 21 LA 67, 70–71; Shister in 17 LA 230, 232. In Terry Poultry Co., 109 NLRB 1095 (1954), an employee could be punished where he left his post to present a grievance in violation of a reasonable and nondiscriminatory plant rule. But spontaneous work stoppages to present grievances under the NLRA have been held protected under the facts of some cases. See NLRB v. Solo Cup Co., 237 F.2d 521 (CA 8, 1956); NLRB v. Kennametal, Inc., 182 F.2d 817 (CA 3, 1950). Also see NLRB v. Washington Aluminum Co., 82 S. Ct. 1099 (1962). As to the right of management to specify a specific location within the plant for union representatives to interview grievants and write up their grievances, see Walker Mfg. Co., 41 LA 1288, 1299 (Whelan, 1963).

[75] "Basic Patterns in Labor Arbitration Agreements," 34 LA 931, 936 (1960); "Grievance Procedure Under Collective Bargaining," 63 Monthly Labor Review 175, 183 (U.S. Dept. of Labor, 1946).

Moreover, regular meetings provide better opportunity for the discussion of mutual problems of policy and for the anticipation of difficulties, thus preventing future grievances.[76] When the agreement provides for regularly scheduled meetings, it might also provide for emergency meetings when either party feels that consideration of a grievance should not be delayed.[77]

Grievance Representatives

Unless restricted by the agreement, both the union and the company are generally free to determine the kind and number of representatives they wish to use,[78] and are likewise free to select the individuals who are to serve as their grievance representatives.[79]

Limitation of the number of representatives who may appear at various hearings or negotiations is a common feature of collective agreements. Such limitation is said to be both legitimate and proper, and to be a proper subject for negotiation between the parties.[80] Sometimes, too, the agreement will impose a limitation upon the right of a party to select its representatives.[81]

Unions most often use "shop stewards" and grievance "committeemen." The steward represents the employee at the initial stages of the grievance procedure. The steward who performs successfully

---

[76] "Grievance Procedure Under Collective Bargaining," 63 Monthly Labor Review 175, 183 (U.S. Dept. of Labor, 1946).
[77] "Basic Patterns in Labor Arbitration Agreements," 34 LA 931, 936 (1960); Cudahy Packing Co., 7 LA 645, 646 (Fisher, 1947).
[78] Ford Motor Co., 1 ALAA ¶67,045 (Shulman, 1944).
[79] For the general right of each party under the NLRA to select its representatives for the purpose of collective bargaining (which of course includes grievance processing) and for some of the situations in which a party might be entitled to veto the other party's selection, see General Electric Co., 71 LRRM 2418 (CA 2, 1969); NLRB v. David Buttnick Co., 62 LRRM 2441 (CA 5, 1966); Standard Oil Co. v. NLRB, 54 LRRM 2076 (CA 6, 1963); Slate Belt Apparel Contractors' Assn., 45 LRRM 2626 (CA 3, 1960). For arbitral recognition of this general right, see Arbitrator Hayes in 53 LA 972, 973–974; Kabaker in 50 LA 634, 636; Kates in 36 LA 682, 685.
[80] Ford Motor Co., 1 ALAA ¶67,045 (Shulman, 1944).
[81] In Kahala Hilton Hotel Co., 44 LA 453, 457 (Burr, 1965), the agreement contained an express limitation. In Corry-Jamestown Corp., 36 LA 682, 685 (Kates, 1961), the agreement was interpreted to prevent the union from designating a representative to serve outside his own department. Another arbitrator found no such restriction in Chardon Rubber Co., 50 LA 634, 636 (Kabaker, 1968). Also see Arbitrator Berkowitz in 55 LA 901, 904. In Holan Div., 52 LA 1078, 1081 (Stouffer, 1969), the agreement was interpreted to restrict participation by the company's attorney at a pre-arbitral stage of the grievance procedure.

the responsibilities with which he is entrusted is an asset to management as well as to the employees whom he represents. As an employee spokesman he has the responsibility of policing the collective agreement, but he also has the responsibility of dissuading employees from pursuing complaints that are without merit.[82] In dealing with management he seeks to effectuate general union policies. Union grievance committeemen usually represent employees in the intermediate stages of the grievance procedure. The grievance committee frequently has the responsibility of determining union policy in connection with grievances.

The management representative closest to the employees and their work is the foreman. The foreman's effectiveness in grievance settlement is determined largely by his own capability and the amount of authority given him; if he is able and sufficient authority is given him, better settlements as a rule will be obtained at the foreman level than at later steps, since the foreman often understands shop problems better than those above him.[83] "Foremen trained by experience, observation, and study of labor and industrial psychology are able to prevent and to rectify most of the ordinary grievances of the workers."[84] Of course, to state this is to state the ideal only. Unfortunately, in numerous plants foremen lack authority, or fail to use it, and "pass the buck" to higher management officials.[85] Many employers, however, conduct training courses for foremen for the purpose of enabling them better to deal with grievances and acquaint them with the applicable company policies.

Many unions and companies conduct training programs for all their representatives. Such training usually covers the provisions of the collective agreement and basic union or company policy. Proper training should develop a feeling of mutual respect and confidence between stewards and foremen; one of its primary purposes should

---

[82] For related discussion, see this Chapter, topic titled "Attitude of Parties to the Grievance Procedure."

[83] "Grievance Procedure Under Collective Bargaining," 63 Monthly Labor Review 175, 179 (U.S. Dept. of Labor, 1946).

[84] Lapp, How to Handle Labor Grievances 109–110 (1945).

[85] "Grievance Procedure Under Collective Bargaining," 63 Monthly Labor Review 175, 179 (U.S. Dept. of Labor, 1946). Some reasons why the "ideal" of foreman-steward settlement often is not attained include personality clashes between foreman and steward, fear by both management and unions that such settlements may establish undesirable precedents, and fear by both the foreman and the steward that they will be reversed by their superiors. The Grievance Process 57–58 (Mich. State Univ. Lab. & Ind. Rel. Center, 1956).

be to foster the attitude that grievances are problems to be solved, not arguments to be won. Training, too, increases employee understanding of the use and objectives of the grievance procedure.[86]

Many plants have industrial relations departments to handle labor relations. Generally it is the function of this department to centralize and unify the company's policy and dealings with the union. Some industrial relations departments handle grievances. Opinion differs as to whether this is desirable. While some feel that it is an aid to grievance processing, others feel that it forces more grievances to the higher stages of the procedure because it cuts into the authority of the foreman.[87]

Right to Union Representation at Early Stage

Unions and management frequently disagree as to whether, in the interest of better relationships, employee grievances should be taken directly to the foreman or first to the union steward and then by the steward to the foreman.

Management often holds the view that the aggrieved employee should go to his foreman alone before going to his steward and that the union should not enter the picture until after the first step of the grievance procedure. It is argued that better relationships are fostered if the individual employee and the foreman discuss the grievance alone. The presence of the steward, it is thought, tends to make the grievance appear more serious than it really is. Management's right to act pursuant to these beliefs, however, is limited by the bargaining duty under the NLRB.[88]

---

[86] These points regarding training programs are stated and discussed in "Grievance Procedure Under Collective Bargaining," 63 Monthly Labor Review 175, 177–183 (U.S. Dept. of Labor, 1946).

[87] Id. at 184.

[88] The NLRB has held that settlements at the first step of the grievance procedure are "adjustments" within the meaning of the Section 9(a) proviso and that the union must have an opportunity to be present. Bethlehem Steel Co., 25 LRRM 1564 (1950). The right to be present may be waived. Globe-Union, Inc., 29 LRRM 1198 (1952). In Westinghouse Electric Corp., 52 LRRM 1385 (1963), the NLRB held that the employer modified the contractual grievance procedure and thus violated the duty to bargain by inviting employees to take grievances directly to their foreman before consulting their union steward. A court disagreed, holding the employer's statement to be only a suggestion that the grievance procedure would operate more smoothly if employees discussed possible complaints with their foreman before a formal grievance arose. Westinghouse Electric Corp. v. NLRB, 54 LRRM 2696 (CA 7, 1963).

On the other hand, unions often take the position that the steward should handle grievances from the start. The employee is believed to need the assistance and moral support of the steward to insure recognition of all of his rights. Unions wish to be able to "push" grievances of employees who are too timid to approach the foreman alone. Moreover, unions say that management benefits by the union's screening of grievances, a process which eliminates complaints that have no merit. Finally, unions feel that settlements by individuals make it possible for foremen to play favorites and that uniform settlements can be had only if the union is present from the outset.

Arbitrators, in turn, have sometimes been directly confronted with the question of when an employee is first entitled to demand union representation in the handling of his grievance. Most of the cases involve the right to pre-grievance union representation in meetings or interrogations in which discipline against the employee is assessed, or is a possibility, or in which the employee has reason to think that discipline might be contemplated. These cases fall roughly into three categories: (1) cases in which the agreement is found to provide, either expressly or by construction, for the presence of a union representative at the pre-grievance stage in question;[89] (2) cases holding there is no right to union representation, unless the agreement provides otherwise, until after discipline has been assessed;[90] (3) cases holding there is a right, even if not traced directly to the agreement, to union representation as early as the investigation stage.[91] Some arbitrators

---

[89] See Arbitrator Holly in 53 LA 226, 227; Stein in 50 LA 451, 452; Petree in 46 LA 283, 286–287; Dworkin in 44 LA 647, 648, 650–652; McNaughton in 40 LA 1100, 1102; Teple in 39 LA 784, 788; Cahn in 28 LA 570, 571–572; Shister in 18 LA 374 at 374. In Armstrong Rubber Co., 52 LA 501, 502–503 (Kotin, 1969), literal compliance with the provision was not required where there was substantial compliance with its underlying intent.

[90] See Arbitrator Keefe in 51 LA 672, 676; Dybeck in 49 LA 101, 105; Bradley in 35 LA 1, 6; Owen in 32 LA 413, 416–417; Gregory in 29 LA 646, 650–651. Also see Arbitrator Wenke in 28 LA 179, 180. In Texaco, Inc. v. NLRB, 408 F.2d 142 (CA 5, 1969), the court held (disagreeing with the NLRB) that the employer's refusal to comply with an employee's request for union representation during an interview concerning alleged theft of company property did not violate the employer's duty to bargain. In Quality Mfg. Co., 195 NLRB No. 42 (1972), the Board noted that following the court decision in "Texaco" the Board "has * * * refused to find 8(a)(5) violations under circumstances involving purely investigatory interviews"; but the Board held that, aside from any duty-to-bargain issue, the employer improperly discharged an employee for insisting that a union representative be present at an interview concerning possible discipline.

[91] See Arbitrator Jones in 50 LA 1253, 1260–1262; Anderson in 33 LA 769, 771; Meyers in 33 LA 57, 60; Reynolds in 19 LA 344, 346–347. Also see Tatum in 40 LA 1095, 1100; Rohman in 40 LA 619, 624. An employer's

have held that an employee cannot be heard to complain that he did not have union representation at pre-grievance stages if he did not request the union's presence.[92]

The question of union representation during a formative stage where the grievance did not initially involve discipline has occasionally arisen. For instance, where an employee questioned management's distribution of overtime, he was held to have the right to union representation during an incipient grievance stage in which the foreman participated.[93] It has been recognized that an employee might need someone to explain his gripe at the outset.[94] However, an employee who was suspected of being under the influence of alcohol was held not entitled to union representation during a breathalyzer test to determine his fitness for work. The arbitrator held inapplicable a contractual provision for union representation when an employee is summoned for possible discipline, since no disciplinary action was taken because of the incident; also held inapplicable in the present situation was a provision stating that an employee who has a complaint may discuss it with his foreman with or without the presence of a union steward.[95]

In any event, it appears clear that arbitrators recognize a right to union representation at least commencing with the first step of the contractual grievance procedure.

Grievance Adjustment by Individual Employees

Much has been written concerning individual employee rights in grievance adjustment and arbitration, and concerning the em-

---

refusal to permit union attendance during employee interrogation was held to present an arbitrable issue in Humble Oil & Refining Co. v. Independent Industrial Workers' Union, 337 F.2d 321 (CA 5, 1964).

[92] Weirton Steel Co., 50 LA 103, 105–106 (Kates, 1968); Erwin Mills, Inc., 43 LA 31, 32 (Strong, 1963).

[93] Braniff Airways, Inc., 27 LA 892, 896–898 (Williams, 1957), where the arbitrator reversed management's action in discharging the grievant for refusing to discuss his "overtime" grievance with the foreman in the absence of a union representative.

[94] See statement by Arbitrator Platt in International Harvester Co., 21 LA 344, 347 (1953). In American Hoist & Derrick Co., 35 LA 1, 6 (1960), Arbitrator Bradley noted a greater need for immediate union representation in some types of cases than in other types. In Reflector Hardware Corp., 49 LA 886, 889 (Kelliher, 1967), a clause making union representation available on certain specified premium days was held not to guarantee availability of union representation during all working hours. Cf., Arbitrator Cole in 40 LA 208, 214.

[95] Bethelehem Steel Corp., 55 LA 994, 995 (Seward, 1970).

ployee's right of fair representation. It is the purpose here to deal only briefly with these matters.[96]

The National Labor Relations Act (NLRA) as amended by the LMRA of 1947 provides in Section 9(a) that the majority union shall be the "exclusive representative" of all employees in the bargaining unit, and provides in Section 8(d) that the duty of the employer and union to bargain includes the duty to confer in good faith with respect to questions arising under the collective agreement. However, a proviso to Section 9(a) states that "any individual employee or a group of employees shall have the right at any time to present grievances to their employer and to have such grievances adjusted, without the intervention of the bargaining representative, as long as the adjustment is not inconsistent with the terms of a collective-bargaining contract or agreement then in effect," and as long as "the bargaining representative has been given opportunity to be present at such adjustment." The enactment of this proviso in 1947 generated much discussion, reflecting two widely differing interpretations.

Under one interpretation individual employees have a statutory right to settle their grievances directly with the employer and no agreement between the union and the employer can deprive them of this right; individual employees have a right to use the grievance and arbitration procedure without the union's assistance or over its veto.[97]

---

[96] For extensive treatment of these matters, see Fleming, The Labor Arbitration Process 107–133 (Univ. of Ill. Press, 1965); Rosen, "The Individual Worker in Grievance Arbitration: Still Another Look at the Problem," 24 Md. L. Rev. 233; Williams, "Intervention: Rights and Policies," Labor Arbitration and Industrial Change 266–295 (BNA Incorporated, 1963); Summers, "Individual Rights in Collective Agreements and Arbitration," 37 N.Y.U. L. Rev. 362 (1962); Aaron, "Some Aspects of the Union's Duty of Fair Representation," 22 Ohio St. L. J. 39 (1961); Cox, "Rights Under a Labor Agreement," 69 Harv. L. Rev. 601 (1956); Lenhoff, "The Effect of Labor Arbitration Clauses Upon the Individual," 9 Arb. J. 3 (1954).

[97] See Summers, "Individual Rights in Collective Agreements and Arbitration," 37 N.Y.U. L. Rev. 362 (1962); Lenhoff, "The Effect of Labor Arbitration Clauses Upon the Individual," 9 Arb. J. 3, 14–16 (1954); Donnelly v. United Fruit Co., 190 A.2d 825 (N.J., 1963); Arbitrator Bauder in 40 LA 780, 783; Arbitrator Volz in 37 LA 356, 358. In the *Donnelly* case, supra, the court recognized a right of individual employees to intervene, with independent representation, in arbitration proceedings between union and employer. For arbitration cases involving attempts of third parties or minority groups of employees to intervene in cases being processed by the union, see Arbitrator Jones in 45 LA 1115, 1122–1123; Sembower in 27 LA 353, 354–355. Related discussion is found in Chapter 7, topic titled "Bilateral Arbitration of Trilateral Conflicts." For a case involving a union's right to complete an arbitration instituted prior to the union's decertification, see Trumbull Asphalt Co., 38 LA 1093, 1097–1098 (Elson, 1962).

Under a second interpretation the Section 9(a) proviso permits (as an exception to the duty to deal exclusively with the union) but does not require the employer to adjust grievances with individual employees. Under this interpretation the statue places a right of control in the employer, who can keep control or who can relinquish it in the collective agreement either (1) by giving individual employees a right to adjust their grievances directly with the employer or (2) by placing the right of grievance adjustment solely in the union.[98]

Some of the uncertainty as to the scope of individual employee rights in grievance adjustment was removed by the U.S. Supreme Court's *Maddox* decision in 1965 and by its *Vaca* decision in 1967, though neither decision expressly discusses the Section 9(a) proviso.[99] Neither decision particularly favors the interests of the individual employee over the interests of the union.

In *Maddox* the Supreme Court held that an employee who had not attempted to use the contractual grievance procedure to enforce his right to benefits under the collective agreement was precluded from instituting court suit against the employer for this purpose. The Court explained:[100]

"As a general rule in cases to which federal law applies, federal labor policy requires that individual employees wishing to assert contract grievances must *attempt* use of the contract grievance procedure agreed upon by employer and union as the mode of redress. If the union refuses to press or only perfunctorily presses the individual's claim, differences may arise as to the forms of redress then available. * * * But unless the contract provides otherwise, there can be no doubt that the employee must afford the union the opportunity to act on his behalf. * * * Union interest in prosecuting employee grievances is clear. Such activity complements the union's status as

---

[98] See Cox, "Rights Under a Labor Agreement," 69 Harv. L. Rev. 601, 621–624 (1956); Black-Clawson Co. v. Machinists Lodge 355, 313 F.2d 179 (CA 2, 1962); Aribtrator Frey in 39 LA 751, 756; Arbitrator Hays in 20 LA 443, 444–445. In North American Aviation, Inc., 44 LA 1102, 1107–1108 (1965), Arbitrator Ross held that a separate "employee grievance procedure" in which employees could represent themselves violated the collective agreement, stating that while Section 9(a) of the statue permits the employer to maintain a separate employee grievance procedure in absence of any contrary commitment, the agreement may require (as this one did) that grievances be processed exclusively through the contract grievance procedure.

[99] Indeed, only in *Maddox* did the Court make even a passing reference expressly to the proviso. That reference is noted hereinbelow.

[100] Republic Steel Corporation v. Maddox, 85 S.Ct. 614, 616; 58 LRRM 2193 (1965).

exclusive bargaining representative by permitting it to participate actively in the continuing administration of the contract."[101]

Vaca directly involved an employee's suit against his union in which he alleged that the union had arbitrarily and capriciously failed to take his case to arbitration. In the wide-ranging majority opinion in this case the Supreme Court recognized that because the contractual grievance and arbitration remedies "have been devised and are often controlled by the union and the employer, they may may well prove unsatisfactory or unworkable for the individual grievant."[102] Furthermore, the Court expressly rejected the notion that the individual employee has an absolute right to have his grievance taken to arbitration regardless of the provisions of the collective agreement:[103]

> "Though we accept the proposition that a union may not arbitrarily ignore a meritorious grievance or process it in perfunctory fashion, we do not agree that the individual employee has an absolute right to have his grievance taken to arbitration regardless of the provisions of the applicable collective bargaining agreement. In L.M.R.A. §203(d), Congress declared that 'Final adjustment by a method agreed upon by the parties is * * * the desirable method for settlement of grievance disputes arising over the application or interpretation of an existing collective-bargaining agreement.' In providing for a grievance and arbitration procedure which gives the union discretion to supervise the grievance machinery and to invoke arbitration, the employer and the union contemplate that each will endeavor in good faith to settle grievances short of arbitration. Through this settlement process, frivolous grievances are ended prior to the most costly and time-consuming step in the grievance procedures. Moreover, both sides are assured that similar complaints will be treated consistently, and major problem areas in the interpretation of the collective bargaining

---

[101] In its footnote to the first sentence of the just-quoted passage, the Court said: "The proviso of §9(a) of the LMRA * * * is not contra; Black-Clawson Co. v. Machinists Local, 2 Cir., 313 F.2d 179." Also to be noted from *Maddox* is the Court's comment that "The federal rule would not of course preclude Maddox' court suit if the parties to the collective bargaining agreement expressly agreed that arbitration was not the exclusive remedy." 85 S.Ct. at 619. The *Maddox* rule was extended to railroad employees in Andrews v. Louisville & Nashville Railroad Co., 92 S.Ct. 1562 (1972). Cf., Glover v. St. Louis-San Francisco Ry. Co., 89 S.Ct. 548 (1969). The *Maddox* rule does not apply to a seaman's wage claims, which can be taken directly to federal court under an early statute or to arbitration under §301. U.S. Bulk Carriers, Inc. v. Arguelles, 91 S.Ct. 409 (1971). The question of whether direct court action on a grievance alleging violation of the Fair Labor Standards Act would be proper even if the grievance were subject to the grievance and arbitration provisions of the agreement was left undecided in Iowa Beef Packers, Inc. v. Thompson, 92 S.Ct. 859 (1972).
[102] Vaca v. Sipes, 87 S.Ct. 903, 914; 64 LRRM 2369 (1967).
[103] 87 S.Ct. at 917.

contract can be isolated and perhaps resolved. And finally, the settlement process furthers the interest of the union as statutory agent and as coauthor of the bargaining agreement in representing the employees in the enforcement of that agreement."[104]

The Court stated that an employee may seek judicial enforcement of his contractual rights if the union has sole power under the agreement to invoke the higher stages of the grievance procedure and if the employee has been prevented from exhausting the contractual remedies by the union's wrongful refusal to process the grievance.[105] As to what is a "wrongful" refusal, the Court stated that "A breach of the statutory duty of fair representation occurs only when a union's conduct toward a member of the collective bargaining unit is arbitrary, discriminatory, or in bad faith."[106] Finally, the Court indicated that an employee bringing suit against the union for alleged breach of the duty of fair representation (by refusing to take his case to arbitration) may and probably should join his Section 301 action against the employer in the same suit, the employer to be liable for damages attributable to the employer's breach of the collective agreement and the union to be liable for any increase in those damages caused by the union's refusal to process the grievance.[107]

---

[104] The Court did not fear for the interests of the individual employee: "Nor do we see substantial danger to the interests of the individual employee if his statutory agent is given the contractual power honestly and in good faith to settle grievances short of arbitration. For these reasons, we conclude that a union does not breach its duty of fair representation, and thereby open up a suit by the employee for breach of contract, merely because it settled the grievance short of arbitration." Id. at 918. Insofar as the Railway Labor Act is concerned, the Supreme Court indicated in the *Burley* cases that in order for a union to bind individual employees in grievance settlements before the National Railroad Adjustment Board it must appear that the employees authorized the union in some "legally sufficient manner," which may be by custom, by union rules in the case of union members, or by the failure of an individual employee with notice of proceedings to assert his rights. See Elgin, Joliet & Eastern Ry. Co. v. Burley cases in 325 U.S. 711, 16 LRRM 749 (1945); 327 U.S. 661, 17 LRRM 241 (1946). In Isaacson, "Labor Arbitration in State Courts," 12 Arb. J. 179, 188 (1957), it was suggested that the *Burley* decisions apply only to cases under the RLA. It may be noted that the Supreme Court did not refer to these decisions in *Vaca*.
[105] 87 S.Ct. at 914.
[106] 87 S.Ct. at 916. In Motor Coach Employees v. Lockridge, 77 LRRM 2501, 2512 (U.S. Sup. Ct., 1971), the Court also considered the required showing to demonstrate a breach of the duty of fair representation.
[107] 87 S.Ct. at 920–921. For an indication as to the effect of *Vaca* and *Maddox* upon lower court actions, see "Arbitration and Federal Rights Under Collective Agreements in 1967," Developments in American and Foreign Arbitration 201–206 (The Bureau of National Affairs, Inc., 1968). Also see discussion by Tobias, "A Plea For the Wrongfully Discharged Employee Abandoned by His Union," 41 U. of Cincinnati L. Rev. 55 (1972).

It is now apparent that individual employees have no inherent right to independent grievance processing and/or arbitration with the employer. However, opportunity for independent processing may be given to employees by the employer (if he has not bargained away his right to do so); and the right to independent processing may be given to employees by the collective agreement. Of course, even apart from the two just-noted possibilities, the union does not always resist an employee's desire for independent processing even though the union may have a contractual right to do so.[108]

Many agreements do appear to give the individual employee a right to present and adjust his grievance independently of the union.[109] Whether a given agreement actually does give such right is of course a matter of construction. Some tribunals no doubt will find the right only if it is clearly indicated by the language of the agreement.[110]

---

[108] See, for example, Maier Brewing Co., 49 LA 14, 18 (Roberts, 1967), where the union and company agreed that the contract had not been violated but where these parties nonetheless gave individual grievants full opportunity, through counsel of their own choosing, to establish otherwise. Of course, where the union is the moving party against an employee there should be no union objection to his representation by counsel of his own choosing. See Pacific Mercury Electronics, 34 LA 91, 92 (Aaron, 1960). Also see Arbitrator Wren in 42 LA 292, 293–294. In Wirtz, "Due Process of Arbitration," The Arbitrator and the Parties 1, 25 (BNA Incorporated, 1958), it is said that arbitrators have generally refused to permit the grievant to be represented by counsel of his own choosing rather than by the union. For instances of such refusal, see Arbitrator Kerrison in 41 LA 736, 737; Short in 38 LA 1076, 1079–1080. Here again, the language of the agreement (and now of course the *Vaca* decision) will be a prime factor in the result.

[109] See Major Collective Bargaining Agreements: Arbitration Procedures 29 (U.S. Dept. of Labor Bull. No. 1425–6, 1966); "Basic Patterns in Labor Arbitration Agreements," 34 LA 931, 932 (1960). For the results of union and company efforts to rectify their initial disregard of the individual grievant's contractual right to attend and participate in grievance sessions, see Flambeau Valley Farms Cooperative, 39 LA 724, 727–729 (Anderson, 1962). With an individual employee's contractual right to file grievances may go the burden of meeting contractual time limits. Publishers' Assn. of New York City, 39 LA 379, 382 (Schmertz, 1962). As to how arbitrators might dispose of settlements between employer and individual employee which conflict with the collective agreement, see Arbitrator Koven in 44 LA 431, 433–434; Schedler in 38 LA 909, 911–912; Blumrosen in 36 LA 251.

[110] For an example of a court's reasoning process in interpreting the agreement in this regard, see Black-Clawson Co. v. I.A.M., 313 F.2d 179, 183 (CA 2, 1963). Cf., Riley Stoker Corp., 7 LA 764 (Platt, 1947). In Local Union No. 12405, U.M.W. v. Martin Marietta Corp., 328 F.2d 945 (CA 7, 1964), the court interpreted the word "union" in the agreement as referring to the international, and the court held that the local union could not compel arbitration over the objection of the international.

Privileges and Protection of Grievance Representatives

In order to facilitate the operation of the grievance machinery, collective agreements frequently give special privileges and protection to union grievance representatives. Also, an area of protection for grievance representatives exists under arbitration decisions recognizing a certain immunity from discipline for their actions in performing their duties as such.

Superseniority

Many agreements provide superseniority for union representatives, assuring their continued employment as long as they hold office.[111] The underlying purpose of superseniority provisions often is to assure the fullest possible union representation at the plant by experienced representatives, and arbitrators have construed superseniority clauses liberally to achieve this objective.[112]

Apart from this objective, however, there is considerable arbitral authority for the principle that superseniority benefits to union representatives are limited to those rights and privileges which are clearly stated in the agreement.[113] Arbitrator Edwin R. Teple has explained:

"Superseniority obviously is a contradiction of the basic principle of seniority * * * and should be carefully limited to the terms by which it is created. It is clearly an exception to the rule which seniority

---

[111] For statements by the U.S. Supreme Court and by the War Labor Board in support of such superseniority, see U.S. Plastics Products Corp., 36 LA 808, 810–811 (Tischler, 1961). The union has a responsibility to notify the employer as to which employees hold union office with entitlement to superseniority. Rex Windows, Inc., 41 LA 606, 607 (Lehoczky, 1963).

[112] See Arbitrator Updegraff in 39 LA 587, 589–590; Tischler in 36 LA 808, 812; Valtin in 35 LA 304, 305. In U.S. Plastics Products Corp., 36 LA 808, 811–812 (Tischler, 1961), the agreement was construed to prevent the employer from transferring committeemen, during reduction in force, out of departments they had been representing. But see Arbitrator Teple in 37 LA 396, 399–400; Shister in 25 LA 856, 857; Lehoczky in 17 LA 291, 293. Also as concerns transfers, it may be noted that some agreements expressly require union consent for the transfer of grievance representatives from one shift to another, and some give the union the right to demand a transfer where grievance handling requires such. See BNA's Collective Bargaining Negotiations and Contracts, pp. 51, 181–183.

[113] See Arbitrator Dworkin in 45 LA 1109, 1114–1115; McCoy in 40 LA 675, 679; Teple in 40 LA 323, 326; Cahn in 37 LA 1017, 1018; Mueller in 37 LA 991, 996; Jaffee in 37 LA 458, 464; Fisher in 33 LA 655, 661. Cf., Roberts in 41 LA 275, 278; Cole in 40 LA 208, 214.

demands, that older employees in point of service are entitled to preference.[114]

Arbitrator Calvin L. McCoy has added that superseniority is a bargaining concession to the union as such, rather than to individuals; thus the exercise of superseniority must be limited to the purpose clearly indicated by the agreement.[115]

By the same token, an employee ordinarily should not be deprived of normal seniority rights by virtue of service as a union representative. Thus, an employer improperly refused to award a vacant job to a union representative (who was entitled to the job by seniority and qualifications) on the ground that her necessary absences from the job to attend to union matters would result in inefficient operations. In this case Arbitrator Ralph C. Hon stated that seniority provisions characteristically involve a compromise with efficiency, and that the need for competent union representatives requires that employees not be prejudiced by reason of their union position.[116]

Plant Access

Many agreements give representatives access to the plant for the purpose of investigating grievances. Furthermore, some arbitrators have considered that such right inheres under a collective agreement even if not expressly given.[117] Thus, nonemployee union representatives, such as the union business agent, may be given reasonable access to the plant. It is essential that union representatives be given opportunity, as management is, to examine all circumstances surrounding grievances.[118]

---

[114] American Monorail Co., 40 LA 323, 326 (1963).

[115] Rola Division, 40 LA 675, 679 (1963).

[116] American Lava Corp., 42 LA 117, 119–120 (1964). Similarly, see Arbitrator Marshall in 54 LA 1123, 1124.

[117] See Collins Radio Co., 36 LA 815, 820–822 (Rohman, 1961), in which the employer was directed to grant union access to a building in which disputed duties were performed; Librascope, Inc., 30 LA 358, 363–364 (Jones, 1958). Contra, Wheland Co., 32 LA 1004, 1006–1007 (Tatum, 1959). As to a right to plant access for the purpose of investigating grievances under the NLRA, compare Adolph Coors Co., 150 NLRB No. 158 (1965), with Westinghouse Electric Corp., 113 NLRB 954 (1955).

[118] For a discussion of the respective obligations of the parties in the investigation of grievances, see Jonco Aircraft Corp., 20 LA 211, 212 (Merrill, 1953). For an example of the intense emotions and turmoil that may be generated by plant access disputes, see Waycross Sportswear, Inc., 53 LA 1061 (Marshall, 1969).

In one case, under an agreement permitting union officers to enter the plant for the purpose of assisting in the adjustment of grievances, the word "plant" was interpreted to mean the "entire working area where employee grievances may arise."[119] Under another agreement giving union representatives the right to investigate grievances in the plant the company had no right to determine unilaterally that a grievance was not bona fide and use that determination to deny access to the plant.[120]

But certain limitations must be observed. In one of the cases just considered, for instance, Arbitrator James C. Hill held that under this type of provision the employer is entitled to know the subject of the grievance for which the union representative seeks entry to the plant.[121] Speaking of the right of entrance, Arbitrator Hill said:

> "There should be a legitimate reason for entering a specific area of the plant. It does not give the Union representative the right to roam the plant at will, and it would be a clear violation of the agreement for the Union to use this opportunity to engage in organizational activities."[122]

As to procedural formalities and requirements, an employer could not require union agents to make advance appointments for plant visits or to give advance notice as to the reason for visits where the agreement gave the right to plant access "for the purpose of ascertaining whether or not this agreement is being observed."[123] Another case held that management could require the union president-steward, while on leave for union business, to sign in at the plant main gate as a "visitor", but could not restrict him to talking to only one employee at a time.[124]

---

[119] Standard Motor Products, Inc., 11 LA 1147, 1153 (Hill, 1949). Also see Buddy-L Corp., 41 LA 185, 188–189 (Sembower, 1963). But in Avco Mfg. Corp., 40 LA 476, 480–481 (Stouffer, 1963), the agreement confined stewards to their own department.

[120] Aluminum Co. of America, 23 LA 317, 320–321 (Prasow, 1954).

[121] Standard Motor Products, Inc., 11 LA 1147, 1152 (1949).

[122] Id. at 1153. Also see Bendix Aviation Corp., 39 LA 393, 394 (Cahn, 1962). As to plant access by nonemployee union organizers under the NLRA, see NLRB v. Babcock & Wilcox Co., 67 S.Ct. 679 (1956). Regarding the scope of the company's obligation to make records available to union representatives under plant access "investigation" clauses, see North American Aviation, Inc., 19 LA 385, 389–390 (Komaroff. 1952).

[123] Associated Hospitals of the East Bay, Inc., 47 LA 858, 860–861 (Koven, 1966).

[124] Manning, Maxwell & Moore, Inc., 37 LA 475, 482–483 (Stutz, 1961).

Special Immunity

Many arbitrators have recognized that union representatives have some immunity, though it is by no means unlimited, against punishment by the employer for their actions in performing their duties as such. There have been numerous cases in which discipline of an employee was set aside or reduced because the "cause" for the discipline (often abusive language in heated exchange with supervision) emerged from or was related to the employee's activities as union steward.[125] However, there have been numerous other cases in which steward status did not shield the individual from discipline even though the incidents leading to it (abusive language, threats, or worse) were directly or indirectly related to the individual's status as union representative and might never have occurred but for such status.[126]

The cases in this area of study do not always fall into neat and reconcilable categories. Indeed, for the most part each case appears to have been decided on its own merits. However, various generalizations have been offered by arbitrators and some of these will noted here to illustrate possible lines of arbitral thought.

In overruling the suspension of a union committeeman for insulting remarks to a foreman, Arbitrator John P. McGury explained:

"If a committeeman, when attempting to discuss pending grievances, while not even on Company time, is given a disciplinary suspension for improper language, the Union and Unionism are being penalized, as well as the committeeman. The danger is that committeemen will become inhibited in their dealings with management, by fear of discipline. * * * Discipline should not be upheld solely on

---

[125] See Arbitrator Larkin in 49 LA 1111, 1114; Teple in 49 LA 346, 350; Solomon in 45 LA 751, 756; Giles in 45 LA 258, 261; Kadish in 39 LA 277, 280–281; Reynolds in 18 LA 772, 773; Komaroff in 17 LA 199, 204; Dwyer in 3 LA 497, 498. Also see Kleinsorge in 46 LA 73, 75; McGury in 44 LA 858, 861. In Bradlees Family Circle Stores, 47 LA 567, 574 (House, 1966), the employer was not permitted to punish a steward for failure to return to work immediately as instructed since he was engaged in legitimate steward duties and had not used excessive time. For other cases involving alleged time infractions, see Arbitrator Holly in 49 LA 269, 271; Komaroff in 17 LA 199, 204.

[126] See Arbitrator Turkus in 51 LA 766, 767; Nichols in 47 LA 672, 674–675; Roberts in 46 LA 486, 489; Luskin in 42 LA 948, 950; Rock in 42 LA 746, 749–750; Murphy in 42 LA 563, 566; Miller in 42 LA 568, 571; Roman in 41 LA 360, 365; Trotta in 38 LA 1226, 1229–1230; Kates in 36 LA 947, 950; Bothwell in 28 LA 543, 547–548. Also see Sinicropi in 53 LA 646, 647, 652; Porter in 48 LA 203, 205; Gorsuch in 40 LA 641, 651–652; Wolff in 32 LA 719, 739.

the basis that insulting remarks were made to a foreman. There should be a further showing that due to the surrounding circumstances, the remarks had an adverse effect on production or managerial authority."[127]

Arbitrator Alex Elson has emphasized the dual status of union stewards and has noted that it requires a delicate balancing of the duties and responsibilities as steward and those to the employer as an employee. Arbitrator Elson explained that the steward "must be free to express himself vigorously and indeed militantly, if the employees are to have an adequate advocate," but, important as is the steward's function, "he is a creature of the collective agreement" and has an "overriding responsibility" to maintain the agreement; discipline may be in order if this responsibility is disregarded.[128] In this particular case Arbitrator Elson held, as have other arbitrators, that a steward is not immune from discipline for encouraging work stoppages in violation of the agreement.[129]

Also emphasizing the dual status characteristic, Arbitrator Byron R. Abernethy accepted that an individual serving in the dual capacity "is properly subject to discipline for his actions as an employee, but is immune from discipline when acting clearly within the scope of his recognized Union duties and responsibilities."[130] Arbitrator Abernethy added, however, that the line between permissible conduct as a union representative and that not permitted an employee is not always so clear that a new and inexperienced steward (as in the case before him) should be expected to recognize it unmistakably, when acting in good faith.[131] It has also been considered that punishment for

---

[127] Bucyrus-Erie Co., 44 LA 858, 861 (1965).
[128] Sinclair Refining Co., 42 LA 131, 134 (1964). In Arden Farms Co., 45 LA 1124, 1130–1131 (1965), Arbitrator Tsukiyama similarly spoke in terms of the "two hats" worn by employees who also serve as stewards.
[129] 42 LA at 135–136. For other cases upholding discipline for encouraging work stoppages, see Arbitrator Miller in 50 LA 562, 564; Roberts in 48 LA 855, 860–861. In Reynolds Metals Co., 52 LA 936, 939–940 (Porter, 1969), a union president could be punished for conducting a union committee meeting during scheduled work hours without permission, since the meeting amounted to a small -scale walkout in violation of the no-strike clause.
[130] Bates Lumber Company, 65-1 ARB ¶8222 (1964).
[131] Id. at page 3801. For instances in which immunity was denied for infractions pertaining to the individual's service as an employee, see Arbitrator Tsukiyama in 45 LA 1124, 1130–1132; Kornblum in 43 LA 838, 842. In General Electric Co., 40 LA 1126, 1156–1157 (1963), Arbitrator Davey sustained the discharge of a union officer for writing an article in the union newspaper maliciously disparaging the employer's product—the misconduct was viewed as that of an employee. In Linn v. U.P.G.W.A. Local 114, 86 S.Ct. 657, 61 LRRM

an individual's actions as an employee is subject to modification if it is tainted by ill will carried over from the individual's activities as a union steward.[132]

A "rule of reason" for determining immunity of union stewards was advanced by Arbitrator Eli Rock in upholding discharge of a steward for threats and blackmail in connection with grievance handling:

"Obviously, the right of a steward to do his job properly must be strictly protected, without fear of retaliation of any kind for the performance of that proper role. Mere militancy or zealousness can never justify punishment; nor can a steward be limited to the language or behavior of the parlor. And as the Union points out, the steward is certainly entitled to be wrong in the issues that he presses or fights over, on behalf of his constituents.

"If the latter were all that was involved here, there would obviously be no problem. Much more is contained, however. Even the average, extremely zealous steward knows that there are some limits on his behavior. He cannot, for example, assault foremen, or call wildcat strikes or counsel employees to disobey Company orders, or do other things which are recognized as being outside the sphere of proper activity for this position. Clearly, a rule of reason is recognized and accepted on the subject, and few, if any, are the stewards who would regard the office as conferring on them the right to resort to the *combination* of extreme activities which were followed by this particular grievant."[133]

In turn, Arbitrator Burton B. Turkus, in upholding the discharge of a union steward for a series of insubordinate acts designed to embarrass and humiliate management in front of other employees, declared:

"Probably no area in disciplinary disputes may pose a more troublesome problem to the parties to a labor agreement than keeping

---

2345 (1966), the Supreme Court held the states are not preempted from giving damages for false and defamatory statements (if made with malice) during union organizational campaigns. But in General Motors Corp. v. Mendicki, 54 LC ¶11,488 (CA 10, 1966), accusations uttered at a grievance hearing were held immune from liability for damages, and in Crown Central Petroleum Corp., 177 NLRB No. 29 (1969), name-calling at a grievance meeting was held not so abusive as to render the spokesman unprotected under the NLRA.

[132] Lawndale Industries, Inc., 46 LA 220, 223 (McGury, 1966). However, the mere fact that an employee's misconduct occurs at grievance or union meetings will not necessarily immunize him from employer punishment. See Lone Star Brewing Co., 45 LA 817, 821 (Merrill, 1965), involving fighting by an employee (not a steward) at a union meeting on company premises; Special Metals Inc., 39 LA 1, 3 (Shister, 1962), involving discipline of an employee (not a steward) for false testimony at a grievance meeting.

[133] Singer-Fidelity, Inc., 42 LA 746, 749 (1963).

the balance true between the right of Union shop stewards and representatives to be accorded a sound and realistic latitude in the method and attitude adopted in presenting grievances to management and their concomitant responsibility and obligation as Union officials to scrupulously refrain from the abuse of such status to cloak patent insubordination and defiant challenge of management's right to manage and direct the work force."[134]

In this case the steward's actions were triggered in part at least by his being sent home early with loss of overtime earnings. As to this, Arbitrator Turkus stated:

"In return for assuming a steward's responsibilities an employee does not receive the right to be high-handedly insubordinate or to urge others not to work as directed by their supervisors. And this is particularly so when a steward is prosecuting his own grievance—one that arises from his own conduct or misconduct in the work place. In these circumstances, his conduct when pressing the grievance must be judged by the same standards that govern the conduct of any other employee.[135]

Pay for Grievance Time

Many employers compensate union representatives and other employees for time spent in handling grievances during working hours.[136] In some large plants it is the practice of management to pay for full-time union stewards.[137]

---

[134] Calmar, Inc., 51 LA 766, 767 (1968).
[135] Id. at 769. In Trans World Airlines, Inc., 39 LA 1131, 1134 (Gilden, 1962), a steward had no immunity for misbehavior in acting on his own behalf at a grievance meeting. In Reynolds Metals Co., 39 LA 584, 587 (1962), Arbitrator Sembower cautioned that a steward should hesitate to represent himself as to his own grievance.
[136] As to the extent and variations of this practice, see "Basic Patterns in Labor Arbitration Agreements," 34 LA 931, 935–936 (1960); "Grievance Procedure Under Collective Bargaining," 63 Monthly Labor Review 175, 184 (U.S. Dept. of Labor, 1946).
[137] Under a proviso to NLRA §8(a)(2) an employer may permit employees to confer with him during working hours without loss of time or pay. Under LMRA §302 employer payments to employee representatives are prohibited, with the express exception of compensation for services as an employee. It is accepted that management may pay union representatives for time spent discussing grievances with management, but question exists as to whether payment may be made for grievance activities other than those of "conferring" with management. Several carefully reasoned arbitral opinions (some after the 1959 amendment of §302) have concluded that employer payments to union representatives for time spent in processing grievances and administering the agreement are legal, though some of these opinions recognized that a court might disagree. See Arbitrator Seibel in 44 LA 866, 867–871; Stark in 36 LA 351, 364–371; Beatty in 36 LA 291, 297–300; Dworkin in 35 LA 228, 234–235; Gregory in 10 LA

Unions take the position that the activity of union grievance representatives benefits management as much as employees. Of course, both parties will agree that it is to the advantage of both if only persons of responsibility act as grievance representatives. Payment for time spent in handling grievances is one way to secure the services of such persons. Grievance pay also facilitates prompt settlement, thereby improving morale and plant efficiency.

Emphasizing that the basic purpose of pay for grievance time is to compensate union officials who help management resolve differences with employees, an arbitrator construed a contractual provision to pay grievance representatives for time lost as not applying to the grievant himself; that arbitrator stated that "it might be very unwise to offer to pay employees for time lost while settling their own grievances."[138] But even where the agreement did not specifically require pay for time spent by employees in discussing their conduct with management prior to possible assessment of discipline, they were held entitled to pay for all time lost from work, the arbitrator stating that they should have been called in during nonworking time.[139] In the latter regard, pay for nonworking time utilized by employees on their own grievances has been denied.[140]

Some arbitrators have held that past practice should determine whether grievance time is to be compensated where the agreement is silent or ambiguous on the matter.[141]

In some cases the employer has not been required to pay union representatives for time spent at arbitration hearings in the absence of a clear and specific contractual requirement for such pay.[142] How-

---

471, 473–474. Also see Arbitrator Willcox in 23 LA 812, 814; Kelliher in 16 LA 734, 735–736.
   [138] American Car & Foundry Co., 2 LA 644, 645–646 (Larkin, 1945).
   [139] Bethlehem Steel Co., 19 LA 261, 262–264 (Shipman, 1952).
   [140] Allied Chemical Corp., 47 LA 686, 690 (Hilpert, 1966); Bethlehem Steel Co., 17 LA 436, 439 (Killingsworth, 1951).
   [141] See Arbitrator Hardy in 49 LA 415, 417–418; Seibel in 41 LA 1042, 1044–1045; Dworkin in 35 LA 228, 233–234; Lehoczky in 27 LA 187, 188; McCoy in 16 LA 240, 241–242; Hepburn in 13 LA 418, 422.
   [142] See Arbitrator Updegraff in 50 LA 1025, 1027 and in 36 LA 1044, 1046; Bothwell in 50 LA 230, 231; Bennett in 43 LA 331, 332; Begley in 38 LA 319, 320; Marshall in 28 LA 107, 108; Campbell in 25 LA 700, 707–708; Spaulding in 21 LA 763, 768; Fulda in 14 LA 775, 780; Coogler in 12 LA 1021, 1022; Gorder in 8 LA 945, 946–948; Lehoczky in 8 LA 33, 35. In some of these cases the arbitrator noted the absence of any clearly established practice to pay for arbitration time.

ever, so definite a provision for such pay has not been required in all cases,[143] especially where there was an established practice for the employer to pay union representatives for arbitration time.[144]

Under an agreement providing that union representatives shall be paid for time spent "conferring with management," time spent researching company records (relevant to grievances) in the absence of management was held to be compensable if the amount of time is "relatively slight and of an incidental nature."[145]

Payment for grievance work is generally made on a straight-time basis.[146] Some agreements, however, provide that grievance representatives "shall not lose pay for time spent" in grievance meetings with management. Under such a provision one arbitrator held that representatives had to be paid a special differential which they would have received had they not been called from work for grievance meetings, even though another provision of the agreement stated that the differential was to be paid only in case of actual performance of differential work.[147] But under a similar provision in an agreement which also provided that grievance conferences should be held during working hours, a minimum of four hours' pay at straight time, in accordance with call-in pay provisions, was held to be sufficient for less than four hours of grievance work performed after working hours; the arbitrator rejected the union demand for payment at the overtime rate.[148]

Various means of control have been used to prevent abuse of grievance-pay practices. Some agreements limit the amount of time that may be spent in such activity;[149] others contain no specific limit,

---

[143] See Buckeye Holmesville Mfg. Co., 53 LA 866, 866–867 (McIntosh, 1969); Modine Mfg. Co., 23 LA 243, 245 (Porter, 1954).

[144] See Arbitrator Smith in 46 LA 637, 639; Dunau in 38 LA 49, 51; Jones in 31 LA 240, 242–243; Dworkin in 22 LA 352, 357; Brown in 21 LA 529, 532.

[145] Standard Oil Co., 16 LA 734, 735–736 (Kelliher, 1951).

[146] "Grievance Procedure Under Collective Bargaining," 63 Monthly Labor Review 175, 184 (U.S. Dept. of Labor, 1946). But see International Harvester Co., 22 LA 196, 197–198 (Cole, 1954). As to applicability of cost-of-living adjustments to grievance time pay see Bethlehem Steel Co., 33 LA 632, 636–637 (Feinberg, 1959).

[147] Bethlehem Steel Co., 10 LA 284, 287–288 (Dodd, 1948).

[148] Ford Roofing Products Co., 5 LA 182, 184 (Wardlaw, 1946).

[149] Similarly, the agreement may expressly limit the pay for grievance activity, or limit the number of individuals who may collect grievance pay. See "Basic Patterns in Labor Arbitration Agreements," 34 LA 931, 935 (1960).

but say that a "reasonable amount" of time will be paid for.[150] Management has been held entitled to require the union to fill out forms, giving a general account of grievance services performed and the time involved.[151] This right is said to accompany management's contractual obligation to pay for such services.[152] Use of such report forms is not considered to be espionage or interference with union activity.[153]

Many companies require union representatives to report to their foreman before leaving work to handle grievances. Where an agreement provided that stewards were to be compensated for earnings lost in handling grievances but did not spell out a procedure to be followed by stewards, Arbitrator Peter Di Leone held that management could require stewards to notify their supervisor when leaving work to handle grievances, and to clock out and in for the period of time away from the steward's work station; provided, that prior notification should not be required in emergencies or if the foreman is not readily available.[154]

Another means of protecting grievance-pay practices from abuse is to provide, in the agreement, that management may inaugurate a grievance at a advanced step of the grievance procedure if abuse is believed to exist.[155] Then, too, such abuse may lead directly or in-

---

[150] Where the agreement by implication provided pay for grievance handling but did not state any limitation, and where past practice was to pay for all time so spent, it was held that the employer could not unilaterally limit the amount of paid time but could challenge in specific instances the reasonableness of the amount of time claimed for grievance activity. Goss Co., 44 LA 824, 826–827 (Pedrick, 1964).

[151] See Arbitrator Cahn in 50 LA 909, 914–915; Seinsheimer in 36 LA 166, 169 (merely saying "union business" did not suffice); Wolff in 33 LA 112, 123; Jaffe in 11 LA 729, 730–731; Shulman in 2 LA 382, 383.

[152] Bell Aircraft Corp., 11 LA 729, 730–731 (Jaffe, 1948).

[153] Ford Motor Co., 2 LA 382, 383 (Shulman, 1944).

[154] Picker X-Ray Corp., 44 LA 463, 465–466 (1965). Arbitrator Di Leone also stated that the prior practice of not requiring stewards to do these things when the union business was within their own department did not preclude management from establishing reasonable procedures to guard against abuse of the right to conduct union business on company time. Id. at 465. In Active Products Corp., 67-1 ARB ¶8261 (Seinsheimer, 1967), a plant rule requiring stewards to clock out and in was held reasonable and enforceable by discipline. In Jenkins Bros., 11 LA 432, 434–435 (Donnelly, 1948), management (with some contractual basis) could require stewards to clock out and in when leaving work to process grievances, but the Arbitrator stated that such action by management may be shortsighted in view of the dissatisfaction which it may cause.

[155] See Fact-Finders Van Fossen, Humphrey & Prifrel in 2 LA 227, 241; Marshall, Spencer & Holly in 1 LA 512, 521–522.

directly to the proper warning or punishment of the grievance representative.[156]

Written Statement of Grievance

There are various reasons why grievances should be presented in writing at an early stage of the grievance procedure, and to do so is the general practice. The written complaint establishes a record of the grievance. By putting the grievance in writing it is less likely to become distorted as it is processed through the grievance procedure.[157] Then, too, if grievances must be stated in writing, those that lack merit often are dropped.

Some persons consider it important to have a written grievance filed at the beginning, or "first step," of the grievance procedure in view of the value of a complete written record.[158] However, many parties prefer informal oral discussion at the first step, considering written grievances to be best suited to the later steps of the procedure. These parties may oppose written presentation of grievances at the first step on the ground that it makes the procedure too inflexible and cumbersome, discourages employees from voicing their complaints, and impedes prompt settlement.[159]

One "interests" arbitrator, recognizing that the presentation of grievances in writing is a well-established practice in industry, granted an employer's request for a provision requiring grievances carried beyond the employee's immediate superior to be presented in writing on simple forms provided by the company.[160] In this connection, a clause requiring that grievances be "filed" at the second step within

---

[156] See Arbitrator Teple in 48 LA 1345, 1348–1349; Cahn in 39 LA 1185, 1185–1186; Wolff in 33 LA 112, 123.
[157] For a related discussion, see Chapter 7, topic titled "Extent of Permissible Deviation From Pre-Arbitral Discussion of Case."
[158] Updegraff, Arbitration and Labor Relations 138 (The Bureau of National Affairs, Inc., 1970); Updegraff & McCoy, Arbitration of Labor Disputes 53 (1946).
[159] For a most interesting program by one company and union for speedy and informal handling of most complaints "at the level of the shop floor, without written grievances," see Ross, "Distressed Grievance Procedures and Their Rehabilitation," Labor Arbitration and Industrial Change 104, 128 (BNA Incorporated, 1963).
[160] New York City Omnibus Corp., 7 LA 794, 820–821 (Cole, 1947).

a specified time was interpreted to require that grievances be stated "in writing" at that step.[161]

In some instances the discussion of grievances not filed in writing as required by the agreement has been held to waive the "written grievance" requirement.[162] One arbitrator, in placing the burden upon management to raise the issue promptly, stated that if management desires to insist upon strict compliance with "written grievance" requirements, it should express its disapproval of oral grievances at the time when they first become a subject of discussion between the parties. "The company's failure to raise the objection at that time constitutes a waiver of that requirement."[163] But another arbitrator ruled otherwise, declaring that "if there is any place in the interpretation of collective bargaining agreements where strict or technical construction is necessary it is in that which provides for the grievance machinery and procedure."[164]

Time Limitations

Promptness is one of the most important aspects of grievance settlement. Failure to settle grievances with dispatch is sure to lead to labor unrest. All parties agree that promptness in the settlement of grievances leads to better labor-management relationships; opinion differs, however, as to the best means of insuring such promptness. While many agreements provide time limits for taking complaints to the grievance procedure as well as time limits for processing grievances through the various steps of the procedure, other agreements contain no such provisions. Some parties feel that time limits provide a safeguard against stalling, and against the accumulation of cases and pressing of stale claims. On the other hand, others believe that the setting of specific time allowances permits a party to stall to the maximum

---

[161] Jones & Laughlin Steel Corp., 16 LA 788, 789 (Cahn, 1951). To similar effect, Ranco, Inc., 48 LA 974, 977 (Gibson, 1967).
[162] See Arbitrator Teple in 45 LA 196, 201; Wolf in 44 LA 107, 109; Greene in 10 LA 567, 568; Gilden in 3 LA 327, 332–333. Also see Dworet in 40 LA 788, 789. The contractual time limit for filing a written grievance was held waived by proceeding without objection in Beaunit Fibers, 44 LA 1040, 1042 (McCoy, 1965).
[163] Lapham-Hickey Co., 3 LA 327, 333 (Gilden, 1946). To similar effect, Royal Paper Products, Inc., 48 LA 636, 638 (Seitz, 1966).
[164] Firestone Tire & Rubber Co., 9 LA 518, 522 (Rader, 1948). For related material, see this Chapter, subtopic titled "Failure to Comply Strictly with Technical Requirements of Grievance Procedure."

allowable time.[165] Even worse, it sometimes operates to bar grievances which should be settled for the sake of improving the relations of the parties.

In the final analysis, prompt settlement of grievances depends, not upon the presence of contractual time limits, but upon a sincere desire of the parties to settle differences. But that time limits do have definite value may be presumed from the fact that numerous agreements contain them. Without question, such limits provide an additional element of order to the grievance procedure.[166]

No set formula is available for the establishment of time limits. Rather, the special circumstances of the parties should determine, in each instance, the nature of the time-limit provisions of their agreement. The agreement may fix time limits for each step of the procedure, or an over-all time limit for complete processing of a grievance, or simply forbid delay. Any of these forms might be coupled with a time limit for the initial submission of grievances. Different limits may be prescribed for the submission of different types of grievances. This was done, for instance, by a fact-finding board recommendation of a five-day limit for filing discharge and pay adjustment disputes, and a 30-day limit for all other grievances.[167]

Some cases hold there is no time limit for filing grievances where the agreement does not specify any.[168] But some arbitrators have held

---

[165] It has been emphasized, however, that grievance processing should not be rushed to the extent that snap judgments are prompted. Lehigh Portland Cement Co., 46 LA 132, 134–135 (Duff, 1965), where the agreement was viewed as anticipating a brief time lapse between filing time and answering time; time limits could not be shortened by employer insistence upon giving immediate answers.

[166] For general discussion of advantages of using time limits, see The Grievance Process 60 (Mich. State Univ. Lab. & Ind. Rel. Center, 1956). Of 400 agreements included in one survey, 81 percent contained time limits for filing grievances and 53 percent contained limits for later stages of the procedure. "Basic Patterns in Labor Arbitration Agreements," 34 LA 931, 932–933 (1960), where variations in time limit provisions are also noted.

[167] Minneapolis-Moline Power Implement Co., 2 LA 227, 241 (Van Fossen, Humphrey & Prifrel, 1946).

[168] See Arbitrator Shister in 47 LA 601, 602; Gundermann in 44 LA 585, 589 (but recognizing an exception where undue hardship results to the other party from delayed filing); Gilden in 6 LA 238, 260 (grievance may be filed at any time during the contract term), and in 3 LA 327, 333; Whiting in 5 LA 477, 478. Also see Havinghurst in 26 LA 688, 692; Copelof in 21 LA 788, 792. Some grievances arise outside the term of any contract, and some that do arise during the contract term are not disposed of during that term. For discussion of the right to process these grievances, apart from any question of time limits, see Chapter 3, subtopic titled "Pre-Contract and Post-Contract Grievances."

that even though the contract does not state a time limit for filing, a requirement for filing within a reasonable time is inferred by the establishment of a grievance procedure.[169] It has been held also that where the contract states no time limit for filing grievances but does state specific time limits for taking grievances to the various steps of the procedure once they have been filed, the evident intent of the contract is that grievances must be filed with reasonable promptness.[170]

Where the absence of strict time limits results in the acceptance of grievances notwithstanding delayed filing, the arbitrator may make the grievance adjustment retroactive only to the date on which the grievance was filed or to some other date short of full retroactivity.[171] In particular, arbitrators can be expected to deny that part of a claim which, if allowed, would result in a loss to one party caused by the negligent delay of the other party in asserting the claim. Whether the arbitrator calls such delay laches, acquiescence, or sleeping on one's rights, the principle involved appears to be generally recognized and applied.[172]

If the agreement does contain clear time limits for filing and prosecuting grievances, failure to observe them generally will result

---

[169] See Arbitrator Killion in 47 LA 1153, 1156–1157 (where an unreported decision by Edgar A. Jones is quoted to the same effect); Scheiber in 43 LA 129, 134–137; Somers in 24 LA 324, 330. Also see Cox in 49 LA 837, 840–841.

[170] See Arbitrator Traynor in 47 LA 767, 775–776; Greenwald in 66-1 ARB ¶8185; Williams in 26 LA 505, 507; Maggs in 19 LA 677, 681, and in 12 LA 311, 316. But see Smith in 32 LA 274, 276. A requirement for reasonably prompt filing was held to exist under a provision calling for expeditious grievance settlement. Kennecott Copper Corp., 35 LA 412, 413–414 (Ross, 1960). In American Bakeries Co., 44 LA 156, 160–161 (1965), Arbitrator Harold D. Jones held that the union could file a grievance and hold its further processing in abeyance pending the occurrence of a similar incident, since the contract did not set time limits for processing grievances from step to step.

[171] See Arbitrator Dworkin in 45 LA 812, 816; Larkin in 45 LA 517, 521–522; Markowitz in 37 LA 140, 143; Lockhart in 16 LA 156, 160–161; Davey in 9 LA 139, 140; Brandschain in 7 LA 785, 787; Gilden in 2 LA 655, 659–660. Also see cases cited in next footnote. But see Appleby in 20 LA 183, 188–189. Of course the agreement may expressly limit retroactivity. See Arbitrator Cole in 39 LA 1148, 1153; Crawford in 37 LA 1046, 1047.

[172] See extensive statement by Arbitrator Lockhart in Lavoris Co., 16 LA 156, 160–161 (1951). For other arbitrators applying the principle, see Kates in 47 LA 1045, 1048; Dworkin in 45 LA 812, 816; Dolnick in 45 LA 357, 361; Markowitz in 37 LA 140, 143; Ross in 32 LA 713, 719; Kelliher in 31 LA 219, 220; Cornsweet in 12 LA 482, 483–484; Wolff in 10 LA 288, 293–294; Lehoczky in 9 LA 659, 660; Brandschain in 7 LA 785, 787; Gilden in 2 LA 608, 612. Also see Seitz in 49 LA 197, 199; Bauder in 40 LA 780, 784; Stouffer in 37 LA 231, 234. Cf., Murphy in 38 LA 1031, 1040–1041.

in dismissal of the grievance if the failure is protested.[173] Thus the practical effect of late filing in many instances is that the merits of the dispute are never decided.[174]

It has been held that doubts as to the interpretation of contractual time limits or as to whether they have been met should be resolved against forfeiture of the right to process the grievance.[175] Moreover, even if time limits are clear, late filing will not result in dismissal of the grievance if the circumstances are such that it would be unreasonable to require strict compliance with the time limits specified by the agreement.[176]

If both parties have been lax as to observing time limits in the past, an arbitrator will hesitate to enforce them strictly until prior

---

[173] E.g., Arbitrator Stouffer in 53 LA 79, 82; Gibson in 51 LA 837, 840; Nathanson in 50 LA 1220, 1222; Krinsky in 48 LA 594, 597; Porter in 47 LA 1057, 1059; Tatum in 47 LA 563, 566; Boothe in 47 LA 336, 339; Strongin in 46 LA 767, 768; Teple in 46 LA 338, 345; Roberts in 46 LA 59, 61; Small in 45 LA 257, 258; Loucks in 37 LA 588, 590; Scheiber in 64-3 ARB ¶9041; Livengood in 27 LA 157, 159; Morvant in 26 LA 732, 735–736; Prasow in 25 LA 225, 228–230; Maggs in 19 LA 677, 680; Cahn in 17 LA 277, 280; Handsaker in 16 LA 369, 372; Holden in 13 LA 387, 390; McCoy in 11 LA 98, 100; Rader in 7 LA 595, 597–598.

[174] One of the relatively few cases in which the merits were reached in spite of a ruling against the grievant on the time issue is Northeast Airlines, Inc., 37 LA 741, 745 (Wolff, 1961), in which time limits were held breached, but a ruling on the merits was issued in the belief that the parties would be aided by the Arbitrator's views. In American Zinc Co., 46 LA 645, 650 (Abernethy, 1966), the company asserted late filing but nonetheless agreed to have a ruling on the merits first, the time limit issue to be ruled upon only if the company should lose on the merits. In Chambers v. Beaunit Corp., 69 LRRM 2732 (CA 6, 1968), an arbitrator's dismissal of a grievance for late filing was held to bar subsequent resort to the federal courts on the merits. However, in M & E Co., 44 LA 76, 83–86 (Lennard, 1965), the arbitrator refused to grant the employer's request to specify in the award (dismissing the grievance for late filing) that the claim could not be pursued before any other tribunal. Where an agreement did not contain any time limit for filing grievances, it was held that a grievance which was dismissed on procedural grounds could be refiled and processed to arbitration. Local 616, IUE v. Byrd Plastics, Inc., 74 LRRM 2550 (CA 3, 1970).

[175] Technical Service Corp., 36 LA 148, 151 (LaDriere, undated); Globe-Wernicke Co., 33 LA 553, 555 (Sanders, 1959). In Stauffer Chemical Company, 63-1 ARB ¶8140 (Hale, 1963), a loophole existed in a time limitation provision since the yardstick for determining when the time has expired could not be applied to the grievance. In Miami Industries, 50 LA 978, 984 (1968), Arbitrator Howlett stated that in raising time issues a party raises an affirmative defense which he has the burden of proof to establish by a preponderance of the evidence.

[176] See Arbitrator Porter in 47 LA 524, 525; Klein in 42 LA 1076, 1082; Hardy in 66-2 ARB ¶8699; Duff in 63-3 ARB ¶9060; Reid in 23 LA 135, 136; Sturges in 16 LA 794, 800; Maggs in 15 LA 934, 935. Also see Kesselman in 50 LA 1223, 1225; Seward in 47 LA 549, 550; Pierson in 13 LA 782, 786.

notice has been given by a party of intent to demand strict adherence to the contractual requirements.[177]

Of course time limits may be extended or waived by a special agreement in writing. Oral agreements have also sufficed for this purpose.[178] Even where an agreement expressly required time limit waivers to be in writing, it was held that the parties' actions may produce a waiver without a writing.[179]

In many cases time limits have been held waived by a party in recognizing and negotiating a grievance without making clear and timely objection.[180] But there are cases holding to the contrary.[181] Where clear and timely objection is made to time limit violations, no waiver will result from subsequent processing of the grievance on the merits.[182] Indeed, it has been suggested that upon making timely objection to delayed filing, the objecting party ordinarily should then discuss the grievance on the merits so that all issues will be ready for presentation to an arbitrator if the case reaches that stage.[183] Under a less expeditious procedure the objecting party may refuse to enter-

---

[177] See Arbitrator Sembower in 52 LA 97, 98–99; Doyle in 50 LA 1157, 1158; Kesselman in 42 LA 884, 888; Biscoe in 9 LA 595, 596; Cornsweet in 9 LA 625, 626; Rauch in 4 LA 170, 173. Also see Killingsworth in 19 LA 186, 187.

[178] See Arbitrator Howlett in 50 LA 978, 984; Seinsheimer in 42 LA 740, 745; Dworet in 41 LA 303, 304.

[179] Jackson Electrical Instrument Co., 42 LA 740, 745 (Seinsheimer, 1964).

[180] E.g., Arbitrator Keefe in 50 LA 453 at 453; Wagner in 49 LA 1036, 1039; Roberts in 49 LA 214, 218; Dybeck in 48 LA 1085, 1087; Krimsly in 48 LA 802, 805–806; Merrill in 47 LA 1120, 1125; Fallon in 45 LA 271, 275–276; Teple in 45 LA 196, 201; Anderson in 44 LA 66, 72; Rice in 44 LA 16, 18; Stouffer in 63-1 ARB ¶8358; Willingham in 62-2 ARB ¶8464; Gorsuch in 41 LA 200, 203–205; Davey in 43 LA 453, 458; Autrey in 38 LA 400, 403; Wood in 32 LA 216, 219; Whiting in 28 LA 398, 400; Platt in 27 LA 685, 687; Klamon in 24 LA 869, 873; Ross in 24 LA 857, 859; Day in 22 LA 775, 778. Cf., Davey in 18 LA 497, 504. While parties gave persistent and prolonged consideration to a grievance over a period of three years, the contractual time limit was held not to bar the claim. Grace Lines, Inc., 39 LA 633, 635–636 (Shaughnessy, 1962). Similarly, see Arbitrator Roberts in 55 LA 210, 216–217. As long as the parties are still discussing the possibilities of settling a grievance at a given step, the time for proceeding to the next step of the grievance procedure might be held not to have started running. See Montgomery Ward & Co., 48 LA 1171, 1172–1173 (Updegraff, undated). However, management's expression of opinion that employees had no valid basis for complaint did not suffice to relieve them of the contractual time limit for filing their grievance. Kroger Co., 36 LA 270, 272 (Stouffer, 1960).

[181] See Arbitrator Tatum in 47 LA 563, 566; Sembower in 44 LA 304, 306–307; Schmertz in 39 LA 379, 381–382.

[182] See Arbitrator Boothe in 47 LA 336, 339; Scheiber in 43 LA 129, 136; Elkouri in 42 LA 153, 156.

[183] North American Aviation, Inc., 17 LA 715, 719 (Komaroff, 1951).

tain the grievance on the ground that it is null and void, forcing the grievant to file a second grievance involving the time issue alone; discussion of the original dispute on the merits would thus be delayed pending final resolution of the time issue.[184]

The particular contractual provision would appear to determine whether Saturdays, Sundays, holidays, and the day of the occurrence are to be counted in computing time.[185] An arbitrator might be inclined toward flexibility in applying a short time limit within which a holiday falls, provided the basic objective of prompt grievance processing is not seriously jeopardized.[186]

Grievances are not always discovered at the time they occur. Some agreements provide specifically that grievances are to be filed within a certain number of days after they "occur or are discovered."[187] Even without such specific provision, arbitrators have held that one cannot be expected to file a grievance until he is aware or should be aware of the action upon which the grievance is based.[188] But time limits "cannot be extended by the excuse that the grievant just didn't think of it sooner."[189] Furthermore, where the employee had knowledge of adverse action but did not speak up, the union will not be heard to say that the time limit should be extended because the union did not know.[190]

A party sometimes announces its intention to do a given act but does not do or culminate the act until a later date. Similarly, a party may do an act whose adverse effect upon another does not result until a later date. In some such situations arbitrators have held that the "occurrence" for purposes of applying time limits is at the later date.[191]

---

[184] Square D Co., 25 LA 225, 230 (Prasow, 1955).
[185] See Arbitrator Ralston in 15 LA 640, 642–643; Ebeling in 11 LA 732, 737; Shulman in 1 ALAA ¶67,040.
[186] See Eimco Corp., 41 LA 1184, 1186–1187 (Dykstra, 1963).
[187] As in International Minerals and Chemical Co., 3 LA 405, 406 (Dwyer, 1946). Also see Bethlehem Steel Corp., 46 LA 767, 768 (Strongin, 1966).
[188] See Arbitrator Block in 48 LA 2, 8–9; Altieri in 42 LA 781, 784; Geissinger in 40 LA 1182, 1183; Donahue in 26 LA 501, 502–503; Holly in 24 LA 268, 271; Platt in 24 LA 141, 143; Willcox in 23 LA 21, 23; Maggs in 19 LA 647, 649; Komaroff in 17 LA 715, 718. Also see Dworkin in 48 LA 83, 86; McCoy in 20 LA 416, 419.
[189] General Fireproofing Co., 48 LA 842, 848 (Teple, 1967).
[190] Ekco Products Co., 40 LA 1339, 1341 (Duff, 1963).
[191] See Arbitrator Krimsly in 55 LA 14, 16; Dworkin in 46 LA 1021, 1027; Solomon in 46 LA 993, 997–999 (here the "occurrence" was at an intermediate point); Tatum in 44 LA 373, 375; Schedler in 38 LA 259, 261; Grant in

For example, where a company changed a seniority date on its records as a correction, a grievance protesting the change was held timely though not filed until nine months later; the arbitrator stated that the basis of the grievance would be the employee's frustrated attempt to exercise seniority rights based upon the old date, rather than the mere change in the company's records.[192]

In this general connection, too, where a grievance protesting a layoff was filed seven days after the employer signed the layoff notice, the filing was held timely although the contract placed a five-day limit on filing grievances; it was said to be reasonable to assume that two days were required for the notice to reach the grievant.[193] In another case the agreement required the company to give its answer to a grievance within ten days, but the arbitrator refused to determine the allowed period on an "hour and minute" basis where the parties had not previously applied their time limits so exactly.[194] The arbitrator in this case also stated that delivery of the company's answer to the U.S. mail was equivalent to delivery to the union.[195] The combined effect of these two cases is that a time limit does not start running against a party until he is actually informed as to the other party's position, and his response will be timely if it is thereafter deposited in the mails within the time limitations period. This is consistent with the above-noted view that doubts as to the interpretation of contractual time limits or as to whether they have been met should be resolved against disposition of grievances by forfeiture.

Under some circumstances a party may be permitted to toll the running of time limits by giving notice to the other party of reasonable basis for delaying the filing of a grievance.[196]

Many arbitrators have held that "continuing" violations of the agreement (as opposed to a single isolated and completed transaction)

---

37 LA 1044, 1046; Komaroff in 26 LA 622, 626, and in 20 LA 789, 792–793; Warren in 18 LA 662, 663–664. Cf., Sembower in 44 LA 304, 307; Komaroff in 19 LA 385, 387. In Square D Co., 25 LA 225, 228–229 (1955), Arbitrator Prasow held that an act occurred on the day it was announced, but there the union itself had clearly recognized the existence of a grievance as of that day.
    [192] Dayton Tire & Rubber Co., 46 LA 1021, 1027 (Dworkin, 1966). Also see Arbitrator Larkin in 52 LA 633, 635–636.
    [193] Torrington Co., 13 LA 323, 325 (Stutz, Mottram & Sviridoff, 1949).
    [194] E. W. Bliss Co., 45 LA 1000, 1002–1003 (Lehoczky, 1965).
    [195] Id. at 1003.
    [196] See American Smelting & Refining Co., 29 LA 262, 265 (Ross, 1957). Also see Monogram Productions, Inc., 13 LA 782, 786 (Pierson, 1949).

give rise to "continuing" grievances in the sense that the act complained of may be said to be repeated from day to day—each day there is a new "occurrence"; these arbitrators have permitted the filing of such grievances at any time, this not being deemed a violation of the specific time limits stated in the agreement (although any back pay ordinarily runs only from the date of filing).[197] For example, where the agreement provided for filing "within ten working days of the occurrence," it was held that where employees were erroneously denied work, each day lost was to be considered a new "occurrence" and that a grievance presented within ten working days of any such day lost would be timely.[198]

Sometimes an agreement will provide that any grievance not appealed from one step to the next within a specified time shall be considered settled on the basis of the last answer. On one occasion this type of provision was applied strictly with the result that a grievance which, by error, had been left unappealed until the time limit had expired was held to have been settled.[199]

If the foreman does not answer within the prescribed time, the grievant may take the complaint to the next step of the procedure. The failure of the foreman to answer will not be interpreted as an admission of the grievance by default (unless the agreement expressly calls for such default), since the burden is on the grievant to carry the complaint to the next step following the lapse of the specified

---

[197] E.g., Arbitrator Boothe in 55 LA 23, 25; Slavney in 49 LA 1028, 1033–1034; Shister in 49 LA 480, 481–482; Williams in 48 LA 44, 45–46; Kates in 47 LA 1045, 1048; Altrock in 47 LA 408, 413; Teple in 1106, 1109–1110; Murphy in 46 LA 289, 290–291; Dolnick in 45 LA 357, 360–361; Fallon in 45 LA 271, 275; Hayes in 44 LA 701, 703; Handsaker in 64-2 ARB ¶8789; McNaughton in 43 LA 1165, 1167; Kornblum in 43 LA 765, 767–768; Stouffer in 62-2 ARB ¶8504; Gillingham in 39 LA 567, 570; Gorsuch in 33 LA 135, 137; Warns in 28 LA 424, 428; Platt in 27 LA 262, 264–265; Cahn in 26 LA 649, 650–651; Seward in 23 LA 538, 540; Justin in 17 LA 303, 309; Gregory in 15 LA 147, 149; Hepburn in 14 LA 387, 388. Cf., Larkin in 47 LA 382, 383–384; Livengood in 27 LA 157, 159; Feinberg in 26 LA 550, 551–552; Aaron in 12 LA 786, 793–794. Retroactivity is not always limited to the date of filing. See Blaw-Knox Company, 50 LA 1086, 1089 (Meltzer, 1968).

[198] Pacific Mills, 14 LA 387, 388 (Hepburn, 1950).

[199] Chrysler Corporation, 1 ALAA ¶67,017 (1945). In several other cases, too, such "default" type provisions have been strictly enforced (in some instances the given provision required company action, which was not taken, in order for the company to avoid a default). See Arbitrator Dworkin in 45 LA 812, 814, 816, and in 44 LA 878, 882–883; Ryder in 41 LA 8, 10 (nor could the issue be revived by filing another grievance, based upon the same incident, in the name of another employee); Duff in 25 LA 534, 537–538; Platt in 25 LA 437, 438. Cf., Sanders in 33 LA 553, 555–556.

time.[200] But it has been emphasized that the foreman should make a decision or comment on each grievance.[201]

Observance of Grievance Procedure

Arbitrators recognize that the grievance procedure, when adhered to, advances peaceful and constructive industrial relations, with resultant benefits alike to labor, management, and the public. Moreover, arbitrators realize that the success of arbitration itself may be jeopardized if the grievance procedure is not carefully followed.

Arbitration awards show that arbitrators expect the parties to pay due respect to the grievance procedure, not only by using it, but also by observing its formal requirements. Such respect is something of a "condition precedent." In some cases it is a condition precedent to an award of requested relief. In these cases the arbitrator takes jurisdiction but, upon learning of the grievant's failure to fulfill the condition precedent, denies relief, in whole or in part. In other cases it is a condition precedent to the assumption of jurisdiction by the arbitrator. The requirement that these conditions precedent be met is somewhat analogous to the requirement by the courts that the administrative remedy, if any, be exhausted before the court will give relief.

Use of Grievance Procedure v. Self-Help

Arbitrators often deny or limit requested relief, notwithstanding the merits of the original complaint, where the grievant has resorted to self-help rather than to the grievance procedure. Many arbitrators have taken the position that employees must not take matters into their own hands but must obey orders and carry out their assignments,

---

[200] See Arbitrator Sembower in 43 LA 165, 168; Emery in 37 LA 1103, 1104; Seligson in 26 LA 393, 394; Boles in 24 LA 295, 299; Updegraff in 3 LA 737, 742–743. The "authority" to refer a grievance to the next step is said to rest with the grievant, not with the foreman. Ford Motor Co., 3 LA 840 at 840 (Shulman, 1946).

[201] Ford Motor Co., 3 LA 840, 841 (Shulman, 1946). Also see Bethlehem Steel Co., 19 LA 521, 522 (Feinberg, 1952). Some agreements require the foreman's response to be in writing. "Basic Patterns in Labor Arbitration Agreements," 34 LA 931, 933 (1960). Absent such provision, an oral response to a grievance within the contractual 5-day time limit was held to suffice and not to be invalidated by a written response after that time limit. Warren Co., 39 LA 395, 398 (Woodruff, 1962).

even if believed to violate the agreement, then turn to the grievance procedure for relief.[202]

The fact that employees acted by "advice of counsel" has been held not to provide a defense or justification for self-help.[203] Nor is a refusal to obey management's orders immunized by the fact that the employee was "caught in the middle" between company and union, though this fact might be reason for reducing the penalty.[204] In regard to reducing the penalty, the offense of disobeying orders has sometimes been considered to have been mitigated somewhat where the initial refusal to obey was followed by obedience.[205]

An important exception to the general rule against resorting to self-help exists where obedience to orders would involve an unusual health hazard or similar sacrifice.[206] This exception is discussed in detail in this book's chapter on Safety and Health.[207]

---

[202] E.g., Arbitrator Roberts in 52 LA 221, 223; Teple in 50 LA 501, 504; Larkin in 49 LA 231, 234; R. R. Williams in 48 LA 980, 982; Duff in 48 LA 485, 486; Florey in 48 LA 32, 34; Wallen in 48 LA 19, 22; Peck in 47 LA 739, 743; Turkus in 47 LA 644, 645; Boles in 47 LA 242, 245; Welch in 47 LA 83, 86; Shipman in 46 LA 885, 887; Dworkin in 46 LA 15, 23; Healy in 45 LA 981, 985; Kennedy in 45 LA 976, 978; McNaughton in 45 LA 663, 666; Bauder in 45 LA 430, 433; Stix in 44 LA 1139, 1142; Daugherty in 39 LA 781, 782–783; Gregory in 29 LA 646, 649; Howlett in 29 LA 404, 407; Warns in 29 LA 412, 413; Donnelly in 29 LA 74, 76–77; Sembower in 28 LA 486, 490; Haughton in 28 LA 394, 397; J. Williams in 27 LA 892, 900; Reynard in 27 LA 400, 403–404; Begley in 25 LA 802, 804; Lyons in 25 LA 727, 729–730; Klamon in 24 LA 839, 845; Boyer in 21 LA 736, 740; Young in 21 LA 145, 150; Ralston in 20 LA 875, 877; Anrod in 20 LA 653, 656–657; Komaroff in 19 LA 712, 715–716; Rosenfarb in 18 LA 418, 428; Maggs in 17 LA 606, 610; Stein in 17 LA 256, 257; McCoy in 16 LA 307, 310; Feinberg in 15 LA 749, 752; Kerr in 11 LA 219, 221–222; Updegraff in 5 LA 561, 563; Kharas in 2 LA 274, 276. Cf., Hebert in 39 LA 419, 430. In most of the above cases the grievant's action in taking matters into his own hands was a significant factor in the arbitrator's decision to deny the grievance or to grant relief in part only. However, the fact that employees may be penalized for resorting to self-help does not constitute a waiver of the union's right to arbitrate the issue which had led to the self-help. Mansfield Tire & Rubber Co., 36 LA 1348, 1351 (Teple, 1961), where the propriety of a contested work assignment was held arbitrable.
[203] Robertshaw-Fulton Controls Co., 36 LA 4, 9 (Hilpert, 1961). Cf., Arbitrator Hebert in 39 LA 419, 430.
[204] See Safeway Stores, Inc., 51 LA 413, 416–417 (Gillingham, 1967); Contra, Costa Readymix, 38 LA 200, 204–205 (Koven, 1962).
[205] See, for example, Tubular Products Co., 28 LA 255, 257 (Stutz, 1957); American Sugar Refining Co., 24 LA 66, 71 (Reynard, 1955).
[206] This exception was expressly noted by many of the arbitrators cited hereinabove as authority for the general rule.
[207] See Chapter 16, topics titled "Refusal to Obey Orders," and "Employee Complaints of Specific Hazards."

Some arbitrators have recognized other possible exceptions to the duty to obey orders, as where the order commands the performance of an immoral or criminal act;[208] or where the order violates the rights or domain of the union itself by interfering with the union's contractual right to investigate and process grievances;[209] or where an order interferes with the employee's proper use of the grievance procedure;[210] or where the order commands a skilled craftsman to perform work wholly unrelated to his craft;[211] or where the order "is *quite clearly and indisputably* beyond the authority of" the company.[212] In certain

---

[208] This possible exception was recognized but did not apply in Temco Aircraft Corp., 29 LA 693, 696 (Boles, 1957). In Univac Div., 48 LA 619, 620–621 (1967), Arbitrator Cahn stated that an employee's personal moral or religious beliefs do not excuse a refusal to obey orders. But exceptions to the general rule might exist as to an order which would humiliate the employee (see Arbitrator McCoy in 34 LA 689 at 689) or which would invade some personal right which the arbitrator considers inviolable (see Arbitrator Williams in 52 LA 57, 59).

[209] See Arbitrator Kinyon in 35 LA 873, 880; McCoy in 16 LA 307, 310–311; Shulman in 10 LA 213, 214. Also see Whelan in 41 LA 1288, 1297–1299; Mittenthal in 39 LA 238, 241; Maguire in 36 LA 1193, 1195–1196. Cf., Porter in 50 LA 1140, 1142; Williams in 39 LA 934, 936–937.

[210] See Arbitrator McNaughton in 40 LA 1100, 1102; Williams in 27 LA 892, 900; Rosenfarb in 18 LA 418, 428. Also see Teple in 39 LA 784, 788–789. In Nuclear Fuel Services, Inc., 53 LA 252, 255–256 (King, 1969), another exception was found where the refusal to obey an order resulted from the company's own failure to honor the grievance procedure.

[211] See Ironrite, Inc., 28 LA 394, 397 (Haughton, 1956); Ford Motor Co., 3 LA 782, 783 (Shulman, 1946). However, Arbitrator Shulman declared that this exception would apply in rare cases only, in 19 LA 237, 238–239, and this limitation was again emphasized by Arbitrator Platt in 30 LA 46, 55. In Sheller Mfg. Corp., 34 LA 689, 692 (McCoy, 1960), a related exception was recognized as to orders which have no reasonable relation to the employee's job duties. Also see Arbitrator Block in 55 LA 690, 693–694. Here again, however, the exception may be viewed as a narrow one. See Arbitrator Solomon in 42 LA 1, 11–12.

[212] Dwight Mfg. Co., 12 LA 990, 996 (McCoy, 1949). Also see Ross Clay Products Co., 43 LA 159, 163–164 (Kabaker, 1964), permitting self-help where the employer acted directly contrary to an arbitration award which had just been issued. Some arbitrators have held that employees need not obey orders to work overtime where the contract permits them to refuse such work. See Arbitrator Sembower in 48 LA 492, 497; McCoy in 48 LA 61, 63; Begley in 27 LA 458, 461–463; Maggs in 17 LA 606, 609–610. Also see Burr in 37 LA 275, 277. Cf., Seitz in 53 LA 200, 202–203; Geissinger in 50 LA 181, 185; Mullins in 44 LA 141, 144; Hilpert in 36 LA 4, 8–10; Wollett in 34 LA 925, 927–928; Young in 21 LA 145, 150; Fuchs in 15 LA 645, 651. In Equitable Bag Company, 52 LA 1234, 1237–1238 (Hayes, 1969), an employee could not be punished for refusing to attend fire-fighting training on overtime, the Arbitrator stating that an employee cannot be punished for refusing to train for a job which he cannot be required to perform (fire fighting as distinguished from fire prevention).

other situations, too, arbitrators have recognized an exception to the general duty to obey management's orders.[213]

Although disobedience to orders or work assignments may be immunized as to those employees who are directly covered by one of the aforementioned exceptions and who are acting individually, this does not mean that otherwise improper group or concert action to force concessions from the employer will be permitted.[214] Even where a fact situation brings one of the exceptions into play, the exception might be deemed to give only personal and individual immunity to employees.[215] Similarly, some actions which may properly be taken by individuals for individual reasons might be improper when taken as group or concert action for a group objective. For example, where employees as a group refused to report for early morning "start up" work, Arbitrator Saul Wallen held the group action improper even assuming that the work was voluntary to the extent that individual employees, for individual reasons, could refuse the work:

"Such individual right to refuse work as may be inherent in the Agreement was intended to be motivated by purely individual reasons, not by a desire to join with others to compel a solution to a problem by group action—or inaction. The settlement of grievances or other disputes during the life of the Agreement is supposed to be accomplished by means of the grievance procedure and arbitration, not by group refusals to perform work. And if the problem is one not campassable by those procedures, it must remain to be handled in negotiations at expiration time."[216]

Union representatives should not instruct employees to disobey management's orders.[217] Indeed, many arbitrators have recognized a

---

[213] See Arbitrator Duff in 55 LA 862, 864–865; Sembower in 55 LA 731, 743; Krimsly in 54 LA 604, 606; Lennard in 54 LA 574, 575–576.
[214] See Arbitrator Mullin in 47 LA 848, 854, and in 44 LA 141, 144; Altrock in 47 LA 621, 627–628; Volz in 43 LA 849, 853–854; Platt in 41 LA 609, 615.
[215] Ibid. To illustrate, employees not affected by a safety hazard would not be justified in using self-help instead of the grievance procedure. Metal Specialty Co., 43 LA 849, 853–854 (Volz, 1964).
[216] Fitchburg Paper Co., 47 LA 349, 352 (Wallen, 1966). Similar results were reached in Pratt & Whitney, Inc., 53 LA 69, 71–72 (Feinberg, 1969).
[217] See Arbitrator Strong in 39 LA 1080, 1081–1082; Abrahams in 37 LA 76, 81–82; Abersold in 37 LA 62, 71–74; Feinberg in 19 LA 43, 46–47; Kerr in 11 LA 219, 221–222; Scheiber in 7 LA 3, 4–7; Shulman in 3 LA 779, 780. An exception has been recognized, however, as to "action falling primarily within the Union's domain." Ford Motor Co., 10 LA 213, 214 (Shulman, 1948). The existence of a grievance procedure, and particularly the availability of arbitration, for resolving a dispute implies a no-strike obligation even if there is no

special responsibility on the part of union leaders to take affirmative action to persuade employees to use the grievance procedure for matters subject thereto in lieu of taking matters into their own hands (as by refusing to obey orders or by striking in violation of a no-strike obligation).[218]

The over-all necessity for observing the grievance procedure is effectively explained in the following statement of Umpire Harry Shulman:

> "Some men apparently think that, when a violation of contract seems clear, the employee may refuse to obey and thus resort to self-help rather than the grievance procedure. That is an erroneous point of view. In the first place, what appears to one party to be a clear violation may not seem so at all to the other party. Neither party can be the final judge as to whether the contract has been violated. The determination of that issue rests in collective negotiation through the grievance procedure. But, in the second place, and more important, the grievance procedure is prescribed in the contract precisely because the parties anticipated that there would be claims of violations which would require adjustment. That procedure is prescribed for all grievances, not merely for doubtful ones. Nothing in the contract even suggests the idea that only doubtful violations need be processed through the grievance procedure and that clear violations can be resisted

---

express no-strike clause in the contract (or if such a clause is too narrow to cover the dispute). See Ingersoll-Rand Co., 51 LA 83, 88 (Teple, 1968); Trailways of New England, Inc., 46 LA 369, 371 (Wallen, 1965); Teamsters v. Lucas Flour Company, 369 U.S. 95, 49 LRRM 2717 (1962).

[218] See Arbitrator Belcher in 53 LA 154, 157–158; Oppenheim in 52 LA 1047, 1050 (where stewards "endorsed" a stoppage by resigning their office and participating in it); Graff in 50 LA 1029, 1032–1034; Turkus in 50 LA 691, 692–694; King in 49 LA 27, 33; Schmertz in 47 LA 1100, 1100–1102; Summers in 47 LA 369, 370; Kennedy in 45 LA 976, 979; Larkin in 45 LA 81, 85; Koven in 43 LA 644, 649; Dworet in 43 LA 608, 609; Davis in 43 LA 182, 189; Markowitz in 41 LA 732, 735; Platt in 41 LA 609, 613–615; Burr in 39 LA 688, 690–691; Volz in 37 LA 401, 406; Koretz in 37 LA 36, 42; Crawford in 36 LA 214, 215; Wallen in 34 LA 325, 328; Bothwell in 33 LA 594, 601; Kelliher in 29 LA 622, 623–624; Howlett 29 LA 495, 497; Sembower in 25 LA 774, 777; Feinberg in 21 LA 421, 424; Laskin in 18 LA 919, 923–924; Seward in 14 LA 986, 988–989; Gilden in 8 LA 758, 769–770; Shipman in 2 LA 194, 198–199. Contra, McCoy in 33 LA 807, 808. For a general discussion, see Leahy, "Arbitration, Union Stewards and Wildcat Strikes," 24 Arb. J. 50 (1969). While there is wide recognition of the special responsibility, examination of the above-cited cases reveals that arbitrators are by no means agreed as to what punishment, if any, may be assessed against union officers for failure to fulfill that special responsibility. For cases involving claims against the union for alleged failure to make reasonable effort to prevent work stoppages, see Arbitrator Kabaker in 50 LA 683, 689–690; Turkus in 50 LA 691, 692–694; Kelliher in 47 LA 610, 613; House in 47 LA 567, 572–574; Platt in 43 LA 785, 788.

through individual self-help. The only difference between a 'clear' violation and a 'doubtful' one is that the former makes a clear grievance and the latter a doubtful one. But both must be handled in the regular prescribed manner."[219]

Umpire Shulman observed further that:

"When a controversy arises, production cannot wait for exhaustion of the grievance procedure. While that procedure is being pursued, production must go on. And someone must have the authority to direct the manner in which it is to go on until the controversy is settled. That authority is vested in supervision. It must be vested there because the responsibility for production is also vested there; and responsibility must be accompanied by authority. It is fairly vested there because the grievance procedure is capable of adequately recompensing employees for abuse of authority by supervision."[220]

Company Obligation to Honor Grievance Procedure

In a number of cases arbitrators have emphasized management's obligation to preserve the integrity of the grievance procedure.[221] For example, in view of the obligation to utilize fully the possibilities of settlement inherent in the grievance procedure, an employer was held to have acted improperly in by-passing the union committee which represented certain grievants and communicating an offer of settlement directly to the grievants themselves.[222]

In another case the company was held to have an obligation to furnish information to the union, upon request, as to how the company had complied with a settlement reached in the grievance procedure so the union could determine if the settlement was carried out.[223]

In another situation, where an arbitrator found that management had a contractual obligation to exhaust the negotiation machinery

---

[219] Ford Motor Co., 3 LA 779, 780–781 (1944).
[220] Id. at 781. However, Umpire Shulman recognized the "unusual health hazard or similar sacrifice" exception to the duty to obey orders. Id. at 782. For a very strong statement as to the obligation of both parties to observe the grievance procedure and preserve its integrity, see Arbitrator Healy in Gregg & Sons, Inc., 45 LA 981, 984–985 (1965).
[221] For a very strong statement as to the company's duty in this regard, see Arbitrator Healy in Gregg & Sons, Inc., 45 LA 981, 984–985 (1965).
[222] Central Franklin Process Co., 17 LA 142, 145 (Marshall, 1951).
[223] North American Aviation, Inc., 17 LA 121, 124–125 (Komaroff, 1951). For related material, see this Chapter, topic titled "Attitude of Parties to the Grievance Procedure."

before resorting to disciplinary action, management's failure to do so was held to be sufficient basis for reinstating discharged employees, although the discharges were otherwise justified.[224] However, absent such contractual requirement the employer need not resort to the grievance procedure before punishing an employee for misconduct.[225]

In a "slowdown" case the arbitrator condemned the company for taking "the law into its own hands" by assessing a wage cut for the slowdown instead of utilizing the "adequate grievance provisions" or other remedies available under the contract (including the right to discipline or lockout employees engaged in the slowdown).[226]

It may be noted that some agreements require maintenance of the status quo pending grievance settlement, both parties being obligated to maintain the conditions prevailing immediately prior to some stated point (such as prior to the incident or prior to filing the grievance).[227]

Exhaustion of Grievance Procedure as Condition Precedent for Arbitration

A limitation by arbitrators of their jurisdiction to cases which the parties have made bona fide efforts to settle can be expected to result in improved handling of grievances at the lower levels. The National War Labor Board learned from experience that settlements through negotiations are encouraged when arbitrators refuse to take jurisdiction over grievance issues until the parties show that they have exhausted all chances of settlement through negotiations.[228] Arbitrators can do this unless the agreement permits direct resort to arbitration.[229]

---

[224] Gloucester, Mass. Fisheries, 1 ALAA ¶67,340 (1946). Also see Arbitrator Miller in 35 LA 757, 780. In San Angelo Packing Co., 52 LA 261, 263 (Sartain, 1969), an otherwise justified discharge was set aside because the employer refused to participate in meetings on the discharge grievance as required by the agreement. Similarly, see Arbitrator Daly in 52 LA 306, 309.
[225] Falls Stamping & Welding Co., 48 LA 107, 113 (Dworkin, 1967). Nor was the employer required to use the grievance procedure instead of direct punishment by virtue of the added fact that the actions for which the employee was punished might have been done in his role as a union officer. Beckett Paper Co., 51 LA 936, 939–940 (Gibson, 1968). Accord, Arbitrator Wolff in 33 LA 112, 123. Contra, Arbitrator Gray in 31 LA 144, 145.
[226] Jacobs Mfg. Co., 29 LA 512, 517–518 (Scheiber, 1957).
[227] See Sealtest Foods, 48 LA 797 at 797 (Valtin, 1966); McCall Corp., 43 LA 951, 954, 956 (Layman, 1964).
[228] Aluminum Co. of America, 12 War Lab. Rep. 446, 455 (1943).
[229] For instance, where the grievance procedure had not been exhausted the dispute was held to be nonarbitrable by Arbitrator Goldberg in 46 LA

A New York court, in granting an employer's motion for a stay of arbitration, spoke of the requirement that conditions precedent be performed prior to arbitration:

"One of the preliminary steps, viz. submission to the grievance committee of the association, was omitted entirely as were other steps in connection with some of the issues tendered for arbitration. No explanation is here given for such omission or neglect. It was incumbent upon the union, under the terms of the contract, to exhaust all other methods of conciliation as provided for therein before it could invoke the remedy of arbitration. Until it complies with the conditions of the contract in respect to all the essential acts on its part to be performed or offers a reasonable and just excuse for non-performance, the union will be enjoined from proceeding with the arbitration."[230]

The critical nature of some disputes leads the parties to stipulate that all pre-arbitral steps are waived and that the dispute is to be taken directly to arbitration.[231] The agreement itself may provide for the direct appeal of such disputes to arbitration, but this type of provision has been held inapplicable to ordinary employee grievances.[232]

A party who refuses to comply or fails to comply properly with the negotiation steps of the grievance procedure will not be permitted to prevent arbitration on the ground that the grievance procedure has not been exhausted.[233] Nor must the grievance procedure be exhausted where to do so would be "futile,"[234] or a "useless and idle

---

1131, 1138; Blair in 39 LA 760, 762–763; Feinberg in 20 LA 675, 678; Komaroff in 19 LA 729, 731–733. Also see Nichols in 51 LA 79, 82–83; Dworkin in 46 LA 941, 945. In Fruehauf Corp., 47 LA 421, 422–423 (Hayes, 1966), an additional issue could not be introduced unilaterally at the arbitration stage.
    [230] In re Picture Frame Workers Union, 8 LA 1063, 1064 (N.Y. Sup. Ct., 1947). If the federal law applies to the case, questions of procedural arbitrability (such as whether the preliminary steps of the grievance procedure have been exhausted or excused) are to be decided by the arbitrator. John Wiley & Sons v. Livingston, 84 S.Ct. 909, 918–919, 55 LRRM 2769 (1964). For related discussions, see Chapter 6, Determining Arbitrability.
    [231] As in Magnode Products Inc., 47 LA 449 at 449 (Hayes, 1966); Calumet & Hecla, Inc., 25 LA 663, 664 (Smith, 1955). Also see Arbitrator Kesselman in 45 LA 201, 203.
    [232] Ford Motor Co., 1 ALAA ¶67,030 (1944). The agreement also provided for direct appeal in New Orleans Steamship Assn., 45 LA 1099, 1101 (Oppenheim, 1965).
    [233] City of Meriden, 48 LA 137, 140–141 (Summers, 1967), involving improper compliance with lower steps. Also, Glass Bottle Blowers v. Arkansas Corp., 35 LA 153, 46 LRRM 2950 (USDC, 1960), and Brynmore Press, Inc., 8 LA 511, 512–514 (Rains, 1947), involving refusal to comply with lower steps.
    [234] Barbet Mills, Inc., 16 LA 563, 565 (Livengood, 1951). Also, In re Roto Supply Sales Co., 28 LA 657, 658 (N.Y. Sup. Ct., 1957).

gesture,"[235] or where compliance with the pre-arbitral grievance procedure has been rendered unrealistic or impossible by plant closure or removal.[236]

Then, too, if an agreement provides only an informal type of grievance procedure, the arbitrator may not be exacting as to the preliminaries necessary to give him jurisdiction. Arbitrator William E. Simkin has stated, for instance, that to give an arbitrator jurisdiction in such a case it is necessary only that the issue be one on which the parties have had some prior discussion and on which the "realistic possibilities" of settlement at the lower grievance steps have been exhausted.[237]

Finally, the right to object that the grievance procedure has not been exhausted may be held waived by agreeing to arbitrate the dispute without raising any issue as to exhaustion of pre-arbitral steps.[238]

Grievance Settlements as Binding Precedents

It is to be expected that a mutual settlement of a grievance by the parties ordinarily will be held binding upon them insofar as the particular instance is involved.[239] It also seems obvious that where a grievance has been settled by mutual agreement of the parties, the same issue that is involved in such "settled" grievance, though appearing in the guise of another grievance, should not ordinarily be subject to arbitration at the request of only one party (or, if the issue does reach arbitration, the prior settlement should constitute a binding precedent). "It is essential to good labor-management relations * * * that grievance settlements not be disturbed in the absence

---

[235] In re Greenstone, 29 LA 161, 162 (N.Y. Sup. Ct., 1957). To similar effect, General Tire & Rubber Co. v. Rubber Workers, 37 LA 496, 49 LRRM 2001 (USDC, 1961).
[236] H. K. Porter Co., 49 LA 147, 153–154 (Cahn, 1967); Sidele Fashions, Inc., 36 LA 1364, 1369 (Dash, 1961).
[237] Reading Street Railway Co., 8 LA 930, 933 (1947).
[238] United Tavern, 16 LA 210, 214 (Slavney, 1951).
[239] Elwell-Parker Electric Co., 48 LA 1361, 1364 (Kates, 1967). Where necessary, a subsequent grievance may be filed on the question of the other party's compliance with the prior settlement. Lockheed Aircraft Service Co., 44 LA 51, 58–59 (Roberts, 1965). Of similar essence, Arbitrator Morgan in 47 LA 756, 759; Turkus in 40 LA 504, 506. Another possible means of enforcing grievance settlements is court action under LMRA §301. See General Drivers, Local 89 v. Riss and Company, 83 S.Ct. 789 (1963); Amal. Meat Cutters & Butcher Workmen v. M. Feder & Co., 224 F. Supp. 739 (E.D. Pa., 1963).

of a conclusive showing of changed conditions."[240] One arbitrator would add that settlements are open to investigation on substantial charge of fraud or grievous error.[241]

Aside from any effect of mutual settlements as binding precedents, such settlements may be accepted by an arbitrator as indicating the proper interpretation of ambiguous contract language. It has been observed, in this regard, that "Where the parties themselves settle a grievance the evidence of intent as to the meaning of a provision carries special weight."[242]

Somewhat different considerations are involved, however, where a grievance has not been mutually settled, but simply has been denied by management at some pre-arbitral step of the grievance procedure and, for various possible reasons, has not been appealed further. If management's denial of a grievance is "accepted" by the union so as to provide the elements of a "settlement" an arbitrator might consider it a binding precedent.[243] But numerous arbitrators have held that the mere failure to appeal a grievance is not per se acquiescence in the disposition of the issue on the basis of management's final answer so as to bar the issue from arbitration in a subsequent case.[244] This

---

[240] Standard Oil Co. (Indiana), 13 LA 799, 800 (Kelliher, 1949). In general accord, Arbitrator McCoy in 49 LA 82, 83; Barnhart in 45 LA 300, 301; Emery in 19 LA 812, 814; Wallen in 17 LA 36, 39–40; Blumer in 7 LA 378, 380. Essentially contra, Raimon in 36 LA 621, 625 (particularly as to lower step settlements); Brandschain in 15 LA 672, 673. Arbitrator J. K. Hayes found no binding precedent in a prior settlement since, he stated, "one settlement does not make for a past practice." Consolidated Aluminum Corp., 53 LA 122, 124 (1969). In Vulcan Mold & Iron Co., 41 LA 59, 60–61 (1963), Arbitrator Brecht held that even where an issue has been arbitrated, the award cannot constitute a bar to the arbitration of similar issues—the earlier award would influence the subsequent arbitrator but would not bar the issue from arbitration.

[241] Tennessee Coal, Iron & Railroad Co., 7 LA 378, 380 (Blumer, 1947). Of course a settlement will not bind future cases if it was entered into with the understanding that it not establish a precedent for any future case, as in Alpha Cellulose Corp., 50 LA 300, 302 (Gilden, 1968). Nor will any precedent exist where it is uncertain whether any settlement was ever reached. See National Cash Register Co., 47 LA 248, 250–251 (Nichols, 1966).

[242] Bendix-Westinghouse Automotive Air Brake Co., 23 LA 706, 710 (Mathews, 1954). Also see Arbitrator Ray in 50 LA 265, 267. But a prior settlement could not operate to amend a clear and unambiguous provision of the agreement in Lukens Steel Co., 35 LA 246, 248 (Crawford, 1960). As to a matter not treated by the collective agreement, a settlement may amount to a special agreement governing future rights of the parties. See Peoples Gas Light & Coke Co., 39 LA 224, 225–226 (Davis, 1962).

[243] See U.S. Steel Corp., 21 LA 26, 30 (Garrett, 1953).

[244] See Arbitrator Merrill in 52 LA 179, 180–181; Stein in 49 LA 288, 289; Dash in 48 LA 314, 316; Teple in 46 LA 1106, 1110; Stouffer in 46

is particularly so where withdrawal of a case from the grievance procedure is done "without prejudice,"[245] or where the withdrawing party
indicates that it intends ultimately to seek an arbitral ruling on the
issue.[246] To insure against the possibility of a binding precedent, a party
apparently is well advised to state some such condition in deciding
not to appeal a grievance further.[247]

Sometimes the collective agreement deals specifically with this
matter. For example, under a clause providing that grievances not
appealed to arbitration were "to be considered settled on the basis
of the decision last made," Arbitrator Harry H. Platt refused to decide
an issue which had been involved in two prior grievances which had
been withdrawn:

> "The present grievance appears plainly to be an attempt to rein-
> state the former grievances which had already been withdrawn by the
> Union. To permit this, in the absence of proof that the earlier with-
> drawal was induced by the Company through fraud, misrepresentation,
> intentional concealment of facts, overreaching or through mutual mis-
> take, would encourage the relitigation of grievances after they had been
> disposed of by the parties in the proper exercise of their discretion.
> This would indeed undermine the grievance procedure and the Umpire
> system. Here, there is no claim or proof that the Company had any-
> thing to do with the Union's decision to withdraw the earlier grievances
> from the procedure and from arbitration. It was a voluntary action
> presumably taken with full knowledge of all the facts, and must be
> held binding on the Union."[248]

Other arbitrators have reached similar results,[249] one of the arbitrators
stating that the only exception "would be a situation in which the
'new' grievance would embrace factors and changed conditions which
would clearly distinguish the latter grievance from the former."[250]
However, some cases have reached a contrary result on the basis

---

LA 578, 581–582; Autrey in 45 LA 783, 787; Jenkins in 45 LA 696, 702;
Fallon in 45 LA 271, 275, 277; Williams in 44 LA 5, 6; Peck in 39 LA
1249, 1251; L. Smith in 23 LA 289, 291; Gilden in 16 LA 811, 816; Blumer
in 6 LA 426, 429. Cf., Ryder in 41 LA 8, 10.
    [245] Ohio Steel Foundry Co., 36 LA 445, 446 (Dworkin, 1961); Greer Hydrau-
lics, Inc., 29 LA 706, 708 (Friedman, 1957).
    [246] Lion Oil Co., 25 LA 549, 552 (Reynard, 1955).
    [247] See Kaiser Aluminum & Chemical Corp., 28 LA 439, 440 (McCoy, 1957).
    [248] Republic Steel Corp., 25 LA 437, 438 (1955).
    [249] See Arbitrator Murphy in 52 LA 869, 874–875; R. Smith in 39 LA
624, 627–629; Duff in 31 LA 297, 299–300; Dworkin in 24 LA 541, 547–548;
Myers in 15 LA 417, 419.
    [250] Babcock & Wilcox Co., 24 LA 541, 548 (Dworkin, 1955).

that the contractual language did not clearly indicate an intention that the underlying issue as well as the individual grievance be deemed settled.[251]

Notice of Intent to Arbitrate

Collective agreements frequently provide that parties who wish to arbitrate disputes not settled by the negotiation steps of the grievance procedure must give notice of desire and intent to arbitrate within a specified period of time.[252] Arbitrators often have held that failure to give the required notice, unless waived by the other party or otherwise excused, renders the dispute nonarbitrable.[253]

The obvious fact that many arbitrators consider a contractual provision for notice of appeal to arbitration to be far more than a mere formality, and indeed to be in effect a statute of limitations, is particularly significant in view of the fact that questions of procedural arbitrability (including time limit compliance) are to be decided by the arbitrator if the federal law applies to the case.[254]

Under an agreement which required written notice of intent to arbitrate, a timely oral announcement of intention was held not to

---

[251] See Arbitrator Merrill in 52 LA 179, 180–181; Barnhart in 45 LA 300, 301–302; May in 25 LA 157, 162.

[252] See Major Collective Bargaining Agreements: Arbitration Procedures 30–31 (U.S. Dept. of Labor Bull. No. 1425–6, 1966). Many agreements also state time limits on the selection of the arbitrator. Id. at 51–52. Where an issue is in arbitration, some agreements toll the time limits for similar grievances pending decision of the representative or "test" case. Id. at 70.

[253] See Arbitrator Hebert in 51 LA 384, 387–389; Stouffer in 49 LA 338, 341–342; Stark in 47 LA 606, 607 (dispute not arbitrable where notice was mailed one day late as indicated by postmark); Feinberg in 46 LA 1185, 1188 (notice must be unequivocal, a conditional notice not sufficing); Geissinger in 44 LA 1190, 1192; Ellmann in 41 LA 97, 99–100; Keeler in 39 LA 772, 776; Burr in 39 LA 668, 670; Seinsheimer in 36 LA 1460, 1463; McCoy in 20 LA 34, 34–35; Emery in 20 LA 865, 866; Handsaker in 16 LA 369, 371; Abersold in 13 LA 266, 267–269; Levy in 6 LA 397, 399–403; Dodd in 5 LA 742, 744–746; Updegraff in 4 LA 458, 461. Where the agreement did not state a time limit for proceeding to arbitration, an implied requirement that a party act within a reasonable time was found by Arbitrator Dworkin in Cleveland Pneumatic Tool Co., 43 LA 869, 872–874 (1964), and in Hydraulic Press Mfg. Co., 39 LA 1135, 1138–1139 (1962).

[254] In John Wiley & Sons v. Livingston, 84 S. Ct. 909, 918–919, 55 LRRM 2769 (1964), the U.S. Supreme Court noted that the lower courts were disagreed as to whether "procedural" conditions to arbitration have been met are to be decided by the court or by the arbitrator. Some of the cases cited by the Court as evidencing the conflict involved compliance with time limits. The Supreme Court held that questions of procedural arbitrability are for the arbitrator rather than the court. For related discussion, see Chapter 2, Legal Status of Arbitration, and Chapter 6, Determining Arbitrability.

be sufficient.[255] However, a timely oral announcement of intent to arbitrate was held sufficient where the agreement did not specifically require written notice.[256] Unless the agreement expressly requires the notice to be in some particular form or requires the use of some particular terminology, substance should govern over form and a notice should be held sufficient if it clearly and unequivocally advises the other party within the time limit that the grievance is being taken to arbitration.[257]

Some agreements provide that within a specified time after notice of intent to arbitrate has been given a joint request is to be submitted asking that an arbitrator act on the dispute. Failure to notify the arbitrator within the specified time may be held to render the dispute nonarbitrable.[258] But if one party fails to meet its obligation in respect to the joint request, that party cannot prevent arbitration on the ground that the other party alone referred the case to arbitration.[259] Where the agreement states no time limit for proceeding to the selection of an arbitrator after notice of intent to arbitrate has been given, considerable delay in selecting an arbitrator might occur without rendering the dispute nonarbitrable,[260] particularly where both parties have been guilty in respect to the delay.[261]

---

[255] Bethlehem Steel Co., 5 LA 742, 746 (Dodd, 1946). Also see Arbitrator Mittenthal in 44 LA 469, 472.

[256] See Ironrite Inc., 28 LA 398, 400 (Whiting, 1956); Lincoln Industries Inc., 19 LA 489, 491 (Barrett, 1952). Also see Arbitrator Roberts in 42 LA 589, 592.

[257] See Arbitrator Anderson in 44 LA 66, 72; Elkouri in 42 LA 153, 156; Mueller in 38 LA 307, 310. Of course, the notice must be given by a party who has a contractual right to take the grievance to arbitration. Fibreboard Paper Products Corp., 46 LA 59, 61–62 (Roberts, 1966).

[258] As in John Deere Harvester Works, 10 LA 778, 781–782 (Updegraff, 1948). Similar results were reached in General Telephone Co., 50 LA 1207, 1210–1211 (Teple, 1968), where a contractual requirement for selection of an arbitrator within a stated time was not met. Cf., Arbitrator Teple in 42 LA 995, 998.

[259] Malone & Hyde, Inc., 5 LA 443, 445–446 (Wardlaw, 1946). Also see Arbitrator Bothwell in 52 LA 1035, 1039–1040. Where both parties were responsible for delay in selecting an arbitrator, the grievance was not forfeited. American Air Filter Co., 54 LA 1251, 1253 (Dolnick, 1970).

[260] See Magma Copper Co., 40 LA 45, 48–49 (Gorsuch, 1962), and cases cited there. Chase Bag Co., 42 LA 153, 155–156 (Elkouri, 1963), held that notice of intent to arbitrate need be given only to the other party within the prescribed time limit, with notice to the appointing agency to be given within a reasonable time thereafter. Also see Arbitrator Koven in 52 LA 805, 807–809. Where timely notice of intent to arbitrate is given, a reasonable time will then be permitted for filing any necessary court action to compel arbitration. Local 198, U.R.C.L.P.W. v. Interco, Inc., 415 F. 2d 1208 (CA 8, 1969).

[261] See General Precision, Inc., 42 LA 589, 592 (Roberts, 1964); Sinclair Refining Co., 38 LA 1251, 1254 (Gilden, 1962).

Although arbitrators are compelled to apply contractual limitations, they may do so with apparent displeasure. Witness, for example, the statement of Arbitrator Bert W. Levy:

"It should be frankly noted that the umpire reaches his conclusion with real regret. 'A time limitation is a summary bar. Its imposition precludes application of principles of equity, of fairness, and of justice, regardless of merit * * *.' But the company in these cases has carefully refrained from any conduct which could properly be deemed a waiver of the strict procedural requirements * * *. There is nothing here to buttress the liberal interpretation which the umpire would much prefer to adopt, no peg upon which he can 'hang his hat.' These grievances must be choked off at this point. It is ruled that they have all been appealed too late * * *."[262]

As might be expected, reasonable excuse for failure to meet notice requirements or the presence of other justification for the arbitrator not to enforce such requirements strictly may prevent a forfeiture of the right of arbitration. In such cases jurisdiction will be assumed and the dispute will be decided on the merits.[263] This was true where the parties in the past had mutually accepted loose interpretation of their contractual time limits.[264] A reasonable excuse may be a good-faith mistake or difference of opinion,[265] or it may be the unavoidable

---

[262] Bethlehem Steel Co., 6 LA 397, 402 (1947). Also see Arbitrator Hebert in 51 LA 384, 387–389; Sembower in 49 LA 302, 309–310.

[263] See Arbitrator Cahn in 49 LA 147, 153–154; Bender in 45 LA 545, 547; Lehoczky in 26 LA 633, 634; Stutz in 19 LA 234, 236; Abruzzi in 18 LA 193, 195–196; Prasow in 17 LA 205, 206; Selekman in 17 LA 7, 8; McCoy in 8 LA 883, 884; Trotta in 8 LA 844, 845; Simkin in 7 LA 276, 278; Brandschain in 4 LA 509, 510–513; Wardlaw in 3 LA 500, 503–504. But see Arbitrator Stouffer in 49 LA 338, 342. In some cases dispute centers upon *when* the time limit started running. In Newspaper Agency Corp., 43 LA 1233, 1235 (Platt, 1964), the contract stated a time limit for giving notice of intent to appeal from awards of local arbitrators to an appeals board (within 5 days after the award has been "rendered"); the time limit was held not to have started running until receipt of an award some 10 days after its date. For related material see this Chapter, topic titled "Time Limitations."

[264] See Arbitrator Wolf in 49 LA 681, 682; Sembower in 48 LA 492, 496; Lehozcky in 26 LA 633, 634. Also see Abruzzi in 18 LA 193, 195–196. Where each party had "sinned" as to observing contractual procedural requirements the arbitrator refused to hold the union strictly to the time limit for proceeding to arbitration. Penn Jersey Boiler & Construction Co., 50 LA 177, 179 (Buckwalter, 1967). Arbitrators have disagreed as to whether the time limit for proceeding to arbitration is extended by continued negotiations toward settlement of the grievance. A "yes" answer was given in Montgomery Ward & Co., 49 LA 271, 272–273 (Updegraff, 1967), but it was "no" in Booth Broadcasting Co., 41 LA 97, 99–100 (Ellmann, 1962). Also on this question, see Arbitrator Geissinger in 44 LA 1190, 1192.

[265] See Bethlehem Steel Co., 7 LA 276, 278 (Simkin, 1947); International Shoe Co., 3 LA 500, 503–504 (Wardlaw, 1946).

absence of an essential party, so as to make the observance of time limits impracticable.[266] Furthermore, a reasonable excuse may be said to exist if it would be futile to request arbitration within the time limit.[267] In one case a request for an extension of time was held adequate to preserve the union's right to appeal a grievance to arbitration where the delay was not unreasonable under the circumstances.[268]

In an estoppel situation, a commitment made but later repudiated by one party was held to be a reasonable excuse for the failure of the other party to comply literally with the notice requirement.[269] Finally, the right to enforce time limits may be waived, as by signing a submission agreement to arbitrate and failing to raise the time issue until the arbitration hearing.[270]

---

[266] Ohmer Corp., 5 LA 278, 280 (Lehoczky, 1946).

[267] Forse Corp., 39 LA 709, 716 (Dworkin, 1962); Manhattan Transit Co., 8 LA 844, 845 (Trotta, 1947).

[268] Carpenter Steel Co., 44 LA 1185, 1186–1187 (Kerrison, 1965).

[269] B. F. Goodrich Co., 8 LA 883, 884 (McCoy, 1947).

[270] National Fireworks Ordnance Corp., 23 LA 289, 291 (Smith, 1954); Lawrence Products Co., 14 LA 310, 311 (Marshall, 1950). But see Arbitrator Seinsheimer in 36 LA 1460, 1463.

CHAPTER 6

DETERMINING ARBITRABILITY

When an existing dispute is taken to arbitration by a joint submission of the parties there ordinarily is no problem of arbitrability since by the submission the parties identify the dispute and agree to its arbitration. A different situation may be presented, however, when one party invokes the arbitration clause of a collective agreement by a demand or notice of intent to arbitrate a dispute which has arisen during the term of the agreement. Here arbitration may be resisted by the other party on the ground that the dispute is not arbitrable.[1] It may be asserted, for instance, that the case does not involve any of the types of disputes that are covered by the arbitration clause,[2] or that while covered by the arbitration clause the dispute is not arbitrable because some condition precedent to arbitration, such as exhaustion of the grievance procedure or timely notice of intent to arbitrate, has not been met.[3]

Where Arbitrability Challenge Might Be Lodged

Challenges to arbitrability are presented either to the arbitrator or to the courts. If an appointing agency is named in the arbitration clause, the challenge may be filed with it. There is no uniformity

---

[1] For extensive categorization and discussion of specific grounds upon which arbitrability might be challenged, see Smith & Jones, "The Impact of the Emerging Federal Law of Grievance Arbitration on Judges, Arbitrators, and Parties," 52 Va. L. Rev. 831, 839 et seq. (1966); Smith & Jones, "The Supreme Court and Labor Dispute Arbitration: the Emerging Federal Law," 63 Mich. L. Rev. 751, 780 et seq. (1965). For additional discussions of arbitrability issues and the roles of courts and arbitrators in the determination of arbitrability, see McDermott, "Arbitrability: the Courts Versus the Arbitrator," 23 Arb. J. 18 (1968); Pirsig, "Arbitrability and the Uniform Act," 19 Arb. J. 154 (1964); Smith, "Arbitrators and Arbitrability," Labor Arbitration and Industrial Change 75 (BNA Incorporated, 1963); Cornfield, "Developing Standards for Determining Arbitrability," 14 Labor L. J. 564 (1963).
[2] For related discussion, see Chapter 3, topics titled " 'Interests' Arbitration Contract Clauses"; " 'Rights' Arbitration Contract Clauses."
[3] See Chapter 5 for discussion of these conditions precedent.

of policy of the various agencies in regard to processing cases and appointing an arbitrator where one party files a challenge to arbitrability. Some of the agencies do appoint an arbitrator in such instances, at least where a minimal showing of an arbitration clause is made, and the party protesting arbitrability is permitted to raise that issue before the arbitrator or the courts.[4]

In deciding where to lodge the challenge to arbitrability, the challenger may be influenced in varying degree by the particular language of the arbitration clause, by the state or federal law that governs the case,[5] and, possibly most important, by the challenger's general attitude toward the arbitration process. Then, too, he might take a passive attitude, forcing the other party to seek enforcement of the arbitration clause by a court or arbitrator, at which stage the challenger will raise the issue of arbitrability.

Determination by the Courts

Although the parties often leave arbitrability questions in the hands of the arbitrator, such questions may be involved when the courts are drawn into the arbitration process. The nature and extent of court participation may depend largely upon the applicable law and the language of the arbitration clause.

The courts may become concerned with arbitrability questions in several ways:[6]

(1) The party challenging arbitrability may seek a temporary injunction or "stay of arbitration" pending determination of arbitrability.

---

[4] For discussion of the policy and procedures of the various appointing agencies (state, federal, and private) where arbitrability is questioned, see Justin, "Arbitrability and the Arbitrator's Jurisdiction," Management Rights and the Arbitration Process 1, 11–15 (BNA Incorporated, 1956). For additional discussion of American Arbitration Association and Federal Mediation and Conciliation Service policy (the rules of both agencies provide for ex parte proceedings), see McDermott, "Arbitrability: the Courts Versus the Arbitrator," 23 Arb. J. 18, 31–33, 37 (1968). Also see "Arbitrability," 18 LA 942, 951 (1951).

[5] See, generally, Chapter 2, Legal Status of Arbitration.

[6] See Chapter 2, Legal Status of Arbitration; McDermott, "Arbitrability: the Courts Versus the Arbitrator," 23 Arb. J. 18, 20 (1968); Smith & Jones, "The Supreme Court and Labor Dispute Arbitration: the Emerging Federal Law," 63 Mich. L. Rev. 751, 753 (1965); Pirsig, "Arbitrability and the Uniform Act," 19 Arb. J. 154 (1964). Also see Note, "Judicial Review of Labor Arbitration Awards After the Trilogy," 53 Cornell L. Rev. 136, 139–144 (1967).

(2) The party demanding arbitration may seek a court order compelling the other party to arbitrate where the applicable law upholds agreements to arbitrate future disputes; the latter party then raises the issue of arbitrability.

(3) The issue of arbitrability may be considered when an award is taken to court for review or enforcement, unless the parties have clearly vested the arbitrator with exclusive and final right of determining arbitrability, or unless the right to challenge arbitrability is held by the court to have been otherwise waived under the circumstances of the case.[7]

When a court is asked to stay or compel arbitration the question of arbitrability ordinarily becomes involved. If such a case is covered by federal law, the court's function is delimited by teachings of the *Trilogy*.[8] Two of the *Trilogy* decisions deal with substantive arbitrability (whether the subject matter of the dispute is arbitrable).[9] In *American Manufacturing* the Supreme Court stated:

"The function of the court is very limited when the parties have agreed to submit all questions of contract interpretation to the arbitrator. It is then confined to ascertaining whether the party seeking arbitration is making a claim which on its face is governed by the contract. Whether the moving party is right or wrong is a question of contract interpretation for the arbitrator. In these circumstances the moving party should not be deprived of the arbitrator's judgment, when it was his judgment and all that it connotes that was bargained for."[10]

In *Warrior and Gulf* the Court stated that "arbitration is a matter of contract and a party cannot be required to submit to arbitration any dispute which he has not agreed so to submit." In its next sentences, however, the Court declared:

"Yet, to be consistent with congressional policy in favor of settlement of disputes by the parties through the machinery of arbitration, the judicial inquiry under §301 must be strictly confined to the question

---

[7] Regarding waiver of right to court review of arbitrability, see this Chapter, topic titled "Delay in Contesting Arbitrability," below.

[8] As to coverage of the federal law and applicability of state law, see Chapter 2, topic titled "The Applicable Law." For a summary of the significant teachings of the *Trilogy* and other Supreme Court decisions affecting arbitration, see Chapter 2, topic titled "Federal Law."

[9] The Supreme Court ruled as to procedural arbitrability in *Wiley & Sons,* treated hereinbelow.

[10] United Steelworkers v. American Manufacturing Co., 80 S.Ct. 1343, 1346, 34 LA 559, 560 (1960).

whether the reluctant party did agree to arbitrate the grievance or agreed to give the arbitrator power to make the award he made. An order to arbitrate the particular grievance should not be denied unless it may be said with positive assurance that the arbitration clause is not susceptible to an interpretation that covers the asserted dispute. Doubts should be resolved in favor of coverage."[11]

In *American Manufacturing* the Supreme Court expressly rejected the *Cutler-Hammer* doctrine that a contract cannot be said to provide for arbitration if the meaning of the provision sought to be arbitrated is beyond dispute.[12] In rejecting that doctrine the Supreme Court stated that the courts are not to weigh the merits of grievances:

> "The courts therefore have no business weighing the merits of the grievance, considering whether there is equity in a particular claim, or determining whether there is particular language in the written instrument which will support the claim. The agreement is to submit all grievances to arbitration, not merely those the court will deem meritorious. The processing of even frivolous claims may have therapeutic values which those who are not a part of the plant environment may be quite unaware."[13]

Under the federal law the question of substantive arbitrability is for the court when asked to stay or compel arbitration, unless the arbitration clause clearly specifies that the arbitrator shall make the determination.[14] However, even though the agreement does not ex-

---

[11] United Steelworkers v. Warrior and Gulf Navigation Co., 80 S.Ct. 1347, 1353, 34 LA 561, 564–565 (1960). The party resisting arbitration might claim that bargaining history shows the parties intended to exclude the disputed matter from arbitration. Courts of Appeals disagree as to whether they should consider such evidence. It was admitted in Petroleum Workers v. American Oil Co., 54 LRRM 2598 (CA 7, 1963), but excluded in A. S. Abell Co. v. Baltimore Typographical Union, 57 LRRM 2480 (CA 4, 1964).

[12] This New York doctrine has since been repudiated there by statutory amendment. N.Y. Civ. Prac. Law §7501 (1963).

[13] United Steelworkers v. American Manufacturing Co., 80 S.Ct. 1343, 1346, 34 LA 559, 560–561 (1960), the Court adding: "The union claimed in this case that the company had violated a specific provision of the contract. The company took the position that it had not violated that clause. There was, therefore, a dispute between the parties as to 'the meaning, interpretation and application' of the collective bargaining agreement. Arbitration should have been ordered."

[14] The concurring opinion to the *Trilogy* states: "Since the arbitration clause itself is part of the agreement, it might be argued that a dispute as to the meaning of that clause is for the arbitrator. But the Court rejects this position, saying that the threshold question, the meaning of the arbitration clause itself, is for the judge unless the parties clearly state to the contrary." 34 LA 572, 573. In Atkinson v. Sinclair Refining Company, 82 S.Ct. 1318, 1320 (1962), the Supreme Court stated that under its decisions "whether or not" a party

pressly leave the determination of arbitrability to the arbitrator and in spite of the fact that the parties have gone first to the court, the court might leave the initial determination to the arbitrator. This was the result, for instance, where arbitrability could not be determined without delving into the merits, the court stating:

"In these circumstances we believe the matter should proceed to arbitration, where the arbitrator may determine the subsidiary facts upon which depend both the merits of the controversy and his jurisdiction to decide it. A finding of jurisdiction, unlike a finding on the merits when jurisdiction is not in question * * * will not be insulated from subsequent judicial review. * * * We believe full recognition of the role of labor arbitration requires court intervention in a case such as this only when it has become absolutely necessary, viz., on a petition to vacate or enforce the award."[15]

Furthermore, the Supreme Court has ruled that questions of procedural arbitrability are for arbitrators to decide and not for the courts. When a court has determined that the subject matter of a dispute is arbitrable (substantive arbitrability), the arbitrator is to decide all procedural questions which grow out of the dispute and bear on its final disposition. The Supreme Court stated that procedural questions, such as whether the preliminary steps of the grievance procedure have been exhausted or excused, ordinarily cannot be answered without consideration of the merits of the dispute.[16]

Determination by the Arbitrator

The determination of arbitrability is often left by the parties to the arbitrator. There are sound reasons for this. The delay and expense of court proceedings are avoided. Moreover, the arbitrator can be

---

is "bound to arbitrate, as well as what issues it must arbitrate, is a matter to be determined by the Court on the basis of the contract entered into by the parties."

[15] Camden Industries Co. v. Carpenters Local 1688, 353 F.2d 178 (CA 1, 1965). For other instances in which courts have found it difficult to consider arbitrability without penetrating the merits, see McDermott, "Arbitrability: the Courts Versus the Arbitrator," 23 Arb. J. 18, 27–29 (1968), where it is also noted that attorneys arguing arbitrability will frequently have difficulty in doing so without delving into some aspect of the merits.

[16] John Wiley & Sons v. Livingston, 84 S.Ct. 909, 918–919, 55 LRRM 2769 (1964), in which the Court also noted that a different ruling would produce frequent duplication of effort by court and arbitrator, and needless delay. In Operating Engineers v. Flair Builders, Inc., 80 LRRM 2441 (U.S. Sup. Ct., 1972), the Court refused to narrow the scope of this ruling as to the arbitrator's jurisdiction to decide procedural questions.

expected to exercise the industrial relations expertise which the parties contemplated when they provided for arbitration.

The collective agreement itself may specifically provide that the arbitrator is to rule on questions of arbitrability as well as upon the merits of the dispute.[17] This provides the surest method for parties to minimize court involvement in the arbitration process.

Further, the parties by special submission or stipulation may authorize the arbitrator, either specifically or impliedly, to rule both on questions of arbitrability and on the merits of the dispute.[18] Where it is clear that the parties have authorized the arbitrator to determine arbitrability, the courts will not readily overturn his ruling on that issue.[19]

Most significant, however, is the fact that even where the parties have not clearly authorized the arbitrator to determine arbitrability, he often does so (as an inherent part of his duty) and they generally accept his conclusions without resort to litigation.

Arbitrators appear generally agreed that the legitimate interests of the parties are adequately served by submitting arbitrability issues to the arbitrator.[20] Furthermore, the hundreds of substantive arbitrability issues that have been decided by arbitrators would appear to indicate general concurrence by arbitrators in the view that "an agreement to arbitrate future disputes of a specified kind vests in a duly appointed arbitrator power to determine whether a particular dispute, with respect to which one party invokes arbitration, is a dispute of that kind."[21]

An American Bar Association committee has stated that "the function of the arbitrator to decide whether or not an allegation of

---

[17] It is not uncommon for the collective agreement to provide expressly for determination of arbitrability by the arbitrator, although a few agreements specify court determination. See Major Collective Bargaining Agreements: Arbitration Procedures 24–26 (U.S. Dept. Labor Bull. No. 1425-6, 1966).

[18] An example is Park-Pitt Building Co., 47 LA 234, 235 (Duff, 1966).

[19] See, for instance, Metal Products Workers Union v. Torrington Co., 358 F. 2d 103, 62 LRRM 2011 (CA 2, 1966); United Steelworkers v. North Range Mining Co., 249 F. Supp. 754 (DC, Minn. 1966); Wiese Rambler Sales Co. v. Teamsters Local 43, 47 LA 1152, 64 LRRM 2139 (Wis. Cir. Ct. 1966).

[20] Smith, "Arbitrators and Arbitrability," Labor Arbitration and Industrial Change 75 (BNA Incorporated, 1963).

[21] Barbet Mills, Inc., 19 LA 737, 738 (Maggs, 1952). Also see comments of Arbitrator Whitley P. McCoy in West Penn Power Co., 24 LA 741, 742 (1955).

non-arbitrability is sound could be compared to that of a trial judge who is asked to dismiss a complaint on motion for a directed verdict or for failure to state a cause of action. This analogy indicates that a preliminary decision relating to arbitrability by the arbitrator *is an inherent part of his duty*."[22] That arbitrators are capable of self-restraint is evidenced by the committee's conclusion, based upon examination of many awards, that "arbitrators generally are well aware of the limitations of their authority and scrupulously try to avoid any transgression of those limitations."[23]

The question arises whether substantive arbitrability must be determined by a court in the first instance where a party, without going to court, challenges the arbitrator's jurisdiction to determine arbitrability. Arbitrator Thomas J. McDermott has concluded that he should not refuse to rule on arbitrability in such case:

"[An arbitrator] would be remiss in his responsibilities as an arbitrator, if he were to refuse to rule on the arbitrability of a given dispute, where the arbitration provisions are of an all inclusive nature and where one party requests that such ruling be made. Obviously, any ruling that he makes is not self-enforcing, and court action will be required for such enforcement, if either party refuses to abide by the award. Should such action take place all parties are well aware that the Courts will be the final source of determining arbitrability."[24]

With regard to procedural arbitrability, it should be recalled that even where challenge to arbitrability is first lodged in the courts, the Supreme Court has held that questions of procedural arbitrability are for the arbitrator rather than the court.[25]

"Trilogy" Arbitrability Criteria and the Arbitrator

Several arbitrators have emphasized that when parties go to an arbitrator on the question of substantive arbitrability, he should exer-

---

[22] "Arbitrability," 18 LA 942, 950 (1951), emphasis added. The Committee's view was relied upon by Arbitrator Gorsuch in Sandia Corp., 40 LA 879, 886 (1963).
[23] "Arbitrability," 18 LA 942, 951 (1951).
[24] Master Builders' Assn. of Western Pa., 45 LA 892, 896 (1965). He cited court decisions supporting his conclusion that he need not wait for a court to rule first as to arbitrability, but other court decisions were cited to the contrary. Id. at 895. For related discussion, see McDermott, "Arbitrability: the Courts Versus the Arbitrator," 23 Arb. J. 18 (1968). Also see Arbitrator Hilpert in 32 LA 1013, 1022. Cf., Arbitrator Summers in 48 LA 137, 139.
[25] See this Chapter, topic titled "Determination by the Courts."

cise his own judgment on the question; that he is not restricted to the criteria established for the courts by the *Trilogy,* and should not decide the issue slavishly on the basis of how a court might decide it.[26] Some other arbitrators, in holding that doubts concerning arbitrability should be resolved in the affirmative, appear to have their eye on the basic *Trilogy* standard of presumptive arbitrability.[27]

May an arbitrator determine a dispute to be nonarbitrable after a court has ordered arbitration under the *Trilogy?* Arbitrator Edgar A. Jones has expressed belief that an arbitrator may do so (though he did not do so in the case before him) since there may be surface indication of arbitrability to justify a court in ordering arbitration whereas the arbitrator in delving deeper into the case may conclude that it was not intended to be arbitrable.[28] Court decisions go both ways on this question.[29]

Procedural Techniques for Ruling on Arbitrability

Sometimes arbitrability is the sole question before the arbitrator, but probably more often he is called upon to rule both on the preliminary issue of arbitrability and, if he finds the dispute arbitrable, also on the merits.[30]

---

[26] See Arbitrator Turkus in 43 LA 1287, 1289; Roberts in 39 LA 1191, 1203–1205; Aaron in 36 LA 1125, 1129. Similarly, Arbitrator Dugan in 46 LA 1018, 1021.

[27] See Arbitrator Morris in 53 LA 246, 248; Kates in 51 LA 741, 742; Ray in 51 LA 284, 286; Yagoda in 48 LA 1040, 1043. Arbitrator Warns clearly had the *Trilogy* standard in mind in 36 LA 380, 381. Many arbitrators have denied that the 1960 *Trilogy* has made them more inclined to decide in favor of arbitrability. Smith, "Arbitrators and Arbitrability," Labor Arbitration and Industrial Change 75 (BNA Incorporated, 1963). An early study supports this denial. See Report of Research & Education Committee, "The Steelworkers' Trilogy and the Arbitrator." Id. at 360–363. For an extensive survey of views of arbitrators and parties concerning the impact of *Trilogy* arbitrability teachings upon arbitrators, see Smith & Jones, "The Impact of the Emerging Federal Law of Grievance Arbitration on Judges, Arbitrators, and Parties," 52 Va. L. Rev. 831, 866 et seq. (1966), where numerous decisions by arbitrators are also examined for indications as to *Trilogy* influence. Authors Smith and Jones concluded that "The total impact upon arbitrators, although real, is difficult to evaluate fully at this time." Id. at 912.

[28] Zoological Society of San Diego, 50 LA 1, 7 (1967). Also see Warrior & Gulf Navigation Co., 36 LA 695, 697 (Holly, 1961).

[29] See "Arbitration and Rights Under Collective Agreements," Problems of Proof in Arbitration 377–378 (The Bureau of National Affairs, Inc., 1967); Smith & Jones, "The Supreme Court and Labor Dispute Arbitration: The Emerging Federal Law," 63 Mich. L. Rev. 751, 761 (1965).

[30] See statistics in "Substantive Aspects of Labor-Management Arbitration," 28 LA 943, 944 (1957).

Where the arbitrator is to rule on both arbitrability and the merits, evidence and argument on the question of arbitrability will be *heard* before the presentation on the merits. But the procedural question remains as to whether the arbitrator should *rule* on arbitrability before any presentation is made on the merits, or whether he should reserve his ruling on arbitrability until the full case has been presented.

One school of thought holds that a ruling on arbitrability should be made before the presentation on the merits. This view was elaborated by Arbitrator Harry J. Dworkin:

> "The Chairman is of the opinion that when a party raises the issue of arbitrability, it is better practice to pass upon this issue at the time it is presented, and before hearing the dispute on the merits, for the reason that whenever possible parties should have the right to an interim decision or ruling on any question presented during the course of the hearing, and that this procedure is preferable to the reservation of the ruling until after the conclusion of the hearing."[31]

Under this procedure only one hearing might prove to be required,[32] but two hearings often are required.[33]

Another view holds that the ruling on arbitrability may be reserved until the full case has been heard. As elaborated by Arbitrator Douglass B. Maggs:

> "The arbitrator may properly reserve his ruling upon arbitrability until after he has heard evidence and argument upon the merits. A contrary rule would cause needless delay and expense, necessitating two hearings whenever the arbitrator needed time to consider the question of arbitrability. Furthermore, in many cases, it is only after a hearing on the merits has informed the arbitrator of the nature of the dispute that he is in a position to determine whether it is of the kind covered by the agreement to arbitrate.

---

[31] Babcock & Wilcox Co., 22 LA 456, 460 (1954). For other instances in which this procedure was used (sometimes by specific agreement of the parties), see Arbitrator Duff in 48 LA 600, 603; Bennett in 45 LA 90, 91; Anrod in 45 LA 34 at 34; Kornblum in 43 LA 765, 766; Dworkin in 39 LA 1135 at 1135; Howard in 34 LA 617, 618. The interim ruling as to arbitrability might be verbal, in which case it will later be restated in a written opinion which also covers the merits. As in Dynamic Manufacturers, Inc., 36 LA 635, 636 (Crane, 1960).

[32] As in Hercules Powder Co., 47 LA 336, 338–339 (Boothe, 1966). In Lockheed Aircraft Service Co., 44 LA 51, 59 (Roberts, 1965), the arbitrator held the grievance to be arbitrable and remanded it to the parties, to be heard on the merits only if the parties could not resolve it.

[33] See Arbitrator McCoy in 45 LA 1055, 1056, and 46 LA 1063 at 1063; Jones in 45 LA 633, 635, and 45 LA 635, 640; Anrod in 45 LA 34 at 34; Stark in 44 LA 1150, and 47 LA 92 at 92.

"* * * This procedure does not, of course, preclude the party who loses from obtaining any judicial review of the arbitrator's decision to which it is entitled by law; to reassure the Company about this I explicitly ruled that its participation in the hearing upon the merits would not constitute a waiver of its objections to arbitrability."[34]

It would seem that the choice between these two procedures should be dictated by consideration of all the circumstances of the particular case. Such a flexible procedure has been used by the Connecticut State Board of Mediation:

"The Board will inform the party protesting arbitrability that it will be permitted to raise that issue at the hearing. The Board will then first hear arguments on arbitrability before it proceeds to the merits of the dispute. The Board makes clear that at the hearing both parties must be prepared to proceed on the merits after the Board has heard them on arbitrability.

"After the issue on arbitrability has been presented, 'the Board will assess the circumstances then obtaining to determine if it will proceed directly to the merits.'

"Under its policy, the Board reserves the right either to require the parties 'to go forward directly on the merits' at the same hearing or to determine that 'the decision on arbitrability should be made first before proceeding on the merits.' "[35]

Some agreements expressly give the arbitrator the option of hearing the arbitrability issue and the merits either together or in separate proceedings.[36] Even without such contractual provision, however, the arbitrator might require a party (against its wishes) to proceed to the merits before the ruling is made on arbitrability.[37] What should

---

[34] Barbet Mills, Inc., 19 LA 737, 738 (1952). Arbitrator Maggs explained his view in greater detail in Caledonia Mills, Inc., 15 LA 474, 476–477 (1950). For other instances in which the ruling on arbitrability was reserved until the merits had been heard (the arbitrator sometimes saying this would minimize delay and costs), see Arbitrator Oppenheim in 52 LA 1164, 1168–1169; Gibson in 51 LA 837, 838; Bender in 45 LA 545 at 545; Boles in 45 LA 502, 503; Singletary in 45 LA 261, 262; Schedler in 35 LA 499 at 499. This approach is suggested also in "Arbitrability," 18 LA 941, 950–951 (1951). For an instance where it was necessary to get into the merits before the arbitrability issue could be decided, see Chesapeake & Potomac Telephone Co., 46 LA 321, 322 (Seward, 1965).

[35] Justin, "Arbitrability and the Arbitrator's Jurisdiction," Management Rights and the Arbitration Process 1, 12 (BNA Incorporated, 1956).

[36] Major Collective Bargaining Agreements: Arbitration Procedures 25 (U.S. Dept: Labor Bull. No. 1425–6, 1966), where it is also noted that most agreements specify use of the same arbitrator for determining arbitrability and merits.

[37] As under the policy of the Connecticut State Board, noted hereinabove, or as the arbitrator did in Union Carbide Nuclear Co., 35 LA 499 at 499

an arbitrator do when a party insists, against the opposition of the other party, upon a ruling as to arbitrability before proceeding to the merits? A panel discussion by the National Academy of Arbitrators indicated that some arbitrators would issue an oral ruling as to arbitrability at the hearing, while some would proceed to the merits (possibly ex parte) despite the objections of one party.[38]

Finally it may be noted that regardless of *when* the ruling on arbitrability is made, it will often be placed in the arbitrator's written decision of the case at a point prior to his discussion of the merits.[39]

Delay in Contesting Arbitrability

The right to contest arbitrability before the arbitrator is not waived merely by failing to raise the issue of arbitrability until the arbitration hearing.[40]

Whether participation in an arbitration hearing on the merits constitutes a waiver of the right to court review of arbitrability may depend upon the terms of an applicable statute or upon the view of the particular court. No uniform rule exists as to this question.[41]

(Schedler, 1960). A "special appearance" to contest arbitrability did not prevent a ruling on the merits where the submission was broad enough to include the merits. Lake Mills Redi-Mix, Inc., 38 LA 307, 312 (Mueller, 1962).

[38] "Procedural Problems in the Conduct of Arbitration Hearings: A Discussion," Labor Arbitration—Perspectives and Problems 1–2, 21–22 (BNA Incorporated, 1964), where all participants indicated, however, that their choice of action might vary with the situation. Also see Arbitrator Merrill in 47 LA 339, 340; Lennard in 46 LA 746, 747, 749–750, and in 46 LA 750 at 750. For discussion as to proceeding ex parte, see Chapter 7, topic titled "Default Awards"; McDermott, "Arbitrability: the Courts Versus the Arbitrator," 23 Arb. J. 18 (1968). The arbitrator did proceed ex parte to the merits in Velsicol Chemical Corp., 52 LA 1164, 1168–1169 (Oppenheim, 1969), and issued a default award against the company, which had refused to introduce evidence or cross examine as to the merits.

[39] As Arbitrator Dworkin did in Babcock & Wilcox Co., 22 LA 456, 460 (1954), and Arbitrator Maggs in Barbet Mills, Inc., 19 LA 737, 739 (1952).

[40] E.g., Arbitrator Williams in 48 LA 44, 46; Dugan in 46 LA 1018, 1021; Young in 20 LA 289, 292; Kerr in 11 LA 219, 220; Rader in 7 LA 595, 598. Cf., Greene in 47 LA 282, 283. As to how far into the arbitration hearing a party may wait before first contesting arbitrability, see Arbitrator Layman in 45 LA 417, 421–422; Sembower in 39 LA 534, 537.

[41] The different results on the question are reflected in Humble Oil & Refining Co. v. Teamsters Local 866, 65 LRRM 3016 (USDC N.Y., 1967); Ficek v. Southern Pacific Co., 57 LRRM 2573 (CA 9, 1964), cert. den. 60 LRRM 2284 (U.S. S.Ct. 1965); National Cash Register Co. v. Wilson, 35 LA 646 (N.Y. Ct. App., 1960). For other material relevant to this question, see Chapter 2, Legal Status of Arbitration.

As a precaution against such waiver, a participant in an arbitration hearing on the merits may expressly reserve the right to court review of arbitrability.[42] Likewise, an arbitrator who calls for evidence and argument on the merits of a dispute before he rules on a challenge to arbitrability may emphasize that "participation in the hearing upon the merits would not constitute a waiver of objections to arbitrability."[43]

---

[42] Under many statutes this precaution would suffice. But under the New York statue it might be inadequate. See McNamara v. Air Freight Haulage Co., 46 LA 768, 61 LRRM 2424 (N.Y. S.Ct., 1966).

[43] Barbet Mills, Inc., 19 LA 737, 738 (Maggs, 1952).

CHAPTER 7

ARBITRATION PROCEDURES AND TECHNIQUES

Source of Procedural Rules

It is difficult to generalize concerning arbitration procedures since rarely do the procedures followed in any given case spring from a single source. Indeed, it frequently happens that in a given case some of the procedure utilized is based upon legal requirements, some upon agreement of the parties, and some upon directive of the arbitrator. Then, too, if the parties have agreed to arbitrate under the rules of some administrative agency, such as the American Arbitration Association, many procedural matters will be governed by the rules of the agency. Accordingly, the reader should bear in mind that the procedures outlined in this chapter do not necessarily apply in all cases, but may be varied significantly for some cases by the applicable law,[1] administrative agency rules, special agreement of the parties, or by the views of the particular arbitrator.

It is highly desirable that arbitration procedures be based, to the extent reasonably possible, upon the wishes of the parties and the judgment of their arbitrator. In this regard, it is significant that most arbitration statutes contain very little detail regarding that part of the arbitration process from the time the arbitrator is selected until his award has been issued.[2] Then, too, even where statutes deal with this part of the process, the parties may be permitted to waive statutory requirements.[3] Likewise, the procedural rules of administrative agen-

---

[1] As to what law may be applicable to the case, and particularly as to the applicability of state law where the case is covered by LMRA §301, see Chapter 2, topic titled "The Applicable Law."
[2] See Chapter 2 for the general content of arbitration statutes.
[3] For instance, see In re Aranson, 6 LA 1033 (N.Y. Sup. Ct., 1946). Also see Chapter 2.

cies ordinarily may be waived by the parties by proceeding without objection when the rules are not observed.[4]

It is the function and responsibility of the arbitrator to determine procedural matters which are not covered by any applicable law or administrative agency rule and upon which the parties have not reached agreement. It is also to be noted that, as between court and arbitrator, the U.S. Supreme Court has stated that when a court has determined that the subject matter of a dispute is arbitrable, procedural questions "which grow out of the dispute and bear on its final disposition should be left to the arbitrator."[5]

In actual practice arbitrators frequently determine what procedure shall be followed in regard to many aspects of the arbitration process.[6] It must be emphasized, however, that the arbitrator should and ordinarily will endeavor to comply with the wishes of the parties whenever they agree on procedural matters.[7] Such agreement may of course be reached at the hearing, but it may have been reached earlier in the submission or the collective agreement.[8]

Control of Arbitration Proceedings

It is generally accepted that the conduct of arbitration proceedings is under the jurisdiction and control of the arbitrator, subject

---

[4] Such waiver is permitted, for instance, by American Arbitration Association Rule 33, 43 LA 1292, 1295.

[5] John Wiley & Sons v. Livingston, 84 S.Ct. 909, 918–919, 55 LRRM 2769 (1964). For related discussion, see Chapter 6, Determining Arbitrability.

[6] The cases and materials throughout this Chapter illustrate this function of the arbitrator. In this regard, too, American Arbitration Association Rule 46 empowers the arbitrator to interpret its rules "insofar as they relate to his powers and duties." 43 LA 1292, 1296.

[7] See subtopic titled "Control of Arbitration Proceedings," below. Also see report of tripartite committee, "Problems of Proof in the Arbitration Process," Problems of Proof in Arbitration 86, 87–88 (The Bureau of National Affairs, Inc., 1967). Where arbitrators failed to follow a procedural requirement specified by the agreement, a federal court remanded the case to them for compliance with the contractual procedure. Smith v. Union Carbide Corp., 60 LRRM 2110, 45 LA 703 (CA 6, 1965).

[8] The submission stated procedural details, for instance, in A.S. Abell Co., 45 LA 801, 806–807 (Cluster, 1965). Of 416 agreements analyzed in one survey, 33 percent contained provisions concerning arbitration procedures (either by stating procedural rules in the agreement, or by stipulating that the procedural rules of the American Arbitration Association, of a specified state, or as established by the arbitrator, are to govern). Major Collective Bargaining Agreements: Arbitration Procedures 59–61 (U.S. Dept. of Labor Bull. No. 1425–6, 1966), where it is also noted that the FMCS has set only a few rules for the conduct of the proceedings.

to such rules of procedure as the parties may jointly prescribe.[9] As to this control by the arbitrator, the reporter of one survey has observed that:

> "In the absence of strict procedural guidelines the arbitrator necessarily has had to assume wide discretion in conducting hearings and in deciding cases. This broad role has been affirmed by the United States Supreme Court. But the arbitrator, it is clear from this survey, has not become a tyrant as a consequence."[10]

Of course a fair hearing is generally the ultimate objective of procedural rules. However, an efficient and orderly hearing is also important to the success of arbitration proceedings. Thus, the arbitrator must give the parties a fair chance to present their case, must satisfy himself that he is being adequately informed by the parties to enable him to decide the case, and at the same time he must provide procedural efficiency to keep the hearing from getting out of hand.[11] This is not always an easy task.

Initiating Arbitration: Submission v. Arbitration Clause

Arbitration may be initiated either (1) by a "submission" or (2) by a demand or notice invoking a collective agreement arbitration clause. Sometimes both instruments are used in a case.

A submission (sometimes called a "stipulation" or an "agreement to arbitrate") is used where there is no previous agreement to arbitrate. The submission, which must be signed by both parties, describes an existing dispute; it often also names the arbitrator (or the method of appointment) and it sometimes contains considerable detail regarding the arbitrator's authority, the procedure to be used at the hearing, and other matters which the parties wish to control.[12]

---

[9] See FMCS Regulations, §1404.8; Code of Ethics and Procedural Standards for Labor-Management Arbitration, §4 of Part II and §5 of Part III. The Code of Ethics is published in 15 LA 961–966.

[10] Eaton, "Labor Arbitration in the San Francisco Bay Area," 48 LA 1381, 1391 (1967). For the possibility of court relief where procedural unfairness is found, see Harvey Aluminum, Inc. v. United Steelworkers, 263 F.Supp. 488 (USDC, 1967).

[11] As to the latter objective, see panel discussion, "The Arbitration Hearing—Avoiding a Shambles," Proceedings of 18th Annual Meeting of National Academy of Arbitrators 75 (BNA Incorporated, 1965); Jones & Smith, "Management and Labor Appraisals and Criticisms of the Arbitration Process: A Report with Comments," 62 Mich. L. Rev. 1115, 1127 (1964).

[12] For example, see the submission in Goodyear Engineering Corp., 24 LA 360, 361–362 (Warns, 1955).

Since collective agreements generally do not provide for the arbitration of "interests" disputes that might arise in the future, the agreement to arbitrate such disputes most often is entered into after the dispute has materialized and at a time when the issues can be defined. In such cases the parties will use one instrument only, which will contain full provision for the arbitration.[13]

However, most collective agreements do provide for arbitration of "rights" disputes involving the application or interpretation of the agreement. Thus there is an "agreement to arbitrate" future disputes that may arise under and during the term of the collective agreement. If a dispute is covered by such an arbitration clause, arbitration may be initiated unilaterally by one party by serving upon the other a written demand or notice of intent to arbitrate; the latter party may reply with a statement covering its position, but the arbitration proceeds regardless of whether any such reply is made.[14] Use of a demand only, with no joint submission, has long been common practice where the collective agreement contains an arbitration clause.[15] Moreover, in such cases no submission will be required to make arbitration enforceable by the courts if the case is covered by state or federal law under which agreements to arbitrate future disputes are specifically enforceable.[16]

However, even where the collective agreement contains an arbitration clause covering a dispute, the parties may choose also to execute

---

[13] For examples of the instrument used in such instances, see A.S. Abell Co., 45 LA 801, 806–807 (Cluster, 1965); River Valley Tissue Mills, Inc., 3 LA 245, 246 (Blair, 1946). Also see submission instruments in 28 LA 477, 478–479; 26 LA 904, 904–905; 25 LA 54, 55.

[14] See American Arbitration Association Rule 7, 43 LA 1292. The FMCS prefers to act upon a joint request, but may act if the parties have agreed that either party may seek a panel of arbitrators. FMCS Regulations, §1404.4.

[15] See "Procedural Aspects of Labor-Management Arbitration," 28 LA 933, 934 (1954 statistics); Updegraff, Arbitration And Labor Relations 138–139 (The Bureau of National Affairs, Inc., 1970); Updegraff & McCoy, Arbitration of Labor Disputes 53 (1946). One survey revealed that: "Opinion on use of the submission agreement varied from 'always,' 'absolutely,' and 'usually prefer it,' to 'almost never,' and 'never had one.' Use of the submission agreement seems to depend more than anything else on the relationship between the parties. Opposition to its use was most frequently based on the ground that it leads to interminable haggling over phraseology, with each side jockeying for a favorable statement. * * * Despite these difficulties, a majoritiy of those interviewed preferred a submission agreement, and stated that they arrive at one successfully in most cases." Eaton, "Labor Arbitration in the San Francisco Area," 48 LA 1381, 1386 (1967).

[16] See Chapter 2, Legal Status of Arbitration.

a submission after the dispute has materialized. Some reasons for doing this are:

1. To expand or diminish the authority of the arbitrator more than provided by the collective agreement.[17]

2. To state precisely the issue to be decided by the arbitrator, and thus to indicate the scope of his jurisdiction more precisely.[18]

3. To state procedural details where the parties desire to control them and the collective agreement contains little or no detail in regard thereto.

4. In arbitration under a statute, to complete any statutory requirements not met by the arbitration clause of the collective agreement.

5. In cases not covered by state or federal law making agreements to arbitrate future disputes specifically enforceable, to provide a contract after the dispute has materialized. Contracts to arbitrate existing disputes are the basis of damage actions under the common law of some jurisdictions and sometimes are made specifically enforceable by statute even where agreements to arbitrate future disputes are not.[19]

6. To confirm the arbitrability of the particular dispute.[20]

7. To provide an additional opportunity to settle the dispute—in negotiating on a submission the parties may find that they are not too far apart for a negotiated settlement of the basic dispute.[21]

It is obvious from the above discussion that any use of a submission depends upon the particular case, and that the particular contents and form of submissions which are used will vary greatly from case to case. Some submissions are very brief, while others are quite detailed.

The arbitration clause of the collective agreement and/or the submission define the limits of the arbitrator's jurisdiction. An award

---

[17] For example, see International Shoe Co., 21 LA 550, 550–551 (Rader, 1953). In E. K. Porter Co. v. United Saw, File & Steel Products Workers, 406 F.2d 643 (CA 3, 1969), the subsequently adopted submission controlled over the collective agreement in reference to the arbitrator's jurisdiction.

[18] See E. I. du Pont de Nemours & Co. 39 LA 1083, 1084 (Begley, 1962); North American Cement Corp., 28 LA 414, 417–418 (Callaghan, 1957). The desired clarity is not always achieved in the submission, and the burden may fall upon the arbitrator to make the initial interpretation of an ambiguous submission in order to determine the scope of his jurisdiction. See Eagle Rubber Co., 35 LA 256, 261–262 (Dworkin, 1960).

[19] See Chapter 2, topic titled "State Law." Also see Updegraff, Arbitration and Labor Relations 142–145 (The Bureau of National Affairs, Inc., 1970); Updegraff & McCoy, Arbitration of Labor Disputes 56–58 (1946).

[20] As in Kraft Foods Co., 15 LA 336 at 336 (Elson, 1950).

[21] See Kagel, Anatomy of a Labor Arbitration 55 (BNA Incorporated, 1961).

may be subject to court challenge if it decides any issue or matter not submitted to the arbitrator by at least one of these instruments, and court relief might be available also if the award fails to decide all issues and matters so submitted.[22] Obviously, care should be exercised by the parties in drafting these instruments and by the arbitrator in responding to them.

Stating the Issue

Arbitration does not utilize formal pleadings similar to those used by courts to determine the precise issue or issues to be resolved. Such formal pleadings would destroy at least some of the simplicity and utility of arbitration. But somewhere in the course of an arbitration proceeding the issue to be resolved by the arbitrator must be specifically stated or pinpointed.

If the parties jointly initiate the arbitration by a submission agreement the issue will ordinarily be stated clearly in that instrument. However, as noted above, frequent practice is to use only a demand for arbitration where the collective agreement contains an arbitration clause covering the dispute.[23]

Although no submission is used, the arbitrator will have jurisdiction of a dispute if it is covered by an arbitration clause in the collective agreement. To illustrate, if the arbitration clause covers disputes over the application or interpretation of the collective agreement, then any such dispute becomes arbitrable when either party serves the other with a demand or notice of intent to arbitrate. This demand or notice will identify the case in general terms at least, but often it does not

---

[22] As to possible court remedies in these situations, see discussion of federal and state law in Chapter 2. Also see Amalgamated Food & Allied Workers v. Great Atlantic and Pacific Tea Co., 415 F.2d 185 (CA 3, 1969); Carr v. Kalamazoo Vegetable Parchment Company, 354 Mich. 327, 331–332 (Mich. Sup. Ct., 1958); In re MacMahon, 4 LA 830, 831 (N.Y. Sup. Ct., 1946); Arbitrator Begley in 39 LA 1083, 1084; Howlett in 38 LA 808, 817.

[23] It may be noted that most collective agreements are silent as to statement of the issue in arbitration, but some do deal expressly with the matter by providing that the parties shall submit a joint statement of the issue or by calling for separate statements from each party (implying that ultimate determination of the issue is for the arbitrator). See Major Collective Bargaining Agreements: Arbitration Procedures 61–64 (U.S. Dept. of Labor Bull. No. 1425–6, 1966). Even where the agreement expressly provided that the issue "shall be mutually agreed upon," a federal court held that arbitration would not be defeated by inability of the parties to agree upon a statement of the issue. Socony Vacuum Tanker Men's Assn. v. Socony Mobil Oil Co., 63 LRRM 2590 (CA 2, 1966).

state the precise issue in dispute.[24] The arbitrator selected for the case has jurisdiction to decide the dispute since it involves the application or interpretation of the collective agreement; but the question remains, what is the precise issue to be resolved by him? The issue, or issues, must be identified or pinpointed. This may be achieved in any of several ways where the parties have not done so sometime prior to the hearing.

Use of Original Grievance

The grievance statement as processed through the grievance procedure often serves as the statement of the issue, especially if the grievance statement is carefully worded.[25] The parties sometimes specifically stipulate that the written grievance is to be the statement of the issue,[26] particularly after they have tried but failed to agree on a specific statement of the issue.[27] The arbitrator himself might turn to the original grievance when the parties have not agreed upon a specific statement of the issue.[28]

Too often, however, the original grievance is too poorly worded to provide a key to the precise issue in dispute.[29] Also, the discussion at the pre-arbitral grievance steps sometimes develops the issue in different or modified channels. To a limited extent this may happen also at the arbitration stage, as in the case wherein Arbitrator Meredith

---

[24] For instance, one Bethlehem Steel arbitrator noted that it had "not been the practice under the Bethlehem Agreement for the parties to formulate 'submissions' defining precisely and exclusively the issues to be resolved." Bethlehem Steel Co., 17 LA 295, 300 (Selekman, 1951). Also see Davy, "The John Deere-UAW Permanent Arbitration System," Critical Issues in Labor Arbitration 161, 190 (BNA Incorporated, 1957). Where no joint submission is used, American Arbitration Association Rule 7 requires the unilateral demand for arbitration (a copy of which goes to the Association) to state "the nature of the dispute and the remedy sought," but this gives only one party's version, which may or may not contain an accurate statement of the issue. 43 LA 1292. The parties sometimes send a joint letter to the Association, in which the issue might be stated. As in Public Service Co., 52 LA 639 at 639 (Klein, 1969).

[25] As in Borden Mfg. Co., 25 LA 629, 630 (Wettach, 1955); Lukens Steel Co., 15 LA 408, 409 (D'Andrade, 1950).

[26] As in Texas Gas Transmission Corp., 27 LA 413 at 413 (Hebert, 1956).

[27] As in Johnson Bronze Co., 34 LA 365 at 365 (McDermott, 1960); New Haven Clock & Watch Co., 18 LA 203 at 203 (Stutz, 1952). The collective agreement called for a similar approach in Bowaters Southern Paper Corp., 52 LA 674, 675 (Oppenheim, 1969).

[28] As did Arbitrator Johnson in 48 LA 1357, 1358; Davey in 43 LA 453, 455; Donnelly in 19 LA 690, 691.

[29] Then, too, cases sometimes reach arbitration without any formal written grievance ever having been submitted. For example, see White Motor Co., 43 LA 682, 683 (McGury, 1964).

Reid noted that "at the hearing the broad issue suggested by the grievance was narrowed very substantially as a result of testimony and argument."[30]

Parties Stipulate Issue at the Hearing

At the commencement of the arbitration hearing the parties may execute a stipulation or submission precisely stating the issue.[31]

The view has been expressed that the issue should be framed as soon as possible, preferably by the parties even prior to the arbitration hearing.[32] As we have noted, the parties sometimes do agree to a statement of the issue either prior to the hearing or at its commencement. Unfortunately, however, the parties frequently are unable to agree upon any specific statement of the issue, and sometimes attempts to do so tend to generate more dispute. Indeed, the parties themselves do not always know precisely what the issue is at the outset of the hearing.[33] Moreover, even when the parties have signed a submission stating the issue it may be ambiguous and in need of clarification.[34]

Likewise, the issue as stated by the parties may be too narrow to dispose of the entire dispute; in such instances the arbitrator may so inform the parties in order that they might authorize him to resolve the dispute fully.[35]

---

[30] Heppenstall Co., 22 LA 84, 85 (1954). For other cases in which the issue as developed at the hearing governed over the grievance statement, see Arbitrator Dworkin in 45 LA 897, 901–902; McCoy in 45 LA 630, 633.

[31] See Arbitrator Roberts in 46 LA 486, 487; Whelan in 23 LA 126, 127; Kelliher in 15 LA 363, 364. Reference to such stipulations does not always reveal the stage of the hearing at which the issue is defined. See Arbitrator Jones in 53 LA 165, 167; Abernethy in 50 LA 760 at 760 (parties agreed to substance of the issue and arbitrator thereafter stated it in his own words); Wagner in 46 LA 81, 82. Sometimes the stipulation is oral. See Arbitrator Roberts in 46 LA 486, 487; Aaron in 16 LA 165, 166.

[32] See Heath, "Defining the Issue and the Remedy," The Arbitrator, the NLRB, and the Courts 352–359 (The Bureau of National Affairs, Inc., 1967). Also see comments by Jones & Smith, "Management and Labor Appraisals and Criticisms of the Arbitration Process: A Report With Comments," 62 Mich. L. Rev. 1115, 1130–1132 (1964).

[33] See Mundet Cork Corp., 18 LA 254, 255 (Reynolds, 1952).

[34] See Zia Co., 52 LA 89, 90 (Cohen, 1969), where both parties signed a reworded submission to clarify the issue; McKinney Mfg. Co., 19 LA 291, 292 (Reid, 1952), where the arbitrator had implied authority to restate the issue contained in the submission.

[35] See American Smelting & Refining Co., 29 LA 262, 264 (Ross, 1957). Absent such broadened authority from the parties, the arbitrator will feel confined to the narrowly stipulated issue. See Arbitrator Roberts in 49 LA 121, 122, 125; Fallon in 48 LA 12, 15–16.

Sometimes the parties agree to a statement of the issue during the course of the hearing.[36] After some testimony has been received the dispute often appears in sharper focus. At an opportune moment the arbitrator may call for a discussion to clarify the issue. Such discussion may produce an agreed statement of the issue—perhaps one worded by the arbitrator and accepted by the parties.

Of course the arbitrator has the privilege at the hearing of calling for discussion or statements to clarify the issue and its scope. Whether he will choose to do this (and if so, at what stage of the hearing) will depend upon his evaluation of its necessity and upon his impression as to whether it will expedite or retard the proceedings. In any event, it has been suggested that arbitrators should not press the parties unduly to arrive at an exact statement of the issue.[37]

Issue Pinpointed by Arbitrator

In many cases the burden of clarifying or pinpointing the issue settles upon the arbitrator. Ordinarily the general nature of the issue or issues underlying the dispute becomes apparent to the arbitrator before the hearing has progressed very far, and he usually has no difficulty in discerning the precise issue or issues after he has studied the entire case.

The parties may specifically request that the arbitrator determine what the issue is.[38] A similar result may be produced by the collective agreement itself, as where the agreement provided that if the parties "fail to agree on a joint submission each shall submit a separate submission and the arbitrator shall determine the issue or issues to be heard."[39]

Sometimes the burden of pinpointing the issue falls to the arbitrator after the parties have attempted without success to agree upon a statement thereof at the hearing.[40] In these instances the parties'

[36] As in Marblehead Lime Co., 48 LA 310 at 310 (Anrod, 1966); Republic Oil Co., 15 LA 895 at 895 (Klamon, 1951).
[37] Sembower, "Halting the Trend Toward Technicalities in Arbitration," Critical Issues in Labor Arbitration 98, 101 (BNA Incorporated, 1957).
[38] See Arbitrator Daugherty in 46 LA 1049, 1049–1050 (parties asked him to frame the issue after the hearing); Larkin in 43 LA 1025 at 1025; Hildebrand in 28 LA 769, 775. Also see Hebert in 45 LA 131, 132–133, 139; Bauder in 22 LA 163 at 163.
[39] Lockheed Aircraft Corp., 23 LA 815, 815–816 (Marshall, 1955). Also see Arbitrator Abernethy in 42 LA 988, 989; Dworkin in 29 LA 29, 31, 35.
[40] See Arbitrator Scheiber in 53 LA 312, 314; Leonard in 48 LA 1296, 1297; Gundermann in 43 LA 907, 909; Kates in 41 LA 937 at 937; Smith

discussion and/or separate statements from each may aid the arbitrator in stating the issue.[41]

In many cases there is no discussion by either the arbitrator or the parties at the hearing specifically directed toward pinpointing the issue, even where it has not been previously defined clearly.[42] In these cases the arbitrator arrives at a precise statement of the issue or issues after he has studied the entire record of the case, including, if available to him, such matters as the original grievance statement and the grievance procedure minutes, the demand for arbitration and any reply of the other party, correspondence of the parties, the transcript of the hearing (or the arbitrator's notes), the parties' exhibits, and the parties' briefs.

Frequently the arbitrator finds that the issue is clearly and accurately stated in a single one of these sources. Again, the arbitrator may conclude that one party's wording of the issue is an accurate statement thereof.[43]

Simultaneous Arbitration of Several Grievances

The question has often arisen whether one party may be compelled by the other to arbitrate several grievances before the same arbitrator in one proceeding. Simultaneous arbitration of grievances has been said to reflect "the best ideals of the whole arbitration process, which are devoted to efficiency, expeditious disposition and economy."[44] A large number of arbitrators obviously agree, for a very

---

in 27 LA 251, 253; Anderson in 20 LA 715, 716. Also see Marshall in 49 LA 69 at 69; Lee in 48 LA 353, 361. In Borden Co., 46 LA 1175 at 1175 (Bellman, 1966), the parties declined to attempt a joint statement of the issue—this left it to the arbitrator. In C & D Batteries, Inc., 31 LA 272, 273, 275–276 (Jaffee, 1958), a party could not defeat the arbitration by walking out upon failure to achieve a joint statement of the issue.

[41] See Arbitrator Abernethy in 51 LA 9, 10; Burr in 36 LA 1132, 1133; Smith in 27 LA 251, 253. Also see Larkin in 46 LA 39, 40.

[42] For some cases which appear to fall within this category and in which the arbitrator pinpointed the issue, see Arbitrator Krimsly in 47 LA 518, 520–521; Rezler in 46 LA 1073, 1074; Kates in 45 LA 153, 154; Marshall in 25 LA 480, 481; Dworkin in 24 LA 73, 74; Cole in 22 LA 868, 869; Merrill in 20 LA 727, 731; Bailer in 19 LA 257, 259; Prasow in 17 LA 25, 26; Healy in 15 LA 764, 765; Gregory in 15 LA 420, 424.

[43] See Magma Copper Co., 51 LA 9, 10 (Abernethy, 1968); Gisholt Machine Co., 23 LA 105, 108 (Kelliher, 1954).

[44] Stewart-Warner Corp., 12 LA 305, 306 (Gregory, 1949). For discussions of the various arguments for and against multiple grievance arbitration, with the "for" arguments prevailing, see Arbitrator Traynor in 51 LA 1001,

strong line of arbitral authority holds that such simultaneous arbitration of all grievances which reach the arbitration stage at the same time can be compelled by either party unless the arbitration clause of the collective agreement clearly and unambiguously provides otherwise.[45]

In adhering to this general rule, many arbitrators have expressly considered and rejected the contention that a different result is required by the contract's use of the singular term "grievance."[46] However, the right to require multiple grievance arbitration has been denied where the contract speaks in the singular *and* there is an adequately established past practice of arbitrating only one grievance at a time.[47] Furthermore, Arbitrator Samuel H. Jaffee has recognized that there may be special circumstances justifying other exceptions to the aforementioned general rule, such as in the following situations: (1) individual grievances involving widely separated plants, with separate contracts, with witnesses located in many places; (2) inordinately large number of grievances; or (3) grievances of a special nature requiring an arbitrator with corresponding specialized experience.[48] Arbitrator Harry J. Dworkin has discerned that multiple griev-

---

1004–1005; Solomon in 50 LA 1070, 1074–1080; King in 46 LA 827, 829–830; Ray in 46 LA 210, 212–214. If the agreement deals expressly with this matter, its terms will of course govern. See Arbitrator Shister in 47 LA 601, 602; Schedler in 40 LA 95, 96.

[45] See Arbitrator Dworkin in 53 LA 239, 244–245; Bothwell in 52 LA 1035, 1041–1043; Traynor in 51 LA 1001, 1004–1005; Solomon in 50 LA 1070, 1074–1080; Cahn in 47 LA 330, 332; King in 46 LA 827, 829–830; Ray in 46 LA 210, 212–214; Singletary in 44 LA 1154, 1156–1158; Holly in 43 LA 570, 572; Hebert in 42 LA 1232, 1237–1239; Jaffee in 41 LA 1017, 1019–1020; Stouffer in 41 LA 424, 426–427; Horlacher in 41 LA 252, 254; Haughton in 39 LA 943, 947; Fisher in 37 LA 724, 725–726; Hawley in 36 LA 751, 752–753; Sembower in 36 LA 96, 98–99; Luskin in 33 LA 859, 860; Fleming in 32 LA 442, 444; Warns in 28 LA 586, 588–589; Feinberg in 23 LA 588, 589–590; Williams in 23 LA 13, 14–15; Rader in 20 LA 441, 442–443; Trotta in 13 LA 878, 879; Gregory in 12 LA 305, 306–307. A federal court has ruled that the question whether grievances are to be resolved in a single or in multiple proceedings should be decided by the arbitrator rather than the courts. Avon Products, Inc. v. Auto Workers Local 710, 67 LRRM 2001 (CA 8, 1967).

[46] Of the arbitrators listed in the prior footnote, all who were confronted with this contention rejected it.

[47] See Arbitrator Marshall in 51 LA 215, 220; Lockhart in 42 LA 65 66–67; Turkus in 39 LA 814, 819–820; Wissner in 38 LA 1045, 1047–1048.

[48] American Brake Shoe Co., 41 LA 1017, 1019–1020 (1963). Various of these possible exceptions have been recognized by other arbitrators. See Arbitrator Bothwell in 52 LA 1035, 1041–1043; Duff in 49 LA 355, 356 (where there was a backlog of 52 cases he limited the number to be heard by a single arbitrator at a hearing to five); Seinsheimer in 44 LA 97, 101 (nature of different cases might require different arbitrators); Taylor in 7 LA 112, 112–113 (simultaneous arbitration of grievances under separate contracts not required).

ance arbitration would not be required if "it is clearly shown that to do so would result in confusion, prejudice or substantial detriment to either party."[49]

Once an arbitrator has been selected a party has little basis for submitting additional grievances to the arbitrator without his consent and agreement by the other party.[50] In this regard, for instance, American Arbitration Association Rule 7 provides that "After the Arbitrator is appointed no new or different claim may be submitted to him except with the consent of the Arbitrator and all other parties."[51]

Advisory Opinions

Arbitrators generally are reluctant to issue advisory opinions or "declaratory judgments."[52] In one case Arbitrator D. Emmett Ferguson ruled, for example, that it was premature to submit to arbitration

---

Where an agreement separated grievances into "general" and "technical" categories, separate arbitration was required for each category. Cambridge Tile Mfg. Co., 66–1 ARB ¶8098 (Nichols, 1966).

[49] Apex Smelting Co., 53 LA 239, 244 (1969). In Appalachian Power Co., 53 LA 1012, 1013 (Reid, 1969), the arbitrator would hear only one of four grievances where the other three had not been processed in accordance with the agreement and hearing them would be "unreasonably burdensome" since the employer was not prepared on them and had no witnesses.

[50] See discussion by Arbitrator Bert L. Luskin in Maremont Automotive Products, Inc., 25 LA 171, 172–173 (1955). Accord, Arbitrator Dworkin in 53 LA 239, 245 and in 41 LA 961, 965. It has also been held that simultaneous arbitration can be required only as to those grievances which can be grouped together in the same letter to the FMCS. Harshaw Chemical Co., 44 LA 97, 101 (Seinsheimer, 1965); Stauffer Chemical Co., 44 LA 41, 42 (Griffin, 1964).

[51] 43 LA 1292. But see Sylvania Electric Products, Inc., 24 LA 199, 201–205, 210 (Brecht, 1954), where under Rule 7 grievances filed at the start of the arbitration hearing were accepted against the objection of one party where they added no new issue, arose from the same action as the grievance specifically identified in the demand for arbitration, and were fully anticipated in that demand. Also, Allied Chemical Corp., 43 LA 996, 997 (Cahn, 1964), would permit cases to be added for a limited period after the parties have exchanged lists of acceptable arbitrators.

[52] See Arbitrator Kamin in 50 LA 1093, 1096; Purdom in 50 LA 940, 947 (he refused to issue a "bush whacking broadside" ruling and confined himself to the narrow issue presented by the evidence); Kabaker in 50 LA 683, 691; Platt in 47 LA 1127, 1130–1131; Duff in 45 LA 225, 227–229; Scheiber in 44 LA 929, 936; Howlett in 44 LA 827, 829 (no ruling on moot question) and in 29 LA 495, 501; Turkus in 64–3 ARB ¶9161 (no ruling on moot question); Kates in 41 LA 937, 942; Crawford in 35 LA 453, 454 (no ruling on moot question); Dworkin in 35 LA 237, 240–241; Eckhardt in 29 LA 861, 862; Ferguson in 27 LA 640, 642; Marshall in 26 LA 74, 78. Cf., Stouffer in 40 LA 898, 901; Seitz in 37 LA 1034, 1036–1037; Haughton in 33 LA 543, 545. For a related discussion, see Shulman, "Reason, Contract, and Law in Labor Relations," 68 Harv. L. Rev. 999, 1022–1023 (1955), reprinted in Management Rights and the Arbitration Process 169 (BNA Incorporated, 1956).

"a hypothetical question" and that "each case must be judged on its own merits when, and if, it arises."[53]

Arbitrator Harry H. Platt has elaborated:

"Grievance determination, in order to be effective, should rest on facts or conclusions drawn from facts and not on speculative and hypothetical situations. Especially in cases like this [challenge as to reasonableness of revised company rule concerning the status of any flight hostess who becomes pregnant or adopts a child], factual differences weigh heavily. The question of whether a rule is fair and reasonable cannot be confidently determined except in the context of a concrete case and upon consideration of the specific circumstances of a particular case in which the rule is invoked and applied. Even a so-called policy grievance should be made as concrete as possible in terms of an actual case rather than in vague and general terms. For, as has often been said, general principles do not decide concrete cases. And equally important is the fact that where a decision is made on a specific grievance or a concrete factual setting, the chances are minimized of the Board reaching unintended conclusions or indulging in generalization."[54]

An arbitrator may be more inclined to issue an advisory opinion if the requesting party demonstrates that it is necessary to protect the party's interests under the contract,[55] or if the arbitrator is convinced that both parties desire one.[56]

The parties may specifically provide by contract for advisory opinions. The Chrysler Corporation, for instance, adopted "an Agreement-provided 'declaratory judgment' procedure for securing determinations of basic issues in advance of actual grievance situations."[57] A disadvantage of such provisions has been said to be that "an actual grievance may present an issue of contract interpretation in sharper focus than a claim stated in general terms."[58]

---

[53] Monarch Machine Tool Co., 27 LA 640, 642 (1956).

[54] Trans World Air Lines, Inc., 47 LA 1127, 1130 (1967), refusing to issue a declaratory judgment. But in National Airlines, Inc., 42 LA 1206, 1208–1209 (Black, 1964), a company grievance seeking a declaration that management had the right to adopt a rule requiring employees to wear safety caps was successful. Also see Northwest Airlines, Inc., 45 LA 565, 570 (Shister, 1965).

[55] See Arbitrator Dworkin in 49 LA 922, 926–927; Williams in 39 LA 1051, 1054; Kharas in 25 LA 755, 758.

[56] See J. B. Williams Co., 47 LA 596, 598–600 (Barnhart, 1966); Rexall Drug Co., 25 LA 830, 835 (Klamon, 1956). However, even where both parties wanted a declaratory judgment for future cases, Arbitrator Samuel S. Kates did not render one. D-V Displays Corp., 41 LA 937, 942 (1963).

[57] Wolff, Crane & Cole, "The Chrysler-UAW Umpire System," The Arbitrator and the Parties 111, 118 (BNA Incorporated, 1958).

[58] Id. at 147 (discussion by a General Motors Umpire, Nathan P. Feinsinger).

Extent of Permissible Deviation From Pre-Arbitral
Discussion of Case

Occasionally one party to an arbitration objects to an alleged attempt by the other party to enlarge the scope of the case by unilaterally injecting new issues, arguments, or claims for the first time at the arbitration stage. In disposing of these objections arbitrators tend to emphasize substance over form in seeking to uncover the real merits of the case.

An arbitrator may refuse to confine the parties rigidly to what occurred prior to the arbitration if the deviation from the pre-arbitral stage does not amount to the addition of new issues, but merely involves a modified line of argument, an additional element closely related to the original issue, the refinement or correction of an ineptly stated grievance, or the introduction of new evidence.[59]

To this extent, new aspects of the dispute may be aired initially at the arbitration stage, unless the arbitration tribunal is serving purely in an "appellate" capacity. For example, in overruling a party's objection to the consideration of an element which was relevant to the dispute but which had not been discussed by the parties prior to arbitration, Arbitrator Benton Gillingham stated that the objection was "based upon an unreasonably and unjustifiably limited and restrictive concept of arbitration" as it is generally conceived and applied in the field of labor relations.[60]

Arbitrator Gillingham explained further:

"* * * arbitration is not strictly comparable to the appeal process in the courts, or in any system of judicial or quasi-judicial agencies, where the appeal process involves a review by a higher authority of a judgment already rendered by a subordinate or inferior agency. To the contrary, arbitration is a process involving the use of a third party to resolve a dispute where the primary parties have been unable to resolve the disagreement. Thus it would appear that arbitration is much more

---

[59] For discussion of use of new evidence at the arbitration stage, see Chapter 8, topic titled " 'New' Evidence at Arbitration Hearing." Also see Chapter 15, topic titled "Post-Discharge Conduct or Charges." Permitting a reasonable amount of deviation at the arbitration stage also enhances the possibility of settlement. See "Settlements at Arbitration Stage," below. The general subject of new issues and evidence at the arbitration stage is also treated by Fleming, The Labor Arbitration Process 144–153 (Univ. of Ill. Press, 1965).

[60] Washington Motor Transport Assn., 28 LA 6, 9 (1956).

nearly analogous to the litigation of a controversy in a judicial or quasi-judicial agency of *initial jurisdiction* * * *."[61]

Arbitrator Robert Feinberg has stated that contentions which do not change the issue should always be available to the parties, although he indicated that he would reject attempts to broaden the scope of the grievance for the first time in arbitration.[62] In turn, Arbitrator Walter Boles has declared that "any arbitrator would be derelict in his duty if, in considering whether or not a given section of a contract was applicable to a matter before him, he limited his inquiry only to points of argument raised before the matter came on to hearing."[63]

Nor will a grievant be bound rigidly at the arbitration stage by an ineptly worded grievance statement, or one which gives an incorrect contractual basis for the claim or cites no contractual provision at all.[64] Formal and concise pleadings are not required in arbitration. A possibly typical view is that which was expressed by Arbitrator Marion Beatty:

> "Employees or their Union officers cannot be expected to draw their grievances artfully. If they have sufficiently apprized the Company of the nature of their complaint and if it is found that the Company has violated any portion of the contract, the employees, in my opinion, are entitled to relief."[65]

---

[61] Ibid. Emphasis added.

[62] Mergenthaler Linotype Co., 15 LA 707, 708 (1950). Also see Arbitrator Doyle in 39 LA 489, 492.

[63] Temco Aircraft Corp., 22 LA 826, 828 (1954), wherein Arbitrator Boles distinguished a prior case in which he refused to hear "an entirely new issue."

[64] See Arbitrator Kates in 51 LA 1098, 1100; Dunau in 50 LA 236, 238–239; Hayes in 48 LA 524, 528; Gorsuch in 48 LA 429, 436; Howard in 48 LA 379, 382; Altieri in 41 LA 47, 48–49; Sembower in 40 LA 1266, 1271; Beatty in 39 LA 1226, 1230; Hebert in 37 LA 42, 46; Miller in 35 LA 757, 778; Hale in 34 LA 827, 833–834; Griffin in 33 LA 847, 850; Jaffee in 27 LA 844, 854; Gorder in 20 LA 880, 882; Coffey in 17 LA 125, 129; McCoy in 16 LA 775, 776. Also see Peck in 39 LA 1249, 1256–1257; Morvant in 39 LA 1220, 1225. While a grievant will be permitted to rely upon a contractual provision not relied upon prior to arbitration, the possibility should be noted that his failure to cite the provision in the grievance statement might be taken as some indication that he did not then believe the provision supported his case. For example, see Wyandotte Chemicals Corp., 41 LA 230, 235–236 (Howlett, 1963). If a jointly signed submission states a precise issue, the arbitrator ordinarily will feel strictly limited to answering that question. E. I. du Pont de Nemours & Co., 39 LA 1083, 1084 (Begley, 1962). But see Western Electric Co., 42 LA 1316, 1319–1320 (Altieri, 1964).

[65] Armour & Co., 39 LA 1226, 1230 (1963). In American Bosch Arma Corporation v. I.U.E. Local 794, 243 F.Supp. 493 (USDC, 1965), the court noted that it has never been required that grievances be submitted in language comparable to that used in formal court proceedings.

A more extensive expression was provided by Arbitrator A. Langley Coffey:

> "Neither is it acceptable as a valid objection, that, because the Union in its written protest, and in claiming that the aggrieved employee has been discriminated against, cites provisions of the contract other than the one upon which jurisdiction rests, it has foreclosed its right to enlarge upon its claim that the discharge was in violation of the contract. Such objections admittedly have standing in places where the record means more than it does in arbitrations. However, where there is no requirement by contract, or otherwise, that either party submit or stand on any formal written protest or answer, formalities are dispensed with in hearings of this kind, and technical objections are brushed aside in an endeavor to get at the facts of a given case, and to do equity and complete justice to the rights of all parties, without let or hindrance, or the entanglements of formal pleadings, procedures or techniques."[66]

If a party materially changes its position from the grievance procedure to the arbitration stage in such a way that the other party is taken by surprise and finds it difficult or impossible to present its case adequately, the arbitrator may take some appropriate action (such as granting a continuance or remanding the case to the parties for further negotiations).[67]

Moreover, if a deviation from what occurred at the pre-arbitral stage actually constitutes the addition of a new issue or dispute that has not been previously discussed by the parties, or the addition of a claim that has not been filed as required by the collective agreement, and if this by-passing of the grievance procedure is objected to by one of the parties, the arbitrator will ordinarily refuse to dispose of

---

[66] Charles Eneu Johnson Co., 17 LA 125, 129 (1950). Even where the agreement limits the arbitrator's authority to a ruling on the specific provision relied upon prior to the hearing, strict enforcement of such limitation might result at most in a postponement of the ultimate consideration of the merits of the dispute. See statement by Arbitrator Seward in Bethlehem Steel Co., 36 LA 441, 442 (1961), and by Arbitrator Stark in Bethlehem Steel Co., 33 LA 285, 290–291 (1959).

[67] See comments of Arbitrator Cahn in Jones & Laughlin Steel Corp., 23 LA 397, 398 (1954); Emery in Texas-New Mexico Pipe Line Co., 17 LA 90, 93 (1951). Even apart from material *changes* in position, an arbitrator will take appropriate action where the grievance statement is too vague to inform the other party as to what is alleged. See Caterpillar Tractor Co., 39 LA 875, 878–879 (Dworkin, 1962). Arbitration proceeded, however, where the employer "was not in fact in the dark or uninformed as to what [the] grievance was all about at the time it came to arbitration." Black, Sivalls & Bryson, Inc., 42 LA 988, 991 (Abernethy, 1964).

the new matter in his award.[68] In this regard, a General Motors Umpire has stated:

> "It is the function of the Umpire to decide questions which the parties themselves have tried to settle without success. New contentions presented for the first time at the Fourth Step are untimely, for their late presentation defeats the avowed aim of the grievance procedure—to settle disputes by collective bargaining whenever possible and to refer to the Umpire only those cases in which collective bargaining has been tried and has failed."[69]

Preparing Cases for Arbitration

Thorough preparation of cases for arbitration is of paramount importance. Ordinarily most or all of the arbitrator's knowledge and understanding of the case is based upon the evidence and arguments presented at the arbitration hearing. Moreover, a party must fully understand its own case in order to communicate it effectively to the arbitrator, and full understanding depends upon thorough preparation.

What is necessary for thorough preparation of any given case will depend largely upon the nature of the case. For instance, in some cases the facts are especially important and each party will concentrate upon proving, largely through testimony of witnesses, that the facts are as that party sees them. In other cases the facts may be less important or not disputed, the controversy being centered upon some other matter, such as the proper interpretation of the collective agreement. Here each party's case may be devoted largely to arguments about how the agreement should be interpreted. In still other cases, economic and statistical data may be especially important.

Thus, the nature of the case should be considered in determining which items of the following "preparation" check list should be emphasized in any particular case. Since not all items are pertinent to every case, no significance lies in the order in which they are listed.

---

[68] See Arbitrator Dworkin in 51 LA 645, 656; Seward in 50 LA 1214 at 1214, and in 17 LA 537, 540; Hayes in 47 LA 421, 422–423; Alexander in 46 LA 184, 186–187; Bothwell in 45 LA 141, 143–144; Grant in 38 LA 153, 156; Meltzer in 27 LA 580, 584; Wolff in 27 LA 448, 453; Rosenfarb in 21 LA 22, 23; Davey in 20 LA 844, 849; Piper in 18 LA 801, 806; Selekman in 17 LA 295, 300. Cf., Koven in 54 LA 677, 680; Brecht in 24 LA 199, 204–206. Also see American Arbitration Association Rule 7(b) which appears to touch upon this matter. 43 LA 1292.

[69] Umpire Decision No. E-276 (1949). Also, Decision No. E-295 (1949).

a) Review the history of the case as developed at the pre-arbitral steps of the grievance procedure.

b) Study the entire collective agreement to ascertain all clauses bearing directly or indirectly on the dispute. Also, comparison of current provisions with those contained in prior agreements might reveal changes significant to the case.

c) So as to determine the general authority of the arbitrator, and accordingly the scope of the arbitration, examine the instruments used to initiate the arbitration. (See "Initiating Arbitration: Submission v. Arbitration Clause" and "Stating the Issue," above.)

d) Talk to all persons (even those the other party might use as witnesses) who might be able to aid development of a full picture of the case, including different viewpoints. You will thus better understand not only your own case but your opponent's as well; if you can anticipate your opponent's case you can better prepare to rebut it.

e) Interview each of your own witnesses (1) to determine what they know about the case; (2) to make certain they understand the relation of their testimony to the whole case; and (3) to cross-examine them to check their testimony and to acquaint them with the process of cross-examination. Make a written summary of the expected testimony of each witness; this can be reviewed when the witness testifies to insure that no important points are overlooked. Some parties outline in advance the questions to be asked each witness.

f) Examine all records and documents that might be relevant to the case. Organize those you expect to use and make copies for use by the arbitrator and the other party at the hearing. If needed documents are in the exclusive possession of the other party, ask that they be made available before or at the hearing. (For other possible means of obtaining such evidence, and for the significance of the other party's refusal to produce it, see Chapter 8.)

g) Visit the physical premises involved in dispute to better visualize what occurred and what the dispute is about. Also, consider the advisability of asking at the hearing that the arbitrator (accompanied by both parties) also visit the site of the dispute.

h) Consider the utility of pictorial or statistical exhibits. One exhibit can be more effective than many words, if the matter is suited to the exhibit form of portrayal. However, exhibits which do not "fit" the case, and those which are inaccurate or misleading, are almost certain to be ineffective or to be damaging to their proponent.

i) Consider what the parties' past practice has been in comparable situations. (For the significance of past practice, see Chapter 12.)

j) Attempt to determine whether there is some "key" point upon which the case might turn. If so, it may be to your advantage to concentrate upon that point.

k) In "interpretation" cases prepare a written argument to support your view as to the proper interpretation of the disputed language. (For the standards or rules used by arbitrators in interpreting contract language, see Chapter 9.)

l) In "interests" or "contract writing" cases collect and prepare economic and statistical data to aid evaluation of the dispute. (For the standards or guides used by arbitrators in "interests" disputes, see Chapter 18.)

m) Research the parties' prior arbitration awards and the published awards of other parties on the subject of the dispute for an indication of how similar issues have been approached in other cases. (Regarding the use of prior awards, see Chapter 11.)

n) Prepare an outline of your case and discuss it with other persons in your group. This insures better understanding of the case, and will strengthen it by uncovering matters that need further attention. Then, too, it will tend to underscore policy and strategy considerations that may be very important in the ultimate handling of the case. Use of the outline at the hearing will facilitate an organized and systematic presentation of the case.

Thorough preparation involves the use of ingenuity to illuminate all the possibilities of the case.[70] Certainly, the arbitrator needs a full picture of the case and he will be interested in all its possibilities to aid him in reaching a sound decision.

Fact Stipulations

An agreed statement of facts can serve well to expedite the arbitration hearing by reducing the number of necessary witnesses and by permitting concentration upon the disputed aspects of the case. This recognized, the parties may come to the hearing with a fact stipulation, or they may enter into one at the hearing.[71]

Sometimes fact stipulations are entered into at the suggestion of the arbitrator, who may recess the hearing to permit the parties to determine whether any facts can be stipulated.[72]

---

[70] For other discussions of case preparation, see Liebes, "Preparing the Case for Arbitration," The Arbitrator, the NLRB, and the Courts 359–366 (The Bureau of National Affairs, Inc., 1967); Kagel, Anatomy of a Labor Arbitration 37–54 (BNA Incorporated, 1961).
[71] See Arbitrator McCoy in 46 LA 1078, 1078–1079; Updegraff in 44 LA 1028, 1029–1030; Kagel in 38 LA 500, 502; Ryan in 17 LA 800 at 800.
[72] As in Inland Container Corp., 28 LA 312 at 312 (Ferguson, 1957).

Need for Hearing

A hearing in the presence of the arbitrator is deemed imperative in virtually all cases. In giving each party full and fair opportunity to be heard, the arbitration hearing simultaneously serves to inform the arbitrator fully regarding all material aspects of the dispute. However, in some cases the parties believe that the arbitrator can be adequately informed without a hearing in his presence, so they submit the dispute for decision entirely on the basis of stipulated facts, written briefs, and sometimes affidavits.[73]

Even where the parties agree to submit their case without a hearing, the arbitrator may not always agree that the case can be properly resolved without a hearing. For instance, where the facts were in issue but the parties nonetheless wanted to submit the case without a hearing (the arbitrator being directed to investigate the facts by interviewing the affected persons), Arbitrator David M. Helfeld convinced the parties that the benefits and safeguards of a hearing were indispensable.[74]

Representatives in Arbitration

It is generally agreed that each party has the right to be represented in arbitration proceedings by persons of its own choosing.[75] As Arbitrator Morton Singer once declared, neither side "may compel the other side to retain or consult with any person other than one of their own free will and choice."[76]

Some parties prefer to be represented in arbitration by the person who served as their spokesman in the pre-arbitral stages of the grievance procedure, since he is thoroughly familiar with the dispute. That

---

[73] For instances where the dispute was submitted to the arbitrator for decision without a hearing, see Arbitrator Merrill in 47 LA 635 at 635; Platt in 18 LA 160, 160–161 and in 16 LA 379 at 379; Komaroff in 16 LA 489, 494. For a detailed procedure which has been suggested for use when parties choose to submit their case to an arbitrator without a hearing, see Kagel, Anatomy of a Labor Arbitration 122–124, 137–138 (BNA Incorporated, 1961).

[74] San Juan Star, 43 LA 445, 445–446 (1964).

[75] For related discussion, see Chapter 5, topic titled "Grievance Representatives," where the generally broad scope of this right under federal law is also noted.

[76] Bronx County Pharmaceutical Assn., 16 LA 835, 838 (1951), where Arbitrator Singer proceeded without one of the parties, who refused to appear in the same room with counsel for the opposition.

person, however, may lack the skill needed to present the case clearly to an outsider who has no background knowledge of the parties or their dispute. Therefore, other representatives such as higher union or company officials may be used to present the case at the arbitration stage. Then, too, attorneys often are used by one or both parties.[77]

Regarding use of attorneys, Arbitrator Benjamin Aaron has aptly observed that an attorney, if he is well-trained and if he understands the nature of collective bargaining and the purposes of arbitration, will have the ability to outline the dispute clearly and simply, to come directly to the point at issue, to present his evidence in an orderly fashion, and to sum up his arguments and relate them to the record made at the hearing.[78] Legal training may be especially important in still other respects if the case is covered by any detailed arbitration statute.

Of course, some laymen possess the ability and experience to present cases very skillfully and effectively. Indeed, as one union consultant has been quoted, "a good union representative" may be "more than an even match for a company attorney."[79]

Some arbitration statutes expressly state that either party has a right to be represented by an attorney and that waivers of this right are subject to limitations stated in the statute. However, if either party plans to be represented by an attorney, the other party as a courtesy may be so informed.[80]

---

[77] See statistics in "Survey of Arbitration in 1964," Proceedings of 18th Annual Meeting of National Academy of Arbitrators 243, 245, 252 (BNA Incorporated, 1965); Fleming, "The Labor Arbitration Process: 1943–1963," Labor Arbitration—Perspectives and Problems 33, 39–40 (BNA Incorporated, 1964); "Survey of Arbitration in 1962," id. at 292, 296, 314; "Procedural Aspects of Labor-Management Arbitration," 28 LA 933, 936–937 (1954 statistics).

[78] Aaron, "Some Procedural Problems in Arbitration," 10 Vand. L. Rev. 733, 748 (1957). Also see Feinsinger, "Collective Bargaining, Labor Arbitration and the Lawyer," id. at 761; Merrill, "A Labor Arbitrator Views His Work," id. at 789, 794; Garrett, "The Role of Lawyers in Arbitration," Arbitration and Public Policy 102 (BNA Incorporated, 1961), summarized in "Current Problems of Arbitration," 35 LA 963, 966 (1961).

[79] Warren & Bernstein, "A Profile of Labor Arbitration," 16 LA 970, 981 (1951). In V. E. Anderson Mfg. Co., 43 LA 174, 175 (King, 1964), the grievant personally expressed concern that the company was represented by an attorney while he was not, but his concern apparently faded when the arbitrator explained that grievant's union representatives were capable and experienced in the presentation of arbitration cases.

[80] Advance notice of intent to use an attorney formerly was specified by American Arbitration Association Rule 20, but this is no longer required. 30 LA 1088; 43 LA 1294.

Privilege to Attend Hearing

Arbitration is a private proceeding and the hearing is not, as a rule, open to the public. However, all persons having a direct interest in the case ordinarily are entitled to attend the hearing.[81] Other persons may be permitted to attend with permission of the arbitrator,[82] or the parties. It would seem that the arbitrator would hesitate to grant such permission against the wishes of the parties.

Limiting Attendance by Witnesses

The arbitrator customarily has authority to require witnesses (except those who are direct parties) to leave the hearing room during the testimony of other witnesses.[83] This is explained by Arbitrator Maurice H. Merrill:

"One of the traditional methods for preserving the purity of testimony, 'the rule' that witnesses be excluded from the hearing chamber during the reception of others' testimony, frequently is invoked in arbitration. Whenever it is sought, I grant it, except, of course, as to the parties. On several occasions, I have observed the effectiveness of this safeguard against the possibility that one witness may be influenced in his testimony by what he has heard some one else say."[84]

Time, Place, and Notice of Hearing

No fixed rule exists for setting the date and locale of arbitration hearings. Ordinarily the arbitrator will meet at any time and place agreed to by the parties, if he can be available. If the parties cannot

---

[81] The problem of what an arbitrator should do when a second union wishes to attend the hearing as observer against the wishes of grievant union in work jurisdiction cases is treated briefly by discussion panel in "Procedural Problems in the Conduct of Arbitration Hearings," Labor Arbitration—Perspectives and Problems 1, 24–25, 32 (BNA Incorporated, 1964). Related discussion is found in topic titled "Bilateral Arbitration of Trilateral Conflicts," below.

[82] See American Arbitration Association Rule 22. 43 LA 1294.

[83] See American Arbitration Association Rule 22, ibid. Also see Douglas Aircraft Co., 28 LA 198, 203–204 (Jones, 1957). Where the arbitration concerns discipline against several employees, all of them are entitled to hear all of the testimony. Economy Forms Corp., 45 LA 430, 432 (Bauder, 1965). Even where the contract expressly provided for exclusion of witnesses except when testifying, the discharged employee's presence at the hearing could not be limited. International Smelting & Refining Co., 45 LA 885, 886 (Kornblum, 1965).

[84] Merrill, "A Labor Arbitrator Views His Work," 10 Vand. L. Rev. 789, 795 (1957). Also see Updegraff & McCoy, Arbitration of Labor Disputes 97–98 (1946). An arbitrator's failure to exclude witnesses as requested by a party apparently will not render his award vulnerable, since it is for the arbitrator to determine the credibility of witnesses. See Transport Workers v. Philadelphia Transportation Co., 283 F.Supp. 597 (DC, 1968).

agree upon these matters, the arbitrator or the administering agency must set them. In this regard, it is generally accepted that the "arbitrator [or agency] should consult the convenience of the parties in fixing the time and place for the hearing but should not allow one party to delay unduly the fixing of a date for the hearing. Written and timely notice of the date, time and place of the hearing should be given."[85]

Under some arbitration statutes the time and place for the hearing are fixed by the arbitrator, who may also be responsible for giving timely notice thereof. In any case, the arbitrator should always take action to insure adequate notice to the parties.[86]

The hearing room itself is ordinarily selected by the parties or by an administering agency. Frequently some "neutral ground" such as a hotel suite is used; this may minimize interruptions that sometimes occur when the hearing is held at the plant. However, some parties prefer to use a conference room at the company since this may reduce costs, will make records and witnesses more quickly available, and will require less time for any visit by the arbitrator to the site of the dispute.

A conference table arrangement (with the arbitrator at the head of the table) is most satisfactory if there are not too many participants. A "courtroom" arrangement tends to be more formal, but it may be preferred if there are numerous participants.

It goes without saying that the hearing room should be well lighted and ventilated, but unfortunately this ideal is not fulfilled in all cases.

Default Awards in Ex Parte Proceedings

Arbitrators sometimes feel compelled to render default awards, akin to the "default judgments" of courts. The justification for ex

---

[85] Code of Ethics and Procedural Standards for Labor-Management Arbitration, Part II, §2. 15 LA 961, 964.

[86] It has been reported that arbitrators (considering that the agreement is basically one between the company and the union, subject only to the union's duty of fair representation) generally are not disturbed by absence of notice to other employees who might be adversely affected if the grievance being processed by the union for some employee or employees is sustained. Fleming, "Due Process and Fair Procedure in Labor Arbitration," Arbitration and Public Policy 69, 71 (BNA Incorporated, 1961), summarized in "Current Problems of Arbitration," 35 LA 963, 964 (1961).

parte proceedings has been explained by Arbitrator Liston Pope in commenting that: "A general arbitration clause in a contract would be rendered meaningless if its implementation depended on the willingness of each party to the contract to present its case, as the party desiring no change in relationships could nullify arbitration simply by refusing to make an appearance."[87]

However, it has also been observed by Arbitrator Joseph Rosenfarb that "our judicial system looks askance at the finality of decisions based on default appearances. The Arbitration process is no exception. Only an unexplained failure to appear, not a delay in appearance, can justify an ex parte proceeding."[88] In this case one party was tardy and the other party requested that the hearing proceed without the tardy party under American Arbitration Association Rule 27 (quoted below); this request was refused by the arbitrator, who rescheduled the hearing for a later date at which time both parties participated.[89]

In cases of willful or deliberate default by one party after due notice, arbitrators have heard testimony and rendered awards as if both parties had participated.[90] Some but not all of these cases have involved state arbitration statutes providing for default awards, or collective agreements which specifically provided for default awards in the event of willful or deliberate default by one of the parties, or application of a provision such as American Arbitration Association Rule 27.[91] Rule 27 provides:

---

[87] Velvet Textile Corp., 7 LA 685, 691 (1947). For similar comment, see McDermott, "Arbitrability: the Courts Versus the Arbitrator," 23 Arb. J. 18, 34–35 (1968). A few agreements expressly authorize the issuance of default awards. See Major Collective Bargaining Agreements: Arbitration Procedures 71 (U.S. Dept. of Labor Bull. No. 1425–6, 1966).

[88] Busch's Jewelry Co., 19 LA 365, 367 (1952).

[89] Ibid. In Flinkote Co., 51 LA 74, 75 (Hardy, 1968), the employer delayed two months in choosing an arbitrator from an FMCS list but he did not thus forfeit his right to show just cause for the disputed discharge.

[90] See Arbitrator Kagel in 52 LA 1189 at 1189; Oppenheim in 52 LA 1164, 1168–1169; Bennett in 44 LA 1174, 1175; Kerrison in 42 LA 62, 62–63; Vadakin in 33 LA 412, 414; Cole in 24 LA 529, 531; Singer in 16 LA 835, 838; Jaffee in 15 LA 715, 720–721; Pope in 7 LA 685, 691; Baskind in 4 LA 719, 720. Cf., Prasow in 39 LA 614, 621.

[91] In Thompson Fuel Service, 42 LA 62 at 62 (1964), Arbitrator Kerrison had no doubt that he could issue a default award where law did not provide to the contrary. But in A.B.C. Cartage & Trucking Co., 42 LA 55, 58–59 (1963), Arbitrator Whelan refused to issue a default award where the case was not covered by American Arbitration Association rules or by any statute expressly authorizing such awards.

"Arbitration in the Absence of a Party—Unless the law provides to the contrary, the arbitration may proceed in the absence of any party, who, after due notice, fails to be present or fails to obtain an adjournment. An award shall not be made solely on the default of a party. The Arbitrator shall require the other party to submit such evidence as he may require for the making of an award."[92]

Federal Mediation and Conciliation Service regulations also provide for ex parte proceedings—the Service has a rule which is very similar in wording to the above-quoted Rule 27 and is identical to it as to substance.[93]

An indication of how an arbitrator might proceed in the absence of one party is provided by Arbitrator Samuel H. Jaffee's approach under American Arbitration Association Rule 27:

"The hearing then proceeded in the absence of * * * any Company representative or of any Company observer. Counsel for the Union remained with his clients and witnesses. These witnesses were sworn in normal course and testified in the usual way, but without the benefit of any cross-examination and in response only to questions of Union counsel, though the arbitrator took it upon himself to ask a substantial number of questions of some of them.

"The findings which follow, and the conclusions based on such findings, of necessity, then, are based upon the evidence received pursuant to the procedure described above. Because of the absence of Company counsel I have examined the evidence with extreme care. The fact that such evidence was uncontradicted did not necessarily mean that it was accepted. Some has been rejected. In evaluating such evidence I have done all I could, within the limitations of the procedure described, to apply such tests and criteria as are applied in courts generally. But the evaluation was of necessity handicapped by the absence of Company counsel, especially, of course, since I had no knowledge of the facts in these cases until evidence was received concerning them."[94]

As Arbitrator Jaffee stated, evaluation of one party's testimony is "of necessity handicapped" by the absence of the other party. This

[92] 43 LA 1294. For statistics regarding the number of ex parte proceedings under Rule 27, see "Procedural Aspects of Labor-Management Arbitration," 28 LA 933, 937 (1954 statistics).

[93] FMCS Regulations. §1404.8.

[94] Aleo Mfg. Co., 15 LA 715, 721 (1950). For another example as to how Arbitrator Jaffee has proceeded ex parte see C & D Batteries, Inc., 31 LA 272, 273–274 (1958), where the defaulting union said it would not honor a default award. It changed heart, however, and participated in a subsequent hearing as to the interpretation of the award. C & D Batteries, Inc., 32 LA 589, 591 (Jaffee, 1959).

handicap possibly could be diminished by making the evidence and argument submitted at the hearing subsequently available to the other party (unless some other procedure is specified by statute or the collective agreement) for its comments thereon within a reasonable time.[95]

Court Enforcement of Default Awards

Court enforcement of default awards may depend upon a variety of factors, such as how the arbitration tribunal was selected, due process considerations, and the applicable law.

Obviously, no arbitration tribunal is entitled to issue a binding decision, ex parte or otherwise, unless the tribunal has been duly vested with jurisdiction over the dispute. Some possible methods for vesting an arbitration tribunal with jurisdiction are (1) joint action by the parties specifically designating the tribunal for a case, a group of cases, or as permanent arbitrator of stated tenure; (2) collective agreement provisions for the designation of the arbitration tribunal, as by specifying the procedures of some appointing agency; or (3) designation of an arbitration tribunal pursuant to court decree compelling arbitration. In proper circumstances a tribunal established by any of these methods can issue enforceable default awards under federal law and under modern arbitration statutes.[96] However, there are ramifications as to method number two.

If the collective agreement specifies a procedure for designation of the arbitration tribunal without the participation of both parties, a tribunal so designated can issue an enforceable default award. For instance, a default award was enforced in an action under LMRA §301 where the neutral was appointed by the Maine State Board of Conciliation and Arbitration under a procedure specified by the collective agreement for use in the event the parties failed to agree upon a neutral within ten days—the court emphasized that the arbitra-

---

[95] A similar approach has been suggested by a group of arbitrators in the Philadelphia area. See Guides For Labor Arbitration 5–6 (Univ. of Pa. Press, 1953).

[96] As to these areas of law and the common law, and as to the applicable law, see Chapter 2. A court enforced a default award by a tribunal established by method number one in Retail Clerks v. Seattle Department Stores Ass'n., 62 LRRM 2706 (USDC Wash., 1966), and in Simons v. New York Herald Tribune, 26 LA 282 (N.Y. Sup. Ct., 1956). Also see Teamsters Union v. Purity Food Co., 14 LA 934 (Conn. Super. Ct., 1950). The default award of a tribunal established by method number three was enforced in Teamsters Local Unions v. Braswell Motor Freight Lines, 392 F.2d 1 (CA 5, 1968). Cases on method number two are cited below.

tion tribunal was designated according to the procedure upon which the parties had agreed in their contract.[97] However, where the agreement makes no provision for designating an arbitration tribunal without the participation of both parties, or where the agreement expressly requires cooperation by both parties, a court may refuse to enforce the default award of an arbitration tribunal designated without the cooperation of both parties.[98]

Furthermore, it is unlikely that a default award even by a properly established tribunal will be upheld by a court if the absent party was not given adequate notice or if other due process considerations were not satisfied.[99] Court enforcement will also be unavailable if the case is covered by the common law rule that executory agreements to arbitrate are unenforceable, but in an increasingly large number of cases that rule will have been displaced by more modern state law or by the federal law under LMRA §301.[100]

Regardless of whether a given default award is legally enforceable, another important consideration lies in the possiblity that the

---

[97] Meat Cutters v. Penobscot Poultry Co., 200 F.Supp. 879, 49 LRRM 2241 (USDC Maine, 1961), in which the court also observed that a party is not required to seek a court order to compel arbitration unless the contract specifies no procedure for designating the arbitrator without the participation of a defaulting party. For other cases in which default awards were enforced where the arbitrator was designated by a procedure specified in the collective agreement without cooperation by a defaulting party, see Steelworkers v. Danville Foundry Corp., 52 LRRM 2584 (USDC Pa., 1963), and Local 149, Boot Workers v. Faith Shoe Co., 49 LRRM 2424, 201 F.Supp. 234 (USDC Pa., 1962), in both of which cases AAA procedures were used as specified by the agreement.

[98] As in Fuller v. Pepsi-Cola Bottling Co., 63 LRRM 2220 (Ky. Ct. App., 1966), the court stating that the proper remedy of the party not in default was a suit to compel arbitration; in re Masters, Mates and Pilots, 52 LRRM 2392 (N.Y. Sup. Ct., 1963), with similar statement by the court. In two "pre-trilogy" cases the court held that it did not suffice that the neutral member of a tripartite board was designated by an appointing agency specified by the agreement (AAA in one case and FMCS in the other) where the defaulting party refused to appoint its member of the board as also specified by the agreement. Industrial Union v. Dunn Worsted Mills, Inc., 36 LRRM 2629 (USDC Rhode Island, 1955); Food Handlers Local 425 v. Pluss Poultry Inc., 43 LRRM 2090 (CA 8, 1958). In light of the "Trilogy" teachings, doubt has been expressed as to the soundness of these two decisions. See McDermott, "Arbitrability: the Courts Versus the Arbitrator," 23 Arb. J. 18, 31–35 (1968); Smith, "Arbitrators and Arbitrability," Labor Arbitration and Industrial Change 75, 78–82 (BNA Incorporated, 1963), both authors discussing court enforcement of awards rendered in ex parte proceedings.

[99] See Farkach v. Brach, 52 LRRM 2334 (N.Y. Sup. Ct., 1963); Goldman Bros., 28 LA 589 (N.Y. Sup. Ct., 1957).

[100] See Chapter 2. Also see B. Z. Wesche Electric Co., 20 LA 216 (Sembower, 1953), which accurately forecast later developments.

award may impose a moral obligation on the losing party and may give the other party a significant moral and psychological victory.

Withdrawal of Cases From Arbitration

Related to the matter of default awards is the withdrawal of the case from arbitration. While the parties may withdraw a case through agreement, we have observed the rendition of default awards in some cases wherein the charged party refused to participate in the hearing.[101] But it is not always the charged party who avoids the case. Sometimes the aggrieved party seeks to withdraw it from arbitration.

It has been suggested that the complainant usually may withdraw the case at any point prior to the arbitration hearing, but that after the hearing has commenced he may not withdraw the case over the objection of the other party unless permitted by the arbitrator.[102] Of course, the collective agreement will govern the matter of withdrawal if it deals with it. Agreement provisions concerning withdrawal of cases after reaching arbitration are in fact fairly common, generally permitting withdrawal only by mutual consent of the parties.[103]

From a strictly legal standpoint, the common law rule that either party may withdraw from arbitration at any time prior to issuance of an award will not apply if the case is covered by the federal law or if the particular state has modified the common law rule.[104]

---

[101] See preceding topic.

[102] See Guides For Labor Arbitration 6 (Univ. of Pa. Press, 1953). For similar views, see Discussion Panel, "Procedural Problems in the Conduct of Arbitration Hearings," Labor Arbitration—Perspectives and Problems 1, 22–23 (BNA Incorporated, 1964). For court decisions holding that the complainant may not withdraw from arbitration proceedings, see Old Dutch Farms, Inc. v. Milk Drivers and Dairy Employees Union Local 584, 222 F.Supp. 125 (USDC, 1963); Simons v. New York Herald Tribune, 26 LA 282 (N.Y. Sup. Ct., 1956). In United Aircraft Corp. v. Canel Lodge 700, 77 LRRM 3167 (U.S.D.C., 1971), the court ordered arbitration at the employer's request where the union had requested arbitration but then had attempted to withdraw the case "without prejudice."

[103] Major Collective Bargaining Agreements: Arbitration Procedures 71 (U.S. Dept. of Labor Bull. No. 1425–6, 1966), also indicating variations as to the precise point after which mutual consent is required. Cases which have reached the umpire at Ford and at Chrysler may not be withdrawn without mutual consent. See discussion panel, "Procedural Problems in the Conduct of Arbitration Hearings," Labor Arbitration—Perspectives and Problems 1, 22 (BNA Incorporated, 1964); Wolff, Crane & Cole, "The Chrysler-UAW Umpire System," The Arbitrator and the Parties 111, 121 (BNA Incorporated, 1958).

[104] Thus a federal court and a state court denied the right of unilateral withdrawal in the "Old Dutch Farms" and "Simons" cases cited hereinabove.

Aside from legal or express contract considerations, the privilege of the complainant to withdraw the case from arbitration may depend upon the peculiar circumstances.[105] For example, a union which submitted an issue to arbitration but then learned that the company had not taken the action complained of was held under such circumstances to be entitled to withdraw the issue "without prejudice" prior to its consideration by the arbitrator.[106]

Arbitrator's Charges When Case Is Cancelled

It has been aptly observed by the Federal Mediation and Conciliation Service General Counsel (whose thoughts are equally applicable to cases not administered by the FMCS) that "A real problem for arbitrators today is the cancellation of a case after he has been selected and a date for hearing set."[107] While emphasizing that efforts by the parties to settle cases "should be seriously pursued right up to the time set for the hearing," that observer straightforwardly recognized that too many cases are scheduled for arbitration with little expectation that they will actually be heard:

"[FMCS] service is free. It is provided by the federal government to those who wish to use it. Accordingly, many companies and many unions have built our easy availability into their dispute-settling machinery and strategy. There is nothing like a threat—'we'll take you to court'—to persuade a recalcitrant party to settle on the courthouse steps. I'm afraid this threat is being used with some regularity. As a result, it is not too uncommon for us or the arbitrator to be notified that a case has been worked out at the eleventh hour—just prior to its scheduled hearing.

"This situation, which you must admit places a great burden on labor arbitrators, all of whom have scheduling problems just like we do, is recognized in our regulations."[108]

---

[105] For related discussion, see Chapter 5, subtopic titled "Waiver of Employee Rights or Signature Requirement" and topic titled "Grievance Adjustment by Individual Employees."

[106] Princeton Worsted Mills, 25 LA 587, 588 (Hill, 1955). Hess Oil & Chemical Corp., 51 LA 445, 448 (Gould, 1968), held that a demand for arbitration could be resubmitted after having been withdrawn where all contractual time limits were still met and where the contract did not deal expressly with withdrawal and resubmission of grievances.

[107] Address of April 8, 1969, by General Counsel Richard P. McLaughlin, titled "Labor Arbitration Today" and published in 70 LRR 428 (quotation from p. 430) under the title "Cost, Time, Training Factors in Labor Arbitration."

[108] Ibid, where he suggested that "perhaps a one-day fee" would be a fair administrative charge where the case is settled a short time before the scheduled hearing date, and where he also suggested that arbitrators give parties advance notice as the arbitrator's policy concerning such charges.

The FMCS regulations as amended in 1968 provide in Section 1404.6(e):

> "The arbitrator is entitled to be compensated whenever he receives insufficient notice of settlement to enable him to rearrange his schedule of arbitration hearings or working hours. In other situations, when an arbitrator spends an unusually large amount of time in arranging or rearranging hearing dates, it may be appropriate for him to make an administrative charge to the parties in the event the case is settled before hearing."

Of course the arbitrator is equally inconvenienced regardless of whether the withdrawal or cancellation of a case could be anticipated by the parties from the outset. It is not surprising, then, that in many cases the arbitrator bills the parties where the arbitration is cancelled after a hearing date has been set.[109] However, in many instances his charges will not in any sense adequately recompense the arbitrator for the full loss of working time and inconvenience suffered by him.

Bilateral Arbitration of Trilateral Conflicts

Underlying some grievances are the conflicting interests of two different groups of employees represented by different unions. These are trilateral situations, with the employer in the middle. Usually the matter involves conflicting work-assignment claims, but not always.[110] Final resolution of trilateral conflicts will be greatly facilitated, of course, if all three affected parties agree to the use of one arbitration proceeding for that purpose. Too often, however, one of the unions rejects this procedure.

In *Carey v. Westinghouse* the U.S. Supreme Court held that the employer was required to arbitrate a work assignment jurisdictional dispute upon demand by only one of the unions. In so holding, the Court said:

> "To be sure, only one of the two unions involved in the controversy has moved the state courts to compel arbitration. So unless the other

---

[109] For statistics as to the practice of arbitrators in this regard, see 1964 and 1962 surveys of arbitration, reported in Proceedings of the 18th Annual Meeting of the National Academy of Arbitrators 243, 247–248 (BNA Incorporated, 1965); Labor Arbitration—Perspectives and Problems 292, 311 (BNA Incorporated, 1964).

[110] Conflicting seniority interests were involved, for instance, in American Sterilizer Co. v. Local 832, 67 LRRM 2894 (USDC Pa., 1968). Also see Associated Brewing Co., 40 LA 680, 682–683 (Kahn, 1963), where trilateral arbitration of a seniority dispute was arranged by all affected parties.

union intervenes, an adjudication of the arbiter might not put an end to the dispute. Yet the arbitration may as a practical matter end the controversy or put into movement forces that will resolve it."[111]

The dissenting opinion responded that the majority decision "not only permits but compels Westinghouse to arbitrate the dispute with only one of the two warring unions" and that this could not bring about a final resolution of the conflict.[112]

Where only one of two affected unions is a party to a pending arbitration proceeding, arbitrators are in disagreement as to whether the arbitrator may invite the second union to participate in the proceeding against the wishes of the union which filed the grievance.[113] Similarly, the efforts of the second union to intervene in the pending arbitration have produced varied results.[114]

Where the union which initiated the arbitration does not oppose its expansion into a trilateral proceeding, arbitrators likewise have had varying views as to whether the arbitrator should take steps beyond a mere invitation to induce the absent union to participate in the proceedings.[115]

---

[111] Carey v. Westinghouse Electric Corp., 84 S.Ct. 401, 406, 55 LRRM 2042 (1964).

[112] 84 S.Ct. at 410. That bilateral arbitration indeed may not resolve the conflict, see Radio Corp. of America, 43 LA 762, 764 (Dunau, 1964). The Supreme Court has indicated that an employer who is not a party to any agreement to arbitrate cannot be forced into a jurisdictional dispute arbitration proceeding agreed to by the disputing unions. The Court explained: "Although this Court has frequently approved an expansive role for private arbitration in the settlement of labor disputes, this enforcement of arbitration agreements and settlements has been predicated on the view that the parties have voluntarily bound themselves to such a mechanism at the bargaining table." NLRB v. Plasterers' Local Union No. 79, 92 S.Ct. 360, 370–371 (1971), in which decision the actual holding was that the employer has a right to participate in NLRB proceedings to determine jurisdictional disputes under Section 10(K) of the NLRA.

[113] Holding the arbitrator has no authority to extend an invitation to the second union, see Arbitrator Helbling in 51 LA 902, 903–905 (citing numerous articles dealing with the pros and cons of the question); Block in 46 LA 865, 868–870 (also citing articles and discussing Supreme Court decisions touching on the question); Koven in 44 LA 1049, 1052; Schedler in 41 LA 665, 666. Also see Lazarus in 42 LA 604, 606. Other arbitrators, however, have concluded that they could extend the invitation. See Lockheed-California Co., 49 LA 981, 985–987 (Francis E. Jones, 1967); Mayfair Markets, Inc., 42 LA 14, 21–24 (Edgar A. Jones, 1964).

[114] See Sinclair-Koppers Co., 52 LA 648, 651–652 (Leonard, 1968); Stardust Hotel, 50 LA 1186, 1188 (Edgar A. Jones, 1968).

[115] Compare Arbitrator R. W. Fleming in E. R. Wagner Co., 43 LA 210, 211–212 (1964), with Arbitrator Edgar A. Jones in National Steel & Shipbuilding Co., 40 LA 625, 630–631 and 40 LA 838, 840–842 (1963). Also see Bernstein,

In the special circumstances of one trilateral conflict the consolidation of pending but separate arbitration proceedings into one trilateral proceeding was required through court action under LMRA §301. Since each of the two unions had a bilateral arbitration pending with the employer, and since the arbitration clause in each of the two contracts was sufficiently broad to permit the employer to submit disputes to arbitration, the employer's motion to consolidate the two proceedings was granted in order to avoid duplication of effort and the possibility of conflicting awards.[116]

In the area of the Railway Labor Act, the U.S. Supreme Court has held that when a union brings a work assignment jurisdictional dispute to the National Railroad Adjustment Board, the Board must dispose of the entire dispute by joining the other union in the proceedings and by considering the contracts (and practices thereunder) of both unions.[117]

Continuances

Arbitrators may grant continuances or adjourn the hearing from time to time upon their own motion or upon joint request of the parties. Moreover, arbitrators do not hesitate to do so upon the application of only one party for good cause shown. Indeed, failure to grant a continuance for good cause may make the proceedings vulnerable to court challenge.[118]

The "good cause" showing is essential since, as Arbitrator David L. Cole has declared, if arbitration proceedings "are to have dignity

---

"Nudging and Shoving All Parties to a Jurisdictional Dispute Into Arbitration: The Dubious Procedure of National Steel," 78 Harv. L. Rev. 784 (1965); Jones, "On Nudging and Shoving the National Steel Arbitration Into a Dubious Procedure," 79 Harv. L. Rev. 327 (1965). In Marvel-Schebler Div., 54 LA 24, 28–30 (1969), Arbitrator Sembower directed the complaining union to arrange with the other union a schedule for hearing the work assignment dispute; he stated that if the other union fails to cooperate and the complaining union does not seek or get court enforcement of an arbitral interpleader, then a hearing on the merits shall proceed between the company and the complaining union and an award shall be issued.

[116] Columbia Broadcasting System, Inc. v. American Recording and Broadcasting Association, 414 F.2d 1326, 72 LRRM 2140 (CA 2, 1969).

[117] Transportation-Communication Employees Union v. Union Pacific Railroad Co., 385 U.S. 157, 63 LRRM 2481 (1966). Arbitrators have concluded that special boards established under the 1966 amendments to the Act similarly must act to dispose of the entire matter in jurisdictional dispute cases. Western Pacific Railroad Co., 50 LA 1013, 1015–1017 (Wyckoff, 1968); Southern Pacific Co., 49 LA 1052, 1054–1058 (Mann, 1967).

[118] See Chapter 2, topic titled "State Law."

and command respect, then no party to a dispute can be allowed to decide when, where and how the hearings are to be conducted."[119] Arbitrator Cole emphasized, however, that for "good cause" he would "always try to accommodate the parties and meet their convenience within reason."[120] In that case one continuance had been granted the absent party, whose request for another continuance was denied as not being for "good cause"; that party's absence from the hearing resulted in a default award.

Not infrequently continuances are requested because of the absence of witnesses. In such instances a continuance ordinarily will be granted, though opposed by the other party, if the arbitrator is convinced that the request for a continuance was made in good faith and that the absence of the witness was without fault on the part of the requesting party.[121]

If a continuance on the ground of absence of witnesses or evidence is requested after the hearing has commenced, in particular where the participants are numerous and have traveled long distances to attend the hearing or where it would otherwise be difficult to arrange a satisfactory time for reconvening the hearing, arbitrators sometimes use a procedure akin to that commonly used by courts. That is, no continuance will be granted upon the ground of absence of evidence (either documentary, witnesses, or otherwise) except upon a statement or affidavit showing the materiality of the evidence and also showing: (1) that due diligence has been exercised and the evidence still has been unavailable; (2) where the evidence is; (3) the probability of securing it within a reasonable time; and (4) that the party making the statement or affidavit believes the evidence to be true. After this is submitted, the opposing party still may avoid a continuance by agreeing to accept the evidentiary facts alleged in the statement or affidavit as having been proved for purposes of the case. Then, too, in arbitration it is sometimes simply agreed that absent evidence may be submitted within a stated time after the hearing (if testimony, in the form of an affidavit or deposition). The opposing party is then given a reasonable opportunity to reply.

In the event the submission or other agreement specifies time limits within which action must be taken, no continuance should be

---

[119] Textile Workers (CIO) v. Upholsterers' Union (AFL), 24 LA 529, 531 (1955).
[120] Ibid.
[121] For example, see Bethlehem Steel Co., 17 LA 676, 677 (Shipman, 1951).

granted which would overreach any applicable time limit (unless extended by agreement of the parties).

Split Hearings

In some cases the parties and the arbitrator agree that the hearing should be divided into two parts, the arbitrator to hear and rule upon some aspects of the case before completing the hearing as to other aspects. For instance, where an alleged contract violation, if established, would have involved possible losses by numerous employees whose individual factual situations were not identical, it was agreed that a decision on the proper interpretation of the contract would be reached "before taking further testimony upon the detailed rights and possible losses of each individual employee * * * because of the length of time which seemed likely to be consumed in testimony upon the individual situations, which time would prove to be wasted if the Board should hold that the Company had not breached the Agreement."[122]

Also, the arbitrator (often on his own) may rule upon some aspects of the case and refer other aspects back to the parties for further negotiations, to be heard and ruled upon ultimately by him only if negotiations fail.[123] Similarly, if an arbitrator concludes after the hearing that additional information is necessary to enable him to reach a decision, he might return the case to the parties for additional fact-finding.[124]

Use of Interim Award

Where the case is divided into phases, as in some of the above situations, the arbitrator may use what he calls an "Interim Award"

---

[122] Fruehauf Trailer Co., 19 LA 159, 160 (Spaulding, 1952). Similarly, Color Corp. of America, 25 LA 644, 651, 657 (Lennard, 1955). Also see Publishers' Association of New York City, 66-1 ARB ¶8284 (Turkus, 1966).

[123] See Arbitrator Kates in 52 LA 396, 403; Porter in 50 LA 33, 35; Jones in 48 LA 1304, 1305; Begley in 44 LA 1212, 1215; Garrett in 44 LA 168, 174–175; Valtin in 38 LA 1166, 1170; Dworkin in 37 LA 323, 330; Rohman in 36 LA 815, 820–822 (the case was returned to him in 36 LA 938); Marshall in 36 LA 71, 78; Shipman in 21 LA 387, 391.

[124] See Arbitrator Dybeck in 53 LA 1215, 1216; Griffin in 53 LA 453, 463–464; Garrett in 53 LA 40, 44; Rohman in 64-1 ARB ¶8209; Smith in 36 LA 1018, 1023; Seitz in 36 LA 86, 91; Warns in 27 LA 290, 293. Another possibility is that he will deny the grievance without prejudice, as in Jones & Laughlin Steel Corp., 23 LA 33, 37 (Cahn, 1954). Also see topic titled "Reopening the Hearing," below.

in disposing of the first phase and a "Supplemental Award" or "Final Award" in disposing of the later phase.[125]

From the legal standpoint, use of "interim" or "partial" awards may be subject to challenge under state law unless authorized by the parties.[126] It would seem, however, that any requirement of authorization might be waived by the parties if they proceed to the issuance of a final award without objection.[127]

Furthermore, if the federal law applies to the case there is some indication in a federal court decision that the arbitrator may have authority to utilize an interim award procedure even without agreement by both parties.[128]

Arbitrator's Express Retention of Jurisdiction

Sometimes the parties jointly request or stipulate the retention of jurisdiction by the arbitrator after issuance of his award, for use in the event the parties are unable to agree as to some specified matter

---

[125] See Arbitrator King in 48 LA 518, 524; Rohman in 64-1 ARB ¶8209; Warns in 27 LA 290, 293; Lennard in 25 LA 644, 651, 657; Shipman in 21 LA 387, 391. In Walker Bros., 41 LA 844, 856 (1963), Arbitrator Crawford issued an Interim Award on the disputed matter pending an NLRB determination of a related "unfair labor practice" issue, a Final Award to be issued after the NLRB decision would become available for study. In Greyhound Lines, Inc., 53 LA 464, 470 (Lennard, 1969), an interim award was issued pending a medical examination of grievant, the final award to depend upon the results of that examination.

[126] See discussion in Updegraff, Arbitration and Labor Relations 280–281 (The Bureau of National Affairs, Inc., 1970); Updegraff & McCoy, Arbitration of Labor Disputes, 1st Ed. p. 122 (1946), 2d Ed. p. 213 (1961). Also for related material, see Chapter 2, topic titled "State Law," and see topic titled "Clarification and Interpretation of Award," below.

[127] See Updegraff and McCoy citations, ibid.

[128] Local 246, ILGWU v. Evans Mfg. Co., 53 LRRM 2455, 40 LA 864 (CA 3, 1963), upholding an arbitrator's authority to issue an interim award directing the company to permit inspection of certain records by the union. The court compared the decision of the U.S. Supreme Court in United Steelworkers v. Enterprise Wheel & Car Corp., 80 S.Ct. 1358, 34 LA 569 (1960), which held that an award need not be set aside for incompleteness merely because the arbitrator neglected to calculate the amount of back pay due the grievant, the Supreme Court ordering that the award be returned to the parties for a determination of back pay by arbitration. For related material, see Chapter 2, topic titled "Federal Law." For subsequent instances in which a court utilized the *Enterprise Wheel* procedure where the parties could not agree on the amounts of back pay due, see Packinghouse & Dairy Workers v. Western Iowa Pork Company, 247 F.Supp. 663 (DC Iowa, 1965); Electric Specialty Co. v. IBEW, 222 F. Supp. 314 (DC Conn., 1963). Cf., IAM v. Aerojet-General Corporation, 263 F.Supp. 343 (DC Calif., 1966), in which the court concluded that a new grievance and arbitration under the collective agreement would be required for determination of the specific employees entitled to back pay under an award.

(such as the amount of damages or back pay, or even as to the appropriate remedy for contract violation).[129] Without indicating any request or stipulation by the parties, numerous arbitrators have stated an express reservation of jurisdiction in rendering their award, to be used if the parties are unable to agree as to the amount of back pay,[130] as to the damages or proper remedy for the contract violation,[131] as to which employees are entitled to payments under the award,[132] or for use if needed for the disposition of other problems which might arise in connection with the execution or implementation of the award.[133] In many of these instances the arbitrator fixed a time limit within which the matter might be returned to him by the unilateral action of a party.

In considering this subject it should be noted that from the strictly legal standpoint there may be some question of the effectiveness of an arbitrator's effort to reserve jurisdiction in light of the possible application of the doctrine that the arbitrator's power is ended in a given case when his award is issued.[134] More often this question

---

[129] See Arbitrator Roberts in 45 LA 929, 932; Wolff in 44 LA 944, 947; Tongue in 44 LA 475 at 475; Cohen in 43 LA 114, 115; Altieri in 41 LA 47, 52; Benewitz in 39 LA 14, 18–19; Wood in 38 LA 148, 149.

[130] See Arbitrator Sembower in 51 LA 582, 589; Jones in 51 LA 421, 428; Howlett in 49 LA 728, 731; Emery in 49 LA 403, 405; Erbs in 49 LA 229, 231; Lugar in 48 LA 463, 478; Davis in 48 LA 441, 445; Lee in 48 LA 353, 364; Bellman in 47 LA 899, 902; McKelvey in 45 LA 1034, 1039; Kabaker in 43 LA 159, 165; Maggs in 33 LA 694, 700.

[131] See Arbitrator Prasow in 50 LA 645, 657; Leonard in 47 LA 661, 666; Leach in 46 LA 897, 902; Anderson in 43 LA 65, 76; Scheiber in 42 LA 483, 490; Black in 42 LA 325, 327; Warns in 41 LA 905, 909; Seligson in 40 LA 540, 544; Shaughnessy in 39 LA 633, 636.

[132] Halle Bros. Co., 42 LA 705, 709 (Kabaker, 1964).

[133] Here a wide assortment of reasons for retaining jurisdiction have been stated by arbitrators. See Arbitrator Eaton in 53 LA 633, 637; Teple in 53 LA 334, 448 and in 52 LA 716, 723; Howlett in 52 LA 997, 1002; Koven in 52 LA 659, 663 and in 51 LA 1285, 1288; Sembower in 52 LA 268, 278; Rauch in. 49 LA 627, 630; Peck in 47 LA 739, 744; Marshall in 43 LA 1118, 1126 (retained jurisdiction used in 43 LA 1137); Seligson in 42 LA 902, 910; Sherman in 42 LA 683, 685; Seitz in 36 LA 86, 91.

[134] See topic on "Clarification or Interpretation of Award," below, and subtopic on "Use of Interim Award," above; Updegraff, Arbitration and Labor Relations 278, 281 (The Bureau of National Affairs, Inc., 1970); Updegraff & McCoy, Arbitration of Labor Disputes, 1st Ed. pp. 120, 123 (1946), 2d Ed. pp. 211, 213 (1961); Textron, Inc., 48 LA 1373, 1377 (Altrock, 1967); New Orleans Steamship Assn., 45 LA 1099, 1104 (Oppenheim, 1965). In Associated Transport, Inc., 50 LA 236, 239 (1968), Arbitrator Dunau advised the parties that the computation and distribution of damages, if the parties could not agree thereon, would "be subject to final and binding arbitration in accordance with the collective bargaining agreement." Arbitrator Seitz has expressed doubt that the "functus officio" doctrine applies to terminate the arbitrator's jurisdiction

is not reached, since under the more frequent practice the award is issued without any mention of reserving jurisdiction. Moreover, it has been observed that where the arbitrator does reserve jurisdiction it usually meets with the approval of the parties and no question is raised.[135]

Transcript of Hearing

A formal written record of the hearing is not always necessary. Use of a reporter appears to be the exception rather than the general practice.[136]

In simple cases the arbitrator can take adequate notes. Likewise, in cases involving contract interpretation only, there being no disputed facts, the arbitrator's notes and the parties' exhibits and/or briefs ordinarily make a transcript unnecessary. However, in complicated or lengthy cases stenographic records may be very helpful, if not indispensable; the transcript will aid not only the arbitrator in studying the case, but also the parties in preparing briefs.[137] The transcript may be

---

where he has issued only an interim or partial award, and has suggested that arbitrators should not hesitate to retain jurisdiction or delay the closing of hearings where the arbitrator believes his adjudicatory function cannot be responsibly discharged on the kind of presentation made by the parties; he added, however, that arbitrators retaining jurisdiction might be well advised to label their awards as interim or partial and in their accompanying opinion state the circumstances which justify a piecemeal approach to fulfillment of their duty. Seitz, "Problems of the Finality of Awards, or Functus Officio and All That," Labor Arbitration—Perspectives and Problems 165, 170–171, 174–175 (BNA Incorporated, 1964).

[135] Updegraff, Arbitration and Labor Relations 281 (The Bureau of National Affairs, Inc., 1970); Updegraff & McCoy, Arbitration of Labor Disputes, 1st Ed. p. 123 (1946), 2d Ed. pp. 213–214 (1961), where agreement by the parties for reservation of jurisdiction is recommended, however, to guard against a possible challenge. In Ohio Power Co., 45 LA 1039, 1049 (Leach, 1965), the company dissent questioned the right of the board to retain jurisdiction. American Arbitration Association's "Arbitration News," No. 8, 1966, published a letter from a union attorney urging that "the retention of jurisdiction is a procedure * * * that should be used only sparingly."

[136] See statistics reported in Proceedings of 18th Annual Meeting of National Academy of Arbitrators 245, 252 (BNA Incorporated, 1965); "Procedural Aspects of Labor-Management Arbitration," 28 LA 933, 937–938 (1954 statistics). For other discussions of transcripts, see Jaffee, "Battle Report: The Problem of Stenographic Records in Arbitration," 20 Arb. J. 97 (1965), not encouraging the ordinary use of reporters; Kagel, Anatomy of a Labor Arbitration 68–69 (BNA Incorporated, 1961), stating strong arguments in favor of using a reporter; Braden, "Problems in Labor Arbitration," 13 Missouri L. Rev. 143, 162 (1948).

[137] In Williams U.S. Super Market, 39 LA 558, 560 (Granoff, 1962), the arbitrator stated that his note taking "necessarily curtailed his desire to concentrate on observing witnesses' demeanor." In Gregory Galvanizing Metal Processing, Inc., 46 LA 102, 104 (Kates, 1966), a party's brief and the arbitrator's notes and recollection presented conflicting versions as to testimony given at the hearing—the arbitrator relied upon his notes and recollection.

invaluable in any court review of the arbitration proceedings.[138] It is said that the palest ink is more accurate than the most retentive memory.

Whether the expense and additional time involved in use of a transcript are justified depends upon the case. Only the parties singly or together can decide. Ordinarily, a reporter will be used if either party so desires.[139] The parties may have the hearing recorded, with the understanding that if the arbitrator finds need for all or portions of the record, it shall be transcribed.[140]

The sharing of the cost of any transcript is a matter for the parties to determine. The cost frequently is shared equally.[141] Each party pays for extra copies it orders. Ordinarily a party not agreeing to use of a transcript and not ordering a copy is not required to share its cost.[142] It has been suggested that otherwise, if sharing of cost is mandatory, "one side may be obliged to curtail its testimony in the interests of economy, while the other might be inclined to prolong the case in order to discourage future arbitration proceedings."[143] One means of mitigating expenses is for one party to provide stenographic services or a tape recorder, in lieu of a formal transcript, to record substantially what transpires.[144] At least one arbitrator has himself recorded the entire proceedings on tape (in addition to taking notes) where no official reporter was being used.[145]

Obviously, the bulk of the transcript will be composed of the opening statements, if any; the testimony of the witnesses; and closing

---

[138] See In re Ruppert, 26 LA 283, 284 (N.Y. Sup. Ct., 1956).

[139] As under American Arbitration Association Rule 21. 43 LA 1294.

[140] American Potash & Chemical Corp., 17 LA 364, 370 (Grant, 1951).

[141] As in Building Owners & Managers Assn. of San Francisco, 22 LA 226, 227 (Ross, 1954); Food Employers Council, 20 LA 724, 725 (Van de Water, 1953). Equal sharing for most cases has been advocated by Updegraff, "Preparing for Arbitration," 22 LA 889, 890. For some indication of transcript costs, see Fleming, The Labor Arbitration Process 48–49 (Univ. of Ill. Press, 1965).

[142] Cleveland Pneumatic Tool Co., 42 LA 722, 727–729 (Dworkin, 1964); Stenzor v. Leon, 24 LA 306, 309 (Calif. Dist. Ct. App., 1955); Mutual Telephone Co., 19 LA 270, 271 (Roberts, 1952). Also see FMCS Regulations, §1404.12; AAA Rules 21 and 24, 43 LA 1294, 1296.

[143] Guides For Labor Arbitration 2 (Univ. of Pa. Press, 1953), authored by a group of Philadelphia area arbitrators.

[144] Moog Industries, Inc., 15 LA 676, 677 (Klamon, 1950). Similarly, see Arbitrator Gibson in 49 LA 1115 at 1115; Roberts in 44 LA 51, 52. Of course such a record probably will not be accepted by the arbitrator as an official record unless both parties agree to such use. See discussion in "Procedural Problems in the Conduct of Arbitration Hearings," Labor Arbitration—Perspectives and Problems 1, 31 (BNA Incorporated, 1964).

[145] Mobil Oil Co., 46 LA 140 at 140 (Hebert, 1966).

arguments, if any. Certain other matters, however, should be included in the record so the transcript will reflect a complete picture of the case. Thus, the arbitrator or tribunal clerk will open the hearing by putting such information as the following into the record:

a) Names of the parties;

b) If there is a special agreement, submission, or stipulation for arbitration, identify it by date and read it into the record (the latter may be done by handing a copy to the reporter with instructions that it be written into the record at that point);

c) The date, hour, and place of the hearing;

d) The name of the arbitrator or arbitrators, and how selected (as by agreement of the parties, appointment by a neutral agency, etc.);

e) Name of the Chairman, if it is an arbitration board (the Chairman is ordinarily selected by the board in executive session immediately prior to opening the hearing—the manner in which the Chairman was designated should be indicated in the record);

f) Announcement of appearances for the parties, that is, the attorneys or other representatives who are to present the case for the parties (state the name, title, and address of each person and state the party for whom he appears—all of this information may be written on a sheet of paper to be handed to the reporter for inclusion in the record, or it may be stated orally by the parties);

g) Name of the reporter;

h) Hours for the hearing, if it is likely to require several days;

i) Any other material information, especially such items as fact stipulations.

After the above information has been read into the record the hearing generally proceeds to the opening statements and on to the introduction of evidence.

In order to avoid cluttering the record, the arbitrator or parties may go "off the record" for comment or discussion which promises to be not material to the record, or for matter on which the spokesman desires not to be committed. It may be then decided that any such matter or any understanding growing out of the discussion should be placed in the record; the hearing would then go "on the record" for this purpose and for continuing with the introduction of evidence.

Both delay and errors in preparation of the transcript can be avoided if parties who intend to read or quote lengthy passages at the hearing furnish extra copies of the material for use by the reporter.[146]

Where witnesses are to be sworn, each witness may be sworn individually immediately prior to his initial testimony, or all persons scheduled to testify may be sworn (if present) when the hearing is opened. Under the latter procedure the reporter should indicate, at the outset of the testimony of each witness, that the witness has been sworn.

Exhibits

Even where no reporter is used, a portion of the evidence will ordinarily be presented and preserved in written form as exhibits. Each party may submit its own exhibits and the parties may also submit exhibits jointly.[147]

Sound observations concerning the use of exhibits have come from Arbitrator Samuel H. Jaffee, who has suggested that parties should "put as much of the evidence as possible in black and white, as simply and plainly and logically as possible," since visible evidence "is often far more persuasive than evidence which one hears and may forget."[148] He also noted that:

> "This is usually the best way of 'educating' an arbitrator. Moreover, it enables the arbitrator to understand the case more quickly and to write the decision faster, and this should reduce arbitration costs."[149]

In offering an exhibit as evidence a party must be prepared to use a witness to identify the exhibit and to put in enough evidence to show its accuracy, in the event that the other party does not indicate a willingness to accept the exhibit for what it purports to be.[150]

Exhibits customarily are introduced into evidence at the point of the hearing where the data in the exhibit is most relevant. While the parties may number their exhibits in advance, the more common

---

[146] For other suggestions for more effective use of the reporter, see Jaffee, "Battle Report: The Problem of Stenographic Records in Arbitration," 20 Arb. J. 97 (1965).

[147] As in Republic Steel Corp., 16 LA 618 (Selekman, 1951), where 19 exhibits were submitted—10 jointly, 1 by the union, and 8 by the company.

[148] Jaffee, "Need for Exhibits in Labor Arbitration," 15 Arb. J. 203, 205 (1960).

[149] Ibid.

[150] Ibid.

practice is to number them when introduced into evidence since the parties do not always know in advance the order in which their exhibits will be submitted. Thus, exhibits generally are numbered in numerical or alphabetical order of introduction. A separate series is used for each party, as well as for joint exhibits. The first exhibit submitted by the company would be identified as Company Ex. #1, the next as Company Ex. #2, and so on. The union's exhibits would be identified as Union Ex. #1, and so on. To avoid confusion parties may choose to use alphabetical designations, A, B, C, etc., to identify one party's exhibits, and to use numbers 1, 2, 3, etc., to identify the other party's exhibits.

Several copies of each exhibit should be prepared in advance to insure a copy for each party, one for personal use by the arbitrator during the hearing, and a copy to be handed to the reporter, if one is used, to be incorporated by reference into the record.

Oath by Arbitrator and Witnesses

Acceptable practice regarding the arbitrator's oath of office and the swearing of witnesses is effectively summarized by American Arbitration Association Rule 24, which provides:

> "Oaths—Before proceeding with the first hearing, each Arbitrator may take an Oath of Office, and if required by law, shall do so. The Arbitrator may, in his discretion, require witnesses to testify under oath administered by any duly qualified person, or if required by law or demanded by either party, shall do so."

Even where the arbitrator's oath is required by statute (it is not required under the common law) it ordinarily may be waived by the parties, and very often is.[151] When the oath of office is taken, the arbitrator swears that he will faithfully and fairly hear and examine the matters in controversy and make a just award according to the best of his understanding.[152] Under the practice of some ap-

---

[151] Even without an express waiver, one will be implied by participating in the hearing without objection. Robinson v. Navajo Freight Lines, 49 LRRM 3048, 38 LA 321 (N.M. Sup. Ct., 1962). For statistics on extent of use of arbitrator's oath, see "Procedural Aspects of Labor-Management Arbitration," 28 LA 933, 936 (1954 statistics).

[152] "Procedural Aspects of Labor-Management Arbitration," ibid; Code of Ethics and Procedural Standards, Part II, §3, 15 LA 961, 964.

pointing agencies the oath of office is written into the instrument of appointment and is affirmed by the arbitrator by signing the instrument in accepting the case.[153]

In adversary proceedings such as arbitration the swearing of witnesses is often preferred, whether required by statute or not (it is not required under the common law). In swearing witnesses, the arbitrator or hearing clerk asks the witness if he solemnly swears that the testimony he is about to give in the case is the truth, the whole truth, and nothing but the truth, so help him God. The witness, with right hand raised, answers, "I do."[154]

Participation by Arbitrator in Hearing

Arbitrators should be informed as fully as possible about the disputes they are to resolve. Accordingly, the arbitrator must feel free to participate personally in the hearing by asking questions, seeking information, and exploring all angles to the extent reasonably necessary to satisfy himself that he has in fact been informed as fully as possible. Arbitrator Harry Shulman emphasized, in this regard, that the arbitrator "should be satisfied that he knows enough to be able to decide the case" and that he "cannot simply sit back and judge a debate. He must seek to inform himself as fully as possible and encourage the parties to provide him with the information."[155]

Similarly, it has been emphasized that while the arbitrator obviously should not take sides, he must be free to ask questions and to explore all angles which he deems necessary to a full understanding

---

[153] See "Procedural Aspects of Labor-Management Arbitration," 28 LA 933, 936 (1957).

[154] Regarding the procedural point at which witnesses are sworn, see topic on "Transcript of Hearing," above. In Aristocrat Travel Products, Inc., 52 LA 314, 316–317 (Koven, 1968), it was held that an employee could be discharged for giving perjured testimony in a prior case involving the earlier discharge of the employee.

[155] Shulman, "Reason, Contract, and Law in Labor Relations," 68 Harv. L. Rev. 999, 1017–1018 (1955), also reported in Management Rights and the Arbitration Process 169, 190–191 (BNA Incorporated, 1957). If the arbitrator does not take the initiative where necessary to adequately explore relevant aspects at the hearing, he may later feel some regret for not having done so. See Halstead Metal Products, Inc., 49 LA 325, 331 (Wagner, 1967). Even where an arbitrator felt constrained to ask some "pointed questions" in an effort to bring out the facts more fully, he later expressed doubt that the whole truth ever came out at the hearing. Gulf Oil Corp., 36 LA 207, 209–210 (Reid, 1960).

of the case "even if they have not occurred to either one or both of the parties."[156]

It has been observed that:

"Where testimony is controverted, it is quite proper for the Arbitrator to take the initiative, if necessary, in reconciling apparent contradictions, or in seeking insight into the motives of those whose testimony is at odds. It is the parties' primary responsibility to present facts and to rebut contrary testimony, but the Arbitrator may also use his office to elicit information or to secure insights where, in his opinion, such procedure is made necessary by the critical nature of the controverted testimony."[157]

Likewise, arbitrators are justified in making an independent study of the entire collective agreement to insure consideration of all provisions that might be relevant to the disposition of the case.[158]

Order of Presenting Case

There is no rigid order in which the parties must present their case in arbitration.[159] The party asserting a claim usually presents its case first, or at least a preliminary or introductory case, but this practice may not be followed where the nature of the issue makes a different procedure preferable. In the latter regard, American Arbitration Association Rule 26 provides:

"The Arbitrator may, in his discretion, vary the normal procedure under which the initiating party first presents his claim, but in any case shall afford full and equal opportunity to all parties for presentation of relevant proofs."[160]

---

[156] Guides For Labor Arbitration 11–12 (Univ. of Pa. Press, 1953). Similarly, see Part II, §4 of Code of Ethics and Procedural Standards for Labor-Management Arbitration, 15 LA 961, 964. Also see Eaton, "Labor Arbitration in the San Francisco Bay Area," 48 LA 1381, 1382–1383 (1967); "Procedural Problems in the Conduct of Arbitration Hearings: A Discussion," Labor Arbitration—Perspectives and Problems 1, 12–13 (BNA Incorporated, 1964); Aaron, "Some Procedural Problems in Arbitration," 10 Vanderbilt L. Rev. 733, 745 (1957).
[157] Guides for Labor Arbitration, id. at 8. For examples of how an arbitrator might participate in the interrogation of a witness, see Allied Chemical Corp., 49 LA 773, 778–780 (Davey, 1967); Booth Newspapers, Inc., 43 LA 785, 789–790 (Platt, 1964).
[158] See Arbitrator Erbs in 50 LA 744, 750; Moore in 37 LA 119, 121; Boles in 22 LA 826, 828. Arbitrator Maxwell Copelof vigorously defended this practice against the charge that it helped the other party make out its case in West Virginia Pulp & Paper Co., 20 LA 385, 391–393 (1953).
[159] For a related discussion, see Chapter 8, topic titled "Burden of Proof."
[160] 43 LA 1292, 1294.

Logically, "the determination of the order of presentation in an arbitration case should depend exclusively on how the facts can best be developed in an orderly way."[161] If the arbitrator can see at the outset of a hearing that one of the parties possesses the basic facts of the case and that the case of the other party will consist primarily of a rebuttal, the arbitrator upon his own initiative or at the request of a party may suggest or require that the party in possession of the basic facts present its case first. This is not uncommon, for instance, in discharge and discipline cases.[162]

After both parties have presented their basic case, each party in turn will be given full opportunity to present its rebuttal case. Indeed, the hearing will not be adjourned until each party has nothing further to add.[163]

Opening Statements and Closing Arguments

Opening statements are brief, generalized statements in clear language designed to acquaint the arbitrator with each party's view of what the dispute is about and what the party expects to prove by its evidence.[164] Occasionally a party will prepare its opening statement

---

[161] Aaron, "Some Procedural Problems in Arbitration," 10 Vanderbilt L. Rev. 733, 739 (1957).

[162] See Aaron, id. at 739–740; Eaton, "Labor Arbitration in the San Francisco Area," 48 LA 1381, 1385 (1967); Douglas Aircraft Co., 28 LA 198, 202–203 (Jones, 1957); Armstrong Cork Co., 18 LA 651 at 651 (Pigors, 1952). But see Latrobe Steel Co., 38 LA 729, 734 (Wood, 1962); Sealtest Dairy Products Co., 35 LA 205, 208–209 (1960). A related matter involves the efforts of a union to call a foreman as its first witness or of a company similarly to call a union representative. See discussion in "Procedural Problems in the Conduct of Arbitration Hearings," Labor Arbitration—Perspectives and Problems 1, 3–4 (BNA Incorporated, 1964). Stating that the arbitrator has the authority to regulate the proceedings and the order of proof, a court held that an arbitrator's refusal to uphold the employer's attempt to call the grievant in a discharge case as its first witness was not basis for refusing to enforce an award reinstating the grievant. Local 560, I.B.T. v. Eazor Express, Inc., 65 LRRM 2647 (N.J. Superior Ct., 1967), where the union had made it clear that it would call the grievant and that the employer would not have to limit its cross-examination to the scope of the union's direct examination. For related discussion, see Chapter 8, subtopic titled "Use of Adverse Witnesses."

[163] The arbitrator should not restrict or limit the rebuttal case of either party. In Harvey Aluminum, Inc. v. Steelworkers, 67 LRRM 2580 (USDC Calif., 1967), an award was vacated because of the arbitrator's refusal to consider certain testimony on the grounds that it should have been presented as part of the employer's case-in-chief and was not proper rebuttal; the employer had the right to assume that the arbitrator would permit the presentation of all material evidence before closing the hearing.

[164] For more extensive comment as to what might be included in opening statements, see Roberts & Dash, "How to Get Better Results From Labor-Management Arbitration," 22 Arb. J. 1, 3, 8–9 (1967).

in written form, with copies to be handed to the arbitrator and the other party. Even when this is done, however, the statement will be presented orally for purposes of emphasis and more effective communication.

Use of opening statements is ordinarily optional with the parties, but often the arbitrator specifically requests that each party make one.[165]

Sometimes both parties make opening statements at the outset of the hearing, before any evidence is introduced by either party. This is especially helpful to the arbitrator since it enables him to grasp more quickly what the dispute is about. Another possibility is that each party will make its opening statement immediately prior to presenting its initial evidence; thus, one party will have made its opening statement and presented its evidence before the other party makes its opening statement. Ordinarily the arbitrator will follow whatever procedure the parties desire, unless he is convinced that some particular procedure is essential for proper presentation of the case.

By making closing arguments after all the evidence of both parties has been presented, the parties

"can render a real service to the arbitrator as well as to themselves by carefully analyzing and synthesizing the important aspects of the case, emphasizing the facts they feel they have proved and placing them in proper relation to the ultimate conclusion at which they seek to persuade the arbitrator to arrive."[166]

The arbitrator will always permit the parties to make closing arguments (though he may limit the amount of time), and he sometimes requests specifically that they do so. Closing arguments and post-hearing briefs sometimes serve much the same purpose, and while the parties sometimes choose to use both they more frequently choose to use either one or the other.[167]

Examining Witnesses

The manner in which witnesses are used, both in direct and cross-examination, may either promote or impede a party's case and it will also affect the character of the arbitration proceeding generally.

---

[165] As in Inland Container Corp., 28 LA 312 at 312 (Ferguson, 1957).
[166] Howard, "Informing the Arbitrator," 10 Vanderbilt L. Rev. 771, 786–787 (1957).
[167] As in William Brooks Shoe Co., 19 LA 65, 67 (Dworkin, 1952).

In this regard, an excellent guide has been offered by Arbitrator Clarence M. Updegraff:

> "Prove your case by your own witnesses. Do not try to establish it by evidence gleaned from people put on the stand by your opponent. They are there to oppose you, not to help you.

> "If you cross-examine the other parties' witnesses, *make it short.* Do not unduly prolong cross-examination in attempts to get damaging admissions. The more questions you ask on cross-examination, the more opportunity you give a hostile witness to repeat the adverse testimony he came to give. Choose most carefully the inquiries you make of such parties. Make them as few as possible.

> "Each party has the right to ask leading questions [so worded as to suggest an answer] when cross-examining hostile witnesses. Each party should save time by asking its own witnesses leading questions, excepting at points where disputed facts are involved. Testimony on controverted matters, should be brought out by questions which do not suggest the answer, if possible."[168]

In contrast to the question-answer method of examining witnesses, it is sometimes best to request that one's own witness tell his story in his own way. Obviously, the latter method is not advisable for the examination or cross-examination of adverse witnesses.

Objections to Evidence

Each party is entitled to object when it believes the other party is seeking to introduce improper evidence or argument at the arbitration hearing. Such objections, when based upon some plausible grounds, can serve a useful function even if overruled, for the arbitrator will have been cautioned to examine the challenged evidence or argument more closely before giving it weight. A party is also entitled to object to evidence he considers irrelevant, for the record should not be burdened with a mass of material having little or no bearing on the issue.

However, objections which have no plausible basis, and those which are repetitious, should be avoided, as has been advised by Arbitrator Clarence M. Updegraff:

> "Do not make captious, whimsical or unnecessary objections to testimony or arguments of the other party. Such interruptions are likely to waste time and confuse issues. The arbitrator, no doubt, will realize without having the matter expressly mentioned more than once, when

---

[168] Updegraff, "Preparation for Arbitration," 22 LA 889, 890 (1954).

he is hearing weak testimony such as hearsay and immaterial statements."[169]

Plant Visits by Arbitrator

Sometimes the arbitrator's understanding of the case can be greatly improved if he personally visits the physical site directly involved in the dispute. Indeed, in some types of cases, such as job evaluation, a plant tour is virtually indispensable.[170]

The values of a plant visit have been elaborated by Arbitrator William E. Simkin:

"The eye is better than the ear in many aspects of disputes, or at least is a valuable supplement to oral or written evidence. A plant visit is a simple device by which the arbitrator can secure a better understanding of the background of a case. In some instances a plant visit either before or during the hearing will serve to avoid voluminous testimony. The award may be more realistic and therefore acceptable because the plant visit fills part of the gap in the arbitrator's knowledge."[171]

Frequently the parties suggest a plant visit by the arbitrator. However, the arbitrator may suggest one if he feels it essential. For instance, Arbitrator Paul Prasow sought and obtained permission from the parties to make first-hand observations where evidence submitted at the hearing failed to reveal clearly the distinction between two job classifications involved in the dispute; as a result of the plant visit much of the confusion caused by the apparently conflicting contentions of the parties was eliminated.[172]

The arbitrator has discretionary authority to make plant visits in cases governed by American Arbitration Association Rule 30, which provides:

"Whenever the Arbitrator deems it necessary, he may make an inspection in connection with the subject matter of the dispute after written notice to the parties who may, if they so desire, be present at such inspection."[173]

---

[169] Updegraff, "Preparation for Arbitration," 22 LA 889, 890 (1954). For another statement as to use of objections in arbitration, see Kagel, Anatomy of a Labor Arbitration 98 (BNA Incorporated, 1961).

[170] For some indication of the practical significance of actually viewing the job in its setting, see Arbitrator Rubin in 47 LA 577, 579; Bothwell in 42 LA 145, 148; Forrester in 16 LA 264, 266.

[171] Simkin, Acceptability as a Factor in Arbitration Under an Existing Agreement 24 (Univ. of Pa. Press, 1952).

[172] Procter & Gamble Mfg. Co., 1 LA 313, 314 (1945).

[173] 43 LA 1292, 1295.

Unless the parties are arbitrating under a provision such as Rule 30, or unless an applicable statute gives the arbitrator similar authority, plant visits by the arbitrator may be deemed improper unless consented to by both parties.[174]

Settlements at Arbitration Stage

Sometimes disputes are settled by the parties after arbitration has been initiated. Some settlements occur prior to the arbitration hearing, and possiblities of settlement may be even stronger after the hearing is commenced.[175] The parties sometimes see the dispute in new light during arbitration, especially upon participating at the hearing. Umpire Harry H. Platt has observed in this regard:

> "Under a system in which grievances are heard by the umpire *de novo* and in the presence of all interested parties to the controversy, it is not unusual for the hearing to disclose an underlying misunderstanding that may have blocked an earlier settlement or uncover new thoughts, new facts, and occasionally new areas of agreement that provide real opportunities for constructive settlements. At Ford, these opportunities are usually not ignored, even though it may be thought that this tends to encourage appeals to the umpire."[176]

Likewise, other parties and arbitrators do not ignore real possibilities for constructive settlements. Some of the available procedures for accommodating further negotiations between the parties include the following:

a) The hearing may be recessed for direct negotiations at the request of the parties or at the arbitrator's suggestion, if accepted by the parties.[177]

---

[174] See Justin, "Arbitration: Proving Your Case," 10 LA 955, 964 (1948); Berizzi Co. v. Krausz, 146 N.E. 436, 239 N.Y. 315, 319–320 (N.Y. Ct. App., 1925).

[175] For related material, see "Extent of Permissible Deviation From Pre-Arbitral Discussion of Case," above, and "Arbitrator's Charges When Case Is Cancelled," also above.

[176] Comments of Umpire Platt in The Arbitrator and the Parties 141, 144 (BNA Incorporated, 1958), in response to statement by the Chairman of the Chrysler Appeal Board, with basically appellate jurisdiction, that cases were not often referred back to the parties for settlement efforts after reaching the Impartial Chairman, but that many cases had been settled by the pre-arbitral meetings of the Appeal Board. See "The Chrysler-UAW Umpire System," id. at 111, 124, 133.

[177] For discussion of this and other settlement procedures, see Simkin, Acceptability as a Factor in Arbitration Under an Existing Agreement 57–65 (Univ. of Pa. Press, 1952).

b) The hearing may be closed with the understanding that the award will be delayed pending negotiations by the parties for a specified time, an award to be issued thereafter only if no settlement is reached.[178]

c) It may be agreed that the arbitrator will rule or comment by an interim decision upon some aspects of the case, referring the unresolved matters back to the parties for further negotiations, to be ruled upon ultimately in a supplemental award by the arbitrator only if the negotiations fail.[179]

Whatever procedure is used, it should be undertaken only by sanction of the parties. If they show no interest in an arbitrator's suggestion for further negotiations he should not attempt to force acceptance.[180] Concededly, an arbitrator

"should not undertake to induce a settlement of the dispute against the wishes of either party. If, however, an atmosphere is created or the issues are so simplified or reduced as to lead to a voluntary settlement by the parties, a function of his office has been fulfilled."[181]

Ordinarily the settlement negotiations themselves are carried on only by the parties, without participation by the arbitrator. However, in some situations the arbitrator may perform a mediation role. Attempts at mediation by ad hoc arbitrators are certainly not rare,[182] and mediation by permanent arbitrators has long been a fairly common practice.[183]

Putting Settlement in Form of Award

When parties settle their dispute during the course of arbitration they often request that the arbitrator set forth the terms of the settle-

---

[178] See Victor Chemical Works, 22 LA 71, 72 (Dworet, 1953), where the parties requested this procedure.

[179] See topic titled "Split Hearings," above.

[180] See Instant Milk Co., 24 LA 756, 758 (Anderson, 1955).

[181] Code of Ethics and Procedural Standards for Labor-Management Arbitration, Part I, §5, 15 LA 961, 963.

[182] See surveys reported in Proceedings of 18th Annual Meeting of National Academy of Arbitrators 243, 245, 252 (BNA Incorporated, 1965); Labor Arbitration—Perspectives and Problems 292, 296, 314 (BNA Incorporated, 1964), indicating that such attempts often are successful. For some arbitral efforts toward a settlement, see Arbitrator Platt in 50 LA 1103, 1104 (interests dispute); Aaron in 15 LA 162, 168 (rights dispute). In Fairbanks, Morse & Co., 32 LA 278, 281 (1959), Arbitrator Howlett resisted the temptation to try mediation, but he recalled Arbitrator Platt's observation that arbitrators are criticized both for having a tendency to mediate and for seldom trying to mediate.

[183] For full discussion of mediation by permanent arbitrators, and citation of articles discussing whether or in what circumstances ad hoc arbitrators should undertake to mediate a settlement, see Chapter 4, topic titled "Mediation by Permanent Arbitrators."

ment in an award. In making such request, they "should give the arbitrator a full explanation of the reasons therefor in order that he may judge whether he desires to make or join in such an award."[184] Unless there is some aspect of the settlement to which the arbitrator cannot subscribe, he ordinarily may be expected to carry out their request.[185]

Briefs

Practice varies considerably regarding use of briefs in arbitration. In many cases no briefs of any type are used. However, use of post-hearing briefs is fairly common,[186] and sometimes prehearing (or hearing) briefs or statements are submitted.[187] Then, too, in some cases both prehearing (or hearing) and posthearing briefs are used,[188] and still other possibilities include use of rebuttal and supplemental briefs.[189]

---

[184] Code of Ethics and Procedural Standards for Labor-Management Arbitration, Part III, §10, 15 LA 961, 966. Part II, §5(c) gives the arbitrator discretion as to giving settlements the status of awards, as does Rule 39 of the American Arbitration Association. In Chase Bag Co., 53 LA 612 at 612 (Larson, 1969), the withdrawal of a case "with prejudice" was confirmed by an award.

[185] A different situation is presented by the so-called agreed case in which the arbitrator is made aware that the company and union have a common view as to the merits of the case but want a hearing for the record, or for some other purpose such as arbitral review of their proposed solution or arbitral consideration of the different view of some individual or group. Some arbitrators will not participate in such proceedings but others will do so as long as they remain satisfied that it will serve some useful purpose and that it is neither intended nor to be anticipated that it will work an injustice. For discussions of this matter and indications as to views, see Fleming, "Due Process and Fair Procedure in Labor Arbitration," Arbitration and Public Policy 69, 87–90 (BNA Incorporated, 1961); Fleming, "Reflections on the Nature of Labor Arbitration," 61 Mich. L. Rev. 1245, 1271 (1963); "Current Problems of Arbitration," 35 LA 963, 965 (1961). Also see Eaton, "Labor Arbitration in the San Francisco Bay Area," 48 LA 1381, 1389 (1967); "Survey of Arbitration in 1964," Proceedings of 18th Annual Meeting of National Academy of Arbitrators 243, 252 (BNA Incorporated, 1965).

[186] For some statistics on use of posthearing briefs, see "Procedural Aspects of Labor-Management Arbitration," 28 LA 933, 938 (1954 statistics, but there is no reason to believe that the extent of use has subsequently decreased).

[187] As in 47 LA 270 at 270; 29 LA 635, 638; 17 LA 412 at 412; 15 LA 792 at 792.

[188] As in 22 LA 251, 252; 18 LA 20, 21; 16 LA 955 at 955.

[189] See 48 LA 1304, 1306; 47 LA 142, 143; 23 LA 706, 707; 16 LA 149 at 149. After initial briefs are in, additional argument should not be transmitted to the arbitrator without prior agreement by the parties or consent of the arbitrator after notice to the other party. For the trouble that may result when this rule is violated, see Bendix-Westinghouse Automotive Air Brake Co., 36 LA 724, 731 (Schmidt, 1961).

Hearing or prehearing briefs outline the party's view of the case as it stands before the hearing; one of their chief advantages is that the hearing may be shortened by their use.[190] The purpose of posthearing briefs is "summarization of the evidence presented at the hearing, together with the arguments of the parties and their comments on the evidence."[191]

No new evidence should be included in posthearing briefs.[192] However, expanded discussion regarding the proper interpretation of the agreement, and citation and discussion of precedents, articles, and the like for the first time in posthearing briefs is not unusual.[193] Occasionally arbitrators find it necessary to confer with the parties or to call them together again for additional hearing when some point of critical importance develops as a result of filing briefs.

Briefs can be of valuable assistance to the arbitrator.[194] Sometimes the arbitrator deems briefs sufficiently advisable that he specifically requests them.[195]

From the standpoint of the parties, the privilege of submitting briefs may be considered essential to a "fair hearing."[196] However,

---

[190] For discussion of the advantages and disadvantages of using prehearing and posthearing briefs, see Simkin, Acceptability as a Factor in Arbitration Under an Existing Agreement 21–23 (Univ. of Pa. Press, 1952). For additional discussion as to use of briefs, see Roberts & Dash, "How to Get Better Results From Labor-Management Arbitration," 22 Arb. J. 1, 4–5, 19–21 (1967); Eaton, "Labor Arbitration in the San Francisco Bay Area," 48 LA 1381, 1386 (1967); Fleming, The Labor Arbitration Process 74–75 (Univ. of Ill. Press, 1965); Jones & Smith, "Management and Labor Appraisals and Criticisms of the Arbitration Process: A Report With Comments," 62 Mich. L. Rev. 1115, 1128, 1131 (1964); "A Colloquium on the Arbitration Process," Labor Arbitration—Perspectives and Problems 82, 95–97, 107 (BNA Incorporated, 1964).

[191] Code of Ethics and Procedural Standards for Labor-Management Arbitration, Part III, §6, 15 LA 961, 966. Sometimes a "short short" brief is submitted, as by one party in Owens-Illinois, Inc., 50 LA 871, 872 (Klamon, 1968), but briefs more often detail the major facets of the dispute.

[192] Code of Ethics and Procedural Standards, ibid. Also see Arbitrator Rock in 43 LA 833, 836; Dworkin in 36 LA 491, 492–493; Sembower in 29 LA 67, 73. Cf., Jenkins in 45 LA 696, 697 fn. 1, 702.

[193] As to advancement of entirely new theories of the case in briefs, see discussion by Fleming, The Labor Arbitration Process 154–157 (Univ. of Ill. Press, 1965). Matters which were first mentioned in a party's posthearing brief and which were not related to any proofs submitted at the hearing were not considered by Arbitrator Stouffer in Tibbetts Plumbing-Heating Co., 46 LA 124, 126 (1966). Similarly, see American Steamship Co., 44 LA 530, 537 (Keefe, 1965).

[194] See comments of Arbitrator Turkus in 49 LA 798, 801; Mathews in 23 LA 706, 707; McCoy in 16 LA 1, 2.

[195] See Merrill, "A Labor Arbitrator Views His Work," 10 Vanderbilt L. Rev. 789, 796–797 (1957).

[196] See Updegraff, "Preparation for Arbitration," 22 LA 889, 890 (1954).

an arbitrator's refusal to accept posthearing briefs was declared by
a Pennsylvania court not to warrant vacating the award either at
common law or under the statutes of that state.[197]

Sometimes the question of what briefs, if any, may be submitted
is handled by stipulation of the parties.[198] Such stipulations will be
enforced by the arbitrator unless modified by mutual agreement.[199]
Where there is no agreement regarding briefs, the arbitrator ordinarily
will acept and consider the brief of either party desiring to submit
one, and the other party may be allowed time to submit a reply
brief.[200] Either party desiring to file a posthearing brief should give
notice at the hearing; if notice is first given after the hearing is closed,
the arbitrator may be more reluctant to accept a brief filed over the
opposition of the other party.[201]

An arbitrator may take unusual steps to permit consideration
of briefs. For instance, where one party requested permission to file
a brief but, because of a misunderstanding by the arbitrator the award
was issued prior to receipt of the brief, the arbitrator secured agreement by the parties to permit issuance of a supplement to the award
to allow consideration of the brief.[202]

When briefs are to be used, a time limit within which they can
be filed will be set by stipulation of the parties or by the arbitrator.
A very common arrangement is for both parties to file (mail) briefs
simultaneously on a specified date.[203] If either party fails to submit
a brief within the specified time, the arbitrator will proceed to decide
the case without waiting for the brief,[204] especially if no request is

---

[197] Technical Employees v. U.S. Steel Co., 22 LA 62, 64–65 (Pa. Com.
Pleas Ct., 1954). The court observed that it "is not at all unusual" for judges
to "decline to accept post-hearing briefs and make an immediate decision." Id. at
65.
[198] As in McInerney Spring & Wire Co., 20 LA 642, 643 (Smith, 1953);
Cedartown Textiles, Inc., 15 LA 573, 574 (Hawley, 1950).
[199] See Sayles Biltmore Bleacheries, Inc., 24 LA 408 at 408 (Livengood,
1955).
[200] See Steinway & Sons, 17 LA 31 at 31 (Justin, 1951).
[201] Of course, it goes without saying that neither the grievant, the union,
nor the company should seek to communicate their views or evidence to the
arbitrator on an ex parte basis. See comments of Arbitrator Jones in Wilshire
Mfg. Jewelers, 49 LA 1079, 1082–1083 (1967).
[202] Crook Paper Box Co., 27 LA 836 at 836 (Compton, 1957); the supplement
to the award did not change the result.
[203] As in Needham Packing Co., 44 LA 1057, 1059 (Davey, 1965).
[204] See Beech-Nut Packing Co., 20 LA 575, 576 (Davis, 1953).

made for more time.[205] However, for reasonable cause the arbitrator may grant a request for more time, especially if the other party after due notice does not object.[206]

Copies of all briefs submitted to the arbitrator should always be submitted simultaneously to the other party.

Closing the Hearing and Time Limit for Rendering Award

Customarily arbitration hearings are deemed "closed" when all evidence and arguments of the parties have been received and the hearing is ready for adjournment with no additional days of hearing being contemplated. However, where briefs or other documents are to be filed after final adjournment of the hearing, it appears clear that the hearing will be deemed "closed" as of the final date for receipt of these items.[207] The point at which an arbitration hearing is deemed "closed" is significant in determining the time within which the award is to be rendered since ordinarily the time commences to run at the point where the hearing is deemed "closed."

Some collective agreements expressly state time limits, often unrealistic, for rendering the award.[208] Both the AAA and the FMCS specify 30 days for rendering the award after close of the hearing or transmittal of final statements, unless otherwise agreed to or required by law; the FMCS regulation adds, however, that failure to render the award within the 30 days will not invalidate it but may affect future appointments of the arbitrator.[209] Time limits for render-

---

[205] See Pan American Refining Corp., 15 LA 464, 465 (Klamon, 1950). In Sheller Mfg. Co., 40 LA 890, 891 (Davey, 1963), the arbitrator rejected the union's request to consider the company brief as "null and void" where it was filed one day late, the arbitrator stating that briefs are only an "aid" to the arbitrator and that the union was not prejudiced by the late filing.

[206] See Needham Packing Co., 44 LA 1057, 1059 (Davey, 1965); Great Lakes Carbon Corp., 16 LA 918, 919 (Livengood, 1951).

[207] See AAA Rules 31, 37; FMCS Regulations, §1404.9. Also, Arbitrator Gill in 46 LA 513 at 513; Geissinger in 46 LA 115 at 115; Graff in 44 LA 237, 239; Schmidt in 36 LA 724, 728; Danbury Rubber Co. v. Rubber Workers, 29 LA 815, 817 (Conn. Sup. Ct., 1958). Cf., Marsala v. Valve Corporation of America, 254 A.2d 469, 472 (Conn. Sup. Ct., 1969).

[208] See Major Collective Bargaining Agreements: Arbitration Procedures 80–82 (U.S. Dept. of Labor Bull. No. 1425-6, 1966).

[209] See AAA Rule 37; FMCS Regulations, §1404.9. Concerning the 30-day limit of these agencies it has been surmised that "there are doubtless many instances in which the arbitrator requests and receives from the parties an extension of time, and there may even be instances of deliberate ignoring of time limits." Jones & Smith, "Management and Labor Appraisals and Criticisms of

ing the award are also specified by some state arbitration statutes. In the absence of a mandatory time limit, the award may be made within a reasonable time.[210]

Tardy Awards

If by agreement of the parties or by the applicable law an award is to be rendered within a specified time, the award might be held invalid if not made within that time and the parties have not agreed to an extension.[211] Under some state statutes the right to object to a tardy award is waived by failure to object prior to its issuance.[212]

Where a case is covered by LMRA §301 there appears to be relatively little likelihood that the award will be invalidated merely because it is rendered late. Consider the view of one federal appellate court, for instance, that where there has been no objection to the delay until after an award is issued and there is no showing of harm due to the delay, the failure to meet a time limit specified either by state statute or by the collective agreement should not be held to invalidate the award.[213] That court explained:

> "In adopting a uniform federal standard, we ought not to accept an arbitration rule which encourages post-award technical objections by a losing party as a means of avoiding an adverse arbitration decision. Rather, we believe it to be a better rule that any limitation upon the time in which an arbitrator can render his award be a directory limitation, not a mandatory one, and that it should always be within a court's discretion to uphold a late award if no objection to the delay has been made prior to the rendition of the award or there is no showing that actual harm to the losing party was caused by the delay."[214]

---

the Arbitration Process: A Report With Comments," 62 Mich. L. Rev. 1115, 1140–1141 (1964), where other pertinent observations are also made on the subject. The Code of Ethics for arbitrators states that the arbitrator "should render his award promptly and must render his award within the time prescribed, if any." Part II, §5(a).

[210] See Danbury Rubber Co. v. Rubber Workers, 29 LA 815, 817–818 (Conn. Sup. Ct., 1958), and authorities there cited.

[211] For extensive discussion, with citation of authorities going both ways under the common law and under state statutes, see Givens, "The Validity of Delayed Awards Under Section 301, Taft-Hartley Act," 16 Arb. J. 161 (1961). Also see Marsala v. Valve Corporation of America, 254 A.2d 469 (Conn. Sup. Ct., 1969).

[212] The Uniform Arbitration Act so provides, for instance. Section 8(b), 27 LA 909, 910.

[213] IAM v. Geometric Tool Co., 406 F.2d 284, 286–287, 70 LRRM 2228 (CA 2, 1968). This result under §301 was predicted by Givens, "The Validity of Delayed Awards Under Section 301, Taft-Hartley Act," 16 Arb. J. 161, 181 (1961).

[214] 406 F.2d at 286, citations omitted.

Similarly, a court refused to invalidate an award rendered after expiration of the contractual time limit since there was no protest prior to its issuance,[215] and a like result was reached even where there was a timely protest but where there was no showing of prejudice from the delay.[216]

Reopening the Hearing

Under accepted practice the arbitrator on his own motion, or upon request of a party for good cause shown, may reopen the hearing at any time before the award is rendered. American Arbitration Association Rule 32 so provides, but cautions that if the agreement states a mandatory time limit for rendering the award and reopening would prevent issuance of the award within that time, the hearing may not be reopened unless the parties agree to extend the time limit.[217]

The Code of Ethics and Procedural Standards for Labor-Management Arbitration provides:

"When hearings are concluded, parties should not attempt to communicate any additional information to the arbitrator. If new evidence becomes available, written application for the re-opening of the proceeding with the reasons therefor should be made to the arbitrator and a copy transmitted simultaneously to the other party."[218]

The reopening of hearings for introduction of new evidence was discussed by Arbitrator Edward A. Levy in reopening a hearing for this purpose:

"Ordinarily where a hearing has been had in which all parties have participated, and have presented all evidence, and have stated on the record that they have nothing further to offer, the matter is deemed to be officially closed for the taking of evidence. However, where certain evidence is evidentiary and of material import and the admission thereof will probably affect the outcome of a cause, is unavailable at the time of the hearing, and if the same is produced subsequently without seriously affecting any substantial right, and it is shown that reasonable grounds existed for its non-production at the time of the hearing, the arbitrator may, in his discretion, reopen the arbitration for the introduction of such evidence only. The reason for this rule is to afford

---

[215] IAM v. Mooney Aircraft, Inc., 71 LRRM 2121 (CA 5, 1969).
[216] Teamsters v. Anchor Motor Freight, Inc., 71 LRRM 3205 (CA 3, 1969).
[217] 43 LA 1292, 1295. Also see Guides For Labor Arbitration 15 (Univ. of Pa. Press, 1953). For related discussion, see "Closing the Hearing and Time Limit for Rendering Award," above.
[218] Part III, §6, 15 LA 961, 966.

to each of the parties full opportunity to present such material evidence as will assist the arbitrator in ascertaining the truth of all matters in controversy."[219]

In one case, Arbitrator George H. Hildebrand refused to reopen the hearing to receive new evidence where the party requesting reopening could not show that the new evidence could be clearly established.[220]

Sometimes the arbitrator, without reopening the hearing, will simply call upon one or both of the parties for additional information,[221] or he might invite further written arguments regarding some aspect of the case.[222]

The Award and Opinion

The award is the arbitrator's decision of the case. Awards usually are short, and they "should be definite, certain and final, and should dispose of all matters submitted."[223]

Except in rare instances awards are issued in writing.[224] Even when an oral award is rendered, the arbitrator usually later reduces it to writing.[225] The written award must be signed by the arbitrator.

---

[219] Madison Institute, 18 LA 78, 81 (1952), an arbitration administered by the New Jersey State Board of Mediation. Also see statements by Arbitrator Krimsly in 51 LA 745, 748; McCoy in 40 LA 727, 730 (reopening to receive data essential for compliance with court order); Morvant in 33 LA 302, 307. Reopenings are also discussed in Problems of Proof in Arbitration 330–332 (The Bureau of National Affairs, Inc., 1967).

[220] Safeway Stores, Inc., 22 LA 466, 467 (1954). In Harmony Dairy Co., 51 LA 745, 748 (1968), Arbitrator Krimsly could not see that any useful purpose would be served by a reopening so the request for one was denied. In Bridgeport Rolling Mills Co. v. Brown, 53 LRRM 2589, 40 LA 1024 (CA 2, 1963), the court held that evidence discovered after the award had been issued came too late for consideration.

[221] As in Paragon Bridge & Steel Co., 45 LA 833 at 833 (Vines, 1965); Full-Fashioned Hosiery Mfrs., 15 LA 452, 454 (Taylor, 1954). For related discussion, see Chapter 8, topic titled "Evidence Submitted After Hearing."

[222] As did Arbitrator Louisell in Donaldson Co., 21 LA 254, 255 (1953).

[223] Code of Ethics and Procedural Standards for Labor-Management Arbitration, Part II, §5(a), 15 LA 961, 965. As to the latter point, however, see topic titled "Split Hearings," above.

[224] Awards may be oral unless a written award is required by the parties or by statute. Oral awards are sufficient under the common law, but if in writing they must be signed. See Chapter 2, subtopic titled "State Common Law." The collective agreement often will require the award to be in writing. See Major Collective Bargaining Agreements: Arbitration Procedures 76–77 (U.S. Dept. of Labor Bull. No. 1425-6, 1966).

[225] See discussion of oral awards in Guides For Labor Arbitration 14 (Univ. of Pa. Press, 1953). Sometimes it is expressly agreed that an oral ruling will be issued at the hearing or as soon thereafter as possible, to be followed later

Awards of arbitration boards must be signed by all members where a unanimous decision is required, otherwise they must be signed by at least a majority unless the agreement or a stipulation expressly permits issuance of an award by the neutral alone.[226]

Often the arbitrator accompanies his award with a written opinion stating the reasons for his decision. The award should be stated separately from the opinion to indicate clearly where the opinion ends and the award begins;[227] in agreeing in advance to accept the arbitrator's award the parties do not necessarily promise to agree with all of his reasoning.

Attitudes vary as to the desirability of reasoned opinions, but a large majority of parties and of arbitrators favor their use.[228]

A well-reasoned opinion can contribute greatly to the acceptance of the award by the parties by persuading them that the arbitrator understands the case and that his award is basically sound. The United States Supreme Court emphasized this function of opinions in encouraging their use by arbitrators:

> "Arbitrators have no obligation to the court to give their reasons for an award. To require opinions free of ambiguity may lead arbitrators to play it safe by writing no supporting opinions. This would be undesirable for a well-reasoned opinion tends to engender confidence in the integrity of the process and aids in clarifying the underlying agreement."[229]

---

by a written opinion and award. As in Cleveland Transit System, 45 LA 905, 905–906 (Kates, 1965); Quaker Oats Co., 35 LA 535, 536 (Valtin, 1960). In Aerosol Techniques, Inc., 48 LA 1278, 1280 (Summers, 1967), an arbitration board directed the immediate reinstatement of the grievant without waiting for issuance of the formal award.

[226] For full discussion, see Chapter 4, topic titled "Tripartite Arbitration Board."

[227] Code of Ethics and Procedural Standards for Labor-Management Arbitration, Part II, §5(b), 15 LA 961, 965. However, where the nature of a case made it difficult to spell out a formal award without considerable repetition of the opinion, the award merely stated that its substance was as indicated in the opinion. C & D Batteries, Inc., 32 LA 589, 595 (Jaffee, 1959).

[228] For statistics, see "Survey of Arbitration in 1964," Proceedings of 18th Annual Meeting of National Academy of Arbitrators 243, 246, 254 (BNA Incorporated, 1965); Warren & Bernstein, "A Profile of Labor Arbitration," 16 LA 970, 983 (1951). A "bare award" may be held to have no force as a precedent even for the same parties. See John J. Nissen Baking Co., 48 LA 12, 17 (Fallon, 1966).

[229] United Steelworkers of America v. Enterprise Wheel & Car Corp., 80 S.Ct. 1358, 1361, 34 LA 569, 571 (1960). Although the arbitrator has no obligation to the courts to accompany his award with an opinion, he may have one to the parties. The Code of Ethics for arbitrators states that it is discretionary with the arbitrator to state reasons for his decision or to accompany the award

Opinions indeed can have significant educational value to the parties and can aid them in adjusting future related problems. In the latter regard Arbitrator Whitley P. McCoy explained in one case:

> "In explanation of my having discussed issues and contentions upon which the ultimate decision is not to be based, I may say that parties do not spend many days of preparation, three days of hearings, and thousands of dollars worth of the time of important officers and attorneys, for the purpose of finding out whether one girl should or should not have got a trivial promotion. They are interested in principles. They are entitled, for their future guidance in various respects, to the arbitrator's findings upon the evidence and the various contentions."[230]

Some parties, however, prefer not to have an opinion for fear that the arbitrator might make comments not germane to the issue and thus possibly stimulate future disputes. Also, reasoned opinions require more of the arbitrator's time, increasing the cost of arbitration. In view of the cost factor the arbitrator may ask the parties to indicate specifically whether they want an opinion.[231]

Thought Processes of the Arbitrator

In a general sense much of this book deals with the decision-making process or the thought processes of the arbitrator. The Authors

---

with an opinion, but that he should comply with the request of either party for an opinion. Part II, §5(e), 15 LA 961, 965. Frequently the collective agreement will require that awards be accompanied by an opinion. See Major Collective Bargaining Agreements: Arbitration Procedures 76 (U.S. Dept. of Labor Bull. No. 1425-6, 1966).

[230] Southern Bell Telephone & Telegraph Co., 16 LA 1, 9 (1951). For other discussions of such matters as the functions of opinions, the mechanics of writing opinions, criticisms of opinions, hazards of dicta, the advancement in the opinion of new theories for deciding the case, and the like, see: Eaton, "Labor Arbitration in the San Francisco Bay Area," 48 LA 1381, 1387–1388 (1967); Roberts & Dash, "How to Get Better Results From Labor-Management Arbitration," 22 Arb. J. 1, 14–16 (1967); Fleming, The Labor Arbitration Process 157–163, 216–217; 220–221 (Univ. of Ill. Press, 1965); "Problems in Opinion Writing: A Panel Discussion," Proceedings of 18th Annual Meeting of National Academy of Arbitrators 1–26 (BNA Incorporated, 1965); Garrett, "Some Potential Uses of the Opinion," Labor Arbitration—Perspectives and Problems 114–124 (BNA Incorporated, 1964); Editorial, "The Hazards of Dicta in Labor Arbitration," 19 Arb. J. 65 (1964); Syme, "Opinions and Awards," 15 LA 953, 956–958 (1950).

[231] See Trailmobile, Inc., 28 LA 710, 711 (Coffey, 1957). In 1963 the American Arbitration Association drafted a waiver-of-opinion form for use where both parties desire an award without a written opinion. This action followed an association survey in which many parties indicated that they would not ordinarily waive the opinion but that an easy opportunity should be available to do so when desired. Arbitration News, No. 2—1963.

do not undertake to deal more specifically with this matter, but they call attention to the writings of others who have touched directly upon the thought processes of arbitrators.[232]

Clarification or Interpretation of Award

It has been said to be "a general rule in common law arbitration that when arbitrators have executed their awards and declared their decision they are functus officio and have no power to proceed further."[233] A detailed statement of this common law rule explains:

> "The authority and jurisdiction of arbitrators are entirely terminated by the completion and delivery of an award. They have thereafter no power to recall the same, to order a rehearing, to amend, or to 'interpret' in such manner as may be regarded as authoritative. But they may correct clerical mistakes or obvious errors of arithmetical computation."[234]

The general common law rule is also the apparent basis for the following provision in the Code of Ethics and Procedural Standards for Labor-Management Arbitration:

> "After the award has been rendered, the arbitrator should not issue any clarification or interpretation thereof, or comments thereon, except at the request of both parties, unless the agreement provides therefor."[235]

---

[232] See Alexander, "Discretion in Arbitration," Arbitration and the Public Interest 84 (The Bureau of National Affairs, Inc., 1971); Fleming, The Labor Arbitration Process 78–106, 159–164, 211 (Univ. of Ill. Press, 1965); Garrett, "Some Potential Uses of the Opinion," Labor Arbitration—Perspectives and Problems 114–124 (BNA Incorporated, 1964); Teele, "The Thought Processes of the Arbitrator," 17 Arb. J. 85 (1962); Seitz, "How Arbitrators Decide Cases: A Study in Black Magic," Collective Bargaining and the Arbitrator's Role 159–164 (BNA Incorporated, 1962).

[233] Mercury Oil Refining Co. v. Oil Workers, 187 F.2d 980, 983 (CA 10, 1951). Accord, Indigo Springs, Inc. v. Hotel Trades Council, 59 LRRM 3024 (N.Y. Sup. Ct., 1965); Jannis v. Ellis, 308 P.2d 750 (Calif. Dist. Ct. App., 1957), citing Sturges, Commercial Arbitrations and Awards §220. Numerous other cases, some going back many years, are cited by Updegraff & McCoy, below. The term "functus officio" is literally translated to mean "a task performed." Black's Law Dictionary, 4th Ed.

[234] Updegraff, Arbitration and Labor Relations 116 (The Bureau of National Affairs, Inc., 1970), where numerous cases are cited. The same statement is contained in Updegraff & McCoy, Arbitration of Labor Disputes, 1st Ed. p. 33 (1946), 2d Ed. pp. 75–76 (1961).

[235] Part II, §5(f). 15 LA 961, 965. A few collective agreements expressly provide for interpretation of awards by the arbitrator. See Major Collective Bargaining Agreements: Arbitration Procedures 75 (U.S. Dept. of Labor Bull. No. 1425-6, 1966); Paragon Bridge & Steel Co., 48 LA 995, 999 (Gross, 1967). More often any agreement to request an interpretation by the arbitrator will

The common-law doctrine of "functus officio" has been modified by statute in some states to permit the arbitrator to modify or correct his award, to the limited extent stated in the statute, upon submission by a court or upon direct application to him by one of the parties.[236] In addition to the more commonly stated grounds for such action by the arbitrator, the Uniform Arbitration Act also permits him to modify or correct his award "for the purpose of clarifying the award."[237] The Act specifies that the application shall be made within 20 days after delivery of the award to the applicant, that prompt notice of the application shall be given to the other party, and that the notice shall inform the latter that he has 10 days within which to serve any objections to the application.[238]

Under the federal law as developed under LMRA §301 the courts may return an award to the arbitrator for clarification or interpretation where it is ambiguous.[239] However, the mere fact that a court may have power to return an award to an arbitrator for interpretation does not necessarily mean that he may undertake to render an interpretation on his own.[240]

---

be reached after the need for an interpretation arises, as in Brass-Craft Mfg. Co., 36 LA 1438 at 1438 (Kahn, 1961). One survey indicated that labor, management, and arbitrators alike appear generally to favor giving arbitrators power to interpret their awards. See Warren & Bernstein, "A Profile of Labor Arbitration," 16 LA 970, 979 (1951).

[236] See Chapter 2, subtopic titled "State Arbitration Statutes." For an example of a proceeding based upon a motion for modification of award under state statute, see Reserve Mining Co., 55 LA 648 (Sembower, 1970).

[237] Section 9. 27 LA 909, 910. For states adopting the Uniform Act, see Chapter 2, ibid. The New York statute does not list "clarification" as one of the grounds, but this ground is possibly included in the intent of the statute. See "An Outline of Procedure Under the New York Arbitration Law," 20 Arb. J. 73, 90–91 (1965).

[238] Section 9, ibid.

[239] Local 494, I.B.E.W. v. Brewery Proprietors, 289 F.Supp. 865 (DC Wisc., 1968); Chemical Workers v. McKesson & Robbins, Inc., 53 LC ¶11,305 (USDC Conn., 1966); Metal Trades Council v. General Electric Co., 61 LRRM 2004 (CA 9, 1965); Todd Shipyards Corporation v. Marine Workers 59 LRRM 2613 (USDC N.J., 1965); Transport Workers v. Philadelphia Transportation Co., 228 F.Supp. 423 (DC Pa., 1964); I.A.M. v. Crown Cork and Seal Co., 300 F.2d 127 (CA 3, 1962).

[240] In Union Local 679 v. Richmond-Chase Corp., 36 LA 881, 882 (Calif. Dist. Ct. App., 1961), the court under the California statute ordered a rehearing by an arbitration board to clarify its award, but the court denied that the board itself had authority to order the rehearing. In Printing Industry of Washington, D.C., 40 LA 727, 728–729 (1963), Arbitrator Whitley P. McCoy stated that upon rendering his award he had lost all power over the case and that the court order subsequently returning the case to him must be looked to for

Where an arbitrator is not fully satisfied that he has authority to issue an interpretation of his award at the request of one party, he will have good cause to consider the suggestion that "he should refuse to comply, but should indicate that he will give consideration to the request if made by both parties."[241]

Remedy Power and Its Use

The remedy power in arbitration has often been considered from two standpoints: (1) whether the arbitrator has the power to utilize the given remedy, and (2) whether the given remedy should be used in the particular case even assuming that the arbitrator has the power to use it.[242] These two matters are the basic concern of the present topic. Discussion of specific types of remedies and remedies for specific types of violations is found throughout this book.[243]

Scope of Remedy Power

In its *Enterprise* decision the U.S. Supreme Court spoke of the remedy power of arbitrators:

"When an arbitrator is commissioned to interpret and apply the collective bargaining agreement, he is to bring his informed judgment to bear in order to reach a fair solution of a problem. This is especially true when it comes to formulating remedies. There the need is for flexibility in meeting a wide variety of situations. The draftsmen may never have thought of what specific remedy should be awarded to meet a particular contingency. Nevertheless, an arbitrator is confined to interpretation and application of the collective bargaining agreement;

---

determining the scope of his new authority. The "functus officio" doctrine was also acknowledged by Arbitrator Purdom in 51 LA 919, 920–924; Sembower in 37 LA 673, 674; Bothwell in 36 LA 979, 980. Cf., Arbitrator Kates in 53 LA 619, 623, and in 43 LA 625, 633; Platt in 47 LA 289, 316.

[241] Guides For Labor Arbitration 15 (Univ. of Pa. Press, 1953).

[242] For extensive discussions of the remedy power in arbitration, see Wolff, "The Power of the Arbitrator to Make Monetary Awards," Labor Arbitration—Perspectives and Problems 176 (BNA Incorporated, 1964); Sirefman, "Rights Without Remedies in Labor Arbitration," 18 Arb. J. 17 (1963); Stutz, "Arbitrators and the Remedy Power," Labor Arbitration and Industrial Change 54 (BNA Incorporated, 1963); Fleming, "Arbitrators and the Remedy Power," 48 Virginia L. Rev. 1199 (1962); Stein, "Remedies in Labor Arbitration," Challenges to Arbitration 39 (BNA Incorporated, 1960).

[243] For instance, the remedy of damages and remedies for mistake are treated in Chapter 10; the injunction remedy is treated elsewhere in Chapter 7; remedies in discharge and discipline cases are treated in Chapter 15; and so on.

he does not sit to dispense his own brand of industrial justice. He may of course look for guidance from many sources, yet his award is legitimate only so long as it draws its essence from the collective bargaining agreement. When the arbitrator's words manifest an infidelity to this obligation, courts have no choice but to refuse enforcement of the award."[244]

This statement of broad but nonetheless restricted remedy power obviously fails to provide a clear and unequivocal guide. This is further illustrated by the fact that one federal court has acted on the view that arbitrators have power to use a given type of remedy unless it is expressly precluded by the agreement,[245] while another federal court does not appear willing to go nearly so far to find remedial authority in the arbitrator.[246]

In the realm of state law broad remedial authority exists in the arbitrator under the Uniform Arbitration Act, which specifies certain grounds for court vacation of awards but which expressly adds that "the fact that the relief was such that it could not or would not be granted by a court of law or equity is not ground for vacating or refusing to confirm the award."[247]

The views of arbitrators themselves differ widely as to how broad their remedial power is or should be.[248] The expressions or actions of some arbitrators reflect the belief that broad remedy power is implied in the arbitrator. For instance, in awarding an increased rate for a changed job, Arbitrator James J. Willingham explained:

"As arbitration is a process to resolve industrial differences without resort to work stoppage, lockout and other economic measures, it necessarily implies power in the arbitrator, exclusive of specific contractual prohibitions, to settle and dispose of the corpus of the grievance. In this case the corpus of the grievance is, in essence, what pay grade is applicable to the jobs with changed content resulting from the banking of machines. Accordingly, the answer to the third issue is that the

---

[244] United Steelworkers of America v. Enterprise Wheel and Car Corp., 80 S.Ct. 1358, 1361 (1960).

[245] Minute Maid Co. v. Citrus Cannery Food Processing Workers, 331 F.2d 280 (CA 5, 1964); IAM v. Cameron Iron Works, 292 F.2d 112 (CA 5, 1961), cert. den. 368 U.S. 926. (1961).

[246] Luggage Workers v. Neevel Co., 325 F.2d 992 (CA 8, 1964); Truck Drivers & Helpers v. Ulry-Talbert Company, 330 F.2d 562 (CA 8, 1964).

[247] Section 12(a)(5), 27 LA 909, 911. For some states that have adopted the Uniform Act, see Chapter 2, subtopic titled "State Arbitration Statutes."

[248] For related discussion, see Chapter 9, subtopic titled " 'Legislation' vs. 'Interpretation.' "

arbitrator is empowered to establish the Labor Grade applicable to the grievance herein."[249]

In rather sharp contrast, consider the view of Arbitrator Harold W. Davey, stated in response to a suggestion that arbitrators have power under the *Trilogy* to achieve justice in situations not contemplated by or not adequately covered by the collective agreement:

> "The present arbitrator does not share this expansive view of arbitral jurisdiction. Arbitrators are constrained by contracts in the same manner as the parties themselves. I do not believe in blank check arbitration of the 'philosopher king' type, as I have made clear in numerous decisions and journal articles.

> "I am fully aware that denial of these grievances, while required on contractual grounds, does not solve the equitability question that both management and the Union recognize in their earlier efforts to work out some mutually satisfactory treatment of the seniority problem posed by the two groups of employees now working in the same warehouse. My authority as arbitrator, however, does not extend to development of a Solomon-like solution to be imposed upon both parties as final and binding. My authority is limited to deciding whether the grievances have contractual merit. The ruling must be that they do not."[250]

If a given type of remedy has been widely used by arbitrators, an exceedingly strong case may be made in support of an arbitrator's right to use the remedy (absent express denial of such right by the agreement or submission). Compensatory damages to employees who have suffered financial loss from the employer's violation of their rights

---

[249] U.S. Slicing Machine Co., 41 LA 1076, 1081–1082 (1963). Similarly, see statements by Arbitrator Somers in 51 LA 822, 836; Summers in 48 LA 760, 763; Turkus in 46 LA 607, 608 and in 44 LA 1219, 1221–1222; and see actions by Gill in 46 LA 513, 517; Howlett in 42 LA 678, 680–682.

[250] Lagomarcino-Grupe Co., 43 LA 453, 460 (1964), holding that employees of Company A who were terminated when its warehouse was closed had no right to carry their seniority with them when they were hired at Company B's warehouse, even though both companies could be regarded as one from a labor relations standpoint and the same union had contracts with both companies. For other arbitrators taking a similarly narrow "contractual" view of the remedy power, see Arbitrator Marshall in 53 LA 1061, 1062; McIntosh in 48 LA 1121, 1121–1122; Shister in 43 LA 1228, 1231 (the arbitrator derives his authority from the contract, is a prisoner of the contract, and is not freed from this imprisonment by the *Trilogy*); Ross in 42 LA 353, 355 (it remains true that grievance arbitration is essentially contractual interpretation—the *Warrior and Gulf* decision "does not enthrone the arbitrator as a law maker nor permit him to impose new obligations or restrictions which cannot fairly be wrung from the contract as the parties negotiated it").

under the agreement provides the most prominent illustration.[251] Arbitrator Alfred Kuhn has declared in this regard:

> "Many—perhaps most—labor-management contracts in this nation do not specifically authorize an arbitrator to award damages. But in hundreds of such contracts year after year arbitrators do, in fact, award damages. This is done with full knowledge of the parties, who in many cases have had decades in which to rewrite their contracts if they did not so intend them. The Arbitrator submits that under those circumstances the authority of an arbitrator to award damages is as truly and integrally a part of the contract as if it were written there in unmistakable English and boldface type."[252]

As just stated, many agreements are silent as to the arbitrator's remedy power where he has found a violation of the agreement.[253] Of course the parties can deal with the matter in the agreement, the submission, or by stipulation at the hearing. While they sometimes act to restrict the arbitrator's remedy power,[254] likely as not any express action that they may take will be to recognize discretionary remedial authority in the arbitrator by authorizing him to determine "what shall the remedy be" in the event a violation is found.[255]

Should the Given Remedy Be Used?

Even some of the arbitrators who believe the remedy power should be very broad are quick to caution that there is "a great difference between the possession of power and the occasion for its exercise," and that arbitrators should proceed with great caution particularly

---

[251] For full discussion of the damages remedy, see Chapter 10, topic titled "Principles of Damages."

[252] Jeffrey Mfg. Co., 34 LA 814, 825 (1960). Similarly as to compensatory damages, see Arbitrator Dworkin in Aetna Portland Cement Co., 41 LA 219, 222 (1963).

[253] One of the apparently few aspects of the remedy power (apart from the common prohibition against adding to, subtracting from, or modifying the agreement) fairly commonly treated in the collective agreement concerns the retroactive application of the award. See Major Collective Bargaining Agreements: Arbitration Procedures 77–80 (U.S. Dept. of Labor Bull. No. 1425-6, 1966).

[254] As in Lone Star Steel Co., 48 LA 1095, 1098 (Jenkins, 1967), where the arbitrator utilized a footnote to suggest what remedy he would have awarded had his authority not been limited. In Globe-Union, Inc., 42 LA 713, 721 (Prasow, 1963), the arbitrator outlined choices open to the parties as to the remedy power, including reservation of the power to themselves.

[255] See Arbitrator Yagoda in 49 LA 823, 826; Rohman in 47 LA 1178 at 1178; Daugherty in 47 LA 554 at 554; Gray in 46 LA 1146 at 1146; Teele in 46 LA 215 at 215, 218. In Taystee Bread Co., 52 LA 677 at 677, 680–681 (Purdom, 1969), the parties stipulated that the arbitrator was free to fashion a remedy as he saw fit based upon the merits and that he was not bound by the restrictive language of the agreement.

in devising new remedies.[256] Arbitrator M. S. Ryder expressed the view that absent restrictive contract language broad remedial power should be deemed to inhere in the arbitrator, but he also offered the following standards for confining the use of remedies to a proper form and scope:

"1. In form the remedy should be one that would appear to most directly effectuate the intent and purposes of that provision in the labor agreement in connection with which the right was contracted.

"2. The party called upon to give remedy should not be subjected to well-founded surprise by the form, nature, extent and degree of the remedy. What is awarded should be within the realm of conceivable and reasonable remedial expectation by the party in error or by other parties were they to be similarly circumstanced.

"3. Remedies that are punitive in monetary or exemplary nature should be avoided, on the ground that parties bargaining collectively in a more or less perpetual relationship should not seek that one or the other partner be punished for a mistake. To so seek and to obtain punishment is putting a mortgage on the future happiness of the joint relationship. * * *

"4. Remedies that are novel in form should be avoided, again for reasons of unexpectedness or possible well-based surprise. A novel remedy might bring with it unforseen contractual and other impacts on one or both of the parties and create uncertainty as to what may result from future submissions to arbitration. The concept of the arbitrator having an 'arsenal' of forms of relief, with the parties in a position of uncertainty rather than expectation, should be avoided in what is a private litigation seeking to resolve a dispute. Suspense in a private relationship might subvert the efficacy of that relationship."[257]

In some cases the arbitrator finds a violation of the agreement but he returns the case to the parties for negotiations as to the remedy. One arbitrator deemed this procedure essential where he had "received

---

[256] Stein, "Remedies in Labor Arbitration," Challenges to Arbitration 39, 45–47 (BNA Incorporated, 1960). Similarly, see Arbitrator Turkus in Shell Oil Co., 44 LA 1219, 1221–1222 (1965) [power is a heady wine which carries with it an equally potent obligation to exercise care in its use].

[257] Comments by Arbitrator Ryder in Labor Arbitration and Industrial Change 68–69 (BNA Incorporated, 1963). In Madison Bus Co., 52 LA 723, 727–728 (Mueller, 1969), the arbitrator stated that although the Union was subjected to arbitration costs as a result of the Company's violation of the agreement, an award for such costs would constitute a novel remedy not within the reasonable expectations of the parties and accordingly would not be granted. But such an award was made in Ralph Rogers & Co., 48 LA 40, 43 (Getman, 1966).

no guidance at the hearing with respect to a remedy should the grievance be sustained."[258] In another case the arbitrator offered the parties a contingent remedy, to be used unless they could agree "upon an alternative solution" within 60 days from the date of the award.[259]

Recommendations by Arbitrator

Many "rights" arbitrators are authorized only to interpret and apply the collective agreement and are denied the power to add to or modify the agreement. In these instances the award must be based upon what is or is not required by the agreement and there is only limited room, if any at all, for application of "equity."[260] For instance, in refusing to follow a prior award based upon equitable grounds Arbitrator Whitley P. McCoy declared:

"I cannot agree with that decision, which was based on so-called 'equitable' grounds. When it becomes customary and legitimate for arbitrators to amend and add to contracts according to their sense of equity, i.e., what the contract *ought* to provide, then I shall fall in line."[261]

However, arbitrators occasionally do make purely advisory recommendations based upon equitable considerations. In some such cases where the grievance could be sustained only by adding to or modifying the agreement or by otherwise exceeding the arbitrator's authority, but where the arbitrator is convinced that the grievance has merit from the standpoint of equity, he will deny the grievance (or he might dismiss it) and at the same time make an advisory recom-

---

[258] United States Steel Corp., 45 LA 104, 107 (Florey, 1965). Also see Arbitrator Platt in 55 LA 170, 182; Talent in 52 LA 93, 97; Feinberg in 45 LA 161, 174. For related discussion, see topic titled "Split Hearings," above.

[259] Lehman Brothers, Inc., 51 LA 1063, 1067 (Hill, 1968). In Ulene v. Murray Millman, Inc., 33 LA 531, 534-535 (Calif. Dist. Ct. App., 1959), an award was not rendered unenforceable merely because it contained an election provision in respect to the remedy.

[260] See Arbitrator Davis in 48 LA 938, 940, and in 46 LA 970, 972; Cole in 48 LA 481, 485; Lugar in 48 LA 463, 478; C. L. McCoy in 46 LA 11, 15; W. P. McCoy in 45 LA 1165, 1166; Kagel in 65-2 ARB ¶8774; Hebert in 45 LA 131, 139, and in 29 LA 469, 473; Autrey in 43 LA 1066, 1070; Davey in 43 LA 453, 460; Dworkin in 43 LA 120, 125-126, and in 21 LA 133, 139; Barrett in 16 LA 466, 472. Cf., Sembower in 41 LA 631, 635-636; Handsaker in 15 LA 209, 210. Certainly, the parties generally want the agreement applied as written. See Eaton, "Labor Arbitration in the San Francisco Bay Area," 48 LA 1381, 1390 (1967).

[261] Esso Standard Oil Co., 16 LA 73, 75 (1951).

mendation as to how he thinks it should be disposed of for the best interests of both parties.[262]

In doing this Arbitrator Joseph Shister explained:

"Since the Arbitration Board must rule according to the so-called 'contractual approach' to the issue, it has no alternative but to deny the grievance. But while the Board's authority to *rule* is so circumscribed, its powers of *recommendation* are considerably broader. For in making such recommendations it can avail itself of the guideposts afforded by what one might term, 'Industrial relations equity.' "[263]

Similarly, where an arbitrator concludes that the dispute essentially involves "interests" rather than "rights" under the existing agreement so that a sustaining award would in effect be legislating for the parties, he may deny the claim, or remand it, with the suggestion that the matter be negotiated by the parties.[264] But the arbitrator may undertake to decide the dispute by "legislating" for the parties if he believes both parties want and have authorized him to do so.[265]

'Injunctions' by Arbitrators

In giving relief through their awards arbitrators have not often spoken literally in terms of "injunction" or "cease and desist."[266] A

---

[262] This approach was taken by Arbitrator Kerrison in 51 LA 761, 764; Reid in 50 LA 951, 955; Stouffer in 47 LA 443, 448; Davis in 46 LA 970, 972; Autrey in 43 LA 1066, 1070; Prasow in 42 LA 1067, 1071; Russell in 41 LA 913, 917; Hebert in 29 LA 469, 476; Roberts in 28 LA 470, 477; Davey in 25 LA 394, 397; Kelliher in 21 LA 444, 446; Anrod in 20 LA 653, 658; Aaron in 15 LA 162, 168. Also see Copelof in 15 LA 229, 233. Similarly, where the grievance is sustained the arbitrator may suggest that the winner not demand the full measure of its rights under the award. See Arbitrator Shister in 49 LA 791, 797; Johnson in 48 LA 835, 837; Summers in 48 LA 760, 762–763.

[263] General Aniline & Film Corp., 25 LA 50, 54 (1955). Cf., Arbitrator Shister in National Carbon Co., 23 LA 263, 264 (1954).

[264] This approach was taken by Arbitrator Seward in 26 LA 646, 648; Klamon in 26 LA 48, 54; Copelof in 18 LA 486, 489; Kelliher in 16 LA 394, 396; Komaroff in 16 LA 303, 307. Cf., Gill in 46 LA 513, 515–517; Dworkin in 46 LA 9, 11. Also see Chapter 9, topic titled "Ambiguity" and subtopic titled " 'Legislation' vs. 'Interpretation' "; Chapter 10, topic titled "Contract Principles."

[265] See Colonial Provision Co., 16 LA 176, 178–179 (Copelof, 1951). For related discussion, see Chapter 3, topic on " 'Rights' Arbitration Contract Clauses."

[266] For some instances in which arbitrators have done so, see Arbitrator Yaffe in 52 LA 1013, 1019; Kornblum in 52 LA 771, 772, and in 35 LA 384, 386; Burns in 47 LA 873, 888; Turkus in 66-1 ARB ¶8284; Scheiber in 40 LA 954, 958; Williams in 37 LA 824, 830. For some arguments against injunctions by arbitrators, see Stein, "Remedies in Labor Arbitration," Challenges to Arbitration 39, 47 (BNA Incorporated, 1960). The reluctance of many arbitrators to issue injunctions or cease and desist orders is illustrated by Arbitrator

relatively infrequent type of relief to be included in arbitration awards is an injunction ordering a party not to do (or to cease doing) some specified act which the arbitrator has ruled violative of the collective agreement. However, the New York Court of Appeals has recognized significant authority in arbitrators to grant such injunctive relief in proper circumstances, the court observing that "Traditionally, arbitrators have been licensed to direct such conduct of the parties as is necessary to the settlement of the matters in dispute."[267]

In the latter case the court upheld an award containing an injunction where the collective agreement did not directly affirm or deny power in the arbitrator to use such remedy, and where nothing short of an injunction would have accomplished the intent of the parties for speedy relief against the prohibited activity.[268] Moreover, the court also held that the New York Anti-Injunction Act did not forbid injunctions by arbitrators even though that Act severely limited the jurisdiction of the courts to issue injunctions in labor disputes.[269]

It is clear that under the federal law the courts can enforce injunctions issued by arbitrators to halt strikes in breach of the collective agreement.[270] Any doubt that the federal courts have jurisdiction to do so in proper cases can no longer have real substance in view of the U.S. Supreme Court's holding in *Boys Markets* that the Norris-LaGuardia Act does not bar court injunctive relief against such strikes.[271]

Holly in 53 LA 226, 227–228; Hilpert in 47 LA 686, 691; Bernstein in 42 LA 931, 935; Gill in 34 LA 176, 178. Also see Kates in 50 LA 191, 194. For related discussion, see this Chapter, topic titled "Remedy Power and Its Use."

[267] In re Ruppert, 29 LA 775, 776–777 (1958).

[268] Ibid. An arbitrator's cease and desist order was also enforced in F. & M. Schaefer Brewing Co., 53 LA 676 (N.Y. Sup. Ct., 1969). The New York arbitration statute does not deal specifically with injunctions by the arbitrator. An arbitrator's injunction was enforced by a court in Illinois, a Uniform Arbitration Act state. In re Ford Motor Co., 41 LA 621 at 621 (Ill. Cir. Ct. Cook County, 1963).

[269] In re Ruppert, 29 LA 775, 777 (N.Y. Ct. App., 1958). To similar effect, In re Griffin, 42 LA 511 (N.Y. Sup. Ct., 1964).

[270] See Pacific Maritime Association v. Longshoremen, 304 F.Supp. 1315 (DC Calif., 1969); New Orleans Steamship Association v. Longshoremen, 389 F.2d 369 (CA 5, 1968); Philadelphia Marine Trade Association v. Longshoremen, 365 F.2d 295 (CA 3, 1966), reversed on other grounds, 88 S.Ct. 201 (1967). The arbitrator's injunction may not be a feasible remedy where quick action is needed unless the agreement provides an expedited arbitration procedure. See comments of Owen Fairweather to N.Y.U. 18th Annual Conference on Labor, 58 LRR 240 (1965).

[271] Boys Markets, Inc. v. Retail Clerks Union, Local 770, 90 S.Ct. 1583,

While arbitrators do not often issue awards which prohibit a party from carrying out some specified act, awards in the nature of "mandatory injunctions" which command a party to take some affirmative action, such as an award ordering the employer to reinstate an employee, are very common in arbitration.[272]

Common Errors in Arbitration

On the basis of its extensive experience in administering arbitration proceedings the American Arbitration Association has concluded that a party may harm its case by the following practices:

"1. Using arbitration and arbitration costs as a harassing technique.

"2. Over-emphasis of the grievance by the union or exaggeration of an employee's fault by management.

"3. Reliance on a minimum of facts and a maximum of arguments.

"4. Concealing essential facts; distorting the truth.

"5. Holding back books, records and other supporting documents.

"6. Tying up proceedings with legal technicalities.

"7. Introducing witnesses who have not been properly instructed on demeanor and on the place of their testimony in the entire case.

"8. Withholding full cooperation from the arbitrator.

"9. Disregarding the ordinary rules of courtesy and decorum.

"10. Becoming involved in arguments with the other side. The time to try to convince the other party is before arbitration, during grievance processing. At the arbitration hearing, all efforts should be concentrated on convincing the arbitrator."[273]

---

74 LRRM 2257 (1970). For more as to the substance of this decision, see Chapter 2, subtopic titled "Other Supreme Court Decisions Affecting Arbitration." For a comprehensive discussion of court enforcement of arbitrator injunctions (written prior to *Boys Markets* but still very useful), see Meyer, "Enforcement of Arbitrator's Labor Injunctions in the Federal Courts," 7 Howard L. J. 17 (1961). Also see Stutz, "Arbitrators and the Remedy Power," Labor Arbitration and Industrial Change 54, 65–66 (BNA Incorporated, 1963).

[272] For other illustrations of the use of mandatory injunctions, see Arbitrator Allen in 50 LA 522, 529; Prewett in 50 LA 344, 347; Teple in 48 LA 819, 825; Keefe in 48 LA 373, 379; Howlett in 46 LA 879, 881–882; Hon in 46 LA 769, 773; Cahn in 46 LA 195, 198; Somers in 43 LA 414, 426; Gross in 42 LA 339, 343.

[273] Labor Arbitration Procedures and Techniques 20–21 (AAA, 1961). For other suggested "don'ts" in arbitration, see Gill, "Gamesmanship in Labor Arbitration," Collective Bargaining and the Arbitrator's Role 148–158 (BNA Incorporated, 1962).

Expediting the Arbitration Machinery

In limited situations, particularly where there is a large accumulation of grievances, the parties may be able to expedite arbitration procedures to their mutual satisfaction and benefit.

For example, an expedited procedure was adopted by one union and employer to cut the costs and time involved in arbitrating a backlog of grievances. Under the expedited procedure: (1) Each party prepares a written statement of the grievance and facts, and submits a copy to the other party. (2) Each party states its thinking as to how the facts fit the contract, again with a copy to the other party. (3) Both parties seek to arrive at a joint statement. Failing that, their diverse views are submitted to the arbitrator. (4) The arbitrator holds a hearing where he asks questions and listens to statements limited to facts and opinions submitted in the aforementioned statements. No posthearing briefs are filed and no opinion accompanies the award unless the arbitrator feels that comments are needed (an award without an opinion would not serve as a precedent under their plan but could be used "as a basis for conversation").[274]

Some of the aforementioned possibilities for expediting arbitration proceedings are included among the following possibilities which have been enumerated by Arbitrator Harold W. Davey: (1) dry run arbitration; (2) prehearing statements; (3) avoidance of "brinkmanship" prior to actual arbitration; (4) greater use of submission agreements; (5) more effective use of factual stipulations and consequent reduced use of witnesses; (6) elimination of transcripts, except under special circumstances; (7) elimination of post-hearing briefs; (8) drastic shortening of opinions; (9) early issuance of award with brief statement of reasoning, followed later by full opinion; (10) greater use of memorandum opinions or even the equivalent of bench rulings; (11) increased use of "instant" arbitration; (12) expanded use of

---

[274] Ingersoll-Rand Co., 42 LA 965, 966–967 (Scheiber, 1964), where it is also noted that 25 grievances were settled during preparation of joint statements and the parties were able to agree upon a statement of facts in 18 of the 19 remaining cases. The arbitrator did write short opinions on most of the 19 cases. No doubt a significant factor in the success of the plan was the fact that Arbitrator Scheiber had long served the parties prior to use of the expedited procedure.

the hearing officer technique for routine cases under guidance of senior arbitrators.[275]

One or more of the above possibilities may have real utility in a particular case. Judgement obviously must be exercised by the parties and their arbitrator in determining which, if any, of the possibilities are desirable and of beneficial promise for the given parties or for the given case.

Tripartite Board Procedures

Tripartite arbitration boards are made up of one or more members selected by management, an equal number selected by labor, and a neutral who serves as chairman. While most of the material in this Chapter applies equally to tripartite boards and to arbitration tribunals composed only of one or more neutrals, the tripartite composition of the former tribunals raises certain other procedural questions. Both tripartite boards and the procedural questions which are particularly applicable to such boards are discussed in detail in Chapter 4.

Procedure of Boards Under Railway Labor Act

Under the Railway Labor Act boards exist or may be established for both "rights" and "interests" disputes. The procedures of these boards, which are of tripartite composition, are likewise discussed in detail in Chapter 4.

---

[275] Davey, "Restructuring Grievance Arbitration Procedures: Some Modest Proposals," 54 Iowa L. Rev. 560, 565 (1969). Each of these suggestions was discussed by Arbitrator Davey. Id. at 566–577.

CHAPTER 8

EVIDENCE

Strict Observance of Legal Rules of Evidence Usually Not Required

It is widely agreed that unless expressly required by the parties in submitting their case to an arbitrator, strict observance of legal rules of evidence is not necessary. As stated by one federal court:

"In an arbitration the parties have submitted the matter to persons whose judgment they trust, and it is for the arbitrators to determine the weight and credibility of evidence presented to them without restrictions as to the rules of admissibility which would apply in a court of law."[1]

Another federal court, in reviewing an arbitration award within the court's jurisdiction under §301(a) of the Labor Management Relations Act, stated that "It is well established that rules of evidence as applied in court proceedings do not prevail in arbitration hearings."[2] This has long been the rule under common law,[3] and it is the rule under most of the state statutes which deal expressly with the matter.[4]

Tripartite committees, set up by the National Academy of Arbitrators to study evidence problems, have agreed that the observance of rules of evidence should not be strictly required in arbitration proceedings.[5]

---

[1] Instrument Workers v. Minneapolis-Honeywell Co., 54 LRRM 2660, 2661 (U.S. Dist. Ct., E.D. Pa., 1963).

[2] Harvey Aluminum, Inc. v. Steelworkers, 64 LRRM 2580, 2581 (U.S. Dist. Ct., C.D. Calif., 1967). As persuasive guides to this effect the Court quoted a state court decision and American Arbitration Association Rule 28. The Court recognized that the parties can require use of legal rules of evidence. Id. at 2582–2583.

[3] See cases cited in 6 C.J.S. 203, n. 52.

[4] See Justin, "Arbitration: Proving Your Case," 10 LA 955, 962–963 (1948). Where a statute is either silent or not specific on the point, the common law ordinarily applies. See Chapter 2, Legal Status of Arbitration.

[5] See proceedings of National Academy of Arbitrators, Problems of Proof in Arbitration, 149–150, 163, 296 (The Bureau of National Affairs, Inc., 1967).

While the parties may expressly require the arbitrator to observe legal rules of evidence, they seldom do so. In fact, they sometimes specifically provide that strict observance of such rules shall not be required.[6]

Parties arbitrating under the rules of the American Arbitration Association are subject to its Rule 28, which provides, in part: "The Arbitrator shall be the judge of the relevancy and materiality of the evidence offered and conformity to legal rules of evidence shall not be necessary."[7] Likewise, the National Railroad Adjustment Board does not require strict adherence to the rules of evidence used by judicial tribunals.[8]

The net result is that in a majority of cases, "any evidence, information, or testimony is acceptable which is pertinent to the case and which helps the arbitrator to understand and decide the problem before him."[9]

In regard to the flexible application of legal rules of evidence in arbitration proceedings, Arbitrator Willard W. Wirtz has concluded that:

"[Arbitrators] have established the pattern of ordered informality; performing major surgery on the legal rules of evidence and procedure but retaining the good sense of those rules; greatly simplifying but not eliminating the hearsay and parole evidence rules; taking the rules for the admissibility of evidence and remolding them into rules for weighing it; striking the fat but saving the heart of the practices of cross-examination, presumptions, burden of proof, and the like."[10]

Flexible arbitral application of formal rules of evidence is particularly justified in regard to those rules of proof which come from the

---

This volume contains extensive discussion, with a wide variety of viewpoints, as to the precise extent to which the various legal rules of evidence should be applied in arbitration. One committee reached a consensus upon some general precepts to aid in gauging the extent of desirable resort to rules of evidence in a given case. Id. at 163–166. Another committee summarized the basic rules of evidence used by courts and made suggestions as to their applicability in arbitration proceedings. Id. at 249–260.

[6] As in Goodyear Engineering Corp., 24 LA 360, 361 (Warns, 1955).

[7] 30 LA 1086, 1089.

[8] Jones, National Railroad Adjustment Board, 24 (1941). This is a finding of the Attorney General's Committee on Administrative Procedure.

[9] Simkin & Kennedy, Arbitration of Grievances (U.S. Dept. of Labor, Div. of Labor Standards, Bull. No. 82, p. 25, 1946).

[10] Wirtz, "Due Process of Arbitration," The Arbitrator and the Parties 1, 13 (BNA, Inc., 1958).

criminal law. The application of these principles of proof in the field of arbitration, which deals with intraplant employer-employee relations, probably should not be accepted in all cases without some consideration of the appropriateness of their use in the determination of rights under collective agreements by arbitrators.[11]

Liberal Admission of Evidence

Although strict observance of legal rules of evidence usually is not required, the parties in all cases must be given adequate opportunity to present all of their evidence and argument. Arbitrators are usually extremely liberal in the reception of evidence, giving the parties a free hand in presenting any type of evidence thought to strengthen and clarify their case. Indeed, Arbitrator Harry Shulman has observed that "the more serious danger is not that the arbitrator will hear too much irrelevancy, but rather that he will not hear enough of the relevant."[12]

An interesting view has been expressed by Arbitrator William E. Simkin in justification of the free reception of evidence:

"One of the fundamental purposes of an arbitration hearing is to let people get things off their chest, regardless of the decision. The arbitration proceeding is the opportunity for a third party, an outside party, to come in and act as a sort of father confessor to the parties, to let them get rid of their troubles, get them out in the open, and have a feeling of someone hearing their troubles. Because I believe so strongly that that is one of the fundamental purposes of arbitration, I don't think you ought to use any rules of evidence. You have to make up your own mind as to what is pertinent or not in the case. Lots of times I have let people talk for five minutes, when I knew all the time that they were talking it had absolutely nothing to do with the case—just completely foreign to it. But there was a fellow testifying, either as a worker or a company representative, who had something that was important for him to get rid of. It was a good time for him to get rid of it."[13]

---

[11] For a similar view with extensive discussion, see Edwards, "Due Process Considerations in Labor Arbitration," 25 Arb. J. 141 (1970).

[12] Shulman, "Reason, Contract, and Law in Labor Relations," 68 Harv. L. Rev. 999, 1017 (1955).

[13] Conference on Training of Law Students in Labor Relations, Vol. III, Transcript of Proceedings 636–637 (1947). The "therapeutic" approach has many adherents, but also some critics. See Problems of Proof in Arbitration 244–247 (The Bureau of National Affairs, Inc., 1967). There have been some party complaints about the looseness of arbitration proceedings in the matter of presentation of evidence. See Smith & Jones, "Management and Labor Appraisals and

It might be noted that the liberal reception of evidence is not as extreme a departure from traditional judicial practice as many persons might believe; it is not unusual for judges who are trying cases without a jury to receive evidence very freely, on the basis that they can determine its weight and relevancy after all the case is in.

The Code of Ethics and Procedural Standards for Labor-Management Arbitration provides that: "The arbitrator should allow a fair hearing, with full opportunity to the parties to offer all evidence which they deem reasonably material. He may, however, exclude evidence which is clearly immaterial."[14] The need is to achieve a satisfactory balance between procedural efficiency and other interests:

> "At the hearing the arbitrator must provide for procedural efficiency, and at the same time assure himself that he is getting all that he needs to decide the case. To be successful at this he must bear in mind simultaneously a number of complex considerations. The attorneys must be allowed to present their cases fully as they see them. Witnesses should be allowed to say what they feel is important, sometimes even when it is technically irrelevant. It is sometimes necessary to be aware of political considerations within the union or among management people involved in the case, or between union and management in the plant or industry."[15]

Some excursions into extraneous matter may help the arbitrator get the background of the case or may help him understand the viewpoints of the parties. Moreover, the relevance of evidence offered in arbitration, though it may appear at first glance not to be germane to the case, cannot always be determined accurately until the entire case has been unfolded.[16] Accordingly, from a procedural standpoint arbitrators sometimes accept evidence while reserving their response thereto until the challenged evidence can be evaluated in the light of the whole record.[17] The objection to the evidence, even if overruled, will serve to caution the arbitrator to examine the challenged evidence more closely before giving it weight.[18]

Criticisms of the Arbitration Process: A Report and Comments," 62 Mich. L. Rev. 1115, 1127–1130 (1964).

[14] Part II, Rule 4(e).

[15] Eaton, "Labor Arbitration in the San Francisco Bay Area," 48 LA 1381, 1391–1392 (1967).

[16] As to this, see an interesting discourse in "Procedural Problems in the Conduct of Arbitration Hearings: A Discussion," Labor Arbitration-Perspectives and Problems 1, 10–11 (BNA Inc., 1964). LA 1048, 1052; Garrett in 16 LA 32.

[17] As did Arbitrator Sembower in 44 LA 593, 599–600; Seinsheimer in 40 LA 1048, 1052; Garrett in 16 LA 32.

[18] For further discussion, see Chapter 7, topic titled "Objections to Evidence."

Actually, the liberal admission of evidence is much less likely to render the proceedings vulnerable to court challenge than is the rejection of competent evidence.[19] Moreover, under some statutes an arbitrator's refusal to hear all relevant evidence is a ground for vacating the award.[20]

But an arbitrator may properly refuse to admit evidence that lacks revelance or probative value, for if no limitation is placed upon the reception of evidence the hearing can too easily go far afield. Moreover, under some circumstances an award may be properly rendered even though certain relevant evidence has not been formally received by the arbitrator. For instance, where data requested by an arbitrator was not submitted within the specified time, the issuance of the award prior to receipt of the requested data was held not to be ground for vacating the award where the court found that the arbitrator had in fact been fully informed as to the facts and issues of the case.[21]

Evidence to Be Heard by Entire Board

It is a general requirement that, where there is a board of arbitration, all evidence must be taken in the presence of all of the arbitrators. This requirement prevails in common-law arbitration[22] and in arbitration under state statutes.[23] It is also a general requirement under American Arbitration Association Rule 28.[24]

It has been held under a state statute, for instance, that an agreement to arbitrate entitles the parties to the considered judgment of arbitrators based upon evidence submitted in the presence of all the arbitrators, and that participation at proceedings at which only three of six arbitrators were present did not constitute a waiver of the re-

---

[19] See Harvey Aluminum, Inc. v. Steelworkers, 67 LRRM 2580 (U.S. Dist. Ct., C.D. Calif., 1967).
[20] The Uniform Arbitration Act so provides. 27 LA 909, 910. Also see Chapter 2, Legal Status of Arbitration.
[21] In re Aranson, 6 LA 1033 (N.Y. Sup. Ct., 1946). But cf. Excel Pharmacal Co., 21 LA 831 (N.Y. Sup. Ct., 1954). For a related discussion, see Chapter 7, topic titled "Default Awards."
[22] Ziskind, Labor Arbitration Under State Statutes 3 (U.S. Dept. of Labor, 1943).
[23] Id. at 15. While still providing that the hearing shall be conducted by all the arbitrators, some statutes provide that a majority may determine any question and render a final award. As, for instance, under the Uniform Arbitration Act, 27 LA 909, 910.
[24] 30 LA 1086, 1089.

quirement that all arbitrators be present for a binding award.[25] However, where it had been agreed that the partisan members of a board of arbitration could be substituted at any time, the award was held binding although one of the arbitrators who signed it had been substituted after the hearing and had not heard the evidence.[26]

It should be noted that the deliberate refusal by a party and its representatives on a tripartite board to attend the hearing may result in the issuance of a default award.[27]

What Type of Evidence Should Be Used

Of course the specific evidence introduced in individual cases will vary greatly from case to case according to the question involved. It is likewise obvious, however, that each general type of case requires a more or less specific type of evidence. In disputes over the setting of general wage rates, for instance, the most important type of evidence is documented statistical and economic data on such matters as prevailing practice, cost of living, ability to pay, and the like.[28]

In discharge or discipline cases the most important evidence generally comes in the form of testimony of witnesses, the facts which led to the disciplinary action being of great importance. If, however, there is not disagreement as to these facts and if the primary issue is one concerning proper punishment, then the past record of the employee and evidence of past disciplinary action taken in similar cases enter the picture in a major capacity.

In contract interpretation cases the history of precontract negotiations and the past practice of the parties in applying the disputed provision may be of great importance.

In some cases visual or pictorial evidence is useful. The arbitrator's understanding of the dispute may be greatly improved, for instance, by his visiting the physical site directly involved in the case.[29] Pictorial evidence may also be provided at the hearing room, as where

---

[25] Buitoni Products, Inc. v. Nappi, 12 LA 667 (N.Y. Sup. Ct., 1949).
[26] West Towns Bus Co. v. Division 241, 35 LA 145, 148 (Ill. App. Ct., 1960).
[27] See Chapter 7, topic titled "Default Awards." Also, Uniform Arbitration Act, 27 LA 909, 910.
[28] In one such case, "No witnesses were heard but counsel for each party argued their positions and commented on the exhibits." Pensacola News-Journal, 49 LA 433 (King, 1967).
[29] For full discussion, see Chapter 7, topic titled "Plant Visits by Arbitrator."

photographs of employees operating machines were submitted to the arbitrator in a job-rating dispute.[30]

Indeed, as long as evidence "fits" and is relevant to the case the unusual nature of the evidence should not bar its admission and consideration. Thus, in one case a significant type of evidence was sound and time recordings of the movements of a diesel locomotive to indicate the extent to which it was being utilized in a certain operation and to compare its efficiency with that of a steam locomotive.[31]

Ordinarily each party has the right to decide in what form it shall present its evidence; thus, one arbitrator refused to require a party to present its evidence through witnesses rather than statements and exhibits.[32]

"New" Evidence at Arbitration Hearing

Evidence is sometimes presented at the arbitration hearing which was not disclosed at the pre-arbitral grievance steps.[33] Some of the considerations involved in an arbitrator's decision to accept or reject such evidence include his great need for all the facts relevant to the case, the need to protect the integrity of the pre-arbitral grievance machinery, and general concepts of fairness. Thus it is not surprising that, in balancing these considerations, such evidence has been accepted in some cases but rejected in others.

It should be emphasized that whatever element of unfairness may be involved in the use of new evidence, it is largely mitigated or eliminated by the fact that arbitrators who accept newly submitted evidence will take any reasonable steps necessary to insure the opposite party adequate opportunity to respond thereto, regardless of whether the evidence had been withheld in good or bad faith.[34] If the arbitrator

---

[30] Brown & Sharpe Mfg. Co., 21 LA 461, 464–469 (Waite, 1953). Also see Westinghouse Electric Corp., 26 LA 836, 842 (Simkin, 1956).

[31] Republic Steel Corp., 24 LA 336, 339 (Platt, 1955).

[32] Sewanee Silica Co., 47 LA 282, 283 (Greene, 1966).

[33] For a related discussion, see Chapter 7, topic titled "Extent of Permissible Deviation from Pre-Arbitral Discussion of Case"; Chapter 15, topic titled "Post-Discharge Conduct or Charges." As to how frequently surprise evidence is encountered, see Eaton, "Labor Arbitration in the San Francisco Bay Area," 48 LA 1381, 1385 (1967).

[34] As to the reaction of surprised parties, "there is no evidence that they feel that the procedural steps which arbitrators have taken to protect their rights to respond to surprise materials have been less than satisfactory." Fleming, The Labor Arbitration Process 153–154 (Univ. of Ill. Press, 1965).

deems it necessary, for instance, he may return the case to the parties
for further consideration in the light of the new evidence or he may
recess the hearing for whatever time necessary to give the surprised
party opportunity to prepare or revise its defense.[35] Such interruptions
of the arbitration hearing can be avoided if parties using new evidence
will submit it to the other party prior to the hearing whenever the
nature of the evidence makes it reasonably foreseeable that the other
party will need time to prepare a response.[36]

A survey conducted by Arbitrator W. Willard Wirtz indicated
that "unless some deliberate attempt to mislead the other party is
disclosed, and particularly if the 'new' evidence or argument appears
substantially material, most arbitrators will be disinclined to rule the
matter out of the proceedings."[37] In this regard, Arbitrator Ralph
Seward has explained that many pre-arbitral grievance meetings "are
informal and deal with the surface of a problem without in any sense
taking real evidence,"[38] and Arbitrator Wirtz has observed that the
"company, for its part, may very reasonably not have made the thorough investigation it will properly consider warranted if the union
ultimately decides to take the case seriously enough to go to
arbitration."[39]

Also justifying the admission of new evidence, a tripartite committee has reasoned:

> "In some situations * * * it is the practice of the parties not
> to present all the evidence during the grievance procedure. In other
> situations the parties may recognize from the outset that a particular
> grievance must be arbitrated and pass quickly through the steps of
> [the] grievance procedure. In cases like these, evidence not disclosed
> prior to the hearing should be admitted. In general, evidence dis-
> covered after the grievance was processed should also be admitted.

---

[35] See Wirtz, "Due Process of Arbitration," The Arbitrator and the Parties
1, 16 (BNA Incorporated, 1958). In Pittsburgh Steel Co., 48 LA 585, 587
(Valtin, 1967), the arbitrator received the new material into evidence and gave
the surprised party an election to have the case remanded or to proceed with
it; the party chose to proceed.
[36] See suggestions of Arbitrator Maurice H. Merrill in Jonco Aircraft Corp.,
22 LA 819, 823 (1954).
[37] Wirtz, "Due Process of Arbitration," The Arbitrator and the Parties 1,
15 (BNA Incorporated, 1958). Also see Arbitrator Livengood in 47 LA 1170,
1171–1172; Kesselman in 46 LA 65, 70; Komaroff in 17 LA 183, 185–186.
[38] Wirtz, "Due Process of Arbitration," The Arbitrator and the Parties 1,
15 (BNA Incorporated, 1958).
[39] Ibid. Also see Arbitrator Sembower in San Gamo Electric Co., 44 LA
593, 600 (1965).

The arbitrator, however, should grant adjournments or take other measures to insure a fair hearing and to protect a party taken by surprise as to evidence concerning a material issue."[40]

The absence of any contract provision restricting acceptance of new evidence has sometimes been emphasized by arbitrators in receiving evidence presented for the first time at the arbitration hearing.[41] But even where an agreement provided that "the facts concerning the case shall be made available to both parties" at an early stage, facts acquired later could be introduced at subsequent steps of the grievance procedure or at the arbitration hearing.[42]

Also, under a contract requiring the employer to furnish all available evidence to the union "and/or" the arbitrator, the withholding of evidence until the arbitration hearing was held not to be improper where the union was granted 10 days to consider the evidence; sufficient time for consideration of evidence was deemed the basic purpose of the provision.[43]

While stating that "it is understandable that the evidence which comes out at the arbitration hearing is more detailed and more complete than that which is produced in the preliminary steps of the grievance machinery," Umpire I. Robert Feinberg considers that delay in presenting evidence "mitigates its relative importance."[44] Moreover, he has refused to accept evidence offered by a party for the first time at the arbitration stage where the evidence was known to the party at the earlier grievance stages and would have expanded the party's claim if admitted at the arbitration stage.[45]

It is the intentional, calculated, withholding of evidence that arbitrators criticize most severely. In this regard, the view of Umpire

---

[40] "Report of the New York Tripartite Committee," Problems of Proof in Arbitration 295, 302–303 (The Bureau of National Affairs, Inc., 1967). Other tripartite committees were likewise in general agreement that new evidence should be admitted into evidence, and that the arbitrator should take reasonable steps to protect the other party. Id. at 104, 142–143, 260–261.

[41] See North American Aviation, Inc., 17 LA 183, 185–186 (Komaroff, 1951); Carbon Fuel Company, 1 ALAA ¶67,327 (1946). The above-quoted tripartite committee took the position that to the extent that the contract specifically requires full disclosure, new evidence should be rejected by the arbitrator. "Report of the New York Tripartite Committee," Problems of Proof in Arbitration 302 (The Bureau of National Affairs, Inc., 1967).

[42] American Steel & Wire Co., 5 LA 193, 206–207 (Blumer, 1946).

[43] Texas Co., 7 LA 735, 739 (Carmichael, 1947).

[44] Bethlehem Steel Co., 21 LA 655, 656 (1953).

[45] Bethlehem Steel Co., 18 LA 366, 367 (1951).

Gabriel N. Alexander is no doubt shared by many arbitrators:

"[S]ound collective bargaining requires frank and candid disclosure at the earliest opportunity of all the facts known to each party. There will undoubtedly be times when facts are not discovered, and therefore not disclosed, until after the grievance has been partially processed, and problem enough is created by those instances. There is not a scintilla of justification for the withholding of information by either party from and after the time it is discovered."[46]

But the calculated withholding of evidence did not result in its rejection by the arbitrator where, from the outset, the attitude of the party from whom it was withheld was such as to put all pre-arbitral steps on an adversary basis, "with both sides primarily pointed at an ultimate arbitration instead of mutual ascertainment of fact, compromise, or some other solution based upon general collective bargaining considerations."[47]

If the arbitration tribunal is serving essentially in an appellate capacity there is obviously strong reason to confine the evidence to what was considered below. In this regard, the rules of the National Railroad Adjustment Board require that "all data submitted in support" of the party's position "must affirmatively show the same to have been presented to the [other party] and made a part of the particular question in dispute."[48]

Requiring the Production of Evidence

Use of Subpoenas

It is generally accepted that unless authorized by applicable statute or by the agreement, the arbitrator has no subpoena power.[49]

---

[46] General Motors Umpire Decision No. F-97 (1950). Arbitrator Peter Seitz chastised both parties for calculated withholding of evidence in Sperry-Rand Corp., 46 LA 961, 966 (1966), and he noted that such practice can be "self-defeating." Also suggesting that the practice "is likely to boomerang," Davey, "The John Deere-UAW Permanent Arbitration System," Critical Issues in Labor Arbitration 161, 170 (BNA Incorporated, 1957).

[47] Bethlehem Steel Co., 6 LA 617, 619 (Wyckoff, 1947).

[48] National Railroad Adjustment Board, Organization and Certain Rules of Procedure, Circular No. 1 issued Oct. 10, 1934.

[49] Problems of Proof in Arbitration 99, 140, 258 (The Bureau of National Affairs, Inc., 1967), where it is also noted that many states do give arbitrators statutory subpoena power (p. 140). For reference to agreements which expressly grant the arbitrator power to call witnesses and to require production of documentary evidence, see Major Collective Bargaining Agreements: Arbitration Procedures 66–67 (U.S. Dept. of Labor Bull. No. 1425-6, 1966). American Arbitration

One observer, however, has suggested "the idea that because the arbitration process is now federal" an argument can be made that even in states which do not authorize arbitrators to issue subpoenas an arbitrator may do so.[50]

Where a subpoena had been issued by an arbitrator pursuant to state statute, a federal court responded as follows when asked to enforce the subpoena:

"Had the arbitrator and plaintiff's counsel utilized the enforcement procedures prescribed by the Federal Arbitration Act, * * * we would not be confronted with the hybrid question of defendant's compliance with a state subpoena. The plaintiff elected to proceed through avenues afforded by state process; it is not now within this Court's prerogative to intervene and enforce that process.

"Procedural niceties and technical obstructionism, however, with rare exception, should not be judicially nurtured; especially, is this true when lawful arbitration procedural remedies are already in progress. * * * This federal Court does have concurrent enforcement jurisdiction and possesses the necessary statutory authority [citing the Federal Arbitration Act] to enforce the procedures attendant upon the orderly consummation of this arbitration hearing. * * * Under this aegis, it will act *sua sponte* to sever the Gordian knot which created the impasse. The defendant shall produce forthwith the disputed file material for an *in camera* inspection by the arbitrator.

"Such a procedure will, of course, deny to the plaintiff-Union its claim of a carte blanche discovery privilege, to peruse the employer's file. Arbitration has never afforded to litigants complete freedom to delve into and explore at will, the adversary party's files under the pretense of pre-trial discovery. * * *

"It must be assumed that the presiding arbitrator is an experienced person well versed in evaluating the alleged claims of the employer, that some files contain classified security information involving national defense or plant security, personal health records and other similar confidential data. All of this should be screened from the file, except where the arbitrator determines it to be relevant evidence in the dispute. Even in the latter instances, proper safeguards should be ordered, such as sealing the record or limiting its access to counsel

---

Association Rule 28 permits the arbitrator to subpoena witnesses and documents when "authorized by law."

[50] Comment of T. L. Tolan, Problems of Proof in Arbitration 143–144 (The Bureau of National Affairs, Inc., 1967). For a more detailed suggestion along similar lines, see Matto, "The Applicability of State Arbitration Statutes to Proceedings Subject to LMRA Section 301," 27 Ohio State L. J. 692, 705–708 (1966).

only, so that no unnecessary harm or prejudice or unnecessary embarrassment may be caused to anyone."[51]

One group has expressed the view that "Even assuming its legality, the use of the subpoena is not to be encouraged. Demands for relevant information by either party should be honored without the formality of a subpoena."[52]

When a subpoena is to be issued, a procedure along the following lines might be utilized: The requesting party will prepare the subpoena and submit it to the arbitrator for his signature; then the arbitrator or the requesting party will cause it to be served (by anyone other than a party to the case); the subpoena may thereupon be challenged as to scope, materiality, or reasonableness.[53]

Evidence Requested by Arbitrator

The absence of the subpoena power is not very important, since the parties usually are willing to provide any data or evidence requested by the arbitrator.[54]

Arbitrators do not hesitate to request the production of data or information if they have reasonable basis to believe that it will be

---

[51] Machinists v. Pratt & Whitney Division, 329 F.Supp. 283, 286–287 (USDC, D. Conn., 1971), the court also upholding the arbitrator's authority to reopen the arbitration hearing in order to issue a subpoena which by oversight the arbitrator had failed to issue earlier in the arbitration proceedings. In Local 757, IBT v. Borden, Inc., 78 LRRM 2398 (USDC, N.Y., 1971), the court refused to enforce a subpoena obtained by a union from a state court, where an arbitrator had already taken the union's request for production of the desired books and records under advisement.

[52] Report of Pittsburgh Tripartite Committee, Problems of Proof in Arbitration 258 (The Bureau of National Affairs, Inc., 1967). The Chicago Tripartite Committee agrees. Id. at 99. This Committee deems use of subpoenas justified in some situations (as where an employee is reluctant to take time off to testify) but of doubtful wisdom in others (as where an employee is required to testify against a fellow employee). Id. at 100.

[53] See Automatic Electric Co., 42 LA 1056, 1057, 1060–1064 (Sembower, 1964); Schultz and Burch Biscuit Co., 42 LA 280, 281–282, 290 (Solomon, 1964). Use of subpoenas may present troublesome time problems, sometimes requiring adjournment of the hearing to a later date. Ibid. The Uniform Arbitration Act authorizes the arbitrator to issue (or cause to be issued) subpoenas and provides for court enforcement. 27 LA 909, 910. The New York statute in addition authorizes issuance of subpoenas by the attorneys of record. New York CPLR §§2308(b), 7505. In Local 757, IBT v. Borden, Inc., 78 LRRM 2398, 2399 (USDC, N.Y., 1971), the court observed that "Under the United States Arbitration Act it is clear that only an arbitrator can issue a subpoena while under state law an attorney of record may issue a subpoena."

[54] See, for example, Clay City Pipe Co., 20 LA 538, 542 (Young, 1952). Also see comments by Arbitrator Fleming, The Labor Arbitration Process 175 (Univ. of Ill. Press, 1965).

germane to the case.[55] While the arbitrator himself often initiates the request for the production of evidence,[56] in other instances he may make the request on the motion of the party who otherwise does not have access to the evidence in question.[57]

One arbitrator has declared that "neither the Company nor the Union should be allowed to withhold relevant and material testimony or other evidence except possibly in special circumstances * * * such as possible criminal incrimination, trade secrets and classified Defense matters."[58] As concerns the "relevant and material" qualification, arbitrators have refused to order the production of evidence for the purpose of uncovering grievances as distinguished from testing the validity of specific claims.[59]

In one case the arbitrator issued "an interim award," during the course of the hearing, "directing the Company to submit certain payroll information to the Union for its use in connection with" the case.[60] Prior to the hearing in another case, an arbitration board of three neutrals issued the following order:

> "Each party shall produce, at least three working days in advance of the hearing, for the use of the other party such specific documents or information in the employment history of either the challenging striker or the challenged replacement on which it expects to rely at the hearing. Further, at the demand of either party made at least five working days in advance of the hearing the other party shall produce such pertinent specific documents as the demanding party believes to be in the possession of the other party."[61]

---

[55] See discussion by Arbitrator Harry J. Dworkin in Chesapeake & Potomac Telephone Co. of West Virginia, 21 LA 367, 369–371 (1953). Under Federal Mediation & Conciliation Service Regulations, Sec. 1404.12, "the expenses of any witnesses * * * produced at the direct request of the arbitrator, shall be borne equally by the parties unless the arbitrator in his award assesses such expenses or any part thereof against any specified party or parties."

[56] See Detroit Edison Co., 43 LA 193, 200 (Smith, 1964); Resistoflex Corp., 19 LA 761, 762 (Levy, 1952).

[57] See Arbitrator Jones in 29 LA 372, 373; Justin in 24 LA 44, 47; Dworkin in 21 LA 367, 369–371; Feinberg in 18 LA 55, 56.

[58] Tectum Corp., 37 LA 807, 810 (Autrey, 1961).

[59] See Santa Clara County & Central California Meat Processors' Assn., 36 LA 42, 43–44 (Wyckoff, 1961); Chrysler Corp., 22 LA 128, 138 (Wolff, 1954).

[60] News Syndicate Co., 18 LA 55, 56 (Feinberg, 1952). Similar action by an arbitrator was upheld in Local 246, I.L.G.W.U. v. Evans Mfg. Co., 53 LRRM 2455, 40 LA 864 (CA 3, 1963).

[61] Yale & Towne Mfg. Co., 39 LA 1156, 1160 (Hill, Horlacher & Seitz, 1962). For the pros and cons of arbitral use of "discovery" procedures similar to those used by some courts, see Problems of Proof in Arbitration 170–171,

While the National Railroad Adjustment Board does not have the subpoena power,[62] its rules of procedure provide that the parties are "charged with the duty and responsibility of including in their original written submission all known relevant, argumentative facts and documentary evidence."[63]

Significance of Failure to Provide Evidence

The significance of a refusal or failure to provide requested data or evidence is indicated by a statement of Arbitrator Saul Wallen:

"An arbitrator has no right to compel the production of documents [it might be otherwise if the arbitration is carried out under an arbitration statute] by either side. He may, however, give such weight as he deems appropriate to the failure of a party to produce documents on demand. The degree of weight to be attached to such failure will depend upon the relevancy of the documents requested to the issues at hand. If the information withheld appears to be strongly pertinent, the withholding of it may be vital in the making of a decision. If it is of doubtful relevancy and merely represents an attempt by one party to probe through the files of another on the mere chance that its position may be generally strengthened thereby, then the failure to produce such records should be disregarded."[64]

The failure of a party to use a person as a witness who should be in a position to contribute informed testimony may create some sort of inference against the party or at least cause the arbitrator to wonder why the person was not called to testify.[65]

218–227, 304, 333–334 (The Bureau of National Affairs, Inc., 1967); Fleming, The Labor Arbitration Process 61–63 (Univ. of Ill. Press, 1965); Sembower, "Halting the Trend Toward Technicalities in Arbitration," Critical Issues in Labor Arbitration 98, 102 (BNA Incorporated, 1957). Also see Arbitrator Merrill in 20 LA 211, 212; Komaroff in 19 LA 385, 390. As to the duty of the company under the NLRA to provide information to enable the union to evaluate grievances that have been filed, see NLRB v. Acme Industrial Co., 87 S.Ct. 565 (1967).

[62] Jones, National Railroad Adjustment Board 25 (1941).
[63] National Railroad Adjustment Board, Organization and Certain Rules of Procedure, Circular No. 1, issued Oct. 10, 1934.
[64] American Telephone & Telegraph Co., 6 LA 31, 43 (1947). A Pittsburgh Tripartite Committee stated that "an arbitrator should be free to draw conclusions from an individual's failure to testify." Problems of Proof in Arbitration 258 (The Bureau of National Affairs, Inc., 1967). Cf. statement of Arbitrator Kornblum, id. at 328–329; Dworkin in 21 LA 367, 371.
[65] See Brass-Craft Mfg. Co., 36 LA 1177, 1184 (Kahn, 1961); Standard Oil Co. (Indiana), 25 LA 32, 36 (Burris, 1955). For related discussion, see this Chapter, topic titled "Failure of Grievant to Testify."

Use of Adverse Witnesses

Except for one limitation, noted hereinbelow, it appears accepted that the arbitrator should not limit the right of parties to call witnesses from the other side.[66]

The limitation referred to above concerns the grievant in discipline cases. There is a definite split of opinion as to whether the company should have any right to call the grievant as a witness.[67]

Question has been raised as to whether a party calls an adverse witness at its peril; opinion differs as to how strictly such party should be held bound by the testimony of an adverse witness.[68]

Failure of Grievant to Testify

The individual grievant is often able to cast light upon the dispute and ordinarily takes the witness stand. Indeed, the arbitrator prefers that he do so, as explained by Arbitrator Russell A. Smith: "* * * I would like to see the grievant on the stand at some point during the proceeding, and I feel a little uncomfortable, frankly, when he is not. I don't know how many other people share that feeling."[69]

---

[66] Problems of Proof in Arbitration 99, 258, 324 (The Bureau of National Affairs, Inc., 1967). However, a suggestion has been made that the calling of witnesses from the other side should not be encouraged. Id. at 99. As a matter of policy, some companies never call bargaining unit members as witnesses. Id. at 233, 328. On the other hand, a party making no effort to call a person to testify might have little standing to complain that the other party failed to use the person as a witness. F. M. Stamper Co., 51 LA 533, 537 (Eaton, 1968). In Jaeger Machine Co., 55 LA 850, 852 (High, 1970), inferences adverse to the union's case were created when the union refused to permit its representative to testify when the employer attempted to call him as a witness.

[67] Problems of Proof in Arbitration 201–202, 228–229, 258, 324–325 (The Bureau of National Affairs, Inc., 1967). Also see panel discussion, "Procedural Problems in the Conduct of Arbitration Hearings: A Discussion," Labor Arbitration—Perspectives and Problems 27 (BNA Incorporated, 1964). For related material, see this Chapter, topic titled "Failure of Grievant to Testify," and see Chapter 7, topic titled "Order of Presenting Case."

[68] See panel discussion, "Procedural Problems in the Conduct of Arbitration Hearings: A Discussion," Labor Arbitration—Perspectives and Problems 28 (BNA Incorporated, 1964). "Ordinarily, a party may not impeach its own witness through his own testimony, except where he is a hostile witness or his testimony can be shown to constitute surprise." Problems of Proof in Arbitration 302 (The Bureau of National Affairs, Inc., 1967), where it is also stated that "A hostile witness is one who manifests so much hostility or prejudice under examination that the. party who has called him is allowed to cross-examine him, i.e., to treat him as though he had been called by the opposite party."

[69] This statement was made in a National Academy of Arbitrators' discussion; a poll was taken in response to Arbitrator Smith's statement, revealing that a "very large majority" of those present shared his feeling. Problems of Proof in Arbitration 232 (The Bureau of National Affairs, Inc., 1967).

It is not unexpected that the failure of a grievant to appear and testify at the hearing of his grievance has in some cases been one of the factors leading to the arbitrator's conclusion that the grievance lacked merit.[70] However, arbitrators sometimes have expressly stated that the failure of a grievant to testify creates no inference against him;[71] even so, an arbitrator may pointedly note that the grievant's failure to testify has left the case against him unrefuted.[72] The latter situation assumes, of course, that the company has adequately established its case by probative evidence.

In most cases a grievant's testimony will be beneficial to his case. It has sometimes happened, however, that "the chief witness against the grievant was the grievent."[73] Furthermore, if the grievant does take the witness stand, he has an "obligation to testify frankly and fully."[74]

A question thus arises whether an employee may refuse to testify in arbitration by the exercise of a privilege against self-incrimination. One survey has indicated that "there is a fairly clear consensus in the arbitration opinions" that the privilege against self-incrimination, "established in the criminal law, has no place, at least as such, in the arbitration of grievance cases (invariably discharge or disciplinary cases)."[75] However, Arbitrator Nathan P. Feinsinger spoke in that survey as follows: "My evaluation of a discharged employee's not testifying has depended on the circumstances. * * * I don't think one

---

[70] See Arbitrator Carmichael in 52 LA 469, 473; Teple in 51 LA 177, 181; Hardy in 48 LA 1036, 1038 (grievant was present but did not testify); Turkus in 41 LA 575, 576 (but Turkus viewed the grievant's silence differently in 45 LA 1050, 1051–1052 since criminal charges were still pending against the grievant); Maggs in 22 LA 761, 764; Klamon in 16 LA 461, 465–466. Also see Cole in 23 LA 64, 65.

[71] See Arbitrator McIntosh in 50 LA 504, 506; Kesselman in 49 LA 692, 696; Altieri in 43 LA 400, 405; Foster in 40 LA 1311, 1313. It has been noted that there may be innocent explanations of failure to testify, as where the individual is "inarticulate, unintelligent, or easily confused." Problems of Proof in Arbitration 201 (The Bureau of National Affairs, Inc., 1967). Parties sometimes stipulate that the nonappearance of the grievant shall not be prejudicial to his interests. As in U.S. Rubber Co., 25 LA 417, 418 (Hall, 1955).

[72] See Arbitrator McIntosh in 50 LA 504, 506; Kesselman in 49 LA 692, 696; McCoy in 26 LA 742, 745–746.

[73] Diebold, Inc., 48 LA 893, 900 (Bradley, 1967). To similar effect, Capitol Mfg. Co., 46 LA 633, 636 (Gibson, 1966).

[74] Clark Grave Vault Co., 47 LA 381, 382 (McCoy, 1966).

[75] Wirtz, "Due Process of Arbitration," The Arbitrator and the Parties 1, 19–20 (BNA Incorporated, 1958), where several unreported arbitration decisions are noted. Also see comments of Arbitrator McGury in 44 LA 658, 662–663; Maggs in 27 LA 709, 712–713; Klamon in 16 LA 461, 465–466.

can generalize here." Arbitrator R. W. Fleming has proposed a set
of rules whose effect would appear to give at least minimal application
in arbitration to the privilege against self-incrimination.[76] Furthermore, Arbitrator Edgar A. Jones has urged that arbitrators should
give consideration to all Fifth Amendment principles, including the
privilege against self-incrimination.[77] Arbitrator Jones' view has been
severely criticized, however, by Professor Harry T. Edwards.[78]

It should be noted that employee discipline for "refusal to cooperate" has been upheld in some court and arbitration cases, even
though the employee based his position on privilege against self-incrimination.[79] This was so, for instance, where an arbitrator upheld
the discharge of an employee for refusal to be fingerprinted in connection with an investigation into the theft of company products.[80]

The Lie Detector

Under the overwhelming weight of arbitral authority employees
are not to be penalized for refusal to take lie detector tests; and where

---

[76] Fleming, The Labor Arbitration Process 185–186 (Univ. of Ill. Press,
1965). Arbitrator Fleming discussed the constitutional privilege against self-incrimination in some detail. Id. at 181–185.

[77] See Thrifty Drug Stores Co., 50 LA 1253, 1260–1263 (Jones, 1968);
Problems of Proof in Arbitration 199–200 (The Bureau of National Affairs,
Inc., 1967). In the circumstances of one case Arbitrator Turkus gave strong
recognition to the privilege against self-incrimination. United Parcel Service,
Inc., 45 LA 1050, 1051–1052 (1965).

[78] Edwards, "Due Process Considerations in Labor Arbitration," 25 Arb.
J. 141, 151, 154–155, 157, 165 (1970). The Jones view is said to be "unrealistic
in terms of providing a reasonable guide for harmonious collective bargaining
between the parties." Id. at 154. The "standard of 'fairness,' which has traditionally been employed by arbitrators as the more flexible replacement for due
process, seems far better suited to the composite needs of all of the parties
to the tripartite collective bargaining relationship." Id. at 169.

[79] See Fleming, The Labor Arbitration Process 182–184 (Univ. of Ill. Press,
1965).

[80] Colgate-Palmolive Co., 50 LA 441, 443–444 (Koven, 1968). In Exact
Weight Scale Co., 50 LA 8, 8–9 (1967), Arbitrator Whitley P. McCoy held
that an employee could not be discharged for refusing to say whether or not
he had violated a company rule, but that back pay should be denied since
the employee could have mitigated damages by answering promptly (he had
finally answered "no," but not until the arbitration hearing). In Trans World
Airlines, Inc., 46 LA 611, 612 (Wallen, 1965), the company was held entitled
to require a hostess to demonstrate that she was not wearing a wig in connection
with enforcement of regulations as to length of hair. Another arbitrator upheld
a broadcasting company's right to require members of its news staff to fill out
a financial interests questionnaire (to prevent conflict of interest problems) against
the charge that the requirement subjected the employee to self-incrimination.
National Broadcasting Co., 53 LA 312, 318–319 (Scheiber, 1969). Also see Arbitrator Johnson in 56 LA 52, 53–54.

an employee does submit to lie detector testing, the test results should be given little or no weight in arbitration.[81] Numerous reasons exist for questioning the use of the polygraph and for doubting the reliability of its results.[82]

Emphasizing the reluctance of arbitrators to rely upon lie detectors, certain specific cases may be noted. Thus, an employee may not be bound by his employment application promise to submit to lie detector tests.[83]

Efforts to strengthen the testimony of other persons against an employee, by causing the accuser to take a lie detector test, have not impressed arbitrators.[84] Even where an accused employee agrees to take a lie detector test, an arbitrator will prefer to rely upon other types of evidence, though the test results may be noted as to their corroborating effect.[85]

Right of Cross-Examination

Arbitrators uphold the right of cross-examination, but probably not as strongly as do courts of law. An arbitrator ordinarily will not accept an offer of evidence if it is conditioned upon nondisclosure to the other party. Thus, for instance, disciplinary action based solely

---

[81] See Arbitrator Gross in 46 LA 756, 761; Epstein in 45 LA 1155, 1158; Eiger in 66-1 ARB ¶8359; Carmichael in 66-1 ARB ¶8310; Kornblum in 44 LA 709, 710–711; Sembower in 44 LA 405, 409; Rice in 44 LA 16, 18–19; Miller in 63-1 ARB ¶8179; Kelliher in 63-1 ARB ¶8106; Walter in 41 LA 442 at 442; Ryder in 39 LA 470, 479; Lewis in 39 LA 332, 335; Duncan in 39 LA 125, 127; Simkin in 33 LA 44, 48. Cf., Maxwell in 63-1 ARB ¶8026. In Allen Industries, Inc., 26 LA 363, 369 (Klamon, 1956), refusal to take a lie detector test was held a "refusal to cooperate" justifying discharge. For a collection of court and arbitration decisions concerning use of the polygraph, and a collection of articles on the subject, see Louis Zahn Drug Co., 40 LA 352, 356–358 (Sembower, 1963). The courts have generally rejected lie detector evidence. Burkey, "Lie Detectors in Labor Relations," 19 Arb. J. 193 (1964).
[82] For a statement of these reasons, see B. F. Goodrich Tire Co., 36 LA 552, 558 (Ryder, 1961).
[83] Lag Drug Co., 39 LA 1121, 1122–1123 (Kelliher, 1962). But an employer was held entitled to require plant guards to take lie detector tests under their agreement in Warwick Electronics, Inc., 46 LA 95, 97–98 (Daugherty, 1966).
[84] See Arbitrator Walter in 41 LA 442 at 442; Maxwell in 39 LA 883, 885; Porter in 39 LA 745, 746–747.
[85] See Owens-Corning Fiberglas Corp., 48 LA 1089, 1091 (Doyle, 1967), where the test corroborated other evidence of innocence; Westinghouse Electric Corp., 43 LA 450, 452–453 (Singletary, 1964), where the test corroborated other evidence of guilt.

on the charge of an employee whose identity the employer was unwilling to reveal was set aside by Arbitrator David A. Wolff, who stated that no matter how meritorious the reasons for nondisclosure may be, it results in a lack of competent proof.[86] Like reasoning applies to employer reliance on allegedly confidential records not available as proof,[87] and to an employee's defense assertions supported by evidence which the union is unwilling to disclose.[88]

In certain limited situations, however, nondisclosure has not resulted in rejection of evidence. For example, Arbitrator George H. Hildebrand accepted reports of professional "spotters," although the bus driver against whom the reports were used was not permitted to confront the spotters or otherwise know their identity, considering that (1) control over bus drivers is essential for the safety of the public and protection of company property, and the spotter system provides the only practical means by which supervision can exert its responsibility in the transit industry; (2) open identification of the spotters would destroy the effectiveness of the system; (3) the spotters, unlike ordinary employees, were trained observers taught to be accurate and objective, having no personal contacts with the employees and having no incentive to falsify facts; (4) the spotters' reports were prepared before the decision to discharge was made; and (5) there was no tangible basis for believing that the company was biased against the grievant.[89]

Arbitrator Hildebrand added a very important qualification, however: "the necessity for the system would not justify its sloppy

---

[86] Murray Corporation of America, 8 LA 713, 714 (1947). To similar effect, Arbitrator Forsythe in 53 LA 511, 513; Haughton in 52 LA 832, 834; Doyle in 48 LA 1089, 1091 (involving anonymous tip); Koven in 42 LA 803, 805; Kates in 36 LA 857, 859; Scheiber in 24 LA 538, 540–541; Bowles in 22 LA 320, 323; Aaron in 13 LA 433, 434. Also see discussion of "absentee evidence" in Wirtz, "Due Process of Arbitration," The Arbitrator and the Parties 1, 16–17 (BNA Incorporated, 1958). Where he did confront grievant at the arbitration hearing, failure to identify the accuser at the grievance meeting was held not to be improper. Cleaners Hangers Co., 39 LA 661, 664, 667 (Klein, 1962). To similar effect, Arbitrator Sembower in 55 LA 731, 735–737, and in 53 LA 841, 844.
[87] Problems of Proof in Arbitration 204 (The Bureau of National Affairs, Inc., 1967), view of West Coast Tripartite Committee.
[88] Berg Airlectro Products Co., 46 LA 668, 672, 675–676 (Sembower, 1966).
[89] Los Angeles Transit Lines, 25 LA 740, 744–746 (1955). In general accord are the views of Arbitrator Brecht in 23 LA 362, 365. Also see Levinson in 37 LA 748, 750, 754; Oppenheim in 29 LA 291, 292; Seward in 19 LA 210, 211.

or unfair use in disciplinary procedure."[90] Thus, even where spotters were identified and testified, Arbitrator Frank Elkouri could not place strong weight on their testimony or written reports since the testimony was shaky and the reports had not been written up promptly.[91]

Some arbitrators are unreceptive to suggestions that the arbitrator interview spotters or other accusers in private,[92] and one arbitrator insists that the spotter be produced, if he is to be relied upon, "even though the consequence would be to destroy his usefulness to the company."[93]

Sometimes the collective agreement itself will indicate the extent to which testimony or proof by professional investigators may be used and the extent to which it must be subjected to cross-examination.[94]

A statement signed by numerous employees making certain assertions as to fact in a disciplinary case was admitted into evidence, over strenuous objections of the company, but could be given "very little weight" since most of the signers did not testify and were not subject to cross-examination.[95] However, the mere fact that a party presented its nondisciplinary case by written statements and exhibits, rather than through use of witnesses subject to cross-examination, was held

---

[90] Los Angeles Transit Lines, 25 LA 740, 745 (1955). Arbitrator Levinson adds still another qualification: "in assessing the degree of discipline," the sworn denial of the accused should be given "the benefit of the doubt" as against the written report of the undisclosed spotter. Twin City Rapid Transit Co., 37 LA 748, 754 (1961).

[91] Twin City Transit, Inc., 65-2 ARB ¶8438 (1965). Where the grievant is confronted with the spotter at the arbitration hearing, the spotter's testimony and report will be accepted into evidence. See Arbitrator Nathanson in 51 LA 120, 126; Schieber in 48 LA 812, 816 (also holding that delayed confrontation of accused by spotter is not improper, since premature confrontations impair future usefulness of spotter).

[92] Discussion Panel, "Procedural Problems in the Conduct of Arbitration Hearings: A Discussion," Labor Arbitration—Perspectives and Problems 21 (BNA Incorporated, 1964).

[93] Id. at 19. In one case a spotter was placed behind a screen where he was visible only to the arbitrator and counsel for the parties. Fleming, "Due Process and Fair Procedure in Labor Arbitration," Arbitration and Public Policy 69, 85 (BNA Incorporated, 1961); Fleming also discussed confrontation cases in general (pp. 82–87).

[94] As in Bee Line, Inc., 20 LA 675, 676 (Feinberg, 1953).

[95] Rich Mfg. Co., 46 LA 154, 161 (Block, 1966). Customer accusations of employee disrespect carried less significance where the customers, though identified, were absent from the arbitration hearing. Penn Jersey Boiler & Construction Co., 50 LA 177, 180 (Buckwalter, 1967).

not to deprive the opponent of a fair hearing where adequate opportunity to respond to the evidence did exist.[96]

The admission of hearsay evidence denies the opposing party opportunity for complete cross-examination. Courts of law ordinarily refuse hearsay testimony for this reason. While arbitrators admit hearsay evidence, they seek to offset the effects of incomplete cross-examination by admitting it only "for what it is worth."[97]

Since the arbitrator has a paramount interest in securing all of the facts, he may refuse to restrict cross-examination to matters brought out in the examination-in-chief, and he can be expected not to place strict limitation upon the number of re-cross or re-direct examinations. As to the first of these points, arbitral consensus appears to be that reasonably wide latitude should be permitted in cross-examination.[98] It has been suggested, however, that the cross-examiner who seeks to go beyond the direct examination area should call the witness as an adverse or hostile witness.[99]

While the parties are allowed considerable latitude in cross-examining witnesses, to reveal conflicts in their testimony and to challenge credibility, arbitrators will not condone use of personal invectives against witnesses.[100]

Evidence Submitted After Hearing

While ordinarily no new data or evidence may be presented after the hearing, in briefs or otherwise, there are exceptions.[101] Sometimes discussion at the hearing indicates need for additional data which are not quickly available, and if the parties desire not to recess or otherwise delay the hearing, they may agree to the submission of the data to the arbitrator after the hearing has been completed. Likewise,

---

[96] Sewanee Silica Co., 47 LA 282, 283 (Greene, 1966), involving change in job classification.

[97] See this Chapter, topic titled "Hearsay Evidence."

[98] Problems of Proof in Arbitration 102, 147, 259, 301 (The Bureau of National Affairs, Inc., 1967).

[99] Discussion Panel, "Procedural Problems in the Conduct of Arbitration Hearings: A Discussion," Labor Arbitration—Perspectives and Problems 1, 9 (BNA Incorporated, 1964).

[100] See Friden Calculating Machine Co., 27 LA 496, 500–501 (Justin, 1956).

[101] See Chapter 7, topic titled "Briefs" and topic titled "Reopening the Hearing."

the arbitrator during or after the hearing has been completed may request posthearing data or information.[102]

Then, too, important evidence sometimes is discovered or first becomes available after the hearing.[103]

Such posthearing data often will be jointly prepared and submitted by the parties. If the data are individually prepared each party ordinarily must be furnished a copy of the other party's data so that comment may be made thereon or so that a further hearing can be requested in case of gross discrepancies.[104]

Weight and Credibility of Evidence

It is within the province of the arbitrator to determine the weight, relevancy, and authenticity of evidence. The general approach of arbitrators in giving weight and credibility to evidence is effectively illustrated by a statement made by Arbitrator George Cheney in reviewing the discharge of an employee. He noted that the case was illustrative of the type of situation in which the facts are to a large extent determined by the weight and credibility accorded to the testimony of the witnesses and to the documentary evidence offered by the parties. He pointed out that, in arriving at the truth in such a case, an arbitrator must consider whether conflicting statements ring true or false; that he will note the witnesses' demeanor while on the stand; and that he will credit or discredit testimony according to his impressions of the witnesses' veracity. Arbitrator Cheney also pointed out that, in determining where the preponderance of the evidence lies with respect to any material point, the arbitrator will take into consideration whether the witness speaks from first-hand information or whether his testimony is largely based on hearsay or gossip. In summarizing, Arbitrator Cheney stated that the duty of the arbitrator is simply to determine the truth respecting material matters in controversy, as he believes it to be, based upon a full and fair consideration of the entire

---

[102] For instance, after receiving posthearing briefs, Arbitrator Russell A. Smith requested additional data in McInerney Spring & Wire Co., 20 LA 642, 643 (1953).

[103] See discussion in Chapter 7, topic titled "Reopening the Hearing."

[104] See Northeast Airlines, Inc., 37 LA 741, 743 (Wolff, 1961); McInerney Spring & Wire Co., 20 LA 642, 643 (Smith, 1953); Simkin, Acceptability as a Factor in Arbitration Under an Existing Agreement 59–60 (Univ. of Pa. Press, 1952); Updegraff & McCoy, Arbitration of Labor Disputes 103 (1946). For related considerations, see this Chapter, topic titled "Right of Cross-Examination."

evidence and after he has accorded each witness and each piece of documentary evidence, the weight, if any, to which he honestly believes it to be entitled.[105]

Arbitrator Clair V. Duff, in turn, has offered some considerations relevant in evaluating testimony:

"Any attempt to sort credible testimony from that which is not worthy of belief is very difficult for at least four basic reasons. They may be briefly stated:

"INTEREST. While having an interest or stake in the outcome does not disqualify a witness, it renders his testimony subject to most careful scrutiny. * * * Few witnesses will deliberately falsify but there is a common tendency to 'put your best foot forward.' This tendency, either consciously or subconsciously, leads many witnesses to remember and express testimony in a way favorable to the result which they hope the Hearing will produce.

"PERCEPTION. Frequently the initial observation is faulty or incomplete because the observer has no prior knowledge that a dispute will develop concerning what he has seen or heard and his casual sensory impression is not sharp and keen.

"MEMORY. The remembrance of an event weeks or months after it occurred is frequently dim and inaccurate and a witness may be confused as to facts which initially he correctly perceived. By lapse of time precise details may elude his memory.

"COMMUNICATION. The manner in which a witness expresses what he saw and heard may fail to communicate exactly his initial perception of the occurrence, so that after listening to the testimony and the cross-examination of the witnesses, the fact-finder may not have had transmitted to him a completely accurate impression of the facts, even though they were initially observed carefully and well remembered by the witness."[106]

Arbitrator Joseph Rosenfarb cautioned that while "both sides might be subject to the unconscious influences of self-interest, personal predilection or antipathy," it is the duty of the arbitrator "to examine the testimony of each witness on its own merits"—Arbitrator Rosenfarb considered that union members are not necessarily prejudiced

---

[105] Andrew Williams Meat Co., 8 LA 518, 519 (1947). Also see Arbitrator Gorsuch in 40 LA 45, 55; Coffey in 28 LA 710, 715. "Demeanor and the spirit of responses are factors in credibility. Reliability or unreliability never lies wholly in the *words* said." Karnish Instruments, Inc., 45 LA 545, 548 (Bender, 1965).

[106] South Penn Oil Co., 29 LA 718, 720 (1957). Also see discussion by Arbitrator Edgar Jones in 28 LA 198, 204–205.

witnesses any more than are supervisors.[107] Arbitrator Samuel Krimsly has cautioned that if grievant's testimony "is colored by bias," employees used as company witnesses also may have "a bias by reason of their employment."[108]

Widely differing versions of the facts are too frequently presented by the parties. Where the testimony is highly contradictory it ordinarily "becomes incumbent upon the Arbitrator to sift and evaluate the testimony to the best of his ability, and reach the best conclusion he can as to the actual fact situation."[109] However, sometimes "It is unnecessary to resolve the substantial conflict in the evidence to obtain an unobstructed view of the scene. By piecing together the parts, the broad outlines of the whole picture emerges."[110] Arbitrator Sidney L. Cahn has observed that, in discipline cases, the truth often "lies somewhere between" the widely conflicting versions of the facts.[111]

In any event, as Arbitrator R. W. Fleming has aptly observed:

"Arbitrators are not equipped with any special divining rod which enables them to know who is telling the truth and who is not where a conflict in testimony develops. They can only do what the courts have done in similar circumstances for centuries. A judgment must finally be made, and there is a possibility that that judgment when made is wrong."[112]

It seems clear that inconsistencies in the testimony of any witness will ordinarily detract much from the testimony's credibility.[113]

---

[107] Poloron Products of Pa., Inc., 23 LA 789, 793 (1955).

[108] Billingsley, Inc., 48 LA 802, 807 (1967), where he added, however, that "nothing in either of these relationships to a matter in arbitration can be taken to mean there is any presumption any witness will lie."

[109] Texas Electric Steel Casting Co., 28 LA 757, 758 (Abernethy, 1957). Also see Arbitrator Williams in 49 LA 210, 212; Klein in 46 LA 974, 977; Wood in 46 LA 75, 80; Morvant in 41 LA 1327, 1329–1330 (stating that it was his "job to unravel this maze of contradictions and extract the core of truth").

[110] Sampsel Time Control, Inc., 18 LA 453, 456 (Gilden, 1951). In Borg-Warner Corp., 47 LA 903, 906 (1966), Arbitrator Larkin suggested that "Where the testimony of two witnesses is directly opposite, the Arbitrator must consider the surrounding circumstances to determine which story can be corroborated."

[111] Republic Aviation Corp., 17 LA 577, 579 (1951).

[112] General Cable Co., 28 LA 97, 99 (1957). In Overly-Hautz Co., 51 LA 518, 524 (1968), Arbitrator Jerome A. Klein declared: "Considering the incredibly conflicting nature of the testimony, one might feel that the parties might have decided to use a ouija board rather than an arbitrator to resolve their impasse."

[113] As in Hawaiian Telephone Co., 43 LA 1218, 1225 (Tsukiyama, 1964); Walter Butler Shipbuilders, Inc., 2 LA 633, 635–636 (Gorder, 1944).

Special Considerations in Discipline Cases

Special considerations are involved in weighing testimony in discharge and discipline cases. Thus Umpire Harry Shulman recognized that an accused employee has an incentive for denying the charge against him, in that he stands immediately to gain or lose in the case, and that normally there is no reason to suppose that a plant protection man, for example, would unjustifiably pick one employee out of hundreds and accuse him of an offense, although in particular cases the plant protection man may be mistaken or in some cases even malicious. Umpire Shulman declared that, if there is no evidence of ill will toward the accused on the part of the accuser and if there are no circumstances upon which to base a conclusion that the accuser is mistaken, the conclusion that the charge is true can hardly be deemed improper.[114]

Similarly, the testimony of a foreman was accepted over that of the employee whom he accused where the foreman had many years of satisfactory service as against seven months' service by the accused and the foreman had never discharged an employee before.[115] Obviously, however, the testimony of the accuser will be subject to doubt and careful scrutiny if there is evidence of ill will on his part against the accused.[116] The same is true if the factual situation otherwise casts doubt on the accuser's version,[117] or if his testimony on its face is not reasonably credible.

Another factor which might be considered by an arbitrator in weighing testimony in discharge and discipline cases is the so-called code which inhibits one member of an organization and frequently one member of an unorganized working force from testifying against another.[118]

---

[114] Ford Motor Co., 1 ALAA ¶67,274, p. 67,620 (1954). In general accord, Pennsylvania Greyhound Lines, Inc., 19 LA 210, 211 (Seward, 1952); Sun Shipbuilding & Dry Dock Co., 1 ALAA ¶67,648 (1947). Also see Arbitrator Crawford in 40 LA 1084, 1086–1087. Arbitrator Schieber agrees that a discharged employee has "a strong incentive for denying" guilt (48 LA 812, 814), but Arbitrator Krimsly reminds that interest in the outcome does not raise any presumption that a discharged employee is lying (48 LA 802, 807).
[115] Jenkins Bros., 11 LA 432, 434 (Donnelly, 1948). For similar results, see Arbitrator Leonard in 48 LA 1187, 1190; Abernethy in 28 LA 757, 758–759; Coffey in 28 LA 710, 715.
[116] As in Bethlehem Steel Co., 2 LA 187, 190–191 (Dodd, 1945).
[117] See FMC Corp., 45 LA 293, 295 (McCoy, 1965).
[118] General Motors Corp., 2 LA 491, 502 (Hotchkiss, 1938). To similar effect, American Smelting and Refining Co., 48 LA 1187, 1190 (Leonard, 1967).

The Best Evidence

A worthy view as to application of the "best evidence" concept in arbitration has been offered by a New York area tripartite committee:

> "*Best Evidence*—Where objection is made to the introduction of evidence of a secondary nature on the ground that it is not the best evidence, the original document should be produced unless it is shown, for reasons satisfactory to the arbitrator, that it is not available. Reproductions of original documents shall be deemed the best evidence unless the authenticity of the purported original document is significantly in question."[119]

A West Coast area tripartite committee suggested that "Failure, without adequate explanation, to produce a more reliable form of evidence should itself be recognized to have evidentiary weight adverse to the profferer of the lesser valued proof."[120]

Formal v. Informal Records

Business records are a frequent source of proof in arbitration. Complete data taken directly from original business records will ordinarily be given more weight than estimates or informal records.[121] However, even informal records kept by the union or by the employees themselves may be given significant weight if the company has kept no formal records of the activity in question.[122]

Burden of Proof

It is very difficult to generalize on the application of the doctrine of "burden of proof" in the field of arbitration.[123] The burden of

---

Also see Problems of Proof in Arbitration 234 (The Bureau of National Affairs, Inc., 1967).

[119] Problems of Proof in Arbitration 299–300 (The Bureau of National Affairs, Inc., 1967). Other tripartite committees expressed similar views. Id. at 92, 252. The West Coast Committee referred to the best evidence rule at law as "a rather narrowly drawn prescription which mandates that 'no evidence other than the writing itself is admissible to prove the content of a writing.'" Id. at 189.

[120] Id. at 189.

[121] See Jonco Aircraft Corp., 22 LA 819, 823 (Merrill, 1954).

[122] See Bethlehem Steel Co., 16 LA 926, 927–928, 931–932 (Feinberg, 1951).

[123] For helpful discussions of the "burden of proof" concept at law, with comments as to its application in arbitration, see Tenneco Oil Co., 44 LA 1121, 1122 (Merrill, 1965); Fleming, The Labor Arbitration Process 68–73 (Univ. of Ill. Press, 1965). Arbitrator Fleming notes: "Part of the difficulty in talking about burden of proof is that the term means several different things and is often used without careful definition. It can mean the burden of pleading [which

proof may depend upon the nature of the issue, the specific contract provision, or a usage established by the parties. In many cases the arbitrator simply gets the facts and decides the issue without any express indication that he is thinking in terms of burden of proof.

Arbitrators have written specifically in terms of burden of proof much more frequently in some types of cases than in other types. For instance, burden of proof considerations have been stressed fairly often in discharge and discipline cases, as well as in cases involving seniority clauses which require consideration of the fitness and ability of employees.[124] In contrast, for example, Arbitrator Harry Shulman emphasized that "notions of burden of proof are hardly applicable to issues of interpretation."[125]

It is probable that in arbitration the "burden of proof" concept is usually more important in its substantive than in its procedural significance. There is, for instance, no required order of presenting evidence in arbitration cases. While the party asserting a claim usually presents his proof first, or at least a preliminary or introductory case, this practice may not be followed where the nature of the issue makes a different procedure preferable.[126]

It may be noted that the burden of going forward with the evidence may shift during the course of the hearing; after the party having the burden of persuasion presents sufficient evidence to justify

---

does not apply in arbitration], the burden of producing evidence, and the burden of persuasion. When used in the sense of burden of persuasion, it involves further questions as to the quantum of evidence, or standard of proof, which will be required to prevail in the particular case." Id. at 68.

[124] See Chapter 15, topic titled "Burden and Quantum of Proof"; Chapter 14, topic titled "Review of Management's Determination: Evidence and Burden of Proof." For some other types of issues in which an arbitrator has spoken specifically in terms of burden of proof, see Arbitrator McIntosh in 52 LA 1026, 1027; Small in 46 LA 1077, 1078; Bothwell in 43 LA 1256, 1262–1263; Pollock in 37 LA 60, 62; Duff in 24 LA 715, 717; Reynard in 24 LA 369, 372–373; Holly in 24 LA 268, 273; Loucks in 24 LA 81, 84; Reid in 19 LA 291, 294; Livengood in 19 LA 205, 207; Cheney in 8 LA 187, 188; Cole in 3 LA 723, 724. For a related discussion, see this Chapter, topic titled "Unsupported Allegations."

[125] Shulman, "Reason, Contract, and Law in Labor Relations," 68 Harv. L. Rev. 999, 1018 (1955). Arbitrator Benjamin Aaron has spoken vigorously against use of "burden of proof" concepts in arbitration (except in certain types of discharge cases), and in this regard has declared: "To insist that the complaining party carries the burden of proof is manifestly absurd. Neither side has a burden of proof or disproof, but both have an obligation to cooperate in an effort to give the arbitrator as much guidance as possible." Aaron, "Some Procedural Problems in Arbitration," 10 Vanderbilt L. Rev. 733, 740–742 (1957).

[126] For full discussion, see Chapter 7, topic titled "Order of Presenting Case."

a finding in its favor on the issue, the other party has the burden of producing evidence in rebuttal.[127]

Unsupported Allegations

Too often a party goes to arbitration with nothing but allegations to support some of its contentions or even its basic position. But allegations or assertions are not proof, and mere allegations unsupported by evidence are ordinarily given no weight by arbitrators.[128]

Sometimes, too, a party will present no direct case at all, but will rely entirely upon cross-examination of the other party's witnesses, or will simply contend that the other party has the burden of proof and has not proved its case. This practice has been severely criticized by arbitrators.[129]

Hearsay Evidence

Evidence of a hearsay character is often presented at arbitration hearings. Arbitrators generally admit such evidence, but qualify its reception by informing the parties that it is admitted only "for what it is worth."[130] One general survey of labor arbitration revealed the following responses as to hearsay evidence:

"On the admission of hearsay into arbitration proceedings the consensus can be described as a collective shrug, a throwing-up of

---

[127] See Arbitrator Whyte in 51 LA 428, 434; Shipman in 42 LA 343, 344; Sembower in 39 LA 341, 346. Also, Problems of Proof in Arbitration 196, 211 (The Bureau of National Affairs, Inc., 1967).

[128] See Arbitrator Hardy in 49 LA 415, 417; Crawford in 47 LA 971, 973 and in 29 LA 837, 841; Sherman in 46 LA 187, 189 (mere surmise or speculation is not evidence); McDermott in 40 LA 487, 488; Beatty in 39 LA 1226, 1231; Justin in 24 LA 45, 47; DiLeone in 16 LA 613, 615; Barrett in 16 LA 466, 468.

[129] See John Deere Waterloo Tractor Works, 20 LA 583, 584–585 (Davey, 1953); Felsway Shoe Corp., 17 LA 505, 509–510 (Justin, 1951). For a related discussion, see Chapter 7, topic titled "Default Awards."

[130] For general discussion of the hearsay rule *and its many exceptions* at law, with suggestions as to treatment of hearsay evidence in arbitration, see Problems of Proof in Arbitration 90–91, 187–189, 212, 249–250, 272–279, 297–298. "Hearsay consists of testimony given by a person who states, not what he knows of his own knowledge, but what he has heard from others." Id. at 249. A more comprehensive definition states: " 'Hearsay evidence' is evidence of a statement that was made other than by a witness while testifying at the hearing and that is offered to prove the truth of the matter stated. A statement offered for some purpose other than to prove the fact stated by it is no hearsay." Id. at 212. For a related discussion, see this Chapter, topic titled "Right of Cross-Examination."

the hands, and a proclamation that it is inevitable. Many responses of both sides indicated that hearsay 'has to come in,' and that the arbitrator 'can't keep it out.' Admission of hearsay is justified to keep arbitration from becoming too cumbersome through procedural wrangling, or by the requirement that every witness who might be brought in be required to appear. It is agreed that the arbitrator must have wide latitude, and that he should let a witness with a grievance 'get it out.' Though the parties should feel that they have had their say in an informal manner, hearsay should be carefully weighed, once admitted, for its probative value. Despite the general fatalism expressed about the admission of hearsay evidence, there was still substantial opposition to its use."[131]

It is impossible to say just what the arbitrator in an individual case will consider hearsay evidence to be "worth." Arbitrator Arthur R. Lewis has observed that "the reasons calling for the existence of a hearsay rule in common law jury actions should at least guide the judgment of the arbitrator in the evaluation of the weight, if any, to be attributed to such evidence in an arbitration proceeding."[132] In many cases very little weight is given to hearsay evidence, and it is exceedingly unlikely that an arbitrator will render a decision supported by hearsay evidence alone.[133] Then, too, hearsay evidence will be given little weight if contradicted by evidence which has been subjected to cross-examination.[134]

A pertinent observation concerning the weight of hearsay evidence was made by Arbitrator Benjamin Aaron:

"[A] competent arbitrator may be depended upon substantially to discount some kinds of hearsay evidence that he has admitted over objection. He will do so selectively, however, and not on the assumption that hearsay evidence, as such, is not to be credited. If, for example, a newly appointed personnel manager, or a recently elected business agent, offers a letter to his predecessor from a third party, the arbitrator is likely to ignore the fact that the evidence is hearsay; if satisfied that the document is genuine, he will give it such weight as its relevancy dictates. On the other hand, hearsay testimony about statements allegedly made by 'the boys in the shop' or by executives in the 'front

---

[131] Eaton, "Labor Arbitration in the San Francisco Bay Area," 48 LA 1381, 1385 (1967).

[132] Continental Paper Co., 16 LA 727, 728 (1951).

[133] In the latter regard, see Arbitrator Schmidt in 35 LA 77, 80; Gorder in 20 LA 880, 885–886; Klamon in 19 LA 571, 574; Cheney in 8 LA 518, 522. Cf., Siegel in 35 LA 103, 108–109.

[134] See, for instance, Howell Refining Co., 27 LA 486, 492 (Hale, 1956). Also see Arbitrator Rubin in 20 LA 483, 484.

office,' though perhaps not excluded from the record by the arbitrator, probably will have no effect on his decision."[135]

Affidavits

Affidavits are sometimes used in arbitration but are subject to the same limitations as other forms of hearsay evidence.[136] In this connection, the Rules of the American Arbitration Association provide that arbitrators serving thereunder may receive and consider the evidence of witnesses by affidavit but should give it only such weight as they deem it entitled to after consideration of any objections made to its admission.[137] A similar approach is taken by the Code of Ethics and Procedural Standards for Labor-Management Arbitration, with the added qualification that the arbitrator "should afford the other side an opportunity to cross-examine the persons making the affidavits or to take their depositions or otherwise interrogate them."[138]

Circumstantial Evidence

Arbitrators sometimes decide cases on the basis of circumstantial evidence. For instance, such evidence was used to sustain the discharge of an employee charged with violation of a no-smoking rule; Arbitrator Jean McKelvey noted that the evidence was purely circumstantial but said that the proof, circumstantial as it was, indicated beyond a reasonable doubt that no person other than the accused could have been responsible for the smoke in the men's room.[139]

In another case the circumstances did not point so definitely to guilt, but a web of circumstances did exist to support the discharge

---

[135] Aaron, "Some Procedural Problems in Arbitration," 10 Vanderbilt L. Rev. 733, 744 (1957).
[136] See, for instance, South Haven Rubber Co., 54 LA 653, 654–655 (Sembower, 1970); Borden Co., 20 LA 483, 484 (Rubin, 1953).
[137] American Arbitration Association Rule 29. 30 LA 1086, 1089. A physician's statement was received and given some weight under this Rule in Karnish Instruments, Inc., 45 LA 545, 550 (Bender, 1965).
[138] Part II, §4(e).
[139] Columbian Rope Co., 7 LA 450, 455 (1947). As to circumstantial evidence of smoking, Cf. Columbus Show Case Co., 44 LA 507, 512–513 (Kates, 1965). Circumstantial evidence was given significant weight by Arbitrator Platt in 47 LA 1015, 1016–1017; Gilden in 47 LA 966, 970; Larkin in 47 LA 903, 906; Sembower in 47 LA 890, 896 (but he stated that "if there is a shred of doubt it should be taken into account"); Boles in 42 LA 954, 958–959; Reid in 38 LA 749, 751; Marshall in 22 LA 573, 575; Klamon in 16 LA 461, 466.

of several employees for instigating an unauthorized strike; the reasoning of Arbitrator Whitley P. McCoy indicates how circumstantial evidence may be found sufficient to support a finding of guilt:

> "Because of the secret nature of the offense of these men, proof is extremely difficult. It does not follow from this that proof may be dispensed with or that mere suspicious circumstances may take the place of proof, as I have indicated in sustaining the grievances of four men. But I think it does follow that something less than the most direct and the most positive proof is sufficient; in other words, that, just as in cases of fraud and conspiracy, legitimate inferences may be drawn from such circumstances as a prior knowledge of the time set for the strike. Unusual actions in circulating among the employees just prior to 9:30, communication of the time set to employees, and signals, however sureptitious, given at that hour. Mere prior guilty knowledge of the time set would not alone be sufficient since presumably many of the employees must have been told the time a half hour, an hour, or several hours in advance. Nor would merely being the first in a department to quit at the stroke of 9:30, standing alone, be sufficient. A wave of the hand, which might as reasonably be interpreted as a signal of good-bye as a signal to the others to go out, as in the case of Hollingsworth, would of itself be insufficient. But these or other suspicious circumstances, in combination, and especially in case of known leaders in the union's affairs, may be sufficient to convince the reasonable mind of guilt."[140]

Arbitrator Joseph A. Jenkins has stated that "Circumstantial evidence is often far more persuasive than direct testimony, particularly when action 'in the nature of a conspiracy' is involved."[141] In this unauthorized work stoppage case, Arbitrator Jenkins found that circumstantial evidence made out a "prima facie case" of guilt, leaving a burden on each individual employee to offer evidence of excuse (such as illness) for not reporting to work.[142]

As a basic safeguard, Arbitrator Clair V. Duff emphasized that an arbitrator in using circumstantial evidence "must exercise extreme care so that by due deliberation and careful judgment he may avoid making hasty or false deductions. If the evidence producing the chain

---

[140] Stockham Pipe Fittings Co., 4 LA 744, 746–747 (1946). For reliance upon circumstantial evidence in other work-stoppage cases, see Arbitrator Jenkins in 48 LA 949, 950–951; Pollack in 42 LA 142, 143; Harter in 7 LA 239, 240.

[141] Lone Star Steel Co., 48 LA 949, 950–951 (1967). Agreeing that circumstantial evidence may have more probative value than direct testimony, Arbitrator Schieber in Grand Union Co., 48 LA 812, 815 (1967).

[142] Lone Star Steel Co., 48 LA 949, 951 (1967).

of circumstances pointing to [guilt] is weak and inconclusive, no probability of fact may be inferred from the combined circumstances."[143]

Or, as Arbitrator Paul M. Hebert stated, use of circumstantial evidence "does not eliminate in any sense the requirement that there must be clear and convincing proof to establish that the offense charged was committed."[144] Certainly, mere suspicion is not enough to establish wrongdoing.[145]

While expressly rejecting for use in arbitration the criminal law rule that circumstantial evidence is inadequate unless it excludes every reasonable theory except guilt, Arbitrator Ralph Roger Williams concluded that the work involved in the case before him was so complicated and the opportunity for errors so broad that circumstantial evidence did not suffice for a charge of deliberate production of defective work.[146]

Evidence Obtained by Allegedly Improper Methods

Labor and management representatives have disagreed as to the admissibility in arbitration of evidence obtained by breaking into an employee's locker, forcible search of his person, secret surveillance, and other such means.[147] The broad question for the arbitrator is said to be that "absent a constitutional right or a right specified in the contract, may the arbitrator reject evidence because the manner in which it has been obtained is reprehensible or distasteful to him or

---

[143] South Penn Oil Co., 29 LA 718, 721 (1957). Also see similar statements by Arbitrator Sembower in 44 LA 593, 601–603; Duff in 44 LA 577, 578.

[144] Reed Roller Bit Co., 29 LA 604, 606 (1957). Also see Arbitrator Block in 55 LA 1221, 1227; Gross in 46 LA 756, 762–763; Bennett in 45 LA 247, 249; Bowles in 24 LA 761, 764; Kadish in 24 LA 102, 104–105; Platt in 21 LA 428, 429.

[145] See Enterprise & Century Undergarment Co., 24 LA 63, 64 (Donnelly, 1955). Also see comments of Arbitrator Prasow in 23 LA 317, 321; Updegraff in 19 LA 413, 416. Cf., actions of Arbitrator Davis in 48 LA 199, 200.

[146] Westinghouse Electric Co., 48 LA 211, 212–213 (1967). Many arbitrators would no doubt agree with Arbitrator Williams' rejection of said criminal law rule for use in arbitration. But see Arbitrator Wildebush in 44 LA 1143, 1149.

[147] See Problems of Proof in Arbitration 105–106, 129–134, 138–139 (The Bureau of National Affairs, Inc., 1967). Labor spokesmen have emphasized the individual's right to privacy and human dignity; management spokesmen have pointed to the necessity for investigative power and they comment that when an employee takes a job, he does so with the knowledge that he must adhere to plant rules and that he may also be required to give up certain rights which he has on the outside. Id. at 106, 108.

because it is his opinion that sound labor-management relations would be better served by such exclusion."[148]

As will be noted from the following discussion, reported arbitration cases reveal that the views of arbitrators, too, may differ significantly as to the use of such evidence, though the inclination to accept and rely upon it appears to be fairly strong.

In a case involving the discharge of a female employee for violating a rule against possession of dangerous knives on company premises, Arbitrator Joseph D. Lohman emphasized that the company guard had obtained knowledge of the employee's possession of the knife through unilateral entry and search of her locker and purse, that she was escorted to the guard office and asked to empty her purse without being told the reason for the inquiry, and that the guard had been instructed not to disclose the reason for the inquiry. Arbitrator Lohman said this tactic bordered on entrapment, and that the employee's locker and purse continued inviolate as the private realm of the individual even though the entire episode was confined to the premises of the company.[149]

Arbitrator Lohman concluded that "Knowledge, even though incriminating, if acquired through such illegitimate procedures, is of questionable validity in bringing action against the individual." The evidence obtained through such procedures was held inadmissible, and consequently the discharge was held unjustified.[150]

However, even where a court had refused to admit certain illegal search and seizure evidence in a criminal action against an employee, the discharge of the employee on the basis of that evidence (which clearly indicated guilt) was upheld.[151] In this case the arbitrator stated

---

[148] Id. at 106.

[149] Campbell Soup Co., 2 LA 27, 31 (1946).

[150] Ibid. Also see Ross-Meehan Foundries, 55 LA 1078, 1080 (King, 1970).

[151] Hennis Freight Lines, 44 LA 711, 713–714 (McGury, 1964). The evidence had been obtained by police through unlawful arrest. In Jones & Laughlin Steel Corp., 29 LA 778, 779 (Stark, 1957), an employee was escorted to the guard office and told to empty his pockets, which he did. The incriminating evidence thus obtained was a factor in his discharge, which was upheld. No contention of illegal search and seizure was apparent in this case; where such contention was made in Lockheed Aircraft Corp., 27 LA 709, 712–713 (Maggs, 1956), the arbitrator stated that constitutional rights as to search and seizure can only be asserted against the government in criminal cases and are not available to employees in discharge cases. But see Arbitrator Williams in Scott Paper Co., 52 LA 57, 59 (1969). For discussion of search and seizure in arbitration and at law, see Fleming, The Labor Arbitration Process 186–190 (Univ. of Ill. Press, 1965). He likewise discusses wiretapping. Id. at 190–194.

that "The company is manifestly entitled to inquire into facts which suggest their employees are involved in the theft of Company property."[152]

Charges of entrapment and improper surveillance have not been readily accepted by arbitrators. In one case employees complained of entrapment where a night foreman, being reasonably suspicious that a poker game was in progress, returned to the plant after he had previously driven away. Arbitrator Harold M. Gilden rejected the contention of entrapment, stating that the foreman's action must be deemed within his general line of duty, and that the situation was to be distinguished from one where a carefully devised plan is formulated and bait is set or invitations extended for the express purpose of capturing persons in the commission of a wrongful act.[153]

A carefully devised plan was formulated and bait was set in one case to apprehend a locker-room thief. The bait (identifiable money) was placed in a locker which was kept under surveillance. Discharge of the thus apprehended employee was sustained.[154]

Evidence obtained by various forms of secret surveillance has been admitted by arbitrators and, where reliable, has been given weight.[155]

A justification for covert procedures in certain circumstances has been stated by Arbitrator M. David Keefe:

"It is, indeed, distasteful that management should have to check on the honesty of employees. Nevertheless, when suspicions are kindled it seems

---

[152] Hennis Freight Lines, 44 LA 711, 714 (McGury, 1964).

[153] Borg-Warner Corp., 3 LA 423, 432 (1944).

[154] United States Steel Corp., 49 LA 101, 102–105 (Dybeck, 1967). Also see Arbitrator Hill in 55 LA 226, 228–230; Alexander in 53 LA 1279, 1280.

[155] See Michigan Bell Telephone Co., 45 LA 689, 694–696 (Smith, 1965), in which evidence obtained by listening in on telephone operators could be used, with possible limitations; Du Mont Laboratories, 44 LA 1143, 1146, 1149 (Wildebush, 1965), in which "peephole" evidence was admitted but found unreliable since the peephole was too small to permit accurate observation; Keystone Asphalt Products Co., 3 LA 789, 793 (Hampton, 1946), in which management made secret visits to the plant to catch employees sleeping on duty and in which the employees were not confronted until conclusive evidence of guilt had been obtained—the discharges were upheld though the arbitrator considered the employer's actions "beneath the dignity of management"; Douglas Aircraft Co., 1 LA 350, 353 (Courshon, 1945), in which employees were caught "red-handed" through surveillance by guards—the offense was thus established but the discharges were set aside due to past laxness in enforcement of plant rules. For general discussion of surveillance, see Black, "Surveillance and the Labor Arbitration Process," Arbitration and the Expanding Role of Neutrals 1 (BNA, 1970).

better to bring the matter to a head, one way or the other, rather than to risk the greater harm of misdirected doubts smoldering to char the esteem in which an innocent person might be held. In any event, the Company has an undeniable right to protect itself against the type of offense herein involved."[156]

Also, he denied that a procedure becomes "entrapment simply because it must be planned."[157]

Recordings made by one party to a telephone conversation without the knowledge of the other party were not admitted into evidence, the arbitrator requiring the person who made the recordings to testify on a recollection basis.[158] Another arbitrator permitted use of evidence obtained against an employee by tape recorder, the arbitrator stating that "the legality of the means by which information has been gathered is for other authorities to determine."[159]

The right to use a closed circuit television camera to observe employees in a room from which the company believed it was losing material through theft was upheld by Arbitrator Richard Mittenthal, who stated, however, that he did not need to decide whether evidence obtained by this method would be admissible in a disciplinary dispute.[160]

It is said that "Arbitrators know that industrial pilferage is a major problem, and there is no disposition to interfere with proper rules to control it."[161] For instance, in one case the right of the company to inspect large purses of female employees as they leave the plant was upheld.[162]

The use of "spotters" in some industries and the admission of their reports and testimony as evidence of rule violations by employees

---

[156] Attwood Corp., 48 LA 331, 334 (1967).
[157] Ibid.
[158] Needham Packing Co., 44 LA 1057, 1095 (Davey, 1965).
[159] Sun Drug Co., 31 LA 191, 194 (Marcus, 1958).
[160] FMC Corp., 46 LA 335, 338 (1966). Arbitrator W. Willard Wirtz has stated that situations of the television camera/pilferage type "present clear 'due process' questions, not constitutional or legal due process, but obvious demands that individual and enterprise interests be balanced * * *." Wirtz, "Due Process of Arbitration," The Arbitrator and the Parties 1, 17 (BNA Incorporated, 1958). In Eico, Inc., 44 LA 563, 564 (Delany, 1965), the employer was held to have violated a maintenance of working conditions clause by installing a closed circuit television system on the production floor; no problems of supervision or operations existed to warrant the employer's action.
[161] Fleming, The Labor Arbitration Process 188 (Univ. of Ill. Press, 1965).
[162] Aldens, Inc., 51 LA 469, 470 (Kelliher, 1968).

is discussed elsewhere in this Chapter under the topic entitled "Right
of Cross-Examination."

Confessions

An arbitrator may ordinarily be expected to give little or no
weight to a signed "confession" if the signature was obtained through
inducements, commitments, or threats.[163] One arbitrator explained:

> "Such methods of obtaining confessions of guilt are patently wrong.
> A confession, to be valid in prosecuting a case must be statements
> given by the suspected person of his own free will and choice. Induce-
> ments and threats invalidate such documents as evidence."[164]

However, where the evidence showed neither "physical nor mental duress procuring the grievant's admissions of guilt, nor promises
of leniency or reward in exchange for such admissions," the admissions
could be used even though statements by security officers that grievant
could be arrested helped induce the admissions.[165] Nor would a confession be deemed the product of duress or coercion merely because it
was made under the pressure of circumstances.[166]

An employee's plea of guilty in public criminal proceedings ordinarily can be accepted in arbitration as an indication of guilt.[167] A

---

[163] See Arbitrator Jacobs in 55 LA 1195, 1202; Babb in 29 LA 272, 277;
Blair in 12 LA 1065, 1067. In Thrifty Drug Stores Co., 50 LA 1253, 1262
(Jones, 1968), confession statements made by an employee in admitting guilt,
but also implicating other employees, were regarded with skepticism; the question
was "whether the statements are so tainted by compulsions created by the manner
of their taking as to make it too speculative for a trier of fact * * * to give
them credence as evidence against those whom they would implicate." But as
to the "Thrifty Drug" decision, see comments by Edwards, "Due Process Considerations in Labor Arbitration," 25 Arb. J. 141, 150–151 (1970).

[164] Kroger Co., 12 LA 1065, 1067 (Blair, 1949).

[165] Weirton Steel Co., 50 LA 103, 104–105 (1968), Arbitrator Samuel S.
Kates stating that he did "not subscribe to the doctrine that purity must always
envelop those engaged in attempting to ascertain the truth, or that subterfuge
or pretence is always improper in a truth-seeking endeavor." In Lucky Stores,
Inc., 53 LA 1274, 1276 (Eaton, 1969), confessions were used although the
employees had not been notified of any right to remain silent, the arbitrator
stating that rules of the criminal law under the Constitution "do not necessarily
apply in the same way to private investigations where there is no agent of
the state present, which is the case here."

[166] Eastern Air Lines, Inc., 46 LA 549, 555 (Seidenberg, 1965).

[167] Although a grievant testified that he had pleaded guilty to criminal charges
only upon advice of an attorney as "the easiest way out" and the way to obtain
a suspended sentence, Arbitrator John F. Sembower declared that "it is not
possible to go behind such a plea." Northwest Airlines, Inc., 53 LA 203, 206
(1969).

plea of nolo contendere is neither an indication of guilt nor of innocence.[168]

The mere fact that a "confession" is purely voluntary does not always endow it with validity. Thus, a confession of strike leadership was given no weight where there was no evidence surrounding the confession to indicate that the employee was in fact a "leader."[169]

Offers of Compromise and Admissions

Offers of compromise and admissions made in attempting settlement of "rights" disputes prior to submission to arbitration may be received but probably will be given very little, if any, weight by arbitrators.[170] It is recognized that a party to a dispute may make an offer with the hope that a compromise can be reached and the dispute ended.[171] Even the mere introduction of such evidence may impair future attempts at dispute settlements. Thus, it has been strongly urged that offers of compromise should not even be admitted into evidence.[172]

While admissions and statements against interest other than those made in settlement attempts may be considered by an arbitrator, he can be expected to recognize that as a matter of law they are not conclusive.[173]

Admissions made by the grievant in the presence of union representatives during pre-arbitral grievance hearings may be given significant weight.[174] This is true also of grievant's admissions at the arbitration hearing itself.[175]

Admissions which have been acted on by others and those that appear in the record of prior proceedings so as to partake of the nature of judicial admissions may be held by arbitrators to be weighty evi-

---

[168] Akers Motor Lines, Inc., 41 LA 987, 990–991 (Woodruff, 1963).

[169] Union Tank Car Co., 49 LA 383, 388–389 (Crawford, 1967).

[170] See Arbitrator Prasow in 25 LA 398, 403–404; Marshall in 24 LA 430, 436; Cornsweet in 14 LA 494, 497. Also see Chapter 9, topic titled "No Consideration to Compromise Offers."

[171] Universal Milking Machine Co., 2 LA 399, 402 (Elson, 1946).

[172] Problems of Proof in Arbitration 93–94, 190, 253, 287–288 (The Bureau of National Affairs, Inc., 1967).

[173] Harley-Davidson Co., 6 LA 395, 397 (Lappin, 1947).

[174] Diebold, Inc., 48 LA 893, 900 (Bradley, 1967); Problems of Proof in Arbitration 93 (The Bureau of National Affairs, Inc., 1967).

[175] Bethlehem Steel Co., 42 LA 307, 309–310 (Hughes, 1964).

dence against the party making them.[176] Thus, where a party assumed a position in an arbitration case which was inconsistent with the position of that party in a prior arbitration case involving the same contract clause, the position taken in the prior case was one of the reasons for a decision against the party in the subsequent case.[177]

While the record of proceedings before a state workmen's compensation commission was ruled inadmissible in a subsequent arbitration hearing as to the employee's capability of performing his job, the arbitrator nevertheless permitted statements made by the employee in the compensation proceedings to be used by the employer at the arbitration hearing for purposes of impeaching the employee as a witness.[178]

Testimony from other proceedings must be evaluated with special care and in the full setting of the prior proceeding. Moreover, Arbitrator Bertram F. Willcox has observed that sometimes even in the same case an apparently damaging admission by a witness will have resulted from a momentary confusion and that the arbitrator should exercise care not to overemphasize any single item of testimony, especially if it is inconsistent with other testimony of the witness and with the rest of the party's case.[179]

Testimony by Persons From Outside

The nature of some cases makes the use of impartial technicians helpful. In such cases, arbitrators sometimes request permission to bring in specialists for impartial study of the disputed matter. This was done by Arbitrator David Wolff who consulted an electrical engineer, in the presence of both parties, as to whether a power failure was a cause beyond the employer's control (so as to relieve him of any obligation for call-in pay).[180] It has also been done in the deter-

---

[176] For instance, see Arbitrator Komaroff in 21 LA 248, 251; McCoy in 6 LA 681, 684. Also see Meltzer in 28 LA 303, 308.

[177] Goodyear Tire & Rubber Co. of Ala., 6 LA 681, 684 (McCoy, 1947). The prior case was also heard by Arbitrator McCoy. Goodyear Tire & Rubber Co., 4 LA 231 (1946).

[178] Vulcan Mold & Iron Co., 42 LA 734, 736–737, 739 (Sembower, 1964).

[179] General Electric Corp., 16 LA 554, 559 (1951).

[180] Chrysler Corp., 21 LA 573, 577 (1953). One group holds the view that the arbitrator should always advise the parties when seeking expert advice and should give them opportunity to comment on the expert's opinion before reaching his decision. View of Chicago Area Tripartite Committee, Problems of Proof in Arbitration 108 (The Bureau of National Affairs, Inc., 1967).

mination of proper incentive rates for new operations.[181] Likewise, Arbitrator Peter M. Kelliher was authorized to secure the services of a handwriting expert in fixing responsibility for errors in shipping orders.[182]

In some cases in which arbitrators consulted outside sources the arbitrator's opinion did not expressly indicate whether he obtained advance permission to do so.[183] In another case the arbitrator's request that the parties procure the services of an outside expert (to study and express an opinion as to a safety-crew size issue) was virtually an order that they do so.[184]

Arbitrator Arthur M. Ross has emphasized that "While an arbitrator may obtain technical assistance, he cannot delegate the decision-making authority which has been conferred upon him individually."[185]

A limitation upon the use of outside testimony was defined by Arbitrator Willard E. Hotchkiss, who accepted but refused to consider testimony of outsiders to the effect that a discharged employee had admitted his guilt to them; Arbitrator Hotchkiss urged that testimony of outsiders, whether or not relevant, should not generally be admitted since the frequent admission of such testimony would tend to retard the growth of healthy industrial relations and would encourage the calling of character witnesses to refute or support the testimony of the outsiders, the building of technical alibis, and other legalistic practices which would prolong hearings at great expense but to no useful purpose.[186]

Opinion Evidence by Expert Witnesses

"The function of a witness is to relate what he has seen and heard, not to draw inferences from these observations or from other

---

[181] Container Co., 6 LA 218, 220 (Whiting, 1946). Similarly, see Simmons Co., 33 LA 725, 727 (Ross, 1959).

[182] Hiram Walker & Sons, Inc., 18 LA 447, 448 (1952). Similarly, see Seaview Industries, Inc., 39 LA 125, 127–130 (Duncan, 1962).

[183] See Arbitrator Vines in 45 LA 833, 837–838; Ross in 33 LA 725, 727; Lehoczky in 32 LA 481, 482. Arbitrator Ross appointed an industrial engineer to make technical studies on disputed matter; the engineer "received excellent cooperation from both parties." Simmons Co., 33 LA 725, 727 (1959).

[184] American Oil Co., 51 LA 484, 489 (Barnhart, 1968).

[185] Simmons Co., 33 LA 725, 727 (1959). In this instance Arbitrator Ross received "a confidential report in full detail" from the technical assistant whom he had appointed; Arbitrator Ross found the report "most helpful" in reaching a decision, which he emphasized was solely his own. Ibid.

[186] General Motors Corp., 2 LA 491, 497, 503 (1938). Cf., Continental Paper Co., 16 LA 727, 728–729 (Lewis, 1951).

facts. This rule does not apply to the 'expert.' The 'expert' is allowed to draw inferences and conclusions because, in theory, his knowledge is superior to that of the person having to resolve the issue, be it judge, jury, or arbitrator."[187]

In addition to the admission of opinion evidence by expert witnesses (generally admitted by courts of law), it is suggested that arbitrators may in their discretion admit any opinion testimony from knowledgeable persons if such testimony might be helpful.[188]

Medical Evidence

A frequent use of medical evidence in arbitration concerns the physical fitness or qualifications of employees for some given type of work or, indeed, for any continued employment at all with the company.[189] Another use of medical evidence concerns verification of illness by doctors' certificates.

Written Statements vs. Oral Testimony

While doctors sometimes testify in person, their testimony is more often offered in the form of written statements or affidavits. It is understandable that where one party's doctor testifies in person, his opinion may carry greater weight with the arbitrator in contrast to the other party's use of only written statements.[190] Of course, the parties may stipulate that written statements of doctors (though not subject to cross-examination) shall be given the same effect as if the doctors had testified.[191] Even without such stipulation the arbitrator might give the statements "full weight" in the absence of other evidence minimizing their significance.[192]

---

[187] "Report of the Pittsburgh Tripartite Committee," Problems of Proof in Arbitration 253 (The Bureau of National Affairs, Inc., 1967). Related statements by other tripartite committees are also available. Id. at 94–95, 114–115, 298.

[188] View of the New York Area Tripartite Committee, id. at 298.

[189] For related material, see Chapter 13, topic titled "Disqualifying Employees for Physical or Mental Reasons"; Chapter 16, topic titled "Physical or Mental Condition as a Safety Hazard"; Chapter 14, topic titled "Employee's Physical and Psychological Fitness." For general discussion of medical and psychiatric testimony in arbitration, see "The Use of Experts in Arbitration," Arbitration and Social Change 135–145, 151–161 (The Bureau of National Affairs, Inc. 1970).

[190] See Arbitrator Kates in 43 LA 61, 64; Stockman in 41 LA 449, 453–454; Russell in 40 LA 229, 230–231. Arbitrators sometimes have stressed the unsatisfactory aspects of presenting medical evidence by written statements. See Arbitrator Leonard in 48 LA 1187, 1190; Boles in 43 LA 484, 487.

[191] As in Southern Cotton Oil Co., 26 LA 353, 356 (Kelliher, 1956).

[192] As in White Motor Co., 28 LA 823, 829 (Lazarus, 1957). The weight of written statements was greatly reduced by other evidence in American Iron & Machine Works Co., 19 LA 417, 420 (Merrill, 1952).

Shall Medical Evidence Be Weighed?

Often both parties submit medical evidence concerning the grievant's physical qualifications, and it is not surprising that the opinion of the grievant's doctor and that of the employer's medical adviser do not always agree. In many cases the arbitrator has not attempted to resolve such conflicts in medical evidence, but has been inclined to uphold the employer if he acted in good faith pursuant to good-faith medical advice from his doctor (some of these arbitrators spoke in terms of upholding the employer's action unless his doctor's advice or its application was unreasonable, capricious, or arbitrary).[193] Arbitrator W. Willard Wirtz, for instance, has stated that the arbitrator can only decide "whether the medical determination was made in a manner and by * * * a procedure indicating that it was fairly and reasonably made."[194] And Arbitrator James A. Doyle has explained:

> "The judgment of the plant physician is entitled to great weight. He is conversant with the requirements of the occupation involved and the risks inherent in such work. It is generally held that where there is a conflict in the views of qualified physicians, whose veracity there is no reason to question, the Company is entitled to rely on the views of its own medical advisers."[195]

In some cases the arbitrator has undertaken to weigh conflicting

---

[193] See Arbitrator Guse in 50 LA 476, 486–487; Doyle in 49 LA 535, 539; Cayton in 47 LA 254, 256; Elkouri in 47 LA 12, 14; Kerrison in 45 LA 724, 726; Stouffer in 66-1 ARB ¶8030; Kates in 43 LA 61, 64; Autrey in 41 LA 519, 523; Stockman in 41 LA 449, 453–454; Russell in 40 LA 229, 230–231; May in 38 LA 1049, 1054; Thompson in 37 LA 581, 584; Kelliher in 37 LA 175, 176 (involving psychiatric opinion); Quinlan in 33 LA 141, 145; Hoel in 31 LA 256, 259–260 (holding also that if the employer has the employee examined by several doctors and receives conflicting opinions, the employer may decide which opinion to follow in absence of error or unreasonableness); Prasow in 24 LA 732, 738 (quoting Arbitrator Gregory); Abernethy in 24 LA 290, 298; Wirtz in 24 LA 274, 275. But an employee under post-operative care of his personal physician has a right to rely upon that doctor's opinion that he is *not yet able* to return to work. International Harvester Co., 22 LA 138, 139 (Platt, 1954). Also see Arbitrator McConnell in 37 LA 575, 580.
[194] International Harvester Co., 24 LA 274, 275 (1955). In Erie Forge & Steel Corp., 47 LA 629, 633–634 (1966), Arbitrator Mullin stated that while the company doctor's opinion is normally controlling, it will not be so where that opinion or its application is arbitrary or capricious. In Crane Co., 47 LA 227, 231–233 (1966), Arbitrator Mullin held that the employer should have had the employee examined again where the employer was confronted with conflicting opinions from company and employee doctors, the most recent examination (by the employee's doctor), having indicated the employee to be fit. Compare, however, Goss Co., 43 LA 640, 643 (Epstein, 1964), where the employer acted upon the opinion of the employee's first doctor but the employee sought to stand on the opinion of his second doctor.
[195] Hughes Aircraft Co., 49 LA 535, 539 (1967).

medical evidence.[196] In thus searching for a preponderance of the evidence, the arbitrator's role has been compared "to that of a lay jury which must decide between conflicting expert testimony."[197]

Although Arbitrator Maurice H. Merrill apparently would to some extent weigh conflicting medical testimony, he has held that where there is "direct conflict in the medical testimony, with nothing to swing the balance preponderantly on one side or the other," the company "is entitled to rely on the views of its own medical advisers, if it has given" the grievant "fair notice and opportunity to overcome those views before reaching a final decision."[198]

Special Factors in Considering Medical Evidence

Whether the arbitrator weighs the medical evidence or only assumes to decide whether the employer's determination was fairly and reasonably made, certain factors or considerations may be present and of special significance to the arbitrator in the given case. For instance, a stale diagnosis may fare poorly against one that is current;[199] medical opinion based upon extensive examination of the employee and observation over a period of time will carry added weight;[200] medical opinion based only upon the notes of another doctor (who examined the employee) may carry limited weight;[201] the opinion of a medical specialist will usually carry added weight,[202] but will not necessarily control over the opinion of a general practitioner.[203] In some types of cases it is imperative that the doctor direct his evaluation to the specific work requirements and environment of the employee's job.

---

[196] See Arbitrator Purdom in 54 LA 1041, 1044–1047; Dworkin in 46 LA 719, 723–724; Boles in 43 LA 734, 737–738, and in 43 LA 484, 487; Wallen in 38 LA 395, 398–399. For instances of at least limited weighing of such evidence, see Leonard in 48 LA 1187, 1191–1192; Roberts in 48 LA 1175, 1178–1179.

[197] United States Steel Corp., 38 LA 395, 399 (Wallen, 1962). Also see Reynolds Metals Co., 54 LA 1041, 1047 (Purdom, 1970).

[198] Ideal Cement Co., 20 LA 480, 482 (1953). Also see Arbitrator Merrill in 19 LA 417, 420; Kelliher in 26 LA 353, 356.

[199] See North Shore Gas Co., 40 LA 37, 43–44 (Sembower, 1963). Also see Arbitrator McDermott in 62-1 ARB ¶8223.

[200] See Pennsylvania Tire and Rubber Company of Mississippi, 69-1 ARB ¶8395 (Williams, 1969). Also see Arbitrator Allen in 50 LA 1152, 1155; Guthrie in 62-2 ARB ¶8369. In A. M. Castle & Co., 41 LA 391, 400 (1963), Arbitrator Sembower relied upon "the clearest, most succinct and unequivocal opinion" from the doctor closest to the case.

[201] See U.S. Pipe & Foundry Co., 36 LA 481, 484 (King, 1960).

[202] See Arbitrator Roberts in 48 LA 1175, 1178–1179; Cahn in 42 LA 1042, 1044; Wallen in 38 LA 395, 399.

[203] See Gulf States Utilities Co., 44 LA 1252, 1260 (Murphy, 1965). Even the testimony of lay witnesses may be relevant and competent in reference to

Where the employee's doctor failed to do this, his opinion stood up poorly against "the judgment of the Company physician and of the Company officials with their knowledge of the job to be done and the hazards involved."[204]

Use of "Neutral" Doctors

Some agreements provide that if the company's doctor and the employee's doctor disagree as to the employee's physical condition, these two doctors shall jointly select a third doctor whose findings shall be controlling. This course of action also might be taken pursuant to an arbitrator's suggestion in the course of the hearing.[205] In a case where there was insufficient evidence to warrant a finding as to the grievant's physical fitness for continued employment, the arbitrator by his award specified a detailed procedure for securing impartial determination of the employee's physical condition.[206]

Doctor's Certification of Illness

A frequent use of medical evidence concerns written certificates from doctors stating that employees named in the certificates were examined on a stated date and were found to be ailing. Arbitrators have held that these certificates, although not conclusive, should be given significant weight in determining whether the absence from work is to be excused due to illness.[207] Such certificates, however, may be

---

an employee's physical ability for work. See North Shore Gas Co., 40 LA 37, 43 (Sembower, 1963). However, even a medical doctor's opinion that grievant might not "psychologically be a good employee" carried little weight with the arbitrator, who commented that the doctor was not a psychiatrist. Whitaker Cable Corp., 50 LA 1152, 1156 (Allen, 1968).

[204] Gulf States Utilities Co., 47 LA 42, 46–48 (Murphy, 1966). To similar effect, Arbitrator Abernethy in 46 LA 645, 653. But an employer did not prevail where it relied solely upon the lay judgment of company officials as against the opinion of the employee's "medical experts." Texlite, Inc., 48 LA 509, 512 (Ray, 1966).

[205] As in Dayton Malleable Iron Co., 43 LA 959, 960 (Stouffer, 1964).

[206] New Tronics Corp., 46 LA 365, 368 (Kates, 1966). The procedure was: (1) the grievant shall cause herself to be examined by professionals of her own choosing; (2) the company, which had not yet had her examined, may have her examined by professionals of its choice; (3) if the above procedure produces a conflict of medical opinion, neutral medical experts are to be selected by the parties, or by the arbitrator if the parties cannot agree; (4) the neutral findings shall be controlling; (5) the expense of neutral experts shall be shared by the parties. In Ideal Cement Co., 33 LA 141, 143, 145 (Quinlan, 1959), medical testimony was sharply divided but sufficient to warrant a finding as to grievant's condition; the arbitrator noted that no provision of the agreement authorized him to appoint a neutral doctor as requested by one of the parties.

[207] See Arbitrator Elbert in 42 LA 582, 584–585; Oppenheim in 29 LA 291, 292; Livengood in 20 LA 451, 453; Seward in 11 LA 909, 912; Griffin in 1 LA 281, 282. Arbitrator Larkin has expressed doubt that such certificates

impeached if shown to have been given as a favor, to have been obtained through misrepresentation, or to have been based upon mistake.[208]

The right of management to *require* a doctor's certificate as proof of illness is discussed in Chapter 17, subtopic titled "Sick Leave."

Protecting Witnesses

In some situations giving testimony in arbitration proceedings may subject the witness to varied risks of retaliation. For instance, employees and supervisors alike may incur the displeasure of the employer as a result of their testimony. Likewise, employees may jeopardize their relations with fellow workers for testifying at the employer's request. When he feels the need, the arbitrator may seek to protect the interests of persons facing this predicament by reminding the parties of the risks involved.[209]

Although the arbitrator cannot insure definite protection if the person does testify, there may be firm basis for a valid grievance or unfair labor practice charges in some situations of retaliation for giving testimony.[210]

A union's action in fining four members for testifying in the employer's favor at an arbitration hearing violated a clause stating that "either party to this agreement shall be permitted to call employee witnesses at each step of the grievance and arbitration procedure." Furthermore, in so ruling Arbitrator Edgar J. Nathan declared:

> "Even apart from such a contract provision, it would seem that any arbitration agreement would necessarily secure the right of both sides to freely call witnesses. Maturity in relations between responsible people and organizations can result in no other course of conduct."

Arbitrator Nathan's award enjoined the union from enforcing any discipline against the four members and ordered it to revoke the fines.[211]

---

are too reliable, especially if submitted to the employer after extensive time has elapsed. Midland-Ross Corp., 49 LA 283, 287 (1967).

[208] See Arbitrator Oppenheim in 29 LA 291, 292; Livengood in 20 LA 451, 453; Courshon in 2 LA 509, 513.

[209] See Guides for Labor Arbitration 9 (U. of Pa. Press, 1953).

[210] See comments of Arbitrator Sembower in Berg Airlectro Products Co., 46 LA 668, 675–676 (1966), and of Arbitrator Jones in Western Insulated Wire Co., 45 LA 972, 975 (1965). Also see Ebasco Services, Inc., 181 NLRB No. 117 (1970).

[211] New York Twist Drill Mfg. Corp., 39 LA 167, 169 (1962).

CHAPTER 9

STANDARDS FOR INTERPRETING CONTRACT LANGUAGE

Ambiguity

Probably no function of the labor-management arbitrator is more important than that of interpreting the collective bargaining agreement. The great bulk of arbitration cases involve disputes over "rights" under such agreements. In these cases the agreement itself is the point of concentration, and the function of the arbitrator is to interpret and apply its provisions.

There is no need for interpretation unless the agreement is ambiguous. If the words are plain and clear, conveying a distinct idea, there is no occasion to resort to technical rules of interpretation and the clear meaning will ordinarily be applied by arbitrators.[1]

An agreement is not ambiguous if the arbitrator can determine its meaning without any other guide than a knowledge of the simple facts on which, from the nature of language in general, its meaning depends.[2] But an agreement is ambiguous if "plausible contentions may be made for conflicting interpretations" thereof.[3] Moreover, it is recognized that whether a document is or is not ambiguous is a matter of impression rather than of definition; and this is obviously so, because each provision may be as clear and definite as language can make it, yet the result of the whole be doubtful from lack of harmony in its various parts.[4]

---

[1] See, for instance, Arbitrator McCoy in 51 LA 1023, 1025; Pollock in 36 LA 391, 392; Klamon in 15 LA 676, 682; Kelliher in 15 LA 46, 49. Cf., Arbitrator Tischler in 33 LA 919, 922. Where the arbitration is subject to court review on matters of law the court may apply this principle. See cases discussed in Marceau, "Are All Interpretations 'Admissible'?" 12 Arb. J. 150 (1957).
[2] 13 Corpus Juris, Sec. 481, p. 520
[3] Armstrong Rubber Co., 17 LA 741, 744 (Gorder, 1952).
[4] Butte Water Co. v. Butte, 138 P. 195, 197 (Mont., 1914).

Most persons experienced in collective bargaining recognize the collective agreement as a comprehensive, but necessarily flexible, instrument which governs the relations between the parties. The very fact that almost all such agreements provide for the arbitration of grievances concerning agreement interpretation suggests that the parties recognize the impossibility of foreseeing and providing for all questions which may arise during the life of the agreement.[5]

As Arbitrator Martin Raphael pointed out, language cannot be tailored to fit precisely the variant meanings which parties to an agreement may have in their minds; language is frequently used which is general in nature and flexible enough to include those meanings which future experience necessitates being filled in. This arbitrator quoted Mr. Justice Holmes: "A word is not a crystal, transparent and unchanged; it is the skin of a living thought and may vary greatly in color and content according to the circumstances and the time in which it is used."[6]

The primary goal of the "rights" arbitrator is to determine and carry out the mutual intent of the parties. An ambiguity in a contract usually means that the parties have failed to express that intent with clarity. Sometimes, however, an ambiguity may mean more. It may mean that there never was any meeting of the minds. When this has been found to be the case, arbitrators have taken various courses of action (see subtopic below, titled " 'Legislation' vs. 'Interpretation' ").

Accepting, then, that the basic function of the "rights" arbitrator is agreement interpretation, an inquiry should be made concerning the techniques, standards, or rules used by arbitrators in executing this function. An analysis of these techniques and standards should be of much value to contract negotiators as well as to parties preparing cases for arbitration. Such analysis will provide guides which, if observed in the drafting of collective agreements, will tend to protect the parties against pitfalls in the use of language.

This study may suggest the desirability of the use by negotiators of skilled counsel in rephrasing the agreement after mutual understanding is reached. While the agreement should be stated in simple language, understandable by the employees, negotiators are not always

---

[5] Loew's Inc., 10 LA 227, 232 (Aaron, 1948).
[6] Yale & Towne Mfg. Co., 5 LA 753 (1946).

capable of expressing their true intent, either in simple language or otherwise. Moreover, negotiators are inclined to read into that which they have written, however ambiguous on its face, the meaning which they have agreed upon, and to lose sight of the problem which may exist for a third party who must read the contract.

It should be emphasized that the courts, when called upon to construe collective agreements, use accepted standards of interpretation of general application.[7]

Arbitrators likewise use these standards of construction. In other words, it should be recognized that all written instruments, constitutions, statutes, and contracts are interpreted by the same general principles, although the specific subject matter may call for strictness or liberality.[8] Accordingly, collective agreements should be drafted with the same care and precision exercised in drafting commercial contracts.[9]

On the other hand, the standards of construction as used by arbitrators are not inflexible. They are but "aids to the finding of intent, not hard and fast rules to be used to defeat intent."[10] Parties probably expect arbitrators to be less circumscribed by rigid rules of construction than the courts, and this helps to protect against harsh and unworkable results.

Sometimes two or more of the rules of interpretation conflict in a given case. Where this is so, the arbitrator is free to apply that rule which he believes will produce the better result.[11] Sometimes, however, a combination of two or more of the standards may be consistently applied in construing an ambiguous word or clause. The statement of Mr. Justice Holmes, that "it is not an adequate discharge of duty for courts to say: We see what you are driving at, but you

---

[7] See Smith v. Bowen, 121 N.E. 814 (Mass., 1919); Mueller v. Chicago & N.W. Ry. Co., 259 N.W. 798 (Minn., 1935); Reichert v. Quindazzi, 6 N.Y.S., 2d 284 (N.Y., 1938).

[8] See Moran Towing and Transportation Co., 1 ALAA ¶67,012, p. 67,015 (Kidd, 1944). This view is practiced by many arbitrators, but there have been occasional expressions of doubt, as in Crescent Warehouse Co., 10 LA 168, 171 (Aaron, 1948). Some parties specifically provide that in making his decision the arbitrator shall be bound by the principles of interpretation used by courts.

[9] For valuable guides to aid the draftsman, see Marceau, Drafting a Union Contract (Little, Brown & Co., 1965).

[10] Republic Steel Corp., 5 LA 609, 614 (McCoy, 1946).

[11] See, for instance, Arbitrator Block in Inspiration Consolidated Copper Co., 50 LA 58, 62 (1968).

have not said it, and therefore we shall go on as before,"[12] would appear to express the attitude of the many arbitrators who strive to determine what the parties were driving at and to effectuate their intent.

It is recognized that there are dangers to collective bargaining both in a mere literal, mechanical approach to agreement interpretation and, at the other extreme, in the indirect rewriting of the agreement by the substitution of the arbitrator's views under the guise of interpretation.[13]

There are, at the extremes, arbitrators who take a strict legalistic view of interpretation and those who recognize few limitations; but it may be safely said that most arbitrators take an intermediate approach, refusing to pay slavish deference to legalisms but also seeking to give effect to the contract which the parties themselves have made.

"Legislation" vs. "Interpretation"

Regardless of the approach taken by the arbitrator, it is to be expected that something of his personality will creep into his decision. The award of the arbitrator is based upon *his interpretation,* not that of somebody else.[14]

The line between interpretation and "legislation" cannot be drawn absolutely and it is inevitable that this line will be crossed frequently. One arbitrator has openly declared that although the arbitration of a dispute must be confined within the scope of the existing agreement, its adjudication necessitates some *legislating* and interpreting to clarify and remove the uncertainties, obscurities, and ambiguities which exist in the agreement.[15]

Some gap-filling is a natural part of the interpretative process. Situations unforeseen when the agreement was written, but falling within its general framework, often arise. Where reasonably possible, arbitrators considering these situations must decide what the parties would have agreed upon, within the general framework of the agree-

---

[12] Johnson v. United States, 163 Fed. 30, 32 (CA 1, 1908).
[13] National Tube Co., 11 LA 378, 380 (Seward, 1948).
[14] Kendall Mills, 8 LA 306, 309 (Lane, 1947). Also see comments of Arbitrator Boehm in 47 LA 667, 668.
[15] Borg-Warner Corp., 3 LA 423, 428–429 (Gilden, 1944). Also see Arbitrator Rice in 8 LA 586, 588–589.

ment, had the matter been specifically before them.[16] As to such situations, one survey of labor arbitration suggests:

> "In such cases there is no true 'intent' of the parties expressed in the agreement itself. What is asked of the arbitrator is that he conceive, or adopt from the arguments of counsel, a theory of the agreement which explains his solution to the matter not covered by the agreement, and which does no violence to the general spirit and intent which have been expressed in the agreement. The arbitrator's task might be described as having to find out what the parties would have intended had they thought to deal with the particular item under dispute, or if they had had time to deal with it. How to accomplish this procedurally becomes a cardinal task of arbitration."[17]

In one such case the agreement expressly specified rail transport for orchestra members, no thought being given to air travel when the agreement was negotiated. When asked to decide whether the musicians could be *required* to fly on overseas trips, Arbitrator Lewis M. Gill declared:

> "[T]he arbitrator's responsibility here is not merely limited to searching for a mutual intent. He is not to throw up his hands and declare himself without authority to decide the case if he concludes that there is not any mutual intent on the point at issue. * * *

> "This contract has the common definition of matters which are subject to arbitration, describing them as 'disputes regarding the interpretation *or application* of the provisions of this Agreement' [emphasis added]. The provisions must be *applied* to the dispute at hand, in a fair and sensible manner—the only restriction on the arbitrator is the usual admonition that his decision must not 'have the effect of modifying or amending any provision of this Agreement.' "[18]

In holding that the members (with certain exceptions) could be required to fly, Arbitrator Gill denied that he was "adding something" to the agreement, but the Union argued otherwise.[19]

---

[16] See Arbitrator E. Jones in 48 LA 1304, 1317–1318; Dworkin in 46 LA 9, 11; Merrill in 44 LA 1121, 1123; Seitz in 44 LA 259, 262; Block in 43 LA 97, 101; Smith in 42 LA 517, 522–523; H. Jones in 35 LA 686, 690; Dash in 33 LA 925, 948; McKelvey in 25 LA 94, 99; Abernethy in 21 LA 129, 131; Hampton in 18 LA 581, 583; Handsaker in 3 LA 383, 389. Also see Fleming, "Reflections on the Nature of Labor Arbitration," 61 Mich. L. Rev. 1245, 1250–1252 (1963); Killingsworth, "Arbitration: Its Uses in Industrial Relations," 21 LA 859, 861–862 (1953).

[17] Eaton, "Labor Arbitration in the San Francisco Bay Area," 48 LA 1381, 1390 (1967).

[18] Philadelphia Orchestra Assn., 46 LA 513, 515 (1966).

[19] Id. at 517. The award withstood court challenge. Local 77, American Federation of Musicians v. Philadelphia Orchestra Association, 252 F. Supp. 787 (USDC, Pa., 1966).

A similar approach was taken by Arbitrator Russell A. Smith when confronted with the question whether seniority rights would survive closure of a plant and transfer of its operations to the employer's other plant, where the employer was covered by a multi-employer contract defining "seniority" as "length of service with the employing company in the plant involved." Arbitrator Smith noted three possible dispositions of the case:[20]

(1) Give the contract language literal meaning, though the negotiators never thought of the consolidation situation. Under this approach the employees of the closed plant would have no more seniority.

(2) View the contract as silent with respect to the consolidation situation and hold the arbitrator to be without jurisdiction to resolve it since he could supply a definite solution only by violating the prohibition against adding to the agreement; he would have to remand the matter to the parties.

(3) Consider it incumbent upon the arbitrator to give meaning to the term "plant" in the event of consolidation, though the present situation was not specifically contemplated in negotiations; this the arbitrator could do as a matter of contract interpretation and application. Under this approach it would be reasonable to derive from use of the "plant" seniority concept a basic intent to grant seniority rights relating to types of plant operations then existing, and not to presume that parties contemplated eradication of seniority rights through consolidation.

Arbitrator Smith utilized the latter approach.[21] In doing so he stated:

"Arbitrators are constantly required and expected to give meaning to contract provisions which are unclear, in situations which were not specifically foreseen by the contract negotiators. So long as this is done by application of principles reasonably drawn from the provisions of the Agreement, and not by treating of a subject not covered at all by the Agreement, arbitral authority is not being improperly assumed."[22]

---

[20] Superior Products Co., 42 LA 517, 522–523 (1964).

[21] It is significant that the plants involved in the projected consolidation had distinctive types of operations; and under Arbitrator Smith's decision, the term "plant" as used in the seniority provision would be construed as establishing two seniority groups, one relating to the type of operations previously performed only at the L plant and one relating to the type of operations previously performed only at the G plant. Thus, employees from the L plant (to be closed) would carry with them what would amount to departmental seniority to perform in the G plant the same type of operations that they had performed in the former location, while the employees who had seniority at the G plant would continue to have a preferential right to the G plant type of operations.

[22] Superior Products Co., 42 LA 517, 523 (1964). Also see Arbitrator Smith in 48 LA 213, 218–219.

However, an arbitrator may refuse to fill "gaps" where he is convinced that to do so "would constitute contract-making" rather than contract interpretation or application.[23] In such cases arbitrators have concluded that the dispute should be resolved by the parties through negotiations; some of these arbitrators in refusing to rule on the merits have spoken in terms of "no meeting of the minds" of the parties.[24]

Which approach is best where an arbitrator is confronted with an issue growing out of an unforeseen situation? Obviously, no given approach is necessarily best for all cases. The arbitrator is justified in ruling upon the merits where a plausible solution is available within the general framework of the agreement or on the basis of an adequately defined past practice. However, where no such solution is available and the arbitrator is convinced that a ruling on the merits would cross the line too far into the area of legislation, or would involve too much guesswork or "shooting in the dark," he is likewise justified in remanding the case to the parties for negotiations. In any case, the arbitrator must give due consideration to contractual limitations upon his authority, for gap-filling would then be improper (unless authorized by the parties for the particular case) if it results in a basic addition to, subtraction from, or modification of the agreement.[25]

Intent of the Parties

The rule primarily to be observed in the construction of written agreements is that the interpreter must, if possible, ascertain and give effect to the mutual intent of the parties. The collective agreement should be construed, not narrowly and technically, but broadly and so as to accomplish its evident aims.[26]

---

[23] Labor Standards Association, 50 LA 1009, 1012 (Kates, 1968).
[24] See Arbitrator Sembower in 54 LA 292, 297–298; Sweeney in 29 LA 188, 191; Garman in 20 LA 199, 201–202; Killingsworth in 12 LA 709, 714, and in 7 LA 70, 74; Copelof in 7 LA 507, 510, and in 6 LA 667, 669. Also see Arbitrator Johannes in 20 LA 362, 363–364; Brandschain in 9 LA 239, 241; McCoy in 1 LA 556, 560. Cf., Arbitrator Lehoczky in 19 LA 766, 767. The "meeting of the minds" requirement is questioned by Arbitrator Sylvester Garrett, "The Role of Lawyers in Arbitration," Arbitration and Public Policy 102, 121 (BNA Incorporated, 1961). For related discussion, see Chapter 7, topics titled "Remedy Power and Its Use" and "Recommendations by Arbitrator"; Chapter 10, topic titled "Contract Principles."
[25] For cases in which the parties did give special authorization for the particular case, see Arbitrator Beatty in 24 LA 424, 425; Ryder in 22 LA 769, 771.
[26] Rentschler v. Missouri Pacific R.R., 253 N.W. 694 (Neb., 1934). Also see Arbitrator Krimsly in 48 LA 1359, 1361.

In determining the intent of the parties, inquiry is made as to what the language meant to the parties when the agreement was written.[27] It is this meaning that governs, not the meaning that can be possibly read into the language.[28]

The "intent of the parties" rule has been elaborated as follows:

"Whatever may be the inaccuracy of expression or the inaptness of words used in an instrument in a legal view, if the intention of the parties can be clearly discovered, the court will give effect to it and construe the words accordingly. It must not be supposed, however, that an attempt is made to ascertain the actual mental processes of the parties to a particular contract. The law presumes that the parties understood the import of their contract and that they had the intention which its terms manifest. It is not within the function of the judiciary to look outside of the instrument to get at the intention of the parties and then carry out that intention regardless of whether the instrument contains ·language sufficient to express it; but their sole duty is to find out what was meant by the language of the instrument. This language must be sufficient, when looked at in the light of such facts as the court is entitled to consider, to sustain whatever effect is given to the instrument."[29]

Language Which Is Clear and Unambiguous

If the language of an agreement is clear and unequivocal, an arbitrator generally will not give it a meaning other than that expressed. As Arbitrator Fred Witney has stated, an arbitrator cannot "ignore clear-cut contractual language," and he "may not legislate new language, since to do so would usurp the role of the labor organization and employer."[30] Even though the parties to an agreement disagree as to its meaning, an arbitrator who finds the language to be unambiguous will enforce the clear meaning.[31]

An arbitrator, as a neutral, is less likely than the parties to commit the error of seeing what one would like to find in written language

---

[27] Brampton Woolen Co. v. Local Union 112 et al., 61 A. 2d 796 (N.H., 1948). Also see Arbitrator Platt in 13 LA 126, 131. Cf., Arbitrator Boles in 20 LA 227, 231.

[28] Autocar Co., 10 LA 61, 63 (Brecht, 1948). Also see Arbitrator Davey in 21 LA 139, 144.

[29] 12 American Jurisprudence, §227, pp. 746–748 (citations omitted).

[30] Clean Coverall Supply Co., 47 LA 272, 277 (1966).

[31] See Arbitrator Leonard in 47 LA 661, 665; Traynor in 47 LA 193, 194–195; Daugherty in 46 LA 95, 98; Autrey in 45 LA 783, 786, 788; Scheiber in 44 LA 883, 887; Shipman in 9 LA 716, 718; Blumer in 5 LA 378, 382; Rader in 4 LA 497, 502; Epstein in 3 LA 412, 414; Updegraff in 2 LA 469, 472; Peifer in 2 LA 66, 67.

rather than what is actually there. Even when both parties declare a provision to be ambiguous, the arbitrator may find it nòt so.[32] On the other hand, language which appears on the surface to be clear sometimes will prove to have a latent or hidden ambiguity.[33]

Arbitrators apply the principle that parties to a contract are charged with full knowledge of its provisions and of the significance of its language.[34] Arbitrator W. Herman Rauch has explained:

"One of the most important facts about the collective bargaining process is that the parties involved are familiar with the employee and the business problems in respect to which they seek agreement. Therefore, when a tentative agreement is reached, both of them know what it was expected to accomplish. Probably more important, however, is the fact that the entire Union membership reviews the terms of tentative commitments and, based on the knowledge which the individual employee has of the matter in question, decides whether those terms are acceptable."[35]

Thus, the clear meaning of language may be enforced even though the results are harsh or contrary to the original expectations of one of the parties.[36] In such cases the result is based upon the clear language of the contract, not upon the equities involved.[37]

Nonetheless, where very broad language has been used an arbitrator might refuse to apply it literally, but apply it restrictively so as to produce the intended result.[38] Also, if an arbitrator finds that as

---

[32] As in Andrew Williams Meat Co., 8 LA 518, 524 (Cheney, 1947). Also see Arbitrator Scheiber in 40 LA 152, 154–155.

[33] As in Carlile & Doughty, Inc., 9 LA 239, 241 (Brandschain, 1947). Also see Arbitrator Platt in 36 LA 561, 566.

[34] See Arbitrator Rauch in 51 LA 561, 565; Kerrison in 45 LA 530, 531; Platt in 7 LA 708, 711; Updegraff in 3 LA 229, 232 (citing law cases), and in 2 LA 469, 472.

[35] Wyman-Gordon Co., 51 LA 561, 565 (1968).

[36] See Arbitrator McDermott in 49 LA 1157, 1159; Erbs in 49 LA 229, 230–231; Stouffer in 46 LA 578, 583; Small in 45 LA 775, 777; Abernethy in 44 LA 183, 188; Ross in 28 LA 557, 558; Shipman in 20 LA 756, 758–759; Copelof in 13 LA 110, 114; Potter in 7 LA 724, 729; Cheney in 6 LA 962, 965; Marshall in 6 LA 838, 843; Prasow in 6 LA 540, 543; Carmichael in 1 ALAA ¶67,096. Also see Kates in 48 LA 773, 775; Olson in 48 LA 197, 198; Singletary in 45 LA 261, 264. Cf., Seitz in 32 LA 513, 516.

[37] See Arbitrator Davis in 48 LA 938, 939–940; Hayes in 48 LA 276, 280; Marshall in 6 LA 838, 843.

[38] See Arbitrator McCoy in 49 LA 255, 256; Seitz in 46 LA 961, 963–964 (he declared that it "is not difficult to make an ass of the law by a too literal reading of words used by the parties in expressing their bargain"); Roberts in 45 LA 291, 292–293; Warns in 36 LA 380, 381; Updegraff in 33 LA 629, 631–632; Lehoczky in 9 LA 656, 657. Also see Gibson in 46 LA 598, 601.

a result of mutual mistake or typographical error the parties used language or punctuation which does not express their true intent, a reformation may be granted so as to effectuate the true intent of the parties.[39]

Interpretation in Light of the Law

Arbitrators strive to give effect to the collective agreement rather than to dismember it, and, whenever two interpretations are possible, one making the agreement valid and lawful and the other making it unlawful, the former will be used. The parties are presumed to have intended a valid contract.[40] Similarly, the public interest may be a relevant factor in contract interpretation.[41]

When parties use language in their agreement which is the same as language of a statute, the meaning given to that language by courts and administrative tribunals may be persuasive upon arbitrators as indicating the proper interpretation of the language.[42]

Normal and Technical Usage

Arbitrators give words their ordinary and popularly accepted meaning in the absence of anything indicating that they were used in a different sense or that the parties intended some special colloquial meaning.[43] For instance, the word "may" has been given its ordinary

---

The switch to daylight savings time has produced a pair of contrasting cases in which the arbitrator's attitude toward literal application of contractual language is worthy of note. See Arbitrator Abernethy in 51 LA 9, 12, and Arbitrator Roberts in 33 LA 752, 753.

[39] See Arbitrator Anderson in 43 LA 730, 732–733; Compton in 27 LA 829, 831; Willcox in 23 LA 21, 24. Also see Emery in 20 LA 865, 867; McCoy in 3 LA 257, 259. Cf., Sembower in 43 LA 722, 726–727. For further development of this matter, see Chapter 10, topic titled "Remedies for Mistake."

[40] See Arbitrator Gorder in 20 LA 880, 889; Horvitz in 9 LA 702, 703; Tischler in 5 LA 282, 283; Shake in 2 LA 445, 452.

[41] Maritime Service Committee, Inc., 49 LA 557, 562 (Scheiber, 1967).

[42] See Arbitrator Reeves in 20 LA 564, 566; Horvitz in 20 LA 318, 320; Platt in 19 LA 457, 458. For extensive discussion of use by arbitrators of substantive rules of law, see Chapter 10.

[43] See Arbitrator Roberts in 48 LA 978, 980; Anrod in 48 LA 310, 312–313; Summers in 48 LA 137, 142; Shipman in 46 LA 1053, 1056; Slavney in 28 LA 532, 534; Prasow in 27 LA 40, 45; Feinberg in 18 LA 227, 231; Shulman in 12 LA 949, 954; McCoy in 12 LA 650, 652; Lewis in 6 LA 202, 203; Kelliher in 5 LA 409, 410; Rader in 3 LA 605, 607.

"permissive" meaning in absence of strong evidence that a mandatory meaning was intended.[44] The words "day" or "workday" ordinarily must be construed as a calendar day, from midnight to midnight.[45]

Trade or technical terms will be interpreted in a trade or technical sense unless clearly used otherwise. For instance, the term "union shop" was applied in the sense commonly used in labor circles instead of in a special sense (which would not have required maintenance of membership) urged by management; the arbitrator declared that if the employer did not intend that which was meant by the term in the parlance of organized labor or did not understand the term, he should not have let it be used in the contract.[46] Under similar reasoning, the term "regular hourly rate" was given its generally accepted meaning in industry.[47] However, an arbitrator gave a medical term its popular meaning after he "conducted his own 'Gallup Poll' " with laymen, who all agreed as to the meaning of the disputed term; he assumed, absent proof to the contrary, that the negotiators were laymen.[48]

Any term not characteristically a trade or technical term will be construed in its natural, usual sense unless the context or evidence indicates that a technical meaning was intended by the parties.[49]

It is said to be "a well recognized rule of construction that a word used by parties in one sense is to be interpreted, in the absence of countervailing reasons, as employed in the same sense throughout the writing."[50] On the other hand, use of two different terms might be held to imply different meanings.[51]

It is also stated that when parties have changed the language

---

[44] See Arbitrator Hogan in 25 LA 243, 246; Reynard in 22 LA 880, 881.

[45] See AMF Western Tool, Inc., 49 LA 718, 723 (Solomon, 1967), and cases cited therein.

[46] Safeway Stores, Inc., 1 ALAA ¶67,096, p. 67,169 (Carmichael, 1944). Also applying a term in its technical sense, Arbitrator Merrill in 47 LA 1120, 1125. Cf., Sullivan in 39 LA 791, 794–795.

[47] R.M.F. Inc., 50 LA 789, 790 (Sherman, 1968).

[48] American Synthetic Rubber Co., 50 LA 25, 30 (Kesselman, 1967).

[49] Walton Laboratories, Inc., 47 LA 375, 377 (Yagoda, 1966); Great Lakes Dredge & Dock Co., 5 LA 409, 410 (Kelliher, 1946).

[50] Vickers, Inc., 15 LA 353, 356 (Platt, 1950). Also see Arbitrator Platt in 48 LA 1213, 1215.

[51] As in Hanz Trucking, Inc., 46 LA 1057, 1062 (Anderson, 1966), where the contract used two different terms in setting up hourly pay rates for the same work performed under different circumstances. Cf., Arbitrator Morvant in 36 LA 496, 500–501.

of their agreement there is a presumption that they intended a changed meaning.[52]

Use of Dictionary Definitions

Arbitrators have often ruled that in the absence of a showing of mutual understanding of the parties to the contrary, the usual and ordinary definition of terms as defined by a reliable dictionary should govern.[53] Trade or technical terms of a particular industry may be given meaning by resort to a special dictionary for that industry,[54] and a labor relations dictionary may be used for general industrial terms.[55]

However, an examination of the entire agreement and its application to the subject matter being considered by the arbitrator may result in the interpretation of words not in the general dictionary sense but in a mutually agreed sense.[56]

Furthermore, it sometimes happens that dictionary definitions can be found to cover opposing contentions.[57] In such situations (and indeed ordinarily) it is desirable that interpretations not rest upon dictionary definitions alone but be additionally supported by other considerations, especially where the persons drafting the agreement were laymen untrained in the precise use of words.[58]

Agreement to Be Construed as a Whole

It is said that the "primary rule in construing a written instrument is to determine, not alone from a single word or phrase, but from the instrument as a whole, the true intent of the parties and

---

[52] See Arbitrator Kates in 46 LA 715, 717, and in 44 LA 861, 865; Prasow in 40 LA 201, 204; Emery in 20 LA 865, 867. Also see Anderson in 48 LA 1104, 1106 (deletion of an express exception is clear intent to abolish the exception). Where two provisions of a contract were contradictory, the one adopted later in point of time was held controlling. National Distillers Products Co., 53 LA 477, 479 (Jones, 1969).

[53] E.g., Arbitrator Traynor in 47 LA 193, 195; Gibson in 46 LA 633, 635–636; Murphy in 46 LA 289, 292; Cahn in 29 LA 597, 603; Hebert in 23 LA 497, 500; Gorder in 20 LA 880, 888; Luskin in 18 LA 459, 461.

[54] Columbian Carbon Co., 47 LA 1120, 1125 (Merrill, 1967).

[55] Wisconsin Porcelain Co., 36 LA 485, 487 (Anderson, 1961).

[56] See Moran Towing and Transportation Co., 1 ALAA ¶67,012 (Kidd, 1944).

[57] As in Atlanta Newspapers, Inc., 20 LA 809, 817 (Dworet, 1953).

[58] See comments of Arbitrator Lockhart in 16 LA 173, 175; McCoy in 12 LA 650, 652, and in 5 LA 492, 494.

to interpret the meaning of a questioned word or part with regard to the connection in which it is used, the subject matter and its relation to all other parts or provisions."[59]

Similarly, "Sections or portions cannot be isolated from the rest of the agreement and given construction independently of the purpose and agreement of the parties as evidenced by the entire document. * * * The meaning of each paragraph and each sentence must be determined in relation to the contract as a whole."[60] This standard requiring the agreement to be construed as a whole is applied very frequently.[61]

Giving Effect to All Clauses and Words

If an arbitrator finds that alternative interpretations of a clause are possible, one of which would give meaning and effect to another provision of the contract, while the other would render the other provision meaningless or ineffective, he will be inclined to use the interpretation which would give effect to all provisions.[62] In the words of one arbitrator:

"It is axiomatic in contract construction that an interpretation which tends to nullify or render meaningless any part of the contract should be avoided because of the general presumption that the parties do not carefully write into a solemnly negotiated agreement words intended to have no effect."[63]

Ordinarily all words used in an agreement should be given effect. The fact that a word is used indicates that the parties intended it to have some meaning, and it will not be declared surplusage if a reasonable meaning can be given to it consistent with the rest of the

---

[59] Riley Stoker Corp., 7 LA 764, 767 (Platt, 1947).

[60] Great Lakes Dredge & Dock Co., 5 LA 409, 410 (Kelliher, 1946).

[61] E.g., Arbitrator Tongue in 49 LA 443, 445; Geissinger in 47 LA 748, 751–752; Erbs in 47 LA 475, 477; Krimsly in 47 LA 159, 161; Anrod in 45 LA 738, 741; Turkus in 40 LA 1248, 1250; Merrill in 29 LA 334, 339–342; Scheiber in 26 LA 117, 120; Ryder in 20 LA 337, 340; Maggs in 11 LA 992, 993; Hampton in 10 LA 487, 493; McCoy in 5 LA 609, 613; Gilden in 1 ALAA ¶67,315.

[62] E.g., Arbitrator Witney in 50 LA 535, 538; Summers in 48 LA 137, 140; Leonard in 47 LA 661, 665; Merrill in 46 LA 1044, 1047; Layman in 45 LA 417, 424–425; Fraker in 42 LA 1073, 1075; Rohman in 40 LA 1217, 1221; Hale in 39 LA 310, 314; Hebert in 29 LA 469, 473; Kelliher in 27 LA 798, 800; Coffey in 12 LA 1117, 1120; Merrill in 11 LA 25, 30; Aaron in 10 LA 227, 233; McCoy in 4 LA 310, 313. Cf., Platt in 9 LA 91, 94.

[63] John Deere Tractor Co., 5 LA 631, 632 (Updegraff, 1946). Also see Arbitrator Scheiber in 49 LA 557, 562–563.

agreement.[64] However, if no reasonable meaning can be given to a word or clause, either from the context in which it is used or by examining the whole agreement, it may be treated as surplusage and declared to be inoperative.[65]

Words may be implied into an agreement with as much force and effect as if expressed therein if, from a consideration of the agreement as a whole, such inclusion by implication is called for.[66] Thus, in one instance the arbitrator decided that the words "job classification" were impliedly meant to precede the phrase "hourly rates of pay."[67]

Avoidance of Harsh, Absurd, or Nonsensical Results

When one interpretation of an ambiguous contract would lead to harsh, absurd, or nonsensical results, while an alternative interpretation, equally consistent, would lead to just and reasonable results, the latter interpretation will be used.[68] Where the extreme positions of both parties would have produced absurd results, an arbitrator rejected both and arrived at his own interpretation of the disputed provision.[69]

To illustrate application of this standard, a provision for paid vacations for employees in the "active employ" of the company on a specified date, provided they met other requirements, would not be interpreted so as to produce the "absurd" result of disqualifying employees absent on such date due to illness or any other valid reason.[70] Likewise, an interpretation was rejected which, if applied, would have placed a premium on contract violation by encouraging unauthorized strikes.[71]

---

[64] Beatrice Foods Co., 45 LA 540, 543 (Stouffer, 1965); Borden's Farm Products, Inc., 3 LA 401, 402 (Burke, 1945).

[65] American Shearer Mfg. Co., 6 LA 984, 985–986 (Myers, 1947). Also see Arbitrator McNaughton in 49 LA 61, 62–63.

[66] J. M. Huber, Inc., 5 LA 100, 103 (Shipman, 1946). Also see Arbitrator Platt in 15 LA 352, 356.

[67] J. M. Huber, Inc., 5 LA 100, 103 (Shipman, 1946).

[68] See Arbitrator Block in 50 LA 58, 62; Duff in 48 LA 513, 516; Anrod in 48 LA 310, 314; Kates in 45 LA 641, 643; Robertson in 37 LA 220, 225; Dworkin in 23 LA 481, 486; Platt in 15 LA 353, 355; Merrill in 11 LA 25, 29; Raphael in 5 LA 753, 757; McCoy in 2 LA 367, 370; Gilden in 1 LA 417, 419.

[69] D-V Displays Corp., 41 LA 937, 942 (Kates, 1963).

[70] Rockwell Spring & Axle Co., 23 LA 481, 486 (Dworkin, 1954).

[71] A. D. Julliard & Co., 2 LA 140, 141 (Copelof, 1946).

Arbitrator Harry H. Platt found arbitral surgery justified where necessary to prevent absurd results:

"Experience teaches that contracting parties are not always absolutely precise, nor can they be expected to be, in their agreement formulations. Not infrequently, words or phrases are unthinkingly included which, if construed according to their literal meaning would produce results in opposition to the main purpose and object of a provision. This is often true when, as here, some of the language used was drafted by others in a different context and in response to other circumstances and policies. In such a case, there can be no doubt as to the right of an interpreter to modify and mitigate—in effect excise—the unpremeditated, unintended language in order to prevent an absurd result and to give effect to the true intention of the parties."[72]

To Express One Thing Is to Exclude Another

Frequently arbitrators apply the principle that to expressly include one or more of a class in a written instrument must be taken as an exclusion of all others.[73] To expressly state certain exceptions indicates that there are no other exceptions.[74] To expressly include some guarantees in an agreement is to exclude other guarantees.[75] Similarly, where an employee had 20 years of service with the company but less than one year in the bargaining unit, the fact that the agreement specifically allowed credit for all service with the company in determining entitlement to vacation benefits was held to indicate that only bargaining unit service could be credited for earning sick leave.[76]

The hazards of this rule of construction, known as *"expressio unius est exclusio alterius,"* in some instances leads parties to use general rather than specific language,[77] or to follow a specific enumeration with the statement that the clause is not to be restricted necessarily to the things specifically listed.

---

[72] Evening News Assn., 50 LA 239, 245 (1968).
[73] See Arbitrator Malkin in 51 LA 1266, 1268; Turkus in 49 LA 155, 158; Sembower in 46 LA 430, 435; Rosenfarb in 18 LA 418, 423; Copelof in 16 LA 685, 688; Hobbs in 10 LA 541, 549; Hampton in 10 LA 487, 494; Potter in 7 LA 81, 84; McCoy in 3 LA 257, 259. Cf., Holly in 24 LA 268, 271; Maggs in 22 LA 761, 762; Gilden in 15 LA 345, 349.
[74] A. O. Smith Corp., 47 LA 654, 661 (Dworkin, 1966); Modecraft Co., 44 LA 1045, 1049 (Jaffee, 1965).
[75] Great Atlantic & Pacific Tea Co., 46 LA 372, 374 (Scheiber, 1966).
[76] A. S. Abell Co., 46 LA 327, 329 (Horvitz, 1966).
[77] Loew's Inc., 10 LA 227, 232 (Aaron, 1948).

Doctrine of "Ejusdem Generis"

It is axiomatic under the doctrine of *ejusdem generis* that where general words follow an enumeration of specific terms the general words will be interpreted to include or cover only things of the same general nature or class as those enumerated, unless it is shown that a wider sense was intended.[78] Arbitrators apply this doctrine.[79]

For instance, it was held that a clause providing that seniority shall govern in all cases of layoff, transfer, "or other adjustment of personnel" should not be construed to require allocation of overtime work on the basis of seniority.[80] The doctrine has been held inapplicable, however, where the specific words preceding the general words embrace all objects of their class since, except for this qualification, the general words that follow the specific enumeration would be meaningless.[81]

Specific v. General Language

Where there is conflict between specific language and general language in an agreement, the specific language will govern.[82]

For example, where a contract contained a general provision stating that the Company should "continue to make reasonable provisions for the safety and health of its employees" and another provision stating that "wearing apparel and other equipment necessary properly to protect employees from injury shall be provided by the Company in accordance with practices now prevailing * * * or as such practices may be improved from time to time by the Company," it was held that the employer was not obligated to furnish rain clothes to employees where such had not been furnished or required in the past;

---

[78] See 12 Am. Jur. 799–780 (Contracts §244).
[79] See Arbitrator Hilpert in 46 LA 752, 755; Leach in 43 LA 888, 890–891; McCoy in 39 LA 530, 533; Bradley in 37 LA 9, 13; Mueller in 35 LA 912, 914; Rohman in 34 LA 781, 784. Also see Sembower in 43 LA 722, 728; Sullivan in 39 LA 791, 794.
[80] Canadian Industries Limited, 19 LA 170, 172 (Hanrahan, 1951).
[81] St. Louis Terminal Warehouse Co., 19 LA 807, 808–809 (Treiman, 1952). Also see Publishers' Assn. of New York City, 46 LA 388, 394 (Moskowitz, 1966).
[82] See Arbitrator Seidenberg in 48 LA 1005, 1010; Geissinger in 47 LA 748, 751; Kates in 46 LA 715, 717; Abernethy in 44 LA 183, 187; Sembower in 39 LA 534, 538; McKelvey in 29 LA 376, 380; Fleming in 28 LA 554, 556; McCoy in 12 LA 530, 531; Wyckoff in 12 LA 462, 469.

the arbitrator said that had the general clause stood alone he would have been required to determine whether the furnishing of rain clothes was reasonably necessary for the safety and health of the employees.[83]

Arbitrators also may be expected to rule that, when an exception is stated to a general principle, the exception should prevail where it is applicable.[84]

Construction in Light of Context

Definite meaning may be given to ambiguous or doubtful words by construing them in the light of the context.[85] "*Noscitur a sociis* is an old maxim which summarizes the rule both of language and of law that the meaning of words may be controlled by those with which they are associated."[86]

Avoidance of a Forfeiture

If an agreement is susceptible of two constructions, one of which would work a forfeiture and one of which would not, the arbitrator will be inclined to adopt the interpretation that will prevent the forfeiture. This principle has been elaborated by Arbitrator George Cheney:

"A party claiming a forfeiture or penalty under a written instrument has the burden of proving that such is the unmistakable intention of the parties to the document. In addition, the courts have ruled that a contract is not to be construed to provide a forfeiture or penalty unless no other construction or interpretation is reasonably possible. Since forfeitures are not favored either in law or in equity, courts are reluctant to declare and enforce a forfeiture if by reasonable interpretation it can be avoided."[87]

In that case a clause requiring retroactive pay for employees unjustly discharged was interpreted as an indemnity (rather than for-

---

[83] Tennessee Coal, Iron and R.R. Co., 12 LA 530, 531 (McCoy, 1949).

[84] Fulton-Sylphon Co., 8 LA 983, 984 (Greene, 1947).

[85] See Arbitrator Gorder in 20 LA 880, 888; Merrill in 11 LA 25, 31; Wallen in 6 LA 179, 182.

[86] Williston, Contracts, §618.

[87] Mode O'Day Corp., 1 LA 490, 494 (1946), wherein numerous court cases were cited. Accord, Arbitrator Mueller in 35 LA 912, 914; Kelliher in 27 LA 798, 800.

feiture) clause not requiring retroactive pay where employees suffer no loss of earnings while off the company payroll.[88]

Precontract Negotiations

Precontract negotiations frequently provide a valuable aid in the interpretation of ambiguous provisions. Where the meaning of a term is not clear, it will be deemed, if there is no evidence to the contrary, that the parties intended it to have the same meaning as that given it during the negotiations leading up to the agreement.[89] In such case, consideration will be given to all of the circumstances leading up to the making of the contract.[90]

The arbitrator must place himself, to the extent possible, in the situation of the parties at the time of the negotiations so as to view the circumstances as the parties viewed them and to judge the meaning of the agreement accordingly. In this regard, the arbitrator might make a special request for complete detail as to bargaining history.[91] Recordings and minutes of bargaining meetings provide important evidence,[92] and in one case a union's "Negotiations Bulletin" was found to provide a "useful clue" in reference to bargaining history.[93] Even where no stenographic record is kept and no notes are taken, the history of negotiations may be relied upon by the arbitrator if he is satisfied as to the accuracy of the oral testimony of persons who attended the negotiations.[94] Not all evidence as to what occurred in negotiations is competent, however; there may be privileged communications not admissible into evidence.[95]

---

[88] Mode O'Day Corp., 1 LA 490, 494 (Cheney, 1946).

[89] See Arbitrator Teple in 47 LA 438, 440; Whyte in 47 LA 26, 30; Bouwhuis in 1 ALAA ¶67,025, p. 67,041.

[90] Kohlenberger Engineering Corp., 12 LA 380, 384 (Prasow, 1949).

[91] See, for instance, Detroit Edison Co., 43 LA 193, 200–210 (1964), in which the parties prepared a comprehensive exhibit at Arbitrator Russell A. Smith's request.

[92] See Arbitrator Grant in 21 LA 704, 706; Komaroff in 19 LA 138, 143; Blumer in 7 LA 512, 514; Blair in 5 LA 446, 448.

[93] Los Angeles Herald Examiner, 45 LA 860, 862 (Kadish, 1965).

[94] See Arbitrator Dolnick in 46 LA 426, 428–429; Hebert in 42 LA 458, 465; Burke in 3 LA 401, 402–403.

[95] See Air Reduction Chemical & Carbide Co., 41 LA 24, 26 (Warns, 1963), in which statements of mediators in assisting parties to reach agreement were held privileged. Accord, Arbitrator Glushien in 55 LA 1130, 1135.

Furthermore, if an agreement is not ambiguous, it is improper to modify its meaning by invoking the record of prior negotiations.[96]

The intent manifested by the parties during negotiations, rather than any undisclosed intent, is considered by arbitrators to be most important. If one party to negotiations is negligent or unreasonable in permitting the use of a term which does not clearly express the meaning intended by that party and if the other party is thus reasonably misled as to the first party's intentions, a contract may be held to exist in accordance with the second party's understanding.[97]

If a party attempts but fails, in contract negotiations, to include a specific provision in the agreement, many arbitrators will hesitate to read such provision into the agreement through the process of interpretation.[98] Arbitrator Edgar A. Jones has explained that "there is a hazard" in making a specific contract demand in negotiations:

> "If the provision gets caught up in a grievance, the Party who proffers the language will have to bear the burden of demonstrating in a later arbitration proceeding that its omission ought not to be given its normal significance. Normally, of course, the plain inference of the omission is that the intent to reject prevailed over the intent to include."[99]

However, where a proposal in bargaining is made for the purpose of clarifying the contract, the matter may be viewed in a different light. Arbitrator Sidney A. Wolff explains:

> "* * * [I]t is fundamental that it is not for the Labor Arbitrator to grant a party that which it could not obtain in bargaining.

---

[96] See Arbitrator Cole in 18 LA 916, 918; Blair in 3 LA 753, 756; Whiting in 3 LA 482, 486. For further discussion, see Chapter 10, topic titled "Parol Evidence."

[97] See Arbitrator Merrill in 46 LA 503, 505 and in 11 LA 25, 31; Emery in 17 LA 632, 635; Wolff in 8 LA 452; Blair in 4 LA 110, 111; McCoy in 1 LA 165, 167. Also see Turkus in 49 LA 155, 158; Bender in 43 LA 263, 266; Garrett in 15 LA 834, 838. Cf., Brandschain in 5 LA 164, 166; McCoy in 1 LA 556, 560.

[98] See, for example, Arbitrator Blair in 55 LA 312, 324; Larkin in 52 LA 993, 995; Dugan in 52 LA 608, 610; Walt in 50 LA 375, 379; Koven in 49 LA 1000, 1004; Roberts in 49 LA 214, 219; Jones in 47 LA 1075, 1077; Block in 47 LA 574, 577; Williams in 46 LA 1071, 1073; Cahn in 45 LA 840, 841; Sartain in 44 LA 102, 104; Smith in 43 LA 193, 203; Forsythe in 41 LA 1333, 1339; Bonebrake in 40 LA 550, 553; Shister in 40 LA 531, 532; Kates in 37 LA 177, 180; McKelvey in 35 LA 602, 603–604, 606; Jaffee in 27 LA 126, 128; Reynard in 24 LA 224, 228; Reid in 21 LA 699, 702–703.

[99] Progress-Bulletin Publishing Co., 47 LA 1075, 1077 (1966). Also see Arbitrator Jones in 48 LA 1304, 1319.

"This restriction, however, has its limitations. If, in fact the parties were in dispute, on the proper interpretation of a contract clause and one of them unsuccessfully sought in collective bargaining to obtain clarification, it would not necessarily follow that the interpretation sought by the unsuccessful party was wrong."[100]

Then, too, a party's unsuccessful attempt to obtain a clause severely restricting the other party does not compel the conclusion that a limited restriction does not inhere in the contract.[101]

The withdrawal or rejection during contract negotiations of a proposed clause spelling out a right has been held not to be an admission that the right did not exist without the clause, where the proponent stated at the time that it would stand firm on the position that the right existed even without the proposed clause.[102] A similar result was reached where withdrawal of a proposal was encouraged by the other party's statement that the proposal was not necessary.[103]

No Consideration to Compromise Offers

In the interpretation of an ambiguous agreement no consideration will be given to compromise offers or to concessions offered by one party and rejected by the other during negotiations which precede arbitration.[104] "[It] is clear that any offer made by either party during the course of conciliation cannot prejudice that party's case when the case comes to arbitration. It is the very essence of conciliation that compromise proposals will go further than a party may consider itself bound to go on a strict interpretation of its rights."[105]

---

[100] Hospital Service Plan, 47 LA 993, 993–994 (1966). For similar or even stronger statements of this limitation, see Arbitrator Krinsky in 54 LA 824, 828; Valtin in 48 LA 797, 799; Traynor in 46 LA 53, 57; Anderson in 43 LA 65, 73; Cole in 36 LA 753, 759. Arbitrator Shister rejected the Company's contention that it merely had been seeking clarification where he found that "the Company was reaching for something radically different from a clarification; it was attempting to change the language of the provision, and was unsuccessful." Sterilon Corp., 40 LA 531, 532 (1963).

[101] Hugo Neu-Proler Co., 50 LA 1270, 1272 (Bailer, 1968); Celanese Corp. of America, 33 LA 925, 950 (Dash, 1959).

[102] See Arbitrator Myers in 42 LA 269, 271 (rejection); Peck in 39 LA 1249, 1252 (withdrawal); Wolff in 21 LA 436, 439 (withdrawal). As to the effect of withdrawal without such assertion of right, contrast the view of Arbitrator Talent in 50 LA 1061, 1068, with that of Teple in 43 LA 338, 341.

[103] Philadelphia Orchestra Assn., 46 LA 513, 514 (Gill, 1966).

[104] See Arbitrator Kates in 39 LA 20, 22; Garrett in 26 LA 812, 824; Prasow in 25 LA 398, 403–404; Gorder in 25 LA 202, 205; Davey in 20 LA 737, 742; O'Rourke in 10 LA 417, 419; Greene in 8 LA 993, 996; Elson in 2 LA 399, 402. Also see Sembower in 41 LA 391, 397.

[105] Fulton-Sylphon Co., 8 LA 993, 996 (Greene, 1947).

Experience and Training of Negotiators

Whether or not an arbitrator will apply a strict interpretation to an ambiguous agreement may to some extent depend upon the training and experience of the negotiators. If the arbitrator finds that they were laymen untrained in the precise use of words and if the contract on its face bears evidence of a lack of precision, he may refuse to apply a strict construction.[106] Under such circumstances the arbitrator might conclude that the writing "should be considered as a somewhat imperfect attempt to embody rules which were better understood than it was possible to express in words."[107]

A less liberal approach is likely to be taken if the arbitrator knows that the negotiators for both parties were experts in drafting collective agreements;[108] or, to state it in other ways, if the arbitrator believes that the negotiators were "capable and shrewd,"[109] or were "sophisticated veterans" of negotiations.[110]

In applying a strict interpretation to a contested provision, Umpire Harry Shulman emphasized that: "The negotiators were not tyros in the art. They were skilled hands who worked hard, intelligently, and alertly. The agreement was not negotiated in a hurry or under pressure. Careful scrutiny was given to the language after agreement was reached on the substance."[111]

Custom and Past Practice of the Parties

One of the most important standards used by arbitrators in the interpretation of ambiguous contract language is that of custom or past practice of the parties. For extensive discussion of this standard

---

[106] As in U.S. Pipe & Foundry Co., 5 LA 492, 494 (McCoy, 1946). Also see Arbitrator Dolnick in 46 LA 426, 429; McCoy in 11 LA 556, 560. Similar liberal construction was utilized in interpreting a strike settlement agreement drafted by a citizens committee in Yale & Towne Mfg. Co., 39 LA 1156, 1157–1158 (Hill, Horlacher, & Seitz, 1962).

[107] Moran Towing and Transportation Co., 1 ALAA ¶67,012, p. 67,015 (Kidd, 1944).

[108] See Arbitrator Burr in 36 LA 1132, 1135; Morvant in 26 LA 526, 528; Anderson in 20 LA 910, 911; Margulies in 19 LA 683, 686; Lane in 8 LA 306, 308.

[109] Carnation Co., 3 LA 229, 232 (Updegraff, 1946). Also see Arbitrator Updegraff in 2 LA 469, 472.

[110] Hilo Transportation & Terminal Co., 36 LA 1132, 1135 (Burr, 1961).

[111] Ford Motor Company, 1 ALAA ¶67,126, p. 67,265 (1945).

of interpretation the reader is directed to Chapter 12, topic titled "Role of Custom and Practice in Interpretation of Ambiguous Language."

Industry Practice

Reference to custom and practice of the industry in which the parties operate may shed light upon the intended meaning of an ambiguous provision.[112] An even stronger guide is supplied when the same agreement has been entered into by one employer with several unions or by one union with several employers. In this situation practice of any of the pairs of parties operating under the agreement may be taken as some indication of the intended meaning of the language used,[113] but the arbitrator would not be bound by such practice.[114]

Where past practice of the parties in the plant and industry practice differ, the plant practice will ordinarily govern.[115] However, if the industry practice is well established, while the plant practice is not adequately established, the arbitrator may follow the industry practice as the better guide.[116]

Custom and practice of an industry other than that in which the parties operate may be accorded little if any weight. A practice which may be necessary and reasonable in one industry might be meaningless or foolish in another industry.[117] However, this is not always so.[118] Nor to be overlooked as a possible guide is practice by industry in general, either in the locality[119] or over a broader area.[120]

---

[112] See Arbitrator Duff in 48 LA 513, 515–517; Fallon in 48 LA 12, 16; Foley in 46 LA 989, 992; McDermott in 46 LA 774, 782; Roberts in 45 LA 291, 292–293; Kornblum in 35 LA 384, 385; Hill in 11 LA 1081, 1082; Wallen in 6 LA 1017, 1022; Wagner in 6 LA 292, 293. Also see Bauder in 46 LA 712, 714; Zimring in 46 LA 411, 413; Young in 21 LA 278, 282.

[113] See Arbitrator Geissinger in 48 LA 1011, 1013–1014; Marshall in 20 LA 297, 299; Sherbow in 17 LA 524, 526; McCoy in 1 ALAA ¶67,186. Also see McDermott in 53 LA 725, 729; Turkus in 46 LA 1112, 1115; Seitz in 43 LA 277, 283–288; Emery in 20 LA 458, 459–460. Cf., Wolff in 38 LA 242, 244–245.

[114] Sidney Wanzer & Sons, 47 LA 708, 711 (Kamin, 1966).

[115] As in New York Seven Up Bottling Co., 24 LA 601, 603 (Cahn, 1955).

[116] As did Arbitrator Loucks in 24 LA 81, 84, 87–88; Maggs in 17 LA 451, 454.

[117] Certain-Teed Products Corp., 1 LA 354, 358 (Gorder, 1946).

[118] See American Synthetic Rubber Corp., 46 LA 1158, 1159–1160 (Dolson, 1966).

[119] See Carnation Co., 38 LA 270, 272 (Peck, 1962).

[120] See Arbitrator Raimon in 48 LA 87, 90; Whyte in 47 LA 26, 29; Stein in 45 LA 1073, 1074. Also see McCoy in 32 LA 643, 644.

Of course, evidence of industry practice will not be given weight if too meager to furnish a reliable guide.[121] Moreover, while evidence of industry custom will be permitted for the purpose of clarifying the meaning of an ambiguous contract, it must not be given weight where the contract is clear and unambiguous.[122]

Prior Settlements as Aid to Interpretation

Sometimes light is shed upon ambiguous provisions by prior settlements by the parties of grievances involving those provisions. It has been suggested, in this regard, that "Where the parties themselves settle a grievance the evidence of intent as to the meaning of a provision carries special weight."[123] In effect, mutual settlements often constitute binding precedents for the parties.[124]

Similarly, even oral agreements of the parties as to the application of ambiguous language may subsequently be given significant weight by an arbitrator in interpreting that language if such oral agreements are clearly proven.[125]

If the agreement is not ambiguous, however, a past settlement which is inconsistent with the clear language of the agreement may be disregarded by an arbitrator in subsequent cases involving that language.[126]

Interpretation Against Party Selecting the Language

It is incumbent upon the proponent of a contract provision either to explain what is contemplated or to use language which does not leave the matter in doubt.[127] Where doubt exists, any ambiguity not removed by any other rule of interpretation may be removed by con-

---

[121] Lehigh Portland Cement Co., 42 LA 458, 466 (Hebert, 1964).
[122] Western Union Tel. Co. v. American Communications Ass'n. C.I.O., 79 N.Y.S. 2d 545 (N.Y., 1949).
[123] Bendix-Westinghouse Automotive Air Brake Co., 23 LA 706, 710 (Mathews, 1954). Also see Arbitrator Emery in 19 LA 812, 814–815; Wallen in 17 LA 36, 39.
[124] For discussion, see Chapter 5, topic titled "Grievance Settlements as Binding Precedents."
[125] See Autocar Co., 19 LA 89, 92 (Jaffee, 1952). Also see Arbitrator Gundermann in 46 LA 520, 522.
[126] International Harvester Co., 19 LA 812, 815 (Emery, 1953).
[127] See Arbitrator Kahn in 44 LA 1196, 1201; Morvant in 36 LA 496, 502; Smith in 21 LA 196, 198. Also see Emery in 17 LA 632, 635.

struing the ambiguous language against the party who proposed it.[128] It is reasoned that the draftsman, by exactness of expression, can more easily prevent doubts as to meaning.[129]

Courts of law, however, apply this rule only if a satisfactory result cannot be reached by any other rule of construction,[130] and it would seem that arbitrators should observe the same limitation.[131] Moreover, the rule will not be applied if there is no ambiguity,[132] or if there are special reasons for refusal to apply it, as where the clause finally used differed substantially from the one originally prepared unilaterally, and both parties approved the final draft.[133]

Further, it has been held that ambiguous language need not be interpreted against the party who proposed it where there is no showing that the other party was misled.[134]

Company Manuals and Handbooks

Company-issued booklets, manuals, and handbooks which have not been negotiated or agreed to by the union are said to constitute "merely a unilateral statement by the Company and not sufficient to be binding upon the Union."[135] It can be expected that arbitrators ordinarily will be inclined to give such publications little or no weight in the interpretation of disputed contractual language.[136]

---

[128] See Arbitrator Anrod in 49 LA 988, 990; Sales in 47 LA 1078, 1080; Jenkins in 45 LA 696, 702; Kahn in 44 LA 1196, 1201; Small in 41 LA 370, 372; Haughton in 39 LA 943, 947; Smith in 21 LA 196, 198; Healy in 11 LA 228, 233; Merrill in 11 LA 25, 32; Wolff in 8 LA 452, 458; Elson in 2 LA 399, 403. Cf., Scheiber in 48 LA 663, 667.

[129] Brown & Sharpe Mfg. Co., 11 LA 228, 233 (Healy, 1948). To similar effect, Arbitrator Small in 41 LA 370, 372.

[130] For cases, see 13 Corpus Juris 545, n. 44.

[131] The limitation was stated in Deep Rock Oil Corp., 11 LA 25, 32 (Merrill, 1948). To similar effect, Arbitrator Kates in 46 LA 317, 320; Krimsly in 42 LA 311, 314.

[132] John Deere Tractor Co., 2 LA 469, 472 (Updegraff, 1945).

[133] Crescent Warehouse Co., 10 LA 168, 171 (Aaron, 1948).

[134] International Harvester Co., 13 LA 133, 135 (McCoy, 1949).

[135] Greer Steel Co., 50 LA 340, 343 (McIntosh, 1968).

[136] See comments of Arbitrator McIntosh, ibid., and those of Arbitrator Hebert in Westinghouse Electric Corp., 45 LA 131, 140 (1965). A company's inter-office memorandum was held not binding on the company where it had not been adopted as a contract between the parties either by formal amendment or past practice. Tenn Flake of Middlesboro, Inc., 55 LA 256, 258 (May, 1970). The right of an arbitrator to consider a company pamphlet and a bulletin containing company rules in interpreting the collective agreement was upheld in United Furniture Workers v. Virgo Mfg. Corp., 257 F.Supp. 138 (USDC, 1966).

Reason and Equity

It is widely recognized that if a contract "is clear and unambiguous it must be applied in accordance with its terms despite the equities that may be present on either side."[137] Arbitrators strive where possible, however, to give *ambiguous* language a construction which is reasonable and equitable to both parties rather than one which would give one party an unfair and unreasonable advantage.[138]

The arbitrator, it has been said, should "look at the language in the light of experience and choose that course which does the least violence to the judgment of a reasonable man."[139]

---

[137] Firestone Tire & Rubber Co., 29 LA 469, 473 (Hebert, 1957). See similar views by Arbitrator Abernethy in 51 LA 9, 13; Erbs in 49 LA 229, 230–231. For other cases and discussion of this principle, see this Chapter, topic titled "Language Which Is Clear and Unambiguous," and Chapter 7, topic titled "Recommendations by Arbitrator."

[138] See Arbitrator Maggs in 17 LA 606, 609; Broadwin in 12 LA 478, 481; Stein in 11 LA 1019, 1020.

[139] Clifton Paper Board Co., 11 LA 1019, 1020 (Stein, 1949).

CHAPTER 10

USE OF SUBSTANTIVE RULES OF LAW

General Considerations

In agreeing to resolve disputes by arbitration, parties choose to substitute a private solution for litigation in courts of law. Since the appointment and authority of the arbitrator are under the control of the parties, they can by the submission agreement expressly regulate (but do not often do so) the extent to which he is to consider applicable law. Thus, for instance, they may expressly direct him to decide the case consistent with applicable law,[1] or they may restrict his authority to interpret the law.[2] Likewise, the parties can provide in the submission agreement the extent to which his decision is to be final. Thus, for instance, they may provide that the award is to be final only with respect to limited areas, such as questions of fact,[3] or they may provide that it is to be final except in case of "gross mistake of law or fact."[4]

Unless the parties specifically limit the powers of the arbitrator in deciding various aspects of the issue submitted to him, it is often presumed that they intend to make him the final judge on any questions which arise in the disposition of the issue, including not only questions of fact but also questions of contract interpretation, rules of interpretation, and questions, if any, with respect to substantive law.

---

[1] As in A. S. Abell Co., 45 LA 801, 807 (Cluster, Gallagher & Kraushaar, 1965); Board of Education of the City of New York, 44 LA 997, 1001 (Stark, 1964).
[2] See Ingalls Shipbuilding Corp., 54 LA 484, 487 (Boothe, 1970).
[3] See submission in Food Employers Council Inc., 20 LA 724, 725 (Van de Water, 1953), which specifically made the award reviewable as to law by the courts.
[4] As in Goodyear Engineering Corp., 24 LA 360, 362 (Warns, 1955).

Over a century ago the U.S. Supreme Court emphasized that arbitration awards are not generally subject to being set aside for errors of law:

> "Arbitrators are judges chosen by the parties to decide the matters submitted to them, finally and without appeal. As a mode of settling disputes, it should receive every encouragement from courts of equity. If the award is within the submission, and contains the honest decision of the arbitrators, after a full and fair hearing of the parties, a court of equity will not set it aside for error, either in law or fact. A contrary course would be a substitution of the judgment of the chancellor in place of the judges chosen by the parties, and would make an award the commencement, not the end, of litigation."[5]

In a 1953 case involving the Federal Arbitration Act, the U.S. Supreme Court stated that: "In unrestricted submissions * * * the interpretations of the law by the arbitrators in contrast to manifest disregard are not subject, in the federal courts, to judicial review for error in interpretation."[6]

The continued vitality of the general rule that awards are not impeachable for errors of law has been recognized by federal and state courts in both statutory and common law arbitration.[7]

---

[5] Burchell v. Marsh, 58 U.S. 344; 17 Howard 344 (1854).

[6] Wilko v. Swan, 74 S.Ct. 182, 187 (1953), citing the Court's 1854 "Burchell v. Marsh" decision. In evaluating this statement, the Ninth Circuit stated that "manifest disregard of the law must be something beyond and different from a mere error in the law or failure on the part of the arbitrators to understand or apply the law"; a manifest disregard of the law "might be present when arbitrators understand and correctly state the law, but proceed to disregard the same." San Martine Compania de Navegacion, S.A. v. Saguenay Terminals Limited, 293 F.2d 796, 801 (CA 9, 1961). For subsequent reference to Wilko v. Swan and its theme of limited judicial review of awards, see Justice Harlan's concurring opinion in U.S. Bulk Carriers, Inc. v. Arguelles, 91 S.Ct. 409, 414 (1971).

[7] Transport Workers v. Philadelphia Transportation Co., 283 F.Supp. 597, 599 (USDC Pa., 1968), arbitration under LMRA; Dallas Typographical Union v. A. H. Belo Corp., 372 F.2d 577, 581, 583 (CA 5, 1967), arbitration under LMRA; Guille v. Mushroom Transportation Company, 229 A.2d 903, 905 (Pa. Sup. Ct., 1967), common law arbitration; Harvey Aluminum, Inc. v. Steelworkers, 67 LRRM 2580, 2583 (USDC Calif., 1967); Raytheon Co. v. Rheem Mfg. Co., 322 F.2d 173, 182 (CA 9, 1963), arbitration under Federal Arbitration Act; In re Dist. 2, Marine Engineers, 51 LRRM 2561, 2564 (N.Y. Sup. Ct., 1962), arbitration under state statute. Kesslen Bros. v. Board of Conciliation, 32 LA 859 at 859 (Mass. Sup. Ct., 1959), arbitration under state statute. For many other cases, see 6 Corpus Juris Secundum, Arbitration and Award, §105, p. 251. For general discussion as to the limited scope of court review of arbitration awards, see Chapter 2, subtopics titled "The 'Trilogy,' " "State Common Law," "State Arbitration Statutes" [very few statutes grant any right of review for mistake of law].

However, it must be added that the courts, under statute or under the common law, are not likely to honor any award which directs a party to commit an act or engage in conduct clearly prohibited by law.[8]

Furthermore, while arbitration awards are generally final insofar as the application of the agreement is concerned, there may be statutory issues (such as unfair labor practice or representation issues) which the award may not undertake to dispose of or concerning which the award may not be the final word even if it does assume to dispose of the issue.[9]

---

[8] See Smith & Jones, "The Supreme Court and Labor Dispute Arbitration: The Emerging Federal Law," 63 Mich. L. Rev. 751, 804 (1965); Cox, "The Place of Law in Labor Arbitration," The Profession of Labor Arbitration 76, 78–79 (BNA Incorporated, 1957); Sturges, Commercial Arbitrations and Awards §61, p. 202 (1930). Also see Employees' Independent Union v. Wyman Gordon Company, 314 F.Supp. 458 (USDC Ill., 1970); Federal-Mogul Corp. v. Auto Workers, 74 LRRM 2961 (USDC Mich., 1970); U.A.W. v. W. M. Chace Co., 262 F.Supp. 114 (USDC Mich., 1966); Western Union Telegraph Co., 10 LA 923, 924 (N.Y. Sup. Ct., 1948), affirmed, 86 N.E.2d 162 (N.Y. Ct. App., 1949) [the result in this case is seriously questioned by Cox, supra, at pp. 87–89]. Where an award does not order an illegal act but is allegedly inconsistent with some "public policy," it is less vulnerable to court attack. As to this and as to the desirability of holding such awards subject to attack, see Jenkins Bros. v. United Steelworkers, 341 F.2d 987 (CA 2, 1965); Local 453, IUE v. Otis Elevator Co., 314 F.2d 25 (CA 2, 1963); Smith & Jones, supra at 804–805; Eaton, "Labor Arbitration in the San Francisco Bay Area," 48 LA 1381, 1388 (1967); Seitz, "The Arbitrator's Responsibility For Public Policy," 19 Arb. J. 23 (1964); Meiners, "Arbitration Awards and 'Public Policy,'" 17 Arb. J. 145 (1962).

[9] As to statutory issues under the NLRA, for instance, see discussion in this Chapter's subtopic titled "The NLRA, the Arbitrator, and the NLRB." Explaining that agreements making awards "final" are not necessarily inconsistent with recognition of the possibility that the loser might seek court review or the possibility that some other tribunal, such as the NLRB, might have jurisdiction to make subsequent rulings on certain aspects of the dispute, see Arbitrator Seitz in Board of Education of the City of New York, 45 LA 680, 686–687 (1965). However, pointing to jurisdictional and procedural differences and suggesting possible national policy differences under the Civil Rights Act of 1964 in comparison with the National Labor Relations Act, a federal court held that an employee could not properly sue under Title VII of the Civil Rights Act after an arbitrator had already rendered a final and binding award against the employee. Dewey v. Reynolds Metals Co., 429 F.2d 324, 332 (CA 6, 1970). The Supreme Court affirmed (without opinion) by an equally divided (4-4) vote. Dewey v. Reynolds Metals Co., 91 S.Ct. 2186 (1971). In a subsequent Title VII suit the Fifth Circuit stated certain conditions (similar to those under the NLRB *Spielberg* doctrine) to be met if the court is to defer to a prior arbitration award. Rios v. Reynolds Metals Co., 467 F.2d 54 (CA 5, 1972). For related discussion, see McKelvey, "Sex and the Single Arbitrator," Arbitration and the Public Interest 1, 23–25 (The Bureau of National Affairs, Inc., 1971); Gould & Kurtz, "Arbitration and Federal Rights Under Collective Agreements in 1970," id. at 239, 268–270.

On the whole, relatively wide discretion is left to arbitrators to deal with the law according to their best judgment. A principal inquiry in this Chapter concerns the extent to which arbitrators do in fact have recourse to substantive law and to decisions of courts and administrative agencies on questions similar to the one before the arbitrator.

The reader will observe that many arbitrators do give consideration to "the law," but the extent of adherence thereto may vary considerably from case to case depending largely upon the source, form, and status of the legal rule or principle before the arbitrator. Thus, specific requirements and restrictions contained in codified law may be given greater weight by an arbitrator than general substantive law principles of agency, contracts, damages, and the like (although these will not be slighted). Clearly defined law will be given more consideration than unsettled and uncertain law or rules based upon controversial views as to what should be the public policy. Decisions by courts of final jurisdiction normally carry more weight than those of lower courts.

Then, too, the extent to which an arbitrator will consider any factor outside the collective agreement may depend upon the degree to which the parties have restricted his authority to the interpretation and application of the agreement, and upon his view as to the effect of that restriction insofar as consideration of "law" is concerned. It is also to be noted that many arbitrators have viewed the role of public enforcement agent to be beyond their authority and function; these arbitrators believe that the *enforcement* of statutes which impose affirmative duties or make conduct illegal in an affirmative sense should be left to the statutory agency which was established for that purpose.

As to fundamental rules of law, in arbitration cases (just as in litigated matters) there frequently is one primary legal basis for the decision, such as a rule of agency, a principle of waiver or estoppel, or some other rule of law. It is true that arbitrators do not often cite legal decisions, but they do take cognizance—in essence judicial notice—of the legal principle concerning the issue under consideration. In the informality of arbitration it seems natural for arbitrators to state such principles without deeming it necessary to cite specific supporting authority.

It should be apparent from the materials contained in the remainder of this Chapter that parties preparing cases for arbitration, and indeed parties concerned with the initial negotiation of collective agreements, may be well advised to take into consideration pertinent laws, legal principles, and court and administrative rulings.

The Authors do not propose to show in this Chapter every situation in which arbitrators have observed or deviated from "the law." Rather, the objective will be to examine the views and practice of arbitrators in sufficient instances to indicate some of the more likely possibilities.

Range of Views as to Application of "Law"

In the present topic the Authors note the individual views of a number of arbitrators to indicate the range of arbitral thinking as to the extent to which arbitrators should consider "law" in resolving disputes. The reader in turn may reach his own conclusions as to the degree to which the various views overlap and/or conflict. It does seem reasonably clear from the materials in the remainder of this chapter, however, that each of the views noted in the present topic has considerable support in arbitral practice.

At the outset it may be observed that probably most arbitrators would agree with the following three points presented by Arbitrator Bernard D. Meltzer at a meeting of the National Academy of Arbitrators, to wit: (1) where the contractual provision being interpreted or applied has been formulated loosely, the arbitrator may consider all relevant factors, including relevant law; (2) where a contractual provision is susceptible to two interpretations, one compatible with and the other repugnant to an applicable statute, the statute is a relevant factor—arbitrators should seek to avoid a construction that would make the agreement invalid; and (3) where the submission makes it clear that the parties want an advisory opinion as to the law, such opinion would be within the arbitrator's role.[10]

However, Arbitrator Meltzer also presented a fourth point, upon which arbitrators disagree. He urged that where there is clear conflict between the agreement and law, the arbitrator "should respect the

---

[10] Meltzer, "Ruminations About Ideology, Law, and Labor Arbitration," The Arbitrator, the NLRB, and the Courts 1, 15, 31 (The Bureau of National Affairs, Inc., 1967).

agreement and ignore the law." He reasoned that parties call upon an arbitrator to construe their agreement rather than to destroy it, and that there is no reason to credit arbitrators with special expertise with respect to the law as distinguished from the agreement. Thus, arbitrators should respect "the agreement that is the source of their authority and should leave to the courts or other official tribunals the determination of whether the agreement contravenes a higher law. Otherwise, arbitrators would be deciding issues that go beyond not only the submission agreement but also arbitral competence."[11]

Arbitrator Meltzer also based his view on certain language of the U.S. Supreme Court in the *Enterprise Wheel* case, wherein the Court stated of the award involved there:

> "It may be read as based solely upon the arbitrator's view of the requirements of enacted legislation, which would mean that he exceeded the scope of the submission. Or it may be read as embodying a construction of the agreement itself, perhaps with the arbitrator looking to 'the law' for help in determining the sense of the agreement."[12]

In sharp contrast to Arbitrator Meltzer's fourth point noted hereinabove, Arbitrator Robert G. Howlett has insisted that: "Arbitrators, as well as judges, are subject to and bound by law, whether it be the Fourteenth Amendment to the Constitution of the United States or a city ordinance. All contracts are subject to statute and common law; and each contract includes all applicable law."[13] Furthermore, Arbitrator Howlett asserted that:

> "There is a responsibility of arbitrators, corollary to that of the General Counsel and the NLRB, to decide, where relevant, a statutory issue,

---

[11] Id. at 16–17. Professor Theodore J. St. Antoine has commented: "I don't wish to seem perverse in urging arbitrators to issue awards that may fly in the face of applicable law. But I just can't see any source of arbitral power to exercise a more extended jurisdiction unless the parties themselves have so provided." St. Antoine, "Discussion," Developments in American and Foreign Arbitration 75, 79 (The Bureau of National Affairs, Inc., 1968). He explained: " * * * the arbitrator in the usual case remains just the 'reader' of the instrument before him. And if, after giving due weight to the presumption of legality, he cannot reconcile the contract and the law, he should render the award compelled by the contract. Nothing * * * would prevent an arbitrator from salving his conscience by including some obiter dicta in his opinion to tell the parties how he thinks the contract and the award will fare if they reach the courts." id. at 82.

[12] United Steelworkers v. Enterprise Wheel & Car Corp., 80 S.Ct. 1358, 1361; 46 LRRM 2432 (1960).

[13] Howlett, "The Arbitrator, the NLRB, and the Courts," The Arbitrator, the NLRB and the Courts 67, 83 (The Bureau of National Affairs, Inc., 1967).

in order that the NLRB, consistent with its announced policy, may avoid a decision on the merits, and the statutory policy of determining issues through arbitration may be fulfilled."[14]

Having given extensive thought to the views of Arbitrators Meltzer and Howlett, Arbitrator Richard Mittenthal advanced the intermediate view that "although the arbitrator's award may *permit* conduct forbidden by law but sanctioned by contract, it should not *require* conduct forbidden by law even though sanctioned by contract."[15] Arbitrator Mittenthal emphasized that arbitrators are "part of a private process for the adjudication of private rights and duties," and that they "should not be asked to assume public responsibilities and to do the work of public agencies."[16]

The latter idea has been vigorously asserted by Arbitrator Peter Seitz:

"If arbitration begins to do the business of the NLRB and the courts, interpreting legislation, effecting national rather than private goals

---

[14] Id. at 78–79. He also stated the arbitrator has a duty to "probe" to determine whether a statutory issue is involved. Id. at 92. Arbitrator James A. Gross has argued strongly that arbitrators should give full consideration to statutory, social, and constitutional claims and not limit consideration to the contract and customs of the parties. Gross, "The Labor Arbitrator's Role: Tradition and Change," 25 Arb. J. 221 (1970).

[15] Mittenthal, "The Role of Law in Arbitration," Developments in American and Foreign Arbitration 42, 50 (The Bureau of National Affairs, Inc., 1968). In Acme Foundry Co., 45 LA 1025, 1027 (1965), Arbitrator Altieri commented: "Whatever the legality of the [contractual] arrangement might be, it would lie outside the power of the arbitrator to compel the Employer to live up to some agreement other than that which he had entered into. The arbitrator does no more than leave the parties where he finds them. The principle, therefore, that an arbitrator may not direct the performance of an illegal act has no application."

[16] Mittenthal, id. at 58. Asked to comment on the Mittenthal view, Arbitrators Meltzer and Howlett each reiterated his own view. See Meltzer, "The Role of Law in Arbitration: Rejoinders," id. at 58–64; Howlett, "A Reprise," id. at 64–75. Still a fourth view, similar to Mittenthal's but with distinctions of consequence to some cases, was presented to the National Academy of Arbitrators at a later meeting. See Sovern, "When Should Arbitrators Follow Federal Law?" Arbitration and the Expanding Role of Neutrals 29 (The Bureau of National Affairs, Inc., 1970). At a yet later Academy meeting the discussion continued, as did the disagreement, as to the extent to which arbitrators should concern themselves with law and public policy in resolving disputes. See Arbitration and the Public Interest 1–83 (The Bureau of National Affairs, Inc., 1971), presenting the views of Arbitrators McKelvey, Wirtz, Jones, Morris, and Feller. A questionnaire sent to 200 Academy members was answered by 79, the answers reflecting an almost equal division in support for the two basic views. Young, "The Authority and Obligation of a Labor Arbitrator to Modify or Eliminate a Provision of a Collective Bargaining Agreement Because in his Opinion it Violates Federal Law," 32 Ohio State L. J. 395, 396 (1971), also indicating how those who responded rate themselves as to knowledge of specific federal statutes.

as a kind of subordinate tribunal of the Board, that voluntarism which is the base of its broad acceptance could be eroded and its essential objectives changed. Arbitration can be weakened by freighting it with public law questions which in our system should be decided by the courts and administrative agencies. Arbitration should not be an initial alternative to Board adjudication. It has been (and should be) a separate system of judicature respecting *private* rights and duties resulting in final decisions—not decisions on *public* matters reviewable by the Board and deferred to if not repugnant to the Labor Act."[17]

Turning next to the matter of arbitral reliance upon fundamental principles of the common law, while not all arbitrators will agree fully, probably most do share the view that "long and generally accepted judicial principles" can serve well in the forum of arbitration.[18] In this regard, Arbitrator John F. Sembower has commented:

"This arbitrator long has been intrigued by how parties to labor arbitrations, while naturally eschewing all intentions of being 'legalistic,' nevertheless so often tread the same time-worn paths of the development of the great common law. Nor should this be surprising, because after all the vaunted Anglo-American common law consists of the vast heritage of experience—the accumulated customs, viewpoints, and usages of ordinary people just like ourselves."[19]

Finally, the Authors call attention to the fact that there have been numerous other expressions by individual arbitrators falling at various points within the broad range of views noted hereinabove.[20]

Statutory Law

Where arbitrators have been specifically authorized by the submission to determine the validity or application of a contract provision under statutory law, or in other cases where it was clear that the

---

[17] Seitz, "The Limits of Arbitration," 88 Monthly Labor Review 763, 764 (1965).

[18] The latter thought was expressed by Arbitrator Israel Ben Scheiber in applying a basic principle of agency law. Trubitz Hardware & Electric Co., 32 LA 930, 935 (1959), stating also that "the avoidance of procedural legalism should not be accompanied by a disregard for such principles of law as have long been our guiding stars."

[19] Caterpillar Tractor Co., 39 LA 534, 537 (1962).

[20] See Arbitrator Coffey in 54 LA 956, 958; Zack in 54 LA 857, 858–859; Stutz in 54 LA 439, 441; Walsh in 53 LA 792, 795–796; Hogan in 53 LA 329, 332–333; Altrock in 48 LA 1244, 1248; Williams in 44 LA 1244, 1245–1246; Summers in 39 LA 374, 378; Kelliher in 38 LA 619 at 619; Hill in 35 LA 840, 844; Horvitz in 20 LA 318, 320; Whitton in 4 LA 288, 292. Also see Fleming, "Reflections on the Nature of Labor Arbitration," 61 Mich. L. Rev. 1245, 1259–1262 (1963).

parties anticipated that the arbitrator would do so, arbitrators have undertaken to make such a determination.[21] In one case a court mandate required the arbitrator to review federal and state law to ascertain the legality of an unusual union shop agreement that was being requested; the arbitrator made an extensive review of relevant law as the basis of his ruling.[22]

Arbitrators have sometimes emphasized that they would not interpret or apply an agreement in a way that would require a party to commit an illegal act.[23] For instance, Arbitrator George H. Young stated that "he cannot bring himself to render an opinion and award, which, if carried out, would result in both parties to the arbitration being guilty of unlawful conduct," and he refused to order the employer to discharge an employee as requested by the union where such discharge would place both the employer and the union in violation of the NLRA.[24]

In making it clear that he would not render an award which would require the performance of illegal acts, Arbitrator Russell A. Smith stated:

> "I recognize, however, that the authority to decide these legal questions is vested in the Board and the courts, not in the Arbitrator. The parties have agreed that my task has been to interpret their agreement. This I have done. My only concern, with respect to the legal issues (aside from their relevance in the matter of contract interpretation) has been whether my award will have the effect of ordering the Company to perform an illegal act."[25]

Moreover, in refusing to award a union security provision which would be illegal under state statute, Arbitrator Clarence M. Updegraff

---

[21] See Arbitrator Seitz in 53 LA 131, 132; Yaffe in 52 LA 1013, 1015, 1017–1018; Teple in 52 LA 716, 717–721; Burns in 47 LA 873, 876, 881–886; Scheiber in 42 LA 469, 470–474; Kagel in 38 LA 500, 505–506. Also see Barnhart in 47 LA 596, 598–601. Where an arbitrator concluded that the submission did not authorize him to determine whether a contract provision conflicted with statutory law, the parties executed an additional submission specifically authorizing him to make the determination. Morton Salt Co., 21 LA 797, 804–805, 813–814 (Hale, 1953).

[22] Aro, Inc., 54 LA 453, 456 (Caraway, 1970). In Plumbers' Union Health & Welfare Fund, 32 LA 661, 663–664 (Callaghan, 1959), the arbitrator held that until a court should rule otherwise, a disputed trust agreement must be considered legal.

[23] See Arbitrator Stein in 44 LA 965, 966–967; Smith in 41 LA 65, 71–72; Young in 40 LA 833, 835; Dworkin in 37 LA 638, 646–647; Anderson in 22 LA 470, 473; Abernethy in 8 LA 62, 65.

[24] Buckstaff Co., 40 LA 833, 835 (1963).

[25] Globe-Democrat Publishing Co., 41 LA 65, 75 (1963).

touched on the question of constitutionality and explained that the validity of the statute must be assumed:

> "No award of this board can give validity to any contract which contravenes the law of any state. If it is indeed true that the Kansas law is ineffective because unconstitutional, that result has not yet been authoritatively declared by a court of last resort. The act must be assumed effective until otherwise determined."[26]

Specific Statutes

Arbitrator David L. Cole has explained that "in any conflict between a collective bargaining agreement and the law with reference to the rights of a returning veteran, it has repeatedly been held that the law must prevail."[27] In a similar note, Arbitrator Thomas P. Whelan held that regulations under the National Security Act were as a matter of public policy superimposed upon the collective agreement when the employer entered into a "security agreement" with the Department of Defense, and that they took precedence over any provisions of the collective agreement that might have conflicted with them.[28]

In times of wage stabilization arbitrators have taken steps to avoid transgression upon wage stabilization legislation.[29] In one case an over-

---

[26] Kansas City Public Service Co., 8 LA 149, 159 (1957), an "interests" arbitration. It has been held that if a contract adopts one of two alternatives permitted by statute, the agreement does not conflict with the statute but simply limits the parties to one of two possibilities under the law. Wilson and Company, Inc., 1 LA 367, 378 (Lohman, not dated).

[27] International Harvester Co., 22 LA 583, 585 (1954). Accord, Arbitrator Hebert in 46 LA 624, 633; Parker in 23 LA 44, 47. For other cases in which arbitrators took note of the statutory rights of veterans, see Arbitrator Bothwell in 54 LA 1055, 1058–1059; Dworkin in 46 LA 1021, 1025–1026; McCoy in 41 LA 716, 717; Updegraff in 37 LA 1009, 1013; Justin in 23 LA 113, 119–124. But see discussion by Mittenthal, "The Role of Law in Arbitration," Developments in American and Foreign Arbitration 42, 47, 51–55 (The Bureau of National Affairs, Inc., 1968); Meltzer, "The Role of Law in Arbitration: Rejoinders," id. at 58, 59–60. For summary and analysis of court decisions on veterans' reemployment rights, see United States Steel Corp., 51 LA 1244, 1248–1249; 51 LA 1253, 1255–1256 (Garrett, 1968). Also see Arbitrator Wolff in 56 LA 312, 314–315.

[28] Wisconsin Telephone Co., 26 LA 792, 806 (1956). As to limitations on statutory regulation of employment in national defense facilities, see U.S. v. Robel, 88 S.Ct. 419 (1967), involving the Subversive Activities Control Act.

[29] See Arbitrator Keefe in 57 LA 1090, 1091; Donnelly in 17 LA 748, 750–751; Warren in 17 LA 353, 354, 361; Lesser in 16 LA 881, 882; Justin in 16 LA 399, 404. Also see Rose in 19 LA 303, 306. For related discussion, see Chapter 18, topic titled "Governmental Wage Stabilization."

time claim was rejected because its allowance would have resulted in a clear violation of the Wage Stabilization Act.[30] However, an arbitrator emphasized that while wage stabilization regulations should be considered in determining wage adjustments, the influence of wage stabilization on an arbitrator's decision should vary "in direct ratio to the certainty, clarity and stage of its evolution."[31]

Arbitrators have disagreed as to whether the agreement or the Fair Labor Standards Act should control where they conflict. Arbitrator Emanuel Stein has held that where the statute is clear, the agreement must be construed and applied in a manner consistent with the statute.[32] However, where a party argued that an adverse decision would conflict with the Fair Labor Standards Act, Arbitrator Harold S. Burr declared that it is the contract language upon which he must focus and rule.[33]

Arbitrators are also in disagreement as to what consideration, if any, an arbitrator should give to Title VII of the Civil Rights Act of 1964 in deciding grievances. In numerous cases arbitrators have undertaken to construe the Act and apply it to the grievance (or at least insure that the decision was not inconsistent with the act).[34] However, in numerous other cases the arbitrator took the view that

---

[30] Monsanto Chemical Company, 1 ALAA ¶67,089 (1944). Also see Arbitrator Stark in 57 LA 1115, 1118. In Clarkstown Cent. School Dist., 58 LA 191, 193 (Markowitz, 1972), the arbitrator refused to rule as to the validity of an increase under wage stabilization, having concluded that the question must be decided by the stabilization agency.

[31] Merchants Bank of New York, 16 LA 901, 904 (Rosenfarb, 1951).

[32] Pennsylvania Electric Co., 47 LA 526, 527 (1966), where Arbitrator Stein rejected the argument that "Fair Labor Standards Act questions should be resolved in another forum." In accord as to the controlling effect of the statute, Youngstown Sheet and Tube Co., 14 LA 752, 756 (Updegraff, 1950). Cf., Arbitrator Krimsly in 47 LA 518, 523.

[33] Hilo Transportation & Terminal Co., 33 LA 541, 543 (1959). Accord, Arbitrator Seward in 17 LA 29, 30; Marshall in 16 LA 335, 337. A number of arbitrators have considered the question whether an increase in the minimum wage under the FLSA may be relied upon by the employer toward fulfilling his obligation to grant a periodic wage increase specified by the agreement. For example, see Arbitrator Andersen in 52 LA 430, 433–435; Merrill in 52 LA 145, 147–148; Gershenfeld in 48 LA 816, 818; Owen in 42 LA 250, 251.

[34] See Arbitrator Hogan in 56 LA 830, 832; Bernstein in 54 LA 1142, 1145; Turkus in 54 LA 165, 166–167, and in 52 LA 707, 708; Purdom in 53 LA 1157, 1159 (arbitrator would be doing a vain and useless act if he rendered a decision contrary to federal law); Davis in 52 LA 112, 115; Nichols in 51 LA 1259, 1262, 1265; Mueller in 51 LA 785, 789–792; Gray in 48 LA 769, 770; Williams in 47 LA 896, 898; Ray in 45 LA 939, 942–943; Seidenberg in 45 LA 923, 925.

his responsibility and authority was to interpret and apply the collective agreement, not the Civil Rights Act.[35]

Standing at some intermediate point of the spectrum, Arbitrator Louis Yagoda stated that arbitrators should not uphold contractual provisions which violate the Civil Rights Act, but that arbitrators (who he said must act on a presumption of validity of the agreement) should take great care that the violation of the Act is unmistakably apparent, and great care that the arbitrator is not substituting himself for the authority, expertise, and procedures which have been established by and are responsive to the statute. As to the latter point, he cautioned: "We are not the Equal Employment Opportunity Commission and should not put ourselves in its place in terms of our rights and ability to enforce the law which they administer."[36]

In another case, Arbitrator Edgar A. Jones explained that in discrimination cases it often is not necessary for an arbitrator to concern himself with public policy factors extraneous to the agreement:

"This is so because there is such a marked identity of issues when an employer's discrimination is alleged to exist in a bargaining unit covered by a collective agreement containing an arbitration provision. The coincident existence of the proscriptions of the Civil Rights Act

---

[35] See Arbitrator Wyckoff in 54 LA 600, 603 (arbitration board did not have the inherent powers of courts or the mediatory powers of the EEOC, and was a creature of the contract which limited its authority); Duff in 54 LA 340, 342–343; Seinsheimer in 49 LA 709, 718 (even if contested practice should be a violation of the Civil Rights Act, the arbitrator's responsibility is only to determine whether the agreement has been violated); Hogan in 49 LA 199, 202 (arbitrator interprets the agreement rather than the law, but he gave dictum that certain action would be improper under Title VII); Davey in 49 LA 105, 109–110 (arbitrator's sole responsibility was to apply the agreement, not the Act); Kahn in 48 LA 727, 733 (arbitrator had no authority to interpret the Act). Also see Lugar in 51 LA 970, 980; Duff in 49 LA 1186, 1188. In 47 LA 1045, 1050, Arbitrator Samuel Kates said he had no jurisdiction to charge that the employer had violated the Civil Rights Act, but in 50 LA 795, 798–799, he said he could consider the Act in construing a contractual provision which the parties had adopted as a result of the Act.
[36] The Ingraham Co., 48 LA 884, 889 (1966). He added that inasmuch as the EEOC had already taken jurisdiction over the legal issue involved in the dispute, it would be futile for him to do so. However, some arbitrators have held that arbitration was not barred merely because the grievant had first gone to the EEOC. McCall Corp., 49 LA 183, 187 (McIntosh, 1967); National Lead Co., 48 LA 405, 407 (Wissner, not dated). For discussion of the different tribunals that might have jurisdiction over a race or sex discrimination case, see Blumrosen, "Labor Arbitration, EEOC Conciliation, and Discrimination in Employment," 24 Arb. J. 88 (1969). As to whether an arbitrator might give weight to the actions of state human rights agencies, see Arbitrator Myers in 54 LA 534, 540; Altieri in 54 LA 441, 443.

superimposes no discrimination policy of the bargaining relationships which has not already been rather widely recognized for some time by arbitrators to be an incident of the employment relationship to be vindicated through the arbitral tribunal created by the parties."[37]

The disagreement among arbitrators as to consideration of federal statutory law also exists where state statutes are concerned. In a number of cases arbitrators have decided disputes on the basis of the collective agreement in the face of a contention that a different result was required under some state statute or regulation, the arbitrator considering it to be his function to apply the agreement rather than to construe or enforce state law.[38] However, in other cases arbitrators have considered state statutes and regulations (often in the face of a contention that the arbitrator had no authority to do so) in deciding the grievance.[39]

In many cases arbitrators have given serious consideration to state statutes regulating the employment of female workers (to protect their health). Employers have been upheld in refusing to assign jobs to females which would require them to lift weights[40] or work hours[41] in violation of state statutes.[42] In some of these cases the arbitrator has been confronted with the contention that the state statute was in conflict with or superseded by the Civil Rights Act of 1964, but

---

[37] Kaiser Foundation Hospitals, 48 LA 1138, 1142 (1967).

[38] Involving a variety of state statutes or regulations, see Arbitrator Kornblum in 46 LA 1203, 1205; Schedler in 39 LA 766, 768; Summers in 39 LA 374, 378; Haughton in 35 LA 330, 335–336; Teple in 33 LA 758, 764; Kleinsorge in 32 LA 769, 772; Shister in 24 LA 786, 787; Seward in 23 LA 606, 607.

[39] Involving a variety of state statutes or regulations, see Arbitrator Zack in 54 LA 857, 858–859; MacLeod in 53 LA 207, 208–210; Block in 51 LA 597, 599; Allen in 50 LA 522, 527; Small in 44 LA 1025, 1028; Duff in 42 LA 533, 535; Donnelly in 35 LA 501, 503; Hampton in 10 LA 487, 489–490.

[40] See Arbitrator Altrock in 52 LA 942, 944–945; Kates in 51 LA 418, 420; Dworkin in 50 LA 669, 671–672; Duff in 49 LA 1186, 1188; Teple in 48 LA 819, 822–824; Steele in 46 LA 931, 935; Geissinger in 46 LA 115, 116–120; Layman in 45 LA 417, 420, 426; Meyers in 44 LA 152, 155; Hawley in 43 LA 289, 294; Roberts in 39 LA 1094, 1096–1097; Kleinsorge in 38 LA 817, 821. Also see Garrett in 36 LA 599, 602.

[41] See Arbitrator Duff in 54 LA 320, 321–322; Davis in 52 LA 112, 115; Cooley in 46 LA 138 at 138; Platt in 24 LA 288, 289. Also see Kates in 55 LA 357, 358. Cf., Buckwalter in 47 LA 260, 261–262, and Roberts in 42 LA 938, 940, both holding that if it is burdensome upon the employer to comply with the statute in adhering strictly to the agreement, such compliance is nonetheless required.

[42] In UAW v. Chace Co., 64 LRRM 2098 (USDC Mich., 1966), the court indicated it would not enforce an award (48 LA 231) would require the violation of state law prohibiting the assignment of work to female employees which would be "disproportionate to" their strength.

often the arbitrator has given the state statute the benefit of any doubt.[43]

Finally, it is of interest to note that even where a given statute does not cover the parties, or does not apply directly to the case, or permits variations through the collective agreement, an arbitrator may find the statute (or cases construing it) a helpful guide if the agreement is ambiguous or contains no method of determining the issue.[44]

The NLRA, the Arbitrator, and the NLRB

Where a dispute involves both statutory issues under the NLRA and interpretation issues under the collective agreement, dual jurisdiction exists in the NLRB and the arbitrator. This dual jurisdiction as reflected by decisions of the U.S. Supreme Court has been summarized by NLRB member Gerald A. Brown:

> "(1) the availability of arbitration does not preclude Board exercise of jurisdiction over unfair labor practices, (2) the availability of a Board remedy does not bar arbitration, and (3) the Board has discretion to refuse to exercise its jurisdiction when in its judgment federal policy would best be served by leaving the parties to contract remedies."[45]

---

[43] See Arbitrator Kates in 55 LA 357, 358 (follow the state statute until a court declares it superseded); Duff in 54 LA 320, 321–322; Davis in 52 LA 112, 115 (state restriction not nullified by Civil Rights Act); Duff in 49 LA 1186, 1188 (arbitrator refused to consider whether state statute was rendered void by Civil Rights Act); Teple in 46 LA 931, 935 (state statute not superseded); Geissinger in 46 LA 115, 116–120 (no conflict found). In Avco Corp., 54 LA 165, 166–167 (1970), Arbitrator Turkus ruled that the state statute regulating hours of work for female employees had been superseded by the Civil Rights Act. For some court decisions holding state female-employee protective statutes to have been preempted by Title VII of the Civil Rights Act, see Jones Metal Products Co. v. Walker, 4 FEP Cases 483 (Ohio Sup. Ct., 1972); Rosenfeld v. Southern Pacific, 3 FEP Cases 604 (CA 9, 1971), involving California statutes. For related discussion, see McKelvey, "Sex and the Single Arbitrator," Arbitration and the Public Interest 1, 9–14 (The Bureau of National Affairs, Inc., 1971).

[44] See Arbitrator Howlett in 52 LA 997, 1000–1001; Larkin in 47 LA 513, 517 (Presidential Executive Order was persuasive though it did not cover the parties); Anderson in 47 LA 356, 364; Moskowitz in 46 LA 388, 394; Dworkin in 45 LA 897, 904; Quinlan in 42 LA 626, 628–630; Aaron in 22 LA 249, 250–251; Ralston in 21 LA 381, 385; Myers in 7 LA 1, 2.

[45] Brown, "The National Labor Policy, the NLRB, and Arbitration," Developments in American and Foreign Arbitration 83, 84 (The Bureau of National Affairs, Inc., 1968). Relevant decisions include NLRB v. Strong, 89 S.Ct. 541 (1969); NLRB v. Acme Industrial Co., 87 S.Ct. 565 (1967); NLRB v. C & C Plywood Corp., 87 S.Ct. 559 (1967); Carey v. Westinghouse Electric Corp., 84 S.Ct. 401 (1964); Smith v. Evening News Association, 83 S.Ct. 267 (1962).

In its *Carey* decision (involving a jurisdictional dispute between two unions and an employer) the Supreme Court held that an arbitrator could act, but should the Board disagree with the arbitrator its ruling would take precedence. The Court also stated that "The superior authority of the Board may be invoked at any time. Meanwhile the therapy of arbitration is brought to bear in a complicated and troubled area."[46]

Arbitrators themselves have long considered that they are not prevented from acting upon contract issues merely because the dispute may also involve statutory issues that can be taken to the NLRB.[47] Similarly, the mere fact that the NLRB had dismissed unfair labor practice charges has not deterred arbitrators from subsequently taking jurisdiction over contract issues involved in the dispute.[48]

When an arbitrator takes jurisdiction of a dispute that involves issues under both the agreement and the NLRA, he may be confronted with the question as to whether or not he should confine himself primarily to the agreement and leave statutory issues to the NLRB. In some cases arbitrators have considered NLRA issues, or have at least considered the Act and NLRB doctrine in deciding contractual issues.[49] Arbitrators appear to be particularly disposed to look to the

---

[46] *Carey* v. Westinghouse Electric Corp., 84 S.Ct. 401, 409, 55 LRRM 2042 (1964).

[47] See Arbitrator Lennard in 46 LA 746, 747–749; Johnson in 45 LA 1182, 1183 (unfair labor practice charge involves breach of law whereas grievance involves breach of the agreement); Rohman in 42 LA 1308, 1310–1311; Miller in 35 LA 757, 783 (filing of unfair labor practice charges does not constitute an election of remedies or waiver of rights under the agreement asserted in grievance filed at same time); Schmidt in 35 LA 455, 457; Stutz, Mottram & Curry in 22 LA 651, 652; Kaplan in 22 LA 201, 207; Updegraff, Klamon & Raymond in 19 LA 609, 611–612.

[48] See Arbitrator McCoy in 51 LA 309, 310; Schedler in 42 LA 345, 346; Sembower in 37 LA 308, 312; Cole in 24 LA 332, 335.

[49] See Arbitrator King in 54 LA 1110, 1113; Updegraff in 48 LA 1171, 1174 (where the matter has not already been taken to the NLRB, the arbitrator is equally qualified to determine whether a given worker is a supervisor under the NLRA); Gundermann in 48 LA 752, 757, 759 (arbitrator expressly ruled that §8(a)(3) of the NLRA had not been violated); Wallen in 48 LA 19, 23 (in view of the NLRB "Spielberg" doctrine arbitrators must be certain that management actions are free from discriminatory taint where an allegation of discrimination does not appear wholly capricious); Seibel in 44 LA 866, 867–872 (arbitrator considered NLRA and LMRDA even though one party denied his authority to do so); Helfeld in 43 LA 445, 448–449 (arbitrator endeavored to decide a §8(a)(1) issue as the NLRB would decide it). For other instances, see Warns in 24 LA 360, 364; Anderson in 22 LA 470, 472–473; Abernethy in 8 LA 62, 65. Where the NLRB has already made findings on an issue, an arbitrator will likely honor those findings. See Arbitrator Lennard in 46

NLRA and to consider NLRB doctrine when confronted with bargaining unit and union security questions under the agreement.[50]

On the other hand, in some other cases arbitrators have refused to consider NLRA issues (or have disclaimed authority to do so), or to consider the Act and NLRB doctrine in deciding contractual issues.[51] Even where the parties had provided, in submitting discharges to arbitration, that the arbitrators "shall consider the standards of strike misconduct as contained in adjudications under the National Labor Relations Act," Arbitrators Alexander, McCoy, Schedler, and Whiting declared that while the word "shall" required them to give decisions under said Act "considerable weight," it did not require them "to follow any of such decisions blindly."[52]

Particularly in regard to allegations of refusal to bargain, many arbitrators have taken the view that their function is to interpret and apply the agreement rather than to enforce affirmative duties under the statute, and they have refused to decide whether the statutory duty to bargain had been violated.[53] In its *Adams Dairy* decision the

---

LA 746, 747–749; Larkin in 44 LA 580, 584–585. Cf., Hebert in 68-1 ARB ¶8175.
[50] See Arbitrator Roberts in 54 LA 108, 111; Howlett in 50 LA 507, 511–513; Turkus in 50 LA 39, 40–41; Christensen in 46 LA 789, 797; Peck in 45 LA 1009, 1011–1015; Stein in 44 LA 965, 966–967; McIntosh in 44 LA 12, 14–15; Hyman in 42 LA 1296, 1299–1301; McCoy in 42 LA 580, 581; Smith in 41 LA 65, 71–75; Young in 40 LA 833, 835; Dworkin in 37 LA 638, 646–647; Copelof in 21 LA 535, 546–547; Appleby in 21 LA 646, 648–650; Davis in 20 LA 575, 578–579; Barrett in 17 LA 53, 55; Broach in 15 LA 861, 862–863.
[51] See Arbitrator Platt in 55 LA 170, 180–181; Kerrison in 54 LA 1196, 1199 (a different result would have been reached had the arbitrator strictly applied NLRA criteria in determining supervisory status); Stashower in 36 LA 478, 480 (arbitrator not necessarily controlled by NLRB criteria); Cahn in 35 LA 154, 156–157 (under submission arbitrator can only decide whether contract was violated, not whether contract violates NLRA); Bowles in 24 LA 761, 764 (arbitrator not bound by NLRB standard of "cause" for discharge of strikers); Simkin in 3 ALAA ¶68,192, p. 70,162 (arbitrator would feel bound by NLRB decisions only if he should take "the narrow view" that he had been selected solely as a substitute for proceedings under the NLRA). Also see Jaffee in 27 LA 844, 850; Warns in 27 LA 179, 181; Cole in 24 LA 332, 335. A survey of 2300 cases administered by the American Arbitration Association revealed 338 with issues which also fell within the NLRB's scope of activities, but in only 54 of the latter cases did the arbitrator in some manner acknowledge NLRB policies. Waks, "The 'Dual Jurisdiction' Problem in Labor Arbitration: A Research Report," 23 Arb. J. 201, 205–207, 226 (1968).
[52] Southern Bell Telephone & Telegraph Co., 25 LA 85, 86–87 (1955).
[53] See Arbitrator Marshall in 54 LA 1295, 1297–1298; McDermott in 53 LA 470, 474–477; Gould in 51 LA 752, 758–759; Larkin in 50 LA 109, 111; Malinowski in 48 LA 1257, 1258–1259; Darragh in 46 LA 310, 315; Hilpert in 45 LA 651, 652–654, and in 38 LA 267, 268–270; Roberts in 44 LA 1109, 1114–1115; Kelliher in 43 LA 267, 269; Smith in 43 LA 193, 209–210; Warns

NLRB itself recognized that statutory refusal to bargain issues may not fall within the scope of an arbitrator's authority. In holding that a union's failure to resort to arbitration did not warrant dismissal of a refusal-to-bargain complaint under the NLRA, the Board explained:

> "The contract subjects to its arbitration procedures only such disputes as concern 'the interpretation or application of the terms of this Agreement.' But in the instant case, the precise union claim, which is the subject of the complaint before us, does not relate to the meaning of any established term or condition of the contract, or to any asserted misapplication thereof by Respondent. It is directed instead at Respondent's denial to it of a statutory right guaranteed by §8(d) of the Act, namely, the right to be notified and consulted in advance, and to be given an opportunity to bargain, about substantial changes in the working conditions of unit employees in respects *not covered by the contract*. As the particular dispute between the Union and Respondent now before us thus involves basically a disagreement over statutory rather than contractual obligations, the disposition of the controversy is quite clearly within the competency of the Board, and not of an arbitrator who would be without authority to grant the Union the particular redress it seeks and for which we provide below in our remedial order."[54]

In another case the NLRB did defer to arbitration by refusing to exercise its jurisdiction where (1) the collective agreement provided for arbitration; (2) the union was challenging a unilateral action by the employer which was not patently erroneous or designed to undermine the union, but rather was based on a substantial claim of contractual privilege; and (3) it appeared that arbitration would resolve both the contract interpretation issue and the intertwined unfair labor practice issue in a manner compatible with the purposes of the NLRA.[55]

---

in 41 LA 905, 908; Seidenberg in 41 LA 314, 315; Graff in 38 LA 869, 877; Ross in 35 LA 695, 697; Dworkin in 35 LA 237, 241. Also see Hebert in 43 LA 307, 316–317; Schedler in 42 LA 345, 346–348; Sembower in 37 LA 308, 312. In Ralph Rogers & Co., 48 LA 40, 43 (1966), Arbitrator Getman did consider it his responsibility to enforce the NLRA duty to bargain, but his remedy was innocuous. For related discussion, see Chapter 13, subtopic titled "The Duty to Bargain: Right of Unilateral Action."

[54] Cloverleaf Division of Adams Dairy Co., 147 NLRB 1410, 1415, 56 LRRM 1321 (1964).

[55] Jos. Schlitz Brewing Co., 175 NLRB No. 23, 70 LRRM 1472 (1969). For extensive discussions of NLRB policy and cases in reference to deferring to arbitration where no award has yet been issued and also in reference to honoring awards that have been issued, see Brown, "The National Labor Policy, the NLRB, and Arbitration," Developments in American and Foreign Arbitration

The latter case was subsequently reaffirmed in a "strikingly similar" case which possibly set a course for the future in that the NLRB deferred to arbitration but expressly retained jurisdiction over the dispute

> "for the purpose of entertaining an appropriate and timely motion for further consideration upon a proper showing that either (a) the dispute has not, with reasonable promptness after the issuance of this decision, either been resolved by amicable settlement in the grievance procedure or submitted promptly to arbitration, or (b) the grievance or arbitration procedures have not been fair and regular or have reached a result which is repugnant to the Act."[56]

Where an award has already been rendered the NLRB under its *Spielberg* doctrine will honor the award if it is found that the arbitration proceedings were fair and regular, that all parties had agreed to be bound, and that the award was not clearly repugnant to the purposes and policies of the Act.[57] But the Board will not defer to the award unless the unfair labor practice issue before the Board was passed upon by the arbitrator.[58]

The NLRB also has stated a policy of honoring arbitration awards in representation cases if the case involves a question of contract interpretation and arbitration machinery established by the parties for settling their own disputes, and if the award meets the Board's standards.[59]

Court Decisions

An arbitrator's willingness to follow a judicial precedent on a question (assuming that he has concluded that he should consider

---

83 (The Bureau of National Affairs, Inc., 1968); Note, "NLRB and Deference to Arbitration," 77 Yale L. J. 1191 (1968); Ordman, "The Arbitrator and the NLRB," The Arbitrator, the NLRB, and the Courts 47 (The Bureau of National Affairs, Inc., 1967); Cushman, "Arbitration and the Duty to Bargain," 1967 Wisc. L. Rev. 612 (1967); McCulloch, "The Arbitration issue in NLRB Decisions," 19 Arb. J. 134 (1964).

[56] Collyer Insulated Wire, 192 NLRB No. 150, 77 LRRM 1931, 1936, 1938 (1971), in which two members dissented to the deferral to arbitration and in which the majority opinion reviewed the history of the Board's accommodation to the arbitration process.

[57] Spielberg Mfg. Co., 112 NLRB 1080, 1082, 36 LRRM 1152 (1955).

[58] See Raytheon Co., 140 NLRB 883, 52 LRRM 1129 (1963); Brown, "The National Labor Policy, the NLRB, and Arbitration," Developments in American and Foreign Arbitration 83, 85–87 (1968). Sometimes arbitrators expressly indicate that they have not undertaken to pass upon NLRA issues. See Arbitrator Platt in 50 LA 239, 248; Larkin in 50 LA 109, 111; Casselman in 44 LA 361, 372; Bowles in 23 LA 812, 814.

[59] Raley's Inc., 143 NLRB 256, 53 LRRM 1347 (1963).

"law" in deciding the case) will depend to a large extent upon the level of the court rendering the decision and upon the unanimity of other decisions on the point. Arbitrators naturally feel constrained to follow decisions of courts of last resort. When the U.S. Supreme Court or the highest tribunal of the state in which the parties operate has ruled on a point, it is likely that an arbitrator will give very serious consideration to the ruling.[60]

On the other hand, if an arbitrator does not agree with a decision handed down by a court other than one of last resort, he may refuse to follow it. Where one arbitrator, for instance, felt that an opinion by a federal district court was contrary to all accepted rules of statutory construction, he refused to follow it, declaring that since it was not a decision of a court of last resort he was not bound thereby.[61]

Moreover, arbitrators are less likely to honor conflicting lower court decisions. Thus, where two federal district courts had ruled one way and two others had ruled otherwise, an arbitrator declared that the parties were without the benefit of authoritative judicial decisions, and he decided the issue without reliance upon any of the precedents.[62]

Regardless of whether an arbitrator feels any obligation to follow court decisions, he may seek assistance from them in his disposition of contract issues.[63]

Administrative Rulings

The weight to be given by arbitrators to rulings of administrative and executive agencies of the government may be determined by a variety of factors, the most important of which is the authority of the agency making the ruling. For instance, rulings and regulations

---

[60] See Arbitrator Gorsuch in 53 LA 784, 790; Williams in 49 LA 261, 263; Hebert in 46 LA 624, 629–632; Scheiber in 45 LA 366, 370–372; Ray in 43 LA 1203, 1206; McDermott in 37 LA 1011, 1015; Cole in 22 LA 583, 584; Anderson in 22 LA 470, 472; Seward in 16 LA 376 at 376; Kallenbach in 6 LA 736, 741.

[61] Dow Chemical Co., 1 LA 70, 74–75 (Whiting, 1945). Also see Arbitrator Edelman in 37 LA 487, 490–491; Seering in 22 LA 108, 110.

[62] Bell Aircraft Corp., 2 LA 22, 24 (Sharkey, 1946). Regarding conflicting court decisions, also see Arbitrator Schedler in 46 LA 697, 698–699; Willingham in 40 LA 173, 177; Howlett in 39 LA 449, 454–455; Sanders in 21 LA 180, 181.

[63] For example, see Arbitrator Sembower in 47 LA 414, 419; McMahon in 47 LA 393, 395; Feinberg in 46 LA 1129, 1130–1131.

of wage stabilization agencies are likely to be given serious consideration, prevailing over a conflicting collective agreement provision[64] and
over bulletins of other government agencies or officials.[65]

While administrative opinions by the Bureau of Veterans Re-
employment Rights have been given weight by some arbitrators,[66] another arbitrator gave no weight to advice from the Bureau to an employer, the arbitrator emphasizing that the Bureau's only function was
to "render aid" to former servicemen.[67]

Official interpretations by executive departments of the government are given significant weight where relevant. Thus, arbitrators
have respected statutory interpretations by the U.S. Department of
Justice[68] and interpretations by the U.S. Department of Labor.[69]

Moreover, executive and administrative rulings or interpretations
in cases similar to the one being considered by the arbitrator may
be relied upon as persuasive, though not controlling, even though the
statute to which the ruling applies does not cover the parties before
the arbitrator. For instance, the interpretation that had been given
the word "day" by officials enforcing the Walsh-Healey Act was persuasive upon an arbitrator in a subsequent case not covered by that
statute.[70]

An interesting view regarding the weight to be given to administrative rulings was expressed by Arbitrator L. F. Sharkey in consider-

---

[64] As in Libby, McNeill & Libby, 5 LA 564, 569 (Prasow, 1946). Also
see Chapter 18, topic titled "Governmental Wage Stabilization."
[65] As in Peabody Coal Co., 5 LA 18, 23 (Fries, 1946).
[66] See Hancock Steel Co., 23 LA 44, 45 (Parker, 1954); Pet Milk Co.,
21 LA 180, 181–182 (Sanders, 1953). Also see Arbitrator Garrett in 25 LA
778, 781–782.
[67] Archer-Daniels-Midland Co., 26 LA 561, 564 (Lindquist, 1955).
[68] See Arbitrator Platt in 54 LA 12, 17; Ruckel in 36 LA 1138, 1140;
Boles in 23 LA 93, 97–98; Barrett in 17 LA 53, 55; Komaroff in 11 LA
395, 397. Rulings by the state Attorney General were relied upon by Arbitrator
Zack in 54 LA 857, 858–859; Kotin in 52 LA 1065, 1067. Also see Quinlan
in 42 LA 1089, 1092.
[69] F. C. Thornton Co., 50 LA 254, 256–258 (Gross, 1967), interpretation
of statute; Warren Foundry & Pipe Corp., 5 LA 282, 283 (Tischler, 1946),
interpretation of executive order. In W. M. Chace Co., 48 LA 231, 232–236
(1966), Arbitrator Ellmann refused to adhere strictly to a state department
of labor guide, which he said was not "law."
[70] Corn Products Refining Co., 7 LA 125, 131–132 (Updegraff, 1947). Also
see Arbitrator Elson in 39 LA 1210, 1212. But see Coffey in 49 LA 1195,
1197.

ing an interpretation of the Selective Service Act made by the Director of Selective Service:

> "The interpretation of an administrative agency is entitled to weight, but it is not decisive especially when it is a newly formulated one and one not long in effect, one on which the actions of men have not been based over a long period of time. In this instance, the opinion of the Director is one man's opinion entitled to respect. It may be persuasive, but it is not controlling. It has not the authority of law. It has not the power to change the provisions of a statute or a contract."[71]

Arbitrator Sharkey thereupon declared that the interpretation of the Director had raised doubts in the minds of honest men and he refused to rely upon it.

Finally, it may be noted that the conclusions and actions of state unemployment compensation commissions have been given very little weight (often none at all) in arbitration proceedings.[72]

Agency Principles

Arbitrators place strong reliance upon the generally recognized principles of agency. Thus, parties are held responsible for the acts of their authorized agents.[73] For instance, the employer has been required to compensate an employee for lost earnings due to the erroneous diagnosis by the employer's doctor of the employee's condition.[74] A union which authorized its Vice President to settle a grievance was held bound by the settlement even though it was rejected by the union

---

[71] Bell Aircraft Corp., 2 LA 22, 24 (1946). Also see Arbitrator Lindquist in 26 LA 561, 564.

[72] See Arbitrator Feller in 54 LA 1231, 1245; Krimsly in 48 LA 802, 807; Seward in 45 LA 1133, 1136; Teple in 45 LA 196, 201; Roberts in 45 LA 65, 67; Bradley in 44 LA 864, 864–865; Jones in 44 LA 445, 446 (procedures, functions, and issues in the two proceedings are different and there is "no functional incongruity" in contradictory decisions from the two proceedings); Crawford in 40 LA 1084, 1088; Slavney in 40 LA 329, 333; Sembower in 39 LA 584, 587; Gundermann in 38 LA 794, 799. But see view of Arbitrator Turkus in 41 LA 575, 576.

[73] See Bethlehem Steel Co., 26 LA 646, 647 (Seward, 1956). For cases dealing with the possibility that one may be the "alter ego" of another so as to impose responsibilities toward third parties on that basis, see Hanz Trucking, Inc., 46 LA 1057, 1060 (Anderson, 1966); Beckering Construction Co., 43 LA 514, 518–519, 524–525 (Howlett, 1964).

[74] Arbitrator Bothwell in 27 LA 404, 406–407; Bowles in 26 LA 370, 373; Anderson in 24 LA 756, 758–759.

membership when submitted for their approval.[75] Commitments made by past union officials have bound their successors.[76]

A principal may be held responsible for the act of his agent within the scope of the agent's general authority even though the principal has not specifically authorized the act in question; it is enough if the principal empowered the agent to represent him in the general area within which the agent acted.[77] On this basis, employers have been held responsible for or bound by various actions of supervisors.[78] Of course, the employer will not be bound by an act of a supervisor or other management representative if no basis exists to establish authority for the act.[79] Thus, an employer was held not bound by an agreement reached between the plant superintendent and the union committee where both the committee and the superintendent knew that it was subject to the approval, never received, of company officials.[80]

Even where no agency authority exists at the time of an act, it may be supplied retroactively by subsequent ratification. Ratification may be express, but it also may be implied by silence after knowledge of the unauthorized act[81] or by actual operation under an unauthorized agreement.[82]

Arbitrators have often been strict in requiring a showing of authorization or ratification by the union membership of any action of a union committee which changes the terms of the collective agreement. "To hold otherwise would mean that a local Union committee

---

[75] Kendall Cotton Mills, 24 LA 684, 687–688 (Dworet, 1955). Also see Arbitrator Dworkin in 49 LA 974, 979–980; McNaughton in 41 LA 1345, 1347; Wallen in 38 LA 522, 523; Rock in 37 LA 465 at 465.

[76] See Arbitrator Kates in 48 LA 865, 867; Morvant in 33 LA 302, 305–306; Shister in 25 LA 50, 53.

[77] Sunset Line & Twine Co., 79 NLRB 1487, 1509 (1948), citing the Restatement of Agency.

[78] See Arbitrator Cantor in 54 LA 1011, 1018; Jones in 54 LA 820, 823–824; Kates in 48 LA 773, 775; McNaughton in 37 LA 958, 960. Also see Graff in 37 LA 1108, 1111. Cf., Beatty in 48 LA 1123, 1124; Horlacher in 41 LA 252, 255.

[79] See Crouse-Hinds Co., 48 LA 606, 608 (Kates, 1967); Simmons Co., 25 LA 426, 429 (Daugherty, 1955).

[80] Kempsmith Machine Co., 5 LA 520, 530 (Marshall, 1946). If a company representative is found to have had authority to commit the company to a settlement, the company will be bound. General Telephone Co. of Illinois, 49 LA 493, 499 (Kesselman, 1967).

[81] Pacific American Shipowners Assn., 10 LA 736, 746 (Miller, 1948). Also see Arbitrator Kennedy in 45 LA 30, 33; Cox in 28 LA 677, 690.

[82] Lafe Pharmacy, 1 ALAA ¶67,469 (1946). Also see Arbitrator Marshall in 47 LA 97, 101.

meeting with management could dissipate the contractual benefits of its membership without its approval."[83]

The Connecticut State Board of Mediation and Arbitration has held that, in view of the customary procedure of collective bargaining by which all matters of high importance, such as annual wage increases, must be submitted to the membership for final approval, a presumption exists against the validity of action taken by a union committee in respect to these matters until proof of authorization or ratification is shown.[84]

Likewise, a shop steward has no authority to bind the union by an agreement altering or creating an exception to the collective agreement, nor has he authority to waive strict performance of the agreement.[85] Nor does a union field representative have authority to change the collective agreement unless such authority is clearly vested in him by the membership.[86]

Such a strict rule, however, would not apply to an action taken in grievance settlements which does not have the effect of changing the terms of the agreement.[87] Moreover, an oral agreement between the company and a union President was held binding though it involved deviation from the seniority provisions of the collective agreement since he had made numerous such agreements in the past without objection from the union.[88]

---

[83] Flintkote Co., 9 LA 976, 977 (Naggi, 1948). In accord with the general proposition, Arbitrator Altrock in 50 LA 845, 850; Witney in 44 LA 624, 628–629; Schedler in 34 LA 860, 861; Thompson in 23 LA 89, 91; Platt in 12 LA 161, 164, and in 11 LA 805, 808; Donnelly, Curry & Clark in 10 LA 55 at 55. Also see Lennard in 49 LA 76, 80–81. Cf., Anrod in 29 LA 848, 852–854; Warns in 28 LA 424, 427–428. In Eagle Manufacturing Co., 51 LA 970, 979 (Lugar, 1968), it was held, somewhat in converse, that a majority of the employees could not excuse employer action contrary to the collective agreement where the employer's action was not approved by the union as the contracting party. For related discussion, see Chapter 5, topic titled "Grievance Adjustment by Individual Employees."

[84] Russell Mfg. Co., 10 LA 55 at 55 (Donnelly, Curry & Clark, 1948). Also see Arbitrator Platt in 40 LA 1089, 1090.

[85] Valley Metal Products Co., 25 LA 83, 84 (Ryder, 1955); Pacific Mills, 2 LA 545, 548 (McCoy, 1946). Also see Arbitrator Whelan in 33 LA 902, 909.

[86] McLouth Steel Corp., 11 LA 805, 808 (Platt, 1948).

[87] See Arbitrator Williams in 45 LA 727, 729, 731; Dykstra in 41 LA 1184, 1188–1189; Morvant in 41 LA 288, 292–293; Kates in 39 LA 327, 332; Valtin in 30 LA 967, 969; Platt in 12 LA 161, 164. Also see Dworkin in 40 LA 1042, 1047; Wallen in 38 LA 522, 523; Kesselman in 28 LA 434, 436.

[88] Lockheed Aircraft Corp., 23 LA 815, 820–821 (Marshall, 1955). Also see Arbitrator Epstein in 45 LA 146, 149–150; Kennedy in 45 LA 30, 33.

An arbitrator will hold a party bound by the act of its agent, though unauthorized, if the party is found to have clothed the agent with "apparent" or "ostensible" authority to act.[89] For instance, a company was so bound where it held out an employers association as its agent by permitting one of its officers to sit on the association's bargaining committee without disclosing an intent not to be bound by the agreement being negotiated on behalf of the association's members.[90] A union was held bound by actions of its officer where the officer, with the union's knowledge, appeared to be speaking for the union and the union failed to openly disavow that action.[91]

The rule that knowledge of an agent is imputed to the principal has been applied by arbitrators. Knowledge held by a union regarding the existence and nature of a grievance settlement may be charged to the employee affected, and the employer relieved from making good any loss suffered by the employee as a result of the union's failure to notify him of the settlement.[92]

Knowledge held by a management representative may be imputed to the employer,[93] and that of a union agent may be charged to the union.[94] In some cases, however, arbitrators have pointed to the limited authority of the agent and have refused to impute his knowledge to the principal.[95]

---

[89] See Arbitrator Sembower in 54 LA 1265, 1267–1268; Krimsly in 52 LA 1125, 1128–1130; Madden in 52 LA 506, 509; Jarvis in 52 LA 197, 199–200; Dworkin in 49 LA 974, 979–980; Roberts in 48 LA 1166, 1170–1171; Fallon in 45 LA 85, 88–89; Anrod in 29 LA 848, 852–853; Cox in 28 LA 677, 690; Marshall in 23 LA 815, 820–821; Myers in 16 LA 584, 585. In Western Condensing Co., 37 LA 912, 915 (Mueller, 1962), an employee was held bound by actions of his wife under this concept. In Maier Brewing Co., 45 LA 1115, 1123 (Jones, 1965), an employer was not permitted to challenge or "probe behind" the apparent authority, upon which the employer could rely, of union representatives to enter into a collective bargaining agreement.

[90] Pope and Talbot, Inc., 1 ALAA ¶67,157, p. 67,324 (1942). Also see Arbitrator Roberts in 49 LA 14, 19; Mintzer in 38 LA 1171, 1172.

[91] Carmen v. BRT, 44 LA 540, 543 (Wallen, 1965).

[92] Ford Motor Co., 1 LA 409, 410 (Shulman, 1945). Also see Arbitrator Warns in 27 LA 179, 182. In Newspaper Agency Corp., 43 LA 1233, 1235 (Platt, 1964), notice to union representatives who resided at points distant (in different states) from the local union and who were not known to be authorized to receive the notice (copies of arbitration decision), was not notice to local union.

[93] Misco Precision Casting Co., 40 LA 87, 90 (Dworkin, 1962); Pope and Talbot, Inc., 1 ALAA ¶67,157 (1942).

[94] Anheuser-Busch, Inc., 33 LA 752, 753 (Roberts, 1959); Boys & Men's Shop, 8 LA 214, 217–218 (Rosenfarb, 1947).

[95] Hawthorn-Mellody Farms, Inc., 52 LA 557, 560 (Kates, 1969), union agent; Wyandotte Chemicals Corp., 36 LA 1169, 1172 (Hilpert, 1961), company agent.

As to imputing knowledge of the individual employee to the union, one arbitrator has taken the view that knowledge of individual union members concerning the employer's policy and practices under the agreement "cannot be without more charged to the Union, for members of a Union are not necessarily agents of the Union."[96] But another arbitrator has declared that as to knowledge of company policy, "the knowledge of the employee must be the knowledge of the Union."[97]

As to the principal's obligation to indemnify his agents, an arbitrator resorted to basic principles of agency law in determining whether an employee was entitled to be indemnified by his employer for monetary loss which the employee suffered in defending legal actions against him growing out of certain things which he did allegedly in the employer's interest.[98]

Contract Principles

Arbitrators may be expected to recognize fundamental principles of contract law, such as those concerning the need for consideration to produce a binding contract,[99] those concerning offer and acceptance,[100] those concerning anticipatory breach,[101] and those concerning the obligation to perform contractual commitments in spite of hardship.[102]

The principle that there can be no binding contract without a meeting of the minds has been applied by arbitrators.[103] Where the

---

[96] Boys & Men's Shop, 8 LA 214, 218 (Rosenfarb, 1947). As to union responsibility for employee actions in breach of the no-strike clause, compare: Booth Newspapers, Inc., 43 LA 785, 790 (Platt, 1964); General American Transportation Corp., 42 LA 142, 144 (Pollack, 1964).

[97] Chattanooga Box & Lumber Co., 44 LA 373, 376 (Tatum, 1965). Accord, imputing to the union an employee's knowledge that the agreement was being violated by the employer, Sinclair Manufacturing Co., 49 LA 310, 313–314 (Nichols, 1967).

[98] Trubitz Hardware & Electric Co., 32 LA 930, 934–935 (Scheiber, 1959).

[99] See Dixie-Portland Flour Mills, Inc., 46 LA 838, 840 (Hon, 1966); United Drill & Tool Corp., 28 LA 677, 685–686 (Cox, 1957).

[100] See Arbitrator Kelliher in 54 LA 647, 648; Eaton in 54 LA 478, 482–483; Hays in 20 LA 406, 408. Also see Solomon in 42 LA 280, 288.

[101] See Metro East Journal, 47 LA 610, 612 (Kelliher, 1966).

[102] See American Iron & Machine Works Co., 18 LA 285, 287 (Horton, 1952). Also see Seng Co., 51 LA 928, 931–932 (Sembower, 1968), in accord as to hardship and also noting that only in extreme cases will impossibility of performance be accepted as an excuse for not performing a contract.

[103] See Arbitrator Sembower in 54 LA 292, 297–298; Shipman in 46 LA 885, 886; Johannes in 20 LA 362, 363; Garman in 20 LA 199, 201–202;

arbitrator finds that there has been no meeting of the minds on a matter he may recommend further negotiations by the parties,[104] unless he construes his authority to be broad enough to empower him to decide the dispute on the merits.[105]

Remedies for Mistake

The remedy of reformation to correct a mutual mistake in a contract is well established at law, and it has been recognized by arbitrators.[106] In fact, a reformation may be granted even where the evidence falls short of what a court of equity would require for contractual reformation if upon consideration of all the evidence the arbitrator is persuaded that fairness and justice, even though not strictly "equity" as it is administered in the courts, requires this kind of relief.[107]

However, arbitrators, like courts, will grant relief only in case of *mutual* mistake; unilateral mistake is not sufficient.[108]

Brandschain in 9 LA 239, 241; Copelof in 8 LA 475, 478; McCoy in 1 LA 556, 560. The "meeting of the minds" requirement is questioned in Garrett, "The Role of Lawyers in Arbitration," Arbitration and Public Policy 102, 121 (BNA Incorporated, 1961). Fraud in the inducement of a contract was basis for voiding it in Hastings Manufacturing Co., 49 LA 297, 299–300 (Howlett, 1967), but the fact that a contractual promise was given under coercive circumstances did not excuse its performance in City of New Haven, 50 LA 661, 663 (Summers, 1968).

[104] For example, see Arbitrator Sembower in 54 LA 292, 297–298; Johannes in 20 LA 362, 364; Brandschain in 9 LA 239, 241; Copelof in 8 LA 475, 478.

[105] See Arbitrator Beatty in 24 LA 424, 425; Ryder in 22 LA 769, 771; Wallen in 6 LA 286, 288; Rice in 8 LA 586, 589. For related discussion and other cases, see Chapter 9, subtopic titled " 'Legislation' vs. 'Interpretation' "; Chapter 7, topic titled "Recommendation by Arbitrator."

[106] For instance, see Arbitrator Anderson in 43 LA 730, 732–733; Whyte in 41 LA 555, 558–559; Tatum in 34 LA 406, 409; Willcox in 23 LA 21, 24. Also see statements by Arbitrator Christensen in 46 LA 789, 797; Seinsheimer in 35 LA 409, 411; Compton in 27 LA 829, 830–831; Duff in 25 LA 534, 536; Tilford in 20 LA 446, 447; Emery in 17 LA 632, 635; Forrester in 17 LA 592, 594.

[107] See Huntsville Mfg. Co., 6 LA 515, 516–517 (McCoy, 1947). Where an arbitrator was not so persuaded, he insisted that "Only under rare, unusual and compelling circumstances should a labor arbitrator exercise authority not expressly conferred upon him by modifying or reforming a labor agreement of long standing." Sidney Wanzer & Sons, 47 LA 708, 710–711 (Kamin, 1966).

[108] See Arbitrator Sembower in 54 LA 1265, 1268; Erbs in 51 LA 606, 611–612; Gould in 50 LA 877, 881; Williams in 48 LA 1185, 1186; Koven in 48 LA 164, 167; Seward in 47 LA 549, 551; Holly in 67–2 ARB ¶8452; Howlett in 43 LA 913, 917–918; Bowles in 23 LA 746, 749; Platt in 7 LA 708, 711–712; McCoy in 3 LA 257, 259. A reformation may be granted to effectuate the true intent of the parties where that intent is not reflected in the agreement

The common prohibition against adding to, subtracting from, or modifying the terms of the agreement by the arbitrator would seem to provide special justification for the refusal to grant a reformation solely on the basis of unilateral mistake. Moreover, this same prohibition dictates against the setting aside of the terms of an agreement merely because its operation has not been up to the expectations of one of the parties or because, at the time of signing the agreement, the full implications of its provisions may not have been realized by one of the parties.[109]

Like reformation of contract, the remedy of rescission for mistake ordinarily is available only under limited circumstances.[110] In particular, a unilateral mistake is not sufficient basis for rescission unless the mistake was basic and the other party knew and took advantage of it.[111]

Another type of "mistake" situation that has arisen in arbitration has involved the payment of money. In one case, for instance, employees recovered sums which their employer owed them but had mistakenly failed to pay.[112]

Where an employer makes a mistake in the employee's favor, the employer may seek to correct it for the future and he sometimes will seek recoupment. It appears clear that the employer will be permitted to correct mathematical or clerical errors in wage computation where the payment has not yet been made; and there is a probability that the arbitrator will find some right of recoupment in the employer as to those erroneous payments which were made before the error was detected.[113] Where the clerical error concerns an employee's rate

---

as a result of typographical error. See Mohawk Beverages, Inc., 50 LA 298, 300 (Moran, 1968). Also see Chapter 9, topic titled "Language Which Is Clear and Unambiguous."

[109] For cases, see Chapter 9, topic titled "Language Which Is Clear and Unambiguous."

[110] For example, see American Airlines, Inc., 48 LA 705, 717–718 (Seitz, 1967).

[111] For a thorough discussion of mistake as a basis for rescission, see Arbitrator Archibald Cox in United Drill & Tool Corp., 28 LA 677, 687–689 (1957), and Arbitrator Douglas B. Maggs in Glendale Mfg. Co., 28 LA 298, 300–301 (1957). Also see Forrester in 17 LA 592, 594; Townsend in 17 LA 472, 478.

[112] A. D. Julliard & Co., 20 LA 579, 582–583 (Maggs, 1953).

[113] See Arbitrator Schurke in 56 LA 1270, 1275 (recoupment of substantial part permitted); Kesselman in 49 LA 493, 498 (recoupment permitted); Walsh

(or its basis) and has continued for some time, the employer still may be permitted to correct it for the future if he acts promptly upon discovery of the error, but the arbitrator may be less inclined to permit recoupment.[114]

Where the employer's error is not of a clerical nature but is in the nature of a "mistake of law" or "mistake of judgment" with full knowledge of all the facts, he may or may not be permitted to correct it for the future[115] but it is unlikely that recoupment will be permitted.[116]

Unjust Enrichment

The principle of unjust enrichment holds that "one shall not unjustly enrich himself at the expense of another."[117] Arbitrator R. H. Marshall has elaborated:

> "The general principle of unjust enrichment is that one person should not be permitted to enrich himself unjustly at the expense of another, but the party so enriched should be required to make restitution for property or benefits received, where it is just and equitable, and where such action involves no violation or frustration of the law."[118]

In some arbitration cases the evidence has supported the application of this doctrine.[119]

---

in 49 LA 206, 210 (recoupment permitted); Kates in 48 LA 773, 775 (dictum); Stouffer in 44 LA 397, 401 (recoupment permitted); Williams in 42 LA 1084, 1086–1087 (practice supported recoupment); McDermott in 41 LA 10, 13–14 (practice supported recoupment); Garrett in 36 LA 385, 387; Duff in 33 LA 564, 566–567 (partial recoupment permitted). Cf., Willingham in 40 LA 442, 444 (no recoupment permitted).

[114] See Arbitrator Dworkin in 45 LA 1015, 1017–1018; Willingham in 40 LA 91, 94; Pigors in 39 LA 640, 642; Coleman in 33 LA 333, 335.

[115] Compare Eastern Airlines, Inc., 48 LA 1005, 1009 (Seidenberg, 1967), with Northern Ohio Telephone Co., 48 LA 773, 775 (Kates, 1966).

[116] See Eastern Airlines, Inc., 48 LA 1005, 1009 (Seidenberg, 1967); Milwaukee Linen Supply Co., 23 LA 392, 394 (Anderson, 1954).

[117] Bouvier's Law Dictionary 3376 (8th Ed.)

[118] Cyclops Corp., 51 LA 613, 616 (1968), also stating that reliance upon the doctrine "must be supported by clear and convincing evidence," which did not exist in that case.

[119] For example, see Cudahy Packing Co., 51 LA 822, 835 (Somers, 1968); Memphis Publishing Co., 48 LA 931, 933 (Cantor, 1967). In American Maize Products Co., 37 LA 673, 675 (Sembower, 1961), the employer was required to pay an employee under the "quantum meruit" principle for the value of services performed by the employee where the employer knew of it and did nothing to halt the work.

The "unjustly at the expense of another" element is not always present when a person receives an apparent "windfall." Thus, Arbitrator Samuel S. Kates upheld the right of a family to double insurance coverage by reason of separate insurance programs covering both spouses furnished by their separate employers; in the absence of a contractual provision to the contrary, the double family benefit was a legitimate result of the family's double employment.[120]

Waiver and Estoppel

Frequently one party to a collective agreement will charge that the other party has waived or is estopped from asserting a right under the agreement.[121] Arbitrators generally do not appear to be concerned with all of the fine legal distinctions between the term "waiver" and the term "estoppel," but they have often applied the underlying principle.[122]

Especially common in arbitration is that species of waiver known in law as "acquiescence." This term denotes a waiver which arises by tacit consent or by failure of a person for an unreasonable length of time to act upon rights of which he has full knowledge.

Arbitrators have frequently held that where one party, with actual or constructive knowledge of his rights, stands by and offers no protest with respect to the conduct of the other, thereby reasonably inducing the latter to believe that his conduct is fully concurred in, the matter will be treated as closed insofar as it relates to past transac-

---

[120] Hawthorn-Mellody Farms, Inc., 52 LA 557, 560–561 (1969). Accord in principle, Arbitrator Williams in 51 LA 589, 592; Nichols in 67–2 ARB ¶8390; Seinsheimer in 66–2 ARB ¶8567. Cf., Bothwell in 68–1 ARB ¶6210; Wallen in 41 LA 1321, 1322. For cases in which a "coordination of benefits" provision was present so as to prevent double benefits, see Arbitrator Shister in 54 LA 335, 337; Klamon in 47 LA 1142, 1149; Uible in 39 LA 136, 138; Graff in 38 LA 245, 248. For cases involving the scope of coverage where both spouses are employed by the same company, see Arbitrator Blistein in 49 LA 612 at 612; Thompson in 32 LA 843, 847.

[121] For related discussion, see Chapter 5, subtopic titled "Waiver of Employee Rights or Signature Requirement."

[122] For instances in which the arbitrator did note legal distinctions between the two terms, see Continental Distilling Sales Co., 52 LA 1138, 1141 (Sembower, 1969), where an issue was decided on the basis of estoppel; Fox Manufacturing Co., 47 LA 97, 101–102 (Marshall, 1966), where there was an express waiver of certain rights for the future.

tions; but repeated violations of an express rule by one party or acquiescence on the part of the other ordinarily will not affect application of the rule in future operations.[123]

One arbitrator has held that the failure to enforce a right does not constitute a waiver unless the other party is misled to his prejudice, damage, or injury, or unless other elements of estoppel are present.[124] While many arbitrators do not appear to require such a strong showing, most do adhere to fairly strict minimum standards: Clear evidence will be required;[125] only one with authority to waive provisions of an agreement may do so;[126] the waiver of one right or provision, standing alone, will not be held to constitute the waiver of another.[127]

Sometimes arbitrators decide issues specifically on the basis of estoppel.[128] For instance, where a company gave an oral assurance on a matter during contract negotiations to induce the union to agree on a contract and end a strike, Arbitrator Whitley P. McCoy held that an estoppel had been created against the company since the union had changed its position, suffering detriment, in reliance upon the assurance. Accordingly, the company was held bound by the oral as-

---

[123] See Arbitrator Howlett in 50 LA 829, 831–832; Nichols in 49 LA 310, 313; Allen in 48 LA 219, 222–223; Myers in 42 LA 269, 272; Emery in 17 LA 90, 91; Maggs in 12 LA 311, 316; Douglas in 10 LA 562, 563; Courshon in 9 LA 484, 490–491; Wolff in 5 LA 333, 336; McCoy in 4 LA 231, 233. Also see Anderson in 47 LA 356, 362–363; Seward in 36 LA 162, 164; Morvant in 24 LA 750, 752. For other cases reflecting these principles, see materials on continuing violations and on negligent delay in filing grievances in Chapter 5, topic titled "Time Limitations"; Chapter 12, topic titled "Custom and Practice vs. Clear Contract Language." Very strong proof is required to establish amendment of the contract by custom. See Chapter 12, subtopic titled "Amendment of Contract."
[124] Allis-Chalmers Mfg. Co., 8 LA 945, 947 (Gorder, 1947). Accord, Bell Aircraft Corp., 24 LA 324, 327 (Somers, 1955).
[125] Mosaic Tile Co., 13 LA 949, 950 (Cornsweet, 1950); Super-Cold Corp., 8 LA 187, 188 (Cheney, 1947).
[126] Republic Steel Corp., 5 LA 609, 618 (McCoy, 1946), and McCoy in 2 LA 545, 548. Also see Chapter 5, subtopic titled "Waiver of Employee Rights or Signature Requirement."
[127] Union Carbide Corp., 46 LA 195, 198 (Cahn, 1966); Stearms Coal and Lumber Co., 1 LA 274, 276 (Dwyer, 1946).
[128] See Arbitrator Sembower in 52 LA 1138, 1141; Berkman in 49 LA 833, 836; Seitz in 48 LA 705, 720–721; Gorsuch in 46 LA 1089, 1096; McCoy in 46 LA 1078, 1081, and in 17 LA 101, 103; Dworkin in 46 LA 1021, 1026–1027; Epstein in 45 LA 146, 150; Seibel in 44 LA 866, 871–873; Scheiber in 42 LA 483, 489; Ross in 34 LA 752, 755; Reid in 21 LA 199, 203; Cahn in 20 LA 130, 136; Forrester in 18 LA 306, 307; Klamon in 17 LA 654, 661; Emery in 17 LA 632, 635.

surance, which limited the number of employees the company could reclassify under a provision of the contract.[129]

Sometimes, too, arbitrators decide issues essentially on the basis of estoppel without so stating specifically and without requiring as clear a showing of the elements of estoppel as might be required by a court of law.[130] In the latter type of cases emphasis is often placed upon equity, with something like a "fair and just result" standard being applied.

An approach similar to the "election" principle of equity courts, limiting a party to the exercise of only one of two inconsistent or alternate rights, was followed by Arbitrator David A. Wolff in not permitting a party to assume the position of "having his cake and eating it too."[131]

Principles of Damages

In empowering the arbitrator to resolve their dispute, the parties generally are considered to have clothed him with authority to grant adequate monetary relief where he finds that the grievance has merit.[132] In this regard, Arbitrator W. Willard Wirtz has emphasized that arbitrators have authority to award money damages for contract violations even though the contract does not specifically provide such remedy. To restrict arbitrators to remedies specifically set forth in the contract would negate arbitration as a method of dispute settlement or would result in cluttering contracts with numerous liquidated dam-

---

[129] International Harvester Co., 17 LA 101, 103 (1951). Similarly, see Arbitrator Kates in 48 LA 865, 867; Schedler in 36 LA 15, 17; Forrester in 18 LA 306, 307. But see Sembower in 51 LA 582, 588; Keefe in 48 LA 373, 376–377; Koven in 48 LA 164, 166–167; Hon in 46 LA 838, 840–841.

[130] See Arbitrator Sales in 47 LA 1078, 1081; Fallon in 45 LA 85, 90; Stouffer in 43 LA 901, 905; Klamon in 21 LA 300, 305; Havs in 20 LA 406, 408; Luskin in 16 LA 237, 238; Miller in 10 LA 736, 746; Rosenfarb in 8 LA 214, 217; Blair in 4 LA 110, 111.

[131] Chrysler Corp., 6 LA 369, 372 (1947). Also see Arbitrator Klamon in 50 LA 574, 591; Cahn in 22 LA 270, 272–273. In Allegheny Ludlum Steel Corp., 33 LA 669, 674–675 (1959), Arbitrator Seward (1) noted that the doctrine of "election of remedies" has been questioned, and (2) drew a distinction between "election" and "mistake" of remedies. As to waiver by acceptance of benefits, see Colonial Baking Co., 32 LA 193, 198–199 (Piercey, 1959).

[132] For related discussion, see Chapter 7, topic titled "Remedy Power and Its Use." Also see Wolff, "The Power of the Arbitrator to Make Monetary Awards," Labor Arbitration—Perspectives and Problems 176 (BNA Incorporated, 1964).

ages provisions which would invite more trouble than they could prevent.[133]

Compensatory Damages

Monetary damages in arbitration should "normally correspond to specific monetary losses suffered."[134] Arbitrator Ralph T. Seward has explained:

> "The ordinary rule at common law and in the developing law of labor relations is that an award of damages should be limited to the amount necessary to make the injured 'whole.' Unless the agreement provides that some other rule should be followed, this rule must apply."[135]

Thus, for example, where an employer violates the agreement by utilizing junior employees, damages will be due only to those employees whose seniority would have entitled them to the work had the employer acted in accordance with the agreement.[136]

---

[133] International Harvester Co., 9 LA 894, 896 (1947). In accord, see Arbitrator Dworkin in 41 LA 219, 222; Seitz in 37 LA 509, 518; Kuhn in 34 LA 814, 825; Reynard in 27 LA 625, 628; Willcox in 23 LA 21, 23; Louisell in 21 LA 254, 259; Emery in 17 LA 721, 722–723. Also see Laskin in 18 LA 925, 926; Wolff in 15 LA 822, 827.

[134] Patterson-Sargent Co., 23 LA 21, 23 (Willcox, 1954). Also see Arbitrator Sembower in 39 LA 821, 822–823; Laskin in 18 LA 925, 926; Emery in 17 LA 721, 723. Cf., Crawford in 52 LA 243, 247. Collective agreements often leave the matter of retroactivity of damages to the arbitrator, but with a limitation on the period of retroactivity. See Major Collective Bargaining Agreements: Arbitration Procedures 77–78 (U.S. Dept. of Labor Bull. No. 1425–6, 1966). Also as to retroactivity of damages, see Lady Baltimore Bakery Co., 47 LA 8, 11 (Koven, 1966). Where a grievant was now deceased, damages were awarded to his estate or next of kin. Phelps Dodge Aluminum 52 LA 375, 382 (Howlett, 1969).

[135] International Harvester Co., 15 LA 1 at 1 (1950). An employee is entitled to be made whole regardless of the employer's financial problems (see Arbitrator MacLeod in 53 LA 207, 215–216, and McCormick in 45 LA 453, 455), but being made whole is all that is required (see Arbitrator Gray in 43 LA 126, 128, and Drake in 32 LA 453, 458–459). In Hillman's, 32 LA 453, 458–459 (Drake, 1959), a new employee was hired at a higher rate than the contractual rate being paid other employees in the same classification; the arbitrator refused to increase the rate of said other employees for the future, but he did award back pay in the amount of the difference between their pay and that of the new employee for the disputed period. As to the back pay award, cf., New Testament, Matthew 20: 1–16 (parable).

[136] See Arbitrator Killion in 49 LA 1073, 1076–1077; Ross in 41 LA 1204, 1208–1209 and in 32 LA 300, 304; Schedler in 38 LA 207, 209; Boles in 35 LA 845, 850; Gilden in 21 LA 105, 108; Marshall in 17 LA 709, 710; Whiting in 11 LA 495, 498; Copelof in 4 LA 786, 787. Also see Wollett in 35 LA 783, 787–788; Kates in 32 LA 492, 501. Cf., Wolf in 50 LA 357, 361; Loucks in 36 LA 1067, 1070; Shipman in 36 LA 855, 856. In Columbus

Arbitrator Maurice S. Trotta has required a showing of injury to justify damages, and where the existence of any such injury was too speculative he refused to award damages.[137] Similarly, other arbitrators generally require a party to prove his claim for damages,[138] and they will deny monetary relief where the existence of any injury is too speculative.[139]

However, damages will not be denied merely because the amount is difficult to determine.[140] When difficulty is encountered, the simplest fair method available for determining the amount will be used.[141] One possible solution in this type of situation is for the arbitrator to make a finding as to liability and provide that, in the light of the difficulty of determining the exact amount of damages, the liability may be discharged by a lump-sum settlement if the parties can reach one. This was done, for instance, where a time-consuming and expensive process of review of records covering a five-year period would have been necessary to determine the exact amount due.[142]

Auto Parts Co., 43 LA 546, 553–554 (Klein, 1964), the company asserted that the named grievants did not have sufficient seniority to make them proper claimants for damages, but this assertion came too late since it was first made in the posthearing brief.

[137] Permutit Co., 19 LA 599, 600 (1952).

[138] See statement by Arbitrator Callaghan in H. J. Madore, Inc., 47 LA 698, 703 (1966). But where the wrongdoer is in a better position to provide evidence as to damages, the arbitrator might place the burden upon him. See Akers Motor Lines, Inc., 51 LA 955, 964 (Dunau, 1968). Also see Arbitrator Feller in 52 LA 229, 232.

[139] See Arbitrator Seidenberg in 53 LA 1288, 1294; Ladar in 43 LA 1126, 1131; Redden in 41 LA 1269, 1282–1283; Morvant in 37 LA 297, 302; Cahn in 36 LA 785, 787; Miller in 35 LA 757, 782; Dworkin in 35 LA 703, 711. In Master Builders' Association, 48 LA 865, 868 (Kates, 1967), an award was made for past damages but not for "contingent damages." As to the latter, the arbitrator stated that his award would be "without prejudice to any subsequent claim for such damages" if future developments should show additional damages to be warranted. In Kroger Co., 34 LA 686, 688 (Warns, 1960), the grievant suffered no monetary loss from the employer's improper assignment and the arbitrator stated that unlike a jury, he had no authority to assess damages for inconvience occasioned by encroachment upon the grievant's free weekend.

[140] Five Star Hardware & Electric Corp., 44 LA 944, 946 (S. Wolff, 1965); Plumbing, Heating & Piping Employees Council, 39 LA 513, 522 (Ross, 1962), the Arbitrator stating: "The wrongdoer must bear the risk of uncertainty. At the same time the plaintiff is obliged to make a reasonable estimate of damages, supported by the evidence in the case."

[141] Eagle-Pitcher Mining & Smelting Co., 6 LA 544, 549 (Elson, 1947).

[142] Corn Products Refining Co., 7 LA 125, 132–133 (Updegraff, 1947). Similarly, see Arbitrator Feinberg in 16 LA 926, 931–932. In Armco Steel Co., 52 LA 108, 112 (Sembower, 1969), the burden of examining past records was minimized by limiting the period of retroactivity for damages.

Where no other solution is available, the arbitrator "is bound to resort to his own good sense and judgment, and after considering all the pertinent facts and circumstances make a reasonable approximation."[143]

In some instances monetary damages have been denied where such damages were not expressly requested in the grievance,[144] but in other instances no such express request was required.[145] Where an express request for back pay is timely made, the awarding of such damages might be implied in an award which merely states that the grievance is sustained.[146]

Damages Payable to Company or Union

The vast majority of arbitral awards for damages are concerned with indemnifying employees. In some cases, however, it is asserted that the company has suffered damages as a result of union violations of the agreement, or that the union has suffered damages as a result of company violations.

Company claims for damages against the union for illicit work stoppages have not been uncommon. Here, numerous arbitrators have held that the arbitrator may award damages for breach of no-strike clauses unless such remedial authority is expressly denied by the agreement (in some of these decisions the arbitrator itemized the elements of damages).[147] A few arbitrators have ruled otherwise, however, hold-

---

[143] American Machine & Foundry Co., 15 LA 822, 827–828 (S. Wolff, 1950). A liquidated-damages approach was similarly used by Arbitrator Dworkin in 50 LA 621, 624; McCoy in 36 LA 1042, 1044. Some collective agreements specifically provide for liquidated damages for violation thereof, as in Capital Decorating Co., 25 LA 424, 426 (Slavney, 1955).

[144] See Arbitrator Daly in 49 LA 64, 66; Seidenberg in 43 LA 33, 35; Haughton in 35 LA 330, 337.

[145] West Virginia Pulp & Paper Co., 39 LA 163, 166–167 (Stark, 1962); Bethlehem Steel Co., 17 LA 295, 300 (Selekman, 1951), where past practice controlled the result.

[146] California Metal Trades Assn., 41 LA 1204, 1207 (Ross, 1963). Also see Dayton Malleable Iron Co., 11 LA 1175, 1179–1180 (Platt, 1949).

[147] See Arbitrator Eaton in 54 LA 1125, 1129–1130; Kates in 53 LA 869, 872–876; Wyckoff in 53 LA 542, 544–545; Jarvis in 52 LA 197, 198, 200; Scheib in 52 LA 74, 78; Vadakin in 51 LA 500, 503–504; McDermott in 50 LA 1018, 1020–1022; Johnson in 50 LA 35, 36; Klein in 49 LA 1043, 1044, 1051–1052; Berkowitz in 42 LA 95, 95–96; Seitz in 37 LA 509, 518–520; Kleinsorge in 33 LA 574, 585; Cahn in 20 LA 476, 476–477; Laskin in 18 LA 925, 926–929; Rains in 7 LA 648, 654–657. The fact that the union did not authorize the stoppage may affect its liability. See Booth Newspapers, Inc.,

ing that express contractual authority is required to empower the arbitrator to award damages for no-strike violations.[148]

Claims for damages in favor of the union as such might involve, among other possibilities, injury to the union through company violation of union representational rights or union security clauses,[149] or damages resulting from contractual violations by the company in connection with plant removals, discontinuance of a department, and the like.[150]

The "De Minimis" Rule

In denying grievances, arbitrators sometimes apply the rule of *de minimis non curat lex,* under which trifling or immaterial matters will not be taken into account.[151] Often in applying this principle the arbitrator concludes that the action complained of is such a slight departure from what is generally required by the agreement that the action must be viewed either as a permissible exception or as not constituting an injury at all.[152] The *de minimis* concept has sometimes been applied, for example, in denying grievances protesting the performance by management personnel of small amounts of bargaining unit work where a unit employee was not readily available.

Application of the *de minimis* rule has been rejected where "the amount has been small but the principle large."[153] And in any event,

---

43 LA 785, 788–790 (Platt, 1964); Publishers' Assn. of New York City, 42 LA 95 at 95 (Berkowitz, 1964). In Bradlees Family Circle Stores, 47 LA 567, 572–574 (House, 1966), damages were awarded against the union for its failure to try to prevent an unauthorized work stoppage. Also see S. J. Groves & Sons Co., 52 LA 74, 78 (Scheib, 1969), for one arbitrator's view as to how quickly a union may reasonably be expected to take effective action to correct such stoppage.

[148] See Arbitrator Dash in 38 LA 509, 513–515; Crawford in 30 LA 1061, 1065; Hildebrand in 28 LA 769, 774; Copelof in 17 LA 610, 623.

[149] See Arbitrator Singer in 49 LA 991, 995–996; Summers in 48 LA 760, 763; Dash in 37 LA 360, 364.

[150] See Arbitrator Lee in 51 LA 884, 891–892; Duff in 46 LA 4, 9; Dash in 36 LA 1364, 1384–1386; Gray in 34 LA 771, 774–776.

[151] As did Arbitrator Hebert in 47 LA 761, 766–767; Morgan in 47 LA 756, 760; Stouffer in 46 LA 557, 559; Cahn in 45 LA 609, 611–612; Heliker in 43 LA 1159, 1162; Bauder in 64–3 ARB ¶9221; Klein in 41 LA 1045, 1049; Swanson in 27 LA 553, 556; Donnelly in 21 LA 681, 682; Shipman in 17 LA 76, 79; Aaron in 15 LA 168, 172; Cheney in 12 LA 422, 426–427.

[152] For a narrow view as to what constitutes a true *de minimis* situation, see Olin Mathieson Chemical Corp., 47 LA 238, 242 (Hilpert, 1966).

[153] Bethlehem-Sparrows Point Shipyard, Inc., 26 LA 483, 490 (Feinberg, 1956). The rule is also said to be inapplicable where a "continuing" activity

Arbitrator Harold W. Davey has explained that no hard and fast mathematical line should be drawn between minimal on the one hand and substantial on the other, but that each case should be decided in terms of its own circumstances.[154]

Punitive Damages

Even though a party is found to have violated the agreement, the arbitrator may be expected to refuse to award any penalty which would in essence be an award of punitive damages, unless, under the circumstances of the case, punitive damages are clearly justified.[155] While noting that some state and federal courts have disagreed as to the power of arbitrators to award punitive damages, Arbitrator Burton B. Turkus added: "Power to award punitive damages is a heady wine, however, which carries with it an equally potent obligation and abiding responsibility to invoke the remedy with great care and extreme caution in the situations where otherwise the ends of justice would be defeated or unconscionably denied."[156] Some arbitrators have felt justified in awarding punitive damages where the contractual

---

is involved, Union Carbide Corp., 46 LA 195, 198 (Cahn, 1966), and where the arbitration involves "a test case brought seriously to obtain a ruling on a disputed point of contractual interpretation," Tenneco Oil Co., 44 LA 1121, 1128 (Merrill, 1965).

[154] John Deere Planter Works, 29 LA 328, 331 (1957). Also see Westinghouse Electric Corp., 43 LA 84, 89–90 (Altieri, 1964), for discussion of the *de minimis* concept and problems of its application.

[155] To illustrate the great reluctance of arbitrators to award damages which the arbitrator considers to be of a punitive nature, see Arbitrator Kamin in 55 LA 118, 131; Turkus in 53 LA 1056, 1060; Williams in 52 LA 49, 51; Caraway in 51 LA 504, 509; Gundermann in 48 LA 1192, 1198; Kelliher in 47 LA 284, 286; Rezler in 46 LA 1073, 1076; Hughes in 46 LA 36, 39; Koven in 44 LA 1049, 1054; McDermott in 42 LA 1003, 1008; Anderson in 42 LA 632, 637; Hanrahan in 41 LA 417, 418–419; Stouffer in 41 LA 132, 137; Volz in 39 LA 1104, 1107; Seitz in 37 LA 509, 519–520; Gill in 37 LA 134, 136. In many of these cases the request that employees be paid damages was denied because it was not shown that any employee had suffered loss due to the employer's violation of the agreement. In A. C. And C. Co., 24 LA 538, 541 (Scheiber, 1955), the arbitrator denied the union's demand that a penalty payment be made by the employer to a charity where no employee had suffered loss from the employer's violation.

[156] Seaboard World Airlines, Inc., 53 LA 1056, 1060 (1969). As to court decisions, one state court held an award of punitive damages unenforceable as contrary to judicial policy, even though the collective agreement authorized the arbitrator to assess punitive damages. Publishers' Assn. v. Newspaper Union, 18 LA 855, 858–860 (N.Y. Sup. Ct., 1952). A federal court held that the arbitrator's remedial power under LMRA §301 includes punitive awards, but that such power is extraordinary and should be reserved for situations which cannot be pacified by other remedies. Sidney Wanzer & Sons, Inc. v. Milk Drivers Union, 249 F. Supp. 664 (N.D. Ill., 1966).

violation was knowing and repeated,[157] or where it was wilful and flagrant.[158]

The good faith of the offending party has sometimes been emphasized by the arbitrator in refusing to award damages where no person was shown to have suffered loss from the violation of the agreement (the arbitrator sometimes terming it a "technical violation" only).[159]

Interest on Award

The question of interest on the principal sum awarded has sometimes arisen. Arbitrator Sanford H. Kadish refused to order payment of interest on his award of holiday pay since neither the collective agreement nor the submission expressly authorized him to order the payment of interest and "it is not customary in arbitrations for the arbitrator to grant interest on claims which he finds owing."[160] A number of other arbitrators have likewise expressly refused to award interest;[161] but interest has been awarded in some instances.[162]

Mitigating Damages—Deduction of Outside Compensation

In awarding back pay to employees in certain types of cases, particularly those involving discharge or discipline, arbitrators commonly specify that the employer's liability shall be reduced by the amount of the grievant's earnings from other employment during the

---

[157] Mallinckrodt Chemical Works, 50 LA 933, 935–940 (Goldberg, 1968). Also indicating that punitive damages would be justified for repeated violations, see Arbitrator Yarowsky in 48 LA 582, 585; Klein in 46 LA 450, 455; Gill in 37 LA 134, 136.

[158] Five Star Hardware & Electric Corp., 44 LA 944, 946 (Wolff, 1965).

[159] See Arbitrator Prewett in 50 LA 344, 347; Larkin in 48 LA 1031, 1034–1035; McDermott in 44 LA 840, 845; Reid in 36 LA 458, 462; Marshall in 36 LA 962, 964–965 and in 6 LA 926, 935; Reid in 29 LA 743, 747; Gray in 26 LA 723, 726; Duff in 24 LA 623, 625. Also see Seitz in 48 LA 609, 614; Horvitz in 22 LA 390, 392; Shister in 17 LA 254, 256.

[160] Intermountain Operators League, 26 LA 149, 154 (1956).

[161] See Arbitrator Willingham in 48 LA 782, 788; Dolson in 45 LA 705, 706; Keefe in 44 LA 530, 540; Crawford in 43 LA 247, 249; Koven in 41 LA 1310, 1313–1314; Di Leone in 41 LA 856, 862; Davis in 39 LA 177, 179. In Westinghouse Electric Corp., 47 LA 621, 629 (Altrock, 1966), a request for interest on back pay awarded in the reversal of discipline was rejected, the arbitrator adhering to the view that interest should be allowed only where the discipline was "willful, capricious, arbitrary and unconscionable."

[162] See Arbitrator Hilpert in 47 LA 686, 690 and in 39 LA 897, 906–907; Whiting in 41 LA 567, 567–568. Going only part way, some arbitrators have awarded interest to commence running from the date of the award. See Arbitrator Killion in 52 LA 1082, 1087; Miller in 35 LA 757, 782.

period in question. Indeed, there is general agreement by courts, arbitrators, and the NLRB that outside earnings properly are deducted from back pay.[163] Many arbitrators also have specified the deduction of unemployment compensation received by the grievant for the relevant period;[164] but in some cases the arbitrator has expressly concluded that he could not or should not do so.[165]

In the view of many arbitrators an affirmative duty may rest upon employees, when wronged by the employer, to take reasonable steps to mitigate the damages. Even where the agreement provided that an unjustly discharged employee "shall be * * * paid for all time lost," Arbitrator Lewis E. Solomon explained that a duty to attempt to mitigate damages existed:

> "It is commonly and generally recognized that the purpose of a contract provision calling for payment of 'all time lost', when disciplinary action or discharge has been found to be without justifiable cause is to compensate and indemnify the injured employee and make him whole for loss of earnings suffered by him as a result of the inappropriate exercise of judgment by the Company. The loss of earnings is usually to be measured by the wages he would have earned for the period they were improperly denied to him, subject, however, to a recognized duty and responsibility reposed in the employee to mitigate, so far as reasonable, the amount of that loss. If, as a result of employee's action or inaction, he has failed to mitigate the loss, then to the degree of such failure he is himself partially responsible."[166]

---

[163] For an indication of National Railroad Adjustment Board practice as to outside earnings, see National Railway Labor Conference, 53 LA 555, 563 (Seward, Howlett & Livernash, 1969).

[164] See Arbitrator Daugherty in 49 LA 58, 61; Dolnik in 48 LA 273, 276; Summers in 48 LA 188, 190; Dworkin in 48 LA 107, 115; Gorsuch in 46 LA 1089, 1096; Kleinsorge in 46 LA 73, 75; Traynor in 45 LA 524, 529; Tsukiyama in 45 LA 336, 338–339; Wolff in 45 LA 295, 299; Bennett in 45 LA 247, 249; Witney in 45 LA 97, 100; Sembower in 44 LA 405, 412; McDermott in 44 LA 115, 118; Lucas in 44 LA 20, 23; Rice in 44 LA 16, 20; Purdom in 43 LA 1106, 1111; Gunderman in 43 LA 907, 911; Tongue in 39 LA 654, 656; Scheiber in 39 LA 621, 624; Wood in 38 LA 148, 150–151. In allowing such deduction in favor of the employer, three of these arbitrators (Rice, Purdom, and Gundermann) ordered the employer to reimburse the unemployment compensation commission.

[165] See Arbitrator Williams in 53 LA 867, 868; Warns in 62–3 ARB ¶8840; Wagner in 38 LA 1091, 1092; Miller in 35 LA 757, 782; Seward in 16 LA 376, 377; Courshon in 9 LA 484, 487–488.

[166] Love Brothers, 45 LA 751, 752, 756 (1965). In Continental Can Co., 39 LA 821, 822–823 (Sembower, 1962), outside earnings and unemployment compensation were deducted where the agreement stated the grievant was to be paid the "amount he would have earned." But see United States Steel Co., 40 LA 1036, 1039–1041 (McDermott, 1963).

Back pay may be wholly or partially denied where the employee fails to take advantage of reasonable employment opportunities.[167] But this view has not always been accepted, as where an arbitrator stated that "while it may be proper to deduct from a back pay award sums actually earned by an employee before reinstatement, or sums received indirectly from his employer, as through unemployment compensation, no authority exists in an Arbitrator to penalize an employee financially for failing to have earnings."[168]

Even the arbitrators who recognize a duty to mitigate damages may apply some limitations, such as requiring the employer to introduce affirmative evidence to show the inexcusable failure of the employee to minimize damages,[169] and not requiring the employee to use more than "ordinary diligence" to obtain other work.[170] Furthermore, the employee may not be required to accept unsuitable or lower rated work during the pendency of his appeal,[171] and he may be given credit for the added expense involved in actually getting and working at interim employment.[172]

In one case the grievant's duty to mitigate damages was satisfied by expanding his prior farm operations. In this case the arbitrator also concluded that only the extra income from farm work during the grievant's regular working hours with his employer should be deducted.[173]

When an arbitrator concludes that the grievant's outside compensation is to be deducted in the computation of back pay, the grievant has a duty to reveal the facts in regard thereto. Some arbitra-

---

[167] See Arbitrator Block in 52 LA 217, 221 (who made an "educated guess" as to time reasonably necessary for grievant to find other work); Elson in 51 LA 1061, 1063; Kamin in 49 LA 47, 51–52; King in 48 LA 972, 974; Keefe in 48 LA 910, 915; Kelliher in 48 LA 734, 739 (grievant had not "really looked for another job"); Howlett in 48 LA 283, 288; McCoy in 46 LA 109, 111; Solomon in 45 LA 751, 756–758; Parker in 23 LA 640, 642; Healy in 11 LA 827, 831–832; Wolff in 10 LA 288, 294; Lappin in 5 LA 161, 164; Vokum in 2 LA 283, 286. Cf., Jones in 41 LA 646, 650.

[168] Shakespeare & Shakespeare Products Co., 9 LA 813, 817–818 (Platt, 1948).

[169] As in Quick Service Laundry & Cleaners, 52 LA 121, 127–128 (Merrill, 1968); Armour & Co., 11 LA 600, 605 (Gilden, 1948).

[170] Standard Transformer Co., 51 LA 1110, 1113 (Gibson, 1968).

[171] See Arbitrator Jones in 45 LA 635, 640; Parker in 23 LA 640, 642; Aaron in 10 LA 162, 164.

[172] Ingalls Shipbuilding Corp., 37 LA 953, 956 (Murphy, 1961).

[173] American-International Aluminum Corp., 49 LA 728, 730 (Howlett, 1967). On this point, also see Arbitrator Howlett in 48 LA 283, 288.

tors have ordered him to submit a notarized statement as to his outside earnings;[174] and in one case arbitral relief was conditioned upon the grievant's authorization of the release of information showing the public assistance payments he had received.[175]

Other Avoidable Damages; Delayed Arbitration

In some cases back pay has been denied or reduced where the grievant could have avoided being wronged by the employer by speaking up to explain his situation and actions, but he failed to do so.[176] The concept of avoidable damages was applied also against the employer in one case, where he was ordered to pay all arbitration costs since the need for arbitration might have been obviated had he explained his position to the union.[177]

An employer's liability for back pay may be reduced by reason of delay in the arbitration process caused or contributed to by the employee or union.[178] However, no reduction was ordered by the arbitrator where there was no evidence to show that delay was caused by either employee or union;[179] and another arbitrator apparently would in no case reduce back pay because of delay caused by the company or the union.[180]

Judicial Notice and Presumptions

The subjects of judicial notice and presumptions could have been considered in the Evidence chapter. The Authors, however, recognize

---

[174] See Arbitrator Buckwalter in 50 LA 177, 181; Jones in 44 LA 175, 182 and in 37 LA 700, 704.

[175] United States Steel Corp., 52 LA 1210, 1212 (Dybeck, 1969), where the agreement called for deduction of "such earnings or other amounts as he would not have received except for such suspension or discharge."

[176] See Arbitrator Stouffer in 51 LA 234, 240–241; McCoy in 50 LA 8, 9; Merrill in 24 LA 522, 526; Wardlaw in 8 LA 248, 250.

[177] Ralph Rogers & Co., 48 LA 40, 43 (Getman, 1966). But see Madison Bus Co., 52 LA 723, 727–728 (Mueller, 1969). In Thorsen Manufacturing Co., 55 LA 581, 585 (Koven, 1970), the arbitrator upheld a discharge but he awarded some back pay because the company unreasonably complicated and prolonged the proceedings, leaving the grievant in doubt as to his status for a substantial period.

[178] Yale & Towne Mfg. Co., 39 LA 1156, 1162–1163 (Hill, Horlacher & Seitz, 1962), where the matter is fully discussed. Back pay was also reduced for this reason by Arbitrator Reid in 54 LA 681, 683; Bothwell in 49 LA 760, 766–767; Solomon in 42 LA 1, 13; Tsukiyama in 38 LA 404, 413. Cf., Stark in 39 LA 163, 166–167.

[179] Acme Fast Freight, Inc., 37 LA 163, 166 (Warns, 1961).

[180] Gulfport Shipbuilding Corp., 43 LA 1053, 1056 (Ray, 1964).

the view of those who believe that these subjects belong to the general topic of legal or judicial reasoning, and they are accordingly considered here.

Judges take judicial notice of widely known facts of commerce, industry, history, and natural science, and of ordinary meanings of words. Similarly, in arbitration many matters are assumed or accepted without discussion or citation of authority. Thus it may be said that arbitrators also take judicial notice.[181] Not surprisingly, some arbitrators have spoken in terms of taking "arbitral" notice, as did Arbitrator David C. Altrock in noting the short supply of electricians in the area at the time.[182]

Of special significance is the practice of arbitrators of taking judicial notice of industry practice affecting some disputed matters.[183] Thus, judicial notice has been taken of the "general understanding that tips, unless guaranteed by the employer, cannot and should not be used in making a 'wage adjustment.' "[184] Another arbitrator took judicial notice of the fact that it is not common industrial practice to use the rate received by the highest paid experimental employees as the base rate on new jobs when production begins.[185]

Arbitrators also may use presumptions as aids in deciding issues. Presumptions, which are related to the matter of judicial notice, result in the prima facie assumption of the truth of a matter. Thus they take the place of evidence on the part of the party in whose favor they operate, and they require the other party to produce evidence or argument to show that that which is presumed is not true.

To illustrate, Arbitrator Mitchell M. Shipman held that in determining the right to benefits under an employee group insurance plan a wife's dependency upon her husband for support is so basic that

---

[181] For instance, see Arbitrator Roberts in 48 LA 978, 980; Kelliher in 46 LA 707, 708; Kerrison in 46 LA 613, 615; Stouffer in 43 LA 901, 905; Dworkin in 43 LA 507, 509; Wildebush in 41 LA 895, 897; Cayton in 39 LA 159, 160; Rock in 36 LA 65, 70; Lockhart in 20 LA 658, 662–663; Ryder in 20 LA 337, 340; Komaroff in 19 LA 10, 13; Wagner in 6 LA 575, 578, and 6 LA 292, 294.

[182] Textron, Inc., 48 LA 1373, 1376 (1967).

[183] See Arbitrator Kerrison in 46 LA 613, 615; Komaroff in 19 LA 10, 13; Maggs in 17 LA 451, 454; Donnelly in 16 LA 914, 915; Platt in 16 LA 317, 319; Cahn in 7 LA 355, 357; Shipman in 7 LA 121, 122. Also see In re Hopkins, 13 LA 716, 717 (N.Y. Sup. Ct., 1949).

[184] Christ Cella's Restaurant, 7 LA 355, 357 (Cahn, 1947).

[185] Pittsburgh Steel Co., 6 LA 575, 578 (Wagner, 1947).

it will be presumed in the absence of proof to the contrary.[186] Presumptions are used frequently in the interpretation of contract provisions. For instance, parties are presumed to have intended a valid contract,[187] to have intended all words used in an agreement to have effect,[188] and to have intended language to have its commonly accepted meaning.[189]

Presumptions may also be used in "interests" matters. Thus, Arbitrator David L. Cole, in determining the amount of wage increase necessary to offset a rise in living costs, ruled that it was "presumptively proper" to consider only the change in living costs occurring after the parties' last wage negotiation, there being a presumption that all pertinent factors were considered in previous bargaining.[190]

Parol Evidence

Under the parol-evidence rule a written agreement may not be changed or modified by any oral statements or arguments made by the parties in connection with the negotiation of the agreement. A written contract consummating previous oral and written negotiations is deemed, under the rule, to embrace the entire agreement, and, if the writing is clear and unambiguous, parol evidence will not be allowed to vary the contract.[191] This is said to be a rule of substantive law which when applicable defines the limits of a contract.[192]

The parol-evidence rule is very frequently advanced and generally applied in arbitration cases.[193] Sometimes the collective agree-

---

[186] Rock Hill Printing & Finishing Co., 21 LA 335, 340 (1953). For other illustrations, see Arbitrator Kabaker in 50 LA 1080, 1082; Gross in 46 LA 882, 884.
[187] See Arbitrator Gorder in 20 LA 880, 889; Horvitz in 9 LA 702, 703; Tischler in 5 LA 282, 283.
[188] John Deere Tractor Co., 5 LA 631, 632 (Updegraff, 1946).
[189] See Arbitrator Anrod in 48 LA 310, 312–313; Summers in 48 LA 137, 142; McCoy in 2 LA 367, 370–371.
[190] New York City Omnibus Corp., 7 LA 794, 802 (1947).
[191] See Wigmore, Evidence, §2400 (2d Ed.); Cohn v. Dunn, 149 Atl. 851, 70 A.L.R. 740 (Conn., 1930). For full discussion of this rule, see United Drill & Tool Co., 28 LA 677, 679–683 (Cox, 1957).
[192] 2 Williston, Contracts, §631 (1920 Ed.).
[193] See Arbitrator Sullivan in 54 LA 1029, 1034; Stouffer in 52 LA 796, 800; Morris in 51 LA 1146, 1149; Murphy in 49 LA 841, 847; Sembower in 49 LA 1, 5; Kates in 48 LA 773, 775; Autrey in 45 LA 783, 786; Abernethy in 44 LA 183, 187; Quinlan in 38 LA 714, 715; Hebert in 29 LA 667, 671;

ment will provide specifically against verbal agreements that conflict with it.[194]

While some might argue that arbitrators should consider any evidence showing the true intention of the parties and that this intention should be given effect whether expressed by the language used or not, the general denial of power to add to, subtract from, or modify the agreement provides special justification for the observance of the parol-evidence rule by arbitrators.

There are exceptions to the parol-evidence rule, however. Thus, a collateral agreement not intended to be reduced to writing or an entirely distinct contemporaneous agreement may be held valid.[195] Moreover, an arbitrator may permit the use of parol evidence to show fraud or mutual mistake at the time of negotiations.[196] Then, too, if the contract is ambiguous, evidence of the precontract negotiations is admissible to aid in the interpretation of the ambiguous language.[197]

It should also be remembered that the parties to a contract may amend or add to it by subsequent agreement, as was elaborated by Arbitrator A. R. Marshall:

"Although the Labor Agreement is the chief instrument that guides the parties in their relationships there frequently arises an occa-

---

Beatty in 26 LA 100, 102; Feinberg in 25 LA 385, 390; Margulies in 19 LA 683, 685; Cahn in 10 LA 577, 578; Cornsweet in 9 LA 598, 599; Leonard in 9 LA 501, 502; Brandschain in 6 LA 603, 609; Lappin in 6 LA 395, 396; Updegraff in 5 LA 747, 749: Whiting in 3 LA 482, 486; McCoy in 3 LA 257, 258. The rule might be held waived if not advanced at the hearing. See American Can Co., 1 ALAA ¶67,165 (1943).

[194] As in Pillsbury Mills, Inc., 14 LA 1045, 1047–1048 (Kelliher, 1950).

[195] See Arbitrator Merrill in 46 LA 503, 505; Cox in 28 LA 677, 680–681; Spillane in 23 LA 574, 580; Gregory in 8 LA 428, 429. Also see Roberts in 50 LA 413, 416–417; Krimsly in 42 LA 311, 313. A party alleging a contemporaneous oral agreement has the burden of proving it by clear and convincing evidence. See Arbitrator Howlett in 52 LA 252, 255; Dugan in 46 LA 1018, 1020–1021; Tongue in 32 LA 708, 711. Also see Yagoda in 48 LA 1040, 1044. Arbitrators have held the collective agreement to be the controlling document where it conflicts with group insurance policies. See Arbitrator Howlett in 43 LA 913, 917; Griffin in 32 LA 3, 5; Stutz in 24 LA 318, 319.

[196] International Harvester Co., 17 LA 592, 594 (Forrester, 1951); Terre Haute Water Works Corp., 5 LA 747, 749 (Updegraff, 1946). Also see this Chapter, topics titled "Remedies for Mistake"; "Waiver and Estoppel."

[197] See Chapter 9, topic titled "Precontract Negotiations." In Brigham Apparel Corp., 52 LA 430, 431 (1969), Arbitrator Andersen acted on the basis that the parol-evidence "doctrine does not preclude the admissibility of evidence designed to explain an ambiguity or to establish the meaning of terms or provisions which have a particular trade or occupational meaning."

sion when it is thought necessary or desirable to clarify, add to, or change the Agreement in some manner. This is what a side agreement does. They are very commonly used because the parties find them useful in some instances and necessary in other cases."[198]

Furthermore, on the basis of very strong proof the collective agreement may be held to have been amended by subsequent practice based upon mutual intent for a definite modification.[199]

---

[198] Fox Manufacturing Co., 47 LA 97, 101 (1966).
[199] See Chapter 12, subtopic titled "Amendment of Contract."

CHAPTER 11

PRECEDENT VALUE OF AWARDS

Diverse views exist concerning the use of prior awards as precedents in the arbitration of labor-management controversies. The Authors propose to develop some of these views and to consider the degrees of precedential force actually exerted by arbitration awards. In order to obtain a more accurate and realistic picture of the use of awards, some consideration will be given to the force of legal decisions under the doctrine of state decisis. A comparison of arbitration awards and legal decisions, it is believed, will lead to helpful conclusions concerning the precise effect of arbitration awards as precedent. It is believed also that the views expressed by individual arbitrators will be especially enlightening.

The reporting of labor arbitration awards has been said to represent a necessary means of making available one of the most hopeful factors in lessening the economic and social cost of industrial disputes.[1] It also has been said that arbitrators are producing a tremendous mass of hard, practical experience in the field of labor relations and that the welfare of the country demands that their expressions of experience be made available to labor and management.[2]

It is obvious, however, that the most logical reason for reporting awards is to make them available for some type of precedential or guidance use in other cases. Publication of awards also is an effective way to help insure accountability of arbitrators. No doubt, an arbitrator will take greater care to make his award clear and his reasoning

---

[1] Statement of John W. Taylor, "Reporting of Labor Arbitration: Pro and Con," 1 Arb. J. (N.S.) 420 (1946). Publication of awards is strongly favored by unions, management, and arbitrators alike according to statistics in Warren & Bernstein, "A Profile of Labor Arbitration," 16 LA 970, 983 (1951).
[2] Statement of Theodore Kheel, "Reporting of Labor Arbitration: Pro and Con," id. at 424. Publication of awards also makes them widely available as university teaching materials.

logical if he knows that the award will be subject to public inspection. The old Holmesian adage that the best test of truth is in the open market would appear to be applicable here. If the product of labor arbitration is worthy, it can survive open-market inspection.

While emphasizing the importance of independent thinking by arbitrators, Arbitrator A. R. Marshall recognized that the reasoning used and the principles enunciated by outstanding arbitrators have had a decidedly good effect on the general caliber of arbitration decisions.[3] Arbitrator Carl A. Warns has stated that "it is obvious that in arbitration as in other fields, respect must be paid to accumulated wisdom and experience."[4] Reported awards have been said to be "live tools, to be used in shaping and applying the collective bargaining agreement."[5] Arbitrator Arthur Ross once commented that "published awards are not binding on another arbitrator, but the thinking of experienced men is often helpful to him."[6] Arbitrator Raymond Roberts, in turn, has stated that prior awards "may be referred to for advice and for statements of the prevailing rule and standards."[7] Numerous other arbitrators have made similar statements.[8] These statements are consistent with the undoubted wisdom of seeking to profit by past experience. Published awards on a matter will, in any event, provide the setting for evaluating related cases.[9]

A highly practical need for the reasoned opinions of prior awards was made clear in the report of an emergency board created under the Railway Labor Act. One conclusion of the board was that the principal cause of the large number of undisposed claims before the First Division of the National Railroad Adjustment Board was that the First Division did not write fully reasoned opinions or encourage such opinions by referees assigned to it. The result was the accumula-

---

[3] Day & Zimmermann, Inc., 51 LA 215, 219 (1968).
[4] Cochran Foil Co., 26 LA 155, 157 (1956).
[5] Justin, "Arbitration: Precedent Value of Reported Awards," 21 LRRM 8, at 8 (1947).
[6] S. H. Kress & Co., 25 LA 77, 79 (1955). Similarly, see Arbitrator Larkin in 47 LA 513, 517.
[7] National Lead Co., 28 LA 470, 474 (1957).
[8] E.g., Arbitrator Whyte in 47 LA 1065, 1072; Tsukiyama in 47 LA 1051, 1053; Teele in 46 LA 215, 218; Lugar in 40 LA 343, 348; Thompson in 29 LA 518, 523; Boles in 26 LA 84, 87; Scheiber in 25 LA 379, 381–382; Reid in 25 LA 146, 149; Livengood in 21 LA 456, 460; Wettach in 19 LA 797, 799; Schmidt in 19 LA 432, 434.
[9] See Statement of Arbitrator John Dunlop in Pratt & Whitney Co., 28 LA 668, 672 (1957).

tion of a vast number of awards of no precedential value and of no assistance in the application of rules interpreted by the awards.[10]

A cogent statement regarding use of prior awards is that of Arbitrator Maurice H. Merrill:

"As to arbitral decisions rendered under other contracts between parties not related to those in the case at hand, usefulness depends upon similarity of the terms and of the situations to which they are to be applied. They must be weighed and appraised, not only in respect to these characteristics, but also with regard to the soundness of the principles upon which they proceed. Certainly, an arbitrator may be aided in formulating his own conclusions by knowledge of how other men have solved similar problems. He ought not to arrogate as his own special virtues the wisdom and justice essential to sound decision. In at least two instances in recent months I have found by investigation that a strong current of arbitral decision had overborne my first impression of the implications of particular language. To yield to this 'common sense of most,' especially as, on examination, the reasoning on which it was based carried plausibility, was neither to evade my responsibility nor to sacrifice my intellectual integrity. Contrariwise, it reduced discriminatory application of similar provisions. It enabled me to make use of the wisdom of others at work in the same field."[11]

Prior awards can be of value to parties engaged in the negotiation of collective bargaining agreements. Knowledge of how specific clauses have been interpreted by arbitrators will help negotiators avoid pitfalls in the use of agreement language. That awards have such value has been recognized, and is one of the important reasons for writing fully reasoned opinions.[12]

The opponents of the precedential use of awards often voice the same type of criticism sometimes directed toward the doctrine of prece-

---

[10] Report to the President by the Emergency Board created July 18, 1947 (Report dated July 30, 1947). In contrast to Division I, Divisions II, III, and IV do prepare fully reasoned opinions. Sometimes arguments before a referee sitting with one of these Divisions will consist largely of debates about the meaning and applicability of particular precedents. See Miller, "The Railroad Adjustment Board," 3 Arb. J. (N.S.) 181 (1948); Garrison, "The National Railroad Adjustment Board: A Unique Administrative Agency," 46 Yale L. J. 567, 581–582 (1937). Also see Daugherty, Whiting & Guthrie, "Arbitration by the National Railroad Adjustment Board," Arbitration Today 93–127 (BNA Incorporated, 1955).

[11] Merrill, "A Labor Arbitrator Views His Work," 10 Vanderbilt L. Rev. 789, 797–798 (1957).

[12] Crane Carrier Co., 47 LA 339, 341 (Merrill, 1966); Deep Rock Oil Corp., 11 LA 25, 26 (Merrill, 1948).

dent in law; i.e., the binding force of prior decisions ties the present
to the past in such a degree as to stultify progress, and the observance
of precedent becomes an end in itself, with the result that justice sometimes is forced to give way to the symmetrical majesty of the decisions.
These antagonists assert that the arbitrator should search for a rule
of reason which will render justice and at the same time permit the
parties to continue "living together"; they say that the desirable rule
is determined in part by the character of the disputants—by their
economic position, their strength or weakness, their importance to the
community, the history of their past relationships, and their objectives
in taking their present stand. These factors require each case to be
decided on its own and explain why two arbitrators dealing with
different parties but similar facts will arrive at seemingly opposing
decisions.[13]

Another argument is that arbitration proceedings are private business matters, involving the presentation of confidential data which
should be kept secret from competitors. In this regard it may be noted,
however, that the private nature of arbitration and the obligation
not to publish or comment publicly on the award without the consent
of the parties are emphasized by the Code of Ethics and Procedural
Standards for Labor-Management Arbitration.[14]

It is also said that one of the great advantages of arbitration,
namely, its high degree of informality, would be lost should the arbitration tribunal be bound by precedent and legalism. One of the strongest
and most bitter statements against giving precedential force to awards
was by Leo Cherne:

> "The effects of publishing domestic arbitration awards are in-
> evitable and inevitably undesirable. The fact of publication itself cre-
> ates the atmosphere of precedent. The arbitrators in each subsequent
> dispute are submitted to the continuous and frequently unconscious
> pressure to conform. A bad award—and there are such in both the
> courtroom and the arbitration tribunal—will have the effect of stimu-

---

[13] See views of Levenstein in "Reporting of Labor Arbitration: Pro and
Con," 1 Arb. J. (N.S.) 420, 426 (1946).

[14] Part I, §8; Part II, §6; Part III, §7. 15 LA 961 et seq. Neither the
FMCS nor the AAA will release any award for publication unless both parties
have consented. Occasionally the collective agreement itself will expressly prohibit
publication without mutual consent of the parties. See Major Collective Bargaining
Agreements: Arbitration Procedures 77 (U.S. Dept. of Labor Bull. No. 1425–6,
1966).

lating other bad ones; a good one, by the weight of precedent, may be applied where the subtleties of fact should urge a different award."[15]

Despite the opposition of such critics, it is now recognized widely that prior awards do have great value. Many employers and unions acknowledge arbitration awards to be a rapidly expanding body of labor-management rules. Parties in arbitration cases very frequently cite and discuss many prior awards of other parties as well as their own.[16] Indeed, parties sometimes specifically authorize or even direct their arbitrator to consider awards of other arbitrators.[17] Parties thus appreciate the great value of using tested experience, and even where collective agreements expressly provide that no decision is to establish a precedent for other cases, actual practice under such provisions may disclose the parties themselves applying decisions to other disputes involving the same point.[18]

Also from the standpoint of the parties, recognition that "the body of recorded decisional precedent in arbitration proceedings is constantly growing" was one reason for preparation of a dissenting opinion by a partisan member of a tripartite board "to guide those who may have occasion in the future to refer to the decision and award as a precedent."[19]

Of great practical significance is the attitude of arbitrators themselves. An extensive survey of labor arbitration disclosed that 77 per-

---

[15] Cherne, "Should Arbitration Awards Be Published?" 1 Arb. J. (N.S.) 75 (1946). For other arguments against use of awards as precedent, see McPherson, "Should Labor Arbitrators Play Follow-The-Leader?" 4 Arb. J. (N.S.) 163 (1949).

[16] For example, see Kankakee Electric Steel Co., 53 LA 178, 181–183 (Sembower, 1969); Dow Chemical Co., 22 LA 336, 341–345 (Klamon, 1954). For many other such instances the reader need merely scan volumes of reported awards.

[17] Burris Mills, Inc., 26 LA 250, at 250 (Whittaker, 1956); Southern Bell Telephone & Telegraph Co., 25 LA 85, 86 (Alexander, et al., 1955). One survey indicated that there is considerable support, particularly from the management side, for the proposition that arbitrators should make greater use of precedent in deciding cases. Jones & Smith, "Management and Labor Appraisals and Criticisms of the Arbitration Process: A Report With Comments," 62 Mich. L. Rev. 1115, 1150 (1964). Union acceptance of the precedent concept is illustrated by the fact that precedents are often used in arbitration under the AFL–CIO internal disputes plan. For instance, see Umpire Cole in 43 LA 255, 257, and in 43 LA 249, 252.

[18] Rosenblatt, "The Impartial Machinery of the Coat and Suit Industry," 3 Arb. J. 224, 226 (1939).

[19] Journal Publishing Co., 22 LA 108, 113 (1954).

cent of the 238 responding arbitrators believed that precedents, even under *other* contracts, should be given "some weight."[20]

Arbitrators are often unwilling to rely solely upon the parties for making precedents available, and such arbitrators "search out" relevant awards on their own.[21] Where one party has cited precedents, the arbitrator may allow the other party time to consider and answer them.[22] Where neither party has cited precedents, the arbitrator may invite both parties to submit any that are considered relevant.[23]

While it might be expected that persons trained in law would be more inclined to adhere to the doctrine of precedent, it is important to note that many of the arbitrators who give precedential force to prior awards are not lawyers. The Authors, like another observer, have received the "distinct impression that laymen in a judicial position are quite as eager as lawyers in pursuing, and quite as contentious in dissecting, the available precedents * * *."[24]

Accepting, then, that prior awards are of some precedential value and realizing that they do have and will continue to have some force as precedent, the Authors turn to inquire into the quantum of force given them and to the probable course of future development. In seeking an answer it is helpful to consider the force given legal decisions under the doctrine of precedent.

Precedent Value of Legal Decisions

Confusion results when one has in mind the inflexible English rule of stare decisis because even in England the force actually given to prior decisions is not always absolute and inflexible. Therefore, for the purpose of this discussion, the Authors speak of the doctrine of precedent as meaning *the force which is given to prior decisions.*

---

[20] Warren & Bernstein, "A Profile of Labor Arbitration," 16 LA 970, 982 (1951).

[21] E.g., Arbitrator Solomon in 49 LA 718, 723; Krimsly in 47 LA 518 522; Merrill in 47 LA 339, 341; McCoy in 47 LA 164, 169; Traynor in 46 LA 53, 57; Hebert in 44 LA 226, 232; Reid in 26 LA 258, 262–263; Thompson in 23 LA 39, 42; Marshall in 22 LA 181, 182–183; Gross in 20 LA 749, 750; Emery in 19 LA 812, 815; Klamon in 19 LA 639, 646; Dworkin in 19 LA 65, 70.

[22] Simmons Co., 15 LA 921, 922 (Elson, 1950).

[23] A. D. Juilliard & Co., 15 LA 934, 938 (Maggs, 1951).

[24] Garrison, "The National Railroad Adjustment Board: A Unique Administrative Agency," 46 Yale L. J. 567, 583 (1937).

A basic difference between the Anglo-American systems of law and the civil law systems is the official nonacceptance of the doctrine of precedent by the civil law systems. But Professors Shartel and Wolff pointed out that the difference between the common law and civil law systems on this point is more apparent than real in that our own courts do not follow precedents as slavishly as many of their utterances would suggest, while the civil law courts do not ignore precedents to the extent that their general theories might indicate. Further, they pointed out that in all of the civil law countries the binding force of precedents is recognized definitely in practice in one situation, termed a settled course of decision. Thus, although a single prior decision is not regarded as binding, a settled course of decision on a point is regarded as controlling.[25] As will appear presently, the precedential operation of labor arbitration awards seems to be something of a hybrid of the civil law and common law approaches.

But how does the doctrine of precedent under the common law system operate? As was indicated above, it does not operate as inexorably as many persons assume. Salmond, in his *Jurisprudence,* considered the English doctrine of precedent.[26] He divided decisions into two classes, authoritative and persuasive. These were said to differ in the kind of influence exercised by each upon the future course of the administration of justice.

The authoritative precedent was defined as one which judges must follow whether they approve of it or not; the persuasive precedent, one which judges are under no obligation to follow, but which is to be taken into consideration and given such weight as its intrinsic merit seems to demand.

Salmond specified as authoritative the decisions of the superior courts of justice in England.[27] A great body of decisions were designated as persuasive, including (1) foreign judgments, and more espe-

---

[25] Shartel and Wolff, "Civil Justice in Germany," 42 Mich. L. Rev. 863, 866–867 (1944). Also see Lloyd, Introduction to Jurisprudence 366–372 (2d Ed., 1965); Bodenheimer, Jurisprudence 290–291 (Harvard Univ. Press, 1962).

[26] Salmond on Jurisprudence §53 (11th Ed. by Glanville Williams, 1957). All additional reference to Salmond by the Authors pertain to said §53.

[27] Salmond also divided authoritative precedents into two kinds, absolute and conditional. Absolute decisions must be followed without question, however unreasonable or erroneous they may be considered to be. On the other hand, courts possess a certain limited power to disregard decisions having merely conditional authority.

cially those of American courts, (2) decisions of superior courts in other parts of the British Commonwealth of Nations, (3) the judgments of the Privy Council when sitting as the final court of appeal from other members and parts of the Commonwealth, and (4) judicial dicta. Thus we see that even in England, where the most extreme adherence to the doctrine of precedent is found, a large body of decisions have persuasive force only.

In America, the doctrine is even more flexible than in England.[28] That the degree of control to be allowed a prior decision varies with the particular case has been emphasized by von Moschzisker, who, after referring to the tenet that stare decisis is based on the premise that certainty in law is preferable to reason and correct legal principles, made the following statement:

> "If the rule demanded absolute rigid adherence to precedents (as in the English House of Lords), then there might be good ground for the persistence among the uninformed of the erroneous idea just referred to, but the proper American conception comprehends *stare decisis* as a flexible doctrine, under which the degree of control to be allowed a prior judicial determination depends largely on the nature of the question at issue, the circumstances attending its decision, and, perhaps, somewhat on the attitude of individual participating judges."[29]

Von Moschzisker also spoke of the situation in which the precedent should be departed from:

> "Therefore, except in the classes of cases which demand strict adherence to precedent, when a court is faced with an ancient decision, rendered under conditions of society radically different from those of today, and when it is sought to have this ancient decision control present-day conditions even though the attending facts in the two controversies be alike, still there is nothing in the doctrine of *stare decisis* to prevent a departure from the earlier decision and (in the absence of a legislative enactment covering the matter) the restatement of the governing rule there laid down, or acted on, to meet the change in the life of the people to serve whose best interests it was originally invoked."[30]

Professor Shartel stated that precedents are not self-effectuating; rather, that they control only to the extent that they are accepted

---

[28] For explanations as to why this should be so, see Cross, Precedent in English Law 12–14 (Oxford Univ. Press, 1961).

[29] Moschzisker, "Stare Decisis in Courts of Last Resort," 37 Harv. L. Rev. 409, 414 (1924).

[30] Id. at 418.

as binding by judges in later cases, and that varying force is attached to different kinds of precedents.[31] An effective summary of the American doctrine of stare decisis is contained in Chamberlain's classic statement:

> "A deliberate or solemn decision of a court or judge, made after argument on a question of law fairly arising in a case, and necessary to its determination, is an authority, or binding precedent, in the same court or in other courts of equal or lower rank, in subsequent cases, where 'the very point' is again in controversy; but the degree of authority belonging to such precedent depends, of necessity, on its agreement with the spirit of the times or the judgment of subsequent tribunals upon its correctness as a statement of the existing, or actual law, and the compulsion or exigency of the doctrine is, in the last analysis, moral and intellectual, rather than arbitrary or inflexible."[32]

The essence of the above discussion of the doctrine of precedent at common law supports the foregoing definition of precedent as meaning *the force which is given to prior decisions.* Confusion naturally results when one seeks to limit the doctrine to one of inflexibility, since, in fact, the weight given to any prior decision is a question of degree.

Authoritative Prior Awards

Although prior labor arbitration awards are not binding in exactly the same sense that authoritative legal decisions are, yet they may have a force which can be characterized as authoritative. This is true of arbitration both by permanent umpires and by temporary or ad hoc arbitrators.

Giving authoritative force to prior awards when the same issue subsequently arises (stare decisis) is to be distinguished from refusing to permit the merits of the same event or incident to be relitigated

---

[31] Shartel, Our Legal System and How It Operates 418–419 (Univ. of Mich., 1951). Professor Shartel indicated the several respects in which the variation in weight of precedents is apparent: (1) As regards the place and court in which the precedent is cited—a decision of the supreme court of state X has a different weight when cited in state X than when cited in state Y; (2) as regards the character of the judicial statement—a unanimous opinion will have more weight than a divided opinion; (3) as regards the scope of acceptance of the view—one supported by general authority will be more forceful; (4) as regards age and confirmation in later cases; (5) as regards the subject matter involved in the previous decision. Ibid.

[32] Chamberlain, The Doctrine of Stare Decisis 19 (1885). Also see Catlett, "The Development of the Doctrine of Stare Decisis and the Extent to Which It Should Be Applied," 21 Wash. L. Rev. 159 (1946).

(res judicata).[33] Where a new incident gives rise to the same issue that is covered by a prior award, the new incident may be taken to arbitration but it may be controlled by the prior award.

Another situation (neither stare decisis nor res judicata) which may be noted is that in which an arbitrator enforces the prior award of another arbitrator.[34]

Permanent Umpires

The most pronounced situation in which prior arbitration awards have "authoritative" type force is that of arbitration by permanent umpires or chairmen. In this regard, Umpire Charles C. Killingsworth offered the following basic thought: "Where a reasonably clear precedent can be found in prior Umpire decisions, the considerations in favor of following that precedent are very strong indeed, in the absence of relevant changes in contract language or a showing that the precedent decision or decisions were erroneous."[35] Umpire Harry Shulman, who served for many years as umpire for the Ford Motor Company and the United Automobile Workers, spoke of precedent in permanent umpire systems as follows:

"[I]n this system a form of precedent and stare decisis is inevitable and desirable. I am not referring to the use in one enterprise, say

---

[33] For an analysis of the judicial doctrines of stare decisis, res judicata, and collateral estoppel, see Timken Roller Bearing Co., 32 LA 595, 597–599 (Boehm, 1958). The issuance of an arbitration award generally bars any subsequent court or arbitration action on the merits of the same event. See Chapter 2, topic titled "Federal Law"; Todd Shipyards Corp. v. Marine & Shipbuilding Workers, 242 F.Supp. 606 (DC N.J., 1965); Hi-Torc Motor Corp., 40 LA 929, 930–931 (Kerrison, 1963); Hall v. Sperry Gyroscope Co., 21 LA 758, 762 (N.Y. Sup. Ct., 1954), where numerous court cases are collected. It is not a res judicata situation, however, where an entirely different issue, different party, or different event is involved in the subsequent litigation. See Arbitrator Koven in 52 LA 314, 315 (different issue); Johannes in 45 LA 413, 416 (different party); Brecht in 41 LA 59, 60–61 (similar issue but different incident).

[34] As did Arbitrator Williams in 54 LA 428, 429–430; Koven in 41 LA 1310, 1311–1313; Platt in 11 LA 1175, 1179–1180; Singer in 6 LA 463, 464–465. Also see Singer in 49 LA 991, 994–996; May in 43 LA 433, 439–441; Shaughnessy in 39 LA 636, 639. As to an arbitrator's authority to enforce his own award, see view stated by Arbitrator Koven in 43 LA 1060, 1063.

[35] Goodyear Tire & Rubber Co., 36 LA 1023, 1025 (1961). In this instance, however, he could not find a clear guide from prior umpire decisions. The authoritative force of prior umpire decisions is illustrated by Bethlehem Steel Co., 43 LA 228, 232 (Crawford, 1964). For illustrations as to how basic principles established by prior umpire decisions are utilized, see Courtaulds North American Inc., 47 LA 609 at 609 (McCoy, 1966); United States Steel Corp., 46 LA 414, 416 (Florey, 1966). Of course, a prior umpire decision is not an authoritative precedent for a distinguishable case. See Bethlehem Steel Corp., 47 LA 270, 272 (Gill, 1966).

United States Steel, of awards made by another arbitrator in another enterprise, say General Motors. * * *

"But the precedent of which I am now speaking refers to the successive decisions within the same enterprise. Even in the absence of arbitration, the parties themselves seek to establish a form of stare decisis or precedent for their own guidance—by statements of policy, instructions, manuals of procedure, and the like. This is but a means of avoiding the pain of rethinking every recurring case from scratch, of securing uniformity of action. * * *

"When the parties submit to arbitration in the system of which I speak, they seek not merely resolution of the particular stalemate, but guidance for the future, at least for similar cases. They could hardly have a high opinion of the arbitrator's mind if it were a constantly changing mind. Adherence to prior decisions, except when departure is adequately explained, is one sign that the determinations are based on reason and are not merely random judgments."[36]

In the full-fashioned hosiery industry prior awards have become a part of the "common law" of the industry. "The Impartial Chairman will hesitate, therefore, to write any decision contrary to the precedents already established."[37] In that industry the principles enunciated in the decisions, not the personage of the Impartial Chairman, are all-important; the mere fact that the person of the Impartial Chairman changes from time to time does not lead to the voiding of past decisions.[38]

---

[36] Shulman, "Reason, Contract, and Law in Labor Relations," 68 Harv. L. Rev. 999, 1020 (1955), reprinted in Management Rights and the Arbitration Process 169, 193–194 (BNA Incorporated, 1956). For more on the important role of precedent in umpireships, see Killingsworth, "Arbitration: Its Uses in Industrial Relations," 21 LA 859, 861–863 (1953); Reilly, "Arbitration's Impact on Bargaining," 16 LA 987, 990–991 (1951); Davey, "The John Deere-UAW Permanent Arbitration System," Critical Issues in Labor Arbitration 161, 174 (BNA Incorporated, 1957); Wolff, Crane & Cole, "The Chrysler-UAW Umpire System," The Arbitrator and the Parties 111, 115, 128 (BNA Incorporated, 1958).
[37] Kennedy, Effective Labor Arbitration 63 (1948). "In fact each decision becomes a part of the National Labor Agreement which provides 'all decisions and rulings of the Impartial Chairman * * * not in conflict with the terms of this Agreement are hereby adopted and shall be binding upon the parties hereto.'" Id. at 62.
[38] Full-Fashioned Hosiery Industry, 2 ALAA ¶67,542 (1946). Somewhat similar to national labor-management arrangements as concerns precedential force of decisions, umpire decisions rendered under the AFL-CIO Internal Disputes Plan have been researched for precedential use: "While it is clear that each complaint made under this plan must rise or fall on its own facts and merits it is also clear that there should be some uniformity in the interpretation of" the Plan. Steelworkers v. Mechanics Educational Soc., 51 LA 1080, 1084 (Kleeb, 1968).

One permanent board of arbitration, Arbitrator Herbert Blumer serving as Chairman, was called upon to render an opinion as to the binding effect of decisions made at grievance meetings or arbitration hearings. After defining "grievance" as referring to a particular complaint and "issue" as referring to the general contractual question that is raised, the arbitrators made the following statement of position:

"(1) A grievance which has been settled in grievance meetings or in arbitration or which has not been appropriately appealed if the proposed settlement has not been accepted, remains settled. This grievance cannot be reinstituted.

"(2) An issue that is settled by the parties in grievance meetings remains settled. Such a settlement, if accepted by both parties, is equivalent to a separate, local agreement. [For full discussion of the precedential effect of grievance settlements, see Chapter 5.]

"(3) Either party may bring an issue to this Board (by the appropriate procedure) even though the party has not appealed the decision on a grievance incorporating the issue. While the given grievance may not be reinstated, another grievance may be processed to the Board in order that the party may secure a final ruling on the issue.

"(4) A grievance even though generally similar to a grievance which has been settled may be processed if it raises an issue which is anyway different from an issue that has been settled.

"(5) An issue which has been ruled on by an umpire prior to the constitution of this Board remains settled unless the ruling is in conflict with the ruling of other umpires entrusted with the same issue. In such a situation, either party is entitled to a ruling from this Board (by following the procedure prescribed in the Agreement) which will dissipate the conflicting arbitration decisions. Further, if the ruling by the umpire is not clear, either party is privileged to process a grievance to this Board so as to secure a clear ruling on the issue. Also, if the ruling of the umpire on an issue appears not to be in line with the rulings of this Board, a grievance dealing with that issue may be processed to this Board. Rulings by this Board on issues have precedence over the rulings made by other umpires. Issues ruled on by this Board shall remain settled and no grievance clearly confined to such issues may be processed to this Board."[39]

Bethlehem Steel Company Umpire Ralph T. Seward has stated that "though he does not consider that he is necessarily bound by

---

[39] Tennessee Coal, Iron & Railroad Co., 6 LA 426, 429 (1945). It was decided that the issue presently involved had been ruled on previously, so the grievance was denied. Also see American Steel and Wire Co., 11 LA 945 at 945 (Seward, 1948).

the decisions of prior umpires, he does believe that a heavy burden of persuasion rests on the party who urges that such prior decisions should be reversed."[40] When this heavy burden is met and a later umpire is convinced that a prior decision is erroneous, it will be reversed.[41]

Then, too, umpires sometimes reverse themselves, as Umpire Seward has.[42] Finally, Umpire Seward has observed that mere dictum statements of other Bethlehem system umpires "are entitled to respect," but are not binding.[43]

In implementing such views as those noted hereinabove, the awards of many permanent umpires are published for the guidance of both unions and management and to discourage the appeal of cases which do not present issues or involve situations different from those previously considered.

Temporary Arbitrators

Prior awards also may have authoritative force where temporary arbitrators are used. An award interpreting a collective agreement usually becomes a binding part of the agreement and will be applied by arbitrators thereafter.[44]

---

[40] Bethlehem Cornwall Corp., 25 LA 894, 897 (1956). For more of Umpire Seward's views on this, see Bethlehem Steel Co., 20 LA 87, 90–91 (1953). Also see Arbitrator McDermott in 46 LA 774, 775–776; Crawford in 41 LA 587, 590.

[41] Bethlehem Steel Co., 24 LA 379, 380–381 (Recommended decision by Alexander, approved by Seward, 1955). Where there was a much more complete presentation of evidence before a subsequent umpire, he modified a prior umpire ruling. United States Steel Corp., 48 LA 1149, 1158–1159 (McDermott, 1967).

[42] See comments of Permanent Arbitrator David L. Cole in International Harvester Co., 21 LA 214, 215 (1953).

[43] Bethlehem Steel Co., 28 LA 351, 352 (1957).

[44] E.g., Arbitrator Altrock in 48 LA 502, 504–505; Schmertz in 47 LA 1100, 1101; Stouffer in 47 LA 464, 468–469; Small in 47 LA 212, 214; Dworkin in 47 LA 217, 223 (Cf. Dworkin in 43 LA 120, 126); Murphy in 46 LA 798, 800–801; Gibson in 46 LA 709, 710–711; Cahn in 46 LA 517, 518–519; Rock in 45 LA 43, 46; Hawley in 43 LA 391, 394; Stein in 43 LA 178, 180–181; Johnston in 42 LA 304, 306–307; Lehoczky in 40 LA 499, 502; Gillingham in 39 LA 567, 574; Wyckoff in 36 LA 1341, 1347; Ross in 32 LA 646, 648–649; Moore in 29 LA 83, 85; Roberts in 28 LA 470, 476–477; Daugherty in 25 LA 426, 428; Kelliher in 16 LA 816, 818; Smith in 12 LA 132, 135; Abernethy in 7 LA 202, 213. For the opposing view, see Baab in 23 LA 562, 567; Wallen in 9 LA 757, 763 (but Wallen did hold prior awards binding in 43 LA 1041, 1042–1043 and in 16 LA 365, 368). Arbitrator Ryder, in 22 LA 605, 606, would give such awards "serious and weighty consideration though not binding."

This was emphasized by Arbitrator Whitley P. McCoy, who declared that where a "prior decision involves the interpretation of the identical contract provision, between the same company and union, every principle of common sense, policy, and labor relations demands that it stand until the parties annul it by a newly worded contract provision."[45] Moreover, Arbitrator McCoy expressed the view that where identical contractual provisions are adopted by joint negotiations of a union with a number of competing companies, an award construing the provision should be given great weight in like cases involving any of the companies.[46]

Arbitrator Russell A. Smith has urged that a proper regard for the arbitration process and for stability in collective bargaining relations requires acceptance by an arbitrator, even though he is not technically bound, of any interpretation of the parties' contractual relations rendered by a previous arbitrator, if in point and if based on the same agreement.[47]

It seems obvious that the binding force of any award ordinarily should not continue after the provision upon which it is based is materially changed or is eliminated entirely from the parties' agreement.[48] However, if the agreement is renegotiated without materially changing a provision that has been interpreted by arbitration, the parties may be held to have adopted the award as a part of the contract.[49] Indeed, the binding force of an award may even be strengthened by such

---

[45] Pan American Refining Corp., 2 ALAA ¶67,937, p. 69,464 (1948).

[46] American-St. Gobain Corp., 39 LA 306, at 306 (1962). Arbitrator Bauder considers that prior awards involving identical contractual language between locals of the same union and divisions of the same company should be given "great, but not controlling, weight." Reynolds Mining Corp., 33 LA 25, 28 (1959). But see Arbitrator Rubin in 35 LA 680, 681.

[47] O & S Bearing Co., 12 LA 132, 135 (1949), where the prior award was not followed, however, since it involved a temporary special agreement rather than the agreement before Arbitrator Smith. In general accord with Arbitrator Smith's suggestion, see Arbitrator Duff in 46 LA 132, 137; Hebert in 46 LA 140, 146; Turkus in 38 LA 679, 680.

[48] Bethlehem Steel Co., 41 LA 624, 626 (Porter, 1963). Similarly, see Arbitrator Dunau in 43 LA 661, 662–664. An award may cease to be binding even before the contract expires if the parties follow a practice inconsistent with the award. Waterfront Employers Assn. of the Pacific Coast, 2 ALAA ¶67,949 (1948).

[49] See Arbitrator Stouffer in 50 LA 208, 212; Dworkin in 43 LA 715, 721; Marshall in 64–1 ARB ¶8292; Geissinger in 41 LA 348, 351; Crawford in 37 LA 711, 715; Uible in 33 LA 816, 819; Justin in 22 LA 721, 725–727; Kelliher in 16 LA 816, 818; Wallen in 16 LA 365, 368; McCoy in 16 LA 217, 218–219. Also see Killion in 37 LA 853, 856–857; Kaplan in 18 LA 777, 779–780. Contra, Kamin in 50 LA 1093, 1095–1096.

enegotiation without change.[50] For instance, while Arbitrator Jules
. Justin apparently would ordinarily give an award of the same
▸arties only "a 'persuasive' force which compels consideration," still,
▾here the parties did not disturb an award in renegotiating their
.greement, he found "no basis or warrant to disturb it."[51]

The parties are free in any case to stipulate as to what preceden-
ial role a forthcoming award shall play.[52]

While Arbitrator Herbert Blumer declared that "it is only fair
.nd reasonable to expect an arbitrator's decision to apply to subse-
₁uent cases of the same nature" and that "the refusal to apply the
.rbitrator's decision to similar cases leaves unsolved and unsettled the
eneral problem covered by the decision," nevertheless he added that
he refusal to apply an award to cases of the same nature is justified
▾here it is shown that any one of the following elements is present:
1) The previous decision clearly was an instance of bad judgment;
2) the decision was made without the benefit of some important
.nd relevant facts or considerations; or (3) new conditions have arisen
₁uestioning the reasonableness of the continued application of the deci-
ion.[53] Other arbitrators have agreed that an arbitrator is justified
₁ refusing to follow an award which he considers to be clearly er-
oneous,[54] or one whose continued application is rendered questionable
▸y changed conditions.[55] Arbitrator Leo Kotin has expressed the view
▸hat a party is not ordinarily justified in seeking an award contrary

---

[50] See Arbitrator Johnston in 42 LA 304, 306–307; Justin in 22 LA 721,
25–727; Wallen in 16 LA 365, 368. Also see Geissinger in 43 LA 1022, 1024.

[51] Federal Bearings Co., 22 LA 721, 725–727 (1954).

[52] For instance, see Arbitrator Beatty in 49 LA 55, 56 (award to govern
ne disposition of pending like grievances); Smith in 42 LA 517, 523 (award
ot to bind other parties to master agreement); Anderson in 19 LA 106, at
06 (award to govern future like grievances). Only a small percentage of collective
▸greements contain any provision as to the precedential effect of awards. See
Basic Patterns in Labor Arbitration Agreements," 34 LA 931, 940 (1960). Some-
₁mes the arbitrator himself will specify that his award is not to have authoritative
recedential force (see Arbitrator Smith in 48 LA 213, 219; Lehoczky in 36 LA
1, 22).

[53] Inland Steel Company, 1 ALAA ¶67,121, p. 67,248 (1944). Arbitrator
▸lark Kerr would add obvious and substantial errors of fact or law and the
▸ck of fair and full hearing as justification for refusal to apply the prior award,
ut he would place the burden of proof upon the party alleging any of these
▸rounds. Waterfront Employers Assn. of Pacific Coast, 7 LA 757, 758 (1947).

[54] See Arbitrator Carter in 52 LA 357, 359; Waldron in 49 LA 314, 319;
Iilpert in 32 LA 1013, 1017; Klamon in 19 LA 779, 787; Komaroff in 15 LA
26, 630–631.

[55] See Braun Baking Co., 43 LA 433, 439–440 (May, 1964); Armstrong
:ork Co., 34 LA 890, 894 (Morvant, 1960).

to a prior decision by submitting (in a different case but with the
same issue) additional evidence to a subsequent arbitrator;[56] but in
several cases the presentation of additional evidence or clarification
of previously presented evidence has produced a contrary award by
the subsequent arbitrator.[57]

An arbitrator understandably may feel less firmly bound by another arbitrator's award if it is not accompanied by a reasoned opinion;[58] and dictum statements of a prior ad hoc arbitrator may carry
little or no weight.[59]

Frequently when prior awards are cited as being authoritative,
the arbitrator will avoid such effect by distinguishing them.[60] Often
the distinction will be clear, but there are cases where the drawing
of a distinction can prove to be troublesome. For instance, in one
case the company cited an award rendered two years earlier in a case
involving the same company but a different union. The arbitrator,
James J. Healy, said that the similarity of the two cases made the
prior award germane; moreover, the question itself was not one of
peculiar relevancy to a particular bargaining unit. But then he stated
that, while the prior decision carried weight in appraising the merits
of the present case, its mere existence did not foreclose the arbitrator
from reaching a different conclusion. Apparently realizing the incon-
sistency, he qualified the latter statement by saying that there was
no adequate opinion in the earlier award and that it was on a slightly
different issue. The arbitrator expressed the dilemma in the following
words:

> "Placing the Company in the position of having two arbitrators
> make different rulings on the same question is repugnant to all parties;
> the very dignity of arbitration is endangered, and, on the surface,
> it would appear that arbitration is dangerously subjective. Therefore,

---

[56] Douglas Aircraft Co., 49 LA 744, 748, 752 (1967), where he also indicated
that this may be justified where production of the evidence was foreclosed by
circumstances beyond the control of the party.
[57] See Arbitrator Jones in 53 LA 477, 480; McDermott in 48 LA 1149,
1158–1159; Cayton in 45 LA 889, 891–892; Murphy in 38 LA 1199, 1207.
[58] See General Dynamics Corp., 53 LA 424, 427 (Roberts, 1969); John
J. Nissen Baking Co., 48 LA 12, 17 (Fallon, 1966).
[59] See Blaw-Knox Company, 50 LA 1086, 1088 (Meltzer, 1968).
[60] E.g., Arbitrator Erbs in 50 LA 744, 750; McCoy in 48 LA 983, 988;
Marshall in 46 LA 617, 620; Koven in 45 LA 955, 957–958; Crawford in
44 LA 924, 926; Boles in 43 LA 258, 261; Valtin in 43 LA 79, 81–83; Davey
in 23 LA 343, 347–348; Abruzzi in 18 LA 193, 195; Kirsh in 6 LA 124,
126; Carmichael in 3 LA 798, 800–801.

it is only after sincere and prolonged deliberation that the undersigned makes the following ruling."[61]

It appears that the fact situations of the cases were enough alike that he did not feel entirely free to deviate from the prior award because to do so would make it appear that arbitration is "dangerously subjective." He concluded, however, that there was sufficient distinction between the cases to justify a refusal to be bound by the prior award.

Persuasive Prior Awards

While prior awards have authoritative force in some situations, the great mass of awards are considered to have persuasive force only.[62] Nothing is settled by saying that prior awards do or do not have the force of precedent. Rather, it is essential that one recognize that the precedential force of prior awards always is a question of degree. The range is broad, including prior awards that have absolutely no persuasive force, through those with varying degrees of persuasiveness, to those which are binding in future like cases. The dividing line cannot be drawn with finality, just as the line between authoritative force and persuasive force cannot be established absolutely. Confusion is avoided by remembering that it is only a question of degree in each particular case. The following analysis is made with these thoughts in mind.

There are many cases where, in varying degree, the arbitrator was persuaded by prior awards; in some of these cases the arbitrator spoke in terms of finding "support" in prior awards, but in either case the effect is the same—the' arbitrator relied upon or otherwise made use of prior awards.[63]

---

[61] Brown & Sharpe Mfg. Co., 7 LA 134, 138–139 (1947). For at least two of the possible courses of action available to a third arbitrator when confronted with the conflicting decisions of two prior arbitrators, see Mallinckrodt Chemical Works, 50 LA 933, 935 (Goldberg, 1968); Board of Education, New York City, 45 LA 43, 44 (Rock, 1965). Also see Arbitrator Wann in 55 LA 510, 513.

[62] Salmond defined the persuasive precedent as one which depends for its influence upon its own merits and upon that alone. Salmond on Jurisprudence §53 (11th Ed. by Glanville Williams, 1957). He also included judicial dicta with the persuasive precedents. Thus it might be said that dicta in prior awards differ from decisions in prior awards primarily in regard to the degree of force exerted by each.

[63] For many cases, see p. 258 of the 1960 edition of this book. For some of the many later cases, see Arbitrator Whitney in 53 LA 1078, 1086; Dworkin

It is easy for an arbitrator to be persuaded by or to rely upon a prior award that is in near agreement with his own views. Moreover, most *careful* awards rely upon principles which will command respect by reason of their logic and the fair result which they yield under the facts. In law we speak of the "reasonably prudent man." Most good awards can be said to incorporate the view of the reasonably prudent man, and it is reasonable to expect other men, in similar cases, to be persuaded to some extent by the awards and their supporting reasoning. In particular, the considered judgment of any widely known and respected arbitrator cannot be dismissed lightly or ignored.[64]

The attitude of one eminent arbitrator confronted by an award of another eminent arbitrator is possibly typified by the late David A. Wolff (Chrysler Umpire) in considering an award of the late Harry Shulman (Ford Umpire):

"The Chairman realizes that, despite the great similarity of contract provisions and their apparent common origin and despite the fact of similarity of parties, location and type of business, there are distinctions which exist and must be observed. The parties are not the same parties. Their practices are not identical. Even their application of the considered contract provisions has varied. Further, while Dr. Shulman and the Chairman both act as umpires they were not selected, nor do they act for, the same parties. The parties making the selections undoubtedly had in mind the known general thinking of each at the time of selections and made the selections on an individual basis. On the other hand, points of similarity may not be disregarded. In addition the Chairman has high regard for Dr. Shulman's sincerity, clarity of thought, and reasoning processes. The Chairman does not propose to unthinkingly adopt Dr. Shulman's determination in another

---

in 52 LA 1158, 1162; Oppenheim in 52 LA 1164, 1166; Bradley in 52 LA 773, 780; Cox in 49 LA 837, 838–839; Seinsheimer in 49 LA 468, 470; Seward in 49 LA 334, 336–337; McIntosh in 48 LA 1121, 1122; Lugar in 48 LA 463, 470–476; Tsukiyama in 47 LA 781, 783; Morgan in 47 LA 756, 760; Merrill in 47 LA 635, 638–639; Wolff in 47 LA 552, 553; Stouffer in 47 LA 464, 469–470; Griffin in 47 LA 257, 258; Whyte in 47 LA 26, 29; Kotin in 46 LA 378, 381; Tongue in 46 LA 374, 377; Murphy in 46 LA 289, 292; Petree in 46 LA 283, 285–286; Klein in 46 LA 203, 208; Wagoner in 46 LA 81, 87–90; Larkin in 46 LA 39, 43; McCoy in 46 LA 11, 15; Leach in 45 LA 1039, 1044; Solomon in 45 LA 751, 758; Wren in 45 LA 244, 245–246; Hebert in 44 LA 226, 231–233.

[64] See statement of Arbitrator Spaulding in 25 LA 181, 185; Reynard in 22 LA 880, 882–883; Gorder in 20 LA 880, 888; Fulda in 18 LA 315, 319; Aaron in 8 LA 261, 272; Levy in 6 LA 397, 402. Also see Stix in 47 LA 870, 873.

case as his own in the instant case. However, to the extent to which he believes it here applicable, he makes use of it with appreciation."[65]

In any event, it would seem that when either party cites an award, the arbitrator cannot disregard it lightly. Good faith and respect for the citing party require the arbitrator at least to consider the contentions of the party.[66] An interesting case illustrating the extreme to which an arbitrator might go in order to consider a prior award relied upon by one of the parties is that in which the hearing was reconvened for that basic purpose.[67] While precedential use of awards occurs primarily in "rights" arbitration, such use is by no means unknown to "interests" arbitration as well. Prior awards are considered fairly frequently in "interests" cases.[68] In some circumstances a prior "interests" award may have special persuasive significance to other parties "similarly facing the same inquiry."[69]

In all civil law countries, as we have noted, the binding force of precedents is recognized definitely in practice in one situation, which is called a settled course of decision. An analogous situation is found in labor arbitration awards. Where there is a settled course of arbitral decision on a point, the principle stated in the decisions is often very persuasive, or at least highly comforting support for a later ruling.[70]

---

[65] Chrysler Appeal Board Case No. 573 (1948).
[66] Even where the parties agreed that their arbitrator was not bound by precedents, he considered those cited by the parties. Meyer's Bakery of Little Rock, 38 LA 1135, 1140 (Hon, 1962). Sometimes the bulk of an opinion will be devoted to the discussion of precedents cited by the parties and researched by the arbitrator. See Watkins Trucking, Inc., 48 LA 1101, 1102–1104 (Klein, 1967). In Bethlehem Steel Co., 43 LA 79, 83 (1964), Arbitrator Valtin stated that he had extensively reviewed the precedents cited by the parties "because he thinks that it is important to make clear what effect is being given them in deciding the present case."
[67] Boston Daily Newspapers, 6 LA 179, 183–186 (Wallen, 1946).
[68] For example, in Patriot News Co., 15 LA 871, 874 (1950), Arbitrator Egan spoke of studying "dozens of arbitration decisions."
[69] Union Railroad Co., 20 LA 219, 224 (Gilden, 1953).
[70] For many cases, see p. 260 of the 1960 edition of this book. For later cases, see Arbitrator Dworkin in 53 LA 394, 398–399; Mueller in 48 LA 1331, 1334; Dammers in 48 LA 1327, 1330; McDermott in 48 LA 1108, 1111; Livengood in 47 LA 1170, 1174; Tsukiyama in 47 LA 1051, 1053; Krimsly in 47 LA 159, 162; Kesselman in 47 LA 154, 157–158; Teple in 46 LA 1106, 1110; King in 46 LA 827, 829; Moskowitz in 46 LA 388, 395; Graff in 46 LA 329, 332–333; Koven in 45 LA 398, 404–406; Witney in 45 LA 97, 98–99; Tongue in 44 LA 475, 477; Solomon in 41 LA 1257, 1267–1268; Brown in 35 LA 560, 566; Hogan in 34 LA 158, 161–163. In Koehring Div., 46 LA 827, 829 (1966), Arbitrator King stated that parties should take notice as to how given provisions have generally been interpreted by arbitrators, and that if a party desires some other meaning, it should negotiate the other meaning into the contract by clear language.

It is unlikely that any such course of decision will be achieved upon faulty reasoning. In this sense, it can be correctly said that "it is not the long line of previous decisions that is determinative," but "the validity of the reasoning behind the principle."[71]

By no means are arbitrators always swayed by cited awards, even awards which are reasonably in point. Arbitrators are alert to distinction between cases.[72] Moreover, when arbitrators cannot agree with the conclusion of cited precedents, they do not hesitate so to state.[73] It is also possible that prior decisions, though sound for their day, will be considered to be out of step with changed times.[74]

When confronted with conflicting prior awards, an arbitrator may reject those which are unconvincing or which fail to set forth with clarity the reasons therefor and he may accept clearly reasoned opinions with the statement that the "reasoning applies with persuasive force to the instant case."[75] Where there are clear lines of arbitral precedent going each way on an issue, the arbitrator will of course use his best judgment as to which line should be applied to the case under consideration.[76]

Sometimes an arbitrator will dismiss cited awards with the statement that he has examined them carefully and has found nothing to alter his thinking on the matter.[77] Then, too, an arbitrator might

---

[71] Bachmann Uxbridge Worsted Corp., 23 LA 596, 602 (Hogan, 1954).
[72] E.g., Arbitrator Killion in 47 LA 435, 437; Sembower in 47 LA 414, 420; Witney in 47 LA 272, 277; Solomon in 46 LA 993, 1004; Kates in 45 LA 120, 124; Townsend in 28 LA 664, 668; Phelps in 28 LA 88, 91; Hebert in 23 LA 497, 502; Abernethy in 23 LA 379, 382; Scheiber in 15 LA 111, 114. In Glidden-Durkee Div., 52 LA 457, 461–463 (1969), Arbitrator Edgett distinguished precedents cited by a party, and he supplied other precedents to "buttress" his finding.
[73] See Arbitrator Bothwell in 52 LA 1035, 1043; Hilpert in 47 LA 129, 140; Autrey in 45 LA 783, 787; Altieri in 43 LA 602, 604; Crane in 36 LA 635, 639; McCoy in 20 LA 34, 36; Handsaker in 16 LA 964, 966; Whitton in 6 LA 714, 716.
[74] As in Southern Airways, Inc., 47 LA 1135, 1141 (Wallen, 1966).
[75] Consolidated Chemical Industries, Inc., 6 LA 714, 716–717 (Whitton, 1947). Similarly, Arbitrator Bellman in 52 LA 1218, 1220; Bothwell in 51 LA 1129, 1133; Lennard in 49 LA 76, 77; Teple in 46 LA 1106, 1110; Tsukiyama in 46 LA 849, 851; Yagoda in 46 LA 692, 696; Merrill in 19 LA 854, 855–856.
[76] See Arbitrator Stieber in 48 LA 1069, 1073; Beatty in 40 LA 544, 547; Valtin in 35 LA 535, 541. In Omaha Cold Storage Terminal, 48 LA 24, 26, 32 (Doyle, 1967), the Arbitrator decided contra to his view in an earlier case with other parties, now having been persuaded by a later line of cases which he considered to be better reasoned.
[77] See Arbitrator Prasow in 44 LA 691, 694, and in 7 LA 67, 69; Cheney in 8 LA 518, 525. Also see Steiber in 46 LA 967, 970.

acknowledge cited awards but give no indication as to their persuasive force upon him.[78]

Because arbitrators recognize that use of their awards may be sought in similar cases, they sometimes caution against the precedential use of a particular award, especially if there are features peculiar to that case which make the award inappropriate as a guide for any other case.[79]

Finally, in the event of court review an award may be strengthened in the eyes of the court if supported by prior awards.[80]

Precedent and Development of Substantive Principles

The controversy over use of awards as precedents is accompanied by a related and integrated controversy regarding development of substantive principles through arbitration. The authors offer in the following discussion their own evaluation of these matters.

The authors are convinced that considerable use of precedents in arbitration is inevitable. They are convinced also that development of substantive principles through arbitration is likewise inevitable— and desirable. Most arbitrators, able though they be, do not possess enough of Solomon's wisdom to justify rule by man instead of rule by principle. Not all cases can best be decided in a vacuum.

The authors agree that the question is "not *whether* principles are being evolved, but *what* they are and *how far* they should carry."[81]

As to "how far" substantive principles should carry, it is obvious that no principle should be promiscuously applied.[82] In any event, general principles should be applied to cases only after careful thought and thorough consideration.

---

[78] See Anaconda Wire & Cable Co., 10 LA 20, 24 (Scheiber, 1948); Lebanon Steel Foundry, 6 LA 633, 634 (Brandschain, 1947).
[79] See Arbitrator Kornblum in 45 LA 885, 889; Seitz in 29 LA 322, 324; Ralston in 20 LA 465, 467; Wolff in 19 LA 430, 431; Prasow in 6 LA 323, 326.
[80] See Bakery Workers Union v. Hall Baking Co., 69 N.E.2d 111, 115 (Mass. Sup. Ct., 1946).
[81] Petshek, "Discussion of Principles Emerging From Grievance Arbitration," 1953 Proceedings of Industrial Relations Research Association 154, 156.
[82] See words of Arbitrator Joseph Shister in Electro Metallurgical Co., 22 LA 684, 686 (1954).

Precedent, the Siamese twin of substantive principles,[83] is totally out of place in some arbitration cases. In other cases only a little use of precedent is justified. In a sense, each collective bargaining relationship is a world of its own—a world which may be given features of infinite variety under the virtually unlimited right of contract enjoyed by Americans. The phrase "each case must be decided on its own" does have a definite place in arbitration.

Still, issues being arbitrated do frequently have counterparts in reported awards. In arbitration as in other important areas of human activity, growth and refinement through use of tested experience is inevitable and desirable. Then, too, from the arbitrator's viewpoint, it is comforting to know that his decision finds support in other awards, or to know at least that it does not vary drastically from what others have decided.

No arbitrator can serve long without becoming aware of the existence of certain more or less generally recognized principles and penetrating propositions. It is questionable whether any arbitrator, and especially the experienced, can always eliminate the influence of what he knows others have done.

It is difficult to determine precisely the extent to which substantive principles are being evolved and applied since, for a variety of reasons, many awards are never published.[84] Frequently where an arbitrator might be inclined to consider precedent, there simply is no reported case similar to that under consideration.[85]

Moreover, many of the awards which are published have little

---

[83] "The appearance of precedent in labor arbitration probably results less from a conscious effort to develop a case law, and more from general recognition of the validity of certain principles for the treatment of similar cases." Holman, "The Back-Pay Issue in Arbitration," I. L. Research, Vol. II, No. 1, pp. 6–8 (1955).

[84] For explanation of the factors which one publisher considers in deciding which awards to publish, of those which are available for publication, see Stewart, "Memo From the Executive Editor," 36 LA vii–viii (1962), where users of LA are also assured that they "can rely on the long experience and mature judgment of BNA's editorial staff to provide full coverage of significant new decisions." Nonetheless, concern has been expressed that the total of all published awards is only a small percentage of those rendered. Jones & Smith, "Management and Labor Appraisals and Criticisms of the Arbitration Process: A Report With Comments," 62 Mich. L. Rev. 1115, 1152 (1964).

[85] See Arbitrator Ray in 55 LA 54, 57; Sherman in 52 LA 561, 564; Roberts in 48 LA 978, 979; Neville in 48 LA 120, 123–124; Dworkin in 44 LA 1274, 1277; Helfeld in 43 LA 445, 446; Scheiber in 40 LA 1061, 1063; Singletary in 29 LA 504, 507; Marshall in 23 LA 228, 233; Merrill in 22 LA 706, 707; Treiman in 19 LA 807, 808; Schmidt in 19 LA 432, 434.

utility as guides for other parties. However, as one spokesman has stated, some decisions, "due to the logic of their problem-solving persuasiveness, are potential candidates for wide application beyond the parties."[86] And, as another observer has begrudgingly admitted, "From the published awards, it is evident that standards have been turned by the lathe of arbitration for a wide range of problems."[87]

The authors readily agree with those who believe that the term "principle" is "abused when it is employed as a synonym for *binding* precedent."[88] However, it should be recognized that regarding the development of principles for widespread application there is not too much concern with the "authoritative" or "binding" force which awards often exert in subsequent cases involving the same parties and the same contract language. Rather, the emphasis falls much more on the "persuasive" or "guiding" force that awards under *other* contracts often exert. Arbitration awards under other contracts *are* important as precedents. A glance through recent volumes of reported arbitration decisions reveals the very frequent citation, discussion, and use of such precedents.

The persuasive or guidance force of prior awards varies widely. Many awards exert little or no force, but some awards are quite useful in other cases, especially where there is a settled course of arbitral decision on a point.

Furthermore, a substantive principle might be revealed through a single well-reasoned decision, which becomes the "leading case" on the point.[89] Then, too, arbitrators sometimes discern substantive principles through a process which might be called "negative inference." For instance, in one case Arbitrator Whitley P. McCoy stated that he had been "unable to find any authority among the thousands of arbitration decisions" for a holding that a certain type of conduct by an employee constitutes a punishable offense.[90] In another case,

---

[86] Petshek, "Discussion of Principles Emerging From Grievance Arbitration," 1953 Proceedings of Industrial Relations Research Association 154, 157.

[87] Manson, "Substantive Principles Emerging From Grievance Arbitration: Some Observations," 1953 Proceedings of Industrial Relations Research Association 136, 137.

[88] Id. at 74 (emphasis added).

[89] For example, see Struthers-Wells Corp., 17 LA 483, 485 (Strashower, 1951), recognizing the leading-case status of a decision of Umpire Harry Shulman; Grand Sheet Metal Products Co., 17 LA 388, 390 (Kelliher, 1951), noting the leading case status of a decision by Arbitrator Irving Bernstein.

[90] U.S. Pipe & Foundry Co., 20 LA 513, 516 (1953). A similar approach was taken by Arbitrator Teple in 45 LA 671, 680; Hebert in 37 LA 42, 49;

388   How Arbitration Works

Arbitrator Edwin R. Teple upheld a company's actions in training employees for duties outside their assigned classification where a study of arbitration decisions revealed no suggested limitation upon the right of management to do so.[91]

In actual practice it is not at all uncommon for an arbitrator to preface the assertion of an established rule or principle with some statement such as "it has become a well-accepted principle," or "it is a general rule that," or "the consensus is," or "the weight of authority is." In doing this arbitrators frequently cite precedents,[92] but just as frequently they cite few or no specific cases to support their assertion that the principle does in fact exist.[93] Possibly the true significance of such statements lies in the fact that the arbitrator was willing to accept arbitration awards as a source of fundamental substantive principles.

Finally, it must be emphasized that a great contribution to industrial stability lies in the probability that many disputes are settled by the parties themselves before reaching arbitration because they are aware of prior awards on the issue involved which point out the objective merits of contentions and which are indicative of results likely to be had through arbitration.

Howard in 23 LA 440, 446; Cheit in 21 LA 293, 298; Williams in 20 LA 784, 787.

[91] Goodyear Atomic Corp., 45 LA 671, 680 (1965).

[92] For many cases, see p. 264 of the 1960 edition of this book. For some of the many later cases, see Arbitrator McDermott in 48 LA 1108, 1111–1112; Gibson in 48 LA 974, 976–977; Livengood in 47 LA 1170, 1174; Merrill in 47 LA 1120, 1125; Whyte in 47 LA 1065, 1069; Tsukiyama in 47 LA 1051, 1053; Kerrison in 47 LA 580, 581; Larkin in 47 LA 382, 384; Kelliher in 47 LA 284, 285–286; Volz in 47 LA 263, 265; McCoy in 46 LA 1063, 1065; Stouffer in 46 LA 654, 659; Tatum in 46 LA 583, 588; Moskowitz in 46 LA 388, 395; Kotin in 46 LA 378, 381–382; Tongue in 46 LA 374, 377; Klein in 46 LA 203, 208; Dworkin in 45 LA 1109, 1115; Williams in 45 LA 877, 879; Witney in 45 LA 97, 98–99; Solomon in 44 LA 161, 165–168.

[93] For many cases, see p. 264 of the 1960 edition of this book. For some of the many later cases, see Arbitrator Geissinger in 50 LA 181, 184; McIntosh in 49 LA 581, 583; Chalfie in 49 LA 117, 120; Keefe in 48 LA 1077, 1081; Graff in 48 LA 1065, 1068; Kabaker in 48 LA 925, 928; Johnson in 48 LA 186, 187; Bailer in 48 LA 157, 160; Hebert in 47 LA 761, 767; McCoy in 47 LA 752, 754; Prasow in 47 LA 726, 734; Mullin in 47 LA 629, 633; Altrock in 47 LA 621, 629; Kelliher in 47 LA 582, 583; Cohen in 47 LA 547, 549; Boothe in 47 LA 336, 338–339; Feinberg in 46 LA 1129, 1131; Shipman in 46 LA 833, 837; Tatum in 45 LA 1030, 1033; Bauder in 45 LA 430, 433; Roberts in 44 LA 919, 920; Block in 43 LA 97, 101; Marshall in 42 LA 945, 946; Autrey in 41 LA 796, 799. However, if the parties themselves allege existence of established principle, they should be prepared to prove it. See comments of Arbitrator Fisher in 27 LA 812, 814; Hill in 25 LA 587, 591.

CHAPTER 12

CUSTOM AND PAST PRACTICE

Unquestionably custom and past practice constitute one of the most significant factors in labor-management arbitration. Evidence of custom and past practice may be introduced for any of the following major purposes: (1) to provide the basis of rules governing matters not included in the written contract; (2) to indicate the proper interpretation of ambiguous contract language; or (3) to support allegations that clear language of the written contract has been amended by mutual action or agreement. In the present Chapter use of custom and past practice for each of these purposes will be discussed.[1]

Custom and Practice as Part of the Contract

Under certain circumstances custom and past practice may be held enforceable through arbitration as being in essence a part of the parties' "whole" agreement. Some of the general statements of arbitrators in this regard may be noted:

Arbitrator Dallas L. Jones: "It is generally accepted that certain, but not all, clear and long standing practices can establish conditions of employment as binding as any written provision of the agreement."[2]

Arbitrator Arthur T. Jacobs: "A union-management contract is far more than words on paper. It is also all the oral understandings, interpretations and mutually acceptable habits of action which have grown up around it over the course of time. Stable and peaceful relations between the parties depend upon the development of a mutually satisfactory superstructure of understanding which gives operating significance and practicality to the purely legal wording of the

---

[1] For other discussions of custom and practice, see McLaughlin, "Custom and Past Practice in Labor Arbitration," 18 Arb. J. 205 (1963); Mittenthal, "Past Practice and the Administration of Collective Bargaining Agreements," Arbitration and Public Policy 30 (BNA Incorporated, 1961); Davis, "Arbitration of Work Rules Disputes," 16 Arb. J. 51 (1961); Aaron, Davis, and Bailer, "The Uses of the Past," Arbitration Today 1–24 (BNA Incorporated, 1955).
[2] Alpena General Hospital, 50 LA 48, 51 (1967).

written contract. Peaceful relations depend, further, upon both parties faithfully living up to their mutual commitments as embodied not only in the actual contract itself but also in the modes of action which have become an integral part of it."[3]

Arbitrator Marlin M. Volz: "[I]t is well recognized that the contractual relationship between the parties normally consists of more than the written word. Day-to-day practices mutually accepted by the parties may attain the status of contractual rights and duties, particularly where they are not at variance with any written provision negotiated into the contract by the parties and where they are of long standing and were not changed during contract negotiations."[4]

Arbitrator Whitley P. McCoy: "Custom can, under some circumstances, form an implied term of a contract. Where the Company has always done a certain thing, and the matter is so well understood and taken for granted that it may be said that the contract was entered into upon the assumption that that customary action would continue to be taken, such customary action may be an implied term."[5]

Arbitrator Maurice H. Merrill: "In the light of the [arbitration] decisions, * * * it seems to me that the current of opinion has set strongly in favor of the position that existing practices, in respect to major conditions of employment, are to be regarded as included within a collective bargaining contract, negotiated after the practice has become established and not repudiated or limited by it. This also seems to me the reasonable view, since the negotiators work within the frame of existent practice and must be taken to be conscious of it."[6]

Numerous other arbitrators,[7] and the U.S. Supreme Court,[8] have expressed similar thoughts.

Statement of such general thoughts, however, does not always decide specific cases. The problem remains: Under what circumstances shall custom be binding for the future? Are all types of matters to be treated as "custom" for this purpose? What of the clash between

---

[3] Coca-Cola Bottling Co., 9 LA 197, 198 (1947).
[4] Metal Specialty Co., 39 LA 1265, 1269 (1962).
[5] Esso Standard Oil Co., 16 LA 73, 74 (1951). In Beaunit Fibers, 49 LA 423, 424 (1967), Arbitrator McCoy emphasized the "under some circumstances" words of limitation.
[6] Phillips Petroleum Co., 24 LA 191, 194–195 (1955).
[7] See Arbitrator Mills in 53 LA 845, 848; Kates in 48 LA 1275, 1276; Koven in 47 LA 353, 355; Schmidt in 44 LA 467, 468; Horlacher in 43 LA 145, 148; E. Jones in 29 LA 372, 375; Prasow in 27 LA 6, 10; Dworkin in 24 LA 614, 618–619; Levinson in 23 LA 277, 280; Gorder in 20 LA 880, 883; Hale in 20 LA 818, 823; Wirtz in 20 LA 276, 280; Updegraff in 20 LA 243, 244; Talbott in 19 LA 628, 629; Marshall in 17 LA 105, 108; Gilden in 17 LA 81, 85; Whiting in 16 LA 115, 117; Hampton in 16 LA 59, 62.
[8] United Steelworkers v. Warrior & Gulf Navigation Co., 80 S.Ct. 1347, 1351–1352 (1960).

two legitimate objectives: (1) the need for industrial stability, which is served by custom, and (2) the need for managerial freedom of action to operate the business efficiently?

Examination of many reported decisions suggests that there are no unanimously accepted standards for determining precisely under what circumstances unwritten practices and custom will be held binding by arbitrators, or for determining what matters may be the subject of such binding practice. Certainly the result reached in any given case may depend in part upon the thinking of the particular person who has been authorized by the parties to decide the case. However, it may be noted that in some of the cases cited above, and in other cases, certain considerations have been stressed.

First, even assuming that a matter is such that it may otherwise be given "binding practice" effect as an implied term of the agreement, it will not be given that effect unless it is well established—strong proof of its existence will ordinarily be required.[9] Indeed, many arbitrators have recognized that, as stated by Arbitrator Jules J. Justin: "In the absence of a written agreement, 'past practice,' to be binding on both Parties, must be (1) unequivocal; (2) clearly enunciated and acted upon; (3) readily ascertainable over a reasonable period of time as a fixed, and established practice accepted by both Parties."[10] However, the mutual acceptance may be tacit—

---

[9] Arbitrator Tsukiyama in 47 LA 781, 783; Seitz in 43 LA 322, 325; Gorsuch in 41 LA 105, 108; Davis in 39 LA 97, 99; Justin in 24 LA 753, 754; Updegraff in 20 LA 243, 244. Also see Yaffee in 50 LA 14, 16–17. The party alleging the existence of a binding practice has the burden of establishing it. Columbian Carbon Co., 48 LA 919, 922 (Ray, 1967).

[10] Celanese Corp. of America, 24 LA 168, 172 (1954). These three requirements (or similar requirements) have been recognized by Arbitrator Mills in 53 LA 845, 848–849; Karlins in 51 LA 551, 555–556 (quoting Arbitrator Solomon); Dolson in 51 LA 281, 283; Anrod in 51 LA 90, 93, 95; Beatty in 49 LA 55, 57; Updegraff in 47 LA 720, 722–723; Scheiber in 46 LA 372, 374 ("Just as the proverbial solitary swallow does not make a spring or summer, so a past practice, to be binding, must be long-continued, well understood, and mutually concurred in by the parties"); Wood in 45 LA 881, 884; Gorsuch in 41 LA 105, 108 (quoting Arbitrator Sembower); Kovenock in 40 LA 300, 304; McDermott in 37 LA 967, 970; Dall in 37 LA 849, 852; Mittenthal, "Past Practice and the Administration of Collective Bargaining Agreements," Arbitration and Public Policy 30, 32 (BNA Incorporated, 1961). Also see Arbitrator Belcher in 52 LA 571, 574; Block in 48 LA 1118, 1120; Cahn in 47 LA 330, 331–332; Doyle in 44 LA 718, 719; Schmidt in 44 LA 467, 468; Hilpert in 36 LA 1169, 1172. In Univac, 54 LA 48, 52 (Volz, 1969), the arbitrator stated that "Leniency by individual supervisors must be distinguished from mutual agreement or acquiescence by the contracting parties in a consistent course of repetitive action."

an implied mutual agreement—arising by inference from the circumstances.[11]

While another factor sometimes considered is whether the activity was instituted by bilateral action or only by the unilateral action of one party,[12] it would seem that the fact of unilateral establishment should not necessarily be given controlling weight.[13]

Where a practice is otherwise found to be binding, question may arise as to its scope. In this general regard, it appears reasonable that the underlying circumstances must be considered to give a practice its true dimensions: "A practice is no broader than the circumstances out of which it has arisen, although its scope can always be enlarged in the day-to-day administration of the agreement."[14]

The question remains as to what types of matters should be given "binding practice" status as an implied term of the agreement (assuming the practice is otherwise adequately established under standards such as those noted hereinabove). One arbitrator suggested that an established practice may be unilaterally discontinued if it involves a "gratuity," but that it is binding if it concerns a "working condition."[15] But another arbitrator doubted the validity of this test and suggested that perhaps the best test, though admittedly inexact, is that

---

[11] See Arbitrator Wood in 45 LA 881, 884; Jones in 44 LA 698, 700; Schmidt in 44 LA 467, 468; Updegraff in 20 LA 309, 311. Awareness of a practice is to be presumed from its long-established and widespread nature. Bethlehem Steel Co., 33 LA 374, 376 (Valtin, 1959). For a discussion of what a party should do to avoid being bound by a practice commenced by the other party, see Donaldson Co., 20 LA 826, 830–831 (Louisell, 1953).

[12] See Arbitrator McCoy in 49 LA 423, 424; Roberts in 48 LA 1166, 1168; Turkus in 47 LA 75, 78; Dugan in 46 LA 1007, 1008; Howlett in 42 LA 385, 388; Seinsheimer in 36 LA 166, 170; Wirtz in 20 LA 276, 280; Cahn in 17 LA 780, 783. Also see Mittenthal, "Past Practice and the Administration of Collective Bargaining Agreements," Arbitration and Public Policy 30, 33 (1961).

[13] See Sterling Furniture Mfrs., 46 LA 705, 706 (Hanlon, 1966); Union Asbestos & Rubber Co., 39 LA 72, 75 (Volz, 1962), both holding a practice as to employee benefits to be binding though unilaterally instituted by the employer. In contrast, in some of the decisions cited in the preceding footnote certain methods of operations unilaterally instituted by management, in the exercise of discretion in the performance of management functions, were held not to constitute binding practices. Thus the critical consideration may be the subject matter of the practice rather than whether it was established by unilateral or bilateral action.

[14] Mittenthal, "Past Practice and the Administration of Collective Bargaining Agreements," Arbitration and Public Policy 30, 32–33 (1961).

[15] Fawick Airflex Co., 11 LA 666, 668–669 (Cornsweet, 1948).

the usage, to achieve contractual status, must concern a "major condition of employment."[16]

The latter arbitrator cited Professors Archibald Cox and John T. Dunlop, who had urged that: "A collective bargaining agreement should be deemed, unless a contrary intention is manifest, to carry forward for its term the major terms and conditions of employment, not covered by the agreement, which prevailed when the agreement was executed."[17] As noted above, the "major condition of employment" test is inexact. From whose standpoint is something "major"? Where is the line to be drawn? Cox and Dunlop included as "major" such things as "basic wages, seniority, and pensions," but they were apparently willing to exclude such matters as job content, work loads, and incentive systems.[18]

The line between practices which are binding and those which are not may well be drawn on the basis of whether the matter involves methods of operation or direction of the working force, or whether it involves a "benefit" of peculiar personal value to the employees (though also involving the employer's purse).

Arbitrators are often hesitant to permit unwritten past practice or methods of doing things to restrict the exercise of legitimate functions of management. For example, such hesitance was evidenced by Arbitrator Whitley P. McCoy:

> "But caution must be exercised in reading into contracts implied terms, lest arbitrators start re-making the contracts which the parties have themselves made. The mere failure of the Company, over a long period of time, to exercise a legitimate function of management, is not a surrender of the right to start exercising such right. If a Company had never, in 15 years and under 15 contracts, disciplined an employee for tardiness, could it thereby be contended that the Company could not decide to institute a reasonable system of penalties for tardiness? Mere non use of a right does not entail a loss of it."[19]

---

[16] Phillips Petroleum Co., 24 LA 191, 194 (Merrill, 1955). Other arbitrators have util᠆᠆᠆d some type of major-minor test: Koven in 47 LA 353, 356; Anrod in 45 I ᠆4, 37–38; Reynard in 25 LA 611, 613; Updegraff in 20 LA 309, 311; Talᵤᵤₜt in 19 LA 628, 629.

[17] Cox and Dunlop, "The Duty to Bargain Collectively During the Term of an Existing Agreement," 63 Harv. L. Rev. 1097, 1116–1117 (1950).

[18] Id. at 1118.

[19] Esso Standard Oil Co., 16 LA 73, 74 (1951). Citing this case with clear approval, see Arbitrator Turkus in 52 LA 493, 496 and in 44 LA 1219, 1223; Ray in 43 LA 395, 399.

One of the most cogent and provocative statements published regarding the binding force of custom was that of Umpire Harry Shulman, in a case involving operating methods and direction of the working force (assignment of work), wherein he urged that past practice not be "enshrined without carefully thought out and articulated limitations":

> "A practice, whether or not fully stated in writing, may be the result of an agreement or mutual understanding. And in some industries there are contractual provisions requiring the continuance of unnamed practices in existence at the execution of the collective agreement. (There are no such provisions in the Ford Agreement or in those of the automobile industry generally.) A practice thus based on mutual agreement may be subject to change only by mutual agreement. Its binding quality is due, however, not to the fact that it is past practice but rather to the agreement in which it is based.

> "But there are other practices which are not the result of joint determination at all. They may be mere happenstance, that is, methods that developed without design or deliberation. Or they may be choices by Management in the exercise of managerial discretion as to the convenient methods at the time. In such cases there is no thought of obligation or commitment for the future. Such practices are merely present ways, not prescribed ways, of doing things. The relevant item of significance is not the nature of the particular method but the managerial freedom with respect to it. Being the product of managerial determination in its permitted discretion such practices are, in the absence of contractual provision to the contrary, subject to change in the same discretion. The law and the policy of collective bargaining may well require that the employer inform the Union and that he be ready to discuss the matter with it on request. But there is no requirement of mutual agreement as a condition precedent to a change of practice of this character.

> "A contrary holding would place past practice on a par with written agreement and create the anomaly that, while the parties expend great energy and time in negotiating the details of the Agreement, they unknowingly and unintentionally commit themselves to unstated and perhaps more important matters which in the future may be found to have been past practice. The contrary holding would also raise other questions very difficult to answer. For example, what is properly a subject of a practice? Would the long time use of a wheelbarrow become a practice not to be changed by the substitution of four-wheeled buggies drawn by a tractor? Or would the long time use of single drill presses be a practice prohibiting the introduction of multiple drill presses? Such restraints on technological change are alien to the automobile industry. Yet such might be the restraints, if past practice were enshrined without carefully thought out and

articulated limitations. Again, when is a practice? How frequently and over how long a period must something be done before it is to be called a practice with the consequences claimed? And how is the existence of the past practice to be determined in the light of the very conflicting testimony that is common in such cases? The Union's witnesses remember only the occasions on which the work was done in the manner they urge. Supervision remembers the occasions on which the work was done otherwise. Each remembers details the other does not; each is surprised at the other's perversity; and both forget or omit important circumstances. Rarely is alleged past practice clear, detailed and undisputed; commonly, inquiry into past practice of the type that is not the result of joint determination or agreement produces immersion in a bog of contradictions, fragments, doubts, and one-sided views. All this is not to say that past practice may not be important and even decisive in applying provisions of the Agreement. The discussion is addressed to the different claim that, apart from any basis in the Agreement, a method of operation or assignment employed in the past may not be changed except by mutual agreement."[20]

Statements by numerous other arbitrators reflect lines of thought similar to the underlying viewpoint of the McCoy and Shulman statements quoted hereinabove.[21]

Arbitrators frequently (but not always) have recognized wide authority in management to control methods of operation and to direct the working forces, which authority includes the right without penalty to make changes *if these do not violate some right of the employees under the written contract.* If a given change or the method of putting it into effect does result in the violation of some contractual right of identified employees, then the arbitrator can be expected to award compensation to the employees for the loss sustained, even if he does not take the further step of ordering management to revert to the prior practice.

---

[20] Ford Motor Co., 19 LA 237, 241–242 (1952). Citing this Shulman statement with clear approval, see Arbitrator Teple in 55 LA 19, 22; Updegraff in 54 LA 869, 871; Solomon in 51 LA 1102, 1107; Eyraud in 49 LA 654, 658; Dugan in 46 LA 1007, 1008; Mittenthal in 46 LA 335, 337, and in 39 LA 65, 67; Turkus in 44 LA 1219, 1222; Ray in 43 LA 395, 399; Scheiber in 42 LA 965, 970–971; Donaldson in 37 LA 528, 531. For additional discussion of this subject, see Shulman, "Reason, Contract, and Law in Labor Relations,' 68 Harv. L. Rev. 999, 1011–1013 (1955), reprinted in Management Rights and the Arbitration Process 169, 184–188 (BNA Incorporated, 1956).

[21] See arbitrators cited in the two preceding footnotes, and see Arbitrator Cahn in 53 LA 809, 810; Roberts in 48 LA 1166, 1168; Turkus in 47 LA 75, 78; Summers in 45 LA 1149, 1151; Updegraff in 45 LA 557, 557–558; Howlett in 42 LA 385, 388. Also see Shister in 54 LA 871, 873. But see Cahn in 51 LA 705, 706.

Numerous cases involving the authority of management to control methods of operation and to direct the working forces are collected in Chapter 13, topics on Control of Quality Standards, Control of Operation Methods (some changes in operation methods may require new rates of pay for jobs affected by the change), Job and Classification Control, Scheduling Work, Determination of Size of Crews, and other such topics. At this point, however, some specific examples may be noted.

For instance, in some cases past practice has not operated to prevent management from changing work schedules,[22] from reassigning work,[23] from determining the number of workers needed on a job,[24] from adding or eliminating job duties within reasonable limits,[25] from eliminating a job,[26] from discontinuing a particular line of business services or activity,[27] from not filling a temporary vacancy,[28] from discontinuing collateral information on seniority lists,[29] from changing the method of using work-progress time cards,[30] from using a formal instead of informal method of determining skill and ability of employees,[31] from rotating certain employees between two operating units to familiarize them with both operations,[32] from changing payday to Friday in order to reduce Friday absenteeism,[33] or from determining

---

[22] See Arbitrator Solomon in 51 LA 1102, 1110; Hebert in 44 LA 226, 233; Howlett in 42 LA 25, 30; Tsukiyama in 41 LA 1115, 1116–1117; Reid in 27 LA 123, 125; Ryder in 24 LA 496, 499–500; McCoy in 16 LA 73, 74–75. Cf., Meyers in 39 LA 93, 95–96.
[23] See Arbitrator Daugherty in 49 LA 234, 236–237; Kesselman in 45 LA 201, 206; Turkus in 44 LA 1219, 1224; Larkin in 43 LA 1064, 1066; Mittenthal in 39 LA 65, 67–68; Beatty in 35 LA 637, 640; Abernethy in 35 LA 353, 356; Blair in 22 LA 701, 703; Shulman in 19 LA 237, 240–242. Cf., Myers in 23 LA 776, 778–779.
[24] See Arbitrator Mittenthal in 42 LA 1188, 1190–1191; Updegraff in 30 LA 115, 117, and in 18 LA 827, 830–831; Marshall in 29 LA 687, 692–693.
[25] See Arbitrator McDaniel in 54 LA 155, 158; Kelliher in 43 LA 1006, 1009–1010; Reynard in 25 LA 611, 613–614; Klamon in 22 LA 336, 342–343, 351; Updegraff in 20 LA 890, 891, and in 18 LA 320, 322–323.
[26] See Arbitrator Warns in 29 LA 324, 326–328, and in 26 LA 155, 160; Warren in 19 LA 283, 286–287.
[27] Detroit Edison Co., 43 LA 193, 209 (Smith, 1964).
[28] Celotex Corp., 43 LA 395, 399–400 (Ray, 1964).
[29] International Harvester Co., 22 LA 191, 192 (Platt, 1954).
[30] W. O. Larson Foundry Co., 42 LA 1286, 1292 (Kates, 1964).
[31] Lockheed Aircraft Corp., 25 LA 748, 751–752 (Williams, 1956). Also see Arbitrator Garrett in 15 LA 840, 841–842.
[32] Mathieson Chemical Corp., 18 LA 620, 624–625 (Smith, 1952). But as to the frequency of shift rotation, see Arbitrator Marshall in 34 LA 345, 349–350.
[33] Glamorgan Pipe & Foundry Co., 46 LA 1007, 1008 (Dugan, 1966).

the frequency of holding safety meetings.[34] But if past practice *supports* management's actions in such matters, it will provide additional reason for upholding management.[35]

In permitting unilateral change by management, arbitrators sometimes have pointed out that the matter may be subject to negotiations if requested by the union, but, if any such negotiations fail to produce agreement, management may exercise its unilateral judgment in making or continuing the change.[36]

In contrast to the above-indicated freedom of management to make changes in the exercise of basic management functions, arbitrators have often ruled custom to be binding where it involved a "benefit" of peculiar personal value to the employees. These cases generally did not involve methods of operation or control of the working force (except perhaps indirectly). Thus, where the benefit was supported by established custom, management was not permitted to discontinue (or in some cases to change) the following "benefits" or "working conditions": wash-up periods,[37] lunch period arrangements,[38] paid work breaks,[39] free coffee or free meals,[40] utilities at discount or nominal charge,[41] bonuses,[42] various other monetary benefits or allow-

---

[34] Ingalls Shipbuilding Corp., 49 LA 654, 657–658 (Eyraud, 1967).
[35] See Arbitrator Snyder in 54 LA 1159, 1162; Holly in 39 LA 496, 500; Reynard in 25 LA 611, 613–614; Whiting in 16 LA 115, 117. Also see McKenna in 48 LA 941, 949.
[36] See Arbitrator Hepburn in 28 LA 467, 467–468; Williams in 25 LA 748, 751–752; Updegraff in 7 LA 943, 945; Whiting in 7 LA 183, 187. It has been suggested also that even concerning changes which management may not be strictly required to discuss, discussion may be "the better practice." Bethlehem Steel Co., 16 LA 68, 70 (Feinberg, 1950). Also see Chamberlain and Kuhn, Collective Bargaining 135–136 (2d Ed., 1965); Chamberlain, "Management's Reserved Rights," Management Rights and the Arbitration Process 118, 145–147 (BNA Incorporated, 1956).
[37] See Arbitrator Holly in 51 LA 549, 551; Duff in 45 LA 277, 279; Anrod in 40 LA 1329, 1331–1332; Killingsworth in 35 LA 929, 930–931; Wirtz in 20 LA 276, 280; Davey in 18 LA 276, 278. Cf., Davey in 49 LA 773, 783–784.
[38] See Arbitrator Kates in 51 LA 490, 493–494; Teple in 40 LA 13, 17; Klamon in 39 LA 964, 974–975; Murphy in 32 LA 228, 233; Wagner in 30 LA 35, 38; Dworkin in 24 LA 614, 619; McCoy in 3 LA 137, 138. Cf., Marshall in 54 LA 311, 314; McIntosh in 33 LA 137, 138–139.
[39] See Formica Corp., 44 LA 467, 468 (Schmidt, 1965); Ingalls Iron Works Co., 32 LA 960, 961 (Reid, 1959).
[40] See Arbitrator Jones in 50 LA 48, 51–52; Wolf in 44 LA 107, 110; Handsaker in 39 LA 1188, 1191; Scheiber in 37 LA 381, 383.
[41] Central Illinois Public Service Co., 42 LA 1133, 1149–1150 (Willingham 1964); Phillips Petroleum Co., 24 LA 191, 195 (Merrill, 1955).
[42] See cases cited in Chapter 13, topic titled "Bonuses," where cases permitting the discontinuance of bonuses are also cited.

ances,[43] maternity leaves of absence,[44] notice to union before discharge for dishonesty is effected,[45] special rights for senior employees,[46] and a wide variety of other "benefits" or "working conditions."[47] In some cases, however, management has been upheld in discontinuing or reducing customary employee benefits.[48] In some of these cases the company in giving the benefit had emphasized that it was to be a gratuity only and not a part of the wage structure, or there was some special justification for discontinuing the benefit.

We have noted that where custom has been enforced the element of "mutuality" has usually been supplied by implication—that is, there has been "implied mutual agreement." In this regard, existing employee benefits usually affect all or at least sizeable groups of employees, and thus are likely to be in the thoughts of union and company negotiators. It may reasonably be assumed that the parties in shaping bargaining demands as to wages and other employee benefits do so with silent recognition of existing unwritten benefits and favorable

---

[43] See Arbitrator Duff in 50 LA 417, 421 (meal and taxi allowance); Kelliher in 48 LA 1022, 1024 (overtime pay); Bernstein in 48 LA 641, 643–647 (overtime pay); Koven in 47 LA 353, 354 (premium pay allowance); Hanlon in 46 LA 705, 706 (paid insurance premiums); Klein in 45 LA 594, 598 (paid insurance premiums); Anderson in 44 LA 66, 73–75 (housing allowance); Rubin in 35 LA 680, 681 (holiday pay); Joseph in 35 LA 374, 377 (right to employee's regular rate when doing lower rated work); Dworkin in 35 LA 228, 233–234 (pay to grievance representatives); Gorder in 20 LA 880, 882–883 (pay for time lost from work while receiving reprimand); Hampton in 16 LA 59, 62 (right to higher rate when substituting on higher-rated work); Gilden in 7 LA 614, 620 (vacation pay).

[44] Northland Greyhound Lines, Inc., 23 LA 277, 280 (Levinson, 1954).

[45] Coca-Cola Bottling Co., 9 LA 197, 198 (Jacobs, 1947).

[46] International Minerals & Chemicals Corp., 36 LA 92, 95 (Sanders, 1960); Fruehauf Trailer Co., 29 LA 372, 375 (Jones, 1957).

[47] See Arbitrator Walker in 55 LA 294, 297–298, 302 (access to vending machines); Kornblum in 52 LA 771, 772 (access to locker and cafeteria); Witney in 51 LA 813, 817 (receiving paycheck during working time); Block in 49 LA 224, 227 (restriction on termination because of age); Summers in 45 LA 1149, 1151–1152 ("short shift" privilege on day before Thanksgiving); Kovenock in 39 LA 907, 909–910 (receipt of paycheck at plant); Volz in 39 LA 72, 75 (furnishing and cleaning of work gloves); Komaroff in 17 LA 395, 398 (free milk).

[48] See Arbitrator Teple in 53 LA 405, 409; Roberts in 48 LA 1166, 1168; Stein in 42 LA 765, 766; Hilpert in 38 LA 267, 268–269; Volz in 37 LA 635, 637–638; McDermott in 36 LA 220, 222; Fallon in 34 LA 59, 62; Kleinsorge in 33 LA 157, 161–164; Reid in 32 LA 960 at 960; Schmidt in 30 LA 593, 595–598; Lynch in 26 LA 749, 750–751; Marris in 24 LA 745, 747–748; Louisell in 20 LA 826, 829–831; Giardino in 19 LA 421, 422; Naggi in 10 LA 804, 805. For cases in which management has been permitted to discontinue bonuses, see Chapter 13, topic titled "Bonuses."

working conditions. This accepted, such matters may well be called "major" (for those who would apply a "major-minor" test).

It may be less plausible to assume that such bargaining demands are shaped with any comparable silent thought as to existing practices regarding methods of operation and direction of the working force—matters legitimately falling within the fundamental areas of basic management responsibility.

In the final analysis, management in most cases is not really oppressed when it is required to continue customary benefits for the remainder of the contract term. Management itself, either unilaterally or by mutual decision, initially agreed to grant the benefits in most cases. In negotiating the collective bargaining agreement management, because of existing benefits, may very well have been faced with tempered wage demands by the employees. On the other hand, in most instances, it does not oppress the employees to deny continuance of established methods of operation or established practice regarding direction of the working force. Management freedom of action in the latter matters, though sometimes considered unjustified by the workers directly affected (frequently a small number), is essential for efficient and progressive operation of the enterprise, and this serves the long-run interests of all the employees as well as management.

The above discussion suggests a test of "employee benefits" vs. "basic management functions," with which test many reported arbitration awards are compatible.[49] Moreover, some of the awards which appear at first glance to be contrary to this test may conform to it upon closer analysis, the award being based in fact upon some clause of the written contract. The test gives the employees the benefit of the doubt as to certain matters and management is given the benefit of the doubt as to others. From this standpoint, too, the test may be deemed "fair" or "just."

---

[49] In some cases the arbitrator has spoken expressly in terms of this distinction between employee benefits and basic management functions as concerns the binding status of practice. See Arbitrator Volz in 54 LA 52, 55–56, and in 39 LA 72, 75; Witney in 51 LA 813, 818–819; Eyraud in 49 LA 654, 657–658; Kates in 48 LA 1275, 1276, and in 44 LA 1217, 1218; Warns in 66–1 ARB ¶8039, p. 3129; Summers in 45 LA 1149, 1151; Kennedy in 45 LA 353, 355; Turkus in 44 LA 1219, 1223–1224; Ray in 43 LA 395, 399–400; Rubin in 42 LA 833, 835–837; Tsukiyama in 41 LA 1115, 1116–1117; Anrod in 40 LA 1329, 1331–1332; Morvant in 39 LA 1020, 1023.

While the above discussion provides some general guides for predicting the extent to which unwritten practice and custom will be enforced by arbitrators, variations will often result from the peculiar facts and circumstances of the individual cases as well as from the thinking of the particular arbitrator making the ruling. It is entirely possible that under very similar circumstances one arbitrator might hold established practice subject to change or discontinuance during the term of the contract only by mutual agreement, but a second arbitrator might hold it subject to unilateral change or discontinuance at any time even without negotiations. Taking an intermediate approach, a third arbitrator might hold the practice subject to unilateral change or discontinuance during the term of the contract, but only after negotiations have failed to produce agreement.[50]

Regulation, Modification, or Termination of Practice as Implied Term of Contract

In a number of cases arbitrators have held a given practice to be binding on management but at the same time have upheld the right of management to regulate and police it against abuse.[51] For example, where management imposed a limitation as to how often employees could take breaks to use the company vending machine, Arbitrator Marlin M. Volz upheld the limitation with the following explanation:

> "[I]nherent in every practice is the principle that it is not to be abused and that, if it is, reasonable corrective action may be taken. It can not be inferred that the other party has accepted or acquiesced in the excesses constituting the abuse so as to make them binding. The employees, no less than management, are under a duty to act reasonably. Both must cooperate and meet the other halfway in following sound industrial practices which will enable the plant to be operated efficiently for the ultimate benefit of the men as well as the Company."[52]

Also, the mere fact that a given employee-benefit practice is binding does not necessarily mean that the administrative arrangements

---

[50] See Ryan Aeronautical Co., 17 LA 395, 398–399 (Komaroff, 1951).

[51] See Arbitrator Miller in 50 LA 974, 976; Kates in 48 LA 1275, 1276, and in 44 LA 1217, 1218; Schmidt in 44 LA 467, 468; Rubin in 42 LA 833, 835–837; Rohman in 40 LA 1217, 1221; Volz in 39 LA 1265, 1269; McIntosh in 33 LA 860, 861–862. Abuse of a practice was one of the factors justifying the termination of the practice by the employer in Kentile Floors, Inc., 55 LA 808, 813 (Cyrol, 1970). Also see Lawson-United Feldspar & Mineral Co., 76 LRRM 1588 (NLRB, 1971).

[52] Metal Specialty Co., 39 LA 1265, 1269 (1962).

by which the company has provided the benefit are frozen.[53] Further-more, in two cases management was permitted to provide substitute parking facilities for employees when the established benefit (parking near work situs) and legitimate management interests came into conflict.[54]

Arbitrators have recognized that an otherwise binding practice may be modified or eliminated where the underlying basis for the practice has changed.[55] The rule was elaborated by Arbitrator Sidney L. Cahn:

"It must be stated as a general proposition that, absent language in a collective bargaining agreement expressly or impliedly to the contrary, once the conditions upon which a past practice has been based are changed or eliminated, the practice may no longer be given effect."[56]

Thus, a 25-year practice of allowing painters ten minutes overtime to clean their brushes could be unilaterally discontinued by management when it eliminated the congestion problem which had been the underlying reason for the practice.[57]

Even absent any such change in the underlying basis of a practice, an impressive line of arbitral thought holds that a practice which is not subject to unilateral termination during the term of the collective

---

[53] Bethlehem Steel Corp., 50 LA 202, 205 (Strongin, 1968), holding that the company could relocate the place of giving medical services by closing a branch dispensary and centralizing all services in one dispensary. For other indications of management control over arrangements in providing employee benefits, see Arbitrator Walker in 55 LA 294, 301–302 (company could reposition vending machines and require employees to use only certain ones); Florey in 48 LA 55, 57 (practice required company to make food service available, but company could decide "how," providing the arrangement be reasonable).

[54] Jervis B. Webb Co., 52 LA 1314, 1315 (Holly, 1969); Beaunit Fibers, 49 LA 423, 424–425 (McCoy, 1967). Exceptions to the requirements of past practice may be justified by special circumstances. See Sterling Brewers, Inc., 53 LA 1078, 1087 (Witney, 1969), where the arbitrator refused to give "slavish adherence" to past practice under the circumstances.

[55] See Arbitrator Kates in 51 LA 490, 493; Crawford in 48 LA 1239, 1242–1243; Kelliher in 48 LA 1000, 1002; Mullin in 47 LA 848, 852–853; Kahn in 42 LA 148, 152; Strong in 41 LA 1038, 1041; Mittenthal in 39 LA 65, 67; Cahn in 34 LA 99, 100. The "maintenance of local working conditions" provisions in steel industry agreements are accompanied by provisions which specifically permit changes by management if the basis for the existence of the local working condition is changed or eliminated. See Arbitrator Garrett in 44 LA 317, 320–321, and in 33 LA 394, 396, 399; Blair in 40 LA 239, 240; Valtin in 36 LA 394, 396.

[56] Gulf Oil Co., 34 LA 99, 100 (1959).

[57] Newport News Shipbuilding & Drydock Co., 48 LA 1239, 1242–1243 (Crawford, 1967).

agreement is subject to termination at the end of said term by giving due notice of intent not to carry the practice over to the next agreement; after being so notified the other party must have the practice written into the agreement to prevent its discontinuance.[58] Arbitrator Richard Mittenthal has explained:

> "Consider first a practice which is, apart from any basis in the agreement, an enforceable condition of employment on the theory that the agreement subsumes the continuance of existing conditions. Such a practice cannot be unilaterally changed during the life of the agreement. For * * * if a practice is not discussed during negotiations most of us are likely to infer that the agreement was executed on the assumption that the practice would remain in effect.

> "That inference is based largely on the parties' acquiescence in the practice. If either side should, during the negotiation of a later agreement, object to the continuance of this practice, it could not be inferred from the signing of a new agreement that the parties intended the practice to remain in force. Without their acquiescence, the practice would no longer be a binding condition of employment. In face of a timely repudiation of a practice by one party, the other must have the practice written into the agreement if it is to continue to be binding."[59]

---

[58] See Arbitrator Jones in 50 LA 48, 51; Guild in 49 LA 94, 96; Dunau in 43 LA 661, 662–664; Koretz in 40 LA 235, 238; Stutz in 14 LA 951, 952–953; Meltzer, "Ruminations About Ideology, Law, and Labor Arbitration," The Arbitrator, the NLRB, and the Courts 1, 35–36 (The Bureau of National Affairs, Inc., 1967); Mittenthal, "Past Practice and the Administration of Collective Bargaining Agreements," Arbitration and Public Policy 30, 56–57 (BNA Incorporated, 1961). Also see Killingsworth in 35 LA 929, 931; McKelvey in 35 LA 602, 606. But see Bernstein in 48 LA 641, 643–647. For NLRB decisions not requiring mutual assent for the discontinuance of a practice after giving due notice of intent not to carry it over to the next agreement, see Murphy Diesel Co., 179 NLRB No. 27 (1970), where the union did not take advantage of opportunity to bargain on the matter after being informed of management's intention to discontinue the practice; Lee Deane Products, Inc., 181 NLRB No. 168 (1970), where there was extensive bargaining before management discontinued the practice. Also see Torrington Co. v. Metal Products Workers, 362 F.2d 677 (CA 2, 1966). There may or may not be a statutory duty to bargain on the discontinuance of a practice. For instance, contrast Hoover Ball & Bearing Co., 187 NLRB No. 56 (1970), with Beacon Journal Publishing Co., 164 NLRB No. 98 (1967). Many arbitrators have taken the view that it is not their function to decide whether any statutory duty to bargain has been violated. See Chapter 10, subtopic titled "The NLRA, the Arbitrator, and the NLRB." In John W. Hobbs Corp., 45 LA 651, 652–654 (1965), Arbitrator Hilpert took this view, but he added that in that case there had been extensive bargaining before management discontinued the practice of supplying work clothing to certain employees. For general discussion of the duty to bargain, see Chapter 13, subtopic titled "The Duty to Bargain: Right of Unilateral Action."

[59] Mittenthal, "Past Practice and the Administration of Collective Bargaining Agreements," Arbitration and Public Policy 30, 56 (BNA Incorporated, 1961). In contrast, repudiation of a practice which gives meaning to ambiguous language in the written agreement would not be significant—the effect of this kind of

Another possible basis for upholding the refusal to continue a practice is a finding that any binding status of the practice ended through the give and take of bargaining.[60] Then, too, the termination of a practice may be based upon its gradual discontinuance over a period of time.[61]

Contract Clauses Regarding Custom

The status of unwritten practice and custom may be dealt with specifically in the written agreement. All binding force of customary practices may be eliminated *if* the contract language is quite strong. Thus, even where a bonus practice was the product of negotiations between company and union and had been paid for several years (but where it was not written into the contract) it could be unilaterally discontinued by the employer since the written contract provided:

> "This contract represents complete collective bargaining and full agreement by the parties in respect to rates of pay, wages, hours of employment or other conditions of employment which shall prevail during the term hereof and any matters or subjects not herein covered have been satisfactorily adjusted, compromised or waived by the parties for the life of this agreement."[62]

But a weaker clause, stating that "this contract expresses the entire agreement between the parties," was held to eliminate automatically only those practices which conflicted with the contract's terms, since practices, the arbitrator said, are not necessarily matters for agreement.[63]

---

practice can be terminated only by rewriting the language. Ibid. Similarly, a practice could not be unilaterally terminated where to do so would defeat rights under a newly adopted contract provision which was premised upon the practice. Kroger Co., 36 LA 129, 130–131 (Updegraff, 1960).

[60] See Arbitrator Kelliher in 54 LA 647, 648; Roberts in 50 LA 125, 127–128; Gundermann in 39 LA 1270, 1273. Also see Stouffer in 45 LA 470, 475. On the other hand, the binding effect of a practice may be confirmed as a result of negotiations. See Leeds & Northrup Co. v. NLRB, 67 LRRM 2793 (CA 3, 1968), where the union had reduced its demands because management withdrew its proposal to modify a practice.

[61] See Bethlehem Steel Co., 37 LA 956, 958 (Seward, 1961). But a practice will not be deemed to have been changed or eliminated merely by a single unprotested departure from the practice. Bethlehem Steel Corp., 48 LA 1205, 1208 (Seward, 1967).

[62] Bassick Co., 26 LA 627, 630 (Kheel, 1956). Also see Arbitrator Autrey in 53 LA 1317, 1319–1320; Dworkin in 44 LA 630, 634; Klein in 42 LA 165, 168; Larkin in 36 LA 160, 162; Edes in 21 LA 398, 400.

[63] American Seating Co., 16 LA 115, 116–117 (Whiting, 1951). Also see Arbitrator Teple in 53 LA 405, 407; Murphy in 32 LA 228, 233. Cf., Lewis in 53 LA 1024, 1027.

Though a contract provided that it "cancels all previous Agreements, both written and oral, and constitutes the entire Agreement between the parties," an arbitrator declared that the provision "has no magical dissolving effect upon practices or customs which are continued in fact unabated and which span successive contract periods."[64] Nor would such a provision negate practices that cast light upon ambiguous contract language.[65]

Some collective agreements contain clauses designed to insure continuance of certain established practices or local working conditions.[66] Of course, under such clauses the question often arises as to when a practice or local working condition exists.[67]

Where a letter of agreement on local practices specifically listed certain practices to be continued, an arbitrator ruled that the omission of other practices from the list did not imply that they could be unilaterally eliminated; rather, the effect of the list was to eliminate need for proof as to the existence of the practices listed. Other usages were not annulled without explicit language supporting their termination.[68]

"A general 'catch-all' provision, designed to freeze general working conditions, cannot be construed to nullify an express provision of the contract."[69] Thus, such a clause was held not to require the employer to continue a customary paid holiday the day before Christ-

---

[64] Fruehauf Trailer Co., 29 LA 372, 374–375 (Jones, 1957). Also see Arbitrator Kates in 52 LA 1146, 1150; Duff in 50 LA 417, 421. Cf., Giardino in 19 LA 421, 423.

[65] See Edmont Wilson, 54 LA 686, 688 (Nichols, 1970); Kelsey-Hayes Co., 37 LA 375, 376–377 (Gill, 1961).

[66] For a variety of such clauses, see Arbitrator Cahn in 52 LA 176, 177; Lee in 48 LA 206, 209; Prasow in 47 LA 1131, 1133, 1135; Stashower in 40 LA 73, 75. For clauses insuring that existing minimum standards will not be lowered, see Arbitrator Keefe in 50 LA 453, 454; Turkus in 35 LA 503, 504. For a Board of Inquiry report as to the history of the steel industry "local working conditions" clause and as to union and employer contentions regarding the effect of the clause upon progress, see Steel Industry, 33 LA 236, 239–240 (Taylor, Perkins & Lehoczky, 1959). In two cases public sector "interests" arbitrators were reluctant to bind public employers by maintenance of practices clauses which would impair management's efforts to achieve efficient and high quality operations. Oscoda Area Schools, 55 LA 568, 573 (Block, 1970); Arlington Education Assn. 54 LA 492, 495–496 (Zack, Fitzgerald & Cohen, 1970).

[67] See Arbitrator Stutz in 52 LA 963, 964; Florey in 40 LA 1201, 1202 (where he quotes "guideposts" for resolving the question under the steel industry clause); Valtin in 35 LA 755, 756.

[68] Bakelite Co., 29 LA 555, 558–559 (Updegraff, 1957). Cf., Sargent Industries, 52 LA 1273, 1275–1276 (Lennard, 1969).

[69] Valley Dolomite Corp., 11 LA 98, 100 (McCoy, 1948). Similarly, see Arbitrator Seward in 45 LA 778, 779; Abersold in 41 LA 193, 199.

mas since the contract specifically listed paid holidays and Christmas Eve was not on the list. The general "custom" clause could not "expand and broaden an already specific provision."[70] Furthermore, such a clause has been construed to refer to such things as employee benefits, and not to restrict basic management functions absent clear indication of such intent.[71]

The agreement may provide that if the employer changes or eliminates established practices, he shall, upon challenge through the grievance procedure, bear the burden to "justify" his action.[72] In one case the agreement provided that past practice should not be considered to control or to prohibit change if the practice contributes to inefficient or uneconomical operations.[73]

Question of Arbitrability

The question of arbitrability in disputes concerning the binding status of custom was not raised in many of the cases cited above. Ordinarily there is little basis for raising the question where the collective agreement contains a broad arbitration clause or where the dispute is taken to arbitration by a joint submission. However, the question of arbitrability of custom disputes has sometimes been raised where the arbitration clause was limited to disputes concerning the interpretation or application of the "agreement." The question was answered in the affirmative in some cases,[74] but not in others.[75]

Role of Custom and Practice in Interpretation of Ambiguous Language

One of the most important standards used by arbitrators in the interpretation of ambiguous contract language is the custom or past

---

[70] Machlett Laboratories, Inc., 26 LA 117, 120 (Scheiber, 1956).

[71] Borden Co., 39 LA 1020, 1023 (Morvant, 1962).

[72] Bethlehem Steel Co., cases in 29 LA 418 and in 17 LA 382. Also see Arbitrator Gill in 23 LA 210, 212. A similar result might be reached even without a specific contract clause. John Deere Waterloo Tractor Works, 18 LA 276, 278 (Davey, 1952).

[73] Mead Corporation, 42 LA 643, 646 (Hawley, 1964).

[74] See Arbitrator Kates in 51 LA 490, 492–493; Handsaker in 39 LA 1188, 1190–1191; Volz in 39 LA 72, 74–75; Crawford in 34 LA 732, 735; Gilden in 7 LA 614, 620–621. Also see Sembower in 54 LA 292, 294–296; Cahn in 17 LA 780, 783.

[75] U.S. Industrial Chemicals Co., 28 LA 401, 402 (Alexander, 1957); M. T. Stevens & Sons Co., 7 LA 585, 587 (Copelof, 1947). Also see Arbitrator Morgan (dissenting) in 50 LA 417, 422; Brandschain in 3 LA 254, 255–256.

practice of the parties. Indeed, use of past practice to give meaning to ambiguous contract language is so common that no citation of authority is necessary. The general attitude of arbitrators is illustrated by Arbitrator Charles C. Killingsworth, who, in noting that the parties had operated under a provision for nearly three years before requesting an arbitrator to interpret it, stated that he had "a context of practices, usages, and rule-of-thumb interpretations by which the parties themselves" had gradually given substance to the disputed term.[76] Nonetheless, in another case Arbitrator Clyde W. Summers added a note of caution when he stated that "In interpreting a collective agreement probably nothing is more capable of constructive use or susceptible to serious abuse as appeals to custom and practice."[77]

Where practice has established a meaning for language contained in past contracts and continued by the parties in a new agreement, the language will be presumed to have the meaning given it by that practice.[78] It has been stated:

"There would have to be very strong and compelling reasons for an arbitrator to change the practice by which a contract provision has been interpreted in a plant over a period of several years and several contracts. There would have to be a clear and unambiguous direction in the language used to effect such a change * * *."[79]

The weight to be accorded past practice as an interpretation guide may vary greatly from case to case. In this regard, the degree of mutuality is an important factor. Unilateral interpretations might not bind the other party.[80] However, continued failure of one party

---

[76] Eastern Stainless Steel Corp., 12 LA 709, 713 (1949).

[77] Standard Bag Corp., 45 LA 1149, 1151 (1965).

[78] See Arbitrator Krimsly in 54 LA 1146, 1148–1149; Rauch in 51 LA 561, 565; Teple in 49 LA 220, 223–224; Smith in 46 LA 637, 639; Prasow in 23 LA 27, 32; Updegraff in 20 LA 243, 247; McCoy in 16 LA 240, 241; Kelliher in 15 LA 85, 87; Copelof in 7 LA 461, 466.

[79] Webster Tobacco Co., 5 LA 164, 166 (Brandschain, 1946). Also see Arbitrator Krimsly in 54 LA 1146, 1149. However, prior practice may be "an unsafe guide" after contract provisions have been changed. Huebsch Originators, 47 LA 635, 639 (Merrill, 1966). Similarly, see Arbitrator Bothwell in 53 LA 584, 585.

[80] See Arbitrator Roberts in 47 LA 916, 920–921 (verbal protest each time company did the act and grievance was ultimately filed after protests were disregarded); Howlett in 44 LA 954, 956 (union lacked knowledge of company's method of payment, so no showing of mutuality); Altieri in 43 LA 651, 660; Hebert in 27 LA 762, 766–767; Baab in 23 LA 562, 569; Updegraff in 11 LA 825, 826; Potter in 7 LA 81, 84. Also see Sullivan in 54 LA 381, 387.

to object to the other party's interpretation is sometimes held to constitute acceptance of such interpretation so as, in effect, to make it mutual.[81]

While arbitrators sometimes refuse to charge a party with knowledge of what is going on in the plant,[82] claims of lack of knowledge often carry relatively little weight. Thus, a party may be "assumed" to know what is transpiring,[83] or it may be held that a party "knew or should have reasonably known" of the asserted practice.[84] Even successor unions sometimes are charged with knowledge of practice under the same contract language as administered by the company and the predecessor union.[85]

Another important factor to be considered in determining the weight to be given to past practice is how well it is established. In this regard, Arbitrator Robert E. Mathews stated that to be given significant weight in contract interpretation, "the practice must be of sufficient generality and duration to imply acceptance of it as an authentic construction of the contract."[86] A "single incident" has been

[81] See Arbitrator Shister in 54 LA 335, 338–339; Boothe in 53 LA 941, 944; Marshall in 53 LA 234, 239 (union reluctantly went along with management's action for a time, then negotiated briefly on it without reaching agreement, then failed to pursue the matter for several years thereafter); Teple in 49 LA 220, 223–224, and in 33 LA 46, 51; Tatum in 44 LA 373, 376; Layman in 44 LA 326, 334 (arbitrator spoke of "tacit recognition" of the practice); Allen in 22 LA 289, 291; Kirsh in 4 LA 584, 586; Prasow in 1 LA 313, 316. Cf., Arbitrator Jones in 53 LA 13, 16–17 (complex method of pay required considerable period of time for various facets to manifest themselves to the employees); Peck in 47 LA 739, 742 (failure to protest trifling matters could not be the basis of a practice).
[82] See Arbitrator Cole in 39 LA 1148, 1152; Scheiber in 36 LA 958, 960; Jones in 24 LA 821, 826–827.
[83] Baer Bros., 16 LA 822, 824 (Donnelly, 1951). Similarly, see Chattanooga Box & Lumber Co., 44 LA 373, 376 (Tatum, 1965), stating that as to prior practice "the knowledge of the employee must be the knowledge of the Union."
[84] Owens-Corning Fiberglas Corp., 19 LA 57, 63 (Justin, 1952). Similarly, see Arbitrator Jones in 44 LA 698, 700; Porter in 22 LA 608, 609. Also see McDermott in 42 LA 1277, 1280.
[85] Wagner Electric Corp., 21 LA 524, 527 (Brown, 1953). Also see Arbitrator Jones in 44 LA 698, 700; Anderson in 29 LA 45, 49–50. The successor union's actual knowledge of a practice and its failure to negotiate a change in contract language is still stronger basis for holding it bound by the practice. See National Cash Register Co., 50 LA 1242, 1246 (Wolff, 1968). Similarly, see Arbitrator Updegraff in 20 LA 243, 247. Cf., Moberly in 51 LA 400, 404.
[86] Sheller Mfg. Corp., 10 LA 617, 620 (1948). Also see Arbitrator Daugherty in 45 LA 494, 495; Kesselman in 45 LA 201, 206; Feinberg in 45 LA 26, 29; Hebert in 27 LA 762, 766–767. Erroneous administrative procedure by one

held not to establish a "practice."[87] However, it seems reasonable that fewer instances would be required to establish a "practice" where the situation arises only infrequently than would be required where the situation arises often.[88] Thus, even a single incident which was "fully parallel" to the situation before the arbitrator sufficed where parallel situations would not likely arise often.[89]

Past practice, to be given significant weight, need not be absolutely uniform. Arbitrator Dale Yoder, for instance, held the "predominant pattern of practice" to be controlling even though there had been scattered exceptions to the "clearly established pattern."[90] On the other hand, a practice as to the rate to be paid in one situation could not control a somewhat similar but distinguishable fact situation, the arbitrator stating: "A practice implies the consistent handling of repetitive and like situations. An arbitrator has no more authority to extend a practice beyond its limits than he has to amend or add to the written contract."[91]

It is obvious that past practice provides no guide where evidence regarding its nature and duration is "highly contradictory."[92] Where such conflict exists the arbitrator will be inclined to rely entirely upon other standards of interpretation.

Custom and Practice v. Clear Contract Language

While custom and past practice are used very frequently to establish the intent of contract provisions which are so ambiguous or so

---

department though carried on for ten years did not bind the company as a practice where no rational basis for the procedure was shown. U.S. Industrial Chemicals Co., 47 LA 651, 654 (McGury, 1966).

[87] Arbitrator Solomon in 49 LA 718, 725; Duff in 43 LA 678, 681; Smith in 22 LA 835, 837. Also see Arbitrator Dybeck in 53 LA 1215, 1216. Two incidents did not suffice in York Bus Co., 24 LA 81, 87 (Loucks, 1955).

[88] See Arbitrator Mullin in 54 LA 593, 596; Kadish in 34 LA 763, 771; Callaghan in 28 LA 414, 417.

[89] Kennecott Copper Corp., 34 LA 763, 771 (Kadish, 1960).

[90] Curtis Companies, Inc., 29 LA 434, 439 (1957). Similarly, see Arbitrator Prasow in 50 LA 645, 657; Rohman in 47 LA 1178, 1181. Also see McDermott in 42 LA 1172, 1179.

[91] General Refractories Co., 54 LA 1180, 1182 (Volz, 1970). Also see Arbitrator Klein in 53 LA 266, 269; Leach in 45 LA 1039, 1045.

[92] Reliance Steel Products Co., 24 LA 30, 32 (Lehoczky, 1954). Also see Arbitrator Gould in 48 LA 1161, 1165; McCoy in 47 LA 648, 649 (practice could not be established by mere general statement without reference to names or dates); Merrill in 44 LA 1121, 1127; Reynard in 27 LA 793, 795.

general as to be capable of different interpretations, they ordinarily will not be used to give meaning to a provision which is clear and unambiguous. For instance, note the following statements:

Arbitrator Jules J. Justin: "Plain and unambiguous words are undisputed facts. The conduct of Parties may be used to fix a meaning to words and phrases of uncertain meaning. Prior acts cannot be used to change the explicit terms of a contract. An arbitrator's function is not to rewrite the Parties' contract. His function is limited to finding out what the Parties intended under a particular clause. The intent of the Parties is to be found in the words which they, themselves, employed to express their intent. When the language used is clear and explicit, the arbitrator is constrained to give effect to the thought expressed by the words used."[93]

Arbitrator Hubert Wyckoff: "[Established practice] is a useful means of ascertaining intention in case of ambiguity or indefiniteness; but no matter how well established a practice may be, it is unavailing to modify a clear promise."[94]

Many other arbitrators have expressed similar views.[95]

A related rule is that a party's failure to file grievances or to protest past violations of a clear contract rule does not bar that party, after notice to the violator, from insisting upon compliance with the clear contract requirement in future cases.[96]

The clear language of the contract has been enforced even where

---

[93] Phelps Dodge Copper Products Corp., 16 LA 229, 233 (1951).

[94] Tide Water Oil Co., 17 LA 829, 833 (1952).

[95] For many cases, see p. 281 of the 1960 edition of this book. For some of the many later cases, see Arbitrator Bradley in 51 LA 185, 188; Shipman in 50 LA 673, 674; DiLeone in 49 LA 357, 359; Solomon in 49 LA 718, 725; Daugherty in 48 LA 1355, 1357; Koven in 47 LA 858, 859–860; Leonard in 47 LA 661, 665–666; Hayes in 47 LA 449, 452; Buckwalter in 47 LA 260, 262; Hilpert in 47 LA 238, 241; Teple in 46 LA 1106, 1108; Hon in 46 LA 825, 827; Stouffer in 46 LA 578, 583; Murphy in 46 LA 289, 293–294; Dworkin in 45 LA 1109, 1113; Ray in 45 LA 868, 873; Hebert in 45 LA 131, 139; Wallen in 44 LA 251, 253–254; Williams in 44 LA 5, 6–7; Howard in 43 LA 573, 577; Witney in 41 LA 206, 209–210; Strong in 38 LA 256, 258–259.

[96] See Arbitrator Dworkin in 52 LA 79, 83; Allen in 48 LA 219, 222–223; Porter in 46 LA 491, 492–493; Murphy in 46 LA 289, 294; Fallon in 45 LA 271, 276–277; Williams in 44 LA 5, 6–7; Block in 43 LA 1248, 1252; Myers in 42 LA 269, 272; Platt in 40 LA 859, 861–862; McDermott in 38 LA 461, 464; Smith in 23 LA 289, 295; Lockhart in 17 LA 497, 503; Feinberg in 15 LA 688, 689; Luskin in 15 LA 918, 921; Maggs in 12 LA 311, 315; Courshon in 9 LA 484, 491; Wolff in 5 LA 333, 336. For discussion of related points, see Chapter 10, topic titled "Waiver and Estoppel."

the arbitrator believed that, on the basis of equity, past practice should have governed:

"In the opinion of the Impartial Tribunal the practice would not have grown up in the first place and would not have been tolerated by the parties if the situation did not justify it. The sudden refusal of the union to continue with a practice that has apparently proved satisfactory for many years, thus precipitating the present dispute, may well be severely criticized as an unreasonable stand not necessary to protect any substantial right of the workers. * * * If it were at all possible the decision should be that the position of the workers is in violation of the contract."[97]

Amendment of Contract

While Arbitrator Harry H. Platt has emphasized that evidence of past practice "is wholly inadmissible where the contract language is plain and unambiguous,"[98] he has also recognized that, on the basis of very strong proof, the clear language of the contract may be amended:

"While, to be sure, parties to a contract may modify it by a later *agreement,* the existence of which is to be deduced from their course of conduct, the conduct relied upon to show such modification must be unequivocal and the terms of modification must be definite, certain, and intentional."[99]

Arbitrator Hamilton Douglas has declared that a party contending that clear language has been modified must "show the assent of the other party and the minds of the parties must be shown to have met on a definite modification."[100] Arbitrator Charles C. Killingsworth required a showing that "both parties * * * have evinced a positive acceptance or endorsement" of the practice.[101] Other arbitrators, too, have required a showing equivalent to mutual agreement to amend the contract.[102]

---

[97] Chicago Association of Dress Manufacturers, 1 ALAA ¶67,234, p. 67,521 (Hodes, 1945).

[98] Penberthy Injector Co., 15 LA 713, 715 (1950).

[99] Gibson Refrigerator Co., 17 LA 313, 318 (1951), emphasis added. Also see comments of Arbitrator Platt in 22 LA 65, 68.

[100] Merrill-Stevens Dry Dock & Repair Co., 10 LA 562, 563 (1948).

[101] Bethlehem Steel Co., 13 LA 556, 560 (1949).

[102] See Arbitrator Mittenthal in 54 LA 716, 719–720; Daugherty in 48 LA 1355, 1357; Wolff in 47 LA 993, 994; Updegraff in 47 LA 720, 722–723; Koretz in 47 LA 495, 500–501; Traynor in 47 LA 193, 195–196; Volz in 46 LA 1208, 1212–1213; Hebert in 46 LA 140, 151; McCormick in 45 LA 453, 458; Fallon in 45 LA 271, 276–277; Williams in 44 LA 5, 6–7; Anrod in

Of course, the parties to a contract may amend it by a subsequent agreement. This result was produced, for instance, by a special "interpretation agreement" of the parties.[103]

Gap-Filling

Arbitrators have sometimes recognized that contract language may cover a matter generally but fail to cover all of its aspects—that is, "gaps" sometimes exist. It has been recognized that established practice may be used, not to set aside contract language, but to fill in the contract's gaps.[104] Similarly, past practice might indicate an exception to the general application of a contract clause.[105]

---

43 LA 1173, 1176; Yagoda in 42 LA 421, 424–425; Roberts in 28 LA 470, 474; Hoban in 27 LA 605, 607; Emery in 17 LA 90, 91. But long, unchallenged practice was deemed sufficient by Arbitrator Lennard in 27 LA 376, 383; Gifford in 25 LA 826, 827; Sherbow in 17 LA 524, 526. Also see Seinsheimer in 49 LA 709, 714–718; Duff in 46 LA 920, 923.

[103] Borg-Warner Corp., 29 LA 629, 633–634 (Marshall, 1957). Also see Arbitrator Marshall in 47 LA 97, 101 (contract amended by subsequent side agreement); Summers in 40 LA 575, 575–576.

[104] See Arbitrator McCoy in 44 LA 246, 250; Roberts in 28 LA 470, 474; Hogan in 25 LA 216, 225; Emery in 17 LA 90, 91; Killingsworth in 17 LA 65, 67.

[105] Standard Brands, Inc., 25 LA 851, 853 (Justin, 1955).

CHAPTER 13

MANAGEMENT RIGHTS

Views Regarding Management Rights

Under the common law, owners of business establishments possess certain freedoms of action, incidental to their legal status, which are commonly called management rights or management prerogatives. The word "right" has been defined by Webster to mean "any power, privilege, or immunity, vested in one by authority, social custom * * * or * * * by the law * * * ." Webster has defined the word "prerogative" to mean the "right to exercise a power or privilege in priority to, or to the exclusion of, others * * * for the exercise of which in theory there is no responsibility or accountability as to the fact and the manner of its exercise."

Two management spokesmen, noting that the term "management prerogative" is as distasteful to union representatives as the term "closed shop" is to many management representatives, have denied that "management prerogative" refers to a divine right to manage. These spokesmen would define the term to refer to "those rights, or that authority, which management must have in order successfully to carry out its function of managing the enterprise."[1]

Management spokesmen generally adhere rigidly to the position that "residual" or "reserved" powers are in management. These spokesmen declare that under the common law an employer, as property owner, may operate his business as he chooses, except where his common law rights have been limited by constitutional legislation or by collective bargaining agreements.[2] Management takes the position

---

[1] Hill & Hook, Management at the Bargaining Table 56 (1945). Also see Phelps, "Management's Reserved Rights: an Industry View," Management Rights and the Arbitration Process 102 (BNA Incorporated, 1956).

[2] See Story, Arbitration as a Part of the Collective Bargaining Agreement 9 (1948); Hill, "Using Management's Rights in Day-to-Day Labor Relations," American Management Association Personnel Series, No. 82, p. 11 (1944).

412

that it need not look to the collective agreement to determine what rights it has reserved to itself, but should look to the agreement only to determine what rights it has ceded away or agreed to share with employees. Thus one management spokesman has defined "the doctrine of reserved rights" as "the simple and understandable view that management, which must have the right to manage, has reserved its right to manage unless it has limited its right by some specific provision of the labor agreement."[3]

As might be expected, labor spokesmen deny that the rights of management are so broad. For instance, while serving as General Counsel of the United Steelworkers of America, Arthur Goldberg expressed that union's view of the reserved rights concept:

"This concept is not only distasteful; it is based on extreme over-simplification of history. It overlooks the degree to which collective bargaining modifies workers' rights—the right to cease work, the right to press a point without regard to any set of rules or guides, the right to improvise concepts of fairness on the basis of the necessities of the moment without commitment to the future. How could management obtain employee acceptance of job evaluation without the union's modification of the inherent right of workers to press wage complaints on whatever ground appears suitable at the moment. No—this wresting away process is not all one way by any means."[4]

He also offered the following position as to management's reserved rights:

"What then are management's reserved rights? These are usually rights reserved in the agreement subject to the substantive clauses of the agreement. Some of these rights relate to subjects excluded from the collective bargaining area by custom, by law, or by express provision. When a contract says that management has the exclusive right to manage the business, it obviously refers to the countless questions which arise and are not covered by wages, hours, and working conditions, such as determination of products, equipment, materials, prices, etc.

"Not only does management have the general right to manage the business, but many agreements provide that management has the

---

[3] Fairweather, "American and Foreign Grievance Systems," Developments in American and Foreign Arbitration 1, 15 (The Bureau of National Affairs, Inc., 1968).

[4] Goldberg, "Management's Reserved Rights: A Labor View," Management Rights and the Arbitration Process 118, 122–123 (BNA Incorporated, 1956).

exclusive right to direct working forces and usually to lay off, recall, discharge, hire, etc.

"The right to direct, where it involves wages, hours, or working conditions, is a procedural right. It does not imply some right over and above labor's right. It is a recognition of the fact that somebody must be boss; somebody has to run the plant. People can't be wandering around at loose ends, each deciding what to do next. Management decides what the employee is to do. However, this right to direct or to initiate action does not imply a second-class role for the union. The union has the right to pursue its role of representing the interest of the employee with the same stature accorded it as accorded management. To assure order, there is a clear procedural line drawn: the company directs and the union grieves when it objects. To make this desirable division of function workable, it is essential that arbitrators not give greater weight to the directing force than the objecting force."[5]

In the past some attempt has been made to draw a line separating matters of interest to the union from those of sole concern to management. Such attempt was made at the President's Labor-Management Conference in 1945, but with no success. There, management members of the Committee on Management's Right to Manage did agree upon a specific classification of management functions. The labor members, however, were unable to accept any such clear-cut classification. They submitted a separate report explaining their position:

"The extensive exploratory discussions of the committee have brought forth the wide variety of traditions, customs, and practices that have grown out of relationships between unions and management in various industries over a long period of time.

"Because of the complexities of these relationships, the labor members of the committee think it unwise to specify and classify the functions and responsibilities of management. Because of the insistence by management for such specification, the committee was unable to agree upon a joint report. To do so might well restrict the flexibility so necessary to efficient operation.

"It would be extremely unwise to build a fence around the rights and responsibilities of management on the one hand and the unions on the other. The experience of many years shows that with the growth of mutual understanding the responsibilities of one of the parties today may well become the joint responsibility of both parties tomorrow.

"We cannot have one sharply delimited area designated as management prerogatives and another equally sharply defined area of

---

[5] Goldberg, id. at 120–121.

union prerogatives without either side constantly attempting to invade the forbidden territory, thus creating much unnecessary strife."[6]

Objective observers appear to share, in part at least, the views expressed by the labor members of the Committee.[7] "Collective bargaining is too dynamic to permit drawing a statutory line between management's prerogatives and the areas of joint responsibility."[8]

Various conclusions have at different times been reached by objective observers concerning how far unions may desire or be inclined to push into management areas:

(A) "Some unions appear constantly to seek a larger share in the governance of the industry while others believe that they should avoid responsibility for the conduct of the business."[9]

(B) "There is no consciousness of invading managerial prerogatives. By the same token there is no area of management which most [unions] would hesitate to put on 'next year's list' if they felt the interests of the union were involved."[10]

(C)   "In the daily shop work of job assignments, skill classification, production standards, and maintenance of discipline, union officers show little desire to join in managing and in initiating action; they prefer to retain their freedom to protest management's decisions and to stay out of the cross fire of criticism and avoid the wounding resentments of their own members.

"Unions have not pushed massively and inexorably into vital policy areas. They have pushed when they could and when it was in their clear interest to do so, advancing when management was careless or weak and retreating when management aggressively resisted them. When unions do enlarge their powers, it is almost always in those areas where they have long been established: wages, hours, and conditions of employment."[11]

In any study of arbitration the view taken by arbitrators in regard to management rights is of great interest and importance. Many arbitrators have expressly recognized that the residual powers are in man-

---

[6] The President's National Labor-Management Conference, Nov. 5–30, 1945 (U.S. Dept. of Labor, Div. of Labor Standards, Bull. No. 77, pp. 57–59, 61, 1946).

[7] See Chamberlain, The Union Challenge to Management Control 156–157 (1948).

[8] Cox & Dunlop, "Regulation of Collective Bargaining by the National Labor Relations Board," 63 Harv. L. Rev. 389, 430 (1950).

[9] Cox & Dunlop, id. at 431.

[10] Chamberlain, The Union Challenge to Management Control 157 (1948).

[11] Chamberlain & Kuhn, Collective Bargaining 92 (1965).

agement.[12] To illustrate the variations in arbitral statements recognizing the "residual" or "reserved" rights doctrine, we may note the following:

> *Arbitrator Harry J. Dworkin:* "It is axiomatic that an employer retains all managerial rights not expressly forbidden by statutory law in the absence of a collective bargaining agreement. When a collective bargaining agreement is entered into, these managerial rights are given up only to the extent evidenced in the agreement."[13]

> *Arbitrator Lewis E. Solomon:* "Collective bargaining agreements, generally, are devised to establish and grant certain rights to employees, which rights they would not otherwise have under common law. It is also a normal and well recognized principle in the interpretation of such Agreements that the rights of management are limited and curtailed only to the degree to which it has yielded specified rights. The right of Management to operate its business and control the working force may be specifically reserved in a labor agreement. However, even in the absence of such a specific reservations clause, as is the case here, those rights are inherent and are nevertheless reserved and maintained by it and its decisions with respect to the operations of the business and the direction of the working forces may not be denied, rejected, or curtailed unless the same are in clear violation of the terms of the contract, or may be clearly implied, or are so clearly arbitrary or capricious as to reflect an intent to derogate the relationship."[14]

> *Arbitrator John Day Larkin:* "Initially, before unions came into the picture, all power and responsibility in all aspects of personnel management were vested in the company and its officials. Except for certain

---

[12] For many instances, see pp. 287–288 of the 1960 edition of this book. For later instances, see Arbitrator Whyte in 54 LA 942, 945; Whitney in 53 LA 1078, 1083–1084; Belcher in 53 LA 410, 412; Talent in 52 LA 93, 96; Graff in 69-2 ARB ¶8610; Dworkin in 51 LA 1174, 1181–1182; Doyle in 50 LA 1157, 1158; Geissinger in 50 LA 792, 793; Larkin in 50 LA 109, 111; Stouffer in 50 LA 17, 19; Solomon in 49 LA 370, 380; Kabaker in 48 LA 925, 928; Hilpert in 47 LA 238, 239–240; Turkus in 47 LA 75, 78; Klamon in 46 LA 459, 468; Ray in 46 LA 91, 94; Block in 45 LA 807, 810; Sarachan in 44 LA 488, 489–490; Oppenheim in 44 LA 274, 279; Kelliher in 43 LA 1006, 1011; Howlett in 42 LA 1321, 1325; Beatty in 40 LA 544, 546–547; Morvant in 39 LA 1020, 1023; Williams in 39 LA 504, 507; Hebert in 39 LA 419, 425; Hale in 39 LA 310, 313; Quinlan in 38 LA 714, 715; Emery in 37 LA 1103, 1104–1106; Roberts in 37 LA 1064, 1067; McIntosh in 37 LA 758, 759; Wolfe in 37 LA 664, 665; Mueller in 37 LA 629, 632; Cobb in 37 LA 466, 467; Bradley in 35 LA 306, 310; Rohman in 34 LA 781, 784; Stockton in 33 LA 219, 223. Also recognizing the general concept, see Krimsly in 48 LA 1359, 1360; Seitz in 47 LA 975, 978; Koven in 47 LA 286, 287–288; Wood in 45 LA 881, 884; Altieri in 42 LA 1316, 1321; Davis in 39 LA 224, 225; Ross in 32 LA 713, 717.
[13] Cleveland Newspaper Publishers Assn., 51 LA 1174, 1181 (1969).
[14] Fairway Foods, Inc., 44 LA 161, 164 (1965). Also see Arbitrator Solomon in 55 LA 997, 1001–1002.

limitations imposed by Federal, state or local legislative enactments, there were no limitations on management's prerogatives. When a union is formed, and a collective bargaining agreement is entered into, the original power and authority of the company is modified only to the extent that it voluntarily and specifically relinquishes facets of its power and authority. * * * In short, the Company does not have to bargain with the Union to get 'rights' which are inherent in the management function; but it may relinquish certain of those rights in the course of bargaining with the Union."[15]

We have noted the management view that management "has reserved its right to manage unless it has limited its right by some *specific* provision of the labor agreement."[16] In many cases arbitrators have in fact spoken in terms of a specific contractual provision (containing either an express or implied limitation) as being necessary in order to limit management's rights. In other cases some arbitrators (at least as to some types of issues, such as subcontracting) have taken the view that limitations upon management rights are not necessarily restricted to those contained in some specific provision of the agreement but may exist as "implied obligations" or "implied limitations" under some general provision of the agreement such as the recognition clause, seniority provisions, or wage provisions.[17]

Also, it has been observed that in practice arbitrators may tend to modify the residual rights theory by imposing a standard of reasonableness as an implied term of the agreement.[18] Certainly, many arbitrators are reluctant to uphold arbitrary, capricious, or bad faith managerial actions which adversely affect bargaining unit employees. Even where the agreement expressly states a right in management, expressly gives it discretion as to a matter, or expressly makes it the "sole judge" of a matter, management's action must not be arbitrary, capricious, or taken in bad faith.[19]

---

[15] National Lead Co., 43 LA 1025, 1027–1028 (1964). Also see Arbitrator Larkin in 55 LA 329, 335; 54 LA 250, 252.

[16] Fairweather, "American and Foreign Grievance Systems," Developments in American and Foreign Arbitration 1, 15 (1968), emphasis added.

[17] For example, see topic titled "Right to Subcontract" in this Chapter. Also see discussion by Arbitrator Seward in Bethlehem Steel Co., 30 LA 678, 682–683 (1958). The term "implied obligations" has sometimes been given a meaning much more restrictive upon management than the term "implied limitations." See discussion in Wiggins, The Arbitration of Industrial Engineering Disputes 73–74 (The Bureau of National Affairs, Inc., 1970).

[18] See discussion in Robert E. McKee, General Contractor, Inc., 39 LA 411, 413–414 (Oppenheim, 1962). Also, again see topic titled "Right to Subcontract" in this Chapter.

[19] See Arbitrator Roberts in 54 LA 896, 900; Sandler in 53 LA 482, 486; Gorsuch in 52 LA 552, 556; Krimsly in 51 LA 49, 53; Merrill in 36 LA 1353, 1355–1356.

It is also to be remembered that numerous arbitrators have accepted the view that under some circumstances unwritten practices
and custom, as to some matters, should be held binding upon both
parties as being in essence a part of their "whole" agreement. Thus
past practice is another possible source of limitation upon management
rights.[20]

Finally, it may be noted that there has been Court of Appeals
recognition and approval of the residual rights doctrine in a LMRA
case.[21] The U.S. Supreme Court also has commented relative to management rights, in the *Warrior & Gulf* case, but the significance
of the Court's comments is not clear.[22] One able arbitrator has suggested that the *Warrior & Gulf* decision "would appear to give
full weight to the reserved rights doctrine" but with the additional
condition that such rights are likewise subject to the willingness of
employees to work under the particular unilaterally imposed conditions.[23] Another able arbitrator has suggested that the decision in effect
rejects the "pristine" or "original" reserved rights doctrine.[24] As to
the NLRB, some of the Board's concepts and policies in regard to
the bargaining duty are at odds with the residual rights doctrine applied by many arbitrators and can produce results different from those
reached by the arbitrator. This will be treated in detail hereinbelow
in the subtopic titled "The Duty to Bargain: Right of Unilateral
Action."

Limitations on Management Rights

In recent decades there has been progressive invasion of once
unchallenged areas of exclusive managerial decision. Many matters

---

[20] For full discussion, see Chapter 12, topic titled "Custom and Practice
as Part of the Contract."

[21] United States Steel Corporation v. Nichols, 229 F.2d 396, 399–400, 37
LRRM 2420 (CA 6, 1956), cert. den. 351 U.S. 950. The "Nichols" case view
as to residual rights was quoted with approval in Gunther v. San Diego &
Arizona Eastern Ry. Co., 198 F. Supp. 402 (S.D. Calif, 1961), reversed on
other grounds, 86 S.Ct. 368 (1965). For arbitral reference to the "Nichols"
case, see Arbitrator Young in 55 LA 933, 935–937, 943; Dworkin in 51 LA
1174, 1181; Sembower in 50 LA 1177, 1181; Altieri in 42 LA 559, 560–562;
Jones in 37 LA 771, 775–776; Ross in 32 LA 713, 717–718.

[22] Steelworkers v. Warrior Navigation Co., 34 LA 561, 565 (1960).

[23] Int'l Smelting & Refining Co., 54 LA 657, 660 (Cahn, 1970).

[24] Killingsworth, "Management Rights Revisited," Arbitration and Social
Change 1, 7–10 (The Bureau of National Affairs, Inc., 1970).

which were once regarded as the "rights" or "prerogatives" of management have ceased to be so characterized. Inroads into management areas have been made by legislation, collective bargaining, and arbitration. Some inroads were noted in the preceding topic. Others will be noted in topics that follow.

Inroads Made by Legislation

Beginning about 1890 and continuing through the years, the enactment of state and federal legislation has restricted, to some extent, the right of management to offer employment upon its own terms. Restrictions are found in laws relating to minimum wages and maximum hours, child labor, health and safety, workmen's compensation, unemployment insurance, yellow-dog contracts, fair employment practices, and the like. Such legislation as the Sherman Act, the Clayton Act, the Robinson-Patman Act, and the Securities Exchange Act, each in its own way, has drained the reservoir of management rights. Much of this legislation was enacted largely and directly in the interest of the public. More direct restriction upon management rights came about through the Railway Labor Act of 1926, the National Labor Relations Act of 1935, the Labor-Management Relations Act of 1947, the Labor-Management Reporting and Disclosure Act of 1959, and the Civil Rights Act of 1964.

The Duty to Bargain: Right of Unilateral Action

The labor relations acts, by stimulating collective bargaining, set the stage for overall restriction of management rights through the provisions of collective bargaining agreements. The original National Labor Relations Act placed on employers a legally enforceable or "mandatory" duty to bargain with duly authorized employee representatives on subjects falling within the terms "rates of pay, wages, hours of employment, or other conditions of employment."[25] The same obligation is continued (and made applicable to unions also) in the Act as amended by the Labor-Management Relations Act.

Cases decided by the NLRB or the courts have held that, in addition to wages and hours, the area of mandatory bargaining may

---

[25] For the concept of mandatory, permissible, and unlawful subjects of bargaining, see NLRB v. Wooster Division of Borg-Warner Corp., 78 S.Ct. 718 (1958).

cover such subjects as holiday and vacation pay,[26] subcontracting,[2] discharges,[28] work loads and work standards,[29] bonuses,[30] pensions,[3] profit sharing,[32] insurance benefits,[33] merit increases,[34] union shop,[3] checkoff of union dues,[36] hiring hall,[37] work schedules,[38] plant rules,[3] rest periods,[40] placing existing practices in the contract,[41] managemen rights,[42] incentive pay plans,[43] company owned houses,[44] stock pur chase plans,[45] production work by supervisors,[46] paid coffee break,[4] accumulation of seniority while employee is in a supervisory status,[4] no-strike clauses,[49] employee discounts,[50] installation of new ma chinery,[51] and transfer of employees to a new location.[52]

The above enumeration of mandatory bargaining subjects is no

---

[26] Singer Mfg. Co., 6 LRRM 405 (1940), enforced, 8 LRRM 740 (CA 7, 1941); Union Mfg. Co., 21 LRRM 1187 (NLRB, 1948).

[27] Fibreboard Paper Products Corp. v. NLRB, 379 U.S. 203, 57 LRRM 2609 (1964). For some limits as to the duty, see Westinghouse Electric Corp. 58 LRRM 1257 (NLRB, 1965). Also see Tellepsen Petro-Chem Constructors, 7 LRRM 1235 (NLRB, 1971).

[28] NLRB v. Bachelder, 8 LRRM 723 (CA 7, 1941).

[29] Woodside Cotton Mills Co., 6 LRRM 68 (NLRB, 1940).

[30] NLRB v. Niles-Bement-Pond Co., 31 LRRM 2057 (CA 2, 1952).

[31] Inland Steel Co., 21 LRRM 1310 (1948), enforced, 22 LRRM 250ᴇ (CA 7, 1948), cert. den., 24 LRRM 2019 (1949).

[32] NLRB v. Black-Clawson Co., 33 LRRM 2567 (CA 6, 1954).

[33] NLRB v. W. W. Cross & Co., 24 LRRM 2068 (CA 1, 1949).

[34] NLRB v. J. H. Allison & Co., 18 LRRM 1369 (1946), enforced, 21 LRRM 2238 (CA 6, 1948), cert. den., 22 LRRM 2564 (1948).

[35] NLRB v. Andrew Jergens Co., 24 LRRM 2096 (CA 9, 1949). The amended NLRA bans closed shops and restricts other forms of union security.

[36] U.S. Gypsum Co., 28 LRRM 1015, 29 LRRM 1171 (NLRB, 1951).

[37] NLRB v. Associated General Contractors, 59 LRRM 3013 (CA 5, 1965).

[38] Hallam & Boggs Truck Co., 28 LRRM 1457 (1951), enforced, 30 LRRM 2602 (CA 10, 1952); Wilson & Co., 5 LRRM 560 (1940), enforced, 7 LRRM 575 (CA 8, 1940).

[39] Timken Roller Bearing Co., 18 LRRM 1370 (1946), enforcement den on other grounds, 20 LRRM 2204 (CA 6, 1947).

[40] National Grinding Wheel Co., 21 LRRM 1095 (NLRB, 1948).

[41] Nat'l Carbon Div., Union Carbide & Co., 30 LRRM 1338 (NLRB, 1952) amended without affecting this point, 32 LRRM 1276 (NLRB, 1953).

[42] NLRB v. American National Insurance Co., 343 U.S. 395, 30 LRRM 2147 (1952).

[43] NLRB v. East Texas Steel Castings Co., 33 LRRM 2793 (CA 5, 1954).

[44] NLRB v. Lehigh Portland Cement Co., 32 LRRM 2463 (CA 4, 1953) Cf., NLRB v. Bemis Bros. Bag Co., 32 LRRM 2535 (CA 5, 1953).

[45] NLRB v. Richfield Oil Corp., 37 LRRM 2327 (DC Cir., 1956).

[46] Globe-Union, Inc., 29 LRRM 1198 (NLRB, 1952).

[47] Fleming Manufacturing Co., 41 LRRM 1115 (NLRB, 1957).

[48] Mobile Oil Co., 147 NLRB 337 (1964).

[49] Shell Oil, 22 LRRM 1153 (NLRB, 1948).

[50] Central Illinois Public Service Co., 51 LRRM 1508 (1962), enforced, 54 LRRM 2586 (CA 7, 1963).

[51] Renton News Record, 49 LRRM 1972 (NLRB, 1962).

[52] Cooper Thermometer Co. v. NLRB, 65 LRRM 2113 (CA 2, 1967).

exhaustive. Nor is it final. Subjects that have been directly held to fall within or without the area of mandatory bargaining might be held otherwise by future decision. In general, the tendency has been to expand the area. For instance, the NLRB has moved significantly in holding economic decisions of management to be mandatory subjects of bargaining if job security or working conditions are affected.[53] However, the NLRB sometimes has encountered stiff Court of Appeals resistance, particularly as to economic decisions to move or terminate all or part of the business.[54] In this regard, it may be noted that in its *Darlington* decision under the NLRA the U.S. Supreme Court did not reach any question as to whether an employer must bargain on a purely economic decision to terminate the business.[55]

Section 8(d) of the NLRA as amended by the LMRA provides, in part, that "* * * to bargain collectively is the performance of the mutual obligation of the employer and the representative of the employees to meet at reasonable times and confer in good faith with respect to wages, hours, and other terms and conditions of employment, or the negotiation of an agreement, or any question arising thereunder and the execution of a written contract incorporating any agreement reached if requested by either party, but such obligation

---

[53] See Dixie Ohio Express Co., 167 NLRB No. 72, 66 LRRM 1092 (1967); NLRB v. Town & Country Mfg. Co., 136 NLRB 1022, 1027 (1962). The NLRB had previously long held that the employer, absent any anti-union motive, was not required to bargain over economic decisions to make technological improvements, to relocate operations, to subcontract, and the like, although there was a duty to bargain about the effects of such decisions on the employees.

[54] NLRB v. Acme Industrial Products, Inc., 76 LRRM 2697 (CA 6, 1971); NLRB v. Drapery Mfg. Co., 74 LRRM 2055 (CA 8, 1970); Morrison Cafeterias Inc. v. NLRB, 74 LRRM 3048 (CA 8, 1970); NLRB v. Transmarine Navigation Corp., 65 LRRM 2861 (CA 9, 1967); NLRB v. Royal Plating and Polishing Co., 60 LRRM 2033 (CA 3, 1965). However, in these cases the court did recognize a duty to bargain about the effects of the employer's decision upon the employees.

[55] Textile Workers Union v. Darlington Mfg. Co., 85 S.Ct. 994, 998, 58 LRRM 2657 (1965), holding that an employer has the absolute right to terminate his entire business for any reason he chooses, including anti-union bias, but that termination of part of a multi-enterprise business will violate the NLRA if the employer is motivated by a purpose to "chill" unionism in the remaining parts of the business and if he reasonably can foresee that the partial closing will have that effect. In a case under the Railway Labor Act a union threatened to strike to force a railroad to amend the collective agreement to require mutual consent in order to abolish existing jobs (the railroad had received public utility commission approval to close certain stations which were little used and wasteful); the Supreme Court held that the union's demand was "not unlawful" under the RLA and that the Norris-LaGuardia Act prevented an injunction against the strike. Railroad Telegraphers v. Chicago & Northwestern Ry., 80 S.Ct. 761, 767, 45 LRRM 3109 (1960).

does not compel either party to agree to a proposal or require the making of a concession * * * ."[56] In general, the duty is to bargain upon request.[57]

Section 8(d) also provides that there is no duty to bargain about proposals to make changes in the collective agreement that would take effect during its term. But in the *Jacobs* case the NLRB held, and was affirmed by the Court of Appeals, that "those bargainable issues which have never been discussed by the parties, and which are in no way treated in the contract, remain matters which both the union and the employer are obliged to discuss at any time."[58] The Board emphasized, however:

> "In so holding, we emphasize that under this rule, no less than in any other circumstance, the duty to bargain implies only an obligation to *discuss* the matter in question in good faith with a sincere purpose of reaching some agreement. It does not require that either side agree, or make concessions. And if the parties originally desire to avoid later discussion with respect to matters not specifically covered in the terms of an executed contract, they need only so specify in the terms of the contract itself. Nothing in our construction of §8(d) precludes such an agreement, entered into in good faith, from foreclosing future discussion of matters not contained in the agreement."[59]

It thus appeared from the *Jacobs* case that any duty to bargain during the term of the agreement could be avoided by use of general waiver or so-called zipper clauses stating that the right to bargain on matters not covered by the agreement is waived or stating that the collective agreement constitutes the complete agreement of the parties. However, the NLRB has developed a doctrine (which has received considerable court support) of narrowly construing such clauses so as to give them very limited effect. For instance, in holding a general waiver or zipper clause insufficient to constitute a waiver

---

[56] As to the general nature of the duty to bargain, see NLRB v. Insurance Agents' International Union, 80 S.Ct. 419, 45 LRRM 2704 (1960).

[57] See NLRB v. Columbian Enameling and Stamping Co., 59 S.Ct. 501, 504, 4 LRRM 524 (1939); NLRB v. Sands Mfg. Co., 59 S.Ct. 508, 514, 4 LRRM 530 (1939). Where a union did not object or request bargaining after being notified by management of anticipated changes, the employer did not violate the bargaining duty by making the changes unilaterally. NLRB v. Humble Oil & Refining Co., 161 NLRB No. 64 (1966). Also see discussion in Butler Mfg. Co., 50 LA 109, 111 (Larkin, 1968); Robertshaw-Fulton Controls Co., 36 LA 4, 12–13 (Hilpert, 1961).

[58] In re Jacobs Manufacturing Company, 94 NLRB 1214, 1219, 28 LRRM 1162 (1951), affd., 196 F.2d 680 (CA 2, 1952).

[59] Ibid.

of the union's right to demand bargaining on a change in the method of handling operations in the employer's shipping room (the employer had refused to discuss the change but had referred the union to the grievance and arbitration procedure), the Board stated that a "union's statutory right to be notified and consulted concerning any substantial change in employment may be waived by contract, but such waiver must be expressed in clear and unmistakable terms, and will not lightly be inferred"; furthermore, the Board reiterated that even where a waiver clause is stated in sweeping terms, it must appear from an evaluation of the negotiations that the particular matter in issue was fully discussed or consciously explored and that the union consciously yielded or clearly and unmistakably waived its interest in the matter.[60]

As previously noted, the duty to bargain in good faith does not mean that agreement must be reached.[61] Where bargaining to an impasse fails to produce agreement on a matter, management is privileged to take unilateral action consistent with its proposals in bargaining.[62] However, unilateral action by an employer on matters "which

---

[60] Unit Drop Forge Div., Eaton, Yale & Towne, Inc., 171 NLRB No. 73, 68 LRRM 1129, 1131 (1968). The dissent would have deferred to arbitration in this case. Also see The Press Co., 121 NLRB 976, 978 (1958).

[61] The NLRB is without power to compel a company or a union to agree to any substantive contractual provision of a collective agreement. NLRB v. Burns International Security Services, Inc., 92 S.Ct. 1571, 80 LRRM 2225 (1972); Porter Co. v. NLRB, 90 S.Ct. 821, 73 LRRM 2561 (1970). In Brotherhood of Loc. Eng. v. Baltimore & Ohio R. Co., 83 S.Ct. 691, 694 (1963), the Supreme Court reiterated that the Railway Labor Act "does not undertake governmental regulation of wages, hours, or working conditions."

[62] In NLRB v. Crompton-Highland Mills, Inc., 69 S.Ct. 960, 961, 963, 24 LRRM 2088 (1949), after a bargaining impasse had been reached but before negotiations had been completely terminated, the employer unilaterally granted a wage increase substantially greater than he had proposed in bargaining; the Supreme Court concluded that "under the circumstances" this was an unfair labor practice, but the Court indicated that it would have been proper for the employer to unilaterally grant the increase proposed by him but rejected by the union in bargaining. For other cases recognizing the employer's right to institute his proposals after bargaining has failed, see NLRB v. Burns International Security Services, Inc., 92 S.Ct. 1571, 1586, 80 LRRM 2225, 2234 (1972); DuQuoin Packing Co., 183 NLRB No. 108 (1970); Television and Radio Artists v. NLRB, 57 LC ¶12,612 (DC Cir., 1968), affirming 163 NLRB No. 55 (1967); United Fire Proof Warehouse, 356 F.2d 494, 497–498 (CA 7, 1966); NLRB v. U.S. Sonics Corp., 312 F.2d 610, 615 (CA 1, 1963); United States Steel Corporation v. Nichols, 229 F.2d 396, 399–400 (CA 6, 1956), cert. den. 351 U.S. 950. Explaining the necessity for this rule, see Schatzki, "The Employer's Unilateral Act—A Per Se Violation—Sometimes," 44 Texas L. Rev. 470, 495–496 (1966); Durbin & Gooch, "Unilateral Action as a Legitimate Economic Weapon: Power Bargaining by the Employer Upon Expiration of the Collective Bargaining Agreement," 37 N.Y.U.L. Rev. 666, 673 (1962). In Allied Chemical & Alkali

are in fact under discussion" has been viewed by the Supreme Court as obstructing bargaining as much as "a flat refusal" to bargain and has been held (absent excusing or justifying circumstances) to be a violation of the bargaining duty.[63]

The significance of collective agreement arbitration clauses (and awards issued thereunder) in relation to the legal duty to bargain has been considered in the courts and by the NLRB. One view is illustrated by the Court of Appeals decision in the "Timken" case. Here the union charged the employer with an illegal refusal to bargain on the subject of subcontracting. The employer claimed the right to subcontract under the management rights clause of the agreement. In holding that the employer's action was not a refusal to bargain the court said that the dispute "was a dispute as to the interpretation of the management clause, and the contract specifically provided that such disputes were to be settled within the grievance procedures and, if they failed, by arbitration." Thus, the court held that the company

---

Workers v. Pittsburgh Plate Glass Co., 92 S.Ct. 383, 402 (1971), the Supreme Court held that benefits for retired workers are only a "permissive" and not a "mandatory" subject of bargaining, and that "a unilateral mid-term modification of a permissive term such as retirees' benefits does not" violate the NLRA duty to bargain.

[63] NLRB v. Katz, 82 S.Ct. 1107, 50 LRRM 2177 (1962). For interpretations giving a limited scope to this decision, see Fairweather, "The 'Fibreboard' Decision and Subcontracting," 19 Arb. J. 76, 77 (1964); Durbin & Gooch, "Unilateral Action as a Legitimate Economic Weapon: Power Bargaining by the Employer Upon Expiration of the Collective Bargaining Agreement," 37 N.Y.U.L. Rev. 666, 699–702 (1962). Business needs may privilege unilateral action, consistent with offers rejected by the union, although no impasse has been reached. Raleigh Water Heating Mfg. Co., 136 NLRB 76 (1962); NLRB v. Bradley Washfountain Co., 192 F.2d 144 (CA 7, 1951). Under the Railway Labor Act the Supreme Court has held that the obligation of both parties in major disputes where the Act's status quo provisions have been invoked "is to preserve and maintain unchanged those actual, objective working conditions and practices, broadly conceived, which were in effect prior to the time the pending dispute arose and which are involved in or related to that dispute," whether or not those conditions are covered in an existing collective agreement; the Court held that a railroad accordingly was precluded from making certain outlying assignments at places in which there previously had been none. Shore Line R.R. v. Transportation Union, 90 S.Ct. 294, 300–301, 72 LRRM 2838, 2842 (1969), the Court not reaching the duty to bargain issue. In World Airways, Inc., 54 LA 101, 105–107 (Roberts, 1969), the arbitrator considered the "Shore Line" decision inapplicable where the employer claimed contractual right for the contested action and the dispute thus involved contract interpretation rather than a major dispute under the RLA. As to permitted unilateral action under the RLA after bargaining has been exhausted, see Brotherhood of Loc. Eng. v. Baltimore & Ohio R. Co., 83 S.Ct. 691 (1963) [employer may put its bargaining proposals as to crews into effect]; Brotherhood of Ry. & S.S. Clerks v. Florida East Coast Ry. Co., 86 S.Ct. 1420 (1966) [within limits employer may make unilateral changes beyond its bargaining proposals].

could lawfully insist on the use of the grievance procedure and ultimately on arbitration to determine whether the management rights clause was broad enough in scope to include subcontracting.[64] Concerning this decision, Professors Archibald Cox and John T. Dunlop explained that it "implies that [the company] could lawfully stand on a favorable arbitration award until the expiration of the contract."[65] Furthermore, they expressed the conclusion that any duty to bargain during the term of the agreement can be channeled into a grievance and arbitration procedure:

"During the term of a collective bargaining agreement, an offer to follow the contract grievance procedure satisfies any duty to bargain collectively with respect to a matter to which the contract grievance procedure may apply. A refusal either to follow the contract procedure or to discuss the issue at large is a violation of Sections 8(a)(5) and 8(b)(3) [of the National Labor Relations Act]."[66]

Under one line of NLRB decisions the duty to bargain can be so channeled,[67] but another line of NLRB decisions holds that unilateral action by an employer can justify NLRB action on refusal to bargain charges despite provision in the agreement for arbitration.[68]

---

[64] Timken Roller Bearing Co. v. NLRB, 161 F.2d 949, 955 (CA 6, 1947), denying enforcement to 70 NLRB 500 (1946). Also see Square D Co. v. NLRB, 322 F.2d 360 (CA 9, 1964).

[65] Cox & Dunlop, "Regulation of Collective Bargaining by the National Labor Relations Board," 63 Harv. L. Rev. 389, 424 (1950).

[66] Cox & Dunlop, "The Duty to Bargain Collectively During the Term of an Existing Agreement," 63 Harv. L. Rev. 1097, 1101 (1950), italics omitted.

[67] For example, see McDonnell Aircraft Corp., 109 NLRB 930, 935 (1954), where the Board stated that the employer had satisfied the bargaining duty by willingness to arbitrate a grievance over unilateral action. For other cases in this line of decisions, see Bemis Bros. Bag Co., 143 NLRB 1311 (1963); Hercules Motor Corp., 136 NLRB 1648 (1962); National Dairy Prods. Corp., 126 NLRB 434 (1960).

[68] For example, see Unit Drop Forge Div., Eaton, Yale & Towne, Inc., 171 NLRB No. 73, 68 LRRM 1129 (1968); Cloverleaf Division of Adams Dairy Co., 147 NLRB 1410 (1964); Beacon Piece Dyeing & Finishing Co., 121 NLRB 953 (1958); John W. Bolton & Sons, Inc., 91 NLRB 989 (1950). For discussion of both lines of cases see Peck, "Accommodation and Conflict Among Tribunals," Southwest Legal Foundation 15th Annual Institute on Labor Law 138–142 (1969). In NLRB v. C & C Plywood Corp., 87 S.Ct. 559, 64 LRRM 2065 (1967), the agreement contained a wage scale to be effective upon signing of the agreement, "with wages closed for the term of" the agreement. However, the agreement gave the employer the right "to pay a premium rate over and above the contractual classified wage rate to reward any particular employee for some special fitness, skill, aptitude or the like." Soon after signing the agreement the employer announced that all members of certain crews would be paid a premium if their crews met certain production standards. The NLRB denied that the agreement gave the employer the right to do this and held

We have noted the NLRB's tendency (1) to hold economic decisions of management (not merely the effects of the decision but the making of the decision itself) to be matters of mandatory bargaining if job security or working conditions are affected, and (2) to construe waiver or zipper clauses narrowly, giving them very limited effect. Neither tendency gives weight to general management rights clauses or to the residual rights doctrine adhered to by many arbitrators. We have also noted a line of NLRB decisions under which the Board may take jurisdiction in unilateral action cases despite the presence of an arbitration clause (or even after an award has been issued). As General Counsel of the National Labor Relations Board, Arnold Ordman compared the approach taken by many arbitrators with that of the Board and he explained:

"In evaluating contractual provisions urged as a defense to unfair labor practice charges involving unilateral action, many arbitrators differ from the Board in their approach.

"The Board's evaluation of the circumstances in which the claim of privileged unilateral action is made usually involves considerations other than the interpretation of a single specific contract provision. Frequently, the claim of privilege is predicated, at least in part, on the presence of a generalized management prerogative clause, the absence of any express contractual prohibition of the particular action taken, or the union's failure to obtain a specific prohibition during negotiations. The Board has developed statutory principles for evaluating these general circumstances. For example, the Board with court approval has held that a waiver of statutory rights must be clear and unmistakable; waiver will not be found merely because a contract is silent on a subject protected by the Act, or because the contract contains a general management prerogative clause, or because the union in contract negotiations failed to obtain contractual protection for its statutory rights.

---

the unilateral change in contractual pay rates a violation of the bargaining duty. The Court of Appeals reasoned that the agreement "arguably" allowed the employer's act and divested the NLRB of jurisdiction over the union's unfair labor practice charge. The Supreme Court upheld the Board's jurisdiction to interpret the agreement in order to determine whether the employer had violated any duty to bargain. In so holding, the Court noted that the agreement did not contain an arbitration clause. In NLRB v. Huttig Sash & Door Co., 377 F.2d 964, 968–969 (CA 8, 1967), even though the agreement did contain an arbitration clause, the court relied on "C & C Plywood" in upholding NLRB jurisdiction to find a bargaining duty violation in the unilateral reduction of wages. That dual jurisdiction technically does exist in the NLRB (to enforce the statute) and the arbitrator (to interpret and apply the agreement) appears clear. See Chapter 10, subtopic titled "The NLRA, the Arbitrator, and the NLRB."

"Many arbitrators, since they are concerned solely with whether there has been a breach of contract, consider it improper for arbitrators to apply the statutory principles developed by the Board or to apply them differently than the Board does. Some arbitrators apply the so-called 'residual rights' theory where management takes unilateral action, holding that management is free to act unless the collective bargaining agreement expressly prohibits the challenged conduct. * * *

*   *   *   *   *

"* * * In short, in a unilateral-action case, a reference to an arbitrator for a decision of the contract question may well either be a futile gesture or lead to a result in conflict with the policies of the Act. Under such circumstances, is there justification for the Board to delay enforcement of the public command to bargain collectively until an arbitration is had?"[69]

General Counsel Ordman's conclusion was that "The exercise of Board discretion to defer to arbitration must be determined on a case-by-case basis."[70]

From the standpoint of an arbitrator *who is limited by the common prohibition that the arbitrator not add to, subtract from, or modify the agreement,* the following categories or possibilities appear most likely when action taken by an employer in the management of the enterprise is challenged by an arbitrable grievance:[71]

(A) The arbitrator may find that the action is prohibited (1) expressly or impliedly by some specific provision of the agreement, or (2) by an "implied limitation" or "implied obligation" under some general provision of the agreement such as the recognition clause, or (3) by the arbitrary, capricious, or bad-faith character of the action, or (4) by some binding past practice deemed a part of the "whole" agreement.[72]

(B) The arbitrator may find that management expressly or impliedly has an affirmative right to take the action under the management rights clause or some other provision in the agreement, or under some past practice.

---

[69] Ordman, "The Arbitrator and the NLRB," The Arbitrator, the NLRB, and the Courts 47, 64–66 (The Bureau of National Affairs, Inc., 1967), citations omitted.
[70] Id. at 67. For discussion and cases reflecting the Board's practice as to deferring to arbitration (both before and after an award has been rendered), see Chapter 10, subtopic titled "The NLRA, the Arbitrator, and the NLRB."
[71] For a different method of classifying cases, and from a somewhat different standpoint, see Simkin, Mediation and the Dynamics of Collective Bargaining 301–305 (The Bureau of National Affairs, Inc., 1971).
[72] For discussion, see topic titled "Views Regarding Management Rights," above.

(C) The arbitrator may find that the action is neither expressly nor impliedly covered by any part of the agreement or by any binding practice, but is an action taken in the good faith management of the enterprise.

No doubt many arbitrators, and certainly those who adhere to the residual rights doctrine, would deny the grievance unless the arbitrator finds that one of the possibilities under category (A) properly applies under the facts. In this general regard, many arbitrators have taken the view that their function is to interpret and apply the agreement rather than to enforce affirmative duties under the NLRA, and they have refused to decide whether any statutory duty to bargain has been violated.[73]

In contrast to the aforementioned possibilities, the essence of NLRB doctrine is "that the contract does not permit unilateral action *without prior discussion* unless the employer's right to take such action is clearly and unmistakably spelled out in the contract."[74]

The NLRB's views as to required bargaining before management makes economic decisions and the Board's requirement that any waiver be express and specific have been criticized by former NLRB Chairman Guy Farmer:

> "A requirement placed on employers to bargain individually and piecemeal over their decisions affecting employment conditions constitutes a non-too-subtle, dramatic shift of bargaining power to unions, in that it requires employer bargaining at the critical time when employer action is essential and delay is costly. Presumably, having been placed in such an advantageous bargaining position, the union will expect some quid pro quo each time management proposes to implement a decision which, by definition, has become negotiable. Depending on the need for promptness, the employer may well find it necessary to give the quid pro quo or to abandon the proposed action, in order to avoid the time-consuming rituals of bargaining as viewed by the Board.

    *   *   *   *   *

---

[73] For cases, see Chapter 10, subtopic titled "The NLRA, the Arbitrator, and the NLRB."

[74] Mittenthal, "The Role of Law in Arbitration," Developments in American and Foreign Arbitration 42, 56–57 (The Bureau of National Affairs, Inc., 1968). Under NLRB doctrine the employer also must bargain before changing wages or terms and conditions of employment established by a collective agreement even though that agreement has expired. See observations in NLRB v. Burns International Security Services, Inc., 92 S.Ct. 1571, 1585, 80 LRRM 2225, 2233 (1972).

"Two unfortunate consequences may be foreseen * * * . First, the added strain on the collective bargaining mechanism will cause a deterioration of the labor-management relationship, which may be manifested in more serious disputes and an increase in the incidence of strikes. Second, the bargaining stalemates which will ensue will have a depressing effect on business expansion and, over the long haul, will retard automation, perpetuate uneconomic business operations and blunt competition. They will tend to convert an essentially flexible industrial economy into a crystallized, inefficient and antiquated system."[75]

As to the possibility of narrowing the area of conflict between arbitrators and the NLRB, one arbitrator has suggested that the evolution of basic principles which command general acceptance "is more likely to be achieved by Board movement toward arbitration concepts than the other way around."[76]

Inroads Through Collective Bargaining

Collective bargaining is said to be "the very mechanism by which organized workers may achieve control and exercise it jointly with management"; and again, "The primary mechanism by which unions may share managerial authority in the corporation is collective bargaining, including both contract negotiations and grievance procedures, supported by the power of the strike."[77]

Restrictions made by collective bargaining agreements upon management rights are not always confined to the area of wages, hours, and conditions of employment. In fact, it is conceivable that such restrictions might invade the entire field of management functions.

---

[75] Farmer, Management Rights and Union Bargaining Power 9–10 (1965). For other severe criticisms of NLRB bargaining doctrine from the management point of view, see O'Connell, "Erosion of Management Rights," 1969 Labor Relations Yearbook 345 (BNA, 1970); O'Connell, "The Drive Toward Joint Participation and Co-Determination," 1967 Labor Relations Yearbook 71 (BNA, 1968); Anderson, "The Duty to Bargain During the Term of the Contract," 1967 Labor Relations Yearbook 242 (BNA, 1968). For severe criticism from a neutral source, see Northrup, Compulsory Arbitration 98–99 (1966).

[76] Mittenthal, "The Role of Law in Arbitration," Developments in American and Foreign Arbitration 42, 57–58 (The Bureau of National Affairs, Inc., 1968). Were arbitrators to make decisions consistent with "Board law" it "would mean the rejection of a method of contract construction which [arbitrators] have helped to develop over the past 25 years and which the parties have accepted by and large. * * * On the other hand, if arbitrators continue on the present course, the division between the arbitrator and Board is likely to widen." Id. at 57. For general discussion of arbitral adherence to legal doctrine, see Chapter 10, topic titled "Range of Views as to Application of 'Law.' "

[77] Chamberlain, The Union Challenge to Management Control 105 (1948).

There is nothing to prevent weaker employers from bargaining, and making concessions, with respect to practically any matter in the area of management functions concerning which stronger unions may wish to have a voice.

Management has been cautioned that the invasion of its rights through collective bargaining may be more far-reaching than appears on the surface, and that its rights often are given away unwittingly:

> *Economist Sumner H. Slichter:* "In actual bargaining, the working rules of trade unions are built up gradually one or two at a time. This leads to an atomistic consideration of their effects, which may cause their effects as a whole to be overlooked."[78]

> *Attorney Robert Abelow:* "Rights are often given away—not taken away. Employers frequently negotiate away their responsibilities by accepting proposals which at the time seem innocuous or not immediately harmful. Being mainly concerned with the immediate problems at hand, employers are prone to make concessions on proposals, the effect of which they do not foresee, or if they do, seem too far off to worry about."[79]

It has similarly been cautioned that where frontal attacks on management rights have not met with success, union negotiators have developed flanking maneuvers which have been more effective. The success of such maneuvers is said to be due to the fact that they are methods of approach which appear on the surface to be reasonable and that their danger to management often is not perceived until too late. These indirect methods of invasion are considered to include (1) mutual-consent clauses, (2) joint committees of labor and management, (3) clauses for the application of strict length-of-service seniority, and (4) unlimited arbitration clauses.[80]

Inroads Through Arbitration

Sometimes belief is expressed that arbitration is a device by which a union may broaden its authority within an industrial enterprise.[81]

---

[78] Slichter, Union Policies and Industrial Management 578 (1941).

[79] Abelow, "The Challenge to Management's Rights," Symposium on Labor Relations Law 260, 263 (Edited by Ralph Slovenko, 1961).

[80] Hill & Hook, Management at the Bargaining Table 61 (1945); Dunn, Management Rights in Labor Relations 111–112 (1946). Also see Abelow, "The Challenge to Management's Rights," Symposium on Labor Relations 260, 263 (1961).

[81] Hill & Hook, ibid; Dunn, ibid. Abelow, id. at 266–268. Also, Chamberlain, The Union Challenge to Management Control 107 (1948). However, it has been reminded that union rights also may be lost through arbitration. Cooper, "Comments," Symposium on Labor Relations Law 285, 287 (1961).

It is said that management rights may be lost through the use of "wide open" arbitration clauses under which the arbitrator is given authority to decide questions raised by the union concerning any matter, whether within or without the scope of the collective agreement. Moreover, warning is given that management rights also may be lost through "the creation of contract ambiguities due to inept use of the English language, which enable an arbitrator to interpret a clause in a manner not intended by the employer."[82] This spokesman also added, however, that management rights may be protected, too, through the arbitration provisions of an agreement.[83]

When an "interests" dispute is submitted to arbitration, there is some substitution of the judgment of the arbitrator for that of the parties. "To the extent that his decision finds in favor of the union, whether in whole or in part, he becomes the instrument by which union power has been extended."[84]

In regard to arbitration clauses, management spokesmen have recommended the use of certain "protective" clauses designed to prevent the invasion of management rights through arbitration. For example, the following clause has been suggested:

"The sole and only function of the arbitrator shall be to decide if there was or was not a violation of an express provision or provisions of the agreement, and in the performance of such function he shall apply the law of the state in which the agreement was executed."[85]

Another suggested clause would state:

"Provided, however, that if such a grievance is carried to arbitration, the Arbitrator shall not substitute his judgment for that of Man-

---

[82] Story, Arbitration as a Part of the Collective Bargaining Agreement 4 (1948).

[83] Id. at 1.

[84] Chamberlain, The Union Challenge to Management Control 107 (1948). For one arbitration board's explanation of the surrender of management rights (and also of the union's right to test its contentions by a show of economic strength) in "interests" arbitration, see Pan American Airways, Inc., 5 LA 590, 595 (Cahn, Snyder & Forge, 1946).

[85] Lamfrom, "Comments," Symposium on Labor Relations Law 283, 284 (1961). For a similar suggestion, see Story, Arbitration as a Part of the Collective Bargaining Agreement 10 (1948). In Worcester Teachers' Assn., 54 LA 796, 806 (1970), Fact-Finder Seidenberg recommended adoption of an arbitration clause prohibiting the arbitrator from adding to, subtracting from, or altering the terms of the agreement, and also providing: "Neither shall the Arbitrator have the power to alter or modify any policy of the School Board or action of the Superintendent of Schools, not clearly inconsistent with the terms of the Agreement."

agement and shall reverse the decision of Management only if he finds that it has acted arbitrarily and without reason, or for the purpose of escaping or defeating any of the other articles of this Agreement."[86]

A variety of protective or limitation clauses have been suggested by management representatives as a response to the "Trilogy" and subsequent decisions of the U.S. Supreme Court.[87]

Management Rights Clauses

While management representatives have sometimes disagreed in the past regarding the advisability of having a management rights clause, such provisions now appear to be widely favored by management.[88]

Management rights clauses vary widely in form and content. The clause may provide simply that "all normal prerogatives of management shall be retained by the Company except as specifically limited or abridged by the provisions of this agreement."[89] Clauses with much more detail as to management's rights are illustrated by the following provision stating specific powers to be exercised by management:

"Section 1. It is expressly agreed that all rights which ordinarily vest in and are exercised by employers such as COMPANY, except such as are clearly relinquished herein by COMPANY, are reserved to and shall continue to vest in COMPANY. This shall include, this enumeration being merely by way of illustration and not by way of limitation, the right to:

"(a) Manage the plant and direct the working forces, including the right to hire and to suspend, discipline or discharge employees for proper cause.

---

[86] Clifton, "Management Functions," N.Y.U. First Ann. Conf. on Labor 89, 97 (1948). A similar clause was involved in DeLaval Separator Co., 18 LA 900, 901–903 (Finnegan, 1952).

[87] See survey by Smith & Jones, "The Impact of the Emerging Federal Law of Grievance Arbitration on Judges, Arbitrators, and Parties," 52 Va. L. Rev. 831, 902–907 (1966).

[88] For a collection of views as to use of management rights clauses, see Cummins Diesel Sales Corp., 34 LA 636, 641 (Gorsuch, 1960). Two surveys of 400 representative agreements disclosed that about 70 percent have management rights clauses. See "Basic Contract Patterns: Management, Union Rights," 1970 Labor Relations Yearbook 42 (BNA, 1971). As a mandatory subject of bargaining, employers may insist that the agreement contain a management rights clause. NLRB v. American National Insurance Co., 343 U.S. 395, 30 LRRM 2147 (1952).

[89] K & T Steel Corp., 52 LA 497, 500 (Simon, 1969). Similarly, see Winnebago County, 53 LA 1305, at 1305, 1307 (Gundermann, 1969).

"(b) Transfer employees from one department and/or classification to another.

"(c) Lay off or relieve employees from duty because of lack of work or for other legitimate reasons.

"(d) Promote and/or transfer employees to positions and classifications not covered by this agreement, it being understood employees in the bargaining unit cannot be forced to take a position outside the bargaining unit.

"(e) Make such operating changes as are deemed necessary by it for the efficient and economical operation of the plant, including the right to change the normal work-week, the number of hours normally worked during the work-week, the length of the normal workday, the hours of work, the beginning and ending time of each shift or assignment, and the number of shifts to be operated.

"(f) Transfer persons from positions and classifications not covered by this agreement to positions and/or classifications covered hereby.

"(g) Maintain discipline and efficiency.

"(h) Hire, promote, demote, transfer, discharge or discipline all levels of supervision or other persons not covered by this agreement.

"(i) Determine the type of products to be manufactured, the location of work within the plant, the schedules of production, the schedules of work within work periods, and the methods, processes, and means of manufacture and the conduct of other plant operations."[90]

The simpler clauses were once favored because of their clear-cut statement of the rule that the employer has all the proprietary rights of management except as restricted by the terms of the agreement.[91] However, as one reaction to the 1960 *Trilogy,* many management representatives now prefer a much more extensive and detailed clause to specify as fully as possible the matters over which management retains full discretion.[92] Indeed, one management spokesman has urged that the desirability of a strong and detailed management rights clause is now "redoubled" as serving a dual purpose: "One is statutory—

---

[90] Southern Aircraft Corp. and Int'l. Union of United Automobile, Aircraft, and Agricultural Implement Workers of America.

[91] See Story, Arbitration as a Part of the Collective Bargaining Agreement 11 (1948); Dunn, Management Rights in Labor Relations 109 (1946).

[92] Smith & Jones, "The Impact of the Emerging Federal Law of Grievance Arbitration on Judges, Arbitrators, and Parties," 52 Va. L. Rev. 831, 897–902 (1966), where detailed clauses favored by management representatives are quoted. For an agreement using *both* the simpler "residual rights" clause and the detailed clause, see Almaden Vineyards, Inc., 56 LA 425, 426 (Kagel, 1971).

protection against the [NLRB] and its duty-to-bargain philosophy—
and the other contractual—protection against the invasion of the
management area through arbitration."[93]

No doubt, a management rights clause may strengthen the employer's position before an arbitrator.[94] It is also clear that during
the term of a collective agreement which contains a broad and detailed
management rights clause the employer may not be required to bargain about some changes upon which, in the absence of such clause,
he might otherwise be compelled to bargain.[95] Another significant purpose of such clauses is to aid union officials in explaining to the membership what the agreement does and does not give them.[96]

Impact of Arbitration Upon Management Rights

The extensive use of labor-management arbitration has resulted
in the evolution of a continually developing private system of industrial
jurisprudence. Included within the growing body of industrial rulings
are many involving management rights issues. While legal principles,
as well as court and administrative board decisions, loom in the background, relatively wide discretion is left to arbitrators to deal with
the law according to their best judgment.[97] It should be recognized,
therefore, that arbitral case law is in itself a separate and distinct
institution. It also should be recognized that the industrial jurisprudence of arbitrators will not always be in absolute harmony with
the course of decisions under the National Labor Relations Act.[98]

The primary objective of the remainder of this Chapter will be
to consider the effective scope of management rights as evidenced and
outlined by arbitration awards.

---

[93] O'Connell, "Erosion of Management Rights," 1969 Labor Relations Yearbook 345, 350, 353 (BNA, 1970).
[94] For example, see National Cash Register Co., 46 LA 317, 320 (Kates,
1966).
[95] See Consolidated Foods Corp., 183 NLRB No. 78 (1970); Cello-Foil Products, Inc., 72 LRRM 1196 (NLRB, 1969); LeRoy Machine Co., 56 LRRM
1369 (NLRB, 1964); The Borden Company, 35 LRRM 1133 (NLRB, 1954).
As to management's right to insist on a clause insuring it the right to take
unilateral action on matters not specifically covered by the agreement, see Long
Lake Lumber Co., 182 NLRB No. 65, 74 LRRM 1116 (1970), holding that
insistence on such a clause was not an unlawful refusal to bargain.
[96] See Phelps, "Management's Reserved Rights: an Industry View," Management Rights and the Arbitration Process 103, 113–114 (BNA Incorporated, 1956).
[97] For extensive discussion, see the first four topics in Chapter 10.
[98] See this Chapter, subtopic titled "The Duty to Bargain: Right of Unilateral
Action"; Chapter 10, subtopic titled "The NLRA, the Arbitrator, and the NLRB."

Control of Operation Methods

In general, arbitrators have recognized broad authority in management (absent clear limitations in the agreement) to determine methods of operation.[99] It has been said that unless restricted by contract, management has the right "to determine what is to be produced, when it is to be produced, and how it is to be produced."[100] Again, unless restricted by the agreement management has the right to determine what work shall be done,[101] to determine what kinds of services and business activity to engage in,[102] and to determine the techniques, tools, and equipment by which work in its behalf shall be performed.[103]

Management must have some discretion as to the method of carrying on its operations. It "should not be put in a straight jacket."[104] A primary function of management is to operate on the most efficient basis.[105] "In the operation of any plant, management has a fixed obligation to see that unnecessary costs are dispensed with and that production programs are changed to meet changing production demands. This is an inherent right * * * ."[106]

---

[99] See general statements by Arbitrator A. P. Roberts in 54 LA 896, 900; Whyte in 54 LA 807, 814; Turkus in 44 LA 1219, 1223; Kamin in 42 LA 173, 175; Markowitz in 41 LA 1087, 1090; Koven in 39 LA 939, 940–941; Raimon in 36 LA 621, 626; Dworkin in 29 LA 787, 792; Kesselman in 28 LA 441, 444–445; R. S. Roberts in 27 LA 736, 742–743; Klamon in 22 LA 336, 351; McCoy in 6 LA 681, 687. Also see Davey in 40 LA 700, 705–706; Fleming in 30 LA 147, 149. For related discussion see Chapter 12, topic titled "Custom and Practice as Part of the Contract." Contract clauses requiring management to discuss or give notice of operational changes have been narrowly construed so as not to impose an undue limitation on management. See Arbitrator Kelliher in 43 LA 267, 268–269; Smith in 43 LA 193, 206–207; Uible in 41 LA 510, 512; Jaffee in 40 LA 114, 117–118.

[100] Torrington Co., 1 LA 35, 42 (Courshon, 1945). Similarly, see Arbitrator Roberts in 54 LA 896, 900; Bauder in 22 LA 163, 165.

[101] Pacific Mills, 9 LA 236, 238 (McCoy, 1947); Gulf Oil Corp., 3 LA 798, 800 (Carmichael, 1946).

[102] Detroit Edison Co., 43 LA 193, 209 (Smith, 1964), also holding that a past practice of engaging in a particular line of activity of itself provides no contractual assurance that it will be continued.

[103] Corn Products Co., 42 LA 173, 175 (Kamin, 1964). Also see Arbitrator Rohman in 44 LA 682, 686.

[104] Shell Oil Co., 44 LA 1219, 1223 (Turkus, 1965); Thompson Mahogany Co., 5 LA 397, 399 (Brandschain, 1946).

[105] See Arbitrator Larkin in 54 LA 250, 252; Turkus in 44 LA 1219, 1223; Eyraud in 36 LA 1388, 1392; McIntosh in 33 LA 860, 861; Dworkin in 29 LA 787, 792; Marshall in 29 LA 687, 692; Kesselman in 28 LA 441, 445; Ridge in 26 LA 422, 426–427; Myers in 10 LA 261, 265.

[106] Youngstown Sheet & Tube Co., 4 LA 514, 517 (Miller, 1946). Also see Arbitrator Gross in 20 LA 749, 750; Klamon in 15 LA 782, 789. However, where the agreement expressly prohibited the employer from using spray equip-

The line of demarcation between "operation methods" and "working conditions" often must be determined. In one case Arbitrator Whitley P. McCoy noted the difficulty which such determination may entail. The agreement of the parties recognized the exclusive right of management to determine methods of operation, but it also restricted the right of management to change working conditions by requiring negotiations with the union before such changes could be made. The employer changed the operations of some employees from a noncontinuous to a continuous basis in the interest of plant efficiency, with the result that the employees were ordered to work through a period previously allowed for washing up. Arbitrator McCoy ruled that the order requiring the employees to work through the wash-up period was proper as an incidental result of the employer's good-faith exercise of the exclusive right to determine methods of operation. He stated the general considerations involved:

> "The distinction between a change in working conditions, which by the terms of the contract must be the subject of negotiation prior to its institution, and a change in methods of operation, which by the terms of the contract is a sole function of management, is not easy to define or even to make clear by example. Abolition or sharp curtailment of an existing practice concerning rest time, wash-up time, paid lunch period, furnishing of shower baths and lockers, matters pertaining to sanitation, safety and health, or such like matter are clearly changes in working conditions. On the other hand, a change from the use of pot heaters to McNeill presses or from noncontinuous to continuous operation is just as clearly a change primarily in methods of operation. The latter changes usually cause, with respect to the individuals affected, some change of their working habits, but they are primarily and essentially changes in methods, not in conditions, and as such are exclusively a management function, subject only to the right of affected employees to resort to the grievance procedure to correct abuses or hardships such as decreased earnings or stretchout. Of course a change that was merely in form one of method, used as a pretext to institute a change of working conditions, would not be justifiable."[107]

---

ment without written consent of the union, the arbitrator enforced the restriction even though such equipment would have been more efficient for the particular job. Claremont Painting & Decorating Co., 46 LA 894, 895–896 (Kerrison, 1966).

[107] Goodyear Tire & Rubber Co., of Ala., 6 LA 681, 687 (1947). Also dealing with the line between "operation methods" and "working conditions," see Arbitrator Kabaker in 55 LA 1306, 1308–1309; Stouffer in 44 LA 1134, 1137–1138; Kovenock in 40 LA 300, 303–304; Koven in 39 LA 939, 940–941;

The right of management to determine the types of machinery and equipment to be used and to determine the processes of manufacture may be stated specifically in the agreement. This right also might be ruled to be included in a clause reserving the right of general management of the plant to the employer.[108] Even if such right is not specified in the agreement, numerous cases expressly or inferentially recognize that it can be exercised as a residual management power except as it has been restricted by the agreement.[109]

As a corollary it follows that the employer has the right to have the employees operate improved machines and perform changed operation methods in good faith up to the level of their productive capacity.[110] Employees may be inclined to resist technological change, for workers who have spent years in a skilled trade are reluctant to risk its disappearance. "The need of the manufacturer to improve production methods is matched by the concern of the employees that they may be thrown out on the streets."[111]

In this general regard, it has been observed that:

"Whenever a job is abolished, a machine discontinued, or work in a department is discontinued, men lose jobs and their seniority rights to jobs are affected. But this involves no wrong of itself; it is merely one of the forms of injury or damage flowing from an act. The primary

Dworkin in 29 LA 787, 792–793; Marshall in 29 LA 687, 692–693; Kesselman in 28 LA 441, 444; Roberts in 27 LA 736, 742–743; Updegraff in 20 LA 890, 891; Hampton in 15 LA 603, 607–608.

[108] For example, see Associated Shoe Industries of Southeastern Mass., 10 LA 535, 537–539 (Myers, 1948). Also see Arbitrator Raimon in 36 LA 621, 626; Healy in 11 LA 703, 705–706; Myers in 10 LA 261, 264–265.

[109] See Arbitrator Dworkin in 45 LA 897, 902; Cahn in 45 LA 609, 610–611; Markowitz in 41 LA 1087, 1090; Kagel in 40 LA 62, 63; Koven in 39 LA 939, 940–941; Eyraud in 36 LA 1388, 1392; Ross in 35 LA 695, 697–698; Updegraff in 30 LA 115, 117, and in 7 LA 943, 945; Beatty in 26 LA 1, 3; Townsend in 17 LA 472, 475. Even where the agreement expressly imposed some requirement or limitation upon management in regard to automation or technological changes, the provisions were narrowly interpreted to apply only to sweeping and fundamental changes. Los Angeles Herald Examiner, 45 LA 860, 861–862 (Kadish, 1965); Mackay Radio & Telegraph Co., 42 LA 612, 617–619 (Koven, 1964).

[110] Associated Shoe Industries of Southeastern Mass., 10 LA 535, 539 (Myers, 1948). To similar effect, Arbitrator Porter in 52 LA 162, 164; Lehoczky in 45 LA 996, 998; Tatum in 41 LA 1147, 1150; Whiting in 38 LA 644, 646; Stouffer in 34 LA 165, 169; Brecht in 17 LA 268, 270.

[111] Associated Shoe Industries of Southeastern Mass., 10 LA 535, 538 (Myers, 1948).

question is whether the act was wrongful. If it was not, then no question can properly arise as to damage."[112]

It has been suggested, too, that the exercise of this management function serves to protect the interests of the employees as well as of the employer, for if the employer is permitted to operate new machinery, "his competitive position will be enhanced, improving his chance to win new business and thereby to provide greater employment."[113] Similarly, an Emergency Board under the Railway Labor Act declared that: "An employment stabilization program based upon rules which freeze existing jobs, bar improvement in work methods and block technological progress reaps more damage than benefit."[114] The Board recommended against a union proposal which would freeze existing jobs, but the Board recommended that the parties take steps to minimize the adverse effects upon employees resulting from operational changes by the employer.[115]

Wage Adjustments Following Changes in Operation Methods

Changes in operation methods, which are largely left within the discretion of management, often necessitate adjustments in wage rates. While the employer has wide discretion in determining operation methods, he is closely restricted in the determination of wage rates for new or changed processes.

The right initially to determine the job rate for a new or altered job may be given to management by the agreement. The following clause is illustrative:

"* * * rates on all new or changed operations shall be temporarily established by the employer * * * . If a grievance arises there-

---

[112] Allegheny Ludlum Steel Corp., 20 LA 455, 457 (McCoy, 1953). Also see Arbitrator Kagel in 56 LA 425, 429; Ross in 35 LA 695, 697–698; Fleming in 30 LA 147, 149; Updegraff in 28 LA 135, 136–137; Roberts in 27 LA 736, 742–744; Beatty in 26 LA 1, 3. However, in Premier Albums of New Jersey, 41 LA 945, 946–947 (Mazur, 1963), it was held that while the employer had the right to introduce new machinery, no worker could be terminated due to the change.

[113] Associated Shoe Industries of Southeastern Mass., 10 LA 535, 539 (Myers, 1948).

[114] Southern Pacific Co. v. Railroad Telegraphers, 37 LA 413, 421 (Platt, Wyckoff & Handsaker, 1961).

[115] Id. at 422–424.

from, the price shall be negotiated * * * . If unable to agree the matter shall be arbitrated in accordance with this contract."[116]

If the agreement does not give the employer the right initially to set the new rate, an arbitrator may require him to bargain before setting a rate. Arbitrator Harry H. Platt, for instance, speaking as chairman of an arbitration board, ruled that, under an agreement recognizing the union "as the sole collective bargaining agency for the employees of the company" and in the light of the continuing legal duty of the employer to bargain during the entire life of the contract, the employer could not unilaterally establish the rate for a new job.[117] However, Arbitrator Arthur M. Ross, speaking as chairman of another arbitration board, ruled that after negotiations had ended in disagreement the employer could install new rates, subject to challenge through the grievance and arbitration procedure, for this "is almost universally the practice in American industry."[118]

Another arbitrator, considering a contract which reserved the direction of the working forces to management and which provided that the company could re-timestudy and adjust piece rates after changes in materials, tools, or methods, expressed the view that management had and should have the right initially to determine job duties and job rates for new or altered jobs, because the "exigencies of production do not permit the problems arising from improved production methods to be settled in advance." This arbitrator noted that in some industries these matters are left initially to management determination, subject to the grievance procedure. He did recognize, however, that

---

[116] Associated Shoe Industries of Southeastern Mass., 10 LA 535, 537 (Myers, 1948). Also see Arbitrator Duff in 46 LA 295, 296; Lehoczky, Fisher & Myers in 32 LA 957, 958–959 (here "interests" arbitrators ordered use of a similar clause); Shipman in 21 LA 387, 389–390; Gilden in 9 LA 931, 937. Absent a specific provision for arbitration of rates of changed jobs, some arbitrators have denied their authority to set the rate. See Arbitrator Erbs in 49 LA 1270, 1274; Gregory in 41 LA 1169, 1174–1176. But a different conclusion was reached by Arbitrator Marshall in 23 LA 228, 233–234. For other cases dealing with the arbitrator's authority to set the rate on changed jobs, see Arbitrator Shister in 47 LA 601, 605–606; Willingham in 41 LA 1076, 1081–1082.

[117] Copco Steel & Engineering Co., 6 LA 156, 164 (1947). To similar effect, Arbitrator Marshall in 23 LA 228, 233; Carmichael in 14 LA 544, 546; Justin in 13 LA 177, 180. But see Lewis in 49 LA 202, 204 (management's right to create new jobs carries with it the right to set a new rate for the job if job is not same as existing classifications); Sizelove in 24 LA 726, 728; Klamon in 15 LA 782, 791. Also see Gregory in 14 LA 802, 805, where past practice strongly influenced the result reached.

[118] Keasbey & Mattison Co., 36 LA 423, 424 (1960).

this "requires the union to have the patience to endure management's determinations until the grievance procedure produces a remedy."[119]

Even where an agreement provided that existing rates should be continued without change, this was held not to preclude management from establishing new piece rates after introducing new equipment which materially changed job duties; Arbitrator Wayne L. Townsend reasoned that the requirement that rates be continued was based upon the assumption that equipment and methods would remain the same and, since that assumption was not borne out by subsequent events, the requirement did not apply.[120]

Many disputes concerning rates for new or changed operating methods have reached arbitration.[121] Arbitrators have recognized certain principles or standards to be considered in determining rates for new or changed operations (these standards are sometimes stated in the agreement). The standards observed by arbitrators should be noted because of their obvious practical importance.[122]

Hourly Rated Employees

The rule generally applied in the case of employees who work for hourly rather than incentive rates is that an increase in hourly rates should accompany any *material* increase in the workload.[123] Where the matter was not specifically covered by the contract, for instance, Arbitrator Whitley P. McCoy ruled that when a change is made in job content, the job should be restudied to determine whether the original workload has been changed sufficiently to necessitate an adjustment in the wage rate. He stated that it does not follow that simply because work has been added to a job there must necessarily be an increase of pay, though presumptively there should be; whether there should be an increase in pay "depends upon whether

---

[119] Diemolding Corp., 2 LA 274, 276 (Kharas, 1945). Also see Thor Corp., 16 LA 770, 772–774 (Baab, 1951). But the view has been expressed that to consider a unilateral action of management as a grievance is not a substitute for negotiation prior to the action. General Motors Corp., 7 LA 368, 371 (Griffin, 1947).

[120] A. C. L. Haase Co., 17 LA 472, 477–479 (1951).

[121] In some cases such disputes have been held nonarbitrable. See Arbitrator Teple in 46 LA 1189, 1194; McDermott in 44 LA 774, 777; Warns in 36 LA 329, 330.

[122] For related material, see this Chapter, topic titled "Production Standards, Time Studies, and Job Evaluation."

[123] For related material, see this Chapter, topic titled "Determination of Size of Crews."

the workload was too light and the increase does not make it too heavy or whether the workload was proper and the increase is material and makes it too heavy."[124]

A similar ruling was made by Arbitrator A. Howard Myers under a contract containing provision for rate revision following workload changes. Arbitrator Myers ruled that not all changes in workload necessitate a revision of wages.

"The theoretical issue arises as to whether every change in workload or equipment, irrespective of competitive conditions and original workload, justifies a rate increase. I think that the answer must be in the negative where, as here, the change results in raising an abnormally slow job rate to a still slow rate, with pay that is not inequitable in terms of comparable rates in this plant or in other plants * * * ."[125]

However, Arbitrator Clarence M. Updegraff appeared unwilling to give so much weight to the factor of a previously light workload where the agreement provided that consideration should be given to the adjustment of rates when the workload is materially increased. He ruled that such a provision does not permit the employer to discount entirely a material increase in the workload on the ground that the previous workload was too light, but that this is one of the factors which, without having a decisive effect, may be taken into consideration as limiting the increase to be granted.[126]

A slight increase in workload does not call for a higher rate.[127] It has been held that changing to new machines which produce more but which require less skill and effort does not constitute such change in the workload as to require revision of rates.[128] Where, however,

---

[124] Goodyear Tire & Rubber Co. of Ala., 6 LA 924, 925 (1947). Similarly, see Arbitrator Marshall in 51 LA 1051, 1054–1055; Shister in 44 LA 992, 995–996; Seinsheimer in 35 LA 113, 116–117. Also see Prasow in 40 LA 966, 969–970; Marshall in 29 LA 687, 692–693; Valtin in 28 LA 530, 531–532. For factors which an arbitrator considered in applying a contractual requirement that employees do "a reasonable day's work," see Arketex Ceramic Corp., 42 LA 125, 130–131 (Seinheimer, 1964).
[125] Verney Corp., 7 LA 27, 29 (1946). To similar effect, Aleo Mfg. Co., 19 LA 647, 649–650 (Maggs, 1952). Also see Arbitrator Markowitz in 52 LA 1306, 1309; Seward in 27 LA 906, 907.
[126] Continental Can Co., 5 LA 247, 250 (1946).
[127] See Arbitrator Strong in 41 LA 1038, 1041; Seinsheimer in 35 LA 113, 116–117; Abernethy in 4 LA 773, 775. As to what might be considered more than slight, see Arbitrator Kelliher in 13 LA 220, 222; Copelof in 5 LA 115, 118.
[128] Central Screw Co., 11 LA 108, 111 (Edes, 1948); E. F. Houghton & Co., 4 LA 716, 717–718 (Cahn, 1946). Also see Arbitrator Wood in 32 LA 216, 220; White in 13 LA 223, 225.

a new machine or operation involves more than a slight increase in duties, skill, responsibility, or hazards, rate revision may be required.[129]

Incentive Employees

"An incentive wage plan is a method of wage payment by which workers receive extra pay for extra production. In establishing wage incentive plans, consideration must be given to (1) the base rate for the job; (2) the amount of work required to earn the base rate; and (3) the relationship between extra work above the base and extra pay for the extra performance."[130]

A standard sometimes applied by arbitrators in reviewing the rates of incentive employees whose workload has been changed is the maintenance of prior earnings.[131] The theory underlying this standard

---

[129] See Arbitrator McIntosh in 54 LA 418, 420; Hertz in 48 LA 577, 578; Rubin in 47 LA 577, 579–580; Roberts in 45 LA 964, 967; Mazur in 41 LA 945, 947; Prasow in 40 LA 565, 568–569; Lehoczky in 38 LA 584, 585; Dworkin in 37 LA 323, 330; Justin in 28 LA 548, 553; Harbison in 21 LA 609, 611–612; Jaffee in 19 LA 452, 454; Reid in 19 LA 358, 361; Copelof in 16 LA 76, 78–79; Gilden in 9 LA 931, 937; Blair in 2 LA 572, 576. Also see Seward in 27 LA 906, 907; Donnelly in 23 LA 782, 783–784; Cahn in 17 LA 277, 278–280; Brecht in 17 LA 268, 271–272; Healy in 8 LA 88, 91. In Southwest Steel Corp., 38 LA 344, 345–346 (Duff, 1962), a temporary (one day) increase in workload required additional pay.

[130] Incentive Wage Provisions; Time Studies and Standards of Production (U.S. Dept. of Labor, Bureau of Labor Statistics, Bull. No. 908–3, p. 1, 1948). For an explanation of several different types of incentives used in industry (productivity incentive, continuity of operation incentive, quality incentive), see Keystone Steel & Wire Co., 55 LA 41, 50 (McKenna, 1970). In Weatherhead Co., 55 LA 837, 840 (Fish, 1970), the arbitrator listed reasons which might justify management in placing a ceiling on incentive production. For cases dealing with union access to incentive system data and records, see Tappan Co., 49 LA 922, 928 (Dworkin, 1967); Hydril Co., 37 LA 279, 282 (Lehoczky, 1961). For labor, management, and neutral views on arbitration of incentive disputes, see "Arbitration of Disputes Involving Incentive Problems," Critical Issues in Labor Arbitration 61–97 (BNA Incorporated, 1957). For other general discussions see Unterberger, "The Arbitration of Wage Incentive Cases," 23 Arb. J. 236 (1968); Davis, "Incentive Problems," Management Rights and the Arbitration Process 50 (BNA Incorporated, 1956); Morrison, "Arbitration of Wage Incentives," 11 Arb. J. (n.s.) 199 (1956); Waite, Seybold & Unterberger, "Problems in the Arbitration of Wage Incentives," Arbitration Today 25-44 (BNA Incorporated, 1955).

[131] See Arbitrator Stouffer in 28 LA 259, 264–265; Copelof in 10 LA 933, 940; Keister in 4 LA 386, 389; Dwyer in 4 LA 355, 358. This standard was given a significant role in the award of a steel industry incentive coordinating committee. See Coordinating Committee, Steel Companies, 53 LA 145, 149 (Simkin, Seward, Garrett, 1969). Also see Arbitrator McDermott in 46 LA 660, 664; Markowitz in 41 LA 1087, 1090; Garrett in 26 LA 812, 822; Townsend in 17 LA 472, 479.

is that incentive employees should be able to earn as much under the new operation as under the old.[132]

Another standard, much less concrete, requires the maintenance of the ratio of earnings to effort expended.[133] Under the "ratio of earnings to effort" standard no change in incentive rates is in order unless there is a change in the amount of incentive effort required per unit of incentive production.[134] Application of this standard means that employees receive increased earnings on that part of increased production that is due to increased work effort, and that management receives the benefit from that part of increased production that is due to mechanical improvements as such.[135]

Use of this standard is illustrated by a case in which the employer ordered an increase in the speed at which a machine was to be operated and simultaneously decreased the incentive rate. Although the decreased rate yielded higher earnings than the employees had received before the increase in machine speed, they demanded that the prior incentive rate be re-established since, even at the higher prior rate, earnings would be increased by a smaller percentage than the increase in effort required to control the machine at the higher speed. The arbitrator found that the increase in machine speed was 19 percent, that the increase in work effort was 16 percent, and that, even if the prior higher rate were used, the increase in earnings would amount only to 11.6 percent. Accordingly, he held the demand of the employees to be reasonable and ordered that the prior rate be re-established.[136]

---

[132] In this regard, there have been a number of cases dealing with management efforts to change from incentive to hourly rates. See Arbitrator Duff in 47 LA 1157, 1159–1160; Lehoczky in 40 LA 875, 878; Horlacher in 38 LA 434, 435–436; Warns in 27 LA 758, 760–761; Davey in 23 LA 490, 493–494; Seward in 17 LA 918, 920–921; McCoy in 13 LA 414, 416–417.

[133] This standard was used by Arbitrator Shipman in 37 LA 669, 670; Lehoczky in 22 LA 450, 452; Scheiber in 10 LA 20, 23–24; Blumer in 8 LA 846, 849; Hampton in 6 LA 579, 582; Whiting in 6 LA 218, 219–220; Dwyer in 4 LA 482, 483.

[134] American Steel & Wire Co., 8 LA 846, 849 (Blumer, 1947).

[135] Carnegie Illinois Steel Corp., 5 LA 712, 720 (Blumer, 1946), where it was also explained that the change in incentive effort is not necessarily the same as the change in work required for the operation. Also see Arbitrator McCoy in 28 LA 129, 131; Shipman in 21 LA 386, 390. Concerning a claim of hourly rated employees to the benefit of increased productivity where less skill was required on new machines, see Marsh Stencil Machine Co., 33 LA 1, 4–5 (Klamon, 1959).

[136] Anaconda Wire & Cable Co., 10 LA 20, 24 (Scheiber, 1948).

Reduction of incentive rates has been allowed where the introduction of new machinery has resulted in increased production without requiring an increase in effort.[137] Moreover, reduction of incentive rates has been ordered where employees controlled production on new machines at a very low level.[138]

It can be expected that no adjustment in incentive rates will be required as long as the change in the workload is slight.[139]

Production Standards, Time Studies, and Job Evaluation

"Whether wages are computed on a time or incentive basis, there is usually some formal or informal determination of the output expected of employees on each operation. This expected production is commonly called the work load or production standard and represents the amount of work required or expected to be done in a given time by the average, qualified operator under normal conditions * * *."[140]

Where the agreement contains no express provisions on the subject, it has been held in many cases that management has the right to set reasonable production standards and to enforce them through discipline.[141] In other cases this general right of management was ex-

---

[137] Jenkins Bros, 11 LA 432, 435 (Donnelly, 1948); Reliance Mfg. Co., 3 LA 677, 679 (Whiting, 1946). Cf., Arbitrator Shipman in 17 LA 650, 653–654. For the imposition of a time limit (within a "reasonable time") for changing incentive rates in response to changes in production methods, see Worthington Corp., 34 LA 497, 503 (Crawford, 1959), where management waited too long to change the rate (producing lower earnings). For an illustration that the incentive premium can lose its appeal to employees, see Jenkins Bros., 33 LA 275, 277 (Donnelly, 1959).

[138] Associated Shoe Industries of Southeastern Mass., 10 LA 535, 538–539 (Myers, 1948); Wolverine Shoe & Tanning Corp., 15 LA 195, 196–197 (Platt, 1950). Concerning the pace at which employees should work when paid on a group incentive basis, see Pittsburgh Plate Glass Co., 36 LA 21, 22 (Lehoczky, Fisher & Myers, 1960).

[139] Schlueter Mfg. Co., 10 LA 295, 296–297 (Hilpert, 1948), where it was ruled, however, that the over-all effect of a succession of minor additions to an operation could be considered; Goodyear Tire & Rubber Co. of Ala., 5 LA 30, 35 (McCoy, 1946). Some agreements expressly provide for change in incentive rates when there is a "substantial" change in operations. For cases involving the application of such provisions, see 28 LA 129, 21 LA 387, 21 LA 84, 20 LA 455, 18 LA 375.

[140] Incentive Wage Provisions; Time Studies and Standards of Production (U.S. Dept. of Labor, Bureau of Labor Statistics, Bull. No. 908-3, p. 37, 1948).

[141] See Arbitrator Bradley in 54 LA 737, 744 (employer could discharge incentive employee who failed to produce enough to earn the federal minimum wage); C. McCoy in 50 LA 917, 921, and in 50 LA 136, 140; Solomon in 50 LA 888, 894–895; McIntosh in 49 LA 581, 583, and in 37 LA 758, 759–760;

pressly or impliedly recognized, but the discipline for failure to meet a production standard did not stand because the standard was unreasonable or because the discipline was for some other reason unjust.[142]

Production standards are commonly determined through time study, but they also may be based on past experience or production records or on "rule of thumb" determination.[143] Management's right to undertake time studies unilaterally has been emphasized,[144] and the union's right to make independent time studies for grievance purposes has also been recognized.[145]

Arbitrators use time study in reviewing rates after operation changes if the parties do not object.[146] Also, they may order or sustain

---

Roberts in 46 LA 1196, 1199–2000; Gilden in 44 LA 393, 394–395; Willingham in 43 LA 1155, 1157–1158; Kates in 42 LA 1286, 1291–1292; Altieri in 38 LA 894, 896; Mueller in 36 LA 1442, 1444–1445 (but discharge was reversed on contract procedural grounds); Schmidt in 33 LA 913, 915; Schedler in 32 LA 865, 867; Bradley in 32 LA 317, 321; Williams in 32 LA 122, 124; Prasow in 31 LA 33, 37; Eckhardt in 30 LA 1048, 1049–1050; Neff in 30 LA 264, 266. In Wallace-Murray Corp., 55 LA 372, 375–376 (Kabaker, 1970), the arbitrator explained that incentive workers may not be performing satisfactorily even though they may be earning their guaranteed minimum hourly wage, the guarantee being intended merely to protect them against complete loss of earnings due to some outside cause such as a mechanical break-down.

[142] See Arbitrator Krimsly in 51 LA 1280, 1283–1284 (production standard was "fraught with statistical distortions"); W. P. McCoy in 42 LA 1162, 1166 (employer may not set production standard on individual employee basis but must set it for the job involved); Teple in 40 LA 866, 872–874; Murphy in 39 LA 130, 133–134; Davis in 38 LA 896, 902 (failure to meet new production standard was due to lack of practice rather than alleged slowdown); Ruckel in 35 LA 584, 586–587 (discipline for failure to make standard must be related to consistency with which employee falls below standard); Maggs in 33 LA 694, 698–700; W. P. McCoy in 33 LA 203, 204–205 (constantly changing standard was unfair and unreliable).

[143] Incentive Wage Provisions; Time Studies and Standards of Production (U.S. Dept. of Labor, Bureau of Labor Statistics, Bull. No. 908-3, p. 37, 1948). For other discussion of principles involved and methods utilized in setting production standards, see Arbitrator Dworkin in 51 LA 101, 105; Altrock in 49 LA 320, 323–324; Sembower in 42 LA 298, 300–302; Nichols in 41 LA 953, 956–957; Lehoczky in 40 LA 33, 36–37; Mueller in 36 LA 1442, 1444–1445; Cahn in 32 LA 640, 641, and in 29 LA 828, 832–833; Meltzer in 32 LA 610, 611–612; Bradley in 32 LA 317, 321. For detailed treatment of time study, see Barnes, Motion and Time Study (5th Ed., 1963); Mundel, Motion and Time Study (3rd Ed., 1960).

[144] F & M Schaefer Brewing Co., 40 LA 199, 200–201 (Turkus, 1963). Also see Arbitrator Roberts in 46 LA 1196, 1199–2000.

[145] Fafnir Bearing Co. v. NLRB, 62 LRRM 2415 (CA 2, 1966); Armstrong Cork Co., 41 LA 1053, 1056–1058 (Shister, 1963). As to the use of company-paid union time study men, see Pittsburgh Plate Glass Co., 34 LA 908, 910–911 (Lehoczky, Fisher & Myers, 1960).

[146] See Simmons Co., 33 LA 725, 727 (Ross, 1959); Container Co., 6 LA 218, 220 (Whiting, 1946).

its use in rate setting where it has been used by the parties for this purpose in the past.[147]

The purpose of time study is to measure the work of an operation. "Each element of the operation is studied and a determination is made of the time required for its performance by a normal experienced operator working with normal effort and without undue fatigue."[148] Concerning the use of time study in incentive rate setting, Arbitrator Paul N. Lehoczky explained:

"* * * in conjunction with job evaluation (which determines relative base rates) it actually evaluates each incentive job in like terms and makes the ideal of 'equal pay for equal work' possible. When properly carried out, all jobs in the plant pay relatively equally well, and an expenditure of extra effort or skill applied to any job pays off equally well."[149]

We have just noted that "job evaluation" is used in determining relative base rates. As stated by one authority, "Job evaluation attempts to determine the worth of each job in relationship to the worth of all other jobs."[150]

A widely used method of job evaluation is the "point" method, under which, in general:

1. Factors are selected (and defined or described) which are common to the range of jobs to be rated (for example, the factors may be learning time, skill, responsibility, judgment decision, physical demand, working conditions, and the like).

---

[147] See Timken Roller Bearing Co., 6 LA 979, 983–984 (Lehoczky, 1947); National Malleable & Steel Castings Co., 4 LA 189, 194 (Gilden, 1946). Cf., Arbitrator Hilpert in 10 LA 295, 296.

[148] Ford Motor Co., 12 LA 949, 951 (Shulman, 1949). Similarly, see Timken Roller Bearing Co., 51 LA 101, 105 (Dworkin, 1968).

[149] Timken Roller Bearing Co., 6 LA 979, 983 (1947), also noting that use of time study in setting new rates may be favored over comparison with rates for similar operations since the establishment of new rates on the basis of existing rates tends to perpetuate existing intraplant inequities.

[150] Lanham, Job Evaluation 3 (1955). Job evaluation "involves several major phases such as securing and analyzing facts about jobs, writing up these facts into descriptions of the jobs, studying these descriptions and evaluating the jobs according to some rating method, and then pricing the jobs in relation to the evaluation." Id. at 5. For other writings on job evaluation, see Wiggins, The Arbitration of Industrial Engineering Disputes 91–121 (The Bureau of National Affairs, Inc., 1970); Unterberger, "Automation and Job Evaluation Techniques," Labor Arbitration and Industrial Change 238 (BNA Incorporated, 1963); Unterberger, "Arbitration of Job Evaluation Cases," 17 Arb. J. 219 (1962); Murphy, "Job Classification Arbitrations Under Bethlehem Steel Agreements," 16 Arb. J. 8 (1961); Johnson, Boise & Pratt, Job Evaluation (1946).

2. Different grades or degrees are specified (and defined or described) for each factor (for example, Grade A, Grade B, and so on), to be used to indicate the extent to which the factor exists in the given job.

3. A point value is assigned to each grade or degree of each factor (for example, Responsibility Factor Grade C may be assigned 45 points).

4. The job evaluator selects the grade or degree of each factor which most nearly describes the requirements for the job as indicated by the facts and evidence.

5. The total point value of the job is then obtained by simple addition.

To illustrate, if it is concluded that Skill Factor Grade A (10 points), Responsibility Factor Grade D (65 points), Judgment Decision Factor Grade B (25 points), and Working Conditions Factor Grade B (20 points) apply to the job, the total point value of the job will be 120 points. A job thus evaluated at 120 points will, by a previously set scale, carry a specified wage rate.[151] When an arbitrator is involved in job evaluation, his task under this system is to determine the applicable grade for each factor on the basis of the evidence and his observations during a plant visit (very important in job evaluation cases). The parties may then determine the total point value of the job and the rate or Labor Grade which that point value calls for under their agreement.

A basic function of job evaluation—determining the true requirements of the job—clearly emerges from the following statement by Arbitrator Paul N. Lehoczky:

"One of the major blocks to the bilateral settlement of job evaluation disputes is rooted in the fact that the parties concerned do not have a common basis for their discussions. In this case, for example, the grievant is strongly influenced by what he knows he brings to the job while the Company insists that only those characteristics listed in the job's description and only to the degree that they are detailed, are of value. In actual application, neither position is wholly correct; many of the grievant's abilities are not required to the degree he thinks they are and conversely, the availability of certain 'extra' ability, over and above what the job description calls for, is frequently essen-

---

[151] For extensive discussion of the point method, see Lanham, Job Evaluation 73–74 (1955); the Lanham study also discusses several other generally accepted methods. For citation of arbitration cases revealing a variety of job evaluation plans, see Wiggins, The Arbitration of Industrial Engineering Disputes 103 (1970).

tial. The job's description, after all, represents a theoretical analysis of what the job has been planned to require and not necessarily what it actually requires. This statement cuts both ways. Your arbitrator knows of many jobs whose descriptions call for degrees of knowledge and skills which the specific occupant could *never* produce nor will he ever be required to produce them."[152]

Arbitrator Lehoczky also emphasized that it is the job, not the man or machine, that is being evaluated:

"Again, two different jobs performed on the same make and model machine tool by the same operator in the same type of department may still carry different wage rates, all because it is the specific job that is being evaluated and not the man or the machine as such. The same lathe, for example, could be utilized for work which could range in value through perhaps five labor grades, from rough turning through the most intricate precision work. For this basic reason, one cannot accept unsupported examples from other plants as 'evidence' of specific job—or factor—values."[153]

Control of Quality Standards

Management has been held to have the right at all times to exercise control over the standards of quality of its products since "a lowering in the degree of quality under a competitive market may have serious and disastrous results."[154] Thus, it has been ruled that management had the right to determine what work was faulty and whether it should be reworked or scrapped where the determination was made by men well qualified and experienced in all departments and where it was the employer's policy to resolve all doubts in favor of the employees.[155]

The "competitive market" has been stressed by Arbitrator Clair V. Duff in sustaining the demotion of an employee for faulty work:

"In managing the Plant and directing the working forces Management has the right and the duty to insure the highest quality standards so that its product can be sold in a competitive market with the resultant benefits to the employer and employees, each of whom has a stake in the success of the enterprise. How this quality-control is to be attained is also the responsibility of Management.

---

[152] Victor Mfg. & Gasket Co., 48 LA 957, 958 (1967).
[153] Id. at 959.
[154] Torrington Co., 1 LA 20, 26 (Courshon, 1945).
[155] Ibid. As to management's right to establish and enforce a quality control program, see Patent Button Co., 43 LA 1208, 1211–1214 (King, 1965).

"* * * We are aware that most industries are becoming more competitive as their respective sales forces contest for a place in the market. Unless quality standards are maintained and unless a Company is in a position where it can provide a high quality product it cannot successfully exist in a competitive economy. Failure to achieve quality in a product not only reduces the benefit to the ultimate consumer but also places the Company in jeopardy with, at least potentially, a resultant disadvantage to itself and to its employees. In not a few industries the competition in quality of final product is as important as price competition."[156]

The company may have a legitimate concern not only with respect to the sale of its product, but also with regard to its reputation and the safety of persons who use its product. In this connection, the grievance of an employee who was discharged for faulty work was denied by Arbitrator Robert G. Howlett, who stated:

"* * * In such situations the manufacturing concern must be in a position to protect its reputation and the quality of its product. A company's failure to do so would redound to the detriment of all persons connected with the enterprise—owners, management and employees."[157]

He stated further:

"The Company necessarily is concerned with the production of good castings and the safety of persons who use its products. If faulty castings are produced by the * * * Company it will not only lose customers but property may be damaged and persons who come in contact with equipment in which its castings are placed may be injured, or even death may result."[158]

Management has the right to formulate and enforce reasonable rules for protecting the quality of its products.[159] Pursuant to such rules, it may in appropriate circumstances discharge or discipline em-

---

[156] American Radiator & Standard Sanitary Corp., 29 LA 167, 170 (1957). Similarly, Arbitrator McCoy sustained the demotion of an employee where management's action was based upon an "honest desire to improve efficiency and the quality of the Company's product." Firestone Tire & Rubber Co., 33 LA 206, 208 (1959).

[157] Valley Steel Casting Co., 22 LA 520, 525 (1954).

[158] Id. at 526. Also see Macomber, Inc., 39 LA 719, 723 (Teple, 1962); Lockheed Aircraft Corp., 31 LA 1036, 1037 (McIntosh, 1958). But in Lockheed Aircraft Corp., 35 LA 684, 685 (Grant, 1960), discharge was commuted to layoff despite serious faulty work, the arbitrator determining that the company must share the responsibility for the failure to inspect the work properly.

[159] Kellogg Co., 55 LA 84, 88 (Shearer, 1970), where management had a rule regulating the length of hair and sideburns to protect its products from hair contamination.

ployees who fail to meet quality standards.[160] Management also has the right to institute an inspection and testing program as declared by Arbitrator Rolf Valtin:

> "Management obviously is free to inspect products and to make sure that quality standards are being met. Inspection is a recognized and commonly followed part of practically every manufacturing process. Equally well-established is the rule that the work of any employee— craft or otherwise—is at all times subject to scrutiny and critical examination."[161]

While management has wide freedom to control quality standards, the fairness of penalties imposed for faulty work may be closely scrutinized by arbitrators.[162]

Job and Classification Control

It is difficult to formulate neat or precise categories in the discussion of cases involving the right of management to establish, eliminate, or combine jobs or job classifications, or cases involving its right to transfer duties between jobs or between job classifications. This is likewise true of cases involving the right of management to assign duties and tasks to workers.

This difficulty springs in part from the fact that the words "job" and "classification" at times are used synonymously and at other times are intended to carry different meanings.[163] In addition, different terminology utilized in the decision of cases involving similar issues (the arbitrator's choice of terminology often conforms to that utilized by the parties in presenting the given case), different meanings apparently intended in the use of similar terminology, failure of cases to define

---

[160] Ibid. Also Patent Button Co., 43 LA 1208, 1214 (King, 1965).

[161] Bethlehem Steel Co., 32 LA 541, 542 (1959).

[162] See Arbitrator Lucas in 44 LA 20, 22–23; King in 43 LA 1208, 1212–1214; McKelvey in 38 LA 586, 592–593; Marshall in 36 LA 1303, 1304; Dworkin in 36 LA 491, 495; Grant in 35 LA 684, 685; Duff in 29 LA 167, 169–170; Graff in 27 LA 656, 659–662; Howlett in 22 LA 520, 524–527; Noel in 19 LA 650, 652.

[163] "There is no question that the word 'job' may have a different meaning from the word 'classification.' Two men may have the same classification, for example, 'painter,' but one may have the job of keeping certain rooms painted while the other has the job of keeping certain equipment painted. On the other hand, the two words are sometimes used synonymously. The question is in what sense did the parties use the word [in their agreement]." Fulton-Sylphon Co., 2 LA 116, 117–118 (McCoy, 1946). Also see Arbitrator Talent in 50 LA 1061, 1066–1067; Herbert in 49 LA 445, 450, and in 27 LA 762, 764–765; Livengood in 20 LA 19, 21; McCoy in 1 LA 121, 124.

clearly the terminology that is used, and other such practices make it virtually impossible to arrange the cases into clearly outlined compartments. The many borderline situations, too, have produced many shadings of arbitral opinion touching upon otherwise basic issues.

For these reasons the Authors urge the reader to keep in mind the close relationship between (and frequent overlapping of) the materials in the subtopics which make up the remainder of this topic.[164]

Establishing, Eliminating, and Combining Jobs and Classifications

The right of management to establish new jobs or job classifications is sometimes specifically stated in the agreement, along with some provision for union challenge of management's actions via the grievance procedure and arbitration. The right also has been recognized as being vested in management except as restricted by the agreement and it likewise might be included within the scope of a general management rights clause.[165] Moreover, under an agreement stating that rates "for any new classifications will be negotiated," management not only had the right but was held to have an implied duty to establish a new classification when the company introduced a new and substantially different machine.[166]

Where job classifications are specifically set up by the agreement, and especially if the agreement is rigid as to classifications, management may not be permitted unilaterally to establish new classifications,[167] but as noted hereinbelow, many arbitrators have rejected the

---

[164] For other important related material, see Chapter 12, topic titled "Custom and Practice as Part of the Contract."

[165] See Arbitrator Laybourne in 50 LA 997, 999–1000; Buckwater in 50 LA 624, 631–632 (but here the contract did restrict the right); Ray in 46 LA 91, 94; Shafer in 45 LA 448, 450; Murphy in 36 LA 1392, 1394; Prasow in 30 LA 444, 448; Platt in 17 LA 697, 700–701; Bowles in 16 LA 955, 957; Reynolds in 8 LA 1041, 1042–1043. Also see Lewis in 49 LA 202, 204; Autrey in 41 LA 1140, 1143; Stouffer in 40 LA 898, 901–902; Sembower in 25 LA 188, 191; Marshall in 23 LA 228, 233–234; Wallen in 22 LA 831, 833; Gaffey in 18 LA 462, 468; Coffey in 12 LA 676, 679–680. Contra as to job classifications (requiring bargaining before their establishment), Donnelly in 18 LA 90, 92; Griffin in 7 LA 368, 371. In some cases the question arises as to what constitutes a "new job." For the answer given in one case, see Allegheny Ludlum Steel Corp., 32 LA 446, 451–452 (Platt & Mittenthal, 1949).

[166] Lockheed-Georgia Co., 48 LA 518, 519, 521 (King, 1967).

[167] See Arbitrator Ray in 45 LA 78, 80–81; Gilden in 13 LA 369, 371; Howard in 13 LA 3, 8. Also see Volz in 46 LA 1208, 1212–1213; Autrey in 42 LA 697, 698, 700–702; Willingham in 35 LA 662, 664; McCoy in 2 LA 319, 321. Cf., Davey in 48 LA 339, 341–342, 348; Wolff in 41 LA 1150, 1151–1152.

view that jobs or classifications are frozen by the mere fact that they are included in the agreement.

Arbitrators often have recognized the right of management, unless restricted by the agreement, to eliminate jobs (and where a few duties remain to reallocate them) where improved methods or other production justification exists and management otherwise acts in good faith.[168]

Arbitrators likewise have recognized management's right, where not restricted by the agreement, to eliminate job classifications (and reallocate the remaining duties) when done in good faith for a justifiable purpose.[169]

In upholding this right of management to eliminate jobs or classifications, Arbitrator Howard S. Block offered the following evaluation:

"The impact of a changing technology upon the work force has posed problems to both management and labor not easy of solution. That this issue has been a persistent and vexing one over the years is indicated by the significant number of arbitration proceedings on

---

[168] See Arbitrator Hilpert in 47 LA 778, 779–780; Bradley in 46 LA 685, 691; Abrahams in 44 LA 359, 361; Volz in 43 LA 353, 355; Marshall in 42 LA 945, 946; Stouffer in 41 LA 927, 931; Seward in 40 LA 850, 851; Seitz in 40 LA 511, 512; McDermott in 40 LA 70, 72; Altrock in 40 LA 65, 66; Raimon in 38 LA 196, 199–200; Di Leone in 37 LA 24, 29; Fleming in 32 LA 836, 837; Warns in 29 LA 324, 326–328; Wettach in 19 LA 797, 799; Sachs in 18 LA 616, 619–620; Gilden in 16 LA 252, 255–256; Klamon in 15 LA 782, 790–791; Copelof in 15 LA 754, 761; Smith in 12 LA 719, 721–722; Pollard in 10 LA 498, 510; Willcox in 10 LA 371, 378; Abernethy in 6 LA 314, 318–319. Also see Sembower in 49 LA 874, 880. Even where a contract contained a job-freezing clause, it was narrowly construed to permit elimination of a job as justified by changes in equipment and method. Anheuser-Busch, Inc., 36 LA 1289, 1295, 1300 (Hill, 1961). But see Arbitrator Nichols in 43 LA 1057, 1058–1060. In Borg-Warner Corp., 35 LA 367, 371–372 (Klein, 1960), the employer could not abolish a job and assign the duties to another employee where the duties continued to exist in significant proportions and substantially in the original form—the job was abolished in name only. Also see Arbitrator Schedler in 41 LA 120, 121–122.

[169] See Arbitrator Roberts in 54 LA 896, 900; Whyte in 54 LA 807, 814–816; Dworkin in 51 LA 1174, 1180–1181, and in 51 LA 1031, 1038–1039; Block in 48 LA 72, 76, and in 46 LA 1027, 1029–1030; Doyle in 48 LA 24, 25–32; Graff in 46 LA 329, 332–335; Horlacher in 64-1 ARB ¶8287; Leflar in 40 LA 769, 772–774; Murphy in 36 LA 1392, 1394–1395; Bothwell in 34 LA 24, 28–29; Updegraff in 33 LA 169, 171; Bauder in 33 LA 25, 28–29; Fleming in 32 LA 115, 116; Ridge in 26 LA 422, 427; Prasow in 25 LA 44, 49; Ryder in 20 LA 764, 767. Also see Witney in 54 LA 197, 203–204. But see Arbitrator Seidenberg in 51 LA 303, 308–309; Dworkin in 47 LA 396, 404; Gilden in 38 LA 799, 802; Davey in 38 LA 20, 28–31; Beatty in 25 LA 838, 840–841; Reynard in 22 LA 880, 882. For related discussion, see this Chapter, topic titled "Assigning Work Out of Bargaining Unit."

this subject dating back to the earliest reported decisions. A review of these decisions reveals that they fall into two fairly distinct categories which seem noteworthy here: (1) One line of cases emphasizes that where a Collective Bargaining agreement sets forth a comprehensive rate structure, the wage rate established for each classification evidences an agreement between the parties as to the wage rate, as well as the classification; these cases then go on to provide that, in general, the terms of this bargained for exchange may not be unilaterally altered. To the extent that some of these decisions regard the classification structure as being unalterably frozen during the life of the Agreement, they do not represent the weight of arbitration authority. (2) A second group of cases holds that the existence in the Agreement of a negotiated rate structure does not guarantee that the classifications will remain unchanged during the term of the Agreement. The reason advanced for this interpretation is that economic necessity in a competitive market makes it essential that management have the degree of flexibility necessary to adapt the work force to changed conditions. Where arbitrators have upheld management's right to eliminate jobs or classifications and reallocate residual job duties, they have stressed that such changes must be made in good faith, based upon factors such as a change in operations, technological improvements, substantially diminished production requirements, established past practice, etc. It is this second line of cases which appears to reflect the present weight of authority on this issue."[170]

In this general regard, the view of an early case that "Combining the duties of classifications recognized in the contract is a different thing from combining the duties or job content of various jobs, or abolishing those jobs," and that the inclusion of classifications and their wage rates in the agreement has the implied effect of freezing such classifications (though not freezing jobs within a classification) for the life of the agreement,[171] has been expressly rejected in later cases.[172]

---

[170] American Cement Corp., 48 LA 72, 76 (1967). For similar general evaluations and conclusions, see Arbitrator Doyle in 48 LA 24, 25–32; Leflar in 40 LA 769, 772–774.

[171] Esso Standard Oil Co., 19 LA 569, 571 (McCoy, 1952).

[172] See Arbitrator Doyle in 48 LA 24, 26–31; Leflar in 40 LA 769, 774; Bothwell in 34 LA 24, 28, and in 32 LA 260, 264. Arbitrator Doyle had previously cited and followed the "Esso" case view, and in subsequently rejecting it he explained: "The prevailing rule is based on the premise that a freezing of classifications by implication would unduly restrict and hamper the Company in making decisions that would improve the economy and productivity of the plant. Such a limitation should not be lightly inferred." Omaha Cold Storage Terminal, 48 LA 24, 31 (1967). In Teple, "Contract Provisions Affecting Job Elimination," 17 Western Reserve L. Rev. 1253, 1264–1267 (1966), cases are cited for the conclusion that neither seniority provisions nor "local working conditions" clauses

Many arbitrators have spoken in terms of combining jobs or job classifications. Again, it often has been held that management has the right, where not restricted by the agreement, to combine jobs or job classifications in determining methods of operation.[173] Arbitrators also have held that management has the right, unless restricted by the agreement, to combine jobs or classifications where there is insufficient work in one (or in each) of them for a normal day's work and where excessive workloads do not result from the combination.[174]

Likewise, in the absence of contractual restriction management has been permitted to abolish two job classifications and establish a new classification following technological change in equipment,[175] or following a change in products.[176]

Inter-Job and Inter-Classification Transfer of Duties

Short of eliminating or combining jobs or job classifications, some of the duties of one job or classification are sometimes transferred to another job or classification. The right of management to require workers in the "receiving" job or classification to perform the work is discussed hereinbelow in the subtopic on "Assignment of Duties and Tasks." At this point, however, the matter is considered primarily

---

(technological improvements or the like often establish a change in the underlying basis of the local condition) are likely to bar the elimination of jobs or classifications. This conclusion is supported also by various cases cited in this topic.

[173] See Arbitrator Marshall in 51 LA 1051, 1055 (right reinforced by general management rights clause); Moskowitz in 44 LA 801, 802; Prasow in 35 LA 63, 66 (seniority rights no bar); Pollock in 34 LA 226, 228–229 (right reinforced by general management rights clause); Regester in 34 LA 209, 212; Quinlan in 33 LA 379, 384–385; Wersing in 23 LA 797, 798–799; Bowles in 16 LA 955, 957–958. Also see Gorsuch in 40 LA 879, 886–888; Bothwell in 32 LA 260, 263. But see Arbitrator McIntosh in 41 LA 997, 999 (clause freezing classifications was strictly enforced); Crawford in 41 LA 285, 286–287 (where contract provided for craft jobs and training programs, management could not combine jobs in such a way as to virtually eliminate the craft system); Coffey in 39 LA 1058, 1059, 1063–1064.

[174] See Arbitrator Florey in 47 LA 1092, 1093; Duff in 40 LA 305, 306; Kesselman in 28 LA 441, 443–445; Somers in 27 LA 466, 467–468; Kelliher in 18 LA 216, 217–218. Also see Crawford in 37 LA 711, 714–715; Hampton in 17 LA 666, 668; Gilden in 16 LA 252, 255–256; Klamon in 15 LA 782, 789–790. Cf., Sembower in 25 LA 188, 190–191.

[175] See Arbitrator Marshall in 43 LA 1118, 1123–1124, and in 43 LA 1137, 1142; Cobb in 37 LA 466, 467–468; Uible in 35 LA 434, 436; Wettach in 19 LA 797, 799. Also see Blair in 36 LA 1097, 1100; Fleming in 32 LA 115, 116–117; Copelof in 15 LA 754, 761.

[176] Square D Co., 46 LA 39, 43 (Larkin, 1966); Hewitt-Robins, Inc., 30 LA 81, 83–86 (Kates, 1958).

(but not exclusively) from the standpoint of the effect of the transfer upon workers in the "giving" job or classification.[177]

In a variety of situations the inter-classification transfer of work has been upheld where no restriction was found in the agreement (in some instances the employer's right of action was reinforced by a general management rights clause).[178] For example, under a contract giving management the right to manage the works and direct the working force and containing no provision expressly prohibiting unilateral changes in job content, Arbitrator Benjamin Aaron held that management could remove from the oiler's job the relatively minor tasks of lubricating and cleaning cranes and assign these duties to crane men, even though said duties were mentioned in the oiler's job description and not in the craneman's; the union could request re-evaluation of the craneman's job if it believed that the added duties justified a higher rate, but it could not prevent management from making the changes in job content.[179]

Under another contract reserving to the company the right to "manage the plant and direct the working force" and stating that "the usual and customary rights of the employer remain unimpaired," Arbitrator Clarence M. Updegraff upheld the transfer of certain unskilled and semi-skilled work from one classification to another, and he explained:

> "In part the union relied upon a contention that since the agreement between the parties includes a list of job classifications with the hourly wage rates agreed for the same that none of the duties of any job classification so listed may be essentially changed since this would indirectly at least alter the compensation for work in the designated classification.

---

[177] For important related discussion, see this Chapter, topics titled "Right to Subcontract" and "Assigning Work Out of Bargaining Unit."

[178] See Arbitrator Daugherty in 49 LA 234, 236–237; Kelliher in 48 LA 1000, 1002–1003; Updegraff in 45 LA 557, 557–558; Smith in 43 LA 193, 206–207; Hebert in 36 LA 186, 192–193; Shister in 35 LA 664, 667; Abernethy in 35 LA 353, 355–357; Beatty in 33 LA 311, 312–313 (operation could be assigned to different craft after the work was simplified by technological improvement); Bauder in 33 LA 308, 310; Aaron in 26 LA 666, 668. But see Dworkin in 43 LA 1188, 1196; Bothwell in 39 LA 833, 844–849. The temporary transfer of work (such as on holidays) merely to effect a savings in labor costs was found improper by Arbitrator Atwood in 55 LA 964, 969; Seinsheimer in 33 LA 14, 18–19; McCoy in 32 LA 848, 849–850.

[179] National Supply Co., 26 LA 666, 668 (1956), where Arbitrator Aaron also noted that the transfer in no way impaired job security.

"The company asserts the position that in the absence of negotiated job descriptions it is within the usual rights, powers and privileges of management to assign duties to one classification and subsequently when efficiency and economy seem to require the same, to take such job duties from a classification which has been discharging them and assign such duties to another classification.

"In this connection it must be observed that innumerable unskilled and semi-skilled duties are commonly found in industrial plants to be within the scopes of duties of several job classifications. It is normally regarded as within the prerogatives of management to transfer unskilled or semi-skilled duties which do not characterize or fall within the scope of characteristically high skilled jobs, to one or another group of skilled, semi-skilled or unskilled workers from time to time as convenience and economy within the plant appeared to make it desirable. This is all within the commonly recognized scope of managerial authority and normally under management clauses is recognized to be proper.

      *   *   *   *   *

"* * * There can be no doubt that normally in industry generally, the assignment and reassignment of unskilled and semi-skilled duties such as those here involved would be entirely and exclusively within the discretion of management in the absence of a clear, express agreement otherwise."[180]

Arbitrator Joseph M. Klamon recognized an "inherent right of management to take a job which initially or originally may require a considerable degree of skill and then to establish a production line in which a fairly complex job becomes essentially routine and repetitive."[181] In that case management was permitted to discontinue the assignment of certain work, after it had become simplified, to skilled workers (who claimed a "proprietary interest in the work") and to assign it exclusively to employees in a lower classification. To hold otherwise, he declared, would deny the company the right to operate with the greatest degree of skill and efficiency; he noted that nothing in the contract prevented the company "from using lesser grades of skill on a job if higher grades of skill are wholly unnecessary to perform such jobs."[182]

Where workers in one classification must suffer layoff or other such consequence as a result of management's transfer of substantial

---

[180] Pure Oil Co., 45 LA 557, 558 (1965).
[181] McConnell Aircraft Corp., 21 LA 424, 427–428 (1953).
[182] Ibid. Also see Arbitrator Koven in 39 LA 939, 940–941; Klamon in 33 LA 1, 4–5.

work from their classification to another, arbitrators have sometimes deemed such transfer a violation of the workers' seniority rights where the transfer was not justified by emergency or other such reason.[183]

But some arbitrators are unwilling to accept seniority as a guarantee that the job or classification will remain unchanged. For instance, in upholding the right of management to transfer work from one classification to another where not expressly restricted by the agreement, Arbitrator Paul Prasow reasoned:

"* * * Seniority protects and secures an employee's rights in relation to the rights of other employees in his seniority group; it does not protect him in relation to the existence of the job itself. By the use of an objective measure, length of service, the rights of one employee are balanced against the other employees' rights.

"The rights inherent in seniority do not themselves guarantee the continued existence of the job, or that it shall be maintained without change in content. Seniority can only stand as a bar to changes in job content if the contract so expressly provides, or if it can be shown that the changes are motivated on the part of management by a desire to evade the seniority clause. * * *

"While it is certainly true that changes in job content of a classification may adversely affect the job opportunities of the employees involved by reducing the amount of work available to them, the problem is still essentially one of jurisdiction, rather than of seniority. It is a well-established principle in industrial arbitration that management has the right, if exercised in good faith, to transfer duties from one classification to another, to change, eliminate or establish new classifications, unless the Agreement specifically restricts this right."[184]

Speaking in terms of the right of management to transfer work from one seniority unit to another, one arbitrator held that management may not do so even though there is no express prohibition in the agreement.[185] But in another case management was permitted to

---

[183] See Arbitrator Dworkin in 34 LA 743, 750–751 (the possibility of future harm sufficed); Livengood in 23 LA 196, 199–202; Gregory in 15 LA 147, 150–151; Ebeling in 14 LA 163, 164–165. Also see Klamon in 32 LA 870, 872–873.

[184] Reynolds Metals Co., 25 LA 44, 48–49 (1955). For similar statements or results, see Arbitrator Hon in 40 LA 259, 262; Holly in 39 LA 496, 499–500; Quinlan in 38 LA 714, 717; Prasow in 35 LA 63, 66; Warns in 33 LA 357, 359–360 (also suggesting that jobs "tailor-made" to the company's requirements are more subject to unilateral change than traditional craft jobs); Bauder in 33 LA 25, 28–29; Updegraff in 29 LA 555, 557; Thompson in 28 LA 374, 376–377; Uible in 25 LA 897, 899; Platt in 17 LA 697, 700–701.

[185] Lukens Steel Co., 15 LA 408, 411–412 (D'Andrade, 1950). In general

transfer work from one seniority unit to another where there was no specific restriction in the agreement and the transfer was made in good faith in the interest of efficiency.[186]

Assignment of Duties and Tasks

In general management is permitted to exercise much more discretion in assigning individual duties and tasks to workers than it is permitted in assigning workers to regular jobs. While the assignment of workers to regular jobs often requires the observance of contractual "seniority" and "fitness and ability" considerations,[187] collective agreements much less frequently contain direct restrictions upon the right of management to assign duties and tasks to workers. Thus, in the latter regard, arbitrators have held that unless the agreement provides otherwise, employees are not entitled to exercise their seniority to select the duties or machines which they particularly prefer within their classification.[188]

In one case Arbitrator Clarence M. Updegraff observed (speaking of hourly rated employees) that "it is assumed throughout industry that the employer has the general right to make reasonable changes from time to time in the job duties of every individual. The employer may decrease or increase the duties as long as the total work load remains in reasonable bounds."[189] This broad right of management in the assignment of duties and tasks is evidenced by numerous other arbitration cases (in some of the cases the right was reinforced by a general management rights clause).[190]

---

accord, though applying a "de minimis" exception, United States Steel Corp., 35 LA 832, 835 (Shipman, 1960). Also see Arbitrator Anderson in 44 LA 873, 877; Seitz in 40 LA 742, 749–753; Myers in 23 LA 776, 778–779.

[186] Douglas & Lomason Co., 23 LA 691, 695 (Bowles, 1954). In general accord, Arbitrator Cahn in 40 LA 865, 865–866; Kelliher in 33 LA 828, 829–830. Also see Daugherty in 49 LA 234, 236–237; Crawford in 36 LA 273, 276, 280; Garrett in 35 LA 541, 543; Prasow in 35 LA 63, 66; Springfield & Seward in 25 LA 366, 368.

[187] See Chapter 14, Seniority.

[188] See Arbitrator Howlett in 42 LA 385, 388; Burris in 41 LA 504, 506; Stashower in 37 LA 591, 593; Bowles in 36 LA 1160, 1162–1163; Beatty in 35 LA 637, 639–640; Montgomery in 26 LA 546, 548; Sanders in 24 LA 160, 162.

[189] St. Joseph Lead Co., 20 LA 890, 891 (1953).

[190] See Arbitrator Witney in 54 LA 197, 203–205; Hebert in 50 LA 458, 460; Madden in 49 LA 487, 488–490; Larkin in 47 LA 382, 384; Clayton in 41 LA 925, 926; Dworkin in 39 LA 801, 805–806; Cahn in 36 LA 822, 823–824; Abernethy in 34 LA 278, 283; Ryder in 29 LA 677, 679; Ridge in 26 LA 422, 426–427; Uible in 25 LA 897, 899; Prasow in 25 LA 44, 48–49;

Certainly, where jobs are classified by titles (if formally classified at all) but the parties have not negotiated a detailed description of job content, management will be permitted wide authority to assign any work which is of the same general type as, or is reasonably related to, or is incidental to the regular duties of the job.[191] However, a change in job duties by adding work which is not related in such ways to the regular duties may be held improper.[192] Even where an agreement expressly recognized a right of management to reassign duties across classification lines the arbitrator cautioned management that a limitation was necessarily implied under the standard of reasonableness—duties must be compatible with the classification to which they are transferred.[193] Nonetheless, where the need is sufficiently strong, employees may be assigned duties or tasks which are foreign to their regular job.[194]

A significant limitation upon the right of management to assign work to skilled tradesmen (as opposed to production workers) was recognized in two decisions by Umpire Harry Shulman—he did not

---

Wallen in 22 LA 831, 833; Klamon in 22 LA 336, 351; Marshall in 20 LA 800, 802; Smith in 18 LA 620, 624; Ryan in 17 LA 800, 803. Cf., Dworkin in 29 LA 787, 792. Regarding the duty of employees to do the work assigned to them and to utilize the grievance procedure rather than self-help if they think an assignment is improper, see Chapter 5, topic titled "Observance of Grievance Procedure."

[191] See Arbitrator Hebert in 49 LA 445, 450–451; Dybeck in 49 LA 86, 89 ("maintenance of local conditions" provision does not limit the level of work load); Whyte in 49 LA 33, 38; Duff in 48 LA 52, 54; Kelliher in 43 LA 1006, 1009–1010; Oppenheim in 40 LA 257, 259; Donaldson in 37 LA 528, 531; Ryder in 29 LA 677, 679; Thompson in 28 LA 374, 376; Uible in 25 LA 897, 899; Reynard in 25 LA 611, 613; Berkowitz in 25 LA 422, 424; Prasow in 25 LA 44, 48–49; Bowles in 23 LA 691, 695; Blair in 22 LA 701, 703; Hawley in 22 LA 157, 161; Dworet in 20 LA 803, 806; Marshall in 20 LA 800, 802; Shulman in 19 LA 237, 238–242; Gaffey in 18 LA 462, 468; Gilden in 17 LA 408, 409; Lesser in 16 LA 505, 507; Kharas in 2 LA 274, 276–277. In some of these cases the agreement contained a management rights clause; in others it did not.

[192] American Zinc Co., 18 LA 827, 830–831 (Updegraff, 1952). Also see Arbitrator Dorsey in 55 LA 1182, 1183; Snyder in 54 LA 1159, 1162–1163. Where an agreement excluded supervisors from the bargaining unit, supervisory duties could not be assigned to unit employees. Arkla Chemical Corp., 54 LA 62, 64–65 (Prewett, 1969). The right to assign workers to tasks outside the plant has sometimes been arbitrated, such assignment being held improper by Arbitrator Stone in 2 LA 552, 553, but held proper by Arbitrator Williams in 53 LA 1308, 1310, and by Anrod (on the basis of practice) in 20 LA 653, 656–657.

[193] Vickers Inc., 47 LA 716, 719 (Keefe, 1966).

[194] See Goodyear Atomic Corp., 45 LA 671, 680 (Teple, 1965), where all employees were required to handle emergency equipment; Glen Rock Lumber & Supply Co., 38 LA 904, 906 (Turkus, 1962), where the task of walking the company watch dog could fall on any employee (except the union steward).

permit the assignment of work which is of a different trade.[195] Some years later Umpire Harry H. Platt "reaffirmed" these decisions, but in doing so he pointed out important exceptions:

"(a) Umpire Opinions A-223 and A-278 are reaffirmed. It is ruled that a skilled tradesman may not be required to do work wholly different from and unrelated to the central skill of his trade. If such bald assignment is attempted because of a shortage of work in his trade or a desire to get the other work done, he may refuse it and take a layoff instead.

"(b) In emergencies, the Company may make assignments across trade lines.

"(c) In cases where the capabilities of tradesmen overlap, work which is within the scope of two or more trades may be assigned to any of the trades within whose normal and proper scope it falls. In determining whether a task falls within the normal scope of more than one trade, due regard must be had for accepted standards in the trades generally and for clearly established in-plant assignment practices which are based on agreement or mutual understanding or which are characterized by acquiescence for a long time, with the consequences that the parties may be assumed to have agreed with reference to them and for their continuance.

"(d) Relatively minor tasks which are complementary to a principal job but which do not require a long period of reasonably continuous work and which are within the capabilities of the principal tradesman on the job and can be performed by him with safety, are incidental work which can properly be assigned to the principal tradesman."[196]

Another set of "standards to determine whether management validly exercised its right to assign * * * challenged work * * * in keeping with the principle of craft integrity" was offered by Arbitrator Louis C. Kesselman:

---

[195] The first case was Ford Motor Co., 3 LA 782, 783 (1946). In the second case, Ford Motor Co., 19 LA 237, 238–239 (1952), he repeated the restriction but emphasized that it was to be narrowly applied. In Champion Papers, Inc., 49 LA 33, 38 (Whyte, 1967), the multicraft assignment of work to craft workers was upheld.

[196] Ford Motor Co., 30 LA 46, 55 (1958). The exception stated in Arbitrator Platt's paragraph (d) was applied by Arbitrator Turkus in 44 LA 1219, 1223–1224; Updegraff in 44 LA 989, 990–991. In Kaiser Aluminum & Chemical Corp., 44 LA 449, 452 (1965), Arbitrator Rohman explained: "A modern development coincidental with automation is the fostering of combination skills. No longer will an individual skilled in that one craft perform work solely of that craft. True, his primary duties will be confined to that craft but, in addition, he will also perform the work of other crafts which are incidental to the necessary completion of that task."

"1) Skilled tradesmen should not be required to do work wholly different from and unrelated to the central skill of their trades;

"2) Intent must not be to destroy jobs or deny any other contract rights and the assignment made must be in good faith and be reasonably related to the efficient operation of the plant;

"3) Greater latitude should be given where there is no economic loss to the employees—no layoffs or denial of overtime work opportunities;

"4) Assignments which are occasional and of short duration rather than permanent should be viewed with greater liberality as reasonable exercises of management prerogatives in overlapping areas of work; and

"5) Borderline work assignments which will be made only when members of classifications, for whom work is central rather than peripheral, are not avaliable should be given more leeway than when permanent reassignments of duties are made.

*   *   *   *   *

"Obviously, there is no craft whose work, tools, and skills are absolutely independent of all other crafts. Principles of craft jurisdiction must be applied with common sense and some flexibility. Judgments may be based upon:

1) the type of tools required
2) nature of the materials being worked on
3) character of the training required
4) level of skill involved
5) generally accepted elements of the trade * * *

No one of these by itself is necessarily controlling. One can only judge on the basis of all the relevant facts, whether a job requires the special skills of a particular trade."[197]

Regarding the assignment of unskilled work to skilled workers, Arbitrator Edgar L. Warren observed that: "While workers in skilled classifications obviously should not be required to do a large amount of unskilled work, some measure of this is a part of every job. The most practical restraint on the amount of unskilled work that a company will assign to highly skilled workers is the cost involved. Few employers would feel that they could afford to have highly paid hourly employees doing chores which could be performed by unskilled

---

[197] Tennessee River Pulp & Paper Co., 45 LA 201, 205 (1965). These standards were quoted and followed by Arbitrator Block in 56 LA 353, 356.

laborers."[198] In another case an added reason was recognized for assigning some associated greasing and lubricating duties to skilled repairmen—they are more likely to spot trouble than other employees with less skill.[199]

In the absence of contractual restrictions on the right of management to assign new duties or reallocate old duties as reasonably required by technological changes, management may be permitted considerable leeway to do so.[200]

Even when there are detailed job descriptions, Arbitrator J. Fred Holly has held that they do not prohibit minor changes in job content, noting that any ban on such changes must be stated in the agreement "in unmistakable language," and that the "purpose of job evaluation and job descriptions is to provide for equitable wage rates, not to provide a control over job content."[201] But the existence of detailed job descriptions, especially if negotiated, may deprive management of the right to make substantial changes in job duties.[202] One arbitrator went a step further, holding that even where there is no written job description management may not make a substantial change in the traditional job content of classified occupations during the life of the contract;[203] however, in subsequently upholding the right of manage-

---

[198] Lockheed Aircraft Service, Inc., 21 LA 292, 293 (1953), upholding the assignment of cleanup work to craftsmen for a short time every few weeks despite the fact that their job descriptions did not mention such work. Also see Arbitrator McDaniel in 54 LA 155, 157–158; Mittenthal in 40 LA 446, 448. But see Willingham in 36 LA 531, 536. In Mosaic Tile Co., 21 LA 278, 282–283 (Young, 1953), clean-up work could not be required of incentive workers, who were distinguished from hourly rated workers on the basis that additional duties do not reduce the earnings of the latter.

[199] United States Steel Corp., 40 LA 414, at 414 (Florey, 1963).

[200] See Arbitrator Shipman in 46 LA 833, 837; Bradley in 46 LA 685, 691; Rohman in 45 LA 758, 761; Oppenheim in 40 LA 923, 926–927; Seward in 26 LA 146, 147; Beatty in 26 LA 1, 2; Updegraff in 20 LA 890, 891. Also see Gorsuch in 53 LA 23, 32; Larson in 29 LA 59, 66–67; Roberts in 27 LA 736, 741–743; Shister in 26 LA 212, 213; Gilden in 23 LA 164, 166–167. But see Doyle in 22 LA 785, 788–790; Hampton in 12 LA 631, 634. For related discussion, see this Chapter, topic titled "Determination of Size of Crews."

[201] United States Steel Corp., 26 LA 325, 326 (1956). Also see Arbitrator Cahn in 53 LA 1130, 1131 ("job description cannot be considered as an agreement in and of itself as to how the job will be performed in the future or that it will continue to be performed without change"); Klamon in 27 LA 784, 786–787; Davey in 23 LA 206, 209; Whiting in 5 LA 304, 306–307.

[202] See Arbitrator Block in 45 LA 807, 810–811; Bowles in 26 LA 415, 421; Ryder in 23 LA 829, 832–834. Also see Livengood in 23 LA 520, 521; Donnelly in 20 LA 586, 588.

[203] Nebraska Consolidated Mills Co., 22 LA 785, 789–790 (Doyle, 1954). For similar results, see Arbitrator Rubin in 44 LA 1264, 1270–1271, 1273; Stouffer

ment to eliminate a contract classification and assign its duties to another classification, that arbitrator acted "on the premise that a freezing of classifications by implication would unduly restrict and hamper the Company in making decisions that would improve the economy and productivity of the plant."[204]

Many cases have spoken in terms of job classifications. In one such case, Arbitrator Marion Beatty upheld the right of management to assign an employee small amounts of work outside his classification, observing that work jurisdictional lines can be very crippling to efficient operations and should not be read into an agreement by inference.[205] While recognizing that management may require employees to perform duties outside their classification for temporary periods, Arbitrator Joseph Shister held that management may not require the performance of such duties as a regular and continual part of their jobs.[206]

It is not unusual, of course, to find duties and tasks which may properly fall within two or more separate job classifications. In this regard, Arbitrator Robert S. Thompson has expressed the following opinion:

> "* * * management may assign tasks which involve minor and occasional variation from job descriptions to employees in different classifications when what is required falls within the skills and other factors which are common to the several classifications. The arbitrator believes that this principle is well established except where there are specific contract provisions otherwise."[207]

---

in 44 LA 1134, 1138; Wolff in 18 LA 853, 854 (he reached a different result in 45 LA 234, 238, where there was a special agreement).

[204] Omaha Cold Storage Terminal, 48 LA 24, 31 (Doyle, 1967). For related discussion, see subtopic titled "Establishing, Eliminating, and Combining Jobs and Classifications," above.

[205] Phillips Petroleum Co., 29 LA 226, 228 (1957). Similarly upholding management's action, see Arbitrator Larkin in 54 LA 250, 252; Solomon in 48 LA 364, 370–372; Morgan in 47 LA 756, 760; Williams in 46 LA 602, 604–605; Hebert in 43 LA 491, 497; Klein in 41 LA 1045, 1049–1050; Beatty in 40 LA 733, 735; Thompson in 28 LA 374, 376–377; Uible in 25 LA 897, 899; Prasow in 25 LA 44, 48–49; Wallen in 22 LA 831, 833. But see Arbitrator Caraway in 54 LA 1080, 1083; Volz in 42 LA 336, 338–339; Teple in 41 LA 815, 818–819; Hale in 32 LA 873, 879–882; Cahn in 32 LA 221, 221–222.

[206] Linde Air Products Co., 20 LA 861, 864 (1953). Also see Arbitrator Donnelly in 20 LA 586, 588; Hampton in 17 LA 666, 668; Feinberg in 16 LA 926, 928–930; Simkin in 8 LA 113, 115–116.

[207] Goodyear Tire & Rubber Co., 28 LA 374, 377 (1957).

In reaching this conclusion Arbitrator Thompson spoke at length of the natual overlapping of duties between classifications:

"It is understandable that in the interests of job security, unions press for inviolability of job classifications. Certainly, practices which permitted more or less discriminate transfer of duties from one classification to another, or the assignment of tasks now to one classification and now to another, would lead to anxieties about the kind and amount of work that might be available to particular employees at different times.

"However, the reality is that there is much overlapping in jobs and their classifications. It would take an almost completely rationalized industry to provide for each worker absolutely distinct jobs. In highly specialized production work, operations are split off from general operations, and there may in consequence be an approach to fairly exclusive jobs one from another. However, in maintenance work duties are by the nature of the needs necessarily more general.

"It is reassuring to be able to place things in neat categories. Is aspirin a drug and therefore to be sold only under a physician's prescription? How about the new tranquillizers? Is there a sharp line between intelligence and stupidity, or a gradually changing quality ranging from genius to idiot?"[208]

When work falls within the job descriptions of two or more crafts or classifications, or is by nature a borderline or overlapping duty of two or more crafts or classifications, or if it has been performed by two or more crafts or classifications in the past, management has been permitted considerable leeway in assigning the work and ordinarily has not been limited to assigning it exclusively to one of the crafts or classifications.[209] However, where work of an overlapping

---

[208] Id. at 376.

[209] See Arbitrator Block in 56 LA 353, 356; Wren in 51 LA 411, 413; Bothwell in 51 LA 41, 44–45 ("in dealing with the problem of work jurisdiction where there are several crafts in a plant, the arbitrator cannot ignore the language contained in other craft union agreements with the Company, or practice in the past in administering the language"); Eyraud in 50 LA 1001, 1003; Seward in 50 LA 1214, 1216; Block in 50 LA 361, 366; McKenna in 48 LA 941, 948; Anrod in 48 LA 310, 313; Duff in 48 LA 52, 54; Uible in 41 LA 510, 512; Sembower in 40 LA 481, 486–487; Oppenheim in 40 LA 257, 258–259; Strong in 39 LA 1207, 1208–1209; Mittenthal in 39 LA 65, 67–68; Quinlan in 38 LA 714, 717–718; Rubin in 38 LA 538, 541–543; Klein in 38 LA 180, 182; Donaldson in 37 LA 528, 530–531; Duff in 36 LA 376, 379; McCoy in 32 LA 848, 851; Prasow in 30 LA 444, 447–448; Klamon in 22 LA 336, 350–351; Cole in 21 LA 814, 815 (when work falls within the job descriptions of two classifications management has the right to decide which shall do it if there is insufficient work to keep both classifications busy). As to claiming a particular share of work over which there is overlapping craft jurisdiction, see

nature had long been assigned to one craft, the mere whim or caprice of management was not a reasonable basis for diverting the work to another craft.[210] Furthermore, work which was the "jugular vein" of one craft and not de minimis could not be assigned to another craft.[211]

Management generally has been held to have considerable discretion in unusual situations to make temporary or emergency assignments of tasks across job or classification lines. For instance, Arbitrator James P. Miller has ruled that in case of emergency or breakdown it is reasonable for an employer to require maintenance employees with certain occupational titles to assist employees with other occupational titles:

> "Many years of experience have proven to me that a plant maintenance crew is somewhat similar to the crew of a ship or a football team. Each member has a designated position or title and spends most of his team time attending to the duties and tasks associated with his designated position. However, when an emergency arises, they all respond as a crew and assist in getting the ship back on an even keel, weathering the storm, or, as in the case of the football team, advancing the ball to the opposing team's goal line."[212]

What Arbitrator Miller thus said in regard to maintenance employees would appear to apply to plant employees generally. For instance, an employer was held to be within his rights in assigning an emergency job which arose on a nonworkday to the only two employees scheduled to work on that day, despite the fact that the work did not fall within the duties of their job classifications. The arbitrator stated that management should have the right to meet unusual situations in this manner unless restricted from doing so by the agreement.[213]

United States Steel Corp., 54 LA 184, 187–188 (Garrett, 1969). In Rayonier, Inc., 36 LA 883, 888 (Christon, 1961), procedures were suggested for harmonious operations where the company had contracts with each of four unions, each contract reserving work within the union's jurisdiction to its members.

[210] Dow Chemical Co., 32 LA 587, 592 (Gorsuch, 1964).

[211] Shell Chemical Co., 47 LA 1178, 1180–1181 (Rohman, 1967).

[212] Youngstown Sheet & Tube Co., 4 LA 514, 520 (1946).

[213] Thompson Mahogany Co., 5 LA 397, 399 (Brandschain, 1946). For other cases permitting such temporary and/or emergency assignments, see Arbitrator Valtin in 49 LA 411, 414–415; Stouffer in 49 LA 169, 172; Dworkin in 49 LA 131, 139; Teple in 44 LA 853, 857; Klamon in 43 LA 982, 994, and in 22 LA 336, 351; Autrey in 39 LA 961, 964; Lehoczky, Fisher & Myers in 36 LA 21, 27 ("interests" arbitration); Ross in 34 LA 752, 755; Sembower in 29 LA 704, 706; Williams in 27 LA 790, 792; Reid in 22 LA 358, 361;

Finally, it should be remembered that while management often has wide authority to assign duties and tasks to employees, they in turn may challenge the fairness of the rate paid for the job after its change.[214] Morever, employees temporarily performing work which is rated higher than their regular work may be entitled to the higher rate for performing the higher rated work.[215]

Hiring of Employees

Except as restricted by statute or the collective agreement management retains the unqualified right to hire or not to hire. Particularly significant statutory restrictions are those against anti-union discrimination under the National Labor Relations Act[216] and those against discrimination because of race, color, religion, sex, or national origin under the Civil Rights Act of 1964.[217] Contractual restrictions upon the right to hire exist most often in seniority or union security provisions (discussed hereinbelow).

Arbitral recognition of management's basic right and control in hiring is illustrated by the following lines of cases: Company rules against hiring spouses or other relatives of present employees have been upheld.[218] Management's right to hire includes the right to set pre-employment standards and to implement them by requiring applicants to give accurate information as to their work and medical history and concerning their record as law abiding citizens.[219] The employer's

---

Hawley in 22 LA 157, 161; Gilden in 19 LA 802, 805; Kelliher in 18 LA 216, 217–218; Hampton in 17 LA 666, 668; Elson in 8 LA 129, 132.

[214] See Arbitrator Dworkin in 39 LA 1065, 1073; Cahn in 36 LA 822, 823–824; Klamon in 22 LA 336, 351. For full discussion, see this Chapter, topic titled "Wage Adjustments Following Changes in Operation Methods."

[215] See Arbitrator Larkin in 35 LA 265, 268; Seward in 32 LA 200, 212–215; Kelliher in 25 LA 64, 65–66; Platt in 16 LA 215, 216; Hepburn in 11 LA 145, 147; Elson in 8 LA 389, 393–394. Cf., Steele in 47 LA 796, 798; Howlett in 35 LA 480, 482–483; McCoy in 8 LA 883, 890–891.

[216] For example, see Phelps Dodge Corp. v. NLRB, 61 S.Ct. 845 (1941), upholding the NLRB's power to require an employer to hire applicants who had been rejected because of their union affiliation even though they had obtained substantially equivalent employment elsewhere.

[217] For example, see Phillips v. Martin Marietta Corp., 91 S.Ct. 496 (1971), holding the Act does not permit one hiring policy for women with pre-school age children and another for men with such children.

[218] See Arbitrator Block in 55 LA 283, 286; McNaughton in 55 LA 258, 260; Davey in 49 LA 105, 109–110; Beatty in 48 LA 1123, 1124; Kates in 45 LA 641, 643.

[219] E.g., see Arbitrator Koven in 55 LA 581, 585; McNaughton in 55 LA 258, 260; Myers in 54 LA 534, 539–540; Duff in 53 LA 597, 600; Holly

right to hire includes the right to hire additional employees even though this may mean less overtime or other reduced opportunities for employees,[220] and has been held to include the right not to hire any new employee to fill a vacancy where the employer had no bids from his employees and there was no contractual requirement for maintaining a certain number of employees within the classification.[221]

Specific restrictions on hiring contained in the seniority provisions of the collective agreement may be to the effect, for example, that the employer may not hire new employees to fill vacancies until the rehiring list of laid-off employees is exhausted,[222] or that the employer must consider present employees for vacancies before hiring new workers.[223]

Where the contract neither explicitly nor by strong implication restricted the right of management to hire new employees, one arbitration board refused to read a restriction into the contract. That board distinguished between the right to hire and the right to promote under a contract which did not specifically restrict management's right to hire but did require the observance of seniority in the event a promotion was made, the arbitrators stating that this "agreement to promote by seniority does not, as such, exclude either explicitly or implicitly the right of the Company not to promote but to hire."[224] Other arbitrators, however, while not speaking in terms of the right to hire, did find a violation of the seniority provisions requiring preferential

---

in 53 LA 503, 506; Cohen in 52 LA 89, 92; McCoy in 47 LA 752, 754–755; Stouffer in 46 LA 654, 658–659; Altieri in 46 LA 559, 562; Lehoczky in 45 LA 513, 515; Kelliher in 45 LA 335, 336; Sherman in 42 LA 323, 324.

[220] See Arbitrator McCoy in 45 LA 1165, 1166; Geissinger in 42 LA 1293, 1295–1296; Larson in 38 LA 1152, 1154; Hale in 33 LA 685, 692.

[221] Connecticut Coke Co., 28 LA 360, 361–362 (Stutz & Mottram, dissent by Curry, 1957). For related material, see this Chapter, topics titled "Vacancies" and "Determination of Size of Crews."

[222] As in San Francisco Chronicle, 21 LA 253 at 253 (Kerr, 1953).

[223] As in Electric Auto-Lite Co., 24 LA 765, 766 (Kahn, 1955).

[224] Travelers Insurance Co., 18 LA 534, 535 (Donnelly & Mottram, dissent by Sviridoff, 1952). Also see Arbitrators Donnelly, Mannino & Mottram in 24 LA 631, 632. For similar results where the contract contained a general management rights clause, see Chrysler Corp., 32 LA 988, 991 (Wolff, 1959), the arbitrators stating that the section on promotions governs the manner in which a vacancy is to be filled *if* it is filled by promotion—it does not restrict management's right to fill the vacancy by a new hire even if a present employee is qualified for the job (past practice also supported this interpretation). In Kansas City Power & Light Co., 52 LA 1087, 1097–1098 (Klamon, 1969), a qualified probationary employee had no standing to protest the hiring of an equally qualified new employee for a vacancy; the contract stated that probationers had no contractual rights prior to becoming regular employees.

consideration of senior employees when the company failed to consider its employees for a vacancy and hired an outsider.[225]

In another situation where the company conceded that its right to hire was qualified by the seniority clause, the company was nevertheless held not required to fill a job opening from present employees when none of them could perform the job without intensive training—it was permitted to hire an already qualified person.[226] In the latter regard, other arbitrators likewise have recognized management's right to hire a new employee where it has no qualified employee for the job,[227] or where other reasonable justification exists for the action.[228] In one case the employer could fill a vacancy by hiring a new employee where the only employees who were qualified to perform the job were on strike and a posting of the vacancy for bids "would have been an idle gesture."[229]

The employer's discretion in hiring may be restricted by a union security clause to the extent that any such clause is legal under applicable state and federal statutes. Where the union security provision is lawful, arbitrators appear to frown upon hiring practices which accomplish by indirection the condition which the provision was designed to prevent, or which prevent the condition which the provision was intended to accomplish.[230] For instance, one employer was ordered to discharge again an employee previously discharged pursuant to a

---

[225] See Arbitrator Marshall in 49 LA 69, 70–71; Yarowsky in 48 LA 582, 585 (under the facts it was a technical violation only); Gilden in 27 LA 544, 546–547; Dworkin in 21 LA 589, 595. Also see Tatum in 41 LA 1027, 1030–1031; Feinberg in 13 LA 991, 999.

[226] Wagner Electric Corp., 20 LA 768, 775 (Klamon, 1953).

[227] See Arbitrator Hertz in 50 LA 463, 465; Marshall in 49 LA 69, 71; Altrock in 48 LA 629, 633; Daugherty in 47 LA 554, 558–559; Merrill in 36 LA 145, 147–148; Stouffer in 35 LA 397, 399; Seward in 31 LA 267, 268–269. Also see Block in 54 LA 460, 461, 467; Sembower in 53 LA 950, 954–955; Singletary in 44 LA 1193, 1194–1195, and in 41 LA 1033, 1037–1038; Kornblum in 40 LA 403, 407. For a contract giving management broad authority to hire persons needed because of their special training, ability, or experience, see Jefferson City Cabinet Co., 35 LA 117, 123 (Marshall, 1960).

[228] See Otis Elevator Co., 5 LA 173, 174 (Davey, 1944).

[229] Allied Chemical & Dye Corp., 16 LA 28, 29 (McCoy, 1951). For legal doctrine concerning management's right to hire and retain workers hired during economic strikes, see NLRB v. Fleetwood Trailer Co., 88 S.Ct. 543 (1967); NLRB v. Mackay Radio & Telegraph Co., 58 S.Ct. 904 (1938). Also, The Laidlaw Corporation, 171 NLRB No. 175 (1968). For arbitration decisions, see Arbitrator Merrill in 55 LA 109; Gorsuch in 53 LA 784; Turkus in 42 LA 823; Hill, Horlacher & Seitz in 39 LA 1156; Crane in 36 LA 635; Weinstein in 34 LA 125; Loucks in 33 LA 777.

[230] See Arbitrator Aaron in 10 LA 227, 232–233; Updegraff in 1 LA 331, 333; Fabinski in 1 LA 15, 19–20.

maintenance-of-membership provision while employed as a production worker and subsequently rehired as an assistant foreman. The arbitrator declared that the rehiring of the worker under these circumstances was a cause of dissention and violated the intent of the maintenance-of-membership provision.[231]

Under contracts providing for union referrals in hiring but containing the requirement that referrals be satisfactory to management, arbitrators have allowed employers considerable discretion in rejecting union-referred candidates.[232] But it has been held that the employer must exercise good faith in reaching his decision.[233] It has also been held that while an employer had discretion in selecting from among those referred by the hiring hall, he could not secure employees through direct hire where the contract did not reserve the right to do so.[234]

Determination of Size of Crews

Many grievances have involved the right of management to determine the number of men to be utilized in a given operation.[235] Crew size determinations may be of a more or less permanent nature, as, for example, where a new operation or new equipment is installed or where management eliminates a job to accommodate reduced production needs and market changes; or such determinations may affect a given crew only temporarily, as where the company does not fill a crew member's position during his brief absence.

It has been held that management has the right unilaterally to determine the size of crews necessary for operation of the plant, either under a general management rights clause,[236] or as a matter of man-

---

[231] Merrill-Stevens Co., 1 LA 15, 19–20 (Fabinski, 1944).

[232] See Arbitrator Latimer in 52 LA 327, 332; Feinberg in 8 LA 593, 595; Reynolds in 3 LA 367, 369. Also see Bennett in 18 LA 764, 766, and Wyckoff in 5 LA 38, 40, both involving "interests" disputes.

[233] Matson Navigation Co., 29 LA 209, 213 (Cobb, 1957). Also see Arbitrator Schmertz in 43 LA 245, 246.

[234] Union Painting Contractors Assn., 42 LA 902, 908–909 (Seligson, 1964). Also see Arbitrator Platt in 50 LA 239, 245. The use of union hiring halls is legal under federal law if not used as an instrument of discrimination. Local 357 I.B.T. v. NLRB, 81 S.Ct. 835 (1961).

[235] It may be noted, too, that one of the most critical "interests" disputes of many years involved crew consist for the railroad industry. See Railroads v. Operating Brotherhoods, 41 LA 673 (Aaron, Healy & Seward, 1963).

[236] See Arbitrator B. Wolf in 47 LA 425, 427; King in 46 LA 70, 71; Sembower in 40 LA 720, 726; T. McDermott in 40 LA 67, 70, and in 34 LA 365, 367; Marshall in 28 LA 252, 254; Updegraff in 12 LA 865, 869.

agement prerogative,[237] so long as no other provision of the agreement is violated by the employer's determination.[238]

Union challenges to management action in determining the size of crews have presented arbitrators with a variety of factors for their consideration, including the following: the union may argue that a contract manning provision limits the company's right of action; it may charge the violation of a clause not specifically related to crew size, such as the recognition clause, seniority or layoff clauses, or clauses concerned with filling vacancies;[239] there may be safety or health considerations, or a question of increased burden on remaining crew members; technological or process changes or changes in operations methods and procedures may result in idle time for employees affected by such changes; or economic and production needs may be a factor.[240] These factors are discussed below.

Does a Crew in Fact Exist?

The preliminary question may arise as to whether a group of men actually constitute a "crew." Commenting in regard to the parties' local working conditions clause, Arbitrator Sylvester Garrett noted that the mere fact that a certain number of men perform a given operation for a number of years does not necessarily establish a local working condition governing crew size; and he continued, "It is the *relationship* between this course of conduct, and some *given set of underlying circumstances* which is important in determining

---

[237] See Arbitrator Teple in 55 LA 19, 22; Hebert in 46 LA 140, 151; Mittenthal in 42 LA 1188, 1191; Hon in 38 LA 1135, 1139; Marshall in 29 LA 687, 692–693; Miller in 10 LA 736, 745. Also see Arbitrator Updegraff in 30 LA 115, 117. The National War Board recognized this to be a management function. American Smelting & Refining Co., 21 War LAB. Rep. 163 (1945).

[238] See Arbitrator King in 46 LA 70, 72; Ross in 33 LA 421, 423; Willingham in 61–1 ARB ¶8069. Some arbitrators would require management's action in reducing the size of a crew to "meet the test of reasonableness." Continental Can Co., 35 LA 602, 607 (McKelvey, 1960). Also see Arbitrator Hoffman in 63–1 ARB ¶8199; Reid in 33 LA 442, 445.

[239] See Arbitrator Daugherty in 45 LA 648, 650; Mittenthal in 42 LA 1188, 1190; Hale in 36 LA 919, 921; Stouffer in 36 LA 245, 248; Bauder in 33 LA 25, 27; Dworkin in 29 LA 787, 789; Stutz in 28 LA 360, 361; Feinberg in 19 LA 523, 525; S. Wolff in 19 LA 487, 488. For related material, see this Chapter, topics titled "Layoff of Employees," "Vacancies," "Control of Operation Methods," "Job and Classification Control"; Chapter 14, Seniority.

[240] In Pittsburgh Plate Glass Co., 33 LA 614, 617–619 (1959), and 36 LA 21, 22–23 (1960), Arbitrators Lehoczky, Fisher, and Myers developed general principles as a guide in determining specific manpower proposals.

whether there has been a recurring response which has evolved as the normal and accepted reaction in dealing with the problem."[241]

In holding that the employer had acted within its rights under the management rights clause when it eliminated two maintenance employees, Arbitrator Thomas J. McDermott stated that employees are not a "crew" simply because employment has been stable for a long period of time and thus manning requirements have remained the same. He further observed:

"Most arbitrators hold to the position that a crew for purposes of local working conditions exists where the employees making up the work force have a relationship that is interdependent to each other. This would mean that, when one member is removed or absent, the remaining workers are required to assume an increased amount of work, or there is a significant change in the type of work they are required to perform. In other words, there must be a relationship between the repetitive nature of the work and the interdependence of members to each other."[242]

Arbitrator Clair V. Duff has cautioned that "The problem of *crew* sizes must be differentiated from the size of a work force in a particular department or other sub-division of the plant which usually fluctuates in size, depending on many circumstances."[243]

In summary, then, to demonstrate the existence of a "crew" in the absence of a contractual definition thereof, it must be shown that (1) an established course of conduct has existed (2) with respect to the assignment of a specific number of employees (3) who have performed in an interdependent manner (4) a particular type of work (5) under a given set of circumstances (6) for a significant period of time.

The above views have been expressed under agreements containing local working conditions clauses. It has been suggested that an even stronger showing as to the existence of a "crew" would be required in the absence of such local working conditions clauses.[244]

---

[241] United States Steel Corp., 33 LA 394, 404 (1959).

[242] Pittsburgh Steel Co., 40 LA 67, 68–69 (1963). Also see Arbitrator Sherman in 47 LA 317, 319; T. McDermott in 46 LA 733, 734; Duff in 39 LA 151, 153. Cf. Arbitrator Crawford in 40 LA 903, 907–908; Porter in 39 LA 921, 925.

[243] Jones & Laughlin Steel Corp., 39 LA 151, 153 (1962).

[244] See Comments of Arbitrator Harry H. Platt in "The Silent Contract vs. Express Provisions," Collective Bargaining and the Arbitrator's Role (BNA, Inc., 1962), p. 147.

The remaining topics discussed below involve established crews.

Limiting Contract Provisions

Of course, a particular crew size may be fixed by a specific contract provision stating the number of men in the crew with the result that management likely would be denied the right to eliminate a member of that crew. This was the arbitrator's ruling despite the fact that new equipment was installed which, absent the clause specifying the crew size, might have justified the reduction.[245]

Somewhat less specifically, a clause may call for "adequate help,"[246] "adequate manpower,"[247] or a "sufficient number" of men.[248] Or the contract may require the employer to schedule the "normal number" of employees,[249] the "standard force,"[250] or the "full crew."[251]

Management's right to determine crew size may be restricted by a contract clause requiring joint determination with the union following any significant change in equipment or method of operation.[252] The right of management to reduce the size of a crew may also be limited by a clause, such as is prevalent in the steel industry contracts, which requires maintenance of established local working conditions unless the underlying basis for the condition is changed.[253] However, the mere existence of a local working conditions clause or one calling for "adequate help," etc., does not necessarily freeze the number of

---

[245] Barton Salt Co., 46 LA 503, 505 (Merrill, 1966); Edition Bookbinders of New York, Inc., 42 LA 1167, 1171 (Altieri, 1964). In both cases the contract was specific as to certain crew complements but not as to others. Also see Arbitrator Flink in 21 LA 653, 654.

[246] Schlitz Brewing Co., 30 LA 147, 148 (Fleming, 1958); Pabst Brewing Co., 29 LA 617, 621 (Fleming, 1957).

[247] Lone Star Brewing Co., 50 LA 458 (Hebert, 1968); Pearl Brewing Co., 42 LA 145, 147 (Bothwell, 1964).

[248] American Pipe & Construction Co., 43 LA 1126, 1134 (Ladar, 1964).

[249] Gulf Oil Corp., 42 LA 294, 297 (Rehmus, 1964); Sherman-Williams Co., 25 LA 879, 881 (Kelliher, 1956).

[250] Keystone Steel and Wire Co., 45 LA 648, 650 (Daugherty, 1965).

[251] Plymouth Oil Co., 36 LA 919, 922 (Hale, 1961); Continental Can Co., 35 LA 602, 603 (McKelvey, 1960).

[252] As in Memphis Publishing Co., 50 LA 186, 190 (Duff, 1967).

[253] See United States Steel Corp., 33 LA 394, 397–404 (Garrett, 1959). Also see Arbitrator Florey in 43 LA 1048, 1050; Crawford in 40 LA 984, 986; T. McDermott in 39 LA 432, 434. Some contracts are silent as to past practices, while other contracts contain local working conditions clauses. On the question whether there is significant difference in results reached by arbitrators under these two types of contracts, see views by Saul Wallen, Lloyd H. Bailer, and Harry H. Platt, "The Silent Contract vs. Express Provisions," Collective Bargaining and the Arbitrator's Role (BNA, Inc., 1962), pp. 117–147.

employees in a crew, since many factors, discussed hereinbelow, singly or in combination may nevertheless justify a change in the size of the crew. Many of the cases involving such contract clauses also involved changes in operations, technological changes, or questions of employee safety, and the like; and the arbitrator's finding that a proper crew had or had not been provided was based upon the evidence presented in the given case.

Technological and Process Changes

Arbitrators are in general agreement that where substantial changes in technology or manufacturing processes have been made management has the right to make changes in the size of the crew, unless restricted by the agreement.[254] This is true even where the contract contains a local working conditions clause, for it is reasoned that the changes in technology or processes cause a change in the basis for the existence of such condition.[255] Of course, the changes must be substantial enough to result in a material reduction in the employees' work load in order to justify the reduction in crew size.[256]

Moreover, there must be a "reasonable causal relationship" between the changes and the reduction in the crew, not only in the substance of the change, but also in the span of time between the change in equipment or process and the change in crew size.[257] Thus, where a series of changes was completed and the employer did not act to reduce the crew size until 10 years later, the arbitrator refused to uphold the reduction.[258]

However, even though there was a substantial span of time between the first of several changes and the reduction in crew size, management was upheld where it acted with "reasonable dispatch following the last of several related changes which rounded out the total

---

[254] See Arbitrator Hebert in 50 LA 458, 461; Altieri in 42 LA 1167, 1171; Hawley in 42 LA 479, 482; Hoffman in 63-1 ARB ¶8199; Joseph in 63-1 ARB ¶8092; Hon in 38 LA 1135, 1140; McKelvey in 35 LA 602, 607; Reid in 33 LA 442, 445.

[255] See Arbitrator T. McDermott in 43 LA 770, 772; Duff in 41 LA 432, 434, and in 41 LA 300, 301-302; Garrett in 62-2 ARB ¶8676, and in 34 LA 127, 135; Alexander in 37 LA 318, 320.

[256] See Arbitrator Dybeck in 51 LA 1303, 1306; Platt in 49 LA 1018, 1026; Florey in 43 LA 1048, 1050; May in 43 LA 433, 440; T. McDermott in 39 LA 432, 435. Also see McKenna in 55 LA 41, 53-54.

[257] See United States Steel Corp., 40 LA 984, 987-988 (Crawford, 1963). Also see Kaiser Steel Corp., 44 LA 353, 357-358 (Bernstein, 1965).

[258] United States Steel Corp., 40 LA 984, 987-988 (Crawford, 1963).

picture of altered circumstances affecting the jobs in question." The arbitrator stated that the changes "are not properly considered as individual and isolated changes but must be viewed in their cumulative effect."[259]

Changes in Type of Operations, Methods, and Procedures

Substantial changes in the type of operations[260] or in the method of operations[261] have been considered justifying factors in upholding management's reduction in the size of crews. Thus, under a contract providing for "the normal number of men . . . required for the then existing conditions," the company was upheld when it eliminated a helper from a crew since a modernization program had made substantial changes in the type of operation and had substantially reduced the quantity of work to be performed by such helper. The work that remained did "not appear . . . to burden unduly" the remaining crew members.[262]

Under a local working conditions clause, an arbitrator held that substantial cumulative changes in warehouse and shipping procedures justified the reduction in crew size; even though instituted over a period of years, the changes were considered to be "part and parcel of the same improvement pattern."[263]

Market Changes

One arbitrator considered market changes an important factor, along with improved and new equipment and procedures, in upholding management's right to reduce the size of crews.[264] Similarly, in the absence of a contractual requirement to maintain crew sizes, where changes occurred in customer's buying habits as well as in methods of operation, which in turn substantially reduced the amount of work available to the employees involved, it was held that the company had the right to reduce the crew size.[265]

---

[259] United States Steel Corp., 41 LA 468, 479–480 (C. McDermott, 1963). Also see Arbitrator Hebert in 46 LA 140, 148; McKelvey in 35 LA 602, 607; Sherman in 34 LA 556, 558.

[260] See Arbitrator T. McDermott in 43 LA 770, 772; Hawley in 42 LA 479, 482; Rehmus in 42 LA 294, 297.

[261] See Arbitrator Fallon in 64–3 ARB ¶9169; Seward in 36 LA 162, 163; Brown in 35 LA 618, 620–621.

[262] Gulf Oil Corp., 42 LA 294, 297 (Rehmus, 1964).

[263] United States Steel Corp., 41 LA 56, 58–59 (Altrock, 1963). Also see Cities Service Oil Co., 42 LA 479, 482 (Hawley, 1964).

[264] Cities Service Oil Co., 42 LA 479, 482 (Hawley, 1964).

[265] Mead Corp., 64–3 ARB ¶9169 (Fallon, 1964).

Production Needs and Reduced Operations

When operations are reduced in order to adapt to production needs, arbitrators appear to be in general agreement that management may reduce the size of crews so long as such action is not barred by the contract or does not create a safety hazard.[266] Thus, when a certain operation had been discontinued, it was held that management had the right to eliminate a job pertaining to such operation and assign the relatively few remaining duties of the job to another crew member.[267]

Work Load and Idle Time

The union frequently challenges the company's action on the basis that a reduced crew results in an excessive work load for the remaining crew members. However, working conditions may be changed significantly by technological or process improvements, by reducing or discontinuing certain operations, or by changes in methods and procedures, and the like. When such factors have resulted in a substantial amount of idle time for the employees in a crew, arbitrators have held that the company could properly reduce the crew and re-allocate whatever duties remain to other employees in the crew.[268] In most of such cases the arbitrator has found that the remaining work allocated to the other crew members did not excessively increase their work load.[269]

If there is a finding that the elimination of a job from the crew has increased the work load of the remaining crew members, some adjustment in their rate of pay may be ordered. Under such circumstances, one arbitrator held that there was an "increase in job content"

---

[266] See Arbitrator Mittenthal in 42 LA 1188, 1190–1191; T. McDermott in 40 LA 487, 489; Seward in 37 LA 83, 84, and in 34 LA 584, 585; Valtin in 36 LA 217, 218; Platt in 31 LA 217, 218.

[267] Pittsburgh Steel Co., 40 LA 70, 72 (T. McDermott, 1962). The arbitrator made no finding regarding the question of excessive work load on the remaining crew.

[268] Pittsburgh Steel Co., 40 LA 70, 72 (T. McDermott, 1962); Reynolds Mining Co., 33 LA 25, 28 (Bauder, 1959). Also see Foster Wheeler Corp., 64–1 ARB ¶8103 (Shister, 1963).

[269] See Arbitrator Herbert in 50 LA 458, 461; T. McDermott in 46 LA 733, 734, and in 34 LA 365, 367; Bothwell in 42 LA 145, 147–148; Rehmus in 42 LA 294, 297; Fallon in 64–3 ARB ¶9169; Marshall in 29 LA 687, 692. One arbitrator found that in fact the work load of the remaining crew was less than it had been before the crew was reduced by reason of reduced operations and improved methods. Midwest Carbide Corp., 35 LA 618, 621 (Brown, 1960).

which was justification under the contract for negotiation of an adjustment in wage rate.[270]

In another situation, where the company was not permitted under the contract to operate with a crew member absent but nevertheless required three members of a four-man crew to perform all the tasks of the crew, the arbitrator directed the company to pay each of those three members an additional sum equivalent to one third of the regular wages the fourth crew member earned, as compensation for the additional work duties performed while he was absent.[271]

Use of Supervisors or "General Help"

The fact that the company assigns supervisors or "general help" to perform work which would have been done by the eliminated crew member may be pertinent in determining whether a reduction in the crew was in fact justified. The weight to be accorded such a factor would be dependent upon the amount and frequency of work performed by personnel outside the crew in question. Thus, where foremen or "general help" have not given inordinate assistance to those remaining in the reduced crew, arbitrators have held that such factor would not be determinative of the decision in the case.[272] However, where the union proved that foremen were persistently performing the work that would have been done by the eliminated crew member, the arbitrator considered that the company by such action tacitly recognized that the crew was short-handed.[273]

Safety or Health Hazard

Management's right to determine the size of work crews has frequently been challenged on the ground that a reduction in the size of the crew has resulted in a safety or health hazard to the remaining employees. This argument has been advanced in the wake of technological changes,[274] introduction of safety equipment and procedures,[275]

---

[270] Mobil Oil Co., 61-4 ARB ¶8069 (Willingham, 1961).
[271] Southwest Steel Corp., 38 LA 344, 346–347 (Duff, 1962). Similarly, Pittsburgh Steel Co., 66–1 ARB ¶8286 (T. McDermott, 1966).
[272] See Arbitrator Kadish in 41 LA 381, 384; Valtin in 35 LA 289, 292–293; Updegraff in 30 LA 115, 116.
[273] United States Steel Corp., 61–2 ARB ¶8527 (Garrett, 1961). Also see Keystone Steel and Wire Co., 45 LA 648, 650–651 (Daugherty, 1965).
[274] See Arbitrator Bothwell in 42 LA 145, 147–148; Duff in 41 LA 432, 434–435, and in 41 LA 300, 301–302; Howlett in 41 LA 230, 236; Garrett in 34 LA 127, 135–136; Reid in 34 LA 442, 445.
[275] See Arbitrator Duff in 43 LA 583, 587; Lehoczky in 43 LA 427, 429; Sembower in 39 LA 341, 346–347; Murphy in 37 LA 501, 503.

changes in operations and methods,[276] changes in production needs and reduced operations,[277] introduction of new production procedures,[278] and the like. However, by far the preponderance of cases involving such changes have held either that there was no sufficient showing of a safety hazard or that there was no increase in the normal and inherent hazard of the job.[279]

It should be observed that in many jobs there are certain normal and inherent risks which cannot be avoided if the jobs are to be performed at all. Thus, in crew safety cases it must be determined (1) whether a safety hazard actually exists, and (2) if so, whether it is an abnormal safety hazard. Of course, such determinations must be made on the basis of the facts in each case.

A crew safety dispute may include the question whether an additional employee would eliminate the alleged safety hazard, or the question of possible increased hazard to an employee left working alone when all the other crew members are eliminated. In a case involving the former issue, Arbitrator Clair V. Duff required the return of an employee to the crew when he found that a genuine safety hazard existed despite the installation of electronic safety devices and other automatic equipment. He held the innovations were not adequate to "insure an equivalent amount of protection which would be furnished if a vigilant employee was also on duty."[280] On the other hand, conditions may be such that the presence of an additional experienced man would still not eliminate the alleged hazard.[281]

In instances where the company has reduced a crew leaving only one man, arbitrators appear to be in general agreement that working

---

[276] See Arbitrator Lehoczky in 43 LA 427, 429; Duff in 41 LA 432, 434–435; Howlett in 41 LA 230, 236; Reid in 33 LA 442, 445.

[277] See Arbitrator Mittenthal in 42 LA 1188, 1191; Seward in 37 LA 83, 84; Valtin in 36 LA 217, 218; Platt in 31 LA 217, 218–219.

[278] United States Steel Corp., 41 LA 300, 301–302 (Duff, 1963).

[279] See cases cited in preceding footnotes, this topic. In only one of these cases was an increased hazard found. Jones & Laughlin Steel Corp., 43 LA 583, 587 (Duff, 1964). Also see American Pipe & Construction Co., 43 LA 1126, 1134–1135 (Ladar, 1964).

[280] Jones & Laughlin Steel Corp., 43 LA 583, 587 (1964). Also see American Pipe & Construction Co., 43 LA 1126, 1134–1135 (Ladar, 1964). In United States Steel Corp., 54 LA 317, 320 (Garrett, 1969), an apprentice could not be substituted for one of the two regular men on a crew, the practice being to use two journeymen for safety reasons and there being no change in conditions to affect the need for two journeymen.

[281] Bethlehem Steel Co., 36 LA 217, 219 (Valtin, 1961). Also see United States Steel Corp., 41 LA 432, 434–435 (Duff, 1963); Brooklyn Union Gas Co., 47 LA 425, 429 (B. Wolf, 1966).

alone is not a "hazard per se."[282] Moreover, where an employee had instructions to request additional help if he felt that it was necessary, the arbitrator found it significant that no such requests had been made.[283] Nor is it felt that such instructions place an "unreasonable psychological or physical burden" on the employee.[284]

Two other aspects of crew size issues, discussed elsewhere in this book, may be noted briefly here. These relate to (1) the obligation of management to provide reasonably safe working conditions; and (2) the obligation of an employee to stay on the job unless a real safety or health hazard exists, and, conversely, the employee's right to be relieved of duty pending correction of abnormally hazardous conditions.[285]

Vacancies

It is generally recognized that in the absence of a contract provision limiting management's rights in regard to filling vacancies, as, for example, a clear requirement to maintain a certain number of employees on a particular job, it is management's right to determine whether a vacancy exists and whether and when it shall be filled.[286]

Moreover, contractual provisions dealing with posting of vacancies but not specifically requiring management to fill vacancies have been narrowly construed. Thus, a contractual provision for posting of "permanent vacancies" was held to apply only if management decides that a vacancy exists; in this instance the company had decided that there was no need to replace a promoted employee, so no vacancy

---

[282] Pickands-Mather Co., 43 LA 427, 429 (Lehoczky, 1964). Also see Arbitrator Mittenthal in 42 LA 1188, 1192; Duff in 41 LA 300, 301–302; Valtin in 36 LA 217, 219.

[283] Pearl Brewing Co., 42 LA 145, 148 (Bothwell, 1964).

[284] Brooklyn Union Gas Co., 47 LA 425, 428 (B. Wolf, 1966).

[285] For discussion on these points, see Chapter 5, topic titled "Use of Grievance Procedure v. Self-Help," and Chapter 16, topic titled "Safety and Health Hazard."

[286] See Arbitrator Roberts in 54 LA 896, 900–901; Kesselman in 52 LA 894, 897–898; Larkin in 44 LA 580, 584; Solomon in 44 LA 161, 164–168; Hardy in 43 LA 1276, 1287; Seinsheimer in 40 LA 819, 821; Murphy in 39 LA 1074, 1077; Crawford in 36 LA 825, 827; Dworkin in 35 LA 649, 653; Fleming in 32 LA 115, 116; Donnelly in 29 LA 162, 166; Livengood in 28 LA 844, 847; Seligson in 25 LA 360, 364; Kelliher in 22 LA 576, 577; Dworet in 22 LA 71, 74. But see Davey in 29 LA 13, 16–17, where the contract made it mandatory to fill vacancies. For related discussion, see this Chapter, topic titled "Determination of Size of Crews."

existed.[287] Under another contract requiring posting and giving preference to senior employees in their given classification, it was held that
neither the posting nor the seniority or classification provisions of the
contract contained any implied restriction on management's right to
determine if a vacancy existed and, if so, whether to fill it.[288] It has
been held also that where insufficient work existed to justify filling
the job of an employee who had retired, management was not required
to post the job and could assign the excess duties occasioned by the
retirement to another employee (subject only to the possibility that
the job of the latter employee may need to be re-evaluated).[289]

Even where a job has been posted for bid, this does not necessarily
guarantee that a vacancy exists and will be filled.[290] In one case management was upheld in permitting a successful bidder to withdraw
his bid and return to his original job even though the latter had in
turn been posted for bid.[291]

The filling of temporary vacancies also has been arbitrated. It
is well established that management has the right, unless clearly restricted by the agreement, to decide whether or not to fill temporary
vacancies occasioned by absences due to illness, vacations, and the
like.[292] Contract provisions stating that temporary vacancies "will"
or "shall" be filled by a stated procedure have been construed merely

---

[287] Sherwin Williams Co., 49 LA 74, 75 (Ray, 1967). Similarly, see Arbitrator
Block in 46 LA 1027, 1029–1030; Seinsheimer in 40 LA 819, 821 (provision
stating that "job opportunities shall be posted for bidding" did not require
management to fill the job of an employee who had resigned).
[288] Fairway Foods, Inc., 44 LA 161, 164–168 (Solomon, 1965). The mere
fact that a job classification has been dormant for a lengthy period does not
mean that it has been abolished. See Ohio Chemical & Surgical Equipment
Co., 40 LA 481, 485 (Sembower, 1963).
[289] Link-Belt Co., 36 LA 825, 827 (Crawford, 1961). Similarly, see Arbitrator
Roberts in 54 LA 896, 900–901.
[290] R. C. Can Co., 52 LA 894, 897–898 (Kesselman, 1969); McCall Corp.,
43 LA 951, 956 (Layman, 1964).
[291] R. C. Can Co., 52 LA 894, 897–898 (Kesselman, 1969), where a prior
agreement existed, however, which would produce a different result if a successful
bidder already has commenced work on his new job.
[292] See Arbitrator Teple in 55 LA 19, 22; Ray in 43 LA 395, 399–400;
Roberts in 41 LA 492, 496; Larson in 38 LA 1152, 1154; Stouffer in 36 LA
245, 249–250; Seligson in 36 LA 266, 267–268; Abernethy in 29 LA 467, 468;
Hebert in 28 LA 538, 541–542; Marshall in 28 LA 252, 254; Hawley in 22
LA 157, 159; Klamon in 16 LA 352, 356. The fact that management may
have elected to fill such vacancies in the past does not bind it to do so in
the future. See Arbitrator Ray in 43 LA 395, 399–400; Roberts in 41 LA
492, 496.

to specify the procedure to be used *if* management decides to fill a vacancy.[293]

Scheduling Work

Collective agreements may deal expressly with the scheduling of work. For example, the agreement may fix or in some respect regulate shifts,[294] or expressly fix the workweek,[295] or expressly provide that scheduling is an exclusive function of management,[296] or in some respect expressly limit the employer's right to schedule work.[297] Another possibility is that the agreement may impliedly restrict management's rights in the scheduling of work, as where certain contract language was construed to prevent management from instituting seven-day continuous shift operations.[298]

Many arbitrators have recognized that except as restricted by the agreement the right to schedule work remains in management.[299] Much of the material in the remainder of this topic deals with the application of this rule, giving some indication as to the scope of management's rights—and limitations thereon—in this area.

In proper circumstances management has been permitted to suspend operations temporarily, eliminate double-time work, reduce the number of shifts, change the number of days to be worked, and the

---

[293] See Arbitrator Hebert in 28 LA 538, 541; Roberts in 25 LA 885, 888; Hawley in 22 LA 157, 159. The posting of schedules and scheduling of employees does not guarantee the number of employees who are to work and require replacements for sick employees. Standard Oil Co., 36 LA 245, 249–250 (Stouffer, 1960).

[294] For example, see Curtis-Wright Corp., 36 LA 629, 629–630 (Crawford, 1960).

[295] For example, see Norfolk Naval Shipyard, 54 LA 588, 589 (Cushman, 1970).

[296] For example, see Celanese Corp. of America, 30 LA 797, 798 (Jaffee, 1958).

[297] For example, see Taylor Stone Co., 29 LA 236, 237 (Dworkin, 1957).

[298] Morse Chain Co., 43 LA 557, 560–561 (Cahn, 1964).

[299] See Arbitrator Solomon in 51 LA 1102, 1107–1108; Kabaker in 48 LA 1365, 1367; Howlett in 42 LA 25, 28–31; Stark in 35 LA 788, 790–792; Hill in 33 LA 320, 322; Shister in 32 LA 77, 80; Kelliher in 29 LA 615, 617; Dworkin in 29 LA 236, 239; Duff in 28 LA 37, 40; Warns in 24 LA 619, 622; Davey in 22 LA 657, 660; Uible in 19 LA 213, 214–215; Rule in 16 LA 328, 330; McCoy in 16 LA 73, 75; Schedler in 13 LA 192, 199; McCreary in 9 LA 834, 839–840; Whiting in 3 LA 482, 485; Korey in 1 LA 430, 432–433. Also see Arbitrator Davidson in 42 LA 51, 53; Scheiber in 40 LA 152, 159; Swauger in 37 LA 883, 886; Willcox in 36 LA 1117, 1119–1120; Coffey in 20 LA 432, 433; Guild in 19 LA 891, 892; Klamon in 15 LA 733, 739; Tischler in 13 LA 396, 398.

like. Thus, where nothing in the agreement clearly guaranteed any particular amount of work each week and the agreement did not otherwise restrict management's right to suspend operations, management could determine whether work should go forward and its decision to close down on a given day was upheld since it acted for a valid reason and not arbitrarily.[300] The elimination of Sunday (double-time) work was upheld even though such work had been regularly scheduled for many years, the arbitrator stating that "While the agreement contains no 'management rights' clause, the scheduling of work is a normal and customary function of management which would not ordinarily be deemed limited or waived except by some express provision of the agreement."[301]

Moreover, where the contract contained no express limitation on work scheduling it was held that management could change from a schedule of two six-hour shifts six days a week to a schedule of one eight-hour shift five days a week; the arbitrator held that the change was not barred either by the contract's reference to six-hour shifts (which he said did not crystallize the workweek but merely provided the framework for overtime computation) or by the provision on preservation of "present practices and policies."[302] Management's right to change from a five-day work schedule to a six-day schedule has similarly been upheld.[303] In upholding such changes arbitrators have spoken of management's right "to schedule the work with a view

---

[300] See Arbitrator Kabaker in 48 LA 1365, 1367–1368 (closing on the day before Christmas and the day before New Year's because of reduced orders); Solomon in 45 LA 388, 396–398 (closing to give holdiay to nonunit employees though this meant unit employees did not work); Davidson in 42 LA 51, 53; Kabaker in 40 LA 970, 972–974 (shortage of materials justified sending certain employees home); Klamon in 36 LA 1031, 1034; Stark in 35 LA 788, 790–792.

[301] New Jersey Brewers' Assn., 33 LA 320, 322 (Hill, 1959).

[302] Kimberly-Clark Corp., 42 LA 982, 986–988 (Sembower, 1964), where the change was discussed with the union prior to being instituted. Similarly permitting management to change from a six-day work schedule to a five-day schedule, see St. Regis Paper Co., 51 LA 1102, 1107–1108 (Solomon, 1968), where there was no express restriction and the contract contained a general management rights clause; the arbitrator distinguished several other cases in which past actions of the parties made out a joint understanding as to scheduling. A "maintenance of standards" clause was held not to prevent management from changing from a 48-hour workweek to a 40-hour workweek in Borden Co., 39 LA 1020, 1023–1024 (Morvant, 1962); but long established differences in a company's summer and winter schedules did constitute a binding "local working condition" under the agreement in Bethlehem Cornwall Corp., 31 LA 793, 795–796 (Valtin, 1958).

[303] Goodyear Tire & Rubber Co., 32 LA 77, 80 (Shister, 1958); Screw Machine Products Co., 3 War Lab. Rep. 553, 556 (1942), where the decision was signed by the public, labor, and management members of the panel.

to optimum efficiency,"[304] and have expressed the view that limitations on the right "ought not be lightly inferred."[305]

The mere fact that a work schedule has been traditionally on a workweek basis of five consecutive days has been held not to establish a vested interest in employees in the continuation of the schedule.[306] Thus, where nothing in the agreement prohibited management's action and where there was a general management rights clause management was within its rights in establishing staggered work schedules,[307] in changing from fixed to rotating shifts,[308] or in adding an extra shift to permit seven-day operations.[309] However, while recognizing management's right to establish work schedules except as restricted by the agreement, Arbitrator Joseph D. Lohman held that management was not privileged to schedule shifts in such a way as to deprive employees of certain rest periods to which they were entitled under the contract.[310] Nor could a company change from fixed to rotating shifts where the change would impair the contractual right of senior employees to their preferred shift and "days off."[311]

One arbitrator was asked to decide whether, in the absence of a contractual provision, an employer had the right to reschedule hours

---

[304] Kimberly-Clark Corp., 42 LA 982, 986 (Sembower, 1964).

[305] St. Regis Paper Co., 51 LA 1102, 1107 (Solomon, 1968).

[306] Calumet & Hecla, Inc., 42 LA 25, 28–31 (Howlett, 1963), where the employer changed from scheduling Monday through Friday and began scheduling employees for five days during the week as required by operational needs; Columbia Steel Co., 7 LA 881, 883 (Blumer, 1947).

[307] Ingram-Richardson Mfg. Co. of Indiana, 3 LA 482, 485 (Whiting, 1946). For other cases construing the contract as not requiring the workweek to be composed of five consecutive days and thus permitting "staggered" or "split" work schedules, see Arbitrator Koven in 49 LA 1000, 1002–1004; Hayes in 47 LA 449, 452; Schedler in 13 LA 192, 199; Blumer in 7 LA 881, 883. Also see Jaffee in 30 LA 797, 799–803; Abrahams in 15 LA 142, 146–147.

[308] Morris P. Kirk & Son, Inc., 27 LA 6, 10 (Prasow, 1956); General Cable Corp., 15 LA 910, 912 (Kaplan, 1950), where there was no management rights clause. In Carnation Co., 34 LA 345, 349–350 (Marshall, 1960), management was bound by past practice as to the frequency of shift rotation.

[309] Minnesota Mining & Mfg. Co., 15 LA 46, 49 (Kelliher, 1950). Also see Arbitrator McCoy in 34 LA 34, 36. Where an agreement established three specific "regular" shifts and contained a general management rights clause, operational requirements were held to justify management's establishment of an "oddball" shift for one employee different from the shifts specified in the agreement. Scott Paper Co., 48 LA 591, 593 (Williams, 1967).

[310] Wilson & Co., 1 LA 342, 347 (1946). Also see Bakelite Co., 29 LA 555, 559 (Updegraff, 1957), involving a change in scheduled lunch periods.

[311] Reynolds Metals Co., 35 LA 800, 802–803 (Ross, 1961). Other contractual rights of employees have likewise been protected against invasion by managerial scheduling actions. See Arbitrator NcNaughton in 50 LA 304, 306; Howard in 45 LA 72, 74.

of work for operations at night and, if so, on what basis of compensation. The arbitrator ruled that there was no question as to the company's right to assign employees to night work, but that it must pay a night-work differential that had been paid in the past.[312] Another arbitrator upheld management's right to schedule Sunday work where not prohibited by the agreement; the reasonableness of management's action was tested from the point of view of the needs of the business rather than the convenience of the employees.[313]

It has been held that, where an agreement is silent as to the workweek insofar as its commencement and end are concerned, the employer may change the day on which the workweek begins if the change is not made arbitrarily and is made in conformance with industry practice in the area.[314] Similarly, where the contract contained no express restriction on the employer's right to determine the starting time for work shifts, the employer has been permitted unilaterally to change the starting and stopping time.[315] Even where the agreement specified the shift starting times, essential pre-shift "start-up" work has justified management in requiring certain employees to report early for the work.[316]

Under agreements which expressly state what is a "normal" or "regular" workweek management often has been permitted consider-

---

[312] Everett Dyers & Cleaners, 11 LA 462, 466 (Myers, 1948). In FMC Corp., 50 LA 261, 263 (Koven, 1968), management could change an employee from an evening schedule to a daytime schedule where the change was for sound business reasons and where management had changed schedules in the past.

[313] Drake Bakeries, Inc., 38 LA 751, 753–754 (Wolf, 1962.) Also see Arbitrator Summers in 39 LA 374, 378. For related discussion, see Chapter 17, topic titled "Accommodation of Employees' Religious Beliefs."

[314] Schulze's Bakery, 5 LA 255, 257 (Wardlaw, 1946). Also see Bethlehem Steel Co., 33 LA 324, 326 (Valtin, 1959). A provision requiring union consent for changing the day on which the workweek begins was strictly enforced in Redi-Gas Service, 48 LA 197, 198 (Olson, 1967).

[315] See Arbitrator Howlett in 44 LA 954, 955; Schedler in 42 LA 345, 346–348; Tsukiyama in 41 LA 1115, 1116–1117; Mittenthal in 41 LA 1050, 1052–1053; Warns in 36 LA 1035, 1036–1037 (contractual requirement to "consult" with union as to change in starting time did not require union consent for a change); Hepburn in 28 LA 467, 467–468; Reid in 27 LA 123, 125. Also see Kates in 50 LA 741, 743; Hayes in 46 LA 129, 131–132. The agreement itself may be construed to give management the unilateral right to make the change (see Arbitrator McIntosh in 49 LA 661, 663, and in 49 LA 659, 660–661), or it may be construed to deny such right (see Arbitrator Meyers in 39 LA 93, 96; Koven in 38 LA 803, 807–808).

[316] Fitchburg Paper Co., 47 LA 349, 351–352 (Wallen, 1966); American Brake Shoe Co., 33 LA 344, 347–348 (Gilden, 1959). Also see Arbitrator Klamon in 21 LA 91, 97. But see Myers in 24 LA 565, 566.

able leeway in making adjustments in the workweek as needed for efficient operations.[317] For example, although an agreement specified a "normal" workweek of Monday through Friday, special production needs justified the scheduling of one employee to a Tuesday through Saturday workweek.[318] Although another agreement provided for a "regular" workweek of five days, management could schedule a four-day workweek during a period of reduced production. The arbitrator stated that the provision for a "regular" workweek was designed to regularize employment and furnish norms from which overtime premiums may be calculated—it cannot be regarded as a guarantee of employment for all or any group of employees for any specific number of hours per day or days per week.[319]

However, even where the agreement specifically provided that there was no work guarantee and expressly reserved the right to management to adjust work schedules to meet operating requirements, it was held that the contractual provision establishing "normal" workday, workweek, and shift hours was violated when the schedule was modified during Christmas and New Year's weeks; the employer was held not to have a right to change the schedule arbitrarily, the arbitrator stating that the employee "adjusts his life" to the "normal routine" and that the employer had not demonstrated satisfactorily that a change from the normal work schedule was necessary.[320]

In the absence of a specific contract provision regarding the right of management to reduce the workweek in lieu of making layoffs, arbitrators have gone both ways on the issue.[321] Thus, one arbitration

---

[317] See Arbitrator Daugherty in 50 LA 1211, 1213 (shut down for one day on three separate occasions); Cayton in 48 LA 570, 572; Hebert in 44 LA 226, 229–230, 233; Summers in 39 LA 374, 377 (although contract spoke of normal Monday through Friday workweek management could use seven-day continuous shift schedules for certain operations); Gamser in 33 LA 610, 613; Boles in 30 LA 465, 469–470; Kelliher in 29 LA 615, 617; Ryder in 24 LA 496, 500.

[318] Universal Foods Corp., 44 LA 226, 229–230, 233 (Hebert, 1965).

[319] Triangle Conduit & Cable Co., 33 LA 610, 613 (Gamser, 1959), the arbitrator stating that the layoff provisions were not violated. Very clear language is required for a guaranteed wage. New York Herald Tribune, 36 LA 753, 761 (Cole, 1960).

[320] Aro, Inc., 34 LA 254, 259 (Tatum, 1960). For other cases in which deviation from the "normal" or "regular" schedule was held improper, see Arbitrator Roberts in 42 LA 589, 593; Crawford in 36 LA 687, 689–690 (employer could not expand workweek to continuous shift where contract spoke of "normal" workweek of 40 hours); Carmichael in 28 LA 20, 33; Reynard in 27 LA 625, 627; Donnelly, Mottram & Curry in 17 LA 463, 465–466.

[321] For a collection of cases in addition to those cited in the succeeding

board held that management had the right to reduce hours of work in the absence of anything in the agreement restricting such right. There the contract defined the normal workweek as five days of eight hours each and set forth the procedure for layoffs in case of reduction in work. Speaking through its Chairman, Herbert Blumer, the board held that the employer was not prohibited from reducing hours per day to seven in lieu of making layoffs, declaring that the clauses defining the normal workday and normal workweek were standard clauses serving ostensibly as a basis for the calculation of overtime, that the working of the hours specified was not made mandatory, and that the agreement said nothing in regard to the necessity of making layoffs in lieu of reducing hours of work.[322]

A different result was reached by another arbitration board, which held that an employer who reduced the workweek of some employees from five to four days was required to apply the "layoff" provisions of the agreement in doing so. The agreement provided for a basic workweek of five days and made seniority govern in case of layoff.[323] In another case a provision defining the "basic working week" as forty hours was similarly held violated by a reduction of the workweek for the purpose of sharing the work, the arbitrator stating that seniority must be honored by the use of layoffs; but he cautioned that the aforementioned provision did not guarantee individual employees forty hours of work and would not limit management's right to reduce the workweek as necessary for plant efficiency or product quality.[324]

Management may be denied the right to make temporary changes in the work schedule where the purpose of doing so is to avoid overtime

footnotes, see this Chapter, topic titled "Layoff of Employees." Some arbitrators have emphasized their conclusion that each case on this issue must turn on its own facts and contractual provisions. See Arbitrator Stouffer in 37 LA 877, 882; Boles in 35 LA 845, 848; Kates in 32 LA 492, 496.

[322] Geuder, Paeschke & Frey Co., 12 LA 1163, 1164–1165 (1949). Also permitting a reduction in the workweek in lieu of layoffs, see Arbitrator Murphy in 52 LA 852, 855–857; Stouffer in 37 LA 877, 881–883; Cahn in 32 LA 746, 748.

[323] United Smelting & Aluminum Co., 13 LA 684, 685–686 (Donnelly & Sviridoff, Mottram dissenting, 1949). Also disallowing a reduction in the workweek in lieu of layoffs, see Arbitrator Hertz in 55 LA 859, 861; Williams in 40 LA 456, 459–460; Boles in 35 LA 845, 848–849. In one such case the arbitrator rejected the employer's contention that "layoffs believed at their inception to be but of brief duration are not layoffs but are matters of scheduling work." Bethlehem Steel Co., 5 LA 578, 588 (Brandschain, 1946).

[324] Motch & Merryweather Machinery Co., 32 LA 492, 497–498, 500–501 (Kates, 1959).

payments. Even under a contract providing that nothing therein should "be interpreted as interfering in any way with the Company's right to alter, rearrange or change, extend, limit or curtail its operations * * * whatever may be the effect upon employment, when, in its sole judgment and discretion, it may deem it advisable to do all or any of said things," it was held that the employer could not change the work schedule for one week where the sole purpose in doing so was to avoid contractual overtime payments.[325] Some arbitrators, however, have held otherwise where the change is made prior to the commencement of the workweek[326] or is made with a full week's notice.[327] Such cases were regarded as not analogous to changes made on short notice.

In the absence of limiting contract language, other arbitrators have permitted management to change work schedules to avoid the payment of overtime, holding that the company is not obligated to provide overtime work.[328]

Finally, it may be noted that the "right" of management to schedule work has been held to carry with it the "duty" to do so; in that case Arbitrator Charles G. Hampton ruled that an employer who abdicates such right by permitting employees to determine their own overtime schedules must be held partly responsible for trouble caused by such schedules.[329]

Emergency Changes in Work Schedule

Arbitrators appear to be generally inclined to allow management a great deal of flexibility, where it is possible to do so under the agreement, in making unscheduled and emergency changes in the work

---

[325] Kennecott Copper Corp., 6 LA 820, 822 (Kleinsorge, 1947). For other awards denying management the right in question, see Arbitrator Hale in 39 LA 310, 314–315; Maggs in 35 LA 249, 254; Beatty in 21 LA 416, 419; Platt in 17 LA 313, 315; Gilden in 12 LA 624, 627; Blumer in 5 LA 402, 406; Trotta in 5 LA 69, 71.

[326] National Zinc Co., 4 LA 768, 772 (Wardlaw, 1946). Also see Arbitrator Autrey in 44 LA 961, 964; Hale in 39 LA 310, 315.

[327] Wilson & Co., 7 LA 601, 602 (Lohman, 1947).

[328] See Arbitrators Stutz & Williams, Curry dissenting, in 27 LA 92, 93; Wolff in 21 LA 210, 214; Uible in 19 LA 213, 214–215. Also see Dworkin in 36 LA 233, 238; Rohman in 34 LA 781, 784; Warns in 24 LA 619, 622; Coffey in 20 LA 432, 433; Sturges in 16 LA 517, 525.

[329] Fulton Glass Co., 10 LA 75, 78 (1948).

schedule if made in good faith and for reasonable cause.[330] Even where the agreement in some respect limits management's right or imposes some obligation upon management in regard to making changes in the work schedule, the limitation or obligation may be held inapplicable if there is an emergency, an act of God, or a condition beyond the company's control.[331] For some general definitions of such terms the reader is directed to the topic in this Chapter titled "Emergencies, Acts of God, and Conditions Beyond the Control of Management."

The right to make some unscheduled changes in the work schedule is implicit in the agreement itself if the agreement contains a provision for reporting pay, as a great number of agreements do. The import is that management has the right to make such changes but the right is accompanied by an obligation to make the contractually specified payment to employees.[332] Moreover, many reporting pay clauses state express exceptions even as to the obligation to pay if the employees are not used because of an emergency or condition beyond the control of management. Thus, in the bulk of the cases the right to make the unscheduled change in work has not been questioned, the dispute centering rather on the company's obligation for reporting pay where employees reported for work but were not used.

Turning next to the consideration of specific cases, we note one arbitrator's ruling that a clause giving management the exclusive right to schedule working hours permits it to make temporary changes in the work schedule without consulting the union. In that case the arbitrator held that the employer was not obligated to pay employees for a half hour waiting period on a day when they were scheduled to work at 10 a.m. but were unable to begin work until 10:30. The

---

[330] See Arbitrator Cole in 36 LA 753, 757–758; Reid in 31 LA 93, 95; Thompson in 28 LA 494, 503; Graff in 26 LA 43, 46–47; Platt in 17 LA 313, 315, and in 7 LA 485, 489; Reynolds in 13 LA 326, 327–328; Stein in 10 LA 579, 581.

[331] See Arbitrator Koven in 51 LA 1151, 1153 (provision requiring notice of layoff applies to normal layoff situations, not to abnormal situation of suspension of operations due to strike); Moran in 51 LA 1069, 1071 (riot justified shutdown though riot was not one of the express contractual exceptions to notice of layoff requirement); Cantor in 51 LA 720, 721 (contract stated no exception to reporting pay but one was implied for civil disorders); Madden in 51 LA 692, 695–696 ("act of God" was only express exception to reporting pay provision but civil disorders justified shutdown); Prasow in 25 LA 794, 797–799; Cornsweet in 16 LA 277, 279. But see Arbitrator Emerson in 32 LA 112, 114 (contract stated no exception for strike and none would be implied).

[332] For a similar conclusion, see Bethlehem Steel Co., 33 LA 285, 291 (Stark, 1959).

call-in pay clause was held not to cover the situation because the employees actually worked and received pay for more hours than were guaranteed by the clause. In sustaining the right of the employer to make temporary changes in the work schedule, Arbitrator R. W. Fleming said:

"This is the usual 'management prerogative' type of clause [speaking of the clause giving the employer the right to schedule working hours]. Experience shows that this clause is inserted in the contract at the instance of management to make clear that it has freedom to do certain things without having to consult with the union. So, in this case, the Company retained the exclusive right to schedule working hours, without consultation with the union. In the opinion of the arbiter the clause cannot fairly be read to mean in addition that the Company, once it has set the working hours, must pay for hours not worked unless failure to work was for reasons beyond the Company's control."[333]

Under an agreement containing a minimum pay guarantee of four hours for employees who report to work and are not put to work and also for employees who, after having been put to work, are laid off before completing four hours of work, but providing that the guarantee should not apply in case of strike, breakdown of equipment, or act of God, Arbitrator Joseph Brandschain ruled that the employer's decision to send employees home when the machine to which they were assigned broke down, rather than to provide them with other work, represented the exercise of a management prerogative which the union was not entitled to challenge in the absence of a contractual requirement that the employer provide alternative work. As to the wisdom of the employer's decision, he said:

"However, in most instances, it might be much wiser from both the point of view of economy of operation and employee morale if a determined effort were made to find other work in these situations, particularly if it is true that preceding foremen used to concern themselves more with this problem. As the union points out, the men suffer the inconvenience and expense of coming to work, packing lunch, and paying for transportation so that management should make every effort to find work for the men to do wherever possible. Still, this is entirely a matter of management policy and not something that management would have to do because of any contract obligation."[334]

---

[333] Libby, McNeill & Libby, 11 LA 872, 874 (1948).
[334] Bethlehem Steel Co., 4 LA 450, 454–455 (1946). For a similar ruling, see Terre Haute Water Works Corp., 5 LA 747, 749 (Updegraff, 1946).

Many times unscheduled changes in work have been made as a direct or indirect result of weather conditions. For instance, under an agreement giving management exclusive authority to schedule production and determine shifts,[335] and under an agreement giving it the right to direct and assign the working force,[336] management was not required to pay employees for scheduled hours not worked when, because of severe weather, employees were dismissed early to permit them to reach their homes safely—despite the fact that sufficient work was available. In other cases, too, weather conditions have been found to present an emergency, an act of God, or a condition beyond the control of management so as to justify unscheduled changes in work or (where it was the issue) to relieve management of any reporting pay or other such obligation.[337] But a different fact situation may result in a different conclusion.[338]

One arbitrator has held that "The decision as to the suitability of weather conditions for certain types of work must be made by Management; this decision should be made on the basis of its best judgment in the light of the immediate circumstances and must be respected provided there is no abuse by Management of its authority."[339] Nonetheless, weather conditions were held not to constitute an emergency so as to relieve management of a reporting pay obligation where the employer's fears of much absenteeism (and thus of inefficient operations) due to a snowstorm proved to be unfounded, the arbitrator determining that the storm was not severe enough to create an emergency.[340]

A power failure was held not to be beyond the control of management where the company had known of the potential danger and

---

[335] Sealed Power Corp., 7 LA 485, 489 (Platt, 1947).

[336] Pan American Airways, Inc., 13 LA 326, 327–328 (Reynolds, 1949).

[337] For example, see Arbitrator Stouffer in 46 LA 1123, 1125–1129 (in snowstorm it sufficed that impossibility of orderly and efficient operations could be reasonably anticipated); Cabe in 38 LA 655, 657 (plant too cold because gas company could not supply enough fuel); Platt in 36 LA 991, 993; Stark in 33 LA 285, 291; Stein in 10 LA 579, 581.

[338] For example, see Arbitrator Jaffee in 52 LA 1023, 1025 (fuel shortage was fault of employer); Krimsly in 51 LA 246, 249 (no imminent danger to employees or equipment); Brandschain in 37 LA 1001, 1003.

[339] Bethlehem Steel Co., 27 LA 482, 485 (Feinberg, 1956), quoting Umpire Stowe in a previous case between the parties.

[340] Westinghouse Electric Corp., 51 LA 298, 300–301 (Altrock, 1968). For cases in which excessive absenteeism (making operations impracticable) was held not to be a condition beyond management's control under the facts, see Arbitrator Alexander in 51 LA 1089, 1092; Leach in 43 LA 888, 890–891.

did not take steps to correct it.[341] Machine or equipment breakdowns have similarly been held not to be beyond the control of management in some cases,[342] but have been held otherwise under the circumstances of other cases.[343]

Under an agreement providing for notice when employees are laid off due to a reduction in force except in emergencies, it was held that a strike by some of the employees was an emergency.[344] It has also been held that an emergency existed when a deliberate slowdown by the employees resulted in an accumulation of stock in one department making continued production impossible.[345] Under a contract not providing for emergencies but stating that employees shall be given one week's advance notice in case of "arbitrary layoff," the employer was not required to give advance notice of layoff when a shipment of materials failed to arrive on time, the arbitrator stating that the situation was an emergency.[346]

Bomb threats and actual or threatened riots or civil disturbances have been deemed conditions beyond the control of management, thus employers have not been required to pay reporting pay or otherwise to compensate employees for time lost when management cancelled scheduled work in view of the circumstances.[347] In the so-called Na-

---

[341] Chrysler Corp., 21 LA 573, 579 (D. Wolff, 1953). Similarly, see Arbitrator Porter in 54 LA 1218, 1219. In other cases, however, power failures have been found to be beyond management's control. See Arbitrator Geissinger in 55 LA 522, 525; Strasshofer in 51 LA 850, 852 (trouble could not be anticipated); Altieri in 41 LA 47, 51.

[342] See Arbitrator Sullivan in 51 LA 1183, 1194 (trouble was foreseeable); Luckerath in 51 LA 873, 875 (failure to make reasonable inspection). Also see Arbitrator Powers in 52 LA 1270, 1272.

[343] See Arbitrator Klein in 44 LA 748, 751–752; Koven in 37 LA 811, 818; Anderson in 36 LA 654, 657.

[344] American Airlines, Inc., 27 LA 448, 450 (S. Wolff, 1956); Owens-Corning Fiberglas Corp., 23 LA 603, 605–606 (Uible, 1954). Strikes were held to create emergencies or conditions beyond management's control by Arbitrator Hebert in 51 LA 312, 319–320 (strike threat); Gorsuch in 49 LA 194, 195–196 (unforeseen strike at supplier plant); Seitz in 33 LA 502, 506. A plant shutdown when some of the company's employees struck did not violate the no-lockout provision in the agreement of other employees. Bell Aerosystems Co., 54 LA 745, 749 (Seitz, 1970). Cf., Arbitrator Wyckoff in 51 LA 603, 605–606.

[345] Lone Star Steel Co., 28 LA 465, 466 (McCoy, 1957). Where a slowdown by some employees made operations impossible a no-lockout clause was not violated when innocent employees were sent home. United States Steel Corp., 42 LA 97, 100–101 (Garrett, 1963).

[346] Lavoris Co., 16 LA 173, 175 (Lockhart, 1951). In National Airlines, Inc., 16 LA 532, 534 (1951), "interests" arbitrator Payne recommended that the new contract provide that no notice be required in emergencies.

[347] See Arbitrator Sartain in 55 LA 1119, 1120; Updegraff in 54 LA 696,

tional Day of Mourning cases involving claims for reporting pay or
other restitution for time lost when management cancelled work on
the proclaimed day of mourning following political assassinations, the
claims have been sustained in some cases but denied in others—some
of the denial awards stressed that the agreement's reference to a five-
day or 40-hour workweek did not constitute either an express or an
implied guarantee of work whereas some of the sustaining awards
stressed that the decision to close was not a matter or condition beyond
the control of management.[348]

It is to be noted that even where a change in the work schedule
is fully justified, the question still may be presented as to whether
the agreement or the circumstances impose a duty upon the employer
to notify the employees of the change, or at least to make a reasonable
effort to give notice; and if such duty does exist, the question may
remain as to whether the effort to give notice was a reasonable one
in reference to those employees who did not actually receive word
of the change and who accordingly reported for work.[349] Many cases
have considered the adequacy of radio announcements as a method
of giving notice. Management's effort to notify employees of schedule
changes by radio announcements was deemed adequate under the
circumstances of some cases,[350] but not adequate in other cases.[351]

697; Duff in 54 LA 408, 411; Feller in 52 LA 736, 740; Moran in 51 LA
1069, 1071; Cantor in 51 LA 720, 721; Madden in 51 LA 692, 695–696.

[348] Claims were sustained by Arbitrator McCoy in 43 LA 1035, 1038–1039;
Suagee in 42 LA 1181, 1183–1184; Kabaker in 42 LA 705, 708; Kornblum
in 42 LA 692, 694. Claims were denied by Arbitrator Wolff in 50 LA 921,
926; Altieri in 43 LA 602, 603–604 (employer was justified in closing restaurant
business since there would be few customers); Bauder in 42 LA 1272, 1274–1275;
Davey in 42 LA 1071, 1072; Prasow in 42 LA 1067, 1070–1071 (arbitrator
did recommend that employees receive part pay); Kesselman in 42 LA 884,
890 (employees were not guaranteed a 40-hour workweek, but he did award
reporting pay to those employees who did not get word of shutdown and reported
for work). In one case it was the union that instituted the day of mourning
and it was held to violate the no-strike clause. American Radiator & Standard
Sanitary Corp., 43 LA 644, 648 (Koven, 1964).

[349] For some cases dealing with these aspects, see Arbitrator Heilbrun in
55 LA 685, 689; Young in 55 LA 396, 402; Duff in 54 LA 408, 410; Larkin
in 52 LA 705, 707; Roberts in 51 LA 276, 278; Klein in 44 LA 748, 752;
Davis in 43 LA 300, 302; Altieri in 41 LA 47, 51.

[350] See Arbitrator Volz in 49 LA 929, 931–932 (employees knew that this
method would be used); Yagoda in 49 LA 856, 861–863; Warns in 38 LA
1064, 1067–1068 (there were many employees to be notified and this method
had been used previously).

[351] See Arbitrator Luckerath in 51 LA 873, 874–875 (normal method was
telephone or visit to employee's home); Altrock in 51 LA 298, 302 (radio
announcement two hours before shift start); Wildebush in 43 LA 919, 932

Emergencies, Acts of God, and
Conditions Beyond the Control of Management

Management's freedom to act may possibly be expanded and managerial obligations may possibly be narrowed if an emergency, an act of God, or a condition beyond the control of management is involved. The collective agreement may expressly state an exception for emergencies, acts of God, or conditions beyond the control of management, or an arbitrator may hold such exception to be inherently and necessarily implied.

Unquestionably, each case must be decided largely on the basis of its own facts and circumstances insofar as determining whether an emergency, an act of God, or a condition beyond the control of management is actually involved. Emphasizing this concerning emergencies, one arbitrator refused to generalize as to what constitutes an emergency, considering it not to be within the arbitrator's province to provide a workable definition of the term "emergency" for future use.[352] Nonetheless, some arbitrators have offered definitions or guides which may be found useful in other cases and which are noted in the present topic with this possibility in mind.

One arbitrator has defined the term "emergency" as "an unforeseen combination of circumstances which calls for immediate action," and he added that it is not an emergency where the situation permits the exercise of discretion.[353] In determining whether a breakdown of equipment constituted an emergency and, if so, whether it was such an emergency as would justify a departure from contractual procedures for distribution of overtime, Arbitrator Louis C. Kesselman expressed the following views:

"Does Management have the power to meet emergencies in an exceptional manner?

"Common sense and the entire pattern of American industrial experience make it necessary to acknowledge that emergencies do develop as a result of factors beyond the control of even the best of Managements and that a Company should not be penalized for taking

---

(radio would not suffice where other methods were specified by the contract); Hoban in 40 LA 1157, 1160–1161.

[352] Coleman Co., 49 LA 431, 432 (Lazar, 1967).

[353] Canadian Porcelain Co., 41 LA 417, 418 (Hanrahan, 1963). For other statements or guides as to what is an emergency, see Arbitrator Suagee in 42 LA 1181, 1183; Killion in 40 LA 513, 521; Koven in 37 LA 811, 817–818.

steps to cope with such unforseen developments even if it necessitates failure to observe all provisions of the contract. However, there are limits and standards which must be observed:

1) Management must not be directly responsible for the emergency
2) The emergency must involve a situation which threatens to impair operations materially
3) The emergency must be of limited time duration
4) Any violation or suspension of contractual agreements must be unavoidable and limited only to the duration of the emergency

*   *   *   *   *

"The breakdown of one of the production lines in the acid plant on June 12 did pose what could broadly be called an emergency because it created a situation which called for quick action. However, the Arbitrator feels that a distinction must be made between: 1) those emergencies which can and should be met within the provisions of the Agreement because the dangers to production etc. are minimal, and 2) those which are so exceptional and so dangerous to the operations of a plant that measures going beyond the Agreement must be taken to cope with the problems."[354]

An "act of God" has been defined by Arbitrator Harry H. Platt as "an act, event or occurrence which is due exclusively to an extraordinary natural force free of human interference and which could not have been prevented by the exercise of reasonable care and foresight."[355]

A "condition beyond the control of management" has been briefly defined as "a condition which could not be reasonably expected and prepared for by the Company."[356] A more detailed definition was given by Arbitrator David A. Wolff:

"Considered in context 'cause beyond the control of the management' cannot mean all causes over which, regardless of reason, the Company exercises no control. Rather, and at most, it must mean either a cause not falling within the general area of the Company's responsibilities or, if falling within this area, a cause which could not be anticipated or, if anticipated, could not have been guarded against at all or except by unreasonably burdensome or unrealistic measures. However, if a cause does fall within this area and could have been anticipated and reasonably guarded against, failure to provide such necessary safeguards, either unintentially or as a cal-

---

[354] Virginia-Carolina Chemical Co., 42 LA 237, 240 (1964).
[355] United States Steel Co., 36 LA 991, 993 (1961).
[356] Gould National Batteries, Inc., 42 LA 609, 611 (Linn, 1964).

culated risk, would not place the cause beyond the control of the management."[357]

Overtime

Although numerous overtime issues have reached arbitration, those which appear to have been arbitrated most frequently concern (1) management's right to require employees to work overtime, (2) management's contractual obligation to equalize overtime opportunities among the employees, and (3) the determination of a proper remedy where management has violated an employee's contractual right to overtime. The present topic discusses these three basic issues.

Right to Require Overtime

Although the right of management to require employees to work overtime has been stated variously, the essence of most decisions is that where the agreement is silent on the subject management has the right to make reasonable demands for overtime work from employees.[358] The thinking of many arbitrators in this regard appears to be that management may require overtime work in the absence of contract prohibition provided that it is of "reasonable duration, commensurate with employee health, safety and endurance, and the direction is issued under reasonable circumstances."[359] Another qualification is that management must be willing to accept reasonable excuses advanced by the employee.[360] Several arbitrators have suggested

---

[357] Chrysler Corp., 21 LA 573, 579 (1953).

[358] See Arbitrator Gibson in 55 LA 1185, 1186–1187; Witney in 54 LA 773, 779; Volz in 53 LA 703, 705–706; Geissinger in 50 LA 1181, 1184–1185; Bothwell in 49 LA 1172, 1175–1176; Epstein in 49 LA 429, 431; Howlett in 67–1 ARB ¶8115; Dammers in 48 LA 1327, 1329–1330; Kabaker in 48 LA 925, 928; Cayton in 48 LA 570, 571–572; Dworkin in 46 LA 15, 20–21; Anrod in 45 LA 738, 740–741; Helfeld in 41 LA 834, 837–842; Barrett in 39 LA 299, 302; Brecht in 39 LA 292, 298; Bradley in 35 LA 306, 310; Hoel in 32 LA 88, 92; Kharas in 25 LA 755, 757; Fleming in 24 LA 526, 528; Douglas in 21 LA 513, 515; Reeves in 20 LA 564, 566; Gilden in 14 LA 146, 149; Seward in 12 LA 810, 811; Kelliher in 12 LA 779, 783; Wolff in 10 LA 98, 100; Platt in 9 LA 735, 740.

[359] Texas Co., 14 LA 146, 149 (Gilden, 1949). Similarly, see Arbitrator Gibson in 55 LA 1185, 1186–1187; Bothwell in 49 LA 1172, 1175; Kabaker in 48 LA 925, 928; Dworkin in 46 LA 15, 20; Anrod in 45 LA 738, 740.

[360] American Body & Equipment Co., 49 LA 1172, 1175–1176 (Bothwell, 1967). Similarly, see Arbitrator Gibson in 55 LA 1185, 1187; Volz in 53 LA 703, 705–706; Howlett in 67–1 ARB ¶8115; Geissinger in 50 LA 181, 184–185; Anrod in 45 LA 738, 741; Barrett in 39 LA 299, 302; Brecht in 39 LA 292, 298; Bradley in 35 LA 306, 312–313; Kharas in 25 LA 755, 758; Fleming in 24 LA 526, 528; Douglas in 21 LA 513, 515. In Fruehauf Corp., 46 LA

that reasonable notice must be given,[361] but the adequacy of notice may be viewed merely as one of the relevant considerations in determining the adequacy of any excuse offered for not working overtime.

Even apart from the frequent recognition of the right to require overtime work as an inherent or residual right of management, arbitrators have often found implied contractual support for or confirmation of the right in provisions recognizing management's right to direct the working forces, in scheduling provisions, in provisions for the distribution of overtime, and the like.[362] In contrast, arbitrators have been reluctant to find any implied contractual prohibition of the right. It has been held, for instance, that the fact that an agreement specifies a "normal" workday as one of a certain number of hours or a "normal" workweek as one of a certain number of days does not prohibit management from requiring employees to work overtime since the word "normal" implies occasional resort to "abnormal."[363] This is said to be especially so where the agreement provides for time and one half for hours over a certain number a week, since the latter provision "clearly recognizes an obligation on the company to pay for overtime, and surely by implication, that workers are obliged to work reasonably necessary overtime unless specifically excused."[364] Also,

---

15, 21 (Dworkin, 1966), flimsy excuses of personal inconvenience did not suffice. In Westinghouse Electric Corp., 47 LA 621, 628 (1966), Arbitrator Altrock stated that "in an atmosphere of concerted action, individual excuses should be subjected to particular scrutiny." Accord, Arbitrator Edes in 51 LA 472, 476; Keefe in 48 LA 1077, 1081. For the NLRB's view that a concerted refusal to work overtime is a strike, see Meat Cutters, Local P-575, 76 LRRM 1273 (1971).

[361] See Arbitrator Volz in 53 LA 703, 705; Howlett in 67-1 ARB ¶8115; Anrod in 45 LA 738, 741; Helfeld in 41 LA 834, 842; Brecht in 39 LA 292, 298.

[362] See Arbitrator Cohen in 55 LA 31, 32; Turkus in 52 LA 493, 496; Keefe in 48 LA 1077, 1081; Cayton in 48 LA 570, 572; Dworkin in 46 LA 15, 21; Anrod in 45 LA 738, 740; Roberts in 41 LA 868, 869; Oppenheim in 40 LA 407, 409–410; Strong in 39 LA 1080, 1082; Bradley in 35 LA 306, 311.

[363] Carnegie-Illinois Steel Corp., 12 LA 810, 811 (Seward, 1949). Accord, Arbitrator Volz in 51 LA 261, 263; Cayton in 48 LA 570, 572; Dworkin in 46 LA 15, 20–21; Cahn in 29 LA 708, 709–710. However, management could not require overtime where an agreement definitely established the length of the workweek by providing that the "eight (8) hour day and forty (40) hour week * * * shall be in effect without revision, during the term of this contract." Connecticut River Mills, Inc., 6 LA 1017, 1019 (Wallen, 1947). To similar effect, Baker & Taylor Co., 1 ALAA ¶67,318 (1944).

[364] Nebraska Consolidated Mills Co., 13 LA 211, 214 (Copelof, 1949). Accord, Arbitrator Anrod in 45 LA 738, 740–741; Bradley in 35 LA 306, 311; Klamon in 21 LA 91, 94. Contra, Maggs in 17 LA 606, 608–609; Lehoczky in 1 LA 468, 470.

there was no implied prohibition of management's right to require overtime in a contract provision stating that "employees refusing over-time will be charged with such overtime for purposes of equalization," the provision being deemed merely to provide a guide for management in administering overtime and not to give employees the right to refuse overtime.[365]

Furthermore, the fact that the employer has been lenient in exer-cising the right to require overtime work or the fact that overtime has been voluntary in the past has not affected management's right to require overtime where the volunteer approach fails to supply suffi-cient workers for needed overtime work.[366]

An agreement may specifically or by implication provide that the employee has an option as to overtime work and that he may ask to be excused from it.[367] Under such a provision it has been held that the employee must ask to be excused if he does not intend to work overtime.[368] Where employees did properly exercise their option not to work overtime, management could not force them to do so by calling the work a work assignment which must be protested under the grievance procedure.[369]

Sometimes the agreement will contain a provision specifically giv-ing management the right to require overtime work of employees.[370] Even so, the right of the employer to punish for refusal to work over-time may be held to depend upon the facts of the case. There may be extenuating circumstances. Thus, Umpire Harry Shulman stated that, while "an employee's refusal to work overtime may be a breach of duty for which he may properly be disciplined, his refusal may be justified and, if justified, is not ground for disciplinary penalty."[371]

---

[365] Roberts Brass Mfg. Co., 53 LA 703, 705 (Volz, 1969). Similarly, see Arbitrator Geissinger in 50 LA 181, 183–184; Anrod in 45 LA 738, 741.

[366] See Arbitrator Volz in 53 LA 703, 706; Turkus in 52 LA 493, 496; Carpenter in 51 LA 287, 288; Bothwell in 49 LA 1172, 1176; Keefe in 48 LA 1077, 1081; Kabaker in 48 LA 925, 928; Cayton in 48 LA 570, 571–572; Dworkin in 46 LA 15, 21; Anrod in 45 LA 738, 742; Strong in 39 LA 1080, 1082. But past practice was held controlling by Arbitrator Rock in 29 LA 482, 484–485; McCoy in 9 LA 374, 374–375.

[367] Lear, Inc., 28 LA 242, 245–246 (Bradley, 1957); West Penn Power Co., 27 LA 458, 462 (Begley, 1956).

[368] Lear, Inc., 28 LA 242, 245–246 (Bradley, 1957).

[369] West Penn Power Co., 27 LA 458, 463 (Begley, 1956).

[370] See Arbitrator Copelof in 13 LA 269, 272; Shulman in 11 LA 1158, 1160; Updegraff in 11 LA 561, 565; Klamon in 2 LA 201, 202.

[371] Ford Motor Co., 11 LA 1158, 1160 (1948).

In that case, it was found that the employee's refusal was justified since the order for overtime work was made shortly before quitting time, and the reason for the refusal was that the employee would miss his usual ride and the use of public transportation would require additional time far out of proportion to the overtime he was asked to work.

Equalization of Overtime

By no means are employees always compelled to work overtime. To the contrary, many employees "prize the opportunity" to work overtime:

> "Many employees prize the opportunity to add to their income by working overtime. Indeed the possibility of earning such extra income has come to be regarded as a vital ingredient of the whole employment package and is often featured as such in company recruitment advertisements. Hence the demand for equitable distribution of overtime work assignments."[372]

However, it has been recognized that where the agreement does not contain any provision guaranteeing overtime to employees, management has the right to determine whether work shall be performed on an overtime basis.[373] It also has been recognized that except as restricted by the agreement, the allocation of overtime (where overtime is to be worked) is an exclusive right of management.[374]

Many agreements do deal with the allocation of overtime. Some leave management little or no discretion in the matter. For example, where the agreement provided that "overtime shall be distributed proportionately among all qualified employees" within a given work group, it was held that day-to-day equalization of overtime was called for.[375] More often the agreement will contain a modified equalization provision calling for equalization of overtime among the employees

---

[372] American Enka Corp., 52 LA 882, 884 (Pigors, 1969).

[373] Continental Can Company, Inc., 53 LA 809, 810 (Cahn, 1969). Similarly, see Arbitrator Zack in 56 LA 751, 752; McDermott in 53 LA 741, 746; Klamon in 46 LA 459, 471; Lanna in 45 LA 451, 453; Emerson in 61–3 ARB ¶8812. For related discussion, see this Chapter, topic titled "Scheduling Work."

[374] Graham Brothers, Inc., 16 LA 83, 85 (Cheney, 1951), citing a War Labor Board case. Also see Arbitrator Morris in 51 LA 1146, 1147–1148; Hilpert in 46 LA 641, 643; Marshall in 20 LA 212, 216.

[375] Mason & Hanger-Silas Mason Co., 36 LA 425, 434–435 (Hale, 1961). Also requiring daily equalization or otherwise leaving little flexibility in the distribution of overtime, see Arbitrator Listerhill in 66–3 ARB ¶8950; Sullivan in 33 LA 335, 338–339; Doyle in 28 LA 100, 101–102.

within the specified equalizaton unit or group "as far as practicable," or "as equally as possible," or the like. Such provisions have generally been held to allow management reasonable flexibility to permit efficient operations—they have been construed to permit equalization over a reasonable period of time.[376] In the latter regard, it has been stated that under an "as equally as possible" provision "no employee has a pre-emptory right to overtime on any particular day that it is available."[377] Under a similar provision, Arbitrator Vernon L. Stouffer said:

> "The decision as to what is as 'equitable a basis as possible' rests with Management, subject to the Union's right to grieve that it was equitably possible for the Company to have given the assignment to employees other than those selected. In so doing the Union has the burden of proving that the Company deliberately or unreasonably bypassed the employee with the lower amount of overtime."[378]

But Arbitrator Morris L. Myers held that "the burden falls on the employer to justify its action" where an employee who already has more overtime than other employees is afforded the next overtime opportunity.[379]

Regardless of where the ultimate burden of proof is held to fall, it is clear that management must remain alert to the underlying objective of equalization provisions. Thus, Arbitrator John F. Sembower cautioned that, while recognizing the need for flexibility, also to be taken into account is "the rule that the general aim of the agreement is for overtime to be equalized, albeit qualified by the Company's doing so with some latitude, and that this imposes a duty upon the Company to meet an appropriate test of diligence under the particular circumstances of each instance."[380]

---

[376] See Arbitrator Bothwell in 54 LA 613, 617–618; Stouffer in 49 LA 933, 939; Kelliher in 49 LA 886, 888; Ray in 49 LA 360, 362–364; Shister in 48 LA 848, 851; Tsukiyama in 47 LA 781, 784–785; Guild in 46 LA 385, 386; Cugna in 68–1 ARB ¶8266; Hardy in 68–1 ARB ¶8091 (past practice refuted the union's contention for day-to-day equalization); Seinsheimer in 64–1 ARB ¶8303; Cahn in 42 LA 830, 831; McCoy in 40 LA 526, 529; Williams in 39 LA 929, 930. But see Arbitrator Sullivan in 33 LA 335, 338–339.

[377] Sundstrand Corporation, 66–2 ARB ¶8700 (Kelliher, 1966). Accord, Duquesne Light Co., 48 LA 848, 851 (Shister, 1967). Also see Arbitrator Kelliher in 49 LA 886, 888.

[378] McCall Corp., 49 LA 933, 939 (1967). Accord, Standard Ultramarine & Color Company, 64–1 ARB ¶8303 (Seinsheimer, 1963).

[379] Vendorlator Mfg. Co., 53 LA 494, 497 (1969), where the agreement provided that "every effort will be made to distribute overtime equally."

[380] Pittsburgh Plate Glass Co., 32 LA 622, 624 (1958). For some guidelines that have been offered for the equalization of overtime, see Arbitrator Stouffer

Arbitrators have recognized various considerations which may be relevant in judging whether management has administered the overtime equalization provision in a reasonable manner. Among others, these include such factors as ability to do the required work,[381] safety and plant protection,[382] and reasonably assured availability.[383] Arbitrators have disagreed as to whether the cost factor is a relevant consideration.[384]

Remedy for Violation of Right to Overtime

Unquestionably the most frequently utilized remedy where an employee's contractual right to overtime work has been violated is a monetary award (generally at the overtime rate) for the overtime in question.[385] In some cases, however, the arbitrator has considered make-up overtime within a reasonable time to be the appropriate remedy.[386]

---

in 49 LA 933, 939–941; Cahn in 35 LA 526, 529. As to the scope of management's obligation to notify employees of available overtime, see Arbitrator Sembower in 55 LA 474, 476–477; Markowitz in 55 LA 384, 385; Geissinger in 55 LA 353, 356.

[381] Myers Drum Co., 55 LA 1048, 1052 (Koven, 1970); Continental Can Co., 51 LA 1086, 1089 (Merrill, 1968). But management cannot insist that ability, if adequate, be as great as that of the employee who normally performs the work. Paragon Bridge & Steel Co., 48 LA 995, 1000 (Gross, 1967).

[382] Airco Alloys & Carbide Co., 51 LA 156, 160–161 (Kesselman, 1968).

[383] Quaker State Oil Refining Corp., 56 LA 848, 851 (Waldron, 1971); Eaton, Yale & Towne, Inc., 54 LA 950, 953 (France, 1970). Cf., Arbitrator Lehoczky in 52 LA 1098, 1100.

[384] Holding it a relevant factor, Arbitrator Guild in 46 LA 385, 386; Bladek in 68–1 ARB ¶8148; Livengood in 22 LA 144, 147. Holding it not relevant, Arbitrator Levin in 54 LA 387, 392; Pigors in 52 LA 882, 885; Merrill in 51 LA 1086, 1088; Gilden in 16 LA 811, 816.

[385] E.g., see Arbitrator Lehoczky in 54 LA 579, 580; Solomon in 53 LA 293, 300; Cahn in 52 LA 1144, 1145–1146; Pigors in 52 LA 882, 886; Chalfie in 52 LA 33, 36; Stouffer in 49 LA 933, 939–941; Marshall in 48 LA 923, 924; Oppenheim in 46 LA 229, 232–233; Teple in 42 LA 1228, 1230–1231; Abernethy in 41 LA 1065, 1067–1070; Dworkin in 41 LA 219, 223; Edes in 37 LA 888, 891; Hale in 36 LA 425, 438–439; Larkin in 35 LA 495, 498; Wissner in 34 LA 811, 814; Hebert in 34 LA 643, 651–652; Sullivan in 33 LA 335, 339; Sembower in 32 LA 622, 629–630; Reynard in 31 LA 494, 496; Kelliher in 26 LA 540, 541. One arbitrator has emphasized that a monetary award is the only proper remedy if the alternative remedy of make-up overtime would unjustly and adversely affect either the grievant or any other employee. Giant Tiger Super Stores Co., 43 LA 1243, 1246 (Kates, 1965).

[386] See Arbitrator Bothwell in 54 LA 613, 617; Edes in 53 LA 616, 619; Stouffer in 49 LA 933, 939–941; Updegraff in 33 LA 365, 366; Shister in 27 LA 634, 636; Justin in 24 LA 168, 172–173; McCoy in 5 LA 30, 32. In Giant Tiger Super Stores Co., 43 LA 1243, 1246 (Kates, 1965), the award was 50 percent back pay and 50 percent make-up overtime. An apportionment was also made in Bridgeport Brass Co., 19 LA 690, 693 (Donnelly, 1952).

In using the make-up overtime remedy one arbitrator stated that in the absence of specific contract language, a monetary award for violation of overtime rights must be based upon a "clearly established past practice or upon a showing that the grievant-claimant actually did suffer damages rather than temporary postponement of an overtime work opportunity."[387] In contrast, another arbitrator has declared that the only proper remedy for violation of overtime rights is a monetary award:

> "Offering an employee an opportunity to make up improperly lost hours at a later date is not an adequate remedy. He is entitled to work those hours at the time they are available, to know when he may expect his turn, and not be expected to work at some time more convenient to the employer, or at the personal whim of a foreman.

> *   *   *   *   *

> "The one sure way of putting an end to foremen's inadvertent errors, or their favoritism in making overtime assignments under the round-robin system, is to hold the Company liable for these breaches of contract by awarding pay to the employee who failed to get his proper assignment."[388]

The latter arbitrator's view was expressed in a case in which the improper overtime assignment had been made to an employee within the overtime equalization unit. But some arbitrators would make a distinction in this regard, considering make-up overtime to be the preferred remedy where the improper assignment of overtime was made within the equalization unit or other group entitled to the overtime but viewing a monetary award as essential where the improper assignment was made to employees outside such unit or group. It is reasoned

---

[387] A. O. Smith Corp., 33 LA 365, 366 (Updegraff, 1959). Also indicating that past practice may be a factor in selecting the remedy, see Arbitrator Bothwell in 54 LA 613, 617, and Stouffer in 49 LA 933, 940; but refusing to consider past practice as a relevant factor, see Arbitrator Abernethy in 41 LA 1065, 1069–1070, and Edes in 37 LA 888, 891.

[388] John Deere Dubuque Tractor Works, 35 LA 495, 498 (Larkin, 1960). Some arbitrators have indicated that they would issue a monetary award if management's action was deliberate but that the make-up overtime remedy might be appropriate (if other considerations permit it) if inadvertent error produced the violation. See Arbitrator Chalfie in 52 LA 33, 36; Stouffer in 49 LA 933, 939; Kates in 43 LA 1243, 1246; Hebert in 34 LA 643, 651–652. Even where the contract specified use of the make-up remedy, a monetary award was used where the violation was deliberate. See Arbitrator Chalfie in 52 LA 33, 36; Hon in 39 LA 216, 220.

that if the overtime was assigned within the entitled unit or group
it is possible to make it up since the employee who received the improperly assigned overtime is charged with it and will receive that
much less future overtime within the unit or group; however, if the
improper assignment of overtime was made to employees outside the
unit or group, it is impossible to make it up since it can never be
recovered and the only logical remedy is a monetary award.[389]

Right to Subcontract

The right of management to subcontract, in the absence of specific contract restriction, has been the subject of numerous arbitration
cases.[390] The basic and difficult problem is that of maintaining a
proper balance between the employer's legitimate interest in efficient
operation and effectuating economies on the one hand and the union's
legitimate interest in protecting the job security of its members and
the stability of the bargaining unit on the other.[391]

In earlier cases, arbitrators generally held that management has
the right, if exercised in good faith, to subcontract work to independent contractors (the work thus to be done by nonemployees of
the employer) unless the agreement specifically restricts the right.[392]

---

[389] For arbitrators approving this distinction, see Arbitrator Bothwell in 54
LA 613, 617–618; Edes in 53 LA 616, 619; Cahn in 52 LA 1144, 1145; Shister
in 48 LA 848, 853; Hebert in 42 LA 525, 531–532; Dworkin in 41 LA 219,
223; Brecht in 41 LA 59, 62–63; Kelliher in 26 LA 540, 541. In one case
where the erroneous assignment was within the entitled group the arbitrator
awarded make-up overtime but specified that it must be upon work which would
not otherwise have been performed at overtime rates. Morton Salt Co., 42 LA 525,
531 (Hebert, 1964). Similarly, see Arbitrator Crawford in 38 LA 70, 73–74.
[390] The arbitrability of subcontracting disputes has also been the subject
of arbitration decisions, many of which are collected in Celanese Corp. of America,
33 LA 925, 936–948 (Dash, 1959). For Supreme Court doctrine as to arbitrability,
see United Steelworkers v. Warrior & Gulf Navigation Co., 80 S.Ct. 1347
(1960). For a general discussion of arbitrability, see Chapter 6. Many arbitration
cases involve the interpretation and application of contract provisions expressly
dealing with subcontracting. Arbitrators have also treated the question of whether
clauses denying management the right to assign work of unit employees to employees outside the unit prohibit the subcontracting of such work to persons
not in the employ of the company at all. See Arbitrator Witney in 51 LA
363, 371; Klamon in 27 LA 57, 73; Aaron in 26 LA 870, 873; Porter in
22 LA 608, 608–609; Cahn in 19 LA 882, 883; McCoy in 12 LA 707, 709.
[391] See Arbitrator Hon in 52 LA 190, 192; Hebert in 43 LA 307, 313;
Larson in 27 LA 233, 235; Lennard in 25 LA 118, 120; Aaron in 16 LA
644, 648.
[392] See Arbitrator Feinberg in 13 LA 991, 1001; McCoy in 12 LA 707,
709; Kelliher in 11 LA 197, 199; Healy in 10 LA 842, 843; Hill in 10 LA
396, 405–406; Copelof in 8 LA 990, 992.

This view is also stated in some of the later cases.[393] The basic reasoning is indicated by the following statement:

> "It is true, of course, that job security, and an opportunity to perform available work, is of concern to a union and that the letting of work to outsiders by an employer may in some instances be said to be a derogation of the basic purposes of their collective bargaining agreement. Nevertheless, it is also true that where the subject has assumed importance in the relations between the parties a provision is generally inserted in the agreement defining their respective rights. It has almost been universally recognized that in the absence of such a provision an employer may, under his customary right to conduct his business efficiently, let work to outside contractors if such letting is done in good faith and without deliberate intent to injure his employees."[394]

Most of the later cases have somewhat modified the above view. Where the agreement does not deal specifically with subcontracting, most of the more recent cases fall into either of two categories: (1) The essence of some cases appears to be that the recognition, seniority, wage, and other such clauses of the agreement limit management's right to subcontract, and certain standards of reasonableness and good faith are applied in determining whether these clauses have been violated.[395] (2) The essence of other cases is that management can subcontract if it does so reasonably and in good faith.[396]

---

[393] See Arbitrator Bladek in 52 LA 670, 672; Stouffer in 49 LA 471, 473; Klamon in 46 LA 459, 468–470; Warns in 30 LA 493, 495–496; Dworkin in 27 LA 704, 709; Marshall in 26 LA 74, 78.

[394] National Sugar Refining Co., 13 LA 991, 1001 (Feinberg, 1949).

[395] Holding that such clauses do limit management but listing standards pointing to the test of good faith and reasonableness, see Arbitrator Dolnick in 54 LA 1251, 1255; Somers in 49 LA 585, 587–588; Williams in 36 LA 714, 716; Larson in 27 LA 233, 235; Lennard in 25 LA 118, 120; Hogan in 21 LA 713, 724–725. Not listing standards but recognizing a general test of reasonableness and good faith, see Arbitrator King in 52 LA 588, 592; Kadish in 40 LA 737, 740; Hill in 30 LA 379, 380; Hebert in 27 LA 413, 419; Aaron in 26 LA 870, 873; Reid in 22 LA 124, 128; Garrett in 17 LA 790, 792–794. Finding a strict limitation in such clauses, see Gundermann in 42 LA 1121, 1122.

[396] Holding that the recognition, seniority, wage, and other such clauses do not restrict management's right to subcontract and basing the award upon factors pointing to the reasonableness and good faith test, see Arbitrator Gould in 51 LA 752, 757; Emery in 51 LA 575, 577; Shister in 49 LA 805, 809; Abrahams in 47 LA 325, 327; Murphy in 43 LA 554, 557; Kates in 40 LA 444, 447; Smith in 39 LA 1213, 1218; Larkin in 38 LA 718, 721–722; McDermott in 36 LA 1147, 1151–1152; Teple in 34 LA 215, 220; Wolff in 29 LA 594, 594–595; Wallen in 28 LA 491, 493–494; Kornblum in 28 LA 270, 273; Gray in 26 LA 723, 725; Kelliher in 24 LA 158, 159–160: Kagel in 24 LA 33, 34–37; Coffey in 20 LA 432, 433–434; Maggs in 19 LA 503, 506; Grant in 19 LA 219, 220.

It appears obvious, however, that the end result ordinarily would be the same regardless of which of these approaches is taken—that is, the right to subcontract depends upon "reasonableness" and "good faith." To illustrate, one arbitrator has emphasized that the recognition, seniority, and wage clauses restrict subcontracting:

> "After a thoughtful consideration of this question the Arbitrator concludes that the Recognition Clause when considered together with the Wage Clause, the Seniority Clauses, and other clauses establishing standards for covered jobs and employees limits the Company's right to subcontract during the term of the Contract. The Contract sets forth standards of wages and working conditions applicable to those employees and those jobs covered by the Recognition Clause. When the contract was signed the employees in the mending room were on the covered jobs, and the Contract contemplated that work normally performed by them would continue to be so performed as long as the work was available. To allow the Company, after signing an agreement covering standards of wages and conditions for mending room jobs and employees, to lay off the employees and transfer the work to employees not covered by the agreed standards would subvert the Contract and destroy the meaning of the collective bargaining relation."[397]

But in this same case, the arbitrator stated some "conditions crucial to the decision" that subcontracting violated the recognition, wage, and seniority clauses of the contract, which "conditions" are similar to some of the standards (outlined below) for determining reasonableness and good faith used by other arbitrators, including those who do not rely upon such clauses.

In the final analysis, the thinking of many arbitrators is probably reflected in the statement that:

> "In the absence of contractual language relating to contracting out of work, the general arbitration rule is that mangement has the right to contract out work as long as the action is performed in good faith, it represents a reasonable business decision, it does not result in subversion of the labor agreement, and it does not have the effect of seriously weakening the bargaining unit or important parts of it. This general right to contract out may be expanded or restricted by specific contractual language."[398]

---

[397] A. D. Juilliard Co., 21 LA 713, 724 (Hogan, 1953).

[398] Shenango Valley Water Co., 53 LA 741, 744–745 (McDermott, 1969). Also see similar rule of reason statements by Arbitrator Gould in 51 LA 752, 757; Valtin in 48 LA 797, 801; Kesselman in 46 LA 1166, 1169; Dworkin in 44 LA 762, 766; Kadish in 40 LA 737, 740. Emphasizing that each subcontracting

Standards for Evaluating Propriety of Subcontracting

It should be emphasized that the standards used by arbitrators in evaluating subcontracting cases are merely guides and are not necessarily conclusive. True, sometimes one factor has been considered decisive of the case. More frequently, however, several factors have been considered and applied in combination. This often means that a weighing process is involved—where some considerations support the subcontracting but others do not, the arbitrator must weigh the counterworking considerations in deciding whether the subcontracting should be upheld.[399] The standards most frequently used are:

1. *Past Practice.* Whether the company has subcontracted work in the past.[400]

2. *Justification.* Whether subcontracting is done for reasons such as economy,[401] maintenance of secondary sources for production and

---

case must be decided on its own, see Arbitrator Seidenberg in 53 LA 819, 823; Somers in 49 LA 585, 587; Kates in 46 LA 444, 447. It may be noted in passing that if subcontracting is found to have been proper, the union might be found to have violated the no-strike clause by refusing to handle subcontracted material. See Arbitrator McDermott in 53 LA 470, 475; Kagel in 24 LA 33, 37–38.

[399] For example, see Arbitrator Seidenberg in 53 LA 819, 823–824; Seinsheimer in 51 LA 842, 846–848; Shister in 49 LA 805, 806–808; Valtin in 48 LA 797, 801. Where the contract states standards to be considered, the arbitrator may feel limited thereto. See Arbitrator Beatty in 48 LA 1025, 1026–1027; Gibson in 45 LA 331, 332.

[400] Past practice was one of the factors considered by Arbitrator Cahn in 54 LA 657, 659; Emery in 51 LA 575, 577; Somers in 49 LA 585, 588; Guild in 45 LA 174, 176; Redden in 36 LA 787, 796–797; McDermott in 36 LA 1147, 1153; Seward in 30 LA 678, 683; Wolff in 29 LA 594, 594–595; Wallen in 28 LA 491, 493–494; Larson in 27 LA 233, 236; Klamon in 27 LA 57, 70; Gray in 26 LA 723, 725; Haughton in 26 LA 432, 454; Lennard in 25 LA 118, 121; Kelliher in 24 LA 158, 159; Blair in 23 LA 171, 173; Cummins in 20 LA 60, 61; Maggs in 19 LA 503, 505–506; Copelof in 13 LA 652, 659–660. Subcontracting was permitted as to perishables, largely on the basis of long past practice, even where the contract expressly prohibited subcontracting without negotiations. Safeway Stores, Inc., 51 LA 1093, 1094–1095 (Koven, 1969). For full discussion of custom and practice generally, see Chapter 12, "Custom and Past Practice."

[401] For cases in which economy was considered along with other factors in upholding subcontracting, see Arbitrator Seidenberg in 53 LA 819, 824; Gould in 51 LA 752, 758; Hebert in 51 LA 660, 664–665; Somers in 49 LA 585, 587–588; Smith in 39 LA 1213, 1219–1220; McDermott in 36 LA 1147, 1152; Wallen in 28 LA 491, 492–493; Kornblum in 28 LA 270, 273; Wolff in 27 LA 174, 178; Aaron in 26 LA 870, 873; Reid in 22 LA 124, 126; Williams in 21 LA 330, 334. For cases in which the economy factor was outweighed by other considerations, see Arbitrator Volz in 51 LA 997, 1001; Seinsheimer in 51 LA 842, 846; Valtin in 48 LA 797, 801; McCoy in 27 LA 671, 674;

manpower aid,[402] augmenting the regular work force,[403] plant security measures,[404] or other sound business reasons.[405]

3. *Effect on the union or bargaining unit.* Whether subcontracting is being used as a method of discriminating against the union and/or whether it substantially prejudices the status and integrity of the bargaining unit.[406]

4. *Effect on unit employees.* Whether members of the bargaining unit are discriminated against,[407] displaced,[408] deprived of jobs previously available to them,[409] or are laid off[410] by reason of the subcontract. Subcontracting may be justified by other considerations even where layoffs will result.[411] Moreover, arbitrators have considered whether layoffs could be anticipated, saying that subcontracting is to be judged by foresight rather than hindsight.[412] Another factor in judging subcontracting is whether unit em-

---

Aaron in 16 LA 644, 648–650. Some arbitrators have stressed that economy in the form of lower labor costs gives little or no support to management's action. See Arbitrator Volz in 51 LA 997, 1001; Gould in 51 LA 752, 758; Warns in 41 LA 905, 907; Smith in 39 LA 1213, 1219.

[402] Dalmo Victor Co., 24 LA 33, 37 (Kagel, 1954). Also see Arbitrator Kadish in 40 LA 737, 741.

[403] Phillips Pipe Line Co., 20 LA 432, 433 (Coffey, 1953); Carborundum Co., 20 LA 60, 61 (Cummins, 1952).

[404] A. D. Juilliard & Co., 22 LA 266, 270 (Kelly, 1954). Cf., Lorraine Mfg. Co., 22 LA 390, 391 (Horovitz, 1954).

[405] See Arbitrator Shister in 49 LA 805, 806–807; Kesselman in 46 LA 1166, 1169–1170; Kadish in 40 LA 737, 741; Smith in 39 LA 1213, 1219; Larkin in 38 LA 718, 722; Seward in 30 LA 678, 683; Hill in 10 LA 396, 405.

[406] See Arbitrator Dolnick in 54 LA 1251, 1256; Seidenberg in 53 LA 819, 824; Larkin in 52 LA 1028, 1030; Volz in 51 LA 997, 1001; Gould in 51 LA 752, 758; Turkus in 51 LA 600, 601; Emery in 51 LA 575, 577; Somers in 49 LA 585, 588; Hebert in 27 LA 413, 420; Aaron in 26 LA 870, 874; Kates in 25 LA 281, 290; Lennard in 25 LA 118, 121; Kelliher in 24 LA 158, 160; Kagel in 24 LA 33, 37; Porter in 22 LA 608, 610.

[407] See Arbitrator Slade in 54 LA 1135, 1139; Bladek in 52 LA 670, 672; Hebert in 27 LA 413, 420; Williams in 21 LA 330, 334; Holly in 19 LA 815, 818.

[408] See Arbitrator Seinsheimer in 51 LA 842, 847; Turkus in 51 LA 600, 601; Wolff in 50 LA 69, 72–73; Somers in 49 LA 585, 588 (there was displacement but it was de minimis); Valtin in 48 LA 797, 801–802; Gray in 26 LA 723, 725–726; Blair in 23 LA 171, 173–174.

[409] Bethlehem Steel Co., 30 LA 678, 679, 683 (Seward, 1958); General Motors Corp., 25 LA 118, 121 (Lennard, 1955).

[410] See Arbitrator Dolnick in 54 LA 1251, 1256; Abrahams in 47 LA 325, 326–327; Kesselman in 46 LA 1166, 1170; Kornblum in 28 LA 270, 273; Haughton in 28 LA 158, 162; Klamon in 27 LA 57, 70–71; Aaron in 26 LA 870, 874; Jones in 24 LA 821, 827; Kelliher in 24 LA 158, 160; Gilden in 22 LA 68, 70.

[411] See Dutch Maid Bakery, 52 LA 588, 592–593 (King, 1969).

[412] Marquette Mfg. Co., 51 LA 230, 234 (Mullin, 1968); Columbus Auto Parts Co., 36 LA 1079, 1081 (Alexander, 1961).

ployees lose regular or overtime earnings,[413] but loss of overtime
often has not been a weighty factor where the agreement did
not contain any overtime guarantee.[414]

5. *Type of work involved.* Whether it is work which is normally
done by unit employees,[415] or work which is frequently the subject
of subcontracting in the particular industry,[416] or work which is
of a "marginal" or "incidental" nature.[417]

6. *Availability of properly qualified employees.* Whether the skills
possessed by available members of the bargaining unit are sufficient
to perform the work.[418]

7. *Availability of equipment and facilities.* Whether necessary equipment and facilities are presently available or can be economically
purchased.[419]

8. *Regularity of subcontracting.* Whether the particular work is frequently or only intermittently subcontracted.[420] In one case the
arbitrator pointed out that the subcontracting had not been so
regular in amount or type of work that additional places could

---

[413] See Arbitrator Seinsheimer in 51 LA 842, 847; Wolff in 50 LA 69,
72; Kesselman in 46 LA 1166, 1170; Reid in 22 LA 124, 126–127.
   [414] See Arbitrator Cahn in 53 LA 809, 810; McDermott in 53 LA 741,
746; Larkin in 52 LA 1028, 1030; Turkus in 51 LA 600, 601; Klamon in
46 LA 459, 471; Lanna in 45 LA 451, 453; Hebert in 27 LA 413, 419; Coffey
in 20 LA 432, 433. But see Larson in 21 LA 267, 270.
   [415] See Arbitrator Amis in 52 LA 901, 903; Shister in 52 LA 40, 43–44;
Seinsheimer in 51 LA 842, 847; Murphy in 43 LA 554, 556; Hebert in 43
LA 307, 313–314; Hogan in 21 LA 713, 725. Even where this factor is in
the union's favor, it may be outweighed by other considerations in the company's
favor. See Arbitrator Seidenberg in 53 LA 819, 823; Shister in 49 LA 805, 807.
   [416] See Arbitrator Seidenberg in 53 LA 819, 824; Wolff in 50 LA 69, 72;
Valtin in 48 LA 797, 802; Seward in 30 LA 678, 683; Maggs in 19 LA 503,
506.
   [417] See Arbitrator Dolnick in 54 LA 1251, 1256; Seidenberg in 53 LA 819,
824; Wallen in 28 LA 491, 494; Kornblum in 28 LA 270, 273.
   [418] See Arbitrator Talent in 52 LA 93, 96 (same result was possible by
using methods within employee skills); Geissinger in 52 LA 37, 39 (volume
of orders exceeded capacity of company workforce); Wagner in 51 LA 435,
439; Mullin in 51 LA 230, 233; Murphy in 43 LA 554, 556; Warns in 41
LA 905, 907; Duff in 29 LA 609, 612–613; Shister in 28 LA 461, 463 (all
employees were working); Larson in 27 LA 233, 235; Wolff in 27 LA 174,
178 (shortage of trained personnel); Klamon in 27 LA 57, 70; Lennard in
25 LA 118, 121; Hogan in 21 LA 713, 725.
   [419] See Arbitrator Shister in 49 LA 805, 807; Murphy in 43 LA 554, 556;
Warns in 41 LA 905, 907; Seward in 30 LA 678, 683; Wallen in 28 LA
491, 492; Wolff in 27 LA 174, 178; Haughton in 26 LA 438, 454; Lennard
in 25 LA 118, 121; Blair in 23 LA 171, 174; Hogan in 21 LA 713, 725;
Holly in 19 LA 815, 818; Grant in 19 LA 219, 220.
   [420] See Arbitrator Hebert in 27 LA 413, 419 (first time the job had been
necessary); Larson in 27 LA 233, 236; Lennard in 25 LA 118, 121 (subcontracted
work was to be done continuously, not intermittently).

have been made available to permanent employees within the bargaining unit.[421]

9. *Duration of subcontracted work.* Whether the work is subcontracted for a temporary or limited period,[422] or for a permanent or indefinite period.[423] Even where it is permanent, however, the harm may be outweighed by the justifications for the subcontracting.[424]

10. *Unusual circumstances involved.* Whether the action is necessitated by an emergency, some urgent need, or a time limit for getting the work done.[425] Also, the subcontracting may be justified because a "special job" is involved,[426] or because it is necessitated by a strike or other such situation.[427]

11. *History of negotiations on the right to subcontract.* Whether management's right to subcontract has been the subject of contract negotiations.[428] Arbitrators have pointed to the union's unsuccessful attempt to negotiate a restriction on subcontracting.[429] However, it has been emphasized that while this factor may support a claim to considerable latitude in subcontracting it cannot imply that there is no restriction at all, for parties may try to solidify or expand existing rights through bargaining.[430]

Another possible standard bears comment. In some cases, an ostensible standard for disapproving subcontracting is the fact of performance of the work on the company's premises. However, review of

---

[421] Temco Aircraft Corp., 27 LA 233, 236 (Larson, 1956).

[422] See Arbitrator Emery in 51 LA 575, 577; Kesselman in 46 LA 1166, 1170; Kadish in 40 LA 737, 741 (subcontracting was episodic and temporary); Larson in 27 LA 233, 235; Maggs in 16 LA 829, 831.

[423] See Arbitrator Seinsheimer in 51 LA 842, 847–848; Valtin in 48 LA 797, 801; Kates in 46 LA 444, 447–448; Lennard in 25 LA 118, 121.

[424] As in Schluderberg & Kurdle Co., 53 LA 819, 823–824 (Seidenberg, 1969).

[425] See Arbitrator Nichols in 53 LA 670, 675; King in 52 LA 588, 593; Wagner in 51 LA 435, 439; Murphy in 43 LA 554, 556; Smith in 39 LA 1213, 1220; Sembower in 36 LA 1173, 1176; Duff in 29 LA 609, 612; Lennard in 25 LA 118, 121; Kelly in 22 LA 266, 270.

[426] See Texas Gas Transmission Corp., 27 LA 413, 419 (Hebert, 1956).

[427] See Arbitrator Updegraff in 36 LA 510, 512; Uible in 23 LA 603, 605–606; Maggs in 16 LA 829, 831.

[428] Bargaining history may, for instance, indicate the intended limits of permissible subcontracting. As in Great Atlantic & Pacific Tea Co., 54 LA 1189, 1191–1192 (Britton, 1970). As to failure to object when put on notice of management's subcontracting intentions, see Continental Oil Co., 52 LA 532, 537 (Abernethy, 1969).

[429] See Arbitrator McDermott in 53 LA 741, 746; Bladek in 52 LA 670, 672; Wolff in 50 LA 69, 70–71; Guse in 45 LA 184, 188–189; Wolff in 27 LA 174, 177–179; Klamon in 27 LA 57, 71–74; Haughton in 26 LA 438, 453–454; Kates in 25 LA 281, 289.

[430] Allis-Chalmers Mfg. Co., 39 LA 1213, 1218 (Smith, 1962).

such cases indicates that the arbitrator was primarily concerned about employee layoff, displacement, or the like, thus the "premises" standard may be of minimal significance.[431]

Although the test of reasonableness and good faith may appear nebulous and uncertain, nevertheless we have observed the emergence of a set of standards or guides by which the arbitrator may determine whether, under all the circumstances of the case, the action of management in subcontracting was reasonable and in good faith. Indeed, the use of flexible guides has an important and time-honored counterpart in the development and use by courts of general guides under the law of agency for determining whether a given relationship is that of "independent contractor.[432] Although the latter guides do not produce automatic results, they are nonetheless very useful. Likewise it does not suffice to say that each subcontracting case must be decided on the basis of its own facts; there must be guides or standards against which to measure those facts, and reported arbitration decisions have provided guides of great utility.

Notice of Intent to Subcontract; Duty to Bargain

The collective agreement may require notice of intent to subcontract.[433] Where the contract was silent as to subcontracting, one arbitrator emphasized that prior notification of planned subcontracting generally should be given,[434] while another arbitrator held that no notice was required.[435]

Notice requirements may be strictly construed. Thus, under a contract stating that when work is contracted out the company will promptly notify the union "of the reason for contracting it out," ad-

---

[431] For cases mentioning the "premises" aspect, see Arbitrator Warns in 41 LA 905, 907; Gray in 26 LA 723, 725–726; Stutz in 24 LA 882, 884; Jones in 24 LA 821, 827–828; Larson in 21 LA 267, 269–273.

[432] See, Restatement of Law of Agency, §220. In some arbitration cases an issue has been whether the relationship involved was in fact that of independent contractor. See Arbitrator White in 57 LA 193, 195; Seidenberg in 51 LA 271, 275; Sembower in 29 LA 67, 72–73; Vokoun in 26 LA 79, 82–83; Wolff in 14 LA 31, 34.

[433] See Arbitrator Duff in 54 LA 1207, 1209; Strongin in 53 LA 993, 996 (failure to give notice did not prejudice union in this instance); Graff in 46 LA 724, 727–729. Contractual notice requirement was not violated by failure to give notice in an emergency. Schlitz Brewing Co., 51 LA 41, 46 (Bothwell, 1968).

[434] Pittsburgh Brewing Co., 53 LA 470, 477 (McDermott, 1969).

[435] Haveg Industries, 52 LA 1146, 1151 (Kates, 1969).

vance notice of intent to subcontract was not required.[436] In another case the parties had a mutual understanding that under their collective agreement the company would give notice and discuss its subcontracting plans with the union before entering into subcontracting arrangements. When this understanding was violated an arbitrator devised a special remedy designed to return the parties as nearly as possible to the status quo ante and to deter future violations of the notice and discussion requirement.[437]

Apart from any contractual requirement for notice and discussion, the U.S. Supreme Court's *Fibreboard* decision holds that in certain circumstances the employer has a duty to bargain about subcontracting under the National Labor Relations Act.[438] In this decision the Court said:

> "We are * * * not expanding the scope of mandatory bargaining to hold, as we do now, that the type of 'contracting out' involved in this case—the replacement of employees in the existing bargaining unit with those of an independent contractor to do the same work under similar conditions of employment—is a statutory subject of collective bargaining under §8(d). Our decision need not and does not encompass other forms of 'contracting out' or 'subcontracting' which arise daily in our complex economy."[439]

In evaluating the scope of *Fibreboard*, one arbitrator has spoken of the Supreme Court's "cautious approach toward recognizing unilat-

---

[436] Electric Autolite Co., 35 LA 415, 420 (Willcox, 1960), the arbitrator emphasizing that the contract used the word "when" rather than "before."

[437] Milprint, Inc., 51 LA 748, 750–751 (Somers, 1968).

[438] Fibreboard Paper Products Corporation v. NLRB, 85 S.Ct. 398, 57 LRRM 2609 (1964).

[439] 85 S.Ct. at 405. In Westinghouse Electric Corporation, 150 NLRB 1574, 58 LRRM 1257 (1965), the NLRB held that the company did not violate the NLRA by failing to consult the union about each of thousands of annual subcontracting decisions where the subcontracting was motivated solely by economic considerations; it comported with traditional methods by which the company conducted its operations; it did not vary significantly in kind or degree from subcontracting of work under established practice; it had no demonstrable adverse effect on employees in the bargaining unit; and the union had an opportunity to bargain about subcontracting practices at general negotiating meetings. But the Board said that bargaining would be required if the subcontracting involved a departure from previously established operating practices, effected a change in conditions of employment, or resulted in a significant impairment of job tenure, employment security, or reasonably anticipated work opportunities for those in the bargaining unit. In Union Carbide Corp., 178 NLRB No. 81, 72 LRRM 1150 (1969), the Board considered the elimination of job classifications to be merely one factor to be considered, and this factor in this instance was outweighed by other considerations. In Hayes-Albion Corp., 190 NLRB No. 18, 77 LRRM 1052 (1971), the layoff of one employee was similarly just one of several factors to be considered, and it was outweighed by other considerations.

eral subcontracting as a mandatory subject for bargaining";[440] another has reminded that the Court "limited the decision to the facts in the case";[441] and a third arbitrator has concluded that the decision does not apply where the agreement contains a subcontracting clause.[442]

In a case in which Arbitrator Arvid Anderson concluded that there was a legal duty to bargain, he also concluded (1) that he had authority to decide whether the employer fulfilled the duty to bargain, and (2) that the employer did fulfill its duty to bargain by giving advance notice of its plan to subcontract and by giving the union an advance opportunity to examine the proposed specifications for the work to be subcontracted—the union did not request bargaining and Arbitrator Anderson considered that it had failed to take advantage of the opportunity to discuss the proposed project.[443]

Arbitral Remedies Where Subcontracting Violated the Agreement

In some cases the arbitrator is asked only to rule on the permissibility of subcontracting, in which case he merely states whether past or contemplated subcontracting is sanctioned by the agreement.[444]

Where the arbitrator is called upon to remedy improper subcontracting he may select one or more forms of relief as justified by the particular case. He may make a monetary award of damages for lost work. Where he does so, the award may simply call for the grievants to be made whole or it may expressly indicate whether payment is to be made at the straight time rate or at the overtime rate.[445] The

---

[440] Hess Oil & Chemical Co., 51 LA 752, 759 (Gould, 1968).

[441] Peet Packing Co., 55 LA 1288, 1296 (Howlett, 1971).

[442] Hughes Aircraft Co., 45 LA 184, 189–190 (Guse, 1965). For other cases in which the arbitrator commented as to the "Fibreboard" decision or considered its applicability to the dispute before him, see Arbitrator Witney in 54 LA 886, 894–895; McDermott in 53 LA 470, 474, 477; Volz in 48 LA 409, 411; Gundermann in 45 LA 177, 181; Guild in 45 LA 174, 175–176.

[443] Milprint, Inc., 44 LA 678, 681–682 (1965). For extensive discussion of the duty to bargain, see this Chapter, subtopic titled "The Duty to Bargain: Right of Unilateral Action." Many arbitrators have taken the view that it is not their function to decide whether any statutory duty to bargain has been violated. For cases, see Chapter 10, subtopic titled "The NLRA, the Arbitrator, and the NLRB."

[444] For example, see West Virginia Pulp & Paper Co., 51 LA 842, 849 (Seinsheimer, 1968); Sealtest Foods, 48 LA 797, 802 (Valtin, 1966).

[445] For cases reflecting these possibilities, see Arbitrator Duff in 54 LA 1207, 1210; Bothwell in 53 LA 627, 631; Kesselman in 53 LA 270, 273; Yaffe in 52 LA 1013, 1018–1019; Crawford in 52 LA 243, 247; Witney in 51 LA 363, 382; Kates in 46 LA 444, 449; Gundermann in 45 LA 177, 183; Dworkin in 44 LA 762, 768; Anderson in 43 LA 65, 74; Prasow in 38 LA 347, 350 (pay was awarded for one half of the hours involved).

proper measure of damages has been said to be what the grievants would have earned rather than any larger amount that the independent contractor's employees were paid for the work,[446] and no damages were awarded where no monetary loss had been suffered.[447]

Awards have sometimes spoken in terms of the employer being required to cease and desist from the improper subcontracting,[448] in terms of the employer being required to cancel improper subcontracts,[449] and/or in terms of an obligation (sometimes qualified) of the employer to give the work to his employees.[450] There also have been instances in which seniority adjustments have been ordered by the award.[451]

Assigning Work Out of Bargaining Unit

Arbitrators have ruled both ways on the question of whether, in the absence of contract provisions to the contrary, management has the right to assign bargaining unit work to employees outside the unit. Many of the decisions have involved the assignment of such work to supervisory employees; others involve professional, clerical, or other salaried workers, or nonunit production or maintenance employees. The cases in which such action has been permitted occasionally, but not always, conflict with those in which the right has been denied. We will consider herein the factors that have been significant in the thinking of arbitrators.

In holding that management has such right, some arbitrators have emphasized the absence of a specific restriction in the contract.

---

[446] Bethlehem Steel Co., 37 LA 499, 500 (Seward, 1961).

[447] Chamberlain Mfg. Corp., 54 LA 1135, 1139 (Slade, 1970).

[448] See Arbitrator Yaffe in 52 LA 1013, 1019; Volz in 51 LA 997, 1001; Keefe in 49 LA 544, 551. But see Bernstein in 42 LA 931, 935.

[449] See Arbitrator Somers in 51 LA 748, 752; Anderson in 43 LA 65, 74; Tsukiyama in 39 LA 676, 684–685; Marshall in 30 LA 449, 455 (company was allowed a reasonable time to comply). In Mullite Refractories, Inc., 13 LA 690, 691 (Donnelly, 1949), it was stated that: "The Board recognizes that many circumstances might make it impossible for the Company to recover the work but the Board also recognizes the obligation of an attempt to do so as resting with the Company."

[450] See Arbitrator Somers in 51 LA 748, 751–752; Keefe in 49 LA 544, 551; McGury in 43 LA 682, 684; Anderson in 43 LA 65, 74–75; Tsukiyama in 39 LA 676, 684–685 (company not required to reinstate uneconomical operation).

[451] See Warrior & Gulf Navigation Co., 36 LA 695, 705–706 (Holly, 1961).

For example, in one case Arbitrator Robert K. Burns stated:

> "A careful examination of the contract fails to reveal any provision that specifically prohibits the Company from making a bona fide transfer, allocation or assignment of work out of the bargaining unit—which is the issue posed in this particular case. In the absence of a specific prohibition or limitation to the contrary it must be assumed that these are reserved and retained powers of management * * *."[452]

Where there likewise was no specific contract restriction and management acted in good faith in assigning the work to nonunit employees, other arbitrators have emphasized in varying degrees certain considerations or justifying circumstances in upholding management's action. Included among such considerations or circumstances are the following fact situations:

1. The quantity of work or the effect on the bargaining unit is minor or de minimis in nature.[453]

2. The work is supervisory or managerial in nature.[454]

3. The work assignment is a temporary one for a special purpose or need.[455]

4. The work is not covered by the contract.[456]

5. The work is experimental.[457]

---

[452] Stewart-Warner Corp., 22 LA 547, 551 (1954). For other cases in which the arbitrator stressed the absence of any clear contractual prohibition (in some of the cases the arbitrator also relied upon a management rights clause), see Arbitrator Kates in 54 LA 692, 696; Klamon in 42 LA 1025, 1040–1041; Yagoda in 42 LA 31, 39; Larkin in 38 LA 718, 722; Hampton in 16 LA 59, 65; Lane in 13 LA 135, 136; Cheney in 7 LA 412, 413–414. Also see Doyle in 52 LA 440, 443–445; Roberts in 44 LA 1109, 1113–1114.

[453] See Arbitrator Altrock in 49 LA 1083, 1085–1086; Drake in 49 LA 243, 246; Graff in 48 LA 1065, 1068–1069; Block in 48 LA 746, 750; Morgan in 47 LA 756, 760–761; Murphy in 46 LA 798, 801; Wood in 45 LA 881, 884–885; Tatum in 45 LA 797, 800; Larkin in 43 LA 1064, 1065–1066; Marshall in 30 LA 710, 713; Mann in 28 LA 728, 731; Donnelly in 21 LA 681, 682; Shipman in 17 LA 76, 79; Gilden in 16 LA 252, 258; Blumer in 5 LA 237, 240.

[454] See Arbitrator Calhoon in 50 LA 107, 109; Hardy in 43 LA 1276, 1287; Klein in 40 LA 1032, 1034–1035; Bothwell in 34 LA 24, 30; Ridge in 26 LA 422, 427; Healy in 23 LA 504, 510–511; Wolff in 23 LA 247, 251; Shipman in 17 LA 76, 78; Kerr in 13 LA 390, 390–391; Uible in 12 LA 893, 895–896.

[455] See Arbitrator Fulda in 13 LA 456, 459; Kerr in 13 LA 390, 390–391; D'Andrade in 12 LA 584, 585.

[456] See Arbitrator Kates in 54 LA 692, 695–696; Rohman in 36 LA 938, 940; Klamon in 36 LA 732, 738–739, and in 19 LA 264, 267; Jones in 30 LA 358, 364; Barrett in 26 LA 853, 854; Hildebrand in 16 LA 950, 953–954.

[457] See Arbitrator Dybeck in 52 LA 880, 882; Coffey in 42 LA 601, 603; Duff in 39 LA 190, 192; Sturges in 18 LA 219, 225–227.

6. Under past practice the work has not been performed exclusively by bargaining unit employees.[458]

7. There is a change in the character of the work.[459]

8. Automation or a technological change is involved.[460] Removal of accounting, payroll, billing, time keeping, and other clerical work from the bargaining unit upon establishment of centralized electronic data processing programs has been upheld in numerous cases.[461] In one such case the arbitrator stated that "utilization of computer technology and centralization of data processing have become very common in American business practice" and that "the Company would be at a competitive disadvantage if it could not make use of these possibilities."[462]

9. An emergency is involved.[463]

10. Some other special situation or need is involved.[464]

---

[458] See Arbitrator Murphy in 46 LA 798, 800; Begley in 46 LA 782, 789; Wood in 45 LA 881, 884; Lugar & Furbee in 43 LA 369, 377–378 (past practice also determined the amount of unit work which could be performed by supervisors); Singletary in 33 LA 94, 97; Feinberg in 14 LA 159, 161. Also see Howlett in 55 LA 1288, 1298.

[459] See Arbitrator Kates in 54 LA 692, 695–696; Stutz in 30 LA 282, 288; Reynard in 24 LA 369, 374.

[460] See Arbitrator Block in 48 LA 746, 750; Cahn in 66–2 ARB ¶8430; Roberts in 27 LA 736, 743. But see Hamm Brewing Co., 28 LA 46, 49 (Lockhart, 1956), where the new machine did not change the job, but only made it more efficient.

[461] See Arbitrator Dworkin in 50 LA 322, 334–337, and in 44 LA 201, 208–210; Altrock in 45 LA 555, 556; Seitz in 43 LA 5, 8; Ross in 42 LA 353, 356–358; Altieri in 41 LA 506, 509; Garrett in 37 LA 302, 305; Feinberg in 35 LA 72, 73; Pigors in 28 LA 791, 796–797. Cf., Platt in 41 LA 124, 126–129; Gilden in 62–3 ARB ¶8944; Anderson in 39 LA 24, 27. Centralization of design engineering work was upheld in United States Steel Corp., 44 LA 1224, 1228 (Florey, 1965), as was centralization of reproduction and stationery operations in Phillips Chemical Co., 39 LA 82, 84–85 (Larson, 1962).

[462] Safeway Stores, Inc., 42 LA 353, 358 (Ross, 1964). Computer monitoring and control of production machines near the production situs may be a significantly different matter. See Arbitrator Seward in Bethlehem Steel Co., 46 LA 730, 732 (1966), and Valtin in Alan Wood Steel Co., 35 LA 157, 159 (1960), both upholding the union. Cf., Killingsworth in Goodyear Tire & Rubber Co., 35 LA 917, 918–919 (1961), in which past practice and de minimis were factors in favor of the company.

[463] See National Cash Register Co., 46 LA 782, 789 (Begley, 1966); Intermountain Chemical Co., 26 LA 58, 61 (Kadish, 1956). Also see Arbitrator McCoy in 19 LA 372, 374.

[464] See Arbitrator Updegraff in 48 LA 400, 401–402 (unit employees were absent); Merrill in 27 LA 748, 754 (need for supervisor's presence); Aaron in 27 LA 332, 334–335 (plant security problem); Aaron in 25 LA 263, 266 (safety problem); Klamon in 20 LA 690, 703 (minor preparations for reopening plant after shutdown due to strike).

Other arbitrators have ruled against the right of management to assign work out of the bargaining unit, even in some cases in which there might have been justification, on the basis that it is not included within the various types of general management rights clauses.[465] Similarly, arbitrators have so ruled on the basis that the recognition,[466] seniority,[467] or job security clause[468] is violated by such action; or that the job, being listed in the contract, is a part of the contract, the action thus violating the contract.[469]

The reasoning underlying this view was elaborated by Arbitrator Saul Wallen, who rejected the management rights clause and applied the seniority provisions of the contract:

> "Job security is an inherent element of the labor contract, a part of its very being. If wages is the heart of the labor agreement, job security may be considered its soul. Those eligible to share in the degree of job security the contract affords are those to whom the contract applies. * * *
>
> "The transfer of work customarily performed by employees in the bargaining unit must therefore be regarded as an attack on the job security of the employees whom the agreement covers and therefore on one of the contract's basic purposes."[470]

However, some arbitrators have agreed that the recognition, seniority, and other such clauses do evidence an intention to restrict the performance of unit work to unit employees, but at the same time they have considered that it is not an absolute restriction. Thus, some of these arbitrators have recognized that the assignment of such work outside the bargaining unit may be proper where there is "good

---

[465] See Arbitrator Hon in 46 LA 769, 772; Selekman in 17 LA 295, 299; Copelof in 12 LA 1074, 1080; Coffey in 10 LA 254, 256–257; Wallen in 8 LA 720, 722–723.

[466] See Arbitrator Peck in 51 LA 1221, 1223; Porter in 48 LA 305, 309; Howlett in 33 LA 188, 193; Lockhart in 28 LA 46, 48–49; Kelliher in 27 LA 631, 633; Feinberg in 21 LA 283, 284; Boyce in 20 LA 681, 683–684; Komaroff in 13 LA 545, 550.

[467] See Arbitrator Jaffee in 50 LA 613, 614; Kelliher in 27 LA 631, 633; McCoy in 19 LA 372, 374; Gilden in 18 LA 346, 351; Killingsworth in 16 LA 111, 113; Copelof in 12 LA 1074, 1080; Wallen in 8 LA 720, 722–723.

[468] See Hamm Brewing Co., 28 LA 46, 48–49 (Lockhart, 1956). Also see Arbitrator Dykstra in 40 LA 466, 468–469.

[469] See Arbitrator Hon in 46 LA 769, 772; Oppenheim in 41 LA 1348, 1350; Reynard in 22 LA 880, 882; Shipman in 21 LA 35, 40–41; Lehoczky in 20 LA 603, 604. In some cases the work was supervisory in nature, but this did not privilege the assignment. See Arbitrator Levy in 19 LA 761, 763; Selekman in 17 LA 295, 300; Pollard in 10 LA 498, 502.

[470] New Britain Machine Co., 8 LA 720, 722 (1947).

cause,"[471] where it is de minimis, [472] where the work is supervisory in nature,[473] or where there is an emergency or some other justification.[474]

Another view as to the proper approach for judging the assignment of bargaining unit work to persons outside the unit was offered in a decision by Arbitrator Russell A. Smith. In that case the agreement recognized management's right "to manage its plants and offices and direct its affairs and working forces." Arbitrator Smith stated that "This 'right' which obviously exists even though the Agreement does not so provide, must be balanced against the interests and rights which the union and bargaining unit employees have under the [recognition, seniority, and wage clauses of the] Agreement." He explained:

"In the opinion of the Umpire, this is not a case of 'absolutes' one way or the other. Rather, it is a case of an appropriate balancing of the legitimate interests of management, the bargaining unit employees, and their union representative. The managerial interest in efficient allocation of work should not have to stop at the boundaries of a defined bargaining unit. On the other hand, the decision to allocate work to employees outside the bargaining unit should be one made in the honest exercise of business judgment, and not arbitrarily, capriciously, or in bad faith."[475]

Other arbitrators, too, have used a similar "balancing of interests" approach.[476]

Sometimes the agreement will specifically prohibit management from assigning work of unit employees to nonunit employees. Where such prohibition exists, absent some justifying circumstance, arbitrators generally hold that such action is not permitted under the contract.[477]

---

[471] Cotton Bros. Baking Co., 51 LA 220, 223–224 (Hebert, 1968); Great Lakes Pipe Line Co., 27 LA 748, 753 (Merrill, 1956).
[472] See Arbitrator Roberts in 52 LA 1183, 1186; Crawford in 41 LA 883, 883–884; McCoy in 19 LA 372, 374.
[473] Crown Zellerbach Corp., 52 LA 1183, 1186 (Roberts, 1969); Kroger Co., 33 LA 188, 193 (Howlett, 1959). Also see Arbitrator Duff in 46 LA 920, 924 (quality testing purposes).
[474] See Arbitrator Peck in 51 LA 1221, 1223; Oppenheim in 41 LA 1348, 1350; McCoy in 19 LA 372, 374.
[475] Chrysler Corp., 36 LA 1018, 1022 (1961).
[476] See Reactive Metals, Inc., 46 LA 978, 981–982 (Gibson, 1966); Safeway Stores, Inc., 42 LA 353, 357 (Ross, 1964).
[477] See Arbitrator McDermott in 55 LA 160, 169–170; Solomon in 49 LA 474, 478–479; Rubin in 48 LA 657, 662; Gamser in 28 LA 70, 71–72; Klamon in 27 LA 692, 696; Emery in 26 LA 397, 398–399; Cole in 24 LA 332, 333; Ralston in 17 LA 669, 670; Hawley in 17 LA 516, 520; Gilden in 16 LA 162, 165; Wardlaw in 10 LA 143, 147.

However, arbitrators sometimes have construed the prohibitory clause narrowly to apply only to the category of nonunit employees specifically stated in the clause or to apply only to assignments at certain locations, and the like.[478]

Where the prohibitory clause is otherwise applicable some arbitrators still may permit the assignment of work out of the unit if there is some justifying circumstance, if the work is supervisory in nature, or if the work is de minimis in amount.[479] But other arbitrators may adhere strictly to the letter of the contract and refuse to permit such action.[480]

Plant Removals

In connection with the foregoing discussion of the assignment of work out of the bargaining unit, the related subject of partial or complete plant removal is noted here. Without discussing the reported arbitration cases that deal with plant removals, the Authors merely note that many of the cases have involved collective agreements containing express clauses on the subject (these express clauses may vary widely, ranging from absolute prohibition of removals to a mere requirement that advance notice be given).[481] However, there are cases

---

[478] See Arbitrator Weatherill in 55 LA 1157, 1158–1159 (the clause expressly restricted the performance of unit work by supervisors or salaried employees but no restriction was stated as to such work by any other category of nonunit employees); Wolff in 54 LA 517, 521; Lewis in 50 LA 1165, 1169–1170 (the clause did not apply to other locations); Dworkin in 46 LA 1065, 1070 (the clause did not apply to radically different work although the end result remained essentially the same); Woodruff in 43 LA 1264, 1265, 1268.

[479] See Arbitrator Solomon in 55 LA 997, 1002–1005 (reclaiming supervisory duties); Garrett in 54 LA 118, 121–123; Duff in 53 LA 958, 959–960 (de minimis); Meiners in 50 LA 553, 555 (supervisors did work of unit employees who refused to cross picket line); Lucas in 48 LA 1180, 1183–1184; Yagoda in 48 LA 124, 132; Gross in 46 LA 1030, 1034 (supervisors did the work during vacation shutdown, as in the past); Guse in 44 LA 727, 730; Casselman in 44 LA 361, 371–372; Hebert in 40 LA 806, 809–810; P. Davis in 39 LA 224, 229; Ray in 36 LA 1141, 1146–1147; Hale in 36 LA 578, 584; Teple in 36 LA 416, 419; Killingsworth in 35 LA 917, 919; Clements in 30 LA 43, 45; Luskin in 28 LA 288, 293 (identical duties had been performed by supervisors in the past); Schedler in 28 LA 349, 350; Crawford in 26 LA 399, 400 (de minimis); Fulda in 24 LA 696, 699; Warren in 19 LA 283, 286–287; Ralston in 16 LA 321, 323–324; Gilden in 1 LA 417, 419.

[480] See Arbitrator Seinsheimer in 44 LA 188, 191–192; Hawley in 28 LA 321, 323; S. Davis in 27 LA 144, 147; Kelliher in 21 LA 657, 658; Jaffee in 19 LA 467, 469–471; Handsaker in 18 LA 476, 477–478; King in 18 LA 156, 158–160. The language of the prohibitory clause may imply that there is to be no de minimis exception. See Arbitrator Williams in 52 LA 49, 50; Tatum in 34 LA 904, 907.

[481] See Arbitrator Platt in 55 LA 170, 178–179; Reid in 53 LA 1219, 1220, and in 45 LA 1104, 1108; Keefe in 48 LA 373, 378; Dash in 36 LA 1364,

in which a removal was challenged even though the agreement did not contain any express restriction on plant removals.[482]

Plant Rules

It is well established in arbitration that management has the fundamental right unilaterally to establish reasonable plant rules not inconsistent with law or the collective agreement.[483] Thus, when the agreement is silent upon the subject, management has the right to formulate and enforce plant rules as an ordinary and proper means of maintaining discipline and efficiency and of directing the conduct of the working force.[484] Management also may establish and enforce plant rules to insure the health and safety of employees or others.[485]

This unilateral right of management to establish plant rules also exists under the various types of management rights clauses.[486] Even

---

1384–1386; Wolff in 36 LA 1074, 1076–1077; Gray in 34 LA 771, 774–776; Kheel in 25 LA 804, 806–807; Brower in 8 LA 1001, 1004–1005. For discussion of plant removal cases, see Dolgen, "The Remedy of Plant Return in the Arbitration of Plant Removal Cases," ILR Research, Vol. xi, Feb. 1966; Feinberg, "Transfer and Sale of Plant Operations in Arbitration," 13 Labor L. J. 625 (1962).

[482] See Arbitrator Lande in 58 LA 653, 657–662; Murphy in 40 LA 1073, 1078–1079; Howlett in 39 LA 449, 458–459; McIntosh in 38 LA 621, 622–623; Kelliher in 38 LA 619, 620; McGoldrick in 28 LA 514, 517–518. Also see Scheiber in 44 LA 979, 986–987. For cases involving the applicability to plant removals of contractual clauses restricting subcontracting, see Metal Textile Corp., 42 LA 107, 110–111 (Rubin, 1964); Selb Mfg. Co., 37 LA 834, 842–843 (Klamon, 1961).

[483] See Arbitrator Robertson in 55 LA 306, 312; Whyte in 54 LA 942, 945–946; Williams in 54 LA 129, 130; Gordinier in 52 LA 731, 733; Teele in 50 LA 112, 114; Turkus in 48 LA 1337 at 1337; Caraway in 47 LA 372, 373–374; Dworkin in 46 LA 1098, 1103; Kesselman in 46 LA 65, 68; McCoy in 44 LA 733, 734; Daugherty in 40 LA 670, 671; Volz in 39 LA 1265, 1268; Kates in 34 LA 581, 583; Updegraff in 11 LA 689, 690; Whiting in 7 LA 150, 153. For general discussion of plant rules and their enforcement, see Daykin, "Arbitration of Work Rules Disputes," 18 Arb. J. 36 (1963); Stessin, "Management Prerogatives and Plant Rule Violations," 14 Arb. J. 3 (1959).

[484] Federal Machine & Welder Co., 5 LA 60, 69 (Whiting, 1946). In accord, Arbitrator Dunne in 55 LA 99, 100; Solomon in 53 LA 878, 883; Platt in 47 LA 1127, 1129; Kotin in 46 LA 481, 484–486; Leflar in 44 LA 104, 105; Kates in 43 LA 1162, 1164; Stouffer in 43 LA 465, 466; Hebert in 39 LA 419, 425; Dworkin in 39 LA 404, 409; Roberts in 37 LA 1064, 1067; Gorsuch in 34 LA 636, 641–642; Friedman in 28 LA 328, 329; Lynch in 27 LA 653, 655–656; Keller in 26 LA 401, 403.

[485] See Arbitrator Hnatiuk in 50 LA 985, 986; Jenkins in 48 LA 1094, 1096; Sembower in 38 LA 443, 450; Logan in 30 LA 252, 253; Yeager in 29 LA 487, 489. For additional cases and related discussion, see Chapter 16, topic titled "Management Rights and Obligations in Safety and Health Matters."

[486] See Arbitrator Erbs in 55 LA 197, 208; Bradley in 47 LA 691, 697; Dahl in 46 LA 356, 357; Wallen in 32 LA 1025, 1027; Stouffer in 26 LA 638, 640; Shister in 20 LA 448, 450–451; Baab in 16 LA 118, 120; McCoy in 12 LA 73, 74–75; Gilden in 9 LA 931, 934; Healy in 6 LA 430, 432.

where an agreement required management to discuss plant rules with the union before being put into effect, Arbitrator Harold M. Gilden observed: "The purpose of the discussion is to ascertain whether the rule itself contains any loopholes, or whether its enforcement will give rise to unexpected problems. After a discussion, the company, at its option, may put the rule into effect, even though union approval is not obtained."[487]

Under an agreement which vested in management the right "to establish reasonable rules for the management of the plant and to maintain discipline among its employees," Arbitrator Maurice H. Merrill held that rules so established must be considered a part of the agreement and that a clause prohibiting the arbitrator from adding to the terms of the agreement did not preclude him from considering established plant rules in determining whether an employee had been properly disciplined. In this case Arbitrator Merrill stated:

"As a practical matter, it is not possible to embody in a collective bargaining contract a complete code of plant rules. Such a code would make the contract too long and cumbersome. It would introduce into collective bargaining new sources of delay and dispute. It would prevent the necessary adjustments and modifications of rules between periods of negotiation."[488]

After plant rules are promulgated, they may be challenged through the grievance procedure (including arbitration) on the ground that they violate the agreement or that they are unfair, arbitrary, or discriminatory.[489] This right to challenge applies also where the agreement expressly gives management the right to establish plant rules.[490] Rules promulgated unilaterally by the employer may be challenged when established—the union need not delay its challenge until employees have been disciplined for violation of the rules.[491]

---

[487] Borg-Warner Corp., 16 LA 446, 453 (1951). Similarly, see Arbitrator McDermott in 48 LA 1149, 1157; Karlins in 44 LA 609, 612. Cf., Traynor in 46 LA 53, 58–59.
[488] American Zinc Co. of Illinois, 20 LA 527, 530 (1953).
[489] See Arbitrator Dolson in 51 LA 281, 283; Dyke in 48 LA 681, 687; Platt in 47 LA 1127, 1129–1130; Whyte in 47 LA 1065, 1069; Kotin in 46 LA 481, 483–484; Leflar in 44 LA 104, 105; Thompson in 30 LA 231, 235; Crawford in 29 LA 731, 733; Crane in 27 LA 717, 720–722; Smith in 27 LA 99, 104–105; Donaldson in 13 LA 943, 945; Courshon in 2 LA 509, 514.
[490] Capitol Mfg. Co., 48 LA 243, 248 (Klein, 1967).
[491] Linde Co., 34 LA 1, 5–6 (Schmidt, 1959).

The test of reasonableness of a plant rule "is whether or not the rule is reasonably related to a legitimate objective of management."[492] Plant rules must be reasonable not only in their content but also in their application; thus, a rule requiring the wearing of safety glasses in the plant could not be applied during lunch periods where the risk of injury was remote.[493]

While it has been held that management's right to supervise employees does not extend to their personal lives after they leave the plant,[494] the employees' personal lives may be governed by plant rules where the conduct or situation in question affects plant operations.[495]

Management should be permitted to change plant rules, if not restricted by the agreement, to meet changed circumstances.[496] However, it has been emphasized that "Sound industrial relations policy dictates that abrupt changes in rules should be accompanied by a gradual educational process."[497] Moreover, new or changed plant rules which curtail employee privileges supported by long established past practice may be subject to challenge.[498]

Upon demand, management must bargain with respect to such rules as affect conditions of employment, and the filing of a grievance challenging a rule might be construed by an arbitrator "as a demand to negotiate on the subject."[499] Even where the agreement gave management a general right to make and modify rules "for purposes of discipline and efficiency," it was held that "after they have once become a subject of mutual agreements, very specific bargaining and

---

[492] Robertshaw Controls Co., 55 LA 283, 286 (Block, 1970).

[493] Bauer Bros. Co., 48 LA 861, 863 (Kates, 1967).

[494] Pioneer Gen-E-Motors Corp., 3 LA 486, 488 (Blair, 1946). For related material, see Chapter 15, topic titled "Conduct Away From Plant."

[495] See Arbitrator Teple in 43 LA 338, 340; Gorsuch in 34 LA 636, 641–642; Platt in 28 LA 583, 585–586; Willingham in 28 LA 411, 413–414; Friedman in 28 LA 328, 330; Kates in 27 LA 540, 542; Keller in 26 LA 401, 402–404; Holden in 24 LA 810, 812–813; Cole in 21 LA 709, 710.

[496] See Florence Stove Co., 19 LA 650, 651 (Noel, 1952). Also see Butler Mfg. Co., 50 LA 109, 111 (Larkin, 1968).

[497] Joy Mfg. Co., 6 LA 430, 434 (Healy, 1946). Also see Arbitrator Turkus in 48 LA 1337, 1338; Smith in 27 LA 99, 105.

[498] See Standard Oil Co. (Indiana), 11 LA 689, 690 (Updegraff, 1948). Also see Arbitrator Dolson in 51 LA 281, 283; Kreimer in 43 LA 337, 338; McCoy in 4 LA 775, 777–779. For related discussion, see Chapter 12, topic titled "Custom and Practice as Part of the Contract."

[499] Federal Machine & Welder Co., 5 LA 60, 68–69 (Whiting, 1946). Also see Borg-Warner Corp., 3 LA 423, 433–434 (Gilden, 1944). For full discussion, see this Chapter, subtopic titled "The Duty to Bargain: Right of Unilateral Action."

agreement are required to make their modification again exclusively a matter of company decisions and announcements."[500]

Posting of Rules

The decision as to whether plant rules are to be posted is a part of the managerial function, and the posting of rules ordinarily is not a condition precedent to management's right to discipline employees for their violation.[501] However, except where the nature of the prohibited activity is such that employees should know it is improper,[502] rules must be communicated to employees in some manner.[503]

Thus, in the absence of posted rules management's freedom of action may be more restricted than it would be if they were posted,[504] and management is under a somewhat greater responsibility to show the absence of discrimination in the discipline of an employee.[505] Especially when management chooses to apply a rule rigidly to the point of meeting its violation with discharge, there should be no doubt in the minds of employees as to the existence and nature of the rule.[506]

Seniority

Management's right of action is very often restricted by requirements of seniority recognition. Chapter 14 is devoted to discussion of seniority concepts and to an examination of the standards utilized by arbitrators in evaluating management actions in the setting of seniority requirements.

---

[500] Ampco Metal, Inc., 3 LA 374, 378–379 (Updegraff, 1946). Also see Arbitrator Sembower in 47 LA 20, 25; Hampton in 5 LA 391, 396.

[501] Bethlehem Steel Co., 7 LA 334, 335 (Killingsworth, 1946); Watt Car & Wheel Co., 4 LA 67, 69 (Blair, 1946). Also see Arbitrator Teple in 50 LA 501, 504 (plant rules need not be in writing); Lovell in 48 LA 498, 501–502; Murphy in 44 LA 459, 461 (there is no one way of either establishing or publicizing a rule); Merrill in 37 LA 862, 864; Schmidt in 35 LA 293, 296.

[502] As in Ashland Oil Refining Co., 28 LA 874, 877–878 (Bradley, 1957); Omar, Inc., 26 LA 641, 642 (Beatty, 1956). Cf., Arbitrator Jenkins in 52 LA 1266, 1269; Harkins in 18 LA 336, 339.

[503] See Arbitrator Mullins in 54 LA 498, 500; Teple in 50 LA 501, 504; Keefe in 48 LA 910, 914; Kates in 47 LA 441, 442–443 (an employer "takes an unnecessary risk of enforcement in failing to put all its shop rules in written form"); Murphy in 44 LA 459, 461; Klein in 43 LA 1268, 1273; Davis in 28 LA 83, 87; Healy in 14 LA 787, 790.

[504] See Arbitrator Keefe in 48 LA 910, 914; Davis in 28 LA 83, 87; Healy in 14 LA 787, 790.

[505] Bethlehem Steel Co., 7 LA 334, 335 (Killingsworth, 1946); Watt Car & Wheel Co., 4 LA 67, 69 (Blair, 1946).

[506] Joy Mfg. Co., 6 LA 430, 434 (Healy, 1946). Also see Arbitrator Teple in 44 LA 820, 822–823. Cf., Lovell in 48 LA 498, 501–502.

Layoff of Employees

In the absence of contractual restriction, it is the right of management to determine the number of employees to be used at any given time and to lay off employees in excess of that number, giving any required recognition to seniority.[507] Recognition of seniority is the most significant type of restriction placed by many agreements upon the layoff right.[508] Clauses requiring advance notice for layoff in order to permit employees to plan ahead are not uncommon, but such a notice requirement ordinarily is not severe from the employer's point of view since he also prefers to plan ahead.[509]

The meaning of the term "layoff," and allegations that employees have been laid off in fact even if not in name or form, are frequent issues in arbitration.[510] Arbitrators have ruled that the term "layoff" must be interpreted to include any suspension from employment arising out of a reduction in the work force, and that the scheduling of employees not to work or the use of the term "not scheduled" by management does not make the occurrence any the less a "layoff."[511] One arbitrator defined "layoff," in the context of a particular clause, as an "actual severance from the Company's payroll, and a break in continuous service."[512]

---

[507] See Arbitrator Blair in 55 LA 312, 324; Murphy in 46 LA 289, 291; Feinberg in 19 LA 523, 525, and in 10 LA 883, 885; Wolff in 19 LA 487, 488. Also see Hebert in 47 LA 941, 946–947; McCoy in 39 LA 268, 269; Reid in 36 LA 458, 462; Nagle in 24 LA 770, 774. Where the contract listed four reasons for layoffs, management could lay off only for those reasons. City of Milwaukee, 55 LA 926, 931–932 (Sembower, 1970). For discussion of the rights of laid off employees, see Arbitrator McCoy in 39 LA 268, 269; Brown in 35 LA 560, 563–564; Whelan in 25 LA 443, 449–451.

[508] Illustrating the strict application of such restriction, see Wayne Pump Co., 35 LA 623, 625 (Horlacher, 1960). For the application of a clause providing for layoff by seniority but authorizing exceptions for special skills, see Trane Co., 44 LA 212, 216 (Markowitz, 1965).

[509] For related discussion, see this Chapter, topic titled "Emergency Changes in Work Schedule." For a clause interpreted to permit very few exceptions to the notice requirement, see Mobil Chemical Co., 50 LA 80, 81–82 (Kesselman, 1968).

[510] See Arbitrator Cohen in 55 LA 981, 985–986; Moran in 51 LA 1069, 1071; Murphy in 46 LA 289, 292–293; Boles in 45 LA 502, 505, 508; Teple in 40 LA 1067, 1069; Prasow in 27 LA 40, 45; Campbell in 26 LA 924, 929–930; Platt in 23 LA 137, 141; McCormick in 22 LA 695, 696–698; Marshall in 22 LA 181, 183; Emery in 19 LA 231, 232–233; Piper in 18 LA 801, 808; Feinberg in 16 LA 71, 72.

[511] See Arbitrator Feinberg in 14 LA 191, 195; Donnelly in 13 LA 684, 686; Brandschain in 5 LA 578, 587. Cf., Williams in 48 LA 767, 768.

[512] Bethlehem Steel Co., 16 LA 71, 72 (Feinberg, 1950). Also see Arbitrator Campbell in 26 LA 924, 929.

Downgrading is often tied to layoffs. It has been held that down-grading "is such an intimate concomitant of layoff" that layoff seniority provisions must be applied in downgrading.[513] Many con-tracts contain provisions permitting employees to accept layoff in lieu of downgrading.[514] Where the contract was silent regarding the right of employees to choose layoff rather than downgrading, one arbitrator held that they are deemed to have such right if downgrading involves a significant reduction in pay.[515]

Numerous cases have arisen involving the observance of seniority in temporary layoffs. Contracts sometimes expressly allow management to disregard seniority in making temporary layoffs.[516] Such agreements generally indicate the maximum period that may be considered tem-porary, such period varying in different contracts from a specified number of hours up to as many as thirty days.[517]

An interesting situation was presented under a contract which required observance of seniority only in case of layoffs for "indefinite" periods. There the employer was permitted to provide one week's work for all employees and then to lay off all employees for one week, rather than to lay off junior employees indefinitely, the arbitration board ruling that the layoffs were for definite, temporary periods.[518]

In cases where the agreement contains no specific exception from the requirement of observing seniority in making "temporary" or

---

[513] Kenworth Motor Truck Corp., 8 LA 867, 869 (Seering, 1947). A similar result was reached in Ford Motor Co., Opinions of the Umpire, Opinion A-30 (1943). But this result was not reached where downgrading was not tied to layoffs. Lockheed Aircraft Corp., 10 LA 222, 226 (Aaron, 1948). Also see Arbitra-tor Mathews in 1 LA 298, 300–301.

[514] As in Tappan Co., 40 LA 149, 150 (Dworkin, 1962); Carbide & Carbon Chemicals Co., 20 LA 205, 206 (Shister, 1953).

[515] Caterpillar Tractor Co., 23 LA 313, 315–316 (Fleming, 1954). Also see Arbitrator McCoy in 47 LA 164, 169–170; Shipman in 15 LA 698, 703. Cf., Garrett in 31 LA 988, 991–992.

[516] As in 38 LA 1, 4; 28 LA 494, 497; 24 LA 88, 89; 15 LA 910, 913; 8 LA 792, 794; 1 LA 544, 545. In Barler Metal Products, Inc., 38 LA 1, 4–5 (Sembower, 1962), it was held that the "temporary" character of a layoff is determined in advance rather than retrospectively.

[517] See cases cited in prior footnote. No specific period was stated in 43 LA 1092, 1093–1094; 18 LA 785, 786; 12 LA 826, 828. Even where the contract fixes a maximum period, a series of temporary layoffs without observing seniority has sometimes been permitted. See Anaconda Aluminum Co., 43 LA 775, 777–779 (Volz, 1964); Alliance Mfg. Co., 37 LA 177, 180 (Kates, 1961).

[518] Whitlock Mfg. Co., 13 LA 253, 254 (Stutz, Mottram & Curry, 1949).

"emergency" layoffs, arbitrators have ruled both ways as to the right of management to disregard seniority in making such layoffs.[519] Some of these cases can be reconciled on the basis of differing contract language, including contractual requirement for notice of layoff, or by distinguishing between "temporary" and "emergency" layoffs.[520]

Issues concerning "temporary" or "emergency" layoffs may be approached, as has been done by Arbitrator Russell A. Smith, "in the light of the well known fact that the common purpose of seniority layoff provisions is to give protection as between classes of employees on the assumption that some of them may properly be suspended under conditions of lack of work, and not to guarantee work." He construed the contract in question as being broadly applicable to temporary as well as permanent suspensions of work (those where there is no immediate prospective need of the services involved), but not as requiring the employer to follow seniority "when the emergency is such that, due to time limitations, it would be either impossible or unreasonably burdensome to give effect to these rules."[521]

The question sometimes arises regarding management's right to reduce the workweek of all its employees in lieu of laying off junior employees. In the absence of a specific contract provision covering

---

[519] Cases requiring observance of seniority: Arbitrator Tatum in 40 LA 1115, 1118–1120; Killion in 40 LA 513, 520–521; Murphy in 38 LA 1199, 1202; Lugar in 35 LA 299, 303; Duff in 30 LA 441, 443; Howlett in 29 LA 724, 726–727; Platt in 23 LA 137, 141; Thompson in 23 LA 89, 92; McCormick in 22 LA 695, 698; Marshall in 22 LA 181, 184; Stutz in 21 LA 400, 401, and in 10 LA 88, 91; Spaulding in 19 LA 159, 163–164; Feinberg in 14 LA 413, 416; Gorder in 13 LA 529, 531; Uible in 12 LA 893, 895; Brandschain in 5 LA 578, 587–588; Whiting in 5 LA 24, 25; Gilden in 1 LA 530, 537. Cases not requiring the observance of seniority: Arbitrator Caraway in 52 LA 368, 372 (past practice supported employer); Klamon in 37 LA 778, 784; Abernethy in 32 LA 345, 350–351; Hebert in 23 LA 497, 500; Garrett in 21 LA 71, 74–75; Prasow in 20 LA 345, 347–348; Marshall in 20 LA 297, 299; Morgan in 18 LA 517, 518; Horton in 18 LA 285, 289; Lockhart in 16 LA 173, 175; Bauder in 14 LA 681, 685; Feinberg in 14 LA 191, 196; Stein in 10 LA 579, 581; Dwyer in 8 LA 506, 509; Elson in 8 LA 129, 134. Also see Howlett in 24 LA 232, 237–238; Healy in 15 LA 192, 194. Observance of seniority in emergency recalls was not required by Arbitrator Platt in 14 LA 970, 976, and in 14 LA 552, 562. Also see Turkus in 48 LA 179, 181. Cf., Dworkin in 22 LA 875, 880.

[520] In at least one instance, however, opposite results were reached within the same month by two different arbitrators applying the same contractual provision to similar fact situations. See International Harvester Co., 9 LA 399, 401 (Hays, 1947), and International Harvester Co., 8 LA 129, 134 (Elson, 1947).

[521] Dow Chemical Co., 12 LA 763, 767 (1949). Also see Kaiser Steel Corp., 48 LA 1199, 1201 (Roberts, 1967).

this issue, arbitrators have ruled both ways.[522] Some of the cases on this issue are discussed elsewhere in this Chapter.[523]

Bumping

Layoff often gives rise to "bumping" issues. Arbitrators have emphasized that, absent any contract provision permitting it, senior employees have no right to bump junior employees merely because the senior employee wants the job of the junior employee—no layoff being involved.[524] However, it has also been emphasized that, in the absence of any contract prohibition, "it is almost universally recognized that senior employees, under a plant-wide seniority system, have the right to bump junior employees from their jobs in order to avoid their own layoff, provided they can perform the work of the juniors."[525] The right to bump in short-term temporary layoff situations may be considerably more limited.[526]

While it is generally accepted that an employee facing layoff may exercise his bumping right laterally or downward, i.e., to a job equal

---

[522] For cases permitting such action, see Arbitrator Murphy in 52 LA 852, 855–857; Stouffer in 37 LA 877, 881–883; Cahn in 32 LA 746, 748; Witney in 30 LA 938, 947; Prasow in 25 LA 794, 797–799; Ebeling in 24 LA 874, 876–877; Slavney in 22 LA 473, 475; Piper in 18 LA 801, 807; Dash in 18 LA 625, 627. For cases not permitting such action, see Arbitrator Hertz in 55 LA 859, 861; Hughes in 40 LA 460, 464; Williams in 40 LA 456, 459–460; Boles in 35 LA 845, 848–849; Kates in 32 LA 492, 500–501; Larkin in 25 LA 308, 312; Ryder in 25 LA 83, 84; Donnelly in 24 LA 846, 848; Cole in 24 LA 311, 313; Davey in 24 LA 88, 91–92; Selekman in 14 LA 1031, 1039. In Wilshire Mfg. Jewelers, 49 LA 1079, 1082 (Jones, 1967), a contractual provision on work sharing was construed to *require* management to reduce hours of employees instead of laying off or discharging some of the employees for lack of work.

[523] See topic titled "Scheduling Work."

[524] See Arbitrator Volz in 48 LA 579, 581–582; Turkus in 39 LA 670, 671; Williams in 39 LA 494, 495. Also see Krinsky in 54 LA 824, 827–828; Carmichael in 64–1 ARB ¶8255. Explaining the purpose of "bumping" and distinguishing it from "transfer," see Borden Ice Cream Co., 37 LA 140, 141–142 (Markowitz, 1961).

[525] Darin & Armstrong, 13 LA 843, 847 (Platt, 1950). Also see Arbitrator Altieri in 43 LA 499, 504; Kornblum in 42 LA 403, 404, 407; Markowitz in 37 LA 140, 141; Larson in 26 LA 532, 535–536; Parker in 22 LA 883, 885; Cornsweet in 14 LA 494, 498; Healy in 11 LA 827, 831. The present ability requirement is obviously important. See Arbitrator Kamin in 50 LA 1093, 1099; Geissinger in 41 LA 348, 351–352; Klamon in 35 LA 128, 132. Although the senior employee is not entitled to training, a reasonable trial period to demonstrate his present ability has sometimes been required in bumping situations. See Arbitrator Prasow in 24 LA 437, 442; McKelvy in 22 LA 167, 170; Kelliher in 22 LA 53, 55; Randle in 17 LA 486, 487. Cf., Tatum in 24 LA 517, 518; McCoy in 23 LA 779, 781.

[526] See Arbitrator Kates in 42 LA 669, 671; Blair in 30 LA 962, 963; Fuchs in 15 LA 172, 179. Cf., Seibel in 22 LA 306, 310.

to his own or a lower classification, arbitrators have ruled both ways on the issue of "upward" bumping. Where arbitrators have denied the right of an employee to bump into a higher-rated classification, they have based their decisions upon one or more of the following reasons:

1. A layoff may not be used as a means of achieving a promotion. The rationale of these cases seems to be that a promotion can be sought only when a vacancy exists; promotions must be governed by the promotion clause of the collective agreement; and since upward bumping would result in a promotion in violation of the promotion requirements of the contract, it cannot be permitted.[527]

2. A showing was made that past practice prohibits upward bumping, or there was no showing of past practice allowing it.[528]

3. The history of contract negotiations indicates an intent to preclude upward bumping.[529]

4. While the contract would permit upward bumping, it does not require that it be permitted, and in the absence of a showing of practice by the parties, the arbitrator cannot sustain a claim to upward bumping.[530]

Some of the arbitrators who have permitted upward bumping have done so upon the basis of one or more of the following reasons:

1. The contract does not specifically prohibit it.[531]

---

[527] See Arbitrator McSwain in 38 LA 430, 433–434; Larson in 26 LA 532, 536; Hall in 25 LA 417, 420–421; Seward in 24 LA 261, 266–267, and in 15 LA 891, 892; Rosenfarb in 23 LA 789, 795–796; Horvitz in 22 LA 736, 737; Abernethy in 14 LA 938, 941. Also see Shulman in 3 LA 863, 865.

[528] See Arbitrator Seward in 30 LA 815, 819; Hebert in 30 LA 1, 8; Warns in 23 LA 220, 222. In Empire-Reeves Steel Corp., 44 LA 653, 657 (Nichols, 1965), past practice permitted upward bumping but only on a limited basis—this controlled the decision.

[529] See Bethlehem Steel Co., 24 LA 261, 266–267 (Seward, 1955).

[530] See Bethlehem Steel Co., 30 LA 815, 819 (Seward, 1958). Where a contract was "highly permissive" as to upward bumping, the arbitrator said that criteria of "productivity, tensions and morale" should be applied in determining whether to permit it in any particular layoff. C. E. Howard Corp., 38 LA 128, 129–130 (Pollard, 1961).

[531] See Arbitrator Burris in 30 LA 886, 892; Marshall in 29 LA 629, 633–634; Cole in 21 LA 214, 216; Low in 20 LA 394, 396. Cf., Seward in 15 LA 891, 892. In Bethlehem Steel Co., 16 LA 478, 483 (1951), Arbitrator Shipman recognized that downward bumping is the general rule, but he held that there should be some exceptions. In Air Reduction Sales Co., 34 LA 294, 296 (Hawley, 1960), the arbitrator said that to deny upward bumping in layoff would seriously restrict departmental seniority rights and might lead to substitution of classification seniority for the broader departmental seniority specified by the contract.

2. The layoff provisions of the agreement are broad.[532]

3. Upward bumping does not conflict with the promotion provisions of the agreement.[533]

4. Past practice of the parties either supports or does not prohibit upward bumping.[534]

In regard to exercising the bumping right, it has been held that senior employees have an obligation to notify management of their desire to exercise bumping privileges,[535] whereupon management has a duty to disclose the jobs that may be bumped into and to inform junior employees of their layoff under the seniority provisions of the agreement.[536] In recalls, management has been held to have the duty of taking the initiative in ascertaining from employees whether they are available for jobs to which their seniority entitles them.[537]

Promotion and/or Transfer of Employees

The term "promotion" usually connotes an upward movement to a better job or a higher rating in the same job. However, it is to be noted that some parties or arbitrators have used the term less specifically, with the result that there has been some overlapping and intermingling of the terms "promotion" and "transfer." The mixed nature of some employee job movements should also be kept in mind: promotions often involve transfers, transfers may involve promotions, but not all promotions involve transfers, and certainly not all transfers involve promotions.

In concluding that the term "promotion" generally indicates movement to a higher job classification, one arbitrator referred to

---

[532] See Arbitrator Volz in 44 LA 694, 697; Burris in 30 LA 886, 892; Low in 20 LA 394, 396; Seward in 14 LA 502, 503–504.

[533] See Aetna Paper Co., 29 LA 439, 441–442 (Warns, 1957). Also see Arbitrator Ebeling in 12 LA 738, 740.

[534] See International Harvester Co., 21 LA 214, 216 (Cole, 1953). Also see Arbitrator Volz in 44 LA 694, 697.

[535] See Union Electric Steel Corp., 13 LA 464, 467 (Blair, 1949); General American Transportation Corp., 15 LA 672, 676 (Brandschain, 1950). Also see Arbitrator Stein in 43 LA 178, 180–181. But see Arbitrator Warns in 34 LA 297, 300; Howlett in 33 LA 524, 527–528 (involving union representatives with superseniority).

[536] Union Electric Steel Corp., 13 LA 464, 467 (Blair, 1949). Also see Arbitrator Stein in 43 LA 178, 180–181; Bradley in 37 LA 9, 11–13. Some arbitrators require the employee to specify the job into which he desires to bump. See Arbitrator Prasow in 27 LA 40, 48; Gilden in 6 LA 803, 813.

[537] The Thor Corp., 13 LA 319, 323 (Baab, 1949).

industrial practice, the practice of the particular parties, and the following definitions contained in a dictionary of labor terms:[538]

"PROMOTION. Transfer of an employee to a higher job classification."

"TRANSFER. Shift of an employee from one job to another within a Company. A lateral transfer is a change in an employee's job within a department, to another machine or to very similar duties."

Also pointing out that the term "promotion" refers to upward movement, another arbitrator stated that the term generally appears "in a context of collective bargaining agreements connoting an upward movement to a higher occupational classification requiring superior skills or greater effort and to which, for such reasons, a higher minimum wage scale is attached." He also noted that the term is "never associated with an outward or lateral movement of employees, to the operation of different machines, or the performances of different work drawing identical wage rates."[539] It has also been held that a lateral or downward movement could not be considered a promotion "even though such a movement may lead to higher pay, a job more to the liking of the worker, and a higher ultimate maximum pay."[540]

However, where an agreement provided that "Promotions to all vacancies" will be made on the basis of seniority and ability, an arbitrator followed the view that movement to a job with clearly better working conditions or from which advancement opportunities are or may be better, may be viewed as a "promotion" even though the

---

[538] Pittsburgh Plate Glass Co., 30 LA 981, 982 (Kelliher, 1958), referring to the CCH Dictionary of Labor Terms. In another case that arbitrator found that the terms "promotion" and "transfer" had been defined by the contract. United States Steel Co., 21 LA 707, 708 (Kelliher, 1953).

[539] Bunker Hill & Sullivan Mining & Concentrating Co., 8 LA 1010, 1011 (Cheney, 1947), where he also stated that permitting an employee to select his job, machine, or place of work "would in effect be confiding the management of the business, and the direction of the working forces to employees to no small degree."

[540] Rochester Telephone Co., 26 LA 231, 234–235, 238 (Thompson, 1956), in which past practice was a factor in the decision. For other cases considering that lateral or downward movements are not promotions, see Arbitrator Mullin in 54 LA 593, 595–596 (the contract expressly spoke of right to bid on "higher rated" jobs); Kates in 40 LA 1212, 1214–1215 (the contract provided that employees shall be "promoted" to fill vacancies and the arbitrator said that "in the absence of extraordinary conditions surrounding the opening for which a lateral or downward bid is made, such a bid * * * generally does not involve a 'promotion' "); Seward in 30 LA 550, 551; Reid in 26 LA 849, 852, and in 23 LA 159, 162; Kelliher in 23 LA 105, 107; Selekman in 12 LA 588, 591.

job does not pay more.[541] Moreover, if the agreement provides for
recognition of seniority in the filling of vacancies but does not use
language which is reasonably clear in linking or limiting job vacancies
and bidding procedures to promotion or advancement, the arbitrator
may hold that employees are entitled to exercise their seniority for
lateral or downward movement.[542]

Management's general right to control promotions, except as limited by the collective agreement, was elaborated by Arbitrator Whitley
P. McCoy as follows:

"When there is no contract provision at all limiting the Company's
rights in selecting men for promotion, the Company's rights, of course,
are unlimited. If the only contract restriction is one against discrimination for Union activity, then that is the only restriction. In other
words, absent a contract right in favor of the employees, or a contract
restriction on a company, the latter may ignore not only seniority but
also even skill, ability, and physical fitness. The employees must obtain benefits at the bargaining table, not from arbitrators. Arbitrators
are bound by the contract under which they are arbitrating."[543]

The right of management to promote employees, however, is frequently qualified by the seniority provisions. The general problems
encountered in the operation of "seniority" and "fitness and ability"

---

[541] Indiana Chair Co., 34 LA 856, 857–858 (Russell, 1960). Also see Arbitrator
Marshall in 36 LA 570, 572; Hawley in 33 LA 719, 721; Pfaus in 24 LA
723, 724; Klamon in 18 LA 701, 711–712. Past practice supported the claimed
right to lateral movement in Picker X-Ray Corp., 42 LA 179, 181–182 (Nichols,
1964). Seniority may not be disregarded by calling a promotion a merit increase.
Bestwall Gypsum Co., 43 LA 475, 481 (Marshall, 1964).

[542] For such holdings, see Arbitrator Hayes in 55 LA 270, 272–274 (but
employee must have a reasonable motive rather than "whim or fancy" for the
move); King in 55 LA 89, 91; Altrock in 47 LA 952, 954–955 (fact that
senior employee was needed more in present job could not defeat his right
to fill vacancy by transfer); Crawford in 44 LA 10, 11–12; Marshall in 41
LA 329, 331; McIntosh in 40 LA 1305, 1307–1308; Slavney in 38 LA 371,
373; Cahn in 36 LA 785, 785–786. But see Arbitrator Doyle in 52 LA 733,
735–736 (contract construed to permit company to fill vacancies by lateral transfer
but not to require it—clear language would be required to give employees a
right of lateral transfer by seniority); McPherson in 48 LA 573, 575–576 (an
express provision would be required to give employees an unqualified right to
exercise seniority for downward movement); Gill in 44 LA 457, 458 (absent
a local practice permitting it, employee could not exercise seniority for lateral
or downward movement); Woodruff in 44 LA 7, 8–9; Pfaus in 24 LA 723,
723–724. In Tenn-Tex Alloy & Chemical Corp., 43 LA 152, 157–159 (Hebert,
1964), the term "any open job" was narrowed in scope by past practice.

[543] New Britain Machine Co., 45 LA 993, 995–996 (1965). Also see Arbitrator
Jones in 50 LA 455, 457–458; Kates in 46 LA 562, 565; Klein in 42 LA
165, 167–168; Bailer in 20 LA 835, 836; Beneduce in 17 LA 568, 569. In
Sun Oil Co., 52 LA 463, 468–469 (Abernethy, 1969), management could select
a junior employee for temporary promotion to a supervisory job expressly excluded
from the agreement.

clauses discussed in Chapter 14 apply here. There are, in addition, some other considerations which should be noted.

Temporary assignments to better jobs, such as may be made while incumbents are on vacation, may be held not to be "promotions" and thus not to require the application of contract seniority provisions governing promotions.[544] To require the recognition of seniority in such cases, it has been said, would impose a handicap and serious detriment to management in its direction of the working force.[545] Moreover, it has been held that management may compel designated employees to accept temporary promotion against their will.[546]

However, management has not been permitted unilaterally to change qualifications customarily required for a job if the change would impair the right of senior employees to be promoted in accordance with the contract's promotion clause.[547] Also, management may not hold a successful bidder on his old job beyond a reasonable time to train his replacement.[548]

The general rule regarding the right of management to transfer employees was stated by Arbitrator David A. Wolff as follows: "Unless restricted by agreement, law, custom, practice, or estoppel, management has the right to effect transfers as a necessary element in the operation of its business."[549] Arbitrator Wolff also considered the right

---

[544] See Arbitrator Prasow in 24 LA 421, 423, and in 17 LA 644, 646–647; D'Andrade in 18 LA 932, 933, and in 12 LA 584, 585; Lohman in 5 LA 695, 696. Also see Cayton in 45 LA 889, 890–891; Oppenheim in 44 LA 274, 279–280; Hebert in 33 LA 348, 350–351; Grant in 20 LA 202, 204. But see Seward in 47 LA 549, 551; Copelof in 20 LA 385, 393. For cases concerned with the application of "fitness and ability" requirements of seniority provisions in temporary promotions, see Arbitrator Daugherty in 38 LA 108, 110–111; Emery in 28 LA 733, 734–735; Warren in 21 LA 228, 231.

[545] Wilson & Co., 5 LA 695, 696 (Lohman, 1946).

[546] See Arbitrator Justin in 27 LA 877, 879–880; Ryder in 24 LA 132, 135–136; Howard in 18 LA 798, 801. Also see Cahn in 16 LA 767, 769. But see McCoy in 20 LA 281, 282; Blair in 8 LA 317, 323. In Bethlehem Steel Co., 37 LA 1099, 1102–1103 (Valtin, 1962), the arbitrator concluded that employees could be required to accept temporary promotion but not permanent promotion. For cases holding that management could require senior employees to accept permanent promotion, see Arbitrator Seinsheimer in 43 LA 1011, 1015–1017, and Kelliher in 23 LA 105, 108–109.

[547] See Arbitrator Howlett in 26 LA 885, 890–891; Stutz in 26 LA 289, 291; Frohlich in 14 LA 12, 16. Also see Gilden in 20 LA 142, 146–147.

[548] Columbus Bolt & Forging Co., 35 LA 215, 220 (Stouffer, 1960).

[549] Chrysler Corp., 6 LA 276, 281 (1947). Also see Arbitrator Howlett in 52 LA 252, 254–255; Gibson in 49 LA 1115, 1117; Klein in 46 LA 450, 454–455; Gorsuch in 40 LA 879, 888; Murphy in 39 LA 1074, 1078–1079; Teple in 35 LA 162, 167; Doyle in 34 LA 179, 180; Sembower in 30 LA 290, 292; Seward in 28 LA 437, 438; Reid in 23 LA 159, 162; Kelliher in 23 LA 105, 107; Feinberg in 14 LA 83, 86; Hepburn in 9 LA 442, 443.

to transfer to be included within the right to direct the working force.[550]

Some agreements explicitly recognize management's right to transfer. While such agreements sometimes make the transfer right subject to other terms of the agreement, it appears that arbitrators generally require any restriction upon the right to be clearly stated.[551] However, management's right to transfer will be restricted to the extent that a limitation is necessary to preserve contractual rights of employees.[552] Thus, for instance, an employer could not require employees to transfer to service outside the unit covered by the collective agreement, for they otherwise might be stripped of rights under the agreement and be required to work under conditions over which they have no control.[553]

A transfer may be effected when the employer requires employees to rotate among jobs within their classification,[554] or to move from one shift to another,[555] or to move from one job to another in a different classification in the same job class,[556] or when the employee is moved to a new machine on the same job,[557] or to a new location for the same job.[558]

---

[550] Chrysler Corp., 6 LA 276, 281 (1947). Also see Arbitrator Stockton in 33 LA 219, 223; Donnelly in 24 LA 399, 400; Kelliher in 23 LA 105, 107.

[551] See Arbitrator Williams in 45 LA 206, 209–210; Fallon in 44 LA 111, 113–114; Dunlop in 42 LA 911, 915; Morvant in 36 LA 1433, 1437; Wettach in 25 LA 629, 634; Singletary in 23 LA 456, 459; Copelof in 23 LA 67, 75; Uible in 11 LA 139, 142–143; Wagner in 8 LA 26, 29.

[552] See Arbitrator Lugar in 48 LA 463, 470–475; Hughes in 42 LA 809, 814; Stouffer in 40 LA 961, 964–965. In Sohio Chemical Co., 44 LA 624, 628 (Witney, 1965), permitting two employees to trade positions was held to violate the intent, if not the letter, of contractual provisions for job bidding; the arbitrator added that the employer could not have ordered the trade.

[553] Corte Construction Co., 48 LA 463, 470–475 (Lugar, 1967), citing other cases in support of Arbitrator Lugar's conclusions.

[554] Simmons Co., 25 LA 194, 198 (Elson, 1955). Cf., Arbitrator Talent in 50 LA 1061, 1066.

[555] Midland Rubber Co., 18 LA 590, 593 (Cheney, 1952). Also see Arbitrator Graff in 69–2 ARB ¶8610. Employees have no right to exercise their seniority for shift preference unless the right clearly exists under a contract provision or past practice. See Arbitrator Pointer in 49 LA 527, 529; Doyle in 44 LA 718, 719; Updegraff in 38 LA 103, 104; Sanders in 36 LA 92, 94–95 (past practice was shown); Platt in 19 LA 199, 200.

[556] Bethlehem Steel Co., 28 LA 437, 437–438 (Seward, 1957).

[557] Gisholt Machine Co., 23 LA 105, 107 (Kelliher, 1954). Also see Arbitrator Stashower in 37 LA 591, 593.

[558] Phillips Petroleum Co., 34 LA 179, 180 (Doyle, 1960).

In the absence of a contract provision to the contrary, it has been held that the employer's right to transfer workers is not conditioned upon the willingness of the workers to be transferred,[559] and that the employer has the right to determine whether a transfer is temporary or permanent.[560] Moreover, management has been held to have the right and duty to transfer an employee if his presence in a given occupation creates some undue hazard for himself or others.[561] Various other justifications have similarly been accepted by arbitrators in upholding transfers required by management.[562] However, the right to transfer as a form of discipline appears to be definitely limited.[563]

Demotion of Employees

The collective agreement may specifically recognize the right of demotion as belonging to management. Also the right may be held to be included within a general management rights clause, as, for example, one giving management the right to select, assign, and direct the working force and to promote and transfer employees.[564] Then, too, the right may be held to remain in management, except as restricted by the agreement, as a residual power.[565] In many cases the arbitrator does not expressly state any particular source of the right to demote, the arbitrator merely upholding management if it has acted

---

[559] See Arbitrator Murphy in 39 LA 1074, 1078–1079; Teple in 35 LA 162, 167; Seward in 28 LA 437, 438; Donnelly in 24 LA 399, 400. Also see Kahn in 44 LA 1196, 1201.

[560] Jones & Laughlin Steel Corp., 23 LA 33, 36 (Cahn, 1954). For some possible tests for distinguishing between permanent and temporary transfer, see Continental Can Co., 37 LA 386, 388–389 (Sembower, 1961).

[561] International Shoe Co., 14 LA 253, 255 (Wallen, 1950). Similarly upholding management, see Arbitrator Guse in 50 LA 476, 487; Teple in 49 LA 649, 651; Siegel in 35 LA 103, 105, 109. Cf., Coles in 48 LA 533, 538–539.

[562] See Arbitrator Teple in 49 LA 346, 350–351 (personality clash between employee and foreman); Williams in 45 LA 229, 233 (incompetence); Holly in 40 LA 1025, 1027 (need for more direct supervision of indifferent employees). But see Arbitrator Wissner in 38 LA 838, 846–847.

[563] See Arbitrator Belcher in 53 LA 410, 413; Johnson in 49 LA 1061, 1062; Kelliher in 47 LA 1162, 1163–1164; Stutz in 30 LA 505, 506; Montgomery in 26 LA 546, 549; Stashower in 16 LA 922, 926.

[564] Drug Products Co., 10 LA 804, 805 (Naggi, 1948). Similarly, see Arbitrator Whyte in 51 LA 192, 195; Duff in 66–3 ARB ¶9060; France in 43 LA 934, at 934, 938.

[565] See E. I. DuPont de Nemours & Co., 17 LA 580, 585 (Cornsweet, 1951). Also see Arbitrator Whyte in 51 LA 192, 195; Whiting in 7 LA 150, 152.

on some reasonable basis in making a demotion.[566] The right to demote, however, has been held to be subject to the limitation that it may not be exercised in an arbitrary, capricious, or discriminatory manner.[567]

The right to demote has sometimes been found to have been contracted away. Such was the case, for instance, under a clause providing that wage rates fixed by the contract should be continued during the term of the contract, since the contractual wage rates were established on the basis of specific individuals.[568] A clause requiring promotions to be made on the basis of ability and seniority was interpreted to require the same for demotions, the arbitrator stating that otherwise the promotion clause would be meaningless as employees could be demoted immediately after promotion.[569] Management was also denied the right to demote under an agreement which was silent with respect to demotion and which provided permanent job status for employees surviving a trial period on the job, the employer being held required to lay off employees in slack periods rather than to demote.[570]

In considering an agreement that was silent on the matter of demotion for lack of qualifications, Umpire Harry Shulman stated that it may be assumed that, in the interest of achieving optimum performance, management may make periodic or sporadic appraisals of its employees and demote those whose performance falls below standard. Elaborating, he said:

> "We may assume further that the obligation to perform satisfactorily is a continuous condition of the maintenance of the better job and that an employee's performance, though once adequate, may fall below standard and merit demotion, either because his own performance has deteriorated or, though it has not deteriorated, because the standard in his occupation has been raised by the greater ability of those around him. Such a demotion would be an instance of the Company's

---

[566] For example, see Arbitrator Seinsheimer in 55 LA 1025, 1027–1029; Gorsuch in 48 LA 429, 437; King in 45 LA 793, 796.

[567] See Arbitrator Roberts in 55 LA 261, 268–270; Whyte in 51 LA 192, 195; Malkin in 49 LA 663, 665; Hawley in 26 LA 245, 248; Hale in 24 LA 470, 483; Shister in 19 LA 671, 673.

[568] National Vulcanized Fibre Co., 3 LA 259, 263 (Kaplan, 1946). Also see Arbitrator Aaron in 9 LA 419, 421.

[569] Raytheon Mfg. Co., 15 LA 291, 295 (Healy, 1950). Also see Arbitrator Roberts in 55 LA 261, 267–270; Hale in 24 LA 470, 483. Cf., Shister in 19 LA 671, 673.

[570] Merrill-Stevens Dry Dock & Repair Co., 10 LA 88, 90 (McCoy, 1948).

continuing interest in the satisfactory performance of each of its jobs."[571]

In downgrading for lack of qualifications shortly after an employee begins performing a different job, management may be required to show by substantial proof that the employee is not qualified and cannot qualify for the job within a reasonable time.[572] Where an employee has occupied a job for a long period of time, it has been held that management must show that the employee is no longer able or willing to perform his job duties.[573] However, it has been held that the mere fact that an employee has been retained in a job for a number of years does not necessarily warrant a finding by the arbitrator that he was qualified for it.[574]

A lack of qualifications has been found by the arbitrator, and demotion therefore considered justified, for example, where a truck

---

[571] Ford Motor Co., Opinions of the Umpire, Opinion A-30 (1943). Also permitting demotion for incompetence or lack of qualifications: Arbitrator Seinsheimer in 55 LA 1025, 1028–1029; McKenna in 54 LA 998, 1007 (mere fact that contract expressly authorizes employee's return to his former job if he is found unqualified at end of trial period does not guarantee that he will be retained in the new job once he passes the trial period); Whyte in 51 LA 192, 195; McDermott in 48 LA 1108, 1111–1112; Gorsuch in 48 LA 429, 437; Duff in 66–3 ARB ¶9060; Block in 47 LA 1001, 1009; King in 45 LA 793, 796; McCoy in 44 LA 1180, 1181; Stouffer in 38 LA 882, 886–887; Uible in 9 LA 77, 80; Abernethy in 7 LA 202, 225. Also see Platt in 47 LA 1015, 1017; Pollard in 10 LA 498, 508 (demotion for incompetence permitted under contract permitting demotion for "cause"). As between demotion or discharge of unqualified employees, an arbitrator may consider demotion to be the solution that gives fair consideration to the legitimate interests of both management and the employee. See Arbitrator Sembower in 53 LA 357, 360; Tsukiyama in 48 LA 218, 222–223; Dworkin in 40 LA 1054, 1060, all involving formerly qualified employees whose abilities have deteriorated. For a like view where the employee does not perform satisfactorily after promotion, see Arbitrator Kamin in 46 LA 539, 543–544; Schedler in 34 LA 860, 863. For the related discussion of failure to meet productions standards, see this Chapter, topic titled "Production Standards, Time Studies, and Job Evaluation." For other related discussion, see this Chapter, topic titled "Disqualifying Employees for Physical or Mental Reasons."

[572] United Aircraft Products, Inc., 10 LA 143, 146 (Wardlaw, 1948). Similarly, see Arbitrator Roberts in 55 LA 261, 269–270; Nicholas in 51 LA 1300, 1302–1303; Howlett in 35 LA 545, 548. Also see Shister in 38 LA 861, 864–865.

[573] Dewey & Almy Chemical Co., 25 LA 316, 322 (Somers, 1955). Also see Arbitrator Moberly in 55 LA 69, 73; McDermott in 48 LA 67, 68–69; Hale in 24 LA 470, 484; Komaroff in 17 LA 784, 789. For cases dealing with the necessity for warning the employee that his work is poor, see Arbitrator McKenna in 54 LA 998, 1008–1009; Burris in 25 LA 32, 36; Kelliher in 18 LA 447, 449; Komaroff in 17 LA 784, 789.

[574] E. I. DuPont de Nemours & Co., 17 LA 580, 586–587 (Cornsweet, 1951). Similarly, see Arbitrator Simon in 53 LA 1181, 1192. Also see Keeler in 36 LA 970, 973–974; Duff in 29 LA 167, 170.

driver's operator's license was revoked,[575] where the employee was unable to perform the job duties satisfactorily,[576] where the employee was physically or psychologically unable to perform the job duties or was unable to perform them safely,[577] and where a leadman displayed racial prejudice in a plant employing many Negroes.[578] In the latter instance, the arbitrator said that the employee's prejudice "made it clear that he could no longer do an effective job as leadman." One arbitrator, however, refused to permit the company to demote an employee for lack of qualifications where the company was aware of the employee's shortcomings at the time of his promotion but promoted him in spite of them. The promotion was not made on a trial basis, and the employee's work was no worse after the promotion than it had been before.[579]

Some arbitrators have held that management may not use demotion as a form of discipline unless the agreement specifically so provides, since such action would violate the contract seniority rights of the employees.[580] It was held in one case, for instance, that manage-

---

[575] Virginia-Carolina Chemical Corp., 18 LA 892, 895 (Hepburn, 1952). In J. A. McMahon Co., 44 LA 1274, 1277–1279 (Dworkin, 1964), an employee's physical condition made him uninsurable and this was a "legitimate" reason for placing him on layoff status under the contract.

[576] See Arbitrator Block in 49 LA 1144, 1147; Malkin in 49 LA 663, 665; France in 43 LA 934, 938; Willingham in 41 LA 40, 46 (employee could not do all elements of job due to fear of heights); Duff in 29 LA 167, 170; Wolff in 27 LA 682, 684; Hawley in 26 LA 245, 248; Morris in 24 LA 745, 746; Cornsweet in 17 LA 580, 586–587.

[577] See Arbitrator Simon in 53 LA 1181, 1192; Killingsworth in 47 LA 146, 150; Murphy in 44 LA 1252, 1263; Porter in 42 LA 137, 138; Autry in 41 LA 519, 523; Tripp in 41 LA 112, 116–117; Ryder in 38 LA 105, 107; Keeler in 36 LA 970, 973–974; Copelof in 7 LA 560, 563–564. Also see Davey in 55 LA 1206, 1214 (demotion upheld though failure to take required training course was due to employee's nervous condition). Cf., Arbitrator Horlacher in 39 LA 107, 110–113 (demotion based primarily upon workmen's compensation medical reports and award). In Simoniz Co., 54 LA 172, 174–175 (Talent, 1969), an employee claimed (unsuccessfully) a contractual right to demotion on the basis of his alleged physical condition.

[578] North American Aviation, Inc., 20 LA 789, 794 (Komaroff, 1953). In Pacific Gas & Electric Co., 48 LA 264, 266 (Koven, 1966), a service man who made improper advances to a female customer could be demoted from his public-contact job.

[579] Bethlehem Steel Co., 18 LA 368, 369 (Feinberg, 1951). Also see Arbitrator Emery in 37 LA 973, 975. For cases dealing with how long a period management may be permitted to determine the fitness of an employee who has been promoted, see Arbitrator Owen in 49 LA 669, 672; Burns in 48 LA 270, 272.

[580] See Arbitrator Moberly in 55 LA 69, 72–73; McDermott in 48 LA 1108, 1111 (also noting the view that disciplinary demotion may be viewed as an indeterminate sentence which has no terminal point and may go far beyond the extent of the penalty warranted by the infraction committed); Kelliher in 48

ment did not have the right to use temporary demotion as a means of discipline for negligence in job performance (as opposed to lack of ability to perform the job), where such discipline was not provided for specifically by the agreement and where the demoted employee's position was temporarily filled by a junior employee in contravention of the seniority clause. The arbitrator said:

> "The company's right to discipline flows from the general managerial prerogative recognized in the management clause. In accordance with established legal construction, the exercise of such general prerogatives is limited by the specific clauses in the labor agreement. Thus, management in exercising its general prerogatives lacks the contractual right to abridge designated contractual privileges of the employees covered by the agreement unless specific provision is made for [such] * * *"[581]

Management has also been denied the right to discipline an employee by demotion where the contract gave the employer the right to discipline employees by various specified means which did not include demotion, on the theory of "expressio unius est exclusio alterius."[582] Management likewise has not been upheld in demoting an employee for occasional carelessness or failure to obey instructions, the arbitrator distinguishing between a lack of ability and temporary poor performance, but recognizing that some form of discipline should be imposed in such a case.[583]

On the other hand, management has been held justified in using demotion as a form of discipline where the employee's refusal to obey a work order was typical of his uncooperative attitude and the contract did not set out any particular methods of discipline,[584] and where

---

LA 454, 456; Kesselman in 47 LA 154, 157–158; Rosen in 47 LA 67, 73; Dworkin in 46 LA 1098, 1105; Blumer in 6 LA 379, 382. Also see Reid in 33 LA 108, 110; Hawley in 26 LA 245, 247–248. Cf., Altieri in 39 LA 1143, 1147. Arbitrators have reached different conclusions as to whether disciplinary demotion is permitted under a clause giving the right to "demote" for "cause." See Arbitrator Crawford in Lukens Steel Co., 42 LA 252, 254 (1963), not permitting it; Updegraff in Macomber, Inc., 37 LA 1061, 1063–1064 (1961), permitting it.

[581] American Steel & Wire Co., 6 LA 379, 382 (Blumer, 1946).

[582] See Reynolds Alloys Co., 2 LA 554, 555 McCoy, 1943). Also see Arbitrator Kelliher in 48 LA 454, 456; Dworkin in 46 LA 1098, 1105; McCoy in 14 LA 882, 883. Also see Chapter 9, topic titled "To Express One Thing Is to Exclude Another."

[583] Republic Steel Corp., 25 LA 733, 735 (Platt, 1955). Similarly, see Arbitrator Moberly in 55 LA 69, 73; Valtin in 28 LA 330, 332.

[584] Lewers & Cooke, Ltd., 30 LA 542, 545 (Cobb, 1958). Also permitting demotion as discipline, see Arbitrator Yagoda in 46 LA 1034, 1038–1039; Altieri

demotion of the employee was deemed necessary as a safety measure.[585] Finally, it has been emphasized that if demotion is used as discipline, the contract's procedural requirements for discipline must be met.[586]

Discharge and Discipline

The right of management to discipline or discharge employees has been dealt with extensively by arbitrators and is a subject to which a separate chapter is devoted in this book. For discussion of discharge and discipline the reader is directed to Chapter 15.

For discussion of nondisciplinary termination of employees the reader is directed to the present Chapter, topics titled "Compulsory Retirement" and "Disqualifying Employees for Physical or Mental Reasons."

Merit Increases

Merit rating is concerned not with what an employee does but with how he does it. Thus, it may be immaterial that some employees receive a higher rate than others doing the same work.[587] Furthermore, in determining eligibility for merit increases, there is no presumption of progress or improvement due solely to passage of time.[588]

The collective agreement may make specific provision for merit increases.[589] In this regard, Arbitrator Dudley E. Whiting observed:

> "It is well established that merit increases are an appropriate subject for collective bargaining, and bargaining thereon frequently results in contractual provisions establishing objective standards for

---

in 39 LA 1143, 1147; Lehoczky in 8 LA 923, 924 (the arbitrator did not speak of "discipline" but the demotion was clearly disciplinary).

[585] See Braniff Airways, Inc., 29 LA 487, 488–489 (Yeager, 1957); Connecticut Power Co., 18 LA 457, 458–459 (Donnelly & Mottram, Curry dissenting, 1952). Also see Arbitrator Tongue in 36 LA 1038, 1041; Morgan in 17 LA 328, 329.

[586] Alexander's Markets, Inc., 51 LA 165, 168, 170 (Levin, 1968).

[587] Bethlehem Steel Co., 21 LA 614, 616 (Feinberg, 1953); International Harvester Co., 14 LA 77, 79 (Seward, 1948).

[588] Ralph C. Coxhead Corp., 21 LA 480, 483 (Cahn, 1953).

[589] As did the agreement involved in Davis Co., 41 LA 932, 933 (Holly, 1963), where the arbitrator emphasized that the word "merit" implies increases, not decreases, in pay under a clause authorizing management to fix wages of individual employees "on a basis of merit."

merit increases or fixing a regular review period or making such increases subject to review or negotiation by the union, or other types of such provisions."[590]

Where a collective agreement specified minimum wage rates for classifications and provided for a ten-cent-per-hour premium over the rates shown "for an employee in any of such classifications who achieves and applies a high degree of proficiency in all phases of his work, as determined by the Employer," Arbitrator Gerald G. Somers held that this specific provision for rewarding meritorious service implied that it was the only means of giving individual merit increases without negotiations.[591] Arbitrator Somers also expressed the view that, absent a clause expressly giving management such right, management cannot unilaterally give individual increases under any agreement which contains a wage schedule.[592]

However, in another case Arbitrator Thomas J. McDermott rejected a union contention that merit increases were no longer a matter of unilateral determination by management (as they had been by past practice) after minimum and maximum salary ranges were written into the collective agreement. Arbitrator McDermott explained:

"It should be noted that the subject of merit increases has long been an appropriate subject for collective bargaining. Therefore, a Union is within its rights when it seeks to negotiate contractual provisions that will eliminate an existing merit wage increase program, modify it, or that will establish contractual procedures for the operation of any such program. However, if the Union fails to negotiate such contractual provisions, it is not within the power of an arbitrator, absent mutual permission of the parties, either to abolish an existing merit increase system or to write procedures into the contract as to how such system will be administered.

*　　　　*　　　　*　　　　*　　　　*

---

[590] Sommers & Adams Co., 6 LA 283, 285 (1947).

[591] J. Gruman Steel Co., 54 LA 521, 522, 524–525 (1970). Also see Valve Corporation of America, 48 LA 869, 871–872 (Johnson, 1967).

[592] J. Gruman Steel Co., 54 LA 521, 525 (1970). Similarly, see Frito-Lay, Inc., 42 LA 426, 428–429 (Lee, 1964). Even where a unilateral right of management to give merit increases on an individual basis is conceded, this does not include the right to give a blanket increase to a group of employees. Atlanta Newspapers, Inc., 43 LA 758, 759–760 (King, 1964). In NLRB v. C & C Plywood, 87 S.Ct. 559 (1967), the contract expressly recognized management's right to give individual merit increases but this did not include the right to give group increases. The case concerned the duty to bargain under the NLRA. For further discussion, see this Chapter, subtopic titled "The Duty to Bargain: Right of Unilateral Action."

"* * * [W]hat the Union negotiated into the 1968 contract was a set of rate ranges to apply to salaried workers in the bargaining unit. Nothing was agreed to that relates to how individual employees would move from the bottom job rate in his class to the upper limit. In the absence of any such contractual language, and in view of the past practice that has prevailed at this plant, this determination still remains a function of management. In such circumstances the conclusions of management with respect to the granting of specific merit increases are not generally subject to successful challenge in arbitration unless it can be shown in individual cases that management acted unfairly, arbitrarily, discriminatorily, or completely unreasonable. This has long been the generally-held principle in arbitration. Thus, the negotiation of the rate ranges did not, as the Union contends, eliminate the merit increase system. The very presence of a rate range requires either that the maximum rate be achieved through a prescribed procedure, usually referred to as automatic progression, or in the absence of joint agreement on such procedure, the movement from bottom to top remains subject to the evaluation of management.

"* * * There is no right in the existing agreement for the Union to insist that the Company negotiate individual merit increase cases. The most that can be required is that, given the requirement in Paragraph 2 of the intent to establish a harmonious relationship, the Company has the obligation to discuss cases with the Union and to explain the Company position. It does not have to secure Union agreement, and it retains the right to make the final determination. As long as that determination was not arbitrary, unfair, discriminatory or very unreasonable it is not subject to being overruled."[593]

Numerous other arbitrators have similarly recognized that where the collective agreement contains no provision regarding the granting of merit increases or where it makes provision for merit increases without stating by whom the initial determination is to be made, the determination of when individual employees should be given merit increases still remains the function of management.[594]

---

[593] H. K. Porter Co., 55 LA 593, 595–596 (1970). In Means Stamping Co., 46 LA 324, 326 (Cole, 1966), the contract stated maximum and minimum rates for classifications and it was held that management could not give merit increases which would result in rates above the specified maximum.

[594] See Arbitrator Seidenberg in 41 LA 314, 315; Wood in 40 LA 143, 145–146; Feinberg in 21 LA 614, 616; Beneduce in 17 LA 568, 569–570; Luskin in 15 LA 180, 181–182; Townsend in 15 LA 4, 12; Updegraff in 10 LA 678, 680; Abernethy in 7 LA 202, 217; Whiting in 6 LA 283, 285; Gorder in 3 LA 1, 3. Also see Kates in 45 LA 153, 155–156; Porter in 40 LA 411, 413; Cahn in 14 LA 96, 102. This right may be held to be included within a general management rights clause (see Arbitrator Platt in 9 LA 91, 94–95), or it may be given specifically to management by the agreement (see Arbitrator Seward in 26 LA 824, 826, and Bernstein in 14 LA 139, 142).

Where management has the right to make this determination (regardless of the source of the right), it appears clear that its conclusions in regard to merit increases are not generally subject to successful challenge in arbitration unless unfair, arbitrary, or discriminatory,[595] or unless the decision is based upon a misconception of existing facts or insufficient evidence.[596] In this general connection, Arbitrator I. Robert Feinberg stated:

> "[M]erit is difficult to prove and the parties themselves, through daily observation of the employee, have usually gained greater knowledge of the employee's abilities and efficiency than the Umpire can ever have. In the absence of detailed proof, a third party is generally not in a position to determine whether an employee has demonstrated increased efficiency or whether the quality of his work has improved. It is recognized that that determination can best be made by the employee's supervisor, who is closest to the employee in these matters."[597]

Under certain circumstances management may be required to review employee merit ratings at reasonable intervals. This was the result under an agreement which, in providing for merit increases, gave management the right to make initial determinations but required management to be "fair,"[598] and it was also the result under another agreement which permitted the company to determine merit increases subject only to the restriction that the determination not be arbitrary or capricious.[599] Of course, as noted above, the contract may specifically provide for periodic review of each employee's rate and record.[600]

---

[595] See Arbitrator Cayton in 50 LA 296, 298; Kates in 48 LA 606, 608; Altrock in 47 LA 126, 128; Stouffer in 40 LA 452, 454–456; Wood in 40 LA 143, 146; McIntosh in 39 LA 799, 800; Feinberg in 21 LA 614, 616; Cahn in 21 LA 480, 482–483 (who considered criteria used by management in evaluating eligibility for merit increases); Bernstein in 14 LA 139, 143; Updegraff in 10 LA 678, 680; Platt in 9 LA 91, 95–96; Abernethy in 7 LA 202, 217.

[596] Bethlehem Steel Co., 21 LA 614, 616 (Feinberg, 1953); Atlas Imperial Diesel Engine Co., 3 LA 1, 4 (Gorder, 1946). In Dahlstrom Mfg. Corp., 39 LA 90, 92 (Duff, 1961), the contract expressly required management to state its reason for refusing a merit increase; the arbitrator said that this "strongly implies that Management's reason must not be arbitrary, capricious or discriminatory. When challenged in Arbitration, the Company should show that its reason is based on evidence and standards that are reasonable, demonstrable and objective."

[597] Bethlehem Steel Co., 21 LA 614, 616 (1953). Similar language was used by Arbitrator Duff in 39 LA 90, 92 ("Management's discretion must be heavily relied upon because no other rule is practicable"); Cahn in 21 LA 480, 483; Warren in 16 LA 508, 509; Bernstein in 14 LA 139, 143.

[598] International Harvester Co., 13 LA 809, 812 (Seward, 1949).

[599] Bethlehem Steel Co., 26 LA 824, 826 (Seward, 1956).

[600] As in Pacific Airmotive Corp., 16 LA 508, 508–509 (Warren, 1951).

Bonuses

Arbitrators have ruled both ways on the question of the right of management, in the absence of contractual limitation, unilaterally to eliminate or alter bonus practices.[601]

In cases where the facts indicated that the bonus had become an integral part of the wage structure, thus constituting a deferred wage payment, arbitrators have held that management may not unilaterally eliminate or alter bonus plans, despite the fact that bonuses were not mentioned in the contract.[602] The presence of several or all of the following types of evidence would tend to indicate that a bonus has become an integral part of wages: long usage; treatment by the company of bonus payments as relevant considerations during contract negotiations, in wage calculations (such as vacation pay), or in hiring; failure of the company to make it clear that the bonus was a gift or gratuity; stability and predictability of the amount of the bonus; relating the bonus to work performed by the employee; payment of the bonus in such a way as to create an expectation by the employees at the end of the year.[603]

On the other hand, in cases where the facts indicated that the bonus was a gratuity given at the discretion of management and not paid as part of wages, management was permitted unilaterally to alter or eliminate the bonus plan in the absence of contractual restriction.[604]

---

[601] For important related materials, see Chapter 12, topic titled "Custom and Practice as Part of the Contract."

[602] See Arbitrator Anrod in 45 LA 34, 37–38; Seitz in 43 LA 892, 894–896; Horlacher in 43 LA 145, 149–151; Ellmann in 42 LA 415, 416; Berkowitz in 41 LA 182, 184; Crawford in 36 LA 1335, 1340, and in 34 LA 732, 739–740; Dash in 22 LA 808, 818–819; Justin in 17 LA 505, 509–510; Prasow in 5 LA 564, 571; Courshon in 2 LA 509, 514; McCoy in 2 LA 483, 490. Also see Stutz in 29 LA 400, 404; Sullivan in 25 LA 165, 170; Lehoczky in 15 LA 618, 622, all involving contract clauses providing for payment of bonuses to employees.

[603] See cases cited in previous footnote. Maintenance of benefits clauses have had some weight in some cases (see Arbitrator Emery in 65-2 ARB ¶8464; Ellmann in 42 LA 415, 416; Berkowitz in 41 LA 182, 184), but not in others (see Stein in 42 LA 765, 766; Singer in 33 LA 139, 140; Klamon in 32 LA 395, 399–400), depending upon other supporting evidence.

[604] See Arbitrator Larkin in 55 LA 329, 335–336; Eaton in 51 LA 533, 536–537; Small in 46 LA 1077, 1078; Singer in 46 LA 472, 472–473, and in 33 LA 139, 140; Stein in 42 LA 765, 766; Russell in 42 LA 417, 419–420; Kelliher in 42 LA 331, 332–333; McIntosh in 38 LA 216, 217; Duff in 34 LA 586, 592, and in 32 LA 388, 392–393; Klamon in 32 LA 395, 399–401; Kheel in 26 LA 627, 628–630; Kharas in 25 LA 853, 855–856; Delehanty in 24 LA 500, 506; Cheney in 8 LA 518, 526; Cahn in 6 LA 654. Under

The presence of several or all of the following types of evidence would tend to indicate that the bonus is a gift: annual consideration and vote by the board of directors as to whether, when, and how much to pay; distribution of bonus checks separately from pay checks; variation in amount or nature of the bonus; payment to all employees without having previously announced a bonus plan; statements posted by the company that bonus payments are discretionary and union acquiescence in some way to such statements.[605]

The development of the concept of the compulsory bargaining obligation, treated earlier in this Chapter, has a bearing on what individual arbitrators will do with respect to this type of matter.

Compulsory Retirement

In the earlier cases on compulsory retirement due to age, arbitrators often stated that it was a general principle that in the absence of specific contractual restriction management has the right unilaterally to establish compulsory retirement plans (in some of these cases the arbitrator expressly denied that compulsory retirement would violate the seniority or discharge provisions of the agreement).[606] However, in upholding compulsory retirement these arbitrators and others (who did not state such general principle) usually have emphasized the fact that the plan under consideration was of long standing; that it had been established and administered without objection from the union; and that it had been administered without arbitrariness, discrimination, or caprice.[607] On the other hand, where the collective

---

particular contract clauses providing for a bonus, a bonus may nevertheless be considered a gratuity. See Cheney in 10 LA 341, 344; Epstein in 3 LA 412, 418. In T & M Rubber Specialties Co., 54 LA 292, 296–298 (Sembower, 1970), the arbitrator concluded that the bonus was not a gratuity but that he could not make an award in favor of the employees since the amount for payment as bonuses had been determined by the board of directors in the past depending on "success of year"; he directed the parties to bargain on the matter.

[605] See cases cited in previous footnote.

[606] See Arbitrator Prasow in 27 LA 153, 156; Shister in 25 LA 50, 52–53; Reynolds in 13 LA 326, 328–329; Gregory in 9 LA 560, 561; Gorsuch in 9 LA 124, 126; Ridge in 7 LA 773, 778; Kirsh in 4 LA 601, 603–604.

[607] Again, see the cases cited in the preceding footnote. For cases in which the arbitrator emphasized these facts while not stating the aforementioned principle, see Arbitrator Prasow in 50 LA 645, 657; Gilden in 46 LA 302, 305, and in 22 LA 732, 735–736; Schedler in 29 LA 541, 543–545, and in 27 LA 669, 671; Shipman in 23 LA 214, 216–217; McConnell in 17 LA 587, 589; Lehoczky in 14 LA 490, 491–492. In United States Steel Corporation v. Nichols,

agreement was likewise silent as to compulsory retirement but where there was no established policy of compulsory retirement which had been accepted in practice by both parties, many arbitrators have held that compulsory retirement violated the seniority, discharge, or discrimination provisions of the agreement.[608]

Notwithstanding the significance which many cases have placed upon the existence or absence of a long standing and applied compulsory retirement policy in determining whether to uphold compulsory retirement, there have been some relatively late cases upholding management's unilateral institution of compulsory retirement (where the agreement did not expressly restrict the right) even though there was no established practice for it.[609]

Finally, we may note that there are some interesting arbitration cases in which the agreement dealt expressly with retirement but left the compulsory vs. voluntary aspect to implication only, or in which

---

229 F.2d 396, 399–400, 37 LRRM 2420 (CA 6, 1956), certiorari denied 351 U.S. 950, the company had a reasonable and nondiscriminatory policy of compulsory retirement going back some years. Then the parties bargained on the question of dealing expressly with the subject in the collective agreement. The court held that their failure to reach agreement did not deprive management of the right to compel an employee to retire under its policy and that the employer did not violate the collective agreement in doing so (the employee had alleged violation of the "proper cause" for discharge provision). For related discussion, see this Chapter, subtopic titled "The Duty to Bargain: Right of Unilateral Action." The "Nichols" case was discussed by Arbitrator Young in 55 LA 933, 935–937, 943; Sembower in 50 LA 1177, 1181; Altieri in 42 LA 559, 560–562; Teple in 39 LA 1003, 1007–1008; Jones in 37 LA 771, 775–776; Ross in 32 LA 713, 717–718.

[608] See Arbitrator Anrod in 56 LA 251, 253–255; Young in 55 LA 933, 942–943; Gorsuch in 51 LA 909, 913–915; Moore in 51 LA 46, 48–49; Sembower in 50 LA 1177, 1180–1182 (contract was not silent but was ambiguous as to compulsory retirement); Block in 49 LA 224, 227–228; Larkin in 47 LA 513, 516–518 (past practice of compulsory retirement not adequately shown, but even if shown the arbitrator stated it would violate seniority provisions of contract); Altieri in 42 LA 559, 561–562; Scheiber in 42 LA 483, 489–490 (most recent practice was not to compel retirement); Teple in 39 LA 1003, 1007–1010; Jones in 37 LA 771, 775–777; Granoff in 37 LA 350, 355; Schedler in 33 LA 84, 87–88; Hepburn in 32 LA 1022, 1025; Ross in 32 LA 713, 717–719, and in 25 LA 77, 79–82; Justin in 9 LA 921, 924–926.

[609] In particular see the comments and holding of Arbitrator Beatty in Packaging Corp. of America, 40 LA 544, 546–547 (1963). Also see Arbitrator Rice in 50 LA 597, 600; Bell in 45 LA 500, 500–502. In Updegraff, Arbitration and Labor Relations 321 (1970), it is stated that "the employer's traditional authority to terminate or retire employees continues to inhere in management unless modified by statute or by a contract." It may be noted that the Age Discrimination in Employment Act of 1967 does not apply to employees under the age of 40 or over the age of 64.

an aspect of the case concerned the question whether an employee may be retained in service after reaching the normal retirement age.[610]

Disqualifying Employees for Physical or Mental Reasons

The material contained in the present topic constitutes only a portion of the Authors' treatment of the subject. For other portions the reader is directed to Chapter 8, topic titled "Medical Evidence," and to Chapter 16, topic titled "Physical or Mental Condition as a Safety Hazard."

There are a great many reported arbitration decisions concerning managerial action in disqualifying employees for physical or mental reasons. While the disqualification often is in the form of termination, it also may be effected by layoff, leave of absence, or a refusal to permit the employee to return to work following an accident or medical leave.

There are many cases upholding management's right to terminate employees whose physical condition renders them unable or unfit to perform their job,[611] and there are cases upholding the disqualification of employees because of mental unfitness (psychiatric problems or mental illness) for work.[612] There are many other cases which have

---

[610] See Arbitrator Shipman in 50 LA 90, 92–94 (agreement provided employee "may" retire at age 65 "or at any time thereafter"); Kates in 46 LA 916, 919–920 (agreement provided that "employment after age 65 shall be with the mutual consent of the company and the union"); Young in 44 LA 45, 50–51 (employer not required to discharge employee who had retired at voluntary retirement age but who had been allowed by employer to return to work); Small in 41 LA 370, 372 (agreement provided "employee may be permitted to remain" in employment after normal retirement age of 65 until attainment of age 70).

[611] For example, see Arbitrator Holly in 51 LA 579, 581; Blair in 44 LA 635, 639–640; Duff in 43 LA 678, 680–682; Epstein in 43 LA 640, 643; Seinsheimer in 43 LA 613, 615; Autrey in 41 LA 796, 799–800; Updegraff in 39 LA 53, 57–58 (employer could terminate four employees, all 65 or older, whose work was too heavy for them to keep up in view of physical disabilities that had developed with advanced age). Also see Kerrison in 45 LA 724, 726 (employer could refuse to permit return to work). But under the facts of some cases the arbitrator considered transfer or demotion, rather than termination, to be warranted. See Arbitrator Roberts in 49 LA 121, 126; Keefe in 45 LA 986, 989–990. For related discussion, see this Chapter, topic titled "Demotion of Employees."

[612] See United States Steel Corp., 46 LA 545, 548–549 (Rock, 1966), upholding refusal to recall; Fischer Scientific Company, 66-1 ARB ¶8011 (Turkus, 1965), upholding discharge. Also see Arbitrator Hazelwood in 56 LA 832, 834. For mental illness cases in which the arbitrator found the employee fit for return to work, see Arbitrator Stouffer in 43 LA 959, 963; Davis in 43 LA 568,

upheld termination because the employee's physical or mental condition rendered his continued employment unduly hazardous to himself or to others.[613]

On the other hand, there are many cases in which the arbitrator required management to return an employee to work where the evidence indicated that the employee was not so affected or disabled as to be unable to perform his job satisfactorily or safely.[614] A similar result has been reached where the employee's condition had existed for a long period of time, during which the employee had performed satisfactorily and safely.[615] In one case management could not terminate an employee who was physically handicapped when hired seventeen years earlier, whose condition was not deteriorating, and who, though a slow worker, had not received any complaint from supervision as to his work.[616]

Significance of Workmen's Compensation Disabilities and Costs

The mere fact that an employee has previously been awarded workmen's compensation for permanent partial disability (or has received compensation under a settlement of his claim) does not per se establish his inability or unfitness for employment so as to justify management's refusal to use him.[617] In one case an employee had

---

569; Guthrie in 38 LA 297, 299. For cases in which mental illness was asserted as a mitigating factor in discharge for misconduct, see Arbitrator Sugerman in 49 LA 564, 568; Coffey in 39 LA 604, 606.

[613] See Chapter 16, topic titled "Physical or Mental Condition as a Safety Hazard."

[614] For example, see Arbitrator McDermott in 48 LA 1271, 1274 (obese employee); Kevin in 45 LA 217, 221; Cobb in 43 LA 599, 600–601; Cahn in 42 LA 1042, 1044 (loss of one eye); Kabaker in 42 LA 513, 517; Berkowitz in 42 LA 374, 376; Scheiber in 41 LA 278, 284; Valtin in 39 LA 918, 920–921; Ross in 24 LA 857, 861–862 (further employment conditioned on employee's taking treatment for his ailment); Williams in 20 LA 784, 787 (no showing that prior ailment was likely to recur); Pollard in 18 LA 889, 892. Also see McNaughton in 50 LA 1277, 1279. Management's action may be especially vulnerable if taken without or in complete disregard of professional medical opinion. See Arbitrator Keefe in 50 LA 965, 968; Dybeck in 48 LA 1085, 1087–1088; McDermott in 37 LA 736, 737.

[615] See Arbitrator Dworkin in 46 LA 719, 723–724; Teple in 42 LA 818, 821–822; Lande in 40 LA 799, 804–805.

[616] American Optical Co., 42 LA 818, 821–822 (Teple, 1964).

[617] See Arbitrator Teple in 53 LA 334, 337 (compensation agency's finding of 25 percent permanent disability was not proof of actual inability to perform work); Ray in 52 LA 55, 56; Somers in 51 LA 137, 140 (arbitrator should take notice of agency's 33 percent disability finding but it is not conclusive as to right

asserted and affirmed in a settlement agreement that "my injuries are serious, disabling and permanent in nature," and that such "permanent disability does seriously affect my ability to perform the type of work for which I am otherwise qualified." The arbitrator declared that this was not conclusive as to the employee's physical status three months later and that the employer improperly refused to permit his return to work where the employer offered no other evidence to establish the employee's inability to work and where the employee's physician certified to his physical capacity to perform the job.[618]

Moreover, where it was found that an employee was otherwise able and fit to perform his job, some arbitrators have not permitted the employer to deny the right to continued employment merely because it could impose workmen's compensation liability on the employer in the future or could increase his insurance rates.[619] However, other arbitrators have indicated that these potential liabilities are relevant though not conclusive considerations in reference to the right to continued employment.[620]

Excessive Absences Due to Illness

All reasonable management readily excuses occasional absences due to illness. However, management may properly seek to guard against false claims of illness.[621] Moreover, it may feel impelled to terminate employees whose genuinely poor condition of health requires excessive absences.

The right to terminate employees for excessive absences, even where they are due to illness, is generally recognized by arbitrators.[622]

---

to return to work); Allen in 50 LA 1152, 1155 (10 percent disability); Emery in 49 LA 403, 404–405 (50 percent disability); Roberts in 47 LA 812, 815, and in 37 LA 729, 731–732; Kiroff in 42 LA 1051, 1055–1056 (50 percent disability); Sembower in 42 LA 734, 736–737, 739; Blumrosen in 42 LA 392, 398–399; Volz in 39 LA 138, 141–142 (35 percent disability); Jaffee in 36 LA 797, 803, and in 19 LA 189, 191; Cayton in 34 LA 149, 152. But see Epstein in 43 LA 640, 643; Crawford in 39 LA 600, 602–603; Stouffer in 34 LA 204, 206–207.
  [618] Goodyear Tire and Rubber Co., 52 LA 55, 56 (Ray, 1968).
  [619] See Arbitrator Kevin in 45 LA 217, 221; Kabaker in 42 LA 513, 517; Berkowitz in 42 LA 374, 376.
  [620] See Arbitrator Somers in 51 LA 137, 143; Seinsheimer in 50 LA 1171, 1176 (management has right "to protect itself"); Stouffer in 34 LA 204, 208.
  [621] For discussion of the steps available to management for this purpose, see Chapter 17, subtopic titled "Sick Leave."
  [622] For example, see Arbitrator Teple in 48 LA 615, 618; Anderson in 46 LA 436, 439–440 (but the employee could not be denied insurance or pension

In this regard, Arbitrator Edwin R. Teple explained:

> "At some point the employer must be able to terminate the services of an employee who is unable to work more than part time, for whatever reason. Efficiency and the ability to compete can hardly be maintained if employees cannot be depended upon to report for work with reasonable regularity. Other arbitrators have so found, and this Arbitrator has upheld terminations in several appropriate cases involving frequent and extended absences due to illness."[623]

Examination of the cases makes it readily apparent that there is no fixed or generally accepted rule as to when the "excessive" absence point is reached—the particular facts and circumstances of the given case often will be considered along with the number of absences, the amount of time involved, and the prospects as to future absences. Moreover, an arbitrator may require considerable tolerance on the part of management where the equities in favor of the employee are strong.[624]

In one case the arbitrator recognized the general right of management to terminate employees for excessive absences due to illness, but he stated that the right "cannot be exercised capriciously or with disregard for the employee's seniority and stake in maturing fringe benefits." He also noted a distinction between "intermittent" absences and "extended" absences, pointing out that an extended absence imposes a lesser burden upon management in that it permits "continuous coverage of the vacancy without taxing the employer with constant uncertainty over the filling of the opening."[625]

Right to Require Physical Examination

Management's good faith right to require job applicants to submit to a physical examination is so basic that it has rarely been an

---

benefits, there being no misconduct); Klamon in 43 LA 703, 714; Duff in 43 LA 678, 680–682 (the contract provided that employees "shall not lose their seniority rights" when off due to illness, but the arbitrator said this did not require that sick leave be extended beyond a reasonable time); Solomon in 41 LA 1257, 1267–1268; McCoy in 39 LA 187, 188 (citing many earlier cases).

[623] Cleveland Trencher Co., 48 LA 615, 618 (1967). Also see statement by Arbitrator McCoy in 9 LA 143, 145.

[624] For example, see Trans World Airlines, Inc., 44 LA 280, 282–283 (Gilden, 1965). Also see Arbitrator McCoy in 44 LA 1040, 1043.

[625] Great Atlantic & Pacific Tea Co., 48 LA 910, 912–913 (Keefe, 1967). Also recognizing the latter distinction, see Arbitrator Hale in 35 LA 469, 477; Soule in 14 LA 153, 155.

issue in arbitration.[626] The utility of physical examinations obviously
is not ended once the applicant has been hired and has commenced
service with the employer—situations arise to warrant physical examinations during the employment relationship.

It is clear from reported arbitration decisions that management
has the right, unless restricted by the agreement, to require employees
to have physical examinations where the right is reasonably exercised
under proper circumstances, such as where an employee desires to
return to work following an accident or sick leave, or following extended layoff, or where an employee has bid on a job requiring greater
physical effort.[627] However, it has been emphasized that "this right
is not an absolute one exercisable at the whim" of management, and
that it "cannot be arbitrarily insisted upon without reasonable
grounds."[628]

Selection and Control of Supervisors

Arbitrators have generally recognized it to be the function and
responsibility of management to run the business and to produce
profits. It is generally accepted as an incident to management's right
to control operations that management must be permitted to select

---

[626] In Conveyor Co., 38 LA 1141, 1143 (Roberts, 1962), the arbitrator
emphasized the "inherent right" to require a physical examination of job applicants, but in that case there was strong evidence that the contract was intended
to prohibit exercise of the right.
[627] See Arbitrator Duff in 52 LA 985, 986–987; Kelliher in 50 LA 351,
352; Johnson in 48 LA 1357, 1358; Keefe in 47 LA 1, 6; McIntosh in 46
LA 530, 532; Bothwell in 45 LA 39, 42; Klein in 43 LA 217, 223–224 (in
view of safety considerations, diabetic could be required to submit to weekly
medical examination at his own expense); Phelps in 42 LA 161, 164; Sembower
in 40 LA 37, 42–43; Klamon in 37 LA 960, 966; Donnelly in 37 LA 456,
458; Stouffer in 32 LA 686, 689; Boles in 31 LA 824, 826; Bothwell in 27
LA 404, 406 (could require physical examination in recall); Stashower in 12
LA 896, 897–898. Also see Whitney in 53 LA 1078, 1086 (under past practice
employees had returned to work on basis of their own doctor's certifications,
but this did not make demand for physical examination by company designated
doctor improper where justified by the circumstances). The fact that the contract
states certain ailments or situations for which a physical examination may be
required does not deprive management of the right to require one in other
proper circumstances. See Arbitrator Block in 50 LA 58, 62; Solomon in 42
LA 1, 8–11. Cf., Klein in 42 LA 1151, 1156–1158.
[628] Conchemco, Inc., 55 LA 54, 57 (Ray, 1970), where reasonable grounds
were not found. Also not finding reasonable grounds for requiring physical examinations, see Arbitrator Cahn in 50 LA 833, 835; Dworet in 37 LA 378,
379 (could not require all employees absent two weeks for whatever reason
to submit to physical examination); Daugherty in 36 LA 104, 105–106 (reasonable
grounds did not exist for requiring psychiatric examination).

and control supervisory personnel without union interference.[629] In the words of Arbitrator Dudley E. Whiting:

> "It is a fundamental principle of American industry that the selection and retention of foremen or other supervisory personnel is the sole prerogative of management * * *. There is no doubt that the union may not, as a matter of right, demand the dismissal or demotion of a foreman and that such a demand is not a proper subject matter for a grievance."[630]

Thus, Arbitrator Whitley P. McCoy held that unless the agreement expressly permits, or the employer waives the jurisdiction issue and submits the dispute on the merits, a demand by the union for discipline or discharge of a supervisory employee ordinarily is not arbitrable, and that even where the arbitrator can exercise jurisdiction in such disputes, he should do so sparingly and only on very clear grounds.[631] Numerous other arbitrators have taken positions in general agreement with this view, either by holding the union's demand to be nonarbitrable,[632] or by holding that the arbitrator has no authority to order management to punish supervisory personnel.[633]

---

[629] For cases illustrating management's broad control and discretion as to supervisory personnel, see Arbitrator Bothwell in 51 LA 1113, 1115 (can pay management personnel on any basis employer desires); Williams in 51 LA 296, 297–298; Sembower in 51 LA 197, 199–200 (employer has right to determine how many persons are to be made supervisors); Shister in 44 LA 992, 993; Seidenberg in 44 LA 145, 147–148 (selection of supervisors is not governed by seniority or other contract provisions); Oppenheim in 43 LA 9, 11; Hawley in 42 LA 79, 82 (need not consider seniority in filling temporary vacancy in foreman position); Williams in 27 LA 432, 436–437 ("Supervisors hold their positions at the will of the company except where the company has specifically yielded its power"); Whiting in 11 LA 1023, 1031. In San Francisco-Oakland Mailers' Union, 69 LRRM 1157 (NLRB, 1968), a union violated the NLRA by fining foremen who by contract were required to be union members, the Board finding that the union had interfered with the employer's choice of representatives for collective bargaining. For arbitral emphasis of management's NLRA right of control over supervisors, see Arbitrator Updegraff in 49 LA 1154, 1155; Purdom in 38 LA 301, 305–306. For the application of contracts which require foremen to be union members but which limit the union's right to discipline them, see Arbitrator Smith in 43 LA 1073, 1075–1083; Rohman in 40 LA 619, 621–624.

[630] King Powder Co., 1 LA 215, 216 (Whiting, 1944). This also was the view of the War Labor Board. Stanoland Oil & Gas, 20 War Lab. Rep. 211 (1944).

[631] Electro Metallurgical Co., 19 LA 8, 8–10 (1952).

[632] See Arbitrator Solomon in 53 LA 878, 884–886; Sembower in 49 LA 752, 757–760; Brecht in 27 LA 806, 810; Cornsweet in 13 LA 949, 950; Selekman in 5 LA 684, 686; Smith in 1 LA 75, 78–79. Also see Coffey in 45 LA 707, 710–712. In San Juan Star, 43 LA 445, 445–446 (Helfed, 1964), the employer did agree to arbitrate the alleged misconduct of two supervisors and the submission agreement specified that they would be discharged if the charges were established (they were not established).

[633] See Arbitrator Geissinger in 50 LA 221, 225–226; Hilpert in 47 LA 686, 690–691; Klamon in 15 LA 32, 35 (only in "very rare and unusual circum-

However, while recognizing management's control over supervisors as a general right, Arbitrator McCoy explained in another case that "in very extreme cases, where a foreman's conduct is beyond the limits of lawfulness or decency, making for an intolerable condition which management itself could not with decency condone, it may become arbitrable," or where there is "a menace to the life and health of the employees while at their work" an arbitrable issue may be presented.[634] In still another case Arbitrator McCoy required an employer to remove from the department a foreman who, on many occasions, had used profanity in the presence of women employees and had addressed obscene remarks to them. In requiring the removal, he said that "management has, by contract (seniority clauses, etc.), given the employees rights to their jobs under decent working conditions."[635]

Furthermore, even where management may not be required to discipline supervisors, it will be required to compensate employees injured by their wrongful acts.[636] Umpire Harry Shulman, for instance, ruled that "to the extent that a foreman or other representative of managerial authority takes action detrimental to an employee and in violation of the parties' contract, the grievance procedure is properly invoked to provide appropriate redress." He added, however, that "what is called for is protection of the employees within their contractual rights as distinguished from mere punishment of the Company's supervisory or other managerial representatives," and that, while punishment of a supervisor may be the only feasible way to stop improper treatment of employees, the Umpire can direct that such improper conduct be stopped, but "how the result is to be achieved is * * * a matter normally left to the Company."[637] In an-

---

stances" should the demand be sustained); Copelof in 10 LA 237, 240; Shulman in 1 ALAA ¶67,011; Whiting in 1 LA 215, 216. Cf., Arbitrator Elson in 39 LA 870, 874–875, where the arbitrator ordered the company to "formalize" the reprimand which the company itself had given a supervisor for violating the agreement.

[634] Goodyear Tire & Rubber Co. of Ala., 5 LA 30, 34 (1946).

[635] Continental Can Co., 1 LA 65, 68 (1945). For other cases involving alleged abusive language by foremen, see Arbitrator Florey in 50 LA 976, 977–978; McNaughton in 40 LA 125, 127; Brecht in 27 LA 806, 809–811.

[636] Profile Cotton Mills, 2 LA 537, 538–539 (McCoy, 1942). Also see Arbitrator Brecht in 27 LA 806, 810–811; Cornsweet in 13 LA 949, 950; Whiting in 1 LA 215, 216; Smith in 1 LA 75, 78.

[637] Ford Motor Company, 1 ALAA ¶67,011, p. 67,012 (1945). Also see Arbitrator Jensen in 38 LA 781, 784 (union is entitled to assurances against future misconduct by supervisor but no right to a public apology from him); Dworet in 35 LA 381, 383.

other case Arbitrator John F. Sembower held a grievance demanding the removal of a foreman not to be arbitrable but he gave the union ten days to submit an amended grievance requesting an arbitrable type of relief.[638]

Accompanying the right of management to control supervisors is the function and responsibility to inform them fully as to their rights, authorities, and duties. It has been held that management must compensate employees for any loss suffered as a result of its failure to instruct and train its foremen fully.[639]

Management's right to discipline or discharge supervisors may be limited by contract.[640] In this regard, where bargaining unit employees acquire rights under the contract and later become supervisors, their discharge presents an arbitrable issue insofar as the union claims a right under the collective agreement for the individual to return to the bargaining unit (the claimed right has been upheld in some cases but denied in other cases).[641]

Awards vary on the question of whether management has a right, in the absence of a specific contractual provision on the matter, to place former bargaining unit employees back into the unit on the basis of seniority accumulated during work in the unit or with accumulated seniority for time spent in supervisory service. For discussion and cases on this issue, see Chapter 14, subtopic titled "Service Outside the Seniority Unit."

---

[638] Reserve Mining Co., 49 LA 752, 757–760 (1967), stating that any amended grievance would be returned to a lower step of the grievance procedure for de novo proceedings from that point.

[639] Standard Oil Co. (Indiana), 11 LA 689, 691 (Updegraff, 1948).

[640] Even the captain of a ship was protected by a "just cause" requirement where he was covered by the collective agreement. Cargo & Tankship Management Corp., 38 LA 602, 612 (Gellhorn, 1962). By the agreement management may accept other limitations upon its rights as to supervisors. For example, see Southwest Airmotive Co., 41 LA 353, 358 (Elliott, 1963). Where employees are temporarily transferred to supervisory positions they may remain covered by the agreement for various purposes. See Bethlehem Steel Co., 39 LA 1101, 1103–1104 (Seward, 1963).

[641] See Arbitrator Somers in 57 LA 58, 60–61; Schurke in 56 LA 712, 720; Elliott in 54 LA 965, 972–973, 981; Keefe in 50 LA 1052, 1056; Gibson in 48 LA 1234, 1236–1239; Marshall in 40 LA 193, 198; Merrill in 29 LA 334, 336; Baab in 28 LA 641, 642–643; Williams in 27 LA 432, 436–437; Duff in 26 LA 919, 920–921, Anrod in 25 LA 452, 455; Emery in 16 LA 48, 50.

CHAPTER 14

SENIORITY

One of the most severe limitations upon the exercise of managerial discretion is the requirement of seniority recognition. Indeed, the effect of seniority recognition is dramatic from the standpoint of employer, union, and employee alike since "every seniority provision reduces, to a greater or lesser degree, the employer's control over the work force and compels the union to participate to a corresponding degree in the administration of the system of employment preferences which pits the interests of each worker against those of all the others."[1]

In the absence of a definition of the term in the collective agreement, seniority "is commonly understood to mean the length of service with the employer or in some division of the enterprise."[2] Seniority "means that men retain their jobs according to their length of service with their employer and that men are promoted to better jobs on the same basis."[3] "It is generally recognized that the chief purpose of a seniority plan is to provide maximum security to workers with the longest continuous service."[4]

It should be kept in mind that "seniority is a relationship between employees in the same seniority unit, rather than a relationship between jobs."[5] As stated by Arbitrator Paul Prasow:

"Seniority protects and secures an employee's rights in relation to the rights of other employees in his seniority group; it does not protect him in relation to the existence of the job itself. By the use of an

---

[1] Aaron, "Reflections on the Legal Nature and Enforceability of Seniority Rights," 75 Harv. L. Rev. 1532, 1534–1535 (1962).
[2] Curtiss-Wright Corp., 11 LA 139, 142 (Uible, 1948). Also see Arbitrator Dworkin in 24 LA 73, 76; Williams in 23 LA 366, 367.
[3] Lapp, How to Handle Problems of Seniority 1 (1946). Also see Arbitrator Dworkin in 24 LA 73, 76.
[4] Darin & Armstrong, 13 LA 843, 845 (Platt, 1950). Also see Arbitrator Williams in 23 LA 366, 367; Reid in 22 LA 379, 381; Cole in 21 LA 231, 232.
[5] Axelson Mfg. Co., 30 LA 444, 448 (Prasow, 1958).

objective measure, length of service, the rights of one employee are balanced against other employees' rights."[6]

Because of the interrelationship between employees with respect to seniority rights, one court permitted intervention by employees in an arbitration involving seniority rights of other employees in the same seniority unit, the court saying that in such a controversy "for every person whose seniority is advanced, someone will be adversely affected by such advancement."[7]

Seniority issues in arbitration arise out of the attempt by the parties to promote their respective interests. In this regard, Arbitrator Walter Gellhorn balanced the interests of management against those of the employees and analyzed the "costs" of seniority to both management and employees:

"To be sure, the full utilization of seniors cannot be achieved without costs. When seniors 'get the breaks,' the more ambitious and capable of the junior men may feel frustrated. Moreover, a management that likes to see a clear line of promotability from within the work force does not welcome the inflexibility that sometimes comes from giving preference to older, perhaps less adaptable workers. But these costs were measured when the contract was made. The parties presumably concluded that the price was worth paying. From the standpoint of the men, they must have concluded that the deferment of youthful hope was offset by the assurance of fair opportunity for veteran employees. From the standpoint of management, they must have concluded that an occasional personal rigidity was offset by the enhanced loyalty and stability that are encouraged by an effective seniority clause."[8]

Arbitrator Carl R. Schedler would add the union as an interested party, aside from its representation of the employees:

"Traditionally, a union considers seniority both as a useful organizing tool and as a basic objective in collective bargaining negotiations. It is, therefore, utilized in invoking what is often considered a latent, if unexpressed, need of workers; and, it is also employed to demonstrate the value of concerted activities as opposed to the results workers can expect from trying to 'go it alone' in dealing with management."[9]

In an arbitration situation involving not only contract interpretation but some "interests" aspects also, Arbitrator Marion Beatty fur-

---

[6] Ibid. Also see statement by Arbitrator Cahn in 54 LA 350, 352; Abrahams in 47 LA 325, 326–327.
[7] In re Iroquois Beverage Corp., 28 LA 906, 907 (N.Y. Sup. Ct., 1955).
[8] Universal Atlas Cement Co., 17 LA 755, 757 (1951).
[9] Schedler, "Arbitration of Seniority Questions," 28 LA 954, at 954 (1957).

ther analyzed the struggle in relation to the application of seniority in the extreme situation. He first considered the objectives of the parties: the union struggling for greater security in tenure for certain workmen and the company trying to avoid a "burdensome seniority system carried to the extreme of shuffling men in the course of one day's work." The objectives of both parties, he felt, were proper. Arbitrator Beatty noted that the company was offering the union a job-standing list which would provide for promotion, reduction in force, and overtime in accordance with strict seniority, but not for such short periods as one day's work. In refusing to award the seniority arrangement requested by the union, he stated:

"I must agree with the company that carrying seniority to the extreme requested by the union would make for a wasteful, cumbersome and uneconomical method of operation. It has in it an element of 'made work' (the few minutes or hours that would be necessary in making the shifts in personnel). It can hardly be denied anymore that made work is economically unsound. If carried to the extreme it would make for much work and little production. Efficiency of operations is something to be desired in every business, it enures to the benefit of all including the public, and an enterprise that cannot operate as efficiently as its competition will suffer the consequences."[10]

Source of Seniority "Rights"

Even prior to the advent of collective agreements employers generally gave job preference to their older employees, not as any binding obligation but as a matter of equity, so long as they could do the required work.[11] However, seniority benefits exist as "rights" only to the extent made so by contract.[12] As stated by Arbitrator Joseph Brandschain:

" * * * whatever seniority rights employees have exist only by virtue of the collective bargaining agreement that is in existence be-

---

[10] Standard Oil Co. (Indiana), 24 LA 424, 426–427 (1954).
[11] Lapp, How to Handle Problems of Seniority 2–3 (1946).
[12] See Arbitrator Geissinger in 54 LA 828, 829; Cahn in 54 LA 350, 352, and in 30 LA 221, 222; Killion in 49 LA 1073, 1076; Volz in 48 LA 743, 744; Roberts in 48 LA 621, 624; Williams in 48 LA 184, 185; McCoy in 45 LA 993, 995–996; Buckwalter in 44 LA 301, 303; Scheiber in 37 LA 330, 332; Mitchell in 37 LA 240, 244; Luskin in 35 LA 378, 380; Kabaker in 35 LA 74, 76; Boehm in 32 LA 595, 600–601; Dworkin in 24 LA 73, 76; Shipman in 21 LA 604, 607. Also see Larson in 54 LA 555, 558; Oppenheim in 46 LA 860, 864; Smith in 42 LA 517, 524. For court recognition of this rule, see Aeronautical Industrial Lodge v. Campbell, 69 S.Ct. 1287 (1949); Trailmobile v. Whirls, 67 S.Ct. 982 (1947).

tween the union and the employer. Such seniority rights depend wholly upon the contract. They arise out of the contract. Before a collective bargaining contract is in existence, there are no seniority rights.

"Therefore, until we have a contract, the employer has the right, which he has always exercised, to shift workers around and promote and demote them. The very purpose of collective bargaining was to constrict such rights of management and, reciprocally, to gain for the workers job-security rights based upon seniority and to insure such rights contractually. Thus, we start with the situation, before the existence of a contract, where the employer has all rights in connection with promotions and transfers and need pay no heed to seniority of the workers, and the workers have no rights to promotions or transfers because of length of service.

"How does this situation change when a collective bargaining agreement is in existence? It changes to the extent that these rights are given up by the employer and given to the workers under the terms of the contract. Therefore, whatever the employer has yielded in his absolute time-established rights of hiring, firing, promoting, and demoting and whatever the workers have gained in the way of seniority rights with respect to these matters must be measured entirely by the contract."[13]

Thus an employee who was laid off prior to the effective date of the first contract between the employer and the union was not entitled to any seniority rights or any other rights provided by the contract, which affected only employees of the company who were in its employ on or after the effective date of the contract.[14]

Seniority rights do not necessarily remain static; they may be modified in subsequent agreements, with the current agreement governing. For instance, in ruling that the seniority rights of a returning veteran (who did not qualify for re-employment rights under federal legislation) were governed by the contract in effect at the time of his return, rather than the contract in effect at the time he entered the armed forces, Arbitrator Harry Shulman stated:

"Seniority rights under a collective agreement are entirely the products of the Agreement. Their characteristics and their effects are determined solely by the Agreement. In the absence of special provisions to the contrary, the collective Agreement creates rights and binds parties only for the term of the Agreement. Nothing in * * * [any

---

[13] Alan Wood Steel Co., 4 LA 52, 54 (1946). Also see Arbitrator Rubin in 43 LA 347, 348; McIntosh in 35 LA 682, 683; Uible in 11 LA 139, 143.
  [14] Acme Galvanizing Co., 19 LA 575, 577 (Gooding, 1952). Also see Kansas City Power & Light Co., 52 LA 1087, 1097–1098 (Klamon, 1969).

of the parties'] Agreements indicates a purpose to single out seniority rights for individual employees and give them a vested effectiveness beyond the period of the Agreement and beyond the power of the parties to modify by later Agreements. Modification of prior seniority provisions in subsequent Agreements is a fairly common feature of collective bargaining. And while it is true that such modifications commonly result in the increase of seniority rights of some employees, they also necessarily result in some decrease or change in the seniority rights of other employees."[15]

Collective agreements generally provide for the recognition of seniority in several, and often many, aspects of the employment relationship. Among these are promotions, layoffs, rehiring, shift preference, transfers, vacations, days off, and overtime work. Indeed, consideration of seniority looms so importantly that it has been said that "one of the principle purposes for entering into a collective bargaining agreement is usually to secure for the employees the prized right of seniority in case of layoff and promotion."[16]

Seniority Units

Seniority rights relate to a specific group or unit. Seniority units are defined by the collective agreement either specifically or by interpretation. Among other possibilities, a seniority unit may be plant-wide,[17] multiplant,[18] departmental;[19] or based upon the bargaining unit,[20] or upon an occupational group or classification;[21] or upon a combination of the foregoing.[22] Then, too, some agreements specify recognition of industry seniority for some purposes.[23]

The seniority unit is basic in the computation of length of service and in the assertion and determination of seniority rights. For example,

---

[15] Ford Motor Co., 23 LA 296, 297 (1954). Recognizing that seniority rights provided for in a collective agreement may be modified by agreement of the union and the employer acting in good faith, see Ford Motor Co. v. Huffman, 345 U.S. 330 (1953). For many other court cases, see annotation in 90 ALR 2d 1003, 1004–1006. Noting various respects in which seniority rights may be neither absolute nor permanent, see Kramer, "Seniority and Ability," Management Rights and the Arbitration Process 41, 41–42 (BNA Incorporated, 1956).

[16] Cournoyer v. American Television Co., 28 LA 483, 485 (Minn. Sup. Ct., 1957).

[17] See for example 30 LA 406; 29 LA 83.

[18] See 11 LA 207. Cf. 25 LA 37.

[19] See 27 LA 685; 25 LA 826.

[20] See 57 LA 366; 21 LA 604.

[21] See 52 LA 372; 24 LA 424.

[22] See 30 LA 326; 30 LA 267.

[23] As in Rueter Worth Dairy Co., 45 LA 111, 114 (Elson, 1965).

where a contract called for promotions on the basis of departmental seniority, provided the senior employee was qualified, the employer was not required to make promotions on the basis of plant-wide seniority where all bidders for the job were from outside the department in which the vacancy existed.[24] In another case, where several bargaining units in the plant each had separate agreements with the employer, employees laid off from one unit were not permitted to exercise their seniority to bump employees in another unit; Arbitrator Mitchell M. Shipman stated that since the contracts did not expressly provide otherwise, there was a presumption that layoffs and promotions "are to be made on an intra-bargaining unit basis, with the employee's seniority or length of service computed on his service within his bargaining unit and applied only among employees therein."[25]

Although seniority often is both acquired and exercised in one unit, the contract may provide (or be so interpreted) that seniority is acquired in one unit and exercised in another. For example, a contract provision stating simply that the employer shall operate "on a departmental and plant wide seniority basis" was construed (in the light of past practice and the history of contract negotiations) to mean that seniority was to be exercised on a departmental basis, but measured by length of service in the plant.[26]

Similarly, seniority rights may be based upon different units with respect to the various aspects of the employment relationship. For instance, a contract may provide that departmental seniority shall govern with respect to layoff and recall, while providing for plant seniority to be exercised in bumping.[27]

Seniority Standing and Determining Length of Service

Ordinarily, seniority is based upon length of service, although the collective agreement may provide for exceptions such as "super-

---

[24] Charles Bruning Co., 25 LA 826, 827–829 (Gifford, 1955). Also see Arbitrator Randle in 17 LA 486, 488.

[25] Tide Water Associated Oil Co., 21 LA 604, 607 (1953). Also see Arbitrator Cahn in 54 LA 350, 352; Shipman in 46 LA 1053, 1056.

[26] McFeely Brick Co., 22 LA 379, 382 (Reid, 1954). Also see Arbitrator Kates in 25 LA 338, 340–341.

[27] Harsco Corp., 30 LA 326, 327–328 (Koretz, 1957). Also see Arbitrator Shipman in 46 LA 1053, 1056; McCoy in 35 LA 692, 694–695; Logan in 29 LA 279, 281.

seniority" for union officers and stewards,[28] denial of seniority for probationary employees,[29] loss of seniority in whole or in part under specified circumstances,[30] and the like.[31] Since seniority, length of service, and their concomitant rights are creatures of contract, it is necessary always to look first to the contract in determining length of service and the seniority standing of employees.

Seniority Standing

The seniority standing of an employee is his position on the "preference" or seniority list in relation to other employees in his seniority unit. An employee's seniority standing may be a problem where, among other situations, another employee in the same seniority unit began to work on the same day but at a different hour, or had the same hiring date but began to work on a different day. Arbitrators seem to be reluctant to draw too fine a line in such situations. For example, in interpreting a collective agreement providing that an employee's continuous length of service should be computed from the date he first began to work, an arbitrator held that the seniority standing of two employees who commenced work on the same day, though on different shifts, was the same. He stated that "The legal as well as the popular meaning of the word 'date' imports the day, month and year without reference to the hour."[32] Another arbitrator further observed that it would be impractical and inconsistent with existing industrial practice to ascertain length of service in units of less than one day.[33]

The contract may be explicit as to the order of seniority. For instance, it may provide not only that seniority is to be computed from the first day worked, but also that new employees are to be registered numerically as they check in on the first day worked with their seniority standing to be in the same order as their names appear on the register. Under such a provision, where two employees were

---

[28] For discussion of superseniority, see Chapter 5, subtopic titled "Superseniority."

[29] For example, see Borden Chemical Co., 32 LA 697, 700 (Prasow, 1959).

[30] See topic titled "Loss of Seniority," below.

[31] Recognizing a potentially broad leeway in the parties to specify seniority or preference rights on bases other than length of service, see United States Borax & Chemical Corp., 41 LA 1200, 1202 (Leonard, 1963).

[32] Bethlehem Steel Co., 26 LA 567, at 567 (Seward, 1956).

[33] Standard Oil Co. of Ind., 3 LA 758, 759 (Whiting, 1946). Cf., Arbitrator Lyons in 42 LA 961, 963–964.

hired on the same day, it was held that (barring any discrimination in the assignment of shifts) the one who "clocked in" on the first shift had more seniority that the other who commenced work on the same day but on the second shift.[34]

Under another contract defining seniority as continuous length of service, but containing no clause specifying a starting point from which length of service should be computed, it was held that where one employee started to work a day before another, the former had the greater seniority since he had the longer service record, even though both were hired on the same day.[35]

Where the seniority of employees was found to be equal, management was upheld in breaking the "tie" by considering the ability of the employees.[36]

Seniority Lists

In the absence of a contract provision requiring the posting of seniority lists, the employer may be held to be under an implied obligation to make proper and reasonable disclosure, upon demand by an aggrieved employee or his union, of the seniority standing of the aggrieved and that of other employees in his seniority unit. In this regard, Arbitrator Ralph T. Seward stated:

"An employee—and the union as his representative—clearly has a right to be informed of the seniority date and length of continuous service credited to him on the Company's records. By the same token, since most seniority issues involve a comparison of the relative rights of two or more employees, the employee—and the union as his representative—has a right to know the seniority dates and length of continuous service credited to the other employees in the seniority unit applicable to him at any given time. The only accurate source of such information is obviously the Company. It has the records. It is initiating the various transfers, promotions, demotions, 'bumps', layoffs, recalls, etc. which are daily causing changes in those records. The information practically obtainable from the employees themselves could never be as accurate, up-to-date or complete as that which the Company can make available. Indeed, some employees might have

---

[34] Robertshaw-Fulton Controls Co., 22 LA 273, 274 (Williams, 1954).
[35] National Biscuit Award, 4 ALAA ¶68,530.1 (Donnelly, 1950).
[36] See Arbitrator Howlett in 50 LA 507, 516; Kahn in 38 LA 1058, 1060–1061; Scheiber in 37 LA 330, 334. In McCall Corporation, 49 LA 183, 186 (McIntosh, 1967), the contract specified that ties should be resolved by a joint committee of the parties; the arbitrator specified a "toss of a coin" if the committee should disagree.

an interest in concealing information as to their own seniority standing in an effort to protect themselves from being 'bumped.' "[37]

The collective agreement may specifically provide for the posting of seniority lists.[38] It may also make provision for challenging the seniority list, often with some stated time limit, and failure of an employee to make a timely protest concerning a seniority date may be deemed a waiver of his right to challenge.[39] Even without a fixed time limit, a waiver may be based upon a failure to protest within a reasonable time after the employee knows or should know that his date is incorrect.[40] However, some arbitrators have been disinclined to cut off an employee's right to challenge an erroneous seniority date.[41] Moreover, even though an employee does not challenge his posted seniority date for several years, an employer may be estopped from refusing to change an admittedly incorrect date where he has consistently treated the employee in accordance with the correct date and not the posted one.[42]

Service Outside the Seniority Unit

The length of service credited to an employee and his seniority standing may be affected by service outside the seniority unit. He may lose or retain previously earned seniority or continue to accumulate seniority, depending upon the wording of the collective agreement and how it is interpreted. Special provision may be made that an employee transferred out of the seniority unit to an exempt job continues to accumulate seniority[43] or retains seniority already earned.[44]

---

[37] Bethlehem Steel Co., 24 LA 699, 702 (1955). Also see Arbitrator Dworkin in 33 LA 60, 66; Platt in 18 LA 907, 909.

[38] As in Pickett Cotton Mills, Inc., 17 LA 405, at 405 (Soule, 1951).

[39] See Arbitrator Shanker in 53 LA 216, 220–221 (also dealing with management's right to correct the list); Merrill in 41 LA 438, 440–441; Wolff in 37 LA 741, 744; Cahn in 30 LA 432, 433–434; Platt in 24 LA 286, 287; Soule in 17 LA 405, 405–406. Employees may challenge incorrect lists at once, not being required to wait until the employee has been adversely treated by the actual application of an erroneous list. Long Beach Oil Development Co., 41 LA 583, 586 (Block, 1963).

[40] See Linde Co., 32 LA 568, 570 (Duff, 1959). Under the circumstances in General Plywood Corp., 36 LA 633, 634 (Porter, 1961), the employee could not reasonably be charged with knowledge of the error.

[41] See Arbitrator Hebert in 51 LA 778, 784; Gross in 41 LA 524, 526–528; Schedler in 41 LA 6, 7. Also see Stouffer in 37 LA 231, 233.

[42] Republic Steel Corp., 25 LA 434, 435 (Platt, 1955).

[43] As in 55 LA 875, 35 LA 932, 29 LA 220, 27 LA 229, 25 LA 452, 24 LA 60, 23 LA 400.

[44] As in 55 LA 1011, 52 LA 383, 41 LA 1200, 37 LA 240, 30 LA 221, 26 LA 195 (could retain seniority up to one year), 26 LA 67.

In cases where there is no specific contract provision governing the seniority rights of employees transferred out of the seniority unit, awards vary. For example, it has been variously held that in such a situation the employee (1) retained seniority previously earned;[45] (2) could not continue to accumulate seniority while outside the unit;[46] (3) continued to accumulate seniority during temporary promotion out of the unit;[47] (4) continued to accumulate seniority while working outside the unit for an extended period;[48] and (5) forfeited all his seniority because he had in effect voluntarily quit.[49] In some of the cases cited in the above categories the result was influenced by past practice.

Many arbitrators agree that an individual generally cannot be credited with seniority for any service performed prior to his entry into the bargaining unit.[50] For example, individuals who had been promoted to supervisory jobs prior to the date of the first contract with the union were held to have no seniority when demoted into the bargaining unit.[51] However, seniority credit for pre-unit service

---

[45] See Arbitrator Marshall in 54 LA 1093, 1095; Elliott in 54 LA 965, 972–973, 981; Leach in 45 LA 1039, 1044–1045; Block in 43 LA 97, 100–101; McDermott in 41 LA 1228, 1230–1231; Feinberg in 40 LA 495, 498–499; Schmidt in 36 LA 1245, 1249; Kates in 36 LA 857, 858; Begley in 32 LA 892, 893; Baab in 28 LA 641, 645; Howard in 23 LA 440, 446; Ryder in 22 LA 769, 771–773; Myers in 22 LA 704, 705–706; Cahn in 22 LA 492, 495; Healy in 14 LA 916, 918; Lohman in 14 LA 537, 540.

[46] See Arbitrator Block in 43 LA 97, 100–101; Schmidt in 36 LA 1245, 1249; Cahn in 29 LA 828, 830, and in 22 LA 13, 17; Marshall in 17 LA 105, 108.

[47] See Arbitrator Caraway in 53 LA 1143, 1145–1146; Volz in 48 LA 743, 744–746; Teple in 45 LA 671, 674; Haughton in 28 LA 315, 317. Also see Hotchkiss in 4 LA 21, 24.

[48] See Arbitrator McDermott in 42 LA 1172, 1177–1179; Mishne in 36 LA 691, 694; Garrett in 28 LA 740, 743, and in 15 LA 834, 836; Byrnes in 25 LA 595, 596–597; Shipman in 21 LA 682, 685; Fulda in 18 LA 315, 317; Roberts in 14 LA 482, 486; Gregory in 8 LA 51, 52; Reynolds in 3 LA 748, 752. Also see Anrod in 34 LA 285, 290; Smith in 23 LA 338, 340. Cf., Garrett in 48 LA 872, 883.

[49] See Arbitrator Shister in 40 LA 531, 532; Kotin in 27 LA 30, 35; Platt in 26 LA 898, 899–901. Also see Gorsuch in 44 LA 802, 806–807, and in 40 LA 388, 391–392; Marshall in 17 LA 105, 108. Acceptance of a supervisory position at another of the company's plants, which had a different bargaining unit, resulted in loss of all seniority in The Colorado Fuel & Iron Corp., 47 LA 1131, 1135 (Prasow, 1966).

[50] See Arbitrator Block in 41 LA 583, 587; Singletary in 41 LA 215, 218–219; Hebert in 37 LA 200, 205; Loucks in 36 LA 1067, 1069; Schmidt in 33 LA 150, 152; Smith in 32 LA 274, 277; Cahn in 30 LA 221, 223, and in 29 LA 828, 830; McKelvey in 27 LA 229, 231–232; Tatum in 24 LA 517, 521.

[51] United States Radium Corp., 36 LA 1067, 1069 (Loucks, 1961).

has been upheld where the agreement referred to seniority in terms of "length of continuous service with the company," or the like.[52]

Extension of Seniority Rights to Different Plant or Successor Employer

Where employees acquire seniority rights under a collective agreement by performing service at a given plant for a given employer and the plant is relocated or closed down, the employees may assert a right to extend or transfer their seniority to another plant of their employer. Likewise, where the business is sold or absorbed by merger, they may assert a right to continue their seniority in the employ of the successor employer.

Closing or Relocation of Plant

While the collective agreement or some special agreement may expressly provide for the transfer of seniority rights to other locations,[53] in the absence of such express provision numerous arbitrators have construed the collective agreement before them as giving seniority rights to be exercised only at the plant location where service was performed which earned the rights, the seniority rights thus not surviving the closing or removal of the plant.[54]

In the widely repudiated and ultimately overruled court case of *Zdanok* v. *Glidden* it was held that seniority rights survived the expiration of a collective agreement and a relocation of the plant.[55] In overruling its *Glidden* decision the U.S. Court of Appeals, Second Circuit, explained:

"We are persuaded that the reasoning of the majority opinion in the Glidden case was erroneous and that erroneous reasoning led to an incorrect result. For example, the basic proposition of the opin-

---

[52] See Arbitrator Alexander in 38 LA 741, 744; Cobb in 38 LA 188, 190–192; Anrod in 34 LA 285, 290; Guild in 26 LA 256, 258. But see Shipman in 21 LA 682, 685.

[53] See C. K. Williams Co., 12 LA 987, 988 (Kerr, 1949).

[54] See Arbitrator McCoy in 46 LA 1063, 1065; Kagel in 45 LA 551, 552–554; Scheiber in 44 LA 979, 984–986; Casselman in 44 LA 361, 369; Turkus in 43 LA 798, 803–804; Davey in 43 LA 453, 459; Howlett in 39 LA 449, 454–456; Kelliher in 38 LA 619, 620; Duff in 37 LA 928, 932. Also see Malinowski in 48 LA 1257, 1260–1261 (economic closing of plant does not violate contract seniority or recognition clauses); Larson in 39 LA 82, 84–85. Cf., Smith in 42 LA 517, 523–524.

[55] 288 F2d 99, 47 LRRM 2865 (CA 2, 1961).

ion, that seniority is a vested right, finds no support in authority, in logic or in the socio-economic setting of labor-management relations. Seniority is wholly a creation of the collective agreement and does not exist apart from that agreement. The incidents of seniority can be freely altered or amended by modification of the collective agreement. Ford Motor Co. v. Huffman, 345 U.S. 330, 73 S.Ct. 681, 97 L.Ed. 1048 (1953). In giving seniority a conceptual status apart from the provisions of the collective agreement and the intentions of the parties the Glidden opinion seriously misconceived the nature of the employment relationship and dealt 'a blow to labor-management relations.' "[56]

Merger or Sale of Company

In its *John Wiley & Sons* v. *Livingston* decision the U.S. Supreme Court upheld the arbitrability of grievances concerning the survival of the seniority and other rights of employees following their employer's disappearance by merger and expiration of their collective agreement, the Court emphasizing that there was a "substantial continuity of identity in the business enterprise" before and after the merger.[57]

After *Wiley* the question remained as to whether not only the arbitration clause, but also other provisions of the predecessor's agreement, must be honored by the successor employer under the National Labor Relations Act. In its subsequent *Burns International Security Services* decision, the Supreme Court, while cautioning that its resolution of the issues "turns to a great extent on the precise facts involved here," held that a successor employer was required to bargain with the union that had represented its predecessor's employees but that

---

[56] Local 1251 UAW v. Robertshaw Controls Co., 405 F2d 29, 33, 68 LRRM 2671 (CA 2, 1968), in which the court cited several articles which had been written in criticism of the "Glidden" decision. Also rejecting the contention that seniority rights are "vested rights" which cannot be cut off or defeated by a relocation of the plant, Charland v. Norge Division, Borg-Warner Corporation, 70 LRRM 2705 (CA 6, 1969); Oddie v. Ross Gear & Tool Co., 50 LRRM 2763 (CA 6, 1962).
[57] 84 S.Ct. 909, 55 LRRM 2769, 42 LA 268 (1964). It has been stated that "Under the *Wiley* doctrine, an arbitration clause of a collective bargaining agreement remains in effect when a successor employer replaces its predecessor by way of merger, purchase, lease, or otherwise, the principal test being whether there is a 'substantial continuity of identity in the business enterprise.'" Gould & Kurtz, "Arbitration and Federal Rights Under Collective Agreements in 1970," Arbitration and the Public Interest 239, 256 (The Bureau of National Affairs, Inc., 1971). As to indicia that an employer is a "successor," see Arbitrator Seligson in 40 LA 540, 543; Kates in 37 LA 980, 982–983; Donnelly in 36 LA 1396, 1399. As to what constitutes a "merger" of companies, see Arbitrator Duff in 51 LA 408, 409–410; DiLeone in 31 LA 976, 978.

the NLRB had improperly ordered the successor to honor the predecessor's collective agreement.[58] The NLRB had relied upon *Wiley*
in holding the successor bound by the predecessor's agreement, but
the Supreme Court distinguished that case:

> "We do not find *Wiley* controlling in the circumstances here.
> *Wiley* arose in the context of a §301 suit to compel arbitration, not
> in the context of an unfair labor practice proceeding where the Board
> is expressly limited by the provisions of §8(d). That decision empha-
> sized 'the preference of national labor policy for arbitration as a substi-
> tute for tests of strength before contending forces' and held only that
> the agreement to arbitrate, 'construed in the context of national labor
> policy,' survived the merger and left to the arbitrator, subject to ju-
> dicial review, the ultimate question of the extent to which, if any,
> the surviving company was bound by other provisions of the
> contract."[59]

In holding that the successor was not bound by the predecessor's
agreement in *Burns,* the Supreme Court stated:

> "In many cases, of course, successor employers will find it advan-
> tageous not only to recognize and bargain with the union but also
> to observe the pre-existing contract rather than to face uncertainty
> and turmoil. Also, in a variety of circumstances involving a merger,
> stock acquisition, reorganization, or assets purchase, the Board might
> properly find as a matter of fact that the successor had assumed the
> obligations under the old contract. * * * Such a duty does not, how-
> ever, ensue as a matter of law from the mere fact that an employer
> is doing the same work in the same place with the same employees
> as his predecessor, as the Board had recognized until its decision in
> the instant case."[60]

There are arbitration cases decided prior to the Supreme Court's
ruling in *Burns,* in which the arbitrator held a successor employer
bound by the predecessor's agreement (although it did not contain
a successors and assigns clause),[61] including an obligation to recognize

---

[58] N.L.R.B. v. Burns International Security Services, Inc., 92 S.Ct. 1571,
80 LRRM 2225 (1972).

[59] Id. at 92 S.Ct. 1581. For the arbitrator's ultimate ruling as to the extent
to which the predecessor's contract was binding on the successor in *Wiley*, and,
in particular, the extent to which seniority rights of the predecessor's employees
survived the merger, see Interscience Encyclopedia, Inc., 55 LA 210, 218–221,
225 (Roberts, 1970).

[60] N.L.R.B. v. Burns International Security Services, Inc., 92 S.Ct. at 1584.

[61] See United States Gypsum Co., 56 LA 363, 385–388 (Valtin, 1971),
where the business remained essentially the same after the change in ownership
and where the arbitrator gave express recognition to the NLRB ruling in *Burns*.
In Kent Enterprises, Inc., 55 LA 777, 781–783 (Roberts, 1970), a seller's contract
was held not binding upon the buyer where the business was substantially altered
after the sale. Similarly, see Arbitrator Roper in 57 LA 1220, 1223.

the seniority rights of the predecessor's employees under that agreement.[62] On the other hand, there are arbitration cases also decided prior to the Supreme Court's ruling in *Burns,* in which the arbitrator held in effect that, absent a successors and assigns clause or a provision explicitly providing for continued seniority (or for benefits based upon seniority) under a successor employer, employees have no right to seniority credit in the employ of a successor employer for service performed with the predecessor company.[63]

Future arbitration decisions as to the continuance of seniority under successor employers obviously will be reached with due consideration of the Supreme Court's decision in the *Burns* case, although some of the language in the Court's opinion may leave the arbitrator uncertain as to its true scope or as to the inferences to be drawn from certain of the Court's language.

Merger of Seniority Lists

Merger of separate companies or consolidation of plants or departments with separate seniority lists may raise the problem of determining precisely how to combine such lists to make a composite list of employees of both operations. An extensive study of this problem and of published and unpublished cases and other experiences reflecting methods and criteria used in the merger of seniority lists was made by Professor Thomas Kennedy, who reported his findings, including those as to the advantages and disadvantages of each method, to the

---

[62] See Interscience Encyclopedia, Inc., 55 LA 210, 218–221, 225 (Roberts, 1970), where the seniority of said employees was continued until their separate identity was lost, and where the arbitrator gave express recognition to the NLRB ruling in *Burns.* Also holding the successor obligated to recognize the seniority of the predecessor's employees, see Arbitrator Williams in 57 LA 1041, 1046–1048; Gooding in 25 LA 66, 67–68.

[63] See Arbitrator Updegraff in 57 LA 227, 229; Cutler in 55 LA 1143, 1146; Killion in 41 LA 1208, 1214; Alexander in 38 LA 741, 744; Luskin in 35 LA 378, 380; Jones in 28 LA 746, 749–750; Cahn in 20 LA 797, 799; Cornsweet in 14 LA 260, 261–262 (the successor employer acquired the business at a bankruptcy sale and the arbitrator stated that the "very essence of a purchase at bankruptcy sale is legally to buy without incurring *any* obligations which the bankrupt may have had"). For cases involving rights of employees under clauses providing that the agreement is to be binding upon successors and assigns of the employer or where the successor himself expressly or impliedly agreed to assume the predecessor's collective agreement, see Arbitrator Duff in 48 LA 600, 603–605; Gundermann in 46 LA 935, 939; Wallen in 44 LA 346, 350; Turkus in 43 LA 798, 799–800; Lyons in 42 LA 961, 962–963; Lynch in 64–3 ARB ¶9096; Crawford in 41 LA 844, 850–853; Anderson in 41 LA 759, 762–763.

National Academy of Arbitrators.[64] The reader is directed to that excellent report for its in-depth consideration of methods of merging seniority lists. The present topic will merely note the methods, identified and analyzed by Professor Kennedy, of making a composite seniority list for purposes of layoff, rehire, promotion, transfer, and the like.[65] Said methods are:

1. *The surviving-group principle.* Here when one company purchases or acquires another company, the employees of the purchasing or acquiring company receive seniority preference over the employees of the purchased or acquired company. The seniority lists are merged by adding the names of the employees of the acquired company to the bottom of the list of the acquiring company.[66]

2. *The length-of-service principle.* Here a combined seniority list is prepared by placing employees on the new list in the order of their length of service regardless of which company or plant the employee worked for prior to the merger or consolidation. All employees are thus treated as if they had always been employed by the same company or plant.[67]

3. *The follow-the-work principle.* Here when companies merge or when plants or departments within a company are consolidated, the employees are given the opportunity to follow their work (if it still can be adequately identified) with the seniority rights to such work protected by continuation of the separate seniority lists.

---

[64] Kennedy, "Merging Seniority Lists," Labor Arbitration and Industrial Change 1–34 (BNA Incorporated, 1963).

[65] Professor Kennedy noted that seniority rights may be divided into two distinct types. One type, termed "benefit seniority," is concerned with benefits such as vacations or retirement pay and usually depends solely on length of service. The other type, termed "competitive-status seniority," is concerned with such matters as layoff or promotion and is not necessarily based solely on length of service. Where the distinction between the two types of seniority is applied, it is necessary to have a seniority list for benefits and another for competitive status; this can result in discrepancies between the two types of seniority. Id. at 2, 29. Also see Arbitrator Spelfogel in 53 LA 1253, 1258–1259; Duff in 48 LA 600, 603–606 (employees of an acquired company were permitted to keep all their benefit seniority but only one half of their competitive-status seniority—a separate list for each type of seniority was specified by the arbitrator); Anderson in 44 LA 311, 314.

[66] For instances in which this method was used either exclusively or in combination with another method, see Seniority Roster, Local 640, IATSE, 53 LA 1253, 1258–1259 (Spelfogel, 1969); Armco Steel Corp., 36 LA 981, 988–989 (Platt, 1961), where group A list was placed near bottom of group B list, group A list being integrated only with group B employees who were on layoff.

[67] For instances in which this method was used either exclusively or in combination with another method, see Arbitrator Spelfogel in 53 LA 1253, 1258–1259; Rohman in 51 LA 717, 718–719; Wagner in 46 LA 589, 598; Kerrison in 45 LA 1018, 1019, 1021; Anderson in 44 LA 311, 315–316; Kahn in 40 LA 680, 685–686; Di Leone in 31 LA 976, 979 (lists "dovetailed" by length of service); Somers in 24 LA 793, 801–803.

If the work becomes merged or its identity is otherwise lost, the seniority lists may be integrated into a single list on a ratio basis representing the amount of work brought to the consolidation by each group of employees.[68]

4. *The absolute-rank principle.* Here employees are placed on the merged seniority list on the basis of the rank they held on their respective prior lists. Thus, the two employees who were first on the two original lists are given the first two places on the merged list (the employee with the longer service gets the first place and the other employee gets the second); the two employees who were second on the two original lists are given the third and fourth places on the merged list; and so on. The ratio-rank principle, noted below, is much more popular than the absolute-rank principle since the ratio-rank method gives due consideration to the rank factor without producing the serious distortions which can occur under the absolute-rank method, as where the groups to be merged are of different size.[69]

5. *The ratio-rank principle.* Here integration of seniority lists may be accomplished by establishing a ratio from the number of employees in each of the groups to be merged and assigning the places on the new seniority list according to this ratio. Thus, if seniority list A has 200 employees and seniority list B has only 100 employees, the ratio is two to one. Therefore, of the first three places on the new seniority list, two are allocated to the first two employees on the A list and one is allocated to the first employee on the B list (as among the three employees, length of service may be used to determine which employee gets each of the first three places); then places 4, 5 and 6 on the new list are allocated to the third and fourth employees on the A list and to the second employee on the B list; and so on, until all the A and B employees are placed on the new list.[70]

In determining which method or combination of methods should be used in the given case (or in determining whether a method agreed to by the parties is fair and should be approved), an arbitrator will of course give intensive consideration to the facts and circumstances of the particular case. Any one of the above methods, particularly

---

[68] This was done in Sonotone Corp., 42 LA 359, 364 (Wolf, 1964), where a group of employees who only brought 70 percent as much work to the consolidation as another group did were credited with 70 percent of their length of prior service and the resultant figure determined their place on a merged (length of service variety) seniority list. Also see Arbitrator Duff in 48 LA 600, 604–606.

[69] In Moore Business Forms, Inc., 24 LA 793, 801–803 (Somers, 1955), the "rank" factor was used in combination with length of service, equal weight being given to (1) overall length of service, and (2) the employees' relative positions on the separate plant lists.

[70] This method was used in combination with other methods by Arbitrator Cole in Pan American World Airways, Inc., 19 LA 14, 20–22 (1952).

the length-of-service method, may possibly be selected for exclusive use in a case.[71] However, it is not unusual for methods to be used in combination.[72] For instance, in merging two pilot seniority lists following the merger of airlines, one-third weight was given to the ratio-rank principle and two-thirds weight to the length-of-service principle; the arbitrator thus considered (1) length of service, and (2) the ratio of pilots in one airline to pilots in the other, but with length of service having greater weight.[73]

Loss of Seniority

Some situations in which seniority rights may be lost in whole or in part have been noted in the preceding topics. It may also be noted that contractual provisions for loss of seniority in designated situations are not uncommon. For example, the agreement may call for loss of seniority in the event of unexcused absence for a specified period,[74] or in the event the employee resigns.[75]

In some instances the agreement will expressly indicate that loss of seniority due to unexcused absences shall also constitute a termination of the employment relationship.[76] Termination of the employee without such express provision has been upheld in some cases as a concomitant of the loss of seniority,[77] but not always.[78]

Seniority Provisions

There are two basic types of seniority provisions. The more rigid type requires the recognition of strict seniority—that is, the employer

---

[71] For example, see City of Green Bay, 44 LA 311, 315–316 (Anderson, 1965). Length of service is given at least some weight in most cases.

[72] For example, see Arbitrator Wolf in 42 LA 359, 364; Platt in 36 LA 981, 988–989; Somers in 24 LA 793, 801–803; Cole in 19 LA 14, 20–22.

[73] Pan American World Airways, Inc., 19 LA 14, 20–22 (Cole, 1952).

[74] See Arbitrator Dworkin in 55 LA 709, 715; Rohman in 49 LA 613, 614–615; Autrey in 43 LA 1066, 1069–1070.

[75] See Simmons Co., 49 LA 950, 952 (Teple, 1967); The Tuttle Press Co., 49 LA 490, 492–493 (R. Seitz, 1967). In Reden Corp., 50 LA 413, 416–417 (Roberts, 1968), the arbitrator enforced a strike settlement agreement under which the accumulation of seniority by strikers was tolled during the period of the strike.

[76] As in Murdock Machine & Engineering Co., 49 LA 613, 614 (Rohman, 1967); Midland-Ross Corp., 49 LA 283, at 283 (Larkin, 1967).

[77] See Arbitrator Stouffer in 47 LA 443, 446–448; Klein in 42 LA 1151, 1161–1162, and in 39 LA 414, 415–416; P. Seitz in 38 LA 278, 279–282.

[78] See Quick Mfg., 43 LA 54, 60–61 (Teple, 1964). Also see Arbitrator Walsh in 49 LA 206, 209.

must give preference to the employee with the longest continuous service without regard to any other considerations.[79] The principal thesis underlying this approach is that, as between a junior man of superior qualities and a senior man of lower qualities, the social claim of the latter should override both the needs of the business and the interest of the public in its efficient operation.[80] The more usual provision, however, is written so as to serve the basic aims of seniority, while recognizing other factors, which basically involve the "fitness and ability" of the employee, in determining preference in employment.[81] Such factors may include skill, ability, aptitude, competence, efficiency, training, physical fitness, judgment, experience, initiative, leadership, and the like.

In regard to this "modified seniority," Arbitrator Harry H. Platt stated:

> "Generally speaking, such modified seniority is acceptable to most unions and employers because it acknowledges the fact that wide difference in ability and capacity to perform the work required exists between employees in a plant and that such differences are a logical and legitimate consideration in determining preference in employment, especially in making promotions and demotions as well as in the reduction of forces."[82]

Modified Seniority Clauses

Modified seniority clauses fall into one of three basic categories:

(1) In one category are those clauses which provide in essence that the senior employee shall be given preference if he possesses fitness

---

[79] See strict seniority provision in Dana Corp., 27 LA 203, 204 (Mittenthal, 1956). In Branch Motor Express Co., 39 LA 795, at 795 (Crawford, 1962), the agreement specified strict seniority except where special training or experience is required, the exception to become effective only by special agreement of the parties.

[80] See Clifton, "Management Functions," N.Y.U. First Ann. Conf. on Labor 89, 97 (1948).

[81] See Darin & Armstrong, 13 LA 843, 845 (Platt, 1950). Some contracts provide for strict seniority for layoffs while calling for consideration of seniority and ability for promotions, as in J. Weingarten, Inc., 42 LA 619, 622 (Rohman, 1964). In New Britain Machine Co., 45 LA 993, 994–995 (McCoy, 1965), the contract merely stated that the employer "will give consideration to seniority"; the arbitrator said this only required good faith consideration of seniority and did not prevent consideration also of ability or physical fitness, or of the employer's own interest in efficient and profitable operations.

[82] Darin & Armstrong, 13 LA 843, 845–846 (1950). Also see comment of Arbitrator Frey in Atlas Powder Co., 30 LA 674, 676 (1958).

and ability equal to that of junior employees.[83] This type of clause might be termed a *"relative ability"* clause, since here comparisons between qualifications of employees bidding for the job are necessary and proper[84] and seniority becomes a determining factor only if the qualifications of the bidders are equal.[85]

The wording of these "relative ability" clauses varies. The contract may provide that seniority shall govern unless there is a marked difference in ability, or unless a junior employee has greater ability. Some clauses provide that seniority shall govern if ability (or other qualifying factors such as physical fitness, competence, etc.) is *relatively equal,* or *substantially equal,* or simply *equal.* Even in the latter regard, however, it has been held that the term "equal" does not mean exact equality, but only substantial equality.[86] Nor does "relatively" equal ability mean "exactly" equal ability.[87] Thus, whether the term used is "equal" or "relatively equal" or "substantially equal," it would appear that only an approximate or near equality of competing employees, rather than an exact equality, should be necessary in order to bring the seniority factor into play.[88] Where the junior employee is substantially superior in ability, however, he may be given preference over a senior employee.[89]

---

[83] For examples of this type of clause, see 56 LA 1206, 1207; 56 LA 399, 401; 56 LA 6, 7; 55 LA 104, 105; 46 LA 1005, 1006; 46 LA 23, 24; 45 LA 444 at 444; 30 LA 674, 675; 29 LA 262, 265; 25 LA 480, 481; 23 LA 322, 323; 21 LA 565, 566.

[84] Alabama Power Co., 18 LA 24, 25 (McCoy, 1952). Relative ability is to be determined in reference to the particular job in question, not in reference to overall ability. New Jersey Telephone Co., 47 LA 495, 500 (Koretz, 1966); Yuba Heat Transfer Corp., 38 LA 471, 474–475 (Autrey, 1962).

[85] See Arbitrator Ross in 34 LA 271, 273; Frey in 30 LA 674, 677; Brecht in 21 LA 565, 568; McCoy in 18 LA 24, 25.

[86] See Poloron Products of Pa., Inc., 23 LA 789, 792 (Rosenfarb, 1955); Combustion Engineering Co., 20 LA 416, 419 (McCoy, 1953). Also see Arbitrator Ross in 34 LA 271, 273; Howlett in 26 LA 885, 889. Cf., Gregory in 9 LA 432, 435.

[87] See Bethlehem Steel Co., 23 LA 532, 534 (Seward, 1954).

[88] See Republic Steel Corp., 1 LA 244, 247 (Platt, 1945). Also see Arbitrator Volz in 47 LA 263, 265 (junior employee "need not be head-and-shoulders better, but his greater ability should be clearly discernible to outweigh the factor of seniority"); Luskin in 46 LA 23, 26–27 (junior employee loses unless there is a definite, distinct, substantial, and significant difference as to ability in his favor); Ross in 34 LA 271, 273 ("if the junior employee is preferred, he should be 'head and shoulders' above the senior").

[89] See Arbitrator Dworkin in 49 LA 390, 395; Volz in 47 LA 263, 265; Luskin in 46 LA 23, 28; Seward in 29 LA 710, 712; Frey in 19 LA 883, 888; Roberts in 19 LA 270, 278–279.

(2) The second basic type of modified seniority clause provides in general that the senior employee will be given preference if he possesses sufficient ability to perform the job.[90] Minimum qualifications are enough under these *"sufficient ability"* clauses.[91] This type of clause may state that preference will be given to the senior qualified bidder, or to the senior employee provided he is qualified or has the "necessary" ability for the job, and the like. Under this type of provision, "it is necessary to determine only whether the employee with greater seniority can in fact do the job."[92] Comparisons between applicants are unnecessary and improper, and "the job must be given to the senior bidder if he is competent, regardless of how much more competent some other bidder may be."[93] Thus, the senior qualified employee will be entitled to preference even though a junior employee possesses greater skill and ability.[94]

(3) The third basic type of modified seniority provision, which may be called a *"hybrid"* clause, requires consideration and comparison in the first instance of *both* seniority and relative ability.[95] The "hybrid" clause ordinarily is worded in such general terms as "seniority and qualifications shall govern," or "due consideration shall be given to length of service, aptitude, and ability," and the like, without indicating the relative weight to be accorded these factors.[96] Arbitrators,

---

[90] For examples of this type of clause, see 56 LA 920, 921; 56 LA 40, 41; 55 LA 813, 814; 52 LA 247, 248; 46 LA 238, 239; 29 LA 29, 31; 27 LA 353, 356; 25 LA 479, 480.

[91] Central Franklin Process Co., 19 LA 32, 34 (Marshall, 1952). In Kingsberry Homes Corp., 53 LA 1345, 1347 (Rauch, 1969), the arbitrator stated that the term "if qualified" must be construed "to mean that the senior employee must have a background of such training, experience, or demonstrated aptitude and physical makeup, as to give a reasonable person cause to believe that this person can be expected to perform the job competently within a reasonable time."

[92] Republic Steel Corp., 1 LA 244, 247 (Platt, 1945). Also see Arbitrator Duncan in 40 LA 364, 366.

[93] Alabama Power Co., 18 LA 24, 25 (McCoy, 1952). Similarly, see Arbitrator Volz in 49 LA 918, 920.

[94] Central Franklin Process Co., 19 LA 32, 34 (Marshall, 1952). Similarly, see Arbitrator Block in 43 LA 1248, 1251–1252.

[95] See Arbitrator Dolson in 50 LA 990, 991, 994; Alexander in 50 LA 397, 399–400; Knowlton in 38 LA 374, 374–375; Davis in 30 LA 862, 870; Cole in 21 LA 183, 185; Cornsweet in 16 LA 280, 283, 285; Frolich in 14 LA 12, 15; Wolff in 11 LA 1190, 1192; Feinberg in 11 LA 743, 744–745. Also see McCoy in 48 LA 983, 988–989; Beatty in 45 LA 267, 268.

[96] In Reliance Universal, Inc., 50 LA 397, 399–400 (Alexander, 1968), the arbitrator held that where the contract listed seniority, ability, and experience as factors to be considered in promotions, the importance of any factor was not to be determined by the order in which it was listed. Accord, Arbitrator Dolson in 50 LA 990, 992.

however, require that fair and reasonable consideration be given to both seniority and relative ability, although the weight that may be accorded to each varies from case to case.

It seems clear that under "hybrid" clauses the relative claims of seniority and of ability must be determined by comparing and weighing against each other the relative difference in seniority of competing employees and the relative difference in their abilities. Thus, in comparing two or more qualified employees, both seniority and ability must be considered, and where the difference in length of service is relatively insignificant and there is a relatively significant difference in ability, then the ability factor should be given greater weight; but where there is a relatively substantial difference in seniority and relatively little difference in abilities, then length of service should be given greater weight. To illustrate, Arbitrator I. Robert Feinberg, giving effect to both factors under a "hybrid" clause, held that a much better qualified junior employee should be given preference over a senior employee who could perform the job, since there was relatively little difference in length of service, thus making relative ability the determinative factor.[97] Conversely, a senior employee whose qualifications were only slightly less but whose seniority was much greater than that of a junior employee has been given preference over the better qualified junior employee, the seniority factor determining the issue.[98]

Determination of Fitness and Ability

Provisions for modified seniority, designed on the one hand to give recognition to the right and responsibility of management to manage the enterprise and on the other hand to protect senior employees, involve some of the most troublesome questions confronting arbitrators. Unions tend to overemphasize seniority and forget merit and ability, while management tends to overemphasize supervision's personal judgment of merit and ability and forget seniority.[99]

Arbitrators have frequently held that, where the agreement makes "fitness and ability" a factor to be considered along with seniority

---

[97] Callite Tungsten Corp., 11 LA 743, 744–745 (1948).
[98] See International Harvester Co., 21 LA 183, 185 (Cole, 1953); International Harvester Co., 11 LA 1190, 1192 (Wolff, 1948). Also see Arbitrator Elliot in 41 LA 353, 359; Ross in 34 LA 472, 475.
[99] Ford Motor Co., 2 LA 374, 375 (Shulman, 1945).

under one of the modified seniority clauses but is silent as to how and by whom the determination of qualifications is to be made, management is entitled to make the initial determination, subject to challenge by the union on the ground that management's decision was unreasonable under the facts, or capricious, arbitrary, or discriminatory.[100] This right to determine ability may be held by management either as a residual management right or as a necessary adjunct to the right to manage the plant and direct the working forces.[101]

A collective agreement containing a modified seniority clause may specifically provide that the employer shall be the judge of the qualifying factors, sometimes also providing for challenge of management's decision by the union through the grievance procedure.[102] However, even where the contract makes the employer the sole judge, arbitrators have held that management's action must not be capricious, arbitrary, or discriminatory, and, some arbitrators have added, must not be unreasonable.[103]

---

[100] For cases where the arbitrator stated these or similar grounds for arbitral review, see Arbitrator Johannes in 56 LA 40, 42–43; Stouffer in 56 LA 6, 10, and in 52 LA 889, 894; Cahn in 52 LA 247, 252 (union need not show that company action was arbitrary, capricious, or in bad faith, it sufficing to show that company made an incorrect factual determination); Anderson in 49 LA 589, 594; Dworkin in 49 LA 390, 394; Oppenheim in 46 LA 860, 863; Klein in 46 LA 203, 208; Kates in 45 LA 743, 747; Schmidt in 44 LA 283, 285; Koven in 42 LA 1093, 1096; Seligson in 41 LA 528, 532; Rohman in 38 LA 132, 143; Hale in 37 LA 801, 805; Maggs in 37 LA 29, 34; Ross in 34 LA 271, 275 (review not limited to arbitrary or capricious action—company decision may be made in good faith but still be unreasonable); Reid in 29 LA 394, 396; Lockhart in 16 LA 525, 529. In some cases arbitrators have spoken in terms of management's decision being subject to challenge on the ground that it is "clearly wrong", or the like. See Arbitrator Beatty in 40 LA 697, 699–700; Caraway in 35 LA 866, 869; Prasow in 27 LA 40, 49; Marshall in 6 LA 838, 841. In still other cases, particularly earlier cases, the arbitrator limited review of management's decision to the narrower ground of arbitratry, capricious, bad faith, or discriminatory action. See Arbitrator Ray in 46 LA 91, 94; Kelliher in 23 LA 105, 109; Carmody in 23 LA 38, 39; Parker in 22 LA 258, 260; Murphy in 18 LA 757, 758–759; Hawley in 17 LA 516, 518–519; Reynolds in 10 LA 624, 626; Ingle in 9 LA 515, 517; Greene in 7 LA 526, 527.

[101] See Arbitrator Stouffer in 52 LA 889, 894; Beatty in 40 LA 697, 699–700; Rohman in 38 LA 132, 143; Hale in 37 LA 801, 805; Britton in 34 LA 788, 792; Dworkin in 29 LA 29, 36; Williams in 25 LA 748, 751; Reid in 23 LA 322, 326; Baab in 20 LA 137, 141; Kerr in 14 LA 163, 167; Reynolds in 10 LA 624, 626.

[102] For example, see 55 LA 813, 816; 53 LA 549, at 549; 30 LA 803, 804; 26 LA 773, 774; 19 LA 402, 403.

[103] See Arbitrator Koven in 53 LA 549, at 549; Peterschmidt in 52 LA 476, 479; Lugar in 45 LA 307, 313–314; Warns in 36 LA 380, 381, 384; Meltzer in 30 LA 803, 807; Disman in 26 LA 773, 778–779; Ralston in 19 LA 402, 405; McCoy in 18 LA 24, 27; Wardlaw in 6 LA 786, 788. Cf., Carmichael in 3 LA 313, 317.

Review of Management's Determination:
Evidence and Burden of Proof

In many cases involving issues of seniority and ability, the arbitrator in reviewing management's determination does not speak in terms of burden of proof but simply considers all the evidence and arguments of both parties and decides from a consideration thereof whether the company's determination should be upheld.[104] On the other hand, in some cases the arbitrator does speak specifically in terms of burden of proof, placing the onus on one party or the other.[105]

There appear to be several basic approaches as to which party should have the burden of proof in cases involving managerial action taken under "relative ability" clauses.[106] In some cases such clauses have been construed to place a relatively light limitation upon the employer and, in effect, to place the burden of proof on the employee. Under this approach, when the union challenges management's determination it must sustain the burden of proving discrimination, caprice, arbitrariness, or bad faith on the part of the employer or that the employer's evaluation of abilities was clearly wrong.[107]

In some other cases such clauses have been construed to place a relatively severe limitation upon the employer and, in effect, to place the burden of proof on him. Under this approach the employer must

---

[104] See for instance, Arbitrator Johannes in 56 LA 40, 42–43; Larson in 55 LA 813, 816–817; Alexander in 50 LA 397, 399–400; Marshall in 43 LA 475, 483–484; Boles in 30 LA 365, 367–374; Ross in 29 LA 262, 265–267; Prasow in 27 LA 40, 49.

[105] See, for instance, Arbitrator Coburn in 56 LA 733, 737; Stouffer in 56 LA 6, 10; Keeler in 45 LA 444, 446. The contract itself may place the burden of proof on one of the parties. For example, see Inland Steel Co., 16 LA 280, 283 (Cornsweet, 1951).

[106] See discussion of "relative ability" clauses supra, topic titled "Modified Seniority Clauses." There are various shadings of opinion within the basic approaches regarding the burden and quantum of proof. In this connection, see Howard, "The Role of the Arbitrator in the Determination of Ability," 12 Arb. J. 14–27 (1957).

[107] See Arbitrator Coburn in 56 LA 733, 737; Stouffer in 56 LA 6, 10; Ray in 46 LA 91, 94; Ingle in 9 LA 515, 517; Marshall in 6 LA 838, 841. Also see Tsukiyama in 55 LA 477, 481; Flannagan in 42 LA 1301, 1306; Dworkin in 39 LA 735, 740; Doyle in 19 LA 47, 49. In some cases, while the arbitrator did not speak in terms of burden of proof, he noted that there was no evidence that the company had acted arbitrarily or in bad faith. For example, see Arbitrator Marshall in 43 LA 475, 484; Disman in 26 LA 773, 779; Jones in 25 LA 600, 604; Brecht in 21 LA 565, 568–569; Wolff in 17 LA 898, 903–904; Hawley in 17 LA 516, 519; Prasow in 17 LA 205, 211–212; Levinson in 16 LA 790, 792; Reynolds in 10 LA 624, 626.

be prepared, when by-passing senior employees, to show, by specific and understandable evidence which relates to capacity for the job in question, that the junior man is the abler.[108] In still other "relative ability" cases, an even heavier burden is, in effect, placed on the employer, and he is required when challenged not only to show greater ability in the junior man to whom he has given preference, but also to show the absence of discrimination and arbitrariness and the presence of good faith.[109]

In cases involving "sufficient ability" clauses,[110] arbitrators have placed the burden on the employer to show that the by-passed senior employee is not competent for the job, and the fact that a junior employee is more competent than the senior employee is irrelevant.[111] Apart from this required showing by the employer under such clauses, if the union specifically alleges discrimination or abuse of discretion, it may be required to prove such allegations by clear evidence.[112]

When a "hybrid" clause is involved,[113] arbitrators appear to place the burden on the employer to show why the ability factor was given greater weight than the seniority factor in by-passing the senior employee.[114]

---

[108] For cases in which the arbitrator required this or a similar showing by the employer, or in which the burden of proof was otherwise clearly placed on management, see Arbitrator Tive in 55 LA 325, 328; Beeson in 54 LA 298, 301; Sullivan in 54 LA 264, 268–269; Jones in 49 LA 275, 277; Williams in 48 LA 530, 531–532; Oppenheim in 46 LA 860, 862–863; Luskin in 46 LA 23, 26–27; Schmidt in 44 LA 283, 285; Hawley in 42 LA 276, 279; Autrey in 38 LA 471, 475–476; Teple in 36 LA 343, 348; Garrett in 22 LA 188, 190; Waite in 19 LA 1, 4; Blair in 16 LA 382, 383; Platt in 13 LA 843, 846; Whitton in 13 LA 666, 668; Brandschain in 5 LA 578, 582; Shulman in 2 LA 374, 375–376.

[109] See Atlas Powder Co., 30 LA 674, 677 (Frey, 1958); Illinois Bell Telephone Co., 14 LA 1021, 1026 (Kelliher, 1950). Also see Arbitrator Reid in 29 LA 394, 397; Klamon in 24 LA 869, 873.

[110] See discussion on "sufficient ability" clauses supra, topic titled "Modified Seniority Clauses."

[111] Pittsburgh Plate Glass Co., 8 LA 317, 329 (Blair, 1947). Similarly, see Arbitrator Amis in 55 LA 432, 434; Altieri in 43 LA 499, 506; Dykstra in 38 LA 906, 908; Hale in 37 LA 801, 806, and in 25 LA 130, 142; Galenson in 25 LA 681, 684; Shister in 25 LA 618, 623; Ross in 23 LA 556, 558; McKelvey in 22 LA 167, 170; Pollard in 16 LA 586, 587. Cf., Dworkin in 39 LA 609, 612–613; Cahn in 29 LA 597, 598.

[112] See Arbitrator Shister in 24 LA 703, 705; Carmody in 23 LA 28, 29; Greene in 7 LA 526, 527.

[113] See discussion on "hybrid" clauses above, topic titled "Modified Seniority Clauses."

[114] Southwestern Bell Telephone Co., 30 LA 862, 871 (Davis, 1958). Also, in International Harvester Co., 21 LA 183, 185 (Cole, 1953), and in International Harvester Co., 11 LA 1190, 1192 (Wolff, 1948), the employer was held not

If "strict" seniority is involved, that is, if the agreement requires the observance of seniority but contains no fitness and ability qualifications, the burden is clearly on the employer to justify a failure to give preference to the senior employee. For example, under a strict seniority clause, an employer passing over a senior but handicapped employee would have the burden of proving that the senior employee is not qualified for the work or that the performance of the work would have injurious effects on him.[115]

Finally, it should be emphasized that the approach taken by any arbitrator as to which party has the burden of proof will depend in great measure upon the terms of the contract and the facts of the case—in one case under one contract in one set of circumstances an arbitrator may decide the issue simply by examining the facts without referring to burden of proof, while in another case under another contract in another set of circumstances the same arbitrator may place the burden of proof on one party or the other.[116] This is by no means a criticism of the arbitrators. Rather, it serves emphatically to bring the problem into focus and to make clear the basic observation that, as a practical matter, whether or not the arbitrator speaks in terms of burden of proof, in most cases when management's determination is challenged both parties are expected to produce whatever evidence they can in support of their respective contentions; and they ordinarily do so. The arbitrator in turn considers all the evidence and decides whether management's determination should be upheld as being reasonably supported by the evidence and as not having been influenced by improper elements such as arbitrariness, caprice, or discrimination.

Factors Considered in Determining
Fitness and Ability

The determination of ability is by no means susceptible to any set formula applicable to any and all circumstances. The precise fac-

---

to have given sufficient weight to the much greater seniority of the senior employee. Also see Arbitrator Sembower in 43 LA 165, 169–170. Cf., Alexander in 50 LA 397, 399–400. In Callite Tungsten Corp., 11 LA 743, 744 (Feinberg, 1948), the employer was upheld where there was little difference in seniority and much difference in ability.

[115] Chrysler Corp., 5 LA 333, 336 (Wolff, 1946).

[116] See, for example, Arbitrator Klamon in 24 LA 869, 873, and 19 LA 639, 646; Platt in 20 LA 460, 462, and 13 LA 843, 846; D. Wolff in 11 LA 1190, 1192, and 5 LA 333, 336.

tors or criteria applicable in one set of circumstances involving one contract may not be proper or sufficient in another situation under another contract. Nevertheless, reported arbitration awards show that in the absence of contract provision for the method to be used or the factors to be considered in determining ability, management has been permitted or required to use a variety of methods and to consider a number of factors, including, in proper circumstances: use of written, oral, performance or aptitude tests; trial period on the job; reliance upon a merit rating plan or upon the opinion of supervision; consideration of production records, attendance or disciplinary records, education, experience, physical fitness, and the like. It has been held that management is entitled to use any method to determine ability so long as the method used is fair and nondiscriminatory.[117]

Technical qualifications for the job in question or a related job are clearly pertinent to management's consideration of an employee's "fitness and ability" for that job. Some of the factors discussed herein, such as the use of tests, technical training, and experience, point to the technical requirements of the job. However, arbitrators generally have permitted or required management to consider other factors as well in determining employees' qualifications. For example, Arbitrator Jerome A. Levinson approved the use of other factors:

"* * * To limit consideration to the one factor of technical knowledge of the job, would appear to be unduly restrictive. * * * [T]he Company could properly consider additional factors in deciding who was qualified for the particular job. * * *

"The criteria used by the Company [education, ability to express himself, alertness, attendance record, flexibility and ability to learn new duties] do not appear unreasonable or arbitrary, as related to the job * * * in this case. They seem to be appropriate and relevant factors for qualification of a man for the duties and responsibilities of this job * * *."[118]

Arbitrator Pearce Davis would impose a duty upon management to consider other matters in addition to technical knowledge, stating:

"In its assessment of comparative abilities, the Company has the right and the duty to prepare, record, and examine *tangible* and

---

[117] See Arbitrator Dworkin in 53 LA 746, 755; Anderson in 49 LA 589, 592; Beatty in 45 LA 267, 268; Graff in 35 LA 169, 172; McCoy in 33 LA 951, 952; Williams in 25 LA 748, 751; Bailer in 19 LA 257, 260; Blair in 8 LA 278, 280.

[118] John Deere Tractor Co., 16 LA 790, 792 (1951).

objective (in so far as possible) evidence concerning such matters as, for example: innate capacity; prior job experience and performance; attendance, health and related factors; tests, if available, such as those to indicate the likelihood of successful performance in the new position."[119]

In any event, the factors considered must relate directly to the question of what the job requires and the employee's ability to meet those requirements. Obviously, the factors used must be consistent with the collective agreement. It is clear that the more objective factors have greater acceptability, and the more of such factors properly considered by management in a given situation, the stronger is the case for the decision reached by it.

The factors most commonly utilized are discussed in detail below. No particular significance is attached to the order in which they appear, and note should also be taken of the possibility that factors other than those considered here may also be pertinent to any given case.[120]

Use of Tests

Even in the absence of specific contract provision, management has been held entitled to give reasonable and appropriate written,[121] oral,[122] performance,[123] and aptitude tests[124] as an aid in determining

---

[119] Southwestern Bell Telephone Co., 30 LA 862, 871 (1958). Also see Arbitrator Justin in 20 LA 468, 474–475.

[120] For example, in addition to other factors used, the necessity of personal interviews with job applicants has been considered. See South Central Bell Telephone Co., 52 LA 1104, 1111–1112 (Platt, 1969); Semling-Menke Co., 46 LA 523, 525 (Graff, 1966).

[121] See Arbitrator Strongin in 56 LA 503, 505; Freund in 55 LA 79, 83; Block in 54 LA 460, 466; Anderson in 49 LA 589, 592; Gorsuch in 46 LA 1116, 1121–1123; Florey in 46 LA 414, 416; Gibson in 45 LA 1003, 1005–1006; Kates in 45 LA 21, 25; Bradley in 38 LA 63, 67; Roberts in 37 LA 49, 52; McCoy in 33 LA 951, 952; Seward in 29 LA 710, 711–712.

[122] See Hammarlund Mfg. Co., Inc., 19 LA 653, 655 (Bailer, 1952). However, oral testing as applied to mechanical skills might not, standing alone, provide a reliable guide since an employee may have skill in performing a mechanical job but lack the ability to communicate the knowledge when questioned orally, and vice versa. Collins Radio Co., 39 LA 436, 440 (Rohman, 1962).

[123] See Arbitrator McDaniel in 53 LA 777, 779–780; Bradley in 38 LA 63, 67–68; Singletary in 29 LA 246, 248–249; Bailer in 19 LA 257, 260.

[124] See Arbitrator Simon in 50 LA 1227, 1231–1232; Uible in 49 LA 735, 737; Bennett in 49 LA 465, 467; Wolff in 47 LA 552, 553; Wagner in 46 LA 81, 91 (citing many cases at 87–90); Dworkin in 43 LA 817, 822; Handsaker in 42 LA 349, 351–352; Frey in 30 LA 674, 677. Management has been held entitled to use aptitude tests to select applicants for training for newly created jobs (Arbitrator Wagner in 46 LA 81, 85; Porter in 44 LA 967, 969), even where the contract provides that the senior employee shall be given a trial period on the job (Nichols in 43 LA 779, 783). For cases discussing the propriety

the ability of competing employees. Moreover, recognizing the company's authority to institute and utilize tests, it has been held that "the company is vested with continuing authority to change its testing methods and procedures in accordance with the exercise of sound judgment."[125] Many arbitrators look with favor upon the use of proper tests in appropriate situations. For example, Arbitrator Harry J. Dworkin noted: "The employment of tests, fairly and objectively administered, would appear to be desirable, and in the interests of the employees, the company, and the union. A sound testing procedure should serve to allay any suspicion among competing employees as to favoritism or discrimination in awarding jobs."[126] Arbitrator David L. Cole declared that use of tests constitutes an "effort to apply some objective measure of qualifications, rather than to leave the determination to the general judgment and subjective reactions of supervision."[127] Arbitrator B. Meredith Reid stated: "In the absence of proof of bias, prejudice, discrimination or injustice, the reasonable exercise of judgment as to ability is helped rather than hindered by the tests in question"—but he cautioned that this approval of the tests was not "open approval for tests of any kind under any circumstances."[128]

Arbitrators generally hold that tests used in determining ability must be (1) specifically related to the requirements of the job, (2) fair and reasonable, (3) administered in good faith and without discrimination, and (4) properly evaluated. In some awards, the arbitrator may find it necessary to discuss all of the above requirements.[129]

---

of aptitude tests for specific jobs, see Tatum in 41 LA 1027, 1031–1032; Graff in 35 LA 169, 171–174; Schmidt in 31 LA 1002, 1005. As for the use of written tests as an aid to demonstrate the aptitude of employees for other jobs in the line of progression, see Strongin in 56 LA 503, 505–506; Koretz in 47 LA 495, 500; McCoy in 34 LA 37, 38.

[125] Celotex Corp., 53 LA 746, 756 (Dworkin, 1969). In Bethlehem Steel Corp., 48 LA 1205, 1208–1209 (Seward, 1967), a "local working conditions" clause precluded management from adding a second entirely different test in addition to the one which could be used under past practice, but management was not precluded from revising the original test.

[126] Mead Containers, Inc., 35 LA 349, 352 (1960). Also see Dworkin in 53 LA 746, 755.

[127] International Harvester Co., 21 LA 183, 184 (1953). Also see Arbitrator Lehoczky in 66–2 ARB ¶8652; Sembower in 27 LA 353, 357 (approving the use of tests but finding the administration of them improper); Marshall in 25 LA 480, 484–485.

[128] Stauffer Chemical Co., 23 LA 322, 326 (1954).

[129] One arbitrator thoroughly examined the testing procedure and the application of its results, noting that management employed a specialist to design and evaluate the tests, that the tests were related to the skills and qualifications

In others, he may discuss one or more, the implication being that the rest of the requirements have been met.

(1) With respect to the first requirement, it has been held that the test must be related to the skill and knowledge required in the job.[130] For example, a written test given to ascertain clerical and arithmetical ability required on the job is a proper aid in determining ability,[131] as is a test requiring performance of duties identical with those actually performed on the job.[132] It has also been held that the employer may not change the requirements of the job through the test,[133] and that he may not include general abstract questions not based upon the type of problems which would actually arise on the job.[134]

(2) A test will probably be considered fair and reasonable if, among other possible characteristics, it covers all relevant factors,[135] the questions are not unduly difficult,[136] and it is given under proper (though not necessarily ideal) conditions.[137] Frequently, the arbitrator will simply state or imply that the test in question has been examined and found to be fair and reasonable.[138]

---

required in the job, that a trained administrator and test examiners gave the tests, and that as an extra precaution against error it was standard procedure to offer each employee an opportunity to take the tests twice. Glass Containers Mfrs. Institute, 47 LA 217, 223 (Dworkin, undated).

[130] See Arbitrator Larkin in 52 LA 633, 638 (citing other cases on the point that a general aptitude test having no relation to the job in question may not be used as a proper guide for denying a senior employee a promotion); Barnhart in 49 LA 1068, 1073; Gorsuch in 46 LA 1116, 1123; Wagner in 46 LA 81, 91; Dworkin in 35 LA 349, 353; McCoy in 34 LA 37, 38–39. In Griggs v. Duke Power Co., 91 S. Ct. 849, 856 (1971), the Supreme Court stated: "Nothing in the [Civil Rights] Act precludes the use of testing or measuring procedures" so long as the tests used "measure the person for the job and not the person in the abstract."

[131] See United States Steel Corp., 46 LA 414, 416 (Florey, 1966); Wallingford Steel Co., 29 LA 597, 599 (Cahn, 1957).

[132] See Arbitrator McDaniel in 53 LA 777, 779–780; Bradley in 38 LA 63, 67–68; Bailer in 19 LA 257, 260.

[133] See Kuhlman Electric Co., 26 LA 885, 890–891 (Howlett, 1956).

[134] See Arbitrator Kates in 56 LA 328, 331; Larkin in 52 LA 633, 638; McCoy in 34 LA 37, 38–39.

[135] See Bendix Aviation Corp., 19 LA 257, 260 (Bailer, 1952).

[136] See Hammarlund Mfg. Co., Inc., 19 LA 653, 655 (Bailer, 1952).

[137] Ibid., where the fact that conditions under which the test was given were not ideal was not sufficient to make the test unfair or unreasonable.

[138] See Arbitrator Uible in 49 LA 735, 737; Gorsuch in 46 LA 1116, 1123; Cahn in 29 LA 597, 599; Ross in 29 LA 262, 265; Reid in 23 LA 322, 325; Lehoczky in 18 LA 413, 414. In Patterson Steel Co., 66–3 ARB ¶8949 (1966), Arbitrator Charles H. Logan found the test "ill conceived, inexcusably unfair, and flagrantly discriminatory" where it dealt with matters far more complex than would ever be encountered on the job.

(3) The test must be fairly administered and graded and uniformly applied.[139] Not only must the test be given to all applicants for the job,[140] but the company may not give the junior employee an unfair advantage by temporarily assigning him to the job shortly before the test is to be given, thus enabling him to learn the practical operation of the machine which is part of the test.[141] A test may be considered questionable if it is so "critical" that it goes beyond determining the type and amount of ability required for the job and selects only the exact number of applicants needed to fill the vacancies.[142] Moreover, where the test is not adopted for uniform application but is devised and given after the promotion has been made or the vacancy filled, in an admitted effort to "reinforce" the company's position, it is entitled to little if any weight since there is too much chance of the test being slanted.[143] In some cases, arbitrators would add the further requirement that the test results must be made available to the union or to the examinees, or they indicated with approval that test results were made available.[144]

(4) The test must be properly evaluated in the light of the contract provisions relating to seniority and job requirements, and it must not be used in a manner inconsistent with the contract.[145] In this regard, where a contract contains a "sufficient ability" clause a test may not be used to determine "relative" ability.[146]

It must be kept in mind that arbitrators generally take the view that while the test may be used as an aid in judging ability or as

[139] See South Central Bell Telephone Co., 52 LA 1104, 1109 (Platt, 1969).
[140] See Bethlehem Steel Co., 29 LA 710, 711 (Seward, 1957); Bendix Aviation Corp., 19 LA 257, 260 (Bailer, 1952). Also see Arbitrator Roberts in 37 LA 49, 52; Cahn in 29 LA 597, 599; Ross in 29 LA 262, 265; Shister in 24 LA 703, 705; Reid in 23 LA 322, 325.
[141] See Joseph T. Ryerson & Son, Inc., 56 LA 1206, 1209 (Caraway, 1971).
[142] See Ball Brothers Co., Inc., 27 LA 353, 357 (Sembower, 1956).
[143] International Nickel Co., 36 LA 343, 349–350 (Teple, 1960). Under the relative ability clause, management was nonetheless upheld in selecting the junior employee since he had greater experience on the job and thus was better qualified.
[144] See Arbitrator Simon in 50 LA 1227, 1233; Bennett in 49 LA 465, 468; Wolff in 47 LA 552, 553; Wagner in 46 LA 81, 91; McCoy in 34 LA 37, 39. Also see Graff in 35 LA 169, 174. One arbitrator would require that the union "be a party to the giving of the tests, the evaluation of the results, and probably to the selection of the tests to be given." Central Soya Co., 41 LA 1027, 1031–1032 (Tatum, 1963). Also see Marshall in 36 LA 570, 573.
[145] See Allegheny Ludlum Steel Corp., 66–3 ARB ¶9071 (Crawford, 1966); American Smelting & Refining Co., 29 LA 262, 265 (Ross, 1957).
[146] See Arbitrator Alexander in 46 LA 801, 805; Kates in 45 LA 21, 25; DiLeone in 41 LA 856, 860; Sembower in 27 LA 353, 357.

a "verification" of ability, the employer may not base his determination of ability solely upon the results of a test but must consider other factors and other evidence.[147]

It has been held that employees are obligated to take required tests even though there is no provision in the agreement therefor.[148] Many arbitrators have ruled that management not only can require bidders to take tests designed to determine ability for the job but also that it is justified in disqualifying any who refuse to take the tests.[149] Thus, it has been emphasized:

"* * * [T]he arbitrator wishes to make it emphatically clear that the Company has the right to require job bidders to take written tests, as well as other job related tests, to determine their qualifications, subject to disqualification if they refuse. The bidder cannot reserve to himself the right to determine which tests he will take and which ones he will refuse. He must comply with this requirement. If the test is not a reasonable one, or is not fairly administered, or if unwarranted conclusions are drawn from the results, the appropriate remedy is through the grievance procedure."[150]

In two instances, the arbitrator apparently considered the equities of the case and held that although the company could disqualify a bidder when he refused to take the test on the erroneous advice of the union, he should be given another opportunity to take the test.[151]

---

[147] See Arbitrator Caraway in 56 LA 1206, 1209; Block in 54 LA 460, 466; Volz in 49 LA 918, 921; Anderson in 49 LA 589, 593–594; Bennett in 49 LA 465, 467; Wolff in 47 LA 552, 553; Strong in 66–1 ARB ¶8306; Beatty in 45 LA 267, 268–269; Kates in 45 LA 21, 25; Gill in 34 LA 71, 75; Frey in 30 LA 674, 677; Seward in 29 LA 710, 712; Cahn in 29 LA 597, 599; Dworkin in 29 LA 29, 36; Howlett in 26 LA 885, 890–892; Reid in 23 LA 322, 325; Lehoczky in 18 LA 413, 414. Arbitrator Harry H. Platt stated that "a determination of how much weight should be given test results, along with other relevant factors, is a matter of judgment," and "when such judgment is exercised honestly and upon due consideration, it is not arbitrary action" even though there may be "room for two opinions." South Central Bell Telephone Co., 52 LA 1104, 1110–1111 (1969).

[148] Equitable Gas Co., 46 LA 81, 91 (Wagner, 1965).

[149] See Arbitrator Dworkin in 53 LA 746, 757, and in 35 LA 349, 353; Johnson in 51 LA 99, 99–100; Anderson in 66–3 ARB ¶8933; McIntosh in 44 LA 720, 721–722; McCoy in 64–3 ARB ¶9258 (holding that employees' refusal meant that they "voluntarily passed up the opportunity to get the job"); Roberts in 37 LA 49, 52–53; Graff in 35 LA 169, 174; Seward in 29 LA 710, 711–712. In some of these cases, the arbitrator found on the evidence that the grievant was not qualified for the job. Cf. American Meter Co., 41 LA 856, 861–862 (DiLeone, 1963).

[150] Vulcan Materials Co., 54 LA 460, 466 (Block, 1970), citations omitted. The arbitrator also considered the fact that the grievants had inadequacies in their ability to perform the job in question. Id. at 466–467.

[151] Celotex Corp., 53 LA 746, 757 (Dworkin, 1969); Standard Oil Co. (Indiana), 11 LA 810, 811 (Updegraff, 1948).

Experience

Experience is distinguishable from both seniority and productivity. It is the extent to which an employee has engaged in a particular job, type of work, or occupation. While the term ability does not necessarily imply prior experience on the particular job, experience is ordinarily considered a tangible, objective factor to be taken into consideration in determining fitness and ability.[152] Indeed, management has sometimes been reprimanded by the arbitrator for failing to take into consideration the experience of a senior employee who has been bypassed.[153]

Various views have been expressed concerning the place of experience in determining fitness and ability. Arbitrator Edwin R. Teple has stated: "Experience usually is, and should be, one of the most important factors in determining ability."[154] Arbitrator Robert G. Howlett noted that "Other things being equal, the man who has had some experience on a job can become a competent employee in the classification faster than the man who has had no such experience."[155] Arbitrator Otto J. Baab expressed the opinion that it is "reasonable to adopt the criterion of actual experience to determine skill and ability,"[156] but Arbitrator Paul N. Lehoczky stated that "experience is not the sole criterion in forming a judgment of ability."[157] Arbitrator Livingston Smith asserted that "experience [is not] in itself a factor in determining fitness and ability save and except to the extent that experience may tend to increase one's skill and ability."[158]

In any event, arbitrators generally give some consideration to experience where it is relevant to the job requirements. It may be one of several factors used, or a major factor, or the sole or determin-

---

[152] See Arbitrator Williams in 48 LA 430, 431–432 (cautioning, however, that experience must not be accorded such "overriding value" as to negate the seniority provision of the parties' agreement); Prasow in 24 LA 437, 441; Baab in 14 LA 512, 515. Also see Arbitrator Dunau in 39 LA 270, 275.
[153] See Arbitrator Owen in 54 LA 434, 435–436; Kates in 45 LA 743, 749; Cole in 21 LA 214, 217–218.
[154] International Nickel Co., 36 LA 343, 349 (1960).
[155] Kuhlman Electric Co., 26 LA 885, 891 (1956). Also see Reliance Universal, Inc., 50 LA 397, 400 (Alexander, 1968).
[156] Thor Corp., 14 LA 512, 515 (1950).
[157] Seagrave Corp., 16 LA 410, 412 (1951). Also see Arbitrator Williams in 48 LA 530, 531–532; Kates in 40 LA 590, 597.
[158] Tin Processing Corp., 17 LA 193, 198 (1951). In Iroquois Gas Corp., 39 LA 161, 162–163 (O'Rourke, 1962), present ability to perform the particular job was a factor in favor of the junior employee where the senior employee admitted that he knew nothing about the particular job.

ing factor. Work experience on the job in question or on a related job could demonstrate an employee's ability to perform the job,[159] with greater weight being accorded to experience on the particular job than on a related job.[160] The weight which the arbitrator gives to experience may depend in large measure upon the emphasis placed on this factor by the parties and upon the evidence, or lack of evidence, concerning other factors relevant to the determination of fitness and ability.[161] Also, the contract language and the fact situation presented to the arbitrator are of prime importance.

Naturally, if experience is not important to the job, little or no weight will be attached to this factor.[162] On the other hand, experience in the work may be a basic requirement for the job, thereby justifying management in giving preference to an experienced junior employee over a senior who lacks experience.[163] Moreover, the employer may be upheld in giving preference to the junior employee where he has had substantially greater experience than the senior,[164] or where the experience of the junior employee is identical with or is more closely related to the work involved than the experience of the senior em-

---

[159] See Arbitrator Johannes in 56 LA 40, 42–43; Stouffer in 56 LA 6, 9–10; Tsukiyama in 55 LA 477, 479–480; Block in 51 LA 896, 898–899; Sembower in 50 LA 445, 449; Alexander in 50 LA 397, 400; Griffin in 29 LA 870, 874; Prasow in 24 LA 437, 441. Management properly may consider related work experience *off* the job, i.e., training courses taken off the job and work experience in a like occupation for another employer. See Arbitrator Sembower in 50 LA 445, 449; Cantor in 48 LA 777, 778; Warns in 36 LA 380, 382.

[160] See Arbitrator Coburn in 56 LA 733, 737; Tsukiyama in 55 LA 477, 479–480 (holding that the junior employee's experience and knowledge ˙which were relevant and related to the job constituted the "material difference" required by contract in the qualifications of applicants, justifying his promotion over the senior employee who lacked such experience and knowledge); Warns in 21 LA 392, 397; Roberts in 19 LA 270, 279.

[161] For various treatment of experience, see Arbitrator Larson in 55 LA 813, 816; Alexander in 50 LA 397, 400; McDermott in 49 LA 1160, 1171; Singletary in 44 LA 1193, 1195; Altieri in 43 LA 499, 504–505; Dunau in 39 LA 270, 273–275; Boles in 28 LA 72, 75–76; Howlett in 26 LA 885, 891; Lehoczky in 16 LA 410, 412.

[162] See Arbitrator Larkin in 56 LA 399, 402–403; Schmidt in 31 LA 1002, 1005–1006; Boles in 28 LA 72, 75–76.

[163] See Arbitrator Coburn in 56 LA 733, 737; Sembower in 50 LA 445, 449–450; Cahn in 18 LA 536, 538. For some kinds of jobs, such as those requiring qualities of leadership, actual experience is given special weight. See Arbitrator Wolff in 54 LA 447, 447–448; Sembower in 50 LA 445, 449–450.

[164] See Arbitrator Stouffer in 56 LA 6, 9–10; Roberts in 47 LA 823, 826–827; Luskin in 46 LA 23, 27–28; Maggs in 37 LA 29, 35; Brecht in 21 LA 565, 568–569; Gilden in 15 LA 636, 638; Platt in 12 LA 6, 7. The fact that the junior employee's experience is more recent as well as more substantial is entitled to weight. See Arbitrator Bradley in 38 LA 63, 68–69; Teple in 36 LA 343, 349.

ployee,[165] or where the job requires extensive training and experience which the junior employee has had and the senior lacks.[166]

Other factors being equal, arbitrators have sometimes held that the senior employee should be given a trial or break-in period on the basis of his having had some experience,[167] even though the junior employee selected by the company had somewhat more experience.[168] In this connection, it should be noted that some arbitrators have distinguished temporary from permanent promotions in judging fitness and ability, and when temporary, the tendency is to emphasize present fitness and ability and hence to give greater weight to experience.[169]

Trial or Break-in Period on the Job v. Training

Agreements sometimes provide for a trial or break-in period on the job to determine ability, and questions in connection with the interpretation and application of such provisions are frequently arbitrated.[170] In the absence of contractual provision, the question arises as to whether management must give the senior employee a trial.[171] Obviously, ability to perform the job, or the lack of it, may be demonstrated by a trial or break-in period on the job. As stated by Arbitrator Carl A. Warns, "The best evidence as to whether an employee

---

[165] See Arbitrator Kennedy in 50 LA 1249, 1252; Dolson in 50 LA 990, 994–995; Stouffer in 50 LA 283, 286–287; Murphy in 34 LA 356, 358–359; Warns in 34 LA 46, 49, and in 21 LA 392, 397; Fleming in 30 LA 237, 239–241; Brecht in 21 LA 565, 568–569. In Lockheed-Georgia Co., 49 LA 603, 605 (Di Leone, 1967), management's reliance upon experience was not upheld since the experience of the junior employee was found to bear little resemblance to the job requirements, and the junior and senior employees were found to be otherwise substantially equal in ability.

[166] See Arbitrator Gill in 48 LA 190, 191–192; Oppenheim in 46 LA 860, 863; Jones in 25 LA 600, 604; Prasow in 24 LA 437, 441–442.

[167] See Arbitrator Klamon in 30 LA 279, 282; Randle in 17 LA 486, 487; Copelof in 16 LA 359, 365 (contractual provision for a trial period); McCoy in 12 LA 682, 685.

[168] See Arbitrator Williams in 48 LA 530, 532 (contractual provision for a training period); Rosenfarb in 23 LA 789, 793–794, and Smith in 17 LA 193, 198 (contractual provision for a trial period); Lehoczky in 16 LA 410, 412.

[169] See Arbitrator Emery in 28 LA 733, 735; Marshall in 23 LA 623, 628; Warren in 21 LA 228, 231.

[170] See, for example, 54 LA 683, 684; 53 LA 1282, 1283; 45 LA 267 at 267; 29 LA 29, 31; 25 LA 661, 662; 24 LA 461, 463; 16 LA 525, 526; 16 LA 359, 361; 9 LA 956, 960; 2 LA 655, 657.

[171] Past practice may be involved. See Arbitrator Flannagan in 56 LA 920, 922, 923–924; Randle in 17 LA 486, 487; Aaron in 15 LA 162, 167; Whitton in 13 LA 666, 670.

can do a job is to give him a fair trial on it."[172] Arbitrator Vernon
L. Stouffer stated that "The purpose of a trial period is to afford
an employee the opportunity to demonstrate that he has the ability
for the job in question or can with some familiarization therewith
achieve the necessary skills within a reasonable period of time to perform the job in an acceptable manner."[173]

There appears to be a close relationship between the use of tests
or other criteria and a trial period on the job—some arbitrators have
expressed the view that the employer should grant the senior employee
a trial period on the job, but not training, to demonstrate his ability
if the test results[174] or other criteria used have been inconclusive in
determining the ability of the senior bidder.[175]

Thus, arbitrators generally are inclined to the view that if there
is a reasonable doubt as to the ability of the senior employee and
if the trial would cause no serious inconvenience, it should be granted,
but that a trial should not be required in all cases.[176] There is a similar

---

[172] Dayton Power & Light Co., 28 LA 624, 626 (1957). Similarly, see I-T-E
Imperial Corp., 55 LA 1284, 1287 (White, 1970).
[173] American Welding & Manufacturing Co., 52 LA 889, 893 (1969). For
discussion of various aspects of trial periods, see Howard, "Senority Rights and
Trial Periods," 15 Arb. J. 51 (1960).
[174] See General Controls Co., 33 LA 213, 217–218 (Thompson, 1959); Linde
Air Products Co., 25 LA 369, 372 (Shister, 1955). Also see Arbitrator Dworkin
in 39 LA 735, 739, and in 29 LA 29, 37, where the contract provision for
a trial period was considered as protecting the employer's interests. Some awards
appear to have treated a trial on the job as something in the nature of a
performance test. See Arbitrator White in 55 LA 1284, 1287; Murphy in 18
LA 757, 760.
[175] See Arbitrator White in 55 LA 1284, 1287–1288; Elliot in 41 LA 353,
359; Rohman in 39 LA 436, 441; McKelvey in 22 LA 167, 170. The same
approach has been taken in cases which involved contract provisions for a trial
period on the job. See Kates in 56 LA 328, 331; Lazarus in 28 LA 823,
828; Cole in 21 LA 231, 234.
[176] See Arbitrator White in 55 LA 1284, 1288; Elkouri in 46 LA 238, 242;
Reid in 29 LA 743, 746–747; Shister in 25 LA 369, 372; Prasow in 24 LA
437, 442; McKelvey in 22 LA 167, 170; Shulman in 2 LA 374, 376. Cf. Arbitrator
Updegraff in 29 LA 50, 52; Murphy in 18 LA 757, 760. In some cases involving
a bumping situation, arbitrators have held that the senior employee is required
to have the "present ability" to perform the work and that he is not entitled
to a trial or break-in period or a training period (some arbitrators citing the
specific language of the bumping clause as requiring present ability, others emphasizing the absence of a provision for a trial, break-in or training period). See
Arbitrator Volz in 44 LA 694, 697; Nichols in 44 LA 653, 656–657; Cahn in
44 LA 24, 24–25; Dworkin in 39 LA 609, 612–613 (citing many cases); McCoy
in 23 LA 779, 781; Updegraff in 16 LA 909, 911–912. Cf. Rohman in 39 LA
436, 441, where the senior had previous experience on the work.

general agreement that the trial period should be a short one,[177] but it also has been held that the trial must be adequate.[178]

From the standpoint of the company also the trial period must be adequate, but the company does not have an unlimited or extended period to determine the fitness of an employee.[179] While most cases involve trial periods of less than thirty days, because of the circumstances some involve greater periods. For example, it has been held that a nine-month trial period ordinarily is too long but was not too long where the employee for seven months of that time was taking a training course which management expected would improve his performance,[180] that the employer is entitled to a reasonable trial period but that eleven months was not reasonable where the employee had received an automatic pay increase six months after his promotion,[181] and that management could remove a senior employee after a five-month trial period where he had four separate opportunities for merit increases but received only one and had consistently been warned about his work and given low ratings during the trial period.[182]

The contract may specify the amount of time for the trial or it may require only "a reasonable qualifying period." In a case involving the latter language, the arbitrator said that no particular number of hours or days must be provided and that "All that is required under this contract is that a long enough period be allowed to demonstrate to management, viewing the employee's performance impartially and reasonably and in good faith, that he can or can not fulfill the requirements of the job."[183]

---

[177] See Arbitrator Williams in 53 LA 160, 162; Prasow in 24 LA 437, 442; Seward in 23 LA 532, 533–534; Kerr in 11 LA 567, 568. In American Oil Co., 53 LA 160, 162 (Williams, 1969), it was held that the "sufficient" ability clause "does not contemplate that the senior employee's fitness and ability be sufficient to perform the job at peak efficiency from the first hour on it, but contemplates a reasonable familiarization (but no training) period on the new job."

[178] See Arbitrator Roberts in 55 LA 261, 269–270; Jones in 53 LA 101, 111 (inadequate supervisory assistance and alleged racial bias); Kates in 44 LA 389, 392; McKelvey in 22 LA 167, 170–171; Copelof in 17 LA 324, 326.

[179] Smith Scott Co., Inc., 48 LA 270, 272 (Burns, 1966).

[180] Koppers Co., Inc., 49 LA 663, 665 (Malkin, 1967), upholding management's removal of the employee since he failed to qualify.

[181] Smith Scott Co., Inc., 48 LA 270, 272 (Burns, 1966), noting also that new hires were given a short qualifying period of a week or two.

[182] Shenango Furnace Co., 46 LA 203, 209–210 (Klein, 1966), noting that the "lengthy trial period tends to negate the probability of any bad faith or prejudice" on management's part.

[183] Decor Corp., 44 LA 389, 392 (Kates, 1965). In Seeger Refrigerator

If the senior employee is obviously unfit or unqualified, as in a situation where the job in question requires a high degree of skill which can be acquired only after a long period of training and there is no evidence that the senior employee has these skills or related skills, then management is not required to give him a trial period and may give preference to the junior employee or new hire who already possesses such skills.[184] The same holds true if there is a contract provision for a trial period.[185] Also, no trial on the job is required where the contract makes seniority controlling only if ability is substantially equal and past service of competing applicants shows the junior to possess qualifications considerably superior to those of the senior applicant.[186] Moreover, it has been held that if management has granted a trial as required by the agreement, it need not continue the trial for the full period specified but may cancel it when the candidate demonstrates his inability to perform the job. As stated by one arbitrator, "When it becomes obvious that an employee is not going to be able to acquire the necessary skills to qualify for the job or by his attitude makes it clear that he is not going to become proficient and fails to exhibit any progress, then the employer is not obligated to continue the trial period."[187]

While circumstances of a given case may require that an employer provide a trial or break-in period on the job, he ordinarily would be under no obligation, unless the contract provides otherwise, to provide training for a senior employee to enable him to achieve the fitness

Co., 16 LA 525, 531 (Lockhart, 1951), interpreting similar language, a minimum of three months was considered necessary because of the circumstances of the case and the nature of the work.

[184] See Arbitrator Block in 54 LA 460, 466–467 (no "reasonable expectation of success on the job"); Marshall in 53 LA 1282, 1287; Kennedy in 50 LA 1249, 1252 (lack of qualification shown by employee's past employment record); Kates in 45 LA 21, 25; Wyckoff in 39 LA 538, 541; Miller in 39 LA 336, 340; Dykstra in 38 LA 906, 909 (unsatisfactory work in jobs requiring less skill than job in question); McKelvey in 22 LA 167, 170. Also see Arbitrator Cahn in 52 LA 247, 249–251; Kornblum in 40 LA 403, 407; Coffey in 39 LA 1117, 1118–1119; Murphy in 34 LA 356, 359; Shister in 25 LA 369, 372; Prasow in 24 LA 437, 442.

[185] See Arbitrator Larkin in 48 LA 1031, 1035; Daugherty in 47 LA 554, 557, 558–559; Singletary in 44 LA 1193, 1195; Dworkin in 39 LA 735, 739, and in 35 LA 391, 396; Merrill in 36 LA 145, 148; Lazarus in 28 LA 823, 828; Platt in 24 LA 79, 80; Cole in 21 LA 231, 234.

[186] Semling-Menke Co., 46 LA 523, 526–527 (Graff, 1966).

[187] American Welding & Manufacturing Co., 52 LA 889, 893 (Stouffer, 1969). Also see Diehl Mfg. Co., 36 LA 1266, 1269 (Kornblum, 1961); Howard, "Seniority Rights and Trial Periods," 15 Arb. J. 51, 59 (1961). Cf. Arbitrator Merrill in 36 LA 145, 148.

and ability called for by the contract.[188] If a senior employee would require such extensive training (in order to qualify for a job) as to make it unreasonable under the contract to expect the employer to provide such training, the employer is justified in giving preference to a junior employee who is already fully qualified.[189] The need for training would seem to indicate a lack of skill and ability.[190]

Where the contract recognizes seniority as a factor, management may not afford training opportunities to junior employees while arbitrarily denying them to senior employees, then promote or retain a junior applicant on the basis of such training.[191] Such action not only may constitute discrimination, but also the seniority clause "might be either nullified or circumvented should the Company provide special and preferential training opportunities for low seniority employees."[192] In two cases, the arbitrators held that training and experience received by junior employees in violation of the contract could not be credited to the juniors in considering relative ability, the contract in one case expressly providing that management would assist senior employees to become qualified for promotion by assigning them to temporary vacancies for training purposes,[193] and the contract in the other expressly precluding temporary assignments exceeding thirty days.[194]

This is not to say that management may not select employees for training under any circumstances. It has been held that management could give training to junior employees where the senior em-

---

[188] See Arbitrator Krimsly in 51 LA 49, 51–52 (some instruction but no training should be given on new machine); Prasow in 47 LA 726, 734; Oppenheim in 46 LA 860, 863; Volz in 44 LA 694, 697; Roberts in 37 LA 49, 53; Kornblum in 36 LA 1266, 1270; Merrill in 36 LA 145, 148; Emery in 28 LA 733, 735; Klamon in 20 LA 768, 774; Lehoczky in 16 LA 410, 412; Greene in 7 LA 526, 527. The agreement may provide for training as in 55 LA 432, 433; 49 LA 953, 954; 48 LA 530, 532.
[189] See Arbitrator Teple in 36 LA 343, 351; Murphy in 30 LA 598, 599; McKelvey in 22 LA 167, 170; Updegraff in 16 LA 909, 911–912.
[190] Poloron Products Co. of Pa., Inc., 23 LA 789, 792 (Rosenfarb, 1955). Also see Glidden Co., 34 LA 265, 268 (Griffin, 1960).
[191] See Arbitrator Kerrison in 29 LA 747, 749; Williams in 28 LA 56, 59; Rosenfarb in 23 LA 789, 793; Waite in 19 LA 1, 4; McCoy in 18 LA 834, 835. Also see Arbitrator Williams in 54 LA 683, 686; Luskin in 46 LA 23, 27; Reynolds in 25 LA 60, 63. Cf. Block in 54 LA 1247, 1250–51 (involving a past practice of training employees in one of two areas but not in both); Emery in 28 LA 733, 736.
[192] Sandvik Steel, Inc., 29 LA 747, 749 (Kerrison, 1957). Also see Arbitrator Williams in 54 LA 683, 686; Luskin in 46 LA 23, 27; Rosenfarb in 23 LA 789, 793.
[193] United States Steel Corp., 36 LA 1082, 1087–1088 (Crawford, 1961).
[194] Kroger Co., 34 LA 414, 418 (Emerson, 1959).

ployee was on sick leave,[195] and that management is not required to make special arrangements for senior employees to take part of a training course and not the rest.[196] Furthermore, in the absence of a contract provision dealing with training, it has been held that management should not be denied a reasonable freedom of discretion in selecting employees for training, particularly in connection with new types of activities, but such selection must not be arbitrary or discriminatory or in conflict with the seniority provisions of the contract.[197]

Where the employer has a policy of providing training for employees desiring to take it, he may not automatically disqualify employees who have not taken such training.[198] That is, the employer may not rely on training so provided as a "conclusive determinant of relative ability" but must affirmatively show that the employees selected are actually better qualified.[199] In one case, the junior employee who took the training was better qualified as a result of the training and experience than the senior employees who refused such training, and he therefore was entitled under the relative ability clause to the promotion.[200] Moreover, the fact that the employee did not take advantage of training offered by the company has been considered a factor against him when he was disqualified at the end of a trial period.[201]

Opinion of Supervision

While the opinion of supervisors regarding the ability of employees is considered important and is entitled at least to some consideration,

---

[195] United States Plywood Corp., 49 LA 726, 728 (Amis, 1967).

[196] Bethlehem Steel Corp., 48 LA 1, 2 (Gill, 1966), where the seniors resisted taking the entire course because it would have required them to work temporarily in a lower classification.

[197] See Purolator Products, Inc., 25 LA 60, 63 (Reynolds, 1955). In Vulcan Materials Co., 49 LA 577, 579–580 (Duff, 1967), it was held that tests used for selecting trainees must be appropriate to ascertain the aptitude of bidders to become trainees. In John Strange Paper Co., 43 LA 1184, 1187 (Larkin, 1965), management was permitted to use a test for screening employees to be given a period of on-the-job training (even though for several years it had given each senior employee a chance at such training) so long as the system of selection was fair, uniform, and nondiscriminatory.

[198] United States Steel Corp., 22 LA 188, 190 (Garrett, 1953). Similarly, Whirlpool Corp., 49 LA 529, 533–534 (Sembower, 1967).

[199] United States Steel Corp., 22 LA 188, 190 (Garrett, 1953).

[200] Patapsco and Back Rivers R.R. Co., 43 LA 51, 53–54 (Seitz, 1964). Similarly, see Kaiser Steel Corp., 42 LA 1109, 1113 (Bernstein, 1964), involving layoff of senior employees who lacked the training which the junior employees had.

[201] See American Oil Co., 50 LA 1227, 1233 (Simon, 1968); National Lead Co., 48 LA 405, 408 (Wissner, undated).

such opinion without factual support will not be deemed conclusive.[202] However, when supervisory opinion is substantiated by objective, tangible evidence, it may be the basis for management's determination as to the relative ability of employees.[203] Such objective evidence may include factors discussed elsewhere in this topic, such as test results, production records, periodic merit ratings, and other documentary material, as well as evidence of prior experience and results of trial periods.

The importance of supervisory opinion was noted by Arbitrator Arthur M. Ross as follows:

"Considerable weight should be given to bona fide conclusions of supervisors when supported by factual evidence. In the first place, a supervisor is responsible for the efficient performance of his unit and has a legitimate concern that the employees be properly assigned to achieve this objective. In the second place, he has a deeper and more intimate acquaintance with the men under his charge than an arbitrator is able to acquire in a brief hearing."[204]

Arbitrator Harry Shulman emphasized the necessity for supporting evidence:

"A supervisor's testimony that he honestly believes one employee to be superior to another with respect to the promotion is certainly a factor to be considered. It is not, however, either conclusive or sufficient. The supervisor must be prepared to state the basis for his belief and to support it, not by repeated assertions but by specific and understandable evidence * * *."[205]

Supervisory opinion has been given controlling weight where management's decision to by-pass the senior employee was based upon

---

[202] See Arbitrator White in 55 LA 1284, 1288; Roberts in 55 LA 261, 269; Platt in 20 LA 460, 462; Hays in 12 LA 317, 322.

[203] See Arbitrator Beeson in 54 LA 298, 301–302; Stouffer in 52 LA 889, 893; Klein in 46 LA 203, 210; Larkin in 45 LA 129, 130–131 (supervisory opinion given great weight in this case which involved job of group leader); Feinberg in 64–3 ARB ¶9087; Tsukiyama in 40 LA 1225, 1227; Wyckoff in 39 LA 538, 541; Waite in 19 LA 1, 4. Also see Arbitrator Ralston in 19 LA 402, 405; Grant in 11 LA 312, 315.

[204] Pacific Gas & Electric Co., 23 LA 556, 558 (1954), cited with approval by Arbitrator Tsukiyama in 55 LA 477, 480 (who emphasized the importance of "first line supervisorial participation" in the selection process); Stouffer in 52 LA 889, 893. Also see Arbitrator Burns in 41 LA 148, 151–152, 154; Burris in 25 LA 32, 36; Cole in 21 LA 214, 218. Arbitrator Ross reaffirmed the above view in the San Francisco News–Call Bulletin, 34 LA 271, 273–274 (1960), stating further: "But it does not follow that a clearly mistaken decision should be left undisturbed merely because it has not been shown to be arbitrary, discriminatory, etc."

[205] Ford Motor Co., 2 LA 374, 376 (1945), cited with approval by Arbitrator Roberts in 55 LA 261, 269; Kates in 45 LA 743, 748.

a composite of the opinions of several supervisors who observed or supervised his work, the opinions being formed on the basis of a variety of incidents in the senior's employment record.[206] In another case, the arbitrator stated that the opinion of management was "what actually controlled his decision" where company officers (president, vice president, etc.) were in almost daily contact over many years with the employees, and thus knew them well and knew the processes and machines well.[207]

Supervisory opinion has been given great if not controlling weight where several levels of supervision, familiar with the work performance of the bidders and with the requirements of the job being bid upon, reach a unanimous decision,[208] and where supervisory opinion is later supported by evidence of an employee's inadequate performance during a trial period.[209] Little if any weight has been accorded supervisory opinion where the company relied upon such opinion concerning one of the bidders while not consulting supervisors of another bidder at all,[210] and where the supervisors consulted had little or no opportunity to observe the men they were rating and were not familiar with the requirements of the job being bid upon.[211]

Merit Rating Plans

Merit rating plans (or performance reviews) involve essentially a documentation, usually periodically made, of supervisory opinion concerning various aspects of the "fitness and ability" of the employees. A merit rating plan may include such factors as quantity and quality of work, knowledge of the job, ability to learn, initiative, acceptance of responsibility, ability to direct others, safety habits and accident record, attitude toward fellow employees and management, attendence, and personal characteristics such as moral character, physical condition and appearance.[212] Other factors may include the quality

[206] See Northwestern Bell Telephone Co., 19 LA 47, 50–51 (Doyle, 1952). Also see Eagle-Picher Mining & Smelting Co., 17 LA 205, 211 (Prasow, 1951).

[207] See Pittsburgh Standard Conduit Co., 32 LA 481, 482–483 (Lehoczky, 1959), where the finding was based upon other factors also, including the use of a test.

[208] See Arbitrator Tsukiyama in 55 LA 477, 480; Wolff in 54 LA 447, 448; Beeson in 54 LA 298, 301–302; Larkin in 45 LA 129, 130–131.

[209] See Arbitrator Stouffer in 52 LA 889, 893; Klein in 46 LA 203, 210; Feinberg in 64–3 ARB ¶9087.

[210] See Northwest Airlines, Inc., 46 LA 238, 241–242 (Elkouri, 1966); International Nickel Co., 45 LA 743, 748 (Kates, 1965).

[211] See Royster Co., 55 LA 432, 434 (Amis, 1970); Ohio Edison Co., 46 LA 801, 805 (Alexander, 1966).

[212] See Western Automatic Machine Screw Co., 9 LA 606, 608 (Lehoczky, 1948).

of pertinent experience and training, special conditions of the job, and achievements which have earned incentive awards or other special recognition.[213]

Arbitrators look upon merit rating plans as an aid in judging fitness and ability. However, while considering performance ratings an important aid, Arbitrator Ralph Roger Williams cautioned against placing exclusive reliance upon them in determining fitness and ability, stating:

> "The word 'fitness' is not synonymous with 'merit'; it means the quality of being suitable to the performance of the regular duties of the job, and includes the employee's habits, industry, energy, ambition, tact, disposition, discretion, knowledge of the duties of the job, physical strength, and related attributes. It means suitability. The word 'ability' means the possession of those qualities of mind, physical strength, and related job attainments which are sufficient, under the usual conditions of the job, to satisfactorily perform the basic and usual duties and tasks of the job. The Company placed too much weight on its past evaluations of the Grievant's job performance. While these performance ratings are important and serve to assist in the employer's evaluation of an employee, they are not all-inclusive."[214]

Merit or performance ratings have been a factor (along with others) accepted and considered by the arbitrator in upholding management's determination of ability under a "relative ability" clause[215] and under a "sufficient ability" clause.[216] However, one employee evaluation system was considered by the arbitrator to be suspect in that "well meaning as it was intended to be, [it] tended to match the traits of each bidder against the others," thus resulting in a comparison of bidders which was not permitted under the "sufficient ability" clause.[217]

An arbitrator's acceptance or rejection of a merit rating plan as a criterion for measuring ability depends upon whether the factors used in the plan and the weights attached to them are consistent with

---

[213] See U.S. Department of Interior, 53 LA 657, 659 (Koven, 1969). Many of the factors noted above are discussed as separate criteria elsewhere in this topic.

[214] American Oil Co., 53 LA 160, 161 (1969), involving a "sufficient ability" clause.

[215] See Arbitrator Volz in 47 LA 263, 265; Tsukiyama in 40 LA 1225, 1227–1228; Grant in 11 LA 312, 315; Gilden in 4 LA 657, 666–667.

[216] Jeffrey Mfg. Co., 29 LA 300, 302 (Seinsheimer, 1957).

[217] Ohio Edison Co., 46 LA 801, 805 (Alexander, 1966).

the collective agreement and the requirements of the job in question.[218] Thus, under a contract providing that seniority should govern where "ability, skill, and efficiency" are substantially equal, management's institution of a performance review plan was upheld since the plan did no more than document on a regular basis supervisory opinion concerning the ability, skill, and efficiency of employees; the arbitrator stated that management could use any method, written or unwritten, to determine the relative ability of employees "so long as that method is not unfair, arbitrary, or based on improper or irrelevant premises."[219] Under another "relative ability" provision, the arbitrator held that some of the factors in the merit rating plan used by the company had no bearing upon an employee's "ability to do the work," and when these were discounted the employees involved were found to have the requisite ability.[220]

Educational Background

Technical training acquired through attendance at trade schools, company- or union-sponsored training programs, and the like obviously is highly pertinent to the determination of fitness and ability if such training relates to the requirements of the job in question. Thus, where a job by nature required at least one course in accounting which the grievant had not taken, the company was held justified

---

[218] See Arbitrator Hogan in 27 LA 816, 819 (improper weight given to certain factors); Hawley in 17 LA 516, 519; Grant in 11 LA 312, 315.

[219] Lockheed Aircraft Corp., 25 LA 748, 750–751 (Williams, 1956), where the union agreed that the company could determine relative ability of employees but objected to the regular documentation of such determination. Accord, Lockheed Aircraft Service Co., 40 LA 1225, 1227–1228 (Tsukiyama, 1963). Also see Acme Steel Co., 9 LA 432, 436–437 (Gregory, 1947), stating that a merit rating plan is preferable to placing "the judgment in the hands of the foremen on an ad hoc basis, with no systematic check on their whims and fancies from top management." As to management's right to place evaluation reports in the employee's personnel file for future use and/or the right of the employee and union to be apprised of their use and to see such reports before some affirmative action is taken which adversely affects the employee, see Arbitrator Gilden in 48 LA 421, 424–425; Leach in 48 LA 299, 304 (where the employee feared that the report was a disciplinary device in the nature of a warning); Gusweiler in 44 LA 200, 201 (upholding management's right to make an efficiency survey, but finding improper the forms used); Morvant in 42 LA 41, 45–47. Also see Mobilization For Youth, 49 LA 1124, 1126–1127 (Wolff, 1967), where a report was orally imparted to supervision, was neither discussed with the employee nor made a part of her personnel record, yet was used to bar advancement.

[220] See Western Automatic Machine Screw Co., 9 LA 606, 608–609 (Lehoczky, 1948). Similarly, American Oil Co., 53 LA 160, 162 (Williams, 1969), under a "sufficient ability" clause. In Merrill Stevens Dry Dock & Repair Co., 17 LA 516, 518–519 (Hawley, 1951), most of the factors were accepted but the company was "urged" to remove imprecise factors from its merit rating plan.

in selecting a qualified new hire.[221] However, where the junior employee's technical training was not related to the job requirements,
the employer was held to have violated the seniority provisions by
awarding the job to him since the senior employee otherwise possessed
substantially equal ability.[222] The same result was reached in another
case even though the junior employee's technical training had potential value for jobs higher in the line of progression, the arbitrator
emphasizing that an employee's qualifications "must be measured a
job at a time."[223]

An employee's formal educational background, that is, high
school and college education as opposed to technical training, may
be a factor in the assessment of fitness and ability if it is pertinent
to the job requirements.[224] Where the contract does not specify a
formal educational requirement for given jobs, arbitrators appear to
have taken several (not necessarily inconsistent) approaches to the
question of whether the employer may consider this factor in determining ability. Thus, it has been variously held that (1) management
may require a high school education where the job is complex and
carries with it automatic progressions through several classifications
involving additional responsibilities;[225] (2) the formal educational
background of the employee may be considered along with other factors;[226] (3) the employer may not automatically disqualify an em-

---

[221] Roosevelt University, 56 LA 604, 607 (Larkin, 1971). Also see United
States Steel Corp., 51 LA 264, 266 (Smith, 1968).
[222] Pennsylvania Power & Light Co., 57 LA 146, 148–149 (Howard, 1971).
As to the need of supervisory testimony to correlate technical training with
the job requirements, see Laupahoehoe Sugar Co., 38 LA 404, 412–413 (Tsukiyama, 1961).
[223] Georgia Kraft Co., 47 LA 829, 830 (Williams, 1966). Also see Realist,
Inc., 45 LA 444, 446 (Keeler, 1965). Progression was not automatic in these
cases.
[224] In Griggs v. Duke Power Co., 91 S. Ct. 849 (1971), it was held that
the employer violated Title VII of the Civil Rights Act of 1964 by requiring
a high school education or the passing of a standardized general intelligence
test as a condition of employment in or transfer to jobs where it was not shown
that such requirements were job-related and where the requirements operated
to discriminate against Negroes.
[225] See Philip Carey Mfg. Co., 30 LA 659, 661 (Warns, 1958). Also see
Arbitrator Kates in 46 LA 1153, 1156–1157; Seibel in 22 LA 446, 449–450.
A different result obtained in West Virginia Pulp & Paper Co., 16 LA 359,
365 (Copelof, 1951), where progression was not automatic.
[226] See Arbitrator Volz in 47 LA 263, 265; Handsaker in 42 LA 349, 351;
O'Rourke in 39 LA 161, 163; Howlett in 26 LA 885, 890. Also see Arbitrator
Cantor in 48 LA 777, 778; Baab in 20 LA 137, 142. In Lockheed-Georgia
Co., 49 LA 603, 605 (Di Leone, 1967), it was found that the superior education
of the senior bidder balanced the experience of the junior so that their overall

ployee for want of a formal education but may consider formal education in evaluating the employee's training and experience;[227] (4) the employer violated the contract by denying a promotion to senior employees solely on the basis that they lacked high school education or its equivalent.[228]

In the latter regard, it has been held that the lack of such formal education alone may not be deemed conclusive evidence of a lack of ability, the arbitrator stating that while the company may establish minimum qualifications for a job, it may not create "exclusionary 'barriers'" which prevent employees from competing for a given vacancy. He stated further: "Though a high school diploma (or equivalent certificate) is some evidence of basic ability to perform a given job, the lack of such 'credentials' cannot, in itself, be deemed to establish, conclusively, the opposite."[229]

The question of ability to read and write in English has arisen in several cases. Where such ability was necessary to the proper performance of the job, management has been held justified in disqualifying the employee who lacks such ability, as in the case in which the senior bidders could not read and write well enough in English to interpret the repair manual and parts list and to make requisitions, all necessary functions of the job.[230] However, in another case communication difficulties were not considered sufficient to outweigh the

---

abilities were substantially equal, entitling the former to the promotion under the "relative ability" clause.

[227] See Union Oil Co., 17 LA 62, 64–65 (Wyckoff, 1951). Similarly, United States Steel Corp., 55 LA 659, 662 (McDaniel, 1970). Also see Arbitrator Brown in 44 LA 92, 94.

[228] See Bridgeport Gas Co., 26 LA 289, 291 (Stutz, 1956). Also see Arbitrator McDaniel in 55 LA 659, 662–663; Dworet in 38 LA 91, 92. In a case where the "really serious issue" was the senior employee's age, the arbitrator disposed of the education factor by finding that the "lack of a formal high school education should not constitute a bar to his being considered" for the job. See CIBA Pharmaceutical Co., 41 LA 14, 17 (Berkowitz, 1963).

[229] United States Steel Corp., 55 LA 659, 662 (McDaniel, 1970). Also see Arbitrator Keeler in 45 LA 444, 447; Brown in 44 LA 92, 95; Gill in 37 LA 14, 14–15 (where the company's concern that the removal of the educational requirement would burden it unreasonably with the giving of trial periods to unqualified employees was considered unfounded due to its testing program). In United States Steel Corp., 42 LA 245, 247 (Altrock, 1964), only minimal weight was given to the fact that the junior employee's schooling was from an "accredited" school, while the senior employee's was not, and since other factors indicated that they were relatively equal in ability, the senior was entitled to the job.

[230] Vulcan Materials Co., 54 LA 460, 466 (Block, 1970). Similarly, see Arbitrator Goodstein in 51 LA 31, 34; Phelps in 32 LA 289, 292–293.

job applicant's meritorious service and his ability to do the basic work
of the job; even though he had a heavy foreign accent and could
read English only slowly, he could read blueprints and had effectively
communicated with a new man he had trained on the job.[231]

Production Records

An employee's production record is objective evidence of his
productivity or output and may be relied upon in whole or in part
(depending upon the circumstances) in determining fitness and ability.[232] One arbitrator asserted that ability "is most assuredly tied up
with productivity" and that productivity must be measured in terms
of both quality and quantity of work.[233] Another stated that "output
reflects not only effort, but know-how, skill and general capability,
and is generally regarded as a proper item to be considered in measuring ability."[234]

Production records may be the sole factor considered where there
is a substantial difference in the productivity of competing employees.
Thus, management's determination of relative ability based solely
upon productivity was upheld where the grievant's production was
considerably below that of other workers,[235] and in another case where
there was a 17 percent difference between the senior and junior employee's production earnings.[236] Management's reliance in part upon
production records has likewise been upheld where the employee consistently failed to make the minimum wage under an incentive system
or where the employee's production record was consistently below the
standard.[237]

---

[231] Lanson & Sessions Co., 50 LA 959, 960–961 (Dahl, 1968). Also see
Gallmeyer & Livingston Co., 20 LA 899, 901–903 (Ryder, 1953).
[232] Regarding the type of data necessary in presenting production records
as evidence of fitness and ability, see Jonco Aircraft Corp., 22 LA 819, 823
(Merrill, 1954). The term "work records" may or may not be broader than
"production records." For cases in which the "work records" of competing employees were a factor, see Arbitrator McDermott in 49 LA 1160, 1170–1172;
Cantor in 48 LA 777, 781; Daugherty in 47 LA 554, 558–559; Hayes in 31
LA 338, 340–341; Brecht in 21 LA 565, 568; Prasow in 17 LA 205, 211.
For a statement regarding the significance of "performance records," see James
N. Travirca, Gen. Contracting Co., 56 LA 1083, 1084 (Logan, 1971).
[233] Universal Mfg. Co., 13 LA 238, 241 (Spencer, 1949).
[234] Worth Steel Co., 12 LA 931, 934 (Bell, 1949).
[235] Byer-Rolnick Corp., 45 LA 868, 872 (Ray, 1965); Universal Mfg. Co.,
13 LA 238, 241 (Spencer, 1949).
[236] Worth Steel Co., 12 LA 931, 934 (Bell, 1949).
[237] See Arbitrator Kesselman in 52 LA 568, 570; Hazelwood in 51 LA 382,
383–384; Abernethy in 23 LA 379, 383; Klamon in 19 LA 639, 646; McCoy
in 11 LA 419, 425–426. Also see Hawley in 33 LA 719, 721.

On the other hand, in situations where there is only a minor difference in productivity of employees, automatic reliance upon productivity alone for the determination of relative ability probably would not be upheld.[238] Moreover, management may not base its determination of ability upon its speculations as to the relative *future* productivity of competing employees.[239]

Attendance Records

Under the various types of seniority clauses, attendance records may be considered at least as one of the factors used in determining fitness and ability, and in some instances may be the sole or controlling factor. In a number of cases an employee's attendance record has been considered as a relevant factor and as tangible and objective evidence in assessing ability and qualifications.[240] An employee's poor attendance record has been the sole or controlling factor where the job involved was critical to operations or otherwise required a high degree of responsibility.[241] Thus, under a contract containing a "relative ability" clause, the promotion of a junior over a senior employee on the basis of their attendance records was upheld where the records showed a "striking" difference in favor of the junior and the job required a high degree of responsibility.[242] In that case, Arbitrator Jacob J. Blair stated:

> "It is well established as a principle that Management has the right to expect and require regular attendance on the job. While it is true that Management has in this instance been extremely negligent in enforcing this right, its negligence does not bar it from applying the right in the case of a promotion. * * *

---

[238] United States Steel Corp., 22 LA 80, 81 (Garrett, 1953).

[239] Wurlitzer Co., 41 LA 792, 795 (Duff, 1963).

[240] See Arbitrator White in 55 LA 1284, 1287 (where the arbitrator exercised an "equitable power" in taking into consideration the attendance factor); Amis in 49 LA 726, 728; Elkouri in 46 LA 238, 241 (but promotion may not be denied as punishment for tardiness); Schmidt in 44 LA 283, 285; Davis in 30 LA 862, 871. Cf. Arbitrator Duncan in 40 LA 364, 366; Edes in 11 LA 108, 109 (where the parties agreed at the hearing that "ability and skill" does not encompass absenteeism). In Lockheed Aircraft Service Co., 40 LA 1225, 1228 (Tsukiyama, 1963), the company was upheld in its determination that the junior employee's superior qualities of leadership (a requirement of the job) outweighed the much better attendance record of the senior employee.

[241] See Arbitrator Kates in 52 LA 1074, 1077–1078; McCoy in 51 LA 857, 858–859 (stating, however, that ordinarily management cannot deny promotions solely on the basis of a poor attendance record); Turkus in 43 LA 946, 950; Blair in 16 LA 382, 383, and in 8 LA 877, 879.

[242] Rogers Bros. Corp., 16 LA 382, 383 (Blair, 1951). Accord, Metal Forge Co., 51 LA 857, 858–859 (McCoy, 1968).

"The action of Management in invoking this right at this time is not arbitrary. True, Management could not discipline * * * [grievant] by layoffs or dismissals for an action which they have condoned over a period of time without prior notice or warning. But the right to discipline and the right of Management to choose between candidates for promotion are distinguishable. * * * Management has the right to invoke the attendance records of two employees contending for a promotion because to do otherwise would condone and even approve a record of irregular attendance at work."[243]

It has also been held that the employer may consider the employee's attendance record in determining whether he is "qualified," even though his numerous absences were due to illness.[244]

However, some arbitrators have held that an employee's attendance record is not a factor to be used in determining the ability or qualifications of an employee. They reason that nothing in the contract permits management to use this factor to pass over a senior employee who otherwise meets the contractual requirements, and, further, that if an employee is guilty of absenteeism, it is a matter of discipline and should have been dealt with at the time the offenses occurred.[245]

In cases involving excused absences for the conduct of union business, it has been held that such absences should not operate as a bar to giving the senior man preference; but the arbitrator appears to have based his decision on past practice,[246] or to have conditioned his award upon the satisfactory performance of the job during a trial period,[247] or upon regular attendance by the employee,[248] reserving explicitly or in effect the right of management to take corrective steps should the employee not perform in an acceptable manner.

Disciplinary Record

If an employee's disciplinary record contains offenses which reflect upon his fitness and ability for a given job, such record may

---

[243] Rogers Bros. Corp., 16 LA 382, 383 (Blair, 1951). Accord, Emhart Mfg. Co., 43 LA 946, 950 (Turkus, 1964), under a "sufficient ability" clause.

[244] See Arbitrator Bailer in 20 LA 835, 836; Levinson in 16 LA 790, 792; McCoy in 11 LA 419, 425–426. Cf. Kelliher in 9 LA 444, 447.

[245] See Arbitrator Duncan in 40 LA 364, 366; Dworkin in 34 LA 852, 854–855; Kelliher in 24 LA 599, 600.

[246] See American Lava Corp., 42 LA 117, 120 (Hon, 1964); Douglas Aircraft Co., Inc., 23 LA 786, 788 (Warren, 1955).

[247] See Marlin-Rockwell Corp., 17 LA 254, 256 (Shister, 1951).

[248] See Goodyear Decatur Mills, 12 LA 682, 685 (McCoy, 1949).

be given some consideration. For example, it has been held that an employee's disciplinary record could be considered since his offenses demonstrated that he lacked maturity, reliability, and a sense of responsibility and hence the ability, merit, and capacity required by the contract.[249] Even where the employee had not been disciplined for his offenses in the past, one arbitrator distinguished between the right of management to discipline at a later date and the obligation of management to promote, stating:

> "When the requirements of the job * * * clearly call for maturity, reliability and a sense of responsibility in addition to technical skill or expertness, it would be less than logical to deny or preclude any consideration at all to offenses directly related thereto simply because such offenses through laxity or forbearance lost vitality as a basis for subsequent disciplinary action."[250]

However, other arbitrators have held that if alleged offenses are not made the subject of discipline at the time they are committed, management may not be permitted to rely upon them later in assessing employee abilities and qualifications.[251] Furthermore, a single offense for which the worker has been disciplined may not be sufficient to compel the conclusion that he is incompetent.[252]

The collective agreement may provide specifically or in effect that the personnel records of the employees be considered by management in determining ability. Under such an agreement, personnel records showing that four written reprimands were issued to the senior employee in connection with his work were considered by the arbitrator to justify management's decision to promote the junior employee.[253]

Employee's Physical and Psychological Fitness

Many contracts specifically include physical fitness as a requirement for job preference.[254] However, even where the contract does

---

[249] Dewey & Almy Chemical Co., 25 LA 316, 318–319 (Somers, 1955). Also see Arbitrator Stouffer in 50 LA 17, 20; Turkus in 43 LA 946, 949; Klamon in 19 LA 639, 646–647.
[250] Emhart Mfg. Co., 43 LA 946, 949 (Turkus, 1964).
[251] See Arbitrator Carlson in 54 LA 151, 155; Kelliher in 24 LA 599, 600; Killingsworth in 19 LA 186, 188.
[252] See Copco Steel & Engineering Co., 13 LA 586, 591 (Platt, 1949). Also see Thompson Bros. Boat Mfg. Co., 55 LA 69, 73 (Moberly, 1970), stating that "inability does *not* mean temporary misconduct or improper work attitudes which more properly should be treated by corrective action."
[253] Inland Steel Co., 16 LA 280, 284 (Cornsweet, 1951).
[254] See, for example, 51 LA 1143, 1144; 30 LA 237, 238; 23 LA 556, 557; 17 LA 486, 487.

not contain the physical ability requirement, it has been said that the term "ability" includes physical (and mental) ability.[255] Health records showing an employee's physical condition have been considered as "tangible and objective" evidence of his fitness and ability;[256] but "old" records as to an employee's physical condition ordinarily may not be relied upon, arbitrators favoring more recent medical evidence concerning such matters.[257]

In the absence of a contract prohibition, management has been held entitled to require employees to take physical examinations, but the right must be exercised properly and not arbitrarily, capriciously, or unreasonably.[258] Management could require such examinations to determine the physical fitness or ability of the employee to perform the work, for instance, before reinstatement or promotion of an ailing employee in a job requiring weight lifting activities,[259] or before transfer or promotion of an employee to a job demanding greater physical effort,[260] or where there is serious doubt as to the employee's ability to perform the work safely because of some physical condition or characteristic.[261]

It would seem to be a corollary to this right that it is the duty of the employer to protect the health of his employees despite their willingness to perform heavier duties. In this regard, Arbitrator Joseph M. Klamon stated:

"* * * Indeed, the Company might incur a legal liability for failure to exercise due care and reasonable judgment to protect the

---

[255] See Arbitrator Simon in 53 LA 1181, 1193; Siciliano in 37 LA 1047, 1050; Jenson in 32 LA 772, 774; Stashower in 12 LA 896, 897. The terms "fitness" and "qualified" also include physical and mental fitness or ability. See Arbitrator Williams in 49 LA 952, 955; Dworkin in 35 LA 391, 394; Tatum in 34 LA 67, 70. Cf. Cahn in 34 LA 426, 427, involving past practice.

[256] See Southwestern Bell Telephone Co., 30 LA 862, 871 (Davis, 1958). Also see Allegheny Ludlum Steel Corp., 42 LA 343, 344 (Shipman, 1963).

[257] See National Lead Co., 42 LA 176, 178 (Seidenberg, 1964); North Shore Gas Co., 40 LA 37, 44 (Sembower, 1963).

[258] See Arbitrator Bothwell in 45 LA 39, 42; Brown in 44 LA 92, 95; Phelps in 42 LA 161, 164; Sembower in 40 LA 37, 42–43. For related discussion, see Chapter 13, subtopic titled "Right to Require Physical Examination."

[259] See Southern Connecticut Gas Co., 48 LA 1357, 1358 (Johnson, 1967); Fulton Glass Co., 31 LA 824, 826 (Boles, 1958). Also see Arbitrator Bothwell in 27 LA 404, 406, involving recall.

[260] See Fairbanks Co., 32 LA 772, 774–776 (Jenson, 1959); Doehler-Jarvis Corp., 12 LA 896, 897–898 (Stashower, 1949).

[261] See Arbitrator McIntosh in 46 LA 530, 532; Brown in 44 LA 92, 95; Klein in 43 LA 217, 224 (periodic examinations upheld); Phelps in 42 LA 161, 164; Klamon in 37 LA 960, 966.

health of operating employees. The ability to perform a job cannot be disassociated from the health hazards involved to male as well as female employees and action the Company takes in this regard is definitely within the inherent rights of Management to operate the plant safely and efficiently."[262]

When the question of physical fitness for a particular job arises, the primary emphasis may be placed on the physical disability of the by-passed employee to fill the job, another employee's greater physical ability for it being secondary.[263] Thus, it has been held that if certain work contributes to or would cause a recurrence of an employee's ill health, he cannot justifiably claim physical fitness for that work.[264] Similarly, a physical defect or limitation which impairs an employee's physical fitness for a particular job has been held to render him deficient in the requisite physical fitness.[265] A like result was reached where the employee's physical condition constituted a hazard to himself, to other employees, or to the plant and equipment.[266] However,

---

[262] See Mengel Co., 18 LA 392, 399 (1952). Also see Arbitrator Johnson in 48 LA 1357, 1358, where the company in requiring a physical examination argued that "it had a responsibility to all employees to give them jobs which would not prove harmful to them"; Kiroff in 42 LA 1051, 1056, where the company's refusal to reinstate an employee was not justified by a mere "feeling" that he might hurt himself.

[263] See Arbitrator May in 55 LA 975, 980–981, where the employee suffered incapacitating injuries in an automobile accident after being promoted; Marshall in 53 LA 1282, 1287, where the company was not required to give a trial period to an employee who lacked the necessary physical coordination and dexterity; Altrock in 51 LA 1143, 1144, stating that physical ability means present, not prospective, ability; Brandschain in 5 LA 579, 581. In Simoniz Co., 54 LA 172, 174–175 (Talent, 1969), the company was upheld in denying an employee's request for demotion to his old job on the ground of physical inability to perform his new job, the arbitrator stating that under the agreement such a request "would be left to management's prerogative to decide."

[264] See Arbitrator Kerrison in 45 LA 724, 726; Singletary in 42 LA 775, 780–781; Dworkin in 35 LA 391, 395; Bailer in 20 LA 835, 836; Spencer in 13 LA 238, 241. Cf. Trotta in 23 LA 800, 803, where there was no conclusive evidence that the new job would aggravate grievant's condition.

[265] See Arbitrator Jaffee in 51 LA 27, 28 (speech impediment justified rejection for group leader job); Murphy in 44 LA 1252, 1263 (epileptic not qualified for hazardous work); Willingham in 42 LA 376, 385; Tatum in 34 LA 67, 70–71; Updegraff in 27 LA 680, 682. It has been emphasized that each case must be decided on its own facts. See Arbitrator Altrock in 51 LA 152, 155–156. For a summary of "the fundamental requirements for the successful incorporation of disabled people into a company's work force," see J. R. Simplot Co., 53 LA 1181, 1188–1189 (Simon, 1969), emphasizing that handicapped workers must be properly placed and stating: "The same standards should be used in evaluating a handicapped person's ability and/or qualifications as related to the job under consideration." The company was held justified in demoting a partially blind employee from a job operating mobile equipment when it became aware of his visual problems. Id. at 1192. For similar statements regarding handicapped persons, see Glass Containers Mfgrs. Institute, 66–3 ARB ¶8999 (Dworkin, 1966).

[266] Allegheny Ludlum Steel Corp., 42 LA 343, 344–345 (Shipman, 1963).

neither the fact that the senior man weighed less than the junior[267] nor the fact that the senior man was older[268] has been considered proof that he was less able to fulfill the physical requirements of the job.

Obesity has sometimes been advanced as a reason for refusal to reinstate an employee following layoff or medical leave, or for refusal to promote a senior employee. Where excess weight or attending physical problems affected the employee's physical fitness for the work, arbitrators have upheld management in denying him that work.[269] However, where obesity has not adversely affected the employee's job performance in the past, management has not been permitted to deny him the work.[270]

In jobs where psychological requirements are important, an employee's fitness in this regard may also be examined. Thus, with respect to a job entailing "psychological strain and stress," Arbitrator Mitchell M. Shipman stated:

> "* * * And, however intangible these psychological requirements may be, they are not to be minimized. * * * Indeed, just as the Umpire must be convinced that [grievant] does have the requisite experience and ability to do the job, so must he be equally convinced that the psychological requirements thereof can also be fully met by him."[271]

An employee's temperament may be such as to disqualify him for a responsible job, as where an employee's nervousness and excitability in moments of emergency were considered grounds for rejecting his bid.[272] Furthermore, management's refusal to recall an employee in accordance with seniority was upheld where his mental

---

[267] See Seagrave Corp., 16 LA 410, 412 (Lehoczky, 1951).

[268] See Combustion Engineering Co., 20 LA 416, 419 (McCoy, 1953).

[269] See Arbitrator Block in 48 LA 2, 9 (accompanying factors of dizziness, hand tremors, and marked nervousness posed a safety threat); Kates in 43 LA 61, 64; Siciliano in 37 LA 1047, 1050. In Keeney Mfg. Co., 37 LA 456, 458 (Donnelly, 1961), conflict of opinion between the conpany's doctor and grievant's doctor resulted in a ruling requiring an examination by a neutral doctor.

[270] See Arbitrator Block in 48 LA 2, 9–10; Dworkin in 46 LA 719, 724; Shulman in 8 LA 1015, 1016–1017.

[271] Bethlehem Steel Co., 18 LA 683, 684–685 (1952). Management failed to prove to Arbitrator Shipman's satisfaction that the senior employee had exhibited anxiety and fear in connection with his work. In Titanium Metals Corp., 49 LA 1144, 1146 (Block, 1967), an employee's fear of heights justified disqualifying him from a job requiring high crane duties after completing a trial period.

[272] See Pacific Gas & Electric Co., 23 LA 556, 558–559 (Ross, 1954). Cf. Arbitrator Lockhart in 16 LA 525, 528–531.

condition was such that he could not perform even the simplest duties without an abnormal amount of supervision.[273]

Sex as a Factor

In cases involving questions of discrimination on the basis of sex, arbitrators have held that management is obligated to determine fitness and ability in relation to the particular job based upon the capabilities of the individual employee and not upon stereotyped ideas of employees' capabilities as a group.[274] It follows that management may not refuse consideration of an employee solely on the basis of sex. Thus, it has been held that the employer discriminated on the basis of sex when he denied contested work to the senior female employee who was found to be qualified for the work physically and on the basis of training, experience, or technical knowledge.[275]

Of course, discrimination in favor of female employees has likewise been held improper, as where preferential work locations were assigned to junior female employees instead of to senior males,[276] where management gave preferential treatment by not assigning the heavy duties of a female employee's job to the female employee,[277] and where a junior female employee was recalled from layoff instead of the senior male for work as a cafeteria helper.[278]

However, management has been upheld in giving preference to junior male employees over senior females where there was adequate justification in the requirements or circumstances of the job or in the qualifications of the individual involved. Such justification has been found in the physical requirements of the job (e.g., heavy weight lift-

---

[273] See White Motor Co., 28 LA 823, 828–829 (Lazarus, 1957).

[274] See, for example, Arbitrator Allman in 55 LA 756, 760; Sembower in 55 LA 193, 195; Mueller in 51 LA 785, 790; Ellman in 48 LA 231, 234, 236–237; Williams in 47 LA 896, 898.

[275] See Arbitrator Dworkin in 57 LA 997, 999; Dolson in 57 LA 549, 552–553; Seitz in 55 LA 895, 896–897; Turkus in 54 LA 165, 166; Mueller in 51 LA 785, 789–792; Forsythe in 48 LA 17, 19; Petree in 42 LA 433, 439; Crawford in 36 LA 1082, 1087–1088. In Gross Distributing Co., 55 LA 756, 759–761 (Allman, 1970), it was found that the company violated the contract when it retained a junior male employee without attempting to determine the senior female employee's physical ability to do the work in question.

[276] Cincinnati Reds, Inc., 56 LA 748, 750 (Kates, 1971).

[277] Sterling Faucet Co., 54 LA 340, 342–343 (Duff, 1970).

[278] Allied Chemical Corp., 35 LA 268, 270 (Valtin, 1960), finding the two employees relatively equal in ability and rejecting "the notion that the male animal suffers from natural handicaps to perform kitchen duties." Also see Creative Industries, Inc., 49 LA 140, 144 (Gershenfeld, 1967).

ing, physical prowess, overtime hours),[279] in standards of morality or propriety,[280] and in the lack of training, experience, or technical knowledge in the female employee.[281] In such cases, it is the justifying factor and not the sex of the individual which disqualifies the employee.

In some instances where there has been doubt concerning the physical ability of the employee to do the work arbitrators have ordered a trial period.[282]

In many of the cases cited in this subtopic, the arbitrator made reference to state antidiscrimination laws, state protective laws for women, and/or to Title VII of the Federal Civil Rights Act of 1964. The latter prohibits discrimination in employment based on sex, in addition to the usual grounds of race, color, religion, and national origin. However, the Act provides that "it shall not be an unlawful employment practice for an employer to hire and employ employees * * * on the basis of * * * religion, sex, or national origin in those certain instances where religion, sex, or national origin is

---

[279] See Arbitrator Sembower in 55 LA 193, 195, and in 43 LA 165, 169; Altrock in 52 LA 942, 944–945; Davis in 52 LA 112, 114–115; Kates in 51 LA 418, 420; Dworkin in 50 LA 669, 671–672; Seinsheimer in 49 LA 709, 714–718 (an employee must be able to do *all* the job); Teple in 48 LA 819, 823–824; Shister in 48 LA 101, 106; Steele in 46 LA 931, 934–935; Layman in 45 LA 417, 423; Goodman in 40 LA 920, 923; Roberts in 39 LA 1094, 1097, and in 35 LA 657, 661; Reid in 36 LA 458, 462 (grievance sustained in theory but denied in fact since there was no work the female employees could perform); Hebert in 34 LA 41, 45. In Sperry-Rand Corp., 46 LA 961, 964–965 (Seitz, 1966), it was held that the company could require female employees to take physical examinations although males were not required to do so, since the jobs in question required physical exertion which "may well be beyond the capacity of some women or dangerous to some." For an illustration of the problems that may be created by totally eliminating sex distinctions in the filling of jobs, see Eagle Mfg. Co., 51 LA 970, 972–973, 983 (Lugar, 1968).

[280] See Arbitrator Gross in 54 LA 303, 305–306 (female properly was denied job of janitress in men's room); Marshall in 52 LA 624, 631–632 (female teacher properly was denied position with bureau of prisons); Shafer in 45 LA 448, 449–450 (male properly was denied job of janitress in women's restroom). Cf. Arbitrator Bernstein in 54 LA 1142, 1144–1146; Crawford in 36 LA 1082, 1083.

[281] See Arbitrator Jones in 57 LA 929, 930; Rauch in 53 LA 1345, 1346–1348 (although the female employee probably had the physical strength and stamina for the job); Merrill in 47 LA 836, 840; Hawley in 43 LA 289, 293–294 (to rearrange duties so that female employee could handle the job would result in discrimination in favor of female employees against male employees).

[282] See Arbitrator White in 55 LA 1284, 1286–1288; Gershenfeld in 49 LA 140, 144 (male employees given trial period on "delicate" work); Ellman in 48 LA 231, 236; Elkouri in 46 LA 238, 242; Sembower in 43 LA 165, 170. In Paterson Parchment Co., 47 LA 260, 262 (Buckwalter, 1966), a training period was ordered where the contract provided for such in bumping.

a bona fide occupational qualification reasonably necessary to the normal operation of that particular business or enterprise * * *."[283]

Prior to the Civil Rights Act, some arbitrators felt bound by the particular agreement and/or the parties' past practice, and separate classifications and separate seniority lists for male and female employees were upheld.[284] In at least one case arising after the Act, where separate lines of progression were maintained in such a way as to provide male employees with experience on higher-rated jobs by means of temporary assignments, the arbitrator directed the employer and the union (which had countenanced the practice) to negotiate integration of the lines.[285]

Subsequent to the Act, many parties incorporated antidiscrimination language into their agreements. Under such a contract, one arbitrator emphasized that "Male and female employees have equal claim to any work opportunity, subject only to their being eligible and qualified," and that "As is clearly apparent, exclusively 'male' or 'female' jobs are no longer recognized, either in law or by contract."[286]

Personal Characteristics of Employee

Personal characteristics of an employee may be considered if they relate directly to his ability to meet the job requirements. For example, it has been held that management may take into consideration the fact that an employee had been guilty in the past of certain "injudicious conduct and conversation" evincing his interest in the cult of nudism, particularly since the job involved not only technical knowledge but also public relations, the arbitrator stating:

"* * * [Grievant's] interest in nudism so expressed itself as to create in management's mind a reasonable doubt as to this employee's discretion and customer-acceptance on the service job for which he

---

[283] Sec. 703 (e). Another statute which may have relevance in this area is the Equal Pay Act of 1963, which amended the Fair Labor Standards Act. For related discussion, see Chapter 10, topic titled "Statutory Law." For some relevant court cases, see Phillips v. Martin Marietta Corp., 91 S. Ct. 496 (1971); Bowe v. Colgate-Palmolive Co., 416 F. 2d 711 (CA 7, 1969); Weeks v. Southern Bell Telephone Co., 408 F. 2d 228 (CA 5, 1969); Caterpillar Tractor Co. v. Grabiec, 2 FEP Cases 945 (USDC, 1970).

[284] See Arbitrator Dworkin in 43 LA 715, 720–721; Eckhardt in 43 LA 460, 462–463; Hawley in 43 LA 391, 394 (employer's procedure had also been upheld in three prior awards under the contract); Marshall in 42 LA 224, 227–228; Talent in 42 LA 182, 184; Goodman in 40 LA 920, 923.

[285] South Pittsburgh Water Co., 56 LA 1242, 1244–1245 (Altrock, 1971).

[286] Glass Containers Corp., 57 LA 997, 999 (Dworkin, 1971).

bid. It should be made clear that such reaction has no necessary relation to the employee's beliefs or personal ideas. It relates directly
to the question of what the job requires and a worker's ability to
meet these requirements. A decision as to this is management's right
and prerogative."[287]

An employee's attitude may be in issue and may be important,
depending upon the nature of the job. It has been held that, in determining whether an employee is qualified for a job, supervision may
evaluate the employee's attitude which may include "conscientious
application, care for materials, concern for others in a group and response to instruction."[288] In another case, the employee's attitude toward the job and spirit of cooperation were said to be included in
the word "qualifications" as used in the seniority provisions; and the
senior employee's uncooperative attitude could properly be considered
in denying him a promotion to a better job.[289] Thus, management
was upheld in giving preference to a junior employee over the senior
where the senior had the experience and aptitude for the job but
lacked the important requisite of a mature and dedicated attitude,[290]
and where the senior employee was found to be "lacking in interest,
effort and basic * * * knowledge" of the job.[291]

However, one arbitrator held that an employee's alleged "surly
and uncooperative" attitude could justify denying a promotion only

---

[287] Gisholt Machine Co., 20 LA 137, 141 (Baab, 1953). Also see Arbitrator
Amis in 49 LA 726, 728 (involving in part the "personal conduct" of an employee); Murphy in 18 LA 757, 760 (involving a "special class of clients");
Pollard in 16 LA 586, 587–588 (the company failing to prove inability to perform
the "human relations" part of a job). In Eagle-Picher Mining & Smelting Co.,
8 LA 108, 111 (Potter, 1947), the filing of a suit by an employee against
his employer was held not to affect his qualifications, the word "qualifications"
being said to relate to physical fitness and ability rather than to "moral"
qualifications.

[288] Swan Rubber Co., 52 LA 59, 61 (Maxwell, 1969), holding that the
company did not discriminate against an employee when it disqualified him,
on the basis of attitude, for a job vacancy to which he had been assigned
for training. Similarly, American Welding & Mfg. Co., 52 LA 889, 893–894
(Stouffer, 1969), where the employee displayed an attitude of unwillingness
to learn, rejecting instruction. In Dewey & Almy Chemical Co., 25 LA 316,
318–319 (Somers, 1955), the arbitrator stated: "A promotion represents a public
recognition of an employee's ability, merit and capacity to do a higher-paid
job. It would be destructive of morale to give such recognition to an employee
who has shown lack of concern for his work and for his fellow employees."

[289] Norwich Pharmacal Co., 30 LA 740, 742–743 (Willcox, 1958). Similarly,
Arbitrator Koven in 42 LA 1093, 1096; Seligson in 41 LA 528, 534 (holding
that management could place strong weight on the factors of cooperation and
ability to get along with others).

[290] Leach Co., 51 LA 382, 383 (Hazelwood, 1968).

[291] United States Steel Corp., 51 LA 264, 266 (Smith, 1968).

if it were shown that efforts had been made, without success, to correct such attitude, and that his attitude detracted seriously from the employee's ability to perform the job.[292]

Special requirements of the job may call for particular attributes (other than technical knowledge) in the employee filling it, justifying consideration by the employer of the employee's ability to meet those requirements. For example, the job may require qualities of leadership,[293] initiative,[294] responsibility for independent judgment or self-reliance,[295] the ability to get along with others;[296] or it may involve dealing with a "special class" of customers,[297] or require that the employee be physically available for emergency work.[298]

Age as a Factor

The conflict between the interests of management and the interests of the employees over the use of age as a factor in denying employment opportunities (particularly in regard to training programs) is evident from the following:

"* * * It is not unreasonable that management should hesitate to invest great amounts of time and money in an apprentice, who because of age will be unable to offer many years of service as a new craftsman. Some 'rules of reason' then properly should be followed. But clearly to favor youth above 'seniority' is to do violence to benefits traditionally provided longer service employees. And, it surely is unreasonable, we believe, to assume that all persons above

---

[292] Bethlehem Steel Co., 19 LA 186, 188 (Killingsworth, 1952).

[293] See Arbitrator Wolff in 54 LA 447, 448; Beeson in 54 LA 298, 302; Cantor in 48 LA 777, 780; Larkin in 45 LA 129, 130–131; Seligson in 41 LA 528, 534.

[294] See Arbitrator Beeson in 54 LA 298, 302; Block in 51 LA 896, 898–899; Cantor in 48 LA 777, 780; Graff in 46 LA 523, 527; Klamon in 19 LA 639, 647. In Penn Controls, Inc., 45 LA 129, 130–131 (Larkin, 1965), where the job of leadman required qualities of leadership and initiative, the senior employee had demonstrated initiative in developing his own business outside of work; but it was held that "the Company has every right first to look to the factors of initiative, efficiency and leadership qualities displayed on the jobs within the plant," and the junior employee was "ahead of" the senior in this respect.

[295] See Arbitrator Wolff in 54 LA 447, 448; Beeson in 54 LA 298, 302; Schmidt in 44 LA 283, 285–286; Klamon in 19 LA 639, 647.

[296] See Arbitrator Block in 51 LA 896, 898–899; Amis in 49 LA 726, 728; McCoy in 45 LA 1028, 1030 (the senior employee was argumentative and the job required a person with an "equable, tactful disposition"); Koven in 42 LA 1093, 1096; Schmidt in 44 LA 283, 285–286; Seligson in 41 LA 528, 534.

[297] See Coca-Cola Bottling Co., 18 LA 757, 759–760 (Murphy, 1952).

[298] See Alabama Power Co., 19 LA 393, 396 (Hawley, 1952), where the grievant lived some distance from town and had no telephone.

a given calendar age are lacking in basic ability or physical fitness for a particular job, and that persons below such age level do possess such qualifications. Such an arbitrary classification, at the very least, fails to give due weight to the fact that people 'age' at radically different rates, both physically and mentally. Moreover, it appears that, historically, seniority and age have been correlative concepts, generally, to determine employee rights under the * * * Agreement.

"* * * The point is that * * * age, per se, reasonably may not be established as a proper basis for barring further consideration of other relevant qualifying factors in the selection of employees to fill apprenticeship or other vacancies * * *."[299]

Thus, it has been held that age may not be used as an automatic bar to consideration of an employee's basic ability for a job.[300] It has also been held that age may not be viewed as necessarily a negative element without a showing that the applicant's age had adversely affected his physical or mental ability in such a way as to render him incapable of meeting the job requirements—but in such event it would be ability and not age per se which constitutes the bar.[301] Such was the ruling in an early case where the job required close attention continuously and a great deal of visual inspection, the arbitrator upholding the employer's determination that a 73-year-old employee did not have the necessary qualifications.[302]

Under the Age Discrimination in Employment Act of 1967, which protects "individuals who are at least forty years of age but less than sixty-five years of age," it is unlawful for an employer "(1) to fail or refuse to hire or to discharge any individual or otherwise discriminate against any individual with respect to his compensation, terms, conditions, or privileges of employment, because of such individual's age; (2) to limit, segregate, or classify his employees in any way which would deprive or tend to deprive any individual of employment opportunities or otherwise adversely affect his status as an employee, because of such individual's age; or (3) to reduce the wage rate of any employee in order to comply with this Act."[303] In one

---

[299] United States Steel Corp., 55 LA 659, 662–663 (McDaniel, 1970).
[300] Ibid.
[301] See United States Steel Corp., 57 LA 237, 251–252 (Clare B. McDermott, 1971), referring to the McDaniel award in 55 LA 659; Scott Paper Co., 49 LA 45, 46–47 (Hogan, undated), stating that "Age may or may not affect ability critically, depending on the man and the job." None of the above cases made reference to the Age Discrimination in Employment Act of 1967.
[302] Emmons Looms Harness Co., 11 LA 409, 411 (Meyers, 1948).
[303] Sec. 4 (a).

case making reference to the Act, the arbitrator upheld the company's maximum age limit of 32 for entering a training program, stating:

"There was no illegal application of age limits which resulted in the grievant's rejection. Federal protection against age discrimination does not extend to persons under the age of 40. Furthermore, an age maximum for entry into a training program of extended duration is a reasonable qualification and is so recognized in the administration of apprenticeship programs generally."[304]

Even prior to the Act, in the absence of any age limitation in the contract and in the absence of any showing that the age of the employee detracted from his ability to perform the job, arbitrators appeared reluctant to permit management to rely upon the age factor as justification for passing over a senior in favor of a junior employee, provided the senior met the job requirements. Thus, arbitrators held that the company could not deny an employee consideration for a job solely because of age,[305] and that the company was arbitrary in barring an employee from an apprenticeship or a training vacancy solely because of age.[306] In some other cases, it was held that under the circumstances of the given case the company could set a *reasonable* age limit for apprenticeships or for a training program.[307]

---

[304] Aro, Inc., 52 LA 372, 375 (Kesselman, 1969). For another case referring to the Act, see American Standard, Inc., 53 LA 1157, 1159 (Purdom, 1969).

[305] See Arbitrator Berkowitz in 41 LA 14, 18 (a 56-year-old employee should be given a physical examination to determine if he is fit for the job); Anrod in 31 LA 994, 999–1000 (age limit of 30 was arbitrary and unreasonable as was barring a 34-year-old employee solely because of age); Gilden in 20 LA 142, 147 (35-year age limit was not justified for the job in question—the real test is physical ability and qualifications).

[306] See Arbitrator Ross in 28 LA 557, 558–559 (48-year-old employee was entitled to the job if equal in ability); Thompson in 28 LA 374, 378–379 (absolute limit excluding employees over 40 from bidding was arbitrary and unreasonable); Kaplan in 19 LA 508, 512–514 (company's denial of 38-year-old senior's bid on ground that he was too old was improper). Also see Arbitrator Edes in 11 LA 108, 109, where the senior employee was younger.

[307] See Arbitrator Thomas J. McDermott in 47 LA 89, 90–91 (age limit of 35 upheld); Wyckoff in 34 LA 756, 759–760 (airline could set an age limit of 60 for training on new and faster aircraft); Kallenbach in 25 LA 716, 721 (age limit of 35 was not unreasonable). Also see Tsukiyama in 37 LA 553, 558–561. While agreeing that a proper age limit would not be unreasonable, Arbitrator Kates found that 30 was too low (46 LA 1153, 1157), and Arbitrator Brown found that 50 was too low (44 LA 92, 95). In Ozark Smelting & Mining Div., 46 LA 697, 698–699 (Schedler, 1966), where the contract stated that a "beginning trainee shall not be over 40," the age limit was liberally construed to mean that an employee is not "over 40" until the day before his 41st birthday, the arbitrator noting conflicting court decisions on the general subject of age.

CHAPTER 15

DISCHARGE AND DISCIPLINE

A significant percentage of cases that reach arbitration involve discharge or disciplinary penalties assessed by management. The present Chapter considers many of the concepts and standards that have been applied by arbitrators in cases of this nature.[1]

Scope of Management Right

In the absence of a collective bargaining agreement it is generally agreed that the only restriction on management's right to discharge and discipline employees is that contained in federal and state labor relations acts or other laws dealing with discrimination.[2] The same

---

[1] For related matter, see Chapter 13, topic titled "Plant Rules." For a full volume on discharge and discipline, see Stessin, Employee Discipline (BNA Incorporated, 1960). For other discussions, see Jones, "Ramifications of Back-Pay Awards in Discharge Cases," Arbitration and Social Change 163 (The Bureau of National Affairs, Inc., 1970); Fisher, "Ramifications of Back Pay in Suspension and Discharge Cases," id. at 175; Kadish, "The Criminal Law and Industrial Discipline as Sanctioning Systems: Some Comparative Observations," Labor Arbitration—Perspectives and Problems 125 (BNA Incorporated, 1964); Teele, "But No Back Pay Is Awarded . . .", 19 Arb. J. 103 (1964); Davey, "The Arbitrator Speaks on Discharge and Discipline," 17 Arb. J. 97 (1962); Holly, "The Arbitration of Discharge Cases: A Case Study," Critical Issues in Labor Arbitration 1 (BNA Incorporated, 1957); Ross, "The Arbitration of Discharge Cases: What Happens After Reinstatement," id. at 21; Myers, "Concepts of Industrial Discipline," Management Rights and the Arbitration Process 59 (BNA Incorporated, 1956); Lazar, Due Process on the Railroads (U. of Calif. Inst. of Ind. Rel., 1953); Notes on Discharge For Cause, Wash. U.L.Q. 92–196 (Vol. 1949 Fall).

[2] See Arbitrator Williams in 50 LA 547, 548; Bell in 45 LA 500, 501; Updegraff in 39 LA 53, 57; Potter in 8 LA 634, 637–638; Whiting in 4 LA 399, 403; Babb in 4 LA 56, 64. Also see Wettach in 25 LA 772, 773; Merrill in 19 LA 417, 419; Coffey in 17 LA 125, 129; McCoy in 8 LA 66, 67. Cf., Blumrosen in 41 LA 76, 78–82. As to statutory restrictions on management, see Levy, "The Role of Law in the United States and England in Protecting the Worker from Discharge and Discrimination," 18 International and Comparative L. Q. 558 (1969). Recognizing that the initiation of discipline is within the province of management, arbitrators have disclaimed the existence of arbitral authority to order the discharge or discipline of an employee. See Arbitrator Hilpert in 39 LA 897, 906; Dash in 38 LA 509, 515. Cf., McCoy in 2 LA 537, 538–539.

result might be reached where a collective agreement exists but contains no express limitation on such right.[3] Where an agreement expressly recognized the right of management to discharge and contained no express limitation upon that right, an arbitrator was unwilling to read a "just cause" limitation into the agreement.[4]

However, many arbitrators would imply a just cause limitation in any collective agreement.[5] For instance, Arbitrator Walter E. Boles held that "a 'just cause' basis for consideration of disciplinary action is, absent a clear proviso to the contrary, implied in a modern collective bargaining agreement."[6] The reasoning is: "If the Company can discharge without cause, it can lay off without cause. It can recall, transfer, or promote in violation of the seniority provisions simply by invoking its claimed right to discharge. Thus, to interpret the Agreement in accord with the claim of the Company would reduce to a nullity the fundamental provision of a labor-management agreement—the security of a worker in his job."[7] Moreover, in at least one case it has been held that management does not have an unrestricted right to discharge at its own discretion even where no bargaining relationship exists, since "the fair and generally accepted understanding of employer-employee relations is that there are obligations on the part

---

[3] See Bohlinger v. National Cash Register Co., 18 LA 595 (N.Y. Sup. Ct., 1952), and cases cited therein.

[4] Hillyer Deutsch Edwards, Inc., 19 LA 663, 664 (Emery, 1952). Also see Arbitrator Berkowitz in 36 LA 331, 332; Warren in 24 LA 680, 683–684; Krivonos in 22 LA 756, 759–760. Cf., Jones in 46 LA 831, 832; Warren in 19 LA 615, 619–621. For a contract limiting challenges of discharge action to "bad faith" discharges, see Arbitrator Somers in 45 LA 655, 656. In the case of In The Round Dinner Playhouse, Inc., 55 LA 118, 128 (Kamin, 1970), the arbitrator took "arbitral notice" that any requirement of "just cause" for termination "is virtually unknown in the theatrical world." In Boscobel Board of Education, 55 LA 58, 60–61 (Wilberg, 1970), the "interests" arbitrator recommended a discharge and discipline clause less restrictive upon management than the usual "just cause" clause.

[5] See Arbitrator Oppenheim in 52 LA 1164, 1166–1167; Eaton in 51 LA 331, 331–333; Volz in 50 LA 1217, 1219; Jones in 48 LA 240, 241–242; Tsukiyama in 42 LA 490, 493; Eiger in 38 LA 778, 780; Ryder in 36 LA 552, 556; Ross in 36 LA 503, 505; Boles in 25 LA 295, 300–301; Maggs in 22 LA 761, 763; Donnelly in 13 LA 747, 749. Also see Dahl in 46 LA 356, 357; Fallon in 45 LA 532, 533–534; Hebert in 25 LA 439, 440–441. Also, a general "just cause" limitation may be found to be implied from some particular provision in the agreement. See Arbitrator Seidenberg in 52 LA 547, 551–552; Sherman in 48 LA 1209, 1212; Merrill in 46 LA 1044, 1046–1047; Morvant in 24 LA 453, 455–456.

[6] Cameron Iron Works, Inc., 25 LA 295, 301 (1955).

[7] Atwater Mfg. Co., 13 LA 747, 749 (Donnelly, 1949), quoting at length from a similar view expressed by Arbitrator Wallen in another case. Id. at 750–751.

of both parties" and that an "obligation on the employer is that an employee shall not be dismissed without cause."[8]

Most collective agreements do, in fact, require "cause" or "just cause" for discharge or discipline. The general significance of these terms was discussed by Arbitrator Joseph D. McGoldrick:

> "* * * [I]t is common to include the right to suspend and discharge for 'just cause,' 'justifiable cause,' 'proper cause,' 'obvious cause,' or quite commonly simply for 'cause'. There is no significant difference between these various phrases. These exclude discharge for mere whim or caprice. They are, obviously, intended to include those things for which employees have traditionally been fired. They include the traditional causes of discharge in the particular trade or industry, the practices which develop in the day-to-day relations of management and labor and most recently they include the decisions of courts and arbitrators. They represent a growing body of 'common law' that may be regarded either as the latest development of the law of 'master and servant' or, perhaps, more properly as part of a new body of common law of 'Management and labor under collective bargaining agreements.' They constitute the duties owed by employees to management and, in their correlative aspect, are part of the rights of management. They include such duties as honesty, punctuality, sobriety, or, conversely, the right to discharge for theft, repeated absence or lateness, destruction of company property, brawling and the like. Where they are not expressed in posted rules, they may very well be implied, provided they are applied in a uniform, non-discriminatory manner."[9]

Some agreements enumerate specific grounds for discipline. It has been ruled that the fact that an agreement specifies certain types of misconduct for which employees may be discharged does not mean that causes not expressly stated may not be used where the grounds enumerated are merely illustrative and not exclusive.[10] Similarly, the

---

[8] Daily World Publishing Co., 3 LA 815, 817 (Rogers, 1946). During negotiations but prior to adoption of their first agreement, the parties agreed to arbitrate the dispute in question. In Government Services, Inc., 40 LA 84, 85 (Schedler, 1963), there was no collective agreement, but in agreeing to arbitrate a discharge the employer was deemed to have accepted a "just cause" standard for the arbitral review. As to the latter point, see Arbitrator Seidenberg in 52 LA 547, 551–552; McIntosh in 43 LA 76, 77–78.

[9] Worthington Corp., 24 LA 1, 6–7 (1955). For other statements defining "cause" or "just cause," see Arbitrator Hon in 44 LA 574, 576; Parker in 21 LA 671, 672; Barrett in 19 LA 489, 493. Agreeing that there is no significant difference between these terms, Arbitrator Buckwalter in 44 LA 1208, 1211; Harris in 29 LA 567, 571. As to the purposes of industrial discipline, see Arbitrator Yagoda in 46 LA 1034, 1039; Howlett in 33 LA 40, 41.

[10] See Arbitrator Wyckoff in 44 LA 552, 553; Altieri in 43 LA 689, 693–694; Updegraff in 9 LA 397, 398; Carmichael in 7 LA 752, 755. Also see Dworkin

listing of certain offenses in written plant rules does not necessarily exclude other offenses as grounds for punishment.[11]

Arbitrators have held that a contract giving the right to discharge for cause and making no reference to other forms of discipline does not deprive management of the right to impose forms of discipline less severe than discharge.[12] Discharge may be too severe a penalty for the offense under the circumstances of the case.

Asserting that discharge "inevitably casts a shadow on a worker's character and reputation," an arbitrator would not permit discharge for lack of work where the agreement required just cause for discharge, the arbitrator stating that layoff is the proper action in case of lack of work.[13] Other arbitrators, too, have held that "discharge" is limited to termination due to fault of the employee.[14]

Probationary Employees

It has been held that where, by the agreement, new employees are not to have seniority rights until completion of a probationary period, and where the agreement is otherwise silent as to management rights with respect to new employees, they may be discharged for any reason except discrimination.[15] Under a somewhat more strict limita-

---

in 48 LA 457, 462–463. But the listing of some grounds was held to exclude others in Pacific Press, Inc., 26 LA 339, 344 (Hildebrand, 1956). Also see Arbitrator Handsaker in 15 LA 616, 618. In Chicago Pneumatic Tool Co., 38 LA 891, 892 (Duff, 1961), the contract specified the right to discharge "for proper cause as agreed to by the parties," but this did not require management to obtain union agreement as to all causes. For a case involving a clause providing that no employee could be discharged "without the consent of the union," see Crawford Clothes, Inc., 19 LA 475, 476–479 (Kramer, 1952).

[11] Mount Whitney Lumber Co., 48 LA 147, 151 (Mullennix, 1967); Farmbest, Inc., 44 LA 609, 612 (Karlins, 1965).

[12] See Arbitrator Solomon in 50 LA 888, 896; Sembower in 43 LA 1197, 1199–1202; Sears in 41 LA 33, 37–38; Strong in 39 LA 859, 860–861; Ross in 36 LA 503, 504; Kleinsorge in 23 LA 711, 713–714; Cornsweet in 17 LA 580, 585; Copelof in 3 LA 122, 125. But in some situations a different result has been reached. See Arbitrator Abernethy in 50 LA 760, 763–766; Sembower in 39 LA 1231, 1235; Copelof in 18 LA 34, 38; Sugarman in 14 LA 16, 23–24.

[13] American Republics Corp., 18 LA 248, 253 (Hale, 1952).

[14] See Arbitrator Howlett in 28 LA 633, 637; Hogan in 23 LA 596, 602; Kelly in 22 LA 266, 268. In Revere Copper and Brass, Inc., 45 LA 254, 255 (McCoy, 1965), the term "non-disciplinary discharge" was suggested for terminations not due to fault.

[15] Joy Mfg. Co., 6 LA 430, 436 (Healy, 1946); Flintkote Co., 3 LA 770, 771 (Cole, 1946). Also see Stone, Labor-Management Contracts at Work 261 (1961); Arbitrator Miller in 42 LA 187, 188–189; Kerr in 6 LA 98, 102 ("inter-

tion placed by an arbitrator upon the right of management to discharge probationary employees, management's action in doing so
would "not be set aside unless it was arbitrary, capricious, or discriminatory"; thus, "the question in such a case goes to the good faith
of the Company, not to the merits of its conclusion."[16]

Where an agreement contained a "just cause" requirement for
discharge and made no reference to any probationary period for new
employees, the requirement was applied fully to new employees.[17] In
another instance where an agreement was entirely silent as to management rights with respect to new employees, another arbitrator likewise
would not read a probationary period into the agreement but he nonetheless would give management wider latitude in determining just
cause for discharge of new employees than allowed in case of employees who have served at least for a short period of time.[18]

Of course the collective agreement may deal expressly with the
discharge of probationary employees, for example, by requiring
"cause"[19] or not requiring it.[20] In the latter situation, problems may
arise concerning the exact limits of the probationary period.[21]

---

ests" arbitration). But see Arbitrator Donaldson in 34 LA 633, 635, and Stutz
in 28 LA 456, 458, both of whom viewed management's right as being considerably
more limited.
    [16] Ex-Cell-O Corp., 21 LA 659, 665 (Smith, 1953). To similar effect, Arbitra-
tor Burns in 48 LA 143, 145; Buckwalter in 44 LA 301, 304; Sembower in
40 LA 757, 762–763; Ross in 38 LA 350, 351–352; Komaroff in 19 LA 565,
569. Also see Cornsweet in 9 LA 625, 630–631.
    [17] Mac Coal Co., 52 LA 1125, 1127 (Krimsly, 1969).
    [18] Park Sherman Co., 2 LA 199, 200 (Lapp, 1946).
    [19] In Ford Motor Co., 48 LA 1213, 1214–1215 (Platt, 1967), the agreement
required cause for discharge after the first 30 days of the three month period
required for an employee to acquire seniority; the arbitrator held the "cause"
required after 30 days to be no different than the "cause" required for discharge
of employees after expiration of the aforementioned three month period. The
arbitrator noted that under previous agreements probationary employees had
been subject to discharge for any reason other than discrimination. The "discrimination" exception had been construed to include reasons of race, union activity,
personal feeling, or sex. Ford Motor Co., 6 LA 853, 854 (Shulman, 1946).
    [20] As in A. S. Abell Co., 49 LA 264, 265–266 (Kennedy, 1967), where
it was held, however, that to be free of the "cause" requirement the discharge
ordinarily must be effected and communicated to the employee within the probationary period. In Pan American World Airways, Inc., 50 LA 722, 724 (Galenson,
1968), the contract gave management the right to discharge probationary employees "at its option," but this did not necessarily mean that the union could
be totally disregarded in the matter.
    [21] For example, see Arbitrator Platt in 48 LA 1213, 1216; Merrill in 47
LA 339, 340–341 (probationary period not extended by strike); Buckwalter in
44 LA 301, 303 (period was 30 working days rather than 30 calendar days
where contract was not specific on the question).

Discharge v. Resignation

When an employee voluntarily resigns, concepts associated with discharge are not generally applicable. Thus, where the employee evidenced clear intent to resign arbitrators have refused to treat the matter as discharge.[22] Moreover, where the facts and circumstances are such as to lead management reasonably to conclude that intent to resign exists, the matter may be treated as resignation even though the individual never actually states any intent to resign.[23]

However, if intent to resign is not adequately evidenced or if a statement of intent to resign is involuntary or coerced, an alleged resignation will be treated as discharge for purposes of arbitral review.[24] A similar result has sometimes been reached where a resignation was made under severe emotional stress[25] or was based upon a mistake concerning material facts.[26]

Also, Arbitrator Maurice H. Merrill has observed that:

"The overwhelming weight of authority holds that there is no voluntary quit by reason of an employee's refusal to perform work to which he is assigned. Unless some affirmation of an intent to quit the job is manifested by the employee, the employer's subsequent refusal to

---

[22] See Arbitrator Turkus in 57 LA 1200, 1206–1208; Hardy in 48 LA 1036, 1040; Russell in 41 LA 913, 917; Doyle in 29 LA 242, 245; Kelliher in 20 LA 618, 619–621; Anderson in 20 LA 715, 717–718; Donnelly in 20 LA 47, 49; Stein in 17 LA 256, 257; Cahn in 16 LA 890, 891.

[23] See Arbitrator High in 53 LA 1103, 1107; Stouffer in 50 LA 46, 48 (employee did tell other employees she was quitting); Scheib in 49 LA 540, 544; Davis in 48 LA 227, 228; Duff in 47 LA 115, 118–119; Davey in 45 LA 599, 603; Kelliher in 30 LA 224, 225; Jaffee in 26 LA 786, 788; Donnelly in 25 LA 608, 610–611; Lewis in 18 LA 808, 809–810; Crawford in 15 LA 282, 290. Cf., Gilden in 18 LA 576, 580; Kelliher in 15 LA 300, 303–304; Platt in 14 LA 462, 465–466.

[24] See Arbitrator Rose in 55 LA 604, 607; Kates in 51 LA 1098, 1102; McNaughton in 51 LA 869, 871; Dolnik in 48 LA 273, 276; McDermott in 46 LA 985, 988; Cahn in 45 LA 1153, 1154; McIntosh in 43 LA 76, 78; Crawford in 42 LA 849, at 849; Kesselman in 29 LA 128, 131–132; Miller in 27 LA 11, 15–18; Klamon in 26 LA 48, 51–52; Browser in 20 LA 868, 870; Killingsworth in 16 LA 683, 684–685; Whiting in 16 LA 170, 172–173; Shipman in 15 LA 698, 702–703; Handsaker in 15 LA 616, 617; Healy in 6 LA 557, 559–560.

[25] See Arbitrator Duff in 57 LA 446, 448; Amis in 51 LA 206, 208; Yagoda in 45 LA 590, 593. But see Ray in 42 LA 1106, 1108. In Weyerhaeuser Co., 42 LA 845, 848 (Tongue, 1964), there was no "quit" when an employee walked off the job to control his anger and not strike his supervisor.

[26] Honeywell, Inc., 51 LA 1061, 1062 (Elson, 1968). In The Tuttle Press Co., 49 LA 490, 492–493 (Seitz, 1967), a resignation was deemed involuntary where it was prompted by the employee's mistaken belief that he had cancer (this was not a discharge or discipline case).

let the employee continue his status constitutes a discharge rather than a resignation."[27]

Moreover, the mere fact that the employee is told to do the work or be deemed to have quit does not appear materially to strengthen management's claim that there was in fact a resignation.[28]

On the other hand, there have been situations in which arbitrators have considered that no intent is required to make a termination a "quit."[29] This was so, for instance, where an employee was terminated under a union security clause.[30]

Sometimes in situations in which an employee has in fact submitted his resignation, he has subsequently attempted to withdraw it. The attempted withdrawal has been upheld in some cases[31] but not in others.[32]

Conduct Away From Plant

The right of management to discharge an employee for conduct away from the plant depends upon the effect of that conduct upon

---

[27] Oklahoma Furniture Mfg. Co., 24 LA 522, 523 (1955), citing numerous cases. For later cases in accord, see Arbitrator Quinlan in 53 LA 521, 524; King in 49 LA 27, 31; Block in 48 LA 1027, 1030; Bellman in 47 LA 899, 901; Tatum in 46 LA 583, 588; Lee in 46 LA 297, 300–301; Witney in 45 LA 97, 98–99, and in 41 LA 386, 389. For related discussion, see Chapter 5, topic titled "Observance of Grievance Procedure."

[28] See Arbitrator King in 49 LA 27, 31; Bellman in 47 LA 899, 901; Lee in 46 LA 297, 300–301; Witney in 45 LA 97, 98–99.

[29] See Arbitrator Bailer in 48 LA 157, 159–160; Hebert in 45 LA 621, 628–629; Willingham in 36 LA 852, 854–855.

[30] New York Times, 48 LA 157, 159–160 (Bailer, 1967).

[31] See Arbitrator Di Leone in 47 LA 332, 336 (notice to quit in the future is not necessarily irrevocable); Tatum in 45 LA 1030, 1033 (employee's tender of resignation is an offer which can be withdrawn prior to its acceptance); Seitz in 41 LA 918, 920–921; Hebert in 38 LA 84, 88–89; Sembower in 34 LA 360, 364–365; Gray in 22 LA 238, 238–239. Also see Bell in 53 LA 1100, 1103 (employee punched out but changed his mind within an hour).

[32] See Arbitrator Kabaker in 50 LA 637, 640 (employee signed "quit form" and company accepted it); Roberts in 47 LA 454, 457 (employee could not withdraw written resignation which had been processed by the company); Marshall in 40 LA 469, 472 (employer had right to choose whether to accept or reject retraction of resignation); Morvant in 38 LA 425, 429 (resignation is effective even without acceptance and employer is not required to permit withdrawal); Dworkin in 29 LA 700, 703–704; Babcock in 7 LA 330, 333; Kaplan in 3 LA 239, 241.

plant operations.[33] In this regard, Arbitrator Louis C. Kesselman explained in one case:

"The Arbitrator finds no basis in the contract or in American industrial practice to justify a discharge for misconduct away from the place of work unless:

"1) behavior harms Company's reputation or product * * *

"2) behavior renders employee unable to perform his duties or appear at work, in which case the discharge would be based upon inefficiency or excessive absenteeism * * *

"3) behavior leads to refusal, reluctance or inability of other employees to work with him * * *."[34]

Arbitrator D. Emmett Ferguson also spoke of the extent to which management may consider conduct away from the plant as the basis for discharge:

"* * * While it is true that the employer does not [by virtue of the employment relationship] become the guardian of the employee's every personal action and does not exercise parental control, it is equally true that in those areas having to do with the employer's business, the employer has the right to terminate the relationship if the employee's wrongful actions injuriously affect the business.

"The connection between the facts which occur and the extent to which the business is affected must be reasonable and discernible. They must be such as could logically be expected to cause some result in the employer's affairs. Each case must be measured on its own merits."[35]

Another arbitrator also stressed that the effect of the employee's outside activity on the employer's business must be reasonably discernible, mere speculation as to adverse effect upon the business not sufficing.[36]

---

[33] For a general discussion of this subject, see Sussman, "Work Discipline versus Private Life: An Analysis of Arbitration Cases," 10 I.L.R. Research 3 (1964). For related material, see Chapter 13, topic titled "Plant Rules."

[34] W. E. Caldwell Co., 28 LA 434, 436–437 (1957). For other general statements, see Arbitrator McMahon in 50 LA 632, 633; Livengood in 45 LA 495, 497. In Eastern Air Lines Inc., 45 LA 932, 936–939 (Ables, 1965), the arbitrator suggested guidelines and procedures for the parties to utilize in disputes involving off-duty misconduct.

[35] Inland Container Corp., 28 LA 312, 314 (1957).

[36] Allied Supermarkets, Inc., 41 LA 713, 714–715 (Mittenthal, 1963), reversing discharge for second instance of "unwed motherhood." A similar result was reached in Movielab, Inc., 50 LA 632, 633 (McMahon, 1968), where the employer introduced no evidence to show adverse effect upon the business as a result of the employee's being convicted (but placed on probation) on narcotics charges. Also see Arbitrator Shearer in 56 LA 469, 473. In Armco Steel Corp., 43 LA 977, 981 (Kates, 1964), the effect of the employee's morals conviction upon

In many cases discharge for conduct away from the plant was held improper because the requirement of adverse effect of the conduct upon the business was not met.[37] However, in many other cases the employee's conduct away from the plant was found to be related to his employment or was found to have an actual or reasonably foreseeable adverse effect upon the business, thus discharge (or in some instances a lesser penalty) was found to be justified.[38]

Off-Duty Misconduct on Company Premises

It appears clear that off-duty employees have a general obligation to observe plant rules while on company premises and that they may be subject to discipline for their misconduct even though the misconduct (which often will adversely affect employee morale, discipline, or other legitimate company interests) occurs while they are off duty and in a nonworking area of the plant such as the company cafeteria or parking lot.[39]

---

the business was uncertain and the employee had long years of service. Conditional reinstatement was ordered, the employer to be permitted to discharge the employee if adverse effect within the plant or adverse outside reactions against the employer should develop as a result of the conviction.

[37] In addition to cases in preceding footnote, see Arbitrator Duff in 46 LA 307, 309 ("romantic exploits at hotel" had no bearing on job as truck driver); Young in 44 LA 133, 140 (taking bankruptcy); Duff in 43 LA 242, 244 (contributing to delinquency of minor); Altrock in 41 LA 460, 463–464 (morals offense); Wyckoff in 37 LA 1040, 1043 (narcotics conviction); Hill in 35 LA 315, 322–323 (invoking Fifth Amendment in Congressional investigation); Brecht in 29 LA 451, 456–459; Kesselman in 28 LA 434, 437 (intoxication); Platt in 23 LA 808, 810–812; Marks in 20 LA 175, 177; Abrahams in 15 LA 42, 45. Also see Thompson in 26 LA 575, 578–579; Healy in 10 LA 637, 641–643; Scarborough in 8 LA 744, 745.

[38] See Arbitrator Florey in 57 LA 725, 730; Johannes in 56 LA 1221, 1226–1227 (incest); Sembower in 53 LA 203, 205–206 (indecent practices of nude photography); Teple in 51 LA 177, 180–181; Wolf in 49 LA 941, 943; Chalfie in 49 LA 117, 120–121 (intoxication); Duff in 47 LA 62, 66 (KKK Acting Grand Dragon); Hughes in 46 LA 857, 859–860 (knife assault); Larkin in 46 LA 346, 348–349 (fight); Ables in 45 LA 932, 936–939; Livengood in 45 LA 495, 497 (bootlegging); Mullin in 45 LA 283, 290–291; Duff in 64–2 ARB ¶8748 (sexual perversion); Granoff in 39 LA 1025, 1028–1029 (employee with sordid private life, whose work required him to enter customers' homes); Volz in 39 LA 245, 248–249; Duncan in 38 LA 1003, 1005 (widespread publicity from bootlegging arrest and grand larceny conviction, reflecting adversely on co-workers and employer); Duff in 38 LA 891, 893 (drug addiction); Roberts in 37 LA 906, 908–909; Ferguson in 28 LA 312, 314; Blair in 27 LA 557, 560–562; Kharas in 26 LA 480, 482–483; Holden in 24 LA 810, 812–813; Granoff in 24 LA 603, 605–606; Cole in 21 LA 327, 328–329; McCoy in 8 LA 647, 652–653; Larkin in 6 LA 58, 59–61.

[39] See Arbitrator Doyle in 50 LA 766, 767–768; Willingham in 50 LA 403, 407; Larkin in 49 LA 1253, 1257; Dworkin in 49 LA 370, 374–375; Block in 48 LA 1099, 1100–1101; Merrill in 45 LA 817, 818, 821 (altercation at union meeting on company premises). Cf., Duff in 48 LA 695, 696–697.

Employer Action Pending Court Hearing
on Conduct of Employee

Where an employee, while on the job, engages in conduct which leads to his arrest, management has been permitted to take action against the employee without waiting for court determination of guilt. In one case the discharge of the employee, effected prior to court trial on the charges, was upheld since the employer established to the arbitrator's satisfaction that the employee was guilty of conduct justifying the discharge.[40] In a number of cases management has been permitted to suspend the employee pending court determination of guilt,[41] but in some cases the arbitrator limited the period of permitted suspension.[42] In one of the latter cases the arbitrator stated that the employer can make his own investigation and if he finds evidence of the employee's guilt, he can assess discipline against the employee (including discharge if the evidence and offense justify it); but if the employer does not do this, he should not continue the suspension for an unreasonable period of time pending court trial.[43]

In cases where an employee is charged with a crime allegedly committed away from company premises, the type of situation in which management may have a right to suspend the employee pending court determination of guilt was summarized by Arbitrator Robert L. Howard:

> "But whether we consider this type of action [that is, suspension pending court determination of guilt] as disciplinary or not, and notwithstanding the presumption of innocence in a criminal proceeding, the employer must have the right to protect his business from the adverse effects flowing from public accusation and arrest for serious crime, supported by a judicial finding of probable cause in a prelimi-

---

[40] Continental Paper Co., 16 LA 727, 728–729 (Lewis, 1951). Also see Arbitrator Maggs in 16 LA 829, 833–835. If the employer does not otherwise have "cause" for the discharge, there should be no discharge merely because the employee was charged with a crime. Yellow Cab Co., 55 LA 590, 592 (Helbling, 1970), where the employee's on-duty assault of a passenger was done in self-defense. In Philadelphia Transportation Company, 49 LA 606, at 606 (Gershenfeld, 1967), completion of the arbitration of a discharge for on-duty misconduct was delayed pending conclusion of court proceedings so as not to prejudice the employee in the criminal action.
[41] See Arbitrator Russell in 34 LA 342, 345; Seitz in 29 LA 442, 445–447; Ryder in 26 LA 570, 571–572.
[42] See Arbitrator Autrey in 54 LA 541, 544–546; Berkowitz in 43 LA 511, 512–514; Oppenheim in 41 LA 1091, 1093–1094; Dash in 22 LA 851, 859–860.
[43] Plough, Inc., 54 LA 541, 544–546 (Autrey, 1970).

nary hearing, when the nature of the charge with its attendant publicity reasonably gives rise to legitimate fear for the safety of other employees or of property, or of substantial adverse effects upon the business."[44]

Arbitrator Howard concluded that in the case before him the violent nature of the criminal offense with which the employee was charged (first degree burglary and assault with intent to rape) could reasonably create feelings of danger and fear among fellow employees and supervisors, so as to interfere with the proper operation of the business and justify the suspension pending court determination of guilt.[45]

Types of Penalties

The type of penalty assessed for wrongdoing usually is either temporary suspension or discharge.[46] Temporary suspension or "disciplinary layoff," as it is sometimes called,[47] results in loss of pay (and sometimes seniority) for the period of suspension, and mars the employee's record. When an arbitrator reinstates a discharged employee without back pay the end result is not unlike suspension.

Warnings are, in a sense, a lesser type of discipline,[48] and as noted elsewhere in this Chapter they are an important factor in evaluating discipline for subsequent offenses.

The right of management to use types of penalties other than those noted above appears to be definitely limited.[49] This is true, for instance,

---

[44] Pearl Brewing Co., 48 LA 379, 390 (1967), where Arbitrator Howard reached his conclusions after studying numerous arbitration decisions.

[45] For other cases upholding suspension pending court decision, see Arbitrator Johannes in 56 LA 1221, 1226–1227; Lennard in 50 LA 274, 277; Johnson in 48 LA 186, 187; Stouffer in 46 LA 124, 126–127; Livengood in 45 LA 498, 499–500, and in 45 LA 495, 497–498. In A. S. Abell Co., 39 LA 859, 862 (Strong, 1962), the employer was held to have improperly suspended an employee pending trial on charges of failing to pay gambling taxes under the Internal Revenue Code. For a collection of cases permitting or not permitting discharge or discipline of employees for absence from work due to jail confinement, see Capitol Mfg. Co., 48 LA 243, 248–249 (Klein, 1967).

[46] Indefinite suspension has been deemed equivalent to discharge. See Penn-Dixie Cement Corp., 29 LA 451, 455 (Brecht, 1957); Harriet Cotton Mills, 27 LA 523, 527 (Barrett, 1956).

[47] See Koppers Co., 11 LA 334, 335 (McCoy, 1948).

[48] See Federal Labor Union v. American Can Co., 21 LA 518 (N.J. Super. Ct., 1953). Also see Arbitrator Roberts in 37 LA 1064, 1068; Louisell in 20 LA 826, 831; Sanders in 20 LA 36, 38. Cf., Teple in 48 LA 1345, 1349.

[49] In some cases, however, arbitrators themselves have utilized various other penalties or remedies in upsetting managerial actions in discharge and discipline cases. See this Chapter, topic titled "Arbitral Remedies in Discharge and Discipline Cases."

in regard to use of demotion or downgrading for purposes of discipline.[50] This is likewise true of transfer,[51] withholding monetary benefits (without actual suspension),[52] requiring employees to present a medical certificate before returning to work after allegedly being sick,[53] and forcing public apologies.[54]

Burden and Quantum of Proof

There are two areas of proof in the arbitration of discharge and discipline cases. The first involves proof of wrongdoing; the second, assuming that guilt of wrongdoing is established and that the arbitrator is empowered to modify penalties, concerns the question of whether the punishment assessed by management should be upheld or modified.[55] The latter is treated below in the topic titled "Review of Penalties Imposed by Management." The present topic deals with proof of wrongdoing.

Discharge is recognized to be the extreme industrial penalty since the employee's job, his seniority and other contractual benefits, and his reputation are at stake. Because of the seriousness of this penalty, the burden generally is held to be on the employer to prove guilt of wrongdoing, and probably always so where the agreement requires "just cause" for discharge.[56]

---

[50] See discussion in Chapter 13, topic titled "Demotion of Employees."

[51] See Chapter 13, topic titled "Promotion and/or Transfer of Employees."

[52] See Arbitrator Dworkin in 36 LA 517, 521–522; Ralston in 18 LA 544, 550; Fearing in 9 LA 505, 508. Cf., Scheiber in 55 LA 1309, 1312. As to the denial of overtime work as punishment, compare the view of Arbitrator Belkin in 53 LA 414, 415–417, with that of Arbitrator Markowitz in 55 LA 384, 386.

[53] See Continental Moss-Gordin Gin Co., 46 LA 1071, 1073 (Williams, 1966).

[54] See Reynolds Metals Co., 22 LA 528, 534 (Klamon, 1954). But see Arbitrator Rauch in 20 LA 823, 826; Kramer in 19 LA 475, 481–482.

[55] See Arbitrator Larkin in 49 LA 882, 886; Lovell in 48 LA 498, 500; Frey in 48 LA 319, 319–320; Doyle in 44 LA 522, 526; Levy in 28 LA 65, 67; Reynard in 27 LA 400, 404; Donnelly in 26 LA 913, 913–914; Howlett in 22 LA 520, 524; Livengood in 20 LA 451, 455; Stutz in 17 LA 701, 702.

[56] Included among the many arbitrators who have held that the burden is upon management to prove wrongdoing are Rohman in 55 LA 435, 437; Solomon in 54 LA 1, 10; Oppenheim in 52 LA 1164, 1169; Howlett in 48 LA 567, at 567; Cahn in 48 LA 132, 135; Nichols in 47 LA 672, 677; Bothwell in 29 LA 781, 783–784; Babb in 29 LA 356, 358; Jones in 28 LA 198, 203; Maggs in 27 LA 709, 711; Jaffee in 27 LA 562, 564; Hale in 27 LA 486, 491; Holly in 27 LA 463, 465; Smith in 25 LA 906, 908; Kelliher in 25 LA 639, 640; McCoy, Schedler & Alexander in 25 LA 270, 274; Somers in 24 LA 728, 729–730; Pollack in 24 LA 401, 405; Reynard in 24 LA 66, 71; Warns in 24 LA 804, 806. But the employee has the burden of proving the

However, the quantum of required proof in this area is unsettled. In some cases proof beyond a reasonable doubt has been required.[57] But in other cases a lesser degree of proof has been required, such as a preponderance of the evidence,[58] or "clear and convincing" evidence,[59] or evidence "sufficient to convince a reasonable mind of guilt."[60]

An arbitrator may require a high degree of proof in one discharge case and at the same time recognize that a lesser degree may be required in others.[61] Similarly, where the proof was not strong enough to support discharge, some arbitrators have nonetheless found it strong enough to justify a lesser penalty.[62]

Concerning the quantum of required proof, Arbitrator Russell A. Smith has observed that: "In general, arbitrators probably have used the 'preponderance of the evidence' rule or some similar standard in deciding fact issues before them, including issues presented by ordinary discipline and discharge cases."[63] But Arbitrator Smith also noted that a higher degree of proof frequently is required where the alleged misconduct is "of a kind recognized and punished by the criminal law," and he concluded:

> "* * * it seems reasonable and proper to hold that alleged misconduct of a kind which carries the stigma of general social disapproval as well as disapproval under accepted canons of plant discipline should be clearly and convincingly established by the evidence. Reasonable doubts raised by the proofs should be resolved in favor of the accused. This may mean that the employer will at times be required, for want

---

validity of the defense or excuse which he asserts in justification of his conduct. See Mississippi Lime Co., 29 LA 559, 561 (Updegraff, 1957). Also see Arbitrator Dunne in 51 LA 174, 177; Jaffee in 27 LA 562, 564–565.

[57] See Arbitrator Cahn in 48 LA 132, 135; Roberts in 46 LA 486, 489; Warns in 24 LA 804, 806; Parker in 21 LA 671, 672–673; Wagner in 7 LA 147, 149. Other instances are cited hereinbelow.

[58] See Arbitrator Erbs in 52 LA 959, 962; McIntosh in 49 LA 39, 39–40; Wildebush in 44 LA 1143, 1148; Levy in 28 LA 65, 67; Hale in 27 LA 486, 491; Pollack in 24 LA 401, 405; Osborne in 21 LA 471, 472; Platt in 1 LA 254, 262–263.

[59] See Arbitrator Dworkin in 27 LA 148, 150; Aaron in 8 LA 261, 268.

[60] Stockham Pipe Fittings Co., 1 ALAA ¶67,460 (1946). Also see Arbitrator Kesselman in 49 LA 692, 695, 697.

[61] See Arbitrator Roberts in 46 LA 486, 489; Graff in 38 LA 1157, 1159; Babb in 29 LA 272, 277; Jones in 28 LA 879, 882–883; Hale in 27 LA 486, 491; Wagner in 7 LA 147, 149–150.

[62] See Arbitrator Hon in 48 LA 891, 893; Sembower in 47 LA 890, 896; Davis in 45 LA 844, 845–847; Rohman in 44 LA 417, 421.

[63] Kroger Co., 25 LA 906, 908 (1955).

of sufficient proof, to withhold or rescind disciplinary action which in fact is fully deserved, but this kind of result is inherent in any civilized system of justice."[64]

In fact, arbitrators have often recognized that proof beyond a reasonable doubt should be required where the alleged offense involves an element of moral turpitude or criminal intent.[65] Moreover, where the offense is of this type management may be required to prove, by a high degree of proof, both the commission of the act and the existence of criminal intent.[66] When, however, the alleged offense is not one that is recognized by the criminal law or does not otherwise involve moral turpitude, Arbitrator Benjamin Aaron has urged vigorously that proof beyond a reasonable doubt should not be required by arbitrators.[67]

In many cases the arbitrator may be able to proceed most realistically along the lines followed by Arbitrators Alexander, Schedler, and Whiting in reviewing discharges for strike misconduct:

"The Arbitration Agreement provides that the Arbitrator shall determine whether there was reasonable cause for the discharge. It does not seem to us that in the making of such determination, we should be bound by a doctrine of the criminal law as to proof beyond a reasonable doubt. We think that the issue we have to decide in any particular case is: Is the employee guilty, and if so, is the act that he committed serious enough to justify discharge?"[68]

Proof in Group Discipline Cases

In a "slowdown" case the evidence was not specific as to the work performance of each individual but the employer was upheld in disciplining all crew members who were on the crew for the full period of the slowdown, the arbitrator stating that "While not every situation would or should lend itself to implicating several employees

---

[64] Ibid.

[65] See Arbitrator Jacobs in 55 LA 1195, 1200–1201; Keefe in 52 LA 709, at 709; Somers in 52 LA 212, 215; Ray in 51 LA 1019, 1021; Jones in 50 LA 1253, 1259; Doyle in 48 LA 1089, 1090; Gross in 46 LA 756, 760; Murphy in 44 LA 897, 901; Altieri in 43 LA 400, 404; Boles in 42 LA 954, 955–956; Ryder in 39 LA 470, 478; Eiger in 38 LA 778, 780; Simkin in 32 LA 44, 47; Bothwell in 29 LA 781, 784; Babb in 29 LA 272, 277; Holly in 27 LA 463, 465; Hale in 24 LA 470, 481–482; Warns in 23 LA 534, 536; Lesser in 11 LA 301, 302–303. Contra, see Arbitrator Purdom in 56 LA 75, 79–82; Block in 49 LA 810, 814; Black in 43 LA 113, at 113.

[66] See Arbitrator Morrissey in 44 LA 257, 259; King in 43 LA 940, 945–946; Holly in 27 LA 463, 465; Somers in 24 LA 728, 729–730.

[67] Aaron, "Some Procedural Problems in Arbitration," 10 Vanderbilt L. Rev. 733, 740–742 (1957).

[68] Southern Bell Telephone & Telegraph Co., 25 LA 85, 87 (1955). Also see Arbitrator Kates in 50 LA 103, 106; Granoff in 17 LA 258, 264.

in slowdown activities, such implications seem justified where [as in the present case] the group involved is small and the focus of delay represents a team effort."[69] Likewise, group discipline of the six members of a boning crew was upheld where each individual denied any responsibility for the bad work which the crew had done but where each individual also refused to testify against any other member of the crew.[70]

On the other hand, some arbitrators have indicated rather clearly that they consider group discipline to be improper in the absence of evidence establishing the guilt of all.[71]

Still another arbitrator considered an intermediate approach to be justified under the circumstances in his case. He rejected the employer's "theory of collective responsibility" for imposing discipline upon several entire crews since (1) not all jobs on the crews contributed equally to production, (2) the make-up of the crews varied from day to day, and (3) the employer's own evidence absolved some of the crew members. However, he also rejected the union's contention that management must produce specific evidence linking each employee to the slowdown in question, and he held that management could meet its initial burden of proof by evidence showing a grievant's presence on a crew with consistent reduction in production rate during the slowdown period.[72]

Review of Penalties Imposed by Management

Several views have been expressed by arbitrators regarding the nature of their function in reviewing disciplinary penalties imposed by management.

---

[69] Kennecott Copper Corp., 41 LA 1339, 1344 (Dykstra, 1963). In Elmira School Dist., 54 LA 569, 570–571 (Markowitz, 1970), the arbitrator applied the New York "Taylor Law" under which public employees absent during a strike were presumed to be strikers and had the "burden of proof" of rebutting the presumption by showing that the absence was not related to the strike. For a similar result apart from statute, see Lone Star Steel Co., 48 LA 949, 951 (Jenkins, 1967).

[70] Marhoefer Packing Co., 54 LA 649, 652–653 (Sembower, 1970). Group discipline for failure to meet production standards was held not to be guilt by association and was upheld by Arbitrator Solomon in 50 LA 888, 897; McIntosh in 49 LA 581, 583–584.

[71] See Arbitrator Williams in 48 LA 211, 213; Gross in 45 LA 53, 55–57; Marshall in 36 LA 1302, 1303.

[72] United States Steel Corp., 49 LA 1236, 1239–1240 (McDermott, 1968), where the decision was made to discipline some individuals but not others.

The view that the determination of the penalty for misconduct is properly a function of management and that an arbitrator should hesitate to substitute his judgment and discretion for that of management was elaborated by Arbitrator Whitley P. McCoy:

"Where an employee has violated a rule or engaged in conduct meriting disciplinary action, it is primarily the function of management to decide upon the proper penalty. If management acts in good faith upon a fair investigation and fixes a penalty not inconsistent with that imposed in other like cases, an arbitrator should not disturb it. The mere fact that management has imposed a somewhat different penalty or a somewhat more severe penalty than the arbitrator would have, if he had had the decision to make originally, is no justification for changing it. The minds of equally reasonable men differ. A consideration which would weigh heavily with one man will seem of less importance to another. A circumstance which highly aggravates an offense in one man's eyes may be only slight aggravation to another. If an arbitrator could substitute his judgment and discretion for the judgment and discretion honestly exercised by management, then the functions of management would have been abdicated, and unions would take every case to arbitration. The result would be as intolerable to employees as to management. The only circumstances under which a penalty imposed by management can be rightfully set aside by an arbitrator are those where discrimination, unfairness, or capricious and arbitrary action are proved—in other words, where there has been abuse of discretion."[73]

Under an agreement requiring just cause, Arbitrator Wilber C. Bothwell held that "the arbitrator should not substitute his judgment for that of management unless he finds that the penalty is excessive, unreasonable, or that management has abused its discretion."[74] Views of similar import have been expressed by many other arbitrators (the "unreasonable, capricious or arbitrary action" standard of review often being stated).[75]

---

[73] Stockham Pipe Fittings Co., 1 LA 160, 162 (1945), where the submission specifically empowered the arbitrator to determine "what disposition" should be made of the dispute. Also see statements of similar import by Arbitrator Larkin in 53 LA 188, 190; Beatty in 41 LA 142, 144 ("an arbitration clause is not an abdication by management of its duties in regard to discipline and discharge and does not grant to the arbitrator authority to redetermine the whole matter by his own standards as if he were making the original decision"); Stouffer in 26 LA 395, 397; Kadish in 25 LA 568, 571; Gilden in 21 LA 105, 107; Reid in 19 LA 724, 727; Prasow in 13 LA 28, 30.

[74] Franz Food Products, Inc., 28 LA 543, 548 (1957).

[75] See Arbitrator Talent in 55 LA 1094, 1098; King in 54 LA 1110, 1113; Dunlop in 52 LA 752, 755; Nathanson in 51 LA 120, 125; Doyle in 50 LA 1157, 1159; Whyte in 47 LA 1065, 1071–1072; Larkin in 47 LA 903, 906;

A less restricted role of the arbitrator in reviewing discipline assessed under agreements requiring cause is apparent under the following view expressed by Arbitrator Harry H. Platt:

> "It is ordinarily the function of an Arbitrator in interpreting a contract provision which requires 'sufficient cause' as a condition precedent to discharge not only to determine whether the employee involved is guilty of wrong-doing and, if so, to confirm the employer's right to discipline where its exercise is essential to the objective of efficiency, but also to safeguard the interests of the discharged employee by making reasonably sure that the causes for discharge were just and equitable and such as would appeal to reasonable and fair-minded persons as warranting discharge. To be sure, no standards exist to aid an arbitrator in finding a conclusive answer to such a question and, therefore, perhaps the best he can do is to decide what reasonable man, mindful of the habits and customs of industrial life and of the standards of justice and fair dealing prevalent in the community, ought to have done under similar circumstances and in that light to decide whether the conduct of the discharged employee was defensible and the disciplinary penalty just."[76]

Here again, views of similar import have also been expressed by arbitrators in other cases.[77]

An arbitrator's view of his function in reviewing discipline may vary according to the nature of the offense. For instance, Arbitrator Robert G. Howlett has stated that an arbitrator should be more hesitant to overrule penalties where the offense is directly related to the company's product than where it involves primarily the personal be-

---

Gibson in 46 LA 633, 636; Altrock in 44 LA 1202, 1204; Meltzer in 28 LA 303, 308; Hale in 27 LA 486, 493; Reynard in 27 LA 400, 404; Dworkin in 23 LA 696, 701; Anrod in 20 LA 653, 658; Luskin in 19 LA 5, 7; Donaldson in 13 LA 943, 945.

[76] Riley Stoker Corp., 7 LA 764, 767 (1947). In Indianapolis Chair Co., 20 LA 706, 709 (1953), Arbitrator W. Howard Mann stated that in reviewing discharge, "The Arbitrator must accept the responsibility of making an actual determination."

[77] See Arbitrator Hayes in 56 LA 924, 926 (quoting the Platt view with express approval); Coffey in 48 LA 1349, 1353; Klein in 46 LA 974, 977; Volz in 45 LA 968, 970–971; Doyle in 44 LA 522, 526–527; Hebert in 41 LA 745, 750 (denying that the arbitrator is merely to determine whether management's action was capricious or arbitrary and declaring that he has a responsibility to determine whether the punishment fits the crime); Turkus in 39 LA 823, 825; Teple in 37 LA 85, 90; Thompson in 36 LA 537, 539. In Capital Packing Co., 36 LA 101, 102 (Seligson, 1961), the arbitrator stated that "a discharge case in arbitration is a hearing in equity, permitting of a flexibility and assessment of mitigating circumstances and factors not available under the more rigorous common law rules."

havior of the employee and is only indirectly related to production.[78] Also, where the safety of the public is a direct factor in a discharge, another arbitrator would require the union to "show that the decision was arbitrary, made in bad faith, or clearly wrong."[79]

On the other hand, Arbitrator Carroll R. Daugherty has offered "a set of guide lines or criteria" to be applied in any given case to determine whether the arbitrator should "substitute his judgment for that of the employer."[80]

Finally, it should be recognized that while arbitrators do not lightly interfere with management's decisions in discharge and discipline matters, this by no means suggests that they fail to act firmly when management's decisions are found to be unjust or unreasonable under all the circumstances. In this regard, Arbitrator Charles B. Spaulding replied as follows where an employer cited awards allegedly to the effect that arbitrators should not interfere with discipline assessed by management where the agreement permits it to exercise judgment:

"Three answers to this line or argument seem appropriate. The first is that arbitrators very frequently do step in and upset the decisions of Management. The second is that, if arbitrators could not do so, arbitration would be of little import, since the judgment of management would in so many cases constitute the final verdict. Finally, the more careful statement of the principle would probably run to the effect that where the contract uses such terms as discharge for 'cause' or for 'good cause' or for 'justifiable cause' an arbitrator will not lightly upset a decision reached by competent careful management which acts in the full light of all the facts, and without any evidence of bias, haste or lack of emotional balance. Even under these conditions, if the decision is such as to shock the sense of justice of ordinary reasonable men, we suspect that arbitrators have a duty to interfere. Since the acts of Management in this case do shock our sense of justice, and since they do seem to have occurred in a situation of emotional tension, in haste, and without a very careful weighing of the facts, we find ourselves inevitably driven to overthrow the decision of this Management."[81]

---

[78] Valley Steel Casting Co., 22 LA 520, 524–525 (1954).
[79] United Air Lines, Inc., 19 LA 585, 587 (McCoy, 1952). Also see Arbitrator Dolson in 46 LA 1161, 1165; Lennard in 30 LA 830, 834–835.
[80] Enterprise Wire Co., 46 LA 359, 362–365 (1966), where he also stated, however, that frequently "the facts are such that the guide lines cannot be applied with precision."
[81] Fruehauf Trailer Co., 16 LA 666, 670 (1951). Also see Arbitrator Autrey in 45 LA 117, 119–120.

Authority of Arbitrator to Modify Penalties

Many agreements give the arbitrator express authority to modify penalties found to be improper or too severe.[82] Also the agreement may give him such authority by implication.[83] Some agreements expressly limit the arbitrator's authority to modify penalties. Under such agreements arbitrators sometimes have sustained discharge where the arbitrator probably would have reduced the penalty but for the limitation upon his authority;[84] but in other instances the denial of arbitral authority to modify penalties has resulted in the reinstatement of employees with no penalty at all even though the employee was guilty of misconduct justifying some punishment.[85]

In one case a party expressed serious doubt as to the wisdom of placing "the arbitrator in a position of making a 'black or white' decision,"[86] and it is not surprising that arbitrators have sometimes considered that any restriction upon their authority to modify penalties must be clearly and unequivocally stated and have narrowly construed contractual provisions purporting to restrict that authority.[87]

Where the agreement fails to deal with the matter, the right of the arbitrator to change or modify penalties found to be improper or too severe may be deemed to be inherent in his power to decide the sufficiency of cause, as elaborated by Arbitrator Harry H. Platt:

> "In many disciplinary cases, the reasonableness of the penalty imposed on an employee rather than the existence of proper cause for disciplining him is the question an arbitrator must decide. This is not so under contracts or submission agreements which expressly prohibit an arbitrator from modifying or reducing a penalty if he

---

[82] For example, see Sundstrand Corp., 46 LA 346, 349 (Larkin, 1966). The parties clothed the arbitrator with this power at the hearing in Dayton Malleable Iron Co., 17 LA 666, at 666 (Hampton, 1951).

[83] See McInerney Spring & Wire Co., 21 LA 80, 82 (Smith, 1953).

[84] See Arbitrator Eaton in 53 LA 1274, 1278; Williams in 52 LA 957, 958; Jones in 48 LA 1092, 1093–1094; Granoff in 40 LA 686, 688–689; Seinsheimer in 39 LA 580, 584.

[85] See Arbitrator Bellman in 47 LA 899, 902; McDermott in 46 LA 985, 989; King in 43 LA 940, 945–946.

[86] Luce Press Clipping Bureau, 40 LA 686, 688, fn. 6 (Granoff, 1963). Arbitral power to modify penalties was generally supported by labor and management representatives in a survey conducted by Eaton, "Labor Arbitration in the San Francisco Bay Area," 48 LA 1381, 1386–1387 (1967).

[87] See Arbitrator Volz in 50 LA 600, 603; Gilbert in 45 LA 580, 584; Dworkin in 36 LA 124, 128. Even a clear restriction upon the arbitrator's authority was stated to be inapplicable under the circumstances in Consolidated Paper Co., 33 LA 840, 846–847 (Kahn, 1959).

finds that disciplinary action was justified, but most current labor agreements do not contain such limiting clause. In disciplinary cases generally, therefore, most arbitrators exercise the right to change or modify a penalty if it is found to be improper or too severe, under all the circumstances of the situation. This right is deemed to be inherent in the arbitrator's power to discipline and in his authority to finally settle and adjust the dispute before him."[88]

Leniency

Modification by an arbitrator of a penalty found to be too severe should not be confused with the exercise of leniency (or clemency). The distinction between these actions was emphasized by Arbitrator Whitley P. McCoy when he recognized the power of arbitrators to modify penalties found on the basis of mitigating circumstances to be too severe for the offense, but at the same time declared that arbitrators have no authority to grant clemency where the penalty assessed by management is not found too severe.[89]

The fact that an arbitrator considers that he has no power of leniency or clemency, and accordingly that he must sustain management's disciplinary action where just cause is found, does not prevent him from *recommending* leniency when he personally feels that it should be considered by management.[90] Inherent in such recommenda-

---

[88] Platt, "The Arbitration Process in the Settlement of Labor Disputes," 31 J. Am. Jud. Soc. 54, 58 (1947). To similar effect as to inherent authority to modify penalties, Arbitrator Feller in 54 LA 1231, 1246; Goetz in 54 LA 546, 550; Koven in 49 LA 190, 193; Autrey in 47 LA 327, 330; Dolson in 46 LA 1161, 1165; Strasshofer in 44 LA 644, 646; Wren in 41 LA 1020, 1023; Sembower in 41 LA 631, 636; Williams in 36 LA 333, 341–342; Levy in 28 LA 65, 69; Wyckoff in 25 LA 634, 637–638; Hebert in 25 LA 439, 442; Hepburn in 9 LA 345, 348. For court recognition of the arbitrator's authority to modify penalties in the absence of an express contractual restriction, see International U. of Dist. 50, UMW v. Bowman Transportation, Inc., 421 F.2d 934, 936 (CA 5, 1970); Gulf States Telephone Co. v. Local 1692, IBEW, 416 F.2d 198, 202 (CA 5, 1969). Also see Lodge No. 12, IAM v. Cameron Iron Works, Inc., 292 F.2d 112, 119 (CA 5, 1961). Cf., Amanda Bent Bolt Co. v. Auto Workers, 79 LRRM 2023 (CA 6, 1971); Truck Drivers & Helpers Union v. Ulry-Talbert Company, 330 F.2d 562, 564 (CA 8, 1964); Textile Workers v. American Thread Co., 291 F.2d 894, 900 (CA 4, 1961).

[89] Chattanooga Box & Lumber Co., 10 LA 260, 261 (1948). Also stating that arbitrators have no leniency power, see Arbitrator Dolnick in 53 LA 990, 991–992; Abernethy in 50 LA 1194, 1198; Daugherty in 50 LA 83, 90; Larkin in 45 LA 156, 159–160; Hughes in 42 LA 307, 310. But see Cahn in 44 LA 1043, 1044.

[90] See Arbitrator Bothwell in 51 LA 1076, 1080; Stouffer in 47 LA 443, 448; Abersold in 42 LA 1251, 1255; Mueller in 36 LA 965, 969; Rosenfarb in 24 LA 674, 675–676; Dworkin in 23 LA 696, 702; Miller in 22 LA 620, 623; Marshall in 22 LA 573, 576; Howlett in 22 LA 520, 527; Kelliher in 21 LA 444, 446; Seward in 17 LA 334, 335.

tions is silent recognition by arbitrators of powers of leniency or clemency in management.[91]

Factors in Evaluating Penalties

Numerous factors may be relevant in the review or evaluation of penalties assessed by management for misconduct of employees. The more prominent of these factors are considered briefly below.

Nature of the Offense: Summary Discharge v. Corrective Discipline

It is said to be "axiomatic that the degree of penalty should be in keeping with the seriousness of the offense."[92] In this regard, Arbitrator Whitley P. McCoy explained:

> "Offenses are of two general classes: (1) those extremely serious offenses such as stealing, striking a foreman, persistent refusal to obey a legitimate order, etc., which usually justify summary discharge without the necessity of prior warnings or attempts at corrective discipline; (2) those less serious infractions of plant rules or of proper conduct such as tardiness, absence without permission, careless workmanship, insolence, etc., which call not for discharge for the first offense (and usually not even for the second or third offense) but for some milder penalty aimed at correction."[93]

As to the less serious offenses, the concept of corrective or progressive discipline has been recognized by arbitrators. Arbitrator M. S. Ryder, for instance, has stated:

> "Further, if the employer so chooses, and it is common practice in industry, the employer may adopt a corrective approach toward penalty, by making second and third offenses of the same nature, or of another nature, cumulative in terms of the degree of severity

---

[91] Arbitrators also have expressly recognized this power in management. See Arbitrator Dolnick in 53 LA 990, 991–992; Luckerath in 48 LA 182, 183; Daugherty in 45 LA 515, 517; Hughes in 42 LA 307, 310; Abernethy in 36 LA 1092, 1096; McCoy in 12 LA 1190, 1192; Gorder in 9 LA 73, 77.

[92] Capital Airlines, Inc., 25 LA 13, 16 (Stowe, 1955).

[93] Huntington Chair Corp., 24 LA 490, 491 (1955). Also recognizing the propriety of summary discharge for serious offenses, see Arbitrator Schmidt in 52 LA 1019, 1021–1022; Keefe in 52 LA 709, 713; Turkus in 51 LA 258, 260; Daugherty in 50 LA 83, 90; Livengood in 47 LA 1170, 1175; Tsukiyama in 43 LA 1218, 1223–1224; Jaffee in 27 LA 768, 772–773; McCoy, Schedler & Alexander in 25 LA 270, 276; Stowe in 25 LA 13, 16; Marshall in 22 LA 573, 576; Seward in 19 LA 210, 212; Updegraff in 17 LA 224, 225. In some of these cases the arbitrator expressly stated that summary discharge is permissible even though the employee has long seniority with a good record.

of penalty imposed for each of the subsequent proven offenses so as to dissuade any further commissions."[94]

However, Arbitrator Robert S. Thompson has cautioned:

"In industrial practice discipline is often 'progressive' or 'corrective' in nature. Warning is tried before suspension; suspension before discharge. Penalties are designed to correct if possible. While theories and practices of 'progressive' or 'corrective' discipline may be in wide use, it does not follow that every Company must, in the absence of contract provisions, adopt such views. Every business and industry has its own peculiar conditions. An Arbitrator should be slow to substitute his own judgment as to the appropriateness of penalties on the basis of theories which seem to have wide appeal."[95]

In fact, there appears to be considerable diversity of arbitral thought in respect to corrective discipline. Without attempting to distinguish or reconcile any cases which appear to conflict, the Authors merely note some of the various views or actions by arbitrators concerning corrective discipline:

1. There are cases in which management was held obligated to use corrective discipline although there was no indication that management had ever approved its use either by the agreement or by unilaterally instituting corrective discipline in the past.[96]

2. It has been said that the formalization of a corrective discipline program is a matter for negotiations by the parties, not for the arbitrator.[97] It also has been said that it "is one thing to determine whether or not a contract permits discharging an employee under given circumstances," but that it "is entirely another matter for an arbitrator to conclude that an employee's discharge violated a contract because of something not in the contract," that is, because of the absence of a corrective discipline program where none is specified by the agreement.[98]

---

[94] Michigan Seamless Tube Co., 24 LA 132, 133–134 (1955). Also see statements by Arbitrator Platt in 25 LA 733, 735; McCoy in 24 LA 490, 492. For futher discussion see comments by Arbitrator Alexander in Management Rights and the Arbitration Process 76, 79–82 (BNA Incorporated, 1956), quoted in significant part by Arbitrator Howlett in 48 LA 283, 287.

[95] Niagara Frontier Transit System, 24 LA 783, 785 (1955), reducing the penalty on the basis of grievant's long seniority.

[96] See Arbitrator Heilbrun in 56 LA 884, 887; Zack in 55 LA 987, 989–990; Teple in 50 LA 541, 544; Nichols in 50 LA 249, 251; Wallen in 48 LA 19, 23; Duff in 45 LA 538, 540; Prasow in 44 LA 669, 672; Dworkin in 40 LA 1052, 1059.

[97] Union Carbide Corp., 46 LA 195, 196–197 (Cahn, 1966), where some corrective discipline had in fact been used.

[98] Aro, Inc., 47 LA 1065, 1070 (Whyte, 1966). In Fruehauf Corp., 47 LA 618, 621 (Levin, 1966), the arbitrator said that until the union approves

3. There are cases in which discharge was upset where the company had a corrective discipline system but failed to abide by it.[99]

4. Where an employer was reluctant to suspend the employee and used counselling and warnings instead (as predischarge measures), this demonstrated a desire to help rather than hurt the employee, an arbitrator said, for which the employer should not be criticized.[100]

5. Where there were "no circumstances to suggest that corrective discipline would rehabilitate the grievant into a satisfactory employee," discharge without corrective discipline was upheld.[101]

6. In adopting a corrective discipline program a company was held not to have surrendered its right to invoke summary discharge for serious offenses warranting such action.[102] Also, the mere fact that an agreement specified the use of corrective discipline for some offenses did not necessarily mean that it must be used for all offenses.[103]

7. In sustaining discharge, arbitrators sometimes have stressed the fact that corrective discipline had been used without avail.[104]

Due Process and Procedural Requirements

Discharge and disciplinary action by management has been reversed where the action violated basic notions of fairness or due process. This was true, for instance, where the employer gave employees no chance to be heard but discharged them summarily upon learning

---

the three-step disciplinary procedure unilaterally instituted by management, the ultimate test for reviewing discipline must be its "reasonableness."

[99] See Arbitrator Belshaw in 49 LA 573, 576–577; Morgan in 45 LA 280, 283; Kates in 43 LA 1031, 1034–1035, and in 39 LA 286, 290–292 (the established sequence should be adhered to in the absence of compelling circumstances otherwise); Dworkin in 41 LA 862, 866. But recognizing the need for flexibility in the administration of corrective discipline systems, see Arbitrator Bradley in 52 LA 538, 544; Krislov in 48 LA 634, 636.

[100] American Cyanamid Co., 51 LA 181, 184–185 (Stouffer, 1968). Similarly, see Arbitrator Stouffer in 51 LA 688, 691. But see Arbitrator Duff in 52 LA 101, 104 (management's continued reliance upon gentle verbal rebukes that were not effective did not adequately warn the employee that his conduct would not continue to be tolerated).

[101] Int'l Telephone & Telegraph Corp., 54 LA 1110, 1113 (King, 1970).

[102] Inland Steel Products Co., 47 LA 966, 970 (Gilden, 1966). Also see statement by Arbitrator Bradley in 52 LA 538, 544.

[103] Alliance Machine Co., 48 LA 457, 462–463 (Dworkin, 1967), upholding the propriety of summary discharge for serious offenses not listed in the corrective discipline schedule.

[104] See Arbitrator Altrock in 48 LA 1224, 1227; Cahn in 47 LA 747, at 747; Stouffer in 47 LA 464, 468; Dworkin in 47 LA 266, 268; Tsukiyama in 45 LA 1124, 1133.

that they had been convicted of larceny by a court.[105] In other situations, too, the failure of management to make a reasonable inquiry
or investigation before assessing punishment was a factor (sometimes
the sole factor) in the arbitrator's refusal to sustain the discharge or
discipline as assessed by management.[106]

One of the factors leading to a reduction of the penalty assessed
by management in one case was the failure to give the employee or
union an opportunity, either at the suspension hearing or in the pre-
arbitral grievance procedure, to question the foreman who was the
employee's accuser.[107] Likewise, procedural unfairness was found
where the employer selected certain employees for discharge out of
a group of illicit strikers without telling the union or the discharged
employees the reason for their being selected until the arbitration hearing.[108] In another case a discharge was set aside where delay in noti-
fying the employee of his discharge made it difficult for him to obtain
witnesses in his own behalf (due to the fact that intoxication was
the offense charged).[109]

Many agreements specify procedual requirements for discharge
or discipline. In many cases arbitrators have refused to uphold management's action in discharging or disciplining an employee where
management failed to fulfill some procedural requirement specified by
the agreement, such as a required statement of charges against the employee, or a notice or investigation requirement, or a requirement for
a hearing or joint discussion prior to the assessment of punishment.[110]

---

[105] United States Steel Corp., 29 LA 272, 277–278 (Babb, 1957), citing
other cases also recognizing the obligation of management to make appropriate
inquiry before discharging employees in such situations. Also see Arbitrator Maggs
in 16 LA 829, 834. Cf., Arbitrator Sembower in 49 LA 439, 441–442.

[106] See Arbitrator Erbs in 55 LA 197, 209 (only one side of the matter
was investigated); Solomon in 54 LA 1, 6–7; Howlett in 52 LA 375, 381–382
(management's failure to make objective investigation did not exonerate the
employees but the penalty was reduced); Bernstein in 50 LA 1263, 1265–1266;
Summers in 48 LA 1278, 1279–1280; Karlins in 44 LA 609, 613–614; Daugherty
in 42 LA 555, 557; Dworkin in 36 LA 124, 128. But see Cahn in 19 LA
674, 676.

[107] Pittsburgh Steel Co., 47 LA 923, 926 (McDermott, 1966). Also see Arbitrator Merrill in 19 LA 417, 419–420 (discharge on the basis of a finding by
the company physician without giving the employee opportunity to present countervailing medical testimony was held improper).

[108] Ross Gear Tennessee Plant, 45 LA 959, 963–964 (Sanders, 1965), the
agreement expressly permitting selective discipline of such strikers.

[109] National Carbide Co., 27 LA 128, 130 (Warns, 1956).

[110] See Arbitrator McDaniel in 56 LA 694, 696–697; Davis in 55 LA 764,
767; Wolff in 55 LA 677, 679–680; Porter in 54 LA 361, 362–363 (contract

However, in numerous other cases compliance with the spirit of such procedural requirements was held to suffice where the employee had not been adversely affected by the failure of management to accomplish total compliance with the requirements.[111] Also, in one case a contractual procedural requirement was held waived by the failure to make a timely objection to the fact that the specified procedure was not followed precisely, the arbitrator also noting that no prejudice resulted to the grievant from the manner in which the discharge was handled.[112]

Postdischarge Conduct or Charges

Some agreements require that all reasons for discharge action be given to the employee at the time of discharge. Under such provisions it has been held that only evidence bearing on the charges made at the time of discharge should be considered in determining the existence of cause for punishment.[113] Even without such specific contractual provision, arbitrators have held that discharge, to use the words of Arbitrator Paul N. Guthrie, "must stand or fall upon the reason given at the time of discharge"; other reasons may not be added when the case reaches arbitration.[114] Arbitrator James T. Burke

---

gave employee right to present evidence before being discharged); Gershenfeld in 52 LA 184, 187; Dolnick in 48 LA 273, 276; Krimsly in 48 LA 257, 261; Sembower in 47 LA 910, 913–914; Griffin in 47 LA 257, 258 (duty to notify union *prior* to discharge); Larkin in 46 LA 1214, 1216; Rohman in 44 LA 417, 420; Kates in 44 LA 389, 391, and in 43 LA 977, 980; Howlett in 40 LA 660, 663 (oral notice did not suffice where contract required written notice); Stouffer in 38 LA 882, 885 (oral notice similarly did not suffice); Merrill in 24 LA 522, 524–526; Platt in 17 LA 412, 417–418.

[111] See Arbitrator Schurke in 56 LA 973, 976; Jaffee in 55 LA 1102, 1103–1104; Kamin in 55 LA 118, 128; Kreimer in 53 LA 342, 344 (oral notice sufficed although contract specified written notice); Dykstra in 52 LA 1213, 1215–1217; Willingham in 52 LA 951, 953; Kates in 52 LA 818, 820; Eaton in 50 LA 807, 808–810 (requirement of notice to union *after* discharge need not be complied with as strictly as must be a predischarge notice requirement); Buckwalter in 50 LA 177, 179; Block in 49 LA 810, 816–817 (violation was merely technical and did not work to employee's disadvantage); Seidenberg in 49 LA 620, 624–625; Stouffer in 46 LA 654, 657–658; Wren in 41 LA 1020, 1021; Daugherty in 34 LA 83, 85. Also see Murphy in 36 LA 1071, 1073.

[112] United Engineering & Foundry Co., 37 LA 1095, 1097 (Kates, 1962).

[113] See Bethlehem Steel Co., 29 LA 635, 640–643 (Seward, 1957); Forest Hill Foundry Co., 1 LA 153, 154 (Brown, 1946).

[114] West Virginia Pulp & Paper Co., 10 LA 117, 118 (1947). To similar effect, Arbitrator Ray in 51 LA 1019, 1022; Roberts in 49 LA 1207, 1210; Williams in 49 LA 210, 213; Summers in 48 LA 188, 190; Jones in 44 LA 175, 181–182; McKelvey in 38 LA 586, 593; Morvant in 35 LA 205, 209; Larson in 32 LA 71, 73; Brecht in 29 LA 451, 457; Healy in 12 LA 108, 115; Burke in 3 LA 607, 608. Also see Somers in 45 LA 655, 658, 661; Kates

reasoned in one of these cases that: "The only relevant evidence are the facts which the person making the discharge was in possession of at the time he acted. A discharge cannot be based upon conjecture, surmise, suspicion, or anything but hard, material, and known facts."[115]

In some other cases the arbitrator did consider postdischarge misconduct or predischarge misconduct of which the company was unaware until after the discharge;[116] in some of these cases the arbitrator purported to qualify such consideration by stating that the misconduct could not be used to justify the discharge but could be used in determining the extent to which the penalty should be modified, if at all.[117] It should also be noted that the discovery of new information or the postdischarge actions of the grievant may equally well be considered in his favor.[118]

Finally, it should be noted that there is a line of cases in which the company's evidence was held inadequate to establish the offense

---

in 43 LA 1031, 1034; Abersold in 37 LA 62, 70; Dworkin in 33 LA 735, 740; Abernethy in 30 LA 1039, 1042–1043. Cf., Peck in 48 LA 953, 956.

[115] Borden's Farm Products, Inc., 3 LA 607, 608 (1945). In San Gamo Electric Co., 44 LA 593, 600 (1965), Arbitrator Sembower concluded that an employer may investigate further in an effort to buttress the action already taken, but not to add an entirely new ground for action or to enlarge the penalty; he also concluded that in the present case the postdisciplinary investigation was well within the employer's original "theory of the case." Also stating that additional evidence as to the facts may be obtained and relied upon by the company after discharge, see Arbitrator Seitz in 41 LA 823, 830–831.

[116] See Arbitrator McKenna in 53 LA 909, 918; McCoy in 47 LA 752, 753 (ordinarily a discharge made for one explicit reason cannot be justified in arbitration for an entirely different reason, but this rule does not apply where the employee has fair opportunity to defend against the additional grounds and the grounds would be reason for another discharge immediately following a reinstatement by the arbitrator); Merrill in 46 LA 1044, 1048 (additional offense at time of discharge formed "part of one connected whole"); Davis in 44 LA 193, 193–194; Daugherty in 39 LA 183, 187; Seitz in 36 LA 706, 709; Simkin in 26 LA 836, 839; McCoy, Schedler & Alexander in 25 LA 270, 274–277; Alexander in 24 LA 353, 355; Updegraff in 17 LA 224, 226–227, and in 14 LA 745, 747. For related matters, see Chapter 8, topic titled " 'New' Evidence at Arbitration Hearing"; Chapter 7, topic titled "Extent of Permissible Deviation From Pre-Arbitral Discussion of Case."

[117] Making this qualified use of postdischarge misconduct, see Arbitrator Kates in 44 LA 507, 513–514; Volz in 43 LA 849, 852; Alexander in 40 LA 935, 936; Gorsuch in 40 LA 641, 651 (saying that postdischarge misconduct may be considered in judging the appropriateness of the penalty just as the employee's past record may be considered); McCoy in 33 LA 807, 808. Making this qualified use of predischarge misconduct of which the employer was unaware, Arbitrator Levin in Sunshine Specialty Co., 55 LA 1061, 1068–1069 (1970).

[118] See Texaco, Inc., 42 LA 408, 411 (Prasow, 1963); Spaulding Fibre Co., 21 LA 58, 58–59 (Thompson, 1953).

for which the employee had been disciplined but was held to be adequate to establish a related lesser offense for which an appropriate penalty (either as assessed by the employer or as reduced by the arbitrator) was in order.[119] In one such case where an employee was disciplined for sleeping on duty, management failed to prove conclusively that the employee was asleep; but Arbitrator Whitley P. McCoy nonetheless upheld the penalty assessed by management since the evidence did establish a related offense:

> "The Association argues that since the Company made no contention that the penalty was imposed for any other reason than being asleep, the Board has no right to justify the penalty unless it finds that he was asleep. I cannot agree with that contention. The penalty was imposed as a result of the facts. * * * Giving a name to those facts is not important. There was a time when the criminal law was so technical that on a given set of facts a conviction of larceny would be set aside on the ground that those facts constituted embezzlement, and vice versa. Arbitration should not be tied up with such technicalities. Cambre did certain things—leaned back in his swivel chair, put his feet on the desk, closed his eyes, relaxed his muscles, leaned his head back against the wall, and assumed the position and appearance of sleeping. Those facts constitute an offense, and I do not think the Board is bound to set a penalty aside merely because the facts fail to prove conclusively that Cambre was asleep."[120]

Double Jeopardy

By application of "double jeopardy" concepts it has been held that once discipline for a given offense has been imposed and accepted it cannot thereafter be increased.[121] The same result has been reached

---

[119] See Arbitrator Turkus in 50 LA 616, 620; Hughes in 50 LA 133, 136; Volz in 45 LA 968, 970; Davey in 42 LA 840, 842; Roberts in 35 LA 939, 943; McCoy in 19 LA 495, 497–498. Also see Arbitrator Sembower in 51 LA 391, 396 (insufficient evidence to support the charged offense but back pay was withheld because grievant at the investigation did not make forthright denial of charge but fostered suspicion against himself); Feinberg in 36 LA 839, 841 (similar result where grievant failed to cooperate at the investigation); Maggs in 36 LA 179, 185.

[120] Esso Standard Oil Co., 19 LA 495, 497–498 (1952).

[121] See Arbitrator Gundermann in 43 LA 907, 910; Sembower in 41 LA 1083, 1085–1086; Dworkin in 40 LA 87, 90; Livengood in 24 LA 356, 358; McCoy in 16 LA 616, 616–617. For other situations in which the double jeopardy concept was applied, see Arbitrator Simons in 55 LA 447, 449 (employee who was discharged and then reinstated after full investigation could not then be discharged again for the same incident); Keefe in 48 LA 910, 914; Ryder in 24 LA 132, 134. Any right to assert the double jeopardy rule was held waived under the circumstances in Kisco Company, Inc., 56 LA 623, 636 (Witney, 1971).

where the original penalty had not been accepted by the employee.[122]

The double-jeopardy concept also has been held applicable where management unduly delays the assessment or enforcement of discipline.[123]

The double-jeopardy concept has been held inapplicable where the preliminary action taken against the employee may not reasonably be considered final.[124] In one case where employees were first suspended for participating in an unauthorized work stoppage and later discharged on the basis of subsequently obtained evidence indicating that they had led the stoppage (a dischargeable offense under the contract), Arbitrator W. Willard Wirtz would not honor a plea of double jeopardy. He stated that the rule of double jeopardy presupposes a full hearing before the first penalty is imposed; since a full hearing of the type assumed by the rule is not customary in industrial disciplinary procedures and was not had in this case when the suspension penalty was imposed, the rule was inapplicable.[125]

The fact that an employee has paid a fine or served a jail sentence for acts committed in connection with his employment does not preclude an arbitrator from taking the acts into account in deciding whether the employer had just cause for disciplining the employee, despite the claim that this amounts to double jeopardy.[126] On the other hand, the mere fact that an employee has been acquitted of criminal charges based upon the incident for which management has

---

[122] United Parcel Service, Inc., 51 LA 462, 463 (Turkus, 1968); R. Munroe & Sons Mfg. Corp., 40 LA 1300, 1302–1303 (Duff, 1963).

[123] See Arbitrator Lehoczky in 53 LA 75, 78; Keefe in 52 LA 663, 666; Hill in 39 LA 203, 206; Schedler in 37 LA 1003, 1006–1007; McCoy in 37 LA 860, 861; Bradley in 28 LA 874, 878 ("Holding the threat of the penalty over the employee for approximately four months is something of a penalty in itself"). Delays of 10 weeks and 30 days were permitted respectively by Arbitrator Strong in 43 LA 31, 31–32; Seward in 12 LA 344, 345. Also see Pollard in 8 LA 234, 245.

[124] See Arbitrator Emerson in 37 LA 1112, 1115 (suspension pending investigation followed by discharge); Schmidt in 35 LA 293, 296 (employee was sent home with instructions to return the next morning for final disposition of his case); Hebert in 35 LA 95, 101; Smith in 32 LA 581, 586.

[125] International Harvester Co., 13 LA 610, 613–614 (1949).

[126] Westinghouse Electric Corp., 26 LA 836, 846 (Simkin, 1956), where the arbitrator also stated, however, that he could consider the previous punishment in determining the severity of the penalty assessed. Agreeing that the employer may punish the employee even if the latter has been punished under the criminal law, see Arbitrator Stutz in 45 LA 350, 351; Scheiber in 45 LA 366, 374; Schmidt in 40 LA 1169, 1173; Mueller in 36 LA 965, 968–969. Also see Arbitrator Seinsheimer in 50 LA 725, 732.

assessed discipline likewise does not preclude an arbitrator from upholding management's action where adequate evidence is presented
to convince him of the employee's guilt of misconduct.[127]

Arbitrators have rejected the claim that consideration of prior
offenses in determining the propriety of the penalty assessed for a
later offense constitutes double jeopardy.[128]

Grievant's Past Record

Some consideration generally is given to the past record of any
disciplined or discharged employee. An offense may be mitigated by
a good past record and it may be aggravated by a poor one. Indeed,
the employee's past record often is a major factor in the determination
of the proper penalty for his offense.

In many cases arbitrators have reduced penalties in consideration,
in part, of the employee's long good past record.[129] On the other hand,
an arbitrator's refusal to interfere with a penalty may be based in
part upon the employee's poor past record.[130] In one case Arbitrator
Morris J. Kaplan held that although neither the incident at the time
of discharge nor any other single incident cited by the employer was
sufficient to warrant discharge, the general pattern of the employee's
unsatisfactory conduct and performance, as established by a series of
incidents over an extended period, was preponderant evidence justi-

---

[127] See Arbitrator Alexander in 53 LA 1279, 1282; Turkus in 50 LA 616,
618–619; Block in 49 LA 810, 814–815; Gershenfeld in 49 LA 606, 608 (the
arbitration hearing must be de novo, but the court acquittal may be introduced
into evidence in support of the employee); Prasow in 39 LA 614, 617; Wyckoff
in 38 LA 93, 96, 99; Simkin in 32 LA 44, 47. Cf., Gomberg in 45 LA 490,
493.

[128] See Arbitrator Davey in 51 LA 127, 134; Sembower in 46 LA 737,
740–741; Porter in 41 LA 890, 892; Pollack in 24 LA 401, 407; Bernstein
in 20 LA 331, 334. Prior offenses are often considered in evaluating the propriety
of penalties. See this Chapter, subtopic titled "Grievant's Past Record."

[129] E.g., Arbitrator Kesselman in 54 LA 145, 151; Scheiber in 50 LA 487,
495; Levin in 47 LA 937, 940; Lee in 46 LA 297, 302; Young in 35 LA
428, 430; Seitz in 33 LA 257, 259; Hebert in 29 LA 604, 608; Dunlop in
28 LA 668, 672; Haughton in 28 LA 394, 398; Thompson in 26 LA 575,
577.

[130] E.g., Arbitrator Howlett in 55 LA 288, 290; Teple in 53 LA 933, 939;
Bothwell in 51 LA 1076, 1080; Stouffer in 51 LA 181, 183; Dworkin in 47
LA 266, 270; Wallen in 46 LA 246, 248; Davis in 44 LA 193, 194; Gilden
in 43 LA 753, 756; Porter in 41 LA 890, 892; Sembower in 30 LA 948,
950; Guthrie in 27 LA 358, 361.

fying discharge.[131] In similar "last straw" situations other arbitrators have also reached similar results.[132]

But there are limitations in the consideration of past offenses. For instance, a distinction should be made between rule infractions that have been proved and mere past "charges." Thus, it has been held that while an employer may have the right to post notations alleging rule infractions on employee records, the failure of the employer to notify employees of alleged infractions at the time of occurrence precludes him from using the notations to support disciplinary action at a later date, since employees should not be required to disprove stale charges.[133] Nor would an arbitrator consider past rule infractions for which the employee was in no way reprimanded,[134] or past warnings which had not been put in such form as to make them subject to a grievance.[135]

If an employee is given notice of adverse entries in his record and does not file a grievance where able to do so, an arbitrator may subsequently accept the entries on their face without considering their merits.[136]

---

[131] Electronic Corp. of America, 3 LA 217, 218–220 (1946).

[132] See Arbitrator Scheiber in 57 LA 981, 992; Howlett in 55 LA 288, 290; Williams in 52 LA 1254, 1257–1258; Koven in 52 LA 448, 450, 451, and in 44 LA 412, 415–416; Dunne in 51 LA 945, 950; McNaughton in 48 LA 1201, 1202, 1204; Singer in 47 LA 948, 951; Sembower in 46 LA 737, 739, Tsukiyama in 45 LA 1124, 1129, 1133; Seward in 45 LA 612, 614; Cahn in 41 LA 887, 888; Oppenheim in 39 LA 652, 653–654; Turkus in 36 LA 639, 640, 643; Hepburn in 32 LA 485, 486; Roberts in 20 LA 274, 275. Cf., Arbitrator Belshaw in 49 LA 573, 577; Teple in 48 LA 558, 562; Davey in 37 LA 605, 616–619; Schmidt in 35 LA 12, 14; Pollard in 8 LA 234, 245. Where there was no present offense, discharge was reversed by Arbitrator McCoy in 45 LA 254, 255; Fallon in 39 LA 855, 858; Dworkin in 29 LA 305, 311.

[133] Consolidated Vultee Aircraft Corp., 10 LA 907, 909 (Dwyer, 1948). Of similar substance, see Arbitrator Lehoczky in 51 LA 540, 545; Sembower in 49 LA 1100, 1109; Lee in 46 LA 175, 180; Block in 46 LA 154, 159; Miller in 42 LA 568, 570–571 ("Past incidents, for which no formal disciplinary action was taken and no official records maintained, and which cannot at a later date be adequately investigated, cannot be accepted" to support discharge); Belkin in 32 LA 86, 88; Scheiber in 24 LA 538, 541.

[134] Western Air Lines, Inc., 37 LA 130, 133 (Wyckoff, 1961). Similarly, see Arbitrator Oppenheim in 48 LA 251, 255.

[135] Duval Corp., 43 LA 102, 106 (Myers, 1964). The recording of warnings given to employees has been held to be a form of discipline which may require proper cause. Federal Labor Union v. American Can Co., 21 LA 518 (N.J. Super. Ct., 1953). Also see Arbitrator Seitz in 54 LA 1185, 1187; Louisell in 20 LA 826, 831.

[136] See Arbitrator Bothwell in 51 LA 1076, 1080; Stouffer in 50 LA 1118, 1121; Edelman in 38 LA 313, 316–317. Cf., Gould in 50 LA 1127, 1129–1131.

Collective agreements sometimes limit consideration of an employee's record to a specified period.[137] The need for a time limitation in the consideration of past offenses may also be recognized even where the agreement does not expressly impose one. Thus, Arbitrator John Day Larkin, while emphasizing the need to consider a grievant's past record, observed:

"In general we should say that in discharge cases the past conduct of the employee in question is of concern to the arbitrator called upon to review Management's disciplinary action. If the employee has an excellent record in the Company's service, the Union is sure to emphasize this. No arbitrator can fail to take note of a good record, the absence of prior warning notice, and other factors which may pertain to the employee's fitness to be continued on his job.

"By the same token, if an employee's past performance has been one of increasing disregard of his responsibilities to his job and to the employer who is paying him, no arbitrator can rightly sweep this sort of evidence under the rug and confine himself to technical evidence pertaining to a particular incident on a particular day. To do so would not add to the cause of good industrial relations. It might do irreparable harm to the arbitration process.

"However, this does not mean that we are to consider everything that is introduced as having equal weight and significance. We sympathize with the position often taken by unions that there should be some limitation on how far back in the record one should be permitted to go in the matter of digging up old scores. Such historic incidents should be close enough in their relation to the problem involved in the immediate case to warrant consideration."[138]

Evidence of past acts showing a course of conduct has sometimes been considered relevant in some types of cases as indicating some

---

In proper cases arbitrators have ordered the removal of matter from an employee's personnel file or have permitted matter ,to remain with the understanding that it not be used against the employee in the future. See Arbitrator Sembower in 54 LA 839, 844; Jenkins in 50 LA 115, 125; Leach in 48 LA 299, 304; Stark in 47 LA 91, 94–96; Meyers in 43 LA 102, 106; Stouffer in 41 LA 315, 317.

[137] For example, see Arbitrator Dybeck in 53 LA 124, 126 (employer was obviously penalized for submitting evidence in violation of such provision); Scheiber in 50 LA 487, 495 (such provision did not prevent consideration of *good* record prior to the limitations period); Kates in 48 LA 833, 834–835 (such provision was narrowly construed); Bradley in 47 LA 994, 999; Aaron in 10 LA 119, 128. As to a provision forbidding the "pyramiding" of penalties, see Arbitrator Shister in 52 LA 1263, 1266.

[138] Borg-Warner Corp., 22 LA 589, 596 (1954). Also regarding "digging up" past matters, see Arbitrator Reynolds in 17 LA 737, 740. In Consolidated Foods Corp., 43 LA 1143, 1148–1150 (Klein, 1964), reduced weight was given to discipline assessed before the union came to the plant.

likelihood that the employee committed the specific act with which he was charged.[139]

Length of Service With Company

Long service with the company, particularly if unblemished, is a definite factor in the employee's favor when his discharge is reviewed through arbitration.[140] Arbitrators have recognized that the loss of seniority may work great hardship on the employee,[141] and that it is not conducive to the improvement of relations between other workers and management.[142]

In one case the fact that a long-service employee was nearing eligibility for retirement was an additional factor in support of reinstatement,[143] but in another case the arbitrator refused to give weight to the fact of approaching retirement.[144]

Knowledge of Rules; Warnings

It has been reported, on the basis of examining over 1000 discharge cases, that one of the two most commonly recognized principles in arbitration of such cases is that there must be reasonable rules or standards, consistently applied and enforced and widely disseminated.[145] Concerning notice of rules, Arbitrator William M. Hepburn stated: "Just cause requires that employees be informed of a rule, infraction of which may result in suspension or discharge, unless con-

---

[139] See Arbitrator Sweeney in 41 LA 1061, 1062; Pedrick in 12 LA 262, 264–265; Gorder in 3 LA 455; Wolff in 3 LA 285. Also see Koven in 48 LA 264, 267. But see Alexander in 46 LA 184, 186; Sembower in 30 LA 948, 950. For discussion, see Fleming, The Labor Arbitration Process 168–170 (U. of Ill. Press, 1965); Wirtz, "Due Process of Arbitration," The Arbitrator and the Parties 1, 20–21 (BNA Incorporated, 1958), noting that caution obviously should be exercised in using evidence of past acts for this purpose.

[140] For instances where this factor was given weight, see Arbitrator Hershenfeld in 49 LA 1262, 1264; Abernethy in 47 LA 184, 192; Drake in 44 LA 234, 237; Prasow in 42 LA 408, 411; Altrock in 41 LA 460, 463–464; Gilden in 29 LA 464, 466; Dunlop in 28 LA 668, 672; Simkin in 24 LA 606, 609.

[141] See Arbitrator Kates in 46 LA 365, 368; Jones in 45 LA 972, 974–975; McCoy in 37 LA 704, 706; Simkin in 24 LA 606, 609; Shipman in 2 LA 194, 195–196.

[142] Argonne Worsted Co., 4 LA 81, 83 (Copelof, 1946). Nonetheless, even long service with the company will not save the job if other factors strongly justify discharge. See Arbitrator Krimsly in 51 LA 745, 747; Porter in 47 LA 104, 105–106.

[143] Brown and Bigelow Co., 44 LA 237, 241 (Graff, 1964).

[144] American Welding & Mfg. Co., 47 LA 457, 463 (Dworkin, 1966).

[145] "Arbitration Awards in Discharge Cases," 28 LA 930, 931–932 (1957).

duct is so clearly wrong that specific reference is not necessary."[146]
In the latter regard it has been held, for instance, that employees
need not be notified of rules against threatening others with loaded
firearms, for "Common sense alone would dictate that a weapon such
as a loaded firearm would not be permitted on the premises of any
employer except in the possession of a duly authorized plant protection
man."[147]

As concerns warnings, evidence as to whether warnings of unsatisfactory conduct were given prior to discharge or discipline generally
is relevant in determining whether the penalty was justified.[148] Where
an employee continues prohibited conduct after having been warned,
the fact that he was warned stands against him.[149] In one case the
employee had been warned repeatedly about leaving his place of duty,
so discharge was upheld even though progressive discipline had not
been used; the arbitrator said that the warnings had apprised the
employee of the seriousness of his misconduct and that there was no
reason to believe that "one more chance" would improve his conduct.[150] On the other hand, failure to give prior warnings may be
one of the reasons for the refusal by an arbitrator to sustain disciplinary
action (particularly discharge).[151]

---

[146] Lockheed Aircraft Corp., 28 LA 829, 831 (1957). Also requiring clear
notice of rules and of the possible penalties for their violation (particularly
where discharge is one of the penalties), see Arbitrator Witney in 48 LA 395,
399–400; Cahn in 48 LA 349, 350; Neville in 48 LA 120, 123; Autrey in
45 LA 117, 119; Maggs in 21 LA 676, 679; Reid in 21 LA 322, 325; Prasow
in 5 LA 109, 111. For related material, see Chapter 13, subtopic titled "Posting
of Rules." In Phillips Petroleum Co., 47 LA 372, 374 (Caraway, 1966), the
company was required to establish that the employee had actual knowledge
of the rule he was charged with violating. In Metromedia, Inc., 46 LA 161,
165–167 (Dworkin, 1965), employees could be disciplined for refusing to sign
a statement acknowledging receipt of a certain plant rule.
[147] Brown & Williamson Tobacco Corp., 50 LA 403, 412 (Willingham, 1968).
Also see Arbitrator Keeler in 45 LA 437, 441 ("a Company does not have
to establish that it had, or that it had communicated specific rules for certain
well-recognized proven offenses such as drunkenness, theft, or insubordination");
Schmidt in 35 LA 293, 296.
[148] Warnings ordinarily need not be in writing unless required by contract.
See Glenn L. Martin Co., 6 LA 500, 507 (Brecht, 1947). Where the contract
does require warnings to be written, the requirement may be firmly enforced.
See Arbitrator Eaton in 53 LA 85, 87–88; Cantor in 46 LA 1041, 1044.
[149] See Arbitrator Abernethy in 40 LA 582, 585–586; Scheiber in 9 LA
765, 766–767, 770; Bowles in 9 LA 447, 449.
[150] Potash Co. of America, 40 LA 582, 585–586 (Abernethy, 1963). But see
Greer Limestone Co., 40 LA 343, 349 (Lugar, 1963), where repeated warnings
followed by repeated noncompliance without discipline was said to have lulled the
employee into believing the warnings were not serious.
[151] See Arbitrator Brown in 56 LA 725, 727; Robertson in 56 LA 512,

Arbitrators have emphasized that no warning is required where the offense is legally and morally wrong.[152]

Lax Enforcement of Rules

Arbitrators have not hesitated to disturb penalties, assessed without clear and timely warning, where the employer over a period of time had condoned the violation of the rule in the past—lax enforcement of rules may lead employees reasonably to believe that the conduct in question is sanctioned by management.[153] Of course, the employer must have known of the prior violations by employees in order to be held to have waived the right to punish an employee who is detected.[154] Another qualification is illustrated by an arbitrator's holding that past condonation of the taking of small quantities of scrap metal did not immunize the attempted theft of large quantities.[155]

Although previously having been lax, an employer can turn to strict enforcement after giving clear notice of the intent to do so.[156] Moreover, the arbitration of a case involving discharge for violation of a rule serves clear notice to the employees for the future that the particular type of misconduct is deemed by the employer to be a dischargeable offense.[157]

Unequal or Discriminatory Treatment

It is generally accepted that enforcement of rules and assessment of discipline must be exercised in a consistent manner; all employees who engage in the same type of misconduct must be treated essentially the same unless a reasonable basis exists for variations in the assessment

---

514; Volz in 50 LA 600, 604; Teple in 48 LA 558, 562–563; Dunlop in 45 LA 535, 537; Wyckoff in 44 LA 552, 553; Spaulding in 39 LA 58, 63; Jones in 37 LA 520, 527–528; Dworkin in 35 LA 17, 23–24; Levy in 28 LA 65, 69; McCoy in 27 LA 160, 162; Wyckoff in 25 LA 634, 637; Marshall in 24 LA 555, 559.
[152] Kroger Co., 50 LA 1194, 1198 (Abernethy, 1968); Glenn L. Martin Co., 27 LA 768, 772–773 (Jaffee, 1956).
[153] See Arbitrator Jacobs in 55 LA 1274, 1277; Springfield in 54 LA 281, 286; Kelliher in 53 LA 428, 429–430; Sembower in 52 LA 1296, 1300; Williams in 49 LA 210, 212; Somers in 48 LA 98, 100–101; Cantor in 46 LA 1041, 1043; Gross in 46 LA 882, 884; Volz in 46 LA 248, 251; Duff in 45 LA 538, 540; Larkin in 45 LA 517, 521; Dworkin in 40 LA 87, 90. But see Stouffer in 53 LA 45, 55–56.
[154] Decar Plastics Corp., 44 LA 921, 923 (Greenwald, 1965).
[155] United States Steel Corp., 48 LA 1114, 1118 (Mittenthal, 1967).
[156] Hartman Electrical Mfg. Co., 48 LA 681, 683 (Dyke, 1967); Fairbanks Morse, Inc., 47 LA 224, 226 (Fisher, 1966).
[157] Universal Match Corp., 42 LA 184, 186 (Coffey, 1963).

of punishment (such as different degrees of fault or mitigating or aggravating circumstances affecting some but not all of the employees).[158] In this regard, Arbitrator Benjamin Aaron has declared: "Absolute consistency in the handling of rule violations is, of course, an impossibility, but that fact should not excuse random and completely inconsistent disciplinary practices."[159]

Where reasonable basis for variations in penalties does exist, they will be permitted notwithstanding the charge of disparate treatment.[160] That variations in penalties assessed do not necessarily mean that management's action has been improper or discriminatory was persuasively elaborated by Arbitrator J. Charles Short:

"The term 'discrimination' connotes a distinction in treatment, especially an unfair distinction. The prohibition against discrimination requires like treatment under like circumstances. In the case of offenses the circumstances include the nature of the offense, the degree of fault and the mitigating and aggravating factors. There is no discrimination, or no departure from the consistent or uniform treatment of employees, merely because of variations in discipline reasonably appropriate to the variations in circumstances. Two employees may refuse a work assignment. For one it is his first offense, there being no prior warning or misconduct standing against his record. The other has been warned and disciplined for the very same offense on numerous occasions. It cannot be seriously contended that discrimination results if identical penalties are not meted out."[161]

Particularly in cases involving illicit strikes or slowdowns, management may vary discipline on the basis of the degree of fault and

---

[158] Arbitrators have frequently refused to uphold variations in punishment where not supported by reasonable basis. See Arbitrator Murphy in 56 LA 880, 883; Quinlan in 54 LA 1035, 1040; Koven in 48 LA 116, 120; Teple in 46 LA 265, 275; Lee in 46 LA 175, 179; Dworkin in 46 LA 161, 167–168; Keefe in 44 LA 530, 538–539; Crawford in 42 LA 849, 850 (although discipline of supervisor is sole right of employer, the failure to punish supervisor as severely for similar offense was a factor in arbitral reinstatement of discharged employee); Dworet in 40 LA 847, 849; Turkus in 39 LA 823, 827; King in 28 LA 775, 779; Reynard in 26 LA 934, 938; Duff in 26 LA 915, 918; Stouffer in 26 LA 638, 640; Somers in 24 LA 728, 731; Kadish in 24 LA 102, 106; Singer in 6 LA 762, 764. But see Cahn in 28 LA 355, 356. In John Deere Tractor Co., 9 LA 73, 77 (Gorder, 1947), the power of leniency was recognized in management "if the leniency shown is not for sinister, malicious, or discriminatory purposes."

[159] Aaron, "The Uses of the Past in Arbitration," Arbitration Today 1, 10 (BNA Incorporated, 1955). Also see Arbitrator Sisk in 48 LA 1286, 1290; Simkin in 26 LA 836, 844.

[160] See Arbitrator Larkin in 49 LA 1253, 1256–1257; Block in 48 LA 1118, 1120; Teple in 46 LA 265, 273; Porter in 45 LA 1007, 1009; Small in 45 LA 257, 258; Pedrick in 15 LA 308, 313. Many other instances are cited hereinbelow in the discussion of penalties for illicit work stoppages.

[161] Alan Wood Steel Co., 21 LA 843, 849 (1954).

is not required to assess uniform punishment against all participants; also, management may punish those who bear greater fault while not punishing other participants at all.[162] Nor is management prohibited from punishing the known leaders of a stoppage or those employees detected in overt activities in connection with the stoppage merely because the company is unable to identify other participants who may have been equally guilty.[163]

Arbitrators have emphasized that in illicit strike or slowdown situations the employer need not deprive himself of the services of all participants but may use selective discipline on the basis of relative fault.[164] Arbitrator Marlin M. Volz commented about this:

"* * * it is unreasonable to require a Company to discharge all the workers participating in a slowdown and thereby lose its experi-

---

[162] See Arbitrator Murphy in 56 LA 880, 882; McDermott in 56 LA 340, 348; Holly in 55 LA 667, 670; Oppenheim in 52 LA 1047, 1049–1050; Turkus in 51 LA 1228, 1235; Altrock in 48 LA 1224, 1227; Roberts in 48 LA 855, 860–861; Krimsly in 48 LA 257, 261–263 (employer can classify degrees of participation and punish different employees on that basis); Hilpert in 47 LA 129, 137; Malkin in 46 LA 982, 984; Duff in 46 LA 120, 124; Stouffer in 45 LA 943, 952–954 (employer may select certain strikers for discipline if basis for selection is reasonable); Autrey in 45 LA 585, 589–590; Wolff in 42 LA 951, 953; Pollack in 42 LA 142, 143–144 (employer may discharge strike leaders and need not prove extent of leadership); Markowitz in 41 LA 732, 735–736; Kelliher in 41 LA 110, 112; Schedler in 40 LA 1209, 1211; Davey in 38 LA 1144, 1148–1149; Klamon in 38 LA 928, 932–933 (union President could be singled out for punishment since he should have attempted to prevent walkout); Marshall in 38 LA 889, 891 (employer could not identify ringleaders but could suspend committeemen who had undertaken responsibility of providing leadership for employees and who had nonetheless participated in slowdown); Pigors in 37 LA 977, 980; Volz in 37 LA 401, 406; Horlacher in 36 LA 660, 663–664 (union declined to identify the strike leaders and employer used fairest method available in selecting employees for discipline); Teple in 33 LA 194, 198 (employer not permitted to "pick and choose" but could single out for punishment those who had lead roles); Smith in 25 LA 663, 674; Short in 21 LA 843, 849–850; Updegraff in 19 LA 601, 602; Morrissey in 15 LA 829, 830; Wirtz in 13 LA 610, 613. Many arbitrators, including some of those just cited, have recognized that union leaders have a special responsibility to promote use of the grievance procedure in lieu of self-help, but arbitrators are by no means agreed as to whether failure to fulfill this responsibility is proper basis for punishment or for variations in punishment. For other cases, see Chapter 5, subtopic titled "Use of Grievance Procedure vs. Self-Help."
[163] See Arbitrator Scheiber in 50 LA 487, 494 (it is inevitable that some of the guilty "get away with it"); Garrett in 50 LA 472, 475–476; Crawford in 49 LA 383, 388; Wallen in 41 LA 1240, 1244.
[164] See Arbitrator Turkus in 51 LA 1228, 1235; Malkin in 46 LA 982, 984; Stouffer in 45 LA 943, 953; Horlacher in 36 LA 660, 663 (to require a uniform penalty against all strikers would make a nullity of the no-strike clause). Also, as a means of protecting itself management is permitted to stagger suspensions, for it cannot be expected to suspend all guilty employees for the same period and thus make a shutdown of operations the price for taking disciplinary action. United States Steel Corp., 40 LA 598, 600 (Seitz, 1963); Bethlehem Steel Co., 39 LA 686, 688 (Valtin, 1962).

enced work force when selective disciplinary action against one or
more key leaders of the slowdown will restore production."[165]

Where all employees on a given shift refused to perform certain work
it was held that management was not required to punish all equally
if doing so would impair production. In permitting management to
order individual employees to perform the work and to send them
home for refusing, Arbitrator Louis Yagoda explained:

> "It is my opinion that management is not under an obligation
> to apply equal punishment to all transgressors, if to do so would cause
> injury to the operations. Discrimination may be validly charged only
> when there is either [a] a demonstrated inconsistency of posture to-
> wards the violations and the violators (such as is present when manage-
> ment tolerates, condones or ignores a series of mis-acts by some and
> then punishes others for committing the same improprieties); or [b]
> when the Employer is responding to an improper ulterior motive or
> animus, using the alleged wrongdoing as a pretext or subterfuge."[166]

Finally, it may be noted that arbitrators themselves have sometimes reduced the penalties of some employees where management
had assessed uniform discipline against all participants but where the
arbitrator found different degrees of fault.[167] In one such case Arbitrator Sylvester Garrett stated that "equality of penalties does not represent equal justice" where management assessed identical penalties
against the victim as well as the aggressor in a fight.[168]

Charges of Anti-Union Discrimination

One arbitrator stated that a charge of discrimination because
of union activities cannot rest upon mere "surmise, inference or conjec-

---

[165] American Radiator & Standard Sanitary Corp., 37 LA 401, 406 (1961).
Even where the agreement provided that disciplinary action taken against employees for illicit strike "shall be applied with equality and impartiality to all
employees," management could punish those who had greater part in the strike
although not punishing all participants. Drake Mfg. Co., 41 LA 732, 735–736
(Markowitz, 1963).

[166] Interchemical Corp., 48 LA 124, 131 (1967). Cf., Arbitrator McCoy
in 37 LA 593, 598–599. In United States Steel Corp., 49 LA 1236, 1241–1242
(McDermott, 1968), management could punish those employees who engaged
in slowdown after formal warning had been given while not punishing violators
prior to the warning, the arbitrator stating that management was engaged in
a rational plan to halt the slowdown.

[167] See Arbitrator Garrett in 51 LA 546, 548; Kates in 36 LA 857, 859–860;
McIntosh in 36 LA 280, 285–286.

[168] United States Steel Corp., 51 LA 546, 548 (1968). In upholding the
different penalties assessed by management against fight participants Arbitrator
Block commented: "The wisdom of a rule calling for identical penalties to all
employees involved in a fight, without regard to culpability, is certainly open
to question." Kaiser Steel Corp., 48 LA 1118, 1120 (1967).

ture."[169] Numerous other arbitrators appear to agree, requiring clear proof to sustain such charges.[170]

However, Arbitrator Ted T. Tsukiyama cautioned that arbitrators have an obligation to examine the evidence with special care where anti-union animus may be involved:

> "Whenever an employee who holds a high union office is discharged, there is always raised the question of a real possibility that the discharge is discriminatory or undertaken in bad faith, that the Company is ridding itself of a zealous unionist under the guise of 'just cause' discharge. In these cases, the arbitrator is obliged to make a thorough search and examination of the entire record to ascertain and satisfy himself that Management has not violated the collective bargaining agreement in this manner."[171]

Management Also at Fault

Where an employee is guilty of wrongdoing but management (ordinarily the supervisor) is also at fault in some respect in connection with the employee's conduct, the arbitrator may be persuaded to reduce or set aside the penalty assessed by management.[172] However, the mere fact that a supervisor was not entirely without fault in an incident was held not to excuse or justify physical assault by an employee, so the employee's discharge was sustained.[173]

---

[169] New York Racing Assn., 43 LA 129, 135 (Scheiber, 1964). Similarly, see Arbitrator Willingham in 49 LA 509, 511.

[170] See Arbitrator Kotin in 49 LA 731, 735 (sharp conflicts in negotiations and a strike do not by themselves constitute prima facie evidence of subsequent discrimination in treatment of union leader); Livengood in 45 LA 495, 498 (that grievant was an active union member is not enough to make out a case of anti-union discrimination); Dworet in 43 LA 1070, 1072; McNaughton in 43 LA 529, 537; Davis in 42 LA 710, 712; Gilden in 39 LA 1131, 1134; Berkowitz in 38 LA 705, 708; McCoy in 33 LA 206, 207, and in 1 LA 447, 448–449; Carmody in 23 LA 38, 39; Maggs in 21 LA 676, 678; Bailer in 20 LA 7, 9; Doyle in 19 LA 111, 122; Scarborough in 2 LA 520, 521. Cf., comments of Arbitrator Kamin in 55 LA 118, 129; Wallen in 48 LA 19, 23; Block in 44 LA 889, 895, in which cases the arbitrator found either that anti-union animus caused or that it contributed to management's action against the employee.

[171] Arden Farms Co., 45 LA 1124, 1130 (1965), where the charge of anti-union motivation was found to be without substance. For a similar statement as to an arbitrator's obligation, see Arbitrator Wallen in 48 LA 19, 23.

[172] See Arbitrator Nichols in 50 LA 95, 98; Fitzgerald in 49 LA 246, 250; Mead in 49 LA 173, 176; Kates in 48 LA 833, 835; Jaffee in 47 LA 1072, 1075; McDermott in 47 LA 923, 926; Reid in 47 LA 559, 562–563; Summers in 47 LA 346, 348; Sembower in 47 LA 208, 211; Wood in 46 LA 75, 80; Novak in 46 LA 33, 35; Roberts in 45 LA 65, 67; Berkowitz in 40 LA 215, 219. But see Schmidt in 52 LA 1019, 1022.

[173] Gerber Products Co., 46 LA 956, 959 (Howlett, 1966).

Arbitral Remedies in Discharge and Discipline Cases

The more common remedies utilized by arbitrators in upsetting managerial actions in discharge and discipline cases have been summarized previously by the Authors as follows:[174] If a penalty of discharge is upset through arbitration, the award often will order reinstatement either with back pay, without back pay, or with partial back pay, and often will further order that other rights and privileges shall remain unimpaired; or the discharge may be commuted to suspension for a specified period, or even to a reduced penalty of only a reprimand or warning. Where a penalty of suspension assessed by management is upset through arbitration, the award usually will either void the suspension completely (sometimes substituting a reprimand or warning), or will simply reduce the length of time the employee is to be deemed suspended—in either event back pay will be ordered consistent with the shortened or eliminated period of suspension.

There are other remedies which, by comparison with those just noted, are less frequently used (some only rarely). Some of these variations in arbitral remedies are:

a) *Loss of seniority.* Some employees have been ordered reinstated on the basis that they not be credited with any seniority for the period between discharge and reinstatement.[175] Loss of some seniority that had accrued prior to the discharge is also a possibility.[176]

b) *Loss of other benefits under the agreement.* In denying seniority credit for the period between discharge and reinstatement, arbitra-

---

[174] Elkouri & Elkouri, "Arbitral Review of Discipline: Variations in Penalties," Symposium on Labor Relations Law 458 at 458 (Symposium edited by Ralph Slovenko and published by Claitor's Bookstore, 1961). The commonly utilized remedies are encountered in many of the cases listed in the present Chapter's Table of Offenses, below.

[175] See Arbitrator Stouffer in 54 LA 228, 232; Caraway in 54 LA 135, 140; Altrock in 51 LA 225, 227; Kates in 50 LA 103, 107; Wren in 49 LA 700, 703; Sembower in 48 LA 152, 157; Seitz in 46 LA 763, 766; Coleman in 34 LA 143, 146; Schedler in 32 LA 677, 680; Belkin in 32 LA 23, 25; McDermott in 30 LA 700, 705 and in 28 LA 804, 808; Wolff in 24 LA 549, 554 and in 3 LA 271, 282; Jaffee in 15 LA 715, 725; Hepburn in 9 LA 345, 349; Courshon in 1 LA 561, 564. Under a strike settlement agreement in Reden Corp., 50 LA 413, 414 (Roberts, 1968), economic strikers did not acquire any seniority for the period of the strike.

[176] See Arbitrator Copelof in 19 LA 437, 439; Hilpert in 10 LA 324, 335; Cheney in 6 LA 211, 213. Also see Merrill in 21 LA 560, 565. Cf., Jaffee in 15 LA 715, 725. Contra, Kelliher in 30 LA 519, 527. Temporary loss of accrued seniority was ordered in Pennsylvania Greyhound Lines, 3 LA 880, 884 (Brandschain, 1946).

tors sometimes have prohibited the accumulation of other agreement provided benefits during said period.[177]

c) *Probation or final warning.* Some discharged employees have been reinstated on a probationary basis (the probationary period often ranging from one to twelve months),[178] or with a final warning that any repetition of the offense will justify immediate discharge.[179]

d) *Reinstatement conditioned upon some special act or promise by employee.* Reinstatement has been ordered on the condition that the employee resign his outside job,[180] that he furnish an indemnity bond required by the employer,[181] that he sign an agreement by which he promises to apply and comply conscientiously with company safety rules,[182] that he reduce his weight from 340 to 215 pounds and quit smoking cigarettes,[183] and that he accept counseling from his pastor or some competent social agency.[184]

e) *Written waiver required.* Where the collective agreement arguably might have required back pay in the event of reinstatement after discharge, a condition to reinstatement was imposed in the form of a requirement that the employee agree in writing to waive back pay.[185]

f) *Reinstatement conditioned upon proof of mental or physical fitness.* Employees discharged for misconduct somehow connected with

---

[177] See Arbitrator Schedler in 32 LA 677, 680; Wolff in 24 LA 549, 554 and in 19 LA 221, 231. Cf., Fearing in 9 LA 505, 509.

[178] See Arbitrator Mullin in 45 LA 560, 565; Kelliher in 30 LA 519, 528; Simkin in 24 LA 606, 610; Lehoczky in 17 LA 283, 285; Copelof in 15 LA 505, 509; Komaroff in 12 LA 233, 238; Scheiber in 10 LA 57, 61; Wardlaw in 8 LA 248, 250; Pollard in 8 LA 234, 245; Cole in 6 LA 958, 960; Updegraff in 3 LA 242, 245. Probationary reinstatement also has been ordered for employees discharged for subnormal production. See Arbitrator Lehoczky in 27 LA 55, 57; Updegraff in 7 LA 191, 195.

[179] See Arbitrator Seinsheimer in 53 LA 1197, 1202–1203; Gordinier in 52 LA 731, 733; Cahn in 44 LA 1043, 1044; Kesselman in 44 LA 289, 294. In General Electric Co., 32 LA 637, 640 (LaCugna, 1959), an employee who had been discharged for absenteeism was reinstated on the condition that the employer could discharge her should she be absent more than twenty working days in any succeeding year.

[180] Kansas City Star Co., 12 LA 1202, 1206 (Ridge, 1949). Also see John Deere Tractor Co., 4 LA 161, 163, 166 (Updegraff, 1946).

[181] Robert Hall Clothes, Inc., 50 LA 840, 845 (Davis, 1968).

[182] Bunker Hill Co., 43 LA 1253, 1256 (Luckerath, 1964). In International Harvester Co., 53 LA 1197, 1202–1203 (Seinsheimer, 1969), the condition required two employees to sign an agreement stating that they would not threaten or molest each other or any other employee, and that violation of the agreement would subject them to immediate discharge.

[183] Taystee Bread Co., 52 LA 677, 680 (Purdom, 1969), where the arbitrator was given broad latitude as to the remedy.

[184] Charleston Naval Shipyard, 54 LA 145, 151 (Kesselman, 1970).

[185] International Harvester Co., 2 LA 158, 163 (Gilden, 1946). To similar effect is an award by Arbitrator Kelliher subsequently cited and quoted by him in Lone Star Steel Co., 30 LA 519, 528 (1958).

physical or psychological disability sometimes have been ordered reinstated on the condition that they be physically and/or mentally fit for the job as determined by physicians or psychiatrists, as the case may be.[186]

g) *Reinstatement conditioned upon the employee's not holding union office.* Under the circumstances of some cases the arbitrator has concluded that the discharged employee should be reinstated, but only on the condition that he not hold union office for a stated period (in some cases the disqualification was to be permanent).[187]

h) *Reinstatement to a different job.* In disciplinary discharge cases where the arbitrator concludes that the grievant should be reinstated but that some strong reason exists for denying him his former job (such reason may involve his physical condition, or a need to screen him from contacts with the public, or personality conflicts, or the like), reinstatement may be ordered to some other job which does not involve the conditions or impediments that disqualify him for his former job.[188] In one case an employee who had been discharged for engaging in a slowdown was ordered reinstated but with the proviso that the company could place him on any job it might wish.[189]

i) *Other variations in remedies.* Yet other infrequently used remedies have been tailored by arbitrators to fit the circumstances of the

---

[186] See Arbitrator Keefe in 48 LA 1369, 1372–1374; Sembower in 46 LA 1014, 1018; Solomon in 42 LA 1, 14; Wallen in 33 LA 788, 791; Stouffer in 32 LA 686, 689–690; Wolff in 26 LA 295, 300. Also see Schedler in 32 LA 677, 680; Pollard in 19 LA 405, 408. Sometimes reinstatement has been similarly conditioned where the employee had been discharged for alleged physical disability (see Arbitrator Teple in 53 LA 334, 338) or for poor workmanship connected with the employee's physical condition (see Arbitrator Kates in 46 LA 365, 368–369).

[187] See Arbitrator Crowley in 54 LA 488, 492; McGury in 46 LA 220, 224; Hayes in 33 LA 103, 107–108; Phelps in 32 LA 690, 695 (the award was modified by a state court in 33 LA 292, 293, by striking the condition against holding union office); Miller in 10 LA 79, 83; Klamon in 7 LA 422, 424; Whiting in 6 LA 965, 968. In Kankakee Electric Steel Co., 53 LA 178, 184 (1969), Arbitrator Sembower stated that he lacked authority to tell the union whom it might choose as representatives but he did "recommend that the Grievant not be given further duties as a grievanceman." Arbitrator Dudley E. Whiting twice imposed the disqualification from holding union office, once for which he was commended and once for which he was castigated. See comments of Arbitrator Whiting in discussion of the remedy power, Labor Arbitration and Industrial Change 70, 73 (BNA Incorporated, 1963).

[188] See Arbitrator Gershenfeld in 49 LA 606, 608; Dworkin in 47 LA 457, 463, in 40 LA 1054, 1058–1060 (personality conflicts), and in 36 LA 491, 495; Keefe in 45 LA 986, 989–990; Tsukiyama in 44 LA 218, 222–223; Stix in 43 LA 824, 825 (discharge converted to suspension and leave of absence until a vacancy occurs in a job which would be proper for grievant); Leary in 10 LA 814, 817–818. Cf., Mueller in 36 LA 965, 969. For related material see Chapter 13, topic titled "Demotion of Employees."

[189] Dirilyte Co. of America, 18 LA 882, 884 (Ferguson, 1952). Cf., Arbitrator Ralston in 18 LA 544, 548–550.

particular discharge or discipline case. Some of these variations include forced apologies,[190] unrecorded suspension,[191] and treating the grievant's mental anguish as a penalty.[192]

Table of Offenses

Many types of conduct have been the "just cause" basis of industrial discipline—discharge or a lesser penalty. Detailed analysis of each individual type of conduct is beyond the scope of this volume. However, to review the more usual grounds for industrial discipline, and to make numerous cases quickly available to the reader, the following table is offered. Two considerations should be emphasized. First, in some cases the arbitrator considers the misconduct sufficiently serious to justify the employer in discharging for the first offense and even in the face of mitigating circumstances. Second, in the vast majority of cases there is no such "automatic" basis for discharge; in these cases all factors relevant to industrial discipline may be considered by the arbitrator in determining whether the employee deserved discharge, some lesser penalty, or no penalty at all—each case is thus decided largely on the basis of its own facts and circumstances.

Included in the table are selected cases. Some of the cases were selected because they discuss one or more of the following: elements of the offense, proof or evidence required, mitigating or aggravating factors. Some were selected because they are especially thoroughly reasoned and/or cite numerous other cases involving the same type of offense. Still other cases were selected because they are relevant to the possible scope of the offense, or because they contain some other aspect of special interest. As to a few of the offenses, cases were selected without regard to the above factors, there being relatively few reported cases on the offense or for the given column in the table. Finally, *it is emphasized that these tables include only a part of the many relevant and useful cases* that have been published in the arbitration reports.

---

[190] Four Wheel Drive Auto Co., 20 LA 823, 826 (Rauch, 1953); Crawford Clothes, Inc., 19 LA 475, 481–482 (Kramer, 1952). But some arbitrators have spoken strongly against forced apologies. See Arbitrator Jensen in 38 LA 781, 784; Dworet in 35 LA 381, 383; Klamon in 22 LA 528, 534.

[191] Fort Pitt Bridge Works, 30 LA 633, 635 (Lehoczky, 1958), in which suspension was upheld but all reference to it was ordered striken from the employees' personnel records. Also see Ironite Inc., 28 LA 394 (Haughton, 1956).

[192] Dayton Steel Foundry Co., 29 LA 137, 142 (Young, 1957); Ashland Oil & Refining Co., 28 LA 874, 878–879 (Bradley, 1957).

Offense	Discharge Upheld	Lesser Penalty Upheld (as assessed by employer)	Penalty Reduced by Arbitrator	No Penalty Permitted
Absenteeism*	57 LA 1107	54 LA 213	54 LA 788	56 LA 159
	57 LA 701	52 LA 69	54 LA 566	51 LA 331
	56 LA 709	46 LA 65	53 LA 623	50 LA 353
	55 LA 1164	40 LA 309	52 LA 731	38 LA 233
	53 LA 594	28 LA 524	51 LA 734	37 LA 484
	52 LA 861	26 LA 176	51 LA 162	36 LA 1042
	52 LA 602		49 LA 848	35 LA 469
	51 LA 1121		44 LA 280	33 LA 146
	51 LA 761		41 LA 862	
	48 LA 615		40 LA 343	
	48 LA 402		31 LA 350	
	47 LA 747		30 LA 231	
	46 LA 436		29 LA 133	
	46 LA 195		29 LA 91	
	45 LA 156			
	45 LA 75			
	42 LA 1251			
	36 LA 1307			
	35 LA 277			
	32 LA 313			
	29 LA 559			
	23 LA 663			
	20 LA 155			
Tardiness	54 LA 343	57 LA 181	53 LA 863	52 LA 923
	52 LA 602	38 LA 43	52 LA 239	51 LA 1110
	49 LA 290	34 LA 581	46 LA 199	49 LA 947
	44 LA 829			49 LA 269
	30 LA 667			47 LA 435
	23 LA 223			27 LA 99
Loafing	55 LA 469	51 LA 174	56 LA 430	53 LA 547
	42 LA 307	50 LA 1118	55 LA 832	52 LA 101
	38 LA 491	49 LA 947	52 LA 965	49 LA 947
		47 LA 1082	38 LA 126	40 LA 730
		43 LA 1143	16 LA 563	36 LA 721
		26 LA 61		28 LA 761
		16 LA 152		19 LA 699
		16 LA 118		17 LA 199

* For related material, see Chapter 13, subtopic titled "Excessive Absences Due to Illness."

Offense	Discharge Upheld	Lesser Penalty Upheld (as assessed by employer)	Penalty Reduced by Arbitrator	No Penalty Permitted
Absence From Work	57 LA 721	55 LA 1128	57 LA 852	55 LA 996
	56 LA 1125	52 LA 221	56 LA 725	53 LA 451
	56 LA 782	47 LA 224	56 LA 673	46 LA 1011
	55 LA 1102	46 LA 180	56 LA 527	45 LA 1066
	55 LA 709	46 LA 65	55 LA 1029	44 LA 958
	54 LA 963	39 LA 324	53 LA 930	41 LA 460
	53 LA 140	37 LA 862	44 LA 889	39 LA 604
	48 LA 276	16 LA 112	43 LA 977	35 LA 863
	47 LA 1065		41 LA 1129	35 LA 734
	47 LA 677		37 LA 619	31 LA 368
	47 LA 266		37 LA 163	28 LA 434
	46 LA 941		34 LA 485	28 LA 33
	42 LA 1151		29 LA 495	23 LA 574
	42 LA 606		28 LA 65	22 LA 138
	38 LA 278		27 LA 446	21 LA 151
	38 LA 130		27 LA 442	20 LA 451
	33 LA 735		27 LA 339	19 LA 471
	32 LA 543		25 LA 614	
	29 LA 322		25 LA 281	
	29 LA 146		21 LA 322	
	27 LA 812			
	25 LA 846			
	24 LA 593			
	23 LA 542			
	21 LA 248			
Leaving Post (Includes early quitting)	56 LA 808	54 LA 947	56 LA 673	54 LA 236
	52 LA 707	52 LA 663	55 LA 832	51 LA 731
	47 LA 104	52 LA 349	53 LA 876	48 LA 667
	44 LA 604	50 LA 375	53 LA 428	46 LA 1131
	44 LA 412	46 LA 885	52 LA 945	46 LA 75
	41 LA 974	42 LA 729	52 LA 375	41 LA 974
	39 LA 1185	42 LA 582	51 LA 127	41 LA 770
	31 LA 501	40 LA 473	47 LA 923	35 LA 873
	27 LA 653	36 LA 517	42 LA 412	27 LA 831
		32 LA 852	38 LA 237	27 LA 407
		31 LA 322	37 LA 619	21 LA 220
			33 LA 840	
			19 LA 607	
			18 LA 184	

Offense	Discharge Upheld	Lesser Penalty Upheld (as assessed by employer)	Penalty Reduced by Arbitrator	No Penalty Permitted
Sleeping on Job	55 LA 1269	54 LA 96	54 LA 726	55 LA 1058
	53 LA 858	47 LA 907	50 LA 437	54 LA 84
	53 LA 288	27 LA 454	45 LA 524	28 LA 874
	51 LA 181	19 LA 495	44 LA 745	27 LA 572
	47 LA 971		43 LA 824	
	38 LA 313		42 LA 840	
	37 LA 437		41 LA 345	
	35 LA 95		35 LA 615	
	30 LA 78		29 LA 528	
	30 LA 121		21 LA 676	
	27 LA 512		19 LA 380	
	22 LA 498			
	20 LA 50			
Assault and Fighting Among Employees	57 LA 327	55 LA 182	57 LA 773	57 LA 824
	56 LA 1150	53 LA 229	57 LA 441	56 LA 224
	56 LA 322	52 LA 810	56 LA 558	53 LA 1210
	55 LA 1069		56 LA 56	53 LA 1152
	55 LA 1061		54 LA 488	52 LA 1142
	53 LA 509		51 LA 1153	51 LA 546
	51 LA 258		50 LA 541	39 LA 897
	51 LA 210		48 LA 1278	29 LA 356
	50 LA 403		47 LA 937	26 LA 874
	50 LA 766		47 LA 346	26 LA 688
	49 LA 1253		46 LA 248	21 LA 122
	48 LA 132		45 LA 817	17 LA 258
	41 LA 1327		44 LA 609	
	40 LA 435		44 LA 115	
	39 LA 1276		40 LA 435	
	39 LA 584		40 LA 45	
	37 LA 1112		36 LA 1250	
	30 LA 948		28 LA 198	
	29 LA 820		26 LA 295	
	28 LA 355		21 LA 32	
	28 LA 312			
	28 LA 303			
	27 LA 557			
	23 LA 645			
	21 LA 186			

Offense	Discharge Upheld	Lesser Penalty Upheld (as assessed by employer)	Penalty Reduced by Arbitrator	No Penalty Permitted
Horseplay	53 LA 188	50 LA 1238	57 LA 1171	45 LA 53
	48 LA 993	44 LA 343	54 LA 281	
	44 LA 921	41 LA 568	48 LA 1278	
	42 LA 689		42 LA 184	
	33 LA 819		40 LA 788	
			30 LA 500	
			30 LA 132	
			28 LA 453	
			25 LA 723	
Insubordination	57 LA 1063	55 LA 869	57 LA 1070	
	57 LA 136	52 LA 221	56 LA 1275	
	56 LA 795	45 LA 408	56 LA 256	
	55 LA 525	40 LA 185	55 LA 1081	
	55 LA 484	34 LA 553	54 LA 135	
	55 LA 481	29 LA 404	53 LA 274	
	54 LA 206	28 LA 37	51 LA 672	
	51 LA 853	22 LA 765	46 LA 813	
	45 LA 663	21 LA 53	45 LA 117	
	45 LA 361		44 LA 421	
	44 LA 385		41 LA 1176	
	41 LA 890		37 LA 448	
	36 LA 639		34 LA 143	
	35 LA 109		32 LA 651	
	34 LA 262		29 LA 414	
	29 LA 728		26 LA 713	
	28 LA 543		25 LA 439	
	27 LA 400		23 LA 284	
	27 LA 148		22 LA 528	
	26 LA 395		19 LA 475	
	26 LA 96		18 LA 82	
	18 LA 849		17 LA 737	
	18 LA 235		17 LA 710	
			17 LA 142	

Offense	Discharge Upheld	Lesser Penalty Upheld (as assessed by employer)	Penalty Reduced by Arbitrator	No Penalty Permitted
Threat or Assault of Management Representative	57 LA 346	55 LA 1069	57 LA 1281	57 LA 770
	57 LA 234	55 LA 421	57 LA 1168	
	56 LA 1245	51 LA 1311	56 LA 101	
	56 LA 908		55 LA 835	
	55 LA 26		54 LA 488	
	52 LA 1019		52 LA 1266	
	52 LA 822		52 LA 423	
	51 LA 633		51 LA 685	
	50 LA 232		50 LA 258	
	49 LA 1086		50 LA 95	
	48 LA 1092		49 LA 941	
	47 LA 833		44 LA 493	
	46 LA 956		36 LA 207	
	45.LA 515		30 LA 763	
	45 LA 398		25 LA 404	
	44 LA 644		19 LA 177	
	44 LA 499		17 LA 710	
	41 LA 575			
	36 LA 947			
	35 LA 293			
	31 LA 675			
	28 LA 757			
	28 LA 51			
	27 LA 148			
	22 LA 255			
Abusive Language to Supervision	54 LA 1	57 LA 1279	56 LA 1037	44 LA 858
	52 LA 781	57 LA 866	55 LA 764	35 LA 887
	47 LA 833	55 LA 1039	54 LA 576	34 LA 383
	43 LA 864	48 LA 319	54 LA 546	27 LA 611
	35 LA 506	47 LA 1017	52 LA 1228	26 LA 713
	35 LA 109	47 LA 672	52 LA 1071	
	33 LA 294	44 LA 254	48 LA 972	
	31 LA 652	38 LA 866	45 LA 65	
	31 LA 52	36 LA 667	40 LA 215	
	21 LA 512	22 LA 528	39 LA 221	
	17 LA 224	21 LA 53	32 LA 23	
			23 LA 284	
			18 LA 82	

Offense	Discharge Upheld	Lesser Penalty Upheld (as assessed by employer)	Penalty Reduced by Arbitrator	No Penalty Permitted
Profane or Abusive Language (not toward supervision)	55 LA 590 55 LA 402 46 LA 633 42 LA 490 34 LA 492 31 LA 52 17 LA 335	47 LA 508 38 LA 1226	57 LA 539 52 LA 51 48 LA 116 46 LA 378 45 LA 538 42 LA 490 41 LA 360 40 LA 717	52 LA 128 51 LA 642 21 LA 122
Falsifying Company Records (including time records, production records)	57 LA 52 53 LA 1008 53 LA 513 52 LA 1263 52 LA 959 51 LA 893 50 LA 431 48 LA 893 48 LA 331 47 LA 966 46 LA 246 44 LA 1043 43 LA 753 39 LA 1086 36 LA 1092 35 LA 265 31 LA 68 25 LA 568 23 LA 534	49 LA 651 48 LA 1022 43 LA 838 40 LA 914	57 LA 709 56 LA 895 52 LA 13 51 LA 805 51 LA 764 48 LA 891 45 LA 844 41 LA 1179 38 LA 1157 37 LA 1108 36 LA 974 36 LA 179 28 LA 879 24 LA 783	57 LA 229 56 LA 274 55 LA 360 55 LA 281 52 LA 1296 52 LA 1285 52 LA 212 50 LA 604 48 LA 251 36 LA 1177

Offense	Discharge Upheld	Lesser Penalty Upheld (as assessed by employer)	Penalty Reduced by Arbitrator	No Penalty Permitted
Falsifying Employment Application	56 LA 673		57 LA 765	57 LA 1053
	56 LA 135		55 LA 283	56 LA 799
	56 LA 11		53 LA 1	54 LA 1192
	55 LA 581		50 LA 161	53 LA 774
	55 LA 258		47 LA 119	44 LA 553
	54 LA 534		46 LA 845	41 LA 178
	52 LA 89		46 LA 233	38 LA 829
	52 LA 451		44 LA 41	37 LA 991
	51 LA 774		29 LA 182	36 LA 1439
	50 LA 53		26 LA 575	32 LA 152
	50 LA 31		21 LA 560	31 LA 1018
	49 LA 297		17 LA 230	24 LA 356
	47 LA 752			
	46 LA 559			
	45 LA 335			
	43 LA 233			
	42 LA 323			
	36 LA 889			
	33 LA 879			
	33 LA 625			
	31 LA 599			
	24 LA 353			
	19 LA 854			
Dishonesty	57 LA 13	37 LA 42	51 LA 869	56 LA 152
	56 LA 168	17 LA 544	49 LA 848	55 LA 562
	55 LA 1089		47 LA 921	42 LA 935
	55 LA 731		46 LA 974	42 LA 446
	53 LA 1197		44 LA 709	39 LA 1
	52 LA 578		25 LA 13	37 LA 1076
	52 LA 314		17 LA 804	33 LA 313
	52 LA 145		17 LA 412	27 LA 629
	51 LA 745			26 LA 934
	51 LA 202			19 LA 413
	49 LA 677			
	48 LA 812			
	47 LA 432			
	42 LA 497			
	37 LA 214			
	32 LA 126			

Offense	Discharge Upheld	Lesser Penalty Upheld (as assessed by employer)	Penalty Reduced by Arbitrator	No Penalty Permitted
Theft	57 LA 369	55 LA 226	57 LA 1189	55 LA 1195
	57 LA 56		56 LA 608	55 LA 1221
	53 LA 1212		52 LA 1276	53 LA 774
	52 LA 1203		52 LA 489	48 LA 1089
	52 LA 847		50 LA 103	46 LA 756
	52 LA 709		48 LA 152	44 LA 405
	51 LA 457		46 LA 974	44 LA 257
	51 LA 257		45 LA 972	43 LA 940
	50 LA 1194		44 LA 897	29 LA 525
	50 LA 504		42 LA 1243	29 LA 272
	49 LA 101		42 LA 849	29 LA 137
	48 LA 1114		36 LA 1062	27 LA 863
	47 LA 903		33 LA 40	26 LA 923
	45 LA 1050		29 LA 781	24 LA 470
	43 LA 1218		29 LA 464	21 LA 832
	42 LA 954		26 LA 480	
	40 LA 533		25 LA 906	
	38 LA 93		24 LA 728	
	36 LA 1360		19 LA 615	
	33 LA 497			
	31 LA 631			
	25 LA 270			
	21 LA 444			
	17 LA 720			
	17 LA 334			
Disloyalty to Government (Security Risk)	30 LA 642	22 LA 709	28 LA 810	39 LA 1280
	27 LA 548		22 LA 751	35 LA 315
	27 LA 265			30 LA 636
	26 LA 792			29 LA 567
	26 LA 609			28 LA 668
	24 LA 852			24 LA 567
	23 LA 715			21 LA 1
	21 LA 532			
	19 LA 40			
	19 LA 39			
	16 LA 234			

Offense	Discharge Upheld	Lesser Penalty Upheld (as assessed by employer)	Penalty Reduced by Arbitrator	No Penalty Permitted
Disloyalty to Employer (Includes competing with employer, conflict of interests)	57 LA 1258 56 LA 973 54 LA 942 53 LA 1247 53 LA 1176 52 LA 1254 49 LA 453 46 LA 1009 44 LA 428 40 LA 1293 40 LA 1126 39 LA 508 39 LA 404 38 LA 600 24 LA 674		44 LA 552 43 LA 46 38 LA 467 34 LA 458 27 LA 540 20 LA 823 18 LA 490 17 LA 179	51 LA 421 43 LA 273 38 LA 456 36 LA 305 33 LA 902 31 LA 547 24 LA 63 20 LA 305 19 LA 125
Moonlighting* (Excluding competing with employer)	57 LA 1267 49 LA 400 41 LA 1126		52 LA 918 52 LA 818	54 LA 381 51 LA 421 43 LA 1106 42 LA 446 37 LA 1095 33 LA 902
Negligence	55 LA 1094 54 LA 1174 49 LA 686 47 LA 994 43 LA 1162 41 LA 591 41 LA 570 40 LA 225 36 LA 261 33 LA 607 31 LA 1036 24 LA 48 21 LA 314 21 LA 105 20 LA 706 18 LA 282	57 LA 1 55 LA 342 54 LA 220 52 LA 957 49 LA 111 48 LA 454 48 LA 299 45 LA 793 43 LA 689 42 LA 257 36 LA 420	57 LA 172 55 LA 499 54 LA 1149 50 LA 571 48 LA 1286 47 LA 559 46 LA 1161 38 LA 586 37 LA 953 36 LA 124 31 LA 1 30 LA 830 27 LA 656 25 LA 634 24 LA 102 21 LA 456	57 LA 538 57 LA 17 54 LA 844 44 LA 377 33 LA 960 28 LA 761 25 LA 736 22 LA 520 20 LA 622 20 LA 465

* For discussion of this subject, see Chapter 17, topic titled " 'Moonlighting' and Outside Business Interest."

Offense	Discharge Upheld	Lesser Penalty Upheld (as assessed by employer)	Penalty Reduced by Arbitrator	No Penalty Permitted
Damage to or Loss of Machine or Materials	57 LA 1155 57 LA 346 53 LA 1279 51 LA 665 50 LA 504 40 LA 1084 38 LA 749 37 LA 158 36 LA 309 27 LA 463 21 LA 314 20 LA 706 17 LA 138	56 LA 645 56 LA 75 48 LA 1227 32 LA 581 26 LA 910 21 LA 105	56 LA 604 25 LA 634 19 LA 650	57 LA 731 56 LA 597 52 LA 1221 48 LA 211 45 LA 53 28 LA 246 19 LA 665
Incompetence* (Including low productivity)	57 LA 1050 57 LA 906 56 LA 916 56 LA 506 56 LA 453 56 LA 165 54 LA 737 53 LA 498 52 LA 552 51 LA 1140 44 LA 61 43 LA 1155 41 LA 200 41 LA 118 39 LA 719 35 LA 794 34 LA 610 30 LA 638 28 LA 710 26 LA 598 26 LA 272 20 LA 353 18 LA 656 18 LA 363	57 LA 85 55 LA 75 50 LA 917 45 LA 689 44 LA 393 33 LA 913 28 LA 162 27 LA 682 26 LA 245 18 LA 457 17 LA 580 17 LA 328	57 LA 1149 52 LA 538 49 LA 620 49 LA 581 46 LA 365 44 LA 522 44 LA 218 41 LA 1184 37 LA 758 31 LA 839 28 LA 330 26 LA 682 19 LA 677 19 LA 151	56 LA 1009 55 LA 231 52 LA 1221 51 LA 1285 48 LA 454 47 LA 723 46 LA 539 35 LA 584 33 LA 275 33 LA 203 30 LA 1048 25 LA 32 23 LA 252 22 LA 819 21 LA 293 20 LA 483 19 LA 585 17 LA 784

* For related material, see Chapter 13, topic titled "Production Standards, Time Studies, and Job Evaluation."

Offense	Discharge Upheld	Lesser Penalty Upheld (as assessed by employer)	Penalty Reduced by Arbitrator	No Penalty Permitted
Refusal to Accept Job Assigmnent*	57 LA 136	57 LA 512	56 LA 924	57 LA 457
	56 LA 1197	56 LA 613	56 LA 884	57 LA 285
	56 LA 1052	55 LA 1302	54 LA 1231	55 LA 944
	54 LA 175	48 LA 32	52 LA 982	54 LA 1114
	53 LA 762	47 LA 739	49 LA 700	52 LA 1234
	51 LA 709	42 LA 1217	48 LA 19	45 LA 293
	49 LA 231	42 LA 173	45 LA 772	44 LA 919
	48 LA 1209	40 LA 997	40 LA 247	41 LA 666
	48 LA 980	38 LA 251	38 LA 200	39 LA 1186
	47 LA 83	33 LA 232	36 LA 78	38 LA 655
	41 LA 88	32 LA 256	34 LA 598	38 LA 443
	40 LA 686	30 LA 199	29 LA 80	37 LA 1116
	40 LA 97	29 LA 412	28 LA 255	36 LA 531
	39 LA 580	29 LA 74	26 LA 915	30 LA 38
	38 LA 852	28 LA 486	20 LA 749	27 LA 523
	37 LA 277	28 LA 394	18 LA 239	23 LA 313
	36 LA 1452	25 LA 802	17 LA 666	22 LA 624
	24 LA 839	20 LA 653	16 LA 939	21 LA 335
	20 LA 875		16 LA 220	19 LA 767
	19 LA 888			16 LA 138
	18 LA 235			
Refusal to Work Overtime†	56 LA 592	55 LA 869	56 LA 758	56 LA 538
	54 LA 832	54 LA 923	52 LA 1290	53 LA 246
	52 LA 752	54 LA 773	52 LA 762	48 LA 492
	44 LA 148	53 LA 69	49 LA 1172	48 LA 61
	40 LA 1189	52 LA 23	42 LA 713	44 LA 565
	36 LA 4	51 LA 287	39 LA 698	37 LA 275
	34 LA 633	51 LA 261	33 LA 708	32 LA 684
	33 LA 871	48 LA 417	27 LA 614	27 LA 599
	33 LA 708	46 LA 15	20 LA 794	27 LA 458
	32 LA 88	44 LA 1139	17 LA 419	24 LA 526
	25 LA 727	38 LA 729		24 LA 163
	17 LA 217	37 LA 338		21 LA 513
		35 LA 193		20 LA 564
		31 LA 796		17 LA 606
		28 LA 242		16 LA 311

* For related material, see Chapter 5, subtopic titled "Use of Grievance Procedure v. Self-Help."

† For related material, see Chapter 13, subtopic titled "Right to Require Overtime."

Offense	Discharge Upheld	Lesser Penalty Upheld (as assessed by employer)	Penalty Reduced by Arbitrator	No Penalty Permitted
Prohibited Strike	57 LA 163	56 LA 351	57 LA 1109	56 LA 1118
	56 LA 340	53 LA 154	55 LA 1214	55 LA 548
	55 LA 667	52 LA 480	53 LA 1165	51 LA 83
	54 LA 633	51 LA 83	53 LA 1061	40 LA 598
	54 LA 30	50 LA 487	52 LA 1131	39 LA 849
	53 LA 619	49 LA 383	49 LA 383	29 LA 644
	51 LA 1228	48 LA 949	46 LA 668	29 LA 635
	50 LA 1131	47 LA 567	44 LA 1057	20 LA 15
	49 LA 697	45 LA 981	41 LA 110	17 LA 11
	48 LA 855	44 LA 339	34 LA 325	
	47 LA 1065	40 LA 598	30 LA 513	
	47 LA 752	33 LA 434	29 LA 681	
	47 LA 129	30 LA 250	24 LA 761	
	41 LA 1100	30 LA 181	19 LA 437	
	40 LA 1209	30 LA 109	18 LA 379	
	39 LA 169	28 LA 782	17 LA 440	
	33 LA 568	28 LA 648	16 LA 939	
	29 LA 622	28 LA 369	16 LA 247	
	25 LA 663			
	21 LA 736			
	20 LA 875			
	19 LA 601			
	16 LA 99			
Misconduct During Strike	56 LA 1301	55 LA 1159	49 LA 1267	56 LA 1118
	50 LA 725	43 LA 450	46 LA 378	52 LA 1249
	47 LA 196		40 LA 616	52 LA 1112
	46 LA 949		39 LA 1273	45 LA 490
	45 LA 366		39 LA 614	42 LA 169
	40 LA 1169		39 LA 441	35 LA 757
	39 LA 614		38 LA 1191	26 LA 186
	38 LA 1182		38 LA 1182	25 LA 470
	26 LA 742		32 LA 899	16 LA 829
	26 LA 250		26 LA 836	
	26 LA 186		25 LA 767	
	25 LA 767		25 LA 343	
	25 LA 556		25 LA 270	
	25 LA 270		19 LA 818	
	22 LA 567		16 LA 722	

Offense	Discharge Upheld	Lesser Penalty Upheld (as assessed by employer)	Penalty Reduced by Arbitrator	No Penalty Permitted
Slowdown	50 LA 1157	53 LA 414	49 LA 581	49 LA 1236
	48 LA 1224	52 LA 162	34 LA 432	49 LA 581
	41 LA 1253	49 LA 1236	29 LA 604	42 LA 1162
	41 LA 607	46 LA 154	21 LA 729	41 LA 1339
	38 LA 644	45 LA 408	18 LA 882	38 LA 896
	37 LA 401	44 LA 393	17 LA 814	37 LA 593
	18 LA 449	41 LA 1339		32 LA 701
	18 LA 370	38 LA 889		29 LA 512
		34 LA 165		21 LA 428
		33 LA 19		17 LA 423
		31 LA 914		16 LA 311
		29 LA 769		
		29 LA 142		
		26 LA 279		
		22 LA 77		
		18 LA 557		
Union Activities	54 LA 1110	52 LA 936	56 LA 1164	57 LA 841
	54 LA 206	50 LA 1183	49 LA 71	56 LA 543
	48 LA 855	50 LA 562	44 LA 889	55 LA 1135
	46 LA 486	41 LA 1288	44 LA 664	55 LA 64
	45 LA 612	36 LA 503	37 LA 471	52 LA 644
	42 LA 746		25 LA 124	49 LA 269
	41 LA 724			45 LA 258
	32 LA 719			44 LA 858
	28 LA 543			38 LA 82
				37 LA 1076
				35 LA 226
				20 LA 325
				17 LA 199
				16 LA 666
				16 LA 536
				16 LA 208
Possession or Use of Drugs	56 LA 1191		57 LA 919	57 LA 884
	43 LA 170			
	38 LA 891			

Offense	Discharge Upheld	Lesser Penalty Upheld (as assessed by employer)	Penalty Reduced by Arbitrator	No Penalty Permitted
Possession or Use of Intoxicants	56 LA 738	32 LA 293	57 LA 637	55 LA 907
	55 LA 306	29 LA 362	57 LA 10	53 LA 1203
	54 LA 1090	26 LA 176	56 LA 837	48 LA 567
	52 LA 1279	16 LA 317	56 LA 789	46 LA 109
	52 LA 764		56 LA 319	18 LA 336
	52 LA 195		54 LA 158	
	51 LA 120		54 LA 145	
	50 LA 173		52 LA 989	
	46 LA 549		52 LA 672	
	45 LA 932		52 LA 653	
	44 LA 308		49 LA 370	
	44 LA 267		49 LA 97	
	42 LA 1251		48 LA 929	
	31 LA 832		44 LA 1043	
	30 LA 94		42 LA 408	
	28 LA 226		41 LA 987	
	25 LA 709		40 LA 935	
	24 LA 810		38 LA 1221	
	23 LA 418		34 LA 14	
	21 LA 367		32 LA 420	
	20 LA 50		28 LA 829	
	19 LA 733		27 LA 128	
	18 LA 671		21 LA 80	
			19 LA 724	
			18 LA 400	
Obscene or Immoral Conduct	56 LA 322	48 LA 264	49 LA 1207	53 LA 1340
	53 LA 1266		45 LA 538	53 LA 1315
	51 LA 453		44 LA 574	51 LA 1019
	44 LA 730		42 LA 490	
	42 LA 806			
	42 LA 490			
	39 LA 1025			
	39 LA 125			
	36 LA 618			

Offense	Discharge Upheld	Lesser Penalty Upheld (as assessed by employer)	Penalty Reduced by Arbitrator	No Penalty Permitted
Gambling	45 LA 1007	51 LA 707	49 LA 1262	52 LA 945
	45 LA 646	29 LA 442	44 LA 1174	45 LA 247
	45 LA 350		37 LA 188	41 LA 823
	40 LA 1323		28 LA 97	39 LA 621
	40 LA 262		22 LA 851	28 LA 97
	39 LA 154		22 LA 210	18 LA 938
	33 LA 174			
	32 LA 44			
	32 LA 26			
	31 LA 191			
	29 LA 778			
	21 LA 788			
	17 LA 150			
	16 LA 727			
	16 LA 461			
Abusing Customers	56 LA 946		53 LA 350	54 LA 1
	52 LA 413		50 LA 177	
	49 LA 895		49 LA 606	
	45 LA 1124		48 LA 91	
	42 LA 497		39 LA 1131	
	30 LA 486			
	30 LA 463			
	27 LA 486			
	27 LA 27			
	21 LA 556			
Attachment or Garnishment of Wages	57 LA 31		55 LA 897	57 LA 314
	55 LA 133		49 LA 569	49 LA 58
	44 LA 87		48 LA 1331	46 LA 822
	39 LA 1040		47 LA 108	44 LA 104
	39 LA 948		46 LA 598	37 LA 85
	37 LA 226		45 LA 885	35 LA 551
	35 LA 343		43 LA 1268	32 LA 50
	30 LA 690		41 LA 631	30 LA 1058
	21 LA 709		36 LA 672	
			35 LA 139	
			31 LA 836	

CHAPTER 16

SAFETY AND HEALTH

Safety and health considerations may arise directly or indirectly out of many labor-management concerns, such as, crew size,[1] the physical or mental condition of an employee, refusal of an employee to obey an order, requirements for special protective clothing or equipment, and the like. Moreover, unions sometimes have contested management's right to require employees to observe a safety rule, and they have grieved that management has not adequately protected the safety and health of the employees. In such cases, arbitrators have generally applied the test of "reasonableness." Indeed, the reader will observe that the golden thread of "reasonableness" runs throughout arbitration decisions on safety and health matters.

Management Rights and Obligations in Safety and Health Matters

Initially, it may be noted that when the agreement is silent on the subject, arbitrators have ruled that management has the prerogative to promulgate and enforce reasonable rules and regulations to insure the safety and health of its employees.[2]

However, many agreements do contain safety and health provisions, and the typical clause may state that management will exert a reasonable effort to protect the safety and health of its employees.[3]

---

[1] See Chapter 13, topic titled "Determination of Size of Crews."
[2] See Arbitrator Hnatiuk in 50 LA 985, 986; Jenkins in 48 LA 1094, 1096; Logan in 30 LA 252, 253; Yeager in 29 LA 487, 489; Kelliher in 29 LA 367, 368; Morvant in 24 LA 453, 457; Brecht in 24 LA 199, 209; Seward in 19 LA 210, 211–212; Short in 18 LA 671, 673–675; Shipman in 10 LA 113, 116. Also see Chapter 13, topic titled "Plant Rules."
[3] See, for example, Arbitrator Wolf in 47 LA 425, 426; Welch in 47 LA 83, 84; Luckerath in 43 LA 1253, 1255; Duff in 43 LA 583, 585; Barrett in 41 LA 211, 212; Dworkin in 40 LA 1285, 1290; Valtin in 39 LA 40, 42.

Under such a clause, arbitrators have ruled that while management must make a reasonable effort toward safety, it is not required to eliminate all possible hazards or to utilize all possible safety precautions.[4]

Another contract clause requiring the company to make every reasonable effort to provide necessary and practicable safety measures was construed as constituting the *minimum* obligation which the company had assumed for the safety and health of its employees; but the company could do more toward that end so long as it acted reasonably.[5]

Similarly, where the contract called for safety rules or devices as should be agreed upon by the joint safety committee, one arbitrator held that the company had an obligation to make, and could enforce by discipline, reasonable provision for the safety and health of the employees even beyond the agreed-upon rules;[6] and another ruled that such a clause did not bar the company from "acting on its own in carrying out its responsibility to provide the employees with a safe place to work," nor did the clause "limit or block the Company's continuing right to take such reasonable safety measures" as would provide for the safety and health of its employees.[7]

Interpreting a "reasonable effort" clause, Arbitrator Harry J. Dworkin listed five specific employer obligations which he reasoned derived from the clause:

> "Under the terms of the contract, it might be reasoned that a specific duty is imposed on the employer to provide (1) a safe place to work; (2) safe machinery, tools, and equipment; (3) competent fellow employees; (4) instructions and warnings as to the dangers involved; and (5) rules for the conduct of the work."[8]

---

[4] See Arbitrator Wolf in 47 LA 425, 428; Murphy in 37 LA 501, 503; Dworkin in 36 LA 902, 912.

[5] See Bethlehem Steel Co., 41 LA 211, 212 (Barrett, 1963); Bethlehem Steel Co., 39 LA 40, 43 (Valtin, 1962).

[6] Bunker Hill Co., 43 LA 1253, 1256 (Luckerath, 1964).

[7] Giant Portland Cement Co., 63-1 ARB ¶8261 (Williams, 1963).

[8] Erie Mining Co., 36 LA 902, 912 (1961). Also see Arbitrator Wolf in 47 LA 425, 428; Murphy in 37 LA 501, 503; Williams in 63-1 ARB ¶8261. In the absence of such contractually derived obligation, it may be noted that while the common law does not impose an affirmative requirement on the employer to take these safety measures, he may be liable for damages if an employee sustains physical injury due to the employer's failure to do so. Of course workmen's compensation legislation goes even further in giving relief to injured workmen. The Federal Occupational Safety and Health Act of 1970 requires employers

Employee Obligations in Safety Matters

The union and employees have a correlative duty in safety and health matters. This duty may be imposed by contract, usually in the form of an agreement to cooperate in promoting safety.[9] It may be imposed by a state safety code.[10] And of course it may be imposed upon the employee by safety rules promulgated under management's prerogative to issue such rules.[11] Moreover, employees have an inherent obligation to protect their own safety and to cooperate in promoting safety.[12]

Safety Rules

While, as noted above, management has the right to issue reasonable safety rules, certain fundamental principles of labor-management relations are pertinent to the question of the reasonableness of such rules. Thus, a safety rule must bear a reasonable relationship to its purpose, i.e., safety and health considerations.[13] Moreover, it must be reasonable in application as well as in content.[14] In this regard, a rule was held to be reasonably and nondiscriminatorily applied where the company required employees working in hazardous areas

---

to comply with specific safety and health standards, and under its "general duty" provisions it requires employers to furnish a place of employment free .of hazards likely to cause death or serious physical harm to employees. Among other provisions, the Act also provides for enforcement: inspections and investigations of employers' work facilities, prompt court action to remedy imminently dangerous conditions, civil and criminal penalties. For an exhaustive analysis of the law, see The Job Safety and Health Act of 1970, The Bureau of National Affairs, Inc., 1971.

[9] See 54 LA 1084, 1086–1087; 51 LA 156, at 156; 50 LA 115, 118; 48 LA 1094, 1095; 47 LA 425, 426; 43 LA 583, 585; 42 LA 1206, 1207; 39 LA 40, 42; 36 LA 970, 971; 32 LA 103, at 103.

[10] As in United States Borax & Chemical Corp., 36 LA 970, 973 (Keeler, 1961).

[11] As in U.S. Plywood-Champion Papers, Inc., 50 LA 115, 121 (Jenkins, 1968); Rome Kraft Co., 61-3 ARB ¶8792 (Hawley, 1961).

[12] See General Electric Co., 31 LA 386, 389 (Sutermeister, 1958). As a corollary, employees should not be penalized for protesting hazards. Reserve Mining Co., 55 LA 648, 652 (Sembower, 1970).

[13] See Arbitrator Black in 42 LA 1206, 1208; Barrett in 41 LA 211, 212, cited and followed by Strongin in 48 LA 765, 766; McDermott in 62-1 ARB ¶8051. Also see Wallen in 47 LA 1135, 1141. A safety rule is not unreasonable merely because its benefits are minor. United States Steel Corp., 40 LA 205, 207 (Florey, 1963).

[14] See Arbitrator Jenkins in 48 LA 1094, 1096; Kates in 48 LA 861, 863; Strongin in 48 LA 765, 767; Black in 42 LA 1206, 1208; Barrett in 41 LA 211, 213. Also see Seitz in 39 LA 1140, 1142.

to wear "hard hats" and safety glasses while it exempted others who worked in an enclosure protecting them from the hazard.[15]

As is true of other plant rules, safety rules must be adequately communicated to the employees in some manner.[16] Finding that adequate notice of a safety rule had been given and that the rule had been violated, an arbitrator may uphold suspension of the offending employee.[17] Discharge may be justified where an employee has persistently disobeyed safety regulations in spite of progressive discipline.[18] In the absence of a contractual restriction on reclassifying employees for safety reasons, violation of safety rules may be a controlling factor in the demotion of an employee.[19]

It would appear that when a rule is in furtherance of safety, there is an even stronger than usual reason to require strict compliance by the employee, with the right to file a grievance instead of resorting to self-help.[20] This is especially so where the company operations are hazardous in themselves.[21]

Arbitrator Alexander B. Porter has ruled that employees may not exercise individual discretion regarding the need to comply with safety rules. He has stated: "Obviously, a safety program based upon permitting thousands of employees to decide when they may safely remove their [safety] glasses would be doomed to fail from the outset."[22]

---

[15] Bethlehem Steel Co., 41 LA 213, 214 (Barrett, 1963).

[16] Oral communication was sufficient where the parties had a history of oral safety rules in Reserve Mining Co., 38 LA 443, 449 (Sembower, 1962).

[17] See Arbitrator Miller in 64-1 ARB ¶8356; Stouffer in 64-1 ARB ¶8018; Duff in 63-2 ARB ¶8675. Arbitrator Bothwell reduced a penalty of discharge to disciplinary suspension due to mitigating circumstances in 36 LA 898, 901, as did Rohman in 45 LA 772, 775, and Marshall in 40 LA 247, 254. Similarly, Arbitrator Dworkin in 47 LA 457, 463, where he gave the company the option to restore grievant to his job or to negotiate with the union on placement in another job.

[18] American Potash & Chemical Corp., 64-1 ARB ¶8356 (Miller, 1963).

[19] United States Borax & Chemical Corp., 36 LA 970, 972-973 (Keeler, 1961).

[20] See situations confronting Arbitrator Murphy in 44 LA 459, 462; Boles in 44 LA 385, 388–389; Bothwell in 36 LA 898, 901; Daugherty in 34 LA 83, 85.

[21] As in 44 LA 459, 462; 34 LA 83, 85; 31 LA 386, 388–389. Insurance may be a factor as in Solar Chemical Corp., 62-2 ARB ¶8651 (Taft, 1962).

[22] Bethlehem Steel Co., 41 LA 1152, 1153 (1963). Similarly, see Arbitrator Bothwell in 53 LA 627, 628, and in 36 LA 898, 901; Hale in 39 LA 385, 389.

Safety rules may not only require observance of certain procedures and practices by employees but they may also impose a duty upon the employee to refrain from working under potentially unsafe conditions.[23]

Refusal to Obey Orders—the Safety Exception

It is a well established principle that employees must obey management's orders and carry out their job assignments, even if believed to violate the agreement, then turn to the grievance procedure for relief.[24] An exception to this "obey now—grieve later" doctrine exists where obedience would involve an unusual or abnormal safety or health hazard.[25] But this exception has been held inapplicable where the hazard is inherent in the employee's job. [26] Moreover, when the exception is invoked, the union must show that a safety or health hazard was the real reason for the employee's refusal.[27]

The exception has been held to apply as well where the employee asserts that if he were to perform as ordered the safety of others would be in jeopardy.[28] However, even assuming that there is a safety hazard sufficient to justify an employee in refusing to do the work, this right of refusal applies only to the employee assigned to do the work; other employees not assigned the work (and not affected by the unsafe condition) would not be justified in resorting to self-help, such as walking off the job, instead of using the grievance procedures.[29]

---

[23] See Arbitrator Lehoczky in 51 LA 344; McCoy in 45 LA 293, 295; Sembower in 38 LA 443, 449; Hawley in 61-3 ARB ¶8792.
[24] See Chapter 5, topic titled "Use of Grievance Procedure v. Self-Help."
[25] See Arbitrator Rohman in 51 LA 709, 711; Jenkins in 50 LA 115, 123–124; Epstein in 49 LA 429, 430; Hopson in 48 LA 788, 793–795; Dworkin in 48 LA 457, 461; Abernethy in 47 LA 184, 191–192; McCoy in 45 LA 293, 295, and in 8 LA 647, 651–652; Roberts in 44 LA 919, 920; Meyers in 43 LA 102, 105; Barrett in 27 LA 523, 526–530; Parker in 22 LA 624, 626, and in 21 LA 410; Shipman in 21 LA 335, 337–338; Elson in 8 LA 826, 831. It should be noted that Section 502 of the Labor Management Relations Act of 1947 provides that the quitting of labor because of abnormally dangerous conditions for work shall not be deemed a strike under the Act.
[26] See Arbitrator House in 48 LA 1082, 1084; Dworkin in 48 LA 457, 461; Meyers in 43 LA 102, 105; Porter in 41 LA 1323, 1326; Anrod in 38 LA 375, 378; Duff in 26 LA 915, 917. Cf. Rohman in 45 LA 772, 775; Gilden in 5 LA 300, 302–304.
[27] See Arbitrator House in 48 LA 1082, 1084–1085; Rohman in 48 LA 963, 965, and in 48 LA 457, 461; Yagoda in 48 LA 124, 131; Mullin in 47 LA 848, 854.
[28] A. M. Castle & Co., 41 LA 666, 670 (Sembower, 1963).
[29] Metal Specialty Co., 43 LA 849, 853–854 (Volz, 1964), citing and quoting from Ford Motor Co., 41 LA 608, 615 (Platt, 1963).

A contract clause may expressly deal with the right of an employee to refuse to do work in abnormally hazardous conditions. Such a clause may give the employee the right, after reporting the alleged hazard to his supervisor, to file a grievance at an advanced step for preferred handling, or to be relieved of the job and, at management's discretion, to be assigned to another available position.[30]

The Range of Arbitral Reasoning

Many grievances have arisen out of discharge or discipline assessed for refusal to obey an order or perform an assignment because of alleged safety or health hazards. Such allegations, countered by management's assertion that no unusual hazard existed, have led arbitrators on a merry chase after an elusive standard or formula for determining when an employee's refusal is justified.[31]

Arbitration decisions are couched in such language as: an "employee's reasonable belief" that unusual danger is involved is enough;[32] the employee "sincerely and genuinely" feared for his life;[33] the "employee's good faith belief of the existence of a hazard does not suffice," but the "hazard must be demonstrated to exist";[34] the employee erroneously but "actually entertained" the fear of danger to his life;[35] if the employee "is sincere in his belief of danger" and "makes a 'reasonable' appraisal of the potential hazards, he is protected in his decision not to act, regardless of whether later on, in fact, it should be established that no hazard existed";[36] the "standard to be applied is not the cowardice or bravery of anyone";[37] "although their fears were based on misconceptions, they were nonetheless real";[38] the employee must obey the order unless there is a "real and imminent danger

---

[30] See, for example, Arbitrator Strongin in 49 LA 1203; Jenkins in 48 LA 1094, 1095; Dworkin in 46 LA 43, 50; Garrett in 45 LA 426, 428; Duff in 43 LA 583, 585.

[31] By definition, a "hazard" is "potential," and determining when the "potential" is sufficient to justify an employee in refusing to obey an order depends upon the facts.

[32] Hercules, Inc., 48 LA 788, 794–795 (Hopson, 1967).

[33] Lone Star Steel Co., 48 LA 1094, 1097 (Jenkins, 1967).

[34] Wilcolator Co., 44 LA 847, 852 (Altieri, 1964).

[35] Allied Chemical Corp., 47 LA 686, 688 (Hilpert, 1966).

[36] A. M. Castle Co., 41 LA 666, 671 (Sembower, 1963). Cf. Dodge Mfg Corp., 49 LA 429, 430–431 (Epstein, 1967).

[37] Goodyear Tire & Rubber Co., 45 LA 772, 775 (Rohman, 1965).

[38] New York Shipbuilding Co., 39 LA 1186, 1188 (Crawford, 1963). Also see Arbitrator Wagner in 49 LA 325, 330.

to life and limb";[39] the fact that a fellow employee is an unsafe driver was "ample reason" for grievant's fears and therefore "valid and reasonable grounds for refusing the assignment";[40] considering the grievants' inadequate training and experience, "the work assignment constituted *for them* an abnormal hazard";[41] although there were some conditions "which required correction and attention in order to maintain the required standards of safety," nevertheless "there were no imminently dangerous conditions which presented a hazard to their safety and health so as to justify them in refusing to work;"[42] although the employee "honestly believed" that there would be unnecessary danger if he complied with the work order, "it was not so clearly and evidently unsafe" that he could disobey after failing to protest through the grievance procedure;[43] the hazards were "neither so compelling nor the opportunities for their correction so hopeless as to require nothing less than an abandonment of the grievance procedure";[44] grievant was "entirely sincere" in questioning the safety of the crew, but his concern was not "well founded";[45] there must be "a reasonable basis" for the allegation that the assignment is dangerous and "at least *prima facie* evidence" that the work is unsafe, but the evidence should be "more than a mere presumption."[46]

Thus, arbitral reasoning appears to range from the purely subjective test of what the particular employee "honestly" or "sincerely" believed as to the presence of a hazard, to the "cold facts" approach of requiring a showing of actual danger with a "real and imminent" hazard to life and limb, and all the shadings between these two extremes.

The "Reasonable Man" Approach

The greatest number of arbitrators appear to take some form of the "reasonable man" approach, i.e., an approach which attempts to ascertain whether the facts and circumstances known to the employee at the time of the incident would have caused a "reasonable

---

[39] Pennsylvania Railroad Co., 45 LA 522, 523 (Seidenberg, 1965).
[40] U.S. Plywood-Champion Papers, Inc., 50 LA 115, 123–124 (Jenkins, 1968).
[41] Bethlehem Steel Corp., 49 LA 1203, 1206 (Strongin, 1968), emphasis added.
[42] International Salt Co., 40 LA 1285, 1291–1292 (Dworkin, 1963).
[43] Duval Corp., 43 LA 102, 105 (Meyers, 1964).
[44] New York Telephone Co., 42 LA 1217, 1223 (Stockman, 1964).
[45] W. P. Fuller & Co., 30 LA 545, 547 (Cobb, 1959).
[46] Marble Products Co., 40 LA 247, 253 (Marshall, 1963).

man" to fear for his safety or health. This view was stated succinctly by Arbitrator Ralph Roger Williams under a contract which required the employee to establish "positively" the claimed health hazard in order to avoid discipline for refusal to obey an order:

> "* * * Hence, if the grievant actually believed that the performance of the assigned task would have created a serious health hazard to him, and if a 'reasonable man' would have reached the same conclusion under the same circumstances, the requirement [of the contract] is met * * *."[47]

Arbitrator Wilber C. Bothwell has summarized the prevailing view as follows:

> "The principle * * * is that an employee may refuse to carry out a particular work assignment if, at the time he is given the work assignment, he reasonably believes that by carrying out such work assignment he will endanger his safety or health. In such an instance the employee has the duty, not only of stating that he believes there is a risk to his safety or health, and the reason for believing so, but he also has the burden, if called upon, of showing by appropriate evidence that he had a reasonable basis for his belief. In the case of dispute, as is the case here, the question to be decided is not whether he actually would have suffered injury but whether he had a reasonable basis for believing so."[48]

Must the Employee Explain His Refusal?

Ordinarily, the employee expresses his fear of danger and thus no question is presented as to whether the burden is on management to elicit or on the employee to express his reasons for refusing to perform an assigned task. The question has been raised in a few cases, however. In the language just quoted, Arbitrator Bothwell appears to place the burden upon the employee to state not only his fears but also his reasons for being fearful and to be prepared to substantiate his statements with evidence.[49]

Another arbitrator apparently would be more demanding of the employer in some circumstances. Thus, where the employee requested additional help for an assigned task but apparently could not articulate his fear, Arbitrator Dan Hopson took the approach that while ideally the duty to speak up should be equal, it does "not seem unreasonable"

---

[47] Jefferson City Cabinet Co., 50 LA 213, 216 (1968).
[48] Laclede Gas Co., 39 LA 833, 839 (1962).
[49] Ibid. Accord: American Radiator & Standard Sanitary Corp., 41 LA 755, 759 (Stouffer, 1963).

to impose a slightly higher standard upon the company to ask the uncommunicative employee why he refused to work.[50] However, Arbitrator John F. Sembower pointed out that the failure of management to ask employees for an explanation does not "excuse them forever from making one."[51]

The burden to explain or clarify may shift from employee to employer as a situation develops. For instance, where the company safety rules provided that an employee should go to his supervisor "If special conditions arise which make [the employee] think it necessary to violate any safety rule in order to do [his] work," it was held that, after the employee raises a question as to the safety of the assignment, it then becomes the supervisor's responsibility to initiate any discussion and to give such advice and explanation as might be required.[52]

Employee Complaints of Specific Hazards

Employee claims of safety and health hazards have been based upon many different circumstances, such as, complaints that plant temperature was too cold,[53] that fumes or dust produced unsafe working conditions,[54] that ventilation was poor and the temperature too high,[55] that it was too drafty,[56] and that excessive noise was detrimental to health.[57] In such cases, arbitrators attempt to distinguish between mere discomfort or displeasure and the situation in which a real threat to employee health or safety is present, the result in any event being dependent upon the facts of the given case.[58]

---

[50] Hercules, Inc., 48 LA 788, 795 (1967). Cf. Eaton, Yale & Towne, Inc., 50 LA 517, 521 (Levy, 1968), where the employee did not express his fears and the company did not inquire; held: insubordination justified the suspension.

[51] A. M. Castle & Co., 41 LA 667, 671 (1963).

[52] Rome Kraft Co., 61-3 ARB ¶8792 (Hawley, 1961).

[53] See 47 LA 332, 335; 46 LA 1131, 1135; 46 LA 920, 922; 41 LA 895, 898; 38 LA 1105, 1108–1109; 38 LA 655, 657; 37 LA 1001, 1003; 34 LA 678, 681; 22 LA 841; 22 LA 835, 837. Also see 41 LA 1144, 1146, where the employee was required to work outside in cold weather.

[54] See 48 LA 1291, 1295–1296; 38 LA 375, 378; 61-2 ARB ¶8394; 31 LA 699, 701. Also see 49 LA 429, 430–431. In United States Steel Corp., 55 LA 61, 62–64 (Dybeck, 1970), an employee could not be punished for refusing to remove a dust respirator while attending a required safety meeting, there being tobacco smoke in the room.

[55] Wilcolator Co., 44 LA 847, 852 (Altieri, 1964).

[56] See 48 LA 1343, 1344; 47 LA 332, 335.

[57] Gallis Mfg. Co., LA 75, 79 (Wood, 1966).

[58] See, for example, Arbitrator Stouffer in 53 LA 45, 55; Kallenbach in 48 LA

Where the employee has refused to cross a picket line of another union due to alleged fear of harm, arbitrators have held such refusal unjustified unless based upon a "reasonable fear of violence."[59]

Defective equipment is another source of employee claims of safety or health hazard.[60] In this regard, it has been observed that the mere fact that defective equipment is operated without accident for some period of time does not mean that there was actually no danger at all.[61] The arbitrator further noted that "any insurance actuarian will state that a hazard which persists long enough has an ever-increasing curve of expectation as to whether a loss will occur."[62]

Lack of experience or training on a job has been another basis for employee complaints of hazard. Thus, it has been held that while an assignment would not normally constitute an unsafe condition for those employees who were trained and experienced in the work, the task could be unsafe and an abnormal hazard where the employees are untrained or inexperienced.[63]

The co-worker's carelessness has been advanced as a reason for refusal of an assignment; an arbitrator's finding that a fellow employee was an unsafe driver was held to be justification for the grievant's refusal to ride with him.[64]

1291, 1295–1296; Duff in 46 LA 920, 922; Anrod in 38 LA 375, 378; Stutz in 22 LA 841; Smith in 22 LA 835, 837. Where the plant was in fact too cold to work in safety, the employees could not be punished for walking off the job. Muter Co., 47 LA 332, 335–336 (DiLeone, 1966); Berger Steel Co., 46 LA 1131, 1136 (Goldberg, 1966); Consider H. Willett, Inc., 38 LA 655, 657 (Cabe, 1962). Also see NLRB vs. Washington Aluminum Co., 82 S. Ct. 1099 (1962).

[59] Gulf Coast Motor Lines, Inc., 49 LA 261, 262–263 (Williams, 1967). Similarly, Arbitrator Seidenberg in 45 LA 522, 523. In Phillips Pipe Line Co., 54 LA 1019, 1024 (Davey, 1970), a contractual safety clause was construed only to cover safety on the job—it did not apply to a picket line situation. In an "interests" case, the arbitrator prescribed protection to be afforded by a telephone company to its employees assigned to work in designated urban areas in which they reasonably fear they are in personal danger of criminal or physical attack. New York Telephone Co., 50 LA 21, 23–24 (McFadden, 1968).

[60] See Arbitrator Hopson in 48 LA 788, 796; Garrett in 45 LA 426, 429; Sembower in 41 LA 666, 670–671; Luskin in 34 LA 504, 506.

[61] A. M. Castle & Co., 41 LA 666, 671 (Sembower, 1963).

[62] Ibid.

[63] Bethlehem Steel Corp., 49 LA 1203, 1206 (Strongin, 1968).

[64] U.S. Plywood-Champion Papers, Inc., 50 LA 115, 123–124 (Jenkins, 1968). Cf. W. P. Fuller & Co., 32 LA 545, 547–548 (Cobb, 1959).

Physical or Mental Condition as a Safety Hazard

Physical or mental conditions giving rise to employer action on safety grounds are varied, including, for example, epilepsy,[65] Parkinson's disease,[66] heart condition,[67] obesity,[68] fainting spells,[69] visual problems,[70] mental disability,[71] diabetes,[72] physical incapacity,[73] and pregnancy.[74] Arbitral disposition of such cases depends mainly upon medical evidence and evidence concerning safety aspects of grievant's condition as it relates to his work.

Management Action: Transfer, Demotion, Layoff, and Termination

The prevailing view of arbitrators would appear to be that management has not only the right but also the responsibility to take corrective action when an employee has a physical or mental disability which endangers his own safety or that of others. Such action may take the form of transfer, demotion, layoff or even termination, depending upon the extent and nature of the employee's disability as well as upon other factors such as the availability of another job which he would be capable of performing.[75]

---

[65] See Arbitrator Morris in 53 LA 578, 583; Gorsuch in 45 LA 616, 620; Murphy in 44 LA 1252, 1263; Hale in 40 LA 18, 26–28; May in 38 LA 1049, 1054; Petree in 38 LA 829, 838; Roberts in 38 LA 826, 828–829; McCoy in 37 LA 503, 505–506. For a discussion of earlier cases, see Florey, "Medical Separation of Epileptics," 17 Arb. J. 175 (1962).

[66] See Arbitrator Tripp in 64-1 ARB ¶8026; Stouffer in 38 LA 156, 160–161.

[67] See Arbitrator Boles in 43 LA 734, 739–740; Rubin in 41 LA 337, 339; Valtin in 39 LA 918, 920–921; Cahn in 62–3 ARB ¶8803 and in 61–3 ARB ¶8747.

[68] See Arbitrator Block in 48 LA 2, 9–10; Kates in 43 LA 61, 63–64; Scheiber in 41 LA 278, 284; Donnelly in 37 LA 456, 458.

[69] See Hughes Aircraft Co., 41 LA 535, 541–544 (Block, 1963).

[70] See Arbitrator Dworkin in 66–3 ARB ¶8999; Scheiber in 41 LA 278, 284; Lande in 40 LA 799, 804–805; Williams in 61–3 ARB ¶8657.

[71] See Arbitrator Dworkin in 45 LA 377, 383, and in 45 LA 384, 387; Guthrie in 38 LA 297, 299–300; Mueller in 37 LA 629, 633–634; Kelliher in 37 LA 175, 176.

[72] See E. W. Bliss Co., 43 LA 217, 223–224 (Klein, 1964).

[73] See Arbitrator Emery in 49 LA 403, 404–405 (leg injury); Luskin in 48 LA 649, 650–653 (back trouble); Florey in 41 LA 597, 598 (impaired sight, hearing, and balance after having had meningitis); Reid in 37 LA 126, 128 (one leg amputated as a result of diabetes).

[74] See Arbitrator Wallen in 47 LA 1135, 1141; Sembower in 38 LA 632, 638–639.

[75] See cases cited in this topic hereinbelow. An important aspect of physical or mental disability cases is the evidence adduced at the hearing. In this regard, see Chapter 8, topic titled "Medical Evidence." For other related discussion, see Chapter 13, topic titled "Disqualifying Employees for Physical or Mental Reasons."

Thus, where an employee sustained a handicap which created a hazard to himself and others in his work, the arbitrator upheld the company's action in transferring him to a different job which he was capable of performing without undue hazard.[76] Such action has been upheld even though the transfer was tantamount to a demotion.[77] However, arbitrators appear reluctant to *require* management, where not obligated by the contract, to offer a disabled employee another, less hazardous job even if it is available,[78] or to create one for him.[79]

When an employee has been on medical leave of absence, the arbitrator may on safety grounds uphold the company's refusal to recall him; but the arbitrator may also rule that if the employee's condition improves in the future so that there would no longer be a safety hazard, he may then seek return to work.[80] For example, in a case involving an employee seeking reinstatement following extended sick leave because of recurrence of his mental illness, Arbitrator Harry J. Dworkin stated:

"* * * An employee who is mentally ill to the point that his employment presents abnormal risks to management and to his fellow employees is obviously not entitled to be returned to his job. A determination that such conditions exist does not forclose reconsideration and reappraisal upon subsequent change in the employee's condition. An employee who is physically or mentally ill may not be forever condemned to be deprived of the right to employment; when the conditions have changed so as to require re-evaluation of the existence of a legitimate reason or basis for denial of employment, he is entitled to further consideration."[81]

---

[76] American Zinc Co., 46 LA 645, 652–654 (Abernethy, 1966); United States Steel Corp., 64–1 ARB ¶8026 (Tripp, 1963).

[77] See Arbitrator Murphy in 44 LA 1252, 1263; Tripp in 64–1 ARB ¶8026. Also see Abernethy in 46 LA 645, 647, 654. For related discussion, see Chapter 13, topic titled "Demotion of Employees."

[78] See Arbitrator Doyle in 49 LA 535, 540; Boles in 43 LA 734, 739–740; Reid in 37 LA 126, 128, and in 34 LA 681, 685. Also see Scheiber in 41 LA 278, 284. Cf., McNaughton in 50 LA 1277, 1279; Cahn in 62–3 ARB ¶8803; Donnelly, Curry & Clark in 20 LA 266, 268.

[79] See Arbitrator Belcher in 52 LA 1152, 1154; Rubin in 41 LA 337, 339; Feinberg in 40 LA 1254, 1258; Hale in 40 LA 18, 26–28. Also see Short in 38 LA 1076, 1083–1084.

[80] See Arbitrator Kates in 43 LA 61, 64–65; Florey in 41 LA 597, 598; Stouffer in 38 LA 156, 160–161.

[81] Ashtabula Bow Socket Co., 45 LA 377, 383 (1965), where he directed further examination of the grievant by an "impartial" psychiatrist; in a supplemental award, 45 LA 384, 387, he reinstated the grievant following such examination but retained jurisdiction of the case for an additional six months "during

Similarly, where an employee has been laid off because there is no available work which he could safely perform due to his physical condition, the arbitrator may approve the continuation of his layoff status subject to his being recalled to a job which may become available in the future and which his seniority and ability may warrant.[82]

Many arbitrators have held that an employee's physical or mental disability may constitute just cause for his termination "if the disability is of such kind and degree as to make unduly hazardous to himself or to others his employment in any job in his employer's facility which he is qualified to fill and which is available to be assigned to him."[83]

Protecting the Employee Himself

In some cases, a prime objective in denying an employee's request for reinstatement in his former job was to protect the employee himself from possible danger even though he was willing to undertake the risk.[84] But in others, the arbitrator stated either that he lacked the authority or that the employer lacked the right to prevent the employee from endangering his life.[85]

---

which period he will be authorized to consider any problems which may arise concerning grievant's employment following his reinstatement."
[82] Glass Container Mfrs. Institute, 66–3 ARB ¶8999 (Dworkin, 1966); Hughes Aircraft Co., 41 LA 535, 541–544 (Block, 1963).
[83] Stauffer Chemical Co., 40 LA 18, 26 (Hale, 1963). Similary, Arbitrator Luskin in 48 LA 649, 650–653; Block in 48 LA 2, 9–10; Stashower in 45 LA 464, 465–466; Rubin in 41 LA 337, 339; May in 38 LA 1049, 1054; Roberts in 38 LA 826, 828–829; Mueller in 37 LA 629, 633–634; McCoy in 37 LA 503, 505–506; Kelliher in 37 LA 175, 176; Reid in 37 LA 126, 128; Merrill in 20 LA 480, 481. Also see Cahn in 42 LA 1042, 1043; Lande in 40 LA 799, 804.
[84] See Arbitrator Luskin in 48 LA 649, 653; Abernethy in 46 LA 645, 653; Block in 41 LA 535, 543; Hale in 40 LA 18, 26–28; Roberts in 38 LA 826, 828–829; Reid in 37 LA 126, 128. In Warner & Swazey Co., 53 LA 643, 644–645 (High, 1969), the arbitrator upheld an employer's refusal to permit an employee to come to work with a splint on his finger because the condition created a safety hazard to the employee.
[85] Arketex Ceramic Corp., 50 LA 1171, 1175–1176 (Seinsheimer, 1967), where the arbitrator ruled, however, that the company could properly discharge the employee (afflicted with silicosis) and rehire him in a nonunit job in order to protect itself from increased insurance premiums; Interwoven Stocking Co., 39 LA 918, 920–921 (Valtin, 1962), where the arbitrator decided that the evidence did not support a finding that termination of grievant (who had had four heart attacks) was necessary in the best interests of the company and that under the contract neither the arbitrator nor the company could decide for the grievant whether he should risk shortening his life by return to work. Cf. Cahn in 61–3 ARB ¶8747.

CHAPTER 17

EMPLOYEE RIGHTS AND BENEFITS

Over the years, the give and take between management and employees has resulted in the establishment of certain employee rights and benefits (such as paid vacations and paid holidays) which are covered by the agreement or which evolved out of a well-established practice. Other rights may be asserted by employees which are more personal in nature and which are less firmly established or not recognized at all in labor-management relations. These asserted personal rights often are indirectly brought to the fore when management enforces a plant rule (such as one dealing with personal appearance), or when management disciplines an employee for refusing to obey a management directive issued pursuant to some contractual right (such as a work-scheduling clause under which the company schedules Sunday work), or when a grievance is filed charging that management has violated some provision of the agreement (such as a maintenance-of-practices clause).

Many employee rights are reflected and sometimes extensively treated in other chapters of this book. Various other employee rights or asserted rights not dealt with elsewhere are collected and discussed in the present chapter. By the same token, not all subjects in this chapter involve employee rights alone. Management, too, has rights and privileges pertaining to these subjects.

As can be readily recognized, in any given area of labor-management relations there may be claim and counterclaim of rights. However, it must also be recognized that many of the asserted employee rights relate more to "the area of traditional and conventional management discretion" concerning operations and production than to "employee rights not so intimately connected with the production process."[1] Thus, while discussion of employee rights in this chapter neces-

---

[1] Eastern Air Lines, Inc., 44 LA 1034, 1040 (Yagoda, 1965).

sarily includes a discussion of management rights, all of the subjects involve considerations which may be of great personal interest to individual employees.

Vacations

Employees have no inherent right to vacations; rather, vacation rights arise out of the contract.[2] Employees, of course, are interested in vacations not only for the rest and relaxation derived from such periods away from work but also for the pay received. The company is also said to have an interest, aside from immediate production needs, in employee vacations. Thus, as stated by Arbitrator Marlin M. Volz:

> "Vacations are for the mutual benefit of employees and employers. The employee who returns to work after a period of rest and relaxation and who has had some free time with his family and to tend to personal affairs is a more valuable man to his employer. * * * A vacation is also one of the economic attractions which a Company offers to its employees to remain on the payroll or to become employees. While a vacation may be regarded as earned or deferred compensation, it may also be considered as an investment by the Company in promoting the longevity of service of its employees and a more productive working force."[3]

Scheduling Vacations

From the employee's standpoint, his right to take his vacation "at a time personally selected is a valuable right";[4] but it is a right that is limited by considerations of business needs. Herein lies the conflict that is reflected in the great number of arbitration cases on scheduling vacations.

It is said that "one of the prerogatives of management [is] to schedule vacations at such time as best meets the needs of the business," and that "in doing so the employer will very often and perhaps

---

[2] See Dover Corp., 48 LA 965, 968 (Volz, 1966); Modecraft Co., 44 LA 1045, 1049 (Jaffee, 1965).

[3] Dover Corp., 48 LA 965, 969 (1966).

[4] Welch Grape Juice Co., 48 LA 1018, 1021 (Altrock, 1967). The length of permitted vacation may be affected by the time when it is taken. See R. D. Werner Company, 55 LA 303, 305 (Kates, 1970), holding that increased vacation benefits under a new contract were not retroactive where the new contract did not expressly provide for retroactivity for employees who had already taken their vacation for the year.

wherever possible also try to do his utmost to meet the wishes of employees."[5] Arbitrator Harold W. Davey elaborated:

"Absent specific contract language, it is generally understood in industrial relations practice that a vacation is an earned equity and is generally to be taken in terms of the employee's preference, subject to the exigencies of the Company's production and maintenance requirements. Where the contract is silent on the specific policy or procedure to be followed, it must be assumed that the employee will request his vacation at a time suitable to his own preferences and that his preferences will be honored to the degree that Company requirements will permit. However, where the contract is silent, it must also be assumed that managerial discretion is greater than in those cases where contract language puts the burden on management to show need for the employee to take his vacation at a particular time, or not to take vacation at a particular time."[6]

Operational Needs—Whether management is given the right by the agreement or possesses it as a residual power, the right to schedule vacations should be exercised with certain considerations in mind. The needs of the business and the maintenance of production are important considerations in vacation scheduling.[7] For instance, under an agreement permitting employees to select their vacation dates whenever practicable, management was permitted to schedule vacations at such times as would not interfere with its operations or increase its costs.[8] Similarly, under a clause providing that "the vacation period shall be selected by the employees by departments in the order of their seniority," but where the contract also reserved exclusively to management the "disposition and number of the working forces," it was held that the vacation desires of the employees should be honored to the extent that this would not unreasonably interfere with orderly plant operations.[9]

---

[5] Sinclair Refining Co., 12 LA 183, 189 (Klamon, 1949). Arbitrator Klamon reiterated (as dictum) this inherent right in Heil Packing Co., 36 LA 454, 458 (1961). Also see Tenneco Chemicals, Inc., 51 LA 699, 701 (Williams, 1968).

[6] Hubinger Co., 29 LA 459, 461 (1957).

[7] See General Cable Corp., 48 LA 1000, 1004 (Kelliher, 1967). For cases dealing with the special problems involved in scheduling extended vacations, see Arbitrator McDaniel in 53 LA 264, 265–266; Strongin in 46 LA 702, 704; Kates in 45 LA 120, 124–125; Tongue in 44 LA 475, 478–479; C. McDermott in 44 LA 906, 909–910; Garrett in 43 LA 790, 795–797 (listing 7 factors to be considered in scheduling EV's); T. McDermott in 42 LA 1002, 1007–1008.

[8] Sinclair Refining Co., 12 LA 183, 190 (Klamon, 1949); National Tube Co., 19 LA 330, 331 (Garrett, 1952). Also see Arbitrator Livengood in 30 LA 225, 229; McKelvey in 25 LA 94, 98. Cf., Emory in 17 LA 461, 462.

[9] Carling Brewing Co., 46 LA 715, 717–718 (Kates, 1966).

However, management may be required to justify denying an employee his preferred vacation time.[10] Thus, under a contract providing that "Vacations will, so far as possible, be granted at times most desired by employees," reserving to the company "the final right to allot vacation periods * * * in order to insure the orderly operation of the plants," it was held that the grievant was improperly denied his choice of vacation time since, contrary to management's contentions, there was available another employee who had been trained to fill the position, and hence there would have been no interference with the "orderly operation of the plants."[11]

Justification was shown under a similar contract clause with the result that the employer could deny the right to take vacations during summer months where business forecasts indicated that work would be at its "peak."[12]

Under an employee preference clause, one arbitrator ruled that management could not reserve certain weeks exclusively for foremen's vacations since the presence of such preference clause in the contract "obligates the Company to give priority to employees' preferences over the foremen's choices where the two conflict, so long as there is no problem about the 'orderly and efficient operation of the plant.' "[13]

In another case, the parties had a practice of having a one-week vacation shutdown, but the grievant was entitled by contract to a second week of vacation. The parties had no established practice and the company had no policy in regard to the second week. Although the contract was silent as to the scheduling of vacations, the arbitrator stated that the company's discretion was limited by the vacation clause according grievant two weeks, which clause could not be "frustrated by arbitrary and unreasonable denial of employee preferences," and that grievant's preference for his second week of vacation should be

---

[10] See Arbitrator Tongue in 44 LA 475, 477, citing many cases; Gill in 36 LA 488, 490; Valtin in 30 LA 899, 900.

[11] United States Steel Corp., 53 LA 222, 224 (McDermott, 1969). Similarly, New York Ship-Building Corp., 43 LA 854, 855–856 (Crawford, 1964). But it has been held that management is not required to recall laid-off employees in order to accommodate vacation preferences. Bethlehem Steel Co., 39 LA 673, 675 (Gill, 1962).

[12] Westinghouse Electric Corp., 40 LA 972, 974 (Cahn, 1963).

[13] Air Reduction Chemical & Carbide Co., 42 LA 1192, 1195 (Kesselman, 1964), distinguishing Armstrong Cork Co., 37 LA 21, 23 (Williams, 1961), on the basis of strong contract language giving management the right to designate vacation time.

granted unless an "adequate reason relating to the operational and production needs of the Company" could be shown.[14]

Where operational needs have been established, arbitrators have permitted management to limit the number of employees who could be on vacation at the same time.[15] But another arbitrator rejected both the company's limit and the union's demand—rather he stated a procedure for determining in a flexible manner the number of men to be on vacation at a given time.[16]

Vacation Shutdown—Umpire Harry Shulman pointed out that some correlation between vacations and what otherwise would be layoffs is not only permissible but also desirable.[17] Under an agreement giving management the right to schedule vacations, the scheduling of vacations to coincide with temporary shutdowns was permitted.[18] There are limitations, however. For instance, where an agreement gave management the right to schedule vacations subject to the requirement that "due consideration" be given to employees' wishes, Umpire Shulman, distinguishing temporary and indefinite layoff, ruled that management could not require employees to take their vacations during a period of indefinite layoff where to do so would destroy the substantive features of a vacation. He reasoned:

> "A vacation is a period of rest between periods of work. A layoff is a period of anxiety and hardship between periods of work. The tremendous difference lies in the assurance of the vacationer that he will return to work at the end of his vacation and the equal assurance

---

[14] National Lock Co., 48 LA 588, 590–591 (Volz, 1967).

[15] See Arbitrator Gilden in 46 LA 887, 890; Seward in 36 LA 584, 585–586. In Reynolds Metals Co., 44 LA 475, 476–477 (Tongue, 1965), the company's limit was raised by the arbitrator. In Laclede Steel Co., 54 LA 506, 507–508 (Kelliher, 1970), management could schedule vacations on an equal basis over the full year and thus eliminate the "summer bulge" of vacations.

[16] Carling Brewing Co., 46 LA 715, 717–718 (Kates, 1966). Also see Mansfield Tire & Rubber Co., 32 LA 762, 766–767 (Shaw, 1959), where the arbitrator was requested to and did formulate a procedure to be followed in scheduling vacations.

[17] Ford Motor Co., 3 LA 829, 831 (1946).

[18] Sefton Fibre Can Co., 12 LA 101, 105 (Townsend, 1948). Also permitting vacation shutdowns, see Arbitrator Feller in 52 LA 257, 259; Williams in 51 LA 699, 700–701 (involving a vacation clause giving management strong rights in the final allocation of vacation periods), and in 39 LA 659, 660–661; Whitton in 39 LA 149, 150–151 (emphasizing the necessity of showing production requirements); Jaffee in 37 LA 458, 464; Livengood in 30 LA 225, 231. Cf., Continental Can Co., 35 LA 836, 840 (Miller, 1960). In Wyman-Gordon Co., 51 LA 561, 565 (Rauch, 1968), past practice strongly supported the two-week vacation shutdown.

of the employee on layoff that he does not know when he will return to work. The basic difference, with its financial, emotional, and psychological implications, is not obliterated by a form of words or by the receipt of income for a part of the indefinite period of layoff."[19]

Other arbitrators have held that, where the contract provides that the employer is to consider the requests of individual employees for particular vacation times, the company may not order a vacation shutdown, since to schedule such a vacation would be to fail to take into account the desires of individual employees as required by contract.[20] However, under "clear, precise, unequivocal" contract language simply stating that "Vacations are to be granted as designated by the Management of the Company," with no reservations, restrictions, or limitations in favor of employee desires, it was held that the company had the right to designate a two-week vacation shutdown.[21]

A vacation shutdown does not necessarily exclude the performance of all work in the plant. Thus, where the contract permitted a two-week vacation shutdown, it was held that the shutdown need not be "total" but that the employer could work employees on essential maintenance, limited receiving and shipping, and limited clerical payroll functions.[22]

Vacation Period Fixed by Contract—Where the agreement fixes the period for taking vacations, the employer has been held not entitled to designate in addition any other vacation period.[23] Employees, too,

---

[19] Ford Motor Co., 3 LA 829, 831 (1946). Cf., Westinghouse Electric Corp., 45 LA 131, 140 (Hebert, 1965). As to scheduling vacations for employees who are already on layoff, see United States Steel Corp., 36 LA 603, 615–616 (Garrett, 1961). In Kentile Floors, Inc., 55 LA 808, 812–813 (Cyrol, 1970), the employees had started applying for unemployment compensation during plant shutdown periods, thus adding to costs; the arbitrator upheld management's right to schedule vacations during plant shutdown.

[20] See Arbitrator Altrock in 48 LA 1018, 1021 (opinion reinforced by past practice); Nichols in 42 LA 1321, 1325–1326; Sembower in 38 LA 389, 392–395 (distinguishing the Shulman award in 3 LA 829); Manson in 35 LA 921, 923–924; Valtin in 35 LA 535, 538–539, and in 33 LA 772, 774; Eckhardt in 32 LA 913, 916–917; Wolff in 32 LA 776, 781; Seward in 30 LA 992, 994; Kelliher in 18 LA 934, 935. Cf., Smith in 15 LA 568, 572–573. But see Williams in 39 LA 1108, 1111; Schmidt in 34 LA 693, 697–698; Garrett in 19 LA 330, 331.

[21] Wisconsin Bridge & Iron Co., 46 LA 993, 1004–1005 (Solomon, 1966). A like result was reached in Vogt Mfg. Corp., 44 LA 488, 489–490 (Sarachan, 1965), where the contract had no provision as to scheduling vacations.

[22] General Cable Corp., 48 LA 1000, 1004 (Kelliher, 1967).

[23] Cone Mills, 29 LA 346, 350 (McCoy, 1957). Cf. General American Transportation Co., 15 LA 481, 484 (Kelliher, 1950). Nor may the employer pay vacation pay to laid-off employees prior to the contractually agreed vacation

have been confined to the fixed vacation period. Thus, under a contract which entitled employees with a year's service to a paid vacation, the employee who completed his year's service after the end of the vacation period fixed by contract was required to wait until the following vacation season to take his vacation.[24]

The contract may state specific requirements for the posting of vacation schedules. Strictly construing such a contract, one arbitrator held improper a notice posted two days after the deadline date and reached the "equitable" solution of setting the vacation period to be the same as in prior years.[25]

Remedy for Forced Vacations—What remedy can be applied by the arbitrator when the company has improperly scheduled and "forced" vacations? One arbitrator awarded "damages" by requiring the company to give the grievants another week's vacation with pay;[26] another awarded another week's vacation but refused to duplicate vacation pay.[27] Another arbitrator, finding that he could not "assign a monetary value to grievants' mental discomfort," refused to grant additional pay in view of the company's good-faith belief that the agreement permitted its action (which apparently had been unchallenged by the union in previous years); but he warned that the company was now on notice and could in the future be required to give the aggrieved employee "either a further vacation on the proper dates or pay-in-lieu thereof."[28]

Vacation Benefits: Deferred Wages or "Refresher"?

Perhaps the confusion of theories as to whether vacations are refreshers or deferred wages can best be approached from the historical view, namely, that originally a vacation was a gratuity "awarded" to faithful employees for past services and to "refresh" them for future

---

period, in view of the practical impact of such action upon the employees' entitlement to unemployment compensation, S.U.B. benefits, and vacations within the agreed period as required by contract. See United States Steel Corp., 36 LA 113, 116 (Garrett, 1961).

[24] Kent of Grand Rapids, Inc., 18 LA 160, 162–163 (Platt, 1952); General Cable Corp., 18 LA 44, 45–46 (Cahn, 1952).

[25] Interstate Industries Inc., 46 LA 879, 881 (Howlett, 1966).

[26] Scovil Mfg. Co., 31 LA 646, 651 (Jaffee, 1958). Also see Arbitrator Valtin in 37 LA 821, 824; Gill in 37 LA 134, 139 (also involving unemployment benefits); Garrett in 33 LA 82, 84.

[27] Chrysler Corp., 32 LA 776, 781 (Wolff, 1959). Also see Arbitrator Sembower in 38 LA 389, 395; Fleming in 31 LA 37, 41.

[28] Bethlehem Steel Co., 31 LA 857, 858 (Seward, 1958). Also see Arbitrator Williams in 39 LA 1051, 1057; Valtin in 33 LA 772, 775.

service. As the collective bargaining process has evolved, vacations and vacation benefits (while still providing rest and relaxation) have become more and more the subjects of bargaining and as such are considered and included in the "wage package," or are at the least bargained against higher wages or other employee benefits. Indeed, vacation provisions often are included in the wage section of the agreement.[29] The so-called trend in decisions toward considering such benefits deferred wages which vest in the employee is the result of recognition of the industrial-relations fact that the parties themselves have bargained for and made vacation benefits a part of the agreement. It is therefore, as usual, to the contract and its bargaining history that one must turn in order to ascertain the status of vacation benefits.[30]

Even though vacation rights may vest in the employee, entitlement to such rights is not absolute but may require compliance with conditions of the agreement such as a minimum length of service (for example, requiring 52 full weeks of employment),[31] or being on the payroll as of a particular date.[32]

The question of vesting of vacation rights has been raised in situations of plant closure or sale of the business,[33] voluntary quit or retire-

---

[29] See, for example, Infant Socks, Inc., 51 400, 402 (Moberly, 1968).

[30] For discussion of various aspects of these and other related concepts and/or collections of cases, see Arbitrator Murphy in 52 LA 837, 839–840; Moberly in 51 LA 400, 402–403; Doyle in 51 LA 349, 350–351; Cox in 49 LA 837, 838–839; Volz in 48 LA 965, 968–969, and in 34 LA 170, 172; McDermott in 43 LA 860, 862; Larkin in 41 LA 513, 514; Cheney in 38 LA 737, 739; Brown in 35 LA 560, 565; Hogan in 34 LA 158, 163–165; Reid in 33 LA 316, 318; Wirtz in 32 LA 156, 168–169; Feinberg, "Do Contract Rights Vest?", Labor Arbitration and Industrial Change 194–205 (BNA Incorporated, 1963).

[31] Great Atlantic & Pacific Tea Co., 43 LA 1, 2 (Turkus, 1964). Also see Arbitrator Moberly in 51 LA 400, 403; Singer in 49 LA 895, 897; Cox in 49 LA 837, 838; Doyle in 39 LA 489, 491; Cheney in 38 LA 737, 739–740; Brown in 35 LA 560, 565; Ross in 33 LA 837, 840.

[32] Barg & Foster, Inc., 53 LA 692, 692–693 (Seitz, 1969). Also see Arbitrator Gilden in 49 LA 646, 648; Davis in 48 LA 938, 940; Turkus in 42 LA 1332, 1334; Doyle in 39 LA 489, 491; Jaffee in 28 LA 838, 841 (who found that because of the plant closure employees' failure to be at work on the eligibility date was not attributable to them). Many arbitrators have found under the particular contract that the "eligibility date" simply is a "cut-off date" for computing vacation pay, and is not a condition precedent for entitlement to vacation benefits. See, for example, Arbitrator Murphy in 52 LA 837, 840; Moberly in 51 LA 400, 403; Markowitz in 38 LA 912, 915; Brown in 35 LA 560, 565; Hogan in 34 LA 158, 163.

[33] In these cases, arbitrators speak in terms of vacation rights as deferred earnings which have vested in the employee; in some instances they point out that vacation pay is by contract based upon the employee's earnings. See Arbitrator

ment by the employee,[34] or death of the employee.[35] In such cases, where the vacation has been fully earned and the employee has fully met all the conditions required by the contract, arbitrators are in general agreement that vacation benefits must be held to have vested in the employee; but where he has not met such conditions, he has been denied vacation benefits.[36]

Strikes as Affecting Vacation Benefits

In the absence of contract language requiring a different result, arbitrators are disinclined to permit employees to benefit in the accrual of vacation credits during time spent on strike, since vacation benefits as deferred wages are part of the pay received for *working* for the company. Arbitrator Marion Beatty has stated:

> "The employer does not reward employees for being absent on strike, but if the Union's position is upheld in this case, the employers will be required to accord these employees vacation pay for time they did not work. The employers here feel aggrieved for being asked, in effect, to subsidize the strike."[37]

The effect of strikes on vacation credits is rarely treated in the contract[38] and is seldom directly covered in the strike settlement agree-

---

Moberly in 51 LA 400, 403; Doyle in 51 LA 349, 350; Reid in 49 LA 421, 422; Markowitz in 38 LA 912, 915; Brown in 35 LA 560, 564–565; Hogan in 34 LA 158, 163–165; Wirtz in 32 LA 156, 168–169.

[34] Where the employee has met contractual requirements prior to quit or retirement, he is entitled to vacation benefits. See Arbitrator Murphy in 52 LA 837, 839–841; Cox in 49 LA 837, 838–839; Altieri in 42 LA 1209, 1211–1213. But where the employee has not met contractual requirements, such as employment on a particular date, he is not entitled to vacation pay. See Arbitrator Seitz in 53 LA 692, 692–693; Gilden in 49 LA 646, 648; Doyle in 39 LA 489, 491. Also see Kabaker in 54 LA 66, 68; Volz in 48 LA 965, 969.

[35] Where the employee has met contractual requirements before death, there is no forfeiture of vacation benefits. See Arbitrator Feinberg in 46 LA 1129, 1130–1131; T. McDermott in 43 LA 860, 862–863; Larkin in 41 LA 513, 515; C. McDermott in 40 LA 1308, 1310–1311; Crane in 38 LA 479, 481. The result was different where strict contract language required employment on an entitlement date. See Arbitrator Erbs in 54 LA 232, 235–236; Davis in 48 LA 938, 940; Seward in 47 LA 258, 259–260; Turkus in 42 LA 1332, 1333–1334. Cf., Kreimer in 44 LA 126, 127.

[36] See citations in the two preceding footnotes.

[37] Motor Car Dealers Assn. of Kansas City, 49 LA 55, 57 (1967), cited with approval by Arbitrator Gorsuch in 53 LA 784, 791. Where it was established to the arbitrator's satisfaction that under past practice vacation credits had been given in all prior strike situations, full vacation time was allowed in Mobil Oil Co., 42 LA 102, 105–106 (Forsythe, 1963), upheld in Local 7-644 OCAW v. Mobil Oil Co., 45 LA 512, 59 LRRM 2938 (CA 7, 1965). Past practice may also deny vacation credits. See Arbitrator Larkin in 42 LA 247, 249; Ross in 33 LA 837, 839.

[38] See Evening News Assn., 53 LA 170, 176 (Casselman, 1969).

ment. Unions have argued that the denial of vacation credits violates strike settlement agreements which require that no penalty be assessed against anyone participating in the strike. Arbitrators, however, have held that the denial of vacation credits where the contract relates such credits to time worked is not to be considered a penalty but is simply an application of the vacation provisions of the contract.[39]

Many cases turn on the question whether a strike is an "excused absence" so as to deprive (or not to deprive, depending upon contract language) employees of vacation credits. For instance, where the contract provided that vacation pay was to be computed on the basis of the employee's earnings for the year and allowing credit for time lost due to illness or other excused absence, it was held that a strike is not an excused absence.[40] Another arbitrator, where the contract provided for prorating vacation pay in case of sick leave or leave of absence, held that a strike "should be treated the same" as a leave of absence.[41] Both arbitrators thus reached the same end result of denying vacation credits for the strike period. The reluctance of arbitrators to credit strike time for vacation benefits in these cases is explained by Arbitrator Russell A. Smith:

"It would seem anomalous that the parties, had they specifically considered the matter, would have intended that working time lost because of direct participation in a strike would be credited as service time whereas [the contract provides that] time lost on authorized leave of absence was not to be credited."[42]

Other cases have involved contracts basing vacation pay on some qualifying phrase such as "time worked,"[43] or "years of service,"[44]

---

[39] See Arbitrator Kates in 47 LA 319, 322; Larkin in 42 LA 247, 249; Smith in 27 LA 251, 255. But see Koven in 52 LA 169, 171, where the strike settlement agreement provided for "retroactivity" of fringe benefits.

[40] Motor Car Dealers Assn. of Kansas City, 49 LA 55, 58 (Beatty, 1967). Also see Arbitrator Wolf in 49 LA 1182, 1185 (discussing the nature of a strike); Smith in 27 LA 251, 254–255. Cf., Ford Motor Co., 33 LA 638, 639–640 (Platt, 1959), involving a somewhat unusual "company policy statement."

[41] Richland Shale Brick Co., 49 LA 113, 117 (Seinsheimer, 1966). Similarly, Arbitrator Smith in 48 LA 213, 217–219; Kates in 47 LA 319, 322; Seligson in 42 LA 929, 930–931, also holding that the company could not adjust the vacation eligibility date by the number of days lost due to a lockout since a lockout is a "voluntary matter" on the employer's part which "prevented the employees from working and accruing the 'continuous' service required by the contract" for vacation eligibility. But see Arbitrator Dworkin in 40 LA 689, 696; Wood in 34 LA 428, 431; both involving different contract language.

[42] Vindicator Printing Co., 48 LA 213, 219 (1966).

[43] Modecraft Co., 38 LA 1236, 1239 (Dall, 1961).

[44] Great Atlantic & Pacific Tea Co., 43 LA 1, 2 (Turkus, 1964).

or "continuous service,"[45] or "employment" by the company,[46] or being "in the employ" of the company,[47] or "scheduled working days."[48] These phrases have been interpreted as requiring the actual rendition of services for vacation eligibility, and as excluding time spent on strike. Thus, a distinction must be made between the bare retention of employment status and the actual performance of services which fulfill eligibility requirements.[49]

Layoff as Affecting Vacation Benefits

Where employees have met eligibility requirements and their vacations have been earned prior to layoff, they have been held to be entitled to vacation benefits in full if fully earned,[50] or on a prorata basis if partially earned,[51] the rationale being that vacation pay is in the nature of additional wages. However, where the laid-off employees were found not to have met the contract's eligibility requirements, they were held not entitled to any vacation benefits.[52]

Sick Leave as Affecting Vacation Benefits

Where the two benefits arose under different contract provisions and were separate and distinct, it was held that the employee should receive both his vacation pay and his sick pay.[53] Similarly, under a contract providing for both vacation and sickness benefits, employees who were on sick leave when the employer closed the plant for a vacation period were held entitled to receive their sickness benefits and to select a different time for their vacations.[54]

---

[45] Evening News Assn., 53 LA 170, 175 (Casselman, 1969). Also see Arbitrator Seligson in 42 LA 929, 931. Cf., Wood in 34 LA 428, 431.
[46] Union Carbide Corp., 49 LA 1180, 1181 (Cahn, 1967); Vickers, Inc., 27 LA 251, 254–255 (Smith, 1956).
[47] San Bruno Sportservice, Inc., 33 LA 837, 838–839 (Ross, 1959).
[48] Lord Mfg. Co., 47 LA 319, 321 (Kates, 1966). Cf., Arbitrator Platt in 33 LA 638, 639–640.
[49] See San Bruno Sportservice, Inc., 33 LA 837, 839 (Ross, 1959), citing and quoting from Safeway Stores, Inc., 22 LA 466, 469 (Hildebrand, 1954); Vickers, Inc., 27 LA 251, 254–255 (Smith, 1956).
[50] See Arbitrator Lugar in 40 LA 129, 131–135, citing and discussing many cases; Reid in 33 LA 316, 318–319; Howlett in 32 LA 278, 282–283 (relying in part on principles of equity).
[51] See Arbitrator Cheney in 38 LA 737, 739–740; Volz in 34 LA 170, 172 (citing cases); Knowlton in 33 LA 428, 431 (permanent layoff). Also see Turkus in 43 LA 1, 2.
[52] See Arbitrator McCoy in 39 LA 1240, 1241–1242; Cheney in 38 LA 737, 740; Caraway in 35 LA 717, 720–721; Pollack in 33 LA 477, 481–482 (permanent layoff).
[53] International Paper Co., 37 LA 1026, 1028–1029 (Bothwell, 1962).
[54] Toledo Scale Co., 25 LA 94, 99–100 (McKelvey, 1955); Derby Gas & Electric Co., 21 LA 745 at 745 (Donnelly, Mannino, & Mottram, 1953).

The earning of vacation credits during time spent on sick leave is another matter, however. Thus, it has been held that an employee who was on paid sick leave for a month was not entitled to vacation credits for the sick leave period, since vacation pay is earned by service; the "test should not be merely whether an employee is receiving payments from the employer," because all payments are "not necessarily 'pay' for the purpose of earning or accruing" vacation credits.[55]

Maternity Leave as Affecting Vacation Benefits

It has been held that time spent on maternity leave is not to be included in computing vacation pay since such leave is directed to job security and is not intended to extend to vacation eligibility.[56]

Holidays

Collective bargaining agreements customarily provide for pay for named holidays not worked.[57] The primary purpose of holiday pay provisions is to insure the employee against the possible loss in earnings when he does not work because of a holiday occurring during the work week.[58] Some contracts explicitly or by clear implication also include pay for holidays which fall on days when the employee would not have been scheduled to work, such as his regular day off or Saturday.[59]

---

[55] San Francisco Newspaper Publishers Assn., 46 LA 260, 262–264 (Burns, 1965). Also see Arbitrator Jaffee in 44 LA 1045, 1049; Reid in 37 LA 126, 129.

[56] American Enka Corp., 48 LA 989, 992 (Pigors, 1966). Also see Arbitrator Witney in 47 LA 272, 277; Gundermann in 39 LA 1270, 1273. Cf., Geissinger in 38 LA 1085, 1088, where ambiguous contract language and past practice resulted in a different award.

[57] For a checklist of various aspects of holiday pay which may be covered in the contract, see Smith, Merrifield and Rothschild, Collective Bargaining and Labor Arbitration 690–691 (Bobbs-Merrill, 1970).

[58] Anaconda Aluminum Co., 48 LA 219, 223 (Allen, 1967). Similarly, see Arbitrator Dworkin in 51 LA 724, 728; Hill in 39 LA 500, 503; Updegraff in 37 LA 1009, 1010, and in 20 LA 323, 324; Pollack in 33 LA 477, 483. For discussion of the history of holiday pay provisions, see Arbitrator Killion in 37 LA 934, 940; Howard in 24 LA 667, 670–672 (also giving examples of types of clauses as well as discussion of work requirements). In R. Herschel Mfg. Co., 35 LA 826, 827 (Ruckel, 1960), the contract stated that the purpose of holiday pay is that no employee shall be deprived "of income he would have been able to earn."

[59] See Arbitrator Dworkin in 53 LA 1165, 1166; Kates in 45 LA 905, 907 (an "interests" arbitration); Goldstein in 43 LA 676, 677; Myers in 42 LA 269, 272; Koven in 40 LA 577, 581; Stark in 35 LA 788, 791–792; Caraway in 33 LA 494, 496; Howard in 24 LA 667, 671; Donnelly in 21 LA 325, 326. Cf. Anderson in 23 LA 392, 394; Seligson in 22 LA 806, 807; Jones in 21 LA 120, 122; Stutz in 21 LA 59, 60.

It is clear that "there is no inherent right to holiday pay, and none exists except as it may be set forth in the labor agreement."[60] As elaborated by Arbitrator Harry J. Dworkin:

> "The right to holiday pay is a creature of contract; it does not exist as a matter of law. To the extent that the parties have seen fit through the orderly process of collective bargaining to stipulate holiday benefits, employees that are covered are entitled to the full measure of the benefits that were bargained for in the contract. It necessarily follows that employees are not entitled to more than the contract provides, nor can contract benefits be expanded beyond the meaning warranted by the language used."[61]

Moreover, it has been declared that "A holiday pay provision is not a guarantee of additional earnings unless it contains specific language to that effect."[62]

When the contract does provide for holiday pay (which, as noted, is the usual practice), it is recognized that such pay is a "fringe benefit" earned by the employee; however, "it is conceived of as being earned by his working a specified qualifying period and also by working specified shifts at agreed time proximate to" the holiday as required by the contract.[63] Thus, while it is recognized as an earned benefit, holiday pay is usually conditioned upon the employee's compliance with contractually stated work requirements.

Work Requirements

Typical of holiday pay provisions are the work requirements upon which such pay is conditioned.[64] Thus, in order for the employee to be eligible for holiday pay, contracts commonly require both a stipulated minimum period of service and work on designated days surrounding the holiday. In the latter regard, the contract may require

---

[60] Gregory Galvanizing & Metal Processing, Inc., 46 LA 102, 105 (Kates, 1966).

[61] Lewall Sportswear Co., Inc., 53 LA 1165, 1169 (1969). To similar effect, see Arbitrator Hunter in 41 LA 991, 993, citing Shapiro in 25 LA 341, 342–343 (both discussing the background and purpose of holiday pay provisions).

[62] Sealtest Foods, 47 LA 868, 869 (Krinsky, 1966).

[63] Kennecott Copper Corp., 36 LA 507, 510 (Updegraff, 1960). Also see Arbitrator Klein in 48 LA 1101, 1102; Kelliher in 47 LA 582, 583; Dworkin in 36 LA 517, 521; Tischler in 33 LA 919, 921 (and cases cited); Tatum in 24 LA 517, 520.

[64] By far the greatest number of holiday pay arbitration cases are concerned with the various aspects of eligibility for such pay—compliance with work requirements, part day absence or tardiness before or after a holiday, and the effect on eligibility of layoff, leave, vacation or strike.

the employee to work *his* last scheduled day before and *his* first scheduled day after the holiday,[65] or the last *regularly* scheduled day before and the first *regularly* scheduled day after the holiday,[66] or the last *scheduled* work day before and the first *scheduled* after the holiday,[67] or the day before *and* the day after the holiday,[68] or the day before *or* the day after the holiday,[69] or the *scheduled full* workday of the plant before and after the holiday,[70] or a specified number of work days during the period before and after the holiday.[71]

The precise language used in the particular contract applied to the facts of a given case ordinarily determines whether holiday pay should be awarded. To illustrate, in the situation where the employee had been in lay-off before and after a holiday, Arbitrator Clarence M. Updegraff drew a distinction between (1) contract language requiring the employee to work on *his* last scheduled day before and *his* first scheduled day after the holiday, and (2) contract language requiring the employee to work on *the* last scheduled day before and *the* first scheduled day after the holiday. Under the first type of clause the employee "would seem to become entitled to the holiday pay upon the showing that he worked faithfully up to the time of the lay-off in which the holiday occurred and returned promptly to work in the first day after the end of the lay-off," while under the second type of clause "obviously he cannot work those days while he is on lay off" and thus would not be entitled to holiday pay.[72]

In a similar vein, Arbitrator Harry J. Dworkin has distinguished the phrase "regular workday" (which appeared in the holiday pay provision under consideration) from "scheduled workday," holding

---

[65] For example, see Arbitrator Jones in 53 LA 477, 478; Keefe in 52 LA 745, 746; Roberts in 48 LA 1281, 1283.

[66] For example, see Arbitrator Teple in 51 LA 481, 482; Davis in 51 LA 1309, at 1309; Klein in 48 LA 1101, at 1101.

[67] For example, see Arbitrator Kelliher in 47 LA 582, 583; Larson in 41 LA 83, 84; Anderson in 33 LA 890, 891. The contract may make a distinction between "scheduled" and "regularly scheduled" work. See Corhart Refractories Co., 47 LA 648, 649 (McCoy, 1966).

[68] For example, see Arbitrator Belsky in 44 LA 910, at 910; Larson in 38 LA 746, 747; McIntosh in 28 LA 693, at 693.

[69] See Young Spring & Wire Corp., 41 LA 991, 993 (Hunter, 1963).

[70] See Price-Pfister Brass Mfg. Co., 25 LA 398, 400 (Prasow, 1955).

[71] For example, see Arbitrator Allen in 48 LA 219, 220 ("actually works during the payroll week in which the holiday falls"); House in 47 LA 567, 568 (three scheduled work days out of five scheduled work days before and after the holiday); Updegraff in 36 LA 507, 508 (a minimum of two shifts during the work week in which the holiday occurs).

[72] Hemp & Co., 37 LA 1009, 1010 (1962), with many citations.

that employees who worked their regular workdays of Friday and Tuesday (surrounding Labor Day) were eligible for holiday pay even though they were scheduled for but did not work overtime on Saturday before the holiday.[73] But where the contract required the employee to work the last "scheduled" workday before and the first "scheduled" workday after the holiday, it was held that Saturday overtime falls within the "scheduled workday" clause as used in the contract and employees who refused to work as scheduled on Saturday were not entitled to holiday pay.[74]

It is generally agreed that the purpose of "surrounding days" work requirements is to prevent employees from "stretching" holidays[75] and to assure a full working force on the day before and the day after a holiday.[76] A significant consequence of the work requirements clauses is that the "failure of an employee to comply with * * * [them] as a condition precedent to holiday pay operates to disqualify him from receiving such benefit."[77]

Part Day Absence or Tardiness on Surrounding Day

Contracts requiring the employee to work the surrounding days in order to qualify for holiday pay are ordinarily interpreted as requiring full days of work so that a part day absence[78] or tardiness[79] may

---

[73] A. O. Smith Corp., 47 LA 654, 660–661 (1966). Similarly, see Arbitrator McCoy in 47 LA 648, 649; Kelliher in 47 LA 582, 584; McCormick in 22 LA 505, 508. Also see Arbitrator Davis in 51 LA 1309, 1310.

[74] Youngstown Steel Door Co., 46 LA 323, 324 (Marshall, 1966). Similarly, see Arbitrator Begley in 44 LA 1212, 1214–1215; Larson in 38 LA 746, 748–749; Crane in 35 LA 389, 390.

[75] For example, see Arbitrator Hill in 53 LA 1206, 1209; Seinsheimer in 49 LA 468, 470; Klein in 48 LA 1101, 1102; Larkin in 41 LA 414, 415; Sembower in 38 LA 632, 634; Cheit in 28 LA 390, 393; Davey in 26 LA 322, 324; Simkin in 21 LA 686, 689; Updegraff in 20 LA 323, 324. Also see General Cable Corp., 37 LA 934, 942 (Killion, 1961), discussing the initial (historical) function and the present day function of the work requirement clauses in the parties' former and present contracts.

[76] For example, see Arbitrator Kates in 46 LA 102, 105; Reid in 40 LA 673, 675; Kleinsorge in 32 LA 769, 771; Cheit in 28 LA 390, 393.

[77] Motch & Merryweather Machinery Co., 51 LA 723, 730 (Dworkin, 1968).

[78] See Arbitrator Keefe in 52 LA 745, 749 ("excused" pass obtained by deception); Dworkin in 51 LA 723, 729–730 (unexcused absence after lunch period); Seinsheimer in 49 LA 468, 470 (employee left early without permission); Bauder in 46 LA 712, 713–714 (employee left early without permission); Koven in 43 LA 885, 887 (employee had a legitimate excuse but refused to state more than "personal" reasons); Reid in 40 LA 673, 675 (wildcat strike); Marshall in 35 LA 117, 120 (union meeting was a form of strike); Kelliher in 34 LA 478, 478–479 (employee left early without permission); Kleinsorge in 32 LA 769, 771 (employee left early without permission).

[79] See Crucible Steel Co., 21 LA 686, 690 (Simkin, 1953); Morgan Bros. Laundry, 14 LA 201, 203 (Fulda, 1950).

serve to defeat an employee's right to such pay. However, if the part day absence[80] or tardiness[81] is contractually or otherwise excused, holiday pay may be awarded. The theory behind the "excused" cases is that the reason for the work requirement is to prevent "stretching" the holiday, and since the employees in these cases demonstrated that they did not try to stretch the holiday they are entitled to holiday pay.[82]

Holidays Falling During Layoff

As stated above, the purpose of holiday pay is to protect the earnings of the employee when a holiday occurs on a day on which he otherwise would have worked. Therefore, since the employee in layoff is not working and would have no earnings, it is said that he would not be entitled to holiday pay in the absence of a contract provision extending such benefits to laid-off employees.[83]

---

[80] See Arbitrator Kesselman in 54 LA 112, 116–117 (permission granted to leave early); Kabaker in 53 LA 431, 432 (permission granted to leave early); Nichols in 48 LA 321, 322 (permission granted to leave early); Summers in 45 LA 1149, 1151–1152 (twenty-year practice of short shift on the day before Thanksgiving); Belsky in 44 LA 910, 911 (contractual exception for illness); Sembower in 38 LA 632, 635 (permission granted to leave early); Autry in 38 LA 400, 403 (permission granted ten days in advance); Cheit in 28 LA 390, 393 (employee left early on the day after the holiday in response to a subpoena); Davey in 26 LA 322, 323 (contractual exception for illness); Copelof in 23 LA 476, 481 (employee had to take his father to the hospital). In one case, Arbitrator Edwin R. Teple held that under the contract language and past practice the company was justified in paying proportional holiday pay on the basis of the number of hours actually worked on the surrounding days. See Trabon Engineering Corp., 49 LA 220, 222–223 (1967), also citing many cases.
[81] See Arbitrator Larkin in 41 LA 414, 415–416 (one employee had car trouble and was one hour late; another missed her usual ride, walked to work, and was twenty-six minutes late—the arbitrator said that these employees did not extend the holiday); Cheit in 28 LA 390, 393 (car pool driver did not appear and employee took a bus); Hayes in 25 LA 753, 754–755 (employee was less than a half hour late on the day after the holiday); Copelof in 23 LA 476, 481 (employee's husband was ill and needed to be given medicine on time). Arbitrator William E. Simkin set out guidelines to aid the parties in future cases involving tardiness before and after a holiday in Crucible Steel Co., 21 LA 686, 691 (1953).
[82] See, for example, Arbitrator Larkin in 41 LA 414, 415; Sembower in 38 LA 632, 634–635; Cheit in 28 LA 390, 393; Fulda in 14 LA 201, 204. As would be expected, absence before a holiday for "personal reasons," without an explanation, did not require that the absence be excused. Houdaille Industries, Inc., 55 LA 1098, 1101 (McDermott, 1970).
[83] See Hemp & Co., 37 LA 1009, 1010 (Updegraff, 1962). Similarly, see Arbitrator Leach in 44 LA 481, 484–487 (discussing many awards); Hunter in 41 LA 991, 993–994; Scheiber in 40 LA 152, 154–155; Pollack in 33 LA 477, 483; Dworkin in 27 LA 507, 510; Shapiro in 25 LA 341, 343; Ralston in 23 LA 49, 51. Cf. Standard Lime & Stone Co., 22 LA 601, 604 (Dworkin, 1954), involving a broad holiday pay provision with no qualifying factors for eligibility.

Most cases involving this issue have been decided on the basis of the work requirements clause[84] or the excused absence clause of the holiday pay provision, the latter excusing the employee from complying with the work requirements in the event of specified circumstances (such as illness) and sometimes adding such language as "or other valid excuse." Thus, in some cases where the contract did not provide for holiday pay for laid-off employees, the arbitrator, basing his opinion upon the excused absence clause[85] or upon the scheduled workday clause[86] of the holiday pay provision, reasoned that the employee had met the basic conditions of the contract and consequently qualified for holiday pay; in some of these cases the arbitrator noted the additional fact that the layoff was of "reasonably" short duration before and after the holiday. However, in other cases the arbitrator rejected the argument that layoff was an excused absence and refused to award holiday pay.[87] Likewise, where the employee in layoff was found not to have met the requirements of the scheduled workday clause, he was denied holiday pay.[88]

It should be noted that arbitrators would disapprove of the situation in which the facts indicate that the layoff was made in bad faith

---

[84] See examples and discussion of work requirements above in subtopic titled "Work Requirements."

[85] Layoff was considered an excused absence by Arbitrator Kates in 42 LA 111, 116 (discussing many cases pro and con); Tischler in 33 LA 919, 923 (citing many cases on various aspects of holiday pay at 921–924); Updegraff in 20 LA 323, 324–325.

[86] For cases in which the employee was found to have complied with the contract requiring work on *his* scheduled workday before and after the holiday, see Arbitrator Wood in 37 LA 103, 106; Prasow in 31 LA 449, 451; Parkman in 28 LA 1, 4; Tatum in 24 LA 517, 519–520. A like result obtained where the plant was closed for short periods surrounding the holidays and the contract required work on *the* scheduled day before and after the holidays in question. See George Otto Broiler Co., 37 LA 57, 60 (Garmon, 1961). In R. Herschel Mfg. Co., 35 LA 826, 829 (1960), Arbitrator Ruckel would have had "no hesitancy in finding for the Union" on the basis of the scheduled workday clause but for another clause stating that the purpose of the holiday pay provision was that no employee should be deprived of income he would have been able to earn; employees in layoff did not lose the opportunity to work as a result of the holiday.

[87] See Arbitrator Scheiber in 40 LA 152, 155–156 (discussing many cases at 154–158); Pollack in 33 LA 477, 483 ("To say that being laid off is to be excused by the company from the necessity of meeting the conditions precedent is preposterous."); Prasow in 25 LA 398, 403; Cahn in 22 LA 18, 19–20.

[88] See Arbitrator Leach in 44 LA 481, 487 (discussing many cases at 484–486); Updegraff in 37 LA 1009, 1010 (past practice also involved); Williams in 37 LA 273, 274–275 (past practice also involved); Pollack in 33 LA 477, 482–483; Prasow in 25 LA 398, 402–403; Ralston in 23 LA 49, 51 (past practice also involved). In all of these cases the contract required the employee to work on *the* scheduled workdays surrounding the holiday.

or was contrived as a means of avoiding the payment of holiday pay.[89]

Of course, the contract may specifically deny holiday pay to employees in layoff,[90] or it may specifically provide for such pay for employees laid off within a specified period of time before the holiday.[91]

Vacation or Leave as Affecting Holiday Pay

Where the contract specifically provides for holiday pay in addition to vacation pay when the holiday happens to occur during an employee's vacation period, arbitrators are in agreement that holiday pay must be allowed.[92] This is so even though the employee reported back to work a day or more late after his vacation,[93] or was guilty of an unexcused absence prior to the vacation period,[94] and even though the contract contained surrounding day work requirements. In the latter regard, the rationale used by arbitrators is that such requirements are intended to meet the employer's manning problems when a holiday occurs during a regular work week and have no application when a holiday occurs during a vacation week.[95]

A vacation shutdown clause may affect the employees' entitlement to holiday pay as it did in a case where the contract also stated that the intent of the holiday pay clause was to pay wages for holidays not worked to employees "who are scheduled to work on the day on which the holiday falls." The employer there scheduled a vacation shutdown during the week when a holiday fell, and the arbitrator refused to award holiday pay, resting his decision "squarely on the

---

[89] See comments of Arbitrator House in 47 LA 567, 571; Hunter in 41 LA 991, 994; Williams in 37 LA 273, 274; Parkman in 28 LA 1, 4–5; Shapiro in 25 LA 341, 343.
[90] See Flintkote Co., 26 LA 526, 527 (Morvant, 1956); Price-Pfister Brass Mfg. Co., 25 LA 398, 400 (Prasow, 1955).
[91] See contract provisions in 53 LA 477, 478; 51 LA 400, 405; 48 LA 915, 917; 47 LA 86, 87; 46 LA 132, 135; 44 LA 817, at 817; 31 LA 449, at 449; 29 LA 173, 175; 27 LA 507, 508; 23 LA 400, 401.
[92] Brooks Foods, Inc., 45 LA 249, 251 (Larkin, 1965), where holiday pay was awarded to employees who had elected to take their vacations during a layoff period, since they satisfied contractual requirements for such pay.
[93] See Arbitrator Saugee in 41 LA 621, 624; Sembower in 39 LA 104, 105–106; Autry in 36 LA 204, 206–207. Also see Olin-Mathieson Chemical Corp., 24 LA 116, 120–121 (Reynard, 1958).
[94] See Bethlehem Steel Co., 27 LA 801, 802 (Seward, 1956); Miami Copper Co., 16 LA 191, 193 (Prasow, 1951), stating also that the arbitrator believed that the employee is "subject to appropriate disciplinary penalty for his unexcused absence."
[95] See Arbitrator Saugee in 41 LA 621, 623; Sembower in 39 LA 104, 105–106; Autry in 36 LA 204, 207; Prasow in 16 LA 191, 193.

restrictive terms of the contract."[96] In another situation, concerned with pay in lieu of vacation, the arbitrator held that an employee on leave of absence who received pay in lieu of vacation could not also receive holiday pay for a holiday occurring during the leave since "a payment in lieu of vacation does not cover any particular time."[97]

The holiday pay issue is also complicated when both layoff and vacation are involved at the same time. Under a contract provision granting holiday pay to employees on vacation in the payroll period in which the holiday occurs, one arbitrator resolved the problem by ruling that a laid-off employee is entitled to pay for a holiday falling within his scheduled vacation period if the vacation is scheduled prior to the layoff, or if the employee is on layoff at the time the vacation is scheduled but returns to work and remains at work until he takes his scheduled vacation; an employee who is not working at the time his vacation is scheduled or prior to the time his vacation occurs is not eligible for pay for a holiday occurring within the vacation period.[98]

The contract may be unclear regarding payment for holidays falling during leaves of absence. If this is the case, the determination of eligibility for holiday pay may turn on such contract provisions as the surrounding days work requirements,[99] or other requirements such as being a "regular" employee, or working during the pay period in which the holiday occurs,[100] or the justifiable absence clause.[101]

In the absence of a specific contract provision for pay for holidays occurring during sick leave or other leaves of absence, arbitrators have been reluctant to award such pay.[102] Even where the contract does

---

[96] Geeco, Inc., 29 LA 658, 662 (Walsh, 1957). Also see Sefton Fibre Can Co., 12 LA 101, 104–105 (Townsend, 1948). Cf. Aladdin Industries, Inc., 18 LA 581, 584 (Hampton, 1952), involving different contract language.

[97] TRW Metals Division, 48 LA 414, 416 (Laybourne, 1967).

[98] United States Steel Corp., 36 LA 603, 616 (Garrett, 1961). Similarly, United States Steel Corp., 36 LA 385, 388 (Garrett, 1960); Firestone Tire & Rubber Co., 14 LA 552, 560 (Platt, 1950). Under contract language identical to the findings made in the Garrett opinion in 36 LA 603, 616, Arbitrator Alexander B. Porter held that the contract applied to employees on sick leave as well as layoff even though the holiday pay provision was "couched in layoff language." Bethlehem Steel Co., 41 LA 624, 627 (1963).

[99] See Mattel, Inc., 23 LA 383, 387 (Warren, 1954).

[100] See Femco, Inc., 50 LA 1146, 1148 (McDermott, 1968); Republic Steel Corp., 21 LA 317, 319–320 (Shipman, 1953).

[101] See Wooster Sportswear Co., Inc., 46 LA 9, 10 (Dworkin, 1965).

[102] See Femco, Inc., 50 LA 1146, 1148 (McDermott, 1968), where the contract provided holiday pay for the "regular" employee, defined as "one having

provide for holiday pay for employees on leave, it has been strictly interpreted. For example, a provision for holiday pay for the employee on sick leave "if his absence due to sickness begins no earlier than the second work day preceding or begins no later than the first work day following the holiday" was strictly applied to deny holiday pay to an employee whose sick leave began earlier than the second work day preceding the holiday.[103]

In some cases where the contract contains no explicit provision on sick leave as affecting holiday pay, the issue may involve the "justifiable excuse" exception to the surrounding days work requirements clause. For instance, where the contract provided that an employee would be ineligible for holiday pay if he was absent on either of the surrounding days "unless such absence is for justifiable cause," the arbitrator held that "an employee on sick leave must be regarded as excused from work or absent for 'just cause,'" thus qualifying for holiday pay.[104] However, although the contract was silent on the matter, the arbitrator held further that it would be "practical and reasonable" and not in conflict with any of the terms of the agreement to "imply a limitation that an employee on sick leave would be entitled to not more than two paid holidays occurring during a three month period of sick leave, providing the employee returns to work upon cessation of her illness."[105]

---

worked in the pay period in which the holiday falls"; the arbitrator said that this provision excluded from holiday pay eligibility employees like the grievant who were on extended leaves of absence. In San Francisco Publishers Assn., 46 LA 260, 265 (1965), Arbitrator Burns held that if the parties had intended to provide holiday pay for employees on sick leave they could have done so just as they provided pay for holidays occurring during regular days off or vacations. Also see Columbia Records, 32 LA 336, 340 (Prasow, 1959), involving past practice.

[103] See Columbus & Southern Ohio Electric Co., 45 LA 1021, 1023 (Schmidt, 1965). Also strictly applying a sickness exception, see Arbitrator Teple in 42 LA 75, 76–77; Shipman in 21 LA 317, 320; Aaron in 15 LA 204, 207. Cf. Kadish in 29 LA 424, 426–427, and Sherman in 24 LA 694, 695, in both of which cases the sickness exception contained no restrictive language.

[104] Wooster Sportswear Co., Inc., 46 LA 9, 10 (Dworkin, 1965). Similarly, see Arbitrators Donnelly, Curry & Mottram in 24 LA 815, 817; Kaplan in 18 LA 777, 779–780. Cf., Arbitrator Warns in 32 LA 516, 521–522. Nor did the employer's obligation to make sick leave payments to the Union's Welfare Fund limit his obligation regarding holiday pay, since the contract expressly provided that the welfare payments shall not be deemed "wages due to the workers." See Dworkin in 46 LA 9, 11. In Printing Industries of New York, 44 LA 124, 125 (Kornblum, 1965), it was held that payment of sick leave pay did not necessarily preclude the requirement of proof of illness to qualify for holiday pay.

[105] Wooster Sportswear Co., Inc., 46 LA 9, 11 (Dworkin, 1965).

An established practice of denying holiday pay to employees on sick leave may lead the arbitrator to deny such pay.[106] Or it may require holiday pay to employees on sick leave.[107]

Holidays Falling on Non-Workdays

Arbitrators appear to be in disagreement on the issue of pay for holidays falling on a non-workday Saturday where the contract designates certain paid holidays without distinguishing between holidays falling within or outside the regular work week.

Thus, on one hand, many arbitrators have held that under such a contract employees are entitled to pay for holidays that fall on Saturdays even though the regular work week is Monday through Friday;[108] they base their rulings upon the lack of ambiguity and upon "the clear, plain and explicit" language of the contract which is "not limited or restricted by any qualifying provision."[109]

On the other hand, many other arbitrators have denied pay for holidays falling on non-workday Saturdays; they have held that while the contract language is unrestricted, it is ambiguous in that it does not contain an express provision that holiday pay should be granted regardless of the day upon which the holiday falls.[110] Some of these arbitrators felt compelled to turn to the "conduct of the parties" or their past practice which gave meaning to the contract; and finding a previously unchallenged practice of not paying for Saturday holidays, these arbitrators refused to grant such pay.[111]

---

[106] See Arbitrator Elkouri in 38 LA 1061, 1064; Warns in 32 LA 516, 521–522; Prasow in 32 LA 336, 340. For cases involving past practice regarding eligibility for holiday pay when the employee is receiving disability pay, see Standard Oil Co. (Indiana), 26 LA 206, 208 (Beatty, 1956); Atlantic Refining Co., 25 LA 100, 104 (Boles, 1955).

[107] See American Smelting & Refining Co., 44 LA 1010, 1014–1015 (Koven, 1965); Atlantic Gummed Paper Corp., 35 LA 680, 681 (Rubin, 1960).

[108] See Arbitrator Goldstein in 43 LA 676, 677–678; Myers in 42 LA 269, 272; Caraway in 33 LA 494, 496; Howard in 24 LA 667, 670–671; Donnelly, Curry & Mottram in 21 LA 325, 326; Anderson in 20 LA 910, 911; Gaffey in 20 LA 734, 737; Phillips in 12 LA 43, 45; Albert in 7 LA 824, 826. In two of these cases the arbitrators awarded holiday pay in spite of consistent past practice of not paying for Saturday holidays. See Myers in 42 LA 269, 272; Donnelly, Curry & Mottram in 21 LA 325, 326.

[109] International Paper Co., 43 LA 676, 677 (Goldstein, 1964).

[110] See Arbitrator Seligson in 22 LA 806, 807; Cheit in 21 LA 98, 101–104; Grant in 18 LA 74, 75–76; Seward in 13 LA 983, 984–985; Trotta in 12 LA 417, 418; Rosenfarb in 11 LA 635, 636–638; Feinberg in 8 LA 334, 336–337; Wallen in 7 LA 745, 746; Scheiber in 7 LA 663, 664–665. Also see Arbitrator Stein in 11 LA 970, 970–971.

[111] See Arbitrator Grant in 18 LA 74, 75–76; Trotta in 12 LA 417, 418; Rosenfarb in 11 LA 635, 637–638; Feinberg in 8 LA 334, 336–337.

The contract may specifically exclude Saturday holidays which are not workdays from the holiday pay clause;[112] or it may specifically include holidays which fall on non-workday Saturdays;[113] or the contract may contain a qualifying clause granting pay for named holidays provided they fall on regularly scheduled workdays.[114] In the latter event, no holiday pay ordinarily would be allowed for holidays occurring outside the regular work week;[115] nor would the employees be entitled to have the Friday preceding a Saturday holiday considered as a paid holiday off.[116]

Strikes as Affecting Holiday Pay

Arbitrators have been generally reluctant to award pay to employees for holidays occurring while they are on strike unless the contract provides otherwise.[117] Thus, in a number of cases where work was available and scheduled during a strike and the contract contained a surrounding days work requirements clause, it was held that employees on strike were not entitled to pay for holidays falling during the strike period.[118] As for holidays falling during a strike occurring in a hiatus period between contracts, the result ordinarily is the

---

[112] As in American Can Co., 33 LA 809, at 809 (Bothwell, 1959); Western Union Telegraph Co., 20 LA 756, at 756 (Shipman, 1953).

[113] As in Lewall Sportswear Co., Inc., 53 LA 1165, 1166 (Dworkin, 1969); Foster Wheeler Corp., 35 LA 788, 789 (Stark, 1960).

[114] As in cases decided by Arbitrator Cayton in 42 LA 843, 844; Anderson in 23 LA 392, 393; Jones in 21 LA 120, at 120; Stutz, Mottram & Mannino in 21 LA 59, at 59; Pigors in 18 LA 356, 357; Gooding in 12 LA 165, at 165.

[115] See cases cited in previous footnote. In Vulcan-Mold & Iron Co., 21 LA 7, 8–9 (Kelliher, 1953), the employer was required to pay for a Saturday holiday despite the contract where there was a past practice of regularly scheduling Saturday work.

[116] Printing Industry of Washington, D.C., 42 LA 843, 844 (Clayton, 1964). Similarly, see Lewall Sportswear Co., Inc., 53 LA 1165, 1169 (Dworkin, 1969). The contract may permit the employer to designate a day to be observed in lieu of certain named holidays, as in Michigan Gas & Electric Co., 45 LA 85, 86 (Fallon, 1965).

[117] See Arbitrator Hill in 53 LA 1206, 1209; Wolff in 50 LA 921, 924; Stieber in 46 LA 967, 970; Kates in 46 LA 102, 104–105; Crawford in 43 LA 213, 214; Forsythe in 42 LA 102, 107; Teple in 42 LA 75, 78–79; Reid in 40 LA 673, 675; Trotta in 24 LA 560, 562–563. But where the contract has no surrounding day work requirements, the result may be different, as in Hellenic Lines, Ltd., 38 LA 339, 341–343 (Yagoda, 1962).

[118] See Arbitrator Kates in 46 LA 102, 104–105; Teple in 42 LA 75, 78–79; Reid in 40 LA 673, 675 (wildcat strike); Marshall in 35 LA 117, 120 (wildcat strike). Also see Bauder in 54 LA 754, 756–757 (holiday pay not due to employees who honored picket line of other employees); Klamon in 25 LA 841, 844. Cf. Keefe in 52 LA 512, 514–515; Davis in 51 LA 1309, 1310.

same.[119] The rulings of the arbitrators are based upon the lack of compliance with the contractual conditions for entitlement,[120] or, in a hiatus period strike, upon the reasoning that the right to holiday pay is a creature of contract and such right does not exist when there is no contract.[121]

Moreover, where the strike had been settled but not all of the employees had been recalled when the holiday occurred, the contractual eligibility requirements were held to apply to disqualify those who had not yet returned to work.[122] In this regard, Arbitrator Samuel S. Kates has stated that despite the original purpose of the surrounding day work requirements "to encourage full staffing of the plant before and after a holiday and to prevent stretching of holiday periods," nevertheless "when a contract states in absolute terms that holiday pay will be allowed only if" such requirements are met, it would be adding to the contract to disregard such requirements.[123]

Where agreements contain a holiday pay clause providing pay for employees on layoff within a certain period of time surrounding the holiday, unions have argued that employees awaiting recall after a strike has ended are entitled to pay under such clause. Arbitrators have ruled both ways on the issue of whether such employees are "laid-off" within the meaning of the contract. Thus, where the contract stated that an otherwise eligible employee who is "laid off for lack of work" will be eligible for holiday pay "if his layoff begins or ends during the holiday week," one arbitrator ruled that employees who after the strike ended were idle while waiting to be recalled "were not laid off for 'lack of work' nor had the Company laid them off

---

[119] See Arbitrator Traynor in 43 LA 539, 545; Kerrison in 37 LA 3, 4; Updegraff in 36 LA 507, 510; Seitz in 33 LA 681, 682–683; Hepburn in 30 LA 671, 674; Trotta in 24 LA 560, 562–563. Also see Sugarman in 36 LA 1276, 1278. But see Universal-Cyclops Steel Corp., 36 LA 1237, 1240–1241 (Crawford, 1961), where a strike settlement agreement extended the old contract.
[120] See Arbitrator Kates in 46 LA 102, 105; Teple in 42 LA 75, 78–79; Reid in 40 LA 673, 675; Kerrison in 37 LA 3, 4; Marshall in 35 LA 117, 120; Kadish in 24 LA 149, 152; Brecht in 19 LA 73, 75.
[121] See Arbitrator Traynor in 43 LA 539, 545; Teple in 42 LA 75, 78; Kerrison in 37 LA 3, 4; Seitz in 33 LA 681, 682–683.
[122] See Arbitrator Kates in 46 LA 102, 105; Updegraff in 36 LA 507, 509–510; Klamon in 25 LA 841, 844.
[123] Gregory Galvanizing & Metal Processing, Inc., 46 LA 102, 105 (1966), where he also emphasized that this was so whether the last scheduled work day was "one day or three days or one week or two weeks or other period before the holiday." In this case it was the day the strike began, which was two weeks before the holiday.

in the first instance," but their idle time resulted from the strike; and they were not eligible for holiday pay for a holiday occurring during the waiting period.[124] However, under a contract clause providing that "employees on layoff two weeks prior to the holiday or two weeks after the holiday shall" be eligible for holiday pay, another arbitrator held that the term "layoff" was broad enough to include employees waiting to be called back to work after a strike; and the employees therefore were held entitled to pay for Labor Day (the strike having ended on August 31st).[125]

Regarding employees laid off because operations were suspended due to another union's strike, it has been held that no holiday pay was due where the contract did not provide for such pay for holidays falling within a layoff period.[126] Moreover, where the contract excused employees from complying with the surrounding day work requirements for certain named reasons or "similar good cause," it was held that employees did not have a "similar good cause" excuse when they did not work the day before a holiday because an illegal strike by other employees forced the employer to shut down the plant.[127] However, where one employee managed to report to work but was told that no work was available and other employees were unable to enter the plant because of picket lines of employees on unauthorized strike, they were held eligible for holiday pay, the arbitrator stating that "whether grievants were stopped at the gate or actually got into the plant, they did all that reasonably could have been required of them

---

[124] E. J. Lavino & Co., 43 LA 213, 214 (Crawford, 1964). Also see Arbitrator Kadish in 26 LA 149, 151–153; Klamon in 25 LA 841, 844. In Mobil Oil Co., 42 LA 102, 107 (Forsythe, 1963), a past practice of not granting holiday pay to employees awaiting recall was held controlling.

[125] St. Regis Paper Co., 46 LA 967, 969–970 (Stieber, 1966); the arbitrator took note of the surrounding days work requirements but found that the exception in the clause noted above applied to the employees in the instant case. Similarly, Torrington Co., 12 LA 211, 212 (Camp, 1949).

[126] See Arbitrator Turkus in 40 LA 140, 142; Hill in 39 LA 500, 503–504; Wolff in 36 LA 1232, 1235. In Rockwell Mfg. Co., 33 LA 77, 79–80 (Scheiber, 1959), an established practice of not paying holiday pay to laid-off employees was held controlling. In Kansas City Bakery Employers Council, 25 LA 91, 93–94 (Walsh, 1955), the contract had no eligibility requirements for holiday pay, and the arbitrator held that the company had an absolute obligation to pay without regard to the company's operations.

[127] Phoenix Steel Corp., 44 LA 927, 928 (Crawford, 1965). Similarly, Schlage Lock Co., 30 LA 105, 107–109 (Ross, 1958), noting that the weight of arbitral decisions declines holiday pay under such circumstances, with citation of cases on both sides of the question at 108–109. Also see Stockton Automotive Assn., 25 LA 687, 689–691 (Whitton, 1955).

and thus their failing to work was because of a 'similar good cause.' "[128]

Loss of Holiday Pay as Penalty for Misconduct

It is generally held that it is improper for the employer to deny holiday pay to an employee as punishment for misconduct or for violation of plant rules if the employee is otherwise eligible for such benefit.[129] However, if the employee by his misconduct or by his violation of plant rules fails to comply with the work requirements of the contract, he disqualifies himself for holiday pay. This was the ruling in a case in which the employees by their wildcat strike on the day before a holiday failed to comply with the surrounding day work requirements clause and thus did not qualify for holiday pay.[130]

Leaves of Absence

"Ordinarily, in industrial relations parlance 'leave', when 'granted', connotes absence from work without the imposition of penalties that might otherwise be suffered for failing to report * * * when scheduled for work."[131]

While a leave of absence status may have important immediate benefits to the employee in terms of pay for time lost and freedom from penalty when absent briefly from work, it may be even more important in terms of future job security (keeping his job open for him and retention of seniority) and future major benefits (disability pensions or retirement benefits) when he must be absent for an extended period of time.[132] From management's standpoint, its interest

---

[128] United States Steel Corp., 46 LA 473, 477 (McDermott, 1966). Similarly, United States Steel Corp., 45 LA 509, 511 (Altrock, 1965). Also awarding holiday pay, see Arbitrator Shipman in 36 LA 99, 100; McIntosh in 32 LA 30, 32–33; Seward in 23 LA 141, 143; in all of these cases the employees reported for work and were sent home or were notified not to report for work because of a strike by other employees, and the contract in the Seward case had a "similar good cause" exception while the contracts in the other two cases contained language to the effect that an employee's absence with company approval or permission was an exception to the work requirements clause.
[129] See Arbitrator Dworkin in 51 LA 723, 728, and in 36 LA 517, 520–522; Reid in 40 LA 673, 674; Sembower in 39 LA 104, 106–107; Anderson in 33 LA 890, 892; Schedler in 32 LA 865, 867–868; Platt in 16 LA 317, 319, and in 13 LA 126, 131–132. Cf. Arbitrator Schmidt in 31 LA 558, 560–561; Smith in 11 LA 1195, 1198–1199; in both of which cases the contract contained language justifying denial of holiday pay as a disciplinary action.
[130] American Brake Shoe Co., 40 LA 673, 675 (Reid, 1963).
[131] Publishers' Assn. of New York City, 32 LA 513, 515 (Seitz, 1959).
[132] See Joyce-Cridland Co., 35 LA 133, 136–137 (Schmidt, 1960).

is not only in the cost of monetary benefits to the employee but also in production problems which may result from the absence of an experienced employee who may be difficult or impossible to replace.[133] Thus, management has a natural interest in promoting regular attendance by employees and in preventing abuse of leave of absence privileges.[134]

It has been held that except as restricted by the agreement, the granting or denial of leaves of absence is a prerogative of management, and the judgment of management will not be disturbed so long as the action taken is not unreasonable or discriminatory.[135] In some cases past practice and custom concerning leaves of absence have determined whether management's action should be upheld.[136] Where leaves of absence were provided for in the contract, with the right reserved to the company to judge the cause for the requested leave, the "arbitrary or discriminatory" test was applied by the arbitrator in determining whether leave had been properly denied.[137]

An employee is not automatically entitled to a leave of absence since this right or privilege exists by virtue of provision in the collective bargaining agreement or a leave plan unilaterally instituted by management or by reason of past practice. For example, one arbitrator held that although the contract provided for sick leave of absence, such leave was not automatic in view of the contractual requirement,

---

[133] See Hudson Pulp & Paper Co., 35 LA 581, 583 (Hill, 1960).

[134] In a case involving discipline for excessive absences, Arbitrator Vernon L. Stouffer stated, "Arbitrators have consistently held that one of the obligations of employment is that the employee report for work inasmuch as successful operation of a plant depends upon regular attendance." Insley Manufacturing Corp., 52 LA 59, 73 (1968). Arbitrator Stouffer also has held that management could discipline an employee for excessive absenteeism even though such absenteeism occurred during authorized medical leaves of absence. Leland Airborne Products, 62-2 ARB ¶8504 (1962). Cf. Arbitrator Schmidt in 35 LA 133, 136–137.

[135] See Arbitrator Roberts in 48 LA 1166, 1167–1168; Dworkin in 45 LA 667, 670; Fallon in 43 LA 670, 673; Waite in 12 LA 661, 662; Wardlaw in 3 LA 108, 110. Also see Elson in 21 LA 502, 511; Tyree in 19 LA 604, 607; Aaron in 15 LA 928, 933. An implied limitation on management was found in contract provisions by Arbitrator Schmidt in 35 LA 133, 136–137.

[136] See Arbitrator Hebert in 45 LA 621, 627–628; Tatum in 44 LA 373, 376; Elkouri in 38 LA 1061, 1063–1064; Levinson in 23 LA 277, 280; McCraw in 19 LA 709, 710; Lesser in 18 LA 528, 531. Also see Cahn in 52 LA 176, 177. For a case involving an attempted but unsuccessful discontinuance of a past practice regarding leaves of absence, see Hillbro Newspaper Printing Co., 48 LA 1166, 1167–1168 (Roberts, 1967). For related discussion, see Chapter 12, topic titled "Custom and Practice as Part of the Contract."

[137] Hudson Pulp & Paper Co., 35 LA 581, 583 (Hill, 1960), holding that denial of leave (requested for the purpose of serving a jail sentence) was not improper.

not complied with by the grievant, for the submission of a written request.[138] Another arbitrator, noting that "The contract language should not be construed or applied so as to defeat its substantive purpose, namely, to make provision for necessary sick leave," held not only that the contract did not require that sick leave requests be granted automatically even though the employee presents a statement from his doctor that sick leave is necessary, but also that the company could "evaluate the factual basis of a sick leave request" and deny the request if it is frivolous and not supported by the facts.[139]

Sick Leave

Provision for sick leave may be negotiated into the contract,[140] or a sick leave plan may be instituted unilaterally by management.[141] In any event, management has a legitimate concern in preventing abuse of sick leave claims and in so doing it may formulate reasonable rules for the documentation of illness,[142] prescribe forms to be filled out by the employee and his doctor,[143] or develop a system for the policing of a sick benefits plan,[144] so long as it is not arbitrary, discriminatory, or unreasonable.[145]

Indeed, it is said that the company has an obligation to guard against fraudulent sick pay claims.[146] Thus, Arbitrator John P. McGury stated that the company has both "the right and the duty to make reasonable inquiries concerning the basis for a sick benefit

---

[138] Doering's Super Valu, 47 LA 364, 368–369 (Lee, 1966). Cf. Arbitrator Teple in 48 LA 615, 618, where the contract provided for six months sick leave as a matter of right without formal application or approval.

[139] The Magnavox Co., 45 LA 667, 669–670 (Dworkin, 1965).

[140] As in The Magnavox Co., 45 LA 667, 668 (Dworkin, 1965).

[141] As in Socony Mobil Oil Co., Inc., 45 LA 1062, 1063 (Kadish, 1965).

[142] See Federal Services, Inc., 41 LA 1063, 1064 (Williams, 1963); General Baking Co., 40 LA 386, 388 (Corsi, 1963). Also see Memphis Publishing Co., 48 LA 554, 557–558 (Oppenheim, 1967).

[143] See Arbitrator Marshall in 52 LA 593, 596; Ryder in 41 LA 1133, 1135; McGury in 38 LA 419, 422.

[144] See Socony Mobil Oil Co., Inc., 45 LA 1062, 1065 (Kadish, 1965).

[145] The reasonableness test was applied in National Airlines Inc., 43 LA 1169, 1171 (1964), where Arbitrator Black held that even though the contract permitted the company to require a physician's certificate to confirm a sick claim, it could do so only when it has reasonable doubts as to the employee's sick claim. Also see Trans World Airlines, 45 LA 1089, 1090 (Gilden, 1965). Where the company's right to require a medical certificate had been the subject of bargaining in the past and had been negotiated out of the agreement, the arbitrator nevertheless ruled that "If the Company has *reasonable* grounds for believing an employee is abusing sick leave the Company has the right to request proof of illness." Galloway Co., 49 LA 240, 242–243 (Gundermann, 1967).

[146] Curtiss-Wright Corp., 36 LA 842, 845 (Seitz, 1961).

claim and it would be extremely impractical if not impossible for these legitimate inquiries to be made without the Company having the right to request the necessary information."[147]

Documentation may also be required under suspicious circumstances, such as absence before a vacation[148] or mass absences on a holiday.[149]

In the absence of a procedure set up by the contract or by company rules, what kind of proof of illness must the employee offer and what kind of proof can the company demand? In one case, the parties had a practice of many years whereby the employee ordinarily told his foreman whether his absence was due to "sickness" and the foreman accepted the explanation if he had no reason to doubt the employee's truthfulness. The parties had no desire to change this practice or to introduce any new rigid requirements. However, Arbitrator Harry H. Platt said that the practice does not mean that the company may never ask for proof of "sickness," and he provided the following guidelines:

> In most cases, it would suffice for the employee to provide an explanation in sufficient detail to enable the supervisor to make a judgment as to whether sick leave is justified.
>
> Some cases require more, but the proof need not be in any particular form, nor must it be the strongest and best proof possible. Verification could be in the following forms:
>
> (a) A doctor's letter would be appropriate but should not be an absolute requirement since there may be illness without the attention of a doctor;
>
> (b) A druggist's prescription might be adequate; or

---

[147] Cities Service Petroleum Co., 38 LA 419, 422 (1961), holding that the company acted reasonably in requiring the employee to sign a "medical waiver" authorizing the disclosure of information by his doctor to the company.

[148] See Marion Power Shovel Co., 43 LA 507, 509–510 (Dworkin, 1964), where the contract did not require medical proof when absence due to illness did not exceed three days and the past practice of the company had been to accept an oral statement by the employee, but the employee "acted improperly in refusing to cooperate" by providing management with information which he had to verify his illness. The arbitrator held that grievant was properly disciplined for his refusal to cooperate.

[149] See Republic Steel Corp., 28 LA 897, 899 (Platt, 1957). Cf. Bethlehem Steel Co., 42 LA 851, 852 (Hill, 1964), where the arbitrator ruled that although grievant's explanation of an absence was open to "suspicion, if not downright disbelief," the company could not condition payment for a holiday upon the employee's proving his preholiday claim of illness at home since there was no practice at the plant of making an employee prove that he had been absent for medical reasons.

(c) A written statement from the employee's wife, neighbor, or fellow worker might suffice.

The nature of the proof must ultimately depend upon the facts and circumstances of each case.[150]

Maternity Leave

Maternity leave may be provided for by the collective agreement;[151] or the granting or denial of such leave may be a matter of past practice.[152] Thus, in one case where the contract had no provision for maternity leave and under past practice the company had treated pregnant employees as "voluntary quit," the arbitrator refused to hold that the termination of the grievant was a discharge (concluding that this was not a case of disciplinary action requiring the application of the "just cause" standard). He stated that to so hold would be tantamount to writing a maternity leave provision into the contract, which he declared would be "grossly improper."[153]

Also relying upon a "long established, important and known practice," another arbitrator held that the company could not discontinue the "practice of granting leaves of absence to pregnant women employees."[154] However, a past practice of requiring pregnant employees to resign was deemed to have been changed by contract provisions (1) preserving the seniority of employees with temporary "physical disabilities," and (2) specifying only four methods of breaking an employee's continuous service (and maternity leave was not one of those methods).[155]

In another case, the arbitrator refused to allow the employer to establish a general rule of no maternity leave, even though the

---

[150] Republic Steel Corp., 28 LA 897, 899 (Platt, 1957), a "mass absences" case. This approach using the above kinds of proof was taken by the company in another "mass absences" case. See Phoenix Steel Co., 51 LA 357, at 357 (Cahn, 1968). Cf. Bridgeport Gas Co., 31 LA 253, 255–256 (Stutz, 1958).

[151] See Arbitrator Mittenthal in 41 LA 713, 714 (the clause requiring one year of service with the company to be operative); McKelvey in 38 LA 11, 12; Teple in 36 LA 132, 133; Myers in 8 LA 827, 828. Concerning sick leave payments during maternity leave, compare Arbitrator Altrock in 57 LA 831, 833–834, with Arbitrator Brown in 57 LA 758, 761.

[152] See Arbitrator Hebert in 45 LA 621, 627–628; Tatum in 44 LA 373, 376; Levinson in 23 LA 277, 280; McCraw in 19 LA 709, 710.

[153] Westinghouse Electric Corp., 45 LA 621, 627–628 (Hebert, 1965). Also see Chattanooga Box & Lumber Co., 44 LA 373, 376 (Tatum, 1965). Cf. National Lead Co., 18 LA 528, 531 (Lesser, 1952).

[154] Northland Greyhound Lines, Inc., 23 LA 277, 280 (Levinson, 1954).

[155] Republic Steel Corp., 37 LA 367, 369 (Stashower, 1961).

contract left to the company the discretion to grant leaves of absence, the arbitrator stating that "that discretion may not be arbitrary, vague or fanciful" but must be exercised "fairly and impartially" not only in the company's interest but with "due regard" to the interests of the employee.[156]

It is to be expected that in the future the resolution of maternity leave issues may be significantly affected by constitutional doctrine and doctrine such as that being developed under Title VII of the Civil Rights Act of 1964. This may be illustrated, for instance, by an arbitrator's emphasis of such doctrine in holding that a school board was not justified in requiring a teacher to take involuntary maternity leave at a point of time sooner than necessary.[157]

Leave for Union Business

Contract provisions for leaves of absence for union business vary greatly, and whether such leave should be granted depends not only upon the particular contract clause but also upon the facts and circumstances involved in each case, with particular reference to the good faith of both parties.[158] While internal affairs of the union and union "secrets" need not be divulged, the employer is entitled to enough information regarding the nature of the union business involved and the probable duration of the absence to permit an intelligent choice as to granting or denying leave.[159]

Leave for "union business" has been held to encompass organizational activity outside the bargaining unit at a plant affiliated with the employer,[160] but it does not include union *political* activity.[161]

---

[156] Gem Electric Mfg. Co., Inc., 11 LA 684, 685 (Wolff, 1948).

[157] Southgate Community School District, 57 LA 476, 477–478 (Heilbrun, 1971). But see East Hartford Board of Education, 57 LA 831, 834 (Altrock, 1971).

[158] See C. & D. Batteries, Inc., 32 LA 589, 594 (Jaffee, 1959), where criteria were discussed in regard to granting leave for union business. As to a second leave at the end of a first leave where the contract provides for "leave of absence for six months" for union business, see Wallingford Steel Co., 54 LA 1130, 1133–1134 (Sherman, 1970).

[159] See Arbitrator Porter in 50 LA 1140, 1144; Anderson in 42 LA 632, 636; Kinyon in 35 LA 873, 881; Jaffee in 32 LA 589, 593–594; Hilpert in 11 LA 569, 572. Arbitrator Jaffee drafted a written form (at the parties request) to be used in requesting leave for union business, in 32 LA 589, 594.

[160] See Arbitrator Porter in 50 LA 1140, 1144; Fallon in 43 LA 670, 675; Anderson in 42 LA 632, 635–636; Kinyon in 35 LA 873, 878–879.

[161] See Husky Oil Co., 37 LA 249, 251–252 (Simpson, 1961); Anchor Duck Mills, 5 LA 428, 430 (Hepburn, 1946). Cf., Arbitrator Updegraff in 8 LA 350, 354.

Under some contracts, arbitrators have approved the action of management in granting leave on a conditional basis.[162] In some cases, past practice of the parties and industry practice have influenced or determined the arbitrator's decision.[163]

Leave for Jury Duty

The vast majority of reported decisions deal not with the right to leave of absence for jury duty but with the resultant pay problems under pertinent contract language on jury duty pay differential. In the absence of such a provision, it has been held that the company is not required to pay jury duty benefits to its employees.[164]

It has been said that the object of such provisions is to "provide competent jurors through the removal of the monetary loss that would otherwise accompany jury service."[165] Thus, employees who are called for jury duty while on vacation[166] or in layoff status[167] have been held not to be entitled to jury duty pay.

The key words in many contracts are "time lost," and where the employee was called to jury service but excused early, the arbitrator held that he had an obligation to return to work since "he could readily have returned to his home, changed to appropriate clothing, and reported for work" for the last half of his shift.[168]

Reconciling jury duty pay provisions to situations in which shift schedules did not coincide precisely with hours of jury duty, Arbitrator Clare B. McDermott held that the "rule of reason" must be applied; and when the hours of jury service come so close before or after the

---

[162] See Husky Oil Co., 37 LA 249, 252 (Simpson, 1961); U.S. Industrial Chemicals Co., 36 LA 400, 404 (Teple, 1961). Cf., Arbitrator Klein in 41 LA 739, 743–744; Stutz in 37 LA 475, 483.

[163] See Arbitrator Fallon in 43 LA 670, 675; Donnelly in 15 LA 611, 612; Martin in 14 LA 574, 591 (an "interests" arbitration); Hilpert in 11 LA 569, 573; Dwyer in 11 LA 1074, 1075.

[164] See Ryder Truck Lines, Inc., 38 LA 113, 115 (Williams, 1961).

[165] Greenleaf Mfg. Co., 32 LA 1, 2 (Edelman, 1959). Also see Arbitrator Freund in 49 LA 901, 905; Mills in 40 LA 1195, 1197.

[166] Columbus Auto Parts Co., 51 LA 1288, 1292 (Klein, 1968).

[167] American Airlines, Inc., 39 LA 500, 503–504 (Hill, 1962). Cf. General Electric Co., 50 LA 852, 860 (Seinsheimer, 1967), involving jury duty performed by employees during a strike called by another union.

[168] Continental Can Co., Inc., 47 LA 683, 685–686 (Dash, 1966), awarding the employee compensation for only one half of each of the five days he was released early from jury duty. Also see Henry Vogt Machine Co., 39 LA 763, 766 (Volz, 1962).

employee's scheduled shift as to give him justifiable grounds for missing that shift, he should be excused and paid jury allowance.[169]

Under a contract providing for pay "If an employee is required to absent himself from the job" for jury service, the employee's need for rest was cited as justification for jury duty pay to an employee who was scheduled to work on the night shift. The arbitrator stated that it was "clear that the Grievant was 'required' to absent herself from the job" in order to obtain needed rest.[170]

The question sometimes arises as to whether time spent in jury service should be included as time worked for purposes of other provisions of the contract. In the absence of a provision specifically covering the issue, it has been held that jury duty does not count as time worked for purposes of computing weekly overtime.[171] One arbitrator, however, held that time spent on jury duty was to be included in computing the employee's vacation time.[172]

Funeral Leave

Cases involving funeral leave provisions have turned upon the precise wording of the funeral leave or "bereavement" pay clause, and arbitrators appear to be inclined toward strict construction of such clauses. Thus, where the contract specifically stated that a certain number of days of paid leave would be allowed to attend the funeral of a member of the employee's immediate family, arbitrators have held that such leave provision includes attendance at the funeral and necessary travel time but does not contemplate absences to aid bereaved relatives or to attend to the estate.[173] Moreover, where the

---

[169] United States Steel Corp., cases at 36 LA 590, 595; 36 LA 595, 597; 36 LA 597, 599 (1961). Arbitrator Ralph T. Seward, while noting that these cases are not binding upon the parties in Bethlehem Steel Corp., 49 LA 334, 336–337 (1967), was "particularly impressed" by Arbitrator McDermott's analysis and wrote that he "joins Arbitrator McDermott * * * in holding that the rule of reason should govern application of the jury pay provision."

[170] Hunt Foods & Industries, Inc., 36 LA 929, 931 (McNaughton, 1961). To similar effect, see Arbitrator Holly in 33 LA 508, 511–512; Schedler in 27 LA 189 at 189.

[171] See Arbitrator Ray in 52 LA 575, 577; Carter in 52 LA 357, 360; Mills in 40 LA 1195, 1197.

[172] Goodyear Aerospace Corp., 51 LA 540, 546 (Lehoczky, 1968).

[173] See Arbitrator Hill in 48 LA 351, 352; Teple in 47 LA 438, 440; Daugherty in 45 LA 494, 495; Luskin in 42 LA 59, 61; Sweeney in 40 LA 223, 224–225; Wolff in 36 LA 1077, 1078; Hays in 34 LA 300, 301. But see Arbitrator McIntosh in 44 LA 739, 740. One arbitrator held that the company could issue a rule requiring the employee to furnish evidence of attendance at the funeral. See Borg-Warner Corp., 47 LA 691, 697–698 (Bradley, 1966).

language used is "pay for time lost" or "paid leave of absence" while attending the funeral of a family member, arbitrators generally have denied such pay when the employee was already on vacation or otherwise not scheduled to work.[174]

However, the arbitrator may favor a somewhat broader construction with regard to that portion of the funeral leave clause which lists the members of the employee's "immediate family." For example, where the contract listed "brother" among other members of the family, the arbitrator, emphasizing the closeness of the relationship between the employee and his step-brother, held that "the latter must be deemed his brother within the meaning of that term as used in the agreement."[175]

Of course, past practice may affect the arbitrator's decision. Thus, in one case where the contract contained no funeral leave clause but did provide for maintenance of working conditions, the arbitrator ruled that the employer was required to continue an established practice of granting up to three days funeral leave.[176] In another case, an existing funeral leave policy, recognized by both parties, of not including payment of such benefits during any period of paid absence from work (such as vacations) was deemed by the arbitrator to have carried over into the new contract provision dealing with paid funeral leave.[177]

Leave for "Personal Business"

As with other leaves of absence, arbitrators have held that management's determination to grant or deny leaves for "personal busi-

---

[174] See Arbitrator McIntosh in 51 LA 517, 518; Tsukiyama in 46 LA 849, 851–852; McCoy in 46 LA 11, 14; Lockhart in 45 LA 644, 645; Roberts in 45 LA 291, 292–293; Davis in 44 LA 937, 939; Turkus in 36 LA 1330, 1332; Updegraff in 33 LA 629, 632; Lanoue in 27 LA 362, 363. Cf. Arbitrator Midonick in 32 LA 385, 386. But where contract language is ambiguous or less specific, or where a conflicting practice is a factor, a different result may obtain. See Arbitrator Yaffee in 49 LA 768, 769–770; Seitz in 37 LA 1034, 1035–1037 (where he discussed two of his earlier awards); Kahn in 37 LA 151, 154–155.

[175] Foremost Dairies, Inc., 43 LA 616, 617 (Greenwald, 1964), citing Arbitrator Cahn in 28 LA 469, 469–470, and Shister in 26 LA 108, 110. To similar effect see Arbitrator Thompson in 43 LA 467, 469–470; Marshall in 40 LA 1230, 1234; Kornblum in 38 LA 1029, 1031; Klamon in 31 LA 603, 606–607. But Arbitrator Dworkin refused to extend the meaning of "brother-in-law" to include the employee's wife's sister's husband. Consumers Power Co., 49 LA 595, 601–603 (1967). Similarly, see Arbitrator Berkowitz in 52 LA 768, 769 (wife's uncle); Davis in 51 LA 289, 290 (stepfather-in-law).

[176] Commercial Motor Freight, Inc., 34 LA 592, 595 (Stouffer, 1960).

[177] Food Employers Council, Inc., 45 LA 291, 292–293 (Roberts, 1965).

ness" must be reasonable and nondiscriminatory.[178] Management must have some information in order to make that determination intelligently, and it is not enough for the employee to state merely "personal business" as his reason for requesting such leave. Thus, Arbitrator Maurice H. Merrill has held that the employer has the right to require the employee to give a reasonably explicit statement of reasons rather than simply stating "personal business."[179] He noted that this may result in a conflict between the employee's right to privacy with respect to his personal life and the employer's interest in discouraging unnecessary absences and insuring efficient operations. However, he found support in the contract for his conclusions, not only in a general leave of absence clause requiring presentation of evidence by the employee to substantiate his request, but also in specific leave clauses relating to jury duty, voting time, and funeral leave, all of which also indicated the necessity of presenting information concerning the employee's personal affairs.[180]

"Moonlighting" and Outside Business Interest

Employees sometimes engage in "moonlighting," i.e., holding a second job during off hours (part time or full time); or they may carry on an outside business interest.[181] In cases involving such "off hours" activity, unions argue for the asserted right of the employee to do what he pleases during his off hours and to use his knowledge and skill to augment his income.[182] It is recognized that the employee may engage in work during his off hours within the limits noted hereinbelow. As stated by Arbitrator Thomas P. Whelan:

> "It is well established that the time of an employee outside his regular hours of work and outside the overtime sometimes incidental thereto belongs to him and may be used for recreation and work,

---

[178] See Arbitrator Merrill in 47 LA 531, 535; Hill in 35 LA 581, 583; Jaffee in 12 LA 95, 97; Wardlaw in 3 LA 108, 110.

[179] Union Carbide Corp., 47 LA 531, 534–535 (1966). Accord, Mead Corp., 51 LA 1121, 1124 (Griffin, 1968).

[180] Union Carbide Corp., 47 LA 531, 533 (Merrill, 1966).

[181] Broadly, the term "moonlighting" may be considered to encompass all remunerative activity engaged in during off hours, whether a second job or a business interest.

[182] For example, these arguments were presented (but to no avail because of the facts involved) in Firestone Retread Shop, 38 LA 600, 601 (McCoy, 1962), and Capital-Chrysler Plymouth, Inc., 53 LA 1247, 1250 (Sembower, 1969), respectively. For related discussion, see Chapter 13, topic titled "Plant Rules," and Chapter 15, topic titled "Conduct Away From Plant."

provided the employee does not engage in practices or occupations that are detrimental or clearly prejudicial to the business and interests with which his duties in the service of his regular employer are connected."[183]

In light of this, the bare fact that an employee holds a second job would not necessarily be grounds for discipline or discharge. Thus, if the primary employer has no set policy forbidding outside employment and it is not shown that the employee's work for that employer has suffered, or if it is not shown that the employee (in a competitive situation) had access to trade secrets, discipline or discharge may be set aside or the penalty may be reduced by the arbitrator.[184]

Balanced against the arguments of the union are the primary employer's right to receive a full measure of productiveness during the employee's hours of work for him[185] and the primary employer's right to loyalty free from the employee's competitive activity or other activity resulting in a conflict of interest.[186] Thus, it has been held that if the employee's second job adversely affects his attendance or work performance or otherwise detrimentally affects his employer, disciplinary action (or discharge in appropriate cases) may be deemed proper.[187]

Moreover, off hours activity may be in indirect competition with the primary employer if the employee works for a competing company, or in direct competition if he himself carries on a business of the same nature as that of his employer. Even where the activity is not competi-

---

[183] Janitorial Service, Inc., 33 LA 902, 907–908 (1959).

[184] As in cases decided by Arbitrator Keefe in 52 LA 1290, 1296 (grievant refused to work overtime so that he could meet the obligations of his second job—penalty reduced because of extenuating circumstances); Kates in 52 LA 818, 820–821, and in 51 LA 1098, 1101–1102 (in both cases, leave of absence was obtained by deceit and the employee went to work for his other employer—reinstated without back pay); Lee in 46 LA 175, 179 (no detriment to the employer was shown—employee reinstated with back pay); Kates in 37 LA 1095, 1098 (employee reinstated with back pay); Whelan in 33 LA 902, 908, and Pigors in 31 LA 547, 551 (in both cases, there was a somewhat competitive situation but there was no rule and no detriment shown to the employer—employee reinstated with back pay); Smith in 17 LA 179, 182–183 (somewhat competitive situation and grievant "did not exhibit the fidelity to his employer which his job required"—reinstated without back pay).

[185] See, for example, Safeway Stores, Inc., 49 LA 400, 402 (Caraway, 1967).

[186] See Arbitrator Caraway in 47 LA 372, 374; Teple in 43 LA 338, 340; Dworkin in 39 LA 404, 409; Gorsuch in 34 LA 636, 642.

[187] See Arbitrator Kates in 52 LA 818, 820–821, and in 51 LA 1098, 1101–1102; Dworkin in 39 LA 404, 409; Keller in 26 LA 401, 403. Also see Arbitrator Hon in 38 LA 965, 971; Jaffee in 37 LA 254, 257–258.

tive, it may result in a conflict of interests.[188] In this regard, where the employee's second job or business interest is prohibited by the contract or by clear company policy and is in direct competition with his employer, or creates a conflict of interest, it is likely that the arbitrator will uphold his discharge,[189] especially where trade secrets are involved.[190]

Arbitrator Whitley P. McCoy has commented upon some aspects of an employee's competitive activity which are "intolerable" to the employer:

"But this is not a mere case of 'moonlighting', that is, holding down another job. It is a case of going into business in competition with his employer, thus creating a conflict of interest. He was in the position of competing in the purchase of * * * [raw materials], and competing in the sales of * * * [the finished product]. At the same time he was in a position to learn of any improvements in materials or processes developed by * * * [the Company], and to adopt them himself. * * * The whole thing created an intolerable situation. I think there was a breach by the grievant of an implied condition of employment.

"I do not consider this discharge as disciplinary. His ownership of a competing business was not, strictly speaking, an offense. But

---

[188] As in Tribune Publishing Co., 42 LA 504, 506–507 (Kagel, 1963), where a drama critic for a newspaper obtained outside work as a press agent for a summer theater.

[189] See Arbitrator Whyte in 54 LA 942, 946–947; Sembower in 53 LA 1247, 1251–1252; Karasick in 53 LA 1176, 1180; Caraway in 49 LA 400, 401–402; Kagel in 42 LA 504, 506–507; Jenkins in 40 LA 1293, 1295; Gorsuch in 34 LA 636, 642–643. Also see Arbitrator Wyckoff in 44 LA 552, 553. For cases holding that the company may promulgate a rule prohibiting outside work in competition with it, see Whyte in 54 LA 942, 945–946; Teple in 43 LA 338, 340–341; Dworkin in 39 LA 404, 409; Gorsuch in 34 LA 636, 642–643; Kates in 27 LA 540, 542; Keller in 26 LA 401, 403. In upholding the reasonableness of such rules, arbitrators have pointed out that the prohibition did not apply to work in other areas of endeavor. See Arbitrator Caraway in 47 LA 372, 374; Jenkins in 40 LA 1293, 1295; Gorsuch in 34 LA 636, 642; Keller in 26 LA 401, 403.

[190] See Arbitrator McCoy in 46 LA 1009, 1010–1011, stating that "the Company had the right to lock the stable door before the horse was stolen," and in 38 LA 600, 601; Dworkin in 39 LA 404, 409–410; Updegraff in 3 LA 113, 115. Also see Caraway in 47 LA 372, 375, where the grievant was reinstated because he had not known of the rule prohibiting outside activity which conflicts with the company's best interest, but he was required to refrain from such activities in the future; Kates in 27 LA 540, 542–543, where the company's right to discharge for violating a rule against working for a competitor was upheld, but the grievant was reinstated (without back pay) because he gave two weeks notice of resignation to his second employer the day the rule went into effect.

it was a condition, created by him, that made his continued employ-ment by the Company intolerable."[191]

Regarding situations involving a conflict of interest, it has been empha-sized that there is no need to prove an actual detriment to the primary employer:

"* * * it is not necessarily required that the employer convinc-ingly establish that a business detriment or financial loss has in fact resulted; it is sufficient if the off-duty relationship is such as would reasonably suggest that the outside employment would lead to a dis-closure to the competitor of information and skills acquired by the employee * * *."[192]

Personal Appearance: Hair and Clothes

The employee has the right to decide what his personal appear-ance will be in private life, away from his place of employment, so long as no harm results to his employer.[193] While the employee's per-sonal appearance in private life may in some circumstances adversely affect the employer, it is primarily the employee's assertion of the aforementioned right at work with which we are concerned here.

Employees tend to resist broad company prohibitions or require-ments which they feel may infringe upon their personal right to dress and to wear their hair or beards as they please. On the other hand, management historically has been concerned with the personal appear-ance of its employees, both from the standpoint of the company's pub-lic "image" and from the standpoint of such safety and health factors as may be involved.[194]

---

[191] Firestone Retread Shop, 38 LA 600, 601 (1962). The employee here was warned and later given an opportunity to sell his business before being discharged. Other aspects of competitive work by employees are discussed by Arbitrator Dworkin in 39 LA 404, 410; Gorsuch in 34 LA 636, 641–642; Keller in 26 LA 401, 403.

[192] Ravens-Metal Products, Inc., 39 LA 404, 409–410 (Dworkin, 1962). Simi-larly, see Arbitrator Gorsuch in 34 LA 636, 643; Keller in 26 LA 401, 403.

[193] See material in Chapter 15, topic titled "Conduct Away From Plant." The Authors do not consider any constitutional law aspects of the present topic. For cases touching on constitutional questions, see Arbitrator Kleinsorge in 55 LA 1020, 1025; Volz in 55 LA 663, 667; Eaton in 55 LA 459, 460; Elson in 54 LA 816, 819; Stutz in 54 LA 439, 441 (leaving constitutional questions to the courts); Steese in 52 LA 1282, 1284.

[194] Weighing these respective positions, Arbitrator Volz recognized the reason-ableness and clarity of one company's grooming regulations, stating further that they represented "a middle ground between the concern of the Company to protect and improve its image with the public and the preference of an employee

Recognizing the employee's right to determine his clothing or hair style, arbitrators nonetheless point out that such right may be limited by the nature of his employment.[195] On balance, arbitrators recognize both the "image" and the safety and health arguments of the employer and his right to regulate the employee's personal appearance for those purposes, but not for the purpose of requiring conformity to the employer's preference on such matters.[196]

It has been noted that "the prevailing theory is that the Company has the right to require its employees to cut their hair and shave when long hair and beards can reasonably threaten the Company's relations with its customers or other employees, or a real question of safety is involved."[197] With regard to the image presented by employees to the public, Arbitrator Philip Neville has elaborated:

"The arbitrator holds to the view that an employer should be free, reasonably to regulate, and to prescribe standards of, personal appearance for its employees so as to require of them a certain degree of conventionality and approximate conformation to the norm. The employer should be permitted, for instance, to prohibit extra long shoulder-length hair or extreme clothing on male employees, full beards on younger men, scanty or sexually exciting dress on the part of female employees. It should be able to expect that its employees will practice personal hygiene and will clothe themselves in a neat manner, at least where the employees meet the public."[198]

However, there must be a showing of a reasonable relation between the company's image or health and safety considerations and the need to regulate employee appearance.[199] Thus, management's right to reg-

---

for self-expression and individuality through hair styling." Pepsi Cola Bottlers, Inc., 55 LA 663, 666 (1970).

[195] See Arbitrator Volz in 55 LA 663, 666; Elson in 54 LA 816, 819–820; Stutz in 54 LA 439, 440; Krinsky in 50 LA 901, 908–909; Johnson in 49 LA 867, 868.

[196] See Arbitrator Krimsly in 54 LA 604, 605; Stutz in 54 LA 439, 441; Bothwell in 53 LA 627, 628; Kotin in 52 LA 1068, 1069; Steese in 52 LA 1282, 1284; Bradley in 51 LA 983, 988–989; Neville in 48 LA 120, 123.

[197] Dravo-Doyle Co., 54 LA 604, 606 (Krimsly, 1970).

[198] Northwest Publications, Inc., 48 LA 120, 122 (1966).

[199] See Arbitrator Eaton in 55 LA 459, 463; Elson in 54 LA 816, 820; Stutz in 54 LA 439, 441; Krinsky in 50 LA 901, 908–909 (particularly where rules "infringe on an individual's personal life"). It must also be established that company rules were adequately communicated to the employees and uniformly enforced. See Arbitrator Neblett in 55 LA 531, 535; Neville in 48 LA 120, 123; Davis in 28 LA 83, 87. In Hillview Sand & Gravel, Inc., 39 LA 35, 40 (Somers, 1962), there were no company rules prohibiting beards, but the arbitrator stated that if the employee's actions caused the company loss, it "would be well within its rights" in suspending him for continual refusal to shave off his beard.

ulate in this area is not absolute. As stated by Arbitrator Leo Kotin:

> "Companies providing a service to the public still have the right to protect their image. To the degree that that image is based upon the appearance of its employees dealing with the public, the company has the right to establish rules and standards of personal appearance. This right has long been recognized by unions. The right, however, is not absolute. Its exercise in any specific manner may be challenged as arbitrary, capricious or inconsistent with the objective for which the right is being exercised."[200]

The Employer's "Image"

The employer's public "image" is a matter of particular concern where the company offers services to the public (as, for example, an airline) or where the employee comes in contact with the company's customers (as a clerk in a store).[201] It has been emphasized that "an employee who deals with the public or who solicits sales has an added responsibility for presenting a pleasing appearance."[202] In such public contact cases arbitrators have permitted discipline or discharge where it was shown that the employee's appearance was detrimental to the company's image.

For example, where a stewardess arrived late for her scheduled flight and was disheveled in appearance, the arbitrator noted that passengers judge the airline primarily by the stewardess who is the main contact between the airline and a "fickle public"; he held that "the appearance of a tardy and disheveled Stewardess on the ramp is conduct prejudicial to the Carrier."[203] Another arbitrator likewise

---

[200] United Parcel Service, 52 LA 1068, 1069 (1968). The points made in this statement apply as well with respect to management's right to regulate for health and safety purposes. Also see Arbitrator Kotin in 53 LA 126, 128, where for the same parties he set forth standards clarifying company rules as to what constitutes satisfactory appearance for employees. In Pacific Gas & Electric Co., 55 LA 459, 464 (1970), Arbitrator Eaton formulated rules to supplant company rules about permissible facial hair.

[201] The employees themselves may recognize this fact. For example, the New York Times Service reported in March 1971 that TWA's pilots had embarked upon a program to help restore the company's earning power; the first step of the program was for the pilots to avoid "extreme styles of personal appearance" and to dress so that "any potential customer" is not offended. The pilots thus expressed recognition that employee appearance and mode of dress can produce an adverse public reaction detrimental to the employer's operations.

[202] Pepsi Cola Bottlers, Inc., 55 LA 663, 666 (Volz, 1970). Similarly, Allied Employers, Inc., 55 LA 1020, 1024 (Kleinsorge, 1970).

[203] Western Air Lines, Inc., 37 LA 130, 133–134 (Wyckoff, 1961), holding, however, that discharge was too severe and reducing the penalty to 7 months suspension without pay. In Trans World Airlines, Inc., 46 LA 611, 612 (Wallen,

stressed the company's image and upheld its right to protect its image of giving better service through its neat, clean employees; he stated that the "vast majority of the public" associates long hair and beards with irresponsibility.[204]

However, in another case where an employee refused to cut his long hair and shave his beard to comply with a company rule, the arbitrator found that the employee worked in an isolated area where contact with customers and other employees was extremely rare, and he further noted that at the hearing the grievant's general appearance was one of "cleanliness and neatness," although his hair was long and he had sideburns and a short van dyke beard. Stating that the rule "as it applied to this grievant working in this location is not reasonable," the arbitrator held that the grievant could maintain the hair style he desired so long as it did not affect his work or that of other employees, or the company's relations with its customers.[205]

The concern of management with its image is keyed to public acceptance of the clothing and hair styles adopted by its employees. As mores change and the acceptability of given attire and hair styles is no longer questioned by the general public, industry has likewise accepted changes. This is effectively illustrated by the evolution of

---

1965), it was held that "management must be accorded the right to verify compliance with clothing, hair length and appearance regulations in a manner which imposes no unreasonable or undignified demands on the employee," and that requiring "such verification is neither improper nor unreasonable"; therefore the airline had the right to require a hostess to demonstrate that she was not wearing a wig.

[204] Western Air Lines, Inc., 52 LA 1282, 1284 (Steese, 1969), upholding discharge for refusal to comply with rule prohibiting long hair and beards. Also upholding discharge, see Arbitrator Dugan in 57 LA 994, 995; Daly in 57 LA 453, 456; Kleinsorge in 55 LA 1020, 1025; Volz in 55 LA 663, 666–667; Johnson in 49 LA 867, 868 (supermarket employee wore his hair long for his second job in a rock and roll band). Also see Casselman in 57 LA 789, 794–795. Upholding or assessing a lesser penalty for refusal to comply with appearance regulations, see Arbitrator Caraway in 52 LA 1117, 1118; Turkus in 51 LA 292, at 292, and in 47 LA 1182, at 1182.

[205] Dravo-Doyle Co., 54 LA 604, 605–607 (Krimsly, 1970). Similarly, see Badger Concrete Co., 50 LA 901, 908 (Krinsky, 1968), but also holding that the company can enforce the rule as to some classes of employees or employees performing certain jobs, for safety or other reasons connected with the company's operations. Id. at 909. Also see Hillview Sand & Gravel, Inc., 39 LA 35, 39–40 (Somers, 1962), observing that an employee can look neat and shave daily (in compliance with a company rule) and still retain a beard. Refusing to uphold the employer's rule or assessment of discipline as to long hair, see Arbitrator Forsythe in 57 LA 1017, 1019 (employee could use wig to cover long hair); Jacobs in 57 LA 963, 969–970; Leonard in 57 LA 821, 824; Somers in 57 LA 410, 414; Strong in 57 LA 197, 199.

acceptability of certain attire of female employees: in the 1930's women were not permitted to wear slacks in some plants because of a possible production hazard in distracting male employees;[206] in the 1940's many plants *required* women to wear slacks to avoid danger involved in working around industrial machinery;[207] in the 1950's and 1960's, slacks for women gained wide acceptability; by 1970 slacks, often in the form of "pant suits" or "pant dresses," came to be viewed by many employers as the preferable attire, gaining approval not only in industrial plants but also in many other business concerns (offices—even some government offices—and retail establishments), hospitals, and airlines (for stewardesses).[208]

One arbitrator has urged: "Custom and fashion in dress and behavior change from time to time, and employees should be permitted to conform reasonably with these changes."[209] So long as no detriment results to the company and no safety or health hazard is involved, conformity to current fashion should not be objectionable if the style followed is not extreme—one can be "in fashion" without resorting to the extremes of fads.[210]

Safety and Health Considerations

Safety, health, and sanitation reasons also have been advanced in imposing restrictions on employees' apparel, hair, or beards.[211]

---

[206] See comments in Mitchell-Bentley Corp., 45 LA 1071, 1073 (Ryder, 1965), involving the wearing of shorts by women workers.

[207] Also for reasons of modesty when women worked, for instance, as welders on elevated platforms. The issue faced in an early case by one arbitrator (decided in the negative) was whether *red* slacks constituted a production hazard because of a tendency to distract male employees. Shulman, Opinions of the Umpire (Ford Motor Co.), Opinion A-117 (1944).

[208] Admittedly, many employers found the pant suits or pant dresses preferable to the "mini" dress which, for instance, led many employers to feel compelled to add "modesty shields" at the front of secretary desks. In School District of Kingsley, 56 LA 1138, 1145 (Howlett, 1971), a school board's notice prohibiting teachers from wearing pant suits was held to be "null and void."

[209] Springday Co., 53 LA 627, 629 (Bothwell, 1969).

[210] A discharged shipping clerk was described as "wearing boots, tight clinging orange-brown pants (with a wide oversized belt and buckle) and a flowing hirsute cranial adornment characteristic of the Beatles." But since his past record was good and since he demonstrated a willingness to cooperate by appearing at the hearing "shorn of his flowing locks, and presenting the very epitome of the more mundane accepted norm," he was reinstated without back pay on condition that he continue to maintain such appearance. American Export-Isbrandten Lines, Inc., 47 LA 1182, at 1182 (Turkus, 1967).

[211] See Arbitrator Mattice in 57 LA 1036, 1038; Elson in 54 LA 816, 819–820; Stutz in 54 LA 439, 441; Bothwell in 53 LA 627, 628–629; Bradley in 51 LA 983, 988–990; Krinsky in 50 LA 901, 908. Also see Arbitrator Davis in

Questions of safety may be raised where loose fitting clothing, dangling jewelry, and long unprotected hair are worn while operating machinery. Management may be expected to object when an employee operating machinery wears a loose shirt with the tail hanging out, or a dangling bracelet or necklace (even a wedding ring may be a hazard in some situations[212]), or long hair, any of which may become caught or entangled in the machinery. In a case involving a safety rule regarding loose apparel and long unprotected hair, management was upheld in refusing to permit an employee to continue work unless he trimmed his beard, Arbitrator Wilber C. Bothwell ruling:

> "It is properly the function of management personnel who directly supervise employees to determine the conditions under which a beard constitutes a safety hazard. The individual employee cannot decide how safety rules are to apply to him, or whether or not he should obey a particular safety rule in a particular situation. * * *

> *   *   *   *   *

> "The arbitrator cannot determine whether a particular beard constitutes a safety hazard. This must be done on a day to day basis by supervision in the industrial plant. Only if such decisions by supervision are clearly unreasonable should the arbitrator intervene."[213]

He stated further: "The employee is not being unreasonably restrained in his conduct or dress so long as there is a reasonable relation between what is required and safety."[214]

A reasonable relation likewise must be shown where health reasons are argued. Thus, an arbitrator found that it was unreasonable of the company to apply a general rule against growing beards to the grievant where the health reasons urged by the company—that beards contributed to dermatitis caused by handling the company's

---

28 LA 83, 87. For general considerations of safety and health matters, see Chapter 16, Safety and Health.

[212] See Bethlehem Mines Corp., 48 LA 765, 766 (Strongin, 1967).

[213] Springday Co., 53 LA 627, 628–629 (1969), where the company did not prohibit the wearing of beards but only regulated them for safety purposes. Another arbitrator would not lay down guidelines as to the point where "face hair becomes hirsute and unacceptable" from a safety standpoint, stating that "each mustache and each pair of sideburns * * * will have to be measured against the safety factor and treated accordingly." City of Waterbury, 54 LA 439, 441 (Stutz, 1970).

[214] Springday Co., 53 LA 627, 629 (1969). A reasonable relationship was not found where the employee (operating machinery) wore a protective cap over his long hair. Challenge-Cook Bros., Inc., 55 LA 517, 520–521 (Roberts, 1970).

product—were found not to apply to the grievant who was a mechanic and had little or no contact with the product.[215]

Employers may attempt to combat employee hirsuteness for sanitation reasons. In one case, the arbitrator recognized that "The maintenance of a [supermarket] meat department, so as to give a clean and sanitary appearance, is essential to its proper operation." But he concluded that sideburns "even somewhat fuzzier" than those worn by the grievant at the hearing did not present a reasonable basis for concern.[216] However, another arbitrator emphasized that "Although hair styles have changed, sanitation needs have not"; and he upheld the discharge of an employee who wore sideburns longer than permitted by the company rule, which the arbitrator held was directed at protecting the company's products from hair contamination rather than at regulating employees' appearance.[217]

Wigs and hair pieces may likewise be the subjects of company rules. In one case, the arbitrator held that for sanitation reasons a meat packing company could prohibit the wearing of wigs and hair pieces in the plant; he placed such items in the same category as hats and other "street clothing" which were barred from the plant by a company rule (the company providing dressing rooms for changing) and by a U.S. Department of Agriculture regulation, such "street clothing" being considered a source of contamination.[218]

Accommodation of Employees' Religious Beliefs

Employees sometimes have complained that their freedom of religion was violated by the scheduling of work on the Sabbath or on other religious holidays. They have urged that they were discriminated against when the employer required them to work on such days or disciplined them for their failure to work. However, at least until 1972, when Title VII of the Civil Rights Act was amended to impose an obligation upon management to make reasonable accommodations for employee religious beliefs (details are noted at the end of this topic),

---

[215] Badger Concrete Co., 50 LA 901, 908 (Krinsky, 1968).
[216] Economy Super Mart, 54 LA 816, 820 (Elson, 1970).
[217] Kellogg Co., 55 LA 84, 88 (Shearer, 1970).
[218] Marhoefer Packing Co., 51 LA 583, 588–590 (Bradley, 1968), with much discussion of evidence comparing natural hair with wigs, and noting in particular that in contrast with natural hair wigs become brittle and break and that dust and dirt settling on a wig can fall off or be blown away more easily.

arbitrators generally had held that the employer was not required to accommodate individual requests for scheduling work so that the employee could observe religious holidays; and discharge or discipline had been upheld where the employee had refused for such reason to work as scheduled.[219]

Arbitrator Clyde W. Summers has stated, "In spite of the high value placed on religious freedom in our society, employers have commonly scheduled work on days which are the sabbath for various employees and are generally considered entitled to dismiss employees who refuse to work for religious reasons."[220] Furthermore, arbitrators have emphasized the company's right to maintain efficient industrial operations, and they have noted the "industrial chaos" which would result if the company were required to accommodate the "individual subjective beliefs" of various employees.[221]

Another aspect of the problem should be noted, i.e., "reverse discrimination." Thus, where the contract contained a provision prohibiting discrimination, it was observed that to treat an employee differently for religious reasons would be to discriminate against other employees in violation of the contract.[222] Also, it has been argued that should the company permit such differential treatment for religious reasons it might be subject to a charge of "reverse discrimination" or favoritism.[223]

In one case, a foreman discontinued a special schedule for one employee when other employees complained that such arrangement was discriminatory; the employee grieved when he was told that he would have to work his regular schedule or become subject to disci-

---

[219] See Arbitrator Turkus in 52 LA 707, 708; Walt in 50 LA 375, 380; Daugherty in 49 LA 204, 206; Garrett in 48 LA 1340, 1342–1343; Cahn in 48 LA 619, 620–621; Summers in 39 LA 374, 378–379; Stark in 29 LA 77, 79; Kelliher in 15 LA 121, 123.

[220] Stanley Works, 39 LA 374, 378–379 (1962).

[221] See Arbitrator Turkus in 52 LA 707, 708; Walt in 50 LA 375, 380; Daugherty in 49 LA 204, 206; Cahn in 48 LA 619, 621. Also see Stark in 29 LA 77, 79. Cf., Spiegal, Inc., 55 LA 653, 657 (Luskin, 1970), involving a de minimus situation.

[222] Avco Lycoming Div., 52 LA 707, 708 (Turkus, 1969); Combustion Engineering, Inc., 49 LA 204, 206 (Daugherty, 1967).

[223] This was a company argument in United States Steel Corp., 56 LA 694, 695 (McDaniel, 1971). The contract in this case, however, contained a requirement that the joint Committee on Civil Rights "shall review matters involving Civil Rights" and the arbitrator set aside the discharge pending such review. Id. at 696–697.

pline.[224] Ruling for the company, the arbitrator stated: "This simply is not a case involving discrimination *against* grievant because of his religious beliefs. Rather, it is he who seeks a special privilege which is not accorded to other employees."[225] But in another case, discipline of an employee for refusal to work on Sunday for religious reasons was held to constitute discrimination in violation of the contract where the company had habitually shown consideration for the religious scruples of other employees in the plant.[226]

May an employer require employees of the same faith to take time off on religious days, imposing upon them the same degree of observance he finds proper for himself? Arbitrator Eva Robbins has answered in the negative, ruling that to do so would be an arbitrary use of the contractual right to relieve employees from duty.[227]

Even prior to the amendment of Title VII of the Civil Rights Act of 1964, the Equal Employment Opportunity Commission guidelines stated that the duty imposed by Title VII not to discriminate on religious grounds "includes an obligation on the part of the employer to make reasonable accommodations to the religious needs of employees * * * where such accommodations can be made without hardship on the conduct of the employer's business." In *Dewey* v. *Reynolds Metals Company* the discharge of an employee who refused to work on Sundays or to induce others to work in his place was upheld, the court ruling that the employer had made "reasonable accommodation" to the employee's religious needs when it gave him the opportunity to secure replacements for his Sunday overtime assignments.[228]

Under Title VII of the Civil Rights Act as amended by the Equal Opportunity Act of 1972, employers must make reasonable accommo-

---

[224] United States Steel Corp., 48 LA 1340, 1341 (Garrett, 1967).

[225] Id. at 1343.

[226] Goodyear Tire & Rubber Co., 1 LA 121, 122–123 (McCoy, 1945). Also see International Shoe Co., 2 LA 201, 205–206 (Klamon, 1946), where the company long had condoned the refusal of an employee for religious reasons to work Saturday overtime—but the arbitrator limited his award to the grievant before him and held that as to new employees and all employees who had previously entered no objection to working Saturday or Sunday, "the company has every right forthwith to discharge any such employee who refuses to work when all other employees are required to work."

[227] Eagle Electric Mfg. Co., 31 LA 1038, 1039 (1957). Also see Eagle Electric Mfg. Co., 29 LA 489, 491 (Gamser, 1957), finding a violation of the seniority provisions under like circumstances.

[228] 429 F. 2d 324 (CA 6, 1970), affirmed by a 4–4 decision of the Supreme Court, 91 S.Ct. 2186 (1971).

dations for employee religious beliefs in the scheduling of work and the like "unless an employer demonstrates that he is unable to reasonably accommodate to an employee's or prospective employee's religious observance or practice without undue hardship on the conduct of the employer's business."[229]

Fraternization, Intermarriage of Employees, Employment of Relatives, Married Employees

Management sometimes promulgates rules prohibiting fraternization among its employees, intermarriage of employees, employment of relatives of its employees, and employment after marriage of certain employees. Arbitrators appear to subject such rules to close scrutiny, but uphold them when justification is shown.

In one case, a company promulgated a rule prohibiting male and female employees from fraternizing after a "love triangle" of employees ended in a shooting incident. Upholding the discharge of an employee who likewise became involved in a love triangle situation, the arbitrator held that the rule was reasonable under the facts.[230] Similarly, discipline was upheld when an airline pilot violated a rule prohibiting dating between male crew members and hostesses, the arbitrator stating that the company has a right to establish and enforce regulations prohibiting practices "which could reasonably result in detriment, damage, and even disaster" in the areas of safety and comfort of passengers in flight, the company's good name, and the reputation of its hostesses.[231]

As to a company policy against hiring or continuing the employment of relatives, it has been held that in the absence of special circumstances or a showing that intermarriage of employees created a particular problem or had an adverse effect upon the operation of the plant, a rule requiring the resignation or termination of one

---

[229] Section 701 (j). As analyzed in the Congressional Record, March 6, 1972, this subsection requires employers to make reasonable accommodations for religious practices "which differ from the employer's or potential employer's requirements regarding standards, schedules, or other business-related employment conditions." That source also states that "The purpose of this subsection is to provide the statutory basis for EEOC to formulate guidelines on discrimination because of religion such as those challenged in Dewey v. Reynolds Metals Company."

[230] Alterman Foods, Inc., 45 LA 459, 460–461 (Woodruff, 1965).

[231] Braniff Airways, Inc., 29 LA 487, 489 (Yeager, 1957).

of the employees could not stand.[232] But another arbitrator upheld a company policy not to hire the spouse of an incumbent employee (male or female) in the interest of a harmonious working relationship in the bargaining unit and to maintain order and efficiency; he placed the burden upon the union to show the unreasonableness of the policy.[233]

A no-marriage policy for airline stewardesses and women employees in other industries has been the subject of many arbitration cases. While upheld as reasonable in earlier cases, arbitrators have been reluctant to uphold such policy in recent years. They cite the fact that "times have changed and views have been altered by experience."[234] In holding such a rule unreasonable in an airline stewardess case, Arbitrator Saul Wallen found that its justification as a safety measure is minimal, its value as a sales promotion device is doubtful, and it is not in conformity with modern attitudes and trends of thought.[235] Even where the contract gave the company the right to terminate six months after marriage, the right was held to be limited to exercising the option by using good faith judgment and discretion (with respect to individual stewardesses) to determine whether the employee's performance of her duties was adversely affected by her marriage.[236]

In another industry, the contract in the case specified certain grounds for the termination of employees but did not include marriage or pregnancy. The arbitrator held that marriage or pregnancy per

---

[232] Hayes Industries, Inc., 44 LA 820, 823 (Teple, 1965), stating that the policy was not clearly stated or consistently followed. Also see Western Air Lines, Inc., 53 LA 1238, 1240 (Wyckoff, 1969).

[233] Studebaker Corp., 49 LA 105, 110 (Davey, 1967). In Phillips v. Martin Marietta Corp., 91 S.Ct. 496 (1971), it was held that the Civil Rights Act of 1964 does not allow for one hiring policy for women and another for men, each having preschool children. The court did say that the existence of such conflicting family obligations, if demonstrably more relevant to job performance for a woman than for a man, could arguably be a basis for distinction under the Act, but that is a matter of evidence tending to show that the condition in question "is a bona fide occupational qualification reasonably necessary to the normal operation of that particular business or enterprise."

[234] Southern Airways, Inc., 47 LA 1135, 1141 (Wallen, 1966). Also see Braniff Airways, Inc., 48 LA 769, 770 (Gray, 1965).

[235] Southern Airways, Inc., 47 LA 1135, 1141 (1966). Also see Arbitrator Gray in 48 LA 769, 770; Kelliher in 48 LA 734, 737–738. Cf. Arbitrator Kahn in 48 LA 727, 733–734. The no-marriage rule has been struck down as violative of the ban on discrimination in employment on account of sex in Sprogis v. United Air Lines, Inc., 3 EPD ¶8239 (CA 7, 1971).

[236] American Airlines, Inc., 48 LA 705, 723–724, 727 (Seitz, 1967).

se was not cause for discharge. However, as a matter of safety and health management may "promulgate certain rules relating to layoff when pregnancy is advanced to a point where hazards arise to the employee, the unborn infant, and perhaps other employees."[237]

Privacy, Dignity, and Peace of Mind

In management's direction of the enterprise, situations sometimes occur in which employees allege an invasion of their right of privacy or an infringement upon their dignity or peace of mind. Employees have invoked such rights in attempts to protect personal aspects of their industrial life in such diverse situations as a safety rule prohibiting the wearing of finger rings,[238] rules against fraternization or intermarriage of employees,[239] the regulation of employees' personal appearance,[240] requirements for giving reasons for leave of absence,[241] and the situations discussed hereinbelow.

Arbitrators have attempted to strike a balance between the personal rights of the employee and the rights of the company in the conduct of the business, considering such factors as whether there was a legitimate business need for management's action or rule,[242] whether there were reasonable safeguards for employee rights,[243] and whether management's action resulted in a substantial change in working conditions.[244]

---

[237] Alwin Mfg. Co., 38 LA 632, 638–639 (Sembower, 1962). Also finding that marriage is not proper cause for discharge, see Tennessee Coal, Iron & RR Co., 11 LA 1062, 1065 (Seward, 1948). Where the contract provided that marriage would not disqualify a stewardess from employment with the company but that pregnancy would, the employer properly discharged a stewardess who had concealed her pregnancy and falsely secured sick leave in Western Air Lines, Inc., 54 LA 600, 603 (Wyckoff, 1970).

[238] Bethlehem Mines Corp., 48 LA 765, 766 (Strongin, 1967), where the arbitrator found the rule to be reasonable, rejecting the union's claim that the rule, as it pertains to wedding bands, infringes upon the employee's religious and moral beliefs.

[239] See this Chapter, topic titled "Fraternization, Intermarriage of Employees, Employment of Relatives, Married Employees."

[240] See this Chapter, topic titled "Personal Appearance: Hair and Clothes."

[241] See this Chapter, topic titled "Leaves of Absence."

[242] See Arbitrator Stutz in 55 LA 910, 915–916; Keefe in 53 LA 525, 530; Scheiber in 53 LA 312, 317–320; Seinsheimer in 52 LA 755, 758; Shister in 50 LA 65, 67–68; Mittenthal in 46 LA 335, 338; Delany in 44 LA 563, 564.

[243] Mead Corp., 51 LA 1121, 1124 (Griffin, 1968); Aldens, Inc., 51 LA 469, 470 (Kelliher, 1968).

[244] See Arbitrator Stutz in 55 LA 910, 914–916 (safety and health clause); Keefe in 53 LA 525, 530 (maintenance of working conditions clause); Delany in 44 LA 563, 564 (maintenance of working conditions clause).

The observations of some arbitrators in regard to claimed rights of privacy, dignity, and peace of mind are noted below in the setting of the particular situations to which they apply.

Disclosure of Information to Employer

Employees sometimes have claimed a right of privacy in resisting the employer's requirement to disclose certain information for company records. However, where such information was reasonably necessary for the proper conduct of the business, management could require the disclosure.

Thus, a company was upheld when it required an employee to disclose his unlisted phone number so that he could be contacted for necessary overtime assignments, the arbitrator stating:

> "It is my opinion that it is not an invasion of privacy for the Company to have an employee's phone number, any more than it could be considered an invasion of privacy to have his home address, or for that matter, to talk to the employee. If being able to call an employee on the telephone could be considered an invasion of his privacy, then so could just talking to him be so considered, and this is obviously just plain unadulterated nonsense."[245]

Another case involved a conflict of interest situation in which a broadcasting company was held entitled to require members of its news staff to fill out a questionnaire regarding financial interests. Regarding the claimed right of privacy, the arbitrator stated:

> "The litmus test of a careful examination makes it clear that the right of privacy is, at best, a limited right which, in general, protects the individual from having his name, picture, actions and statements commercially made public and exploited without his consent. This right, however, only safeguards him from the publication of his private statements or actions."[246]

It was held that the rule was a reasonable method of supervising employees and did not trespass upon their right of privacy since there was no public disclosure of private facts and the information was sought for the legitimate and limited business reason of insuring the absence of bias in reporting the news.[247]

---

[245] Wyandotte Chemicals Corp., 52 LA 755, 758 (Seinsheimer, 1969).
[246] National Broadcasting Co., 53 LA 312, 317 (Scheiber, 1969).
[247] Id. at 317–320, where the question of self-incrimination was also discussed. Also see Scheiber, "Tests and Questionnaires in the Labor-Management Relationship," 20 Labor L. J. 695, 697–702 (1969).

Name Tags

In two cases, arbitrators considered the question of whether management can require employees to wear their surnames on their uniforms. One case involved city police while the other involved service employees of a gas company. In both, the union argued that adding the employee's surname to his uniform was a change in working conditions and that the employer was required to bargain on the issue. In both cases, the union also argued that the wearing of surnames on their uniforms would subject the employees (and their families) to harrassment and an invasion of their privacy. The arbitrator in the police case found (1) that the duty to bargain had been complied with, (2) that while individual officers and their families had received harrassing, threatening, and indecent phone calls, the evidence did not support a conclusion that increased harrassment resulted from the use of name tags, and (3) that there was a reasonable basis for issuing the name tag order (i.e., to improve the police-community relationship).[248]

The arbitrator in the gas company case, finding no legitimate business need, stated:

> "The protested surname display constitutes a recognizable and material change in the working conditions of employees which can believably be expected, under entirely plausible and predictable circumstances, to have adverse reactions on the peace-of-mind, personal security and family privacy of at least certain individuals, thereby subjecting them to unjustifiable and avoidable hardship and inconvenience—if not outright personal hazard."[249]

Observing Employees at Work

It has been said that "Management is properly concerned with the employee's work performance, what he does on the job and whether he obeys the plant's rules and regulations."[250] Such matters are regularly noted by supervisors. However, employees have sometimes alleged that management has gone beyond the proper limits of its right to observe them for the aforementioned purposes.[251]

---

[248] City of Boston, 55 LA 910, 915–916 (Stutz, 1970), where the arbitrator, notwithstanding such findings, stated that if harrassment should increase, and the increase can be attributed to the name tags, the union would have sound basis for demanding that the use of name tags be abandoned.

[249] Michigan Consolidated Gas Co., 53 LA 525, 529 (Keefe, 1969).

[250] FMC Corp., 46 LA 335, 338 (Mittenthal, 1966).

[251] For related discussion, see Chapter 8, topic titled "Evidence Obtained by Allegedly Improper Methods."

Thus, in one case employees complained that intensive observations by a production engineer in cooperation with the foreman created undue "alarm and annoyance" and "fear and apprehension." The arbitrator found that the engineer was performing a proper management function, and he noted that "Although emotional tranquility is a condition much to be desired in labor relations, it is not one of the rights guaranteed by law or by the contract between the parties."[252]

In two cases involving the installation of closed circuit television to observe workers arbitrators reached opposite conclusions. In one, where there had been loss of material and equipment, the company was upheld, Arbitrator Richard Mittenthal stating:

> "One of the supervisor's principal functions is to observe employees at work. Surely, such supervision cannot be said to interfere with an employee's right of privacy. The same conclusion should apply in this case. For all the Company has done is to add a different method of supervision to the receiving room—an electronic eye (i.e., the television camera) in addition to the human eye. Regardless of the type of supervision (a camera, a supervisor, or both) the employee works with the knowledge that supervision may be watching him at any time. He has a much better chance of knowing when he is being watched where there is no camera. But this is a difference in degree, not a difference in kind. For these reasons, I find there has been no interference with the employee's right of privacy."[253]

A maintenance of working conditions clause was crucial to the other case, in which there was no indication of any need to supplement the already adequate supervision.[254] Ruling that the television cameras must be removed, Arbitrator Hubert T. Delany stated:

> "While I do not base my opinion on the Union's argument of the employees' legal 'right of privacy,' nor on the argument advanced by it on unlawful 'surveillance' and 'spying,' I do agree that this

---

[252] Picker X-Ray Corp., 39 LA 1245, 1246 (Kates, 1962). Similarly, F & M Schaefer Brewing Co., 40 LA 199, 200–201 (Turkus, 1963), upholding management's right to conduct time studies and finding that in doing so management was "neither 'spying on employees' nor improperly 'maintaining them under surveillance.' "

[253] FMC Corp., 46 LA 335, 338 (1966), emphasizing that an individual's right of privacy serves to protect him against the publication of his *private* statements or *private* actions and that an employee's actions during working hours are not private actions.

[254] EICO, Inc., 44 LA 563, 564 (1965).

argument cannot be totally overlooked since I find that the TV equipment does vitally affect the employees' working conditions."[255]

Secret surveillance has been upheld in two cases, one of which involved the right of the employer to hire private checkers (whose identity need not be revealed) to follow and check the work performance of delivery truck drivers.[256] The other case involved a telephone company's use of remote listening devices to monitor secretly the telephone operators' performances. There, the union argued that "policy reasons" exist "for preventing any information gathered by secret and remote observations to be used for disciplinary purposes," explaining that such use would produce tensions upon the subject employees and that their performance would vastly improve if they were assured that such surveillance would not be so used. However, Arbitrator Russell A. Smith stated that such considerations "are more pertinent for collective bargaining than to the arbitral forum," and he commented:

> "I do not mean to suggest that 'policy considerations' will under no circumstances be relevant to a determination of the extent of management's right to make use of techniques for keeping employees under surveillance. Modern electronics has produced a variety of possibilities which, if used to the fullest extent, could disclose, surreptitiously, an employee's every move and every conversation while in the plant, whether directly work related or not. This could, allegedly, be the 'Brave New World' of Huxley or Orwell's world of 1984! Some of these developments in employee surveillance might well raise the important question whether there is not, indeed, a 'right of privacy' which employees may invoke to protect some, at least, aspects of their industrial life."[257]

But he said that in the case before him no such issue was actually presented for decision and he made no determination as to the existence or extent of the grievant's right of privacy.[258]

---

[255] Id. at 563, and he found that while the company must have a good deal of discretion in carrying on its operations, use of the TV system imposed an "appreciable and intolerable burden" on the employees.

[256] Kroger Co., 40 LA 316, 317–318 (Reid, 1963). The union had argued that the "secret agents" following the drivers in unmarked cars on unfrequented highways at night put the drivers under an "intolerable strain." Id. at 317. For discussion on the evidential use of "spotters," see Chapter 8, topic titled "Right of Cross Examination."

[257] Michigan Bell Telephone Co., 45 LA 689, 695 (1965).

[258] Id. at 696.

Checking Out

It has been held that the right of employees to absent themselves from their work area to use restrooms or for rest periods was not violated by the employer's requirement that they sign a "check-out" list; the arbitrator found that the rule was not unreasonable and that the evidence did not establish that management had invaded the employees' privacy by using the lists as a basis for improper questions regarding personal habits of individual employees.[259] Similarly, a requirement that employees sign a slip to be placed in a special box when their foreman is unavailable to give them permission to leave was held reasonable since it implemented a long standing rule that employees must obtain permission to leave their work places.[260]

While the company may require "clocking out and in" when an employee leaves his (or her) work station for personal reasons, the application of such rule must be reasonable and nondiscriminatory. So stated Arbitrator John W. Teele, who found the rule before him to be unreasonable to the extent that it was a "source of embarrassment" to female employees who were required to have their male foremen note the reason for the "clock-out." He also found the rule to be discriminatory in that it was applied unevenly in different parts of the plant.[261] While the company was ordered to revoke the rule, it was given an opportunity (after a waiting period of thirty days) to devise an alternate method of accounting for restroom time or to reinstate the "clock-out" method but with proper safeguards to eliminate discrimination, protect the individual's privacy, and avoid undue embarrassment.[262]

Another arbitrator likewise did not quarrel with the company's right to issue a check-out rule directed at abuse of relief privileges, but he found the rule before him to be unreasonable in that it was vague and imprecise in several important respects; he stated further that even if the rule could be assumed to achieve its objective of elim-

---

[259] Elgin Instrument Co., 37 LA 1064, 1068 (Roberts, 1961), where employees had abused the rest period privilege.

[260] Certain-Teed Products Corp., 38 LA 46, 48 (Sembower, 1962).

[261] Gremar Mfg. Co., 46 LA 215, 219 (1965). Concerning the invasion of privacy issue, he stated: "Whether the routine involved an invasion of personal privacy probably boils down to a matter of degree, and it is sufficient, perhaps, to find affirmatively as to embarrassment." He cited other cases dealing with check-out rules and drew certain general conclusions from them. Id. at 218–219.

[262] Id. at 220.

inating abuses, "it does so at a considerable price in terms of actual or threatened invasion of modesty and the ordinary amenities."[263]

Inspecting Employee Lockers, Purses, or Briefcases

In several cases, where management had serious problems with thefts or other reasonable cause, a rule or practice requiring employees to submit purses, briefcases, or lockers for inspection was upheld.[264] The arbitrator in a purse case emphasized that employees are entitled to reasonable safeguards but have a duty to cooperate. He found that the company took all reasonable procedural precautions to protect the employee's privacy and dignity when the security guard exhibited her badge and asked the employee to come to a closed room where the inspection would be made only by the female security guard.[265]

Another arbitrator cautioned that the company must not act in a discriminatory, capricious, arbitrary, or unreasonable fashion but must have a reasonable basis for its search of employee lockers—in this case, the company's search for missing company property was a reasonable basis and the manner of conducting the search was proper.[266]

Use of Personal Radios

It has been stated that "Absent any privilege on the part of the employees which would amount to a contractual right to bring radios into the shop and using them in an unrestricted manner," the company can promulgate rules absolutely or partially restricting employee use of personal radios in the plant so long as such rules are not arbitrary,

---

[263] Detriot Gasket & Mfg. Co., 27 LA 717, 722 (Crane, 1956). In one case, the employer approached the problem of loitering in restrooms and defacing of toilet doors by removing the doors to the toilets, later agreeing to replace them when the union agreed to cooperate in trying to prevent such loitering and defacing. The case went to arbitration when a modest employee, who felt the doorless toilets were "not decent or proper," was discharged for leaving his department to use the restroom (with doors intact) in another department. He was reinstated without back pay (a loss of 6½ months). See Chris-Craft Corp., 45 LA 117, 118–119 (Autry, 1965).

[264] See Arbitrator Kelliher in 51 LA 469, 470; Shister in 50 LA 65, 67–68; Williams in 39 LA 934, 936–937. In Fruehauf Corp., 49 LA 89, 90–91 (Daugherty, 1967), a past practice of inspecting outgoing employees' lunch buckets for possible pilfered company property was found to support the company in searching incoming employees' buckets for liquor on a preholiday shift where drinking on the job had been a problem on such shifts in the past.

[265] Alden's, Inc., 51 LA 469, 470 (Kelliher, 1968).

[266] International Nickel Co., 50 LA 65, 68 (Shister, 1967).

unreasonable, or discriminatory.[267] Thus, a company restriction on use of radios may be found proper if it is based upon adequate reasons such as insuring the quality and quantity of production and promoting safety in the shop.[268]

Management's right in this regard may be limited somewhat where there is a well established practice of allowing employees to play their radios. Thus, it has been held that in the absence of misuse of the radios or adverse effect on the employees' work, the company was not justified in discontinuing a long-time practice of playing radios although it could promulgate reasonable rules to control the type of program as well as the volume of sound.[269]

While one arbitrator ruled that the company was unreasonable in imposing an absolute ban on radios in a plant which had a "well established traditional right of employees to play radios," he also ruled that the company has "ULTIMATE authority to ban employee radios when such a ban appears to be—after suitable alternatives have been tried—the only practical ('reasonable') solution."[270]

In another case where permission had always been required to bring in radios, the arbitrator held that "the practice existed only subject to management permission, modification, or prohibition," and that the employer could properly refuse to permit it to spread to a newly opened building.[271] That arbitrator stated that "it is relevant that the use of personal radios seems to come closer to the area of

[267] Anaconda Aluminum Co., 51 LA 281, 283–284 (Dolson, 1968), finding no established practice to support the alleged right and finding that the company's restrictions were reasonable and proper, but also finding that the rules were discriminatorily applied.

[268] Ibid. Accord, McGraw-Edison Power Systems Div., 53 LA 1024, 1027 (Lewis, 1969), also adding that use of radios in areas where customers are present can lead to an unfavorable customer reaction. Also see Eastern Air Lines, Inc., 44 LA 1034, 1040 (Yagoda, 1965).

[269] Minnosota Mining & Mfg. Co., 49 LA 332, 334 (Jensen, 1967), where there was a 20-year practice of permitting radios during nonworking time; Bangor Punta Operations, Inc., 48 LA 1275, 1276 (Kates, 1967), where the practice of playing radios during working time was recognized but the company could also substitute "piped-in" music or company provided radios at reasonable locations.

[270] Square D Co., 66-1 ARB ¶8134, p. 3493 (Kahn, 1963), finding that a "reasonable procedure" would include efforts by supervision to discuss the problem of objectionable radio playing with the offending employee, and if that failed to discuss it with the union.

[271] Eastern Air Lines, Inc., 44 LA 1034, 1038, 1040 (Yagoda, 1965), where the contract contained a clause maintaining privileges so long as they are not abused.

traditional and conventional management discretion concerning productive factors and influences, than to that of employee rights not so intimately connected with the productive process."[272]

Coffee Making by Employees; Free Coffee

As to employee use of coffee-making equipment in work areas, management has been held entitled to prohibit such use in the absence of an express recognition of the privilege in the agreement or a showing of a well-established practice.[273] In a case where the contract had a maintenance of practices clause and there was an established practice of employees brewing their coffee, it was held that the company violated the contract by installing coffee vending machines and requiring the removal of employees' coffee-making equipment; but the company could impose requirements for "orderly and reasonable use of the equipment for coffee and related beverage making" and could require employees using this equipment to be responsible for "orderly housekeeping practices and any abuses of excessive time use on the equipment."[274]

Where there is an established practice of supplying free coffee to employees during coffee breaks and/or lunch periods, arbitrators have held that the employer may not unilaterally discontinue such practice,[275] but that the company may change the manner in which it supplies the coffee.[276]

Dangerous Weapons on Company Property

The company has a duty to protect the health and safety of its employees, which duty includes "maintaining the right kind of en-

---

[272] Id. at 1040.

[273] Benson Manufacturing Div., 52 LA 571, 574 (Belcher, 1968), finding that the alleged practice was not approved but was intermittent and sometimes surreptitious; Ohio Power Co., 50 LA 501, 504 (Teple, 1967), stating that "The kind of equipment which can be brought onto the Company's premises, and the use of Company time to operate such equipment, would appear to be well within the general authority and control of management" unless the agreement expressly recognizes the particular privilege.

[274] Sheridan Machine Co., 37 LA 831, 832–833 (Gomberg, 1961), also holding that management could "protect itself against the erosion of its rights" by employee extension of the coffee-making privilege to using sandwich grills and frying and cooking pans.

[275] Beech-Nut Life Savers, Inc., 39 LA 1188, 1191 (Handsaker, 1962); Cushmans Sons, Inc., 37 LA 381, 383, 385 (Scheiber, 1961).

[276] Pillsbury Co., 34 LA 615, 616 (McIntosh, 1960).

vironment where employees can be trusted not to commit acts of violence against other employees."[277] To this end it may promulgate and
enforce rules dealing with dangerous weapons.[278] Thus, discharge or
discipline has been upheld when an employee was guilty of infraction
of a no-weapons rule.[279]

Even where there is no express written rule prohibiting firearms
or knives on company premises, the company can prohibit them and
can discipline employees for bringing such weapons to company
premises. "Some conduct is so obviously contrary to good sense, notice
of that fact by all employees may be assumed."[280] But where "conditions of permissiveness" existed, the arbitrator reduced discharge to
five months disciplinary suspension, emphasizing that if the company
had warned the employees about a new rule prohibiting firearms and
if there had been a "line of demarcation between the * * * permissiveness and a new strict policy," discharge would have been upheld.[281]

Company Liability for Employee's
Damaged or Stolen Property

When an employee's equipment or personal property is damaged
or stolen while on company premises (most cases have involved tools),

---

[277] Albritton Engineering Corp., 46 LA 857, 859 (Hughes, 1966). Also see
Michigan Standard Alloy, Inc., 53 LA 511, 513 (Forsythe, 1969).

[278] See Brodie Industrial Trucks, Inc., 50 LA 112, 114 (Teele, 1968); Campbell Soup Co., 2 LA 27, 31 (Lohman, 1946).

[279] See Arbitrator Ryder in 53 LA 1028, 1029–1030; Williams in 53 LA
545, 546–547; Willingham in 50 LA 403, 412 (many cases cited); Teele in
50 LA 112, 114–115; Larson in 61-3 ARB ¶8665. But the evidence of such
infraction must be convincing. See Michigan Standard Alloy, Inc., 53 LA 511,
513 (Forsythe, 1969). In Navy Exchange, 52 LA 1142, 1144 (Williams, 1969),
it was found that grievant was not the aggressor but drew a knife in a "defensive
posture."

[280] Ross-Meehan Foundries, 55 LA 1078, 1080 (King, 1970), nevertheless
holding that discharge was too severe under the peculiar circumstances (grievant's
son had been shot by a fellow employee), and reinstating grievant with only
2 days disciplinary suspension. In accord with the above-quoted statement, see
Brown & Williamson Tobacco Corp., 50 LA 403, 412 (Willingham, 1968).
Discharge was upheld in International Harvester Co., 50 LA 766, 767–768 (Doyle,
1968), citing many cases; Inland Container Corp., 28 LA 312, 314 (Ferguson,
1957). Reducing discharge to a long suspension in the absence of a rule, see
Owens-Corning Fiberglas Corp., 54 LA 419, 420 (Reed, 1970); American Synthetic Rubber Corp., 46 LA 1161, 1163–1165 (Dolson, 1966), involving other
charges as well. For cases where the company alleged a work-related incident
occurring off the company premises, see International Paper Co., 52 LA 1266,
1269 (Jenkins, 1969); Bird & Son, Inc., 30 LA 948, 950–951 (Sembower, 1958).

[281] Bright-O Inc., 54 LA 498, 500 (Mullin, 1970).

he sometimes claims entitlement to recompense from the company. In a few cases the company was held liable for the loss.[282] In many other cases the company was not held liable.[283] The elements argued by the parties or considered by the arbitrator in these cases included: (1) whether the contract's safety and health provision was applicable, (2) whether a bailment relationship existed between the parties, (3) whether the company had exercised reasonable care or had been negligent in regard to the employee's property, (4) whether the contract contained language express or implied to impose liability upon the company, and (5) whether there had been contract negotiations on the subject.

Most arbitrators have rejected the contention that the safety and health provision of the contract applies in cases where an employee's equipment or personal property is stolen or damaged while on company premises. Arbitrator Edwin R. Teple stated that such provision "clearly relates to the employees themselves, and not to their equipment or personal possessions."[284] Arbitrator Marion Beatty felt that "to apply provisions of the working agreement to issues here is reaching way out, for it would take an extremely liberal interpretation of the working agreement to read into it a duty of the Company to insure against loss of the personal effects of an employee under any circumstances."[285] Arbitrator Rolf Valtin stated that it "would be a strained interpretation" of the safety clause to hold the company responsible for the safekeeping of all personal belongings stored in company-provided lockers.[286] And Arbitrator Donald A. Crawford wrote: "Nor do safety clauses as used in labor agreements generally provide for damage suits unless there is a specific provision to that effect."[287]

---

[282] See Arbitrator Amis in 54 LA 430, 432; Lennard in 49 LA 76, 79–80; Cohen in 43 LA 114, 115; Handsaker in 22 LA 482, 483–484; Luskin in 14 LA 641, 644.

[283] See Arbitrator Teple in 55 LA 700, 703–704; Kesselman in 54 LA 240, 242–243; Jenkins in 53 LA 963, 964; Gorsuch in 69-2 ARB ¶8750; Cahn in 51 LA 636, 638; Hampton in 50 LA 348, 350–351; Leonard in 66-1 ARB ¶8362; Block in 47 LA 574, 575; Beatty in 41 LA 727, 729; Valtin in 37 LA 195, 196, and in 32 LA 124, 125–126; Crawford in 36 LA 1136, 1137.

[284] Standard Products Co., 55 LA 700, 704 (1970). Accord, Arbitrator Kesselman in 54 LA 240, 243; Stouffer in 46 LA 106, 108. Also see Fruehauf Corp., 50 LA 348, 350 (Hampton, 1968).

[285] Trans World Airlines, Inc., 41 LA 727, 729 (1963), where the union argued for the application of the safety and health provision and a general provision requiring cooperation between the company and the union.

[286] Bethlehem Steel Co., 32 LA 124, 126 (1959).

[287] Curtiss-Wright Corp., 36 LA 1136, 1137 (1961), where an employee claimed damages for the cost of replacing eyeglasses broken because of the company's alleged negligence regarding defective machinery.

However, Arbitrator Melvin Lennard stated: "While I believe that it is true general safety clauses are designed primarily to safeguard the health and personal security of employees, such clauses should not be held to exclude *all* items of personal property." He postulated that eyeglasses, hearing aids, and items of clothing actually being worn by the employee while at work "seem almost to be extensions of the employee's person," that such items as well as tools the employee is required to furnish make possible the proper performance of the employee's work, and that management and employee interests in having the job well done "form one of the bases for interpreting" the safety clause to cover such personal effects and employee-owned tools. On this basis he concluded: "* * * I believe that when the present employer agreed [in the contract] to 'make reasonable provision for the safety and health of its employees at the plant,' it undertook to do that for both the personal health and safety of employees and also for their clothing being worn, their eyeglasses, hearing aids, etc., and also for tools which the employer requires the employee to bring in and work with."[288] However, he cautioned that nothing in his decision "should be construed as holding or even suggesting that this employer is, or must become, an insurer of employees' tools," but that his decision was directed to the company's obligation to observe an adequate standard of care where locked tool boxes were left on the plant premises in the exclusive custody of the employer while their owners were away from the plant.[289]

The applicability of bailment concepts is sometimes considered by arbitrators in determining the responsibility of the company for the safekeeping of employee property left or stored on plant premises. In this regard Arbitrator Louis C. Kesselman noted two schools of thought, with arbitrators of one school suggesting that "a bailment relationship for the mutual benefit of both parties has been created by the Company's requirement that the mechanics furnish their own hand tools for the Company's benefit and by the Company's awareness of and acquiescence to having the tools stored on its premises due to the physical problem of removing them each night." Under this rationale, he said that if a bailment relationship does exist in a given case, it is then proper for the arbitrator to determine whether the company has been negligent in safeguarding the property in question.

---

[288] Sargent-Fletcher Co., 49 LA 76, 78 (1967).
[289] Id. at 80.

Arbitrators of the other school of thought, which Arbitrator Kesselman endorsed, reason as follows: (1) The arbitrator's duty is to interpret the parties' agreement, which is the law in every case before him. (2) A bailment relationship is a legal one which may or may not be incorporated into the contract—if it is, it should be enforced by the arbitrator. (3) If a bailment relationship is not a part of the contract, the arbitrator has no authority to enforce it or to rule on the question of negligence because such a ruling cannot be enforced by him.[290]

Some arbitrators have cited the company's negligence in ruling for the employee,[291] while other arbitrators have found for the company since it had made a reasonable effort to protect the employee's property.[292] Arbitrators have also looked to the contract and, finding nothing there to impose liability on the company, have denied the grievance or found it nonarbitrable (some referring the grievant to a civil court of law).[293] In some cases it was emphasized either that

---

[290] Commercial Motor Freight Co., 54 LA 240, 243–244 (1970), citing arbitrators for both lines of reasoning.

[291] See Arbitrator Lennard in 49 LA 76, 79–80 (company did not provide a locked area for tool boxes or a system to safeguard tool box keys left with the guard); Cohen in 43 LA 114, 115 (others had access to locked storage area); Handsaker in 22 LA 482, 483–484; Luskin in 14 LA 641, 644. In Plough, Inc., 54 LA 430, 432 (Amis, 1970), the contract required the company to furnish and maintain satisfactory lockers, and while grievants were out on strike the company emptied their lockers (piling the contents in boxes) to make lockers available for employees hired to replace the strikers. The arbitrator held that the company failed to exercise reasonable care and therefore was required to compensate the grievants for damage to and loss of their property. Arbitrators Lennard in 49 LA 76, 79, and Cohen in 43 LA 114, 115, commenting on the advantage to the company from the presence of employee tools on the premises, noted that the company's obligation varies from exercising greater care when the employee's property is in its exclusive custody to exercising lesser care when the custody is shared or is almost exclusively in the employee himself.

[292] See Arbitrator Teple in 55 LA 700, 704 (fence with barbed wire on top, locked gate, guards); Gorsuch in 69-2 ARB ¶8750; Stouffer in 46 LA 106, 108; Valtin in 37 LA 195, 196 (new locks on locker-room doors, janitors instructed to keep doors locked, employees invited to report suspicious behavior, locker rooms included in rounds of plant guards); Valtin in 32 LA 124, 125–126. In Fruehauf Corp., 50 LA 348, 350–351 (Hampton, 1968), where a company rule held employees responsible for 50 percent of the value of company tools lost while in their possession, it was ruled that since the employer and employees each took reasonable security precautions neither was required to compensate the other for loss of tools by theft.

[293] See Arbitrator Teple in 55 LA 700, 703 (stating that he "firmly believes that the Company cannot properly be held to be an insurer of property of employees left or stored upon the plant premises unless the collective agreement contains express terms imposing such broad liability"); Kesselman in 54 LA 240, 243–244; Jenkins in 53 LA 963, 964; Cahn in 51 LA 636, 637–638 (finding a bailment relationship and a possible *legal* obligation on the company, but

contract language protecting the employees was sought unsuccessfully by the union in negotiations or that the problem of tool thefts was so widely recognized in the industry that the parties would have provided protection if they had so intended.[294]

Union Bulletin Boards

Most collective bargaining agreements contain clauses stating that the company will provide a bulletin board for the posting of union notices, usually specifying notices of union meetings, elections, social activities, and general union business (or "official" union business). Such clauses also may contain a proviso that the notices must be "approved," or "signed," or "notated" by the company. In some cases disagreement has arisen between company and union as to whether company approval was wrongly withheld or whether the notices the union sought to post were proper notices within the meaning of the contract.

In this regard, the employer has been upheld on refusing approval of a list of wages paid at another of the company's plants and at a rival company's plant (the bulletin including some controversial and political material which the company alleged would involve it in an unfair labor practice suit),[295] an announcement of the terms of a strike settlement at another company,[296] and a letter which praised and defended the union's activity but derogated and maligned the company.[297]

---

no contract violation); Stouffer in 46 LA 106, 108; Crawford in 36 LA 1136, 1137; Beatty in 41 LA 727, 729 (rejecting the union's bailment argument).

[294] See Arbitrator Jenkins in 53 LA 963, 964; Yagoda in 48 LA 1040, 1043–1044 ("Silence on this subject has significance here as an absence of intent, because of the fact that the subject of protection of employees of this kind against loss of tools is a well-known one to negotiators in this industry. It has been dealt with in other contracts by the same Union bargainers"); Block in 47 LA 574, 575; Leonard in 66-1 ARB ¶8362 (contract provision obligating the company to replace employee tools that "have been broken, lost or worn out in the performance of work for the Company" held not to apply to stolen tools in view of union's unsuccessful attempt in two previous negotiations to have the term "stolen" inserted in the clause).

[295] Reynolds Metals Co., 13 LA 278, 280 (Kleinsorge, 1949).

[296] Danly Machine Co., 13 LA 499, 500–501 (Luskin, 1949), finding that "the announcement contained material that is not customarily and generally considered an official Union announcement of the kind and character usually posted on bulletin boards where the bulletin boards are controlled by the Company."

[297] General Electric Co., 31 LA 924, 925 (LaCugna, undated). The contract provided that company approval would "not be unreasonably withheld," and

The company has also been upheld in disciplining employees who have deliberately disobeyed an order of management not to post certain materials on the union bulletin board, such as materials of a political and controversial nature.[298] In another case discharge was upheld when an employee (after being warned) repeatedly posted on the union bulletin board items which were "inflammatory and defamatory," such as a notice charging that the company practiced favoritism and nepotism in job promotions. To the employee's contention that his right of free speech was being violated, the arbitrator stated:

"In my opinion, although an employee while at work in his employer's plant may not be muzzled, he nevertheless has no unhampered right to voice opinions about his employer at the plant during his working time of such kind and in such manner as clearly to tend to disrupt employee morale or interfere with the orderly and efficient operation of the plant."[299]

In two cases where the contracts provided for union bulletin boards for the posting of "official" notices but did not require company approval, it was held that the company could remove or require the union to remove a notice containing the names of non-union employees of the company. The arbitrator in one of these cases considered the notice as detrimental to work discipline and likely to create an inflammatory response.[300] The arbitrator in the second case found that the list of names was not "official business" of the union, and he found further:

"[T]he postings tended to incite prejudice, animosity, hatred, discrimination and intimidation against certain employees of the Company because of their Non-Union affiliation. * * * Such conclusion

---

the arbitrator found that the company's refusal to approve the letter was not unreasonable in view of its controversial and derogatory tone.
    [298] Cyprus Gardens Citrus Products, Inc., 50 LA 1183, 1186 (Christon, 1968), stating that "The substance of the particular material which the Union posted was completely unrelated to the plant's operations, or to the Union's activities, either in or out of the plant." Also see Bethlehem Steel Corp., 53 LA 228, at 228 (Seward, 1969), where, after express warning, an employee deliberately violated a long-standing company rule barring the posting of notices without management's permission.
    [299] Beaver Precision Products, Inc., 51 LA 853, 854–855 (Kates, 1968), where there was no express contractual provision pertaining to bulletin boards, but the company as a matter of practice provided some for the union's use. Also finding no denial of the right of free speech, see Union Carbide Corp., 44 LA 554, 561 (Stouffer, 1965).
    [300] Quaker Oats Co., 64-3 ARB ¶8986 (Bauder, 1964).

is not predicated on a baseless assumption—any ordinary, reasonable man could predict such a resulting effect."[301]

On the other hand, even though the contract provided for company approval of notices to be posted, it has been held that the company does not have "an unrestricted right to edit and reject" union notices, and it may not arbitrarily, unreasonably, or capriciously withhold its approval; the arbitrator stated, however, that the company can "reject and refuse to approve for posting notices which contain statements that are derogatory to it and its Supervision, those containing obscene or immoral statements, and those which are patently detrimental or disloyal to the Company, its Management and/or its business." The notice in this case announced a meeting to hear a report of contract negotiations at another plant of the employer, and the arbitrator noted that while the company may have considered the purpose of the meeting to be adverse to its interests, it was not warranted in rejecting the notice.[302]

Another arbitrator, ruling on a company approval clause, stated that "The Company can not be arbitrary or capricious in making its determination of whether to post a particular notice * * * but has the right to exercise some judgment concerning its approval or willingness for posting a notice."[303] The case before him resulted from the return of two supervisors to the bargaining unit (contributing to the layoff of unit employees). The notice in question charged that such action violated the agreement and further charged that the action was taken by the company in order to cause a wildcat strike so that it could discharge strike participants, thereby breaking the union. However, the notice advised that the union had not authorized a wildcat strike and would fight the employer's action through legal means. The company's reason for not posting the notice was that it was inflammatory, but it offered to post it if objectional portions were omitted. The arbitrator, commenting that the notice had some "rather harsh words" concerning the company's action, held that the notice

---

[301] Union Carbide Corp., 44 LA 554, 561 (Stouffer, 1965). In Warren City Mfg. Co., 7 LA 202, 206 (Abernethy, 1947), the new contract dropped the company approval requirement and the arbitrator interpreted the bulletin board provision strictly, stating that the contract does not give the company authority to refuse to post "union material submitted by the union" or to remove from bulletin boards "union material posted there by the authorized officials of the union."
[302] Conn Organ Corp., 42 LA 1198, 1200 (Stouffer, 1964).
[303] Fruehauf Corp., 54 LA 1096, 1098 (Marshall, 1970).

was union business within the meaning of the union bulletin board provision and that its "main purpose seemed to be to avert a work stoppage." He concluded that the company should have posted the notice, noting that the company could have posted a notice of its own to the effect that it was not encouraging a wildcat strike.[304]

In other cases, it has been held improper to reject a notice of a meeting at which a strike vote would be taken,[305] a union version of the plant seniority list,[306] and a notice requiring union members to report any management contacts with respect to promotion out of the unit,[307] all of which were viewed as union business.

Thus, the cases noted above indicate that notices for posting on union bulletin boards (1) may not stray in subject matter from the reasonable concept of what constitutes union business at the particular plant, (2) may not be of such a nature as to have a detrimental effect upon employee morale, or of such nature as to inflame employees against each other or against the employer, (3) may not contain statements which defame the employer or are patently detrimental or disloyal to him, and (4) may not be rejected if the notices clearly are matters of "union business" even though they approach being inflammatory or adverse to the company's interests.

Change in Time or Method of Pay

Changes in the time or method of payment of wages sometimes lead to disputes between unions and employers. However, arbitrators agree that unless restricted by the contract the employer may change the time of payment of wages. Thus, arbitrators have upheld a change from weekly to biweekly paydays even though paydays had been weekly for many years.[308] Likewise, the employer was upheld in changing the day of the week on which employees were paid despite the fact that employees had been paid on a particular day for many years.[309]

---

[304] Id. at 1098–1099.

[305] Fairchild Engine & Airplane Corp., 16 LA 678, 681 (Jaffee, 1951).

[306] Lennox Furnace Co., 20 LA 788, 789 (Johannes, 1953).

[307] Walker Mfg. Co. of Wisconsin, 31 LA 80, 81–82 (Luskin, 1958).

[308] See Arbitrator Roberts in 50 LA 125, 127–128; Florey in 66-1 ARB ¶8323 (not a local working condition protected by contract); Barrett in 30 LA 100, 104.

[309] See Arbitrator McCoy in 51 LA 577, 578–579 (payday held not to be a "condition of employment" within the meaning of the contract provision requir-

In cases where the company changed the method of paymen
from cash to checks (with arrangements to permit employees to cash
their checks), and where there was no contractual restriction, arbitrators permitted the company's action even though payment had been
in cash for many years.[310] However, in another case, past practice
was found to be the decisive factor in denying the company the right
to change from hand delivery on company premises to mail delivery
of payroll checks. The arbitrator said that this function was not one
which fell within the scope of the management rights clause as it
was not a question of scheduling production or determining processes
of manufacturing. He concluded: "As to their pay fully accrued, employees have rights as creditors, so that decision as to the place where
check delivery is to be made is not the exclusive function of
management."[311]

---

ing bargaining on all conditions of employment); Dugan in 46 LA 1007, 1008
(finding no binding past practice); Gorsuch in 40 LA 417, 422; Kadish in
30 LA 964, 966.

[310] United States Steel Corp., 36 LA 220, 221–222 (McDermott, 1961);
Diamond Alkali Co., 38 LA 1055, 1057 (Rubin, 1962), stating: "Nor is the
method of wage payment, whether in cash or by check, a type of benefit guarded
by the principle of accepted past practice."

[311] Manitowac Shipbuilding, Inc., 39 LA 907, 909 (Kovenock, 1962). Also
see Peoples Gas Light & Coke Co., 39 LA 224, 225–226 (Davis, 1962), where
a "firmly established" past practice was "created" based upon a grievance settlement under which the employer agreed to pay "cash supper allowance," thus
precluding the employer from changing to check payments for the period of
the current contract.

CHAPTER 18

STANDARDS IN ARBITRATION OF "INTERESTS" DISPUTES

Do Standards Exist?

The nature and proper scope of "interests" arbitration, as well as the function of the arbitrator in such arbitration, are discussed in Chapter 3. There it is also noted that one of the important reasons why arbitration of "interests" issues is viewed with suspicion by many persons is the belief that there is an absence of definite criteria or standards to govern the arbitrator. But there are, in fact, a number of standards that can be used and often are used. Many of these standards were used by the National War Labor Board. Not only did the Board give a great impetus to the process of arbitration, but it gave also an impetus to the use of many of these standards.

Sometimes the parties will specify, in their stipulation for arbitration, the standards to be observed.[1] Even if the parties do not stipulate the standards to be observed, the arbitrator generally will make an award based upon one or several of the commonly accepted standards. In such case the selection of the standards used is still determined by the parties, though less directly, since an arbitrator generally will not apply any given standard unless evidence has been introduced to support its application.

The standards used by arbitrators are not pulled out of the air—nor are they artifically created. They are, generally speaking, the very same ones that are used by the parties in their negotiations.

---

[1] As in 16 LA 933, 935; 12 LA 608, 609–610; 11 LA 118, 120. For discussion of the pros and cons of this practice, see Handsaker, The Submission Agreement in Contract Arbitration (U. of Pa. Press, 1952). It has been emphasized that only the parties, not an arbitrator, should place limitations in the collective agreement concerning the standards that may be observed by future "interests" arbitrators. United Traction Co., 27 LA 309, 317–318 (Scheiber, 1956). Also see Arbitrator Cornsweet in 15 LA 263, 273.

But if the arbitrator and the parties all use the same bargaining criteria, how can arbitration successfully resolve disputes where the parties' bargaining has failed? It can do so because the arbitrator is much more likely to be objective and to weigh impersonally the evidence adduced with respect to the various criteria.

Admittedly, most of the criteria are nebulous; but they are equally so whether applied by the parties or by the arbitrator. They are still the same standards regardless of who applies them, and in no case is it possible to determine whether their application is entirely correct. In this regard, one Emergency Board stated:

> "This Board does not believe that there is any mechanical formula by which wages can be determined by these parties in collective bargaining or recommended by an Emergency Board seeking to encourage a settlement. But the Board does believe there are a number of wage standards, many of which have been discussed by the parties, which may be applied to facilitate and to check the judgment of neutrals."[2]

Since a certain amount of risk of misapplication of standards cannot be avoided in any case, it may be better for the parties to resort to arbitration when an impasse is reached in negotiations than for them to pay the price of a strike which would be costly to labor, to management, and also to the public.

Without question the most extensively used standard in "interests" arbitration is "prevailing practice." This standard is applied, with varying degrees of emphasis, in most "interests" cases. In a sense, when this standard is applied the result is that disputants indirectly adopt the end results of the successful collective bargaining of other parties similarly situated. The arbitrator is the agent through whom the outside bargain is indirectly adopted by the parties. That the parties may thus indirectly adopt the collective bargain of others is well illustrated by the statement of one arbitration board, which, in applying the "pattern" standard, said through its Chairman, Clark Kerr:

> "* * * There is no magic formula for wage adjudication. Consequently one of the compelling considerations must be what has happened in free and successful collective bargaining. This indicates how experienced bargainers have evaluated the wage influencing factors which have evidenced themselves, and what they consider to be 'just'.

---

[2] Railroads v. Nonoperating Unions, 34 LA 517, 524 (Dunlop, Aaron & Sempliner, 1960).

"Arbitration of primary disputes over the terms of a new contract is a substitute for successful bargaining, and the 'pattern' or 'package' indicates what might have evolved from successful bargaining had the parties acted like others similarly situated. Attention to the 'pattern' or 'package,' rather than adherence to any rigid formula, also reduces the risks of parties entering wage arbitration, but also should encourage their own free settlement. It tends to afford equality of treatment for persons in comparable situations. It also provides a precise, objective figure, rather than an artificially contrived rate."[3]

The existence of standards lends a degree of predictability to "interests" arbitration, but the arbitrator is anything but a mere automaton. Even with points of reference agreed upon, his discretion is quite broad. He must determine the weight to be given to each of the standards applied in the given case, since rarely is the number of standards under consideration limited to one. His freedom to weigh the standards, to "mix the porridge," so to speak, means that the results will depend upon the way he applies the standards.[4] It may not often be possible or desirable for the arbitrator to make a strict application of the standards. Rather, they must be applied with the end in view of providing a solution that will be satisfactory enough to both sides to be workable. The circumstances of the parties must always be kept in mind by the arbitrator. His task is to determine

---

[3] Pacific Gas & Electric Co., 7 LA 528, 534 (1947). Also see statement by Arbitrator Roumell in 56 LA 209, 216; Edes in 53 LA 372, 374–375; Gundermann in 39 LA 249, 253. For broader discussion, see Chapter 3, topic titled "Arbitrator's Function in 'Interests' Disputes."

[4] "While there are familiar objective wage criteria to guide an arbitrator in a task of this kind, there is an area of discretion left to him in deciding which criteria are most appropriate or controlling. And persons with equal intelligence and integrity might of course differ as to the applicability of any one or number of criteria or as to the weight to be given to them." Houston Chronicle Publishing Co., 56 LA 487, 491 (Platt, 1971). Upholding the arbitrator's right to decide which standards are to be accorded weight in the given case, see In re Hopkins, 13 LA 716 (N.Y. Sup. Ct., 1949). Where the submission limited him to consideration of five specified factors and required him to indicate how each of the factors affected his award, Arbitrator I. Robert Feinberg explained his authority as follows: "As the arbitrator reads the stipulation, he is required to determine whether a wage increase is justified by considering only the factors listed therein. On the other hand, it does not appear that all of the factors must necessarily be considered of the same or equal importance. Rather, their relative importance is for the Arbitrator to determine. He is merely cautioned not to consider any other factors." H. Boker & Co., 12 LA 608, 610 (1949). Where the New Jersey Public Utilities Disputes Act provided that decisions should be based on the five standards set forth in the Act, so far as applicable to the matter in dispute, a decision could not be based on consideration of only one of the five standards. In re New Jersey Bell Telephone Co., 15 LA 238, 244 (N.J. Sup. Ct., 1950).

what the parties before him, as reasonable men, should have agreed upon by negotiation.

No single standard is available for universal application in all industries and under all circumstances. Arbitrators generally apply a combination of standards, the combination varying from case to case. Each party will advance standards believed to support its position in the given case. Standards that may be applicable in times of prosperity or inflation might be of little value during depressions. The number of standards entitled to be given consideration, and possibly some weight, varies from only one in some cases[5] to as many as 10 or 12 in other cases.[6]

Sometimes no indication will be given as to the standards considered in arriving at the award.[7] At other times it is difficult to tell from an award the weight given by the arbitrator to any particular standard. Only a few of the standards can be said to be basically objective. The weighing and balancing process is illustrated by the statement of Arbitrator Benjamin S. Kirsh, who, in speaking of the case before him, said:

"The adjudication of the various factors which are material to this determination have been carefully and conscientiously weighed by the arbitrator. This case involves a just and equitable evaluation of the totality of the considerations herein described and requires that each material factor be given its proper weight, with the final award representing a fair determination of the entire issue."[8]

Whether this process leads to an award based upon "compromise" is problematical. Often an arbitrator will consciously strive to avoid such a result, and he may deny specifically that the award involves "splitting the difference."[9] In the final analysis, the weight to be accorded a standard in any given case is, or should be, the result of the evidence submitted by the parties in respect to its applica-

---

[5] As in Waterfront Employers Assn. of Pacific Coast, 5 LA 758, 759 (Kerr, 1946).
[6] See Los Angeles Examiner et al., 20 LA 30, 31–32 (Kerr, 1952); San Francisco Employers Council, 7 LA 35, 38 (Wyckoff, 1946).
[7] See American Overseas Airlines, Inc., 6 LA 226 (Lewis, 1947).
[8] Baker & Co., 7 LA 350, 353 (1947). Also see statement by Arbitrator Block in 55 LA 568, 579; Seinsheimer in 54 LA 1069, 1074; Schmidt in 52 LA 1301, 1304; Florey in 51 LA 994, 996; Platt in 50 LA 1103, 1115; Dworkin in 42 LA 548, 553–554; Ross in 29 LA 96, 100; Shipman in 26 LA 651, 659; Kerr in 20 LA 30, 32.
[9] See Billings Contractors' Council, 33 LA 451, 454 (Heliker, 1959); Reliable Optical Co., 7 LA 257, 258 (Rosenfarb, 1947).

tion. The burden is upon the parties to submit evidence which is both factual and material, for arbitrators can be expected to be "unwilling to enter into the field of speculation."[10]

The remainder of this Chapter is largely devoted to a considera- tion of each of the standards used with some frequency in "interests" arbitration. Many of the standards to be considered are of greatest value in the arbitration of disputes involving wages or other "finan- cial" issues. In this regard, the reported arbitration awards indicate that a high percentage of "interests" arbitrations involve wage or re- lated matters, although other types of issues have also been submitted to "interests" arbitration.[11]

Arbitrators tend to apply those standards which are sufficiently recognized in practice to warrant acceptance by the parties. The fact that a given standard is advanced in collective bargaining or arbitra- tion does not of itself mean that the standard has been accepted with- out disagreement or qualification by economists. It is not the arbi- trator's function to set forth a systematic theory of wages or working conditions. This does not mean, however, that arbitrators do not at times consider the theoretical economic effects that may result from the application of a standard.

Prevailing Practice—Industry, Area, Industry-Area

In giving effect to the prevailing practice, an arbitrator relies upon precedent, adopting for the parties that which has been adopted by other parties through collective bargaining or, as sometimes is the case, as a result of arbitration awards. An award based upon applica- tion of this standard is not likely to be too far from the expectations of the parties, since most persons in the business community have long accepted the idea that there should be no basic inequalities among comparable individuals or groups.[12]

If the terms of employment of a given employer are below the standard set by the prevailing practice of comparable employers and

---

[10] St Louis Public Service Co., 8 LA 397, 405 (Holland, Anderson & Hollings- worth, 1947). Also see Arbitrator Seinsheimer in 54 LA 1069, 1072; Feinsinger in 16 LA 501, 504.

[11] For an enumeration of these other issues and for citation of cases in which they were submitted to arbitration, see Chapter 3, topic titled "Purpose and Subjects of 'Interests' Arbitration."

[12] See Ross, Trade Union Wage Policy 74 (1948).

if no basis exists for a differential, an arbitrator may conclude that an inequality exists. Many arbitration awards have undertaken to eliminate inequalities, such as inequalities between related industries,[13] inequalities within an industry,[14] inequalities between comparable firms or work within a specific area,[15] and inequalities within the plant itself.[16]

Application of the prevailing-practice standard may involve difficulties. First, what is to be the basis of comparison? For instance, is it to be the entire industry, the particular industry within the area, or industry in general within the area? After it is decided which prevailing practice is to be used, then just what that practice is must be determined. Finally, there remains the problem of applying the practice to the particular company involved in the case. While difficulties may be encountered, they are not insuperable. The application can be made.

In many cases strong reason exists for using the prevailing practice of the same class of employers within the locality or area for the comparison. Employees are sure to compare their lot with that of other employees doing similar work in the area; it is important

---

[13] See Arbitrators Cole, Aaron & Wirtz in 19 LA 76, 83; Sullivan in 18 LA 599, 608; Jackson, Healy & Dennis in 7 LA 630, 641; Feinberg in 7 LA 30, 32–33; Wallen, Cahn & Donahue in 4 LA 251, 259–260; Strong, Wolfe & Borgmann in 3 LA 41, 81–84.

[14] See Arbitrator Platt in 56 LA 487, 491; Wallen in 43 LA 1094, 1099; Shipman in 26 LA 651, 665; Whiting, Dash & Larkin in 25 LA 506, 521; Hogan in 25 LA 23, 27; Howard in 23 LA 429, 435–436; Colby in 23 LA 422, 426; Cole in 22 LA 371, 375–376; Hays in 20 LA 75, 80–81. Parties sometimes seek to avoid inequalities within an industry by adoption of "most favored nation" clauses designed to equalize benefits within the industry. For cases dealing with the interpretation and application of such clauses, see Arbitrator Cole in 49 LA 551; Scheiber in 49 LA 557; Brecht in 42 LA 1097.

[15] See Arbitrator Barstow in 54 LA 981, 987; Zack in 54 LA 492, 493; Kane in 13 LA 255, 260; Stein in 11 LA 1115, 1115–1116; Cole in 9 LA 577, 578–579; Bitker, Arps & Runge in 8 LA 961, 963–964; Wolff in 4 LA 800, 802.

[16] See Arbitrator Platt in 56 LA 487, 491; Young in 51 LA 1134, 1138; Wallen in 43 LA 1094, 1099–1100; Dworet in 27 LA 343, 346; Shipman in 26 LA 651, 661; Kleinsorge in 23 LA 733, 743; Copelof in 10 LA 133, 138; Jacobs, Clothier & Meyer in 8 LA 9, 16; Strong in 7 LA 673, 677; Cahn, Snyder & Forge in 5 LA 590, 597; Fly in 4 LA 689, 693. Where the salary structure within a hospital had been established by careful study and with the advice of experienced consultants, an arbitrator would not lightly undertake to restructure the salary relationships within the hospital. Palo Alto-Stanford Hospital Center, 50 LA 700, 705 (Mann, 1968), where the arbitrator stated, however, that under the evidence he was unable to find an imbalance in the internal salary structure.

that no sense of grievance be thereby created.[17] Unions have found, for instance, that the imposition of different wage scales upon the same class of employers in the same locality causes trouble both from employers and union members.[18] Sometimes, however, one party will insist upon industry-wide terms while the other party insists upon an area comparison.

If the parties cannot reach agreement as to the basis of comparison, the responsibility is that of the arbitrator to determine, from the facts and circumstances of the case as indicated by the evidence, the appropriate basis for comparison. In the final analysis it may well be that the prevailing practice which properly should be used for the comparison is that of the employer's competitors, whether within or without the area, or that of other firms or industries so situated that there is a sufficient similarity of interests between them and the employer in question for it to be reasonable to use their practice as the standard; comparison with others similarly situated within the industry or area thus may be the crux of the matter.[19]

In the newspaper industry several arbitrators have made some use of comparisons with newspaper operations in other comparable cities across the nation, this "national comparable cities" approach being said by one arbitrator to be relevant in view of the widely recognized similarities in newspaper operations across the nation.[20] In public sector disputes the comparison often has been made with similar occupational groups in comparable cities within the area (this standard is specified in some public sector arbitration statutes).[21]

[17] Condé Nash Publications, Inc., 1 ALAA ¶67,168, p. 67,355 (1942). Also see statement of Arbitrator Deibler as quoted in Houston Chronicle Publishing Co., 56 LA 487, 490 (1971).

[18] Slichter, Basic Criteria Used in Wage Negotiations 28 (1947).

[19] In this regard, see, generally, Cummins Sales, Inc., 54 LA 1069, 1070–1071 (Seinsheimer, 1970).

[20] Houston Chronicle Publishing Co., 56 LA 487, 491 (Platt, 1971). For a collection of other newspaper cases in which greater or lesser use was made of the "national comparable cities" standard, see Dallas Publishers, 50 LA 367, 369–370 (Elkouri, 1968), where some problems involved in the use of the standard are also noted. In A. S. Abell Co., 45 LA 801, 804 (Cluster, Gallagher & Kraushaar, 1965), the standard was used for news and editorial employees but comparisons with local wage rates were used for other employees of the newspaper. The "national comparable cities" standard has also been used in the local transit industry. See Arbitrator Platt in 50 LA 1103, 1105, 1113; Kates in 45 LA 905, 910; Crawford in 45 LA 58, 60–61. But area comparisons were utilized in Des Moines Transit Co., 38 LA 666, 672 (Flagler, 1962).

[21] See Arbitrator Roumell in 55 LA 716, 722–723; Barstow in 54 LA 981, 986; Young in 51 LA 1134, 1136; Saltonstall in 51 LA 208, 209–210; Siegel in 50 LA 1036, 1041–1042.

As to whether the comparison ordinarily should be limited to similar occupational groups, one arbitration board expressed the following view:

> "It should be emphasized that in determining appropriate salaries the basis for comparison is what is paid for work in a particular profession. If the school district were hiring Engineers, Accountants, Physicists, and the like, salaries paid for those professions would presumably apply. Thus a comparison of starting salaries for teachers, who have traditionally been several thousand dollars behind the average of the other professions, may indicate the disadvantageous position of the profession in attracting competent college graduates, but it does not control in determining what should be the proper rate for entry into that profession.

> "The same theory holds true in the Association's argument that teachers' starting salaries should be competitive with those of other professions such as Child Welfare Supervisors, or even callings such as police privates, police sergeants, bricklayers, or plumbers. Each occupation has its own rationale for wage determination, not least of which is supply and demand and control thereover.

> "It is not the duty of this Panel to rectify years of inequity among various callings, or to impose its judgment as to the relative worth of one trade or profession over another."[22]

However, in another case the arbitrator stated that an appropriate guide in judging the pay of municipal police officers assigned to and paid directly by private concerns "are wage rate comparisons with other skilled craftsmen and semi-professionals employed to render highly responsible and skilled services in the private sector of the economy."[23]

If the case involves the setting of terms for an entire industry, the comparison may be with a similar industry. In determining

---

[22] Arlington Educational Assn., 54 LA 492, 494 (Zack, FitzGerald, Cohen, 1970).

[23] Town of Tiverton, R.I., 52 LA 1301, 1303 (Schmidt, 1969). Moreover, the mere fact that an occupational group across the public sector has been underpaid in the past does not mean that "interests" arbitrators will disregard the occupation's claim to fair and equitable recognition for the future. For example, see Arbitrators McDermott, Zollner & Hutskow in 52 LA 233, 234–235; Florey in 51 LA 994, 995–996; Handsaker in 51 LA 879, 882; Seitz in 47 LA 1036, 1039. In this general regard, it also may be noted that some public sector arbitration statutes clearly are not intended to restrict comparisons absolutely to the same occupational group. See the Michigan statute quoted below in the topic titled "Standards in Public Sector Disputes."

whether a significant and close relationship exists between two industries a wide variety of factors may be considered. Such relationship has been found to exist between two industries on the basis of the following factors: "Both are engaged in handling essentially the same products. There is a marked similarity of operations, job titles, job classifications, job duties, and products handled. There is considerable overlapping of union representation * * *. There is competition between the two industries for raw materials as well as for employees. The products of one industry are used almost exclusively by the other."[24] The telephone industry has been found related to the telegraph industry on the basis of the following factors: their products are similar, frequently interdependent, and partially competitive; skills required in key jobs are similar; and requirements in many auxiliary occupations, such as clerical and accounting, are virtually identical.[25]

In any use of area practice, the geographical limits of the appropriate area must be determined.[26] Also, if the prevailing practice of industry in general within the area is to be used, there is the task of selecting the firms whose practice is to be considered in determining the prevailing area practice.[27] Arbitrators frequently use for the comparison the prevailing practice of the particular industry (or public sector occupational group) in question, as opposed to industry in general, within the area.[28]

Where each of various comparisons had some validity, an arbitrator concluded that he should give the greatest weight to those com-

---

[24] Yakima Cement Products Corp., 3 LA 793, 795 (Prasow, 1946).

[25] Western Union Telegraph Co., 4 LA 251, 259–260 (Wallen, Cahn & Donahue, 1946). For guides developed by the National Wage Stabilization Board (1946) for determining whether industries were related, see Policy Statement of that Board at 2 LA XIII.

[26] Frequently the metropolitan area or the state is used. In consideration of national wage stabilization policy the National War Labor Board favored area comparison for the establishment of wage rates. Basic Steel Cos., 19 War Lab. Rep. 568 (1944).

[27] Comparison with rates for industry in general within the area may be deemed of relatively little value unless adequate data is submitted with respect to the kind of industries being cited and the skill levels of the employees involved. See Florida East Coast Ry., 41 LA 1001, 1008–1009 (Platt, Bok & Guthrie, 1963). For other considerations that may be relevant in making inter-industry comparisons, see Railroads v. Nonoperating Unions, 34 LA 517, 530–532 (Dunlop, Aaron & Sempliner, 1960).

[28] E.g., see Arbitrator Roumell in 56 LA 209, 214, and in 55 LA 716, 722; Barstow in 54 LA 981, 987; McCoy in 29 LA 7, 11; Howard in 23 LA 429, 432–434; Stutz in 20 LA 718, 719; Feinberg in 18 LA 55, 59; Warren in 17 LA 353, 354–355.

parisons which the parties themselves had considered significant in free collective bargaining, especially in the recent past.[29]

The selection of the employers whose practices are to determine the standard must, in wage cases, be followed by an analysis of jobs for comparability. Mere job titles often are not reliable and are by no means conclusive. "The range of duties assigned to a single worker has not been as standardized among plants as is widely assumed. The varying ages and types of equipment, the differing scales of operation between large and small plants, and the different techniques of various managers are factors making for different job contents among firms producing roughly similar goods."[30] It is incumbent upon the parties to supply reliable job descriptions in order to establish a basis for comparison.[31]

After the prevailing practice has been determined, it must be applied to the particular company involved in the case. This is not difficult where issues involve matters other than wage rates, as, for example, where the issue is the number of paid holidays. But the application of prevailing wage rates is not so simple. There may be reasons why the employer in question should not pay the prevailing rates. These reasons, which for the sake of convenience the Authors choose to call the "minor" standards, include such matters as relative general differentials of skill and training, responsibility, steadiness of employment, hazards of the employment, and fringe benefits, as well as established geographical differentials and wage leadership (these "minor" standards are discussed below).

Consideration of some of the numerous types of issues which have been resolved on the basis of prevailing practice indicates the very broad application that is given to the standard by arbitrators, emergency boards, and fact-finding boards in private sector and public sector disputes alike. In addition to basic wage rates, the following types of issues have been resolved in some cases largely (and sometimes

---

[29] Rochester Transit Corp., 15 LA 263, 270 (Cornsweet, 1950). Also see Arbitrator Horlacher in 27 LA 295, 296; Donnelly in 22 LA 192, 195; Gilden in 16 LA 539, 541. But see Platt in 56 LA 487, 489–491. For related discussion, see topic titled "Past Practice and Bargaining History," below.

[30] Dunlop, "The Economics of Wage-Dispute Settlement," 12 Law & Contemp. Prob. 281, 283 (1947). Also see Arbitrator Hepburn in 26 LA 381, 382–383.

[31] Illustrating that a misleading picture may result in wage comparisons where job descriptions are incorrect, see City of Marquette, 54 LA 981, 986–987 (Barstow, 1970).

entirely) on the basis of the prevailing-practice standard: holidays,[32] vacations,[33] sick leave,[34] hospitalization benefits,[35] pensions and retirement,[36] meal periods,[37] rest periods,[38] union security provisions,[39] length of workday or workweek,[40] shift differentials,[41] work schedules and shifts,[42] overtime provisions,[43] premium pay for Sundays and holidays,[44] length of contract term.[45] In addition to issues such as those just enumerated, a variety of other "interests" issues in the public sector have been resolved with the aid of the prevailing-practice standard.[46]

Differentials and the "Minor" Standards

As stated above, there may be reasons why a differential should exist between the wage terms of an employer and those of other employers (or between different groups of employees within the same company) with whom a comparison is made in applying the prevailing-practice standard.[47] In this regard, the arbitrator in one public sector dispute commented:

---

[32] See 55 LA 716, 53 LA 372, 52 LA 1301, 21 LA 494, 17 LA 353, 16 LA 933, 11 LA 1037, 9 LA 540, 4 LA 780.

[33] See 55 LA 716, 53 LA 372, 47 LA 482, 24 LA 835, 18 LA 415, 17 LA 353, 9 LA 666, 6 LA 98, 5 LA 170.

[34] See 53 LA 372, 21 LA 356, 17 LA 152, 11 LA 450, 7 LA 845, 2 LA 95.

[35] See 54 LA 796, 21 LA 356, 11 LA 450, 2 LA 624.

[36] See 25 LA 54, 19 LA 538, 13 LA 813, 13 LA 46.

[37] See 17 LA 353, 4 LA 548.

[38] See 17 LA 353, 7 LA 845, 2 LA 227.

[39] See 57 LA 613, 55 LA 671, 54 LA 901, 53 LA 372, 45 LA 801, 18 LA 112, 17 LA 833, 16 LA 611, 6 LA 567.

[40] See 52 LA 1301, 49 LA 1229, 47 LA 482, 27 LA 343, 19 LA 358, 18 LA 903, 9 LA 566, 5 LA 504, 2 LA 582.

[41] See 54 LA 901, 53 LA 372, 50 LA 700, 9 LA 865, 8 LA 488, 5 LA 71, 4 LA 489.

[42] See 43 LA 875, 9 LA 282, 5 LA 781.

[43] See 52 LA 1301, 4 LA 604, 4 LA 548.

[44] See 8 LA 700, 6 LA 269, 2 LA 227.

[45] See 56 LA 209, 50 LA 700, 47 LA 482, 45 LA 58, 27 LA 468.

[46] For example, see Arbitrator Roumell in 55 LA 716, 723–726; Schmidt in 52 LA 1301, 1302–1304; Duff in 51 LA 1072, 1074. The standard has been utilized, too, in awarding "rights" arbitration provisions for public employees. See Arbitrator St. Antoine in 55 LA 671, 672; Barstow in 54 LA 981, 984; Wolf, Feinberg & Stockman in 49 LA 1212, 1226–1228; Wallen in 48 LA 1044, 1049; Dunlop in 42 LA 1114, 1118–1119.

[47] Economist Sumner H. Slichter classified wage differentials as follows: "1. Differentials which equalize the attractiveness of jobs in different occupations, industries, and places. 2. Differentials which reflect the efficiency of men in different occupations and of individuals within an occupation." Slichter, Basic Criteria Used in Wage Negotiations 41 (1947).

"What happens in one community is not necessarily going to follow in another community. It depends on many circumstances. Wages are only one part of bargaining. There may be fringe benefits. Certainly, the financial situation varies from community to community and should be considered in each instance. There may be a question of working conditions. It is noted for example that in [the present case] the working conditions [of firemen] do leave something to be desired because the department is undermanned causing a potential safety hazard. This may not be the situation in other communities. Such a situation may justify more of an increase than normally."[48]

Sometimes an arbitrator is asked to institute a new differential, and sometimes to perpetuate a differential that has existed in the past. Differentials serve a constructive purpose when supported by sound reasons.

Skill and Training—Arbitrators recognize that wages should be to some degree responsive to the general level of skill and experience required in the plant. For instance, where an employer had a "young shop," composed of workers with relatively less experience and therefore less skill as compared with the average in the industry, the factors of skill and training were given consideration as a proper basis for some differential.[49] In another case it was held that a differential should be reduced but not entirely eliminated where a lesser degree of skill was required to produce a tannery company's product than was required in other tanneries; the quality of leather and the consequent skill required to produce it were found to be superior in the other tanneries to the quality and skill prevailing in the company's plant.[50]

Emphasing that a differential may be warranted for employees whose work requires special skill or responsibility, an Emergency Board for the railroad industry stated that the single wage rate in each craft resulted in an inequity in pay among mechanics with reference to the performance of the more skilled and responsible assignments. The Board recommended the negotiation of a wage differential for the latter assignments, and thus a "move in the direction of removing a

---

[48] City of Southgate, 54 LA 901, 913 (Roumell, 1970).

[49] Reliable Optical Co., 7 LA 257, 259 (Rosenfarb, 1947). Also see Arbitrator McCoy in 20 LA 610, 613; Reynolds in 16 LA 933, 937. Differentials between different groups within the same company are justified by differences in skill required. See Arbitrator Kagel in 28 LA 600, 604–605; Feinsinger, Dunlop, Aaron & Coman in 17 LA 68, 70; Townsend in 16 LA 53, 56.

[50] Moench Tanning Co., 8 War Lab. Rep. 54, 60 (National War Labor Board, 1943).

pay inequity in the existing wage structure which will otherwise become more serious with continuing technological change."[51]

Responsibility—Differentials have been justified, in part at least, on the basis of greater responsibility placed upon one group of employees as compared to that placed upon another.[52]

Steadiness of Employment—Differences in the steadiness of employment may justify differences in wage rates. Wage rates for seasonal workers and workers who otherwise have limited job security frequently are set above those of workers with steady employment.[53] This principle was held to justify a rate differential in favor of construction workers as against utility workers even though both were employed on the same work project, weight being given to the fact that utility workers have much greater continuity of employment.[54]

Hazards and Other Undesirable Conditions of Work—Differentials often justifiably exist in favor of employees who perform hazardous work or who work outside during inclement weather or under other undesirable conditions.[55]

Geographic Differentials—Although the individual worker does not always understand why higher wages should be paid to another worker doing the same work but in a different area, there is believed to be sound reason for geographic differentials, as simply stated by one arbitration board: "* * * [E]veryone knows our country cousins, workmen, professional men, all, on the average, earn less than urbanites; and need less. They get on the whole more comforts, services, and commodities for their dollars."[56]

The existence of past wage uniformity between components of a given industry in adjoining areas and the fact that the two areas

[51] National Railway Labor Conference, 53 LA 555, 561 (Seward, Howlett & Livernash, 1969).
[52] See Arbitrator Black in 41 LA 372, 375 (a difference in the number of duties that employees have may justify a difference in wage rates); Dworet in 27 LA 343, 347; Ross in 22 LA 226, 227–228; Blair in 13 LA 454, 455. Also see Healy in 17 LA 636, 637; Stauffer Chemical Co., 15 War Lab. Rep. 264 (1944).
[53] See Arbitrator Rubin in 23 LA 4, 5; Simkin in 6 LA 860, 865; Taylor in 6 LA 830, 834; Prasow in 3 LA 793, 796.
[54] Consolidated Edison System Cos. of New York, 6 LA 830, 834–835 (Taylor, 1947).
[55] See Arbitrator Blair in 13 LA 454, 455; Prasow in 3 LA 793, 796; Fly, Black & Harper in 3 LA 165, 170–171. Also see Hepburn in 26 LA 381, 382.
[56] Chesapeake & Potomac Telephone Co., of Baltimore, 7 LA 630, 641 (Jackson, Healy & Dennis, 1947).

may tend to constitute a single labor market for that industry may be held insufficient reason for requiring employers in the industry in one of the areas to grant the same wage adjustment granted in the other area if differences in the economies of the two areas far outweigh the similarities.[57]

Even if the cost of living were the same in all places, geographic differentials could still be justified on the ground that they cause labor and capital to flow into areas where they are most needed. Employment opportunities are diminishing in many rural regions and increasing in the cities, and movement of labor from rural to urban areas may be stimulated by relatively high urban wage rates. Capital, on the other hand, often needs to be encouraged to move from a high to a low wage area.[58] In a number of cases arbitrators have recognized the need for geographic differentials and have ordered their institution or continuance.[59]

Fringe Benefits—Basic wages are not the only "money" benefits that employees may receive. Terms of employment include other pecuniary benefits, such as pensions, holidays and vacations with pay, sick leave, shift premiums, social and health insurance, and bonuses. These fringe benefits must be taken into account in making wage comparisons.[60] If the fringe benefits offered by an employer are substantially more favorable to employees than those of the employers whose

---

[57] Associated General Contractors, 9 LA 201, 221 (Aaron, 1947).
[58] Slichter, Basic Criteria Used in Wage Negotiations 37 (1947).
[59] See Arbitrator Feinberg in 18 LA 46, 53; Hays, Cole & Stein in 11 LA 276, 284; Leiserson, Bushnell & Wirtz in 9 LA 865, 877; Aaron in 9 LA 201, 221; Hepburn in 8 LA 691, 694; Jacobs, Clothier & Meyer in 8 LA 9, 14–15. However, geographic differentials have been reduced or eliminated where changed conditions justified such action. See Basic Steel Industry, 18 LA 112, 117–118 (W.S.B., 1952); New Jersey Bell Telephone Co., 14 LA 574, 588 (Martin, Lewis & Lesser, 1950).
[60] That fringes should be included was emphasized in Des Moines Transit Co., 38 LA 666, 672–673 (Flagler, 1962), where data pertaining to nine selected fringe benefits was secured from each of the ten companies with which comparison was being made. However, fringe benefits were disregarded where the parties failed to provide evidence about the comparability of the benefits. Cummins Sales Inc., 54 LA 1069, 1072 (Seinsheimer, 1970). In City of Marquette, 54 LA 981, 987 (Barstow, 1970), the arbitrator noted that many fringe benefits "are extremely difficult to translate into dollar terms," but he was "unable to determine any clear evidence of imbalance among fringes" of similar occupational groups in the area, and he concluded that the fringe benefits being compared were "roughly similar in total value" although "differences in detail abound." In City of Providence, 47 LA 1036, 1038 (Seitz, 1966), the arbitrator found that there was such a "wide diversity of working conditions and fringes among the cities ranked" that the prevailing practice standard itself was rendered of little utility.

prevailing practice is being used for comparative purposes and if these favorable provisions are not counterbalanced by other provisions which are less favorable than the prevailing practice, a differential in basic wage rates may be justified in favor of the employer who offers the superior fringe benefits.[61]

In one public sector case a school board asserted that the smaller class sizes and fewer clerical duties of its teachers constituted working conditions "sufficiently preferable to offset any difference in salary compared to other communities." The arbitrators stated, however, that it was unrealistic to attach a specific dollar figure to the value of such working conditions and that, in any event, such working conditions did not justify the employer in asking its teachers to absorb increases in the cost of living for which other teachers in the area had received adjustments.[62]

Wage Leadership—A differential which has existed in the past by virtue of the employer's position as a wage leader may be the basis of an award of wage rates higher than those paid by prevailing practice.[63] Companies which in the past have set the prevailing wage may be looked to for further leadership when the trend is toward a higher level of wages.[64] It has been emphasized, however, that the lead occasionally passes from one company to another and that wage adjustments need not always wait upon agreement of the parties who usually provide the lead.[65]

In a case involving employees of Dallas, Texas, newspapers the union declared that Dallas is a dynamic city whose explosive economic and industrial progress in recent years had benefited the Dallas publishers; the arbitrator agreed that in view of Dallas' economic growth and vitality, the union was not totally unjustified in looking to the publishers for wage leadership.[66]

---

[61] See Arbitrator Kliensorge in 23 LA 733, 742; Kerr in 7 LA 528, 535; Simkin in 6 LA 860, 867, 881. Cf., Randle in 18 LA 280, 281.

[62] Arlington Education Assn., 54 LA 492, 494–495 (Zack, Fitzgerald & Cohen, 1970).

[63] See Arbitrator Donnelly in 26 LA 904, 907; Whiting in 11 LA 1023, 1033; Cornsweet in 8 LA 597, 606. But see Kerr in 7 LA 528, 532. A related question arising out of wage leadership is whether the leader's rate should be included in the sample used for determining the prevailing rate.

[64] But the leader may be relieved of this responsibility if its ability to pay becomes weak. Des Moines Transit Co., 38 LA 666, 674 (Flagler, 1962).

[65] Tribune Publishing Co., 28 LA 477, 480 (Ross, 1957).

[66] Dallas Publishers, 50 LA 367, 373 (Elkouri, 1968).

Historical Differentials—Arbitrators are sometimes reluctant to eliminate historical differentials[67] or those which initially were established by collective bargaining.[68] This reflects a hesitancy to disturb a stabilized situation except on compelling grounds.[69]

Economist Sumner H. Slichter pointed out that some may argue that long-established relationships between wages in several occupations, plants, or localities should be maintained because the quality of labor tends to adjust itself to the wage structure, which means that employers who pay wages above the prevailing rate attract a better class of workers, and the retention of customary differentials merely serves to compensate those with superior ability. He pointed out further, however, that in a rapidly changing world the argument that traditional wage relationships should be preserved has very limited validity.[70] Nonetheless, where a historical parity had existed between the pay of policemen and firemen, an arbitrator acted firmly to maintain it.[71]

If There Is No Prevailing Practice

The question sometimes arises as to how arbitrators should treat demands for contract terms sufficiently unprecedented that no "prevaling practice" is available. It might be urged that demands for improved contract terms should not be rejected on the sole ground that they are unprecedented, since the adoption of a contrary principle would seriously impair the usefulness of arbitration as a method of

---

[67] See Arbitrator Crawford in 45 LA 58, 61; Seibel in 43 LA 410, 411, 414; Ross in 29 LA 96, 99; Pierson in 17 LA 152, 158; Kerr in 14 LA 111, 112, and in 11 LA 458, 461; Dwyer in 5 LA 513, 515–516; Cahn in 3 LA 729, 732. Also see U.S. Smelting Co., 18 LA 676, 677 (Wage Stabilization Board, 1952). Cf., Arbitrator Cheney in 5 LA 220, 222; Wasservogel in 4 LA 548, 575.

[68] See Arbitrator Dworkin in 42 LA 548, 555; Holly in 39 LA 207, 212; Donnelly in 26 LA 904, 907; Cornsweet in 15 LA 263, 270–271; Horvitz in 3 LA 318, 320. Also see McCoy in 20 LA 610, 613.

[69] Newark Call Printing & Publishing Co., 3 LA 318, 320–321 (Horvitz, 1946). In Houston Chronicle Publishing Co., 56 LA 487, 490–491 (Platt, 1971), the importance of not making too large an award (though such award be otherwise justified to fully eliminate an inter-city or inter-employer inequity) was stressed in view of the need to protect "intra-plant harmony." Similarly, see Arbitrator Elkouri in 50 LA 367, 368–369.

[70] Slichter, Basic Criteria Used in Wage Negotiations 40 (1947). Where the validity which a historical differential once had has disappeared, the situation may be viewed as a present inequity. Atlanta Newspapers, Inc., 43 LA 1094, 1100 (Wallen, 1964).

[71] City of Southgate, 54 LA 901, 910–911 (Roumell, 1970). To similar effect, Arbitrator Gillingham in 53 LA 361, 363.

settling labor disputes. It is clear, however, that arbitrators will require a party seeking a novel change to justify it by strong evidence establishing its reasonableness and soundness. Moreover, the absence of prevailing practice may be taken to show that a demand has not yet been adequately justified by labor within the industry or area.[72] Arbitrators generally agree that demands for unusual types of contract provisions preferably should be negotiated. This view was elaborated by Arbitrator Whitley P. McCoy, speaking as Chairman of a board of arbitration:

> "We believe that an unusual demand, that is, one that has not found substantial acceptance in other properties, casts upon the union the burden of showing that, because of its minor character or its inherent reasonableness, the negotiators should, as reasonable men, have voluntarily agreed to it. We would not deny such a demand merely because it had not found substantial acceptance, but it would take clear evidence to persuade us that the negotiators were unreasonable in rejecting it."[73]

New provisions, however, are often included in the recommendations of fact-finding boards. These agencies frequently enter upon policy considerations and considerations of public interest, and they recognize the need for leadership in the introduction of innovations.[74]

Cost of Living

The cost-of-living standard is frequently advanced in collective bargaining and arbitration during periods characterized by pronounced changes in living costs.

The use of this standard has an obvious appearance of fairness, but it is not without criticism. For instance, it is said that a rising cost of living means that the demand for goods at existing prices is outrunning the supply and that increases in wages would simply aggravate the problem except as they reflect increased production through improvements in technique or in employee efficiency.[75] One

---

[72] See Fifth Avenue Coach Co., 4 LA 548, 579 (Wasservogel, 1946).
[73] Twin City Rapid Transit Co., 7 LA 845, 848 (1947). Also see Arbitrator Cole in 11 LA 450, 453–454; Hepburn in 3 LA 194, 196.
[74] For instance, see Minnesota State Highway Patrol, 56 LA 697, 699 (Gleeson, 1971); General Motors Corp., 1 LA 125, 137 (Garrison, Eisenhower & Stacy, 1946).
[75] Slichter, Basic Criteria Used in Wage Negotiations 15 (1947).

answer given to this criticism is that the readjustment of wages has been the result rather than the primary cause of increased living costs. Price rises, it is said, are due to many complex causes.[76] A criticism which labor registers against the cost-of-living standard is that its rigid application would result in a stationary real wage rather than a higher standard of living.[77] But in spite of these criticisms, the very frequent use of this standard is strong evidence that it is generally regarded to be of much value, and in recent decades it has held an important place in the national economy.[78]

In applying the cost-of-living standard arbitrators rely heavily upon the index issued monthly by the Bureau of Labor Statistics of the United States Department of Labor. This index reflects the cost of living as of a date about six weeks prior to its issuance.[79] By use of the index it is possible to measure changes in retail costs of services and commodities and the resulting effect upon the purchasing power of the income of workers in the larger cities. Essentially, the index is the ratio of the current cost of a specified market basket of goods and services to the average cost of the same market basket during some designated past period. The base period for the Bureau of Labor Statistics Consumer Price Index is the average for the year 1967 (1967 = 100), but it should be noted that the base period is updated periodically.[80]

The Bureau of Labor Statistics does not hold that its index is an exact measurement of changes in the cost of living, but arbitrators can be expected to give it considerable weight. For example, it was held in one instance to be an appropriate measure of the change in living costs although the union claimed that it underestimated the change and the company claimed that it overestimated the change;

---

[76] Satter, "Principles of Arbitration in Wage Rate Disputes," 1 Ind. & Lab. Rel. Rev. 363, 367 (1948).

[77] This criticism led one arbitrator to largely disregard the cost-of-living standard, the arbitrator saying that the "uncritical use of the cost-of-living formula often involves the false assumption that all is well when real wages remain constant." 195 Broadway Corp., 7 LA 516, 519 (Meyer, 1947).

[78] The case in its favor was strengthened in 1951 by the Wage Stabilization Board's adoption of it as a ground for wage increases without the need of official approval.

[79] For one type of interpretative problem that this time gap can produce, see Duriron Co., 54 LA 124, 127–128 (Kates, 1969).

[80] Historical data based upon prior base periods is available from the Bureau of Labor Statistics. Tentative plans for a comprehensive revision of the Consumer Price Index to begin in 1970 and to be completed in 1975 were announced by the Commissioner of Labor Statistics in 1969.

neither party presented sufficient evidence to support an adjustment of the index figures, which the arbitrator said at least carried apparent and official certitude.[81]

The latest index available at the time of the arbitration is ordinarily used in the determination of the cost-of-living adjustment to be paid employees until the next wage review; this is so even though such review is not expected to take place until several months later. Thus, in setting wages for a six-month period, one arbitrator said that "greater emphasis must obviously be placed on known facts than on guesses" as to the index level during the next six months.[82] But a wage increase in excess of that indicated to be justified by the index may be awarded where the amount granted does not exceed "the amount which the Arbitrator finds on the record as a whole is presently justified to offset increases in living costs * * *."[83] Moreover, in one case the arbitrator declared that the employees (teachers) were entitled to "an increase that will both maintain their present real income and afford them some protection against the continuing rise in the cost of living, which appears likely to occur during the period of the next agreement."[84]

Many arbitration awards have granted wage improvements on the basis, in part at least, of the application of the cost-of-living standard.[85] Often, however, its effect has been modified by the application at the same time of other standards. In the latter regard one arbitration board refused to guarantee that the employees would be "insulated in toto" against all of the rise in cost of living, the board stating:

"To rest wage rate raises upon cost of living rises as the sole measuring rod means wages will rise with commodity rises as the

---

[81] R. H. Macy & Co., 9 LA 305, 308 (Shulman, 1947).
[82] Waterfront Employers Assn. of Pacific Coast, 5 LA 758, 761 (Kerr, 1946). To similar effect, Arbitrator Feinberg in 18 LA 55, 58–59.
[83] Waterfront Employers Assn. of Pacific Coast, 9 LA 172, 181 (Miller, 1947). Also see Arbitrator Dworet in 27 LA 343, 346.
[84] Worcester Teachers' Assn., 54 LA 796, 800 (Seidenberg, 1970). Where an arbitrator awarded a "firm two year contract" the wage increase he granted was based in part upon "anticipated increases in living costs." The New York Times, 15 LA 332, 333 (Dunlop, 1950).
[85] E.g., Arbitrator Roumell in 56 LA 209, 216; Barstow in 54 LA 981, 988 ("governmental units have a responsibility to cushion their employees to the extent possible against short term cost-of-living changes"); Seidenberg in 54 LA 796, 799–800; Elkouri in 50 LA 367, 374; House in 43 LA 29, 30; Ross in 29 LA 96, 98; McCoy in 29 LA 7, 10; Kagel in 28 LA 600, 606; Dworet in 23 LA 629, 640; Shulman in 22 LA 297, 299; Platt in 18 LA 686, 690; Marshall in 15 LA 878, 880; Sonnenschein in 13 LA 40, 44; Hays in 11 LA 276, 280.

thermometer goes up on a hot day. If wages are to be raised solely because commodity prices go up, wages should go down with falling commodity prices, as the mercury goes down to zero in a freeze; unless, like the human elbow joint, the system is created to flex upward, and only upward."[86]

An appropriate base period must be selected in applying the cost-of-living standard. The base period that is selected determines the real wage that is to be maintained by the standard. Generally the date of the last arbitration award or of the parties' last wage negotiations is used as the base date.[87]

The determination of any adjustment to be made on the basis of a change in the cost of living requires a comparison of the percentage of change in the cost of living with the percentage of change in wages between the base period and the date of the wage adjustment.[88]

In determining whether wages have kept pace with the cost of living, basic wage rates, rather than take-home pay, are generally used for the comparison.[89] The use of take-home pay for the comparison would lead to a distortion of the normal relationship of earnings to hours worked.[90] In making the comparison some changes in wages have been held not to be material. Among these are increases resulting from increased skill and effort,[91] increases granted for the sole purpose of eliminating inequities within the industry,[92] and pay raises for length

---

[86] Chesapeake & Potomac Telephone Co. of Baltimore, 7 LA 630, 640 (Jackson, Healy & Dennis, 1947).

[87] See Los Angeles Transit Lines 11 LA 118, 130 (Aaron, 1948); New York City Omnibus Corp., 7 LA 794, 802 (Cole, 1947). But a date other than that of the last negotiations may be selected as the base period. For some years after World War II, for instance, January 1, 1941, was often used by arbitrators. The use of this date was initiated by the National War Labor Board of World War II. Bethlehem Steel Corp., 1 War Lab. Rep. 325 (1942). The 1941 date was deemed clearly outmoded in Publishers Assn. of New York City, 22 LA 35, 41–42 (Seward, Slocum & Meany, 1954), a later date having been established under a subsequent governmental wage control program.

[88] For more detail about the mechanics of determining and applying the percentage increase in cost of living, see Dallas Publishers, 50 LA 367, 374 (Elkouri, 1968).

[89] Waterfront Employers Assn. of Pacific Coast, 5 LA 758, 761 (Kerr, 1946); Bee Line, Inc., 1 ALAA ¶67,161 (1946).

[90] Waterfront Employers Assn. of Pacific Coast, 9 LA 172, 177 (Miller, 1947); Waterfront Employers Assn. of Pacific Coast, 5 LA 758, 761 (Kerr, 1946).

[91] McGlynn Hays Industries, Inc., 10 LA 360, 361 (Lesser, 1948).

[92] Atlantic & Gulf Coast Shippers, 6 LA 700, 704 (Kleinsorge, 1947).

of service or promotions.[93] The following, on the other hand, may be taken into consideration in making the comparison: Increased earnings of incentive workers which result from a simplification of the work or any other increase not the result of increased efforts of the workers;[94] reclassification adjustments general enough to affect the whole wage structure and thus to be considered general increases instead of merit increases.[95] The use of basic wage rates instead of take-home pay for the comparison eliminates from consideration vacation, holiday, and other fringe benefits granted to employees since the base date.[96]

The cost-of-living standard may be expected to be used much less generally as a basis for wage reductions than as a basis for wage increases.[97] In one contract, for instance, the parties provided for adjustments to maintain the relative purchasing power of the employees against rises in the cost of living, but they provided that "In no event will a decline in the Index * * * cause a reduction in the scale of wages."[98] The social and ethical reasons that can be used to support the application of the standard in times of rising costs are not so readily applicable when costs are on the decline. Rather, these considerations support the constant efforts of labor to attain a higher standard of living. At least, "insofar as a drop in the cost of living is the result of technological progress, it does not furnish a sound reason for wage cuts"; it calls, instead, for a rise in real wages.[99]

However, a governmental wage stabilization agency did require that escalator clauses negotiated after January 25, 1951, provide for downward as well as upward revision of wage rates. It is also interesting to note that a fact-finding board for the basic steel industry, in refusing to recommend a general wage increase, cited, as one of the factors given consideration, the fact that in the prior year the cost of living had declined slightly.[100] Thus while a decrease in the cost of living may not be strong reason for wage reductions, it may

---

[93] Trans World Airlines, Inc., 19 LA 308, 323 (Wenke, Boyd & Sharfman, 1952); Fifth Ave. Coach Co., 1 ALAA ¶67,423 (1946). Also see Arbitrator Stutz in 20 LA 718, 719–720; Lesser in 17 LA 914, 916.

[94] Associated Dress Mfrs. Assn., 6 LA 24, 27 (Copelof, 1946).

[95] Puget Sound Navigation Co., 11 LA 1100, 1107 (Haughton, 1948).

[96] See Bee Line, Inc., 1 ALAA ¶67,161 (1946).

[97] See Puget Sound Navigation Co., 13 LA 255, 258–259 (Kane, 1949).

[98] Koppel Photo Co., 56 LA 1085, 1086 (Zack, 1971).

[99] Slichter, Basic Criteria Used in Wage Negotiations 18 (1947).

[100] Basic Steel Industry, 13 LA 46, 79 (Daugherty, Cole & Rosenman, 1949).

have a greater relevance in determining whether new wage increases are justified.

Escalator and Wage Reopening Clauses

Many collective agreements contain "escalator" clauses which provide for automatic changes in wage rates in response to specified changes in the cost of living.[101] The use of such a clause may justify a longer basic term for the agreement.[102]

An alternative to use of escalator clauses is to provide for wage reopening during the term of the agreement.[103] A wage reopening clause may provide for the negotiation of new wage terms when the cost of living changes by a specified percentage, when there has been a "substantial" change,[104] or simply at specified intervals.[105]

In the arbitration of contract reopening disputes the cost-of-living standard is relevant in many instances. Furthermore, in some reopening disputes the arbitrator asserted the authority to consider all relevant standards, unless restricted by the agreement or the submission, all wage determining factors being deemed equally applicable whether it be a reopening or a new contract dispute.[106] However,

---

[101] Another possibility is to provide for automatic wage adjustments at specified intervals, as in Koppel Photo Co., 56 LA 1085, 1086 (Zack, 1971). For the matters that should be covered in escalator clauses, see Tile Contractors Assn. of Northern Calif., 25 LA 9, 11 (Ross, 1955). Also see Arbitrator Platt in 50 LA 1103, 1111.
[102] See Port Authority of Allegheny County, 45 LA 58, 62 (Crawford, 1965).
[103] See City of Marquette, 54 LA 981, 988 (Barstow, 1970). Of 1717 contracts examined in one survey, nearly 500 contained provisions for renegotiation of economic issues during the contract term and about 15 percent of these provided for arbitration should negotiations fail. Major Collective Bargaining Agreements: Arbitration Procedures 101 (U.S. Dept. of Labor Bull. No. 1425-6, 1966), indicating also that demands for general wage changes were the predominant issues subject to arbitration. For other statistics as to use of reopening (and escalator) clauses, see Stieber, "Voluntary Arbitration of Contract Terms," Arbitration and the Expanding Role of Neutrals 71 (The Bureau of National Affairs, Inc., 1970).
[104] Concerning what might be considered "substantial," see Arbitrator Lesser in 17 LA 914, 916; Justin in 17 LA 31, 33; Granoff in 16 LA 944, 949.
[105] See Major Collective Bargaining Agreements: Arbitration Procedures 101 (U.S. Dept. of Labor Bull. No. 1425-6, 1966).
[106] See Arbitrator Platt in 56 LA 487, 491; Wallen in 43 LA 1094, 1099 (stating that a "de novo" wage determination was permitted); Dworkin in 42 LA 548, 553; Shipman in 26 LA 651, 659; Shulman in 22 LA 297, 298-299; Lesser in 17 LA 114, 116. Also see Ross in 35 LA 185, 187-188; Dash in 14 LA 662, 669-670. In Rose-Derry Ohio, Inc., 49 LA 40, 43 (Kates, 1967), a clause permitting wage reopening when the cost-of-living index changes 2.5 percent was deemed to specify the time of reopening but not to specify how much of a wage adjustment may be negotiated when a reopening is triggered.

in other instances the arbitrator recognized the limitation that weight may be given only to those factors for which the evidence indicates there has been a change since the agreement was signed (this sometimes has been called the "erosion doctrine," limiting the function of reopening to "restoring the bargain" which the parties made when the agreement was signed).[107]

Living Wage

The living-wage standard is related to, but not the same as, the cost-of-living standard. The living-wage standard is in some respects based upon the ideal that the standard of living of American workers should be raised to the highest level possible,[108] but a more realistic basis for it is the belief that "employees are entitled to wages and salaries sufficient to enable them, through the exercise of thrift and reasonable economy, to maintain themselves and families in decency and comfort and to make reasonable provision for old age."[109] In advancing the living-wage theory, a union may be expected to insist that no privately owned industry should be permitted to insure its solvency or to consider a return upon its investment at the expense of its employees nor to require them to subsidize its investment by compelling them to accept wages or working conditions below normal standards of decency.[110] A similar position may be advanced in public sector disputes.[111]

An important difference exists between the cost-of-living and the living-wage standards. While the cost-of-living standard is used to keep the standard of living of employees in status quo, the living-wage standard (which is not directly tied to changes in the cost of living) is invoked to raise the wages of employees to the point that will allow them a decent standard of living. Application of the living-wage

---

[107] See Arbitrator Roberts in 36 LA 171, 177; Dworet in 23 LA 629, 639–640; Gray in 21 LA 13, 14; Livingston in 9 LA 632, 636; Miller in 9 LA 172, 175–176; Kerr in 5 LA 758, 759. Also see Luskin in 36 LA 201, 203–204; Hogan in 25 LA 23, 24, 29; O'Connell in 20 LA 437, 439.

[108] Atlantic & Gulf Coast Shippers, 6 LA 700, 702 (Kleinsorge, 1947).

[109] San Francisco Employers Council, 7 LA 35, 38 (Wyckoff, 1946). Similarly, see Arbitrator Singer in 47 LA 482, 486.

[110] Such a position was taken by the union in St. Louis Public Service Co., 8 LA 397, 402 (1947).

[111] See Arbitrators Zack, FitzGerald & Cohen in 54 LA 492, 494; McDermott, Zollner & Hutskow in 52 LA 233, 234–235; Florey in 51 LA 994, 995–996.

standard may well result in a wage increase greater than that which is indicated by the change in cost of living.

The "budget approach" is sometimes used by parties advancing the living-wage standard. A similar approach underlies the state and federal minimum wage laws. Generally speaking, budgets have been used primarily as background and supplementary material rather than as a specific criterion in the formulation of wage demands.[112] But in some cases unions have relied directly upon the budget approach. A board of inquiry for the meatpacking industry, for instance, was asked to give serious consideration to the "City Worker's Family Budget" issued by the Bureau of Labor Statistics. The board stated that a budget approach to wage determination was not invalid or unprecedented and that the union could properly offer it for consideration as a criterion for resolving the dispute. The board concluded, however, that a proper application of the budget approach to that dispute would require more information than the parties had supplied or could supply from their limited study of the subject up to that date, and more than the board could obtain from governmental or other sources.[113]

This illustrates a major disadvantage of the living-wage standard; namely, its indefiniteness.[114] What may be considered a decent standard of living is largely dependent upon time and circumstances. The aforementioned board also concluded that even with the necessary information, a number of broad policy decisions would have to be made by agreement of the parties. The most important of these decisions were said to be:

"(1) whether the size of the family alone * * * or the composition of the family, including size and other characteristics, should be used; (2) whether the necessary income should come only from earnings of the employee or whether income from all sources should be consid-

---

[112] See Meat Packing Industry, 9 LA 978, 998 (Feinsinger, Davis & Schaefer, 1948). Also see Arbitrator Kleinsorge in 24 LA 38, 43.

[113] Meat Packing Industry, 9 LA 978, 992, 998–999 (Feinsinger, Davis & Schaefer, 1948).

[114] In Port Authority of Allegheny County, 50 LA 1103, 1112–1113 (Platt, 1968), the parties referred to the City Worker's Family Budget but the arbitrator deemed it of little significance to the case. He commented: "To properly evaluate this criterion would involve consideration of many collateral questions to which there are no answers in the record. Indeed, as Professor Alfred Kuhn observed in his monograph on Arbitration in Transit, the living wage criterion, because of its vagueness and intangibility, provides a sort of glittering generality which 'has never been and does not seem destined to become an important wage determinant in the transit industry.'"

ered; (3) whether income from earnings should be computed on the basis of 2,080 hours (52 × 40 hours) at straight-time, without incentive earnings or 'fringe' benefits, * * * or on the basis of earnings from overtime plus incentive earnings and 'fringe' benefits, as well as straight-time earnings; (4) whether the resulting increase should be related only to the job performed or should also vary with number of dependents of individual employees."[115]

It is recognized that budgetary experts are not in agreement as to the composition of an adequate budget. One arbitrator declared that the particular budget submitted to him had "served the purpose more of a goal to be attained over a period of time than the next step in the improvement of the living standards" of America's wage earners, and that the actual attainment of the budget could be had "through full and efficient production and distributive justice." He concluded that the budget could not, at that time, "serve as the sole, or even a significant, basis for wage adjudication."[116] Similarly, where teachers asserted that their salaries should be "commensurate with the standard of living" in their community, the arbitration tribunal stated that this "should be a goal rather than a controlling criterion."[117]

It can be expected that as long as the living-wage argument is presented only in general terms, giving arbitrators no specific basis of application to the concrete problems before them, the standard will be given little effect in awards.[118] However, there are public sector cases in which the arbitrator did find the presentation adequate to give some weight to the living-wage standard.[119]

Ability to Pay

Although it is a generally recognized principle that large profits do not alone justify demands for wages substantially higher than those which are standard within an industry and that small profits do not

---

[115] Meat Packing Industry, 9 LA 978, 998–999 (Feinsinger, Davis & Schaefer, 1948).

[116] Pacific Gas & Electric Co., 7 LA 528, 530 (Kerr, 1947). Also see Arbitrator Kleinsorge in 24 LA 38, 43.

[117] Arlington Education Assn., 54 LA 492, 494 (Zack, FitzGerald & Cohen, 1970).

[118] See Atlantic & Gulf Coast Shippers, 6 LA 700, 702 (Kleinsorge, 1947). Also see Arbitrator Coke in 12 LA 870, 884.

[119] See Arbitrators McDermott, Zollner & Hutskow in 52 LA 233, 234–235 (police); Florey in 51 LA 994, 996 (police); Singer in 47 LA 482, 486 (sanitarium employees).

justify the payment of substandard wages,[120] the ability-to-pay criterion is of great importance in the determination of wage rates and other contract benefits. This importance lies largely in the fact that, while an employer's ability to pay is not, in and of itself, a sufficient basis for a change in wages, it is a significant element properly to be taken into account in determining the weight to be attached to other criteria.[121]

The ability-to-pay standard has been advanced more frequently by management than by labor. For this reason, it has been suggested that perhaps it should be called the "inability-to-pay" standard.[122] Regardless of title, however, the standard has been advanced by management to resist wage demands on the ground of inability to pay, and it has been advanced by labor to support demands for higher wages on the ground of ability to pay. In advancing this criterion, labor may argue that, when the trend is toward higher wage levels, leadership should be taken by employers best able to afford it.[123]

To determine wages exclusively on the basis of ability to pay would lead to wage scales that vary from company to company, and would require a new determination of the wage scale with each rise or fall in profits. The existence of unequal wage levels among different companies would be incompatible with union programs for the equalization of wage rates among companies in the same industry or area. If inability to pay were used as the sole or absolute basis for wage cuts, inefficient producers would receive the benefit of having a lower wage scale than that of efficient ones, regardless of the fact that the value of the services rendered by the employees of each is the same.[124] Indeed, arbitrators have expressed the view that to use the ability-to-pay standard as the sole basis for a wage increase would in effect involve a decision by the arbitrator as to how business revenues should be distributed among stockholders, employees, and the

---

[120] See Third Avenue Transit Corp., 1 LA 321, 325 (Hays, 1946); Galveston Model Laundry, 26 War. Lab. Rep. 224 (1943).

[121] General Motors Corp., 1 LA 125, 145 (Garrison, Eisenhower & Stacy, 1946). Also see statement by Arbitrator Prasow in 27 LA 468, 473.

[122] Slichter, Basic Criteria Used in Wage Negotiations 25 (1947).

[123] A General Motors fact-finding board considered the earning capacity and the good prospects for high profits of the corporation as one basis for its taking leadership in the establishment of a wage pattern for American industry. General Motors Corp., 1 LA 125, 137–138 (Garrison, Eisenhower & Stacy, 1946).

[124] The employer paying lower scales would, of course, ultimately tend to get less efficient labor.

consuming public; arbitrators do not feel themselves competent to rule on such a broad issue of social and economic policy.[125]

One board of arbitration indicated three different degrees of weight which may be given to the ability-to-pay factor. Speaking through its Chairman, John T. Dunlop, that board outlined the three situations as follows: (1) "In the case of properties which have been highly profitable over a period of years, the wage rate would normally be increased slightly over the levels indicated by other standards"; (2) "in the case of persistently unprofitable firms, the wage rate would normally be reduced slightly from the levels indicated by other standards"; (3) "in the case of the companies whose financial record over a period of years falls between these extremes, the wage rate level would be determined largely by other standards."[126]

There have been many instances where the "unfavorable" financial condition of the employer resulted in the granting of smaller increases (or none at all) than otherwise would have been allowed had there been no inability to pay.[127] In one instance a reduction in wages was granted because of the employer's precarious financial position, even though there had been a large increase in the cost of living since the last wage increase. In ordering the reduction, the arbitrator said:

> "The Arbitrator is mindful of the fact that the recommendation of a reduction in wage rates at this time, while the general trend is towards the granting of increases, is a very serious and unpopular recommendation. However, the Arbitrator is convinced that, if the property can be saved, it should result in long-range benefits to the employees and that the seniority accumulated by many of the present employees of the Company will be conserved, enabling them to reap the benefits thereof when profitable operations are again resumed."[128]

---

[125] International Harvester Co., 1 LA 512, 517 (Marshall, Spencer & Holly, 1946).

[126] Twin City Rapid Transit Co., 10 LA 581, 594 (1948).

[127] E.g., see Arbitrator Platt in 50 LA 1103, 1114–1115; Singer in 48 LA 289, 291; Stutz in 40 LA 282, 284; Flagler in 38 LA 666, 673–674; Fallon in 37 LA 270, 272; Bothwell in 34 LA 398, 402; Jones in 28 LA 40, 43; Scheiber in 27 LA 309, 315; Hogan in 25 LA 247, 251; Abruzzi in 23 LA 334, 336; Stein in 10 LA 813, 814; Albert in 10 LA 18, 19; Taylor in 9 LA 666, 683–684; Rosenfarb in 7 LA 257, 259; Brissenden in 6 LA 639, 643; Blair in 3 LA 370, 371, and in 3 LA 245, 248.

[128] Trailways of New England, Inc., 7 LA 319, 321 (Copelof, 1947). The decision appears to have been well advised, for a few months later the arbitrator found the Company's financial position to be sufficiently improved to permit a restoration of the prior wage rate. Trailways of New England, Inc., 8 LA 363, 365 (Copelof, 1947). A wage reduction was ordered because of the employer's precarious position in Tynan Throwing Co., 20 LA 614, 615 (Bailer, 1953).

An arbitrator may give recognition to an employer's weak financial position by ordering that a needed increase be made gradually.[129] Sometimes an arbitrator will award an increase but will recognize the inability-to-pay factor at least to the extent of limiting or denying retroactivity,[130] or of ordering a review of the employer's financial situation after a specified period.[131] Thus appropriate relief can be granted to the employer based on operations under the award during the specified period.[132] But mere temporary inability to pay generally is not sufficient to cut down an increase warranted by other criteria. Moreover, consideration generally will not be given to short-run variations in profits.[133] Thus, for example, extensive nonrecurring losses charged to current operations were rejected as the basis for a lower wage adjustment.[134] A probable future decline in ability to pay sometimes will be taken into account by arbitrators "as a moderating influence on the amount of the increase recommended."[135]

Inability to pay may be given slight consideration where the employer's rates are substandard or inequitable in comparison with other rates in the industry or area.[136] While there is a duty to stockholders

---

[129] See Arbitrator Roumell in 56 LA 209, 218; Brecht in 21 LA 356, 359; Lesser in 17 LA 914, 917; Justin in 9 LA 468, 471.

[130] See Florida East Coast Ry., 41 LA 1001, 1014 (Platt, Bok & Guthrie, 1963); Felt Companies, 16 LA 881, 883 (Lesser, 1951). The National War Labor Board considered ability to pay in determining retroactivity of its orders, James L. Whitaker, 14 War Lab. Rep. 401 (1944), and it also considered this factor in certain special cases, such as where an employer was unable to pay because of inability to get sufficient oil to operate profitably, Consumers Oil & Refining Co., 9 War Lab. Rep. 407 (1943).

[131] International Braid Co., 6 LA 911, 913 (Brown, 1947).

[132] Associated Food Shops, Inc., 7 LA 870, 872–873 (Baskind, 1947).

[133] Florida East Coast Ry., 41 LA 1001, 1011–1013 (Platt, Bok & Guthrie, 1963); Twin City Rapid Transit Co., 10 LA 581, 594 (Dunlop, 1948). A railroad emergency board explained the "interaction between wages and ability to pay," stating in part that: "Financial distress or high profits do not tend in large-scale industry to affect wages in the very short period. The relationship between wages and financial conditions in large-scale industry is typically more gradual. Erosion of financial conditions and the decline in long-run prospects, or a series of profitable years with continuing good prospects, influence wage setting. The financial experience of the railroads over a series of recent years and their prospects for the next several years are most significant to current decisions on wages." Railroads v. Nonoperating Unions, 34 LA 517, 534 (Dunlop, Aaron & Sempliner, 1960).

[134] United States Sugar Co., 5 LA 314, 319 (France, 1946).

[135] Greyhound Bus Co., 1 LA 596, 609 (Simkin, Freidin & Wallen, 1946). To similar effect, Arbitrator Murray in 11 LA 1132, 1134–1135.

[136] See Arbitrator Donnelly in 27 LA 85, 87; Brecht in 21 LA 356, 359; Meyers in 20 LA 258, 259; Cole in 9 LA 577, 580; Frankenthaler in 8 LA 478, 480. Also see Raines in 19 LA 464, 466.

to make profits, there is also a duty to employees to pay "fair" wages.[137] It has been said that a company "does not expect price concessions from suppliers because of inability to pay, and must recognize its duty to its employees to pay them fair wages."[138] If, however, an increase in wage rates would put the rates above the industry or area standard, the inability-to-pay factor will be given considerable weight.[139]

Sometimes an increase in wage rates, if granted, would endanger the solvency of the employer. While the basic risk of business belongs to management, not to the employees,[140] "high wage rates have no value to employees when layoffs are caused thereby."[141] Arbitrators give consideration to the reason for the absence of profits. If the reason is managerial inefficiency, the employees are not likely to be penalized by the denial of wage increases to which they are entitled.[142] The theory here is that if the employer goes out of business new management may put the company on a paying basis.[143] But, if the reason lies in causes beyond the control of management or if it is a matter of strong competition by large firms against small firms, the arbitrator will be less likely to risk the possibility of bankruptcy of the employer. In making a wage award, one arbitration board said: "We assume, without deciding, that any wage increase will put the company out of business." Then the board explained its severe but interesting view as follows:

> "On the record before us, the employer has no better claim to continue in business upon the basis of a subnormal payroll than the employees have to seek wage increases upon the basis of the size of the employer's past profits or the amount of his assets.

---

[137] See Arbitrator Stutz in 40 LA 282, 284 ("employees should not be expected to underwrite the employer's losses"); Donnelly in 27 LA 85, 87; Strong in 7 LA 673, 676; Meyer in 4 LA 604, 634.

[138] Birmingham Electric Co., 7 LA 673, 676 (Strong, 1947). To similar effect, Arbitrator Kleinsorge in 23 LA 733, 740.

[139] Western Union Telegraph Co., 4 LA 251, 263 (Wallen, Cahn & Donahue, 1946).

[140] Capital Transit Co., 9 LA 666, 684 (Taylor, 1947); Atlantic City Transportation Co., 9 LA 577, 580 (Cole, 1948).

[141] Prairie DuChien Woolen Mills Co., 10 LA 73, 75 (Rauch, 1948). To similar effect, Arbitrator Hogan in 25 LA 247, 250–251; Abruzzi in 23 LA 334, 336; Bailer in 20 LA 614, 615; Simkin in 18 LA 631, 645; Brown in 11 LA 984, 990–991.

[142] See Western Union Telegraph Co., 4 LA 251, 264 (Wallen, Cahn & Donahue, 1946). Also see Arbitrator Donnelly in 27 LA 85, 87.

[143] See discussion in Centinela Valley Taxicab Co., 28 LA 40, 42–43 (Jones, 1957).

"Never have the wages of the employees of this company been related to profit or loss contingencies. The company and its employees have never been partners or joint venturers in this enterprise. Over the many years when the company made sustained and substantial profits, the employees were not offered a share in the benefits. And now, when it is claimed that the company faces losses, it is not perceived why the employees should be asked to share any of the burden.

"We therefore conclude that these wages should be fixed without regard to the financial condition of the company or its ability to continue in business."[144]

Some arbitrators, however, take the view that "a clear showing that proposed increases would destroy a business or cause the discontinuance of a service would ordinarily be an important and perhaps a controlling factor in an arbitration decision."[145]

Proof of Inability to Pay

Employers who have pleaded inability to pay have been held to have the burden of producing sufficient evidence to support the plea. The alleged inability must be more than "speculative,"[146] and failure to produce sufficient evidence will result in a rejection of the plea.[147] The payment of reasonable dividends to stockholders and of reasonable salaries to top management has been held to render invalid a plea of inability to pay.[148] Management should be prepared to disclose its profit and loss statements in support of a plea of inability to pay. Arbitrators should provide any safeguards needed to protect the confidential nature of such evidence. Failure of management

---

[144] California Street Cable Ry. Co., 7 LA 91, 94 (Wyckoff, 1947). The National War Labor Board sometimes granted increases despite employer contentions that any increase would force the company out of business. Title Guarantee & Trust Co., 9 War Lab. Rep. 457 (1943).
[145] Georgia Power Co., 8 LA 691, 695 (Hepburn, 1947). To similar effect, Arbitrator Tyree in 13 LA 384, 386.
[146] Restaurant-Hotel Employers' Council of San Diego, 11 LA 469, 477 (Aaron, 1948).
[147] See Arbitrators Platt, Bok & Guthrie in 41 LA 1001, 1013; Justin in 7 LA 241, 243; Feinberg in 6 LA 636, 639; Copelof in 3 LA 437, 442. From the standpoint of the duty to bargain under the National Labor Relations Act, substantiating evidence to support a plea of inability to pay need not always be furnished, but refusal to furnish such evidence on request is one of the factors which may be considered in determining whether the employer has refused to bargain in good faith. Truitt Mfg. Co. v. NLRB, 76 S.Ct. 753, 38 LRRM 2042 (1956).
[148] Employees Transit Lines, Inc., 4 LA 748, 752 (Copelof, 1946).

specifically to plead inability to pay may be considered sufficient to establish ability to pay up to the maximum demanded by the union.[149]

Public Utility Ability to Pay

Special considerations are involved in the application of the ability-to-pay standard in public utility disputes. It is recognized that, since a public utility produces a basic necessity of life and since the public regulatory body must assure the opportunity for a fair return, capacity to pay generally will exist, potentially at least, and that almost any conceivable level of wages could be paid and a "fair profit" still returned to the stockholders. However, not only "fair wages" and "fair profits" are involved—a "fair price" to the consumer also enters the picture—thus ability to pay should not be made the primary consideration in determining public utility wage rates.[150]

An arbitrator may give some weight to the fact that a company is unable, under the terms of its franchise, to seek an increase in the price of its service to the public. This was done by one arbitrator despite the contention of the union that it should not be made a party to the "straitjacket" in which the company had placed itself.[151] On the other hand, an arbitrator may refuse to grant the request of a public utility that any wage increase awarded should be conditioned on the company's securing a rate increase for its services. Arbitrator John T. Dunlop, speaking as Chairman of a board of arbitration, explained the view behind such refusal:

> "* * * In public utilities, including the railroads, there appears to be a long tradition of separation of wage and rate setting. This does not mean that rates and prices are irrelevant to wage setting, but rather that wage rates have tended to be fixed with some general reference to financial capacity and then these costs in turn have been taken into account by the rate or fare making body. Such has been the actual relation between collective bargaining or emergency boards determining wage rates and the Inter-State Commerce Commission setting railroad rates and fares. The transit industry has tended to follow an analogous practice.
>
> "The majority of the Arbitration Board believes it can follow no other precedent in this case. * * * When the Arbitration Board has fixed the wage rates, the appropriate fare making body should

---

[149] Oil Industry, 1 LA 168, 176 (Graham, Eliel & Beyer, 1946).
[150] Pacific Gas & Electric Co., 7 LA 528, 531 (Kerr, 1947).
[151] New York City Omnibus Corp., 7 LA 794, 809 (Cole, 1947).

then set fares, in accordance with proper standards, including the wage rates set by this Arbitration Board as costs. No other procedure in the fixing of wages and fares, which are necessarily interdependent, by different bodies can be workable."[152]

Public Sector Ability to Pay

Special considerations are likewise involved in the application of the ability-to-pay standard in public sector cases. In these cases the employer often does not have sources of revenue apart from the taxing power, which has various limitations including the need for public support.[153]

Where a city-owned hospital did have sources of revenue over and above the taxing power, Fact-Finder George T. Roumell specified that a recommended wage increase should be made gradually in consideration of the hospital's "somewhat dismal" financial picture, but he explained his refusal to give greater weight to the hospital's plea of inability to pay:

"The point is that we are in a period of inflation. Public employees have made great strides in attempting to bridge the gap in their wages between those of private sector and themselves. Such an attempt becomes even more dramatic in a city like Flint where a large percentage of the work force is employed by an employer paying very substantial wages, namely the General Motors Corporation. What private employers have been finding is that because of increased wage demands they have been faced with a profit squeeze. It has caused reappraisals in management techniques in order to continue to produce profits. Such an approach should also occur in public employment. This is particularly so when dealing with a hospital that does have sources of revenues over and above taxing powers. Bluntly put, Hurley Hospital must act like any other employer in recognizing inflationary trends and the normal request for wage increases that are occurring all over

---

[152] Indianapolis Railways, Inc., 9 LA 319, 330 (1947). In recognition of the problem implied here, it has sometimes been suggested that the whole job should be done by the same agency; i.e., that the rate making body should also have jurisdiction to determine wage rates. It has also sometimes been suggested that wage awards should bind the utility commission. In any event, one arbitrator in effect asked that the regulatory commission grant a rate increase to accommodate the wage increase granted by his award. See Twin City Rapid Transit Co., 16 LA 749, 760 (Platt, 1951).
[153] In Hamtramck Board of Education, 54 LA 162, 162–163 (Gould, 1969), the dispute was submitted by the parties with the understanding that the neutral should not make any recommendations which would result in a deficit budget for the public employer.

the country and meet the increases by a review of its labor needs and its management techniques."[154]

In another case Fact-Finder Richard I. Bloch noted the dilemma of a Board of Education, as employer, which was confronted by wage demands from teachers in spite of recent defeats of tax proposals for school purposes:

"The Board of Education is placed squarely in the middle in all these financing problems. On the one hand, they must provide for the citizenry the best possible education for the children of the area. On the other hand, they must answer to those same citizens for the use of the tax dollars. Unfortunately, millage issues seem to be the area where already-overtaxed voters get their revenge. Unless the Oscoda area constituents soon realize the importance of their support, their children will have no classrooms in which to learn. The burden of supporting the capital expenditures of a school system should not fall totally upon the teachers, although some restraint in wage demands is advisable."[155]

In granting a wage increase to police officers to bring them generally in line with police in other communities, an arbitration board recognized the financial problems of the city resulting from temporarily reduced property valuations during an urban redevelopment program; but the board stated that a police officer should be treated as a skilled employee whose wages reflect the caliber of the work expected from such employees, and the board declared that it "cannot accept the conclusion that the Police Department must continue to suffer until the redevelopment program is completed."[156] However,

---

[154] Hurley Hospital, 56 LA 209, 219 (1971). Also see statements by Arbitrator Edes in 53 LA 372, 383; Cahn in 52 LA 971, 972. In Palo Alto-Stanford Hospital Center, 50 LA 700, 716 (Mann, 1968), the arbitrator spoke in terms of balancing and giving fair recognition to the interests of the employees and the hospital employer, and also to the interests of the public "in high quality, economical, and essential hospital care."

[155] Oscoda Area Schools, 55 LA 568, 578 (1970). Also see statements by Arbitrator Seidenberg in 54 LA 796, 799 ("the salaries must come from public revenues which are not limitless, and while teachers should not be expected to subsidize the community in its efforts to obtain quality education, their salary requests must be viewed in light of the total county demands for public funds"); Zack in 54 LA 492, 495; Kerrison in 52 LA 1169, 1176 (noting budget limitations and the fact that the budget had been approved at the polls); Teple in 52 LA 800, 802 (community refused to support higher levy needed for teacher salary increase—the arbitrator recommended no increase for balance of school year since the employer had no source of revenue for payment of any increase, the arbitrator rejecting a suggestion that an increase be paid even if the school must close early for lack of funds).

[156] Borough of Turtle Creek, 52 LA 233, 235 (McDermott, Zollner & Hutskow, 1968).

the board did give definite weight to the city's budget limitations by denying a request for improved vacation benefits, additional insurance, a shift differential, and for a cost-of-living escalator clause.[157] In another case, involving police officers and firemen, an arbitrator awarded a 6 percent wage increase (which he recognized as the prevailing pattern in private industry) in spite of the city's financial problems; he did limit the increase to this figure, though a larger increase was deserved, in order to keep the city within the statutory taxing limit and in light of the impact of the award upon the wages of other city employees.[158]

In some cases neutrals have expressly asserted an obligation of public employers to make added effort to obtain additional funds to finance improved terms of employment found to be justified.[159] Also, in one case the neutral refused to excuse a public employer from its obligation to pay certain automatic increases which the employer had voluntarily contracted to pay, the neutral ordering the employer to "take all required steps to provide the funds necessary to implement" his award in favor of the employees.[160]

Competition

A factor which often must be given consideration in "interests" arbitration is the competitive nature of the employer's business. In

---

[157] Id. at 235, 237. In City of Uniontown, 51 LA 1072, 1074 (Duff, 1968), some improved fringe benefits were awarded to police department employees in lieu of awarding a salary increase larger than that necessary to place them "on parity with salaries paid by municipalities of comparable size."

[158] City of Easton, Pa., 51 LA 879, 881–882 (Handsaker, 1968). In City of Mount Vernon, 49 LA 1229, 1232–1233 (McFadden, Gould & Karow, 1968), involving police and firemen, fact-finders would "not ignore" the city's ability to pay, but they declared that they must make recommendations that are fair and equitable to the employees, the public employer, and the public itself, and they added: "In the final analysis, the City * * * must raise whatever revenues are necessary in the manner which it deems best. The electorate must then pass on these decisions and, inferentially, this Board's recommendations." The fact-finders construed the New York public employee statute as contemplating budgetary action subsequent to fact-finding and they suggested that the budgetary action already taken by the city should not be deemed so final as to preclude implementation of the board's recommendations. For another case where the neutral balanced the interests of the employees (firemen), the city (particularly as to financial resources), and the public, see Arbitrator Dunlop in 42 LA 1114, 1118–1119.

[159] See Arbitrator Gleeson in 56 LA 697, 699 (the parties should urge the Legislature to appropriate funds); Roumell in 54 LA 901, 908–910; Seitz in 47 LA 1036, 1040.

[160] City of Cleveland, 57 LA 781, 787–789 (Dworkin, 1971).

some respects this is related to the ability-to-pay standard. In other respects it is related to the prevailing-practice standard. For these reasons it is generally not considered as an independent standard. Where, however, an employer is engaged in a highly competitive business or is faced with special competitive problems, the arbitrator may specifically point out the competitive nature of the employer's business as a factor to be given special consideration in setting contract terms (sometimes even justifying a wage reduction).[161]

Wage "Patterns"

The "pattern" may be defined as a particular kind of solution of collective bargaining issues which has been used on a wide enough scale to be distinctly identified. The pattern standard is obviously closely related to the prevailing-practice standard and could reasonably be considered merely as one of its aspects. However, it is often spoken of as if it were a distinct criterion.

A "pattern" in wage arbitrations is often stated in terms of a specific number of cents per hour, or it may be stated as a percentage wage increase. For instance, the pattern standard would recognize that where companies or industries A, B, and C have granted general wage increases of 10 cents per hour, related company or industry D should grant a 10 cent increase also. In the application of this standard stress is placed upon the granting of the same amount or percentage of increase granted by others, rather than upon the granting of the same total wage that is paid by comparable employers.

A limited number of key wage bargains, or even only one, might set a pattern for a large part of American industry. Recognition of this fact was one of the factors which strongly influenced a fact-finding board for the Basic Steel Industry to refuse to grant a general wage increase; it was felt that any increase granted would probably be urged as a pattern to be followed in other industries, which, considering

---

[161] See Arbitrator Black in 41 LA 372, 375; Gundermann in 39 LA 249, 253; Kleinsorge in 24 LA 38, 44; Donnelly in 23 LA 843, 844; Hogan in 23 LA 762, 773; Knowlton in 22 LA 653, 654; Bailer in 20 LA 614, 615; Gellhorn in 18 LA 774, 775; Simkin in 18 LA 631, 644–645; Singer in 9 LA 567, 569; Wolff in 8 LA 194, 195; Kirsh in 7 LA 350, 353; Whiteacre in 6 LA 749, 750–751.

the best interests of the general economy at that time, would not have been desirable.[162]

Among other possibilities, the pattern observed may be a national pattern for industry in general,[163] or a national pattern for the particular industry or for related industries,[164] or it may be the pattern for general industry in the area,[165] or for the particular industry in the area.[166] The national pattern may be rejected where a grant of the national figure would upset the trend set by the local area pattern.[167]

Arbitrator Clark Kerr stated that arbitrators should give great weight to "patterns" or "packages" of wage increases, such as those established during the various rounds of increases after World War II, since "rightly or wrongly" such patterns had been established and widely applied in free collective bargaining.[168] While in many cases the full amount of the pattern figure has been granted, in others the pattern factor has been just one of several considered, with the result that the increase granted was not the exact pattern figure.[169] Then,

---

[162] Basic Steel Industry, 13 LA 46, 52 (Daugherty, Cole & Rosenman, 1949). Illustrating that a pattern may be accepted on its face value, one emergency board, in applying the established pattern, said that "we need not consider the multiple factors in wage determination that entered into the establishment thereof." New York Harbor Carriers v. Railroad Marine Harbor Council, 35 LA 628, 632 (Whiting, Roberts & Coburn, 1960). In Pacific Maritime Assn., 35 LA 185, 189 (Ross, 1960), it was emphasized that there are some bargaining topics which are affected by variations in local conditions and cannot be satisfactorily handled by a blanket, industry-wide approach.

[163] As where an arbitrator recognized a "pattern of increases" of about 6 percent to have been "widespread in American industry." City of Easton, Pa., 51 LA 879, 880 (Handsaker, 1968). Also see Arbitrator Platt in 50 LA 1103, 1114.

[164] See railroad emergency boards in 53 LA 555, 41 LA 1001, 35 LA 628, 34 LA 517, 28 LA 110, 17 LA 236, 6 LA 334. Also see 26 LA 14.

[165] Viloco Machine Co., 3 LA 867, 870–871 (Ziegler, 1946). A settlement by a large employer in a given area may have strong impact upon other industries within that area, as did a General Motors settlement. Hurley Hospital, 56 LA 209, 213–215 (Roumell, 1971).

[166] See Arbitrator Ross in 29 LA 96, 99; Howard in 23 LA 429, 434; Haughton in 14 LA 655, 660–661. It could even be a pattern for one company only, as where a pattern resulting from agreements between an employer and several unions was applied to some of his employees represented by still another union. Memphis Publishing Co., 26 LA 381, 382 (Hepburn, 1956). Similarly, see Arbitrator Joseph in 48 LA 425, 428–429.

[167] Jamaica Buses, Inc., 4 LA 225, 227 (Cahn, 1946).

[168] Pacific Gas & Electric Co., 7 LA 528, 534 (1947).

[169] See Arbitrator Roumell in 56 LA 209, 213–214; Healy in 8 LA 124, 126–127; Pollard in 8 LA 134, 136; Kirsh in 7 LA 350, 353. In Labor Standards Assn., 36 LA 171, 178 (Roberts, 1960), departure from the "pattern" was denied lest an inequity be created.

too, under the circumstances of some cases the "pattern" may be rejected entirely.[170]

"Patterns" do not always call for wage increases. Rather, the "pattern" may be for wage decreases,[171] or, when the economy so justifies, for maintenance of the status quo.

In one railroad emergency board proceeding the use of the industry "pattern" was vigorously challenged by the railroad shopcrafts, which insisted that their wage claims should be considered on their merits regardless of the terms to which other railroad unions had agreed. The emergency board responded:

> "Again, as earlier stated, this Board is trapped in the 'pattern' dilemma faced by the parties and by many previous Emergency Boards. The Organizations are asked to accept a general wage increase which was established at bargaining tables at which they were not represented, a wage increase agreement which is thus not of their making. The frustration of the Organizations at being locked into an established pattern is understandable, but, equally understandable is the Carriers' unwillingness to break and upset * * * a wage agreement voluntarily negotiated in good faith at an earlier date. Late settlements above a pattern earlier established penalize employees involved in the earlier voluntary negotiations. This is destructive of the broader system of collective bargaining in the industry. Until and unless the structure of bargaining is modified in the industry there can be no improved approach to this difficult problem. Under these circumstances this Board cannot recommend departure from the wage pattern already in effect for some 77 percent of all railroad employees."[172]

However, the board did say that special increases could be given, without breaking the "pattern", based upon factors peculiar to the shopcrafts:

> "To the extent and degree mutually satisfactory modifications of [work] rules are negotiated, appropriate wage adjustments could be made. Wage increases justified by modifications in rules which, through improved organization of work, contribute to efficiency, productivity, and cost reduction would not be incompatible with earlier wage settle-

---

[170] See E. Cummings Leather Co., 25 LA 247, 250 (Hogan, 1955).

[171] As in Cheney Brothers, 21 LA 159, 163–165 (Scheiber, 1953). Also see Arbitrator Kleinsorge in 24 LA 38, 44.

[172] National Railway Labor Conference, 53 LA 555, 559–560 (Seward, Howlett & Livernash, 1969). For a vigorous effort by an employer to escape the "pattern," see Florida East Coast Ry., 41 LA 1001, 1010–1013 (Platt, Bok & Guthrie, 1963). Though historically following the prevailing "pattern," the employer escaped it in Franklin Woolen Mills, 37 LA 270, 272 (Fallon, 1961).

ments. On the contrary, the Board is of the opinion that negotiations of this character should be encouraged in the industry."[173]

Productivity

The productivity standard is frequently advanced for consideration by arbitrators of wage disputes. Proponents of this standard urge that increases in productivity should be reflected by increases in wages. It has been recognized that there is a close relationship between the general level of productivity and the general level of wages,[174] and that both an increase in wage rates and a reduction in hours may be warranted by increased productivity measured in terms of added output per man-hour.[175]

There is a question, however, as to the extent to which increases in productivity in specific industries should be used as the basis of wage increases within those industries. In one case the union advanced figures to show that productivity had been rising over an extended period of time within the plant, and argued that real wages should be increased commensurately. The arbitration board considered productivity to be an "influential but not decisive" factor, and speaking through its Chairman, Clark Kerr, said:

> "Normally wages rise somewhat more rapidly in those industries where productivity is rising rapidly and less rapidly where productivity is rising slowly or not at all or even declining. Thus productivity is an influential but not controlling factor. For the whole economy it is of more significance, perhaps, than for the individual plant or industry. Real wages can rise significantly in the long run only as physical productivity increases. To tie wages rigidly in each minor segment of the economy to changes in physical productivity in that segment would, however, cause greater distortion as between and among progressive, static and regressive industries than could be sustained."[176]

---

[173] National Railway Labor Conference, 53 LA 555, 560 (Seward, Howlett & Livernash, 1969).

[174] Slichter, Basic Criteria Used in Wage Negotiations 21 (1947). In a December 1970 speech to the National Association of Manufacturers, Secretary of Labor Hodgson noted the growing interest in improving what might be termed the quality of life and he suggested that the problem is whether this can be achieved without sacrificing something in the quantity or quality of goods and services; in his view, increased productivity or production efficiency is the answer.

[175] General Motors Corp., 1 LA 125, 130 (Garrison, Eisenhower & Stacy, 1946).

[176] Pacific Gas & Electric Co., 7 LA 528, 530 (1947). Some weight was also given to productivity by Arbitrator Kagel in 28 LA 600, 606; Hogan in

In another case a fact-finding board for the Basic Steel Industry stated the belief that wage rates in a particular industry should not be tied directly to productivity in that industry but rather should be related to the general industrial rise in productivity; moreover, the board said that any excesses of productivity in any one industry over the general average should provide primarily the means of reducing the prices of the products of that industry.[177]

Increases in productivity can result in increased wages, decreased prices, increased profits, or some combination of the three. If the increase in output per man-hour is due to greater effort and greater skill, there would appear to be no doubt that the gain should accrue to the benefit of the employees. But if the increase is the result of technological progress or better management, several considerations must be taken into account.

It was pointed out by Economist Sumner H. Slichter that changes in wages affect the attitude of employees toward the productivity of the enterprise in which they work and that they will be more likely to cooperate with management to increase productivity if some of the gains of that increase are passed on to them. On the other hand, he recognized two disadvantages of directly passing such gains to the employees: (1) Increase in wages in such cases would introduce unjustified inequalities into the wage structure of the community; and (2) industry as a whole would be prevented from producing the largest possible product, since the rise of wages in the industries where labor productivity is increasing most rapidly would tend to prevent them from reducing their prices to consumers and thus from expanding output and employment. However, he concluded that between raising wages and lowering prices, both of which are likely to follow technological change, the adjustment of the economy to technological

---

23 LA 762, 774; Cole in 22 LA 371, 378; Shulman in 22 LA 297, 299; Gilden in 20 LA 219, 223–224; Guthrie in 20 LA 93, 98–99; Coke in 12 LA 870, 883–884; Bushnell in 3 LA 687, 704. Also see Platt in 56 LA 487, 488. No weight was given to this factor where the evidence was skimpy. Atlanta Newspapers, Inc., 39 LA 207, 209 (Holly, 1962).

[177] Basic Steel Industry, 13 LA 46, 50 (Daugherty, Cole & Rosenman, 1949). Also see Arbitrator Hays in 20 LA 75, 82–83. Cf., Basic Steel Industry, 18 LA 112, 117 (W.S.B., 1952). In Railroads v. Nonoperating Unions, 34 LA 517, 533 (Dunlop, Aaron & Sempliner, 1960), the board stated: "The relevance of increases in productivity to wage rates in a particular industry depends in part upon the ratio of labor costs to total costs; the competitive character of the industry, which influences whether such gains are transmitted rapidly into price and quality changes; the methods of wage payment; and other factors."

progress through higher wages is more favorable to employment and to technological advance than adjustment through falling prices.[178]

While arbitrators may give weight to the productivity factor when increased production is used as the basis of a demand for an increase, it appears that they are not likely to give the factor much consideration when an employer defends against an increase by alleging that his employees have a lower per capita output than is standard. For instance, low productivity has been held not to justify the denial of a pattern increase, for the reasons that employees' efficiency and output are largely within the control of the employer and that the employer should be able, by extending the incentive system, to put the business on a "reasonable competitive basis" in relation to production costs.[179]

A board of arbitration held that an allegedly great reduction in labor efficiency, which the board found to be true to some extent, did not justify the denial of a cost-of-living increase where the inefficiency and high costs in the industry were caused by a variety of factors, including out-of-date technology, high cost of materials, and a shortage of skilled craftsmen.[180] In another case the arbitrator granted a cost-of-living increase without giving weight to the employer's complaint that productivity was low, on the ground that there was a failure to establish a decline in productivity after the execution of the contract.[181]

Numerous reasons exist for the refusal of arbitrators to make productivity a decisive factor in wage determination. The rate of change in productivity varies from firm to firm and even from department to department within a plant. Thus exclusive use of the productivity standard for wage adjustments would soon lead to a chaotic wage structure within a single plant or industry.[182] Moreover,

---

[178] Slichter, Basic Criteria Used in Wage Negotiations 22–23, 43, 48 (1947).

[179] Watson Elevator Co., 8 LA 386, 389 (Copelof, 1947). In Dallas publishers, 50 LA 367, 373 (Elkouri, 1968), the employees failed to establish any special claim to a wage increase based upon their productivity, but the arbitrator acknowledged the economic vitality of the city in which they work to be another type of productivity that had some relevance, under the facts, to the request for increased wages.

[180] Associated General Contractors, 9 LA 201, 226–227 (Aaron, 1947). Also see Arbitrator Abernethy in 22 LA 88, 93.

[181] Waterfront Employers Assn. of Pacific Coast, 9 LA 172, 178 (Miller, 1947).

[182] Dunlop, "The Economics of Wage-Dispute Settlement," 12 Law & Contemp. Prob. 281, 286–287 (1947).

the measurement of productivity presents highly difficult problems of economic analysis and statistical measurement,[183] although assistance may be available under the United States Department of Labor productivity measurement program (which issues industry indexes of output per man-hour).[184] Even after a change in productivity has been measured, the problem still remains of determining whether it was caused by increased skill and effort of employees or by better management or improved technology. The arbitrator also must face the problem of assigning a value to the change in productivity—evidence of changes in productivity is not readily transformed into cents-per-hour wage adjustments.[185]

A powerful factor giving impetus to consideration of productivity as an element in determining wage increases came into being with the agreement of General Motors Corporation in 1950 to grant an annual "improvement factor" increase, amounting to four cents per hour. The figure was based on an estimated three percent annual improvement in productivity throughout all industry, a figure which the company stated it expected to surpass.[186] The 1971 General Motors agreement specified improvement factor increases (ranging from 11 cents to 22 cents per hour depending on the employee's wage rate) and stated: "The improvement factor provided herein recognizes that a continuing improvement in the standard of living of employees depends upon technological progress, better tools, methods, processes and equipment, and a cooperative attitude on the part of all parties in

---

[183] Id. at 287–288. For an example of the difficulty involved in proving productivity changes, see Waterfront Employers Assn. of Pacific Coast, 9 LA 172, 177–178 (Miller, 1947). Also see Arbitrator Horlacher in 27 LA 295, 299; Fact-Finders Platt, Gemrich & Arsulowicz in 18 LA 686, 690.

[184] See Indexes of Output Per Man-Hour, Selected Industries, 1939 and 1947-66 (Bureau of Labor Statistics Bull. No. 1572, 1967).

[185] Dunlop, "The Economics of Wage-Dispute Settlement," 12 Law & Contemp. Prob. 281, 288 (1947). Also see New York Shipping Assn., 20 LA 75, 82–83 (Hays, 1952); San Diego Gas & Electric Co., 12 LA 245, 255–256 (Aaron, 1949).

[186] Regarding the influence elsewhere of this General Motors step, see Union Railroad Co., 20 LA 219, 224 (Gilden, 1953). While granting an increase partly on the basis of the "annual improvement factor," an arbitrator emphasized that an increase on the basis of this factor is not due automatically in every case, but that the factor is one of the considerations to be taken into account along with other factors. Printing Industries of Indiana, Inc., 29 LA 7, 11 (McCoy, 1957). In Labor Standards Assn., 36 LA 171, 178 (Roberts, 1960), the union sought to introduce a productivity factor which had been adopted in other industries, but the arbitrator stated that "it has never been integrated into the wage bargain of these parties and should not be imposed by an arbitrator."

such progress. It further recognizes the principle that to produce more with the same amount of human effort is a sound economic and social objective."

Take-Home Pay

Maintenance of take-home pay emerged at the end of World War II as a means of "cushioning the shock" of the transition from an economy of war to one of peace.[187] Sudden and extensive reductions in weekly earnings throughout industry as a result of reduction of hours, especially overtime, became a matter of national concern at the end of the war while living costs were still rising. Labor demanded wage increases to maintain take-home pay as hours of work were reduced. In considering these demands, arbitrators and fact-finding boards were guided by the national wage-price policy laid down in executive orders, regulations under the Wage Stabilization Act, and an address by the President to the nation. This national wage-price policy recognized that wage increases were necessary as a means of cushioning the shock of the war-peace conversion but that wage increases which would necessitate price increases would have dangerous inflationary tendencies. On the other hand, the policy recognized that business as a whole was in a very favorable earning position and thus could, and should, make substantial wage increases without seeking price increases.[188]

The maintenance of take-home pay standard has been given consideration in numerous cases. Although it generally has not been the only one considered, it has been responsible at least for a part of the increase granted in those cases.[189] In the application of this standard,

---

[187] Another type of situation in which need may exist to "cushion the shock" concerns automation. For example, see New York Shipping Assn., 36 LA 44 (Stein, 1960), which was an "interests" arbitration to determine whether and to what extent royalties should be paid by ship owners to cushion the labor displacement impact of the use of cargo containers.

[188] General Motors Corp., 1 LA 125, 127–128 (Garrison, Eisenhower & Stacy, 1946).

[189] E.g., see Arbitrator McCoy in 29 LA 7, 10–11; Gooding, Fitzgibbon & Slavney in 21 LA 307, 309; Tolley, McKelvey & Turkus in 19 LA 538, 551–553; Payne in 15 LA 524, 525–526; Cole, Horovitz & Edwards in 12 LA 507, 515; Dunlop in 10 LA 581, 596; Gellhorn, Paley & Miller in 4 LA 502, 506; Copelof in 3 LA 566, 569; Wallen in 3 LA 639, 645; Witte, Kerr & Starr in 1 LA 333, 338–339; Garrison, Eisenhower & Stacy in 1 LA 125, 130, 133.

potential[190] or probable[191] loss of take-home pay may be considered as well as present loss.

Application of other standards may preclude the maintenance of take-home pay. For instance, lack of ability to pay was deemed a sufficient reason for permitting the discontinuance of overtime work without at the same time granting a wage increase to maintain take-home pay.[192]

Several arguments may be advanced against use of this standard. Since a reduction in hours means that less labor is being sold, should not the total amount paid for labor drop accordingly? If the principle of relating total wages to the number of hours worked is sound when hours are increasing, is it not sound when hours are decreasing? Moreover, should not workers be encouraged to leave rather than remain in industries and places where a labor surplus exists?[193]

It has been suggested that the heavy penalty rates required for overtime work by the Fair Labor Standards Act and by most collective agreements will keep such work to a minimum in time of peace, and hence that the maintenance of take-home pay will not often need to be considered.[194] It may be reasonable to expect, however, that the standard will be given consideration in any instance where, in the absence of a wage increase, a sudden and extensive reduction in earnings within a specific industry or within a large segment of industry generally would result from a reduction of hours.

This, for instance, was the situation where a railroad emergency board was asked to recommend a 40-hour week in lieu of the then existing 48-hour week for approximately one million non-operating railway workers. The board recognized 40 basic hours per week with time and a half for overtime to be the prevailing practice in American industry, a practice which had been put into effect not only in industries covered by the Fair Labor Standards Act but to a steadily increasing extent in industries excluded from the Act. The board recom-

---

[190] F. W. Woolworth Co., 4 LA 502, 506 (Gellhorn, Paley & Miller, 1946).

[191] General Motors Corp., 1 LA 125, 133 (Garrison, Eisenhower & Stacy, 1946).

[192] Roberts Pressure Valve Co., 8 LA 665, 667 (Singer, 1947). Also see Railroads v. Operating Unions, 14 LA 688 (McDonough, O'Malley & Watkins, 1950).

[193] Slichter, Basic Criteria Used in Wage Negotiations 20–21 (1947).

[194] Id. at 19.

mended the adoption of a 40-hour week, and, in connection therewith, it recommended that all basic rates of pay then in effect be increased by 20 percent to provide the same basic earnings for 40 hours of work as had been received for 48 hours.[195]

Past Practice and Bargaining History

The past practice of the parties has sometimes, although infrequently, been considered to be a standard for "interests" arbitration. This standard is of special significance when parties are engaged in their initial negotiations. It was stated in one instance by Arbitrator Clark Kerr:

> "The arbitrator considers past practice a primary factor. It is standard form to incorporate past conditions into collective bargaining contracts, whether these contracts are developed by negotiation or arbitration. The fact of unionization creates no basis for the withdrawal of conditions previously in effect. If they were justified before, they remain justified after the event of union affiliation. It is almost axiomatic that the existing conditions be perpetuated. Some contracts even blanket them in through a general 'catch-all' clause."[196]

Arbitrators may require "persuasive reason" for the elimination of a clause which has been in past written agreements.[197] Moreover, they sometimes order the formalization of past practices by ordering that they be incorporated into the written agreement.[198]

In arbitrating the terms of a renewal contract, one arbitrator would consider seriously "what the parties have agreed upon in their

---

[195] Railroads v. Non-operating Unions, 11 LA 752, 761–763 (Leiserson, Cole & Cook, 1948). A subsequent board recommended a reduction in the workweek of certain operating railroad employees but did not recommend a requested 20 percent wage increase to maintain take-home pay. The board noted the award for the non-operating employees but distinguished the cases on the following grounds: (1) the rates of the operating employees were already higher than those of employees in other industries, whereas the non-operating rates had been lower; (2) the requested increase was not justified in view of the railroads' financial condition. The board did, however, believe an increase of 18 cents an hour to be justified. Railroads v. Operating Unions, 14 LA 688, 707–708 (McDonough, O'Malley & Watkins, 1950).

[196] Luckenbach Steamship Co., 6 LA 98, 101 (1946). Also see St. Paul Department Stores, 2 LA 52 (Johnston, Gydeson & Harmon, 1946).

[197] Minneapolis-Moline Power Implement Co., 2 LA 227, 230, 240 (Van Fossen, Humphrey & Prifrel, 1946).

[198] Sosna Bros., 6 LA 846, 850 (Rosenfarb, 1947); F. W. Woolworth Co., 4 LA 502, 508 (Gellhorn, Paley & Miller, 1946). Also see Arbitrator Roumell in 54 LA 901, 914; Singer in 47 LA 482, 486 (ordering continuation of an unwritten practice); Sanders, Begley & Gilden in 28 LA 182, 196.

past collective bargaining, as affected by intervening economic events * * *."[199] The past bargaining history of the parties, including the criteria that they have used, has provided a helpful guide to other "interests" arbitrators.[200]

Pre-Arbitration Negotiations

It has been said that the award in a wage dispute seldom falls outside the area of "probable expectancy" and that this area is the normal resultant product of the parties' negotiations and bargaining prior to submitting their differences to arbitration.[201] In this regard, too, one arbitration board concluded:

> "An examination of the wealth of evidence submitted in this matter in conjunction with the provisions of settlement worked out by the parties indicates that the most satisfactory award which the Board could render would be one in general agreement with those terms on which the parties were able at one time to substantially agree. Obviously, these terms are not what either party wanted. They represent compromise by both parties. However, since the general terms indicate a meeting of the minds, the Board considers that they hold the basis of a just award."[202]

While observing that an "interests" arbitrator usually can make a more useful award if he has knowledge of the bargaining positions of the parties prior to the arbitration stage, one group of arbitrators suggested that if at least one of the parties wishes to exclude consideration of pre-arbitral offers it may be sound policy for the arbitrator

---

[199] United Traction Co., 27 LA 309, 315 (Sheiber, 1956).

[200] This aid was used, as specified by a public sector arbitration statute, in Hurley Hospital, 56 LA 209, 212–215 (Roumell, 1971). It was used in private sector arbitration by Arbitrator Elkouri in 50 LA 367, 370; Gunderman in 39 LA 249, 251; Flagler in 38 LA 666, 671; Luskin in 36 LA 201, 202–203; Abernethy in 22 LA 88, 92.

[201] Justin, "Arbitrating a Wage Dispute Case," 3 Arb. J. (n.s.) 228 (1948). Also see Arbitrator Simkin in 18 LA 631, 643. It is also said that parties sometimes agree upon contract terms but for political reasons want an arbitrator to order them. "Current Problems of Arbitration, American Unionism," 29 LA 880, 883 (1958).

[202] Durso & Geelan Co., 17 LA 748, 749 (Donnelly, Curry & Clark, 1951). Also see Arbitrator Siegel in 50 LA 1036, 1042–1043; Black in 41 LA 372, 375–376. In "many instances intangible factors such as the indicated bids or offers by the parties in private bargaining * * * will be of considerable importance" in the arbitrator's consideration of the case. Backman, Economic Data Utilized in Wage Arbitration 3 (1952). In Palo Alto-Stanford Hospital Center, 50 LA 700, 701 (Mann, 1968), the submission agreement expressly confined the arbitrator to the limits of the parties' original proposals. Similarly, see Arbitrators Cluster, Gallagher & Kraushaar in 45 LA 801, 806.

to do so lest future bargaining be inhibited.[203] However, the members of one board of inquiry declared that type of tribunal to be of such nature that tentative agreements, as well as offers and counter offers, of the parties during the negotiation stage could not be ignored completely by the board even though one of the parties protested any consideration of such matters.[204]

Public Interest

The question arises as to how far arbitrators should go in considering the public-interest aspects of "interests" disputes. The public, although not a direct party, has a vital interest in the settlement of some disputes. Fact-finding boards do give strong consideration to the public welfare in making recommendations. For instance, a fact-finding board for General Motors Corporation would recommend only such wage increases as it believed would not have inflationary price consequences.[205] A fact-finding board for the Basic Steel Industry considered the public interest to be one of the two major inquiries which should be made in determining whether a wage increase should be granted. In denying any increase, the board placed strong emphasis on its belief that a wage increase for the steel industry would be used as a pattern for other industries and might well cause price dislocations with adverse effects on the general economy.[206]

The public interest is an important consideration in public utility disputes (see next subtopic), and equally so in disputes directly involving the public sector.[207] For example, the "interest and welfare

---

[203] Guides for Labor Arbitration 9–10 (1953), by a group of arbitrators in the Philadelphia area.

[204] Rochester Transit Corp., 19 LA 538, 541–542 (Tolley, McKelvey & Turkus, 1952). In Cummins Sales, Inc., 54 LA 1069, 1072 (Seinsheimer, 1970), the arbitrator gave significant weight to the employer's offer in negotiations.

[205] General Motors Corp., 1 LA 125, 128 (Garrison, Eisenhower & Stacy, 1946).

[206] Basic Steel Industry, 13 LA 46, 52 (Daugherty, Cole & Rosenman, 1949). In Chesapeake & Potomac Telephone Co. of Baltimore, 7 LA 630, 640 (Jackson, Healy & Dennis, 1947), an increase sufficient to offset the full rise in the cost of living would not be granted where to do so would contribute further to inflation. Cf., Basic Steel Industry, 18 LA 112, 136 (W.S.B., 1952).

[207] See this Chapter, subtopic titled "Public Sector Ability to Pay" and topic titled "Standards in Public Sector Disputes." It has been stated that public policy must be considered much more in public sector disputes than in those in the private sector. Jones, "The Role of Arbitration in State and National Policy," Arbitration and the Public Interest 42, 60 (The Bureau of National Affairs, Inc., 1971).

of the public" is a factor specified by state statute to be given consideration by arbitrators of "interests" disputes in the public sector.[208]

Public Utility Disputes

The public-interest standard is often invoked for public utility disputes. Two considerations are generally involved. The first is that services of public utilities, being constantly consumed necessities of life, should be made available to consumers at a fair price. Since wages paid by a utility will directly affect the cost of its services to the public, the amount of any wage increase granted may be affected by the arbitrator's conclusion about the probable effect of the increase upon the price of the service involved. The arbitrator will keep in mind the needs of the consumers.[209]

The second consideration recognizes that the public has a paramount interest in continuity of operations of public utilities. The public expects utilities to provide uninterrupted service. Indeed, in one case the arbitrator stated that "most of the unions and most of the employees engaged in the essential public utilities" had "long recognized that their responsibilities required uninterrupted service to the public."[210]

Since public utility employees are under a very strong obligation not to strike, there has been considerable public discussion of the need for a wage policy which will assure equitable treatment to these employees, and emphasis usually has been placed upon the desirability of assuring them rates and conditions of work which are as good as or better than those available for comparable work anywhere in the area.[211]

In recognizing these several considerations, Arbitrator George W. Taylor stated that, while a meritorious argument is presented, it is difficult to put them into practice in specific terms.[212] But Arbitrator Clark Kerr declared that an effort should be made to assure utility

---

[208] See City of Birmingham, 55 LA 716, 721 (Roumell, 1970); Town of Tiverton, R.I., 52 LA 1301, 1302 (Schmidt, 1969).

[209] See Arbitrators Platt, Gemrich & Arsulowicz in 18 LA 686, 690; Holland, Anderson & Hollingsworth in 8 LA 397, 402; Kerr in 7 LA 528, 530–531; Taylor in 6 LA 830, 836.

[210] Capital Transit Co., 9 LA 666, 679 (Taylor, 1947).

[211] Consolidated Edison System Cos. of New York, 6 LA 830, 834 (Taylor, 1947).

[212] Ibid.

workers "both as high or higher absolute levels and as favorable or more favorable relative changes in wages as other workers generally in the community."[213] Another arbitrator expressed preference for the view that utility employees should expect to enjoy substantially the same wages, hours, and working conditions—no better and no worse—as those enjoyed by other workers living in the area; thus utility employment should be made to conform to local conditions, not to blaze new trails.[214]

As noted in Chapter I, some states have enacted antistrike laws for their public utilities (some of these laws have subsequently been repealed and/or merged into broader statutes including public sector coverage). In some instances these states have also specified standards to be observed in the compulsory arbitration of public utility disputes, the objective appearing to be to insure that utility employees shall have the same wages, hours, and working conditions as those prevailing for comparable workers.

The Nebraska provisions are of interest in this regard. The Nebraska Act (the coverage of which was expanded in 1969 to include disputes involving governmental service) provides for a Court of Industrial Relations, which is empowered to establish or alter the scale of wages, hours of work, or conditions of employment. In respect to the standards to be applied by the Court, the following is provided by the Act:

> "* * * In making such findings and order or orders, the Court of Industrial Relations shall establish rates of pay and conditions of employment which are comparable to the prevalent wage rates paid and conditions of employment maintained for the same or similar work of workers exhibiting like or similar skills under the same or similar working conditions. In establishing wage rates the court shall take into consideration the overall compensation presently received by the employees, having regard not only to wages for time actually worked but also to wages for time not worked, including vacations, holidays, and other excused time, and all benefits received, including insurance and pensions, and the continuity and stability of employment enjoyed by the employees. Any order or orders entered may be modified

---

[213] Pacific Gas & Electric Co., 7 LA 528, 531 (1947). To similar effect, Consumers Power Co., 24 LA 581, 584 (Smith, Howlett, Sorensen, 1955).

[214] Cleveland Electric Illuminating Co., 8 LA 597, 600, 605 (Cornsweet, 1947). While this view had been advanced earlier by Lee H. Hill, a management spokesman, in the instant case it was approved, but interpreted differently, by both the labor and employer arbitrators.

on the court's own motion or on application by any of the parties affected, but only upon a showing of a change in the conditions from those prevailing at the time the original order was entered."[215]

This Nebraska statutory requirement for the use of the prevailing-practice standard (including the recognition of appropriate differentials) illustrates again the standard's value and acceptability.

Governmental Wage Stabilization

In times of wage stabilization "interests" arbitrators, emergency boards, and fact-finders must take cognizance of governmental stabilization regulations that may apply to the parties. In some cases awards or recommended terms have been made subject to approval by wage stabilization authorities.[216] Sometimes arbitrators have ordered one party to join the other in seeking such approval.[217] Then, too, the arbitrator might examine stabilization regulations and reach his own conclusion as to the permissibility of requested increases.[218]

Where the parties in submitting a case to "interests" arbitration specified that the arbitration board should seek wage stabilization approval (if necessary) of any increase ordered, the arbitrators stated that the wage stabilization program was just one factor to be considered along with others in determining the amount of any wage adjustment.[219] Another arbitrator declared that while wage stabilization regulations should be taken into account in determining wage adjustments, the influence of wage stabilization on an arbitrator's decision should vary "in direct ratio to the certainty, clarity and stage

---

[215] Nebraska Revised Statutes 1943, Sec. 48-818 as amended in 1969. The Wisconsin statute provides that the specific enumeration of standards shall not be construed as precluding the consideration of other factors normally taken into consideration in the determination of wages, hours, and working conditions through voluntary collective bargaining or arbitration. See Sec. 111.57, Subchapter III of Chapter 111, Wisconsin Statutes.

[216] See Los Angeles Standard Rubber, Inc., 17 LA 353, 354, 361 (Warren, 1951); Felt Companies, 16 LA 881, 882 (Lesser, 1951).

[217] See Durso & Geelan Co., 17 LA 748, 750–751 (Donnelly, 1951). Also see Arbitrator Hays in 20 LA 75, 76.

[218] See Frederick Loeser & Co., 16 LA 399, 404 (Justin, 1951). In one case the arbitrator did this at the request of the parties after they had agreed as to increases. City of Cheboygan, Michigan, 57 LA 1090, 1091 (Keefe, 1971). Also see Macy's New York, 57 LA 1115, 1118 (Stark, 1971), where the arbitrator ruled as to the permissibility under wage stabilization regulations of certain automatic wage increases. But see Arbitrator Markowitz in 58 LA 191, 193.

[219] North American Aviation, Inc., 19 LA 76, 77 (Cole, Aaron & Wirtz, 1952).

of its evolution."[220] It may also be noted that at times the President's Council of Economic Advisors has adopted wage guidelines and has urged their observance by industry to aid the control of inflation.[221]

Standards in Public Sector Disputes

The standards or criteria utilized by neutrals in private sector "interests" cases have also been utilized in public sector cases.[222] Indeed, the general utility of using private sector standards in public sector "interests" disputes is underscored by the action of various states which have expressly ordered the use of such standards for public sector disputes. The Michigan Police and Firemen's Arbitration Act provides, for example:

"Sec. 9. Where there is no agreement between the parties, or where there is an agreement but the parties have begun negotiations or discussions looking to a new agreement or amendment of the existing agreement, and wage rates or other conditions of employment under the proposed new or amended agreement are in dispute, the arbitration panel shall base its findings, opinions and order upon the following factors, as applicable:

"(a) The lawful authority of the employer.

"(b) Stipulations of the parties.

"(c) The interests and welfare of the public and the financial ability of the unit of government to meet those costs.

---

[220] Merchants Bank of New York, 16 LA 901, 904 (Rosenfarb, 1951). For related discussion, see Chapter 10, topic titled "Statutory Law."

[221] In Port Authority of Allegheny County, 45 LA 58, 59 (Crawford, 1965), use of the guidelines was rejected, the arbitrator stating that "There is no evidence that the national guidelines for wage increases have ever been applied in collective bargaining or arbitration in this industry, and this is not the time for innovation."

[222] Many of the more recent citations for standards discussed elsewhere in this Chapter are public sector cases. For other writings which give some consideration to standards for public sector "interests" cases, see Doering, "Impasse Issues in Teacher Disputes Submitted to Fact Finding in New York," 27 Arb. J. 1 (1972); Block, "Criteria in Public Sector Interests Disputes," Arbitration and the Public Interest 161 (The Bureau of National Affairs, Inc., 1971); Jones, "The Role of Arbitration in State and National Policy," id. at 42; Garber, "Compulsory Arbitration in the Public Sector: A Proposed Alternative," 26 Arb. J. 226 (1971); Bain, "Third-Party Settlements in Education," 26 Arb. J. 41 (1971); Drotning & Lipsky, "The Outcome of Impasse Procedures in New York Schools Under the Talyor Law," 26 Arb. J. 87 (1971); Wollett & Chanin, The Law and Practice of Teacher Negotiations (The Bureau of National Affairs, Inc., 1970); Loewenberg, "Compulsory Arbitration and the Arbitrator," 25 Arb. J. 248 (1970).

"(d) Comparison of the wages, hours and conditions of employment of the employees involved in the arbitration proceedings with the wages, hours and conditions of employment of other employees performing similar services and with other employees generally:
"(i) In public employment in comparable communities.
"(ii) In private employment in comparable communities.

"(e) The average consumer prices for goods and services, commonly known as the cost of living.

"(f) The overall compensation presently received by the employees, including direct wage compensation, vacations, holidays and other excused time, insurance and pensions, medical and hospitalization benefits, the continuity and stability of employment, and all other benefits received.

"(g) Changes in any of the foregoing circumstances during the pendency of the arbitration proceedings.

"(h) Such other factors, not confined to the foregoing, which are normally or traditionally taken into consideration in the determination of wages, hours and conditions of employment through voluntary collective bargaining, mediation, fact-finding, arbitration or otherwise between the parties, in the public service or in private employment."[223]

Note that one of the criteria listed in the Michigan statute is the "lawful authority of the employer." This consideration has special relevance to the public sector. Other considerations which likewise are not normally relevant in private sector cases will no doubt be recognized for special application in public sector cases in the course of the fuller development of that area in the future. A few of the possibilities as to special considerations are reflected, for instance, in the following statements or actions by neutrals in public sector cases already decided.

As to police officers, Arbitrator Peter Seitz has stated that:

"* * * if the exacting requirements of police work are to be met in the near and more distant future, at least two conditions must be recognized: the level of pay must be high enough to attract able and promising young people who will be able to withstand the lure of higher wages at less dangerous work in plants in the surrounding

---

[223] Michigan SLL 32:262c. Section 9 of the Act is also quoted in City of Birmingham, 55 LA 716, 721 (Roumell, 1970). For a statute which emphasizes the "comparable practice" standard (with recognition of appropriate differentials), see Town of Tiverton, R.I., 52 LA 1301, 1302 (Schmidt, 1969).

communities in the general labor market and the compensation system should be one that will maintain the highest possible morale and esprit de corps in the present force."[224]

Another arbitrator "adopted the principle that Police Department personnel should receive compensation which is sufficient to maintain reasonable standards of health and decency without the necessity to hold alternate employment."[225]

In reference to firemen, Arbitrator John T. Dunlop pointed out that "The City has a fiscal interest in maintaining the quality and morale of its firefighting forces since the fire insurance rates to business and the attractiveness of doing business in Providence are influenced in part by the costs of fire protection."[226]

Considerations underlying a fact-finder's recommendations for increases in teacher salaries were to keep the school district in a competitive position to recruit new teachers, to attract competent experienced teachers, to hold valuable teachers now serving the school district, to give recognition to advanced degrees and training, and to recognize the constantly increasing costs of advanced training to the teacher.[227]

The need to keep public sector employers competitive to obtain and keep well-qualified employees likewise has been a consideration in other cases.[228]

---

[224] City of Providence, 47 LA 1036, 1039 (1966). In City of Birmingham, 55 LA 716, 723 (Roumell, 1970), the arbitrator stated that police officer compensation "should receive relative improvement as compared to other types of employees because of the changing duties and responsibilities of their jobs."

[225] City of Uniontown, 51 LA 1072, 1073 (Duff, 1968). However, this arbitrator could find no compelling reason to classify police department employees as a special group entitled to more holidays or vacation time than other city employees. Id. at 1075. Agreeing that "moonlighting" by police officers should be discouraged by an adequate police wage, Arbitrator Seitz in 47 LA 1036, 1039.

[226] City of Providence, 42 LA 1114, 1119 (1963).

[227] Whitesboro Teachers Assn., 51 LA 58, 61 (Bickal, 1968). Also see Arbitrator Young in 51 LA 1134, 1135–1138.

[228] See Arbitrator McDermott, Zollner & Hutskow in 52 LA 233, 234–235 (police); Young in 51 LA 1134, 1135–1136 (teachers); Florey in 51 LA 994, 995 (police); Singer in 48 LA 289, 291 (nursing home).

CHAPTER 19

ARBITRATION'S PLACE AS AN
INDUSTRIAL INSTITUTION

Arbitration in practice is a distinct institution, the product of a collectively bargained compromise between the alternatives of resort to courts of law, which are not well adapted to the needs of labor-management relations, and resort to work stoppages, which are wasteful and costly to both parties. While arbitration is a distinct institution, however, it would be totally unrealistic to deny the close relationship now existing between it, especially "rights" arbitration, and our formal legal system. Indeed, labor arbitration has drawn heavily from the standards and techniques of that system. In this connection, the Authors believe that on the whole sound judgment has been exercised by arbitrators in effectively utilizing established legalisms without paying slavish deference thereto.

Arbitration is an avenue traveled by thousands, indeed millions, of industrial disputants. It is a vital force in establishing confidence and minimizing confusion at all levels of the labor-management relationship and is a major constructive force in the collective bargaining process itself. Arbitration should not, however, be expected or totally relied upon to create either good contracts or cooperative human relationships—it is a supplement to, rather than a substitute for, conscientious grievance processing and genuine collective bargaining.

Finally, the Authors desire to emphasize their firm conviction that not only has arbitration been an exceedingly useful social and industrial institution but that it will become even more so in the future, both in the private sector and in the public sector.

TOPICAL INDEX